S0-DGE-475

EXPLORING THE *LONGUE DURÉE*

EXPLORING THE *LONGUE DURÉE*

Essays in Honor of Lawrence E. Stager

edited by

J. DAVID SCHLOEN

Winona Lake, Indiana
EISENBRAUNS
2009

Printed in the United States of America.

www.eisenbrauns.com

Library of Congress Cataloging-in-Publication Data

Exploring the Longue Durée : essays in honor of Lawrence E. Stager / edited by J. David Schloen
p. cm.
Includes bibliographical references.
ISBN 978-1-57506-161-0 (hardcover : alk. paper)
1. Palestine—Antiquities. 2. Israel—Antiquities. 3. Middle East—Antiquities. 4. Bronze age—Palestine. 5. Iron age—Palestine. 6. Palestine—History—To 70 A.D. 7. Middle East—History—To 622. 8. Excavations (Archaeology)—Middle East. 9. Bible. O.T.—Antiquities. 10. Bible. O.T.—Criticism, interpretation, etc. I. Schloen, J. David, 1962– II. Stager, Lawrence E.
DS111.E97 2009
933—dc22
2008046887

The paper used in this publication meets the minimum requirements of the American National Standard for Information Sciences—Permanence of Paper for Printed Library Materials, ANSI Z39.48-1984. ♾™

Lawrence E. Stager
Dorot Professor of the Archaeology of Israel and Director of the Semitic Museum at Harvard University
Director of the Leon Levy Expedition to Ashkelon

CONTENTS

PREFACE

LAWRENCE STAGER turned sixty-five in 2008. In a long academic career at the University of Chicago and Harvard University, he has taught many students who are now active researchers and teachers in biblical and Levantine archaeology. As one of those students, I am glad to honor Larry's achievements at this milestone in his impressive career, which is far from over. His influence and his personal relationships as a teacher and colleague can be seen in the fifty essays collected in this volume, offered by a diverse group of friends and former students who explore a wide range of topics, time periods, and methods. These essays, ranging from archaeology to biblical interpretation to philology, and ranging from nitty-gritty description to sweeping theorization, provide a good index of his exceptionally wide circle of intellectual interests and friendships.

The large number of Larry Stager's friends and admirers can be attributed, not just to his charm and the force of his personality, which are considerable, but to the intellectual appeal of his scholarly work and the unique combination of skills and temperament he brings to his research. He has had a major impact on the archaeology of the Levant, both with regard to specific interpretations for which he has argued—concerning ancient agriculture and horticulture, families and households in ancient Israel, the role of seaports and maritime trade in the Bronze and Iron Ages, the migration of the Philistines and other Sea Peoples, the nature of the kingdom of David and Solomon—and, perhaps more importantly, with regard to the way he asks the questions and marshals data and theory to answer them. Many students and specialists, in all manner of settings, in the United States, Israel, and elsewhere, have experienced Larry's personal warmth and illuminating insights. It is therefore with warm feelings of respect and admiration that several dozen of us offer these essays to him in celebration of a long and productive career.

Larry Stager was born on January 5, 1943, in Kenton, Ohio, county seat of rural Hardin County in the western part of the state, about fifty miles northwest of Columbus. He grew up on a farm and attended school in the tiny town of Dunkirk. He is descended from a long line of farmers who had migrated westward from Pennsylvania. He is the first of his family to attend college—and for Larry, college was a world away from the environment in which he was reared. An outstanding student in his high school, he was recruited by the Harvard Club of Dayton, Ohio, who were on the lookout for talented young Ohioans to send to Harvard University. Larry enrolled at Harvard in 1961 and was introduced to biblical archaeology by leading scholars of the subject, graduating with a B.A. *magna cum laude* in 1965. He continued his studies at Harvard under the tutelage of G. Ernest Wright and Frank Moore Cross, among others, earning his M.A. in 1972 and his Ph.D. ("with distinction") in 1975, with a thesis entitled: "Ancient Agriculture in the Judaean Desert: A Case Study of the Buqêᶜah Valley in the Iron Age."

From Harvard, Larry went to the Oriental Institute of the University of Chicago, first as an instructor (1973–1974) and then as assistant professor (1974–1976), associate professor (1976–1985), and full professor (1985–1986) of Syro-Palestinian archaeology. In 1986, he returned to Harvard University, to an endowed chair, as the inaugural Dorot Professor of the Archaeology of Israel and (since 1987) as the director of the Harvard Semitic Museum. He continues to serve in those capacities. With him since his student days has been Susan J. Simmons, whom he married in June 1970. They have two children, Jennifer (born 1978) and David (born 1983).

Since his undergraduate days, Larry has been active in archaeological fieldwork in the Mediterranean region. From 1966 to 1971 he served as an area supervisor at Tell Gezer, the leading American project in Israel at that time. From 1970 to 1973, he was a field supervisor at Tell el-Ḥesi, while also conducting a survey of ancient agricultural terraces from Hebron to Samaria (1972–1973) and a survey and soundings in the Buqêᶜah Valley (1972) to gather data for his doctoral dissertation. From 1974 to 1980 he was the co-principal investigator (with Anita Walker) of the American Expedition to Idalion, Cyprus, serving as field director there from 1971 to 1974. He then turned his attention farther west, directing the Punic Project at Carthage in Tunisia from 1975 to 1980, where he excavated the *tophet*, a burial precinct in which was found evidence of child sacrifice. In 1985, he initiated the Leon Levy Expedition to Ashkelon in Israel, which he has directed ever since. Thanks to the generous support of the late Leon Levy and his wife Shelby White, the latter expedition is one of the largest and lengthiest excavation projects in Israel and, indeed, the entire Middle East. At Idalion, Carthage, and most of all at Ashkelon, Larry Stager has brought together large teams of specialists and students and has trained dozens of field archaeologists, many of whom now direct their own excavation projects.

Among other honors, Larry was chosen to give the Schweich Lectures on Biblical Archaeology sponsored by the British Academy in London in October 2004, and he was recently named a Corresponding Member of the Austrian Academy of Sciences. Over the course of his career, he has served as a trustee of the William F. Albright Institute of Archaeological Research in Jerusalem and of the Archaeological Institute of America (of which he was vice-president in 1986–1988), and as a member of the editorial boards of the *Bulletin of the American Schools of Oriental Research*, *Eretz-Israel*, and *The New Encyclopedia of Archaeological Excavations in the Holy Land.*

The essays in this volume span a broad range of topics, reflecting the research interests of the wide variety of scholars of different ages, countries, and specialties who contributed to it. Chapter 1 is my own personal reflection on Larry's scholarly contribution in the context of North American biblical archaeology. The remaining chapters are arranged alphabetically by author. Some of them, especially those of his former students, draw directly upon Larry's theoretical work, invoking his model of "port power" (chapters 7, 43, 44) and his ideas about kinship and "patrimonialism" in ancient Israel (chapters 2, 5, 47). Others discuss archaeological phenomena that have figured prominently in Larry's research over the years, such as ancient horticulture (chapter 16), Iron Age houses and villages (chapters 12, 21, 33), and features and finds related to the site of Ashkelon in Israel, where Larry has directed excavations since 1985 (chapters 3, 6, 11, 13, 14, 28, 31, 32, 36, 49). The remaining chapters are a fascinating sample of research in biblical studies (chapters 8, 18, 20, 22, 24, 26, 45; most with a sociological emphasis, as in Larry's work), in nonbiblical philology (chapters 9, 35, 38, 39, 40, 41), and in the archaeology of Israel and the eastern Mediterranean region in the Bronze and Iron Ages (chapters 4, 10, 15, 17, 19, 23, 25, 27, 29, 30, 34, 37, 42, 46, 48, 50).

All of the contributors to this volume have my deepest gratitude for the excellence of their articles and their responsiveness during the editorial process. I am grateful especially to Philip King, who not only contributed to the volume but first broached with me the idea of doing a festschrift for Larry and then supported the project at every stage along the way. Paul Mosca and Michael Sugerman suggested the title and cover design, for which I thank them.

I am grateful to Shelby White and the Leon Levy Foundation for subsidizing the production of the volume. A special word of thanks goes to my student Leann Pace, who labored long checking bibliographic references and doing preliminary copy-editing, and to Eudora Struble, who stepped in at the end to assist with proof-reading the volume. Finally, to James Eisenbraun and his staff at Eisenbrauns Inc., I am grateful for friendly encouragement and assistance in producing this book.

J. David Schloen
Chicago, Illinois October 2008

CONTRIBUTORS

Tristan J. Barako
Providence Pictures

Dror Ben-Yosef
Haifa University

Manfred Bietak
University of Vienna

Elizabeth Bloch-Smith
St. Joseph's University

Aaron J. Brody
Pacific School of Religion

Aaron A. Burke
U. of California, Los Angeles

Susan L. Cohen
Montana State University

Michael D. Coogan
Stonehill College

Frank Moore Cross
Harvard University

William G. Dever
University of Arizona

Trude Dothan
Hebrew University

Alexandra S. Drenka
Hebrew University

Avraham Faust
Bar-Ilan University

Israel Finkelstein
Tel Aviv University

Gerald Finkielsztejn
Israel Antiquities Authority

Seymour Gitin
W. F. Albright Institute

Ram Gophna
Tel Aviv University

Sophocles Hadjisavvas
Cyprus Dept. of Antiquities

Baruch Halpern
Pennsylvania State University

Paul D. Hanson
Harvard University

Timothy P. Harrison
University of Toronto

Ronald Hendel
U. of California, Berkeley

Larry G. Herr
Canadian University College

Theodore Hiebert
McCormick Theological Seminary

John S. Holladay
University of Toronto

Jeremy Hutton
Princeton Theological Seminary

Vassos Karageorghis
Leventis Foundation

Philip J. King
Boston College

Karin Kopetzky
University of Vienna

Thomas E. Levy
U. of California, San Diego

Shmuel Liphschitz
Kibbutz Palmachim

David Lipovitch
University of Toronto

Aren M. Maeir
Bar-Ilan University

Nicolò Marchetti
University of Bologna

Mario A. S. Martin
University of Vienna

Daniel M. Master
Wheaton College

Amihai Mazar
Hebrew University

Alan Millard
University of Liverpool

Paul G. Mosca
University of British Columbia

Nadav Na'aman
Tel Aviv University

Lorenzo Nigro
University of Rome

Dennis Pardee
University of Chicago

Émile Puech
École Biblique, Jerusalem

Itamar Singer
Tel Aviv University

Piotr Steinkeller
Harvard University

Ephraim Stern
Hebrew University

Michael Sugerman
University of Massachusetts

Ron E. Tappy
Pittsburgh Theological Seminary

David Ussishkin
Tel Aviv University

Karel van der Toorn
University of Amsterdam

David Vanderhooft
Boston College

Samuel R. Wolff
Israel Antiquities Authority

Assaf Yasur-Landau
U. of California, Santa Cruz

Adam Zertal
Haifa University

ABBREVIATIONS

AA	*American Anthropologist*
AAAS	*Annales archéologiques arabes syriennes*
AASOR	Annual of the American Schools of Oriental Research
AB	Anchor Bible
ADAJ	*Annual of the Department of Antiquities of Jordan*
ADPV	Abhandlungen des Deutschen Palästinavereins
AfO	*Archiv für Orientforschung*
AHw	*Akkadisches Handwörterbuch*, by W. von Soden
AJA	*American Journal of Archaeology*
AmAnt	*American Antiquity*
ANET [3]	*Ancient Near Eastern Texts Relating to the Old Testament*, edited by J. B. Pritchard (3d ed.; Princeton, 1969)
AnOr	Analecta Orientalia
AOAT	Alter Orient und Altes Testament
AoF	*Altorientalische Forschungen*
ARA	*Annual Review of Anthropology*
ARM	Archives royales de Mari
BA	*Biblical Archaeologist*
BAH	Bibliothèque archéologique et historique
BAR	*Biblical Archaeology Review*
BARIS	British Archaeological Reports, International Series
BASOR	*Bulletin of the American Schools of Oriental Research*
BASORSup	Bulletin of the American Schools of Oriental Research Supplement
BCH	*Bulletin de correspondance hellénique*
BCHSup	Bulletin de correspondance hellénique, Supplément
BDB	*A Hebrew and English Lexicon of the Old Testament*, by F. Brown, S. R. Driver, and C. A. Briggs
BHS	*Biblia Hebraica Stuttgartensia*
BiOr	*Bibliotheca Orientalis*
BMB	*Bulletin du Musée de Beyrouth*
BMC	*British Museum Catalogue*
B.P.	before present
BSA	*Annual of the British School at Athens*
BSASup	British School at Athens Supplementary volume
BSOAS	*Bulletin of the School of Oriental and African Studies*
BTAVO	Beihefte zum Tübinger Atlas des Vorderen Orients
BWANT	Beiträge zur Wissenschaft vom Alten und Neuen Testament
BZAW	Beihefte zur Zeitschrift für die alttestamentliche Wissenschaft
CA	*Current Anthropology*
CAD	*The Assyrian Dictionary of the Oriental Institute of the University of Chicago*
CAJ	*Cambridge Archaeological Journal*
CAT	*The Cuneiform Alphabetic Texts from Ugarit*, by M. Dietrich, O. Loretz, and J. Sanmartín (Münster, 1995)
CBQ	*Catholic Biblical Quarterly*
CChEM	Contributions to the Chronology of the Eastern Mediterranean
CHANE	Culture and History of the Ancient Near East
CIS	Corpus Inscriptionum Semiticarum
COS	*The Context of Scripture*, ed. W. W. Hallo and K. L. Younger (3 vols.; Leiden, 2003).
CRAIBL	*Comptes rendus de l'Académie des inscriptions et belles-lettres*
CTA	*Corpus des tablettes en cunéiformes alphabétiques*, by A. Herdner (Paris, 1963)
DJD	Discoveries in the Judaean Desert
EA	el-Amarna text
EB	Early Bronze Age
EI	*Eretz-Israel*
ESI	*Excavations and Surveys in Israel*
ET	English translation
Gk.	Greek
HALAT	*Hebräisches und aramäisches Lexikon zum Alten Testament*, by L. Koehler and W. Baumgartner (Leiden)
Heb.	Hebrew
HSM	Harvard Semitic Monographs
HSS	Harvard Semitic Studies
HTR	*Harvard Theological Review*

HUCA *Hebrew Union College Annual*
IAA Israel Antiquities Authority
IEJ *Israel Exploration Journal*
IJNA *International Journal of Nautical Archaeology and Underwater Exploration*
INJ *Israel Numismatic Journal*
JADIS Jordan Antiquities Database and Information System
JAOS *Journal of the American Oriental Society*
JARCE *Journal of the American Research Center in Egypt*
JAS *Journal of Archaeological Science*
JBL *Journal of Biblical Literature*
JCS *Journal of Cuneiform Studies*
JESHO *Journal of the Economic and Social History of the Orient*
JFA *Journal of Field Archaeology*
JHS *Journal of Hellenic Studies*
JNES *Journal of Near Eastern Studies*
JPOS *Journal of the Palestine Oriental Society*
JRA *Journal of Roman Archaeology*
JRASup Journal of Roman Archaeology Supplementary Series
JSOT *Journal for the Study of the Old Testament*
JSOTSup Journal for the Study of the Old Testament Supplement Series
JSS *Journal of Semitic Studies*
JSSEA *Journal of the Society for the Study of Egyptian Antiquities*
KAI *Kanaanäische und aramäische Inschriften*, by H. Donner and W. Röllig (2d ed.; Wiesbaden, 1966–69)
KTU *Die keilalphabetischen Texte aus Ugarit*, by M. Dietrich, O. Loretz, and J. Sanmartín (Kevelaer, 1976)
LB Late Bronze Age
LAPO Littératures anciennes du Proche-Orient
LXX Septuagint
MB Middle Bronze Age
MDAIK *Mitteilungen des Deutschen Archäologischen Instituts, Abteilung Kairo*
MDOG *Mitteilungen der Deutschen Orient-Gesellschaft zu Berlin*
MSL *Materialien zum sumerischen Lexikon*
MT Massoretic Text
NC *The Numismatic Chronicle*
NEA *Near Eastern Archaeology*
NRSV New Revised Standard Version of the Bible
NWS Northwest Semitic
OBO Orbis biblicus et orientalis
OIC Oriental Institute Communications
OIP Oriental Institute Publications
OIS Oriental Institute Seminars
OLA Orientalia Lovaniensia Analecta
PEQ *Palestine Exploration Quarterly*
PSD *The Sumerian Dictionary of the University Museum of the University of Pennsylvania*
QDAP *The Quarterly of the Department of Antiquities in Palestine*
RA *Revue d'assyriologie et d'archéologie orientale*
RB *Revue biblique*
RLA *Reallexikon der Assyriologie und vorderasiatische Archäologie*
RN *Revue numismatique*
RSF *Rivista di studi fenici*
SAOC Studies in Ancient Oriental Civilization
SAHL Studies in the Archaeology and History of the Levant
SBLDS Society of Biblical Literature Dissertation Series
SEL *Studi epigrafici e linguistici sul Vicino Oriente antico*
SHCANE Studies in the History and Culture of the Ancient Near East
SIMA Studies in Mediterranean Archaeology
SMEA Studi Micenei ed Egeo-Anatolici
SWBA Social World of Biblical Antiquity
TA *Tel Aviv*
TAVO *Tübinger Atlas des Vorderen Orients*
Ug. Ugaritic
UF *Ugarit-Forschungen*
UT *Ugaritic Textbook*, by C. Gordon (Rome, 1965)

UZK	Untersuchungen der Zweigstelle Kairo
VT	*Vetus Testamentum*
VTSup	Supplements to Vetus Testamentum
WBC	Word Biblical Commentary
ZA	*Zeitschrift für Assyriologie und vorderasiatische Archäologie*
ZAW	*Zeitschrift für die alttestamentliche Wissenschaft*
ZDMG	*Zeitschrift der Deutschen Morgenländischen Gesellschaft*
ZDPV	*Zeitschrift des Deutschen Palästina-Vereins*
ZPE	*Zeitschrift für Papyrologie und Epigraphik*

Publications of Lawrence E. Stager

1969 An Inscribed Potsherd from the Eleventh Century B.C. *BASOR* 194:45–52.

1971 Climatic Conditions and Storage in the Persian Period. *HTR* 64:448–50.

1973 Excavations in the Dhali Region, Cyprus. *AJA* 77:213.

1973 (with M. C. Marvin and A. M. Walker) Report on a Colloquium at M.I.T. *Archaeology* 26:63.

1974 (with A. M. Walker and G. E. Wright, editors and contributors) *American Expedition to Idalion, Cyprus: First Preliminary Report, Seasons of 1971 and 1972*. BASORSup 18. Cambridge, Mass.: American Schools of Oriental Research.

1974 El-Bouqeiᶜah [in Chronique Archéologique]. *RB* 81:94–96.

1974 Idalion and the War. *ASOR Newsletter* 6:1–4.

1974 (with M. C. Marvin and A. M. Walker of the Cambridge Archaeology Seminar) *Reconstructing Complex Societies: An Archaeological Colloquium*, ed. C. B. Moore. BASORSup 20. Cambridge, Mass.: American Schools of Oriental Research.

1975 Carthage: The Punic Project. *ASOR Newsletter* 3–4:10–11.

1976 Achor; Agriculture. In *The Interpreter's Dictionary of the Bible—Supplementary Volume*, ed. K. Crim. Nashville, Ky.: Abingdon.

1976 Farming in the Judean Desert during the Iron Age. *BASOR* 221:145–58.

1976–80 *Oriental Institute Annual Report* 1975–76; 1976–77; 1977–78; 1978–79; 1979–80 [reports on the Punic Project at Carthage]

1977 Carthage 1977: The Punic and Roman Harbors. *Archaeology* 30:198–200.

1977 (with H. Hurst) A Metropolitan Landscape: The Late Punic Port of Carthage. *World Archaeology* 9: 334–46.

1978 Excavations at Carthage 1975, The Punic Project: First Interim Report. In *Preliminary Excavation Reports: Bâb edh-Dhrāᶜ, Sardis, Meiron, Tell el-Ḥesi, Carthage (Punic)*, ed. D. N. Freedman, 151–90. AASOR 43. Cambridge, Mass.: American Schools of Oriental Research.

1980 The Rite of Child Sacrifice at Carthage. In *New Light on Ancient Carthage*, ed. J. G. Pedley, 1–11. Ann Arbor, Mich.: University of Michigan Press.

1981 Highland Village Life in Palestine Some Three Thousand Years Ago. *Oriental Institute News and Notes*, March 1981.

1981 (with S. R. Wolff) Production and Commerce in Temple Courtyards: An Olive Press in the Sacred Precinct at Tel Dan. *BASOR* 243:95–102.

1982 The Archaeology of the East Slope of Jerusalem and the Terraces of the Kidron. *JNES* 41:111–21.

1982 Carthage: A View from the Tophet. In *Phönizier im Westen*, ed. H. G. Niemeyer, 155–66. Madrider Beiträge 8. Mainz am Rhein: Philipp von Zabern.

1982 The Rise of Horticulture in the Levant. *Oriental Institute News and Notes*, January 1982.

1983 The Finest Olive Oil in Samaria. *JSS* 28:241–45.

1983 Harran in History and Tradition. *Oriental Institute News and Notes*, May 1983.

1984 Carthago Ha Phinikit-Hanamal Hamiskhariveh "Tofet" [in Hebrew]. *Qadmoniot* 17:39–49.

1984 (with S. R. Wolff) Child Sacrifice at Carthage—Religious Rite or Population Control? *BAR* 10/1:31–51.

1984 Phoenicisch Karthago de Handelshaven en de Tofet. *Phoenix* 28:84–113.

1985 The Archaeology of the Family in Ancient Israel. *BASOR* 260:1–35.

1985 Archaeology, History and the Bible: The Israelite Settlement in Canaan. In *Biblical Archaeology Today: Proceedings of the International Congress on Biblical Archaeology, 1985*, ed. J. Amitai, 83–87. Jerusalem: Israel Exploration Society.

1985 The Firstfruits of Civilization. In *Palestine in the Bronze and Iron Ages: Papers in Honour of Olga Tufnell*, ed. J. N. Tubb, 172–188. London: Institute of Archaeology, University of London.

1985 Merenptah, Israel and Sea Peoples: New Light on an Old Relief. *EI* 18:56*–64*.

1986 (with D. L. Esse) Ashkelon 1985–1986. *ESI* 4–5:2–6.

1987 (with D. L. Esse) Ashkelon 1985–1986. *IEJ* 37:68–72.

1988 Archaeology, Ecology and Social History: Background Themes to the Song of Deborah. In *Congress Volume: Jerusalem, 1986*, ed. J. A. Emerton, 221–34. VTSup 40. Leiden: Brill.

1989 (with A. M. Walker) *American Expedition to Idalion, Cyprus 1973–1980.* OIC 24. Chicago: Oriental Institute, University of Chicago.

1989 A Personal Remembrance of Yigael Yadin As Biblical Archaeologist and Historian. *EI* 20:xiv–xvi.

1989 The Song of Deborah: Why Some Tribes Answered the Call and Others Did Not. *BAR* 15/1:51–64.

1990 Chapters 1 and 2 ("In the Footsteps of the Philistines" and, with D. L. Esse, "Ashkelon Excavations: The Leon Levy Expedition") in *Ashqelon: 4,000 and Forty More Years* [in Hebrew], vol. 1, ed N. Arbel. Tel Aviv: Graph-Or Daphtal.

1990 Shemer's Estate. *BASOR* 277/278:93–107.

1990 Das Silberkalb von Aschkelon. *Antike Welt* 21/4:271–72.

1991 When Canaanites and Philistines Ruled Ashkelon. *BAR* 17/2:2–19.

1991 Why Were Hundreds of Dogs Buried at Ashkelon? *BAR* 17/2:20–37.

1991 Eroticism and Infanticide at Ashkelon. *BAR* 17/2:38–57.

1991 *Ashkelon Discovered: From Canaanites and Philistines to Romans and Moslems.* Washington, D.C.: Biblical Archaeology Society.

1991 Painted Pottery and Its Relationship to the Weaving Crafts in Canaan during the Early Bronze Age I. *EI* 21:83*–88*.

1991 Silbernes Kalb in Aschkelon entdeckt. *Bibel und Kirche* 46/3:127–29.

1991 Un Veau d'argent découvert à Ashqelôn. *Le Monde de la Bible* 70:50–52.

1992 The Periodization of Palestine from Neolithic through Early Bronze Age Times. In *Chronologies in Old World Archaeology* (3d ed.), vol. 1, ed. R. Ehrich, 22–41. Chicago: University of Chicago Press.

1993 Ashkelon. In *The New Encyclopedia of Archaeological Excavations in the Holy Land*, ed. E. Stern, 1:103–12. New York: Simon and Schuster.

1993 In Memoriam: Douglas L. Esse. *BAR* 19/1:20–21.

1993 Toward the Future: It's Just a Matter of Time. In *Biblical Archaeology Today, 1990: Proceedings of the Second International Congress on Biblical Archaeology, Jerusalem, June–July 1990*, vol. 2, 746–55. Jerusalem: Israel Exploration Society and Israel Academy of Sciences and Humanities.

1994 (with I. Carmi et al.) The Dating of Ancient Water-Wells by Archaeological and ^{14}C Methods: Comparative Study of Ceramics and Wood. *IEJ* 44:184–200.

1994 (with M. D. Coogan and J. C. Exum, co-editors) *Scripture and Other Artifacts: Essays on the Bible and Archaeology in Honor of Philip J. King.* Louisville, Ky.: Westminster John Knox.

1995 (with B. L. Johnson) Ashkelon: Wine Emporium of the Holy Land. In *Recent Excavations in Israel: A View to the West*, ed. S. Gitin, 95–109. Archaeological Institute of America Colloquia and Conference Papers 1. Dubuque, Iowa: Kendall/Hunt.

1995 Benjamin Mazar (1906–1995). *BAR* 21/6:22–23, 77.

1995 The Impact of the Sea Peoples in Canaan (1185–1050 B.C.E.). In *The Archaeology of Society in the Holy Land*, ed. T. E. Levy, 332–48. New York: Facts on File.

1996 Ashkelon and the Archaeology of Destruction: Kislev 604 B.C.E. *EI* 25:61*–74*.

1996 The Fury of Babylon: Ashkelon and the Archaeology of Destruction. *BAR* 22/1:56–69, 76–77.

1997 (with M. Faerman et al.) DNA Analysis Reveals the Sex of Infanticide Victims. *Nature* 385:212–13.

1998 Forging an Identity: The Emergence of Ancient Israel. In *The Oxford History of the Biblical World*, ed. M. D. Coogan, 123–75. New York: Oxford University Press.

1999 The Fortress Temple at Shechem and the "House of El, Lord of the Covenant." In *Realia Dei: Essays in Archaeology and Biblical Interpretation in Honor of Edward F. Campbell, Jr.*, ed. P. Williams and T. Hiebert, 228–49. Atlanta: Scholars Press.

1999 Jerusalem and the Garden of Eden. *EI* 26:183*–94*.

2000 Another Mould for Cakes from Cyprus: In the Queen's Image. *Rivista di Studi Fenici* 28:6–11.

2000 (with J. A. Greene and M. D. Coogan, co-editors) *The Archaeology of Jordan and Beyond: Essays in Honor of James A. Sauer.* SAHL 1. Winona Lake, Ind. Eisenbrauns.

2000 Jerusalem As Eden. *BAR* 26/3:36–47, 66.

2001 (with P. J. King) *Life in Biblical Israel*. Louisville, Ky.: Westminster John Knox.

2001 Port Power in the Early and the Middle Bronze Age: The Organization of Maritime Trade and Hinterland Production. In *Studies in the Archaeology of Israel and Neighboring Lands in Memory of Douglas L. Esse*, ed. S. R. Wolff, 625–38. SAOC 59. Chicago: Oriental Institute, University of Chicago.

2002 (with R. D. Ballard et al.) Iron Age Shipwrecks in Deep Water off Ashkelon, Israel. *AJA* 106:151–68.

2002 The MB IIA Ceramic Sequence at Tel Ashkelon and Its Implications for the "Port Power" Model of Trade. In *The Middle Bronze Age in the Levant: Proceedings of an International Conference on MB IIA Ceramic Material, Vienna, 24th–26th of January 2001*, ed. M. Bietak, 353–62. CChEM 3. Vienna: Österreichische Akademie der Wissenschaften.

2003 The Patrimonial Kingdom of Solomon. In *Symbiosis, Symbolism, and the Power of the Past: Canaan, Ancient Israel, and Their Neighbors from the Late Bronze Age through Roman Palaestina*, ed. W. G. Dever and S. Gitin, 63–74. Winona Lake, Ind.: Eisenbrauns.

2003 Phoenician Shipwrecks in the Deep Sea. In *Sea Routes from Sidon to Huelva: Interconnections in the Mediterranean 16th–6th c.* B.C. (Proceedings of the International Symposium held at Rethymnon, Crete, September 29–October 2, 2002), ed. N. Stampolidis, 233–47. Athens: Museum of Cycladic Art.

2005 Phoenician Shipwrecks and the Ship Tyre (Ezekiel 27). In *Terra Marique: Studies in Art History and Marine Archaeology in Honor of Anna Marguerite McCann*, ed. J. Pollini, 238–54. Oxford: Oxbow.

2006 Biblical Philistines: A Hellenistic Literary Creation? In *"I Will Speak the Riddles of Ancient Times": Archaeological and Historical Studies in Honor of Amihai Mazar*, ed. A. M. Maeir and P. de Miroschedji, 375–84. Winona Lake, Ind.: Eisenbrauns.

2006 Chariot Fittings from Philistine Ashkelon. In *Confronting the Past: Archaeological and Historical Essays on Ancient Israel in Honor of William G. Dever*, ed. S. Gitin, J. E. Wright, and J. P. Dessel, 169–76. Winona Lake, Ind.: Eisenbrauns.

2006 (with F. M. Cross) Cypro-Minoan Inscriptions Found in Ashkelon. *IEJ* 56:129–59.

2006 The House of the Silver Calf of Ashkelon. In *Timelines: Studies in Honour of Manfred Bietak*, vol. 2, ed. E. Czerny et al., 403–10. OLA 149. Leuven: Peeters.

2006 New Discoveries in the Excavations of Ashkelon in the Bronze and Iron Ages [in Hebrew]. *Qadmoniot* 39:131.

2006 Yigael Yadin and Biblical Archaeology. In *In Memory of Yigael Yadin, 1917–1984: Lectures Presented at the Symposium on the Twentieth Anniversary of His Death*, ed. J. Aviram, 13–27. Jerusalem: Israel Exploration Society.

2007 (with P. A. Mountjoy) A Pictorial Krater from Philistine Ashkelon. In *"Up to the Gates of Ekron": Essays on the Archaeology and History of the Eastern Mediterranean in Honor of Seymour Gitin*, ed. S. W. Crawford et al., 50–60. Jerusalem: W. F. Albright Institute of Archaeological Research and Israel Exploration Society.

2008 Ashkelon. In *The New Encyclopedia of Archaeological Excavations in the Holy Land*, vol. 5, *Supplementary Volume*, ed. E. Stern. Jerusalem: Israel Exploration Society.

forthc. (with M. Bietak and K. Kopetzky) Stratigraphie comparée nouvelle: The Synchronisation of Ashkelon and Tell el-Dabᶜa. In *Proceedings of the Third International Congress on the Archaeology of the Ancient Near East (ICAANE 3)*, ed. P. de Miroschedji and J.-P. Thalmann.

forthc. (with R. J. Voss) A Sequence of Tell el-Yahudiyah Ware from Ashkelon. In *Tell el-Yahudiyah Ware from Egypt and the Levant*, ed. M. Bietak. Vienna: Österreichische Akademie der Wissenschaften.

1. Lawrence Stager and Biblical Archaeology

by J. David Schloen

Twenty years ago, in the autumn of 1988, I met Lawrence Stager for the first time, in a class on "Biblical Archaeology" that he taught at Harvard. Looking back at my notes from that course, I am struck by the extent to which his lectures—not so much the facts he presented as the issues he emphasized and the questions he raised—reflected a creative and compelling intellectual vision. At the time, being new to the field, I had no idea that I was being treated to a fresh and illuminating perspective on many of the old chestnuts of biblical archaeology, a perspective that drew upon broad reading in history, anthropology, sociology, and philosophy, and was neither incoherently eclectic nor dogmatically narrow and reductive.

In hindsight, I can see that Stager had, quite early in his career, achieved a rare balance between theory and data, making them talk to one another in new ways in order to enhance our understanding of the ancient past. His love of archaeological fieldwork, and his savoring of particular finds, was apparent from the moment he began speaking, both in the classroom and in private conversation—with the bonus that his discourses were spiced with funny stories about the people and places involved. But he would readily move from the particularities of fieldwork and data to abstract sociological and economic concepts borrowed from diverse sources. He did this, not to seem more "scientific," or to mystify and make more impressive inherently banal observations, but in order to explain the burgeoning archaeological evidence. He saw the need in biblical archaeology, in particular, for greater engagement with comparative ethnohistorical data on such phenomena as kin-based social and political organization, premodern agricultural practices, long-distance trade, etc., coupled with a conceptual framework that would indicate the suitability of a given comparison for the Bronze and Iron Age Levant and the further implications of a particular ethnographic or historical analogy for an overall model of ancient Levantine society.

In pursuing this agenda, Stager was and is strongly influenced by the approach of Fernand Braudel, the great French historian of the *Annales* school, whose book on *The Mediterranean and the Mediterranean World in the Age of Philip II* and other works provide conceptual tools that Stager eagerly embraced. In particular, Braudel's concept of *la longue durée*, the long-term environmental and geographical factors that slowly but surely shape historical and cultural developments, often more powerfully than the ephemeral events on which traditional historiography had lavished its attention, resonated with Stager and other archaeologists of his generation. In the context of biblical archaeology, this led him to study Israelite society from the ground up, in terms of its physical setting and resources, its farming and herding practices, its houses and family structures, and its demographic features on both local and national scales. All of these are brilliantly treated in his influential 1985 article on "The Archaeology of the Family in Ancient Israel" and are given more extensive treatment in his 2001 book (co-authored with Philip King) on *Life in Biblical Israel*.

With respect to the ancient economy, Stager has followed Braudel in stressing the powerful effects of long-distance interregional trade, especially maritime trade, as a mechanism for the reorientation of production and settlement in the agricultural and horticultural hinterlands of the Levant. As early as the third millennium B.C.E., in his view, the inland inhabitants of the southern Levant produced large quantities of olive oil and wine that were shipped to Egypt via coastal port cities such as Ashkelon, the site he has been excavating for more than twenty years. Anonymous economic processes produced a systemic integration of widely separated settlements without conscious planning or top-down political control. Stager elaborated this economic model in an influential 2001 paper on "Port Power in the Early and the Middle Bronze Age." Its great virtue is that it makes clear predictions about the distribution of settlements and artifacts that can be tested empirically, especially because it involves a long-term time scale—on the order of centuries and even millennia—that is amenable to archaeological investigation.

In some respects, however, Stager diverges from the Braudelian tendency to downplay short-term events (*l'histoire événementielle*) in favor of the slowly moving trends of *la longue durée*. Stager's affinity for explanatory generalizations that span broad regions and time periods is tempered by his fascination with concrete particulars—the products and ideas of individual human beings. More than most archaeologists, he has always made extensive use of biblical and other textual evidence in his research, hearing in such sources unique human voices expressing views and values that cannot be explained exclusively (and perhaps not at all) by environmental and material factors. Stager's research has therefore largely avoided the taint of materialist reductionism that plagues so many archaeological treatments of ancient social and economic development.

In this respect, he remains connected to the tradition of biblical archaeology in which he was trained. Steeped in the Bible as a farmboy in Ohio, he came to Harvard in the 1960s and studied with G. Ernest Wright, Frank M. Cross, Yigael Yadin, Roland de Vaux, and others. He was immersed in and became intimately familiar with the dominant approach in American biblical archaeology, which stemmed from William F. Albright, the teacher of Wright, Cross, and many others. In this approach, archaeology was not an end in itself; it was not an independent discipline but was a tool, together with textual studies, for reconstructing the history and culture of Israel. But that history and culture were too often understood by the older generation of biblical archaeologists in terms of individual great men and great events, with the result that much excavated evidence was ignored as attention was focused on the all-too-rare remains of datable historical events and personages.

Over the years, Stager has sought a mediating position between the two poles of reductionist materialism, which emphasizes underlying anonymous processes and structures, and idealist event-history, which seeks explanations for historical trends (if at all) in a mental or spiritual realm far removed from the practical realities of daily life. In so doing, he joins a quest that has animated many perceptive scholars for a century or more, who have sought models of explanation that can do justice both to individual human *agency* and to collective social *structure* (to put it in the terms used in sociological literature). The agency-structure linkage has received little sustained attention in biblical or Near Eastern archaeology; however, explanatory models of human behavior, social organization, and social change ultimately incorporate some view or other of the relationship between individual agency and social structure. In my view, the best models incorporate agency at the very heart of the model, framing the analysis of repeated patterns of behavior in terms of typical motivations for action on the part of individuals who have particular beliefs about the world. Max Weber's "patrimonial" model of premodern political organization, adopted by Stager for ancient Israel (e.g., in his 2003 article on "The Patrimonial Kingdom of Solomon") is just such a motivational model that explains the linkage between the typical choices of individual agents, based on their understanding of their social situation, and the long-term patterns of behavior evident in social institutions and architectural and artifactual remains.

In particular, Stager attempts to relate the unique particulars revealed in individual artifacts and idiosyncratic textual narratives to general explanations by finding intersections between the different temporal scales—long-term, medium-term, and short-term—that were articulated by Fernand Braudel. This approach is nowhere more illuminating than in Stager's treatment of religious iconography and architecture, as in his 1999 article on "Jerusalem and the Garden of Eden." In the realm of religious action and religious symbolism, it is clear that all three temporal scales interact and must all be addressed in order to understand the data at our disposal. On one level, the level of event-history, the construction of a temple or the inauguration of a cult is a datable event that resulted from the decision of a ruler who was responding to a variety of political, economic, and perhaps even religious impulses. On the medium-term time scale of economic and demographic analysis, religious establishments and sacrificial systems have an economic cost that can be calculated and a social function that can be elucidated in the context of a more general model of how power is legitimated and social order is maintained. And on the temporal scale of the *longue durée*, religious symbolism and its expression in architecture and artifacts are rooted in enduring cosmologies, which are themselves anchored in human experience of the natural environment, as in the case of Iron Age Jerusalem and its echoes of the primordial Garden of Eden.

Here, especially, Stager finds common ground with his intellectual ancestors in biblical archaeology, many of whom had a keen interest in the development of Israelite religion in its wider Near Eastern context. He has continued and broadened this emphasis, bringing to bear new data while preserving and extending the style of investigation pioneered by his academic forebears. It is clear that Stager's goal is to improve and in some cases correct the tradition of biblical archaeology, but not fundamentally reject it or forget its achievements. In fact, in recent years he has become a vocal champion of older views of the Davidic monarchy, to take one example, defending the traditional chronology and the historicity of the United Monarchy against revisionist scholars.

The striking range of topics Stager has addressed and the contrasting modes of his research—from the mundane mechanics of farming to magnificent representations of the divine, from sweeping models of trade to painstaking descriptions of individual artifacts—bespeak an unusual balance of contrasts that not only marks his scholarship but, for those who know him, reflects his personality. He is a man who is simultaneously earthy and refined; capable of forceful bluster when the occasion demands it and also of great tact and sensitivity. His tastes are both high and low; he is both traditional and radical; his enthusiastic embrace encompasses all kinds of people and ideas. And to a remarkable degree, what makes him interesting as a person is what makes him interesting and insightful as a scholar. He savors particulars but reaches for generalizations, injecting into the tedium of data collection the thrill of discovering something of larger significance that sheds light on human experience.

Most of all, his gift as a friend and as a scholar is the gift of story-telling. From the whirl of events and observations he can be counted on to draw a narrative that makes sense of what he has seen and heard, always with a humorous twist. In so doing, he transforms what in other hands would be dry and meaningless particulars, or sterile and abstruse concepts, braiding them into a coherent story that, if not always convincing, is usually provocative and always entertaining.

The power of narrative imagination, selecting and synthesizing details into a larger scheme, is no doubt what brought a landlocked Ohio farmboy to the Mediterranean Sea, where he has excavated at Idalion in Cyprus, Carthage in Tunisia, and Ashkelon in Israel—not to mention Gezer and Tell el-Ḥesi, and a seaborne excursion with Robert Ballard to study Iron Age shipwrecks in the deep sea. Those of us who have had the privilege of digging with him have seen a master at work, able to spot items of significance and make from mute fragments a compelling tale.

2. Solomon's Patrimonial Kingdom: A View from the Land of Gilead

by Tristan J. Barako

A few years ago, the dedicatee of this volume colorfully referred to the "pummeling" received by kings David and Solomon at the hands of biblical "minimalists" and revisionist Israeli archaeologists (Stager 2003:63). Since then, the barrage has continued (e.g., Finkelstein and Silberman 2006, esp. pp. 161–62), but few body blows have been landed (Coogan 2006). In defense of the "maximalist" paradigm, Stager combined evidence contained within the biblical text with archaeological data to demonstrate that the Solomonic kingdom should still be sought in such tenth-century B.C.E. strata as Megiddo VA–IVB, Taanach IIB, Hazor X, and Gezer VIII. This kingdom was patrimonial in origin and structure, as evidenced, for example, by the administrative districts created by Solomon (1 Kings 4:7–19). Contrary to numerous eminent biblical historians (but cf. Aharoni 1979: 280), Stager argued that these districts closely followed preexisting tribal boundaries and were not a bureaucratic imposition of the United Monarchy.

The sixth district listed in 1 Kings 4 was located in the northern Transjordan and had as its center Ramoth-gilead (v. 13), a site sometimes identified with Tell er-Rumeith. Thanks to generous funding from the Shelby White–Leon Levy Program for Archaeological Publication, I will publish the excavations conducted at Rumeith.[1] My preliminary analysis of these excavations and of the biblical texts relating to the northern Transjordan corroborates Stager's reconstruction of the Solomonic kingdom.

Biblical Texts

Various texts in the Hebrew Bible report that the tribes of Reuben, Gad, and the half-tribe of Manasseh settled in the Transjordan (Numbers 32, Deut. 3:12–17, Josh. 13:15–33, 1 Chron. 5:23–26). Within and among these texts there are numerous discrepancies in detail; moreover, these tribal territories are vaguely defined as compared to those in the Cisjordan (Boling 1988:347–48). Nevertheless, the half-tribe of Manasseh consistently receives the regions of northern Gilead and Bashan, the latter of which included Argob. The boundaries of northern Gilead, which are never clearly delineated by the biblical writers, appear to have been the Jabbok River on the south, the Yarmuk River on the north, the Jordan River on the west, and the desert to the east (see figure 1). Bashan was north of the Yarmuk, west of the Sea of Galilee and the Jordan, south of Mount Hermon, and east of Jebel Druze.

The clans headed by Manasseh's sons, Machir and Jair, are singled out for having led the conquest of these regions. More specifically, Jair is credited with taking villages and renaming them, appropriately, *ḥawwōṯ yāʾîr*.[2] They were located either in Bashan (Deut. 3:14, Josh. 13:30) or Gilead (Num. 32:41; see also Judg. 10:4 and 1 Chron. 2:22), in a region that most likely corresponds to the Plain of Irbid between the mountains of ʿAjlun and the Yarmuk River (Weippert 1997:25; MacDonald 2000:123). The *ḥawwōṯ yāʾîr* were assigned to the provincial official (נצב) Ben-geber, who administered Solomon's sixth district and had his seat at Ramoth-gilead (1 Kings 4:13). Ben-geber's portfolio included also the sixty well-fortified cities that had once belonged to Og, King of Bashan (Deut. 3:4–5). These cities were allotted to the half-tribe of Manasseh, either through Jair (Deut. 3:3–5, 13–14) or Machir (Josh. 13:29–31).

There is, therefore, considerable territorial consistency between the tribal allotment of half-Manasseh and Solomon's sixth administrative district (Kallai 1986:64; contra Wright 1967:67). As far as this district is concerned, it appears that the "premonarchic clan and tribal allocations remained intact" (Stager 2003:68). They were not replaced by a rational bureaucratic system that promoted loyalty to the royal household at the expense of kin-based sodalities. Some of the aforementioned consistency is to be expected given that three of the five key texts (Deuteronomy 3, Joshua 13, and 1 Kings 4) are commonly attributed to a single scribal circle, the "Deuteronomistic School" (Dtr). The fourth and fifth texts (Numbers 32 and 1 Chronicles 5), however, were products of the Priestly Writer and the Chronicler,

---

[1] Larry Stager was instrumental in the establishment of the White-Levy Program and currently serves on its board. Dozens of archaeologists working in the Middle East and eastern Mediterranean regions have benefited from this program—few more so than I.

[2] The word חוות, singular חוה, is otherwise unattested. It appears only in connection with Jair's conquest and related texts, thus its precise meaning is unclear. Arabic *ḥiwāʾ*, which means "circle of tents or houses," is a probable cognate (Rainey 1975:109); thus חוות is usually rendered as "villages."

respectively.[3] Despite the obvious borrowings among four of the five texts,[4] there are good reasons to believe that much of the source material behind them was diverse and early. For instance, Num. 32:39–42, which describes the capture of Gilead by Manassite clans, is sometimes regarded as a Yahwistic, or even pre-Yahwistic, tradition (for references, see Budd 1984:338–42). Also, many biblical scholars believe that 1 Kings 4:7–19 is based on an archival list from the reign of Solomon (for references, see Stager 2003:67) or even from the reign of David (B. Mazar 1960:71; Ottosson 1969:219–20 [esp. v. 19]).

There is, however, one significant difference between the sixth district and the tribal allotment of half-Manasseh: Ramoth-gilead is the provincial seat of the former, but does not appear anywhere among the toponyms of the latter (Kallai 1986:273). In fact, Ramoth-gilead appears in the list of places of refuge (Deut. 4:43; Josh. 20:8) and the list of Levitical cities (Josh. 21: 38) within the *territory of Gad* (Deut. 4:43 and Josh. 20:8; see also Ottosson 1969:33). The location of Ramoth-gilead, therefore, is critically important in determining the degree of correlation between Solomon's sixth district and the territory of half-Manasseh.

Historical Geography

Three sites are commonly associated with Ramoth-gilead: er-Ramtha, Tell er-Rumeith, and Tell el-Ḥuṣn (see figure 1). The apparent preservation of the word *rāmōt* (= "heights") in the first two toponyms is the primary supporting evidence for these candidates. Chance excavations beneath the modern town of Ramtha produced Iron Age pottery, thus strengthening its identification with Ramoth-gilead (Glueck 1951:97). The site appears to fit the bill in terms of geography as well: it is located on the modern-day border between Syria and Jordan—that is to say, in northern Gilead, one of the regions assigned to half-Manasseh. According to Glueck, however, Ramtha falls short in terms of topography: the site does not dominate the surrounding plain in a way that would befit Ramoth-gilead's pivotal role in the wars between Israel and Aram-Damascus (see below).[5]

Several kilometers south of Ramtha is Tell er-Rumeith (map reference 247/212). Rumeith was strategically situated at the junction of the King's Highway and an east-west route linking Irbid to Mafraq (MacDonald 2000:201). The main mound is a rocky outcrop, about 50 m in diameter, that rises approximately 10 m above the surrounding plain (see figures 2 and 3). From the summit there are commanding views of the region, including Ramtha to the north and Irbid some 18 km to the west (Glueck 1951:98). Under the joint sponsorship of the American Schools of Oriental Research and the Pittsburgh Theological Seminary, Paul W. Lapp directed two seasons of excavation at the site in 1962 and 1967 (P. Lapp 1963; 1968; 1975; N. Lapp 1989; 1993). The 1962 sounding uncovered scant Iron Age, Hellenistic, Roman, Byzantine, and Islamic period remains east of the main mound. The absence of substantial architecture in this area indicated only transient occupation. In 1967, excavations were concentrated on the mound proper, where an Iron Age fort was found. A quarter or more of the fort was cleared, revealing coherent architecture and well-stratified ceramic assemblages dating to the late tenth, ninth, and eighth centuries B.C.E. (= Strata VIII–V; see below).

Numerous historical geographers and archaeologists, including Lapp, identified Ramoth-gilead with Tell er-Rumeith (for example, Glueck 1951:98–99; Noth 1959:50–51; Simons 1959:21, 207; Mittmann 1970:225; Aharoni 1979:441; for further references, see MacDonald 2000:202). The site meets the following criteria: (1) the modern name resembles the ancient toponym; (2) it is located in northern Gilead, which was part of the sixth Solomonic district; (3) it occupies a prominent position in the plain; and (4) its occupational history (tenth through eighth centuries B.C.E.) correlates well with events in the region as known from biblical accounts (see P. Lapp 1975: 119). Regarding the last point, Tell er-Rumeith appears to have been established in the tenth century B.C.E. (Stratum VIII), which is the approximate time when Ramoth-gilead became a provincial center (1 Kings 4:13).

[3] It is often noted that the verse containing the late appearance of the half-tribe of Manasseh in this chapter (v. 33) betrays a Deuteronomistic influence (see, e.g., Noth 1968: 235; Levine 2000:495).

[4] There are major differences between the Chronicler's version and earlier accounts of the Transjordanian settlement. Here it is worth noting only that, according to 1 Chron. 5:23, the half-tribe of East Manasseh resided in Bashan as far north as Mount Hermon.

[5] The author visited Ramtha and found that there were excellent views from the summit, particularly to the south and the east. Unfortunately, the modern town almost completely covers the ancient site, making it difficult to determine its size. Nonetheless, the topography suggests that the tell is large.

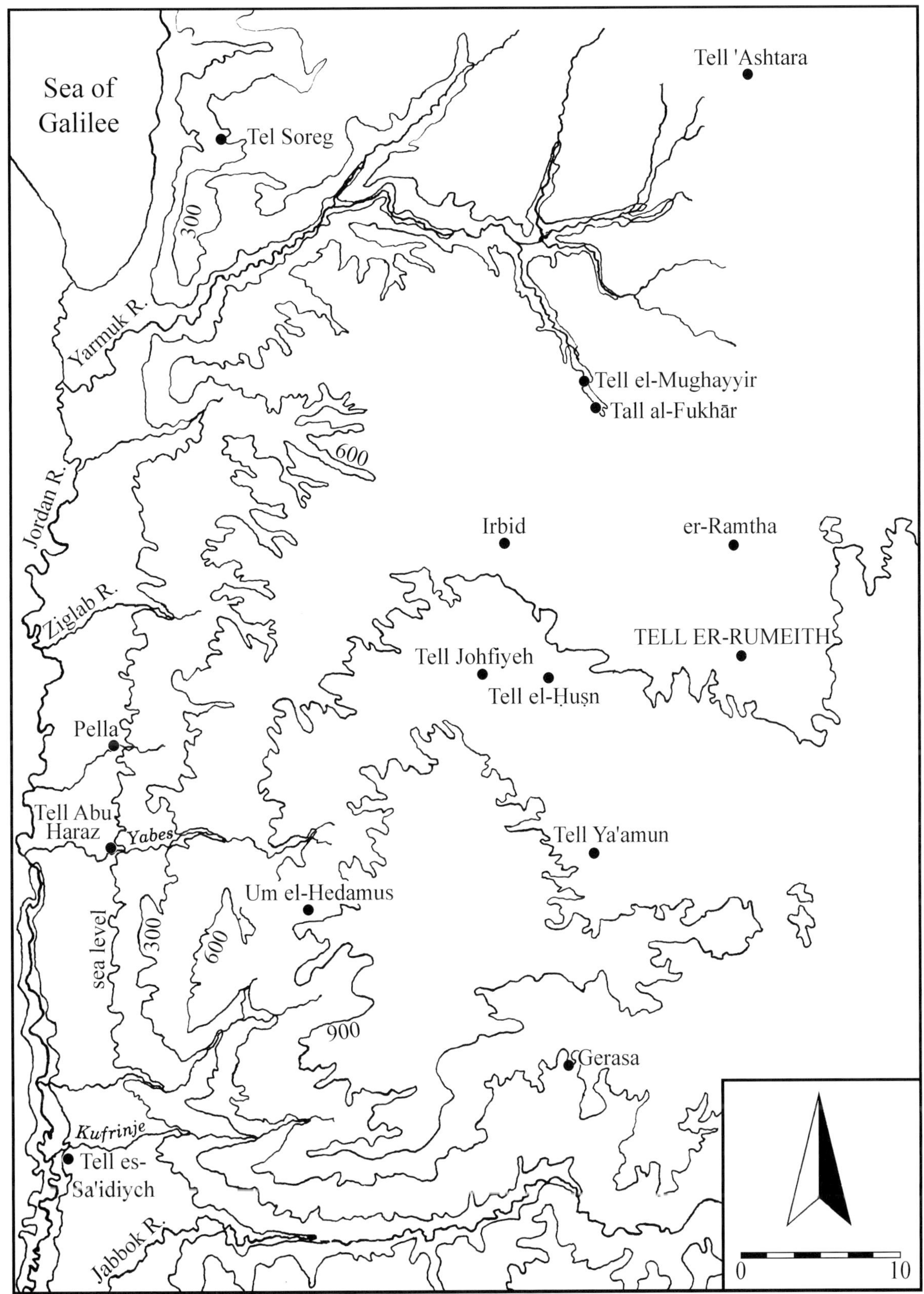

Figure 1. Excavated Iron Age sites in Gilead and Bashan

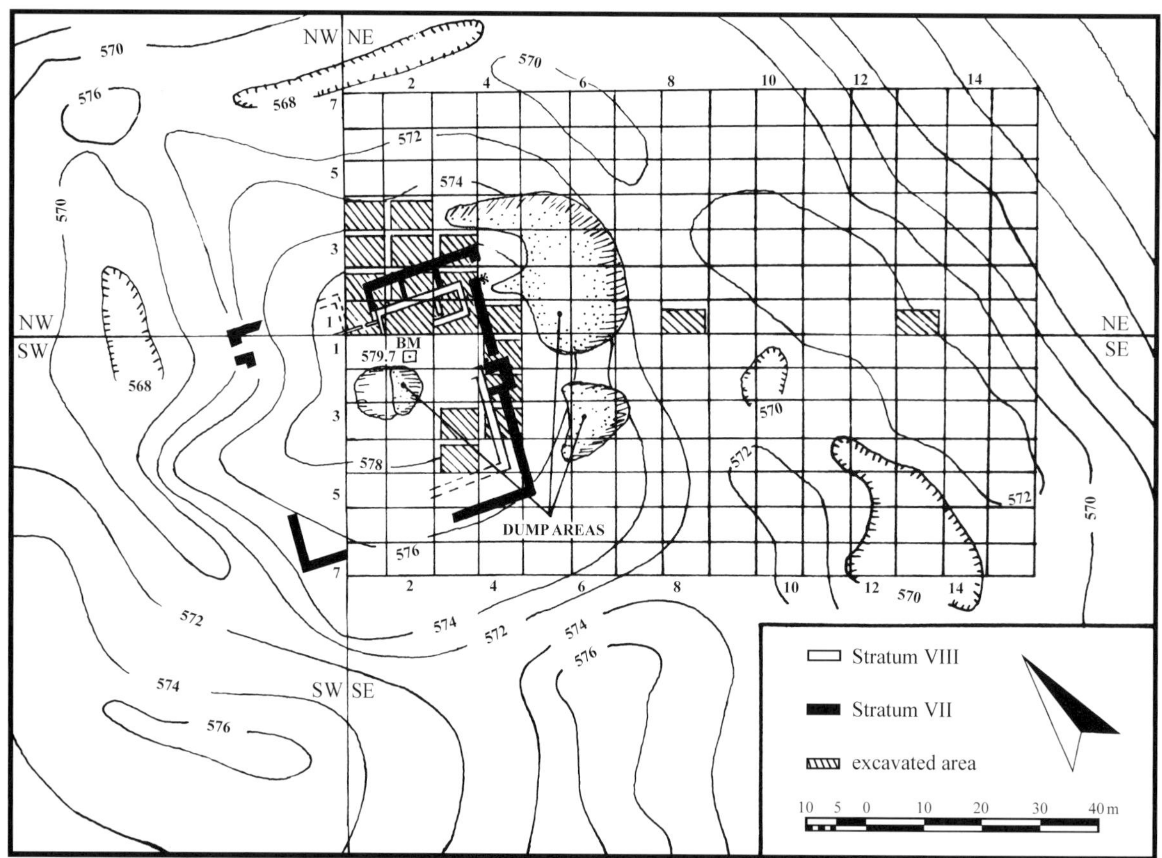

Figure 2. Tell er-Rumeith, Strata VIII and VII (adapted from P. Lapp 1975:pl. 29)

Figure 3. Tell er-Rumeith (view to south)
Photograph by P. Lapp

The main problem has to do with size. The prominence of Ramoth-gilead in the struggle between the kingdoms of Israel and Aram-Damascus during the ninth century B.C.E. (1 Kings 22:1–40; 2 Kings 8:28–29, 9:1–13) indicates a site larger than Rumeith (N. Lapp 1989:497). The Stratum VIII fort covered little more than a tenth of a hectare (see figure 2). Even the expanded fort of Stratum VII (ninth century B.C.E.), including extramural buildings, was probably no more than 0.2 ha in area. For this reason, many scholars favor the more imposing Tell el-Ḥuṣn (e.g., Abel 1967:430–31; Lemaire 1981).

Tell el-Ḥuṣn is a large tell site located approximately 9 km southeast of Irbid (and ca. 12 km west of Tell er-Rumeith) in a fertile plain that connects northern Gilead with the Hauran. There has been no systematic excavation of the upper tell because of the modern cemetery that covers most of the summit; however, a surface survey (Glueck 1951:163) and a salvage excavation at the base of the mound (Leonard 1987:359, 388–89, fig. 16) have both produced Iron Age pottery. Tell el-Ḥuṣn, therefore, meets the criteria of geography and chronology. The most compelling evidence, as indicated above, is its size: at approximately 5 ha, the upper tell alone is many times larger than Rumeith.

No other sites have been plausibly identified with Ramoth-gilead. All three feasible candidates (that is, er-Ramtha, Tell er-Rumeith, and Tell el-Ḥuṣn) share the following features: (1) they are located in northern Gilead, more specifically, in the Plain of Irbid; (2) they have produced Iron Age pottery, either through excavation or survey; and (3) they occupy (to varying degrees) commanding positions above the surrounding plain.[6] Tell er-Rumeith's diminutive size, as noted above, precludes it from serious consideration. Perhaps it was instead one of the "sixty great cities with walls and bronze bars" administered by Ben-geber (1 Kings 4:13; see N. Lapp 1989:497). Tell el-Ḥuṣn is sufficiently large but lacks toponymic continuity. As for Ramtha, if the Iron Age settlement beneath the modern town is indeed extensive, then it may prove to be the strongest candidate.

Although there is disagreement about the identification of Ramoth-gilead, there is consensus regarding its general location, namely, the Plain of Irbid. This observation brings us back to the problem mentioned above: Ramoth-gilead was a place of refuge and a Levitical city within the territory of Gad; however, it was also the center of Solomon's sixth district, which is based on the tribal territory of half-Manasseh. According to the oldest traditions, the initial tribal allotment of Gad was centered to the north of the Arnon River (Num. 32:34–36). Later texts, however, situate Gad as far north as the Sea of Galilee (Josh. 13:24–28). It is likely that pressure from the kingdoms of Moab and Ammon forced the Gadites to resettle to the north at the expense of Reuben and also, perhaps, of half-Manasseh (de Geus 1992). Whoever compiled the lists of places of refuge and Levitical cities must have had this northern location of Gad in mind. The historical geography of Gad vis-à-vis Ramoth-gilead strengthens the argument that these lists date to the eighth century B.C.E. or later (for references, see Spencer 1992a; 1992b).

Based on the biblical evidence, then, the history of Ramoth-gilead may be summarized as follows. It was initially in the territory of half-Manasseh; it was the center of Solomon's sixth district, which was based on this tribal territory; and it later became a part of the territory of Gad, at which time it served as a place of refuge and Levitical city. The archaeological data, broadly speaking, bear out these historical developments.[7]

Archaeological Evidence

The archaeological investigation of Gilead and Bashan is meager in comparison with the other side of the Jordan. Still, there have been two major surveys of Gilead (Glueck 1951; Mittmann 1970) and systematic excavations at a handful of Iron Age sites in both regions. Glueck's extensive surveys of the Transjordan in the 1930s and 1940s included the region of Gilead, wherein he located 65 Iron Age sites. He did not differentiate between Iron I and II pottery; thus his results are useful only for tracking very broad paleodemographic changes in the region.

[6] Eusebius's location of Ramoth-gilead on the Jabbok River (146:4–5), which does not comport with the biblical evidence, is generally disregarded (Glueck 1951:96, n. 119; MacDonald 2000:201).

[7] Only the first two developments, which correspond to the Iron I–IIA periods, are considered here. The third, which concerns the late Iron Age and (possibly) the postexilic period, is beyond the scope of the present study.

A more methodologically rigorous survey of Gilead was carried out by Mittmann in the 1960s. Using greater chronological precision, he produced data that have illuminated the Israelite settlement in the northern Transjordan (see table 1). Most conspicuous is the nearly fivefold increase in the number of sites from the Late Bronze Age (n = 15) to the Iron Age I (n = 73; Mittmann 1970; see also Finkelstein 1988: 114–17). The increase is more prominent in the hilly ᶜAjlun region to the south, where the number of sites jumped from three (LB) to 42 (Iron I). To the north, in the flatter and more hospitable Plain of Irbid, the increase was more modest, from 12 to 31. This explosion of rural sites and thus of population in Gilead is almost certainly related to the settlement of Israelites, more specifically, the tribe of half-Manasseh. During the Iron II period, the number of sites decreased by roughly a third, to 49, but increased slightly in the Plain of Irbid from 31 (Iron I) to 34 (Iron II) (Mittmann 1970; see also Finkelstein 1988: 116–17).

Since the time of Mittmann's survey, there have been a number of smaller-scale surveys in Gilead (Banning et al. 1987; 1989; Bartl et al. 2001; Kamlah 2000; Lenzen and McQuitty 1988; Mabry and Palumbo 1993; Yassine et al. 1988). Most of the new site identifications that resulted have been incorporated into the *Tübingen Atlas* map series (*TAVO*) and the "Jordan Antiquities Database and Information System" (JADIS). In the *TAVO* map that corresponds roughly to the region of Gilead (Zwickel 1990:map 6), there are approximately 200 Iron Age sites.[8] Of these sites, 151 had Iron I pottery and 136 had Iron II pottery. According to JADIS, there are 46 LB II sites in the three sectors (1–3) that approximate the area of Gilead and 188 Iron I sites. Again, the increase was more dramatic in the ᶜAjlun region (from 15 to 103 sites) than in the Plain of Irbid (24 to 75). The number of sites decreased slightly to 178 in the Iron IIA/B and dropped further to 167 in the Iron IIC period. It seems that the wars between Israel and Aram-Damascus (1 Kings 22:1–40; 2 Kings 8:28–29, 9:1–13; Amos 1:3) and the Neo-Assyrian conquest (2 Kings 15:29; Nimrud K 2649/III R 10, 2, ND 400 and ND 4301 + ND 4305, translated in Tadmor 1994) did not significantly affect the settlement density of Gilead during the Iron II period.

Table 1. Survey Results in the Region of Gilead

Source	*LB II*	*Iron I*	*Iron II*	*IIA/B*	*IIC*
Mittmann	15	73	49		
TAVO		151	136		
JADIS	46	188		178	167

Few sites with Iron Age strata have been excavated in northern Transjordan.[9] North of the Yarmuk, pottery and/or architecture from both Iron I and Iron II were found at Tel Soreg (Kochavi 1989:6–9) and at Tell ᶜAshtara (biblical Ashtaroth; Abou Assaf 1968; 1969). South of the Yarmuk, salvage excavations at Irbid (Dajani 1966; Lenzen, Gordon, and McQuitty 1985) and at Tell el-Ḥuṣn (Leonard 1987) yielded evidence for settlement during Iron I and II. Excavations at Tell el-Mughayyir (Ibrahim and Mittmann 1987), Johfiyeh (Lamprichs 2003), Tell Yaᶜamun (Rose et al. 2003), and Khirbet Um el-Hedamus (Mabry and Palumbo 1993) suggest that these sites were inhabited more intensively during the Iron II than the Iron I. At Tall al-Fukhār, there was an occupational gap between Iron IB and IIC (Strange 1997). The site with the best stratified sequence from a wide exposure of Iron Age settlement is Tell er-Rumeith. For this reason, Rumeith will become (once published) the type-site for Iron Age Gilead. What follows is a preview of the publication, especially of Stratum VIII, which has been tentatively dated to the tenth century B.C.E.

The defense wall of the earliest fort (Stratum VIII), which was excavated on the northern and eastern sides of the mound, appears to have been constructed in casemate fashion (figures 4 and 5). Both the inner and outer walls were thick (between 1.25 and 1.5 m), made of mudbrick, founded on bedrock, and preserved in places to a height of nearly 2 m (figure 4). The entrance on the northern side of the fort was formed by a narrow gap in a thin, recessed curtain wall (= NE 1-1-44). If the excavated sections of the defense wall are any indication, then the fort's dimensions were approximately 37 × 32 m. The full extent of the eastern defense wall (ca. 32 m) was exposed after the southeastern corner was located by means of a probe in SE 4-4. The estimated length of the northern defense wall (ca. 37 m) is based on the assumption that the gate is at the midpoint.

[8] The significantly larger number is attributable in part to the inclusion of additional regions covered by this map, namely, the northern Jordan Valley (Ibrahim, Sauer, and Yassine 1976), and Bashan (north of the Yarmuk River).

[9] Numerous sites with Iron Age strata have been excavated, however, in the northern Jordan Valley (for example, Pella, Tell Abu Haraz, Tell es-Saᶜidiyeh, Tell Mazar, and Deir ᶜAlla). But this region is geographically distinct from the highlands of Gilead and Bashan.

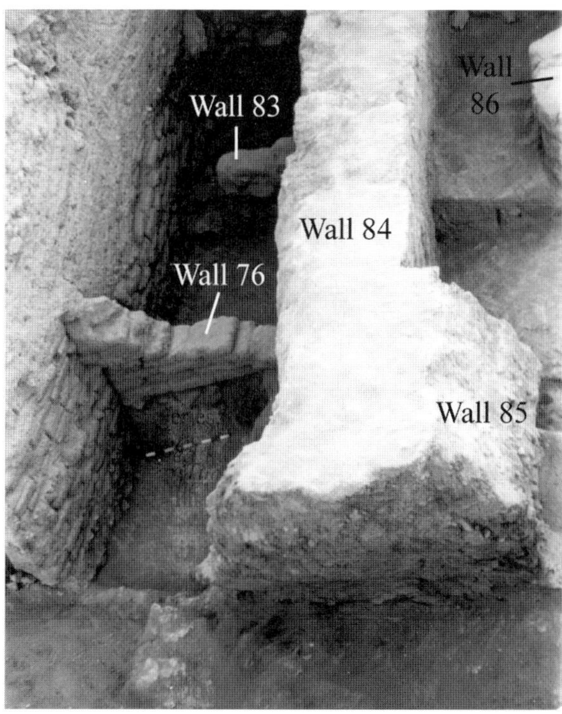

Figure 4. Stratum VIII defense wall in NE 3-1 (view to west)
Photograph by P. Lapp

Inside the wall, the limited amount of architecture uncovered included thick mudbrick walls (e.g., NE 3-2-65), tabuns (NE 2-1-114 and 115), bins (NE 2-1-121 and 122), and superimposed floors (NE 1-1-62 and 63). No extramural buildings were found in Stratum VIII. The small assemblage of pottery found on and between the floors of Stratum VIII, particularly in Square NE 3-1, was tentatively dated by Lapp to the tenth century B.C.E. Apparently this date was the result of field reading and a preliminary analysis carried out by the late James Sauer. Final dating awaits further study of all the Iron Age pottery (Strata VIII–V) to be carried out by the author (Barako, in prep.).

A destruction layer half a meter thick, comprised mostly of burnt mudbrick debris, covered Stratum VIII. The excavators dated this destruction to the early ninth century B.C.E. and provisionally attributed it to Ben-Hadad I, king of Aram-Damascus (1 Kings 15:20 = 2 Chron. 16:4). The transfer of the site from Israelite to Aramean control was detected in the pottery of Stratum VII, said to be "distinctly in the Syrian tradition" (P. Lapp 1975:116). Stratum VII also was surrounded by a casemate wall (see figure 2). The external wall was newly built from stone and the internal wall was a reuse of the Stratum VIII mudbrick defense wall. The thick destruction layer found along the entire defense line may be the result of an Israelite incursion, either by Jehoshaphat and Ahab (1 Kings 22:1–40) or by Ahaziah and Jehoram (2 Kings 8:28–29, 9:1–13), during the mid-ninth century B.C.E. (N. Lapp 1993). Both Stratum VI (ca. 800 B.C.E.) and Stratum V (733 B.C.E.) also ended in destruction, the latter probably wrought by Tiglath-pileser III (2 Kings 15:29). Thereafter, Rumeith lay abandoned until the Hellenistic period.

Conclusions

As Stager has shown, the patrimonial model is an indispensable tool for understanding the structure of Israelite society (King and Stager 2001:4–5, 202). This model can also be applied to Iron Age Gilead, where there was considerable territorial continuity between the tribal allotment of half-Manasseh and the sixth Solomonic district. Tribal affiliations, founded on the bedrock of the patrimonial household, were thus incorporated into the administrative system of Solomon's kingdom.

Although the capital of this district was probably not Tell er-Rumeith, it is still possible to view this site against the backdrop of the United Monarchy. As mentioned above, it is likely that Rumeith was one of the sixty well-fortified cities allotted to Ben-geber, the royal official in charge of the sixth district. In a broader context, the establishment of a fort in the tenth century B.C.E. in northern Gilead is not surprising when one considers the events that followed, for the kingdoms of Israel and Aram-Damascus spent the better part of the next hundred years vying for control of this region.

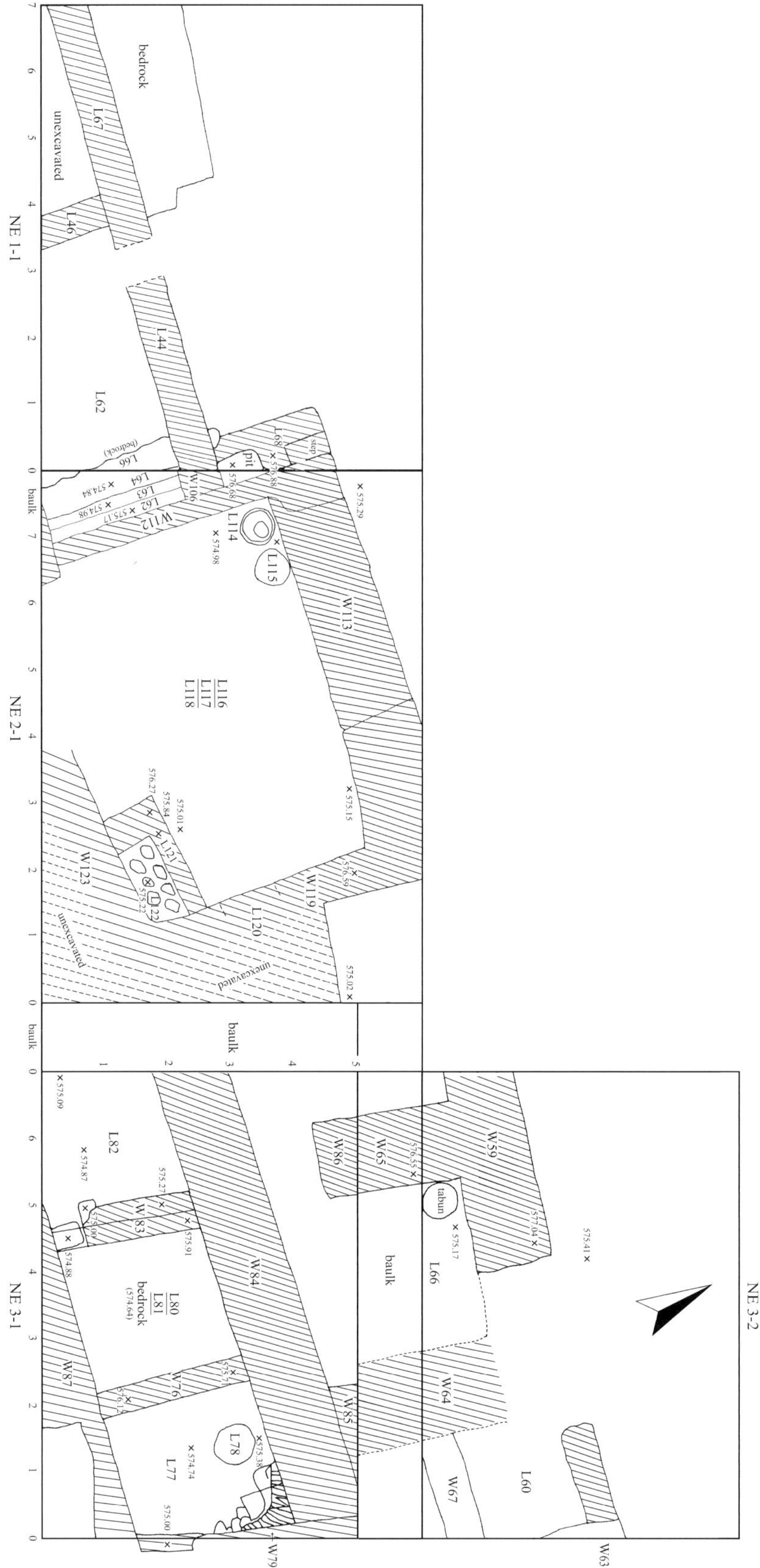

Figure 5. Stratum VIII of Tell er-Rumeith in the northeast quadrant

Bibliography

Abel, F. M.
1967 *Géographie de la Palestine*. Paris: Gabalda.

Abou Assaf, A.
1968 Tell-ᶜAschtara in Südsyrien; Erste Kampagne 1966. *AAAS* 18:103–20.
1969 Tell-ᶜAschtara, 2. Kampagne 1967. *AAAS* 19: 101–8.

Aharoni, Y.
1979 *The Land of the Bible: A Historical Geography*. Translated by A. F. Rainey. 2d ed. Philadelphia: Westminster.

Barako, T. J.
in prep. *Tell er-Rumeith: An Iron Age Border Town in the Land of Gilead; The Excavations Directed by Paul W. Lapp, 1962, 1967*. ASOR Archaeological Report Series. Boston: American Schools of Oriental Research.

Banning, E. B., R. Dods; J. McCorriston, S. Monckton, and P. Sheppard
1987 Report on the Wadi Ziqlab Project 1986 Season of Excavations. *ADAJ* 31: 321–42.

Banning, E. B., R. Dods, J. J. Field, S. L. Maltby, J. McCorriston, S. Monckton, R. Rubenstein, and P. Sheppard
1989 Wadi Ziqlab Project 1987: A Preliminary Report. *ADAJ* 33:43–58.

Bartl, K., F. al-Khraysheh, and R. Eichmann
2001 Palaeoenvironmental and Archaeological Studies in the Khanāṣirī Region/Northern Jordan. Preliminary Results of the Archaeological Survey 1999. *ADAJ* 45:119–34.

Boling, R. G.
1988 *The Early Biblical Community in Transjordan*. SWBA 6. Sheffield: Almond.

Budd, P. J.
1984 *Numbers*. WBC 5. Waco, Tex.: Word.

Coogan, M. D.
2006 Assessing David and Solomon: From the Hypothetical to the Improbable to the Absurd. *BAR* 32/4:56–60.

Dajani, R. W.
1966 Four Iron Age Tombs from Irbed. *ADAJ* 11:88–101.

Finkelstein, I.
1988 *The Archaeology of the Israelite Settlement*. Jerusalem: Israel Exploration Society.

Finkelstein, I., and N. A. Silberman
2006 *David and Solomon: In Search of the Bible's Sacred Kings and the Roots of the Western Tradition*. New York: Free Press.

Geus, C. H. J. de
1992 Gad (Person). In *The Anchor Bible Dictionary*, ed. D. N. Freedman, 2:864–65. New York: Doubleday.

Glueck, N.
1951 *Explorations in Eastern Palestine*. Vol. 4, part 1. AASOR 25–28. New Haven, Conn.: American Schools of Oriental Research.

Ibrahim, M., and S. Mittmann
1987 Tell el-Mughayyir and Khirbet Zeiraqoun. *Newsletter of the Institute of Archaeology and Anthropology, Yarmouk University* 4:3–6.

Ibrahim, M., J. A. Sauer, and K. Yassine
1976 The East Jordan Valley Survey, 1975. *BASOR* 222:41–66.

Kallai, Z.
1986 *Historical Geography of the Bible: The Tribal Territories of Israel*. Jerusalem: Magnes.

Kamlah, J.
2000 *Der Zeraqōn-Survey 1989–1994. Mit Beiträgen zur Methodik und geschichtlichen Auswertung archäologischer Oberflächenuntersuchungen in Palästina*. ADPV 27/1. Wiesbaden: Harrassowitz.

King, P. J., and L. E. Stager
2001 *Life in Biblical Israel*. Louisville, Ky.: Westminster John Knox.

Kochavi, M.
1989 The Land of Geshur Project: Regional Archaeology of the Southern Golan (1987–1988 Seasons). *IEJ* 39:1–17.

Lapp, N. L.
1989 Rumeith (Tell el). In *Archaeology of Jordan*, vol. 2, part 2, *Field Reports, Sites L–Z*, ed. D. Homès-Fredericq and J. B. Hennessy, 494–97. Akkadica Supplementum 7. Leuven: Peeters.

1993 Rumeith, Tell er-. In *The New Encyclopedia of Archaeological Excavations in the Holy Land*, ed. E. Stern, 4:1291–93. New York: Simon and Schuster.

Lapp, P. W.
1963 Tell er-Rumeith. *RB* 70:406–11.
1968 Tell er-Rumeith. *RB* 75:98–105.
1975 Excavations at Tell er-Rumeith. In *The Tale of the Tell*, ed. N. Lapp, 111–19. Pittsburgh: Pickwick.

Lamprichs, R.
2003 Tell Johfiyeh: Ein eisenzeitlicher Fundplatz in Nordjordanien und seine Umgebung; Erste Ergebnisse der Ausgrabungskampagne 2002. *UF* 34:363–452.

Lemaire, A.
1981 Galaad et Makîr: Remarques sur la tribu de Manassé à l'est du Jourdain. *VT* 31:39–61.

Lenzen, C. J., R. L. Gordon, and A. M. McQuitty
1985 Excavations at Tell Irbid and Beit Ras, 1985. *ADAJ* 29:151–59.

Lenzen, C. J., and A. M. McQuitty
1988 The 1984 Survey of the Irbid/Beit Ras Region. *ADAJ* 32:265–305.

Leonard, A.
1987 The Jarash–Tell el-Ḥuṣn Highway Survey. *ADAJ* 31:343–90.

Levine, B. A.
2000 *Numbers 21–36: A New Translation with Introduction and Commentary*. AB 4a. New York: Doubleday.

Mabry, J., and G. Palumbo
1993 Wadi El-Yabis: The 1990 Excavations and Survey Season. *Syria* 70: 218–20.

MacDonald, B.
2000 *"East of the Jordan": Territories and Sites of the Hebrew Scriptures*. American Schools of Oriental Research Books 6. Boston: American Schools of Oriental Research.

Mazar, B.
1960 The Cities of the Territory of Dan. *IEJ* 10: 65–77.

Mittmann, S.
1970 *Beiträge zur Siedlungs- und Territorialgeschichte des nördlichen Ostjordanlandes*. Wiesbaden: Harrassowitz.

Noth, M.
1959 Gilead und Gad. *ZDPV* 75: 14–73.
1968 *Numbers: A Commentary*. Translated by J. D. Martin. Philadelphia: Westminster.

Ottosson, M.
1969 *Gilead: Tradition and History*. Coniectanea Biblica, Old Testament Series 3. Lund: Gleerup.

Palumbo, G., ed.
1994 *The Jordan Antiquities Database and Information System: A Summary of the Data*. Amman: Department of Antiquities of Jordan and American Center of Oriental Research. [*JADIS* was updated by S. Savage in 2003; see http://amon.nic.gov.jo/antiq/]

Rainey, A.
1975 Notes on Some Proto-Sinaitic Inscriptions. *IEJ* 25:106–16.

Rose, J. C., M. El-Najjar, N. Turshan, C. Hunton, and K. Rolf
2003 Tell Yaᶜamun. *AJA* 107:457–58.

Simons, J. J.
1959 *The Geographical and Topographical Texts of the Old Testament: A Concise Commentary in XXXII Chapters*. Studia Francisci Scholten Memoriae Dicata 2. Leiden: Brill.

Spencer, J. R.
1992a Refuge, Cities of. In *The Anchor Bible Dictionary*, ed. D. N. Freedman, 5:657–58. New York: Doubleday.
1992b Levitical Cities. In *The Anchor Bible Dictionary*, ed. D. N. Freedman, 4:310–11. New York: Doubleday.

Stager, L. E.
2003 The Patrimonial Kingdom of Solomon. In *Symbiosis, Symbolism, and the Power of the Past: Canaan, Ancient Israel, and Their Neighbors from the Late Bronze Age through Roman Palaestina*, ed. W. G. Dever and S. Gitin, 63–74. Winona Lake, Ind.: Eisenbrauns.

Strange, J.
1997 Tall al-Fukhār 1990–1991: A Preliminary Report. In *Studies in the History and Archaeology of Jordan*, vol. 6, *Landscape Resources and Human Occupation in Jordan through the Ages*, ed. G. Bisheh, M. Zaghloul, and I. Kehrberg, 399–406. Amman: Department of Antiquities.

Tadmor, H.
1994 *The Inscriptions of Tiglath-Pileser III, King of Assyria: Critical Edition, with Introductions, Translations and Commentary*. Jerusalem: Israel Academy of Sciences and Humanities.

Weippert, M.
1997 Israélites, Araméens et Assyriens dans la Transjordanie septentrionale. *ZDPV* 113:19–38.

Wright, G. E.
1967 The Provinces of Solomon (1 Kings 4:7–19). *EI* 8:58–68.

Yassine, K., T. M. Kerestes, B. G. Wood, and J. M. Lundquist
1988 An Archaeological Survey of the Three Reservoir Areas in Northern Jordan, 1978. In *Archaeology of Jordan: Essays and Reports*, ed. K. Yassine, 209–55. Amman: Department of Archaeology, University of Jordan.

Zwickel, W.
1990 *Eisenzeitliche Ortslagen im Ostjordanland.* BTAVO 81. Wiesbaden: Ludwig Reichert

3. The Dolphin Jug: A Typological and Chronological Assessment

by Manfred Bietak and Karin Kopetzky

This contribution is dedicated to Larry Stager, with whom we enjoyed a wonderful collaboration in our "stratigraphie comparée" project and whose ability to share and to inspire we greatly admire. We also would like to thank him for all the help, kindness, and friendship he has given us. May our collaboration endure for a long time to come.

In 1921, during his work at the pyramid of Amenemhat I in Lisht-North (figure 1), A. C. Mace excavated several shaft tombs, which had already been robbed in antiquity (Mace 1921). One of these, Tomb 879, consists of a shaft and three horizontal chambers at its bottom, each one originally containing a single burial, although only two coffins were found. In the disturbed rubble of this tomb a jug was found that is related to Tell el-Yehudiyeh Ware. It is known in the literature as the "Dolphin Jug" (Kantor 1965:23–24).

Unfortunately, the exact location of the jug was not recorded precisely and the tomb robbers had moved the offerings in a way that has made the reconstruction of its original context impossible. It is also not known whether the three chambers were cut simultaneously or one by one, and how precisely they are related to one other. But the robbery seems to have occurred soon after the deposition because the material in the shaft appears to be homogeneous (Bourriau 1996). The shaft of the tomb was cut from the floor of an extension of a late Middle Kingdom or early Second Intermediate Period house (figure 2). This was clarified by Felix Arnold in a more recent

Figure 1. Map showing excavation sites of vessels mentioned in the text

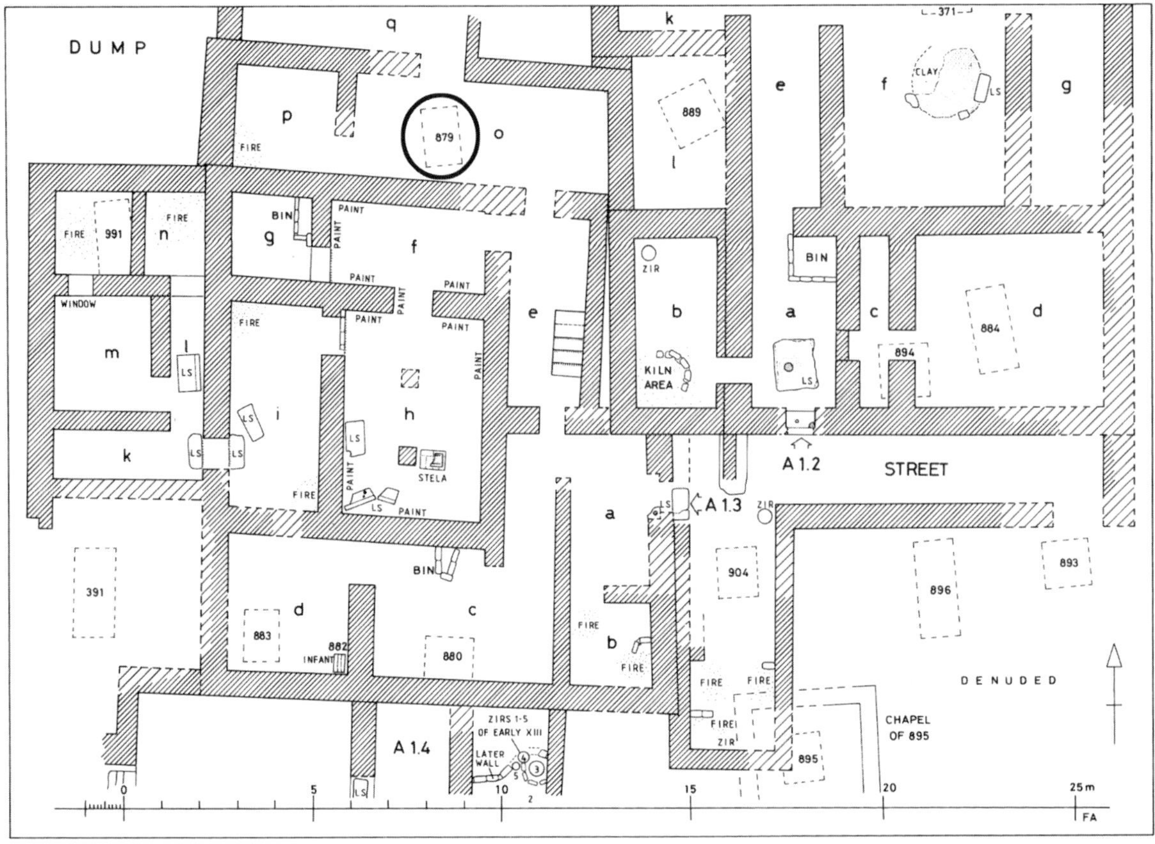

Figure 2. House A 1.3 at Lisht with Tomb 879 (circled)
after F. Arnold 1996:16, fig. 4

excavation: "The mouth shaft was cut from the floor level of the house into a dump of the late Twelfth Dynasty, located north of the house" (F. Arnold 1996:17).

This is an important statement, for it suggests that the shaft and the objects of the tomb postdate the Twelfth Dynasty. "Since the shaft was probably dug some time after the addition of the rooms o-p (the next to last building phase of the area), the tomb in all likelihood dates to the end of the occupation period of the house, i.e. the early Second Intermediate Period (about 1670–1610 B.C. according to the high chronology or 1640–1610 B.C. according to the low chronology). The shaft may actually have been used for the burial of the owner of the house" (F. Arnold 1996:17). Arnold also thinks that the Dolphin Jug originated either from the dump of the house or from a burial contemporary with the later use of the house. He believes that the jar might have been dumped as waste into the open shaft of the tomb, which must already have been robbed at that time. This is highly unlikely because such luxury ware is found normally in tombs and not in settlement dumps, especially since the jug was nearly complete (Allen et al. 1994:35).

The importance of this jug was first recognized by Helene Kantor, who dated it to the Thirteenth Dynasty and compared it with parallels from the Middle Bronze Age Levant (Kantor 1965). This jug and its associated pottery were first published by Barry Kemp and Robert Merrillees (1980:220–225) and later, in more detail, by Janine Bourriau (1996). It was also investigated using neutron activation analysis by Patrick McGovern (Allen et al. 1994:35–40). In accordance with the pottery associated with it, Bourriau dates the jug to the early Thirteenth Dynasty, up to the reign of King Awibre Hor (Bourriau 1996:116), which is thus still within the late MB IIA period (for the relationship between the Middle Bronze Age culture of the Levant and the dynastic chronology of Egypt, see Bietak 2002 and Cohen 2002).

In the following, we shall see that the Dolphin Jug should be dated slightly later than Bourriau's date. Since it is not clear whether the pottery collected with it from Tomb 879 originates from the same period as the jug itself, we shall, in our study, reanalyze the individual pieces according to their own value in order to determine whether their time periods, compared with parallels from other contexts, indeed correspond to the period of the Dolphin Jug, or whether there are indications that the tomb was occupied longer than was initially presumed.

The jug itself has a squat piriform body with a very high and pronounced shoulder (figure 3). Its short neck is delineated from the body by a ledge and it ends in a rim, which is rolled to the outside. A tri-coil loop handle sits completely on the shoulder of the vessel without attachment to the neck. The base is missing and is reconstructed with a base ring (Bourriau 1996:104). Bourriau's accurate drawing suggests that the lower part of the body may have been shaped in a mold, based on the fingertip impressions at the base. If the base had been fashioned on a wheel from one lump of clay, a spiral mark would likely have obliterated the finger-pinching done at the beginning of production. The upper part was most probably fashioned on a speedily rotating wheel, while the neck, including the ledge at its base, was manufactured separately like a small ring stand and then glued onto the central opening of the shoulder. There is an indentation in the wall below the zone of the ledge.

On the natural light-red burnished surface of this vessel are two registers of black figures set off from the light-red background. All of them look toward the left. Concerning the technique, we rely on the accurate description provided by Janine Bourriau (1996). The figures were painted on the light-red burnished surface with a manganese iron pigment, according to a chemical examination (Bourriau 1996:104). The outlines and the patterns within the bodies of the figures were incised afterwards, according to Bourriau. The outlines do not exactly match the outlines of the painted bodies. The surfaces of those figures were also highly burnished, probably in a second burnishing process (Bourriau 1996:105). Although the body of the jug was fired in a highly oxidizing environment, the black bodies of the figures suggest that they were covered during the firing process with a thin layer of some material that would flake off after the jug was taken out of the kiln. This was a very rare technique at the time; it anticipates the Greek black-figured ware. After firing, the outlines and patterns were filled in with a paste of calcium carbonate (Bourriau 1996:105).

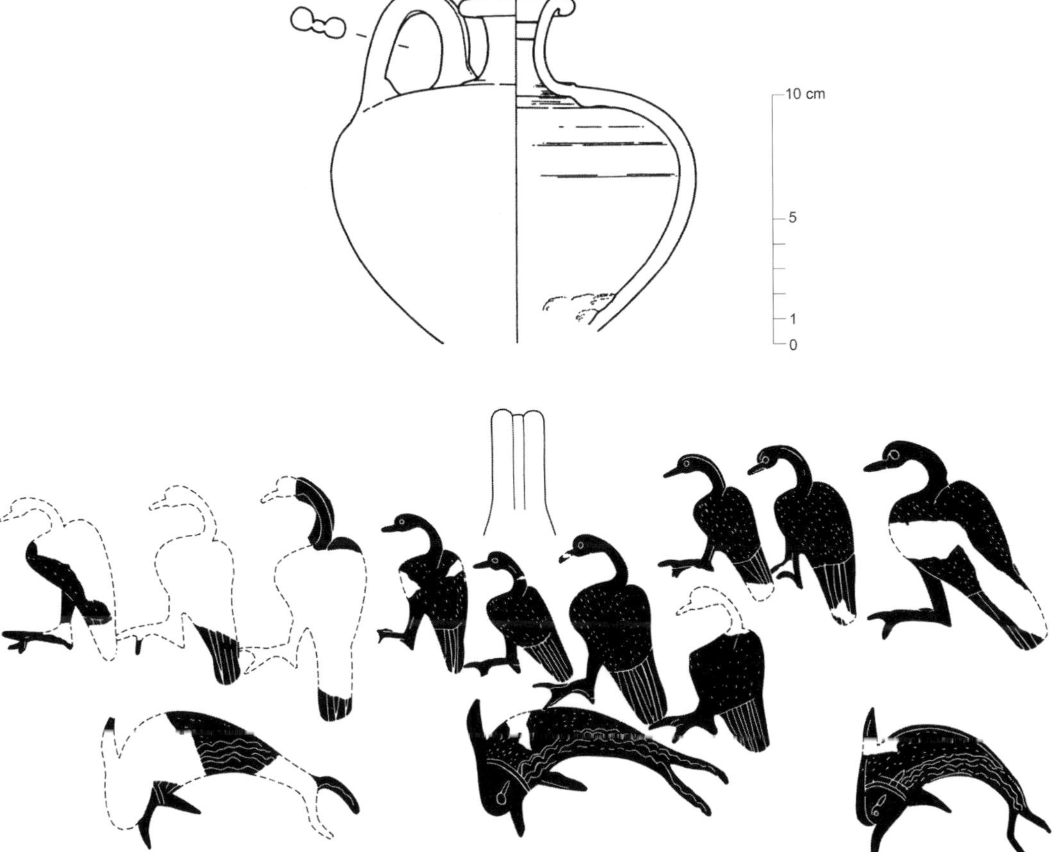

Figure 3. The "Dolphin Jug" from Tomb 879 at Lisht
MMA no. 22.1.95; after Bourriau 1996:103, fig. 2; 105, fig. 4

The lower register consists of three dolphins shown in the act of flipping out of the water, with their midsections bent upwards and their heads downwards. The lower parts of their bodies are filled with parallel wavy lines, the upper part with dots. The heads are set off with double lines.

The upper register consists of ten birds, also black-burnished and incised. The birds are divided into three groups, each group on top of a dolphin. There are two three-bird groups and one four-bird group. They have ascending invisible baselines. In one case, one group ascends above the other. The last bird is the largest. In the four-bird group a smaller bird was added behind the larger one.

The birds have thick, bent feet and relatively small heads. Their bodies are filled with dots. Their eyes, like those of the dolphins, are realistically outlined. The feathered tails show, in a linear fashion, the feathers' outlines. The birds can be identified most probably as geese. They were correctly identified already by Helene Kantor (1965); McGovern's identification of them as storks or cranes (Allen et al. 1994:32) is unlikely because some of them clearly have palmated feet.

Close Parallels in Technique and Style

The Dolphin Jug belongs to a rare ceramic type from the Levant. We know of only three other objects that can be considered close parallels:

1. A large krater (figure 4) was found recently in a multiple burial at Sidon (Doumet-Serhal 2004:140, fig. 88, S/1785a). On its shoulder is a frieze of five jumping dolphins with their heads downwards and facing right. They were painted and drawn on a burnished light-colored surface above stylized representations of waves (Doumet-Serhal 2006:40–43). The bodies are painted black and outlined with an incision, similar to the dolphins on the Lisht jug. There is also a ledge around the neck of the vessel.

Tomb 7, dated by Claude Doumet-Serhal to her Phase 5, contained at least three individual burials. Among the pottery found in this tomb are flaring carinated bowls, which are not known before the transitional MB IIA/B period,[1] as well as monochrome and bichrome painted juglets, which Manfred Bietak has called "painted Tell el-Yahudiyeh juglets" (Bietak 1986:347). They appear in Tell el-Dabᶜa not earlier than Phase E/3 (Bagh 1988:43; 2002:89–101). Pieces with bichrome paint have also been found in Tel Dan Stratum XII, Phase 4, from the transitional MB IIA/B period (Ilan 1996:161, fig. 4:4, 5) and in a tomb of the early MB IIB in Kfar Szold (Epstein 1974:16, fig. 1:5).

The most recent piece among these burial objects from Sidon is a piriform Tell el-Yehudiyeh juglet with four vertically incised segments. At Tell el-Dabᶜa, these juglets appear at the beginning of the Hyksos period in Phase E/2 (Bietak et al. 2001:176, fig. 4). Thus, Tomb 7 might have been in use for a longer time period.

2. The same technique of decoration can be found on a bowl from Tel Akko, which also shows black-burnished incised waves on a red-burnished surface (we would like to thank E. S. Marcus for this information). Unfortunately, this piece was found on the surface.

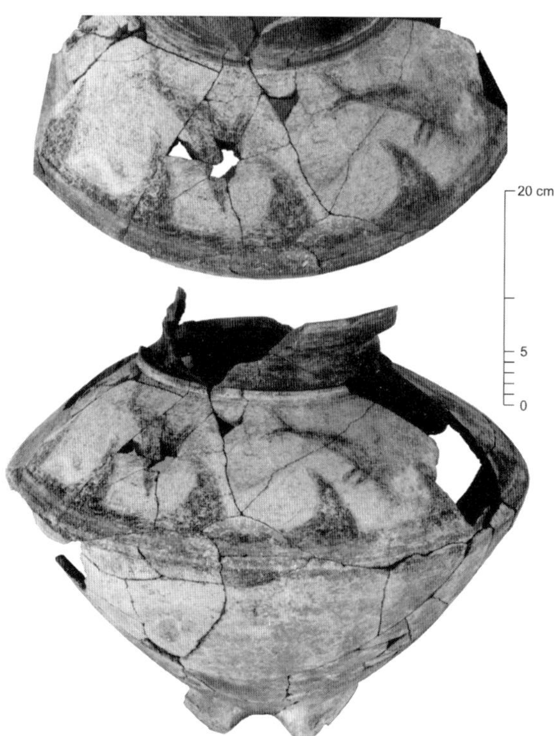

Figure 4. The dolphin krater from Sidon S/1785/197
after Doumet-Serhal 2006:41, fig. 15, 42, fig. 16

3. The third parallel (figure 5) is the nearly complete shoulder of a small juglet, recently published by Sarah Ben-Arieh (Ben-Arieh 2004:93, fig. 2.61:29). It was found in Tomb 510 at Tell Beit Mirsim. This burial cave was mainly occupied during the MB IIB

[1] For early parallels, see J. Kaplan 1955:9, fig. 2:14 (Tel Aviv Tomb 16); Albright 1933:50, pl. 4:9 (Tell Beit Mirsim Stratum F); Maeir 1997:302, fig. 4.2:2 (Tel Hazor Tomb 1181, last burial); Tufnell 1975–76:fig. 2:1, 2 (Ruweise Tomb 66).

and MB IIC periods and even later.[2] The juglet seems to originate from the earlier period of occupation of this cave. On the surface of the juglet are visible the faded remnants of three red (probably burnished) and incised birds, looking left, and one lotus flower.

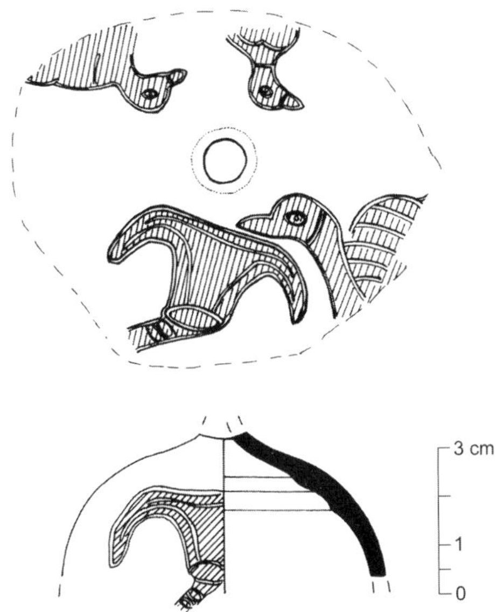

Figure 5. Juglet from Tell Beit Mirsim Tomb 510
IAA no. 84-1281; after Ben-Arieh 2004:93, fig. 2.61:29

Parallels Based on Motifs

The aforementioned juglet from Tell Beit Mirsim is a link to the Tell el-Yehudiyeh juglets with incised figural design. Although not produced by exactly the same technique as the jug from Lisht, Tell el-Yehudiyeh juglets with similar designs have been excavated at Tell el-Dabᶜa. These juglets (see figure 6) appear in burials of Phase E/3, with some degenerated late versions at the beginning of Phase E/2 (ca. first half until middle of the seventeenth century B.C.E.; Bietak 1991:125, pl. 800:1, 2). They have piriform bodies. One has a candlestick rim (Bietak and Hein 1994:232, no. 283); the others have rolled or everted rims, insofar as the rim is preserved (figure 6:1–4). None has a ledge around the neck. Most have a button base, which is sometimes degenerated; one has a ring button. Most of those juglets have a bipartite handle but three already have strap handles (figure 6:1–3). Only one brown-burnished juglet with incised lotus flowers (figure 6:5) shows the same type of tri-coil strap handle as the Dolphin Jug. Unfortunately, it is a stray find. Normally, this type of handle—a transition from bi- and tripartite handles to strap handles—is typical for the beginning of the MB IIB period at Tell el-Dabᶜa and can only be found on vessels from Phases F and E/3.

Nearly all examples of this class were locally produced and are either brown- or black-burnished. In Egypt, such juglets or fragments of them have also been found at Haraga, Touna, Abydos, and Thebes, and one fragment was found at Kerma in the Sudan (M. Kaplan 1980:fig. 126e, f, h, i, j). Other examples of such jugs with figural design were found at Byblos (figure 7:1); in Tomb 1 from Niveau X of Tell el-Ghassil in Lebanon (figure 7:2); and in Tomb 5 at Toumba tou Skourou on Cyprus (figure 7:3). They are close in style and have the same motifs (M. Kaplan 1980:327, fig. 126g). They may have been produced of Levantine clay.[3] There are some more examples from northern Lebanon and Palestine with only very rough designs, which may be seen as an imitation of those from Egypt, Byblos, and Cyprus (M. Kaplan 1980:fig. 127e, f).

The motifs show mainly birds and lotus flowers, either alone (Bietak and Hein 1994:232, no. 283) or in combination. While the heads of the birds show similarities to the Lisht jug, albeit with the beak drawn more upwards, the legs are drawn only with a single line and are longer and not folded like those of the Lisht birds. The wings are set off from the body and either filled with dots (figure 6:1–3) or, in the latest example, with lines (figure 6:4). Nevertheless, there is a relationship between this Tell el-Yehudiyeh Ware with figural design and the Dolphin Jug family, as shown by the example from Tell Beit Mirsim (figure 5). A link between the two groups is the jug from Toumba tou Skourou (figure 7:3), which also shows the band of lotuses like the Byblos example (figure 7:1), although the birds have folded legs with double outlines and their bodies are filled with dots, as on the Lisht jug. The birds of the Toumba tou Skourou specimen face to the right, but all have their heads turned around. The birds between the lotuses are turned 90° upwards (M. Kaplan 1980:fig. 127g). Because the Byblos jug (in the Louvre) also has the lower row of lotuses tied together with hanging gar-

[2] In this tomb, scarabs from the Eighteenth, Nineteenth, and Twenty-first/Twenty-second Dynasties were also found. These might have come from Tomb 500, according to B. Brandl (2004:142), and were later used in LB II and Iron II.

[3] The Byblos juglet was examined by M. Bietak in the Louvre (courtesy of the Louvre Département des Antiquités Orientales). It seems to be made of Levantine clay. The Toumba tou Skorou juglet is missing today; however, it was seen by Michal Artzy from the University of Haifa, who classified it as consisting of Levantine clay. There is another example from Byblos (fig. 127a), which seems to be from a provincial workshop.

lands, one may suspect that both are from the same workshop in Byblos, which had contact with the workshop that produced the Sidon krater (figure 4).

The three juglets from Tell el-Dabᶜa also have lotus flowers at the base, linked together with hanging garlands, and the bodies of the birds are also filled with dots (figure 6:1–3). But the legs of these birds consist of a single line and show, as usual at this site, no bend. The similarity in style of the three juglets from Tell el-Dabᶜa, as well as, in a more general sense, the similarity of the other figural incised juglets at this site with the examples from Byblos (figure 7:1) and Cyprus (figure 7:3), shows that both workshops were in close contact in the time of Phase E/3; that is, during the first half of the sixteenth century B.C.E., shortly before the period of Hyksos rule.

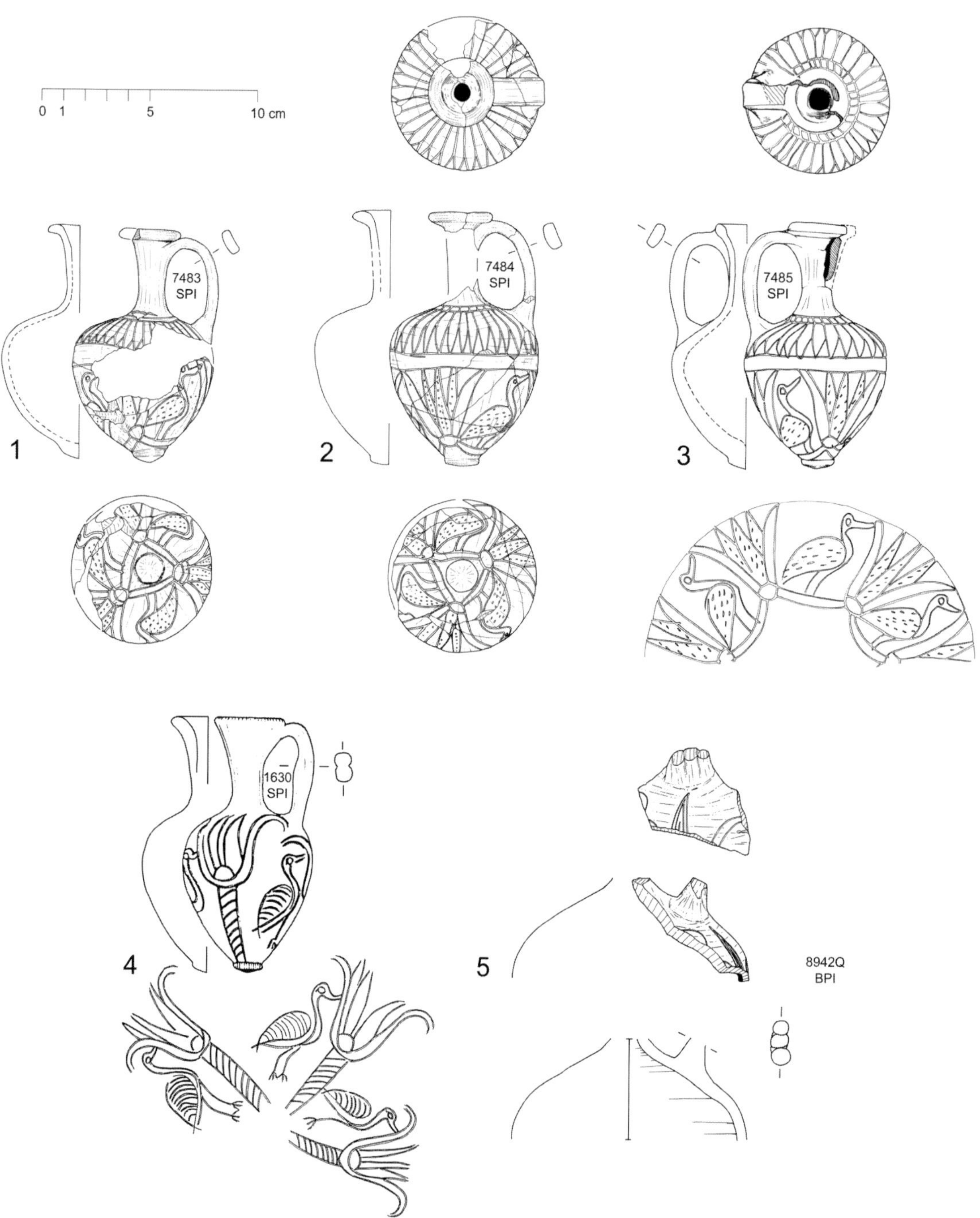

Figure 6. Juglets with birds and flower decoration from Tell el-Dabᶜa

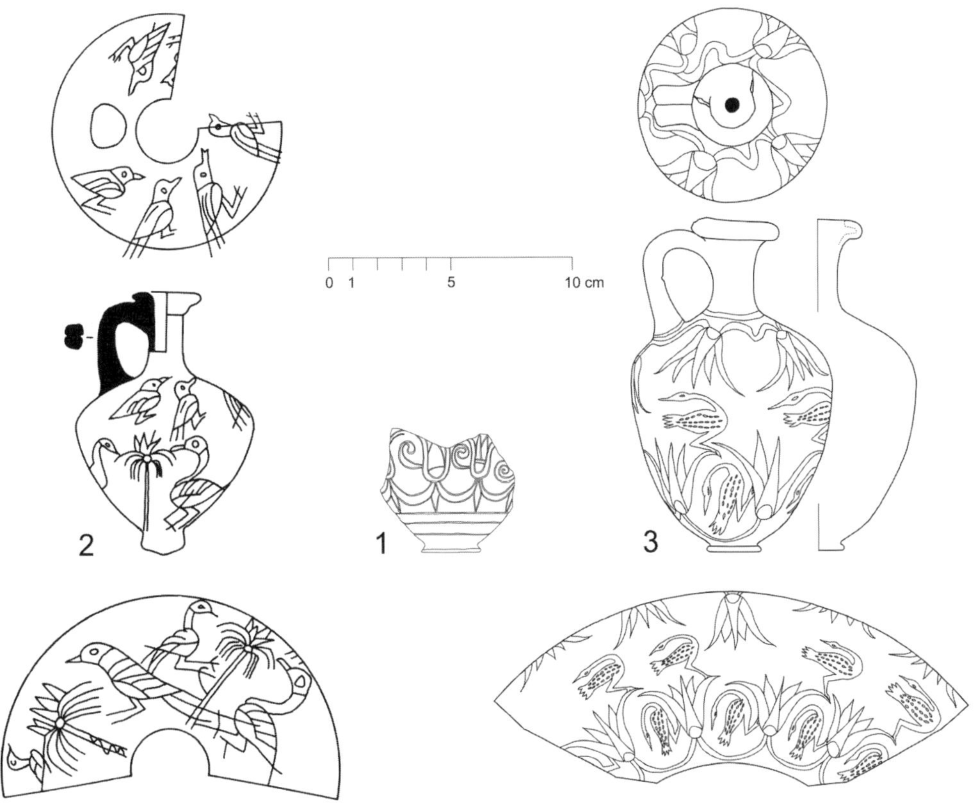

Figure 7. Juglets with faunal and floral decoration from Lebanon and Cyprus
1 after Montet 1928:pl.148 **2** after Doumet-Serhal 1996:197, pl. 15:2 **3** after Negbi 1978:144, ill. 1, 3, 4

Figure 8. Dolphins and fish on Minoan vessels
1 after Warren and Hankey 1989:242, pl. 12c **2** and **3** after Marinatos and Hirmer 1959:pls. 4, 11

The Origin of the Dolphin Motif in the Levant

Dolphins are an unusual decorative feature in the Levant. That we now have a similar frieze from Sidon produced with the same technique can be considered an especially fortunate coincidence (Doumet-Serhal 2004:fig. 3a–e). The white outlines and the wavy pattern in the lower body of the dolphins on the Dolphin Jug from Lisht, as well as the unnaturally forward position of their back fins, have been compared correctly with the dolphin paintings on Minoan pithoi, especially Pithos XIIb from Pachyammos with typical Middle Minoan III decoration (figure 8:1).[4] There is a difference, however, in the angle of the back fin: on the Lisht jug it matches the angle of the head in the front, while it is more clearly set off on the Minoan pithoi.[5]

The combination of at least two distinctive iconographic features in the depiction of the dolphins on the Lisht jug and on the Minoan pithoi cannot be dismissed lightly (Allen et al. 1994). There are no imports or evidence of contact between Egypt and Crete in this period, so the question arises how and when this motif could have been transmitted (Kemp and Merrillees 1980:220–225).

Is it a coincidence that in both Crete and the Levant the fish motif of Middle Minoan II (figure 8:2, 3) is succeeded by the dolphin motif of Middle Minoan III?[6] In the Levant, the fish motif appears in the lowest register on early Tell el-Yehudiyeh juglets of the late MB IIA. Of particular importance for us is the big jug in orange/red-burnished ware from the Tabet Collection in the Louvre (AO29886; figure 9:1), which is squat but is more double-conical in shape than piriform. Its handle is tripartite in triangular composition and is loop-shaped, affixed entirely on the shoulder and detached from the neck. It has a ring base. Its surface color is very similar to the Dolphin Jug. It has three zones of geometric white-incised decoration, filled with punctate impressions. In the lowest part are stylized fish (Nigro 2003:359, fig. 24).

Also found in Egypt are two black-polished incised Tell el-Yehudiyeh jugs of the Levanto-Egyptian Group, Type Piriform I-a, made of Levantine clay. One was found at Tell el-Dabᶜa (figure 9:2). It features five zones of geometric decoration, the lowermost consisting of a frieze of jumping fish (Bietak 1991:29, pl. 4). The handle is a tripartite loop handle detached from the neck, which is broken off. The jug was found in a stratified context in Phase G/2 in a late MB IIA layer (advanced Thirteenth Dynasty, ca. second half of the eighteenth century B.C.E.).

The other example is a sherd found by the excavations of the German Archaeological Institute under Dieter Arnold in Dahshur (figure 9:3). Although only a sherd, it displays a frieze of fish on top of a running spiral decoration near the base of a big jug (Arnold and Stadelmann 1977:pl. 4b). This combination indicates Minoan inspiration.

The transmission of the fish motif to the Levant can be explained now by the contacts that led to the dissemination of Kamares Ware in Middle Minoan IIB. Kamares Ware appears at Tell el-Dabᶜa in Phase G/4 (Walberg 1991; MacGillivray 1995) and at the same time in Ashkelon (Stager 2003:357; Bietak et al. in press), where Kamares Ware was found together with sealings of the late Twelfth and early Thirteenth Dynasty, between Ashkelon Phases 14 and 13, in a context that dates to the early Thirteenth Dynasty. Kamares Ware also appears in this period in Beirut in the Kharji tombs (Saidah 1993–94:pl. 17).

It seems possible, therefore, that during Middle Minoan IIB/IIIA there were sufficient contacts with the Levant to transmit the idea of the dolphin frieze to the coast of Lebanon. It is no coincidence that it was a locally made krater in Sidon that became the carrier of the motif because in Pachyammos dolphins appear on similar vessels. Despite the neutron activation analysis of the Dolphin Jug from Lisht, which suggests southern Levantine clay (Allen et al. 1994: 39), there is reason to believe that the Dolphin Jug was also produced in Lebanon, most likely in the same workshop as the Sidon krater. It is important now to assess the exact date of the Dolphin Jug.

Parallels to the Form from Tell el-Dabᶜa

Most of the dated parallels originate from Phases F and E/3 at Tell el-Dabᶜa. They share the same form but lack the incised and painted motifs. There is, however, no perfect parallel; there is always at least one attribute that does not match. The features crucial to the relative dating of the Dolphin Jug are:

---

[4] For the literature and discussion, see Kemp and Merrillees 1980:220ff.; Walberg 1986:64; Warren and Hankey 1989: 136. The most recent discussion is Höflmayer 2005:36–42.

[5] The dolphins on the Late Minoan wall paintings in the so-called Queen's Megaron have a much more realistic design, with the back fin in the correct position. Also, those dolphins show a dark wavy stripe with a double outline along the lower third of the body.

[6] For the fish motif, see Marinatos and Hirmer 1959:71, pl. 4 top (Kamares cup with a fish frieze moving right); p. 72, pl. 11 (pithos with frieze of fish in Kamares style on top of running spirals, in register below three wavy lines). For the dolphin motif, see Buchholz and Karageorghis 1973:69, 307, with literature; Walberg 1986:87, fig. 103.

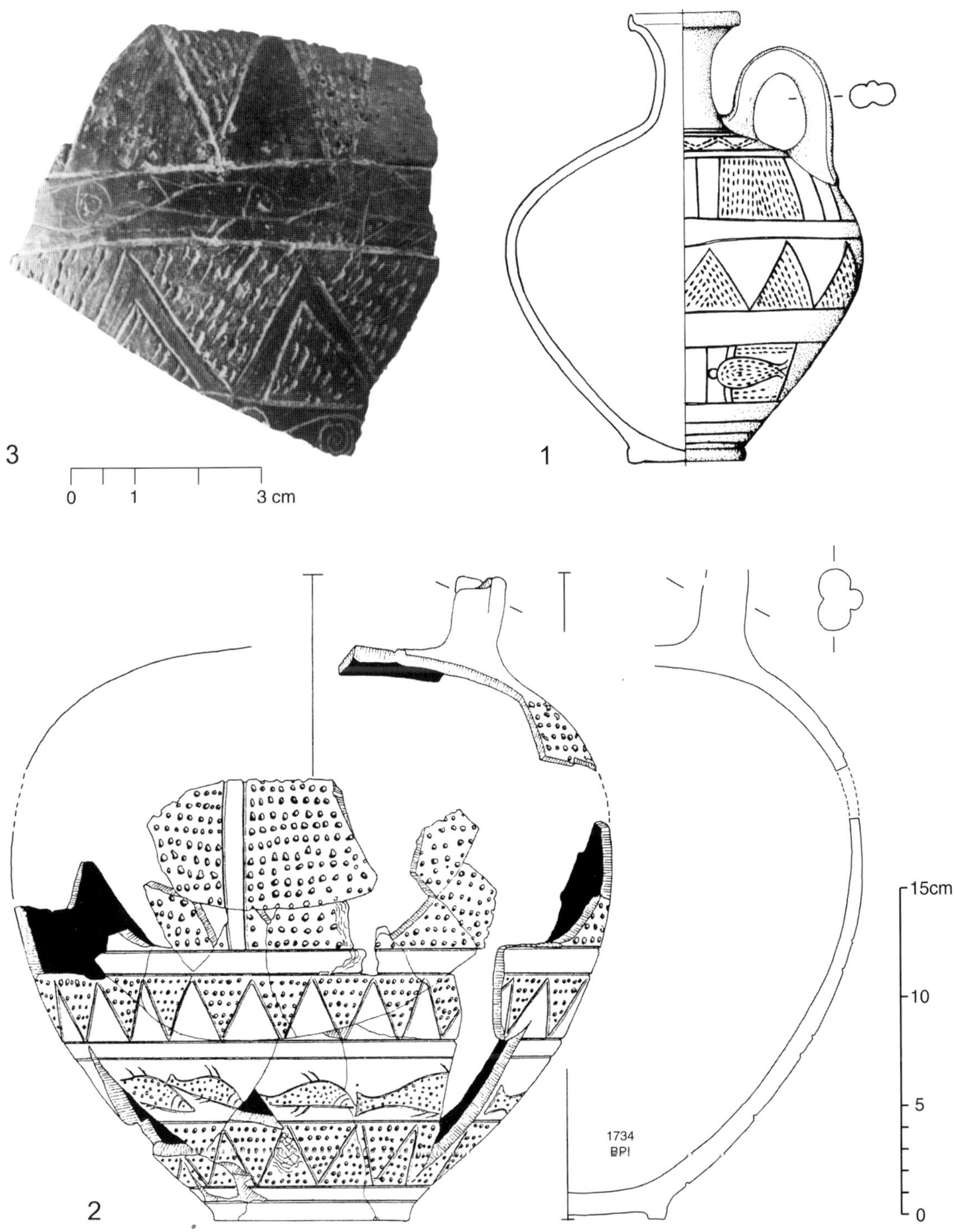

Figure 9. Tell el-Yehudiyeh jugs with fish

1 after Nigro 2003:359, fig. 24 **2** after Bietak 1991:29, pl. 4 **3** after Arnold and Stadelmann 1977:pl. 4

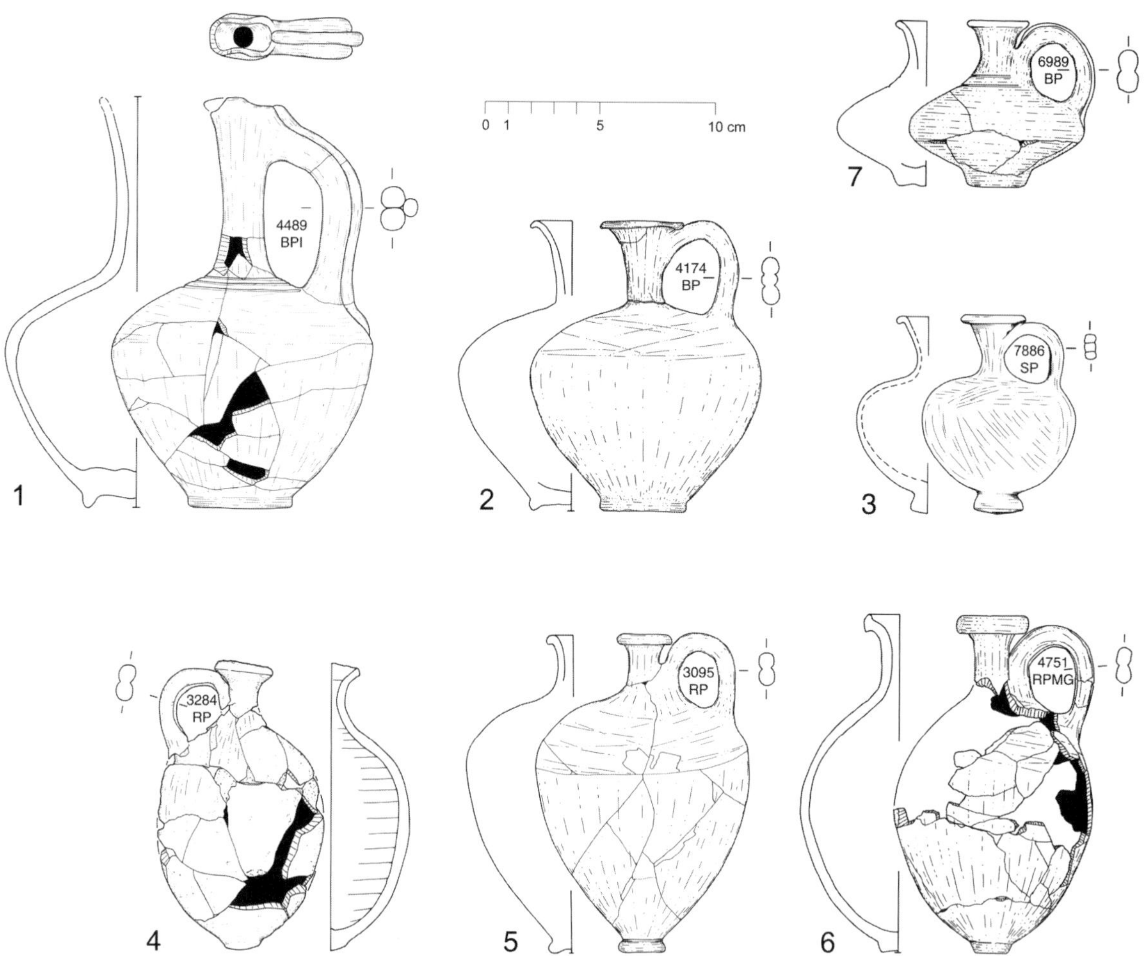

Figure 10. Monochrome juglets from Tell el-Dabᶜa

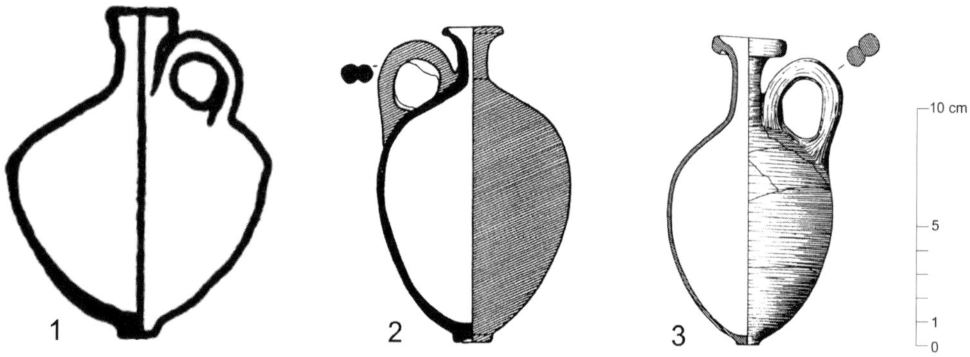

Figure 11. Juglets with loop-shaped handles from Tel Aviv (no. 1), Sidon (no. 2), and Kamid el-Loz (no. 3)
1 after Kaplan 1955:10, fig. 2:2 **2** after Doumet-Serhal 2004:130, fig. 73 **3** after Miron 1982:pl. 24:2

1. *Tripartite strap handle.* Typologically, this kind of handle lies in the middle of the development from a tripartite handle to a double handle. In the original tripartite version, the coils are put together in a triangular fashion, with the middle coil often slightly thinner and added along the median line of a bipartite coil handle (figure 10:1; Aston 2002:81, fig. 14:4).[7] The tripartite strap handle appears first in Phase F at Tell el-Dabᶜa (figure 10:2) and it lasts until Phase E/3 (figure 10:3). The examples are equally distributed between the two phases; some can only be attributed to a range that includes both phases (Forstner-Müller 2003:pl. 78:4; Aston 2004:148, fig. 507–514).[8]

2. *Loop-shaped handle on the shoulder of the jug, detached from the neck.* This appears first in a few examples in Phase G (figure 10:4; Kopetzky 1993:pl. 5:6), has a floruit in Phase F (figure 10:5, 6; Bietak 1991:72, pl. 37:4; Forstner-Müller 2003:pl. 45:7; Kopetzky 1993:pl. 37:11; Aston 2004:141, pl. 129: 459; 129, pl. 117:389, 390 [TD4901]),[9] and has a few occurrences in Phase E/3 (figure 10:7; Bietak 1991: 83, pl. 44:3, 4; Kopetzky 1993:71 no.1 [right]). More precisely, one may say that such handles exist on large jugs already in the MB IIA period, but they do not appear on smaller pieces until the end of MB IIA. In burials at Tell el-Dabᶜa, parallels can be found from the end of MB IIA, in Phase G/1–3 (see figure 10:4; Kopetzky 1993:pl. 5:6 [TD3284]) until Phase F (figure 10:5; Aston 2004:141, pl.129:459; Kopetzky 1993:pl. 37:11 [TD4751]),[10] and rarely in Phase E/3 (figure 10:7).

Juglets with loop handles have been found outside Tell el-Dabᶜa on the coast at Tel Aviv (figure 11:1; Kaplan 1955:10, fig. 2:2) as well as at Sidon (figure 11:2; Doumet-Serhal 2004:130, fig. 73/S/1715), Ruweise (Guigues 1938:53, fig. 77e), and Kamid el-Loz (figure 11:3; Miron 1982:pl. 24:2, Tomb 100).

3. *Rolled rim.* This feature appears from Phase F onwards (Forstner-Müller 2002:183, fig. 17:6; Kopetzky 1993:pl. 5:6; Aston 2004:142, pl. 463) and lasts throughout the Second Intermediate Period (Bietak 1991:292, pl. 270:3). At Tell el-Dabᶜa, it is a feature of the MB II B–C.

4. *Motif of incised birds.* Despite the stylistic and technological differences in the bird representations on the Dolphin Jug from Lisht, as discussed above, juglets with the motif of incised birds are restricted at Tell el-Dabᶜa to Phase E/3, with a few degenerated examples at the beginning of the following Phase E/2 (figure 6:4; Bietak 1991:pl. 80:1, 2).

Figure 10 shows typical examples from Tell el-Dabᶜa that demonstrate most of the attributes of the Dolphin Jug, such as the rolled rim, tripartite strap handle with a high loop positioned on the shoulder and detached from the neck, squat piriform body, and ring base (although the latter is only a reconstruction, albeit a highly likely one—see Bourriau 1996:104).

Figure 10:2 (TD4174) is a jug found in a burial from Phase F (Kopetzky 1993:pl. 8:1).[11] Its shape and attributes are very similar to that of the Dolphin Jug. Its body is squat piriform, 12 cm high; the rim is everted (nearly rolled). The base is formed as a broad and shallow ring. The tri-coil handle of the MB IIA, when the coils were positioned in a triangular way, has given way to a tripartite strap handle. The brown burnishing of the surface is of a high quality; the fabric is Levantine (IV-2).

Figure 10:3 (TD7886) was found in a burial dated to Phase E/3. It also has a tripartite strap handle.[12] This small piriform juglet is 8.5 cm high. It has a rolled rim, a tripartite loop handle that touches the neck and the rim, and a button base. It is black-burnished and of local production (Nile D).

Figure 10:5 (TD3095) was found in a warrior burial of Phase F (F/I–d/23 Tomb 1). It is a piriform juglet, 13.3 cm high, with a rolled rim and a small ring base. The double loop handle arches from the base of the neck to the shoulder. The vessel was an import from the Levant and had a red-burnished surface with a metallic gloss.

Figure 10:6 (TD4751) comes from an undisturbed infant burial dated to Phase F (F/I–k/23 Tomb 33). This nearly ovoid jug, 14 cm high, has a kettle rim, a small ring base, and a double loop handle. Its surface is red burnished with a metallic shine, the fabric is Levantine (IV-2).

---

[7] The jug with cut-off spout shown in figure 10:1 comes from F/I–k/20 Tomb 28, which has been dated by M. Bietak (1989:37*–39*) to Phase b/3=F.

[8] There are chronological changes: while TD4174 (fig. 136:507) dates to Phase F, TD4479 belongs to an ensemble that dates most probably to Phase E/3; and A/IV–h/3 Tomb 6, in which were found TD7902 (fig. 136:509), TD7888 (fig. 136:510), TD7887 (fig. 136:512), TD7886 (fig. 136:513), and TD7894 (fig. 136:514), dates to Phase E/3-2.

[9] The vessel was found in one of the soundings dug by E. Naville, therefore the date given by Aston is insecure.

[10] The burial from which TD3095 originates has been dated to Phase b/3=F by M. Bietak (1984a:341f).

[11] The stratigraphic attribution of F/I–i/22 Tomb 34 has been changed to Stratum b/3 = Phase F.

[12] TD7886, from A/IV–h/3 Tomb 6, dates to Phase E/(3)-2. Publication of this tomb is in preparation by Irmgard Hein.

Figure 10:7 (TD6989) comes from a jar burial of Phase E/3 (F/I–l/23 Tomb 21). It is a small, biconical juglet, 7 cm high, with a small rolled rim, a broad ring base with a pointed middle, and a double loop handle sitting on the shoulder of the vessel. At the base of the neck, two parallel horizontal grooves are visible. The brown-burnished juglet is of Levantine production (IV-2).

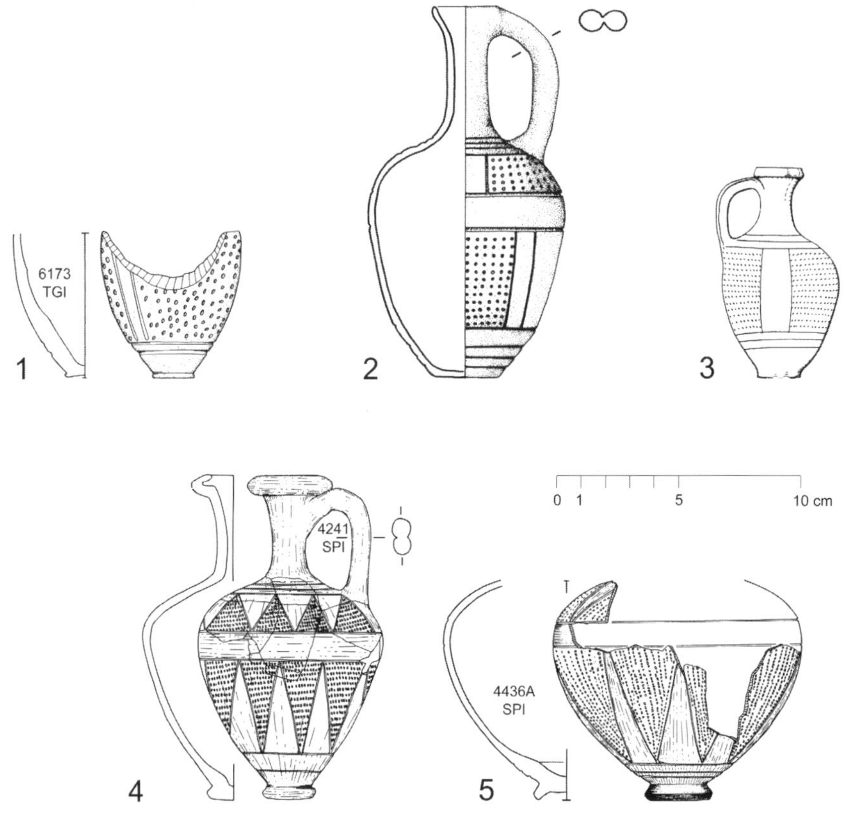

Figure 12. Tell el-Yehudiyeh juglets with rectangular zones of incrustations and Piriform 1c
1, 4, 5 Tell el-Dabʿa juglets **2** Ebla juglet; after Nigro 2003:349, fig. 7 **3** Byblos juglet; after Dunand 1954:198, 8521

Figure 13. Excavation photograph of juglets from Tomb 879 at Lisht
after Kemp and Merrillees 1980:pl. 31

Contextual Discussion

Among the preserved material from Tomb 879 at Lisht are also fragments of four other Tell el-Yehudiyeh juglets. One of them (figure 13, upper row, second from left) has only the lower part of a piriform body and its ring base preserved. Above two horizontal grooves, two rectangular segments are visible; they are filled with incrusted dots and were probably incised with a comb. Juglets with similar decoration have been found at Tell el-Dabᶜa (figure 12:1), Ebla (figure 12:2), and Byblos (figure 12:3).

The Tell el-Dabᶜa piece (TD6173, F/I–k/19) was discovered at the bottom of what was most likely once an open water tank, which is associated with the palace building from Phase G/4. On that piece, two parallel horizontal grooves are visible above a small ring base. While the incisions of the segments were done one at a time by hand, the surface shows no traces of burnishing. This imported juglet dates either to Phase G/4, when the palace was in use, or to the following Phase G/1-3, when the water tank was filled. At Tell el-Dabᶜa, Tell el-Yehudiyeh juglets with handmade incisions are found only in the late MB IIA, in Phases G/4 through F, while those decorated with the help of a comb are not found before Phase F. Thus, the latter technique is considered an MB IIB feature at the site.

Another parallel (figure 12:2; Nigro 2003:349, fig. 7) was found in a burial at Ebla from Mardikh Phase IIIB1. This vessel has a piriform body, a double handle, and a flat base. The decoration shows a broad horizontal band along the maximum diameter of the vessel. This band separates two zones of alternating segments of burnished rectangles from incised ones. The incisions were done with a comb, which makes this jug a bit younger than the Tell el-Dabᶜa vessel. Lorenzo Nigro and Nicolò Marchetti equate Mardikh IIIB1 with the first half of the MB IIB period in Palestine (Marchetti and Nigro 1997:29, table 1).

A third vessel comes from Byblos (figure 12:3; Dunand 1954:198, fig. 205:8521). Unfortunately, this piece is not well stratified, but it is equipped with a double handle, possibly a ring base, and three incised rectangular segments above two horizontal grooves. It seems that here again a comb was used for creating the incisions. Its rim was formed as a gutter or an inserted rim, a detail that occurs at Tell el-Dabᶜa from Phase G/1-3 until the beginning of the Hyksos period in Phase E/2.

Such an inserted rim can be found also on a nearly complete Tell el-Yehudiyeh juglet retrieved among the burial goods from Tomb 879 at Lisht (figure 13, lower row, right). It belongs to our Piriform 1c group (Bietak 1985:13f.). This type of juglet with an inserted rim, a double handle, and a small ring base appears in the tombs of Tell el-Dabᶜa from Phase F through Phase E/2 (figures 12:4 and 12:5). Two more probable fragments of such juglets come from Tomb 879 (figure 13, upper row, first and fourth from left).

Figure 14. Egyptian-style pottery from Tomb 879 at Lisht
after Kemp and Merrillees 1980:pl. 27

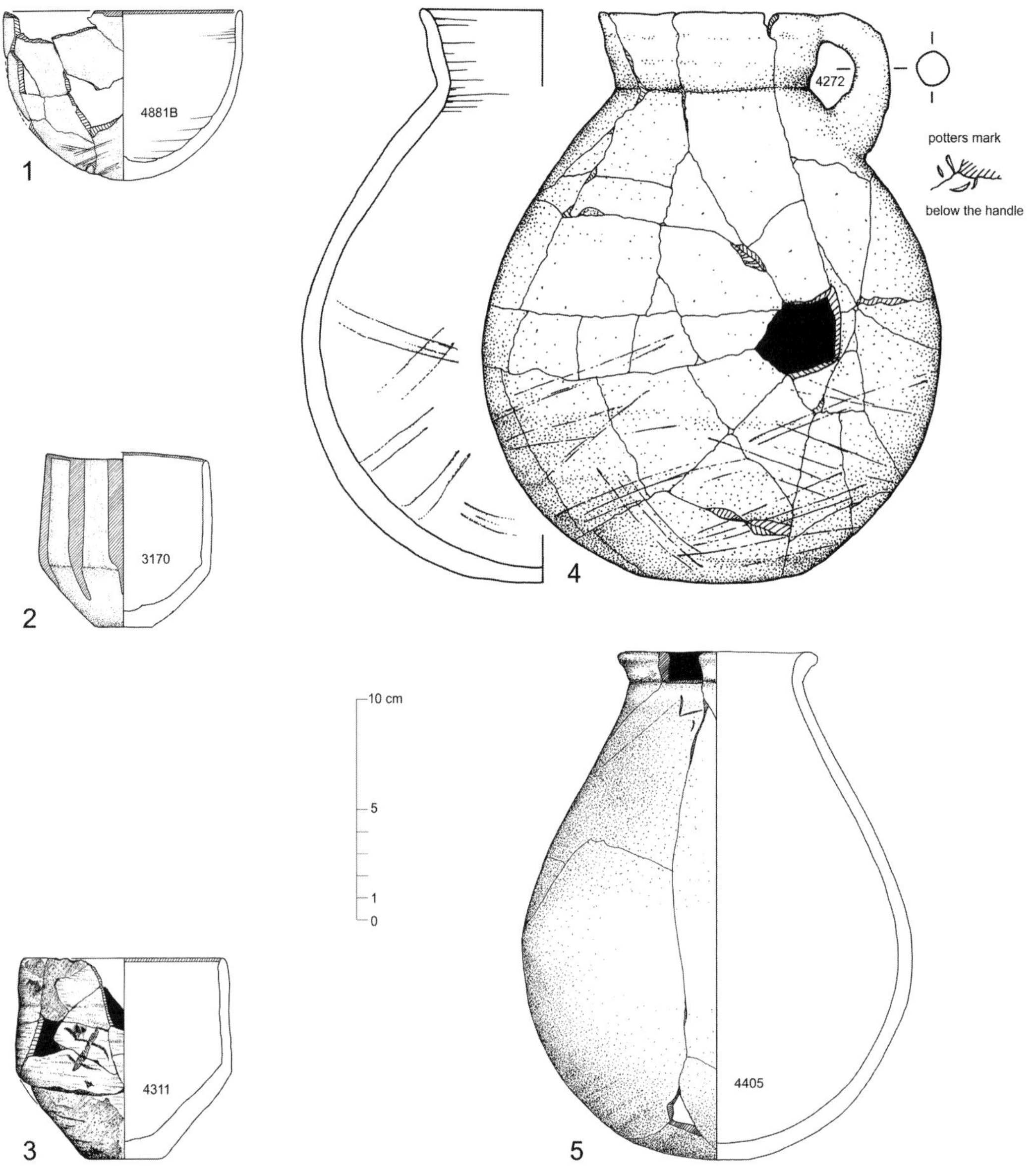

Figure 15. Egyptian-style pottery from Tell el-Dabᶜa

Among the Egyptian-style pottery from Tomb 879 are several miniature vessels. Such models appear in Egyptian tombs already in predynastic times. At Lisht they are quite common in the burials of the Twelfth and Thirteenth Dynasties, but at Tell el-Dabᶜa no miniature vessels have so far been found in or around tombs before the very end of Phase G/1-3 (Kopetzky 1993:pl. 21:3 and pl. 21:4).[13]

Bourriau's assumption that the hemispherical cup (figure 14, upper row, second from left) might be of

[13] For the same pieces, see Aston 2004:207, pl. 195:732, 733. Most of the other pieces that he dated to Phase G/1-3=c are either of another date or do not belong to the typical miniature vessels at the site. For example, TD6388 (pl. 194:721), TD6377 (pl. 196:739), and TD6386 (pl. 196:740) are from F/I–m/18 Tomb 13, which dates to Phase b/3-2=E/3. TD3250 and TD2521 (Aston 2004:210, pl. 198:754 and 755) do not belong to the group of dipper juglets but are rather to be called juglets and thus are not miniature vessels. The model dishes with "triangular" rim, TD4842 and TD5805 (Aston 2004:207, pl. 195:730, 731) are too big to be called "model" vessels, with diameters between 11 and 18 cm. They appear in Phases H through G/1-3 in the settlement material. TD4824 comes from a waste pit, not an offering pit.

Nile B_1 fabric (Bourriau 1996:113) is supported by the results of the analysis from the Tell el-Dabᶜa settlement material. The highest percentage of I-b-1 cups has been found there in Phases G/1-3 and F, where half of the hemispherical cups were produced using this fine Nile clay (Kopetzky 2005:64). The vessel indices of hemispherical cups, which Dorothea Arnold (1982:60–62) and Manfred Bietak (1984b: 480–82) have used for the material of Dahshur and Tell el-Dabᶜa, give secure results only when one is dealing with a larger quantity of vessels. Dating on the basis of only one cup is risky; at Tell el-Dabᶜa there are always exceptions to the norm, like a cup (figure 15:1) from a burial of Phase F-(E/3), which has a vessel index of 146 (Kopetzky 1993:97f.; F/I–l/22 Tomb 29). In figure 16 one can see that cups with such an index fit into Phases H through E/3.

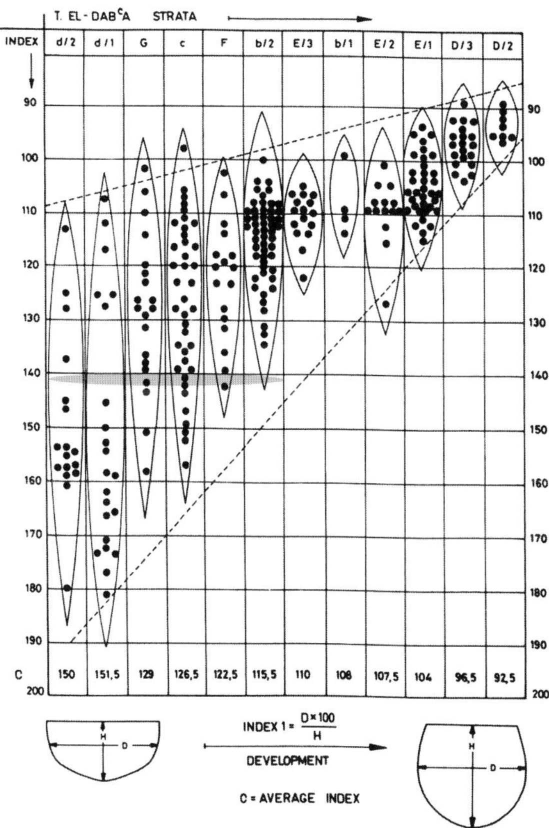

Figure 16. Tell el-Dabᶜa cup seriation

As Bourriau (1996:113) has stated, the so-called flat-bottomed cup (figure 14, middle row, fifth from left) does not belong in the group of cups with a flat base that have been found in the Hyksos phases of Tell el-Dabᶜa. The vessel is more likely a carinated cup with a direct rim and a flat base. At Tell el-Dabᶜa this kind of vessel appears in Phases G/1-3 and F. They are made of fine Nile clay. Either they are painted with red vertical strips below the rim (figure 15:2 [TD3170]; Aston 2004:13, pl. 1:5)[14] or they are plain (figure 15:3 [TD4311]; Kopetzky 1993:pl. 10:7; see also Aston 2004:13, pl. 1:4).[15]

Bourriau identified a jug (figure 14, middle row, third from left) and a jar (figure 14, bottom row, fourth from left) from Tomb 879 as made of Marl C fabric. The jug fragment belongs to a type of vessel of which two complete examples and several fragments have been found at Tell el-Dabᶜa (figure 15:4). One of the jugs comes from a burial of Phase G/1-3 (Kopetzky 1993:pl. 19:3; see also Bader 2001: 198, pl. 65a and Aston 2004:75, pl. 63:201). The other comes from a pit in a settlement area, which dates to Phase G/1-3–(F) (Bader 2001:195, pl. 64j; A/IV–h/6 Pit 14).[16] Additional fragments of such jugs appear in the settlement material from Phase H through the beginning of the Hyksos period (Phase E/2).

The jar type with a round base and a shaped rim (figure 15:5) was produced at Tell el-Dabᶜa from Phase M of ᶜEzbet Rushdi (Bader 2001:106, pl. 22m) until the middle of the Hyksos period (Phase E/1) (Müller 2008:156, pl. 72:53). Dorothea Arnold (1982:62–64) had already observed, while working on the material from Dahshur, that there is a development of these jars from a globular body in the late Twelfth Dynasty to a bag-shaped body in the Thirteenth Dynasty and Second Intermediate Period. This development is mirrored in the settlement pottery from Tell el-Dabᶜa, where globular jars are common in Phase M with the last examples in Phase G/1-3, while bag-shaped vessels have their first appearance in Phase H, with their floruit in Phase G/1-3 (Kopetzky 2005:211), continuing until the first half of the Hyksos period.

After comparing the material from Tomb 879 at Lisht with the pottery found at Tell el-Dabᶜa and in the Levant, the Dolphin Jug must be assigned a more

---

[14] TD3170 is dated to Phase b/3=F. Carinated cups with red-painted vertical strips appear at Tell el-Dabᶜa only in Phases H through F. They are present neither in the layers of ᶜEzbet Rushdi nor in the Hyksos levels (see Kopetzky 2005:71f.).

[15] TD4311 was found in the entrance pit of F/I–j/22 Tomb 29 where it was lying under and between the bones of two donkeys that where sacrificed during the burial ceremony in Phase G/1-3.

[16] Bader dates this pit to Phase G/4–G/1-3. Such an early date is not very likely, for this pit contained also a fragment of a Tell el-Yehudiyeh juglet of Type 1a or 1b. At Tell el-Dabᶜa, Type 1a starts with Phase G/1-3 while Type 1b exists in Phases F and E/3 (see Aston 2004:75, pl. 63:202).

recent date than Bourriau (1996:116) has suggested (she suggests the period of King Awibre Hor, who ruled around 1760 B.C.E. according to Beckerath's chronology). In terms of the stratigraphy of Tell el-Dab^{c}a, the Dolphin Jug belongs typologically and contextually to a time no earlier than Phase F and no later than Phase E/3. This is a transitional period, when the last types of the classical Middle Kingdom pottery vanish and a local development of vessels towards what is later called "classical Hyksos pottery" begins. The same phase shows the last appearance of MB IIA pottery and the advent of the new MB IIB types. In historical terms, Phases F and E/3 should be equated with the period of an independent kingdom at Avaris (Bietak 1984c), the time of the Fourteenth Dynasty (ca.1710–1650 B.C.E.).

Bibliography

Albright, W. F.
1933 *The Excavation of Tell Beit Mirsim.* Vol. 1, *The Bronze Age Pottery of the Fourth Campaign.* AASOR 13. New Haven, Conn: American Schools of Oriental Research.

Allen, S. J., J. Bourriau, G. Harbottle, and P. E. McGovern
1994 The Archaeological Origin and Significance of the Dolphin Vase As Determined by Neutron Activation Analysis. *BASOR* 296:31–43.

Arnold, D., and R. Stadelmann
1977 Dahschur: Zweiter Grabungsbericht. *MDAIK* 33: 15–20.

Arnold, Dorothea
1982 Keramikbearbeitung in Dahschur 1976–1981. *MDAIK* 38: 25–65.

Arnold, F.
1996 Settlement Remains at Lisht-North. In *House and Palace in Ancient Egypt: International Symposium in Cairo, April 8 to 11, 1992*, ed. M. Bietak, 13–21. UZK 14. Vienna: Österreichische Akademie der Wissenschaften.

Aston, D. A.
2002 Ceramic Imports at Tell el-Dab^{c}a during the Middle Bronze IIA. In *The Middle Bronze Age in the Levant*, ed. M. Bietak, 43–87. CChEM 3. Vienna: Österreichische Akademie der Wissenschaften.
2004 *Tell el-Dab^{c}a.* Vol. 12, *A Corpus of Late Middle Kingdom and Second Intermediate Pottery.* UZK 23. Vienna: Österreichische Akademie der Wissenschaften.

Bader, B.
2001 *Tell el-Dab^{c}a.* Vol. 13, *Typologie und Chronologie der Mergel C-ton Keramik: Materialien zum Binnenhandel des Mittleren Reiches und der Zweiten Zwischenzeit.* UZK 19. Vienna: Österreichische Akademie der Wissenschaften.

Bagh, T.
1988 Bemalet MB IIA and Bemalet Tell el-Yahudiyeh Ware fundet i Aegypten. M.A. thesis, University of Copenhagen.
2002 Painted Pottery at the Beginning of the Middle Bronze Age: Levantine Painted Ware. In *The Middle Bronze Age in the Levant,* ed. M. Bietak, 89–101. CChEM 3. Vienna: Österreichische Akademie der Wissenschaften.

Ben–Arieh, S.
2004 *Bronze and Iron Age Tombs at Tell Beit Mirsim.* IAA Reports 23. Jerusalem: Israel Antiquities Authority.

Bietak, M.
1984a Eine Palastanlage aus der Zeit des späten Mittleren Reichs und andere Forschungsergebnisse aus dem östlichen Nildelta. *Anzeiger der Phil.-hist. Klasse* 121:313–49.
1984b Problems of Middle Bronze Age Chronology: New Evidence from Egypt. *AJA* 88:471–85.
1984c Zum Königreich des ^{c}ꜣ-zh-R^{c} Nehesi. *Studien zur altägyptischen Kultur* 11:59–78.
1985 Archäologischer Befund und Historische Interpretation am Beispiel der Tell el-Yahudiya-Ware. In *Akten des vierten Internationalen Ägyptologenkongress, München 1985*, ed. S. Schoske, 2:7–34. Studien zur altägyptischen Kultur Beihefte 2. Hamburg: Buske.
1986 Tell el-Jahudija-Keramik. *Lexikon der Ägyptologie* 6:331–48.
1989 Servant Burials in the Middle Bronze Age Culture of the Eastern Nile Delta. *EI* 20: 30*–43*.
1991 *Tell el-Dab^{c}a.* Vol. 5, part 1, *Ein Friedhofsbezirk der Mittleren Bronzezeitkultur mit Totentempel und Siedlungsschichten.* UZK 8. Vienna: Österreichische Akademie der Wissenschaften.
2002 Relative and Absolute Chronology of the Middle Bronze Age: Comments on the Present Stage of Research. In *The Middle Bronze Age in the Levant*, ed. M. Bietak, 29–42. CChEM 3. Vienna: Österreichische Akademie der Wissenschaften.

Bietak, M., I. Forstner-Müller, and C. Mlinar
2001 The Beginning of the Hyksos Period at Tell el-Dab^{c}a: A Subtle Change in Material Culture. In *Contributions to the Archaeology and History of the Bronze and Iron Age in the Eastern Mediterranean: Studies in Honour of Paul Åström*, ed. P. M. Fischer, 171–81. Österreichisches Archäologisches Institut Sonderschriften 39. Vienna: Österreichische Akademie der Wissenschaften.

Bietak, M., and I. Hein, eds.
1994 *Pharaonen und Fremde: Dynastien im Dunkel.* Ausstellungskatalog des Historischen Museums der Stadt Wien. Vienna: Museen der Stadt Wien.

Bietak, M., K. Kopetzky, and L. E. Stager
in press Stratigraphie comparée nouvelle: The Synchronisation of Ashkelon and Tell el-Dabᶜa. In *Proceedings of the Third ICAANE Conference in Paris, 2001*, ed. P. de Miroschedji and J.-P. Thalmann. Paris.

Bourriau, J.
1996 The Dolphin Vase from Lisht. In *Studies in Honor of William Kelly Simpson*, ed. P. der Manuelian, 101–16. Boston: Museum of Fine Art.

Brandl, B.
2004 Scarabs, Seals, an Amulet and a Pendant. In *Bronze and Iron Age Tombs at Tell Beit Mirsim*, ed. S. Ben-Arieh, 123–88. IAA Reports 23. Jerusalem: Israel Antiquities Authority.

Buchholz, H. G., and V. Karageorghis
1973 *Prehistoric Greece and Cyprus: An Archaeological Handbook*. Translated by F. Garvie. London: Phaidon.

Cohen, S. L.
2002 *Canaanites, Chronologies, and Connections: The Relationship of Middle Bronze Age IIA Canaan to Middle Kingdom Egypt*. SAHL 3. Winona Lake, Ind.: Eisenbrauns.

Doumet-Serhal, C.
1996 *Les fouilles de Tell el-Ghassil de 1972 à 1974: Étude du Matériel*. BAH 146. Beirut: Institut français d'archéologie du Proche-Orient.
2004 Sidon (Lebanon): Twenty Middle Bronze Age Burials from the 2001 Season of Excavation. *Levant* 36:89–154.
2006 Sidon: Mediterranean Contacts in the Early and Middle Bronze Age, Preliminary Report. *Archaeology and History in Lebanon* 24:34–47.
2008 The British Museum Excavation at Sidon: Markers for the Chronology of the Early and Middle Bronze Age in Lebanon. In *The Bronze Age in Lebanon: Studies on the Archaeology and Chronology of Lebanon, Syria and Egypt*, ed. M. Bietak and E. Czerny. CChEM 17. Vienna: Österreichische Akademie der Wissenschaften.

Dunand, M.
1954 *Fouilles de Byblos*. Vol. 2, *1933–1938*. Paris: Geuthner.

Epstein, C.
1974 Middle Bronze Age Tombs at Kfar Szold and Ginnosar. *ᶜAtiqot* 7:13–39 [in Hebrew], 2*–3*.

Guigues, P. E.
1938 Lébéᶜa, Kafer-Ğarra, Qrayé: Nécropoles de la région Sidonienne. *BMB* 2:27–72.

Höflmayer, F.
2005 Die absolut Datierung der späten Mittelbronzezeit und der frühen Spätbronzezeit in der Ägäis. M.A. thesis, University of Vienna.

Ilan, D.
1996 Middle Bronze Age Painted Pottery from Tel Dan. *Levant* 28:157–72.

Kantor, H. J.
1965 The Relative Chronology of Egypt and Its Foreign Correlations before the Late Bronze Age. In *Chronologies in Old World Archaeology*, ed. R. W. Ehrich, 1:1–31. Chicago: University of Chicago Press.

Kaplan, J.
1955 A Cemetery of the Bronze Age Discovered near Tel Aviv Harbour. *ᶜAtiqot* 1:1–12.

Kaplan, M. F.
1980 *The Origin and Distribution of Tell el-Yahudiyeh Ware*. SIMA 62. Göteborg, Sweden: Åström.

Kemp, B. J., and R. S. Merrillees
1980 *Minoan Pottery in Second Millennium Egypt*. Mainz: Zabern.

Kopetzky, K.
1993 Die Datierung der Gräber der Grabungsfläche F/I von Tell el-Dabᶜa anhand der Keramik. M.A. thesis, University of Vienna.
2005 Die Chronologie der Siedlungskeramik der Zweiten Zwischenzeit aus Tell el-Dabᶜa (Ägypten). Ph.D. diss., University of Vienna.

Mace, A. C.
1921 Excavations at Lisht. *Bulletin of the Metropolitan Museum of Art* 16/11/2:5–19.

MacGillivray, J. A.
1995 A Minoan Cup at Tell el-Dabᶜa. *Ägypten und Levante* 5:81–84.

Maeir, A. M.
1997 Tomb 1181: A Multiple-Interment Burial Cave of the Transitional Middle Bronze Age IIA–B. In *Hazor*, vol. 5, *An Account of the Fifth Season of Excavation, 1968*, ed. A. Ben-Tor et al., 295–340. Jersualem: Israel Exploration Society.

Marchetti, N., and L. Nigro
1997 Cultic Activities in the Sacred Area of Ishtar at Ebla during the Old Syrian Period: The *Favissae* F.5327 and F.5238. *JCS* 49:1–44.

Marinatos, S., and M. Hirmer
1959 *Kreta und das mykenische Hellas*. Munich: Hirmer.

Miron, R.
1982 Die "Mittelbronzezeitlichen" Gräber am Nordhang des Tells. In *Kāmid el-Lōz, 1971–74*, ed. R.

Hachmann, 101–22. Saarbrückner Beiträge zur Altertumskunde 32. Bonn: Habelt.

Montet, P.
1928 *Byblos et l'Égypte: Quatre campagnes de fouilles 1921–1924*. BAH 11. Paris: Geuthner.

Müller, V.
2008 *Tell el-Dab^ca*. Vol. 17, *Opferdeponierungen in der Hyksoshauptstadt Auaris (Tell el-Dab^ca) vom späten Mittleren Reich bis zum frühen Neuen Reich*. 2 vols. UZK 29. Vienna: Österreichische Akademie der Wissenschaften.

Negbi, O.
1978 Cypriote Imitations of Tell el-Yahudiyeh Ware from Toumba tou Skourou. *AJA* 82:137–49.

Nigro, L.
2003 The Smith and the King of Ebla: Tell el-Yahudieh Ware, Metallic Wares and the Ceramic Chronology of Middle Bronze Syria. In *The Synchronisation of Civilisations in the Eastern Mediterranean in the Second Millennium* B.C., vol. 2, ed. M. Bietak, 345–63. Denkschriften der Gesamtakademie 29. CChEM 4. Vienna: Österreichische Akademie der Wissenschaften.

Saidah, R.
1993–94 Beirut in the Bronze Age: The Kharji Tombs. *Berytus* 41:137–222.

Stager, L. E.
2002 The MB IIA Ceramic Sequence at Tel Ashkelon and Its Implications for the "Port Power" Model of Trade. In *The Middle Bronze Age in the Levant*, ed. M. Bietak, 353–62. CChEM 3. Vienna: Österreichische Akademie der Wissenschaften.

Tufnell O.
1975–76 Tomb 66 at Ruweise near Sidon. *Berytus* 24:5–36.

Walberg, G.
1986 *Tradition and Innovation: Essays in Minoan Art*. Mainz: Zabern.
1991 Finds at Tell el-Dab^ca and the Middle Minoan Chronology. *Ägypten und Levante* 2:115–20.

Warren, P., and V. Hankey
1989 *Aegean Bronze Age Chronology*. Bristol, England: Bristol Classical Press.

4. Assyrians Abet Israelite Cultic Reforms: Sennacherib and the Centralization of the Israelite Cult

by Elizabeth Bloch-Smith

The Assyrian conquest of the northern kingdom of Israel by Tiglath-pileser III, Shalmaneser V, and Sargon II supplied a rationale for Judahite cultic reform, and Sennacherib's subsequent campaign in 701 B.C.E. expedited its implementation. Sennacherib's devastating campaign may have done more to promote centralization of the Israelite cult than any priestly, prophetic, or royal initiative before or after.

Past studies of the Assyrian impact on Israelite religion largely overlook the repercussions of the military campaigns (Cogan 1974; Holloway 2002). Over a thirty-five-year period, the Assyrians devastated fortified cities and towns from Dan to Beersheba. Cultic centralization in the capital city, which was probably the only major political and administrative city left standing, was the most feasible and logical response. Largely by process of elimination, Jerusalem emerged as the *de facto* cultic center. Sennacherib also supplied a financial incentive and stimulus to centralize the cult. The heavy tribute exacted in order to save Jerusalem had stripped the kingdom, including the doors of the Jersualem temple, of valuable commodities (2 Kings 18:16). A centralized cult would concentrate resources in Jerusalem and refill the temple coffers to restore that structure to its former gilded glory (Claburn 1973; Evans 1980:162). This hypothesis, attributing to the Assyrian conquest of the region a significant role in Israelite religious reforms, harks back to the scholarly practice of attributing cultural change or discontinuity to "foreign invasion."

Repercussions of the Assyrian advance into the region began with the campaign of Tiglath-pileser III in 734 B.C.E. The cumulative effect of the campaigns over more than thirty years, with their inexorable advance toward Jerusalem, presaged Jerusalem's inevitable doom. In his initial foray into the area, Tiglath-pileser III proceeded as far south as Gaza, destroying Philistine and Judahite strategic sites along the way, including the "city of Gezer," as depicted in a scene carved in relief at his palace at Nimrud (Younger 2000a:288, 290, 291; Barnett and Falkner 1962:24, pl. 62). In the following year, Assyria conquered and subjugated territory to the north of Samaria, as described in both the Bible and the Assyrian royal annals: 2 Kings 15:29 lists towns in upper Galilee and Assyrian Annals 18 and 24 add towns in lower Galilee (Younger 2000a:286–92).[1] The northern kingdom of Israel was reduced to a rump state and the conquered territory was reconfigured into Assyrian provinces.

Kings Shalmaneser V and Sargon II completed the dissolution of the northern kingdom with the 722 B.C.E. siege and conquest of Samaria (2 Kings 17:3–6, 18:9–11; Great "Summary" Inscription; Nimrud Prism). In addition to Samaria, Sargon II claims to have vanquished cities as far south as Philistine Gaza, as recorded in the Great "Summary" Inscription, and to have turned against Judah, calling himself "subduer of the land of Judah which is far away" (Younger 2000b:296–97, 298). Assyria's might, capabilities, and proclivities were evident to all.

Against this backdrop of Assyrian imperial expansion, King Hezekiah of Judah likely initiated efforts to centralize the cult before Sennacherib's campaign to the region. According to 2 Chronicles 29–30, the pious Hezekiah initiated the reforms in his first regnal year; 2 Kings 18 mentions the reforms but with no indication of their timing. Biblical testimony does not resolve the relative chronology, but centralizing the cult in Jerusalem under royal patronage effectively secured complete control of the society and its resources in Jerusalem—a prudent move for a king preparing to rebel against Assyria (Borowski 1995).

While details vary, both the Assyrian and biblical sources mention Sennacherib's Levantine campaign and siege of Jerusalem during the reign of Hezekiah. The Bible acknowledges that "King Sennacherib of Assyria marched against all the fortified towns of Judah and seized them" (2 Kings 18:13), while Sennacherib boasts that he "besieged forty-six of his fortified walled cities and surrounding smaller towns, which were without number" and deported more than 200,150 people (Cogan 2000:303). Both kings acknowledge that a ransom was paid to spare Jerusalem, although neither dwells on this (2 Kings 18:14–16; Cogan 2000:303). The salient fact is that numerous fortified towns and cities fell to the Assyrians but Jerusalem emerged unscathed.

[1] Younger's translations of the Assyrian annals use the arrangement of fragments proposed by Tadmor (1994). Rainey and Notley (2006:229–45) provide an excellent summary, with maps, of both the biblical and Assyrian sources.

Archaeological Evidence of the Assyrian Conquest

Archaeological evidence clarifies and in some ways modifies this picture. Although the Assyrian conquest undeniably affected Judahite policy, the scale of the conquest was more modest than the Assyrians claimed. Selected fortified cities and administrative centers were devastated, others were partially destroyed, and some apparently capitulated; but sites in the central highlands around Jerusalem show no evidence of battle or submission. The following discussion accepts excavators' interpretation of "destruction" rather than "Mrs. O'Leary's cow" or some other cause for collapse or burning. Even if willfully destroyed, the Assyrians may not have been the agents; Arameans and Egyptians are also candidates.

According to both their own and biblical testimony, the Assyrians defeated, spoiled, and destroyed towns as they subjugated the territory of Israel, Philistia, and Judah. In Summary Inscription 13, Tiglath-pileser III claims, "[the land of Bit Humria,] all [of whose] cities I leveled [to the ground] in my former campaigns, [...] I plundered its livestock, and I spared only (isolated) Samaria" (Younger 2000a: 292).

Not all settlements suffered the same fate, however. In spite of Assyrian assertions, archaeology reveals selective targeting of prominent sites and no wide-spread destruction of small towns or villages. Assyrians attacked strategically located, fortified sites along the major highways and at critical road junctions. They utterly devastated some sites while at others they merely wrecked the city gate. Compromising a city's fortifications may have sufficed in order for the population to concede defeat, or it may have ignominiously marked a city that had surrendered. Some cities apparently capitulated, with the result that they and their fortifications were left intact. Sites to be utilized by the Assyrians as administrative centers, such as Megiddo and Samaria (and perhaps Ramat Raḥel), were not physically compromised. Elsewhere, the Assyrians selectively destroyed city gates and fortifications, palaces, and storehouses rather than destroying the entire city. This discriminating devastation likely undermined confidence and disrupted, if it did not end, a city's function as a military, administrative, and/or financial hub. Once fortified towns fell, settlers abandoned their peripheral villages.

Given the Assyrian propensity to brag about their military exploits, it is surprising that we lack textual records of the conquest of certain prominent sites such as Megiddo and Lachish. While some sites may have been omitted from conquest lists, the Megiddo and Lachish examples serve as reminders that the extant texts do not tell the full story.

Neither archaeological nor textual evidence identifies the attacking or destroying army at every site. In the majority of cases, an Assyrian king's claim to have conquered and destroyed a city, in some cases with corroborating biblical testimony, identifies the conquering king. Archaeologically, pottery from the last third of the eighth century B.C.E. is indistinguishable from the pottery at the very end of that century (701 B.C.E.), but a consensus has emerged regarding the *lmlk* stamped jars, which are attributed to an initiative of Hezekiah king of Judah in anticipation of his rebellion against Assyria. Accordingly, storage jars with handles stamped *lmlk*, "belonging to the king," the greatest number of which were found at Lachish and the second-greatest number in Jerusalem, provide an archaeological marker of the 701 B.C.E. destruction levels (Naᵓaman 1979).

There are differences of opinion about whether the *lmlk* stamp, in its initial form, continued to be used after the reign of Hezekiah; so there are different interpretations of the chronological significance of its absence (Vaughn 1999:140; Zimhoni 1990:18). For example, in several cases, including Tell Beit Mirsim, Tell Ḥalif, and Beersheba, a prosperous, fortified village or town was destroyed, was reoccupied on a much-reduced scale, and was subsequently destroyed again or abandoned. The current consensus holds that Sennacherib destroyed these towns in 701 B.C.E., but Jeffrey Blakely and James Hardin attribute these destructions to Tiglath-pileser III a few decades earlier (Blakely and Hardin 2002; Finkelstein and Naᵓaman 2004).

While disagreements such as this lead scholars to debate whether to attribute particular destruction levels to Tiglath-pileser III, Sargon II, or an early rather than a later Sennacherib campaign (Grayson 1992: 1089), it is nonetheless clear that settlements from Dan to Beersheba succumbed to the Assyrians within a relatively short period and that many of the most prominent cities were physically destroyed. By 701 B.C.E., many settlements, especially border towns, had fallen. However, the center of the Judahite kingdom survived; throughout repeated devastating campaigns, Jerusalem endured.

Site Destructions Attributed to Tiglath-pileser III

Archaeological evidence of Assyrian conquest and subjugation begins with the campaigns of Tiglath-pileser III in 734–32 B.C.E. The Assyrian army advanced south along the coast to Gaza and the "city of the Brook of Egypt" (Summary 8; Tadmor 1994:

176–79) destroying—according to archaeologists—Akko, Shiqmona, Dor, Tell el-Qudadi, Ashkelon (Annals 18 and 24), and Gezer. In the territory of the northern kingdom of Israel, Tiglath-pileser III claims to have devastated all the cities of Israel, sparing only Samaria (Summary 13; Tadmor 1994:81–83, 201–3) and he boasts of the numbers of prisoners taken from towns in lower Galilee that had belonged to the "House of Omri" (Annals 18 and 24). The Bible also lists settlements in the Galilee, "the land of Naphtali," which fell to the Assyrians, including Kedesh and Hazor, although Dan is conspicuously missing from the list (2 Kings 15:29).

From the so-called Syro-Ephraimite War or Damascus Campaign, strategic Israelite sites at which destruction levels have been attributed to Tiglath-pileser III include Dan, Hazor, Chinnereth (Tell el-Oreimeh), plus Beth Shean, Tel Reḥov, and Megiddo in the Jezreel and Beth Shean valleys, as well as Bethsaida and ᶜEn Gev along the border with Geshur-Aram. The Assyrians entirely destroyed Hazor but only selectively damaged the sites of Dan, Chinnereth, Beth Shean, and Dor. Many sites with destructions that are attributed to Tiglath-pileser appear neither in Assyrian lists nor in biblical accounts.

Tiglath-pileser III's army campaigned south along the coast to Gaza, turning inland to attack the site of Gezer. **Tel Kudadi** guarded the entrance into the Yarkon River estuary. Destruction of portions of the fortress's offset-inset walls and gate is attributed to Tiglath-pileser III (Avigad 1993:882). **Gezer** strategically sits at the opening of the Ayalon Valley and the junction of the Via Maris with a road that leads up into the highlands to Jerusalem. Assyrian lanceheads and arrowheads testify to the destruction of the fortified administrative center of Stratum VI. Affluent residences in Fields II and VII, Palace 8000, the upper gate and casemate wall, and the lower gatehouse all burned and collapsed in the Assyrian assault on the city (Dever 1993:505; 1997:399).

In the Galilee and Golan, Tiglath-pileser III targeted strategic, fortified centers: Dan and Hazor in the north, and Chinneret and ᶜEn Gev on the shores of the Sea of Galilee. At **Tel Dan Stratum II**, destruction by fire in the gate, ImmadiYo's house, Building No. 9235, and the altar room, annex, and pillar room in the sacred precinct testify to sudden devastation in the second half of the eighth century B.C.E. Walls collapsed and mudbricks burned red. The destruction was widespread but not complete; habitation and city life continued elsewhere at the site (Biran 1994:204–6, 253). At **Hazor Stratum V**, strengthened fortifications, including a new watchtower (Area B), proved useless in stopping the Assyrian invasion. The invading army destroyed the entire city (Yadin 1993:601; Ben-Tor 1997:4–5). At **Tel Chinnereth/Tell el-Oreimeh**, on the western shores of the Sea of Galilee, pottery from the second half of the eighth century found in the burned mudbrick filling the two-chamber gate and passageway testifies to its sudden and complete destruction (Fritz 1993:300). On the eastern shore of the Sea of Galilee, the Assyrians completely burned **ᶜEn Gev 2 Stratum III**, a well-fortified, economic center (B. Mazar 1993: 411; Kochavi 1997:223).

Coastal sites also succumbed to the Assyrian assault. Either Tiglath-pileser III or Sennacherib defeated the late eighth-century walled city of **Akko** (Dothan 1993a: 21–22). **Shiqmona**'s houses and olive-pressing installations of Town D were destroyed in the second half of the eighth century. B.C.E. (Elgavish 1993:1375). At **Tel Dor**, as at Chinnereth, destruction appears limited to the city gate, in this case, a massive four-chambered gate. Compared to Chinnereth, more extensive portions of the site have been excavated but still show no city-wide destruction (Stern 2000:115).

Tiglath-pileser III's troops allegedly ravaged sites in the Jezreel and Beth Shean Valleys. In a reappraisal of the earlier excavations, the destruction of **Beth Shean Upper Stratum V** has been attributed to Tiglath-pileser III. Recent excavations at the site uncovered an elaborate version of a "four-room house" (Area P) that burned and collapsed in the Assyrian assault (A. Mazar 1997:73–74). At **Tel Reḥov Stratum III**, individuals killed in the assault on the city (Area A) and the collapse of the towering mudbrick wall testify to the Assyrian devastation (A. Mazar 1999:42f.*; 2002:40*). In the "chariot city" of **Megiddo Stratum IVA, Level H-3**, the Assyrians spared the public buildings (excavated by the University of Chicago), perhaps for their own reuse, but torched a residential area (excavated by Tel Aviv University). Burned debris indicative of destruction was found in some but not all of the contiguous rooms abutting the city wall. Surprisingly, the conquest of Megiddo is not mentioned in extant Assyrian annals (Finkelstein, Ussishkin, and Halpern 2000:143–50, 598).

Not every settlement was burned or lay desolate and abandoned following Assyrian incursions into the region. Small, nonstrategic sites from north to south, such as Tel Par in the Akko Valley, the apparently unfortified Rosh Ha-ᶜAyin, Horvat Eli (located 3 km northwest of Shiloh), and even the fortified site of Naḥal Barqai in the Philistine plain, are sites that continued through the end of the Iron Age without obvious disruption (Gal 1995:33; Hizmi 1998:51f.*, 74–75; Avner-Levy and Torge 1998:40, 58–59; Givon 1995:88–90; 1999:67f.*, 73–74). At some sites, such as Yoqneam Stratum XII, a diminished, and in many cases impoverished, population remained (Ben-Tor 1993:807). Other sites, such as the farming village of Tel Hadar Stratum I in the vicinity of ᶜEn Gev on the eastern shore of the Sea of Galilee, were abandoned (Kochavi 1993a:551–52).

Site Destructions Attributed to Shalmaneser V and Sargon II

Biblical passages, the Babylonian Chronicle, and Sargon's "Great" and "Small" Summary Inscriptions record Assyria's subjugation of Israel and Philistia.

Shalmaneser V and Sargon II besieged the capital city of Samaria and "plundered . . . the entire land of Bit Humria" (Millard 2000:467; Younger 2000b: 296, 297). Destruction levels at Dothan, Shechem, and Tell el-Farᶜah (North) bear witness to the devastating finale. In contrast, the capital city of Samaria, which like Megiddo was an Israelite hub that was to be transformed into an Assyrian administrative center, was left largely intact (Tappy 2001:222–26, 572–75). Other towns, such as the heavily-fortified Khirbet Marjameh in eastern Ephraim, far from a major route, were not destroyed but were abandoned (A. Mazar 1982:171–74; 1993:965–66). Philistine towns were spared physical destruction although Sargon II claims to have vanquished and laid siege to cities as far south as Philistine Gaza, as recorded in the Great Summary Inscription, as depicted on palace wall reliefs, and marked with a memorial stele at Ashdod (Tadmor 1971).

Either Tiglath-pileser III or Sargon II destroyed **Dothan Level 2** (Ussishkin 1993:373) and the fortified **Shechem Stratum VII**. At Shechem, the Assyrians burned Courtyard House 1727 in Field VII (Campbell 1993:1353). Sargon II burned the fortified town of **Tell el-Farᶜah (N) Stratum VIId** with its "palace" and residential areas (Chambon 1984:39–47, plans 4 and 5; 1993:439–40).

In Philistia, the fortified acropolis of **Tel Miqne (Ekron) Stratum II** likely surrendered as the city shows no signs of violent conquest (Dothan and Gitin 2005:7). The approximately three thousand individuals buried in mass graves at **Ashdod Stratum VIII** are considered casualties of Sargon II's conquest of the city (Bachi and Ben-Dov 1971; Dothan 1993b:100). Whether or not this was the work of Sargon II, the city of Ashdod itself does not appear to have been physically destroyed (Finkelstein and Singer-Avitz 2004; Ben-Shlomo 2003); however, the nearby port of **Tel Mor Stratum II**, which was fortified with a casemate wall, was ravaged (Dothan 1993c:1074).

Site Destructions Attributed to Sennacherib

Sennacherib campaigned in the region in 701 B.C.E., about ten years after Sargon II's last visit. King Hezekiah of Judah's alliance with Egypt and/or Babylonia (2 Kings 18:21; 20:12–13), both of which were enemies of Assyria, his incursions into Philistine territory (2 Kings 18:8), and his holding hostage the Assyrian vassal King Padi of Ekron prompted Assyrian retribution (see Cogan 2000:303). In that devastating war against Judah, Jerusalem was spared but many other important Judahite sites fell to the Assyrians. By their reckoning, Assyria "besieged 46 walled cities and surrounding smaller towns, which were without number" (ibid.). The Bible concurs, acknowledging that Sennacherib "marched against all the fortified towns of Judah and seized them" (2 Kings 18:13).

Attribution of destruction levels to Sennacherib rests on the Lachish pottery sequence and Assyrian textual and iconographic references to southern Levantine conquests. Stone-carved reliefs in Sennacherib's Nineveh palace confirm his conquest of Lachish. With this knowledge, Olga Tufnell in 1950, followed by Miriam and Yohanan Aharoni in 1976, dated the late eighth-century pottery in the destruction level of Lachish Stratum III to Sennacherib's 701 B.C.E. campaign and then established pottery correlations with other sites (Tufnell 1950:76–79; Aharoni and Aharoni 1976). Based on comparable assemblages, excavators maintain that Sennacherib destroyed Philistine Tel Miqne II; the Shephelah sites of Tel Batash III, Beth Shemesh II, Tel ᶜErani VI, Lachish III, Tell el-Ḥesi VIIIa, Tell Beit Mirsim A2, and Tell Ḥalif VIB, plus Khirbet Rabud B-II, Tel Sera VI, Tel Beer Sheba II, and perhaps Arad VIII.[2]

Sennacherib appears to have secured the Judahite sites in the lowlands, the Shephelah foothills, and the northern Negev in order to encircle the highlands and isolate Jerusalem. Sennacherib has been credited with destroying only two highland sites, Hebron and Ramat Raḥel, but neither has yielded definitive destruction deposits. At Hebron (Tell er-Rumeide), the destroyed house preceded a building with *lmlk* handles that was not destroyed and so may predate Sennacherib (Stern 2001:10; Eisenberg and Nagorski 2002:83ff.*, 102–3). A destruction of such limited scope have been due to a localized event rather than an attacking army. Sennacherib allegedly destroyed Ramat Raḥel Stratum VB near Jerusalem, but the site lacks burned and collapsed deposits indicative of destruction. Rebuilding is evident but destruction is unproven (Dessel 1997:402; A. Mazar 1990:424; Y. Aharoni 1964:58–60, 119).

That Sennacherib encircled Judah but did not penetrate the highlands remains a hypothesis based upon a very limited number of sites. Jerusalem, Gibeon, and Tell en-Naṣbeh, as well as Ramat Raḥel, show no sign of Assyrian assault or destruction. Un-

[2] Blakely and Hardin add Tel ᶜEton (Tell ᶜAitun) to the list of sites that were destroyed by Tiglath-pileser III, then sparsely resettled, and finally destroyed by Sennacherib. Although O. Zimhoni dated the pottery from a probe on the tell to the mid-eighth century, Blakely and Hardin consider the similarity of the overall sequence to events at Tell el-Ḥesi, Tel ᶜErani, and elsewhere to be determinative (2002: 35). Excavators at Tel ᶜEton in the summer of 2006 found evidence of destruction at several places on the tell but lacked sufficient evidence to attribute this destruction to a particular campaign (A. Faust, pers. comm.).

fortunately, excavation reports of other highland sites such as Bethel, Beth Zur, and Gibeah, all excavated before 1965, lack the necessary information either to support or to challenge this hypothesis.

Widespread disruption and abandonment of settlements is undeniable, as demonstrated by both excavations and surveys, but the impression of a total destruction of sites throughout Judah is unsustainable. The textual record of both Assyria and Judah foster the impression of rampant destruction. For the Assyrians, this was in order to tout their military prowess. For the Judahites, it was to extol the miraculous deliverance of Jerusalem.

This is not to minimize the impact of Sennacherib's campaign: many Shephelah forts, the bulwark against foreign armies traversing coastal roads, fell to the Assyrians. Jerusalem, the capital city and so a prize conquest, lay vulnerable and open to attack. Controlling the northern Shephelah sites secured Assyria's eastern flank from attack by Judah while Sennacherib focused his fury upon Ekron, the city that had initiated the rebellion which prompted the punitive campaign (Rainey and Notley 2006:242; Cogan 2000:303). Conquering the Shephelah forts also effectively isolated Jerusalem, precluded Egyptian military assistance to Judah, and halted east-west commerce. As in earlier Assyrian campaigns, some cities, such as Tell Beit Mirsim, Tel Batash, and Beth Shemesh, were only partially destroyed, targeting only the area of the city gate and other public buildings. Lachish, however, like Hazor, suffered total destruction.

The "LMLK Research Website" (*http://www.lmlk.com/research/lmlk_corp.htm*) has compiled a list of more than 800 *lmlk*-stamped handles, which are considered a marker of the Hezekian rebellion. Among the sites where the greatest numbers of *lmlk* stamps were found, Jerusalem (281 stamps), Ramat Raḥel (164 stamps), Gibeon (92 stamps), and Tell en-Naṣbeh (88 stamps)—all in the Jerusalem vicinity—showed no signs of destruction, while the Shephelah site of Lachish, with the single greatest number of examples (415 stamps), and perhaps Beth Shemesh (71 stamps), fell to the Assyrians. It seems that Hezekiah correctly anticipated Sennacherib's battle plan but was unable to withstand the onslaught.

The route of Sennacherib's third campaign in the region began at Joppa, continued south through the Shephelah to Lachish, and from there one contingent headed north to besiege Jerusalem and perhaps a second contingent returned to the coast to counter an Egyptian offensive (Rainey and Notley 2006:241–42). In extant texts, Sennacherib does not claim to have burned or otherwise destroyed Ekron (Tel Miqne) or even Lachish, although excavations have shown that the Tel Miqne Stratum II walled acropolis was destroyed (Dothan and Gitin 1993:1056; 1997:33) and Lachish was reduced to ruins. The Assyrian textual accounts are therefore woefully incomplete for this campaign.

The Assyrians systematically destroyed the Judahite Shephelah forts that guarded the passes into the highlands and Jerusalem. Excavation results are summarized here from north to south.

Tel Batash Stratum III, a Sorek Valley site that sits astride the road from the coast up to Beth Shemesh and Jerusalem, had been fortified with a newly rebuilt gate and double wall. Sennacherib's troops selectively destroyed parts of the town—the Area C inner gate but not the monumental outer gate, an Area H public building that likely functioned as an administrative center or governor's headquarters, and a governmental storehouse that contained dozens of "Judean-type" storejars with *lmlk* seal impressions in Area D. Other structures displayed no evidence of destruction and continued in use into Stratum II (Kelm and Mazar 1985:104–5; 1995:119, 126–27, 131–35).

The fortified site of **Beth Shemesh Stratum II** likely served as a regional administrative center. The lack of seventh-century pottery in the current excavation has prompted the excavators to attribute the destructive conquest in Fields B and E to Sennacherib in 701 B.C.E. In the Area B building, situated near the city gate, olive oil was produced and many royal and private stamped jar handles were found in the building and its vicinity (Bunimovitz and Lederman 1993:252; 2000:106*; 2001:99*–100*; *http://www.tau.ac.il/humanities/archaeology/projects/bethshemesh_proj.html*).

Tel ᶜErani Stratum VI, on Naḥal Lachish along the Ashkelon–Hebron road, fell to the Assyrians in 701 B.C.E. Numerous sling stones in Area A testify to the assault (Yeivin 1993:418–19, 421; Brandl 1997:257).

Lachish Stratum III, strategically located in the Naḥal Lachish alongside the route leading from the coastal plain up into the Hebron hills, was completely and utterly destroyed in 701 B.C.E. In this fortified settlement with a palace-fort compound, every area excavated has revealed evidence of burning and destruction. Private houses in Area S that contained stamped and unstamped *lmlk* jars lay buried under collapsed walls and roofs (Ussishkin 2004:83–90, 88ff.*; Barkay and Ussishkin 2004:453). Armor scales, sling stones, spearheads, hundreds of arrowheads, Assyrian bronze helmets, and a dagger were retrieved from the conflagration in the city gate (Ussishkin 2004:518–19). The Assyrian siege ramp and counter-ramp within the city, plus metal chains and perforated stones for upsetting and bashing the siege engines, mark the point of attack (Ussishkin 2004:695–742). While the Bible omits mention of the Assyrian destruction of Lachish, it does note that the king of Assyria and his troops encamped there (2 Kings 18:14, 17; Isa. 36:2; 37:8; 2 Chron. 32:9).

Continuing south through the Shephelah and encircling the highlands, the Assyrians attacked **Tell el-Ḥesi Sub-Stratum VIIIa** (formerly Sub-Stratum VIIa). At this fortress, which had upper and lower fortification walls with an intervening steep slope, the thick layer of ash, charcoal, and mudbrick debris covering the architectural remains in Field I Areas 41 and 51 may represent an assault by Sennacherib, or perhaps Tiglath-pileser III (Blakely and Hardin 2002:33, 52).

Tel Sera Stratum VI, an impressive complex of mudbrick buildings constructed with ashlar masonry foundations, was burned late in the eighth century, perhaps at Sennacherib's hand (Oren 1993:1332–33; 1997:1).

At **Tell Beit Mirsim Stratum A2**, the attacking army burned and destroyed sectors of this large, fortified site—the east and west gates, the fortress in the center of town, and public and private buildings in the southeast quadrant of the mound—but, as noted by the excavator: "Most of the town escaped destruction at this time" (Greenberg 1993:180; Albright 1943:66–67).

Tell Ḥalif Stratum VIB, fortified with a modified casemate wall and external glacis, guarded the route leading from Egypt and the southern coast up into the highlands toward Hebron and Jerusalem. At the end of the eighth century, a "massive conflagration" in domestic contexts at the northern and southern ends of the site, in casemate wall rooms in Fields II, III, and IV, and in additional probes around the tell demonstrate that Sennacherib ravaged the entire settlement (Seger 1983:12–15; 1993:558).

At **Khirbet Rabud** (Debir), destruction debris in rooms adjoining the city wall is attributed to an Assyrian attack (Kochavi 1993c:1252).

Sennacherib headed south and east to the administrative center of Beersheba and perhaps to the fortress at Arad. Iron Age Beersheba sits at the junction of roads leading north to Mount Hebron, south to Kadesh Barnea and Elat, east to the Judean Desert and the Dead Sea, and west to the coast. Based on pottery similarities with Lachish Stratum III, it appears that Sennacherib's troops also violently destroyed **Beersheba Stratum II** (Y. Aharoni 1973:107; Aharoni and Aharoni 1976). The Assyrians burned and toppled the casemate wall to the left of the gate (though not to the right), the well-stocked storehouses to the right of the gate, and pillared houses in the western quarter of the town (Y. Aharoni 1973:5, 13, 107; Beit-Arieh 1973:31–37). The "huge conflagration" was "recognizable everywhere . . . masses of brick and debris cover the floors" (Y. Aharoni 1973:5).

At Arad, the original excavation team contended that **Arad Stratum VIII** fell to Sennacherib or the Edomites in 701 B.C.E., stating that "some 90 percent of the pottery in this stratum resembles that from Lachish III and Beersheba stratum II" (Y. Aharoni 1981:149; M. Aharoni 1993:82); however, repeated challenges to the excavators' stratigraphic sequence call into question these historical conclusions (see Finkelstein 1994:170 for references).

Not all sites succumbed to the advancing Assyrians. Some sites continued without disruption, indicating that the Assyrians targeted easily accessible strategic towns located along major routes. At fortified towns in the interior, such as Gibeon and Tell en-Naṣbeh in the hills north of Jerusalem, life and industry continued uninterrupted through the Iron II period. Even the hilltop fort of Khirbet Abu et-Twein, situated in the western slopes of the Hebron hills overlooking the Shephelah, showed no signs of disruption from the eighth century into the sixth–fifth centuries (A. Mazar 1982:174–76).

Not unexpectedly, small farmsteads escaped Assyrian wrath. Examples from the highlands of Samaria in the north to Hebron in the south, as well as examples from the Shephelah, illustrate this phenomenon: no farmstead or hamlet known to exist in the late eighth century appears to have been burned or razed.

Two farmsteads on the western slopes of the Samaria hills, El-Bira 1 and 2, began operation "during the 8th–7th centuries B.C.E., but probably continued in use through the Persian period" (Faust 2003:92, 94).

In the Rephaim Valley outside Jerusalem, the terraced farm of Er-Ras functioned through the eighth and into the seventh century. This farming village consisted of pillared houses, numerous agricultural installations including oil and wine presses, plus isolated structures (Vaughn 1999:144–45; Feig 1996; Feig and Abd Rabu 1996).

Near Wadi Fukin in the Hebron hills, a large farmstead with a pillared house and courtyard with a tower functioned from the eighth into the sixth century (Amit 1991:147).

These sites demonstrate some continuity in highland rural settlement from the eighth century to the sixth century. It is clear that in the wake of Sennacherib's campaign, not everyone fled from their property, was deported by the Assyrians, or was relocated by the Judahite administration (Halpern 1991:27).

While some Shephelah and highland farmers stayed on their farms, survey data do indicate a widespread abandonment with some regional variation. Settlement in the Judean hills peaked in the eighth century B.C.E. and declined thereafter, particularly in the southernmost highlands (Ofer 1994). A similar pattern prevailed in the vicinity of Shechem (Campbell 1991:96–97). Within the Shephelah, as expected, Sennacherib's impact was greatest in the western reaches. From Iron IIA–B to Iron IIC, urban sites (tells) decreased by 65 percent, smaller settlements by 62.5 percent, and farmsteads by 70 percent (Dagan 2004:table 38.5). A survey of the upper Ayalon Valley in the region of Gezer found a reduction in the number of small unwalled settlements from the eighth century (82 percent) to the seventh century (42 percent), not as dramatic a decrease as in the Shephelah (Shavit 2000:189–230). However, in the vicinity of Tell eṣ-Ṣāfī (Gath), sixteen sites have yielded tenth- to eighth-century pottery, but not one has pottery of the seventh–sixth century (Dagan 2002:84*; Finkelstein 1994:172–73; Finkelstein and Naʾaman 2004:60–79).

Conclusion

An archaeological survey of destructions attributed to the Assyrians shows that, contrary to their own boastful assertions, they did not implement a scorched-earth policy throughout the entire region. Their armies traversed major roads destroying forts and administrative centers at strategic road junctions. The Assyrians left the major routes (reconstructed by Dorsey 1991) only twice, once to conquer the valuable coastal cities of Shiqmona and Dor in the north, and a second time to destroy the system of forts guarding Judah's southern and western borders. Except to attack the capital cities of Samaria (with nearby Dothan, Shechem, and Tell el-Farʿah [N]) and Jerusalem, the Assyrian armies avoided the highlands. To subjugate the population, Assyrian policy apparently called for the complete devastation of a small number of well-fortified strategic sites, such as Hazor and Lachish, combined with the partial demolition of other sites, focusing on city gates and nearby structures and on administrative buildings. Peripheral villages and farmsteads were not physically destroyed, although many were abandoned.

The Assyrian impact on the Israelite cult has long been a topic of discussion, but the specific impact of the Assyrian military campaigns on Israelite cultic centralization has not received much attention. Within a few decades, beginning with Tiglath-pileser III's devastating campaign in 734 B.C.E. and culminating with Sennacherib's campaign in 701 B.C.E., Israelite, Philistine, and Judahite forts and administrative centers succumbed to Assyrian might. By 701 B.C.E., the Assyrians had secured the major Shephelah and northern Negev forts guarding the routes to Jerusalem.

That the Judahite capital city of Jerusalem managed to survive the Assyrian campaigns even after Hezekiah's treasonous behavior (2 Kings 18:7–8) in rebelling against Assyria, annexing Philistine territory, and holding hostage the loyal Assyrian vassal Padi of Ekron, served to enhance Jerusalem's status as Yahweh's chosen city. As an unintended consequence of Assyrian imperial policy, therefore, their military campaigns facilitated Hezekiah's efforts to centralize the cult in Jerusalem.

Bibliography

Aharoni, M.
1993 Arad: The Israelite Citadels. In *The New Encyclopedia of Archaeological Excavations in the Holy Land*, ed. E. Stern, 1:82–87. New York: Simon and Schuster.

Aharoni, M., and Y. Aharoni
1976 The Stratification of Judahite Sites in the Eighth and Seventh Centuries B.C.E. *BASOR* 224:73–90.

Aharoni, Y., ed.
1964 *Excavations at Ramat Raḥel: Seasons 1961 and 1962.* Rome: Centro di Studi Semitici.
1973 *Beer-Sheba.* Vol. 1, *Excavations at Tel Beer-Sheba, 1969–1971 Seasons.* Tel Aviv: Institute of Archaeology, Tel Aviv University.
1981 *Arad Inscriptions.* Jerusalem: Israel Exploration Society.

Albright, W. F.
1943 *The Excavation of Tell Beit Mirsim in Palestine.* Vol. 3, *The Iron Age.* AASOR 21–22. New Haven, Conn.: American Schools of Oriental Research.

Amit, D.
1991 Farmsteads in Northern Judea (Betar Area), Survey. *ESI* 10: 147–48.

Avigad, N.
1993 Kudadi, Tell. In *The New Encyclopedia of Archaeological Excavations in the Holy Land*, ed. E. Stern, 3:882. New York: Simon and Schuster.

Avner-Levy, R., and H. Torge
1998 Rosh Ha-ʿAyin. *ESI* 19: 40*, 58–59.

Bachi, G., and M. Ben-Dov
1971 Area D. In *Ashdod*, vols. 2–3, *The Second and Third Seasons of Excavations, 1963, 1965, Soundings in 1967*, ed. M. Dothan, 86–124. ʿAtiqot English Series 9–10. Jerusalem: Israel Department of Antiquities and Museums.

Barkay, G., and D. Ussishkin
2004 Area S: The Iron Age Strata. In *The Renewed Archaeological Excavations at Lachish (1973–1994)*, vol. 2, ed. D. Ussishkin, 411–503. Tel Aviv: Institute of Archaeology, Tel Aviv University.

Barnett, R. D., and M. Falkner
1962 *The Sculptures of Aššur-Nasir-Apli II (883–859 B.C.) Tiglath-Pileser III (745–727 B.C.) Esarhaddon (681–669 B.C.) from the Central and South-West Palaces at Nimrud.* London: British Museum.

Beit-Arieh, I. B.
1973 The Western Quarter. In *Beer-Sheba*, vol. 1, *Excavations at Tel Beer-Sheba, 1969–1971 Seasons*, ed. Y. Aharoni, 31–37. Tel Aviv: Institute of Archaeology, Tel Aviv University.

Ben-Shlomo, D.
2003 The Iron Age Sequence of Tel Ashdod: A Rejoinder to "Ashdod Revisited" by I. Finkelstein and L. Singer-Avitz. *Tel Aviv* 30:83–107.

Ben-Tor, A.
1993 Jokneam. In *The New Encyclopedia of Archaeological Excavations in the Holy Land*, ed. E. Stern, 3:805–11. New York: Simon and Schuster.
1997 Hazor. In *The Oxford Encyclopedia of Archaeology in the Near East*, ed. E. M. Meyers, 3:1–5. New York: Oxford University Press.

Biran, A.
1994 *Biblical Dan*. Jerusalem: Israel Exploration Society and Hebrew Union College-Jewish Institute of Religion.

Blakely, J. A., and J. W. Hardin
2002 Southwestern Judah in the Late Eighth Century B.C.E. *BASOR* 326:11–64.

Borowski, O.
1995 Hezekiah's Reforms and the Revolt against Assyria. *BA* 58:148–55.

Brandl, B.
1997 ᶜErani, Tel. In *The Oxford Encyclopedia of Archaeology in the Near East,* ed. E. M. Meyers, 2:256–58. New York: Oxford University Press.

Bunimovitz, S., and Z. Lederman
1993 Beth-Shemesh. In *The New Encyclopedia of Archaeological Excavations in the Holy Land*, ed. E. Stern, 1:249–53. New York: Simon and Schuster.
2000 Tel Bet Shemesh, 1991–1996 [in Hebrew]. *ESI* 20:105*–8*, 143–47.
2001 Tel Bet Shemesh, 1997–1999 [in Hebrew]. *Ḥadashot Arkheologiyot* 113:98*–100*, 144–47.

Campbell, E. F.
1991 *Shechem*. Vol. 2, *Portrait of a Hill Country Vale: The Shechem Regional Survey*. Atlanta: Scholars Press.
1993 Shechem. In *The New Encyclopedia of Archaeological Excavations in the Holy Land*, ed. E. Stern, 4:1345–54. New York: Simon and Schuster.

Chambon, A.
1984 *Tell el-Farᶜah*. Vol. 1, *L'âge du fer*. Paris: Éditions Recherche sur les Civilisations.
1993 Farᶜah, Tell el- (North). In *The New Encyclopedia of Archaeological Excavations in the Holy Land*, ed. E. Stern, 2:433–40. New York: Simon and Schuster.

Claburn, W. E.
1973 The Fiscal Basis of Josiah's Reforms. *JBL* 92:11–22.

Cogan, M.
1974 *Imperialism and Religion: Assyria, Judah and Israel in the Eighth and Seventh Centuries B.C.E.* Society of Biblical Literature Monograph 19. Missoula, Mont.: Scholars Press.
2000 Sennacherib's Siege of Jerusalem. In *The Context of Scripture*, vol. 2, *Monumental Inscriptions from the Biblical World*, ed. W. Hallo, 302–3. Leiden: Brill.

Dagan, Y.
2002 Survey of the Tel Ẓafit Region [in Hebrew]. *Ḥadashot Arkheologiyot* 114:83*–85*, 102–3.
2004 Results of the Survey: Settlement Patterns in the Lachish Region. In *The Renewed Archaeological Excavations at Lachish (1973–1994)*, vol. 5, ed. D. Ussishkin, 2672–90. Tel Aviv: Institute of Archaeology, Tel Aviv University.

Dessel, J. P.
1997 Ramat Raḥel. In *The Oxford Encyclopedia of Archaeology in the Near East*, ed. E. M. Meyers, 4:402–4. New York: Oxford University Press.

Dever, W. G.
1993 Gezer. In *The New Encyclopedia of Archaeological Excavations in the Holy Land*, ed. E. Stern, 2:496–506. New York: Simon and Schuster.
1997 Gezer. In *The Oxford Encyclopedia of Archaeology in the Near East*, ed. E. M. Meyers, 2:396–400. New York: Oxford University Press.

Dorsey, D.
1991 *The Roads and Highways of Ancient Israel*. Baltimore: Johns Hopkins University Press.

Dothan, M.
1993a Tel Acco. In *The New Encyclopedia of Archaeological Excavations in the Holy Land*, ed. E. Stern, 1:17–24. New York: Simon and Schuster.
1993b Ashdod. In *The New Encyclopedia of Archaeological Excavations in the Holy Land*, ed. E. Stern, 1:93–102. New York: Simon and Schuster.
1993c Mor, Tel. In *The New Encyclopedia of Archaeological Excavations in the Holy Land* , ed. E. Stern, 3:1073–74. New York: Simon and Schuster.

Dothan, T., and S. Gitin
2005 Tel Miqne-Ekron: Summary of Fourteen Season of Excavation 1981–1996 and Bibliography 1982–2005 [unpublished pamphlet]. Jerusalem: Albright Institute and Hebrew University.

Edelstein, G., and I. Milevski
1994 The Rural Settlement of Jerusalem Re-evaluated: Surveys and Excavations in the Rephaim Valley and Mevasseret Yerushalayim. *PEQ* 126:2–23.

Eisenberg, E., and A. Nagorski
2002 Tel Hebron (Er-Rumeidi) [in Hebrew]. *Ḥadashot Arkheologiyot* 114:91*–92*, 112–13.

Elgavish, J.
1993 Shiqmona. In *The New Encyclopedia of Archaeological Excavations in the Holy Land*, ed. E. Stern, 4:1373–78. New York: Simon and Schuster.

Evans, C. D.
1980 Judah's Foreign Policy from Hezekiah to Josiah. In *Scripture in Context: Essays on the Comparative Method*, ed. C. D. Evans, W. W. Hallo, and J. B. White, 157–78. Pittsburgh Theological Monograph Series 34. Pittsburgh: Pickwick.

Faust, A.
2003 The Farmstead in the Highlands of Iron Age II Israel. In *The Rural Landscape of Ancient Israel*, ed. A. Maeir, S. Dar, and Z. Safrai, 91–104. BARIS 1121. Oxford: Archaeopress.

Feig, N.
1996 New Discoveries in the Rephaim Valley, Jerusalem. *PEQ* 128:3–7.

Feig, N., and O. Abd Rabu
1996 Jerusalem, Khirbet er-Ras. *ESI* 15:74–75.

Finkelstein, I.
1994 The Archaeology of the Days of Manasseh. In *Scripture and Other Artifacts: Essays on the Bible and Archaeology in Honor of Philip J. King*, ed. M. D. Coogan, J. C. Exum, and L. E. Stager, 169–87. Louisville, Ky.: Westminster John Knox.

Finkelstein, I., and L. Singer-Avitz
2004 "Ashdod Revisited"—Maintained. *Tel Aviv* 31: 122–35.

Finkelstein, I., D. Ussishkin, and B. Halpern, eds.
2000 *Megiddo* [Tel Aviv]. Vol. 3, *The 1992–1996 Seasons*. Tel Aviv: Institute of Archaeology, Tel Aviv University.

Finkelstein, I., and N. Naʾaman
2004 The Judahite Shephelah in the Late Eighth and Early Seventh Centuries B.C.E. *Tel Aviv* 31:60–79.

Fritz, V.
1993 Chinneret, Tel. In *The New Encyclopedia of Archaeological Excavations in the Holy Land*, ed. E. Stern, 1:299–301. New York: Simon and Schuster.

Gal, Z.
1995 Tel Par. *ESI* 15:33.

Givon, S.
1995 Naḥal Barqai 1993. *ESI* 15:88–90.
1999 Naḥal Barqai 1996–1997 [in Hebrew]. *Ḥadashot Arkheologiyot* 110:67*–68*, 87–88.

Grayson, A. K.
1992 Sennacherib. In *The Anchor Bible Dictionary*, ed. D. N. Freedman, 5:1088–89. New York: Doubleday.

Greenberg, R.
1993 Beit Mirsim, Tell. In *The New Encyclopedia of Archaeological Excavations in the Holy Land*, ed. E. Stern, 1:177–80. New York: Simon and Schuster.

Halpern, B.
1991 Jerusalem and the Lineages in the Seventh Century B.C.E.: Kinship and the Rise of Individual Moral Liability. In *Law and Ideology in Monarchic Israel*, ed. B. Halpern and D. Hobson, 11–107. JSOTSup 124. Sheffield, England: Sheffield Academic Press.

Hizmi, Ḥ.
1998 Ḥorbat ʿEli [in Hebrew]. *ESI* 18:51*–52*, 74–75.

Holloway, S. W.
2002 *Aššur is King! Aššur is King! Religion in the Exercise of Power in the Neo-Assyrian Empire*. CHANE 10. Leiden: Brill.

Kelm, G. L., and A. Mazar
1985 Tel Batash (Timnah) Excavations: Second Preliminary Report (1981–1983). In *Preliminary Reports of ASOR-Sponsored Excavations, 1981–83*, ed. W. E. Rast, 93–120. BASORSup 23. Winona Lake, Ind.: Eisenbrauns.
1995 *Timnah: A Biblical City in the Sorek Valley*. Winona Lake, Ind.: Eisenbrauns.

Kochavi, M.
1993a Hadar, Tel. In *The New Encyclopedia of Archaeological Excavations in the Holy Land*, ed. E. Stern, 2:551–52. New York: Simon and Schuster.
1993b Malḥata, Tel. In *The New Encyclopedia of Archaeological Excavations in the Holy Land*, ed. E. Stern, 3:934–36. New York: Simon and Schuster.
1993c Rabud, Khirbet. In *The New Encyclopedia of Archaeological Excavations in the Holy Land*, ed. E. Stern, 4:1252. New York: Simon and Schuster.
1997 ʿEin-Gev. In *The Oxford Encyclopedia of Archaeology in the Near East*, ed. E. M. Meyers, 2:223–24. New York: Oxford University Press.

Mazar, A.
1982 Three Israelite Sites in the Hills of Judah and Ephraim. *BA* 45:167–78.
1990 *Archaeology of the Land of the Bible, 10,000–586 B.C.E.* New York: Doubleday.
1993 Marjameh, Khirbet. In *The New Encyclopedia of Archaeological Excavations in the Holy Land*, ed. E. Stern, 3:965–66. New York: Simon and Schuster.

1997 Four Thousand Years of History at Tel Beth-Shean: An Account of the Renewed Excavations. *BA* 60:62–76.
1999 Tel Reḥov [in Hebrew]. *Ḥadashot Arkheologiyot* 109:42*–43*, 59–60.
2002 Tel Reḥov 1998–2001 [in Hebrew]. *Ḥadashot Arkheologiyot* 114:38*–40*, 43–45.

Mazar, B.
1993 ᶜEn Gev. In *The New Encyclopedia of Archaeological Excavations in the Holy Land*, ed. E. Stern, 2:409–11. New York: Simon and Schuster.

Millard, A.
1997 The Babylonian Chronicle. In *The Context of Scripture*, vol. 1, *Canonical Compositions from the Biblical World*, ed. W. Hallo, 467–68. Leiden: Brill.

Naʾaman, N.
1979 Sennacherib's Campaign to Judah and the Date of the *LMLK* Stamps. *VT* 29:61–86.

Ofer, A.
1994 "All the Hill Country of Judah": From a Settlement Fringe to a Prosperous Monarchy. In *From Nomadism to Monarchy: Archaeological and Historical Aspects of Early Israel*, ed. I. Finkelstein and N. Naʾaman, 92–121. Jerusalem: Israel Exploration Society.

Oren, E. D.
1993 Seraᶜ, Tel. In *The New Encyclopedia of Archaeological Excavations in the Holy Land*, ed. E. Stern, 4:1329–35. New York: Simon and Schuster.
1997 Seraᶜ, Tel. In *The Oxford Encyclopedia of Archaeology in the Near East*, ed. E. M. Meyers, 5:1–2. New York: Oxford University Press.

Rainey, A. F., and R. S. Notley
2006 *The Sacred Bridge: Carta's Atlas of the Biblical World.* Jerusalem: Carta.

Seger, J. D.
1983 Investigations at Tell Ḥalif, Israel, 1976–1980. *BASOR* 252:1–23.
1993 Ḥalif, Tel. In *The New Encyclopedia of Archaeological Excavations in the Holy Land*, ed. E. Stern, 2:553–59. New York: Simon and Schuster.

Shavit, A.
2000 Settlement Patterns in the Ayalon Valley in the Bronze and Iron Ages. *Tel Aviv* 27:189–230.

Stern, E.
2000 *Dor—Ruler of the Seas*: *Nineteen Years of Excavation at the Israelite-Phoenician Harbor Town on the Carmel Coast*. Jerusalem: Israel Exploration Society.
2001 *Archaeology of the Land of the Bible*. Vol. 2, *The Assyrian, Babylonian, and Persian Periods, 732–332 B.C.E.* New York: Doubleday.

Tadmor, H.
1971 Fragments of an Assyrian Stele of Sargon II. In *Ashdod*, vols. 2–3, *The Second and Third Seasons of Excavations, 1963, 1965, Soundings in 1967*, ed. M. Dothan, 192–97. ᶜAtiqot English Series 9–10. Jerusalem: Israel Department of Antiquities and Museums.
1994 *The Inscriptions of Tiglath-Pileser III King of Assyria*: *Critical Edition with Introduction, Translations and Commentary*. Jerusalem: Israel Academy of Sciences and Humanities.

Tappy, R. E.
2001 *The Archaeology of Israelite Samaria*. Vol. 2, *The Eighth Century B.C.E.* HSS 50. Winona Lake, Ind.: Eisenbrauns.

Tufnell, O.
1950 Excavations at Tell ed-Duweir, Palestine, Directed by the Late J. L. Starkey, 1932–1938. *PEQ* 82:65–80.

Ussishkin, D.
1993 Dothan. In *The New Encyclopedia of Archaeological Excavations in the Holy Land*, ed. E. Stern, 1:372–73. New York: Simon and Schuster.
2004 *The Renewed Archaeological Excavations at Lachish (1973–1994)*. 5 vols. Tel Aviv: Institute of Archaeology, Tel Aviv University.

Vaughn, A.
1999 *Theology, History, and Archaeology in the Chronicler's Account of Hezekiah.* Archaeology and Biblical Studies 4. Atlanta: Scholars Press.

Yadin, Y.
1993 Hazor. In *The New Encyclopedia of Archaeological Excavations in the Holy Land*, ed. E. Stern, 2:594–603. New York: Simon and Schuster.

Yadin, Y., and S. Geva
1986 *Investigations at Beth Shean: The Early Iron Age Strata*. Qedem 23. Jerusalem: Institute of Archaeology, Hebrew University of Jerusalem.

Yeivin, Z.
1993 ᶜErani, Tel. In *The New Encyclopedia of Archaeological Excavations in the Holy Land*, ed. E. Stern, 2:417–19 and 421. New York: Simon and Schuster.

Younger, K. L.
2000a Tiglath-pileser III. In *The Context of Scripture*, vol. 2, *Monumental Inscriptions from the Biblical World*, ed. W. Hallo, 284–92. Leiden: Brill.
2000b Sargon II. In *The Context of Scripture*, vol. 2, *Monumental Inscriptions from the Biblical World*, ed. W. Hallo, 293–300. Leiden: Brill.

Zimhoni, O.
1990 Two Ceramic Assemblages from Lachish Levels III and II. *Tel Aviv*17:3–52.

5. "Those Who Add House to House": Household Archaeology and the Use of Domestic Space in an Iron II Residential Compound at Tell en-Naṣbeh

by Aaron J. Brody

This preliminary view of the archaeology of the family at Tell en-Naṣbeh initiates a broader program of research on Iron Age II households at the site, which was probably the biblical town of Mizpah. By studying the artifacts excavated by the Pacific School of Religion's expedition to Naṣbeh in the 1920s and 1930s in their original architectural contexts, I will explore lifeways in a fortified village from the vantage point of the extended household. Because the extended or joint family was the foundation of ancient Israelite society, this will provide insight into a microcosm that shaped social, economic, and religious elements of biblical culture. This vantage point gives an opportunity to view Israelite (specifically Judahite) society from the bottom up, rather than depending on the royal or elite view typically preserved in the Hebrew Bible for the period of the United and Divided Monarchies. It also serves to correct the archaeological bias toward elite contexts found in numerous Iron II excavations that have focused primarily on monumental structures and large urban centers.

It is an honor and a privilege to dedicate this research to Larry Stager, whom I have known now in many roles, as my teacher, adviser, mentor, dig director, and colleague. Larry's research on the agriculture and lifeways of ancient Israelites has broken new ground in our field. His 1985 article on the archaeology of the family, in which he presented his view of the underlying structures of biblical society and their reflexes in the material culture of the period, is still fundamental after more than twenty years (Stager 1985). The following research is a small token of my appreciation.

Tell en-Naṣbeh

The site of Tell en-Naṣbeh was excavated by a team from the Pacific School of Religion under the direction of W. F. Badè. The site is located 12 km northwest of Jerusalem. It is the most prominent tell in the small territory of Benjamin. In five seasons, from 1926 to 1935, two-thirds of the 3-ha site was uncovered, along with tombs located outside the tell. Badè died in the year following the final season, having published several interim reports and a manual of archaeological field methodology based on his work at Naṣbeh (Badè 1934). The artifacts and accompanying documentation were further processed and analyzed back in Berkeley by a small team of researchers under the direction of C. C. McCown, Badè's New Testament colleague, who was also an archaeologist. The results were published in two final report volumes (McCown 1947; Wampler 1947).

Thomas McClellan (1984) was the first researcher to reinterpret some of the confused stratigraphy at the site based on the original documentation housed at the Badè Museum at the Pacific School of Religion. McClellan's work concentrated on the organization and layout of the settlement in the Iron II period. Later, Jeffrey Zorn, for his dissertation research, reanalyzed all of the phases of occupation at the site, from the Early Bronze I through the Roman period, using the original notes, photographs, and architectural plans in the Badè Museum (Zorn 1993b). He established that Tell en-Naṣbeh has five main strata. Stratum 5 consists of pits and tombs cut into the bedrock dating to the Early Bronze I. Stratum 4 follows after a long gap, and consists primarily of features such as silos and cisterns cut into the bedrock during the Iron I. Stratum 3, which is a fortified village or town primarily made up of pillared houses and several fortification systems, is divided into three subphases that date to the Iron IIA–IIC. Stratum 2 consists of larger four-room buildings from the Babylonian/early Persian period. Stratum 1 is an ill-defined phase from the Hellenistic/Roman periods (Zorn 1993a; 1993b). Zorn has subsequently published numerous articles on Tell en-Naṣbeh, particularly on aspects of the Iron II and Babylonian/early Persian Strata 3 and 2 (see *http://www.arts.cornell.edu/jrz3/pdf_files_of_collected_works.htm*).

Zorn's detailed research on the stratigraphy of Tell en-Naṣbeh provides a phased architectural framework from which to begin an interpretive program of household archaeology at the site. The original excavation notes, or millimeter cards, from the Badè expedition record diagnostic ceramics and small finds in their original contexts (Badè 1934:34–38, 40–41), so we can study the material according to the rooms and features (bins, cisterns, silos, etc.) in which it was found, and we can use Zorn's stratigraphic analysis to determine which rooms and features were contemporaneous. This is virtually impossible to do using the data as presented in the two final report volumes from the site, in which the stratigraphy is mixed and very little contextual information is supplied for artifacts (McCown 1947; Wampler 1947).

To date, very few field projects or synthetic studies in the southern Levant have focused on the methods and theories of household archaeology that allow for research questions concerning family structure, room use and function, household activity areas, and the division of gendered space (see Stager 1985; Daviau 1993; Lederman 1999:120–38; Ilan 2001; Schloen 2001; Hardin 2001; 2004; Meyers 2003; Gadot and Yasur-Landau 2006; for recent studies in household archaeology, see Bermann 1994; Allison 1999; Nevett 1999; Barile and Brandon 2004). Because the household was the most basic social, economic, and even judicial unit in ancient Israel and the broader ancient Near East (Wright 1992:763–64; Blenkinsopp 1997; Meyers 1997; McNutt 1999; Schloen 2001), archaeological research on ordinary houses is critical for understanding these wide ranging issues in their broader contexts.

Research on the material remains of households at Tell en-Naṣbeh is essential for understanding the function of the site in the Iron Age II, despite our understandable hesitation about using materials that were excavated seventy to eighty years ago. The more recent excavations at Tel Halif and the research of James Hardin have provided remarkable insights into the use of space in a single Iron II four-room house based on a detailed spatial analysis of its ceramics, small finds, and microartifacts (Hardin 2001; 2004).[1] Stratum 3 at Tell en-Naṣbeh is not as well documented, but it provides a much larger area for contextual artifact analysis, which makes possible an understanding of lifeways, not just in one house but in several domestic compounds, and allows for comparisons between numerous contemporaneous households. The excavated area at Naṣbeh assigned to Stratum 3 contains 32 three-room and three+-room houses and 10 four-room and four+-room houses (Zorn 1993b:119–21). A similar household analysis can be conducted for Stratum 2, the Babylonian/early Persian phase, but that lies beyond the scope of this paper.

Household Compound

For the moment, I have chosen one household compound to investigate through an analysis of its material cultural contents. This compound will serve as a test case for the application of my method over a broader range of contemporary households at Naṣbeh in the Iron II period (Zorn 1993b:114–62). It consists of a row of three typical agglutinated three-room houses flanked by a two-room building on their northwest and an atypical three-room house to the southeast. I chose to focus on this particular compound for three reasons. First, this compound has often been selected in previous studies of Iron Age pillared houses to illustrate typical three-room houses (Stager 1984:fig. 9g; Holladay 1992:fig. HOU.01.B). Second, three-room houses are the most common type in Stratum 3 at Naṣbeh (Zorn 1993b:137–38). And, finally, there is very little evidence of later construction on top of this house compound or of robbing of its walls.[2]

The compound is located in the southwestern area of the site and consists of a two-room structure in the northwest, three standard three-room houses, and an atypical three-room house in the southeast (see figure 1).[3] The five building units all share common walls and they are bounded by fairly well-defined streets to the north, west, and south, and by an unexcavated "rubble heap" on the east. The five buildings include sixteen rooms, one bin, and two cisterns. These rooms and features were excavated and recorded as separate loci. The two-room structure has a broad room in back, Room 609, and a large room in front, Room 607, which has been interpreted as a courtyard (Zorn 1993b:649).[4] The two-room structure shares its southern wall with a three-room pillared house that has a broad room, Room 610, at its rear, and two long rooms separated by pillars, Rooms 608 and 588, adjacent to the street. A small room, Room 606, is located in the front of Room 608. A small rectangular space, Bin 355, lies within Room 588 and appears to block the entrance to Cistern 359 beneath it (Zorn 1993b:652–53). This three-room house shares its

[1] The author would like to thank J. Hardin for providing him with a copy of his dissertation.

[2] Four "Roman ribbed-ware" sherds were registered among the finds from the compound: two in Room 609 and one in Bin 355 and Room 575. This later material was likely washed into the area from higher up on the tell, or it may have been deposited by modern plowing of the site, which was used for agricultural purposes before and after the excavation.

[3] For a detailed discussion of the architecture and stratigraphy of each individual building, numbered from north to south 142.02, 142.03, 159.04, 159.05, and 159.06, see Zorn 1993b:649–53, 736–41.

[4] Zorn thinks most three- and four-room houses in Stratum 3 contained their own courtyards (1993b:142), an interpretation followed by Schloen (2001:175–80). Based on the architectural and artifact evidence presented below, I suggest that the open courtyards for this compound were located in the two outermost buildings and the three three-room houses were entirely roofed over. The two courtyards would have been used communally by the extended family that inhabited the three three-room houses.

south wall with another three-room pillared house, which has a broad room, Room 612, at the rear and two long rooms in front, Room 584 and 580, divided by pillars. This building's southern wall is shared with the next three-room house, which has a broad room, Room 579, in the rear. Its northern long room is broken up with a small Room 577 in front and larger Room 578 in back; the second long room, Room 576, is over Cistern 354. The final, atypical three-room building is made up of three broad rooms: Room 575, separated by pillars from Room 581, and Room 513.

Almost every wall foundation has one row of stones ca. 31–47 cm wide (figure 1). This construction feature is a hallmark of Stratum 3 buildings. Following Zorn's measurements, the width of these single-stone walls averages 43 cm and ranges from 36 to 50 cm (Zorn 1993b:123). Later phases in Stratum 3 show rebuilds with broader walls that use two rows of stones, with widths averaging 71 cm and ranging from 54 to 88 cm (ibid.). Carol Kramer's research on traditional village houses in Iran that had stone foundations and mudbrick superstructures indicates that a second story requires foundations about a meter thick (Kramer 1982:99). Accordingly, it is likely that our compound did not have any second-story rooms (contra Schloen 2001:176–80).

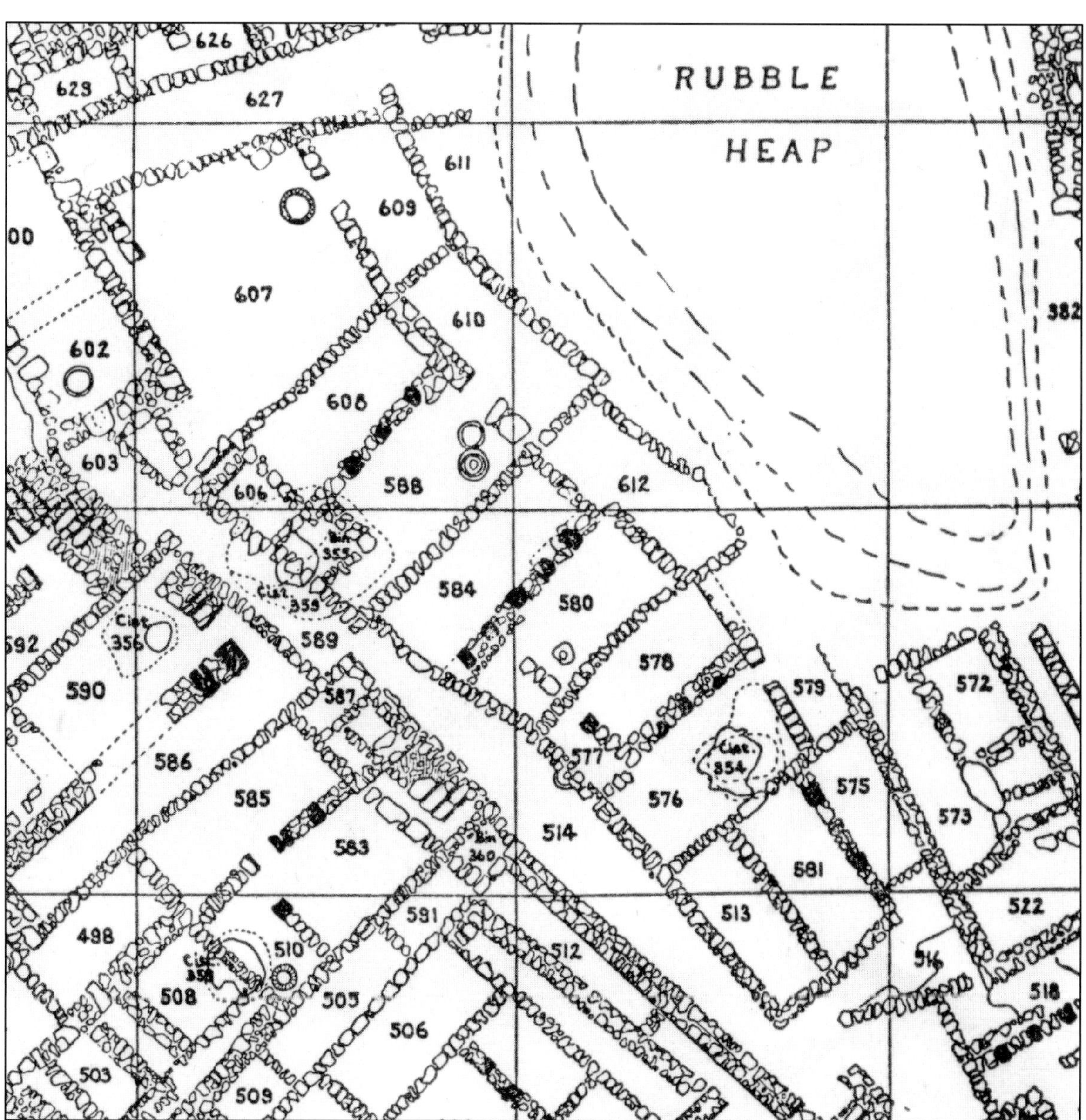

Figure 1. Iron II household compound at Tell en-Naṣbeh (each square is 10 × 10 m)

Courtesy of the Badè Museum at the Pacific School of Religion

Artifacts from the Compound

For the sixteen rooms and one bin that make up the compound, 413 artifacts were registered and recorded on object cards. Unfortunately, either no remains were recorded for Room 606 or the object cards have been misplaced, therefore its finds could not be included in this study. Finds from the two cisterns are not included in the study; their existence and location may be important for the interpretation of room function, but analysis of their artifacts was not considered essential. Three rooms, Rooms 607, 608, and 588, have remains recorded for a "sublevel" that I have included separately from the "Level I" finds from the same loci. All three of these rooms abut one another. These sublevels may represent subfloor fill, floor buildup, or floors on which lay collapsed ceiling material.[5] Unfortunately, no interpretations of this nature were recorded in the field notes.

Not all of the 413 artifacts have been tabulated (tables 1 and 2). Handles and bases were generally not included in the counts because one is never sure whether a rim, handle, and base attributed to a given ceramic category are from the same vessel or from three different vessels of the same type; however, a handle or base was included if it was the only example in a given ceramic category or if it was determined to be from a different vessel type than represented by rims in a given category. Four later sherds, described in note 2, were not included in the sample.

While the field treatment of the pottery from Naṣbeh was outstanding for its time, some of Wampler's terminology has to be updated. For example, "zirs" are categorized as pithoi, "plates" as bowls, and "pitchers" as jugs (see Wampler 1947). Drawings provided on the object cards were compared with their original typological designations, and on occasion, pieces were reassigned to a different vessel type based on current understandings and terminology. Of Ruth Amiran's (1969:15) thirteen broad ceramic categories, ten are represented by the pottery finds from rooms in the compound. These include bowls, chalices, kraters, cooking pots, pithoi, jars, jugs, juglets, pilgrim flasks, and lamps (table 1).[6] Small finds represent a range of artifact and ecofact types, mostly falling into the broad categories of tools, weaving and sewing implements, items of personal adornment, weapons, cultic items, and animal bones and shells (table 2).

Pottery

Most of the ceramic types can be assigned to one of three basic groups based on interpretation of vessel function: cooking, consumption/serving, and storage (Lederman 1999:126; Hardin 2001:133–38; King and Stager 2001:64–67, 142–46). The "cooking" group is made up of cooking pots;[7] the "consumption/serving" group by bowls, kraters, jugs, and pilgrim flasks; and the "storage" group by various types of pithoi and jars, including storage jars, conical jars, and holemouth jars. I have left chalices out of the coding process because we are not sure whether they were used for drinking liquids, offering libations, or burning incense, or served all three functions. In any case, their numbers are small and statistically insignificant. Lamps do not fit into any of the three functional categories and are treated separately. Juglets were further divided into dipper juglets and container juglets (Hunt 1987:203–4) and were tallied in the consumption/serving or storage groups accordingly.

The absolute amount of pottery in any of the three groups differs by room, so the relative percentages of the three groups within a given room are the most meaningful figures to be compared (see table 3). For example, Room 609 has fifteen vessels categorized in the three groups: one for cooking; three for consumption/serving; and eleven for storage. Therefore, 1 of 15 (7 percent) of the vessels is in the cooking group; 3 of 15 (20 percent) are in the consumption/serving group; and 11 of 15 (73 percent) are in the storage group.

The percentages by functional category are presented in table 3 and are diagrammed spatially in figures 2–4. Note that Room 579 has been left out of these figures because its tallies are based on only three vessels—one from each functional category, as it happens—so its statistics do not provide us with any meaningful information.[8]

[5] In his *Manual of Excavation in the Near East*, Badè notes that "at Tell en-Naṣbeh the remains of charred timbers were occasionally found under masses of roof clay, usually made of soft limestone, pounded into fine particles and mixed with water" (1934:61). Unfortunately, he does not detail where these collapsed ceilings were discovered, which is not surprising in an excavation manual, and he died before he could write the site's final report.

[6] No goblet, amphoriskos, or pyxis was found among the pottery in the compound.

[7] Cooking jugs and griddles are also found at Naṣbeh but are not represented in the sample from the chosen group of buildings.

[8] Zorn notes that Room 579 was only partially excavated (1993b:739). This may have been due to its proximity to the large "rubble heap" shown on the site plan (McCown 1947:insert map).

Table 1. Pottery from Rooms in the Tell en-Naṣbeh Compound

Room	*Bowl*	*Chalice*	*Krater*	*Cooking pot*	*Pithos*	*Jar*	*Jug*	*Juglet*	*Pilgrim flask*	*Lamp*
513	7	—	—	5	5	16	1	3	2	2
575	2	—	—	1	4	4	—	1	1	1
576	9	1	—	1	1	8	—	3	—	2
577	2	—	—	1	—	1	2	—	—	1
578	5	—	—	1	1	8	1	3	1	1
579	—	—	—	1	—	1	1	—	—	—
580	4	—	—	1	2	5	1	—	—	1
581	2	—	—	3	2	2	2	—	—	1
584	—	1	—	1	1	3	1	—	—	—
588	3	—	1	2	2	2	1	—	—	1
588 sub	2	—	—	2	—	—	1	—	—	—
607	6	1	1	1	3	10	—	2	—	2
607 sub	1	—	—	—	1	2	—	—	—	—
608	6	—	—	3	1	5	1	—	—	1
608 sub	5	1	—	1	—	1	2	1	—	2
609	1	—	—	1	4	7	1	1	—	—
610	4	—	—	—	1	2	1	—	—	2
612	2	—	—	1	1	1	—	2	—	—
Bin 355	2	—	—	2	2	4	1	—	—	1

Note: Finds are from Level I of the rooms unless indicated as "sub" for Sub-Level I.

Table 2. Small Finds from Rooms in the Tell en-Naṣbeh Compound

Room	*Small finds*
513	Phoenician jug; iron nail; stone bead; leg of bowl/figurine?; 2 pillar-figurine bases; ceramic "face" from decorated vessel; animal figurine leg; stone socle; basalt mortar leg; 2 flint slingstones; 1 limestone slingstone; animal mandible; horse-and-rider frag.; pillar-figurine torso; animal bone; 2 animal teeth; 2 boar's tusks
575	ceramic basin frag.?; basalt rubbing stone
576	limestone cosmetic bowl; flint sickle blade; fenestrated stand frag.; basalt smoothing stone; whetstone; flint hammerstone; animal tusk sawn in half; ceramic jar stopper
577	basalt pestle frag.; flint slingstone; mollusk shell; basalt spindle whorl
578	ceramic funnel; carnelian bead; iron arrowhead; horse-and-rider figurine; mollusk shell pendant
579	round basalt frag.; 2 bronze earrings
580	iron punch; stone basin (on plan)
581	ceramic basin frag.; bone pendant; black stone bead; bone spatula; iron arrowhead; bronze frag.; bronze earring; flint smoothing stone; flint burnishing stone; basalt pestle; animal horn
584	animal figurine torso
588	bone spatula frag.; zoomorphic vessel frag.; flint slingstone frag.; fossil shell; bronze needle; 2 iron "nails"; stone basin (on plan); olive press basin (on plan)
588 sub	—
607	basalt spindle whorl; 2 flint slingstones; basalt grinding stone frag.; iron arrowhead; stone basin (on plan)
607 sub	—
608	iron arrowhead; iron rod; ceramic button base frag.
608 sub	pillar figurine frag.
609	ceramic funnel; bronze fragment; iron rod; dark-brown bead; limestone spindle whorl
610	ceramic ring stand; iron knife frag.; limestone grinding stone; pillar figurine frag.
612	—
Bin 355	clay basin frag.; animal bone

Note: Finds are from Level I of the rooms unless indicated as "sub" for Sub-Level I.

Table 3. Relative Percentages of Pottery by Functional Category

Room	*Cooking*	*Consumption/Serving*	*Storage*
513	13% (5/39)	31% (12/39)	56% (22/39)
575	8% (1/13)	31% (4/13)	62% (8/13)
576	5% (1/22)	50% (11/22)	45% (10/22)
577	17% (1/6)	67% (4/6)	17% (1/6)
578	5% (1/20)	40% (8/20)	55% (11/20)
579	33% (1/3)	33% (1/3)	33% (1/3)
580	8% (1/13)	38% (5/13)	54% (7/13)
581	27% (3/11)	36% (4/11)	36% (4/11)
584	17% (1/6)	17% (1/6)	67% (4/6)
588	18% (2/11)	45% (5/11)	36% (4/11)
588 sub	40% (2/5)	0% (0/5)	60% (3/5)
607	4% (1/23)	30% (7/23)	65% (15/23)
607 sub	0% (0/6)	33% (2/6)	67% (4/6)
608	19% (3/16)	44% (7/16)	38% (6/16)
608 sub	10% (1/10)	80% (8/10)	10% (1/10)
609	7% (1/15)	20% (3/15)	73% (11/15)
610	0% (0/8)	62% (5/8)	38% (3/8)
612	14% (1/7)	57% (4/7)	29% (2/7)
Bin 355	18% (2/11)	55% (6/11)	27% (3/11)

Note: Finds are from Level I of the rooms unless indicated as "sub" for Sub-Level I.
Results are rounded to the nearest percentage. Actual counts are shown in parentheses.

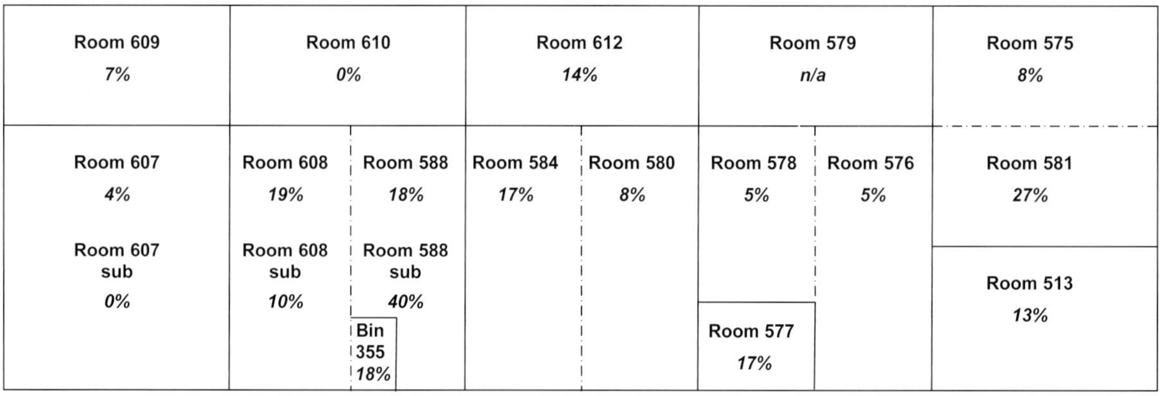

Room 609 *7%*
Room 610 *0%*
Room 612 *14%*
Room 579 *n/a*
Room 575 *8%*
Room 607 *4%*
Room 608 *19%*
Room 588 *18%*
Room 584 *17%*
Room 580 *8%*
Room 578 *5%*
Room 576 *5%*
Room 581 *27%*
Room 607 sub *0%*
Room 608 sub *10%*
Room 588 sub *40%*
Room 513 *13%*
Bin 355 *18%*
Room 577 *17%*

Figure 2. Schematic plan of rooms showing percentages of pottery in the "cooking" category

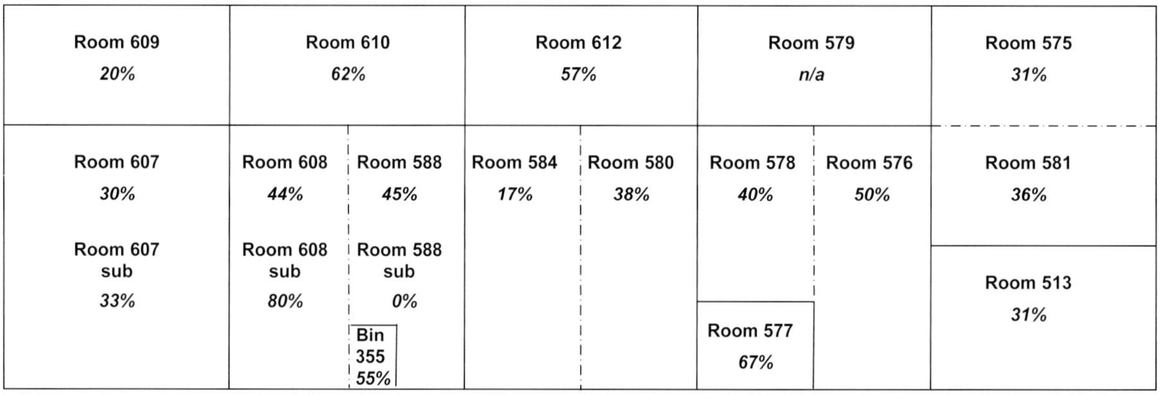

Room 609 *20%*
Room 610 *62%*
Room 612 *57%*
Room 579 *n/a*
Room 575 *31%*
Room 607 *30%*
Room 608 *44%*
Room 588 *45%*
Room 584 *17%*
Room 580 *38%*
Room 578 *40%*
Room 576 *50%*
Room 581 *36%*
Room 607 sub *33%*
Room 608 sub *80%*
Room 588 sub *0%*
Room 513 *31%*
Bin 355 *55%*
Room 577 *67%*

Figure 3. Schematic plan of rooms showing percentages of pottery in the "consumption/serving" category

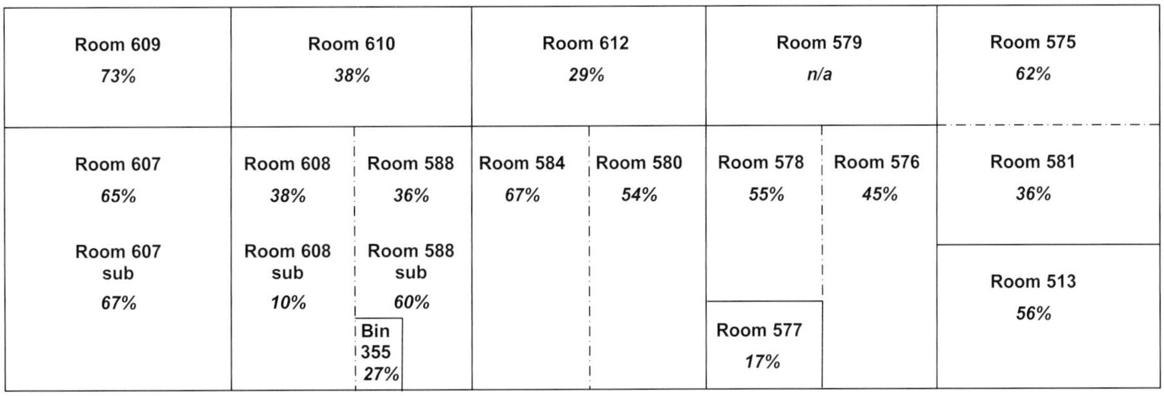

Room 609 73%	Room 610 38%			Room 612 29%		Room 579 n/a		Room 575 62%
Room 607 65% Room 607 sub 67%	Room 608 38% Room 608 sub 10%	Room 588 36% Room 588 sub 60%	Bin 355 27%	Room 584 67%	Room 580 54%	Room 578 55% Room 577 17%	Room 576 45%	Room 581 36% Room 513 56%

Figure 4. Schematic plan of rooms showing percentages of pottery in the "storage" category

The highest proportion of cooking vessels is 40 percent, in Room 588 Sub-Level I; but this may be misleading because there were only five vessels in this locus, two of which were cooking pots. It is possible that Room 588 was used as a kitchen in Sub-Level I and then changed function in Level I (this is discussed below). The next highest proportions of cooking pots are 27 percent in Room 581; 19 percent in Room 608 Level I; 18 percent in Room 588 Level I; and 18 percent in Bin 355, a feature small enough that it was more likely used for storage than cooking. Rooms 608, 588, and Bin 355 are all in the same three-room house and it is unlikely that all three loci were used as kitchens.

Unfortunately, no clay ovens (tabuns) were recorded in any of the rooms or features of the entire compound, which would have helped us to pinpoint a kitchen (Zorn 1993b:table B.3.1). Cooking pots make up 17 percent of the vessels in Rooms 584 and 577; 14 percent in Room 612; and 13 percent in Room 513. The remaining seven rooms and one sublevel have less than 10 percent of their ceramics made up of cooking pots. Interestingly, the one room that has consistently been interpreted as a courtyard, Room 607, has only 1 cooking vessel out of 23 (4 percent) in Level I, and none in its Sub-Level I locus.

Ethnoarchaeological studies in traditional Middle Eastern villages show that cooking is typically done outdoors in the courtyard during the hottest months (Kramer 1979:156; Hardin 2004:75). This may suggest that Room 581 at the opposite end of the building compound also was a courtyard, as it is our most likely kitchen.[9] In the northern wall of Room 581 is a long stone that is likely the threshold of an entrance into Room 576 (see figure 1) and opens directly into the opening for Cistern 354, providing easy access to water for food preparation and cooking. The next highest representations of cooking vessels are in the two long rooms, Room 608 and Room 588, and in Bin 355 in our northernmost three-room house. These numbers may indicate a kitchen used seasonally, perhaps in the winter. Out of the three, Room 608 is the most likely kitchen as Room 588 has one of Stratum 3's two *in situ* olive-pressing vats (Zorn 1993b:146) and Bin 355 seems too cramped to serve as a kitchen. It is possible that Rooms 584 and 577 were used as seasonal kitchens, although Room 577 is fairly small: its interior measuring only two square meters. Thus, I would suggest that Rooms 608 and 581 served as kitchens, perhaps as winter and summer kitchens respectively.

The coding of the consumption/serving group produced interesting results, as vessels in this category are usually associated with the living space in a household (Kramer 1982:102; Hardin 2001:226–27). Living rooms are typically where the nuclear family shared meals, slept, and entertained. Rooms with greater than 50 percent of their ceramics in this group include two of the broad rooms, Rooms 610 and 612; two of the smallest spaces, Room 577 and Bin 355; and the Sub-Level I locus of Room 608, a long room. The presence of 80 percent consumption/serving type ceramics in this lower level in Room 608 may indicate a shift in use from living room to kitchen, as marked by the ceramics in its Level I, as discussed above. If we discount Room 577 and Bin 355 as living spaces, based primarily on their diminutive size, then broad rooms 610 and 612 stand out as the living areas in two of the three room houses. It is probable that Room 579, the broad room of the third three-room house, was also a living room. Unfortunately, Room 579 was only partially excavated and the three ceramic finds from this locus are too few to indicate how the room functioned.

[9] Zorn has also suggested that Room 581 is a courtyard based on architectural analysis (1993b:740).

It is important to note that rooms in the outermost two-room building and the atypical three-room building had relatively low percentages of pottery in the consumption/serving group. This suggests that living rooms were not present in these outermost structures of the compound.

Because storage was vital to the survival of ancient families, it is not surprising that pottery classified in the storage category is present in high percentages in the compound. In six rooms, Rooms 609, 607, 584, 578, 575, and 513, 55–73 percent of the pottery consists of storage vessels. Four out of six of these rooms are in the two outermost buildings of the compound, suggesting that their major use was for storage. The remaining two rooms with a high percentage of storage ceramics are long rooms, Rooms 584 and 578, in the central and southern three-room houses. These houses' other long rooms, Rooms 580 and 576, also have large percentages of storage vessels, 54 percent and 45 percent respectively. In addition, the Sub-Level I locus of Room 588 has 60 percent storage types, although, as we have seen, this level may represent a former kitchen, a room function that also requires a fair amount of storage.

Lamps

The distribution of lamps is important to note and may be taken, with caution, as an indication of roofed space (Hardin 2001:250). Lamp finds are absent from Rooms 609, 612, 584, and 579 (four out of sixteen loci). They are fairly evenly distributed throughout the remaining rooms and the bin, with one or two examples found in each. This includes lamps in Rooms 607 and 581, which have been interpreted above as courtyards. If this functional interpretation is correct, the presence of lamps may suggest that the courtyards were used after sunset.

Small Finds

I have broken down small finds into five broad categories, which account for the majority of these artifacts: tools, weaving and sewing implements, items of personal adornment, weapons, and cultic items. Tools include ground-stone, flaked-stone, and metal objects as well as ceramic funnels and basins. Spindle whorls, bone spatulas, and a bronze needle make up the weaving and sewing category. Personal adornment is represented by stone beads, several bronze earrings, and a bone-and-shell pendant. Weapons found in the remains of the buildings include iron arrowheads and slingstones. Cultic items are represented by clay figurines (animal, horse-and-rider, and female pillar figurines), a fenestrated stand, a fragment of a zoomorphic vessel, and the "face" from a decorated vessel.

Unlike ceramics, small finds tend to be uncovered in limited quantities, so I did not treat them by the percentage they represented out of registered finds, or out of the group of small finds, but rather simply by presence/absence. The highest number of tools, five, is found in Room 576. The concentration of five stone tools in Room 576 and a sawn animal tusk suggests that this space was used as a workshop. I have counted the "cosmetic" palette from Room 576 as a tool, since it is actually a diminutive limestone mortar and even in its broken state could have been reused for grinding small quantities of a wide range of products. My suggestion above, based on ceramic finds, that Room 581 served as a kitchen is further supported by the presence of a basalt pestle and a ceramic basin, which may have been used for milling grain (Amiry and Tamari 1989:19). The remaining small finds categorized as tools are found fairly evenly distributed across the compound, one or two to a room. Only three rooms, Rooms 608, 612, and 584 did not have any tools.

Weaving and sewing items were not found in great number. Only Room 588 had more than one find, with a bone spatula and a bronze needle in its sub-level remains. Room 588 has one of the only *in situ* olive-oil pressing basins; it may be suggested based on the small finds that this space was used for weaving seasonally when not used for pressing olives. One stone whorl was found in each of Rooms 609, 607, and 577, and one bone spatula in Room 581. It is interesting that no loom weights were found in any of the rooms across the compound.

Artifacts related to personal adornment are rare. Except for one bead found in Room 609, they are all concentrated in the two southernmost buildings of the compound. The largest group of jewelry, a bead, bone pendant, and earring, was found in Room 581. As this space has been interpreted as a kitchen, a room type in the southern Levant that is typically associated with women's productive tasks (Meyers 1997:24–26), it is probable that this jewelry belonged to women in the extended household. Two bronze earrings, perhaps a pair, were found in Room 579; a bone-and-shell pendant in Room 578, and a single bead in 513.

Weapons, most likely related to the destruction of the compound, were found fairly evenly distributed in the western rooms.[10] Three slingstones were con-

[10] Zorn (1993a:143) posits that Stratum 3 came to a "non-violent end," an interpretation that is contradicted by the

centrated in Room 513, and two slingstones and an iron arrowhead in the courtyard Room 607. The remaining slingstones and iron arrowheads were found individually in Rooms 608, 588, 578, 577, and 581.

Cultic items, our final category of small finds, are found clustered in only one space, Room 513. Otherwise they are found one to a room, in six different rooms (Rooms 610, 608 Sub-Level I, 588, 584, 578, and 576) in each of the three-room houses. While the ceramics in Room 513 suggest its use in storage, its two pillar figurine bases, one pillar figurine torso, animal figurine leg, horse-and-rider fragment, and sculpted face from a ceramic vessel may be interpreted as representing finds from a shrine. It is probable that the Phoenician trefoil-mouth jug found in Room 513, the only one from the site and the only imported vessel found in the compound, was used in ceremonies associated with these cultic finds (Brody forthcoming). The two boars' tusks from the room may have had a sacred function, although they may have been stored for a profane use as well.

Conclusion

Ethnoarchaeological research in villages in the modern Middle East has shown that the function of rooms in a given household can change over time (Watson 1979; Kramer 1979:157; 1982:96–97; Horne 1994: 177–83; Kamp 2000:91). This "recycling" of architectural space occurs as the family or extended family grows and changes and its needs shift (for historic and archaeological correlates see Stone 1981). These same studies of modern traditional villages show that room use is typically multifunctional and may vary by season.

These factors make the attempt to delineate room-use functions from archaeological remains that much more difficult. Additional complicating factors that must be considered are the length of time a house or building was occupied; in which season it is destroyed or abandoned; and the effects on the site of later settlement, erosion, animal activity, and modern plowing and stone-robbing. The difficulties in interpretation may be overcome through careful excavation and sampling, especially with the aid of microartifact analysis (Hardin 2001:125–27; 2004:74–79). With older excavations we must use a much broader, macroscopic approach, largely dictated by the original collection strategies and records.

We are fortunate that the main records of the finds from the excavations at Tell en-Naṣbeh, the object or millimeter cards, were separated by room and feature, and even by level. The information on these cards, when combined with Zorn's rephasing of the site, allows for interpretation of room use and function based on ceramics and small finds.

I have chosen one compound made up of five connected structures to test the viability of household archaeology in Stratum 3 at Tell en-Naṣbeh. The coding of the ceramics from these structures suggests that cooking took place primarily in Rooms 581 and 608, which have been interpreted as summer and winter kitchens respectively. It is possible that Room 584 was used as a kitchen, or had been a seasonal kitchen and then was reused as a storeroom.

Living rooms, interpreted from their high percentage of pottery used for consumption and serving, are found in the broad rooms at the rear of two of the three-room houses. These rooms, Rooms 610 and 612, have virtually identical interior dimensions of 1.88 × 5.16 m, yielding an area of 9.70 m^2. This figure has closer parallels to living spaces in southwestern pueblos, calculated by Watson as 6.00, 6.50, 9.41, 10.76, and 16.00 m^2, than with rooms in traditional village houses in Iran, whose living rooms averaged 18.2 m^2 (Watson 1979:296). Kramer's calculations for the average size of living rooms in the village she researched in Iran are also large in comparison, averaging 22.4 m^2, a calculation that includes the thickness of the walls (Kramer 1979:table 5.1). The figure is smaller in Horne's study of a village in eastern Iran, where the size of living rooms averaged 13.2 m^2 (1994:table 10). It is possible to explain the larger areas of living rooms in traditional Iranian villages as a result of the historically recent growth in the size of the nuclear family in the Middle East (Stager 1985: 21; King and Stager 2001:41). Presumably, broad room 579 at Tell en-Naṣbeh was also a living room; unfortunately, it was only partially excavated and its ceramics were too few to code.

Storage rooms are concentrated in the two buildings that flank the three three-room houses. These include the broad room Room 609 and its accompanying courtyard, Room 607. Use of courtyards for storage is quite common in modern traditional villages, as is their use for stabling animals. The fact that courtyard Room 607 has a large stone basin supports its identification as a stable, as this basin may have been used as a watering trough (figure 1). It is possible that long room Room 580 also served as a stable because its ceramics are not weighted heavily towards any of the three functional categories (Stager 1985:12–15; Holladay 1992:310–12). Rooms 575 and 513 in the southernmost building have high percentages of storage vessels, and the concentration of

presence of slingstones and iron arrowheads in this one compound.

cultic small finds in Room 513 indicates that it also contained some sort of shrine. Long rooms 584 and 578 from two of the three-room houses were also used for storage. It is probable that the small spaces in Room 577 and Bin 355 were storerooms, since their areas would be too cramped for other types of activities.

The concentration of stone tools in long room 576 suggests that one of its functions was as a workshop. Room 588 has one of the only *in situ* olive-pressing vats uncovered in Stratum 3. Due to the scarcity of contemporary presses at the site, it is likely that the room served the needs in olive harvest season not just of the family and its neighboring kinfolk, but also of a larger section of the town (A'amiry 1987:127–28). Small finds in the same room of a bone spatula and bronze needle suggest that outside of the olive season the space was used in cloth production.

It is reasonable to suggest, based on the data presented and ethnographic parallels, that a nuclear family inhabited the broad room of each of the three-room houses in the compound (A'amiry 1987:145–46; Kamp 2000:85). The shared walls of these houses and the communal functions of what have been identified as storerooms, kitchens, workshops, and courtyards, suggest that the compound as a whole was the residence of one extended or joint family, a minimal *bêt ʾāb*, made up of three nuclear families and their dependents linked both physically and by bonds of kinship.[11]

This conclusion supports the view of Stager and Schloen, who believe that extended families lived in both rural and urban household compounds (Stager 1985:18–22; Schloen 2001:167–68). The evidence from Tell en-Naṣbeh contradicts Avraham Faust's view that Iron II pillared households in urban settlements (walled towns) were the abodes of nuclear, as opposed to extended, families (Faust 2000:19–22). I have presented artifactual evidence that shows that nuclear families had their own living spaces in the broad rooms of three-room houses but also shared resources in the other rooms of the compound, an important trait of the extended family. Perhaps it was extended families like those at Tell en-Naṣbeh that the prophet Isaiah, a contemporary social observer, criticized as "those who add house to house" (Isa. 5:8).

[11] I am interpreting the communal aspect of room use based on the fact that the pattern of function of domestic space is not fully replicated among the five individual building units, let alone the three three-room houses. Although each three-room house has its living space in the broad room at its back, the long rooms show a variety of patterns of use, discussed in detail above. The outermost two-room building and atypical three-room building have a concentration of courtyard and storage space, while the religious activities of the compound were focused in one sideroom, Room 513.

BIBLIOGRAPHY

A'amiry, S. M. A.
1987 Space, Kinship and Gender: The Social Dimension of Peasant Architecture in Palestine. Ph.D. diss., University of Edinburgh.

Allison, P. M., ed.
1999 *The Archaeology of Household Activities*. London: Routledge.

Amiran, R.
1969 *Ancient Pottery of the Holy Land: From Its Beginning in the Neolithic Period to the End of the Iron Age*. Jerusalem: Massada.

Amiry, S., and V. Tamari
1989 *The Palestinian Village Home*. London: British Museum.

Badè, W. F.
1934 *A Manual of Excavation in the Near East: Methods of Digging and Recording of the Tell en-Naṣbeh Expedition in Palestine*. Berkeley, Calif.: University of California Press.

Barile, K. S., and J. C. Brandon, eds.
2004 *Household Chores and Household Choices: Theorizing the Domestic Sphere in Historical Archaeology*. Tuscaloosa, Ala.: University of Alabama.

Bermann, M.
1994 *Lukurmata: Household Archaeology in Prehispanic Bolivia*. Princeton, N.J.: Princeton University Press.

Blenkinsopp, J.
1997 The Family in First Temple Israel. In *Families in Ancient Israel*, ed. L. Perdue, 48–103. Louisville, Ky.: Westminster John Knox.

Brody, A. J.
forthc. Phoenician Pottery from Tell en-Naṣbeh: Interregional Trade in the Iron IIB–IIC Southern Levant. In *The House that Gitin Built: Studies in Honor of Seymour Gitin*, ed. J. E. Wright, J. P. Dessel, and R. A. Mullins. Boston: American Schools of Oriental Research.

Daviau, P. M. M.
1993 *Houses and Their Furnishings in Bronze Age Palestine: Domestic Activity Areas and Artefact Distribution in the Middle and Late Bronze Ages*. Sheffield, England: JSOT Press.

Faust, A.
2000 The Rural Community in Ancient Israel during Iron Age II. *BASOR* 317:17–39.

Gadot, Y., and A. Yasur-Landau
2006 Beyond Finds: Reconstructing Life in the Courtyard Building of Level K-4. In *Megiddo*, vol. 4, *The 1998–2002 Seasons*, ed. I. Finkelstein et al., 563–80. Tel Aviv: Institute of Archaeology, Tel Aviv University.

Hardin, J. W.
2001 *An Archaeology of Destruction: Households and the Use of Domestic Space at Iron II Tel Halif*. Ph.D. diss., University of Arizona.
2004 Understanding Domestic Space: An Example from Iron Age Tel Halif. *NEA* 67/2:71–83.

Holladay, J. S.
1992 House, Israelite. In *The Anchor Bible Dictionary*, ed. D. N. Freedman, 3:308–18. New York: Doubleday.

Horne, L.
1994 *Village Spaces: Settlement and Society in Northeastern Iran*. Washington, D.C.: Smithsonian Institution.

Hunt, M.
1987 The Tell Qiri Pottery. In *Tell Qiri: A Village in the Jezreel Valley; Reports of the Archaeological Excavation 1975–1977,* ed. A. Ben-Tor and Y. Portugali, 139–223. Qedem 24. Jerusalem: Hebrew University of Jerusalem.

Ilan, O.
2001 Household Archaeology at Arad and Ai in the Early Bronze Age II. In *Studies in the Archaeology of Israel and Neighboring Lands in Memory of Douglas L. Esse*, ed. S. Wolff, 317–54. SAOC 59: Chicago: Oriental Institute, University of Chicago.

Kamp, K.
2000 From Village to Tell: Household Ethnoarchaeology in Syria. *NEA* 63/2: 84–93.

King, P. J., and L. E. Stager
2001 *Life in Biblical Israel*. Louisville, Ky.: Westminster John Knox.

Kramer, C.
1979 An Archaeological View of a Contemporary Kurdish Village: Domestic Architecture, Household Size, and Wealth. In *Ethnoarchaeology: Implications of Ethnography for Archaeology*, ed. C. Kramer, 139–63. New York: Columbia University Press.
1982 *Village Ethnoarchaeology: Rural Iran in Archaeological Perspective*. New York: Academic.

Lederman, Z.
1999 An Early Iron Age Village at Khirbet Raddana: The Excavations of Joseph A. Callaway. Ph.D. diss., Harvard University.

McCown, C. C.
1947 *Tell en-Naṣbeh*. Vol. 1, *Archaeological and Historical Results*. Berkeley, Calif.: Pacific School of Religion and American Schools of Oriental Research.

McClellan, T. L.
1984 Town Planning at Tell en-Naṣbeh. *ZDPV* 100: 53–69.

McNutt, P. M.
1999 *Reconstructing the Society of Ancient Israel*. Louisville, Ky.: Westminster John Knox.

Meyers, C.
1997 The Family in Early Israel. In *Families in Ancient Israel*, ed. L. Perdue, 1–47. Louisville, Ky.: Westminster John Knox.
2003 Engendering Syro-Palestinian Archaeology: Reasons and Resources. *NEA* 66/4:185–97.

Nevett, L. C.
1999 *House and Society in the Ancient Greek World*. Cambridge: Cambridge University Press.

Schloen, J. D.
2001 *The House of the Father as Fact and Symbol: Patrimonialism in Ugarit and the Ancient Near East*. SAHL 2. Winona Lake, Ind.: Eisenbrauns.

Stager, L. E.
1985 The Archaeology of the Family in Ancient Israel. *BASOR* 260:1–35.

Stone, E.
1981 Texts, Architecture and Ethnographic Analogy: Patterns of Residence in Old Babylonian Nippur. *Iraq* 43:19–33.

Wampler, J. C.
1947 *Tell en-Naṣbeh*. Vol. 2, *The Pottery*. Berkeley, Calif.: Pacific School of Religion and American Schools of Oriental Research.

Watson, P. J.
1979 *Archaeological Ethnography in Western Iran*. Viking Fund Publications in Anthropology 57. Tucson, Ariz.: University of Arizona.

Wright, C. J. H.
1992 Family. In *The Anchor Bible Dictionary*, ed. D. N. Freedman, 2:761–9. New York: Doubleday.

Zorn, J. R.
1993a Naṣbeh, Tell en-. In *The New Encyclopedia of Archaeological Excavations in the Holy Land*, ed. E. Stern, 3:1098–1102. New York: Simon and Schuster.
1993b Tell en-Naṣbeh: A Re-evaluation of the Architecture and Stratigraphy of the Early Bronze Age, Iron Age and Later Periods. Ph.D. diss., University of California, Berkeley.

6. More Light on Old Reliefs: New Kingdom Egyptian Siege Tactics and Asiatic Resistance

by Aaron A. Burke

It is a pleasure to celebrate the career of Lawrence E. Stager by adding to the discussion of New Kingdom Egyptian reliefs and their importance for the archaeology and history of the Levant, building upon Larry's own contribution to this subject (Stager 1985).[1]

Although some scholars have identified such reliefs as part of a "more or less historical narrative" (Gaballa 1976:127–28), others have taken a more minimalist approach concerning their historical value. Donald Redford, for example, has suggested that the "'post-Kadesh' war reliefs," which depict the siege of Levantine towns, do not constitute a reliable source for the reconstruction of historical details of "individual campaigns" (Redford 1992:186). While it is essentially correct to state that these illustrations do not add historical detail to the brief textual accounts that accompany them, they do supply an important source of information about sieges in the Levant during the Late Bronze Age, contributing to our understanding of the cultural practices of the period. To a lesser extent, the reliefs also illustrate Egyptian siege tactics.

I will attempt, therefore, to demonstrate that a nuanced study of these reliefs yields further insights into both Levantine and Egyptian customs, specifically as they pertain to the conduct of warfare during the Late Bronze Age. Even though various stock motifs were obviously employed in the carving of these reliefs, several distinct themes related to Egyptian New Kingdom siege warfare can be recognized among the motifs used. When these themes are supplemented by Egyptian New Kingdom sources that record sieges, such as Thutmose III's annals, the nature of Egyptian siege tactics and Asiatic responses to them can be quite well understood.[2]

Several observations must be noted that are fundamental to the arguments set forth in this article. First, while New Kingdom reliefs that depict the siege of Asiatic towns do employ the repetition of stock motifs, these motifs were used in regularly defined combinations. Thus, as I shall demonstrate, these combinations very nicely illustrate the progression of a successful Egyptian siege.

Second, while scholars often assume that those conducting a siege, in this case the Egyptians, had the upper hand over those being besieged, the preponderance of historical data from the pregunpowder era suggests that defenders had a better chance of thwarting a siege than historians and archaeologists often assume. It is easy to place undue emphasis on a selected set of textual sources, such as the writings of the biblical prophets, the Assyrian annals, or accounts of Alexander the Great's campaigns, when attempting to assess the probable success of a besieging army. Such sources are useful only to illustrate the effects of a successful siege. Too few accounts are preserved of failed, protracted, or aborted sieges to provide a balanced picture of the frequency with which sieges succeeded. Indeed, archaeological and historical evidence over the course of thousands of years suggests that sieges were often thwarted.

Convincing evidence of this can be drawn, for example, from the work of Aeneas Tacticus (1990), a fourth-century B.C.E. Greek author whose work remains mostly unknown to Near Eastern scholars. A comparison of the prescriptions set forth in Aeneas's *How to Survive under Siege* (hereafter *Siege*) with the details of Asiatic towns and their defenders shown in New Kingdom reliefs, demonstrate the value of his work. Aeneas's writing should be regarded as a collection of ancient wisdom on the art of siege warfare, much of which can probably be traced back to the conduct of siege warfare in the Near East during the Bronze Age.

Finally, it must be remembered that what is *not* portrayed in any of the Egyptian reliefs or textual accounts is a failed siege. This bias in the Egyptian sources has resulted in the widespread assumption that the offensive force always had the upper hand. As will be shown in what follows, this does not appear to have been the case in the Late Bronze Age Levant.

[1] Stager's work was done in conjunction with that of the late Frank Yurco (1977; 1986) during the years that Stager was at the Oriental Institute in Chicago. Yurco also attempted to shed light on the identity of ancient Israel using evidence from New Kingdom reliefs (Yurco 1990; 1997).

[2] I have chosen the term Asiatic to avoid using the term Canaanite, because the towns depicted in these reliefs fall within a larger geographical region than Canaan proper. Similarly, because some of these towns had ethnically mixed populations, it is not possible to refer to their inhabitants simply as Amorites.

Motifs in New Kingdom Siege Scenes

Four primary motifs were used in Egyptian New Kingdom siege scenes to represent the activity of Asiatics within their besieged towns (see table 1).[3] These include Asiatics (1) praying with upraised arms, (2) making offerings, (3) defending their town with a variety of weapons, and (4) lowering children from the city wall.

Despite the manner in which they are rendered, these motifs should not be thought to depict events that occurred simultaneously or took place atop the walls in plain sight of the Egyptian army. Egyptian artistic conventions must be taken into account; the artist does not distinguish activities that took place within the city from those that occurred atop the walls. The activities related to religious practices probably took place within the city itself. These scenes are especially significant because they are the only depictions of Asiatic religious customs that we possess from the Late Bronze Age, unless examples of banquet scenes are also construed as cultic ceremonies (see Ziffer 2005).

The first motif, which consists of Asiatics with upraised arms, was obviously employed to depict Asiatics praying to their gods, presumably in order that their city would survive the Egyptian siege. A parallel for praying and grieving atop city walls is found in the Kirta Epic, where King Kirta is commanded by the god El (ᵓIlu) to:

Climb to the summit of the tower,
  yes, climb to the summit of the tower,
    mount the top of the wall.
Raise your hands heavenward,
  sacrifice to the Bull, your father ᵓIlu.
Bring down Baᶜlu with your sacrifice,
  the Son of Dagan with your game.

[Pardee 1997a:334]

Thanks to another Ugaritic text we are even able to describe the specific rituals associated with climbing to the "top of the wall" during a siege. This text (RS 24.266) has been identified as a "Prayer for a City under Siege" (Pardee 1997b:283). Following the prescriptions for sacrifice are the words of the prayer that was to be recited:

O Baᶜlu, if you drive the strong one from our gate,
  the warrior from our walls,
A bull, O Baᶜlu, we shall sanctify,
  a vow, (O) Baᶜlu, we shall fulfill;
  a firstborn, (O) Baᶜlu, we shall sanctify,
  a *ḥtp*-offering, (O) Baᶜlu, we shall fulfill,
  a *ᶜšrt*-feast, (O) Baᶜlu, we shall offer;
To the sanctuary, (O) Baᶜlu, we shall ascend,
  th(at) path, (O) Baᶜlu, we shall take.

[Pardee 1997b:284–85]

This prayer illuminates in a profound way the principal iconographic evidence for Asiatic religious worship, namely, the Egyptian reliefs discussed here.

The second motif illustrates individuals, presumably Asiatic priests, raising incense burners (or chalices?) to Baal in the manner described in the texts above. Only one individual is usually shown in a given relief in which the motif was used, which also supports the suggestion that this individual should be identified as a priest.[4] However, the priests were not depicted in a way that distinguishes them from other male inhabitants of the town. The priests are also never depicted alone; rather, they are followed by one or more worshippers whose hands are raised in supplication. Unfortunately, it is impossible to determine whether the vessels held by the priests in these reliefs are metal or ceramic.

The third motif consists of Asiatics brandishing various sorts of weapons against Egyptian soldiers who have either surrounded the town or have begun to scale the fortifications. Although in most scenes the individuals are depicted wielding the same type of weapon, other scenes reveal a more nuanced picture of siege warfare at this time. In some scenes, for example, weapons brandished by the Asiatic defenders include not only spears, bows, and shields, but even stones and sails. The dropping or throwing of stones reveals a level of desperation among the defenders that is not evident with the use of the other weapons. This activity may also support the conclusion that protracted sieges often left the defenders with a limited supply of missiles. Conspicuously absent from this motif is any evidence for the use of the sling by Asiatic defenders. Although the reason for this is impossible to determine, we may speculate that this was due to the inherent difficulty of using this weapon within the confined area atop the city wall.

An unusual feature that appears in some of these reliefs, such as in the scenes of the siege of Dapur (see Wreszinksi 1935:pls. 78 and 109), is what appears to be a sail. It is depicted as a triangular sheet flying from a mast above the city (see figure 2). Its purpose was

[3] While the reliefs examined include many of the Canaanite siege scenes of the New Kingdom, this paper does not attempt to provide an exhaustive study of such scenes.

[4] See Wreszinksi 1935:pls. 94 and 95 for an example of several priests with incense burners.

Table 1. Motifs in Scenes of the Siege of Asiatic Towns in New Kingdom Reliefs

Pharaoh	*Town name*	*Wreszinski plate(s)*	*Upraised arms*	*Making offerings*	*Defending with weapons*	*Lowering children*	*Gate fallen*
Sety I	Yenoam	36	x	x	–	–	–
		A massive battle with chariots is depicted to the right of the city.					
	"fort of Sile"	39	–	–	–	–	–
		Town is untouched.					
Ramesses II	Kadesh 1	53	x	–	bows	–	–
		Scene shows siege in progress.					
	Kadesh 2	84, 101			shields, bows, spears, daggers, sail	–	–
	Sibat	56	x	x	shield	–	–
		Town has two ramparts.					
	ꜣIkati	56	–	–	*n/a*	–	–
		Window askew.					
	Kwt ꜣIsr	55a (lower left)	–	–	–	–	–
		Upper part of scene is too damaged to read.					
	ꜣItr	55a (upper right)	x	[x]	shield	–	–
	ꜥkꜣ	55a (lower right)	–	–	–	–	x
	[...]rd	55	x	–	–	–	–
		Name is damaged.					
	Mutir	55	–	–	*n/a*	–	x
	damaged	54a (lower right)	–	–	*n/a*	–	x
	Krmyn	54a	x	x	–	–	–
	[...]mw	54a (upper left)	*n/a*	*n/a*	?	–	–
		Name is damaged; only the lower portion of the scene is legible.					
	I[pk]	54a (upper right)	x	x	shield	–	–
		Name is damaged; town erased.					
	ꜣIy	54	x	–	spears	–	–
		Upper portion of scene is missing; towns's troops are seen marching in.					
	unnamed	57a	x	–	–	–	–
	unnamed	57	x	[x]	–	child	–
		Lower portion of scene is damaged.					
	Dapur	78, 109	x	x	stones, spears shields, bows, sail	–	–
		Spears (pl. 78) or arrows (pl 109) through mast of sail; women hanging from walls (pl. 109).					
	Mutir	71	–	–	–	–	–
	Satuna	66–67	–	–	bows	–	–
		Defenders mistakenly shown as Libyan.					
	unnamed	65	–	–	–	–	x
		Landscape shown with trees cut down.					
	unnamed	163–164a	x	x	bow	x	–
	unnamed	165–168	–	–	–	–	–
		Scene is damaged.					
Merenptah	Ashkelon	58	x?	x	–	teen and child	–
		Siege ladders are shown in this scene.					
Ramesses III	*unnamed*	94–95	x	x	spears, sickle sword, hot oil?, sail	–	–
		Cutting down trees; axes on gate.					
	towns in the "land of Amurru"	146–47	x	x	spears, sail	–	–

Source: Wreszinski 1935. Brackets [**x**] indicate damage to a portion of the relief.

apparently to defend against arrows shot into the city by the besiegers. Arrows are shown stuck in the sail in one scene of the Dapur siege (ibid., pl. 109); but spears, which can be identified due to the absence of fletching,[5] are shown in the other (ibid., pl. 78). The Egyptian artists were evidently confused about the purpose of the sail because spears could not have been thrown so far and high. This confusion is understandable since it is unlikely that the artists personally witnessed the siege. When the sail is shown pierced by arrows, both Asiatics and Egyptians are shown using bows, although the Egyptians are also accompanied by a few spear-wielding Asiatics. However, when the sail is shown catching spears, the defenders themselves are seen wielding only spears and rocks, and no bows at all are present in the scene, except for that of the larger-than-life pharaoh off to the side.

Another sail is depicted in the illustration of Kadesh at Abu Simbel (Wreszinksi 1935:73). In this relief, the defending Asiatics brandish spears, which they hold vertically—a clear indication that the siege had not yet begun—while a sail flies above their city-without any missiles stuck in it. The defenders are prepared for an attack that has not yet been launched.

The appearance of a sail in these siege reliefs has not to my knowledge received special attention, but it finds a striking parallel in the treatise of Aeneas Tacticus in the fourth century B.C.E., who refers to the use of sails to thwart incoming arrows, among other things (*Siege* 32.1, 8–10). Such a device certainly shielded defenders against incoming arrows but it would also have screened the defenders so they could move along the wall without being seen, as for example during Alexander's siege of Tyre (Arrian 2.21.1–7). These Egyptian reliefs provide the earliest evidence for this practice, which was in use as early as the thirteenth century B.C.E.

While the identification of the three motifs discussed above is fairly straightforward, the fourth motif is more ambiguous. It depicts children (identified as such by the relatively smaller size of the figures, who are usually also depicted naked) being lowered over the sides of the city walls by male Asiatic inhabitants of the besieged cities. This is the rarest motif in the ensemble of siege scenes, suggesting that this practice was less often observed during sieges.

Because of the enigmatic nature of this motif, it has been the subject of some debate among scholars. Sarah Morris, for example, has suggested that it is the earliest evidence for Canaanite child sacrifice (Morris 1995:231–32). Child sacrifice was certainly practiced during the Iron Age among the Phoenicians, the descendants of the Late Bronze Age Canaanites, as has been demonstrated textually by Paul Mosca (1975) and archaeologically by Lawrence Stager (1980).[6] But the New Kingdom Egyptian reliefs do not necessarily depict child sacrifice in Canaan during the Late Bronze Age. None of the Asiatic males shown releasing these children was equipped to offer a sacrifice. Merely dropping them would not have constituted a religious act of sacrifice by Canaanite standards. Sacrifices had to be burned and/or cut (see Mosca 1975). Since neither an offertory fire nor a knife is evident in these scenes, the sacrificial interpretation seems unlikely. If the artist had intended to depict a child sacrifice, he would more likely have shown this occurring within the city rather than over the sides of the walls.

A more appropriate parallel for the motif discussed by Morris is to be found on an ivory plaque from Ugarit, which depicts an individual pointing a dagger at the head of a prisoner while grasping his hair in his other hand (see, e.g., Yadin 1963:208). Nevertheless, I agree with Morris that the origin of the Phoenician rite should be sought among the Canaanites of the Late Bronze Age, and it would not be difficult to imagine the evolution of the sacrifice of the "first-born," the "*ḥtp*-offering," and/or the "*ʿšrt*-feast" into child sacrifice over time and under certain conditions.

There is also evidence from the annals of Thutmose III that supports a straightforward interpretation of these scenes as depictions of children being lowered to safety over the town walls. During the Battle of Megiddo at the start of Thutmose's reign, it appears that Asiatics fled before the Egyptian army into the walled town of Megiddo and the gates were closed behind them; however, some lagged behind and could not enter because the gate had been closed. As they reached the walls, efforts were made to hoist them up into the city using garments (Lichtheim 1976:32). It is possible, therefore, that the motif of Asiatics lowering children over the walls during the last stages of a siege was an effort to depict parents lowering their children to safety once the defenses had been breached, reversing the operation of raising stragglers into Megiddo during Thutmose III's siege.[7]

---

[5] Fletching, the use of feathers at the end of an arrow to stabilize its flight, is characteristic of depictions of arrows in New Kingdom scenes.

[6] I thank my colleague, Sarah Morris, for calling her article to my attention in the course of preparing this article.

[7] For a much later example of this, see the episode of the apostle Paul being lowered out of Damascus through an opening in the wall in an effort to avoid the city's gates, which were being watched by his enemies (Acts 9:23–25).

Employment of Motifs in Themes of Siege Warfare

In order to understand what these four motifs were intended to convey, it is necessary to consider the four identifiable combinations or themes in which these motifs were employed. These four themes reveal four discrete stages through which an Egyptian siege of an Asiatic town progressed: (1) the town prior to the start of a siege; (2) a town in the throes of resisting an Egyptian siege; (3) the final moments of a failing resistance; and (4) an abandoned, perhaps destroyed, town following a siege.

The first of these themes, depicting the town prior to the onset of the siege, is characterized by the relative insignificance of the Egyptian army in comparison to the town itself (figure 1). The focus appears to be the prayers of the Asiatic defenders. There is no evidence within the scene that indicates that a siege is underway. This fits with the idea that early New Kingdom siege tactics relied on blockades rather than brute force. This was the case, for example, at Sharuhen and Megiddo (Hoffmeier 1989:183). The motif always employed in this theme is that of the Asiatics with arms raised in prayer. Occasionally, they are accompanied by a male figure, probably a priest, who looks heavenward and raises an incense burner in front of the town's supplicants.

The offering of such prayers has often been mistaken by Egyptologists to be a sign of Canaanite submission and thus an indication of a completed siege. But the act of prayer should be viewed from the perspective of Asiatics as a sign of continued defiance, revealing their hope that their gods would indeed still deliver their city. This is especially likely in light of the fact that the motif occurs in each of the first three themes and never occurs in the fourth theme that presents the destroyed town. Prayer must, therefore, be viewed as an act of resistance, because it occurs in all three themes that depict stages of the siege prior to the destruction or abandonment of the city.

The Asiatics in these scenes seem to be carrying out West Semitic (Amorite) religious rites, which as noted above, may well have followed the liturgy of the Ugaritic prayer for a besieged city. The theme is also reminiscent of Moses raising his arms during the battle between the Israelites and the Amalekites (Exod. 17:8–13). The only noteworthy variant to the very standardized employment of this theme is the addition in one scene of a town's troops (those of ʾIy) returning to it in anticipation of the siege that would follow (Wreszinksi 1935:pl. 54).

The second theme, which presents the second stage of Egyptian siege warfare, shows armed Asiatic resistance to a siege that is fully underway (figure 2).

Figure 1. An undamaged town (here Yenoam) prior to the start of a siege
after Wreszinksi 1935:pl. 36

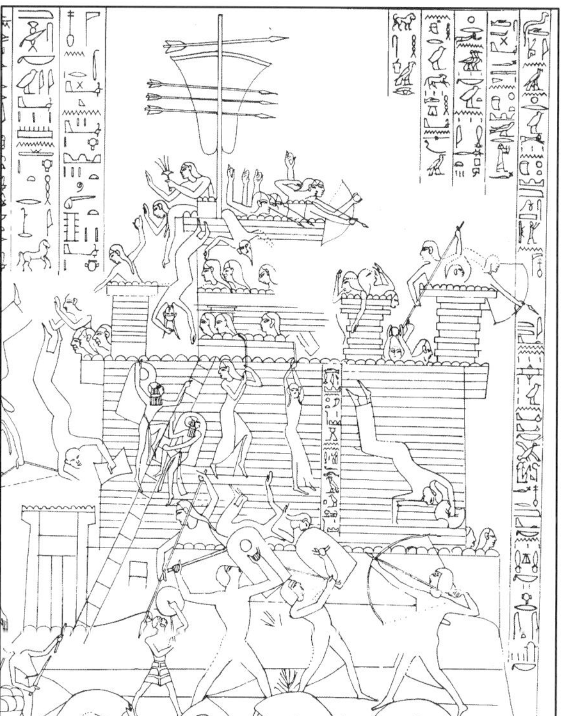

Figure 2. A town (here Dapur) resisting a siege
after Wreszinksi 1935:pl. 109

The first three themes represent a process of motif accretion, whereby a new motif is added to the previous theme, thus forming a new theme and illustrating the progress of events. In the case of the second theme, for example, different signs of armed resistance are added to depictions that include, as in the first theme, individuals with arms raised praying and priests raising incense burners before worshipers.

In the second theme, armed resistance to the Egyptian siege is illustrated in its varied forms, from the simple act of brandishing shields (sometimes simply clutched in the hands of Asiatics falling from the walls) to the firing of arrows, hurling of spears, and throwing of stones. Usually, only one of these means of defending the town is shown in order to depict Asiatic resistance, but in the most dramatic example of such resistance, the siege of Dapur (figure 2), every form of armed resistance possible was employed, from stone to sail.

In the third theme that I have identified, the siege has reached a critical turning point in which Egyptian victory is seen as imminent by the inhabitants of the town. Egyptians are sometimes shown scaling ladders that have been raised against the town wall for the final assault, as in the siege of Ashkelon (figure 3), but the Asiatics are no longer shown brandishing weapons to resist the attack, despite the fact that the siege operation is still underway. Instead, the town's inhabitants stand with their arms raised in prayer (first motif) behind their priest(s), who raise(s) an incense burner heavenward (second motif) as children are lowered over the walls of the city (fourth motif). How was the motif of the child descending outside the wall intended to be understood within the progression of the siege? As I have argued above, it would seem that the Asiatics are attempting to lower their children over the walls to aid their escape from Egyptian soldiers who had by now entered the city, fearing that their children would be sold into slavery in Egypt or a distant land.

Figure 3. A desperate town (here Ashkelon) in the final moments of a siege
after Wreszinksi 1935:pl. 58

The fourth and final theme is that of the devastated Asiatic city (figure 4), showing the successful culmination of an Egyptian siege. In this theme an abandoned town is often illustrated by means of a collapsed gateway (specifically by its fallen lintel), a symbol of the Egyptian conquest. It is striking that no additional efforts were made to depict this stage. This may be due to the nature of Egyptian siege tactics, which did not necessarily entail the complete destruction (that is, burning or leveling) of conquered cities (Hoffmeier 1989). The Egyptian reliefs would appear to support James Hoffmeier's argument that the lack of specific references to the destruction of Canaanite towns during the early Eighteenth Dynasty, especially before the reign of Thutmose III, indicates that the Egyptians did not pursue a policy of eradicating the fortifications of Levantine towns, as a number of scholars have claimed (e.g., Gonen 1984), because in the siege reliefs each conquered town's walls are shown still standing.

Although each of the sieges depicted in New Kingdom reliefs appears to have culminated in an Asiatic defeat, the focus was intended to be the nature of Asiatic resistance rather than Egyptian siege tactics.

Figure 4. An abandoned town (here ꜥkꜣ) symbolized by a fallen lintel
after Wreszinksi 1935:pl. 55a

As I have discussed elsewhere (Burke 2008:25–46), the offensive and defensive siege tactics in use during the Middle and Late Bronze Ages are not only textually attested but are visible in the archaeological record, which provides evidence of both the weaponry and the casualties of such warfare. The Egyptian reliefs are exceptional in providing a narrative of the successive stages of siege warfare and, at each stage, the besieged Asiatics' actions and culturally determined modes of resistance, from prayers to their gods, to vigorous fighting with all the means at their disposal, to a final desperate concern for the safety of their children. The four artistic themes we have examined, and the four basic motifs used in them, are thus a valuable iconographic source for the study of Late Bronze Age warfare in the Levant and the human and cultural reality expressed within it.

The Conduct of Egyptian Siege Warfare during the New Kingdom

Unfortunately, these New Kingdom scenes reveal little about the specific Egyptian tactics that precipitated the various Asiatic responses discussed above. Egyptian archers and slingers are depicted firing into the besieged city, which is something that is not described in texts. In a few instances, soldiers are seen hacking at town gates with their axes. But Egyptian siege practices are otherwise rarely depicted. Curiously, only scaling ladders are ever shown raised against a town's walls, despite the fact that iconographic sources from the First Intermediate Period and the Middle Kingdom demonstrate that the Egyptians were familiar with both the siege tower (Gaballa 1976:fig. 3) and the mantelet (Newberry 1894:pl. 5). To understand these scenes they must be placed within the context of Egyptian siege practices, which are attested in textual sources.

The absence of depictions of Egyptian siege tactics combined with the lack of textual detail regarding Egyptian sieges at the start of the Eighteenth Dynasty have led scholars like Donald Redford (1992:219) to suggest that before the Ramesside period, New Kingdom siege techniques were unimpressive. Sieges undertaken during the reign of Ahmose, which would have included actions against Avaris[8] and Sharuhen, he has called "notoriously inept" (ibid., 138–139), presumably because of the long duration of these sieges. But it is impossible to formulate such definitive conclusions on the basis of the absence of siege scenes of the Ramesside type during the early New Kingdom. Would one likewise refer to Assyrian battlefield tactics as notoriously inept because we lack depictions of Shalmaneser III's defeat of the Levantine coalition or the fact that four attempts were required before he succeeded?

In light of the pervasiveness of this view of Egyptian siege tactics, several factors must be taken into consideration when assessing the Egyptian capacity for siege warfare during the New Kingdom. In the first place, towns in the Levant were by the end of the Middle Bronze Age exceedingly well prepared to withstand siege warfare, being encircled with massive ramparts and walls (Burke 2008:47–84). Only the smallest and most recently founded settlements had poor defenses. It should not be surprising, therefore, that the Egyptians were unable to subdue the southern Levant in a *blitzkrieg* following the fall of Sharuhen. As it is, over a period of decades they were quite successful. It is in this period, probably in the early fifteenth century B.C.E., that we must date the destruction of at least 26 towns in Canaan, which all evidence indicates should be attributed to the Egyptians (see Weinstein 1981).

While the Egyptian advance was probably delayed at first by what remained of Middle Bronze Age fortification systems,[9] the Egyptians also faced sporadic resistance in open battles, as occurred at Megiddo. But after the Battle of Megiddo, the Canaanites seem to have been unable to come to the aid of their neighbors during what were no doubt a number of protracted Egyptian sieges lasting several years. Moreover, Egyptian siege tactics no doubt improved year by year throughout this early period, perhaps

---

[8] A close reading of "The Autobiography of Ahmose son of Abana" suggests that the expulsion of the Hyksos from Avaris involved a protracted siege that included various actions in and around the city itself, which may have lasted for some time (for a recent translation, see Redford 1997:15).

[9] It is impossible to adequately address here Rivka Gonen's contention that most Late Bronze Age settlements in the southern Levant were unfortified (1984). But it must be remembered that the inherent difficulty in distinguishing between late Middle Bronze and early Late Bronze Age remains is partly to blame for the confusion regarding the nature of Late Bronze Age defenses. To date, no one has provided an extensive review of the archaeological data relevant to this question. At this point, therefore, I would only suggest, in the wake of my detailed assessment of Middle Bronze Age fortifications (Burke 2008), that the data are far more ambiguous than Gonen suggested. Gonen's suggestion may, in fact, have served as the impetus for the subsequent and misleading assertion by Ram Gophna (1977), Israel Finkelstein (1992), and Shlomo Bunimovitz (1992) that even the Middle Bronze Age rampart fortifications lacked fortification walls. For a review of the problems inherent in that notion, see Burke 2008:12–15.

aided by lessons learned in their Nubian campaigns. It is quite possible, in fact, as Hoffmeier and a number of other scholars have contended, that Canaan only became Egypt's military objective after the subjugation of Nubia, which began during the last half of the sixteenth century B.C.E. (see Hoffmeier 2004: 124–25). Thus, it was only during the reign of Thutmose III that the Egyptian conquest of Canaan was fully accomplished, building on the earlier subjugation of key centers that controlled access to Canaan, namely, Avaris and Sharuhen. The Egyptians' rapidly growing aptitude for siege warfare, which reached its apex during Thutmose's reign, resulted in an impressive campaign against the extremely distant city of Carchemish, during which he had boats hauled from the Lebanese coast overland in order to cross the Euphrates River (Redford 1992:153–55).

A final factor that must be taken into account when considering the slow pace of the Egyptian imperial advance through the Levant is the considerable advantage enjoyed by the besieged, for which there is extensive historical evidence. Abundant classical sources support the conclusion that the besieged inhabitants of fortified towns often survived sieges and outlasted their besiegers (see examples in Kern 1999). The extreme length of the siege of Sharuhen, which lasted three years (Lichtheim 1976:13), shows that the defenders could hold out for a very long time and their Egyptian besiegers could not succeed (at least in this case) without unusual persistence. Although the Egyptians eventually succeeded in subduing Sharuhen, the first two years of the siege must be considered Canaanite victories because this siege would actually have constituted at least three separate engagements, in the spring and summer each year, with a hiatus in the winter (see Redford 1992:129). If indeed Tell el-ᶜAjjul is to be identified with Sharuhen—and I would argue that it is[10]—evidence of the town's resistance to the Egyptian siege, specifically their efforts to establish a clandestine exit from the site, is found in two tunnels, the so-called Upper and Lower tunnels, that were dug from the exterior, eastern edge of the fosse on ᶜAjjul's eastern side (figure 5). Since all other functions of these tunnels can be ruled out (irrigation, burial chambers, etc.), they were most likely used to allow the besieged inhabitants of the site to escape secretly into the countryside and perhaps to smuggle in provisions and spies (Burke 2008:232ff.).

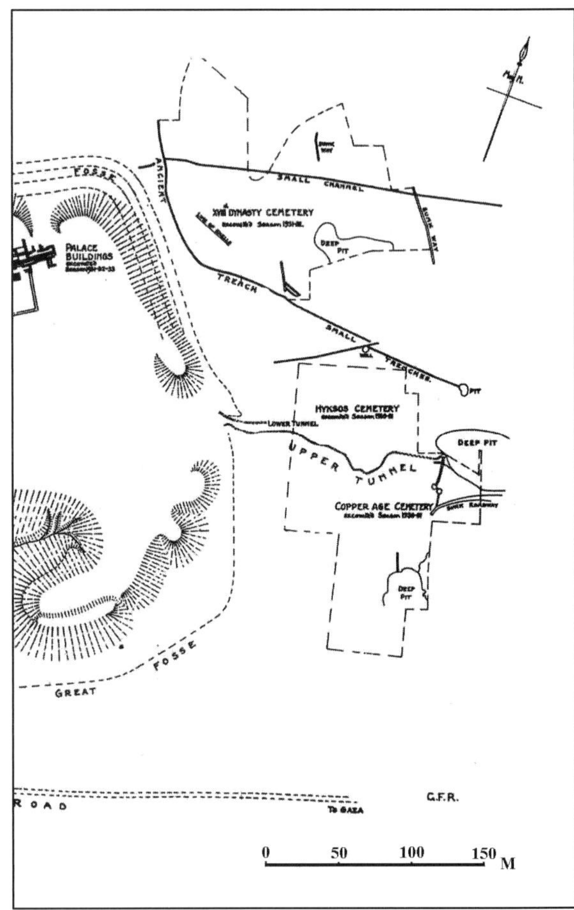

Figure 5. Plan of Tell el-ᶜAjjul showing the location of "escape" tunnels (*after Petrie 1931:pl. 45*)

What, then, accounts for the overall success of Egyptian siege tactics after the reign of Thutmose III? It is often assumed that success is not the result of direct assault; hunger and disease must have overtaken the besieged, who had to choose between starvation and surrender. But none of the defenders of these Asiatic towns is depicted as starving or emaciated. The evidence concerning siege warfare in antiquity suggests that it was ultimately a numbers game that involved three main variables: time, the availability of resources inside the city, and the size of the attacking force. Although it is usually assumed that time was on the side of the besieging army, this is clearly not the case when one considers that the army had a limited supply of food, most of which was drawn from the countryside during the period

[10] For the clearest argument for the identification of Tell el-ᶜAjjul as Sharuhen, see Kempinski 1974. Although some details of Kempinski's argument could be further refined, ᶜAjjul is the best candidate in the southern region. Tell el-Farᶜah (South) was smaller, more poorly defended, and situated in a marginal region farther from the main communication and transportation routes. The identification of ᶜAjjul with Sharuhen is further supported by the presence there of an Eighteenth Dynasty administrative center (see E. F. Morris 2005).

between spring and fall, the only time of the year during which it was possible to conduct a successful siege. (There is no evidence that ancient armies ever planted and harvested their own crops.) All the while, the besieging army would have had to guard its rear in the event that allies of the besieged city came to its aid.[11]

The main reason we view sieges as spelling the inevitable doom of the besieged is the relatively high success rate of numerically overwhelming forces mustered by massive imperial armies fielded by large political entities such as New Kingdom Egypt, and later by the Assyrian, Babylonian, and Achaemenid empires. The overwhelming number of troops available in imperial armies allowed them a more predictable degree of success in siege warfare. As Israel Eph^cal has noted, this is because large numbers of attackers could do more than just prevent escape from the encircled town; they could mount frontal assaults on the town walls and gates and sustain heavy casualties in order to break through, rather than waiting to starve the inhabitants into submission (Eph^cal 1983:92–96; also 1997:50). A large disparity in numbers between attackers and defenders must have made resistance by towns of average and below average size seem completely futile. Empires could also muster the necessary logistical support to impose extremely successful blockades that could guarantee that an extended siege would succeed.

Despite the fact that an empire's reputation would have become established after years of repeated success, many of their smaller adversaries appear to have remained convinced that defeats like those experienced by their neighbors were not inevitable, if they could form proper alliances, as in the Battle of Qarqar against the Assyrians. Those who had not yet been consolidated within the empire often concluded, rightly or wrongly, that their own resistance was the primary reason for the empire's failure. But it was often the case that an empire's resources were diverted into other theaters of operation, depriving them of the requisite numerical superiority to conduct successful sieges in certain regions at certain times.

In addition to using their numerical superiority in direct assaults, information about Egyptian siege practices gleaned from the annals of Thutmose III, specifically the account of the Battle of Megiddo, shows that Egyptian tactics focused on the enforcement of blockades, for which large numbers of troops were also important. During the siege of Megiddo, for example, the Egyptians "measured the town, surrounded (it) with a ditch, and walled (it) up with fresh timber from all their fruit trees" (Lichtheim 1976:33). In a short time, perhaps as little as thirty-seven days (Goedicke 2000:91), the very large force of Canaanites trapped in the city acknowledged their desperate situation and surrendered. On the one hand, they would have realized that the large number of individuals inside the city would quickly consume Megiddo's resources. On the other hand, they would have seen that there was no way to penetrate the Egyptian blockade in order to obtain supplies or call upon allies (if any were left) to attack the Egyptians from behind.

Rather than appearing inept, Thutmoses III's actions—following his decision to march through the Aruna pass—should be viewed as exceptionally apt. Similarly, the Egyptian strategy to take Sharuhen decades earlier cannot be considered a failure or an indication of an army inept in the conduct of siege warfare, despite the fact that the siege lasted three years. We do not know enough about the tactical concerns of the Egyptians (e.g., other towns that they might have engaged) and the sorts of casualties they may have incurred or anticipated incurring during a direct assault at the early stages of this siege. In the end, they won the war, despite what might seem to be slow progress in this particular siege.

Another observation related to Egyptian siege practices reveals that Egyptian cultural values may have governed their choice of tactics, if not their overall battlefield strategies, which therefore suggest a uniquely Egyptian approach to warfare. These values are reflected in Egyptian officers' autobiographies, which do not focus upon battlefield prowess and the killing of countless enemy troops (as the pharaohs themselves do in their self-portrayals). Instead, the autobiographies emphasize the recovery of loot, including live captives—hence the depiction of children escaping from besieged cities in order to evade capture and enslavement. Even the killing of enemy soldiers was described in the context of looting the spoils. Ahmose the son of Abana bragged after the siege of Sharuhen that he had "brought spoil from it: two women and a hand" (Lichtheim 1976:13). Severed hands were collected as an indication of how many enemies one had killed in battle, so in a sense the hands themselves were part of the physical spoils of war. The central part played by the acquisition of loot in the conduct of Egyptian warfare

[11] That such concerns were a reality for an army during the course of a siege is especially evident from Alexander's failed siege of Pellium in Illyria in 335 B.C.E. (see Arrian 1.5.5ff.). During the circumvallation of this town an ally of Clitus, the Illyrian ruler Alexander was pursuing, arrived behind Alexander's force, thus engaging Alexander's army and enabling Clitus to escape.

is nowhere more evident than during the Battle of Megiddo. Because Egyptian soldiers were consumed with acquiring loot rather than defeating the stunned and fleeing Canaanite army, the open battle developed into a siege:

> Now if his majesty's troops had not set their hearts to plundering the possessions of the enemies, they would have [captured] Megiddo at this moment, when the wretched foe of Kadesh and the wretched foe of this town were being pulled up hurriedly so as to admit them into their town. . . .
>
> Then their horses were captured, and their chariots of gold and silver became an easy [prey]. Their ranks were lying stretched out on their backs like fish in the bight of a net, while his majesty's valiant army counted their possessions. Captured was the tent of that wretched [foe], which was worked [with silver]...Then the entire army jubilated...[They lauded] his majesty and extolled his victory. Then they presented the plunder they had taken: hands, living prisoners, horses, chariots of gold and silver and of [painted work].
>
> [Lichtheim 1976:32–33]

Thus it seems that renewed consideration must be given to uniquely Egyptian traditions of warfare, particularly during the early New Kingdom, which included the high value placed on the collection of loot by the army. From this perspective, the success of the Egyptian army after the Amarna period was increasingly limited, insofar as most Egyptian soldiers would have measured success by the quantity of booty collected. The theme of the collection of booty figures much less prominently in battle narratives (e.g., the Battle of Kadesh and Merenptah stele) and private tomb paintings after the mid-fourteenth century B.C.E. The majority of "tribute" scenes in New Kingdom private tombs date from the mid-fifteenth to the mid-fourteenth centuries.

The strong emphasis placed upon the collection of loot in early New Kingdom warfare also casts the debate about the nature of Egyptian empire in a different light, allowing us to reconcile diametrically opposed views of Egyptian imperial ambitions. Some have seen the Egyptian empire as a matter of rational economic interest and others have stressed its ideological nature. If "looting" was a supreme value, with all that it meant culturally in terms of one's status and authority, we can view the empire as motivated equally by economic and ideological factors. On the one hand, Shmuel Aḥituv (1978) has correctly noted that the quantities of goods taken from the Levant are not commensurate with the collection of regular tribute. On the other hand, Nadav Na'aman (1981) is also correct in saying that the sources we possess, both iconographic and textual, emphasize the presentation of "tribute." But this tribute is more appropriately characterized as plunder or loot, because it was not a regular tax imposed upon a vassal. In most Egyptian depictions, the terms are not distinguished (see note in *ANET*[3] p. 248).

In my view, the key conceptual difference between tribute and loot is that tribute was intended to maintain the empire whereas loot served primarily to motivate the troops to perform their duties. This distinction is more than hairsplitting; it reflects a distinctly Egyptian view of warfare. On the one hand, the Egyptian pharaohs were motivated to expand Egyptian rule into the Levant to create a buffer against foreign incursions, whether Amorite, Hittite, or Hurrian, and they funded this expansion through the collection of tribute. On the other hand, soldiers of all ranks seem to have been induced to participate primarily through the prospect of collecting loot, which could enhance their social rank. The reduction in the number of tribute scenes in tomb reliefs as well as the reduction in references to plunder during the late New Kingdom may reflect an abandonment of this policy in favor of an increasingly disciplined and directly paid army that, in the end, incorporated mercenary troops, such as the Sherden.

Conclusion

In recent years, the study of warfare in the ancient Near East has begun to move beyond the cataloguing of weapons, the study of fortifications, and rudimentary attempts to discern tactics and strategies. Increasingly, warfare is recognized as an important topic in the study of ancient cultures for the very reason that warfare is itself "always an expression of culture" (Keegan 1993:12). While Egyptian scenes of Asiatic towns under siege are quintessentially Egyptian in the style of their execution and must be interpreted through an Egyptian cultural lens, to appreciate them fully they must still be viewed through the cultural perspective of the foreigners who are depicted as resisting the Egyptian attack. By considering the defenders' perspective on the siege they were experiencing, which the Egyptian artists themselves took pains to portray, I am attempting to correct and refine the dominant understanding of these scenes. For example, Donald Redford has argued that the Dapur scene "telescopes the action" so that "Egyptian shock troops mount ladders; the defenders resist; finally they capitulate and burn incense in supplication" (Redford 1992:187, pl. 18). But, as I have suggested, the order of these events must be reconstructed from the perspective of the besieged Asiatics because their activities were the focus of these scenes. Redford is right to say that war reliefs, such as those of Ramesses II, "do not permit an analysis into individual campaigns" (ibid., 186), but when those reliefs are placed within the appropriate cultural context they reveal distinctive features of Asiatic resistance to siege warfare. Furthermore, they provide us with a clear basis for understanding the obstacles faced by the Egyptians as they advanced through Canaan in the Late Bronze Age and thus enable us to appreciate more fully the extent of Egyptian efforts throughout this process.

Bibliography

Aeneas Tacticus (Aeneas the Tactician)
1990 *How to Survive under Siege*. Translated by D. Whitehead. Oxford: Clarendon.

Aḥituv, S.
1978 Economic Factors in the Egyptian Conquest of Canaan. *IEJ* 28:93–105.

Arrian
1976–1983 *Anabasis Alexandri*. Translated by P. A. Brunt. 2 vols. Loeb Classical Library. Cambridge, Mass.: Harvard University Press.

Bunimovitz, S.
1992 Middle Bronze Age Fortifications in Palestine as a Social Phenomenon. *Tel Aviv* 19:221–34.

Burke, A. A.
2008 *"Walled Up to Heaven": The Evolution of Middle Bronze Age Fortification Strategies in the Levant.* SAHL 4. Winona Lake, Ind.: Eisenbrauns.

Ephᶜal, I.
1983 On Warfare and Military Control in the Ancient Near Eastern Empires: A Research Outline. In *History, Historiography and Interpretation*, ed. H. Tadmor and M. Weinfeld, 88–106. Jerusalem: Magnes.
1997 Ways and Means to Conquer a City, Based on Assyrian Queries to the Sungod. In *Assyria 1995: Proceedings of the Tenth Anniversary Symposium of the Neo-Assyrian Text Corpus Project, Helsinki, September 7–11, 1995*, ed. S. Parpola and R. M. Whiting, 49–53. Helsinki: The Neo-Assyrian Text Corpus Project.

Finkelstein, I.
1992 Middle Bronze Age "Fortifications": A Reflection of Social Organization and Political Formations. *Tel Aviv* 19:201–20.

Gaballa, G. A.
1976 *Narrative in Egyptian Art*. Mainz am Rhein: Philipp von Zabern.

Goedicke, H.
2000 *The Battle of Megiddo*. Baltimore: Halgo.

Gonen, R.
1984 Urban Canaan in the Late Bronze Period. *BASOR* 253:61–73.

Gophna, R.
1977 Fortified Settlements from the Early Bronze and Middle Bronze II at Tel Poran. *EI* 13:87–90, 293* [in Hebrew].

Hoffmeier, J. K.
1989 Reconsidering Egypt's Part in the Termination of the Middle Bronze Age in Palestine. *Levant* 21: 181–93.
2004 Aspects of Egyptian Foreign Policy in the Eighteenth Dynasty in Western Asia and Nubia. In *Egypt, Israel, and the Ancient Mediterranean World: Studies in Honor of Donald B. Redford*, ed. G. N. Knoppers and A. Hirsch, 121–141. Probleme der Ägyptologie 20. Leiden: Brill.

Keegan, J.
1993 *A History of Warfare*. New York: Knopf.

Kempinski, A.
1974 Tell el-ᶜAjjûl—Beth-Aglayim or Sharuhen? *IEJ* 24:145–52.

Kern, P. B.
1999 *Ancient Siege Warfare*. Bloomington, Ind.: Indiana University Press.

Lichtheim, M.
1976 *Ancient Egyptian Literature*. Vol. 2, *The New Kingdom*. Berkeley, Calif.: University of California Press.

Morris, E. F.
2005 *The Architecture of Imperialism: Military Bases and the Evolution of Foreign Policy in Egypt's New Kingdom*. Probleme der Ägyptologie 22. Leiden: Brill.

Morris, S. P.
1995 The Sacrifice of Astyanax: Near Eastern Contributions to the Siege of Troy. In *The Ages of Homer: A Tribute to Emily Townsend Vermeule*, ed. J. B. Carter and S. P. Morris, 221–45. Austin, Tex.: University of Texas Press.

Mosca, P. G.
1975 Child Sacrifice in Canaanite and Israelite Religion. Ph.D. diss., Harvard University.

Na'aman, N.
1981 Economic Aspects of the Egyptian Occupation of Canaan. *IEJ* 31:172–85.

Newberry, P. E., ed.
1894 *Beni Hasan*. Vol. 2. Archaeological Survey of Egypt. London: Kegan Paul.

Pardee, D.
1997a The Kirta Epic. In *The Context of Scripture*, vol. 1, *Canonical Compositions from the Biblical World*, ed. W. W. Hallo, 333–43. Leiden: Brill.
1997b Ugaritic Prayer for a City Under Siege. In *The Context of Scripture*, vol. 1, *Canonical Compositions from the Biblical World*, ed. W. W. Hallo, 283–85. Leiden: Brill.

Petrie, W. M. F.
1931 *Ancient Gaza*. Vol. 1, *Tell el Ajjūl*. British School of Archaeology in Egypt 53. London: British School of Archaeology in Egypt.

Redford, D. B.
1992 *Egypt, Canaan, and Israel in Ancient Times*. Princeton, N.J.: Princeton University Press.
1997 Textual Sources for the Hyksos Period. In *The Hyksos: New Historical and Archaeological Perspectives*, ed. E. D. Oren, 1–44. University Museum Monograph 96. Philadelphia: University Museum, University of Pennsylvania.

Stager, L. E.
1980 The Rite of Child Sacrifice at Carthage. In *New Light on Ancient Carthage*, ed. J. G. Pedley, 1–11. Ann Arbor, Mich.: University of Michigan Press.
1985 Merenptah, Israel and Sea Peoples: New Light on an Old Relief. *EI* 18:56*–64*.

Weinstein, J. M.
1981 The Egyptian Empire in Palestine: A Reassessment. *BASOR* 241:1–28.
1991 Egypt and the Middle Bronze IIC/Late Bronze IA Transition in Palestine. *Levant* 23:105–15.

Wreszinksi, W., ed.
1935 *Atlas zur altägyptischen Kulturgeschichte*. Vol. 2. Leipzig: Hinrichs.

Yadin, Y.
1963 *The Art of Warfare in Biblical Lands in the Light of Archaeological Study*. Translated by M. Pearlman. New York: McGraw-Hill.

Yurco, F. J.
1977 Merenptah's Palestinian Campaign. *JSSEA* 8:70.
1986 Merneptah's Canaanite Campaign. *JARCE* 23: 189–216.
1990 3,200 Year Old Picture of Israelites Found in Egypt. *BAR* 16/5:21–38.
1997 Merneptah's Wars, the "Sea Peoples," and Israel's Origins. In *Ancient Egypt, the Aegean, and the Near East: Studies in Honour of Martha Rhoads Bell*, ed. J. Phillips, 1:497–506. San Antonio, Tex.: Van Siclen.

Ziffer, I.
2005 From Acemhöyük to Megiddo: The Banquet Scene in the Art of the Levant in the Second Millennium B.C.E. *Tel Aviv* 32:133–67.

7. Cores, Peripheries, and Ports of Power: Theories of Canaanite Development in the Early Second Millennium B.C.E.

by Susan L. Cohen

SIGNIFICANT changes in political and economic organization mark the beginning of the second millennium B.C.E. in Canaan. In addition to increased urbanization and political development, the era saw an increase in Canaanite interactions with polities located throughout the Levant. This interaction, fueled in part by the rise of the Middle Kingdom in Egypt, was matched by a growing number of international contacts throughout the eastern Mediterranean.

Although substantial evidence of these international interactions has been found in the Levant, the data are considerably more scarce concerning Middle Bronze Age Canaanite participation in the international scene and the resultant developments within Canaanite society. In contrast to the data available from other eras—for example, the Late Bronze Age shipwrecks at Kaš or the Iron Age ships excavated off the coast of southern Canaan and Egypt—no shipwreck or ship's cargo has been found that dates to the Middle Bronze Age. Nor is there textual evidence that unequivocally mentions Canaanite locales in connection with maritime or other international trade at this time.[1] But the presence at Canaanite sites of imported artifacts that were most probably transported along maritime routes suggests that Middle Bronze Age Canaan did participate, albeit to a limited degree, in the burgeoning international trade in the eastern Mediterranean, and it is quite likely that this trade contributed to Canaanite economic and cultural development.

Perhaps because of the general paucity of evidence for Canaanite participation in international trade, comparatively little work has focused on the means by which trade influenced the development and organization of Canaanite socioeconomic systems, other than to note in very general terms that the reurbanization that characterizes the Middle Bronze Age in Palestine was, to a large extent, sparked by international trade in the eastern Mediterranean (e.g., Dever 1987; 1993; 1997; Gerstenblith 1983). Trade is often cited as a major factor in the increased social and economic complexity that developed in Canaan, but the mechanisms involved in the actual exchange are themselves rarely examined. Furthermore, studies of the development of international trade as a whole rarely trace the effects of this activity on the subsequent internal development of the individual societies that participate in the trade.

Although the data are, admittedly, rather scarce, it is suggested here that sufficient evidence exists to shed light on the development of social and economic systems in Canaanite society, as they adjusted in response to demands arising from trade. Further, it is posited that the repercussions of Canaanite participation in, or proximity to, international trade in the eastern Mediterranean in the early second millennium B.C.E. can be traced at several levels, each of which can be examined through the application of a different theoretical model. These levels are: (1) the *interregional level* of Canaanite development stemming from interaction with other polities, analyzed according to a "core-periphery" paradigm; (2) the *intraregional level* of economic systems and networks within Canaan that adjusted to accommodate the rise of international trade, analyzed by means of Stager's "port-power" model; and (3) the *local level*, analyzed in terms of "urban-rural" interaction, in which individual settlements or small groups of settlements, often far removed from the actual exchange itself, reacted to the demands placed on them by broader structural changes in Canaanite society.

Trade and Canaanite Development

The term "trade" is subject to multiple interpretations and definitions. While one of the most common definitions simply refers to the movement of goods from region to region or polity to polity, this is not sufficiently precise about the mechanisms by which the goods were transferred. For example, a broad definition of trade as "the reciprocal traffic, exchange or movement of materials or goods through peaceful human agency" (Renfrew 1969:52) implies a level of equality in the interaction and so fails to allow for an asymmetrical distribution of power and goods. Conversely, an alternative definition of trade as the "procurement of materials from a distance, by whatever

[1] While the Mit Rahina inscription, dating to the reign of Amenemhet II (ca. the first third of the nineteenth century B.C.E.), specifically recounts the details of a maritime expedition to somewhere in the Levant (Altenmüller and Moussa 1991), the destinations of the two ships mentioned in the text are most probably not to be located in Canaan, nor is it clear that this expedition was specifically for the purpose of trade and exchange (for further discussion of the inscription, see Cohen 2002; Marcus 1998).

mechanism" (Renfrew 1977:72) does not rule out the use of violent means to acquire desired items, and thus could include military campaigns or tribute (see also Knapp 1985:8). Therefore, for the purposes of this study, trade is defined as the movement of goods and materials between locations and polities, which, while allowing for the existence of unequal power and exchange that may influence the nature of the transaction and the quantity of goods exchanged, does not include forceful procurement or acquisition of the desired items.

For the purpose of examining the impact of trade on Canaanite organization and development, it is also significant to note that trade "ramifies much more widely into the institutional structure of a society than is suggested by any degree of diffusion" (Adams 1974:240). In other words, trade itself, in addition to being an exchange of commodities, is also a significant factor in the developmental processes occurring within any given society that participates in this exchange, including those areas outside the immediate exchange locations. Trade, whether maritime or land-based, has repercussions far beyond the simple movement of goods. Economic systems shift to adapt to demands for trade items, while the distribution and availability of goods, and the power structures based on their acquisition, clearly affect social and political organization and development. As noted above, this significance is displayed on the macro level by core-periphery interactions, at an intermediate level by the development of local systems designed to fuel markets and supplies, and at the micro level by the various subsistence and other strategies adopted or adapted by individual groups to deal with the changing nature of the larger systems and their effect on local development.

Interregional Analysis: Cores and Peripheries in International Trade and the Development of Canaanite Systems

Derived from Immanuel Wallerstein's "World Systems Theory," first set forth in 1974, the core-periphery approach examines the relations between and within economic systems and the way in which those systems are structured (Rowlands 1987:4).[2] Cores, or centers, are identified as those places that control the development of technological skills and production and utilize a state ideology to defend their interests in these matters. Conversely, peripheries lack those attributes and, in addition, are "modified to meet external demands for raw materials" desired by the centers (Rowlands 1987:4). The core, therefore, is "the center of most advanced industrial production based on raw materials and semi-finished products imported from the periphery, which in exchange obtains some of the manufactures of the center" (Ekholm and Friedman 1979:43). The periphery is the area or areas where the bulk of the materials and goods are acquired or produced, and from which they are sent to the core region.[3]

It should also be noted, however, that the relationship between core and periphery is not simply defined by the exchange of goods and/or raw materials, but also involves unequal degrees of social and economic complexity, labor, and organization (Sherratt and Sherratt 1991:355). In other words, it is the core's interest in the periphery that provides some of the impetus for the periphery to modify its social, economic, and political organization to meet the demand for these materials. The Levantine coast in the early second millennium B.C.E., and Palestine in particular, can be understood as a "peripheral" region potentially affected by several "cores" (see discussion in Kohl 1987:16). This outside interest in Canaan and in Canaanite products would have affected the subsequent development of Canaanite society.

Following the core-periphery approach, it would be expected that changes in settlement patterns in the peripheral region—Canaan—would reflect a demographic shift as the region began to respond to external demands for its goods and resources. Further, it would be expected that, in order to cope with these demands, the peripheral region would begin to develop social, economic, and political systems capable of meeting them. Throughout the region, one would expect to see an increasing buildup of settlement networks, particularly in key strategic communication or transport routes, an increased agglomeration of population in those same areas, and larger centers with an increasing diversity of capabilities—in short, an urbanizing complex society.[4]

[2] Although Wallerstein (1991:93) specifically dictated that World Systems Theory could not apply to societies prior to 1500 C.E., considerable effort has been devoted to modifying this model to make it applicable to systems in the ancient world (see, e.g., Kohl 1987; Rowlands et al. 1987), resulting in the model used in this study.

[3] The traditional products of Canaan include timber, bitumen, other resins, wine, and olive oil, as well as people and animals. Most of these commodities, with the exception of people and animals, were in short supply in the traditional "core" societies such as Egypt and Mesopotamia, and thus, by necessity, had to be obtained from regions outside their traditional borders.

[4] In a case study of urbanization in Canaan in the Early Bronze Age, D. Esse (1989; 1991) identified this process as

In general, the data from Canaan support these predictions. Both the distribution of artifacts and the patterns by which settlement in Canaan developed in the early second millennium B.C.E. indicate changes in organization that were concurrent with the rise of international exchange in the eastern Mediterranean. Imported materials and manufactured goods found at sites in Canaan are evidence of international contact during this period. Such items were still relatively rare in the southern Levant in comparison to what has been found at major sites in the northern Levant, which includes artifacts whose point of origin must be located in Egypt that were most likely transported via maritime routes (see Marcus 1998 for a summary of the textual and archaeological data). This provides support for the idea that Canaan was a peripheral region among the integrated economic systems of the eastern Mediterranean. By definition, a periphery's interaction with a core is marked by asymmetrical power and exchange relationships; goods and materials leave the periphery in far greater quantities than they arrive. Moreover, at the beginning of the second millennium, Canaan was still in an early phase of its urban growth and organization; the impetus from the core and the activities generated by the increased international trade in the eastern Mediterranean would have spurred this development. But at its inception, little exchange with Canaan itself would have occurred until the local systems were sufficiently developed to provide a viable trading partner.

This suggestion is also borne out by the systemic development discernible within Canaan. With few exceptions, survey data indicate a change in settlement pattern in the early second millennium B.C.E., marked by an increase of settlement on the coastal plain and in river valleys (Gophna and Ayalon 1980; Gophna and Beck 1981; Gophna and Portugali 1988). Sites with fortifications built or founded in this era are likewise concentrated along the coast or in strategic locations on transport or communication routes (Cohen 2002:fig. 14; Gophna 1984:30). An increase of settlement along water and other transportation routes is also noted for regions in the interior, such as the Jordan Valley (Maeir 1997:210).

Intraregional Analysis: "Port Power" and the Development of Internal Systems in Canaan

Although they were dominant politically, and no doubt militarily, the core regions did not necessarily control the production of the resources they most desired, as in modern system relations. Indigenous networks in peripheral regions can develop without foreign interference and without unfamiliar systems being imposed from outside. Control over production and movement of materials desired by the cores could well have been exercised by regional systems within Canaan.[5] The organization of those regional systems within the periphery is the second, intraregional, level of development in Canaan.

The basic premise of the port-power model, as set forth by Lawrence Stager, is that coastal societies in Bronze Age Palestine "developed a distinctive set of characteristics when linked to long-distance maritime commerce" (Stager 2001:625).[6] These include the integration of coastal settlements with the interior of the region through a series of east-west transport systems in which economic power is controlled by large urban coastal sites. Within this analytical framework, regional integration is organized dendritically, such that the smaller sites in the interior funnel goods through intermediate markets to the large coastal centers.[7] From there, these goods entered the international systems of trade and exchange, in which the urban centers participated (Stager 2001:625).

The port-power model highlights economic power and structure, particularly as it develops in response to the specific demands of foreign trade and maritime commerce.[8] Economic power is tied to the port of

"secondary state formation," in which the demands for resources by a stronger and more sophisticated polity instigated the development of a "secondary state" in the targeted region. While the term "state" is misleading, as it implies a single monolithic entity, which clearly does not conform to the political organization of Canaan in the second millennium B.C.E., Esse correctly highlights the fact that contact between regions of differing power, resources, and organizational systems will invariably have some effect on the subsequent development of the lesser power, as it seeks to conform or adapt to the demands from and/or influence of the stronger power.

[5] The importance of long-distance interaction for local development was noted also by Marfoe (1987:31) in his examination of third millennium societies in the Levant.

[6] It should be noted that while Stager first proposed the port-power model in connection with Early Bronze Age Canaanite society, he believes it can apply to other eras as well (Stager 2001:633).

[7] In contrast to the idea of a dendritic settlement system (see Cohen 2002), it should be noted that in his study of maritime trade in the Levant, Marcus (1998:248) suggested that the regional networks followed a synaptic pattern of settlement development, in which the system has two focal points, the coastal site and an inland central place based on agriculture, which could interact with the settlements of the interior. In either case, however, the system is oriented asymmetrically, with the focus toward the coastal areas.

[8] Because of this heavy emphasis on economic factors, it should be noted that the port-power model does not fully

trade, which then directs the system and influences, but does not exercise immediate or direct control over, the production of the desired goods and materials from the hinterlands (Stager 2002:361). The port-power model, like the core-periphery model, emphasizes uneven power relationships and an asymmetrical organizational structure.[9] In the interregional core-periphery model the cores are the dominant partner, able at times to dictate terms to their peripheries. In a similar fashion, the intraregional port-power model envisions a system in which a large urban center located at the nexus of the periphery and the core is able to dominate and influence the local systems within the periphery. These systems develop in part in response to the ports' demands on regional production, and thus their economic development and continued growth are influenced by interests generated from the larger region's interaction with outside polities and forces.

Using this concept of port power as an analytical model on the intraregional level, therefore, it is possible to identify trends in settlement that would be expected in Canaanite development. The model predicts that the greatest variety and highest quantity of foreign imports (or other indicators of trade and economic power) would be concentrated in the major coastal centers. These indicators would decrease in number and variety at sites farther down the system, declining to almost none at the regional interior sites. The model also predicts that the local systems of settlement and growth would reflect the development of this asymmetrical power relationship, with increased numbers of smaller sites around the larger centers, and also a system or network of sites, decreasing in size, stretching into the areas in which the desired resources could be acquired.

In general, excavation of Middle Bronze Age sites in Palestine has yielded few foreign imports, especially when compared to material found in strata of other eras, and few of these imports necessarily indicate the existence of international trade. An exception to this is a series of forty-seven Egyptian bullae, used to seal clay jars prior to the shipment of commodities, found in a sealed fill at Ashkelon (Stager 2002:353). The prosaic nature of the sealings implies an exchange of subsistence commodities, which tend to be heavier and bulkier than "preciosities" used in gift exchange or trade in luxury goods; this discovery does provide some evidence of Canaanite participation in foreign commerce. Although there is some disagreement regarding the point of origin of the bullae, and whether they are Egyptian or locally made (Stager 2002:353), the bullae themselves indicate the exchange of goods. If Egyptian, the bullae may represent a small amount of goods exported from Egypt to Palestine, which is in keeping with an asymmetrical relationship between core and periphery. Conversely, if they are of local origin, this could be an indication of a small amount of goods being shipped from Canaan, which may reflect the early developmental stage of Canaanite exchange systems within the core-periphery system. Regardless of their origin, their presence at the site points to an exchange of goods between Canaan and Egypt, as well as illustrating the role of the urban port centers in Canaan as the point of exchange.

Other foreign imports found at early second millennium Canaanite sites are relatively scarce. In general, their distribution is confined to sites located along the coasts, or, in some cases, at large inland urban centers situated on clear transport and communication routes linked with coastal regions. Foreign, imported pottery and other objects have been found at such large coastal sites as Ifshar (Paley and Porath 1997), Ashkelon (Stager 2002), and Tell el-ᶜAjjul (Petrie 1931; Stewart 1974), as well as the large inland centers of Gezer and Megiddo.[10] Although limited in both diversity and quantity, these finds illustrate both the skewing of foreign contact toward the major centers and the coast, and the narrow geographical extent to which exchange items spread throughout Canaan.

The small amount of imported material in Palestine stands in sharp contrast to the hundreds of thousands of store-jar sherds of southern Levantine origin (McGovern and Harbottle 1997) excavated at the site of Tell el-Dabᶜa (ancient Avaris) in the Egyptian Delta. These represent perhaps as many as two million "Canaanite" jars (Bietak 1996:20). They were found in levels dating to the later phases of the Twelfth Dynasty and into the Thirteenth (Bietak 1991; 1997).[11] Although it is entirely possible that

address issues of social or political organization; other approaches must be utilized to examine these aspects of Canaanite development.

[9] Dendritic systems are, by definition, systems of economic exploitation (Smith 1976), as the asymmetrical organization of settlement both facilitates and sustains an unequal balance of power.

[10] For a detailed discussion of second millennium evidence for maritime trade and transportation relating to Canaanite sites, see Marcus 1998:244–45.

[11] Levantine ceramic material has been found at other sites in Egypt as well, such as Dahshur and Lisht. Imports from the Canaanite periphery to Egypt began in the early years

some of these vessels reached their destination via land routes, the sheer number of jars, which most probably contained wine or oil, combined with their weight and bulk, suggests that maritime routes were utilized in this exchange.[12] While this trade appears heavily unidirectional in favor of Egypt, it should again be noted that an uneven distribution of trade is to be expected within both core-periphery and port-power scenarios. The core's interest in the products of the periphery would result in an increased volume of material reaching foreign sites, while the major centers in Canaan would have received most of the material benefits of such contact. Different indicators must be utilized, therefore, to examine the effects of these interactions on individual sites.

Local Analysis: Urban-rural Interaction within Canaan

The analysis of Canaanite development on the local level attempts to gauge the effects of international exchange on local systems and/or individual communities, where indigenous social and economic networks were already in place at the beginning of the early second millennium B.C.E. (Cohen, in press). It is to be expected that these sites would have been affected, even if only tangentially, by changes in the cultural landscape, and would have adjusted their social and economic strategies to adapt to the demands placed on them by the regional systems, which themselves developed in response to external stimuli.

Clearly, as illustrated by the data outlined above, the immediate material effect of Canaanite involvement in foreign trade was limited, because the imported goods seem to have reached only those who resided in the larger cities located at key nodes of the major routes. To date, the archaeological record has revealed relatively few foreign imports at smaller sites in the interior. Yet it is important to note that the resources required for trade would have been located in the vicinity of these small sites, which also probably supplied a large percentage of the human resources necessary to produce the desired materials. It would, therefore, be incorrect to assume that, simply because the visible material benefits of international trade did not reach smaller sites, the overall system, including rural village sites, was unaffected by the maritime trade or the subsequent economic and social restructuring that would have accompanied it.

Without visible indicators of international trade, identifying its repercussions on the local level is problematic. In general, however, it can be argued that increased standardization, whether in animal husbandry or ceramic production, as well as production and consumption of other resources, would mark a local site's increasing interaction with regional systems. Furthermore, demand for bulk commodities, such as oil, wine, or foodstuffs would have led to a standardization of the containers in which these goods were transported. For example, evidence from Tell el-Ḥayyat indicates changes in ceramic production and distribution (Falconer 1994:133) in which decentralized production of utilitarian pottery at the village level shifts to a more regionally based ceramic production, distribution, and exchange (Falconer 1985:257). As the Middle Bronze Age progressed, standardization in pottery increased, with a concurrent decrease in local pottery production.

While evidence for these changes at small sites on the local level is limited, standardization of technologies and increased evidence for regional distribution indicate a rural society affected by systemic changes in the region. The preexisting systems at local sites adapted to meet changing circumstances and demands, which themselves were generated by changes in the larger systems throughout the regions. The external demand for Canaanite commodities from the cores, which fueled the regional systems' demand on their hinterlands, would have had a significant effect on the development and organization of rural Canaan, and would have created a mutual relationship between urban centers and their rural hinterlands.

---

of the Twelfth Dynasty and continued throughout the second millennium B.C.E. (Arnold et al. 1995:30).

[12] Evidence for large, single-cargo shipments of Levantine goods in bulk in later eras can be found in the seventh-century B.C.E. shipwrecks found off the coast of Egypt (see Ballard et al. 2002).

Bibliography

Adams, R. McC.
1974 Anthropological Perspectives on Ancient Trade. *CA* 15:239–58.

Altenmüller, H., and A. M. Moussa
1991 Die Inschrift Amenemhets II. aus dem Ptah-Tempel von Memphis: Ein Vorbericht. *Studien zur altägyptischen Kultur* 18:1–48.

Arnold, D., F. Arnold, and S. Allen
1995 Canaanite Imports at Lisht, the Middle Kingdom Capital of Egypt. *Ägypten und Levante* 5:13–32.

Ballard, R., L. E. Stager, et al.
2002 Iron Age Shipwrecks in Deep Water off Ashkelon, Israel. *AJA* 106:151–68.

Bietak, M.
1991 Egypt and Canaan during the Middle Bronze Age. *BASOR* 281:27–72.
1996 *Avaris, the Capital of the Hyksos: Recent Excavations at Tell el-Dabᶜa*. London: British Museum.
1997 The Center of Hyksos Rule: Avaris (Tell el-Dabᶜa). In *The Hyksos: New Historical and Archaeological Perspectives*, ed. E. Oren, 87–139. Philadelphia: University Museum, University of Pennsylvania.

Broshi, M., and R. Gophna
1986 Middle Bronze Age II Palestine: Its Settlements and Population. *BASOR* 261:73–90.

Cohen, S. L.
2002 *Canaanites, Chronologies, and Connections: The Relationship of Middle Bronze Age IIA Canaan to Middle Kingdom Egypt*. SAHL 3. Winona Lake, Ind.: Eisenbrauns.
in press Continuities and Discontinuities: A Re-Examination of the Intermediate Bronze Age–Middle Bronze Age I Transition in Palestine. *BASOR*.

Dever, W. G.
1987 The Middle Bronze Age: The Zenith of the Urban Canaanite Era. *BA* 50:149–77.
1993 The Rise of Complexity in the Land of Israel in the Early Second Millennium B.C.E. In *Biblical Archaeology Today, 1990: Proceedings of the Second International Congress on Biblical Archaeology*, ed. A. Biran and J. Aviram, 98–109. Jerusalem: Israel Exploration Society.
1997 Settlement Patterns and Chronology of Palestine in the Middle Bronze Age. In *The Hyksos: New Historical and Archaeological Perspectives*, ed. E. Oren, 285–301. Philadelphia: University Museum, University of Pennsylvania.

Ekholm, K., and J. Friedman
1979 "Capital" Imperialism and Exploitation in Ancient World Systems. In *Power and Propaganda: A Symposium on Ancient Empires*, ed. M. T. Larsen, 41–58. Mesopotamia 7. Copenhagen: Akademisk.

Esse, D.
1989 Secondary State Formation and Collapse in Early Bronze Age Palestine. In *L'urbanisation de la Palestine à l'âge du bronze ancient: Bilan et perspectives des recherches actuelles, Actes du Colloque d'Emmaüs (20–24 octobre 1986)*, ed. P. de Miroschedji, 1:81–96. BARIS 527(i). Oxford: British Archaeological Reports.
1991 *Subsistence, Trade, and Social Change in Early Bronze Age Palestine*. SAOC 50. Chicago: Oriental Institute, University of Chicago.

Falconer, S. E.
1985 Village Pottery Production and Exchange: A Jordan Valley Perspective. In *Studies in the History and Archaeology of Jordan*, vol. 3, ed A. Hadidi, 251–59. Amman: Department of Antiquities of Jordan.
1994 Village Economy and Society in the Jordan Valley: A Study of Bronze Age Rural Complexity. In *Archaeological Views from the Countryside: Village Communities in Early Complex Societies*, ed. G. M. Schwartz and S. Falconer, 121–42. Washington, D.C.: Smithsonian Institution.

Gerstenblith, P.
1983 *The Levant at the Beginning of the Middle Bronze Age*. American Schools of Oriental Research Dissertation Series 5. Philadelphia: American Schools of Oriental Research.

Gophna, R.
1978 Archaeological Survey of the Central Coastal Plain, 1977. *Tel Aviv* 5:136–47.
1984 The Settlement Landscape of Palestine in the Early Bronze Age II–III and Middle Bronze Age II. *IEJ* 34:24–31.

Gophna, R., and E. Ayalon
1980 Survey of the Central Coastal Plain, 1978–1979: Settlement Pattern of the Middle Bronze Age IIA. *Tel Aviv* 7:147–50.

Gophna, R., and P. Beck
1981 The Rural Aspect of the Settlement Pattern of the Coastal Plain in the Middle Bronze Age II. *Tel Aviv* 8:45–80.

Gophna, R., and M. Kochavi
1966 An Archaeological Survey of the Plain of Sharon. *IEJ* 16:143–44.

Gophna, R., and J. Portugali
1988 Settlement and Demographic Processes in Israel's Coastal Plain from the Chalcolithic to the Middle Bronze Age. *BASOR* 269:11–28.

Kohl, P.
1987 The Ancient Economy, Transferable Technologies and the Bronze Age World-system: A View from the Northeastern Frontier of the Ancient Near East. In *Centre and Periphery in the Ancient World*, ed. M. Rowlands, M. Larsen, and K. Kristiansen, 13–24. Cambridge: Cambridge University Press.

Maeir, A.
1997 The Material Culture of the Central Jordan Valley during the Middle Bronze II Period: Pottery and Settlement Pattern. 2 vols. Ph.D. diss., Hebrew University of Jerusalem.

Marcus, E.
1998 *Maritime Trade in the Southern Levant from Earliest Times through the Middle Bronze IIA Period.* Ph.D. diss., University of Oxford.
2002 The Southern Levant and Maritime Trade during the Middle Bronze IIA Period. In *Aharon Kempinski Memorial Volume: Studies in Archaeology and Related Disciplines*, ed. E. Oren and S. Aḥituv, 241–63. Studies by the Department of Bible and Ancient Near East 15. Beer-Sheva, Israel: Ben-Gurion University of the Negev Press.

Marfoe, L.
1987 Cedar Forest to Silver Mountain: Social Change and the Development of Long-Distance Trade in Early Near Eastern Societies. In *Centre and Periphery in the Ancient World*, ed. M. Rowlands, M. Larsen, and K. Kristiansen, 25–35. Cambridge: Cambridge University Press.

McGovern, P., and G. Harbottle
1997 "Hyksos" Trade Connections between Tell el-Dabᶜa (Avaris) and the Levant: A Neutron Activation Study of the Canaanite Jar. In *The Hyksos: New Historical and Archaeological Perspectives*, ed. E. Oren, 141–57. Philadelphia: University Museum, University of Pennsylvania.

Paley, S. M., and Y. Porat
1997 Early Middle Bronze Age IIa Remains at Tell el-Ifshar, Israel: A Preliminary Report. In *The Hyksos: New Historical and Archaeological Perspectives*, ed. E. Oren, 369–78. Philadelphia: University Museum, University of Pennsylvania.

Petrie, W. M. F.
1931 *Ancient Gaza.* Vol. 1, *Tell el Ajjūl*. British School of Archaeology in Egypt 53. London: British School of Archaeology in Egypt.

Renfrew, C.
1969 Trade and Culture Process in European Prehistory. *CA* 10:151–69.
1975 Trade as Action at a Distance: Questions of Integration and Communication. In *Ancient Civilization and Trade*, ed. J. A. Sabloff and C. C. Lamberg-Karlovsky, 3–59. Albuquerque, N.M.: University of New Mexico Press.
1977 Alternative Models for Exchange and Spatial Distribution. In *Exchange Systems in Prehistory*, ed. T. K. Earle and J. A. Ericson, 71–90. New York: Academic.

Rowlands, M.
1987 Centre and Periphery: A Review of a Concept. In *Centre and Periphery in the Ancient World*, ed. M. Rowlands, M. Larsen, and K. Kristiansen, 1–11. Cambridge: Cambridge University Press.

Rowlands, M., M. Larsen, and K. Kristiansen, eds.
1987 *Centre and Periphery in the Ancient World.* Cambridge: Cambridge University Press.

Sherratt, A., and S. Sherratt
1991 From Luxuries to Commodities: The Nature of Mediterranean Bronze Age Trading Systems. In *Bronze Age Trade in the Mediterranean*, ed. N. H. Gale, 351–86. SIMA 90. Jonsered: Åström.

Smith, C. A.
1976 Exchange Systems and the Spatial Distribution of Elites: The Organization of Stratification in Agrarian Societies. In *Regional Analysis*, vol. 2, *Social Systems*, ed. C. A. Smith, 309–374. New York: Academic.

Stager, L. E.
2001 Port Power in the Early and the Middle Bronze Age: The Organization of Maritime Trade and Hinterland Production. In *Studies in the Archaeology of Israel and Neighboring Lands: In Memory of Douglas L. Esse*, ed. S. R. Wolff, 625–38. SAOC 59. Chicago: Oriental Institute, University of Chicago.
2002 The MB IIA Ceramic Sequence at Tel Ashkelon and Its Implications for the "Port Power" Model of Trade. In *The Middle Bronze Age in the Levant: Proceedings of an International Conference on MB IIA Ceramic Material, Vienna, 24th–26th of January 2001*, ed. M. Bietak, 353–62. Vienna: Österreichische Akademie der Wissenschaften.

Stewart, J. R.
1974 *Tell el-ᶜAjjūl: The Middle Bronze Age Remains.* SIMA 38. Göteborg: Åström.

Wallerstein, I.
1991 World System versus World-Systems: A Critique. *Critique of Anthropology* 11:189–94.

8. THE SOCIAL WORLDS OF THE BOOK OF JOB

by Michael D. Coogan

THE book of Job is a literary work, presenting on one level an imaginary, a fictional world. But on another level its authors[1] also reflect the realities and values of their own world. Hence there are two overlapping social worlds in the book of Job.

The Narrative Context

As is generally the case with wisdom literature throughout the ancient Near East, the book of Job gives no explicit indication of chronology either in the narrative framework or in the dialogues: Job is, deliberately perhaps, a kind of "Everyman." Moreover, the book is neither clear nor consistent about Job's social setting.

Early postbiblical Jewish tradition situated Job in the era of the ancestors of Israel, narrated in the Bible in Genesis 12–50. Thus, the Septuagint, in its addition to the last chapter of the book of Job, informs us that Job was a grandson of Esau; according to the *Testament of Job*, Job's second wife was Jacob's daughter Dinah. This chronology is based on biblical tradition itself.

From the first introduction of Job in the book, to the epilogue, there are allusions to the Genesis traditions. Like Noah (Gen. 6:9),[2] Abraham (Gen. 17:1; 20:6), and, above all, Jacob (Gen. 25:27), Job is *ʾîš tām*, "a perfect man, a man of integrity."[3] Like Abraham (Gen. 25:8 [LXX]) and Isaac (Gen. 35:29), Job dies old and "full of years" (Job 42:17),[4] and his lifespan is suitably patriarchal.[5] Also, as in the distant past, the unit of currency is the *qĕśîṭâ* (Job 42:11, Gen. 33:19).[6]

Job's lifestyle also fits that of the ancestral narratives in Genesis. Like Isaac (Gen. 26:14), Job has a large retinue of servants (Job 1:3).[7] Like all of the patriarchs, Job has large flocks and herds (Job 1:3, 14–17; 31:20, 42:12; see Gen. 12:16; 24:35; 30:43; 32:5, 7, 13–15). Moreover, as in Genesis, especially in the Priestly tradition, two of the preferred names for the deity in the poetic dialogues are El (55 times in Job) and Shadday (31 times).[8] The name Yahweh is used only in the prose framework narrative and in the introductions to the divine speeches in Job 37–41.[9] This has a twofold effect: Job and his friends are depicted as worshippers of the pre-Israelite ancestral deity El, known under various titles, and the issues raised by the book are made more universal.[10]

---

[1] I use the plural to avoid the naïve implication that the book of Job in its present form is the product of a single writer; that model of how texts are formed is frequently inapplicable to ancient literature, including the book of Job.

[2] Job is also linked with Noah in Ezek. 14:14, 20, another ancient witness to an early date for the narrative chronology of the book.

[3] The exact phrase occurs only in Job 1:8; 2:3; and Gen. 25:27 in the Bible.

[4] Similar but not identical phrasing is used elsewhere only in Chronicles.

[5] According to Job 42:16 (MT), Job lived 140 years after the events described in the book; in some Greek manuscripts the number is 170, and the length of his entire life was 240 years, which would mean that he was 70 years old at the beginning of the book. Although numbers are notoriously unstable in textual transmission; the implicit rationale behind the numbers is that Job's remaining years were double those that had preceded his troubles, just as his possessions were doubled.

[6] This obscure word is used elsewhere only in Josh. 24:32.

[7] *ʿăbuddâ rabbâ,* a phrase found only in these two places in the Bible.

[8] In Job, half of the times when Shadday is used, it is a parallel term with *ʾel* (e.g., Job 5:17; 8:3), or occurs in close proximity to it (e.g., Job 21:14–15, 19–20). This recalls the full title El Shadday (Gen. 17:1, 28:3, 35:11, 43:14, 48:3; Exod. 6:4). Another commonly used term for the deity in Job is *ʾĕlōah,* which occurs 41 times.

[9] The only exception is Job 12:9, which with many scholars I take to be a gloss derived from Isa. 41:20; compare Job 19:21. Note further that some Hebrew manuscripts have *ʾĕlōah*, and that the entire verse, along with the preceding half-verse, is missing in the best Greek manuscripts. Even in the formulaic concluding addition to the search for Wisdom, *ʾădōnāy* is used instead of *yhwh* (Job 28:28).

[10] This broader context is also hinted at by the few place names in the book. Job is from Uz (Job 1:1, Gen. 22:21), a place somewhere in southern Transjordan. The same locale is suggested by the presence of the Sabeans (Job 1:15; see also 6:19), probably from northern Arabia. Eliphaz is from Teman (Job 2:11), associated with Edom (Gen. 36:24, Amos 1:12), and Bildad is from Shuah (Job 2:11), also to the east of Israel (Gen. 25:2, 6); Naamah, Zophar's place of origin, cannot be located. Elihu, although in my view a later interpolation, is from Buz (Job 32:2), associated with Edom in Jer. 25:23; see also Gen. 22:21. Perhaps significantly, many of these places are associated with Abraham as well, by means of genealogy. In any case, these place names provide little more than a general setting: the book of Job is no more representative of life in Uz in Edom in the distant past than is the book of Judith of life in Judah during the eighth century B.C.E.

The postbiblical placement of the character Job in the ancestral period is therefore a correct interpretation of allusions in the book itself, allusions which intended readers to adopt the same narrative chronology.[11]

The Social World of the Authors

In contrast to the implicit setting of the narrative chronology, the social world of the authors is that of the Israelite agricultural town, not that of the seminomadic ancestors of tradition. Unlike the patriarchs, Job is evidently not a pastoralist; he is rather a wealthy agriculturalist, living in a house, much like Danel of the Ugaritic texts, with whom he is linked in Ezekiel (14:14, 20), along with Noah, also a "man of the soil" (Gen. 9:20).

Both the framework prose narrative and the poetic dialogues of the book of Job are, at first glance, inconsistent in the vocabulary used for the *mise-en-scène*. In the prologue and epilogue, both Job and his children live in houses (*bêt*; Job 1:4, 10, 13, 18–19; 42:11). In the dialogues, the same word is used both for Job's own dwelling (Job 19:15) and for those of his neighbors (Job 7:10; 15:28; 20:19, 28; 21:9; 22:18; 24:16; 27:18). Yet more than a dozen times, several words for "tent" are also used (principally *ʾōhel*, also *miškān*). This usage should not be taken literally, however, to mean that Job himself (Job 5:24, 11:14, 19:12, 22:23, 29:4) or his neighbors (Job 8:22; 15:34; 18:6, 14, 21; 21:28) were seminomadic pastoralists, like Abraham, Isaac, and Jacob. Some of these references to tents should be understood as poetic convention, in which words for "tent" are formulaic parallels to words for "house"; note the parallels *bêt* / *ʾōhel miškĕnôt* in Job 21:28, and *bêt* / *miškĕnôt* in 39:6 (see also Prov. 14:11; Judg. 20:8). As such, the various words for "tent" often simply mean "dwelling" more generically.[12] In some cases, too, both *ʾōhel* and *miškān* have the further nuance of extended family or household (e.g., Job 18:21; 20:26; 22:23; 29:4 [note 29:5]; 31:31), as indeed does *bêt* (e.g., 21:21).

Thus, in the poetic dialogues, the dwellings of Job and of his contemporaries are permanent structures, or houses, and those houses are clustered in towns.[13] The towns have public squares and gates (Job 5:4; 29:7; 31:21), in which legal and other public business takes place (19:18; 30:28). The towns have as at least one of their systems of leadership that of elders (Job 12:20; see also 29:8), who can function as judges (32:9). There are also priests and other ritual personnel (Job 12:19), and perhaps even a tophet (17:6).[14] The inhabitants of these towns raise the typical crops of Israelite farmers (see King and Stager 2001:93–103)—wheat and barley (Job 31:40; see also 5:26), olives and grapes (15:33; 24:6, 11), in fields that they plow (4:8; 31:38) with oxen (1:14). They also engage in animal husbandry, involving both large cattle (Job 6:5; 21:10; 42:8) and small (21:11; 30:1; 31:20). At least some of them are literate, as two references to writing indicate (Job 19:23; 31:35). On the horizon of this world, but seldom mentioned and thus as it were at a distance, is urban life. There are cities (Job 15:28; 24:12),[15] and there are kings (3:14; etc.), as well as military combat (notably 39:21–25; see also 19:6, 12).

Job is the *paterfamilias* of a socioeconomic unit that includes not just his wife and children, but also other dependents, including servants (*nĕʿārîm*: Job 1:15–17; 29:5); male and female slaves (*ʿăbādîm*: 19:16; 31:13; *ʾămāhōt*: 19:15; 31:13); resident aliens (*gēr*: 31:32; *gārê bêtî*: 19:15); orphans (22:9; 29:12; 31:17, 21; in 31:18 Job describes himself as the orphan's "father"); widows (22:9; 29:13; 31:16); and other needy persons (see further below; in 29:16 Job describes himself as "father" to the *ʾebyônîm*).

In Job's household the status of women is complicated. On the one hand, Job's unnamed wife (he is apparently monogamous, unlike Abraham and Jacob) is mentioned only three times in the entire book. In Job 2:9, she gives her famous short speech urging her husband to "'bless' God and die" (see further Coogan 1990:135; Seow 2006:148–50). Her role as a mother

[11] Throughout the book of Job, there are repeated allusions to and even quotations of a wide range of biblical traditions; for a selection, see Driver and Gray 1921:lxvii–lxviii. These multiple allusions and quotations suggest that the book of Job is to be dated relatively late in the formation of biblical traditions. See also nn. 21 and 23 below.

[12] Likewise, *nāweh*, originally "pasturage," can also be a more general term for "dwelling place" (Job 5:3; 8:6); in fact, it is a parallel word for *ʾōhel* in 5:24 and 18:15.

[13] Unlike the typical Iron Age multiple-family dwelling as described by Stager (1985:18–23), Job's children seem to have lived at some distance from each other and from their father; see Job 1:4–5, 18.

[14] As Habel (1985:277) suggests, at the very least the word *tōpet* may be a pun. The principal manuscripts of the Targum to Job translate it as "Gehenna," and this interpretation is followed by NJPS; most modern scholars identify the word as a hapax legomenon from a root meaning "to spit." In either case, the verse is not entirely clear or grammatical, and is frequently emended.

[15] In Job 29:7, Job described himself exiting the gates of the *qāret*; this word is a biform of the more frequent *qiryah*, which occurs in Job 39:7. Both should probably be translated "town" rather than "city."

is unexplored in the Masoretic Text; she is not even mentioned in the epilogue, which recounts how "Job had seven sons and three daughters" (42:13) to replace those whose deaths had been related in the prologue (1:18–19).[16] In Job 19:17, Job mentions his wife[17] in passing, as he describes his alienation from his society. The last reference to his wife is part of a self-imprecation in the context of a long negative confession. Job declares that if he has ever committed adultery,

> May my wife grind for another,
> May others kneel over her. (Job 31:10)

What Job calls for is a rough retributive justice: his punishment should be the same as the crime that he has been guilty of, namely, someone else will sleep with his wife, because adultery is an offense against husbands. The status of the wife, to say nothing of her feelings as her loss of integrity (in theory) becomes the means of punishing Job, while not without precedent in biblical tradition, is to modern readers both shocking and an illustration of the many differences between ancient and modern ethics.[18]

In contrast to the treatment of Job's wife is the status of his daughters, especially those belonging to the replacement set of children. In general, in Job's world the birth of a son was a cause for special celebration (Job 3:3; see also Jer. 20:15). Yet Job's daughters are given more attention than their brothers.[19] They are mentioned explicitly[20] only in the prologue (Job 1:2, 13, 18), as are their replacements in the epilogue (42:13–15), but the latter reference is notable on several counts. First, the daughters are named (see further Coogan 1990:145–46), unlike either Job's wife or even his sons. Second, we are told of their extraordinary beauty, also probably intimated in their names: Jemimah ("dove"), Keziah (an exotic aromatic), and Keren-happuch ("horn of eye-makeup"). Third, contrary to general ancient Near Eastern and biblical practice, the daughters are given an inheritance equal to that of the oldest son. The only good parallel to this unusual bequest is in the Ugaritic epic of Kirta. Like Job, Kirta's first offspring die. In blessing Kirta at his second marriage, El promises that his wife will produce a new set of sons and daughters. The daughters are apparently named (the text is broken) and of the youngest, El declares that he will make her firstborn (*bkr*; *CAT* 1.15 iii 16). This would certainly include a share in the inheritance, like that given by Job to his daughters. Although some modern commentators (e.g., Mitchell 1987:xxx; Pardes 1992:153–54) see in Job's action evidence of his consciousness having been raised by the immediately preceding theophany, it is more likely epic convention (see Coogan 1990:144–47).

Social Values

Just as the primary setting of the book of Job is that of its authors, so too throughout the book the social values of ancient Israelite society are presented both implicitly and explicitly. Job's world, and that of his friends, is one in which there are established ethical principles, detailed in several important passages.

Two of these passages contain accounts of how wrongly the wicked act. In a typical accusation (Job 22:5–9), Eliphaz accuses Job of having required pledges of collateral without cause, so that, like the complainant in the Meṣad Hashavyahu Ostracon (*KAI* 200; see also Amos 2:8), his kin ("brothers") are left without covering because their clothes have been their collateral. Instead of feeding the hungry and providing for widows and orphans, Job has apparently allowed might to prevail over right, so that only the powerful and elite have rights to the land. We the readers know that these accusations are without merit; like Job's other friends, Eliphaz has reached a logical conclusion based on his premise that because there is divine justice only the wicked suffer: if Job is suffering he must have committed wrong.

Job 24 provides another negative catalogue of the Israelite ethical code. The chapter is difficult because the subjects of the verbs are often unclear—is it the wicked, or their victims? And although Job is identified as the speaker (Job 23:1), this chapter belongs to the apparently disrupted third cycle of the dialogues; the viewpoint of Job 24:13–24 is so inconsistent with Job's stance elsewhere in the book that many scholars attribute these words to Bildad, whose final speech in 25:2–6 is uncharacteristically short as it stands (for a

---

[16] Beginning a process of enhancing the role of Job's wife, the Septuagint has a long addition to her brief speech in the Hebrew text of Job 2:9. In it she bitterly laments the loss of her children, "the labor pains of my womb, for whom I toiled in distress for nothing." Subsequent tradition names her Sitis, derived from the Greek form of the name of Job's hometown, Uz.

[17] And apparently his children as well, if *bĕnê biṭnî* means "sons of my belly" and not "sons of my [mother's] belly"; see further Clines 1989:448–49; Coogan 1990:141–42.

[18] For similar treatment of women as sexual objects to be manipulated by men, see for example Gen. 12.11–16, 19.8, Judg. 19:24. For a modern critique of the value system, see Good 1990:315.

[19] To be sure, in the poetic dialogues, the children in general get only scant attention. See further Coogan 1990.

[20] *bānîm* in at least one case may be collective (Job 8:4; see also 1:5) and include the daughters, but formally it is masculine.

brief summary of scholarly views, see Newsom 2003: 161, 165–66). For my purposes here, these issues are tangential: the chapter clearly describes how the wicked act, regardless of whether or not God is understood as punishing them, and thus again give us a summary of ethical principles.

In Job 24, the norms that the wicked violate include respect for the property of others, both real estate and livestock, and especially those of the orphan, the widow, and the needy. In fact, the society where the wicked hold sway is one in which these powerless individuals have no food, clothing, or shelter, but are forced to give up their children as collateral, as they work as day-laborers. That is because the wicked are murderers, thieves, and adulterers,[21] denizens of the night.

Job replies to these accusations and distinguishes his conduct from that of the wicked in two remarkable speeches in chapters 29 and 31. In 29:12–16, he describes how he was honored by both young and old at public assemblies for his charity:

> I rescued the poor man who cried out,
> the orphan who had no other helper.
> The blessing of the destitute came upon me,
> and I made the widow's heart sing for joy.
> I clothed myself in righteousness, and it clothed me,
> my justice was a cloak and a head-covering.
> I was eyes to the man who was blind,
> and feet to the man who was lame.
> I was a father to those who were needy,
> and I investigated the case of the person
> I didn't even know.

Here Job presents himself as one who, unlike the wicked described earlier, had a special concern for the powerless and afflicted—he was their "father" and so they had become part of his household. As such, he looked out for their legal rights.

This same concern for the powerless is expressed in more detail in Job 31. As has often been observed, this passage is reminiscent of the protestation of innocence in the Egyptian Book of the Dead (125; see *COS* 2.12); the illustration that often appears with the text of the incantation shows the heart of the dead person being weighed on a scale, an image possibly alluded to in Job 31:6:

> May he weigh me on the scales of righteousness,
> and may God know my uprightness.[22]

Job 31 consists of a series of rhetorical questions followed by self-imprecations. He catalogues his innocence, and in doing so gives us yet another picture of the ideals of ancient Israel. He has respected his neighbor's[23] marriage (31:9–12). He has judged fairly the complaints of his slaves, recognizing, remarkably, that they too are human (31:13–15). He has provided for the poor, widows, and orphans, even incorporating them into his household (31:16–20), and defending them in public (31:21–22). Likewise, he has opened his doors to the stranger (*gēr*; 31:32). In fact, he has gone further: he has trusted only in God, not in wealth or in other deities such as the moon god (31:24–28).

Job, then, has complied fully with the requirements of Israel's covenant: exclusive worship of God and respect for the neighbor. Despite the narrative conceit that would make Job a contemporary of the ancestors of Israel, the book that bears his name is in fact a fully Israelite work, reflecting life in biblical Israel and the values that shaped it.

---

[21] The same words for murder (*rṣḥ*), theft (*gnb*), and adultery (*nʾp*) in Job 24:14–15 occur in the Decalogue (Exod. 20:13–15) and are almost certainly an allusion to it, as in Jer. 7:9 and Hos. 4:2.

[22] *tummātî*, as in Job 2:3, 9 a reference to Job as an *ʾîš tām* (Job 1:1, 8; 2:3).

[23] *rēaʿ(* (Job 31:9), another likely allusion to the Decalogue (see n. 21 above).

Bibliography

Clines, D. J. A.
1989 *Job 1–20.* WBC 17. Dallas: Word.

Coogan, M. D.
1990 Job's Children. In *Lingering over Words: Studies in Ancient Near Eastern Literature in Honor of William L. Moran*, ed. T. Abusch et al., 135–47. HSS 37. Atlanta: Scholars.

Driver, S. R., and G. B. Gray
1921 *A Critical and Exegetical Commentary on the Book of Job.* International Critical Commentary. Edinburgh: T. and T. Clark.

Good, E. M.
1990 *In Turns of Tempest: A Reading of Job, with a Translation.* Stanford, Calif.: Stanford University Press.

Habel, N. C.
1985 *The Book of Job: A Commentary.* Philadelphia: Westminster.

King, P. J., and Stager, L. E.
2001 *Life in Biblical Israel.* Louisville, Ky.: Westminster John Knox.

Mitchell, S., trans.
1987 *The Book of Job.* San Francisco: North Point.

Newsom, C. A.
2003 *The Book of Job: A Contest of Moral Imaginations.* New York: Oxford University Press.

Pardes, I.
1992 *Countertraditions in the Bible: A Feminist Approach.* Cambridge, Mass.: Harvard University Press.

Seow, C. L.
2006 Job's Wife. In *Engaging the Bible in a Gendered World: An Introduction to Feminist Biblical Interpretation in Honor of Katharine Doob Sakenfeld*, ed. L. Day and C. Pressler, 141–50. Louisville, Ky.: Westminster John Knox.

Stager, L. E.
1985 The Archaeology of the Family in Ancient Israel. *BASOR* 260:1–35.

9. Telltale Remnants of Oral Epic in the Older Sources of the Tetrateuch: Double and Triple Proper Names in Early Hebrew Sources, and in Homeric and Ugaritic Epic Poetry

by Frank Moore Cross

CHARACTERISTIC of epic poetry is the use of multiple names and epithets—traditional elements used in oral composition to fit metrical or parallelistic prosodic patterns. In the following paragraphs I wish to examine (1) multiple names of identical (or interchangeable) persons, tribes, or places in Greek epic; (2) multiple names of gods and places in Ugaritic epics; and finally, (3) multiple names, tribes, and places preserved in what I have called the Epic Sources, the J and E strands of the Tetrateuch.[1]

My motivation in examining these multiple names and epithets of the Tetrateuch is not to attack the Documentary Hypothesis, which in the last two centuries has been used successfully to partition prose sources, but rather to examine the extraordinary use of double and triple names in the older prose sources of the Tetrateuch, and to argue for their origin in old epic poetry, which stands as an ultimate source or sources behind the surviving prose documents.

The Iliad

I assume that the Iliad was, in its original form, an epic poem orally composed and sung to the accompaniment of music. This understanding, often referred to as the Parry–Lord theory, has slowly gained adherents, and it seems certain that the Iliad either was orally composed and only secondarily written down, or, less likely, was composed in writing using as its basis a large reservoir of oral formulae (see Parry 1930; 1932; Lord 1964; 1968; 1991; Nagy 1996). The following are examples of multiple names appropriate to oral epic:

1. Ilios and Troy (Τροίη) are two names of the city-state used interchangeably by the bard.[2] Perhaps the names had slightly different meanings in the prose of the Mycenean era; in any case, for poetic purposes they are the same great city. Note that the older form of the name Ilios is Wilios (ϝιλιος), which best fits the hexameters of epic verse where Ilios occurs.

2. The same is true for the Greek warriors who besieged Troy. They are named, interchangeably and without geographic distinction, Achaeans, Danaans, and Argives.[3] Latacz remarks, "All three names were thus retained as synonymous metrical variants. All denoted the same thing: the Greeks" (Latacz 2004:133–35). Each name has a different quantitative metrical value: Δάναοι ∪ ∪ —; Ἀργέιοι — — —; Ἀχαιοι ∪ — —. The variants were thus welcomed by the bard in composing orally his hexameters.

3. Ἀλέξανδρος || Πάρις. Alexander, a Greek name, and Paris, an Anatolian name, enter the epic in Book 3 of the Iliad (Alexander in 3:16 and often; Paris in 3:39 and often). They are alternative names for the same person, a hero of Troy, son of Priam. This extraordinary juxtaposition of names is introduced without explanation. It is initially puzzling to modern newcomers to Homer but was not troubling to the audience of Homer, who were accustomed to the metrical requirements of orally composed epic verse.

4. Σπάρτη || Λακεδαίμων are names used indifferently in Homer for the dwelling place of Menelaus.

5. Ἀθήνη || Τριτογένεια are two names used for the same goddess (Book 1:194 and often; Book 4: 515; 8:39; 22:183). "Tritogeneia" may be judged an epithet, although it is not used in the Iliad in combination with the name Athena.

6. Ἐφυρη (Book 6:153, 210) || Κόρινθος (Book 2. 570; 13:664). In Book 6, Ephyrē is explicitly the name of the city, not the goddess-founder.

[1] I must acknowledge my great debt to my colleague at Harvard, Dr. Richard J. Saley. He has carefully read proof and corrected many errors, and checked references. I am also indebted to Prof. Ronald Hendel for his critical reading of my paper and pertinent bibliographical suggestions.

[2] Joachim Latacz (2004:99) notes: "Greek Troy poetry could only welcome the availability of two names for the same geographic entity since both names, with their different metrical forms, made it much easier to work this fabled city into hexameters. . . . It is after all a principle of Greek hexameter poetry . . . that where variant names exist for the same object and make hexameters easier to compose, they will be gratefully exploited."

[3] Compare Gregory Nagy's (1981:83) statement that: "In Homeric diction, this name Akhaioí functions as the synonym of Danaoí and Argeîoi . . ."

Other examples could be cited, but these should suffice to illustrate the argument. Moreover, such variant names of heroes, places, tribes, and gods are closely related to the formulaic epithets of heroes and gods that are the building blocks of orally composed epic hexameters.

Ugaritic Epic

The myths and epics of Ugarit are composed with poetic formulae and patterns that point to original oral composition. Unlike the Greek formulae designed to fit Greek hexameters, Ugaritic (and Hebrew) consist of pairs, and less frequently, triads, of parallel cola, expressing one idea. Within the cola are formulaic pairs (or triads) of stock synonyms (or antonyms), chosen to achieve symmetrical verse.[4] Indeed, Ugaritic epic poetry features grammatical, lexical, and prosodic parallelism. See my discussion of Ugaritic poetry in "Prose and Poetry in the Mythic and Epic Texts from Ugarit" (Cross 1974; see also Aitken 1989).

A colophon is found in *KTU* 1.6 vi 54–57 which certifies that the Ugaritic text was dictated by a chief singer, a priest:

sapiru ʾilimilku šbniyyu
lamīdu ʾattanu prln rabbu kāhinīma
rabbu nāqidīma
ṯāʿiyu niqmadda milku ʾugarīti . . .

Scribe: ʾIlimilku, the Šbnite.
Adept (Singer):[5] ʾAttanu Prln, the chief priest,
the chief shepherd.
Donor : Niqmaddu, king of Ugarit . . .

There is good evidence that parallelistic poetry had its origins in oral composition, and that parallel formulae were an aid to the singer of tales. Parallelism is found in a large number of epic and lyric traditions. Evidence is collected in the late Roman Jakobson's groundbreaking paper, "Grammatical Parallelism and Its Russian Facet" (Jakobson 1966).[6]

Examples of formulaic pairs follow. I have cited only one passage for each in Ugaritic texts; in most cases, multiple examples exist.

[4] Attempts to discover meter, quantitative meter, word counting, or stress meter have failed to gain a consensus despite persistent attempts, including my own. But there is symmetry in Ugaritic verse, if undefined (see Cross 1974).

[5] For *lmd*, vocalized either *lummād* or *lamīd*, "trained singer" (Greek ἀοιδός), compare 1 Chron. 25:7, *mᵉlūmmᵉdê šîr*, "trained in song"; Isa. 50:4, *lᵉšôn limmûdîm*, "tongue of skilled," that is, "those trained in (musical) tradition."

[6] This was the first publication of this paper in English. See also Whallon 1969:117–172; Geller 1979; and Oinas 1978.

1. *ʾil* || *mlk*, "El || King" (*KTU* 1.6 i 35–36; compare Psalm 95:3).

2. *ʾilm* || *dr ʾil*, "gods || family/council of El" (*KTU* 1.15 iii 18–19).

3. *rpʾi ʾar*[*ṣ*] || *qbṣ dt*[*n*], "shades [lit. 'healthy ones,' a euphemism] || clan of DTN" (*KTU* 1.15 iii 14–15).

4. *ʾar (yrḫ)* || *yrḫ*, "light [of the night] || moon" (*KTU* 1.24:37–38; compare Job 31:26).

5. *kṯr wḫss*, "Kôthar wa-Ḫāsis" (*KTU* 1.4 vii 20). This is a frequent double-named epithet of the craftsman of the gods, counterpart of Greek Hephaistos. The name *ḫss* may stand alone (*KTU* 1.4 i 24–25) and *hyn* is a title of the same god, parallel to *ḫāsis*. The phenomenon of two names of a god or goddess, joined with the conjunction *wa–*, is frequent. Examples are *ʾaṯrt wrḥmy*, *nkl wʾib*, *gpn wʾugr*, *qdš wʾamrr*, and *ẓẓ wkmṯ*. The names Kôthar, Athirat, and Nkl are frequently used alone as well as in combination with another epithet. Qudšu too may be used separately, as can Amraru; for example:

qdš.yʾuḫdm šbʿr
ʾamrr kkbkb lpnm

Qudšu took up a torch,
Amraru like a star before.
[*KTU* 1.4 iv 16–17]

This bicolon is instructive. The phenomenon of joined names demands explanation. The solution, I believe, is to assume that the Ugaritic bard originally took the two names of the divine messenger, belonging to a formulaic pair, each in one colon of a bicolon. However, he was free in many cases to combine the two names with the conjunction *wa–*, hence *qdš wʾmrr*, when the singer wished to construct a longer element fitting into one line of the bicolon. In any case, double divine names, combining an "A-word"with a "B-word," was a device widely used in Ugaritic epic verse to lend symmetry.

6. *ʾaṯrt* || *ʾilt* (*KTU* 1.4 iv 49) and *ʾaṯrt ṣrm* || *ʾilt ṣdynm*, "Athirat of the Tyrians || Ilat of the Sidonians" (*KTU* 1.14 iv 38–39). The same goddess is meant, the mother of the gods.

7. *zbl bʿl* || *rkb ʿrpt*, "Prince Baal || Cloud-rider" (*KTU* 1.2 iv 8).

8. *ʾalʾiyn bʿl* || *ʾalʾiy qrdm*, "Conqueror Baal || Conqueror of warriors" (*KTU* 1.3 iv 7–8).

9. *ym* || *nhr* (*zbl ym*) || *ṯpṭ nhr*, "Prince Sea || Judge River" (*KTU* 1.2 iv 16–17, 22, etc.). "Sea" and "River" are variant names in epic poetry, not distinct entities; cf. Pss. 24:2; 89:26; Jon. 2:4.

10. *hd* || *bʿl*, "Haddu (= Hadad) || Baal" (*KTU* 1.12 ii 53–55). Baal, "Lord," originally an epithet of West Semitic Haddu, has become a proper name and dominant on the Levantine coast.

11. *ṯr ʾil* || *ltpn*, "Bull El || Kindly One" (*KTU* 1.6 iv 10–11).

12. *bn ʾil* || *pḫr kkbm*, "sons of El || assembly of stars" (*KTU* 1.10 i 3–4; compare Job 38:7).

Older Sources of the Tetrateuch

Unlike formulae constructed to fit the hexameters of Greek epic, West Semitic epic verse and Hebrew lyric verse were constructed of poetic cola, utilizing formulaic pairs (rarely triads) of words or phrases, especially names that at least in origin functioned in composing oral poetry. Examples that follow are pairs of names drawn from both prose and ancient poetry. When these double names appear in the prose of the early sources that I have called the "Epic Sources,"[7] one searches for an explanation.

1. *Yaʿaqōb* || *Yiśrāʾēl*, "Jacob || Israel." On the surface this duplication is unexpected. The use of these two names, especially in parallel in poetry, is to be noted. Although an explanation is given for the change of names (Gen. 25:26; 32:29), the names are not changed; both names persist in early poetry and continue in use in prophetic poetry. The etiologies of the two names are surely secondary, partly to explain the meaning of the two names, partly, we suspect, to answer the question as to the duplication. The extensive use of the two names originates in parallelistic formulae of orally composed poetry. The actual historical origins of the names are lost in the mists of time. Compare in poetry: Gen. 49:2, 24; Num. 23:7, 10, 21, 23; 24:5; Deut. 33:10; Isa. 40:27; 41:8, 14; 42:24; 43:22; etc. In Deut. 33:5, we find *Yešūrûn* || *Yiśrāʾēl*. However, in a different tradition, see Deut. 33:28, *Yiśrāʾēl* || *Yaʿaqōb* (where the "A-word" and "B-word" are reversed). To this list may be added a passage in Exod. 19:3b that stands close to poetry, with the pair *bêt Yaʿaqōb* ("house of Jacob") parallel to *bənê Yiśrāʾēl* ("sons of Israel").

2. *Sînay* || *Ḥōrēb*, "Sinai || Horeb." This pair does not—in the received text—appear in parallelistic poetry. However, the distribution of the two terms, apparently with no geographic distinction, is most noteworthy. The P and J sources use Sinai as the name of the mountain where Moses receives his primary revelation. The E source in Exodus uses the expression הר האלהים חרבה once (Exod. 3:1) and twice uses simply חרב (Exod. 17:6; 33:6, both geographically ambiguous). In two passages, the E source has הר האלהים (Exod. 8:5 and notably 24:13). In the central pericope where J and P call the mountain סיני, the E source refers to the mountain simply as (ה)הר, once הר האלהים, never חרב (Exod. 3:12; 19:2b, 14, 16, 17; 20:18; 24:4, 12, 17, 18; 32:1, 15, 19). It is only in Deuteronomy that the mount of revelation is invariably called Horeb.

The easiest explanation of these phenomena is to suppose that a redactor has avoided obvious and direct conflict of the names of the mountain in his prose sources. I would argue further that the two names may be traceable back to an epic formulaic pair. Unhappily, the only poetic passage surviving that refers to the mount is the old poem in Deuteronomy 33, which has a different triad in verse 2:

יהוה מסיני בא
וזרח משעיר למו
הופיע מהר פרן

Yahweh came from Sinai,
and dawned from Seir upon us;
he shone forth from Mount Paran.

However, all three names—Sinai, Seir, and Paran—apply to the southeastern mountains, which in epic lore may have been interchangeable in formulae. Compare also the couplet in the old hymn preserved in Habakkuk 3: "God (*ʾElōah*) comes from the south (Teman), the Holy One from Mount Paran" (cf. "Yahweh Teman" at Kuntillet ʿAjrud).

3. *Yahweh* || *ʾElōhîm*. These alternative names of the god of Israel are one of the main bases for the partition of the J Document and the E Document in the Tetrateuch. But the partition is not perfect.

[7] See already my remarks in Cross 1973 and the more extensive discussion (and reply to critics) in Cross 1998:22–52.

Rarely, *Yahweh* appears in an E document (e.g., Gen. 27:7b) and *ʾElōhîm* in a J context (e.g., Gen. 7:9). Various devices have been used to explain these "anomalies." In Gen. 27:7b, the appearance of *Yahweh* in an E context has been attributed to a JE redactor, a redactor critics often resorted to when the partition of the Epic sources does not conform to theory. In Gen. 7:9, some scholars propose that the reading is to be assigned to RJ/RJE (i.e., to a secondary, later J source, or to the redactor who combined J and E). Other examples could be adduced.

In Genesis 2 and 3, we find the expression *Yahweh ʾElōhîm* some twenty times. The combination then disappears from the Pentateuch (save in Exod. 9:30).[8] Critics have proposed that *ʾElōhîm* is a secondary addition of a redactor.[9] Other proposals have been made. More conservative commentators have attempted to explain the double name as pointing to the special sovereignty of God revealed in the creation and fall, but this is ad hoc, indeed, anachronistic, reflecting the theology of a much later era.

I am not inclined to view the double name as arising in epic poetry; the double divine names in Ugaritic literature normally are connected by the conjunction *wa–*, for example, Kôthar wa-Ḫāsis et al. (see above). In the Psalter, Book 2 (Pss. 42–72) and Book 3 (Pss. 73–89) show a strong preference for *ʾElōhîm*, although *Yahweh* does appear sporadically. It is clear that revision by a redactor (or editor) has taken place.

4. *ʾĒl* || *ᶜElyôn* || *Šadday*. These three names appear as a formulaic triad in the archaic Oracles of Balaam in Num. 24:15–16. *ʾĒl Šadday* is, of course, the double name chosen by the P tradent as the divine name revealed to the patriarchs (Gen. 17:1; 28:3; 35:11; 48:3) before the definitive revelation of the name Yahweh to Moses (Exod. 6:2). However, this epithet also appears probably in the old poem in Gen. 49:25 (reading *ʾĒl* with the Septuagint). The name *Šadday* (of doubtful pointing[10]) appears alone (without *ʾĒl*) in three old poetic contexts: in the Balaam Oracle (Num. 24:4, 16) and in an ancient section of Psalm 68 (v. 16). The composer of Job, presumably archaizing, uses the name frequently. Other double names appear in the Epic sources: *ʾĒl ᶜÔlām* (Gen. 21:33), probably to be assigned to J, and *ʾĒl ᶜElyôn* (Gen. 14:18, 19, 20, 22), probably to be assigned to a special source. The name *ᶜElyôn* appears alone in Deut. 32:8–9 in a cosmogonic stanza:

> When the Most High (*ᶜElyôn)* gave the
> nations their inheritance,
> When he separated the children of men,
> He set the boundaries of the peoples
> According to the number of the sons of
> God (*bᵉnê ʾᵉlōhîm*).[11]
> Yea, the portion of Yahweh is his people,
> Jacob the lot of his inheritance.

Here *ᶜElyôn* has been taken by some as a creator god distinct from Yahweh. This was certainly not the understanding of the Deuteronomist who included the old poem in his history. Moreover, the parallelistic triad of names in the Balaam Oracle suggests that we are dealing with an *ʾĒl* epithet. This is confirmed by the appearance in the Sefîre Treaty of the pair *ʾĒl wa–ᶜElyôn* in the list of divine witnesses. The pair is listed after the tutelary (or executive) gods and before the great natural pairs summarizing the powers of the cosmos, "the olden gods."[12] Most of the pairs of gods consist of a male deity and his consort; however, *ʾĒl* and *ᶜElyôn* obviously are not god and consort. Rather, we are inclined to pair them with the phenomenon found in Ugaritic epic: *ʾaṯrt wrḥmy*, *nkl wʾib*, *gpn wʾugr*, *qdš wʾamrr*, etc., that is, two epithets of the same god, namely *ʾĒl*, joined with the conjunction.

5. *ʾōhel môᶜēd* || *miškān*. This formulaic pair (in both the singular and the plural) appears already in Ugaritic epic verse:

> *tiʾty ʾilm l ʾahlhm*
> *dr ʾil l mšknthm*
>
> The gods enter into their tents,
> the council of El to their encampments.
>
> [*KTU* 1.15 iii 18–19]

[8] 4QEx[c] and the Samaritan Pentateuch have אדני יהוה. The Septuagint reads του θεου.

[9] See recently Friedman 2003:35n; the same solution belongs to the classic *The Hexateuch* (Carpenter and Harford-Battersby 1900:vol. 2, p. 3, n. 4c).

[10] See Cross 1973:52–54. Compare the personal name *Šᵉdê-ʾûr*.

[11] On the reading בני אלהים, which appears in the Septuagint as well as in a manuscript of Deuteronomy from Qumran (4QDeut[j]), see Skehan 1954:12–15. See also the official publication edited by Julie Anne Duncan (1995).

[12] See my article "The 'Olden Gods' in Ancient Near Eastern Creation Myths and in Israel" in Cross 1998:73–83.

Again, we find the formula in *KTU* 1.17 v 31–33:

> *tbᶜ kṯr lʾahlh*
> *hyn tbᶜ lmšknth*
>
> Kôthar leaves for his tent,
> Hayyan leaves for his encampment.

The same formulaic language is echoed in the archaic poetry of the Balaam Oracle in Num. 24:5:

> מה טבו אהליך יעקב
> משכנתך ישראל
>
> How goodly are your tents, O Jacob,
> your encampments, O Israel.

In the P strata, the terms *miškān* and *ʾōhel môᶜēd* are both used of the tent constructed according to divine directions in the wilderness. Their distribution is remarkable. The term *miškān* is used exclusively in Exodus 25 to Exod. 27:19; the term *ʾōhel môᶜēd* is used from Exod. 27:21 to Exodus 30. In Exod. 35:11; 39:32, 33; and 40:22, 24, the inner curtain and its contents are called the *miškān,* the outer two curtains the *ʾōhel.* However, there is apparently mixed tradition in 40: 34–38. In v. 34, it is said that the "cloud (*ᶜānān*) covered the *ʾōhel môᶜēd* and the *kᵉbôd Yahweh* filled the *miškān*." In v. 35, it is said that Moses was not able to enter the *ʾōhel môᶜēd* because the cloud (*ᶜānān*) settled or "tabernacled" (see Cross 1973:298ff.) on it. In vv. 36 and 38, it is presumed that the cloud of Yahweh is on the *miškān* (not the *ʾōhel môᶜēd*). One is inclined to believe that old documents in the hands of the Priestly tradents, one or more using tent language (*ʾōhel môᶜēd*), another preferring tabernacle terminology (*miškān*), stands behind the strange mixture. We must postulate that there has been a harmonistic resolution of the tension between the *ʾōhel môᶜēd* language in one document and the *miškān* terminology in alternate tradition(s). In this case, in old tradition the two terms were alternate names of the Tent of Yahweh. That *ʾōhel* and *miškān(ôt)* constituted a formulaic pair in early Hebrew poetry and in Ugaritic epic poetry supports this conclusion, as does the tradition of Nathan's oracle in 2 Samuel 7: "For I have not dwelt in a temple from the day I brought the children of Israel from Egypt unto this day, but I moved about in a tent (*ʾōhel*) and tabernacle (*miškān*)."

6. *Rᵉᶜûʾēl* || *Yitrô*, "Reuel || Jethro." The name of the father-in-law of Moses in J tradition is Reuel (Exod. 2:18; Num. 10:29) but he is Jethro in E tradition (Exod. 3:1; 4:18 [bis]; 18:1, 2, 5, 6, 9, 10, 12). He is called the father-in-law of Moses and the priest of Midian in both traditions. These are different names that hardly constitute a formulaic pair. On the other hand, compare the paired names Paris and Alexander in the Iliad (mentioned above).
7. *Yehôšūᵃᶜ* || *Hôšēᵃᶜ*, "Joshua || Hoshea." The name *Hôšēᵃᶜ bin Nûn* appears only in P tradition in Num. 13:8 and 16, and in the Deuteronomistic notice at the end of the old poem in Deut. 32:44. It is a rare variant of the ubiquitous name Joshua. In Num. 13:16 an explanation is given for the dual name of Moses's successor—that Moses changed his name—an obviously ad hoc explanation. The variant names do not constitute a formulaic pair but are merely a transparent variant in (oral?) transmission.
8. *ᶜĒśāw* || *ʾEdôm*, "Esau || Edom." This is an authentic formulaic pair. In Gen. 36:1 (P), Esau is identified explicitly with Edom. Similarly, in Gen. 36:9 and 43, Esau is described as the father of the Edomites. In Gen. 25:25 (J), we are told that *ʾadmônî*, the "red one"—a play on the name Edom—was first-born, but he was given the name Esau.

Other examples of the survival of formulaic pairs in the prose documents that constitute the Tetrateuch could be adduced; however, these I have listed should suffice to show that remnants of epic poetic pairs survive in the prose sources of the Tetrateuch. Formulaic pairs have been separated, one element in one prose source, another in an alternate prose source. Often, we may speak of an "A-word" selected by one tradent (J) and a "B-word" selected by the other prose source (E). The attempt to solve the problems of the double (or triple) names in the Tetrateuch has been overlooked owing to the presumption, surviving until today, that the Pentateuch was a written document, without ancestry, a prose composition independent of the oral documents which we expect to have been composed in the poetic traditions of early Israel.

Can we really suppose that Israel alone had no singers of tales? Can we really suppose that the documents of the Tetrateuch were prose creations without a background of oral epic poetry, unlike the literary history preserved by bards of surrounding nations? I think not. The survival of poetic formulaic pairs in the lyric poetry of early Israel, and in formulaic pairs surviving in epic sources, strongly undergirds the argument that Israelite prose documents of the Tetrateuch drew heavily on older epic traditions, and that a telltale poetic residue survives in them.

Bibliography

Aitken, K. T.
1989 Word Pairs and Tradition in an Ugaritic Tale. *UF* 21:17–38.

Carpenter, J. E., and G. Harford-Battersby, eds.
1900 *The Hexateuch according to the Revised Version: Arranged in Its Constituent Documents by Members of the Society of Historical Theology, Oxford.* 2 vols. London: Longmans, Green.

Cross, F. M.
1973 *Canaanite Myth and Hebrew Epic: Essays in the History of the Religion of Israel.* Cambridge, Mass.: Harvard University Press.
1974 Prose and Poetry in the Mythical and Epic Texts from Ugarit. *HTR* 67:1–15.
1998 *From Epic to Canon: History and Literature in Ancient Israel.* Baltimore: Johns Hopkins University Press.

Duncan, J. A.
1995 4QDeut[j]. In *Qumran Cave 4*, vol. 9, *Deuteronomy, Joshua, Judges, Kings*, ed. E. Ulrich, F. M. Cross, et al., 75–91. DJD 14. Oxford: Clarendon.

Friedman, R. E.
2003 *The Bible with Sources Revealed: A New Look into the Five Books of Moses.* New York: HarperCollins.

Geller, S. A.
1979 *Parallelism in Early Biblical Poetry.* HSM 20. Missoula, Mont.: Scholars.

Jakobson, R.
1966 Grammatical Parallelism and Its Russian Facet. *Language* 42:399–429.

Latacz, J.
2004 *Troy and Homer: Towards a Solution of an Old Mystery.* Oxford: Oxford University Press.

Lord, A. B.
1964 *The Singer of Tales.* Harvard Studies in Comparative Literature 24. Cambridge, Mass.: Harvard University Press.
1968 Homer as an Oral Poet. *Harvard Studies in Classical Philology* 72:1–46.
1991 *Epic Singers and Oral Tradition.* Ithaca, N.Y.: Cornell University Press.

Nagy, G.
1981 *The Best of the Achaeans: Concepts of the Hero in Archaic Greek Poetry.* Baltimore: Johns Hopkins University Press.
1996 *Homeric Questions.* Austin, Tex.: University of Texas Press.

Oinas, F. J., ed.
1978 *Heroic Epic and Saga: An Introduction to the World's Great Folk Epics.* Bloomington, Ind.: Indiana University Press.

Parry, M.
1930 Studies in the Epic Technique of Oral Verse-Making: I. Homer and Homeric Style. *Harvard Studies in Classical Philology* 41:73–147.
1932 Studies in the Epic Technique of Oral Verse-Making: II. The Homeric Language as the Language of an Oral Poetry. *Harvard Studies in Classical Philology* 43:1–50.

Skehan, P. W.
1954 A Fragment of the "Song of Moses" (Deut. 32) from Qumran. *BASOR* 136:12–15.

Whallon, W.
1969 *Formula, Character, and Context: Studies in Homeric, Old English, and Old Testament Poetry.* Washington, D.C.: Center for Hellenic Studies and Harvard University Press.

10. Merenptah's "Israel," the Bible's, and Ours

by William G. Dever

One of current biblical scholarship's liveliest debates has to do with defining "earliest Israel," that is, locating it historically (if at all) in both the textual and the archaeological records. Until recently, the most pertinent nonbiblical datum was the well-known inscription of the Egyptian Pharaoh Merenptah that mentions "Israel," which is securely dated to ca. 1210 B.C.E. Now, however, several studies have attempted to correlate Merenptah's "Israel" with the growing body of archaeological evidence from the thirteenth–twelfth centuries B.C.E. that documents a complex of some three hundred hill-country settlements in central Canaan.

The discussion on early Israel is brought up to date and thoroughly documented in my book *Who Were the Early Israelites and Where Did They Come From?* (Dever 2003). But it was Larry Stager who initiated this discussion in a brilliant article in 1985 entitled, "The Archaeology of the Family in Ancient Israel" (Stager 1985a) as well as in an article on Merenptah, our subject here, in the same year (Stager 1985b). Then in 1998 Stager offered an authoritative survey of the more current archaeological evidence in *The Oxford History of the Biblical World*, in an article entitled "Forging an Identity: The Emergence of Ancient Israel" (Stager 1998). I am delighted to offer to Larry Stager, a longtime colleague and friend, this further investigation of the Merenptah datum in the light of its recent archaeological context.

Merenptah's "Israel"

Merenptah's "Hymn of Victory" celebrates the Pharaoh's triumph over a series of enemies in Canaan, among them the peoples of places like "Tehenu/ Canaan" (both specified); "Hurru" (the Hurrian empire in Syria); "Hatti" (the Neo-Hittite entity in northern Syria); and "Israel." It also mentions several specific Canaanite cities, such as "Ashkelon," "Gezer," and "Yanoam." Egyptologists have long noted that the references to enemies that are countries or states are preceded in every case by the determinative sign for "foreign country" (the throw-stick plus the three-hills sign). But the term "Israel," the sole exception, is preceded by the determinative sign for a "people" or nonstate entity (the throw-stick for foreigners plus the man+woman over plural strokes). Kenneth Kitchen, an acknowledged authority, describes this as:

> the mark in numberless instances of a people-group, and not a settled state with an urban center. So far as Merenptah's soldiers, record-keepers and this stele's scribe were concerned, this "Israel" was a people-group in western Palestine, and neither a land nor a mini-state. . . . The logic of the situation leaves only the hill-country to which "Israel" may be assigned.
>
> [Kitchen 2004:271f.]

A standard translation is that of J. A. Wilson in *Ancient Near Eastern Texts* (*ANET*[3] p. 378):

> Desolation is for Tehenu; Hatti is pacified;
> Plundered is the Canaan with every evil;
> Carried off is Ashkelon; seized upon is Gezer;
> Yanoam is made as that which does not exist;
> Israel is laid waste, his seed is not;
> Hurru is become a widow for Egypt!
> All lands together, they are pacified.

There have been innumerable analyses of the poetic structure of the "Victory Stele," with consequent differences in the interpretation of its meaning and historical significance. Similarly, the phrase describing Israel's "seed" as having been wiped out has been subjected to exhaustive critical scrutiny.[1] None of this need concern us here, however, since the meaning of the key term "Israel" is unambiguous, as all Egyptologists have maintained since Petrie's discovery of the "Victory Stele" at Thebes over a century ago. Furthermore, as Kitchen and many others have pointed out, the term "Israel" not only is preceded by the determinative for "people" rather than "country/ state," but is a gentilic (Kitchen 2004:271f.). Thus, the only correct reading is "the Israelite people."

That would seem to be the end of the discussion, but unfortunately it is not. Elsewhere, I have characterized the biblical "revisionists" as naïve postmodernists who have unwittingly borrowed an epistemology according to which there is no knowledge. As Baruch Halpern (1995) has cogently observed, the revisionists are not simply "minimalists"; their intent is to erase Israel from history altogether.[2] And, of

[1] The literature is vast, but for convenient orientation and references see McNutt 1999:35–45; Hasel 1998; Noll 2001: 162–64; Stager 1985b. Fundamental Egyptological sources are Redford 1992:247–57; Kitchen 1994:71–77; 2004.

[2] I have also leveled the charge of nihilism in my book *What Did the Biblical Writers Know and When Did They*

course, the revisionists must perforce begin their campaign right at the beginning, with Israel's supposed origin. There cannot have been an "early Israel," for that would prove inconvenient for their agenda. Lest this charge seem too extreme, let me cite here some revisionist distortions of the Merenptah reference to "Israel."

In his book *Prelude to Israel's Past: Background and Beginnings of Israelite History and Identity*, Niels Peter Lemche (1998b:75) acknowledges that for a hundred years the Merenptah stele has been considered correctly as concrete proof of an Israel in Palestine around 1200 B.C.E. But in his more radical book, *The Israelites in History and Tradition*, Lemche declares that the traditional reading is irrelevant: "The victory stele of Merneptah, however, does not confirm the date of the Hebrew conquest of Palestine: in fact, it has no bearing on that topic" (Lemche 1998a:36). He argues that "the inscription's use of determinatives is inconsistent," quoting G. W. Ahlström (I presume). Yet Kitchen has demonstrated that the Egyptian scribe was not careless or inconsistent. And the archaeological "facts on the ground," discussed below, confirm that Egyptian intelligence was remarkably precise. The differences implied by the use of differing determinatives in the Merenptah stele correspond exactly to what we now know of the several political entities listed in the inscription. Israel *was* different.

Thomas L. Thompson, always the most extreme of the revisionists, goes even further than Lemche. He simply disposes of the issue of ethnicity, stating that: "Ethnicity, however, is an interpretive historiographical fiction. . . . Ethnicity is hardly a common aspect of human existence at this very early period" (Thompson 1997:12).

Thompson elaborates by declaring that ethnicity is only a modern attempt to describe societal relationships and collective decisions. But "the physical effects [material culture remains—*WGD*] of such collective decisions are often arbitrary and are, indeed, always accidental" (Thompson 1997:12). Of the Merenptah inscription that mentions "Israelites," Thompson opines:

> The sharp boundaries that the use of the terms "Canaanite" and "Israelite" makes possible are wholly unwarranted. "Canaan" appears on the Merenptah stele and has been shown to be paired with "Israel" as his spouse. They are the metaphorical parents of three towns destroyed by the Egyptian army. [ibid.]

At an international symposium in 2000 in Copenhagen, where Thompson and I opposed each other, he went so far as to suggest that while the Merenptah inscription does mention "Israelites," that is only a coincidence. The Egyptian scribe invented these peoples and their names and by accident came up with the same ethnic designation that we have in the Hebrew Bible. This line of argument is patently absurd and is readily refuted on both philological and archaeological grounds.[3]

Subsequently, Thompson collaborated with Ingrid Hjelm on an article entitled "The Victory Song of Merenptah, Israel and the People of Palestine" (Hjelm and Thompson 2002).[4] In their treatment of the Merenptah inscription, Hjelm and Thompson advance four basic arguments:

1. The inscription is poetry, not history, so it is irrelevant for the historical question of Israelite origins. There was no Egyptian victory in Canaan, so nothing else in the inscription matters. Of course, one may ask how Hjelm and Thompson know this. In fact, there is some specific evidence for Egyptian destructions in Canaan in this horizon, and precisely at Ashkelon and Gezer, which are the sites singled out for mention in the inscription.[5]

Know It? What Archaeology Can Tell Us about the Reality of Ancient Israel (Dever 2001:28–52 *et passim*).

[3] If Thompson were correct that ethnicity is "often arbitrary . . . always accidental," then none of the social-scientific disciplines would be viable, for they all depend upon our ability to discern patterns and purpose in culture. Archaeology, in particular, seeks the "material correlates of behavior"—an impossible task if there is no patterning in culture and history. The topic of archaeology and ethnicity is especially timely and the literature is vast. See, provisionally, Killebrew 2005. See also my forthcoming chapter in the Eric M. Meyers Festschrift, "Ethnicity and the Archaeological Record: The Case of Early Israel."

[4] Here and elsewhere, Thompson avoids using "Israel" as an ethnic label, even for the period of the Israelite monarchy, when he refers to "the province of Samarina" (adopting the Neo-Assyrian usage) or more often "Syria's marginal southern fringe" (Thompson 1999:9, 235, 252; 1997: 176–78, 183, 184). See also Lemche 1998a:51–54.

[5] As I (and others) have argued, whether or not Merenptah actually defeated his enemies in Canaan, or even campaigned there, is irrelevant for our purposes, since the reference to "Israel" stands on its own. Nevertheless, in our excavations at Gezer, Stratum 15 does show signs of major disruptions in the late thirteenth century B.C.E., which can hardly have been caused by Israelites or Philistines. This would provide a context for the pectoral of Merneptah found by Macalister (Dever 1986:50f.). The evidence from Ashkelon is now published in Stager et al. 2008:256. If Yurco and Stager are correct, the Egyptian relief showing the siege of Ashkelon, now redated from Rameses II to Merenptah, may have some historical basis (see Stager 1985b).

2. The term *Ysr*ʾ*el* in the inscription, universally translated by Egyptologists as "Israel," can just as easily refer to any number of other entities. Hjelm and Thompson (2002:13f.) offer as many as five alternatives: "Sharon," "Yeshurun," "Asher," "Asher'el," and "Jezreel."[6]

3. In any case, *Ysr*ʾ*el* here refers to the whole population of Hurru (Canaan), not some putative "Israel" (ibid., p. 16). Again, how do they know that?

4. In any case, "Israel" is only "an eponym . . . a literary reality," not "a specific people in history" (ibid., p. 17).

Happily, Kitchen, with his formidable Egyptological expertise, has refuted all of Hjelm and Thompson's tortured arguments, particularly their notion that the term "Israel" can just as easily be translated in other ways. He also effectively disposes of their assertion that the poetic and metaphorical character of the hymn negates any historical significance. The presence of rhetoric and its ideology has no bearing on the historical element; to think otherwise is simply to miss the point of Egyptian usage (Kitchen 2004: 268). Finally, Kitchen demonstrates, with copious documentation from numerous other inscriptions, that the significance of the determinative sign for "people" that accompanies the term "Israel" cannot be explained away by the "carelessness" of Egyptian scribes (Kitchen 2004:28–71).

At least we have to acknowledge that Hjelm and Thompson's arguments here are consistent with Thompson's (and the other revisionists') ideological program in their other voluminous publications, in which they insist that there was no "early Israel." The most notoriously anti-Israel of the revisionists, Keith Whitelam, insists that the attempt to write the history of this nonpeople is not only impossible but illegitimate. All along, it is the history of the "Palestinian peoples" that biblical scholars and archaeologists should have been writing (Whitelam 1996).[7]

One final revisionist scholar may be cited here. In a 1996 contribution to a volume of essays on ethnicity and the Bible, Diana Edelman, like some others who have adopted the postmodern notion that ethnicity equals racism, rejects the very category (Edelman 1996). As for the data often cited by archaeologists, Edelman, despite having gained considerable field experience herself, nevertheless insists that "there are no *artifactual* [italics hers] remains that can consistently be used to understand a group's ethnicity" (p. 26). It is not surprising, then, that Edelman seeks to dispense with the textual data as well. She repeats the old canard that the term "Israel" in the Merenptah stele may mean something else, in this case "Jezreel," citing only Eissfeldt's long-discredited reading (p. 35; cf. Kitchen 2004:270f.). She also repeats the error, so well refuted by Kitchen and others, that the determinative sign for "people" may not mean anything because Egyptian scribes used these signs "loosely, mistakenly" (p. 35). Thus, apparently, even texts do not help to determine "ethnicity"—and certainly not those of the Bible, in the opinion of Edelman and the other revisionists. So let us turn to that issue.

Virtually all the scholars who devalue the Merenptah reference to "Israel" are biblical scholars (although by no means do the majority of biblical scholars agree with them). One archaeologist, however, has joined the minimalists. Israel Finkelstein, who literally wrote the book on early Israel in his 1988 work *The Archaeology of the Israelite Settlement* (Finkelstein 1988), now insists that in the three hundred or so early Iron Age hill-country villages that he himself put on the map, there was no ethnic group that we can positively identify as Israelites. When his book was first published, Finkelstein accepted the caution of reviewers like myself concerning the use of the term "Israelite" in this period; then he adopted my term "Proto-Israelite"; and finally he rejected the term "Israelite" altogether. He argues that the distinctive Iron I material culture traits that we both recognize on the Late Bronze/Iron I horizon are more the result of environmental and socioeconomic factors than they are reflective of any new ethnic self-consciousness. It is all about "lifestyle," he concludes. But Finkelstein does not seem to understand that lifestyle *is* "ethnicity"—it is what makes "us" different from "them." In any case, in his 2001 popular book with Neil Silberman, *The Bible Unearthed*, (Finkelstein and Silberman 2001), he reverts to the term "Israel."[8]

The Hebrew Bible's "Israel"

One of the recurring motifs of the skepticism of the biblical revisionists concerning ethnicity is that Merenptah's "Israel," as well as the "early Israel" of archaeologists, has nothing whatsoever to do with bib-

[6] For rebuttal, see Kitchen 2004:270f.

[7] Other reviewers also correct identify "the political agenda that dominates this book" (Sommer 1998:85) and conclude that it "comes close to being a political manifesto" (Levine and Malamat 1996:288).

[8] For references, see Dever 2001:40f.; 2003:194f.

lical Israel.[9] Of course not; but that is irrelevant. "Israel" of the settlement horizon in the thirteenth to eleventh centuries B.C.E. is obviously different from the state of "Israel" and its population during the monarchy in the tenth to early sixth centuries. Even the biblical writers knew that.

In the Bible's "prehistory"—that is, in the narratives about the patriarchs and the Exodus-Conquest—the writers sometimes use the term "Hebrew" rather than "Israel." Then, in describing the earliest phases of the settlement in Canaan, "Canaanite" peoples like the inhabitants of Shechem and Gibeon are said to have joined the emergent Israelite confederation with few apparent barriers. The Israelite "tribes" are by no means unified in the stories in Joshua and Judges, and their lack of solidarity probably stems from an ethnic identity that was still fluid. Some even spoke different dialects, as the famous shibboleth/sibboleth incident of Judges 12:5–6 reveals. Even later, during the monarchy, Uriah, a "Hittite," is a prominent career officer in David's army. There is much other evidence to show that, at least originally, the ethnic designation "Israelite" was neither self-evident in meaning nor exclusive, and that it became so only much later. "Early Israel," as many now maintain, was a motley crew.[10]

To be sure, the later Deuteronomistic writers do speak of "all Israel." But they are assuming an ethnic homogeneity that even then may not have been factual. It is significant that 1 Sam. 13:34 uses the gentilic "Hebrew" and the phrase "all Israel" in parallel. Moreover, the term "all Israel" is used so paradigmatically that it may be largely hyperbole, just as we speak in everyday parlance about "all Americans," despite our awareness of the enormous diversity of the U.S. population.

In light of the foregoing, the revisionist's insistent depreciation of the ethnic designation "Israelite" in the Merenptah inscription—our earliest, best-dated, and least-biased reference to Israel—appears to be more a reflection of ideology than honest, fair-minded scholarship. As for the reluctance on the part of some of these scholars to use the term "Israel" even for later periods, we need only point out that by the ninth century B.C.E., "Israel" is the designation used by Israel's neighbors and enemies—no hesitancy there about ethnic labels, much less a "biblical bias." The Tel Dan inscription in Aramaic refers to a "king of Israel" (whether David or not). The Moabite Stone also speaks of a "king of Israel," in the case of Omri. Finally, the earliest of the cuneiform texts that describe the first encounter of the Assyrians with the petty states in the west, Shalmaneser III's account of the Battle of Qarqar in 853 B.C.E., mentions "Ahab, King of Israel."[11]

Our "Israel"

That leaves us with the "Israel" of modern scholarship, in particular the Israel of the Iron Age (not a "Persian" or "Hellenistic" Israel) that is so well attested archaeologically. Elsewhere, I have written extensively on the general question of the date and the historicity of the biblical sources, assessed on the basis of the context now supplied by archaeology (see Dever 2001); and in *Who Were the Early Israelites and Where Did They Come From?* (Dever 2003), I have discussed at length the specific question of Israelite origins, adducing virtually all the current archaeological evidence and interpretive theories (see also Noll 2001 and Killebrew 2005).

Having previously presented in full the empirical data for the existence of an "early Israel" (my "Proto-Israelites"), here I need only raise the question of how or indeed whether *this* "Israel" may correspond to that of the Merenptah stele. To do that, we need first to summarize what we can actually know from the passage in the stele that describes "Israel," whatever its literary structure and its historical veracity. The following are the salient points, all of which I believe are obvious to any dispassionate observer:

1. There was an ethnic group in Canaan sometime before ca. 1210 B.C.E. who called themselves "the Israelite people" and who were known as such to Egyptian intelligence.

2. These people were sufficiently numerous and well established that they were perceived as a threat to Egyptian hegemony in the region.

3. These peoples were not, however, organized into city-states, much less state-like entities, unlike the other peoples listed, a fact reflected in the unique determinative sign with the gentilic.

---

9 This notion is ubiquitous; see, e.g., Davies 1992:61–63; Thompson 1992:310f.; Lemche 1998a:36–38; Whitelam 1996:209, 210, 228; Edelman 1996:35–42.

10 See Dever 2003:181f.; Killebrew 2005:149–96. Note that the fluidity in ethnic identity in Iron I and even into early Iron II does not contradict the continuity in material culture during that time span (see below). The two overlap but are not necessarily identical.

11 For references, see Dever 2001:29, 30, 163–66.

4. These Israelites were distinct socioeconomically and politically from the general Canaanite ("Hurru"/Hurrian) population, and specifically from the population of city-states like Ashkelon and Gezer along the coastal plain and Yanoam in Galilee. The central hill-country is conspicuously empty on a map of Merenptah's campaigns in Canaan (regardless of whether these were real or imaginary).[12]

Skeptics like the biblical scholars discussed above typically argue that there is not enough information in the Merenptah stele to specify anything about who these "Israelites" actually were or to ascertain whether they have anything to do with later "biblical Israel." These, however, are arguments of which we can easily dispose.

First, although the information derived from the Merenptah stele is minimal, it tells us all that we need to know about the Israelites at this juncture. And, however cryptic, all the information conveyed by Egyptian intelligence is correct. Earliest Israel was a loosely organized "tribal" confederation somewhere in central Canaan at this time: a group of people contiguous with the indigenous population, but already beginning to distinguish themselves as a separate ethnic group, and on an evolutionary scale far short of state-level development.

What is significant here is that all of this information about "early Israel," derived independently from a source far removed from the nationalist biases of the biblical writers, is corroborated by the archaeological data that we have accumulated in the past two decades or so. Yet the revisionists, despite paying lip-service to archaeology, have never responded to the vast body of data that I and many other archaeologists have presented. They only demonize archaeologists as "credulous" or worse.[13] Some have likened these revisionists to secular fundamentalists whose minds are made up and who do not wish to be confused by facts. Nevertheless, the Merenptah inscription's facts and the archaeological facts converge at all the salient points, and it is just such convergences that place us on firm historical ground.

The second answer to the revisionists' unwillingness to connect Merenptah's "Israel" to later biblical Israel obviously has to do with cultural and historical continuity and how these are perceived. To give skeptics the benefit of the doubt, there is indeed no textual continuity. The Merenptah text dates to the late thirteenth century B.C.E., while the earliest relevant biblical texts (the Pentateuch/Tetrateuch, the Deuteronomistic History, and the early prophetic writings) are from the late eighth century at best—a gap of some five centuries.[14] Even if the gap is partially bridged by presuming earlier oral tradition embedded within our canonical sources, that gap is considerable.

What few biblical scholars seem to realize is that it is archaeology that bridges the gap. We have a complete and continuous archaeological record from the late thirteenth through the early sixth century, with not even a generation missing. And if from about the eighth century onwards this continuous Iron II culture is "Israelite" (as even some of the revisionists must admit), then its immediate predecessor in Iron I was also "Israelite"—or, at the very least, as I have suggested, "Proto-Israelite," to err on the side of caution.[15] Merenptah's "Israelites" are the authentic progenitors of the biblical Israelites. Yet I can find very few biblical scholars who are aware of the distinctive archaeological assemblage and its striking continuity through the Iron Age.

As Baruch Halpern (1997) has observed, we are still plagued by two monologues rather than the dialogue that some of us have advocated for years.[16] The revisionists seldom cite the numerous archaeological handbooks that are now available to any interested reader.[17] Their agenda becomes increasingly ideo-

---

[12] We have noted Kitchen's recognition of this fact. See also Redford 1992:275; Ahlström 1986:40–42; Finkelstein 1988:28f. Even Lemche (19989a:38) acknowledges this. See further Dever 2003:201–8.

[13] See Dever 2001:30–40. The rhetoric only escalates in Thompson 2001 and Lemche 2000. Lemche dismisses me as a "rustic," but he has much more difficulty refuting my charge of postmodernism, as extended and carefully documented by James Barr (2000:102–78). See further Hagelia 2002.

[14] Both biblical scholars and archaeologists have tended recently to lower the dates of J, E, and Dtr by as much as two to three centuries (see, conveniently, Schniedewind 2004). The Persian or Hellenistic date advocated by the revisionists is not justified, however.

[15] On my "Proto-Israelites," see Dever 2003:194–200 *et passim*. I am not the first to use the term, however. Both Norman Gottwald and P. Kyle McCarter preceded me with a sort of off-hand use of the term, but it was I who first employed the term in a deliberate archaeological sense. Many of my archaeological colleagues in Israel urge me to drop it now that a consensus is emerging that there *was* an "early Israel."

[16] My own calls for such a dialogue go back to 1974; see my *Archaeology and Biblical Studies: Retrospects and Prospects* (Dever 1974).

[17] These include Weippert 1988; Mazar 1990; Ben-Tor 1992; Levy 1995. The most egregious example of this lack of attention to basic information is provided by Davies, who in his book *In Search of "Ancient Israel"* (Davies

logical—political rather than scholarly. And as the rhetoric escalates, the facts on the ground are obscured. The "deconstruction" of the Merenptah inscription, our earliest reference to the early Israelites, is just another sad example of the inroads that postmodernism has made into the field of biblical criticism, which was once a historical discipline. Fortunately, mainstream biblical scholarship, buttressed by old-fashioned positivists (shall we say "empiricists") like Lawrence Stager, help us to hold the middle ground.

Conclusion

I seem to have been the first to charge that the biblical revisionists are really thinly disguised postmodernists. Now, however, James Barr—arguably the dean of British Old Testament scholars—has agreed with me specifically and has in fact gone well beyond my original critique (Barr 2000:102–78). I can only conclude that in their deprecation of the Merenptah datum on early Israel, the revisionists are simply behaving like typical postmodernists. Otherwise, I am at a loss to explain their recalcitrance in the face of the overwhelming evidence, both textual and archaeological. Consider how similar are the basic tenets of the two schools:

1. A contrarian attitude. This is Lyotard's much touted "incredulity toward all metanarratives," in this case the grand metanarrative of the Western cultural tradition, the Bible.
2. A preference for novel, even exotic, "readings of all texts" (and, in this case, artifacts). The only legitimate technique is "deconstruction"; the text can mean anything—except, it seems, what it appears to mean.
3. "All readings are political," postmodernism's most typical mantra. "Reading" is not about truth at all, for there is none, but rather about race, class, gender, politics, and power.
4. In any case, "all claims to knowledge are simply social constructs." Therefore following Foucault, "all history is fiction."

This is not the place to offer a full-scale refutation of postmodernism, even in its revisionist guise. There is, however, a growing literature that suggests that it is becoming passé in real intellectual circles.[18] If that is true, then devotees of Hayden White-style "metahistory" like Davies, Thompson, Lemche, Whitelam, and the other revisionists, will soon be as obsolete as their Merenptah.

1992) cites Mazar only once, in a footnote explaining that Mazar's handbook deals with the Iron Age and is thus irrelevant to Davies' "Persian-period Israel" (p. 24 n. 4). Here, as too often, the presupposition trumps the evidence.

[18] See, for instance, the devastating critiques in Gress 1998 and especially Windschuttle 1996. Recently, however, John Collins (2005)—as much a modernist as I am—has conceded ground to the revisionists, arguing that they have had considerable influence on American biblical scholarship.

Bibliography

Ahlström, G. W.
1986 *Who Were the Israelites?* Winona Lake, Ind.: Eisenbrauns.

Barr, James
2000 *History and Ideology in the Old Testament: Biblical Studies at the End of the Millennium.* Oxford: Oxford University Press.

Ben-Tor, A., ed.
1992 *The Archaeology of Ancient Israel.* New Haven, Conn.: Yale University Press.

Collins, J. J.
2005 *The Bible after Babel: Historical Criticism in a Postmodern Age.* Grand Rapids, Mich.: Eerdmans.

Davies, P. R.
1992 *In Search of "Ancient Israel."* JSOTSup 148. Sheffield, England: Sheffield Academic Press.

Dever, W. G.
1974 *Archaeology and Biblical Studies: Retrospects and Prospects.* Evanston, Ill.: Seabury-Western Theological Seminary.
2001 *What Did the Biblical Writers Know and When Did They Know It? What Archaeology Can Tell Us about the Reality of Ancient Israel.* Grand Rapids, Mich.: Eerdmans.
2003 *Who Were the Early Israelites and Where Did They Come From?* Grand Rapids, Mich.: Eerdmans.

Dever, W. G., ed.
1986 *Gezer.* Vol. 4, *The 1969–71 Seasons in Field VI, the "Acropolis."* Jerusalem: Nelson Glueck School of Biblical Archaeology.

Edelman, D. V.
1996 Ethnicity in Early Israel. In *Ethnicity in the Bible,* ed. M. G. Brett, 25–55. Leiden: Brill.

Finkelstein, I.
1988 *The Archaeology of the Israelite Settlement.* Translated by D. Saltz. Jerusalem: Israel Exploration Society.

Finkelstein, I., and N. A. Silberman
2001 *The Bible Unearthed: Archaeology's New Vision of Ancient Israel and the Origin of Its Sacred Texts.* New York: Free Press.

Gress, D. L.
1998 *From Plato to NATO: The Idea of the West and Its Opponents.* New York: Free Press.

Hagelia, H.
2002 Review or Response? A Critical Evaluation of Thomas L. Thompson's Review of William G. Dever. *Scandinavian Journal of the Old Testament* 16:314–18.

Halpern, B.
1995 Erasing History: The Minimalist Assault on Ancient Israel. *Bible Review* 11/6:26–35, 47.
1997 Text and Artifacts: Two Monologues? In *The Archaeology of Israel: Constructing the Past, Interpreting the Present,* ed. N. A. Silberman and D. Small, 311–41. JSOTSup 237. Sheffield, England: Sheffield Academic Press.

Hasel, M. G.
1998 *Domination and Resistance: Egyptian Military Activity in the Southern Levant, ca. 1300–1185 B.C.* Probleme der Ägyptologie 11. Leiden: Brill.

Hjelm, I., and T. L. Thompson
2002 The Victory Song of Merenptah, Israel and the People of Palestine. *JSOT* 27:3–18.

Killebrew, A.
2005 *Biblical Peoples and Ethnicity: An Archaeological Study of Egyptians, Canaanites, Philistines, and Early Israel, 1300–1100 B.C.E.* Society of Biblical Literature Archaeology and Biblical Studies 9. Atlanta: Scholars Press.

Kitchen, K. A.
1994 The Physical Text of Merenptah's Victory Hymn (The "Israel Stela"). *Journal of the Society for the Study of Egyptian Antiquities* 24:71–76.
2004 The Victories of Merenptah, and the Nature of Their Record. *JSOT* 28:259–72.

Lemche, N. P.
1998a *The Israelites in History and Tradition.* Louisville, Ky.: Westminster John Knox.
1998b *Prelude to Israel's Past: Background and Beginnings of Israelite History and Identity.* Translated by E. F. Maniscalco. Peabody, Mass.: Hendrickson.
2000 Ideology and the History of Ancient Israel. *Scandinavian Journal of the Old Testament* 14:165–93.

Levine, B. A., and A. Malamat
1996 Review of Keith W. Whitelam, *The Invention of Ancient Israel: The Silencing of Palestinian History. IEJ* 46:284–88.

Levy, T. E.
1995 *The Archaeology of Society in the Holy Land.* New York: Facts on File.

Mazar, A.
1990 *Archaeology of the Land of the Bible, 10,000–586 B.C.E.* New York: Doubleday.

McNutt, P. M.
1999 *Reconstructing the Society of Ancient Israel.* Louisville, Ky.: Westminster John Knox.

Noll, K. L.
2001 *Canaan and Israel in Antiquity: An Introduction.* Biblical Seminar 83. London: Sheffield Academic Press.

Redford, D. B.
1992 *Egypt, Canaan, and Israel in Ancient Times.* Princeton, N.J.: Princeton University Press.

Schniedewind, W. M.
2004 *How the Bible Became a Book: The Textualization of Ancient Israel.* Cambridge: Cambridge University Press.

Sommer, B. D.
1998 Review of Keith W. Whitelam, *The Invention of Ancient Israel: The Silencing of Palestinian History. Middle East Quarterly* 5.

Stager, L. E.
1985a The Archaeology of the Family in Ancient Israel. *BASOR* 260:1–35.
1985b Merenptah, Israel and Sea Peoples: New Light on an Old Relief. *EI* 18:56*–64*.
1998 Forging an Identity: The Emergence of Ancient Israel. In *The Oxford History of the Biblical World*, ed. M. D. Coogan, 123–75. New York: Oxford University Press.

Stager, L. E., J. D. Schloen, and D. M. Master, eds.
2008 *Ashkelon.* Vol. 1, *Introduction and Overview (1985–2006).* Winona Lake, Ind.: Eisenbrauns.

Thompson, T. L.
1992 *Early History of the Israelite People: From the Written and Archaeological Sources.* Leiden: Brill.
1997 Defining History and Ethnicity in the South Levant. In *Can a "History of Israel" Be Written?*, ed. L. L. Grabbe, 166–87. JSOTSup 245. Sheffield, England: Sheffield Academic Press.
1999 *The Mythic Past: Biblical Archaeology and the Myth of Israel.* London: Random House.
2001 Methods and Results: A Review of Two Recent Publications. *Scandinavian Journal of the Old Testament* 15:306–25.

Weippert, H.
1988 *Palästina in vorhellenistischer Zeit.* Munich: Beck.

Whitelam, K. W.
1996 *The Invention of Ancient Israel: The Silencing of Palestinian History.* London: Routledge.

Windschuttle, K.
1996 *The Killing of History: How Literary Critics and Social Theorists Are Murdering Our Past.* New York: Free Press.

11. Linchpins Revisited

by Trude Dothan and Alexandra S. Drenka

Larry Stager has been a friend and colleague for many years, during which we have worked on parallel excavations at Ekron and Ashkelon, both cities of the Philistine Pentapolis. We have often enjoyed comparing the results of our respective excavations, as in the case of the bronze linchpin found at Ekron (T. Dothan 2002:11–14) and a larger and more elaborate one found by Larry at Ashkelon (Stager 2006:171–72). These are the only two linchpins currently known from archaeological excavations in Israel.

This paper introduces a fragmentary bronze head of unknown provenance that has recently come to our attention (figure 1).[1] We believe that this object is functionally related to the Ekron and Ashkelon linchpins. Its identification, reconstruction, and dating must rely exclusively upon its stylistic and technical features. Based upon the comparative analyses undertaken below, we propose a probable cultural framework for this piece. Prior to describing the bronze head, we shall briefly review the thoroughly studied anthropomorphic linchpins from the Ekron and Ashkelon excavations, emphasizing the features relevant to our discussion.

The Ekron linchpin (reg. no. 2381) was found in Building 350, a monumental public building with cultic connotations in Field IV, Stratum V, which is dated to the first half of the eleventh century B.C.E.[2] The cultic character of the building was determined on the basis of architectural features and finds.[3] The double-headed linchpin (figure 2), found in its entirety, is of cast bronze. It is 10 cm long and 1.0–2.2 cm wide, indicating that it was originally placed in the wheel of a full-sized chariot, and may be the earliest evidence found so far for Philistine chariots.[4] The function of the linchpin is well illustrated in the depiction of the Ramesseum Chariot (figures 3 and 4).[5] The termination of the undecorated lower part is slightly curved, while the double-headed upper part is reminiscent of the Janus of classical mythology. The antithetical heads, covered by a flat cap, rest upon a single neck, which in turn rests upon a horizontal ring. A horizontal perforation on the neck, between the two heads, was probably intended for the insertion of a cord. Stylistically, the antithetical heads and flat cap strongly resemble the sphinxes that decorated wheeled ceremonial stands from Cyprus and are clearly Aegean in origin (T. Dothan 2002:11; Matthäus 1985:pl. 108).

The Ashkelon linchpin (reg. no. 47971; figure 5) was found in Room 503 in Philistine Bichrome Phase 9, dated to the eleventh century B.C.E., in Grid 50, Square 59, Layer 483 (Stager 2006:171). This context is roughly contemporary to that of the Ekron find. The Ashkelon linchpin, 17.4 cm long, is also complete. The lower part consists of a rounded, undecorated shaft that tapers to a point. The upper part is elaborately modeled and represents an upper torso, long neck, and anthropomorphic head with an outspread headdress or coiffure. The elongated neck is decorated with a "necklace" or a "corslet." The head in the Ashkelon linchpin has prominent facial features consisting of a long nose and bulging eyes. The elaborate hairstyle portrays hair falling in a circular pattern at the back, below five tightly wound horizontal bands. The loop at the back is attached from head to headdress. A cord or strip of leather tied to the loop would probably have held the linchpin securely in place.

The Ashkelon bronze linchpin allows us to reconstruct the original appearance and define the function of the bronze head under discussion, which was made by solid-cast technique and modeled in the round (figure 1). It is broken at the neck; the length of the

[1] The bronze head is courtesy of the Wolfe Family Collection, Jerusalem, and registered as B-00-2. We thank L. Alexander Wolfe, who recently brought the anthropomorphic figure to our attention, for allowing us to study and publish it.

[2] The linchpin was found in Room C, Threshold 23018. For general information on Philistine monumental Building 350, see T. Dothan 2002:1–4; 2003:194–96.

[3] Monumental Building 350 incorporates architectural elements and installations such as a megaron-style entrance, round pebbled hearth, and *bāmāh*. In Rooms B and C, mudbrick *bāmôt* were found and a unique assemblage of bronze (see note 6) came from room B, and iron artifacts (iron knife Object No. 2576, and iron "ingot" Object No. 2173) and a bronze cauldron handle (Object No. 2174) were found in room C (see T. Dothan 2002).

[4] The three miniature eight-spoked bronze wheels (Object No. 2246) found in Stratum VA, Room B, Building 350, in close proximity to the linchpin, are reconstructed as parts of a small-scale wheeled stand.

[5] Ellis 1966:fig. 4. Two linchpins are depicted in the Ramesseum, one with the top shaped like a human face facing outward, with long hair and a circular object above it; the other, with a human figure from the hips up (see also T. Dothan 2002:13).

Figure 1. Bronze head (scale 1:1)
Photographs by Z. Radovan. Drawings by P. Arad.

surviving portion is 3.7 cm. Except for the missing shaft, the figure is relatively well preserved.[6] The head displays well-defined facial features: a partly eroded hooked nose and a mouth with parted lips separated by a groove; the eyes are asymmetrically positioned and deeply incised. Above the eyes are prominent, semicrescent eyebrows. The ears, which continue the line of eyebrows, are each somewhat differently rendered: the left ear is accentuated with a vertical groove and thus is slightly wider than the right ear, which lacks such treatment. The clearly depicted earrings differ from one another in size, shape, and decoration. The left earring is oval and ornamented with two shallow depressions, while the right earring is elongated, with two parallel incisions and one shallow depression. We may assume that apparent disparities in the position and proportion of the eyes, ears, and earrings are not intentional.

The head wears high, slightly concave, cylindrical headgear (circular cross-section; 9 mm long; diameter 10.7–13 mm). It has an oval knob at its top that appears to have been broken in antiquity and polished. An additional feature may have once adorned the headgear. The concave shape of the headgear recalls the outspread coiffure or headdress of the Ashkelon example. The head is set on an elongated neck, which is now broken (preserved length 13 mm; shaft is circular in cross-section, diameter 10.5–12.2 mm). The surface of the break has apparently been carefully smoothed, like the knob atop the head. We assume that the object was reused, perhaps as a pendant. The neck is ornamented with a necklace composed of spiral wires (oval cross-section; diameter 2.0–2.4 mm) that encircle the neck at least seven times. This decoration is reminiscent of the bands above the head and around the elongated neck of the Ashkelon linchpin. Of special interest is the loop at the back of the head (diameter 9.5 mm; 6.7 mm wide; 2.4 mm thick), which consists of three joined wires (circular cross-section; each 2.4 mm thick). As in the case of the Ashkelon example, this loop would have been used to hold the linchpin in place.

Despite the striking similarity between the two main features—the loop at the back and the long neck

[6] L. A. Wolfe provided information on the condition of the object at the time of acquisition: it was heavily encrusted with green and red patches of corrosion.

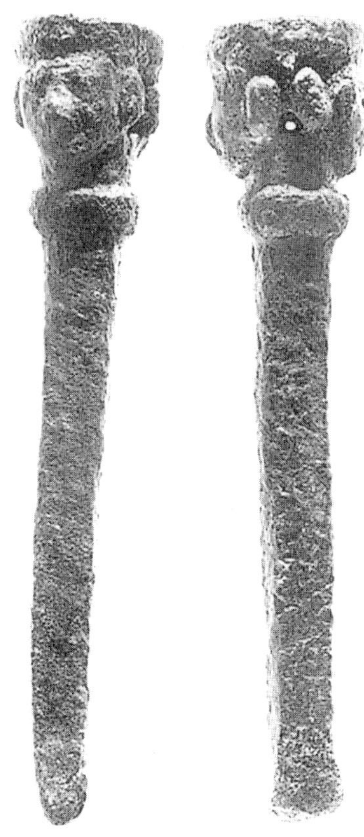

Figure 2. Bronze linchpin from Ekron

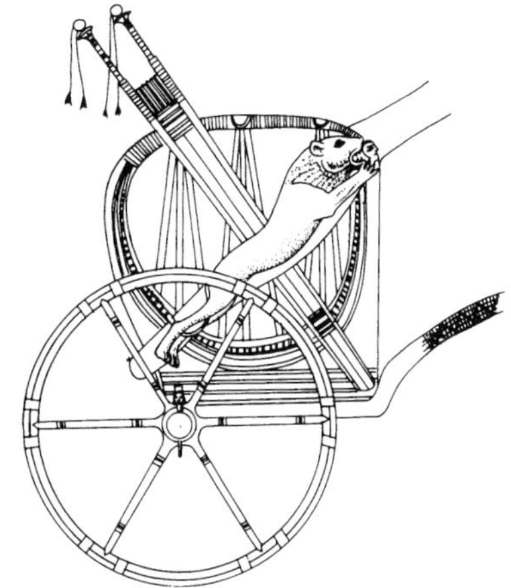

Figure 3. Wheel with linchpin from Ramesseum Chariot
after Ellis 1966:fig. 4

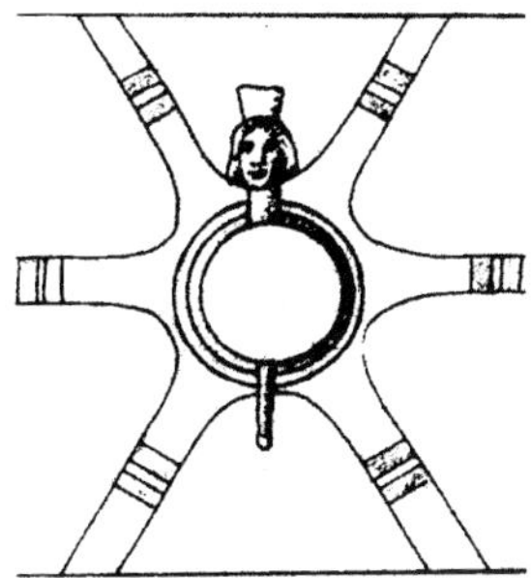

Figure 4. Close-up of Ramesseum Chariot linchpin

with horizontal bands—the bronze head under discussion and the Ashkelon linchpin differ in style and technique (figure 6). This is most obvious in the deeply incised eyes of the former and the bulging eyes of the later. Larry Stager has noted the similarity between the bulging eyes and long nose of the Ashkelon bronze linchpin and the applied clay pellets used to depict the eyes and nose on the terracotta "Ashdoda" figurines.[7] The elongated neck is also reminiscent of the "Ashdoda" deity, modeled in the Aegean tradition (T. and M. Dothan 1992:155; T. Dothan 2002:11; Stager 2006:172). In addition, the distinctive long necks of both the clay and metal figures are decorated with horizontal bands. In Ashdoda figurines, the neck has painted red and black horizontal lines, while in the case of the Ashkelon linchpin, a kind of necklace is depicted. The necklace adorning the long neck of our bronze head is composed of horizontally coiled wires. Both the Ashdoda figurines and the bronzes discussed here appear to portray a similar type of neck adornment.

Typologically, the bronze head under discussion closely resembles a well-defined Canaanite type of solid-cast figurine typical of the Late Bronze Age (Negbi 1976; 1989). The continuation of this type into the Iron Age is perhaps best represented by the figurine of the enthroned "god" from the cache of bronze objects found in the Upper City at Hazor.[8]

[7] For a comprehensive discussion of the Ashdoda-type figurines, see M. Dothan 1971:129–30.

[8] It was found in Area B, under the floor of a cult structure of Stratum XI, dated to Iron Age I. According to Yadin (1975:257), the cache of bronze objects, placed in a jug (Locus 3283), was a foundation deposit or votive. In her detailed reevaluation of the Hazor hoard, O. Negbi stated: "[I] agree with A. Mazar that the figurine under discussion [Hazor enthroned 'god'], like a few other *objets d'art* found in early Israelite contexts, could have been imported from the Canaanite production centres." In addition, the continuity of the Canaanite metallurgical tradition into the early Iron Age is confirmed by numerous bronze artifacts found in eleventh-century contexts, for example, hoards from Megiddo Stratum VI and tombs at Beth Shean and Tell es-Saᶜidiyeh (Negbi 1974:159–72; 1989:362).

It is of particular interest that the three anthropomorphic linchpins belong to different stylistic types. The Ekron double-headed "Janus" has parallels from Cyprus and the Aegean world. The Ashkelon linchpin head has been interpreted as a leading goddess of the Philistines (Stager 2006:172; T. Dothan 1982: 234–37). The new example introduced in this paper evinces strong Canaanite influence. We have identified it as the top part of a linchpin, based upon its similarities to the Ashkelon linchpin.

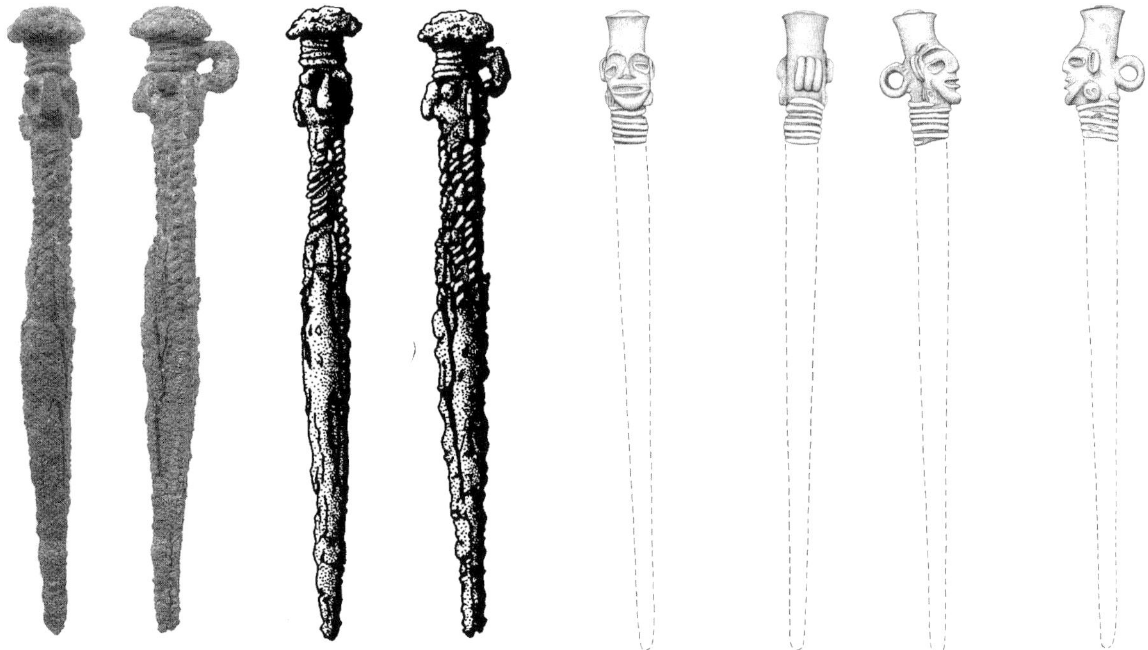

Figure 5. Bronze linchpin from Ashkelon

Figure 6. Possible reconstruction of the bronze head

Bibliography

Dothan, M.

1971 *Ashdod.* Vols. 2–3, *The Second and Third Seasons of Excavations, 1963, 1965, Soundings in 1967.* ᶜAtiqot English Series 9–10. Jerusalem: Israel Department of Antiquities and Museums.

Dothan, T.

1982 *The Philistines and Their Material Culture.* New Haven, Conn.: Yale University Press.

1993 A Double-headed Bronze Linchpin from Tel Miqne/Ekron [in Hebrew]. *EI* 24:62–67.

2002 Bronze and Iron Objects with Cultic Connotations from Philistine Temple Building 350 at Ekron. *IEJ* 52:1–27.

2003 The Aegean and the Orient: Cultic Interaction. In *Symbiosis, Symbolism, and the Power of the Past: Canaan, Ancient Israel, and Their Neighbors from the Late Bronze Age through Roman Palaestina*, ed. W. G. Dever and S. Gitin, 189–213. Winona Lake, Ind.: Eisenbrauns.

Dothan, T., and M. Dothan

1992 *People of the Sea: The Search for the Philistines.* New York: Macmillan.

Ellis, R. S.

1966 A Note on Some Ancient Near Eastern Linch Pins. *Berytus* 16:41–48.

Matthäus, H.

1985 *Metallgefässe und Gefässuntersätze der Bronzezeit, der geometrischen und archaischen Periode auf Cypern: mit einem Anhang der bronzezeitlichen Schwertfunde auf Cypern.* Munich: Beck.

Negbi, O.

1974 The Continuity of the Canaanite Bronzework of the Late Bronze Age into the Early Iron Age. *Tel Aviv* 1:159–72.

1976 *Canaanite Gods in Metal: An Archaeological Study of Ancient Syro-Palestinian Figurines.* Tel Aviv: Institute of Archaeology, Tel Aviv University.

1989 The Metal Figurines. In *Hazor*, vols. 3–4, *An Account of the Third and Fourth Seasons of Excavation, 1957–1958*, ed. Y. Yadin et al., 348–362. Jerusalem: Israel Exploration Society and Hebrew University of Jerusalem.

Stager, L. E.

2006 Chariot Fittings from Philistine Ashkelon. In *Confronting the Past: Archaeological and Historical Essays on Ancient Israel in Honor of William G. Dever*, ed. S. Gitin, J. E. Wright, and J. P. Dessel, 169–76. Winona Lake, Ind.: Eisenbrauns.

Yadin, Y.

1963 *The Art of Warfare in Biblical Lands in Light of Archaeological Study.* Translated by M. Pearlman. New York: McGraw-Hill.

1975 *Hazor: The Rediscovery of a Great Citadel of the Bible.* New York: Random House.

12. Cities, Villages, and Farmsteads: The Landscape of Leviticus 25:29–31

by Avraham Faust

The relationship between the study of material culture, as revealed by archaeology, and the biblical text has received a great deal of scholarly attention. In most cases, archaeological finds are used to illustrate the text or to answer biblically driven questions. But after well over a century of searching the archaeological record for correlations with the Bible, it seems that this approach, worthy in itself, has been exhausted. A different approach, one that uses the archaeological finds as the starting-point for archaeological inquiry, can bring new insights, not only into the societies that existed at the time but also into the world behind the biblical text.

The case study to be discussed here is the Jubilee and the settlement system of ancient Israel in the late Iron Age. This study grew from my long-term research project on Iron Age rural settlements (see Faust 1995a; 1995b; 1997a; 1997b; 1999a; 1999b; 2000a; 2000b; 2003a; 2003b). It did not initially aim to illuminate the Bible; the correlations between the archaeological data and the biblical text emerged only after the analysis of the finds had advanced.

I will begin by presenting the biblical data from Leviticus 25:29–31 and noting the difficulties in the prevailing interpretations. This will be followed by a short discussion of the archaeological evidence regarding the rural settlements of late Iron Age Israel. We will then see how familiarity with the latter solves the problems in the text.

The Law of the Jubilee

The law of the jubilee has received a great deal of scholarly attention. The dating of this law, the background for its development, and the question of whether it was ever applied, have all been discussed (e.g., Lowenstam 1958b:578–82; Wenham 1979: 317–24; Milgrom 2001:2241–48; Wright 1992; Fried and Freedman 2000:2257–70). In brief, the jubilee is "the fiftieth year occurring at the end of the seven sabbatical cycles of seven years each, in which all land was returned to its ancestral owners and all Israelite slaves were freed" (Schifman 1996:549). The jubilee is mentioned and described in Lev. 25:8–17, 23–56; 27:16–25; and Numbers 36:4.

Whether the law was ever applied does not concern us here because a law, even a utopian one, relates to an existing reality and is set against a "real" background. As King and Stager write:

> For our purposes, then, it matters little whether the biblical accounts are "true" in the positivistic sense of some historians and biblical scholars. It is enough to know that the ancient Israelites believed them to be so. The stories must have passed some test of verisimilitude, that is, having the appearance of being true or real. In this sense the biblical account and many other ancient accounts, however self-serving and tendentious, become grist for the cultural historian's mill. [King and Stager 2001:7]

Although this is said in reference to biblical stories, it is also true with respect to the biblical laws. In the words of the classicist Oswyn Murray:

> It does not matter whether the stories which it uses are true, as long as they are believed to be true. And even a forgery is an important piece of evidence for the period that perpetrated it, since it reveals more clearly than a genuine article the conceptions and beliefs about the past of the age that created it. This principle of unconscious revelation through representation . . . is one of the most powerful tools in the modern historian's study of mentalities. [Oswyn Murray, quoted in King and Stager 2001:8]

The Jubilee and בתי החצרים *in Leviticus 25*

Let us examine the settlement terminology used in Leviticus 25, especially in verses 29–31. Generally speaking, the law of jubilee prescribes that the land shall return to its original owner in the fiftieth year. Lev. 25:29–31, however, refers to the fate of houses, and it is those verses we wish now to discuss. We shall first present them in Hebrew (MT) followed by the English translation.

> וְאִישׁ כִּי-יִמְכֹּר בֵּית-מוֹשַׁב עִיר חוֹמָה וְהָיְתָה גְּאֻלָּתוֹ עַד-תֹּם שְׁנַת
> מִמְכָּרוֹ יָמִים תִּהְיֶה גְאֻלָּתוֹ. וְאִם לֹא-יִגָּאֵל עַד-מְלֹאת לוֹ שָׁנָה
> תְמִימָה וְקָם הַבַּיִת אֲשֶׁר-בָּעִיר אֲשֶׁר-לֹא (קרי: לוֹ) חֹמָה לַצְּמִיתֻת
> לַקֹּנֶה אֹתוֹ לְדֹרֹתָיו לֹא יֵצֵא בַּיֹּבֵל. וּבָתֵּי הַחֲצֵרִים אֲשֶׁר אֵין-לָהֶם
> חֹמָה סָבִיב עַל-שְׂדֵה הָאָרֶץ יֵחָשֵׁב גְּאֻלָּה תִּהְיֶה-לּוֹ וּבַיֹּבֵל יֵצֵא.

> If anyone sells a dwelling house in a walled city, it may be redeemed until a year has elapsed since its sale; the right of redemption shall be one year. If it is not redeemed before a full year has elapsed, a house

that is in a walled city shall pass in perpetuity to the purchaser, throughout the generations; it shall not be released in the jubilee. But houses in villages that have no walls around them shall be classed as open country; they may be redeemed, and shall be released in the jubilee. [Lev. 25:29–31, NRSV]

We shall comment on one word in this translation later. The main question to address is why, according to these verses, there is a difference between houses in walled "cities" (עיר אשר לו חומה or עיר חומה) and houses in "villages" (בתי החצרים). Many translations and interpretations have touched upon this question. Most scholars have understood these verses simply as contrasting walled cities with unwalled villages, as in the NRSV translation given above (see, e.g., Noth 1965; Porter 1976; Wenham 1979; Bess 1963; Kuchman 1996; Milgrom 2001; as well as Joosten 1996; Budd 1996; Snaith 1967; Wright 1992; and Hartley 1992). The mere existence of a city wall is seen indirectly, and sometimes even directly, as the most important legal element determining the fate of the house. Many scholars have therefore opined that the law differentiates not only between urban and rural sectors but also between houses in walled versus unwalled towns. Houses in the latter had the same fate as these in the rural sector (e.g., Noth 1965:190; Kuchman 1996:193).

But why is there a difference in the legal status of houses in towns as opposed to villages? Many scholars believe that this was because Israelite laws concerning land applied to the rural sector only while older Canaanite law still dominated the urban sphere (Noth 1965:190; Porter 1976:202; Bess 1963:81f.; Joosten 1996:156; Wright 1990: 125), presumably because there was, throughout the Iron Age, a sizable Canaanite segment in the urban sector (Hartley 1992:439; from a different perspective, see also Faust 2000a; 2005; Finkelstein 1999). Others believe that it was a result of changes in the ownership of land among the urban population (Lowenstam 1958b:580; Weinfeld 2000:176) and even served as "a barrier against the tendency toward socioeconomic development, which led to the appropriation of walled cities from the laws of jubilee and redemption" (Kuchman 1996:193; my translation).[1] Wright (1992: 1027) suggests that the "primary intention of the redemption and jubilee provisions was to preserve the economic viability of families through the secure possession of their inherited land"; unlike "city houses," "village dwellings were treated as part of the rural scene." This distinction is elaborated by Milgrom (2001:2198f.). While also connecting the urban law with Canaanite law, Milgrom stresses that redemption was not relevant for houses but only for land, which is why in a walled city the house belonged (after a year) to the purchaser in perpetuity.[2] A house in a village, in contrast, was regarded as part of the land (Milgrom 2001:2199f.). Following Philo (*The Special Laws* ii 116), Milgrom believes that the village houses were "farm buildings" and that the "villages are the residences of the farmers and are inseparable from the land they work" (Milgrom 2001: 2200).

As we will see below, it appears that Milgrom correctly identifies the essence of the law, which connects the houses of the חצרים with fields (as the wording of the law indeed states, but contrary to most other interpretations). But he does not supply a good explanation for why houses in a village have the same fate as the land. After all, houses in villages were built within nucleated settlements and not directly on the agricultural land (see Dar 1986; Amit 1991; Riklin 1997; Faust 1995a; 1997a; 2000b).

Clearly, previous scholars have understood the geographical terminology in the following way: the city that is mentioned in the verses as "a walled city" is indeed a city surrounded by a wall. The חצרים are unwalled villages, hence the translation "houses in villages that have no walls around them." Moreover, many scholars have explicitly cited the mere existence of a wall as the most important factor in differentiating between a city and a village in the biblical period: cities were surrounded by a fortification wall while villages were unwalled (Drinkard 1996:186; Blenkinsopp 1997:54; Frick 1970:44–45; Uffenheimer 1968:207–8). Some have even referred to it as the only factor (e.g., Drinkard 1996). This differentiation seems to be supported by the frequent combination of עיר and חצריה, which is understood as the city and its (daughter) villages. Some have therefore assumed that when a settlement name includes the חצר component (e.g., חצר שועל in Josh. 19:3), it is a daughter village of one of the walled cities (e.g., Frick 1970:44–45).

We have seen that many scholars agree that the reason for the difference between urban and rural settlements is that the Canaanite law of land ownership was dominant in urban settings. For our pur-

[1] This is a problematic explanation because the law does not serve as a barrier against this development but rather acknowledges and even accepts it (as viewed by Lowenstam 1958b:580, see below). For a more complex suggestion, see Kuchman (1996:191–92).

[2] As to why it was possible to redeem the house at all, Milgrom's answer is that it results from the "merciful foundations of the jubilee legislation" (Milgrom 2001:2199).

poses, however, the question of whether the law regarding the city reflects Canaanite law, or specific social circumstances, or some combination of the two, is a minor issue in the discussion of Lev. 25:29–31. Regardless of whether they invoke Canaanite law, all of the scholars cited above agree that Leviticus differentiates between the rural sector (villages and hamlets) and the fortified urban sector, and that the houses in these two sectors had different fates.

The Problem

This prevailing interpretation suffers from several drawbacks, in my opinion. First, the contrast in the verses is not between walled cities and unwalled towns or villages. That dichotomy results from what I believe is a mistranslation of the Hebrew text that stems from a misunderstanding of the terminology and the geographical and social reality behind it. The word translated as "city" is עיר. In Biblical Hebrew, however, עיר can refer to a settlement of any size (see Portugali 1984:284f.; Bendor 1996:99f. and n. 103; Schloen 2001:160; Kempinski 1987:59; Hulst 1976: 268–72; Zevit 2001:625). This is shown by verses like Deut. 3:5, where עיר is used to designate both fortified settlements and unfortified ones. The same is true in 2 Kings 17:9 and 18:8, where עיר is used for settlements ranging from fortified cities to simple watchtowers (see also Num. 13:19). The word therefore does not differentiate between a city and a village but between a settlement and something that is not a settlement.

In Lev. 25:29–31, that which is not a settlement is called בתי החצרים, while the term עיר encompasses both cities and villages. A similar, though not identical, dichotomy can be seen in Deut. 28:3: "Blessed shall you be in the עיר, and blessed shall you be in the field"; and also in Deut. 28:16: "Cursed shall you be in the עיר, and cursed shall you be in the field." These verses contrast the עיר (traditionally translated as "city") with farmland; that is, the settlement as a place of dwelling is contrasted with the open field. Returning to Leviticus, it is clear that these verses contrast settlements and בתי החצרים —something that is not a settlement.

Why have scholars missed the contrast in Lev. 25:29–31 between settlements and nonsettlements and have seen instead a contrast between cities and villages? Presumably, it is because this text appears to dichotomize walled cities and unwalled בתי החצרים. In many historical periods, cities were walled while villages were not, so biblical scholars have assumed that the presence of a wall is the major factor in the dichotomy. It is clear, however, that the contrast between city and village does not derive from the language of the law, but is an interpretation resulting from the importance attributed to the wall by modern scholars.

As we have seen, the assumed dichotomy between city and village has even led scholars to posit two legal systems, one for cities (based on Canaanite law) and one for villages (based on Israelite law). But this distinction is not supported by the biblical text or by our current understanding of the social development in Iron Age Israel. The notion of two different legal systems was put forward only because interpreters have not found any other way to explain why there is a different law for houses in "cities" than for houses in "villages" (as they interpret the law).

To be sure, the wall around the settlement clearly has a legal significance, but previous interpretations of Lev. 25:29–31 do not explain the importance of the wall. Why would there be a different law for a house in a walled city as opposed to an unwalled settlement? It could be argued that the law itself has created this dichotomy, imposing a theoretical distinction with no basis in reality. A different reading of the law, however, drawing upon the rich archaeological information we now possess, makes sense of the distinction. An examination of the Israelite settlement system of the late Iron Age enables us to understand these verses.

Rural Settlements in the Iron Age II

The archaeology of ancient Israel used to concentrate on the large sites—a tendency that some scholars characterize as "tell minded" (Ahlstrom 1982:25) and have reproached for its "urban bias" (London 1989). Rural sites were not given much attention. For example, Herzog (1992), in his seminal and oft-quoted work on settlement and fortification planning in the Iron Age, referred to various types of settlements, from capital cities to administrative centers to smaller provincial towns. But this is where he stopped. He did not discuss any nonurban settlement. The "lower" end of the settlement continuum was simply ignored by the vast majority of scholars. The lack of data led Holladay (1995:373, 375, 392), in an important paper on Iron Age society, to refer to walled towns like Tell Beit Mirsim and Tell en-Naṣbeh as "villages," probably because these were the smallest and simplest Iron II settlements with which he was familiar. But many rural sites have been excavated in recent years, mainly in salvage excavations (see, e.g., Dar 1986; Riklin 1997; Amit 1991; Covello-Paran 1996; see also Faust and Safrai 2005), and the accumulating data enable us to draw various conclusions regarding the rural sector (Faust 1995a; 1995b; 1997a; 1997b; 2000a; 2000b; 2003a; 2003b). Broadly speaking, there are three types of rural sites: large villages, small villages (hamlets), and farmsteads. This is not the place for a lengthy summary of the evidence from the rural sector, but one observation is of great importance for the present discussion, namely, that almost all excavated Iron II villages were surrounded by a boundary wall, a phenomenon evident also in some single-occupation sites that were only surveyed and never excavated. This is the situation, for example, at Khirbet Jamain (Dar 1986), Beit Aryeh (Riklin 1997), Khirbet Jarish (Amit 1991), Khirbet Malta (Covello-Paran 1996), Khirbet Kla (Eitam 1980), Mevasseret Yerushalayim (Edelstein and Kislev 1981), Kurnet Bir et-Tel (Finkelstein, Lederman, and Bunimovitz 1997:447), and many other sites. It is this observation that led to the development of the ideas expressed in this article.

Iron Age Villages and Biblical Terminology

The existence of boundary walls around Iron Age villages sheds new light on the distinction between the עיר with a wall and places with no walls. As already stated, the word עיר refers to a settlement of indeterminate size and not to a "city" in the modern sense of the word. In Lev. 25:29–31 the word has been interpreted as representing the urban sector because these verses stress the existence of a wall, which modern scholars have assumed must pertain to the urban sector as opposed to the rural sector. But if all settlements, urban and rural alike, were surrounded by a boundary wall, there is no reason to assume that the phrase עיר חומה ("walled settlement") is meant to differentiate between cities and villages. The dichotomy was therefore not between walled cities and unwalled villages, as the latter hardly existed, but between any walled settlement, city and village alike, and the בתי החצרים, which are neither a settlement nor walled. The reference to a wall is not a legal criterion but merely a reflection of the reality that all settlements were surrounded by a wall of some kind. Lev. 25:29 should therefore be translated: "if anyone sells a dwelling house in a walled settlement [or simply "a settlement," because the word "walled" was added just for descriptive purposes], it may be redeemed until a year has elapsed since its sale."

The exceptions to the law are the בתי החצרים. These are not regarded as settlements, so what are they? A close examination of the archaeological record is very helpful in this matter and, in conjunction with a careful reading of the text, can solve the problem. Archaeological investigation has shown that there were habitation sites in Iron Age Israel that did not constitute "settlements." I am referring to isolated farmsteads in which there lived only one family and not a larger community. Such farmsteads are known from all over the country (Faust 2003), including the region of Samaria (Hizmi 1996) and especially its western slopes (Finkelstein 1978; 1981; Faust 2003; Faust 2006; Dar 1982; Yeivin and Edelstein 1970), the Hebron hill country (Amit 1992), and the area around Jerusalem (Seligman 1994; Feig 1995; Maitlis 1993; Faust 1997b). They were isolated structures located on agricultural land amid agricultural installations such as cisterns and terraces. It is these farmsteads that were the houses of the unwalled חצרים in Leviticus 25, in contrast to the houses found within walled settlements.

Such an interpretation of Lev. 25:29–31 does not result simply from reconstructing the settlement system on the basis of the archaeological evidence, but also from the wording of the biblical text itself. Verse 31 specifically states that these houses "shall be classed as open country" (note that the word translated here as "country" can also be translated as "field" and in the original is identical to the word used in Deut. 28:3 and 16, cited above). This is why "they may be redeemed, and they shall be released on the jubilee." Unlike houses in walled settlements (villages included), the houses in isolated farmsteads could not be separated from the agricultural lands on which they sat, which is why they are grouped with agricultural fields in the law of the jubilee and shared the same fate.

Although this is true with respect to Iron Age farmsteads in general, it is even more clearly the case for farmsteads in the vicinity of Jerusalem. These were somewhat different in form from the farmsteads in other parts of the country because the farmhouse stood alone in the field between installations, terraces, and additional buildings, in contrast to farmsteads in other regions, where the house was part of a larger architectural complex that included additional structures, installations, and a courtyard (Faust 1997b; 2003b).[3]

The archaeological evidence, therefore, sheds light on the biblical terminology and allows us to under-

[3] The differences between the farmsteads in the vicinity of Jerusalem and those in the rest of the country apparently stemmed from the high density of settlement around Jerusalem, which was Judah's primary city. This density had reduced security problems in the area and turned animal husbandry into an insignificant branch of the economy (see Faust 1997; 2003).

stand the law properly. We no longer need to assume that the law in Leviticus 25 knew of, and accepted, a separate (Canaanite) legal system for urban settlements. The same principle applied in all cases. A house in a settlement (any settlement) could be bought and sold because it stood by itself and was not encumbered by the land on which it stood and thus by legal procedures regarding the land.[4] Farmland, on the other hand, was to be returned to its original owner in the jubilee year. Lev. 25:21–23 is an appendix to the main jubilee law (which focuses on land), clarifying the disposition of houses. Houses within walled settlements were not exempted from the jubilee due to the existence of a Canaanite population or different social processes, but simply because these houses were not tied to particular plots of farmland and it was only the land (and not houses) that returned to its original owner in the jubilee. The only houses affected by the jubilee law were the בתי החצרים because, unlike houses within settlements, they were not regarded as independent property but as part of the fields on which they stood, and it was impossible to return a field to its original owner while the house remained in the hands of the buyer.

Additional Implications

We have seen that the biblical text of Lev. 25:29–31 can be understood in relation to the settlement system of the late Iron Age. This implies that this settlement reality lay in the background of the biblical law of the jubilee, however artificial or utopian that law may have been. The law of the jubilee is part of the Holiness Code (H), but there is little agreement regarding the date and social background of the Holiness Code, or the precise relationship between it and other textual sources. A variety of views have been espoused, placing it in various contexts in the Iron Age and Persian period (Knohl 1987; Eissfeldt 1965:236–39; Milgrom 1991: 3–35; also Sun 1992 and Milgrom 1992, with additional references). H is usually associated with the Priestly source (P), but there is no agreement regarding the date of P either, which has been attributed to various contexts—preexilic, exilic, and postexilic—from the Iron Age to the Persian period (Eissfeldt 1965:207–8; Rofé 1994; Clines 1993:580; Hurwitz 1974; Wenham 1979:13; Weinfeld 1979:28–33; Friedman 1987; Milgrom 1991:12–13; Schwartz 1999:32–33).

The close match between the law of the jubilee and the settlement reality of the late Iron Age seems to support a late Iron Age dating (at least for H). But it is not sufficient to show that the settlement reality of this period is compatible with the law. In order for this correlation between archaeology and the Bible to be of any value in dating the biblical text, it needs to be shown that the settlement reality of other periods (i.e., the Babylonian "exilic" period and the Persian period) could not have been the cultural background of these verses. While a lengthy discussion is beyond the scope of the present paper, suffice it to say that the exilic period is by no means a likely background, especially in Judah, because the countryside was devastated, especially near Jerusalem (Stern 2001; Faust 2003a; Faust and Safrai 2005). This was not the period in which farmsteads flourished.

As for a background in the Persian period, this also seems unlikely because the countryside was much less populated than during the Iron Age. The entire Persian period lay in the shadow of the collapse of the Iron Age society (see Faust 2004; 2007 for a detailed discussion of the settlements of the Persian period). Furthermore, it is very tempting to ascribe the description of the חצרים, which are part of the fields, to the unique situation in the late Iron Age in the area around Jerusalem, where farmhouses and other structures were scattered in the fields and were not concentrated into complexes as in other regions.

On the other hand, the text can also be understood quite well against the background of the more normal type of Iron Age farmsteads found throughout the country, and not only with regard to those near Jerusalem. And in any case, this can be only a preliminary attempt to date the text on the basis of its archaeological background because the information we currently possess concerning the Persian period is still incomplete and we need to study that period more thoroughly before any conclusions can be reached.[5]

Summary and Conclusions

Triggered by the discovery that Iron II villages were surrounded by boundary walls, research is being directed toward the cultural, social, and even legal implications of this reality. And this leads to a new look at the jubilee. It is debated whether this law was ever

[4] It was possible to redeem a house within a year, but this is probably due, as Milgrom suggests, to the "merciful foundations of the jubilee legislation" (above). After a year the house belonged to the purchaser in perpetuity.

[5] Theoretically, it is possible that the law of the jubilee was written in the Persian period in reference to the remembered reality prior to the destruction of Jerusalem, but should this be the case, for all practical purposes we could consider such a law to be reflective of the late Iron Age.

implemented, but that does not concern us here because even a utopian law reflects a real background. An examination of the settlement reality of the Iron II period, followed by a detailed re-reading of the text, enables each type of data to illuminate the other.

Together, the archaeological and textual data present us with a coherent picture. Most studies of Lev. 25:29–31 have not correctly identified the meaning of the law. Scholars have assumed that the text distinguishes houses in cities from those in villages, and this requires them to explain why there is a different law for each. Explanations have included the suggestion that Canaanite law was practiced in the Israelite urban sector or that the difference was a result of socioeconomic processes. But neither of these suggestions is supported by our current understanding of the sociodemographic processes that took place in the period of the monarchy (Faust 2005) and they contradict both the language and the spirit of the text—and they do not take into account the archaeological finds. Furthermore, biblical scholars have ignored the most important clue supplied by the text itself, which explains that the houses of the חצרים are classified with the agricultural fields.

Understanding the settlement situation in the Iron Age II, when all settlements, cities and villages alike, were surrounded by boundary walls, enables us to understand the meaning of the text and the rationale of the law. Verses 29–31 do not differentiate between cities and villages: the term עיר refers to any settlement, villages included. The חצרים are not settlements and are therefore not villages or nucleated settlements but rather isolated farmsteads. The distinction in the text is between houses in settlements and scattered farmhouses (and as we shall presently see, this distinction is also secondary). Walls are mentioned because all settlements, both cities and villages, were walled, and this differentiated them from farmsteads.

The differential treatment of houses in two contexts is not due to the coexistence of two legal systems, one for the city and one for the village. The difference is between the legal status of houses versus farmland. The houses of the חצרים were part of the farmland because they had no existence without it, which is why they had the same status as land, unlike other houses. This is the intention of verse 31: to limit the special status of houses (that they can be owned by their purchasers in perpetuity) by stating that the houses of the חצרים were different because they had the same status as the land of which they were a part. After all, it was inconceivable to let the purchaser keep the farmhouse while the farmland was returned to the original owner.

The law of the jubilee deals with returning land to its original owner. The verses discussed in this paper are a sort of qualification stating that the law does not apply to houses. The status of houses is different and a transaction involving a house is final (after a year). The last verse (31) is meant to qualify the qualification and make clear that farmhouses, although technically houses, have the same status as the land, from which they are inseparable. In modern language, Lev. 25:29–31 should therefore be read:

> If anyone sells a dwelling house in a settlement [lit. a walled settlement][6], it may be redeemed until a year has elapsed since its sale. If it is not redeemed before that time, a house in a settlement shall pass in perpetuity to the purchaser, and it will not be released in the jubilee. But farmhouses, with no walls around them,[7] are classed as fields; and may therefore be redeemed, and they shall be released in the jubilee.

Appendix: חצר *in the Bible and the Ancient Near East*

The חצר in the Bible and the ancient Near East has received a great deal of scholarly attention. The terms חצר and חצרים are used in many places in the Bible and in other sources. The biblical examples are usually considered to reflect two different Semitic words which have come to be spelled the same way in Biblical Hebrew. One of these words, which is irrelevant for our discussion, refers to the area around a house, an enclosure or courtyard (*BDB* s.v. חצר (I); Kadari 1968:221; Hamp 1986:134–35; Clines 1996:296). This word reflects the Proto-Semitic root ḤṬR (cf. Aramaic חוטרא), which denotes a fenced area or pen (Lowenstam 1958a:273–74; Malamat 1962:143–50; 1963:183).

The second word, which is relevant for the present discussion, refers to a small unwalled site (*BDB* s.v. חצר (II); Kadari 1968:222; Hamp 1986:133–35). According to Malamat (1963:183), it reflects Proto-Semitic ḤṢR, which means "settlement" or habitation, in the sense of a dwelling for people and not for animals. There is no doubt that this is a "settlement form" that lies at the bottom of the settlement spectrum (Lowenstam 1958a:272; Portugali 1984:282). In the following we will discuss only this meaning.

In many instances in the Bible and in other sources (e.g., the Mari archives), the term חצר is mentioned in relation to seminomads (e.g., Jer. 49:28–33; Isa. 42: 11), and this may be reflected in the relatively wide-

[6] The "wall" is stressed in the law because it refers to a visible phenomenon that served to distinguish nucleated settlements—urban or rural communities—from isolated farmsteads.

[7] This is also a descriptive clause.

spread use of the word as part of settlement names in the inheritance of the tribe of Simeon (Malamat 1963:184). According to Lowenstam: "In the חצרים, which are settlements that are more than nomad camps but are not yet walled cities, dwelt mainly people who subsided on grazing, such as the Ishmaelites" (1958:273). Interestingly, Gophna (1963; 1964; 1966; 1970) describes חצרים which he discovered in the northern and western parts of the Negev. These are extremely small sites that existed for brief periods. It appears that these were indeed settlement sites of nomads, and are worthy of the name חצר (in this meaning).

But חצרים existed throughout the country. On 80 percent of the occasions in which a חצר is mentioned in the Bible, it is described as being close to a settlement (עיר); for example, in the topographical lists in the book of Joshua (Portugali 1984:283). It seems, therefore, that חצרים existed throughout the country. This wide dispersion accords well with the fact that חצר, in the meaning discussed in this paper, cannot be equated only with the settlements of nomads but corresponds to small sites with one or two structures, such as farmsteads.

It is likely that the word חצר (from Proto-Semitic ḤṢR) has two separate meanings: (1) a type of settlement of nomads in pastoral zones, as seems to be represented both in Mari and in the Bible; and (2) a type of habitation in agricultural zones. In contrast to what is often thought, the latter were farmsteads and not villages (see Faust 1995a; 2003b). The idea that חצרים were farmsteads was suggested some time ago, though not as part of a detailed discussion but more as an assumption (Edelstein and Gibson 1983:23; for a more detailed analysis, see Edelstein and Milevski 1994:17–19; Maitlis 1993:99 explicitly connected the two, although his entire discussion is problematic).

Basically, חצר denotes an isolated structure (or several isolated structures) in the countryside. In most cases it relates to farmsteads, as in Leviticus 25, and perhaps also to placenames in the inheritance of the tribe of Simeon, which should perhaps be understood as "the farmstead of Shual" and "the farmstead of Susa." The same word was used to describe sporadic settlements of seminomads in the Mari texts and in Isaiah and Jeremiah. However, Biblical Hebrew does not distinguish the socioeconomic role or origin of the inhabitants but describes all isolated structures with the same word. From the typological perspective of modern scholarship the word has two distinct meanings, denoting either a farmstead or structures built by seminomads (perhaps in the process of settling down). In Biblical Hebrew, however, there is only one meaning: an isolated structure or structures in the open country.

Acknowledgments:

I would like to thank Prof. Abraham Malamat, Prof. Shmuel Vargon, and Mr. Avi Shveka for reading and commenting on earlier drafts of this paper. The responsibility for the ideas expressed in this article, and for any mistake or error, is of course mine alone. I would like to thank the Dr. S. Krauthammer Chair in Archaeology and the Moskowitz and Straus Cathedras, all at Bar-Ilan University, for their assistance. A shorter and somewhat different version of this paper appears in Hebrew in *Studies in Bible and Exegesis Presented to Moshe Garsiel*.

Bibliography

Ahlström, G. W.
1982 *Royal Administration and National Religion in Ancient Palestine*. Leiden: Brill.

Amit, D.
1991 Khirbet Jarish. *ESI* 9:157–58.
1992 Farmsteads in Northern Judea (Betar Region Survey). *ESI* 10:147–48.

Bendor, S.
1996 *The Social Structure of Ancient Israel: The Institution of the Family (Beit ʾAb) from the Settlement to the End of the Monarchy*. Jerusalem: Simor.

Bess, S. H.
1963 Systems of Land Tenure in Ancient Israel. Ph.D. diss., University of Michigan.

Blenkinsopp, J.
1997 The Family in First Temple Israel. In *Families in Ancient Israel*, ed. L. Perdue, 48–103. Louisville, Ky.: Westminster John Knox.

Budd, P. J.
1996 *Leviticus: Based on the New Revised Standard Version*. The New Century Bible Commentary. Grand Rapids, Mich.: Eerdmans.

Clines, D. J. A.
1993 Pentateuch. In *The Oxford Companion to the Bible*, ed. B. M. Metzger and M. D. Coogan, 579–82. Oxford: Oxford University Press.

Clines, D. J. A., ed.
1996 *A Dictionary of Classical Hebrew*. Sheffield, England: Sheffield Academic Press.

Covello-Paran, K.
1996 H. Malta [in Hebrew]. *Ḥadashot Arkheologiyot* 106:39–41.

Dar, S.
1982 Ancient Agricultural Farms Near Wadi Beit-ᶜArif [in Hebrew]. *Nofim* 16:47–60.
1986 Hirbet Jemein: A First Temple Village in Western Samaria [in Hebrew]. In *Shomron Studies*, ed. S. Dar and Z. Safrai, 13–73. Tel Aviv: Hakibbutz Hameuchad.

Drinkard, J. F.
1996 Cities. In *The HarperCollins Bible Dictionary*, ed. P. J. Achtemeier, 186–88. San Francisco: Harper.

Edelstein, G., Y. Gat, and S. Gibson
1983 Food Production and Water Storage in the Jerusalem Area [in Hebrew]. *Qadmoniot* 16:16–23.

Edelstein, G., and M. Kislev
1981 Mevasseret Yerushalayim: The Ancient Settlement and Its Agricultural Terraces. *BA* 44:53–56.

Edelstein, G., and I. Milevski
1994 The Rural Settlement of Jerusalem Re-evaluated: Surveys and Excavations in the Rephaim Valley and Mevasseret Yerushalayim. *PEQ* 126:2–23.

Eissfeldt, O.
1965 *The Old Testament: An Introduction*. Translated by P. R. Ackroyd. Oxford: Blackwell.

Eitam, D.
1980 The Production of Oil and Wine in Mount Ephraim in the Iron Age [in Hebrew]. M.A. thesis, Tel Aviv University.
1992 Khirbet Khaddash: A Royal Industry Village in Ancient Israel [in Hebrew]. In *Judea and Samaria Research Studies: Proceedings of the First Annual Meeting, 1991*, ed. Z. H. Ehrlich and Y. Eshel, 161–82. Jerusalem: Reuven Mas.

Faust, A.
1995a The Rural Settlement in the Land of Israel during the Period of the Monarchy [in Hebrew]. M. A. thesis, Bar-Ilan University.
1995b Settlement on the Western Slopes of Samaria at the End of the Iron Age [in Hebrew]. In *Judea and Samaria Research Studies: Proceedings of the Fourth Annual Meeting, 1994*, ed. Z. H. Erlich and Y. Eshel, 23–30. Kedumim-Ariel: The College of Judea and Samaria.
1997a The Family Structure in Iron Age II Villages [in Hebrew]. In *The Village in Ancient Israel*, ed. S. Dar and Z. Safrai, 131–46. Tel Aviv: Eretz.
1997b The Impact of Jerusalem's Expansion in the Late Iron Age on the Forms of Rural Settlements in its Vicinity [in Hebrew]. *Cathedra* 84:53–62.
1999a Differences in Family Structure Between Cities and Villages in the Iron Age II. *Tel Aviv* 26:233–52.
1999b The Social Structure of Israelite Society during the Eighth–Seventh Centuries B.C.E. according to the Archaeological Evidence [in Hebrew]. Ph.D. diss., Bar-Ilan University.
2000a Ethnic Complexity in Northern Israel during Iron Age II. *PEQ* 132:2–27.
2000b The Rural Community in Ancient Israel during Iron Age II. *BASOR* 317:17–39.
2003a Judah in the Sixth Century B.C.E.: A Rural Perspective. *PEQ* 135:37–53.
2003b The Farmstead in the Highlands of Iron II Israel. In *The Rural Landscape of Ancient Israel*, ed. A. Maeir, S. Dar, and Z. Safrai, 91–104. Oxford: Archaeopress.
2004 Social and Cultural Changes in Judah during the Sixth Century B.C.E. and Their Implications for Our Understanding of the Nature of the Neo-Babylonian Period.*UF* 36:157–76.
2005 *Israelite Society in the Period of the Monarchy: An Archaeological Perspective* [in Hebrew]. Jerusalem: Yad Ben Zvi.
2006 Farmsteads in the Foothills of Western Samaria: A Reexamination. In "*I Will Speak the Riddles of Ancient Times": Archaeological and Historical Studies in Honor of Amihai Mazar on the Occasion of his Sixtieth Birthday*, ed. A. M. Maeir and P. de Miroschedji, 2:477–504. Winona Lake, Ind.: Eisenbrauns.
2007 Settlement Dynamics and Demographic Fluctuations in Judah from the Late Iron Age to the Hellenistic Period and the Archaeology of Persian Period Yehud. In *A Time of Change: Judah and Its Neighbours in the Persian and Early Hellenistic Periods*, ed. Y. Levin, 23–51. London: T. & T. Clark.

Faust, A., and Z. Safrai
2005 Salvage Excavations as a Source for Reconstructing Settlement History in Ancient Israel. *PEQ* 137:139–58.

Feig, N.
1995 The Agricultural Settlement in the Jerusalem Area in Iron Age II. In *Recent Innovations in the Study of Jerusalem*, ed. Z. Safrai and A. Faust, 3–7. Ramat Gan, Israel: Rennert Center for Jerusalem Studies.
1996 New Discoveries in the Rephaim Valley, Jerusalem. *PEQ* 128:3–7.

Finkelstein, I.
1978 Rural Settlement in the Foothills and the Yarkon Basin [in Hebrew]. M.A. thesis, Tel Aviv University.
1981 Israelite and Hellenistic Farms in the Foothills and in the Yarkon Basin [in Hebrew]. *EI* 15:331–48.
1999 State Formation in Israel and Judah: A Contrast in Context, A Contrast in Trajectory. *NEA* 62: 35–52.

Finkelstein, I., Z. Lederman, and S. Bunimovitz
1997 *Highlands of Many Cultures: The Southern Samaria Survey*. Tel Aviv: Institute of Archaeology, Tel Aviv University.

Frick, F. S.
1970 The City in the Old Testament. Ph.D. diss., University of Michigan.

Fried, L. S., and D. N. Freedman
2000 Was the Jubilee Year Observed in Preexilic Judah? In *Leviticus 23–27: A New Translation with Introduction and Commentary*, ed. J. Milgrom, 2257–70. New York: Doubleday.

Friedman, R. E.
1987 *Who Wrote the Bible*. NewYork: Summit Books.

Gophna, R.
1963 "Ḥaṣerim" Settlements in Northern Negev [in Hebrew]. *Yediot* 27:173–80.
1964 Sites from the Late Iron Age between Beer-Sheba and Tell el Farᶜa [in Hebrew]. *Yediot* 28:236–46.
1966 Iron Age *Ḥaṣerim* in Southern Philistia [in Hebrew]. *ᶜAtiqot* 3:44–51.
1970 Some Iron Age II Sites in Southern Philistia [in Hebrew]. *ᶜAtiqot* 6:25–30.

Hamp, V.
1986 Ḥaṣer. In *Theological Dictionary of the Old Testament*, ed. G. J. Botterweck and H. Ringgren, 5:131–38. Translated by D. Green. Grand Rapids, Mich.: Eerdmans.

Hartley, J. H.
1992 *Leviticus*. WBC 4. Dallas, Tex.: Word.

Herzog, Z.
1992 Settlement and Fortification Planning in the Iron Age. In *The Architecture of Ancient Israel from the Prehistoric to the Persian Periods*, ed. A. Kempinski, R. Reich, H. Katzenstein, and J. Aviram, 231–74. Jerusalem: Israel Exploration Society.

Hizmi, H.
1996 H. Eli [in Hebrew]. *Ḥadashot Arkheologiyot* 106:74–75.

Holladay, J. S.
1995 The Kingdoms of Israel and Judah: Political and Economic Centralization in the Iron Age IIA–B (ca. 1000–750 B.C.E.). In *The Archaeology of Society in the Holy Land*, ed. T. E. Levy, 368–98. London: Leicester University Press.

Hulst, A. R.
1976 עיר ᶜIr Stadt. In *Theologisches Handwörterbuch zum Alten Testament*, ed. E. Jenni and C. Westermann, 2:268–72. Munich: Kaiser.

Hurvitz, A.
1974 The Evidence of Language in Dating the Priestly Code: A Linguistic Study in Technical Idioms and Terminology. *RB* 81:24–56.

Joosten, J.
1996 *People and Land in the Holiness Code: An Exegetical Study of the Ideational Framework of the Law in Leviticus 17–26*. Leiden: Brill.

Kadari, M. Z.
1968 *Thesaurus of the Language of the Bible* [in Hebrew]. Jerusalem: Konkordantsyah Tanakhit.

Kempinski, A.
1987 Review of *The Archaeology of the Period of the Settlement of Judges*, by I. Finkelstein [in Hebrew]. *Qadmoniot* 77–78:59.

Knohl, I.
1987 The Priestly Torah versus the Holiness School: Sabbath and the Festivals. *HUCA* 58:65–117.
1995 *The Sanctuary of Silence: The Priestly Torah and the Holiness School*. Minneapolis: Fortress.

Kh. er-Ras
1982 Kh. er-Ras [in Hebrew]. *Ḥadashot Arkheologiyot* 77:28–29.

King, P. J., and L. E. Stager
2001 *Life in Biblical Israel*, Louisville, Ky.: Westminster John Knox.

Kuchman, M.
1996 Leviticus [various entries; in Hebrew]. In *Leviticus*, ed. M. Weinfeld. Tel Aviv: Davidson.

London, G.
1989 A Comparison of Two Contemporaneous Lifestyles of the Late Second Millenium B.C. *BASOR* 273:37–55.

Lowenstam, S. E.
1958a Ḥaṣer, Ḥaṣerim. *Encyclopedia Biblica* 3:273–74.
1958b Jubilee. *Encyclopedia Biblica* 3:578–82.

Maitlis, Y.
1993 The Ḥaṣer in Nahal Zimri: The Land-Use System Near Jerusalem at the End of the First Temple Period [in Hebrew]. *Shomron and Benjamin* 3:91–99.

Malamat, A.
1962 Mari and the Bible; Some Patterns of Tribal Organization and Institutions. *JAOS* 82:143–50.
1963 "Ḥaṣerim" in the Bible and Mari [in Hebrew]. *Yediot* 27:181–85.

May, N.
1997 Givᶜat Homa [in Hebrew]. *Ḥadashot Arkheologiyot* 107:93–94.

Mazar, A., D. Amit, and Z. Ilan
1996 Hurvat Shilhah: An Iron Age Site in the Judean Desert. In *Retrieving the Past: Essays on Archaeological Research and Methodology in Honor of Gus W. Van Beek*, ed. J. D. Seger, 193–211. Winona Lake, Ind.: Eisenbrauns.

Milgrom, J.
1991 *Leviticus 1–16: A New Translation with Introduction and Commentary*. New York: Doubleday.
1992 Priestly ("P") Source. In *The Anchor Bible Dictionary*, ed. D. N. Freedman, 5:454–61. New York: Doubleday.
2001 *Leviticus 23–27: A New Translation with Introduction and Commentary*. New York: Doubleday.

Noth, M.
1965 *Leviticus: A Commentary*. Translated by J. E. Anderson. London: SCM Press.

Porter, J. R.
1976 *Leviticus*. Cambridge Bible Commentary. Cambridge: Cambridge University Press.

Portugali, Y.
1984 ᶜArim, Banot, Migrashim and Haserim: The Spatial Organization of Eretz-Israel in the 12th–10th Centuries B.C.E. according to the Bible [in Hebrew]. *EI* 17:282–90.

Riklin, S.
1993 ᶜOfarim [in Hebrew]. *Ḥadashot Arkheologiyot* 100:45–46.
1997 Beit Aryeh [in Hebrew]. *ᶜAtiqot* 23:7–20.

Rofé, A.
1994 *Introduction to the Composition of the Pentateuch* [in Hebrew]. Jerusalem: Academon.

Scheftelovitz, N., and R. Oren
1996 *Trial Excavations in the Kh. el-Bira Region* [in Hebrew]. Tel Aviv: Ramot.
1997 Kh. el-Bira. *ESI* 19:42*–43*.

Schifman, L. H.
1996 Jubilee. In *The HarperCollins Bible Dictionary*, ed. P. J. Achtemeier, 549. San Francisco: Harper.

Schloen, J. D.
2001 *The House of the Father as Fact and Symbol: Patrimonialism in Ugarit and the Ancient Near East*. SAHL 2. Winona Lake, Ind.: Eisenbrauns.

Schwartz, B. J.
1999 *The Holiness Legislation: Studies in the Priestly Code* [in Hebrew]. Jerusalem: Magnes.

Seligman, J.
1994 A Late Iron Age Farmhouse at Ras Abu Maᶜaruf, Pisgat Zeᵓev A. *ᶜAtiqot* 25:63–75.

Snaith, N. H.
1967 *Leviticus and Numbers*. The Century Bible, New Edition. London: Nelson.

Stager, L. E.
1976 Farming in the Judean Desert during the Iron Age. *BASOR* 221:145–58.

Stern, E.
2001 *Archaeology of the Land of the Bible*. Vol. 2, *The Assyrian, Babylonian and Persian Periods, 732–332 B.C.E.* New York: Doubleday.

Sun, H. T. C.
1992 Holiness Code. In *The Anchor Bible Dictionary*, ed. D. N. Freedman, 3:254–57. New York: Doubleday.

Uffenheimer, B.
1968 Urbanization as a Religious and Social Problem for the Prophets [in Hebrew]. In *Town and Community: Proceedings of the Twelfth Conference of the Israeli Historical Society*, 207–26. Jerusalem: Israeli Historical Society.

Weinfeld, M.
1979 Literary Creativity. In *The World History of the Jewish People: The Age of the Monarchies, vol. 5, Culture and Society*, ed. A. Malamat, 27–70. Jerusalem: Masada.
2000 *Social Justice in Ancient Israel and in the Ancient Near East*. Jerusalem: Magnes.

Wenham, G. J.
1979 *The Book of Leviticus*. The New International Commentary on the Old Testament. London: Hodder and Stoughton.

Wright, C. J. H.
1990 *God's People in God's Land: Family, Land, and Property in the Old Testament*. Grand Rapids, Mich.: Eerdmans.
1992 Jubilee, Year of. In *The Anchor Bible Dictionary*, ed. D. N. Freedman, 3:1025–30. New York: Doubleday.

Yeivin, Z., and G. Edelstein
1970 Excavations at Tirat Yehuda [in Hebrew]. *ᶜAtiqot* 6:56–67.

Zevit, Z.
2001 *The Religions of Ancient Israel: A Synthesis of Parallactic Approaches*. London: Continuum.

13. Destructions: Megiddo As a Case Study

by Israel Finkelstein

Larry Stager has been a close friend since our unforgettable days together under the leadership of Yigael Yadin at the Institute of Advanced Studies of the Hebrew University in 1983–1984. One of Larry's most impressive achievements in the field was the excavation of the late seventh-century B.C.E. destruction layer at Ashkelon. This was the theme of a typical Stager article in 1996—an excellent combination of archaeology and text, written from the broadest scope possible (Stager 1996).

The exact nature and meaning of "destruction" has never been fully deliberated on in the archaeology of the Levant. The word is used quite freely to describe ashy layers found in a dig. The fact of the matter is that not every ashy layer represents destruction, that not all destructions entail heavy conflagration, and that not all destructions are of the same nature.

A real destruction of a settlement should be defined by the presence of at least two of the following features:

1. A black layer with charcoal, representing burnt beams, on the floor, usually overlaid with a thick ashy layer.

2. A thick accumulation of collapse—of bricks or stones—on the floor. This accumulation can at times be as much as one meter or more deep. In the case of bricks and a strong fire, the bricks may turn red or even white.

3. In most cases, an accumulation of finds, mainly broken pottery vessels, on the floors.

Megiddo features four destruction layers in a relatively short period of ca. 400 years, between the mid-to-late twelfth century and the late eighth century B.C.E. Since the site was thoroughly excavated, in each case the evidence comes from several sectors of the mound (in two of the cases discussed below from the entire tell) and therefore provides a relatively detailed, reliable picture on the fate of the city. This makes Megiddo an excellent "laboratory" for the study of destructions: their magnitude, their vertical dimension, and their horizontal extent. And the rich assemblages of pottery associated with the Megiddo destructions make it easy to compare them to contemporary events in neighboring sites. One can therefore deal with both the diachronic (local) and synchronic (regional) aspects of the Megiddo destructions. The only problem is that in some cases the University of Chicago's reports do not deal with destructions. Still, sporadic brief references to fire and collapse and the many pictures published in the reports compensate for this shortcoming.

The Destruction of Stratum VIIA

Stratum VIIA, the last layer of Late Bronze Megiddo, was exposed in all four areas dug by the University of Chicago in 1935–1939: in Areas AA, BB, CC, and DD; and in four areas of the current Tel Aviv University-led excavations: Areas F, G (which is part of the University of Chicago's Area AA), K, and M.

The University of Chicago Excavations

Loud (1948:29) described a violent destruction of the palace in Area AA, which he associated with the end of Stratum VIIB. Ussishkin (1995:241–46) argued convincingly that this is the destruction of Stratum VIIA. The palace was destroyed in a heavy conflagration that left an accumulation of fallen stones a meter-and-a-half thick, with another accumulation of fallen bricks on top (see figure 1 below). Mudbricks in the upper parts of the walls, which were found still standing, were "baked" (Loud 1948:fig. 71–72; see the schematic section in Ussishkin 1995:fig. 6, 2–3).

The situation in Area BB was more complicated. There was only one floor in the cella of Temple 2048, dated by Loud to Stratum VIIB with a reuse in Stratum VIIA (picture in Loud 1948:fig. 254). Mazar (1985:97; see also Kempinski 1989:77–83; Ussishkin 1995:256) showed that the pottery assemblage from the temple-hall (Kenyon 1969:54) should be dated to Stratum VIA. Loud (1948:105) mentions "the destruction of the temple" and a "partially burned lime floor" adjacent to the platform at the back of the temple-hall—both in relation to Stratum VIIB. Yet the pottery from the temple-hall seems to indicate that these remains, too, should be associated with the destruction of the settlement of Stratum VIA (see below). This would mean that no clear destruction of Stratum VIIA was observed in Area BB.

Loud's short description of the results in Area CC, which featured domestic buildings, and in Area DD, where more monumental structures were exposed, does not mention evidence for destruction. This, of course, may be due to the brevity and nature of his description, but it is still significant because the published pictures too show no evidence for destruction.

The Tel Aviv University Excavations

The excavation in the Late Bronze gate (Area G) revealed evidence for the last days of the Late Bronze city, including data on its destruction (Ussishkin 1995). Area F of the current excavations is located nearby, in the lower terrace of the mound. The excavation unearthed remains of a massive Late Bronze II building with two phases (Levels F-9 and F-7; Ilan et al. 2000). The remains were disturbed by later activities, which could have blurred the stratigraphic situation; still, it is indicative that no destruction layer was found.

The results of the excavation in Area M in the center of the mound show that the *Nordburg* excavated by Gottlieb Schumacher should be dated to the Late Bronze II (Finkelstein et al. 2006), with its final days in Stratum VIIA. The excavations of 2004 and 2006 uncovered a room of the *Nordburg* (Level M-6) with pottery vessels smashed on the floor; no evidence for fire was observed. The excavation of this room revealed an accumulation of almost a meter of unburned brick collapse. Whether the collapse took place in the final days of Stratum VIIA or the walls were pulled down in the early days of Stratum VIB is not clear.

Interesting data pertaining to the end of Stratum VIIA was collected in Area K, a sectional trench in the southeastern edge of the mound, which revealed remains of domestic nature. Level K-6 seems to equal Stratum VIIA. Traces of destruction were observed, in the sense that some vessels were found broken on the floors. There was no collapse and evidence for fire could be seen in limited spots only.

The destruction of Stratum VIIA can be summarized as follows: evidence for violent conflagration and thick collapse was traced solely in the area of the palace. Lesser pieces of evidence of destruction were found in the gate (which, in fact, is part of the palace complex), in the *Nordburg* (another large building of palatial nature), and to a certain extent in Level K-6. There are no clear data for Areas CC and DD and no destruction was observed in Areas BB of the University of Chicago and in Area F of the current excavations. It seems, then, that the main targets for the assault on the city of Stratum VIIA were the elite quarters. The domestic sectors were touched too, but to a lesser degree.

Figure 1. The palace of Stratum VII at Megiddo

The excellent preservation of the walls hints that they were buried in a thick brick collapse (from Loud 1948:fig. 71).

Stratum VIIA was destroyed in the 1130s B.C.E. This is indicated first and foremost by the base of a statue of Ramesses VI found by the Oriental Institute team in Area CC (Breasted 1948). This find, though retrieved from a problematic stratigraphic context, must have originated in Stratum VIIA (Singer 1988–89; Ussishkin 1995; Finkelstein 1996a). Ussishkin (1995) suggested that Stratum VIIA was destroyed by a group of Sea Peoples; an assault by a local unruly group in the chaotic days of the late twelfth century B.C.E. is also possible.

The Destruction of Stratum VIA

Evidence for the destruction of Stratum VIA was unearthed by all excavators, in almost every area of excavations.

The Schumacher Excavations

Gottlieb Schumacher noted the fierce collapse and conflagration that sealed his *vierte Schicht* (fourth stratum), which is equivalent to the University of Chicago's Stratum VIA. A layer of destruction that he found under the *Palast* (the University of Chicago's courtyard and Gate 1567 to Palace 1723) was labeled the *brandstätte* (area of conflagration). It yielded a rich assemblage of finds, particularly a group of bronze items (Schumacher 1908:85–88; Watzinger 1929:26–31). The same *brandstätte* was detected by Schumacher above the *Mittelburg* (1908: 88–90, taf. 20).

The University of Chicago Excavations

The Oriental Institute's team uncovered Stratum VIA in all four areas dug in 1935–1939 (AA to DD) and reached its easy-to-detect remains in other areas on the mound, excavated in the early phase of the dig. In Area AA, Building 2072—which probably served as the palace of the city of Stratum VIA—and the less monumental buildings to its west, were destroyed by a heavy conflagration, which left charred wooden posts (Loud 1948:45), wooden roof beams (Harrison 2004:29–30), and a large number of pottery vessels *in situ* (Loud 1948:fig. 85; Kempinski 1989:pl. 6; Harrison 2004:fig. 19). Dramatic evidence for this destruction crushed skeletons, charred wooden posts, a hoard of bronze vessels, and a large number of vessels on the floors—was uncovered in the domestic quarter in the south (Area CC; see two letters of Lamon cited by Harrison 2004:3–4 and pictures of the finds in Kempinski 1989:pls. 4–5; Esse 1992; Harrison 2004:fig. 71–74, 82–83, 94, 97). In contrast, Area BB revealed only "miserable walls making no sense whatsoever" (Loud diaries, cited by Harrison 2004:4), although it has become clear that Temple 2048 was destroyed at the end of Stratum VIA (see above). No destruction is mentioned in the short description of Area DD, but one locus (5194) yielded a concentration of pottery vessels (Harrison 2004:fig. 122).

Yadin's Excavations

Destruction debris of Stratum VIA with many pottery vessels and a hoard of small objects was unearthed in soundings under Palace 6000 (Yadin 1970: 77–79; Zarzecki-Peleg 2005a:10–17, figs. 1–15). Burned remains of this stratum were also traced in soundings in the northern gate area and under Gallery 629 (Yadin 1970:91).

The Tel Aviv University Excavations

Evidence for the fierce destruction of Stratum VIA was detected in almost every excavation area (F, H, K, L, and M). In Area F, located in the lower mound, pottery vessels were found on the floors of Level F-5 (Ilan et al. 2000:97–99). No evidence for conflagration or collapse debris was found, but the remains were detected close to the surface of the mound

Figure 2. Destruction layer of Level M-4 at Megiddo (Stratum VIA)

which means that much of the evidence could have been washed away or ploughed away. In Area H, the 2006 excavations uncovered a destruction layer of Level H-9, with pottery crushed on the burned floors and thick debris of collapse (the bricks turned red and white in the heavy conflagration). A large courtyard building that had been destroyed in a violent fire was unearthed in Level K-4 (in the southeastern sector of the mound) with collapse debris of burned bricks up to one meter thick (Gadot et al. 2006). A rich assemblage of pottery (Arie 2006) and several crushed skeletons were found on the floors. Evidence of destruction by fire, a thick brick collapse, and pottery on the floors were found in Level L-5 (Cline 2006). Finally, evidence for a violent destruction by fire, including an extraordinary thick collapse of burned bricks, was unearthed in Level M-4 in the center of the mound (see figure 2 above).

There can be no doubt that the whole city of Stratum VIA was completely annihilated by a terrible fire that left debris of burned bricks up to one meter and more thick, as well as hundreds of pottery vessels on the floors (Arie 2006). The high temperature of the conflagration turned the bricks red, thus it is easy to trace the remains of this layer in many places on the surface of the mound where the University of Chicago's excavations ended by removing the remains of Stratum V. In certain locales, piles of burned bricks can still be seen on the surface, for instance under City Wall 325 of Stratum IVA in the eastern sector of the mound (see figure 3 below).

It seems that the destruction of Stratum VIA was followed by a short occupational gap. The next phase in the Megiddo settlement sequence (Stratum VB) features a drastic change in both material culture and layout of the city—from the second-millennium B.C.E. conventions of Stratum VIA to the Israelite traditions of Stratum V (Finkelstein 2003). Similar destruction layers were detected in contemporary strata in the north, such as Yokneam XVII, Beth Shean Upper VI, and Tel Hadar IV (Finkelstein 2003). At first glance, the pottery assemblages from these strata seem to be identical, but a more thorough study (Arie 2006:227–31) revealed certain differences, which may attest to slight chronological differences in their end-phase.

The date and agent of this destruction have been fiercely debated—King David in ca. 1000 B.C.E. (e.g., B. Mazar 1951:23), or Sheshonq I in the second half of the tenth century (already Watzinger 1929:58, 91), or an earthquake in the mid-eleventh century B.C.E. (Kempinski 1989:89–90 after Lamon and Shipton 1939:7; see the summary of the different opinions in Harrison 2004:11–13). Without repeating outdated arguments, suffice it to say that the ^{14}C dates of samples taken from Level K-4 put the destruction of Stratum VIA sometime in the mid-tenth century B.C.E. (Boaretto 2006; Finkelstein and Piasetzky 2006a). The agent of destruction will be discussed below.

Figure 3. Larry Stager standing near a heap of collapsed and burned bricks under the city wall of Stratum IVA

The Destruction of Stratum VA-IVB

Evidence for the destruction of this stratum was found by the University of Chicago team, by Yadin, and by the current Megiddo Expedition. Schumacher describes evidence of destruction by fire in the *Palast* (Gate 1567 of the University of Chicago) in the southern sector of the mound (1908:95; Ussishkin 1994:419). This structure is associated by most scholars with Palace 1723 of Stratum VA-IVB. Franklin (2006) argues that the gate was in use in the days of Stratum IVA. In that case, the evidence for fire may belong to the end of Stratum IVA.

The University of Chicago Excavations

The Oriental Institute's team exposed Stratum VA-IVB in large areas on the mound (Franklin 2006). Evidence for destruction seems to be partial. The clearest data come from vessels crushed on floors in Area AA, where "pottery was abundant in many of the rooms" (Loud 1948:45 and figs. 99, 102), and from a similar situation in Buildings 10 and 51 unearthed in Area C in the eastern sector of the mound

Figure 4. Destruction of Stratum VA-IVB at Megiddo (Lamon and Shipton 1939:fig. 11)

(Fisher 1929:69 and figs. 17, 44; Lamon and Shipton 1939:7 and figs. 10–11; see figure 4 above). No evidence for a heavy conflagration is mentioned in the report or seen in the pictures. A heap of burned remains, with ashes and charcoal and a collection of small finds, was unearthed by Schumacher nearby, in the shrine of Building 338 (Ussishkin 1989). Ussishkin dated the building to Stratum VA-IVB while others have followed the University of Chicago's dating of Building 338 to the time of Stratum IVA (e.g., Mazar 1990:414; Franklin 2006). Palace 1723 and Building 1482 excavated in the southern part of the mound did not yield evidence for destruction. But the palace was found under the floor levels and therefore such evidence could have been eradicated when the stones of the building were robbed for reuse. Building 1482, originally constructed in Stratum VA-IVB, was apparently cleaned and reused in Stratum IVA (Lamon and Shipton 1939:27; Finkelstein et al. 2000: 313).

Yadin's Excavations

Vessels found crushed on the floors of the northern rooms in Palace 6000 (Yadin 1970:75; Zarzecki-Peleg 2005a:figs. 20–29) seem to indicate that the building was destroyed and then abandoned.

The Tel Aviv University Excavations

Palace 6000 has now been fully unearthed, with no evidence for destruction by fire (Cline 2006). No evidence for destruction was found in the excavation of Area K (Level K-2; Lehmann et al. 2000). Area H provided evidence for partial destruction of Level H-5, probably to be equated with Stratum VA-IVB, in the shape of a thin layer of fallen bricks, some ashes, and a number of restorable vessels.

It is clear that Stratum VA-IVB suffered destruction, since many excavated areas yielded evidence for crushed vessels on the floors. But the city was not put to the torch and was not completely annihilated. Certain parts of the mound did not show evidence for destruction and no brick collapse and evidence for conflagration of the type found in Stratum VIIA and especially in Stratum VIA have been traced. The pottery evidence seems to indicate a short occupational gap after the destruction of Stratum VA-IVB and before the recovery of the city in the days of Stratum IVA (Finkelstein 1999:63–64).

Contemporary strata in the north also yielded evidence for destruction. I refer to Yokneam XIV (Zarzecki-Peleg 2005b:107), Taanach IIB (see picture in Frick 2000:129), the Jezreel compound (Ussishkin and Woodhead 1997:70), Rehov IV (Mazar et al.

2005:237), etc. Taanach and Jezreel never fully recovered from this destruction and at Rehov the next city was limited to the upper mound (Mazar et al. 2005).

For many years scholars dated the destruction of Stratum VA-IVB and its contemporaries to the late tenth century and associated it with the campaign of Sheshonq I to Canaan (e.g., Yadin 1970:95; Stager 2003:64–67). But circumstantial archaeological considerations, such as the similarity in building techniques between Megiddo VA-IVB and Samaria (Franklin 2005) and the similarity between the pottery assemblages of Megiddo VA-IVB and the Jezreel compound (Zimhoni 1997:38–39), led me to the conclusion that this wave of destructions took place in the middle of the ninth century, and that they were inflicted by Hazael of Aram-Damascus (Naʾaman 1997). Radiocarbon dates from several sites in the north indeed show that the Iron IIA horizon contemporary to Stratum VA-IVB at Megiddo (Rehov IV, Rosh Zayit, and Hazor IX) came to an end in the middle of the ninth century B.C.E. (see summaries in Finkelstein and Piasetzky 2006a; 2006b; for Rehov IV, see Mazar et al. 2005:252).

The Destruction of Stratum IVA

In the 1920s, Stratum IVA at Megiddo was unearthed in almost the entire area of the upper mound. No evidence for destruction by fire—neither in the public buildings nor in the domestic quarters—is mentioned in past reports, unless the shrine in Building 338 and the destruction of Gate 1567 are dated to this phase instead of Stratum VA-IVB (see above).

The Tel Aviv University Excavations

Evidence for the end of Stratum IVA was unearthed in two areas: in Level L-2, the northern stables complex (for the function of the buildings as stables see Cantrell 2006; Cantrell and Finkelstein 2006); and in Level H-3, in the northwestern sector of the mound. A large sector of five stables of the northern complex was unearthed, with no evidence for fire. The upper parts of the walls (and probably the roofs) collapsed into the buildings. A thick layer of whitish fallen bricks was identified in every aisle of the pillared buildings (figure 5).

Figure 5. The northern stables of Stratum IVA at Megiddo
White-color bricks from the upper parts of the walls seen in the sections.

Figure 6. Destruction of Level H-3 (Stratum IVA) at Megiddo

It seems that the upper parts of the walls, which were made of bricks, were intentionally pulled down after the buildings went out of use. This evidence fits what we know about the excavation of another sector of the northern stables and the southern stables by the University of Chicago. No evidence for destruction by fire was found.

The only piece of evidence for destruction in the city of Stratum IVA comes from domestic buildings in Level H-3, in the northwestern sector of the mound (figure 6). A destruction layer with brick collapse and many crushed and intact vessels was found there (Joffe et al. 2000).

All scholars agree that the city of Stratum IVA was taken over by Tiglath-pileser III in 732 B.C.E.

Destructions That Never Were

The current excavations at Megiddo unearthed a few additional ashy layers dating to the time-span discussed here which do not display the necessary evidence for destruction listed in the beginning of this article. The floors of Level H-7 of the Iron Age IIA, which were uncovered in the northwestern sector of the mound, revealed such ashy lines. They do not cover the entire area and are not associated with any other evidence for destruction. In Area M in the center of the mound, a flat layer of ashes a few centimeters thick, which appears in almost every square, was labeled Level M-5 (figure 7). It covers the leveled

Figure 7. Ashy line of Level M-5 at Megiddo under floor and destruction layer of Level M-4 (Stratum VIA)

brick collapse of the *Nordburg* (Level M-6, Late Bronze II) and underlies Level M-4 (University of Chicago's Stratum VIA) of the late Iron I. It should probably be dated to the early Iron I (Stratum VIB of the University of Chicago team). Very few architectural remains are affiliated with this layer, which most probably represents an open activity area.

In many cases such ashy accumulations represent no more than areas where fire was used, for example to burn the debris remaining in a threshing area (Mahler-Skalsky and Kislev forthcoming). In other cases, they represent activity areas within buildings. Recent excavations carried out by Ruth Shahach-Gross of the Weizmann Institute of Science and the author at Atar Haro'ah near Sede Boqer—one of the more elaborate early Iron IIA sites in the region—revealed evidence pertaining to this phenomenon. Two rooms ("casemates") were cleared. One had no ashy layer at all. The other had a thin layer of charcoal with a somewhat thicker layer of gray, ashy material on top of it on one side of the room; no such layers were detected on its opposite side. There was no sign of fire in the collapse of the walls. It seems that the site was abandoned and that the walls and roof gradually collapsed into the rooms. The charcoal and ashy accumulation may belong to an activity area—some sort of an installation or fire-place—inside the room (Shahach-Gross and Finkelstein 2008).

To sum up this matter, black lines and thin accumulations of ashes do not represent destructions if they are not accompanied by the other pieces of evidence listed above.

The Megiddo Destruction Scale

The Megiddo data can serve as a basis for establishing the "Megiddo Destruction Scale," which may then be used to scale most cases of destruction layers in other sites. From bottom to top these would be:

Scale 1 Destruction, Megiddo IVA

Partial destruction of a city with no occupational gap following it. Parallels can be found at the following sites:

Ashdod VIII–VI of the Iron IIB: Evidence for destruction is local and fragmentary (Finkelstein and Singer-Avitz 2001:246).

Hazor IX of the Iron IIA: Yadin (1972:143) described a "thick layer of ashes" at the end of Phase IXa (also Yadin et al. 1960:4–5), while later, the Hazor team (Yadin et al. 1989:36) referred only to "traces of burning" in Area A. Still later, in their summary of the evidence from Area A, Ben-Tor and Ben-Ami (1998:11–12) described an ash layer which "may attest to a destruction . . . it may be that the ash layer encountered in Stratum IXb (IXa?) is of a local, apparently industrial nature and not necessarily the result of a military conquest of Hazor."

Hazor VII: Describing Area A, Yadin stated that this stratum was "utterly destroyed by fire" (1972: 169; see also Yadin et al. 1960:16, which relates to a destruction, but almost no fire). No word on a violent destruction can be found in *Hazor III–IV* (Yadin et al. 1989); in fact, at least in Area B the report argues for architectural continuity (ibid., p. 100). Indeed, Ben-Tor's summary table for his excavations in Areas A and M (1996:75) clearly reflects this continuity. Either the destruction was partial or there was no destruction at all.

Scale 2 Destruction, Megiddo VIIA and VA-IVB

A more severe destruction, with evidence for conflagration and/or collapse, sometimes followed by a short abandonment. Parallels can be found at:

Rehov V of the Iron IIA: Mazar et al. (2005) describe destruction by fire. But the city recovered after a very short period of time and continued almost unchanged until the final destruction of the lower city at the end of Stratum IV.

Hazor VA of the Iron IIB: The citadel area was completely destroyed (Yadin et al. 1958:19; Yadin et al. 1960:30, 49; Yadin 1972:190; Yadin et al. 1989:191). Ben-Tor's (1996:75) summary table of his excavations in Areas A and M also relates to a total destruction by fire.

Scale 3 Destruction, Megiddo VIA

Complete annihilation of a settlement with evidence for a heavy conflagration, wall and roof collapse, and large assemblages of finds on the floors. An occupational gap of some sort follows. Parallels contemporary to the four Megiddo chronological horizons mentioned in the beginning of this paper can be found at:

Lachish VI of the Late Bronze III: The site was totally destroyed and then deserted for ca. two centuries (Ussishkin 2004:70); the Lachish countryside was also devastated (Dagan 2004:2679–80; Finkelstein 1996b).

Hazor XIII of the Late Bronze II (somewhat earlier than the late twelfth century B.C.E. layers such as Megiddo VIIA and Lachish VI; Beck and Kochavi 1985). The whole site was devastated (Ben-Tor 1998), followed by an occupational gap of over a century (Finkelstein 2000; for a different post-destruction scenario see Finkelstein 2005).

Beth Shean Lower VI of the Late Bronze III: Violent destruction with one-meter-thick brick collapse (Mazar 1993:217).

Yokneam XVII of the late Iron I: Complete devastation with over one meter accumulation of burned bricks and charred wooden beams, followed by a possible occupational gap (Zarzecki-Peleg 2005b: 22–23, 35, pictures in pp. 30–32).

Rehov IV of the Iron IIA: Total destruction followed by the desertion of the lower mound (Mazar et al. 2005).

Beth Shean S-1 (Lower V) of the Iron IIA: Destruction in severe fire "that caused the mudbricks to melt to white powder" (Mazar 2006:31, see also 35).

Tell es-Safi temporary Stratum IV of the late Iron IIA: Total destruction, with ashes and thick accumulation of collapse debris; the city never recovered from this event (Maeir 2004 and personal communication).

Beth Shean P-7 of the Iron IIB: Destruction by fierce fire (Mazar 2006:33; pictures in Mazar and Sumakai-Fink 2006).

Lachish III of the Iron IIB: The site was completely destroyed, with evidence for a heavy conflagration and collapse (Ussishkin 1982:54).

Beersheba II of the Iron IIB: Severe, total destruction, with evidence for fire and collapse (Aharoni 1973:5).

Other Scale 3 destruction layers that do not date to any of the four chronological horizons discussed in this article include:

Shiloh V of the mid-Iron I: The site was devastated by a violent fire and never recovered from this event (Finkelstein 1993:388–89).

Ashkelon 604 B.C.E.: Total devastation of the entire site, followed by a gap of almost a century, until the Persian period (Stager 1996).

Lachish II of the Iron IIC: The site was completely destroyed and put to the torch in 586 B.C.E., followed by an occupational gap of a century or two (Ussishkin 2004:93–94, 97).

The Destroyer and His Aims

Ancient cities could be destroyed in a military raid, such as a punitive campaign by a neighboring power or a campaign aimed at long-term conquest and domination, or in an attack by a small unruly group, or in an earthquake (for the latter see Marco et al. 2006). The aim of the destroyer could have been total annihilation of a settlement or a takeover in order to establish a new administration in the conquered city. In the latter case, the destroyer, who would have been interested in the continued exploitation of the settlement and its population, would probably aim to destroy only the elite quarter. A destroyer interested in inheriting a settlement and possibly co-operating with its elite groups, might want to leave the public buildings undamaged.

As I have already mentioned, Megiddo provides comprehensive information from different parts of the mound, information which may indicate the aims of the destroyer. In the case of Stratum VIIA, the part of the mound that was completely annihilated is the palace in Area AA. Other sectors were damaged to a lesser degree. In the case of Stratum IVA, the public buildings were left undamaged while the domestic quarters were attacked. In the case of Stratum VA-IVB also, most of the data on the destruction comes from the domestic quarters; the evidence from the two palaces is partial and does not allow one to draw firm conclusions.

Three of the four destruction horizons described above include events of different scales. It seems that in most cases the level of destruction inflicted on a city depended more on the specific, local aims of the destroyer—which depended, in turn, on the location and function of the relevant city and the post-takeover plans of the destroyer—than solely on his identity.

This can clearly be seen in two cases. The Megiddo VA-IVB destruction horizon was probably the result of the assault by Hazael, king of Aram-Damascus, on the northern kingdom of Israel (Naʾaman 1997). Hazor (Stratum IXa) seems to have been partially damaged and so too was Jezreel (Ussishkin and Woodhead 1997:70) and seemingly also Dan. Destruction layers with no evidence for conflagration were detected at Megiddo and Yokneam (for the latter see Zarzecki-Peleg 2005b:107); it seems that the destroyer of Stratum VA-IVB at Megiddo was interested in the departure of the population but not in the destruction of the city by fire. Rehov and

Beth Shean in the north and Gath in the south were completely destroyed in a heavy conflagration. It seems, then, that Hazael devastated the area of Beth Shean (possibly in conjunction with the assault on the Gilead; see 2 Kings 10:32–33), while the damage in the Jezreel Valley was less dramatic. The king of Damascus may have planned to exploit the fertile valley and establish his own administration in places such as Megiddo and Jezreel. The damage at Hazor and Dan seems to have been limited because he may have planned in advance to use these cities as his strongholds in the north (for possible Aramean domination of Hazor in the late ninth century see Finkelstein 1999). Beyond the borders of the northern kingdom, Gath was probably the major target of Hazael's assault because of its standing as the most powerful city in the southern lowlands. The annihilation of Gath must have opened the way for a Damascene domination in this region. Yet, many of Hazael's goals may have not been fulfilled because Damascus was weakened a short while later by Assyria.

The Megiddo IVA horizon represents the Assyrian takeover in the north. At Megiddo only the domestic area was hit, while at Hazor the destruction was more comprehensive. Beth Shean was completely devastated. The evidence from other northern sites is not clear (see, e.g., Biran 1994:260 for Dan and Stern 2000:131 for Dor), although it seems that the destruction at Samaria was partial (Naʾaman 1990:209). In the south, the Assyrian campaigns wreaked total devastation on Lachish and Beer-sheba, while the damage at Ashdod was partial.

The Assyrians must have planned their conquests carefully. Certain cities in the north, such as Hazor and Beth Shean, were destroyed, while much of Megiddo, mainly the stable compounds, was spared. The Assyrians may have wished to use the stables in the first phase after the takeover (on the importance of the Megiddo stables in the international economy of the eighth century B.C.E., see Cantrell and Finkelstein 2006). The walls of the stables were pulled down a short while later, possibly in the days of Sargon II, when Assyria was able to purchase its horses directly from Egypt and when Megiddo was remodeled to serve as the capital of an Assyrian province (Peersmann 2000). In the south the Judahite centers were ravaged, while Ashdod, which was important for the Assyrian economy, was spared (for remains of an Assyrian administration center recently uncovered at Ashdod, see Kogan-Zehavi 2005).

The Assyrian records speak about the siege and takeover of cities (see Ephʿal 1997), as well as destructions (e.g., Tiglath-pileser III's devastation of the Damascene countryside and Esarhaddon's assault on Sidon—Pritchard 1969:283, 290). A combination of detailed textual evidence about an Assyrian conquest and good archaeological record exists for a few places only and therefore is not enough to draw firm conclusions. Yet, it is noteworthy that Sargon II specifically mentions the rebuilding or reorganization of Samaria and Ashdod, while Sennacherib does not refer to a similar policy in Judah.

In the Megiddo VIIA horizon, too, some sites were completely annihilated (Lachish VI, Beth Shean Lower VI), while others were only partially destroyed (Megiddo VIIA). The attack on the city of Stratum VIIA concentrated on the palace area; the cult compound and the domestic quarters did not suffer violent destruction. In this case, the identity of the destroyer and his goals are not clear. This could have been a razzia by a group of Sea Peoples (see Ussishkin 1995), or a band of *ʿapiru*, or an attack by a neighboring city-state. A well-organized military attack by Twentieth Dynasty Egypt on an important center such as Megiddo seems unlikely.

The only case of a total annihilation of an entire region is that of Megiddo VIA and its contemporaries. The whole area of the northern valleys was hit and the cities utterly destroyed. I refer to Megiddo VIA, Yokneam XVII, Taanach IB (Finkelstein 1998), Beth Shean Upper VI, and Tel Hadar IV (Kinneret was abandoned). This is a unique phenomenon which calls for an explanation.

A recent study conducted at Megiddo (Marco et al. 2006) did not find enough support for Kempinski's suggestion (1989:89–90, following Lamon and Shipton 1939:7) that the city was destroyed in an earthquake. One needs to turn then to human-inflicted catastrophe.

The destroyer of the Megiddo VIA settlement horizon, which I would see as a revival of the Canaanite city-state system (Finkelstein 2003), aimed at a total desolation of these cities. It seems that the destroyer had no interest in exploiting their agricultural output or in their commercial advantages. The theory of a destruction by King David (recently Harrison 2004: 108) is based on an uncritical reading of the biblical text and should therefore be neglected. A Sheshonq I destruction suggested by the author (Finkelstein 2002) raises problems regarding the nature of Egyptian campaigns in Canaan (Ussishkin 1990:72–73) and may be somewhat too late for the date of this devastation, which has recently been determined by radiocarbon studies. Hence a takeover by the emerging highland Israelite entity seems to be the best solution, or at least the less problematic one. This fits Arie's (2006:227–31) study of the pottery of the Megiddo IVA horizon in the north, which raises the possibility that the collapse of the late Iron I settlement system in the northern valleys did not come in one blow but was rather a gradual process that took several years or even decades. A gradual early Israelite assault on the urban centers in the valleys, but not necessarily on the rural sector (Finkelstein 2003), also fits the outcome of the events: the next phase material culture horizon in the region, represented by the Iron IIA strata of Megiddo VB, Rehov VI, Taanach IIA and their contemporaries, opens a new era, with different traits in both material culture and settlement layout—that which continues undisturbed into the Israelite, Omride horizon of Megiddo VA-IVB and its contemporaries.

Is there a textual echo to these groundbreaking events in the northern valleys? The answer takes me back to Larry, who suggested almost twenty years ago (Stager 1988) that the Song of Deborah, seen by many as one of the oldest sources in the Hebrew Bible (e.g., Coogan 1978), depicts the victory of the highland Israelites over the Canaanites in the lowlands. Larry may have been right—not for twelfth-century events, but rather for tenth-century clashes that took place on the eve of the rise of the northern kingdom of Israel. Vague memories of such clashes could have been kept in the northern "Book of Saviors" that was written in the north in the eighth century B.C.E. and was later incorporated into the Judahite Deuteronomistic book of Judges (Richter 1966; Knauf 2000:396; Guillaume 2004:37–38).

Acknowledgments:

This study was carried out with the help of the Chaim Katzman Archaeology Fund and the Jacob M. Alkow Chair in the Archaeology of Israel in the Bronze and Iron Ages, Tel Aviv University.

Bibliography

Aharoni, Y.
1973 *Beer-sheba.* Vol. 1, *Excavations at Tel Beer-sheba 1969–1971 Seasons.* Tel Aviv: Institute of Archaeology, Tel Aviv University.

Arie, E.
2006 The Iron Age I Pottery: Levels K-5 and K-4 and an Intra-Site Spatial Analysis of the Pottery from Stratum VIA. In *Megiddo,* vol. 4/1, *The 1998–2002 Seasons,* ed. I. Finkelstein, D. Ussishkin, and B. Halpern, 191–298. Tel Aviv: Institute of Archaeology, Tel Aviv University.

Beck, P., and M. Kochavi
1985 A Dated Assemblage of the Late Thirteenth Century B.C.E. from the Egyptian Residency at Aphek. *Tel Aviv* 12:29–42.

Ben-Tor, A.
1996 The Yigael Yadin Memorial Excavations at Hazor: Aims and Preliminary Results of 1990–1992 Seasons [in Hebrew]. *EI* 25:67–81.
1998 The Fall of Canaanite Hazor: The "Who" and "When" Questions. In *Mediterranean Peoples in Transition: Thirteenth to Early Tenth Centuries B.C.E.,* ed. S. Gitin, A. Mazar, and E. Stern, 456–67. Jerusalem: Israel Exploration Society.

Ben-Tor, A., and D. Ben-Ami
1998 Hazor and the Archaeology of the Tenth Century B.C.E. *IEJ* 48:1–37.

Biran, A.
1994 *Biblical Dan.* Jerusalem: Israel Exploration Society.

Boaretto, E.
2006 Radiocarbon Dates. In *Megiddo,* vol. 4/2, *The 1998–2002 Seasons,* ed. I. Finkelstein, D. Ussishkin, and B. Halpern, 550–57. Tel Aviv: Institute of Archaeology, Tel Aviv University.

Breasted, J. H.
1948 Bronze Base of a Statue of Ramses VI Discovered at Megiddo. In *Megiddo,* vol. 2, *Seasons of 1935–39 (Text),* ed. G. Loud, 135–38. OIP 62. Chicago: University of Chicago Press.

Cantrell, D. O.
2006 Stable Issues. In *Megiddo,* vol. 4/2, *The 1998–2002 Seasons,* ed. I. Finkelstein, D. Ussishkin, and B. Halpern, 630–42. Tel Aviv: Institute of Archaeology, Tel Aviv University.

Cantrell, D. O., and I. Finkelstein
2006 A Kingdom for a Horse: The Megiddo Stables and Eighth-Century Israel. In *Megiddo,* vol. 4/2, *The 1998–2002 Seasons,* ed. I. Finkelstein, D. Ussishkin, and B. Halpern, 643–65. Tel Aviv: Institute of Archaeology, Tel Aviv University.

Cline, E. H.
2006 Area L (The 1998–2000 Seasons). In *Megiddo,* vol. 4/1, *The 1998–2002 Seasons,* ed. I. Finkelstein, D. Ussishkin, and B. Halpern, 104–23. Tel Aviv: Institute of Archaeology, Tel Aviv University.

Coogan, M. D.
1978 A Structural and Literary Analysis of the Song of Deborah. *CBQ* 40:143–65.

Dagan, Y.
2004 Results of the Survey: Settlement Patterns in the Lachish Region. In *The Renewed Archaeological Excavations at Lachish (1973–1994)*, vol. 5, ed. D. Ussishkin, 2672–90. Tel Aviv: Institute of Archaeology, Tel Aviv University.

Ephᶜal, I.
1997 Ways and Means to Conquer a City, Based on Assyrian Queries to the Sungod. In *Assyria 1995: Proceedings of the Tenth Anniversary Symposium of the Neo-Assyrian Text Corpus Project, Helsinki, September 7–11, 1995*, ed. S. Parpola and R. M. Whiting, 49–53. Helsinki: Neo-Assyrian Text Corpus Project, Helsinki University.

Esse, D. L.
1992 The Collared Pithos at Megiddo: Ceramic Distribution and Ethnicity. *JNES* 51:81–103.

Finkelstein, I.
1993 The History and Archaeology of Shiloh from the Middle Bronze Age II to Iron Age II. In *Shiloh: The Archaeology of a Biblical Site*, ed. I. Finkelstein, S. Bunimovitz, and Z. Lederman, 371–93. Tel Aviv: Institute of Archaeology,Tel Aviv University.
1996a The Stratigraphy and Chronology of Megiddo and Beth-shan in the Twelfth–Eleventh Centuries B.C.E. *Tel Aviv* 23:170–84.
1996b The Philistine Countryside. *IEJ* 46:225–42.
1998 Notes on the Stratigraphy and Chronology of Iron Age Taᶜanach. *Tel Aviv* 25:208–18.
1999 Hazor and the North in the Iron Age: A Low Chronology Perspective. *BASOR* 314:55–70.
2000 Hazor XII–XI with an Addendum on Ben-Tor's Dating of Hazor X–VII. *Tel Aviv* 27:231–47.
2002 The Campaign of Shoshenq I to Palestine: A Guide to the Tenth-Century B.C.E. Polity. *ZDPV* 118:109–35.
2003 City-States and States: Polity Dynamics in the Tenth–Ninth Centuries B.C.E. In *Symbiosis, Symbolism and the Power of the Past: Canaan, Ancient Israel, and Their Neighbors from the Late Bronze Age through Roman Palaestina*, ed. W. G. Dever and S. Gitin, 75–83. Winona Lake, Ind.: Eisenbrauns.
2005 Hazor at the End of the Late Bronze Age: A Reassessment. *UF* 37:341–49.

Finkelstein, I., and E. Piasetzky
2006a The Iron I–IIA in the Highlands and beyond: ^{14}C Anchors, Pottery Phases and the Sheshonq I Campaign. *Levant* 38:45–61.
2006b ^{14}C and the Iron Age Chronology Debate: Rehov, Khirbet en-Nahas, Dan and Megiddo. *Radiocarbon* 48/3:373–86.

Finkelstein, I., and L. Singer-Avitz
2001 Ashdod Revisited. *Tel Aviv* 28:231–59.

Finkelstein, I., D. Ussishkin, and R. Deutsch
2006 Western Area M (The 1998–2000 Seasons). In *Megiddo*, vol. 4/1, *The 1998–2002 Seasons*, ed. I. Finkelstein, D. Ussishkin, and B. Halpern, 66–80. Tel Aviv: Institute of Archaeology, Tel Aviv University.

Finkelstein, I., O. Zimhoni, and A. Kafri
2000 The Iron Age Pottery Assemblages from Areas F, K and H and Their Stratigraphic and Chronological Implications. In *Megiddo*, vol. 3/1, *The 1992–1996 Seasons*, ed. I. Finkelstein, D. Ussishkin, and B. Halpern, 244–324. Tel Aviv: Institute of Archaeology, Tel Aviv University.

Fisher, C .S.
1929 *The Excavation of Armageddon*. Chicago: University of Chicago Press.

Franklin, N.
2005 Correlation and Chronology: Samaria and Megiddo Redux. In *The Bible and Radiocarbon Dating: Archaeology, Text and Science*, ed. T. E. Levy and T. Higham, 310–22. London: Equinox.
2006 Revealing Stratum V at Megiddo. *BASOR* 342: 95–111.

Frick, F. S.
2000 *Tell Taannek 1963–1968*, vol. 4/2, *The Iron Age Cultic Structure*. Birzeit: Palestinian Institute of Archaeology.

Gadot, Y., M. Martin, N. Blockman, and E. Arie
2006 Area K (Levels K-5 and K-4, the 1998–2002 Seasons). In *Megiddo*, vol. 4/1, *The 1998–2002 Seasons*, ed. I. Finkelstein, D. Ussishkin, and B. Halpern, 87–103. Tel Aviv: Institute of Archaeology, Tel Aviv University.

Guillaume, P.
2004 *Waiting for Josiah: The Judges*. London: T. & T. Clark.

Harrison, T. P.
2004 *Megiddo*. Vol. 3, *Final Report on the Stratum VI Excavations*. OIP 127. Chicago: Oriental Institute, University of Chicago.

Ilan, D., N. Franklin, and R. S. Hallote
2000 Area F. In *Megiddo*, vol. 3/1, *The 1992–1996 Seasons*, ed. I. Finkelstein, D. Ussishkin and B. Halpern, 75–103. Tel Aviv: Institute of Archaeology, Tel Aviv University.

Joffe, A. H., E. H. Cline, and O. Lipschitz
2000 Area H. In *Megiddo*, vol. 3/1, *The 1992–1996 Seasons*, ed. I. Finkelstein, D. Ussishkin, and B. Halpern, 140–60. Tel Aviv: Institute of Archaeology, Tel Aviv University.

Kempinski, A.
1989 *Megiddo: A City State and Royal Centre in North Israel*. Munich: C. H. Beck.

Kenyon, K. M.
1969 The Middle and Late Bronze Age Strata at Megiddo. *Levant* 1:25–60.

Knauf, E. A.
2000 Does "Deuteronomistic Historiography" (DTRH) Exist? in *Israel Constructs Its History: Deuteronomistic Historiography in Recent Research*, ed. A. de Pury, T. Römer, and J.-D. Macchi, 388–98. JSOTSup 306. Sheffield, England: Sheffield Academic Press.

Kogan-Zehavi, E.
2005 An Assyrian Building South of Tel Ashdod. *Qadmoniot* 38:87–90.

Lamon, R., and G. M. Shipton, eds.
1939 *Megiddo*. Vol. 1, *Seasons of 1925–34, Strata I–V*. OIP 42. Chicago: University of Chicago Press.

Lehmann, G., A. Killebrew, and Y. Gadot
2000 Area K. In *Megiddo*, vol. 3/1, *The 1992–1996 Seasons*, ed. I. Finkelstein, D. Ussishkin, and B. Halpern, 123–39. Tel Aviv: Institute of Archaeology, Tel Aviv University.

Loud, G., ed.
1948 *Megiddo*. Vol. 2, *Seasons of 1935–1939*. Chicago: University of Chicago Press.

Maeir, A.
2004 The Historical Background and Dating of Amos vi 2: An Archaeological Perspective from Tell es-Safi/Gath. *VT* 54:319–34.

Mahler-Slasky, Y., and M. Kislev
forthcoming. Food Remains from Area X. In *Aphek*, vol. 2, *The Acropolis*, ed. M. Kochavi, Y. Gadot, and E. Yadin. Tel Aviv: Tel Aviv University, Institute of Archaeology.

Marco, S., A. Agnon, I. Finkelstein, and D. Ussishkin
2006 Megiddo Earthquakes. In *Megiddo*, vol. 4/2, *The 1998–2002 Seasons*, ed. I. Finkelstein, D. Ussishkin, and B. Halpern, 568–75. Tel Aviv: Institute of Archaeology, Tel Aviv University.

Mazar, A.
1985 The Emergence of the Philistine Material Culture. *IEJ* 35:95–107.
1990 *Archaeology of the Land of the Bible 10,000–586 B.C.E.* New York: Doubleday.
1993 Beth Shean in the Iron Age: Preliminary Report and Conclusions of the 1990–1991 Excavations. *IEJ* 43:201–29.
2006 Beth-Shean from the Late Bronze Age IIB to the Medieval Period: A Summary. In *Excavations at Tel Beth-Shean 1989–1996*, vol. 1, *From the Late Bronze Age IIB to the Medieval Period*, ed. A. Mazar, 26–47. Jerusalem: Institute of Archaeology, Hebrew University of Jerusalem.

Mazar, A., H. J. Bruins, N. Panitz-Cohen, and J. van der Plicht
2005 Ladder of Time at Tel Rehov: Stratigraphy, Archaeological Context, Pottery and Radiocarbon Dates. In *The Bible and Radiocarbon Dating: Archaeology, Text and Science*, ed. T. E. Levy and T. Higham, 193–255. London: Equinox.

Mazar, A., and A. Sumaka'i-Fink
2006 Area P: Description of the Stratigraphy and Architecture. In *Excavations at Tel Beth-Shean 1989–1996*, vol. 1, *From the Late Bronze Age IIB to the Medieval Period*, ed. A. Mazar, 202–68. Jerusalem: Institute of Archaeology, Hebrew University of Jerusalem.

Mazar, B.
1951 The Stratification of Tell Abu Hawam on the Bay of Acre. *BASOR* 124:21–25.

Naʾaman, N.
1990 The Historical Background to the Conquest of Samaria (720 B.C.). *Biblica* 71:206–25.
1997 Historical and Literary Notes on the Excavations of Tel Jezreel. *Tel Aviv* 24:122–28.

Peersmann, J.
2000 Assyrian Magiddu: The Town Planning of Stratum III. In *Megiddo*, vol. 3/2, *The 1992–1996 Seasons*, ed. I. Finkelstein, D. Ussishkin, and B. Halpern, 524–34. Tel Aviv: Institute of Archaeology, Tel Aviv University.

Richter, W.
1966 *Traditionsgeschichtliche Untersuchungen zum Richterbuch*. Bonn: P. Hanstein.

Schumacher, G.
1908 *Tell el-Mutesellim*. Vol. 1, *Fundbericht*. Leipzig: J. C. Hinrichs.

Shahach-Gross, R., and I. Finkelstein
2008 Subsistence Practices in an Arid Environment: A Geoarchaeological Investigation in an Iron Age Site, the Negev Highlands, Israel. *JAS* 35:965–82.

Singer, I.
1988–1989 The Political Status of Megiddo VIIA. *Tel Aviv* 15–16:101–12.

Stager, L. E.
1996 Ashkelon and the Archaeology of Destruction: Kislev 604 B.C.E. *EI* 25:61*–74*.
1988 Archaeology, Ecology and Social History: Background Themes to the Song of Deborah. In *Congress Volume: Jerusalem, 1986*, ed. J. A. Emerton, 221–34. VTSup 40. Leiden: Brill.
2003 The Patrimonial Kingdom of Solomon. In *Symbiosis, Symbolism, and the Power of the Past: Canaan, Ancient Israel and Their Neighbors from the Late Bronze Age through Roman Palaestina*, ed. W.G. Dever and S. Gitin, 63–74. Winona Lake, Ind.: Eisenbrauns.

Stern, E.
2000 *Dor, Ruler of the Seas: Nineteen Years of Excavation at the Israelite-Phoenician Harbor on the Carmel Coast.* Jerusalem: Israel Exploration Society.

Ussishkin, D.
1982 *The Conquest of Lachish by Sennacherib.* Tel Aviv: Institute of Archaeology, Tel Aviv University.
1989 Schumacher's Shrine in Building 338 at Megiddo. *IEJ* 39:149–72.
1990 Notes on Megiddo, Gezer, Ashdod and Tel Batash in the Tenth to Ninth Centuries B.C. *BASOR* 277/278:71–91.
1994 Gate 1567 at Megiddo and the Seal of Shema, Servant of Jeroboam. In *Scripture and other Artifacts: Essays on the Bible and Archaeology in Honor of Philip J. King*, ed. M. D. Coogan, C. J. Exum, and L. E. Stager, 410–28. Louisville, Ky.: Westminster John Knox.
1995 The Destruction of Megiddo at the End of the Late Bronze Age and Its Historical Significance. *Tel Aviv* 22:240–67.
2004 A Synopsis of the Stratigraphical, Chronological and Historical Issues. In *The Renewed Archaeological Excavations at Lachish (1973–1994)*, vol. 1, ed. D. Ussishkin, 50–119. Tel Aviv: Institute of Archaeology, Tel Aviv University.

Ussishkin, D., and J. Woodhead
1997 Excavations at Tel Jezreel 1994–1996: Third Preliminary Report. *Tel Aviv* 24:6–72.

Watzinger, C.
1929 *Tell el-Mutesellim.* Vol. 2, *Die Funde.* Leipzig: J. C. Hinrichs.

Yadin, Y.
1970 Megiddo of the Kings of Israel. *BA* 33:65–96.
1972 *Hazor, with a Chapter on Israelite Megiddo.* London: Oxford University Press.

Yadin, Y., Y. Aharoni, R. Amiran, T. Dothan, I. Dunayevsky, and J. Perrot
1958 *Hazor.* Vol. 1, *An Account of the First Season of Excavation, 1955.* Jerusalem: Magnes.
1960 *Hazor.* Vol. 2, *An Account of the Second Season of Excavation, 1956.* Jerusalem: Magnes.

Yadin, Y., Y. Aharoni, R. Amiran, A. Ben-Tor, M. Dothan, T. Dothan, I. Dunayevsky, S. Geva, and E. Stern
1989 *Hazor.* Vols. 3 and 4, *An Account of the Third and Fourth Seasons of Excavation, 1957–1958.* Jerusalem: Israel Exploration Society.

Zarzecki-Peleg, A.
2005a Tel Megiddo during the Iron Age I and IIA–IIB: The Excavations of the Yadin Expedition at Megiddo and Their Contribution for Comprehending the History of the Site and Contemporary Sites in Northern Israel [in Hebrew]. Ph.D. diss., Hebrew University of Jerusalem.
2005b Stratigraphy and Architecture. In *Yoqne^cam*, vol. 2, *The Iron Age and the Persian Period*, ed. A. Ben-Tor, A. Zarzecki-Peleg, and S. Cohen-Anidjar, 5–232. Jerusalem: Institute of Archaeology, Hebrew University of Jerusalem.

Zimhoni, O.
1997 *Studies in the Iron Age Pottery of Israel: Typological, Archaeological, and Chronological Aspects.* Tel Aviv: Institute of Archaeology, Tel Aviv University.

14. The Late Iron Age II Incense Altars from Ashkelon

by Seymour Gitin

Three incense altars made of *kurkar* (sandstone) were uncovered in the 1992 and 1994 excavation seasons of the Leon Levy Expedition to Ashkelon directed by Lawrence E. Stager of Harvard University.[1] Although only one of the altars (no. 1) was found *in situ* in a late Iron Age II context, the other two (nos. 2 and 3) are also assigned to this period on the basis of the stratigraphic and comparative data. Both were found in secondary use in walls dating to the Persian period at the earliest (see figures 9 and 10), and therefore must have been used as altars in a prior occupation phase. The best candidate is the late Iron Age II, for three reasons: there is a gap at Ashkelon between the late Iron Age II and the Persian period (Stager 1993:107);[2] the altar found *in situ* is securely dated to the late Iron Age II (see figure 8); and there is no evidence of such altars in any earlier period at the site. The comparative data of the other 21 altars found in Philistia also provide a date in the late Iron Age II, that is, the seventh century B.C.E., with two exceptions.[3]

[1] I thank the Leon Levy Expedition to Ashkelon for permission to publish the altars and the Expedition staff for providing the details of the context in which the altars were found and for the photographs reproduced in figures 5–10. Thanks also go to Marina Zeltser for the drawings in figures 1–3 and to J. Rosenberg for the updated altar distribution map in figure 4. Special thanks go to Edna Sachar for her meticulous copy-editing. The three altars are stored in the Expedition's laboratory at Ashkelon.

[2] The excavator reports that "the Persian period strata overlay the Philistine strata"; no evidence has been found for occupation between the 604 B.C.E. destruction of the Philistine city and the beginning of the Persian period (Stager 1993:107). Relevant aspects of the Ashkelon stratigraphy and recording system are described in *Ashkelon 1* (Stager, Schloen, and Master 2008).

[3] The corpus of 21 altars includes 19 from Tel Miqne-Ekron (Gitin 2002:figs. 4–5); one from Timnah (Mazar and Panitz-Cohen 2001:pl. 75:11); and one from Yavneh (Zwickel 2007). The two exceptions are one from Tel Miqne-Ekron found in a post-Stratum IV/pre-Stratum IC context, that is, pre-seventh century B.C.E., but no earlier than the first quarter of the tenth century B.C.E. (Gitin 2002: 114, fig. 5:3, n. 15), and the example from Yavneh, which, although the site is located in the northern part of Philistia, may belong to the northern tradition of Israel. In any event, this altar may be dated typologically to the tenth century B.C.E. (comparable with, for example, May 1935:pl. 12: 2982–2983), but the pottery with which it was found has been dated to the ninth century B.C.E. (Nava Panitz-Cohen, personal communication).

Altar no. 1: Reg. no. 39567; Grid 50, Square 58, Layer 262, Feature 31, Bucket 139; excavated in 1992 (figures 1, 6, and 8).

Dating and context: Period XII (Grid 50 Phase 7), seventh century B.C.E., *in situ* on roof collapse of "Counting House" Building 234.

Description: Block form (length: 24.25 cm; width: 20 cm; height: 18.75 cm), roughly finished. No horns, deep groove, thick rounded band (4 cm high), rim (4.5 cm high). Well-formed depression on top (16 cm long, 14.4 cm wide, 2 cm deep). Freestanding.

Altar no. 2: Reg. no. 43844; Grid 38, Square 84, Feature 341, Bucket 19; excavated in 1994 (figures 2, 7, and 9).

Dating and context: Period XI (Grid 38 Phase 13), pre-sixth century B.C.E., in secondary use in Persian/Hellenistic period Wall 341.

Description: Block form (length: 22.5 cm; width: 21 cm; height: 32.5 cm), roughly finished. One partial knob, deep groove, rounded band. Slight shallow depression on top. Engaged on two contiguous sides.

Altar no. 3: Reg. no. 41072; Grid 50, Square 59, Feature 302, Bucket 55; excavated in 1992 (figures 3, 5, and 10).

Dating and context: Period XI (Grid 50 Phase 6), pre-sixth century B.C.E., in secondary use in Persian-period Wall 302.

Description: Shaft form (length: 35 cm; width: 34 cm; height: 43.5 cm), roughly finished. No horns, wide rim (7 cm high). Top broken. Engaged on one side.

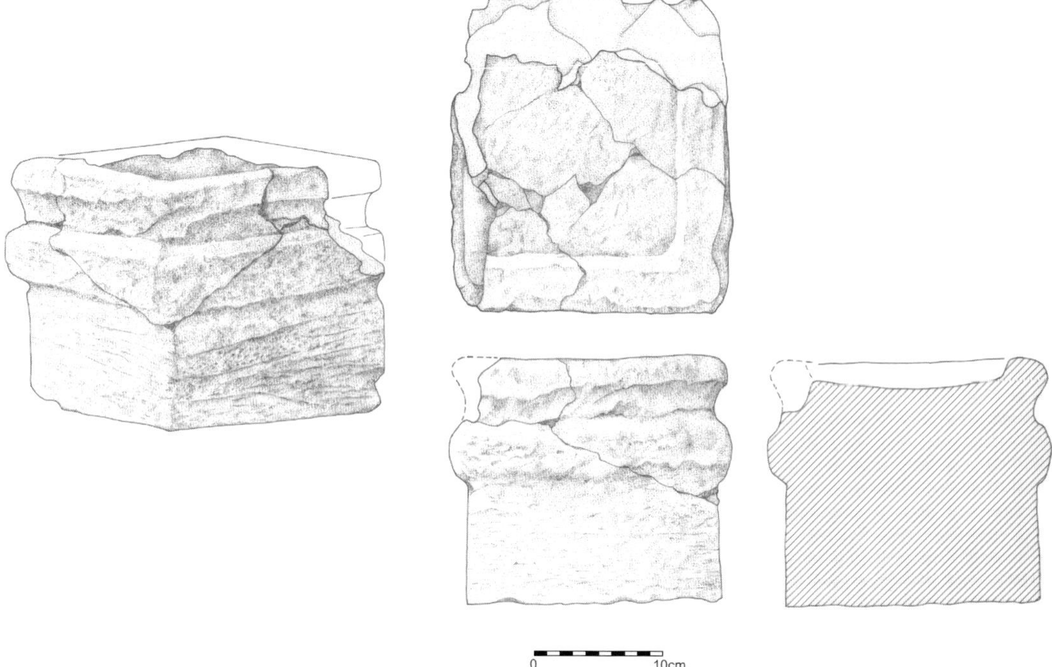

Figure 1. Ashkelon altar no. 1

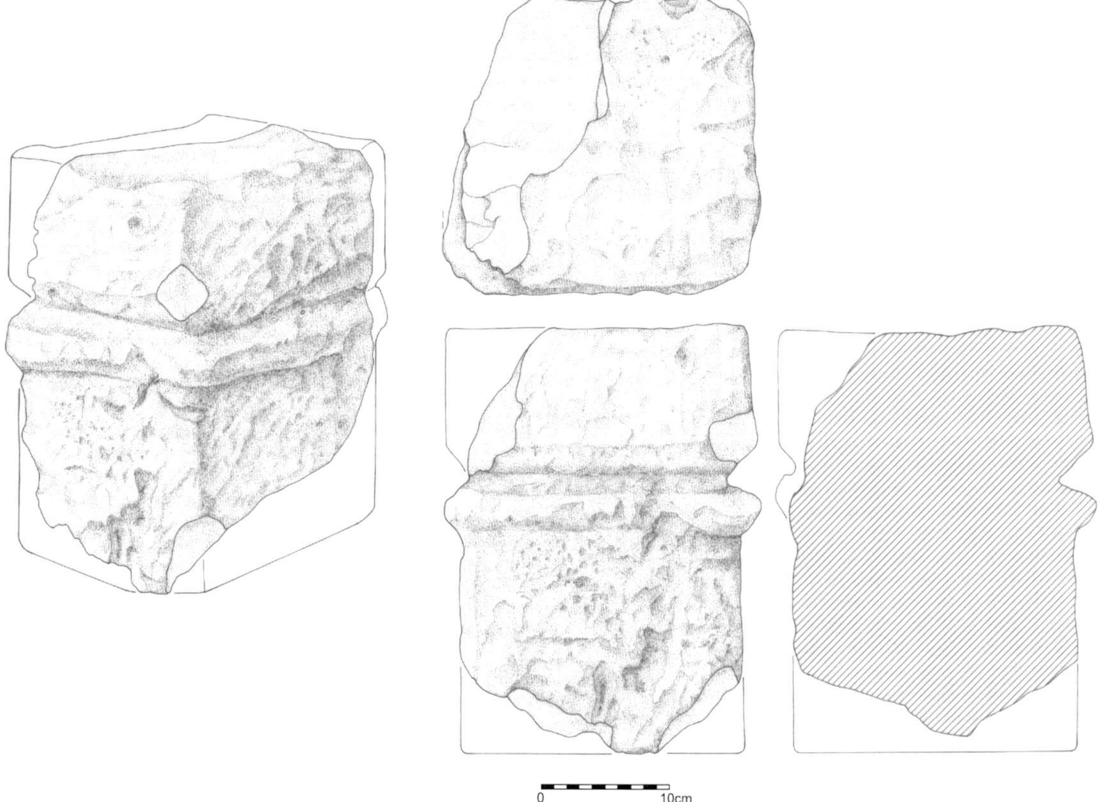

Figure 2. Ashkelon altar no. 2

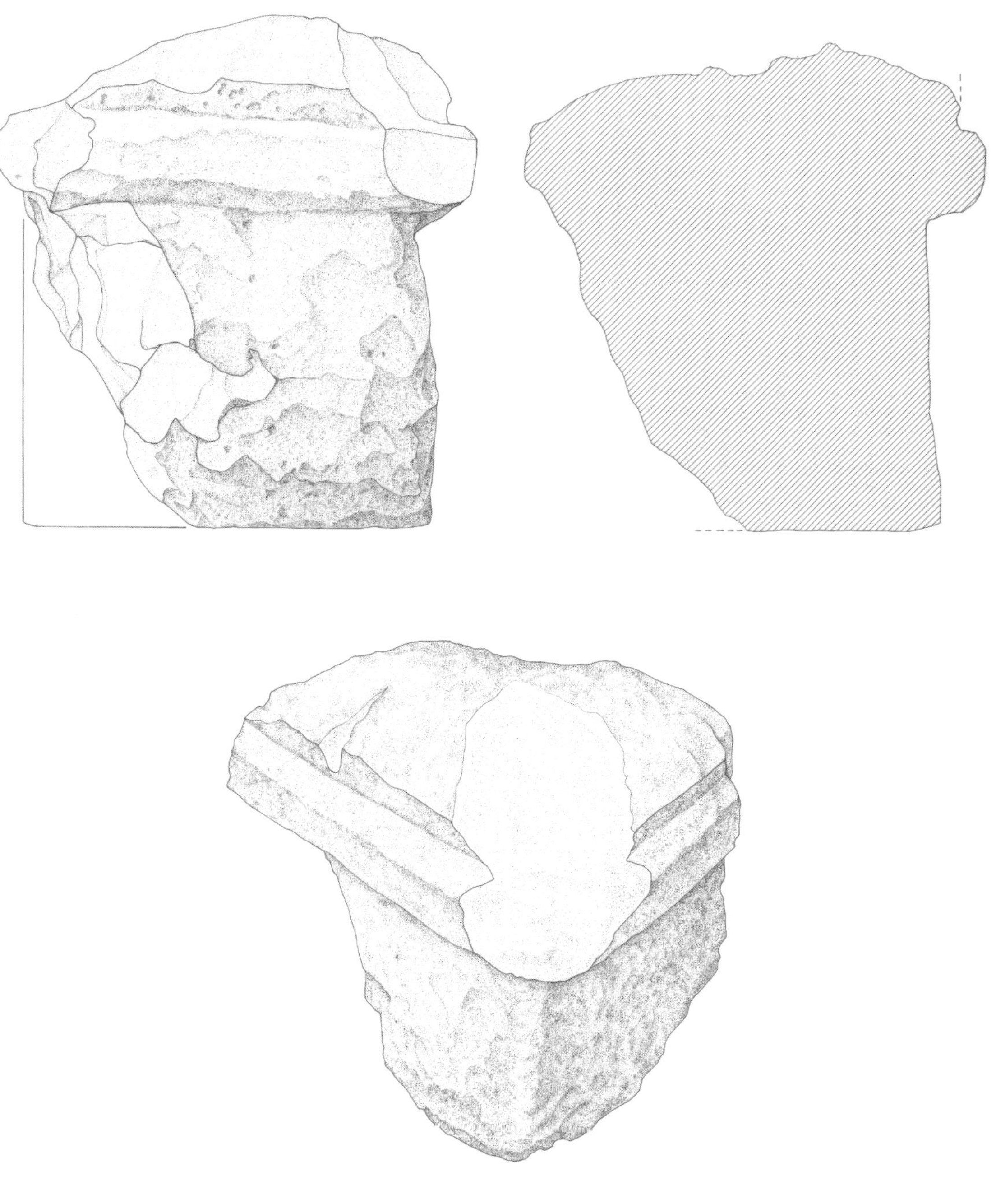

Figure 3. Ashkelon altar no. 3

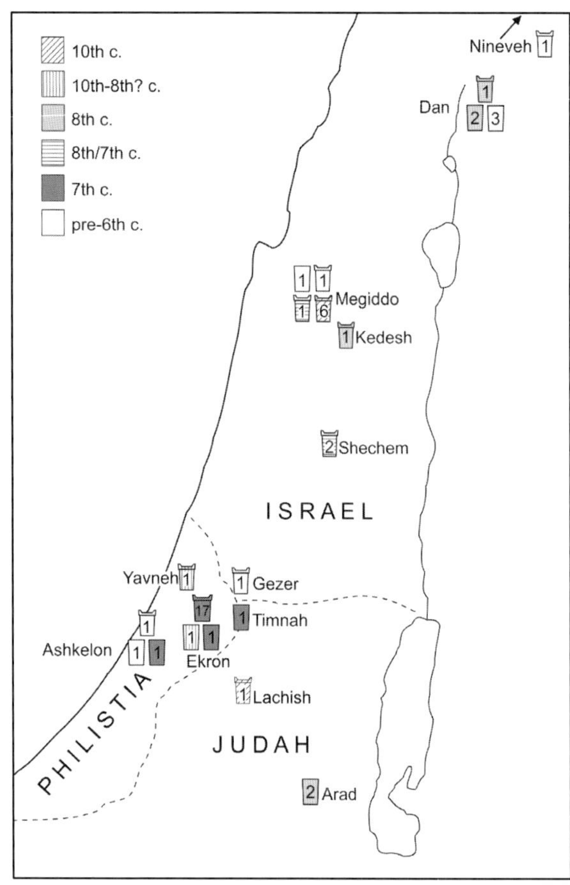

Figure 4. Distribution of Iron Age II altars (tenth to seventh centuries B.C.E.)

horned (34) unhorned (13)

The Ashkelon altars are part of an assemblage of 47 horned altars and altars without horns that have been found at 12 Iron Age sites: 24 in Philistia, 19 in Israel, three in Judah, and one in Assyria (see figure 4), representing, respectively, 51.1%, 40.4%, 6.4%, and 2.1% of the corpus (Gitin 2002:109).[4] The primary Iron Age altar form with four horns is represented by 34 of the corpus of 47 altars. This form derives from the Late Bronze Age II terracotta tower-models known from Syria (Müller-Pierre 1992:40–41), and its functional definition as an object on which incense was burned is supported by the Near Eastern textual evidence of the tradition of burning incense to the gods on tower roofs (Gitin 2002:99). This tradition was carried over into the Iron Age, when the practice of burning incense on a four-horned altar was adopted in Israelite religious ritual, as attested in the biblical accounts of the desert Tabernacle (Exod. 30:1–4, 7; Lev. 4:7) and the temple of Solomon (1 Kings 1:22; 2 Chron. 26:16), and supported by the archaeological evidence from Israelite sites dated to Iron Age IIA–B, the tenth–eighth centuries B.C.E. (Gitin 1989:table 1:6–9, 11–17, 19–20, 36–37). The tradition of burning incense on rooftops is also known in Judah in the Iron Age IIC (Jer. 19:13), and the findspot of Ashkelon altar no. 1 is an example of this ritual.

In this article and in the author's presentation of the altar corpus in earlier studies, the identification of these objects as incense-burning altars—which is consistent with the chain of textual and archaeological evidence from the Bronze through the Iron Age—has been adopted as a form designation (Gitin 1989; 1992; 2002).[5] This is the all-inclusive category by which four-horned and related altars are analyzed and typologically classified, without excluding the possibility that substances other than incense were burned on them.[6]

Although the Ashkelon altars were probably produced locally from the *kurkar* in the area—just as the Ekron altars were made of local limestone[7]—the

[4] Figure 4 is an updated version of the distribution map of 45 altars in Gitin 2002:fig. 6 and of the earlier original corpus of 37 altars presented in Gitin 1989:table 1. Recent excavations at Khirbat al-Mudayna in Jordan have produced at least two stone altars from the Moabite temple destroyed in the seventh century B.C.E., one of which is described as having been used for burnt offerings and the other for burning incense (Daviau and Dion 2002:42–43). The inclusion of these examples in this author's altar corpus awaits their detailed publication.

[5] This definition is supported by a broad scholarly consensus (e.g., Albright 1929:53; May 1935:12; McCown 1950: 210; de Vaux 1965:286–87; Milgrom 1971:767), with some adding or implying the qualification that other substances could also have been burned on these altars (e.g., Shiloh 1979:150; Dever 1983:573; Nielsen 1986:38, 46–47; Holladay 1987:265, 272). Haran, who had previously been part of this consensus (1957:778–79), has more recently argued for the burning of other substances (1993:239–41), and even for the exclusion of the possibility that the four-horned altar was used to burn incense at all (1995:33–35, 37). Haran's arguments, however, lack supporting evidence and are based on untenable *a priori* judgments of biblical texts and on a misunderstanding of the economic realities of the Iron Age II, of cultic folk practices, and of the archaeological data; they have been refuted in Gitin 2002: 103–12.

[6] For example, the altar corpus includes the small limestone altars without horns from Arad, the top surfaces of which yielded burnt fat residue (Aharoni 1967:247), a four-horned altar from Ekron, the top surface of which yielded an organic residue (Gitin 1992:49*, n. 49), and related forms like the three altars from Ashkelon.

[7] The source of the limestone was in all likelihood the quarries located some 500 m to the east of Ekron and visible from the tell.

source of the altar tradition in Philistia must have been in the northern kingdom of Israel, where the closest parallels for the Ashkelon altars originate and where altars played a decidedly more important role than in the southern kingdom of Judah.[8] The north has produced 19 examples and the south only three (figure 4). The appearance of these altars in Philistia in the seventh century B.C.E., at a time when they are hardly in evidence in either Israel or Judah,[9] and after centuries of Philistine interaction with the Israelite kingdoms, during which such altars were absent in Philistia, may be explained as a result of the impact on Philistia of the Neo-Assyrian Empire in the late eighth century B.C.E. Having conquered the nation-states of the eastern Mediterranean basin, Assyria took direct control of the Levant, transforming its conquered territories into provinces and vassal states and creating the *pax Assyriaca*, a period for the most part of political stability and economic growth and prosperity.[10] As a result of the Assyrian policy of population transfers following the destruction of the northern kingdom of Israel, northern Israelite craftsmen could have brought the tradition of altar-making to Ashkelon and Ekron (Gitin 1989:61).[11] As at Ekron, the sudden appearance of these altars in Philistia in general can be understood as a result of the process of acculturation, generated by the continuing exposure to foreign influences (Gitin 1998:162–63). This process was significantly accelerated in the seventh century B.C.E., when Philistine cities like Ashkelon and Ekron became Assyrian vassal city-states, with Ashkelon developing into a major commercial entrepôt (Stager 1996:65*) and Ekron the largest olive oil production center yet uncovered in antiquity (Gitin 1998:173).

The main typologically significant features of the altar are body shape, horns, rim, groove, and band. The altar rim can be equated with the *karkov* and the band with the *zer* in the description of the Tabernacle altar in Exod. 27:5 and 30:3. One of the Ashkelon altars (no. 3) is shaft-shaped with a wide rim (figure 5) and the other two are block-shaped—one with a deep groove, a thick rounded band, and a slightly everted rim (no. 1, figure 6) and the other with a knob representing a debased horn, a deep groove, and a rounded band (no. 2, figure 7).

Figure 5. Ashkelon altar no. 3 (shaft-shaped)

Generally, altars with a T-shaped shaft and a pronounced rim reflect the earlier tenth century B.C.E. tradition of horned altars at Megiddo. The block form introduced in the ninth century becomes the dominant

[8] The clustering of altars in the north and their paucity in the south may indicate a propensity in the kingdom of Israel for less centralized religious ceremonial practices than in Judah, or possibly a dual system combining centralized and decentralized worship. A centralized worship tradition may have been stronger in the south because of the focus on the traditional centers of worship of the Tabernacle and the temple of Solomon. The high percentage of altars at Ekron in the seventh century B.C.E. and their closer typological relationship to northern forms also supports the conclusion that they derived from the northern tradition, the source of which itself may have been in Syria (Gitin 2002: 96). The single example from Nineveh (Thompson and Hutchinson 1927:108, pl. 56:335) and the period with which it is associated suggest that it might have been an import from Israel or made by an Israelite craftsman among the ten tribes of Israel deported to Assyria following the destruction of Samaria (Ephᶜal 1979:188–89). For a typological discussion of the Ekron altars in support of this conclusion, see Gitin 1989:61*–63*.

[9] The exceptions from Judah are two altars without horns from Arad (Aharoni 1967:pls. 46–47).

[10] With Assyria in full control of the Levantine littoral, Philistia, which was vital to Assyrian political and commercial aspirations, was treated leniently and was awarded "favored nation" status. The king of Assyria, Sennacherib, transferred the towns of Judah that he had plundered to his loyal Philistine rulers: Mitinti, king of Ashdod; Padi, king of Ekron; and Sillibel, king of Gaza (Pritchard 1969:288). According to another text, Ashkelon, too, received territory in Judah (Luckenbill 1926–1927:143 [312]). On Ekron's "favored nation" status in the late Assyrian Empire, see Naᵓaman 1998:223; for a historical summary of the period of the *pax Assyriaca*, see Hallo and Simpson 1971:123–42.

[11] For the practice of transferring groups of Assyrian captives to different parts of the empire in general, see Ephᶜal 1979:188–89.

type throughout the remainder of Iron Age II (Gitin 1989:62).[12] Although none of the Ashkelon altars has an exact parallel from the seventh century or earlier, typologically they belong to the final phase of altar development. The widest range of examples from this last typological phase, which occurs in the seventh century B.C.E., is found at Ekron in the degenerate forms with highly profiled but truncated horns or small, less profiled, pointed, or flat-topped projections or small knobs (Gitin 2002:figs. 4:1–8, 5:1–2, 4–7). The development of the overhanging wide rim parallels that of the horns. By the seventh century B.C.E., rims usually appear on altars that have highly profiled, truncated horns (Gitin 2002:figs. 4:7, 5:2, 6).

Figure 6. Ashkelon altar no. 1 (block-shaped)

Two of the Ashkelon altars are exceptions—altar no. 2 without a rim, but with a debased knob-like horn (figures 2 and 7); and altar no. 3, with an overhanging rim, but with no indication of any type of horn, although most of top surface has been broken away (figures 3 and 5). The grooves generally follow the same development as the rims and were probably formed by the stone-cutting technique that produced the effect of the wide overhanging rim. However, two of the altars from Ashkelon (nos. 1 and 2) do have grooves, although they lack the wide overhanging rim (for this feature on altars from Ekron, see Gitin 2002:fig. 4:4, 9).

In the early stages of altar typology, the band, too, probably resulted from the stone-cutter's technique for fashioning the shaft and groove. Although the shaft shape generally gave way to the block form and grooves for the most part disappeared, bands continued to appear throughout the sequence, probably fashioned for their own sake, as on nos. 1 and 2 from Ashkelon (for this feature on altars from Ekron, see Gitin 2002:figs. 4:1, 5, 11, 5:1, 4).

Figure 7. Ashkelon altar no. 2 (block-shaped)

Other characteristics of the altars have important implications for understanding cultic practice at Ashkelon. If an altar is unfinished on one or more sides, it must have stood against or have been fitted into a wall, corner, or installation; that is, it was engaged and had a fixed position. If an altar is finished on all sides, it may have been freestanding and movable, although some freestanding altars may have had a fixed position, for example, very large and/or heavy freestanding altars that would have been difficult to move (for examples from Ekron, see Gitin 2002:fig. 5:6–7). That a freestanding altar was in a fixed position may also be determined by context, if it was found *in situ*.[13] Two of the Ashkelon altars are engaged (nos. 2 and 3) and must have had a fixed position, while the freestanding altar (no. 1), which was apparently portable, had at least a designated position on the roof, as indicated by its findspot (figure 8).[14]

[12] However, one of the Ashkelon altars (no. 3) and some examples from Ekron (Gitin 2002:figs. 4:7, 10, 5:1–2, 6) retain the shaft form as late as the seventh century B.C.E.

[13] Compare the two freestanding altars from Arad that clearly had a fixed position in the temple, indicated by their context (Aharoni 1967:pls. 46–47), and one example from Ekron that had stood in its own niche (Gitin 1995:fig. 4:8).

[14] This is a good example of a freestanding, portable altar that was used in a fixed position—made of dense *kurkar*, it would have been quite heavy to shift.

Figure 8. Altar no. 1 *in situ* on top of roof collapse of Building 234 in the massive 604 B.C.E. Babylonian destruction layer at Ashkelon.

The latter shows that there were portable altars both at Ashkelon and at Ekron.[15]

One definitive conclusion that may be drawn from this evidence is that there were at least three fixed places of cultic worship at Ashkelon at which a ceremonial practice involving burning incense or some other substance took place. Although there is no supporting physical evidence, it is possible that there was another such fixed place of worship, based on Herodotus's report that the temple of Astarte in Ashkelon was destroyed during the Scythian invasion (*Histories* 1:105) in the seventh century B.C.E.

Figure 9. Altar no. 2 in secondary use in Persian/Hellenistic-period Wall 341

In addition, the evidence suggests that, as mentioned above, portable incense altars were used in religious practices at Ashkelon as at Ekron in the seventh century B.C.E. Coming at the very end of the four-horned altar sequence in the late Iron Age, these small, portable altars may have adumbrated the predominant use of portable altars in the form of small limestone chests with four legs in the sixth century B.C.E. Found in the hundreds in Israel and throughout

[15] Twelve portable altars were found at Ekron (Gitin 2002: fig. 4). The only other portable altar from the seventh century B.C.E. in Philistia is the small votive altar from Timnah (Mazar and Panitz-Cohen 2001:pl. 75:11). If the four-horned ceramic altar from Yavneh belongs to the assemblage of Philistine altars, this lightweight example should also be considered portable (Zwickel 2007). However, since it came from a *favissa* and its original context is unknown, it could also have had a fixed position, like the freestanding altar from Ashkelon (no. 1) and the freestanding altar that stood in its own niche from Ekron (Gitin 1995:fig. 4:8). Also, the small portable altars in the tabernacle and the temple of Solomon had fixed positions. The small altars from Tel Dan are made of basalt and may have been too heavy to have functioned as portable altars (Biran 1981:144, pl. 19:3).

the ancient Near East, the ubiquity in size, form, and decoration of these portable chest-like altars may reflect the influence of foreign cultic practices (Stern 1982:186–87, 190–94). The earliest examples come from the late Iron Age II at Beersheba (Stern 1973:pls. 29–30, 52), ᶜEn Ḥaṣeva (R. Cohen and Yisrael 1995:226), and Khirbat al-Mudayna in Jordan (Michelle Daviau, personal communication).

The Ashkelon altars and the literary evidence also suggest the possible coexistence of both centralized and decentralized religious practices at Ashkelon. The purported Astarte temple at Ashkelon mentioned by Herodotus might indicate a centralized worship system, and the three Ashkelon altars may represent elements of a decentralized cultic system. Such a dual system existed at Ekron, with its central sanctuary in Temple Complex 650 and decentralized worship represented by the large number of incense altars found throughout the city (Gitin 2002:114–15).

In order to appreciate fully the role of the three incense altars in the wider context of cultic practice at Ashkelon in the late Iron Age II and its relationship to cultic practices in Philistia as a whole, this evidence must be integrated into a general study of all of the late Iron Age II cultic artifacts from Ashkelon, which are currently being prepared for publication in the Ashkelon final report series. These include Phoenician-type figurines (see Press 2007), Egyptian objects (e.g., a bronze statuette of Osiris and seven bronze *situlae*, each depicting a procession of Egyptian deities in relief, including Min or Amen-Re, and an offering table with two baboons sitting at opposite corners and a falcon and jackal at the other two corners—Stager 1996:68*–69*), amulets, and special ceramic vessels like chalices and votives. These comparative data will greatly enrich our understanding of Philistine cultic practices in the major urban center of Philistia in the late Iron Age II.

Figure 10. Altar no. 3 in secondary use in Persian-period Wall 302

Bibliography

Aharoni, Y.
1967 Excavations at Tel Arad: Preliminary Report on the Second Season, 1963. *IEJ* 17:233–49.

Albright, W. F.
1929 Unsigned review of H. M. Wiener, *The Altars of the O.T. JPOS* 9:50–54.

Biran, A.
1981 To the God Who Is in Dan. In *Temples and High Places in Biblical Times: Proceedings of the Colloquium in Honor of the Centennial of the Hebrew Union College—Jewish Institute of Religion, Jerusalem, 1977*, ed. A. Biran, 141–51. Jerusalem: Nelson Glueck School of Biblical Archaeology.

Cohen, R., and Y. Yisrael
1995 The Iron Age Fortress at ᶜEn Ḥaṣeva. *BA* 58:223–35.

Daviau, P. M., and P.-E. Dion
2002 Moab Comes to Life. *BAR* 28/1:38–49, 63.

Dever, W.G.
1983 Material Remains and the Cult in Ancient Israel: An Essay in Archaeological Systematics. In *The Word of the Lord Shall Go Forth: Essays in Honor of David Noel Freedman*, ed. C. Meyers and K. O'Connell, 571–87. Winona Lake, Ind.: Eisenbrauns.

Ephᶜal, I.
1979 Israel: Fall and Exile. In *The World History of the Jewish People*, vol. 4/1, ed. A. Malamat, 180–92. Jerusalem: Massada.

Gitin, S.
1989 Incense Altars from Ekron, Israel and Judah: Context and Typology. *EI* 20:52*–67*.
1992 New Incense Altars from Ekron: Context, Typology and Function. *EI* 23:43*–49*.
1995 Tel Miqne-Ekron in the Seventh Century B.C.E.: The Impact of Economic Innovation and Foreign Cultural Influences on a Neo-Assyrian Vassal City-State. In *Recent Excavations in Israel—A View to the West: Reports on Kabri, Nami, Tel Miqne-Ekron, Dor, and Ashkelon*, ed. S. Gitin, 61–79. AIA Colloquia and Conference Papers 1. Dubuque, Iowa: Kendall/Hunt.
1998 Philistia in Transition: The Tenth Century and Beyond. In *Mediterranean Peoples in Transition: Thirteenth to Early Tenth Centuries* B.C.E., ed. S. Gitin, A. Mazar, and E. Stern, 162–83. Jerusalem: Israel Exploration Society.
2002 The Four-Horned Altar and Sacred Space: An Archaeological Perspective. In *Sacred Time, Sacred Space: Archaeology and the Religion of Israel*, ed. B. M. Gittlen, 95–123. Winona Lake, Ind.: Eisenbrauns.

Hallo, W. W., and W. K. Simpson
1971 *The Ancient Near East: A History*. New York: Harcourt Brace Jovanovich.

Haran, M.
1957 Altar [in Hebrew]. In *Encyclopaedia Biblica*, vol. 4, ed. U. M. D. Cassuto, 763–79. Jerusalem: Bialik Institute.
1993 "Incense Altars"—Are They? In *Biblical Archaeology Today, 1990: Proceedings of the Second International Congress on Biblical Archaeology, Jerusalem*, ed. A. Biran and J. Aviram, 237–47. Jerusalem: Israel Exploration Society.
1995 Altar-ed States: Incense Theory Goes Up in Smoke. *Bible Review* February 1995:30–37, 48.

Holladay, J. S.
1987 Religion in Israel and Judah under the Monarchy: An Explicitly Archaeological Approach. In *Ancient Israelite Religion: Essays in Honor of Frank M. Cross*, ed. P. D. Miller, P. D. Hanson, and S. D. McBride, 249–99. Philadelphia: Fortress.

Luckenbill, D. D.
1926–1927 *Ancient Records of Assyria and Babylonia*. 2 vols. Chicago: University of Chicago Press.

May, H. G.
1935 *Material Remains of the Megiddo Cult*. OIP 26. Chicago: University of Chicago Press.

Mazar, A., and N. Panitz-Cohen
2001 *Timnah (Tel Batash)*. Vol. 2, *The Finds from the First Millennium* B.C.E. Qedem 42. Jerusalem: Hebrew University.

McCown, C. C.
1950 Hebrew High Places and Cult Remains. *JBL* 69: 205–19.

Milgrom, J.
1971 Altar. In *Encyclopedia Judaica*, vol. 2, 760–68. Jerusalem: Keter.

Müller-Pierre, B.
1992 Un modèle de tout en terre cuite du Moyen-Euphrate. *La Revue du Louvre et des Musées de France* 1:35–41.

Naᵓaman, N.
1998 Two Notes on the History of Ashkelon and Ekron in the Late Eighth–Seventh Centuries B.C.E. *Tel Aviv* 25:219–27.

Nielsen, K.
1986 *Incense in Ancient Israel*. VTSup 38. Leiden: Brill.

Press, M. D.
2007 Philistine Figurines and Figurines in Philistia in the Iron Age. Ph.D. diss., Harvard University.

Pritchard, J. B., ed.
1969 *Ancient Near Eastern Texts Relating to the Old Testament*. 3d ed. Princeton: Princeton University Press.

Shiloh, Y.
1979 Iron Age Sanctuaries and Cult Elements in Palestine. In *Symposia Celebrating the 75th Anniversary of the Founding of ASOR (1900–1975)*, ed. F. M. Cross, 147–57. Cambridge, Mass.: American Schools of Oriental Research.

Stager, L. E.
1993 Ashkelon. In *The New Encyclopedia of Archaeological Excavations in the Holy Land*, vol. 1, ed. E. Stern, 103–12. Jerusalem: Israel Exploration Society.
1996 Ashkelon and the Archaeology of Destruction: Kislev 604 B.C.E. *EI* 25:61*–74*. Jerusalem: Israel Exploration Society.

Stager, L. E., J. D. Schloen, and D. M. Master, eds.
2008 *Ashkelon.* Vol. 1, *Introduction and Overview (1985–2006)*. Winona Lake, Ind.: Eisenbrauns.

Stern, E.
1973 Limestone Incense Altars. In *Beer-sheba*, vol. 1, *Excavations at Tel Beer-sheba, 1969–1971 Seasons*, ed. Y. Aharoni, 52–53. Tel Aviv: Institute of Archaeology, Tel Aviv University.
1982 *Material Culture of the Land of the Bible in the Persian Period, 538–332 B.C.* Warminster, England: Aris and Phillips.

Thompson, R. C., and R. W. Hutchinson
1927 The Excavations on the Temple of Nabu at Nineveh. *Archaeologia* 79:103–48.

Vaux, R. de
1965 *Ancient Israel.* Vol. 2, *Religious Institutions.* New York: McGraw-Hill.

Zwickel, W.
2007 Clay Altar. In *In the Field of the Philistines: Cult Furnishings from the Favissa of a Yavneh Temple*, by I. Ziffer and R. Kletter, 22. Tel Aviv: Eretz-Israel Museum.

15. Palmachim–Giv^cat Ha^ɔesev: A Navigational Landmark for Ancient Mariners?

by Ram Gophna and Shmuel Liphschitz

The excavations at Ashkelon by the Leon Levy Expedition, directed by Lawrence E. Stager, revealed the first evidence of a substantial Early Bronze Age site on the southern coast of Israel. Until that time, it had been assumed that Ashkelon was founded in the Middle Bronze Age, as were other well-known sites along the coast (Stager 1993). Prior to these excavations, and in the years since, scant traces of EB I occupation (second half of the fourth millennium B.C.E.) have been discerned at a series of sites along the coast of Israel: Megadim, Atlit, Jaffa, Palmachim, Yavneh Yam, Afridar (Ashkelon), and Tell Sakan (Gophna 1969; 1994; 2002; Gophna and Liphschitz 1996; Wolff 1998; Braun et al. 2001; Miroschedji et al. 2001; Sharvit et al. 2002). These sites, which have only been partially published, attest to some kind of maritime activity along the southern littoral of Israel during the second half of the fourth millennium B.C.E.

In this short note we wish to present another tiny and enigmatic, but until now neglected, site on the Palmachim coast (Gophna 1974; Braun et al. 2001), which can contribute not only to our knowledge of the dispersal of EB I sites along the coast, but also to our understanding of navigational practices in this early period.

The Site

The site lies on the northwestern edge of a high *kurkar* (local sandstone) bluff known locally as Givᶜat Haᵓesev ("Grassy Hill"), 0.50 ha. in area, where Epipaleolithic flint tools have been collected in the past. The bluff is located to the north of Kibbutz Palmachim, ca. 300 m from the present-day Mediterranean coast and 100 m from the southern bank of Nahal Soreq near its estuary (figures 1–4). Shmuel Liphschitz, a member of Kibbutz Palmachim, first recognized the EB I site in 1966, when a bulldozer exposed a layer of thick black ash containing a small scattering of EB I sherds, ca 0.50 m below a thin sand dune and surface vegetation. In 1970, the site was further damaged by a bulldozer, revealing a 50-meter-long, north-south section. In the southern face of the section two long ashy lenses were visible, ca. 0.50 m thick and 8.0–9.0 m long. In the center of the lenses was white ash; along the margins was blackened sand. Tiny cracked pebbles and a small number of sherds could be discerned at the edges of the lenses and below them upon the stabilized sand dune. Below the sand dune was red *hamra* soil.

In the northern face of the section uncovered by the bulldozer, two courses of *kurkar* stones were visible, 3.5 m long and 0.40 m high, which may have been a wall. The stones rested upon an ashy layer, and above them was a thick layer of black ash containing a few EB I sherds (figure 3).

Several years later, a small, drop-shaped, Egyptianized bottle and a hemispherical EB I bowl were found together, intact, at the foot of the exposed section where they had fallen after heavy rains (Braun et al. 2001:80; Gophna 2002:fig. 25:4).

During a recent visit to the site, the authors were able to delineate the approximate circumference of the archeological site on the northwestern edge of the hill by tracing the sterile sand and *hamra* layers around the revealed remains. The tiny site can thus be estimated at 100–200 square meters in area.

This one-period site of apparently very short duration is located ca. 1300 m to the east of the EB I settlement site of Palmachim Quarry, which was first

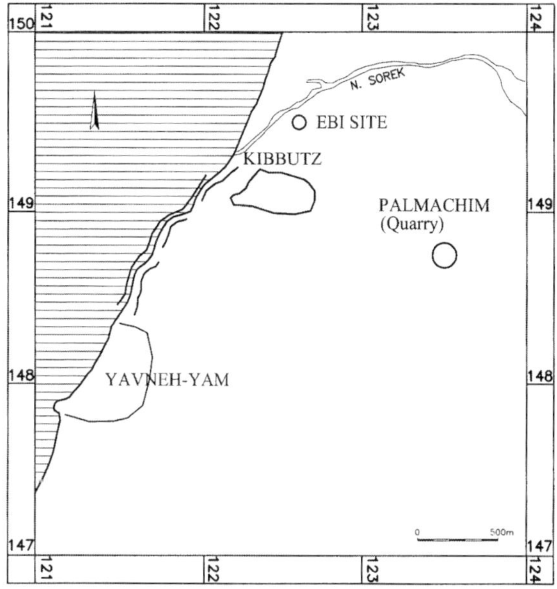

Figure 1. Location of Palmachim–Givᶜat Haᵓesev on the estuary of Nahal Soreq

excavated by Ram Gophna in 1971 and then extensively excavated by Eliot Braun in 1989–90 (Gophna 1974: 46–50; Braun 1992; Braun et al. 2001). The few pottery sherds can be correlated with the latest stage of the EB I occupation at Palmachim Quarry.

Figure 2. Aerial photograph of the hill of Givᶜat Haᵓesev on the estuary of Nahal Soreq, looking north.

The Pottery (figure 5)

As mentioned above, only a small number of pottery sherds were collected from the exposed sections at the site (apart from the two intact vessels mentioned above). Nonetheless, among them were several types of vessels that can be defined as *fossile directeurs* for a dating in the late EB I. Apart from the hemispherical bowl (no. 1), which is generally attributed to the EB I horizon, two rims (nos. 2 and 3) represent a well-known late EB I bowl type with a flat rim, sometimes red-slipped (see Tel Dalit Stratum V, in Gophna 1996:fig. 39:7–9; Arad Stratum IV, in Amiran et al. 1978:pl. 8:1–3). The holemouth jar with intermittent plastic rope decoration (no. 4) is also common in late EB I contexts (see Palmachim Quarry trial excavation 1971, Stratum I, in Gophna 1974:pl. 2:9–10; Arad Stratum IV, in Amiran et al. 1978:pl. 8:16–17). It appears that a late EB I date for our tiny site corresponds well with the latest history of the neighboring site of Palmachim Quarry (Stratum I), and was therefore contemporary with it.

The Egyptianized bottle from the section (Braun et al. 2001:80) accords well with the evidence of Egyptian connections discerned in Braun's excavations at Palmachim Quarry.

Figure 3. The northern face of the section exposed by a bulldozer in 1970.

Figure 4. The sandstone bluff called Givᶜat Haᵓesev, looking north from Kibbutz Palmachim.

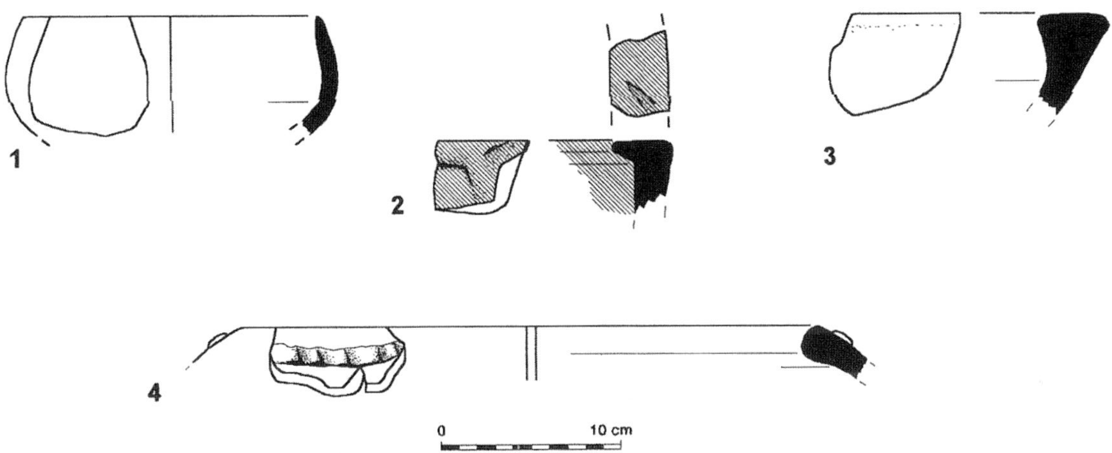

Figure 5. EB I pottery recovered from the exposed section.

Discussion

The question arises, what was the nature of this enigmatic site? Its location on a hill overlooking the mouth of Nahal Soreq suggests to us that this single-episode site served as a navigational landmark to signal mariners sailing along the coast. Navigation in this early period took place during the daytime (Raban 1998), so the heavy ash remains may be explained as the remnants of bonfires used to direct boats to safe anchorage and shelter from storms in the sandy estuary of Nahal Soreq—smoke signals during the day or fires at night to aid mariners in difficulty. The use of navigational landmarks to bring mariners to safe harbor is supported by evidence from the Carmel coast during the Late Bronze and Iron Ages (Artzy 2003).

This signaling from a high bluff near the sea coast would have been a local initiative on the part of the inhabitants of the EB I settlement of Palmachim Quarry, within the framework of their participation in the seafaring activities and seaborne trade that took place along the southern coast as early as the fourth millennium B.C.E. (Prag 1986; Marcus 2002). If our assumption is correct, this site can be added to the accumulating evidence of maritime relations between Egypt and Canaan during the fourth millennium B.C.E. (Prag 1986; Gophna and Liphschitz 1996; Gophna 2002)

In conclusion, the small size of Palmachim–Givᶜat Haᵓesev, its short duration, its location on the sandy estuary in proximity to both Palmachim Quarry and the seacoast, the evidence of fierce burning of organic material, and the meager finds with no evidence of any industrial activity such as the metallurgy in evidence at Ashkelon-Afridar (Golani 2004), lead us to suggest its identification as a navigational landmark for ancient mariners plying the southern coast of Israel during the late EB I, along the coastal trade routes that stretched between the eastern Nile Delta in the south and the Phoenician coast in the north (Prag 1986; Marcus 2002).

Acknowledgments:

We are deeply indebted to the late Professor Avner Raban, with whom we consulted and who heartily encouraged us to put forward the idea presented here in this note. We also wish to thank Shelley Sadeh for the English editing of the article.

Bibliography

Amiran, R., U. Paran, Y. Shiloh, R. Brown, Y. Tsafrir, and A. Ben-Tor
1978 *Early Arad*. Vol. 1, *The Chalcolithic Settlement and Early Bronze Age City*. Jerusalem: Israel Exploration Society.

Artzy, M.
2003 Mariners and Their Boats at the End of Late Bronze Age and the Beginning of the Iron Age in the Eastern Mediterranean. *Tel Aviv* 30:232–46.

Braun, E.
1992 Palmaḥim Quarry: 1989/1990. *ESI* 10:21–23.

Braun, E., E. C. M. van den Brink, R. Gophna, and Y. Goren
2001 New Evidence for Egyptian Connections during a Late Phase of Early Bronze Age I from the Soreq Basin in South-Central Israel. In *Studies in the Archaeology of Israel and Neighboring Lands in Memory of Douglas L. Esse*, ed. S. R. Wolff, 59–98. SAOC 59. Chicago: Oriental Institute, University of Chicago.

Golani, A.
2004 Salvage Excavations at the Early Bronze Age Site of Ashqelon, Afridar. *ᶜAtiqot* 45:9–62.

Gophna, R.
1969 An Egyptian Flint Knife from Yavneh-Yam [in Hebrew]. *ᶜAtiqot* 5:80, 10*, pl. 20:5.
1974 The Settlement of the Coastal Plain of Eretz-Israel during the Early Bronze Age [in Hebrew]. Ph.D. diss., Tel Aviv University.
1996 *Excavations at Tel Dalit, An Early Bronze Age Walled Town in Central Israel*. Tel Aviv: Ramot Publishing House, Tel Aviv University.
2002 Elusive Anchorage Points along the Israel Littoral and the Egyptian-Canaanite Maritime Route during the Early Bronze Age I. In *Egypt and the Levant: Interrelations from the Fourth through the Early Third Millennium B.C.E.*, ed. E. C. M. van den Brink and T. E. Levy, 418–21. London: Leicester University Press.

Gophna, R., and N. Liphschitz
1996 The Ashkelon Trough Settlements in the Early Bronze Age I: New Evidence of Maritime Trade. *Tel Aviv* 23:143–53.

Marcus, E.
2002 Early Seafaring and Maritime Activity in the Southern Levant from Prehistory through the Third Millennium B.C.E. In *Egypt and the Levant: Interrelations from the Fourth through the Early Third Millennium B.C.E.*, ed. E. C. M. van den Brink and T. E. Levy, 403–17. London: Leicester University Press.

Miroschedji, P. de, M. Sadeq, D. Faltings, V. Boulez, L. Naggiar-Moliner, N. Sykes, and M. Tengberg
2001 Les fouilles de Tell es-Sakan (Gaza): Nouvelles données sur les contacts Egypto-Canaanéens aux IVe–IIIe millénaires. *Paléorient* 27/2:75–104.

Prag, K.
1986 Byblos and Egypt in the Fourth Millennium B.C. *Levant* 18:59–74.

Raban, A.
1980 The Silting and Development of Mediterranean Harbors in Antiquity. In *Oceanography: The Past; Proceedings of the Third Congress on the History of Oceanography held September 22–26, 1980*, pp. 750–64. Woods Hole, Mass.: Springer.

Sharvit, J., E. Galili, B. Rosen, and E. C. M. van den Brink
2002 Predynastic Maritime Traffic along the Carmel Coast of Israel: A Submerged Find from North Atlit Bay. In *In Quest of Ancient Settlements and Landscapes: Archaeological Studies in Honour of Ram Gophna*, ed. E. C. M. van den Brink and E. Yannai, 159–66. Tel Aviv: Ramot Publishing House, Tel Aviv University.

Stager, L. E.
1993 Ashkelon. In *The New Encyclopedia of Archaeological Excavations in the Holy Land*, vol. 1, ed. E. Stern, 103–12. Jerusalem: Israel Exploration Society.

Wolff, S. R.
1998 Tel Megadim (Tel Sahar). *ESI* 20:23*–24*.

16. Wine for the Elite, Olive Oil for the Masses: Some Aspects of Early Agricultural Technology in Cyprus

by Sophocles Hadjisavvas

The recent discovery of a Late Bronze Age winepress installation at Alassa and the excavation of an impressive fourth-century B.C.E. olive press at Idalion have radically changed our understanding of ancient agricultural technology on Cyprus and beyond.[1] Pliny (*Natural History* 14:150) reflects the importance of wine and olive oil in antiquity in a two-line statement: *Duo sunt liquors humanibus corboribus gratissimi: intus vini foris olei* ("There are two liquids most pleasant to human bodies, wine inside and oil outside"). In this respect, Cyprus was blessed by nature, and Strabo, the celebrated geographer of antiquity, in Book 14 of his *Geographica* (completed about 23 C.E.), describes the island of Cyprus as follows: "In fertility Cyprus is not inferior to any one of the islands, for it produces both good wine and good oil, and also a sufficient supply of grain for its own use, and possesses extensive copper mines at Tamassos." In emphasizing wine and oil, Strabo seems to speak directly of Bronze Age realities, though his description fits the island throughout its long history.

Wine for the Elite

Winemaking was known in Cyprus long before Strabo wrote his *Geography*, and this fact is confirmed by archaeological evidence. Macrobotanical remains that attest to the presence of vines on the island have been found in two Neolithic sites and in almost all Chalcolithic sites from all over Cyprus. Thus, the earliest archaeologically documented evidence dates back to the middle of the fifth millennium B.C.E. Grape pip imprints were discovered in two sites of the Early and Middle Bronze Age, as well as in later Late Bronze Age sites. The particular shape and size of the pips enabled archaeobotanists to distinguish between the wild grapevine and the cultivated *Vitis vinifera* (Zohary and Spiegel-Roy 1975: 321); so while the earlier incomplete specimen is of uncertain identification, the later pip is classified as belonging to a cultivated species of vine.

It is quite possible that the wild species *Vitis sylvestris* existed on the island along with the olive, long before the first human inhabitants. It is rather difficult to make any assumptions concerning the time and the circumstances under which the wild vine was cultivated. Chemical analyses provide evidence, however, of wine production as early as the Chalcolithic period (3900–2500 B.C.E.). As with the case of the olive, a more intensive cultivation of the vine began during the Late Bronze Age in order to meet the ever-increasing needs of the emerging elites.

To this day, however, there is no direct evidence of the methods used for wine production prior to the Late Bronze Age. Archaeologists have not discovered large deposits of fruit, which would have been

Figure 1. Rock-cut installation (possible winepress)

[1] I share with Larry Stager many interests in the archaeological field: ancient agriculture, Phoenician studies, and Late Bronze Age settlements are but a few. From a long list of possible topics, the one appearing in the title of this small contribution was considered the most appropriate for the occasion for two main reasons. First, because the wine and the olive are two of our favorite subjects; second, because of Idalion, the place we first met and collaborated in the field at a very early stage of our respective archaeological careers.

crushed for the extraction of the juice to be drunk as wine after fermentation. There are, however, some primitive rock-cut installations that could have been used for wine production, but their dating is obscure (figure 1).

We may obtain some idea about winemaking installations from scenes of everyday life that appear on the shoulders of different types of vases dating to the Early and Middle Bronze Ages. One such deep bowl of Red Polished III Ware was found in Kalavasos (Todd 1986:41–42). The Middle Bronze Age bowl (ca. 1900 B.C.E.), bears a composition that the excavator interpreted as a winepressing scene. A fragmentary human figure seems to be standing in a trough and he/she may be treading grapes. This interpretation is by no means certain.

A much better and more realistic scene appears on a richly decorated Red Polished jug that was discovered in a tomb in the village of Pyrghos some years ago (figure 2). The jug is provided with a double cutaway neck and two vertical handles from rim to shoulder. A large number of everyday life scenes rendered in the round occupy the entire shoulder of the vase. The most notable are a plowing scene, a woman holding an infant, women preparing bread, a donkey carrying goods, and a prominent figure sitting on a chair (Hadjisavvas 2001). Another more complex group represents several figures possibly treading grapes for the production of wine. A human figure, his extended hands supported by the two vertical handles of the jug, is standing within an oblong, spouted trough. A circular basin used as a receptacle is placed below the projecting spout to receive the treaded product. Another human figure is standing behind the basin, its hands holding a jug with cutaway spout in the basin.

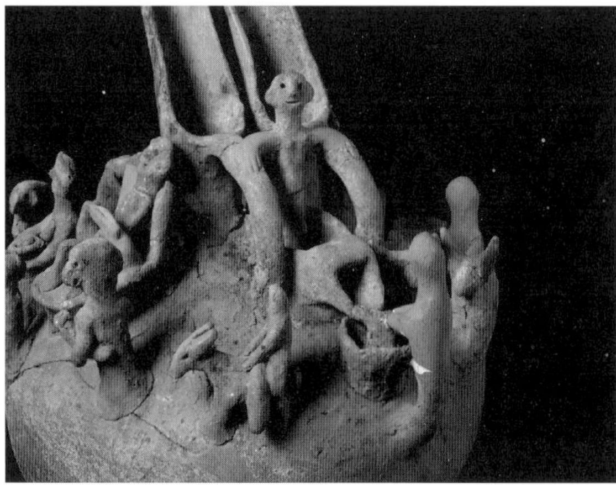

Figure 2. Red Polished double-necked jug

The human figures in combination with the placement of the treading trough and the receptacle hint at the presence of a winepressing installation. The iconography of the Cypriot vase is almost identical to a vintage and treading scene from a painting in the Tomb of Nakht dated ca. 1372–1350 B.C.E. from the Valley of the Nobles in Thebes (Younger 1966:38). The Egyptian painting, however, shows three standing figures in the treading trough, while the remaining features are identical to the Cypriot vase. Naturally, a painting affords many more possibilities for detailed representation than modeling in clay.

A recent acquisition of the Cyprus Museum, from the former Desmond Morris collection, represents a Red Polished model of a grape-treading installation. This object was discussed in detail by Karageorghis (2003:67–79) so it will not be discussed here.

Wine-producing installations are similar to olive oil installations but some slight differences may clarify their identity. Deep pressing troughs are associated with wine production, although their use in olive oil installations is possible. Such is the spouted circular trough from the Late Bronze Age settlement near the Larnaca Salt Lake (Hadjisavvas 1992). Komnos in Crete also produced a couple of similar troughs (Blitzer 1993:168, figs. 2 and 3).

There is little doubt that the lever press was used for the production of wine as well as for the production of olive oil. For the latter, this use was established on archaeological evidence at least from as early as the Late Bronze Age. The LB site of Alassa-Palaiotaverna, situated in the Troodos Mountains, produced the earliest evidence for the use of the lever press in wine production. The winepress was found in Building III, mostly used as a storeroom for large pithoi but also as workshops. This structure is associated with Building II, the second largest administrative Late Bronze Age building excavated so far in Cyprus (figure 3). Such an association of administrative buildings with industrial ones is known from Kalavasos-Agios Dimitrios, Maroni-Vournes as well as from Enkomi and Ugarit, at least as far as olive oil production is concerned (Callot 1987; South 1989; Cadogan 1992; Hadjisavvas 1992).

Building III was constructed on two levels; each series of rooms seems to have been built on a different level following the variations of the ground. The lower series of rooms is of considerable interest. In the easternmost room there is a semicircular structure, its surface covered with pithoi sherds, which is connected with a channel of a depth of 17–30 cm cut in the leveled bedrock and terminating in a pit 1.20 m in diameter. The rock-cut channel is at first uncovered for a length of about two meters, suddenly disappears under a dividing wall and then opens into the pit. The whole arrangement is suggestive of a winepress (figure 4). The presence of a stone counterweight on the eastern side of the room further strengthens this suggestion. On the northern part of the building, a large pithos entirely sunk in a rock-cut pit was found with a stone in its bottom. The pithos is nearly two meters deep, its interior stained with a brownish-red color (figure 5), similar to the wine vessel from Godin Tepe in the Zagros Mountains, which led to a new methodology for investigating organic remains (Feigl 1989; Biers et al. 1990).

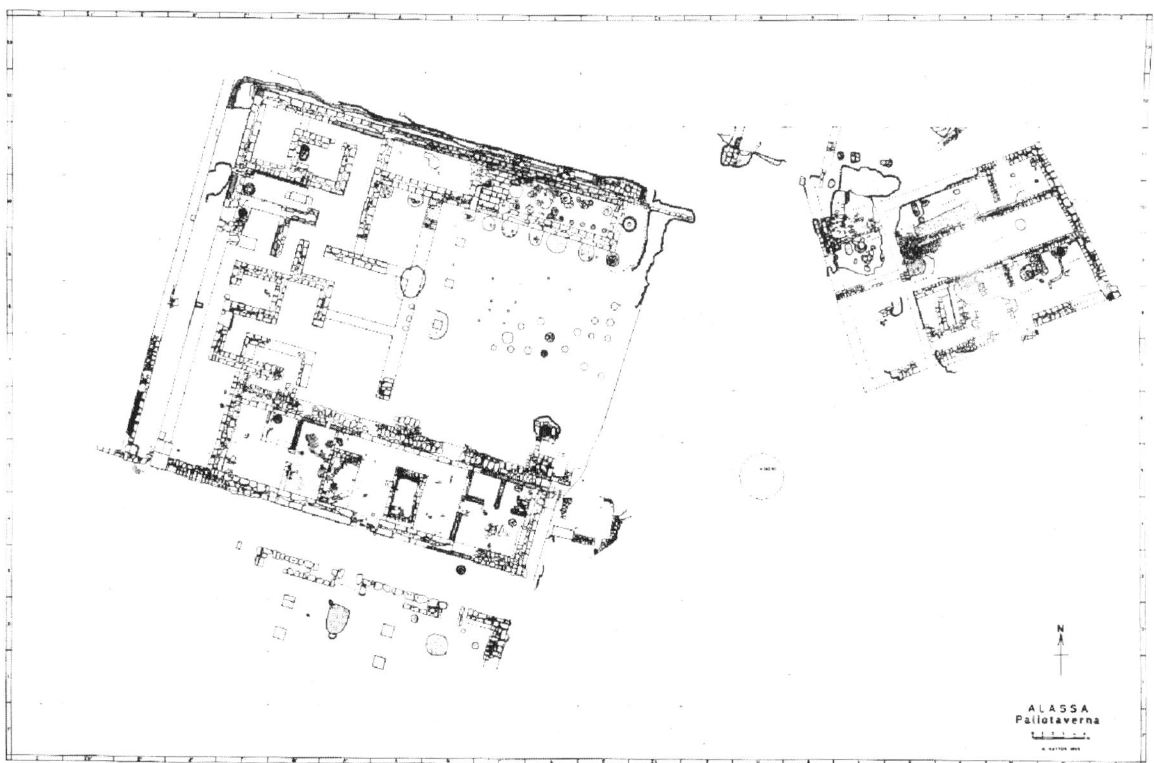

Figure 3. Alassa-Palaiotaverna, Buildings II and III

Figure 4. The "winepress" at Alassa-Palaiotaverna

The positioning of Building III just opposite Building II justifies its interpretation as an auxiliary structure to house the industrial needs of the elite people residing in the Building II. The alignment of Building III is not in accord with that of Buildings I and II and this could explain its later dating. It is contemporary with the last phase of the extension and remodeling of Building II, dating to the LC IIIA period. It is also feasible, however, to suggest that the contours of the hill slope dictated its alignment.

We may conclude this part by adding some notes on the social status of the occupants of Building II,

Figure 5. The wine pithos at Alassa-Palaiotaverna

who were the consumers of the wine produced in Building III. There is little doubt as to the presence of a stratified society at Alassa-Palaiotaverna and this is manifested by the ashlar Building II, ranked second in size only to Bâtiment 18 and the pre-"Horned God" building at Enkomi (Negbi 2005:table 4). The architecture and function of Building II, in its final phase during the LC IIIA period, closely resemble the Aegean palaces. It has a spacious reception hall with a freestanding hearth surrounded by pilasters. It is provided with storage facilities while its bathroom is embellished with a clay bathtub (Hadjisavvas and Hadjisavvas 1997). Alassa, too, produced the largest collection of seal impressions on pithoi, all with a strong Aegean influence (Hadjisavvas 2001). Were the occupants of Building II of the so-called Sea Peoples, who probably came from the Greek mainland after the collapse of the Mycenean city-states?

In the lower city of Alassa, at the locality of Pano Mandilaris, some strainer jugs were found (Hadjisavvas 1991). In a slightly later period they appear in Philistia, where William F. Albright, followed by Trude Dothan, has interpreted them as "beer-jugs." These jugs are thought to be a novelty in the region introduced by the Sea Peoples (Dothan 1982). McGovern, however, disagrees with this identification, considering them rather to be "wine-jugs" (McGovern 2003:227).

Figure 6. "Beer" jugs from Alassa-Pano Mandilaris

Olive Oil for the Masses

Olive oil was produced on the island of Cyprus as early as the beginning of the second millennium B.C.E. Large-capacity installations, however, which leave material evidence of oil production, date to the Late Bronze Age, and more precisely to the LCIIC period (Hadjisavvas 1992:115–16). There is little doubt that their appearance in all major LB sites coincides with the process of urbanization closely related to the specialization of labor. Their presence is combined with immense storage facilities unseen in the record of previous archaeological horizons. Storage facilities are usually confined within the so-called ashlar buildings, identified as administrative, while the pressing installations are housed in nearby auxiliary buildings. This is the case at Agios Dimitrios (South 1989). At Maroni-Vournes, the main ashlar building houses the olive press, while a nearby building designated as the West Structure provides additional storage (Cadogan 1992). The large number of installations of both public and private character, in conjunction with the storage facilities at the two sites, provides an insight into the structure of the Late Bronze Age economy in Cyprus. It seems that olive oil production was the principal occupation of the inhabitants of Maroni and Kalavasos, although copper production is more often highlighted. Archaeologists usually spend little effort to understand the significance of agricultural products compared to metallurgy. Agriculture, however, was more important in a subsistence-based economy. The role played by Cyprus in the production and trade of olive oil has only recently been properly appreciated. In the past, only one aspect, that of metallurgy, was considered as a prime contributor toward social stratification (see Hadjisavvas 1996).

Figure 7. Oil amphora from Salamis Tomb 3

The period between the Late Bronze Age and the Cypro-Classical is characterized by the lack of direct evidence concerning olive oil production. Most of the information we have derives from excavations in cemeteries. The importance of olive oil in the Cypro-Archaic period is attested at Salamis and Kourion by the presence of a number of oil containers placed in rich burials, which are identified as royal. They represent a type of Plain White amphora with raised shoulder handles and narrow base. One of them (figure 7), found in Salamis Tomb 3, bears an inscription in the Cypriot syllabary that reads "[of] olive oil" (Karageorghis 1973:38). This type of amphora is found in almost all excavated built tombs of the Cypro-Archaic period and there is little doubt about its use as an oil container. It was continuously used for the same purpose throughout the Cypro-Classical period and even during the early Hellenistic period in a more slender form. It is mainly found in association with olive oil installations (Hadjisavvas 1992). Some handles of this type of amphora come from the seabed off Salamis and off Kourion, which indicates its use as a transport amphora as well.

The site of Tel Kabri in northern Israel produced fragments from at least 80 similar restorable amphorae (Kempinski 2002:fig. 5:84) Neutron activation analysis and petrographic analysis indicated that they were Cypriot imports. The presence of incised signs and red-painted Cypriot symbols on two of the vessels further confirms this identification. If all these amphorae were used for the export of Cypriot olive oil, then the role played by Cyprus in the production and trade of olive oil in the archaic period should be reconsidered. The mere fact that olive oil was exported to an important oil-producing region like Palestine (Eitam 1993; Gitin 1996) is not only an indication of overproduction but also of the quality and perhaps the lower price of the Cypriot product.

Other factors, however, could be suggested to explain this paradox, such as the biannual fruiting tendency of the olive, which leads to periodic regional shortages. It is likely that trade in oil was intensified during the Cypro-Archaic and Cypro-Classical period, either to meet the demands of the emerging new powers of the region, or as compulsory shipments as part of the tribute paid to the kings of Assyria, Egypt, and Persia.

During the fourth century B.C.E., the growth of production is manifested in a series of innovations in oil-producing installations. The most important novelty was the circular crushing basin, which made possible the use of animal power for the first time. To cope with the increased production from this mill, twin presses were employed in the second stage of the production. The apogee of this chain of improvements is manifested at the site of Idalion at a time when the kingdom was under the supremacy of the Phoenician kings of Kition.

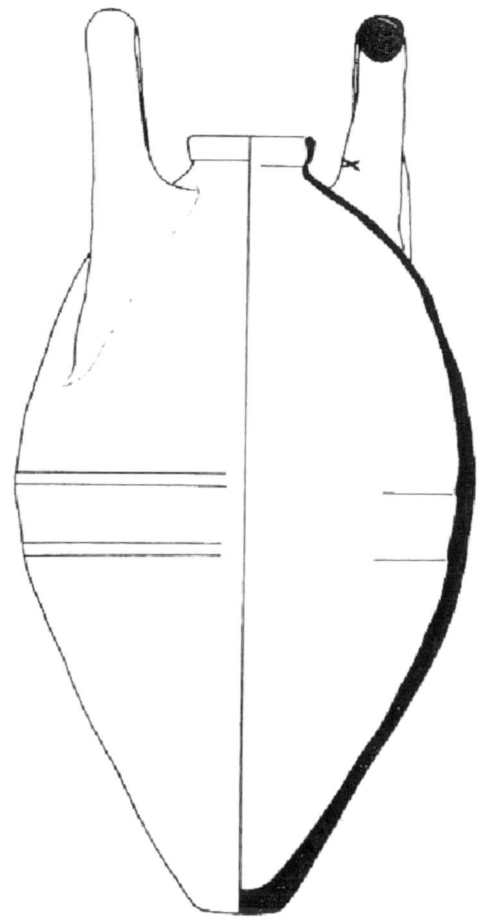

Figure 8. Cypriot "basket-handle" amphora from Tel Kabri in northern Israel

Excavations undertaken since 1991 by the Cyprus Department of Antiquities on the northwest slope of the hill known as Ampileri under the direction of Dr. Maria Hadjikosti have resulted in the recovery of a Phoenician administrative center dated to the fourth century B.C.E. The identification is supported by two groups of Phoenician inscriptions found on the floor of three rooms of the building (Hadjikosti 1997).

The presence of an olive press on the hill of Ampileri–West Terrace was known as early as the 1890s. Max Ohnefalsch-Richter, who was excavating the site at that time, discovered part of an olive mill and this information came through a publication of his wife Magda Ohnefalsch-Richter (1913). In 1973, the American Expedition to Idalion opened a number of trenches on the West Acropolis in order to investigate the fortifications but did not touch the press, which lay only a few meters to the east of their trenches (Stager and Walker 1989). It was twenty-seven years later, during the 2000 excavation season, that Maria Hadjikosti rediscovered the olive press, which proved to be the most impressive ever excavated on the island of Cyprus and beyond (Hadjisavvas 2001a:755–58, figs. 31–33). The press proper and its auxiliary spaces occupy an area of 110 square meters adjacent to the west wing of the administrative building, but at a lower level. Some of its principal elements, such as one of the three circular press beds and the *cupa* of the crushing plant, had been removed in the past.

From the crushing plant or plants, only two fragments from the basin (*cupa*) survived. One was found to the west, opposite the press installation, while the second was found on the floor of the doorway leading to the "washing area." The first fragment is 49 cm high and preserves part of the 10-cm-thick *labrum*. It also preserves part of the concave interior surface. The second fragment was not excavated and because it is lying upside down, no measurements could be taken. Both fragments are made of the same type of dense calcarenite and most probably belong to the same *cupa*.

Figure 9. The second millstone as it was found

Two well-preserved lentoid millstones belong also to the crushing plant. They were found two meters apart, the first one in the center of an open space neighboring the "washing area." The second millstone was found at the extreme west end of the southernmost pit hosting a row of weight stones (figure 9). The two millstones (*orbes*) are identical, having a flat side with a diameter of 89 cm. The maximum thickness is 40 cm. They are provided with a central square perforation with a side of 15.5 cm on the flat side reaching 17.05 on the convex side. The damage on the flat side of both stones caused by the rotary motion provides evidence for the presence of a 25-cm-high central column (*columella*) in the crushing basin. The identical sizes of the millstones in combination with the traces left by the rotary motion are indicative of the mode of operation of the crushing plant. It is obvious that the millstones were operating in pair in a classical-type *trapetum*.

A third millstone of the same type and having approximately the same measurements, where preserved, was found in a central pit that contained a row of weight stones. In order to be used as a Type 1b weight stone, the millstone had been slightly modified (Hadjisavvas 1992:fig. 115).

To cope with the increased output of the crushing plant, four presses were working from time to time. Originally, three press beds rested on a 79-cm-high stone-built bench. The 1.50-m-wide bench ran parallel to a corridor space separating the administrative building from the olive press. The northernmost press bed, now missing, had been removed from its original position. The remaining two are *in situ* (figure 10). They are circular, with a diameter of 1.13 m, and are 22–23 cm high. Both are provided with a circular channel ending in a projecting spout. The two limestone press beds are set 39 cm apart and 40 cm from the eastern wall. The two spouts project over a rectangular basin measuring 2.47 × 0.95 m. Vertically arranged rectangular slabs of gypsum confine its inner walls, while its bottom is made of packed earth. Impressions from the bases of large collecting vessels were found on the earthen bottom of the basin, just under the projecting spouts. Some mudbricks recovered within the basin were most probably used for supporting the collecting jars. A similar basin only 1.40 m in length was found north of the previous one and was originally used for collecting the output of the now-missing press bed. Its construction is similar to the first one but slabs of gypsum cover its bottom.

A third rectangular basin perpendicular to the first one was excavated to the south, running parallel to the south wall of the press room. Its inner walls are damaged but slabs of gypsum cover its bottom. A rectangular press bed was found lying on the top of the basin. It is made of a dense calcarenite slab, measuring 1.01 × 1.07 m and it is 15 cm thick. It is provided with channels running parallel to its three sides joining into a spout at one side over the basin. It has all the characteristics of the Late Bronze Age press beds excavated at Maroni, Enkomi, and Ugarit (Hadjisavvas 1992; Clot 1987).

Three rectangular pits, 2.67 m long and 0.8–1.0 cm wide, with a depth ranging from 50 to 55 cm, were formed on the longitudinal axis of the press beds. The pits are perpendicular to the first two basins described above. The pits were formed by the construction of three long parallel stone-built platforms. The southernmost is 1 m wide, the middle one 1.2 m wide, while the northernmost is 2 m wide. This inconsistency is explained by the nature of the slope on which the platforms were founded. Rectangular limestone slabs cover the tops of the platforms. The long rectangular pits were constructed in order to receive three rows of pyramidal or basket-shaped weight stones. The platforms were used to facilitate the suspension of the weight stones on the wooden lever.

Five weight stones were found in the southernmost pit, four in the middle one, and five in the northernmost. All of them were found resting in their original position. They vary in height from 71 to 88 cm, while their measurements at base level vary from 47 to 66 cm × 18 to 40 cm. They are made of dense calcarenite or gypsum and they still preserve traces of the chisel used for their manufacture. All weights belong to Type 1b of the Cypriot classification (Hadjisavvas 1992:64). They have a horizontal and a vertical perforation in order to facilitate their suspension on the lever. Two similar weight stones were found in the corridor area, east of the press proper, where river stones cover the floor. Most probably they were used for the needs of a fourth press, in which case the lever was running parallel to the south wall of the press room but perpendicular to the rectangular press bed.

In the adjacent area, just outside the pits housing the first two groups of weight stones, three more weight stones were found in horizontal position. They all belong to Type 1a of the Cypriot classification and are similar to weight stones recovered in workshops at Kition and misinterpreted as anchors (Frost 1970:fig. 2, nos. 1, 2, 6, 8, 9, 11). They are much lighter than the ones found *in situ*. Their presence, in combination with the rectangular press bed, all hint to the existence of an earlier olive press at the site most probably dating to the Late Cypriot period.

In the central pit housing the four weight stones and at the place of the fifth one, the excavators found a circular wellhead 47 cm in diameter. The depth of the well is estimated at around 20 m, 5 m of which contained water. The wellhead was found closed with a circular slab of limestone.

Figure 10. The Idalion olive-press room seen from the east

The mode of operation of the olive press at Idalion was quite simple. The three massive wooden levers were anchored in recesses, on the eastern wall of the press room attached to the bench on which the three pressing beds originally stood. The suspension of each weight stone was possible with the help of four persons standing in pairs on the platform on both sides of the pit. The tops of the weight stones protruded a few centimeters above the pit to allow a wooden bar to be inserted in the horizontal hole of the weight stone. The length of each of the three parallel levels is estimated to 6.5 m. The olive pulp after being crushed was placed in sacks piled on the press beds. The liquid resulting from the pressing was conveyed into large open jars placed just under the projecting spouts.

There is no evidence whatsoever for the third stage of olive oil production, namely, the separation of the oil from the watery lees. Perhaps the primitive method of skimming the floating oil using a ladle or a small vessel was applied.

The olive press was roofed and it occupied part of a much larger building complex, provided with a washing area as well as an area to the west for housing the crushing plant. The washing area is situated to the south of the press proper. Its floor is made of three successive layers of large limestone blocks, in such a way as to absorb the water. Quantities of olive pits were found within this area.

The olive press of the administrative center of Idalion has been dated by its excavator, based on the currently available evidence, to the end of the Classical or the beginning of the Hellenistic period. It is so far the earliest of its type on the island and the most complete. Most of its elements were found on their original position, which enable its thorough investigation. What is obvious is its high capacity, comparable only with the much later Roman factory-like presses of North Africa or Dalmatia.

By the fourth century B.C.E., the consumption of olive oil was not the prerogative of the ruling elite alone, as it was during the prehistoric period. The large number of installations combined with their increased productivity is proof of mass consumption. But the close association of the press with the Phoenician administrative building provides further support to our earlier suggestion that olive oil production was under the direct control of either ruling elites or religious institutions (Hadjisavvas 1992). The recovery of much earlier press elements could indicate the existence of an earlier press working under the direct control of the kings of Idalion.

The discovery of a classical *trapetum* at Idalion dating at least to the first half of the fourth century B.C.E. reopens the discussion concerning the earliest appearance of the mill, which revolutionized production techniques. Thus far, the earliest stratified evidence for the use of a *trapetum*-type mill comes from the Macedonian town of Olynthos. The destruction of that town in the year 348 B.C.E. provides a *terminus ante quem* for the use of the mill during at least the middle of the fourth century B.C.E (Robinson and Graham 1938:337–43). In light of the Idalion discovery, we can now suggest either a parallel invention or a very close relation between Macedonia and Cyprus before Alexander's expedition to the East.

Bibliography

Biers, W. R., and P. McGovern, eds.
1990 *Organic Contents of Ancient Vessels: Materials Analysis and Archaeological Investigation.* MASCA Research Papers in Science and Archaeology 7. Philadelphia: University Museum, University of Pennsylvania.

Blitzer, H.
1993 Olive Cultivation and Oil Production in Minoan Crete. In *Oil and Wine Production in the Mediterranean Area*, ed. M. C. Amouretti and J-P. Brun, 163–75. BCHSup 26. Paris: Boccard.

Cadogan, G.
1984 Maroni and the Late Bronze Age of Cyprus. In *Cyprus at the Close of the Bronze Age*, ed. V. Karageorghis and J. D. Muhly, 1–10. Nicosia: A.G. Leventis Foundation.
1992 The British Museum's Work at Maroni. In *Studies in Honour of Vassos Karageorghis*, ed. G. K. Ioannides, 123–26. Nicosia: Hetaireia Kypriakōn Spoudōn.

Callot, O.
1987 Les Huileries du Bronze Récent à Ougarit: Premiers éléments pour une étude. in *Ras Shamra-Ougarit*, vol. 3, *Le Centre de la Ville (38e-44e campagnes, 1978–1984)*, ed. M. Yon, 197–212. Paris: Éditions Recherche sur les Civilisations.

Dothan, T.
1982 *The Philistines and Their Material Culture*. New Haven, Conn.: Yale University Press.

Eitam, D.
1993 "Between the [olive] rows, oil will be produced, presses will be trod..." (Job 24:11). In *Oil and Wine Production in the Mediterranean Area*, ed. M.C. Amouretti and J-P. Brun, 65–90. BCHSup 26. Paris: Boccard.

Feigl, M.
1989 *Spot Test in Organic Analysis*. 7th ed. Amsterdam: Elsevier.

Frost, H.
1970 Some Cypriot Stone-Anchors from Land Sites and from the Sea. *Report of the Department of Antiquties, Cyprus* 1970:14–24.

Gitin, S.
1996 Tel Miqne-Ekron in the Seventh Century B.C.: City Plan Development and the Oil Industry. In *Olive Oil in Antiquity: Israel and Neighbouring Countries from the Neolithic to the Early Arab Period*, ed. D. Eitam and M. Heltzer, 219–42. Padova: Sargon.

Hadjikosti, M.
1997 The Kingdom of Idalion in the Light of New Evidence. *BASOR* 308:49–63.

Hadjisavvas, S.
1991 LCIIC to LCIIIA without Intruders. In *Cypriot Ceramics: Reading the Prehistoric Record*, ed. J. A. Barlow, D. L. Bolger, and B. Kling, 173–80. University Museum Monograph 74. Philadelphia: University Museum, University of Pennsylvania.
1992 *Olive Oil Processing in Cyprus: From the Bronze Age to the Byzantine Period.* SIMA 99. Nicosia: P. Åström.
1994 Alassa Archaeological Project 1991–1993. *Report of the Department* of *Antiquities, Cyprus* 1994:107–14.
1996 Alassa: A Regional Centre of Alasia? In *Late Bronze Age Settlement in Cyprus: Function and Relationship*, ed. P. Åström and E. Herscher, 23–38. Studies in Mediterranean Archaeology and Literature Pocket-book 126. Jonsered: P. Åström.

Hadjisavvas, S., and I. Hadjisavvas
1997 Aegean Influence at Alassa. In *Cyprus and the Aegean in Antiquity: From the Prehistoric Period to the Seventh Century A.D.: Proceedings of an International Archaeological Conference, Nicosia, 8–10 December 1995*, pp. 143–48. Nicosia: Department of Antiquities of Cyprus.
2001 Seal-impressed Pithos Fragments from Alassa: Some Preliminary Thoughts. In *Contributions to the Archaeology and History of the Bronze and Iron Ages in the Eastern Mediterranean: Studies in Honour of Paul Åström*, ed. P. M. Fischer, 61–67. Vienna: Österreichisches Archäologisches Institut.
2001a Chronique des fouilles et découvertes archéologiques à Chypre en 2000. *BCH* 125:743–77.
2003 Cyprus and the Mediterranean World ca. 1600–600 B.C. In *Sea Routes from Sidon to Huelva: Interconnections in the Mediterranean 16th–6th c. B.C.*, ed. N. Stampolides, 88–102. Athens: Museum of Cycladic Art.

Karageorghis, V.
1973 *Excavations in the Necropolis of Salamis*. Vol. 3. Nicosia: Department of Antiquities of Cyprus.
2002 Cypriote Antiquities Repatriated. *Report of the Department of Antiquities, Cyprus* 2002:67–79.

Kempinski, A.
2002 *Tel Kabri: The 1986–1993 Excavation Seasons.* Tel Aviv: Institute of Archaeology, Tel Aviv University.

McGovern, P. E.
2003 *Ancient Wine: The Search for the Origins of Viniculture*. Princeton: Princeton University Press.

Negbi, O.
2005 Urbanism on Late Bronze Age Cyprus: LC II in Retrospect. *BASOR* 337:1–45.

South, A.
1989 From Copper to Kingship: Aspects of Bronze Age Society Viewed from the Vasilikos Valley. In *Early Society in Cyprus*, ed. A. G. Peltenburg, 315–24. Edinburgh: Edinburgh University Press.

Stager, L. E., and A. M. Walker
1989 *American Expedition to Idalion, Cyprus: 1973–1980.* OIC 24. Chicago: Oriental Institute, University of Chicago.

Todd, I. A.
1986 *Vasilikos Valley Project*. Vol. 1, *The Bronze Age Cemetery in Kalavasos Village*. Goteborg, Sweden: P. Åström.

Younger, W.
1966 *Gods, Men and Wine*. Cleveland, Ohio: Wine and Food Society.

Zohary, D., and P. Spiegel-Roy
1975 Beginnings of Fruit-Growing in the Old World. *Science* 187:319–27.

17. The Dawn of an Age: Megiddo in the Iron Age I

by Baruch Halpern

How were Canaanite centers incorporated into ancient Israel in the eleventh–tenth centuries B.C.E.? The subject is now a dull one, reviewed, summarized, and revised almost without surcease since the late nineteenth century. In the last fifteen years, its attraction for scholars has flagged. The events in question are datable by various scientific methods, but understanding them requires two other elements: a familiarity with texts, as in all historical archaeology, combined with what C. Wright Mills (1959) once called "the sociological imagination." Dates and even sizes of sites lack explanatory power in themselves; they only furnish a framework within which explanation is possible. Social processes are more diagnostic of the incorporation of new cultural traits.

Most students of the history of ancient Israel are depressingly familiar with the theories about the transition into the Iron Age I. The first theory, of course, was that of a massive conquest. Nineteenth-century textual scholarship devoted much time to parleying alleged contradictions or even hints in the text into prehistory—for example, the Leah tribes entered at one point, the Rachel tribes at another, and so on. The method resembled that applied earlier by scholars such as Niebuhr (1811–1812) to Roman and, later, Greek history (Müller 1970 [1825]).

But based on the indications of less speculative textual study, particularly of the account of individual successes and failures of Israelite tribes in occupying their territories (Judges 1), and adding a Weberian twist, Albrecht Alt introduced the theory of pastoralist "infiltration" into the hills. The "infiltration" precipitated conflict with agrarians, in what was at the time considered the inevitable confrontation between herders and farmers. The final stage in the process was the taking of towns by the pastoralists, particularly in the lowlands. This led to the inauguration of a United Monarchy of Israel and Judah under the kingship of Saul (Alt 1953a; 1953b).

Another model was introduced by George Mendenhall (1962) and consolidated by Norman Gottwald (1979). In their view, lowland peasants took to the hills to flee urban oppression. Although Mendenhall and Gottwald dated Israel's emergence to the twelfth century, they relied principally on evidence from the Amarna archive of the fourteenth century, about "rebels" known as Habiru, which they equated with king-hating "Hebrews" (Mendenhall 1962; Gottwald 1978; cf. Loretz 1984). Unfortunately, the Amarna evidence is cloaked in the rhetoric of relations with an imperial center, such that one's enemies, even governors of city-states, could be called Habiru, which is to say "subversives" (Halpern 1983; Moran 1987).

Supporting Alt, on the basis of survey data, Israel Finkelstein proposed in his dissertation that Israelites arrived as settlers, starting first in the easternmost reaches of the central hill country (Finkelstein 1983). That the process was a combination of all these processes is a view associated particularly with the name of Volkmar Fritz, who emphasized the symbiotic relations of the settlers with post-Late Bronze Age populations (1987; 1990; 1994). All views not based on a naive reading of the Book of Joshua agree that highland populations descended on lowland towns. This seems to have been the case, although at varying dates.[1] North of Philistia, the Book of Kings *assumes* Solomon's later incorporation of these sites. Yet no known Israelite takes them (and thus we can be certain that David didn't—Halpern 2001). Indeed, taken quite literally, the biblical conquest accounts themselves claim, however improbably, that Joshua controlled the countryside, but that it was only after his death that Israelites supplanted local inhabitants, especially in the lowlands (Halpern 1992). In general, every model we have presupposes Israelite hill pastoralists, partly sedentarizing, overwhelming urban Canaanite centers along the trade routes.

The process of upland polity articulation culminated in the mid-to-late eleventh century, when the kinship system of highland populations was waxing and maturing, intermarriage with lowland populations was probably increasing, and a certain degree of circumscription was going on in the hills (for the latter, see Coote 1990).[2] In part, these phenomena reflect the fact that interregional trade was at a nadir, with Egypt's empire decisively on the wane. The issue of drought as a factor has often been mooted, most generally in connection with Ramesses III's aid to the Hittites, but also in connection with lower Nile levels and apparent drought in Mesopotamia in the

[1] See the ground-breaking study of David Ilan (1999) and, for a summary of all these positions, Fritz 1990; 1994.

[2] For arguments from pottery and other archaeological indicators for the identity of the upland and lowland populations, see W. G. Dever 1987; 1990; 1993; 1995.

succeeding half-century (Stiebing 1989; Neumann and Parpola 1987). Yet the transition from the end of Late Bronze into the later stages of the Iron I remains a puzzle. In Philistia, colonizers arrive shortly after 1200 B.C.E. (against Finkelstein 1995, see Halpern 2001:454–60 from a textual and monumental perspective, Mazar 1997 from a pottery perspective, and Stager 1995 from a political and archaeological perspective). But why the later dwindling of other urban centers? Megiddo may prove no template for other sites, but based on Egyptian withdrawal and the temporary interdiction of long-range overland trade, it offers one example to be considered, an example with clear parallels at Amarna, in the records of other ancient societies, and, truth be told, in the descriptive rather than theoretical writings of Karl Marx (2003).

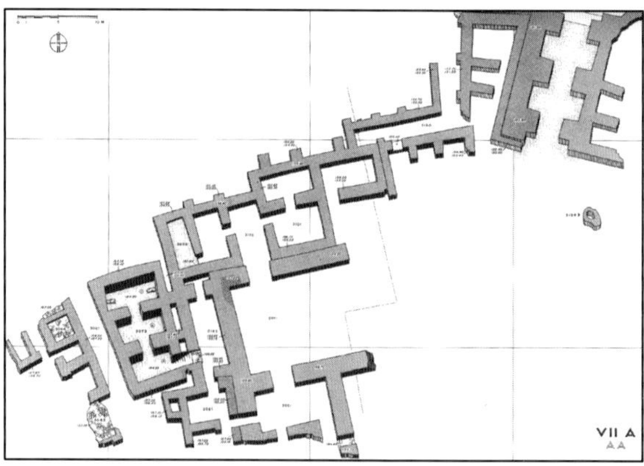

Figure 1. Plans of Megiddo palaces (Area AA) in Strata X–VII and of Temple 2048 (from Loud 1948)

Courtesy of the Oriental Institute of the University of Chicago

At Megiddo, the palace of Stratum X (figure 1) by the acropolis gate is extensive (we now know that Middle Bronze settlement existed at the foot of the existing tell, at least on the north: Franklin 2006; Peersman 2006). Brian Hesse relates (in conversation) that there was camel in a sample from a LB I level in Area N, below the tell in the northwest. Although extraordinary, this is not inconsonant with what one might expect in light of the archaeological demography of that era, in which Megiddo was an almost unrivaled hub of trade before the revival of other sites in LB IIA. In any event, the Middle Bronze levels at the foot of the tell, and perhaps earlier materials, are now buried beneath 3–4 m of colluvium from the nearby hills. But the palace sees marked expansion, consolidation, and the thickening of its walls in Stratum IX (figure 1). Stratum IX follows or just precedes Thutmosis III's taking of the site (Halpern 2000:540–42). It is probably in this stratum, too, that Migdol Temple 2048 was constructed, as in monumentality it seems to be of a piece with that of the palace and of the rampart that was constructed around the site either late in Stratum X or early in Stratum IX (contra Epstein 1965:213; Kempinski 1989:83; Kenyon 1969:49–53).[3] Certainly, the plethora of imported fine wares characterizing Stratum IX indicate ready access to the coast, and probably the eastern Jezreel, and fit neatly into the context of Egypt's focus on Megiddo as an administrative node.

The palace of Stratum VIII, with its extensive treasure trove, succeeds to its predecessor's space, suggesting continuity, while expanding in area (Loud 1948:22–25). At this time, a massive public structure was erected above and just within the earthen rampart of Stratum IX on the lower tell (Ilan, Franklin, and Hallote 2000:86–92). The latter may have functioned as a reception area, or as a sort of customs house. The next palace, of Stratum VIIB, burnt down after 1200 B.C.E., without the site generally being destroyed (see Ussishkin 1995 for the theory that the VIIB palace was merely the lower floor of that of VIIA). And the destruction of the VIIA palace is normally dated around 1140 B.C.E. Those defending this date assume that the base of the statue of Ramses VI, found "under a wall of Stratum VIIB" in Room 1832 of Area CC (Breasted 1948:135 and fig. 409), was misstratified, and was really found in Stratum VIA; they assign its origin to VIIA (as Harrison 2004:9, with bibliography), although phases of Stratum VII were not reliably distinguished in Area CC (see Loud 1948:114). Notably, a basalt offering table found in the remains of the VIII palace in Area DD (and still on the surface there) seems to have parallels in our Area M, in the Schumacher Trench, in LB II (Loud 1948:114 and fig. 411; Schumacher 1908:taf. 16, 20), though in each case survival from Stratum IX is possible. Temple 2048 continued in active use in these strata, though its walls were significantly thinner, and its earlier projecting towers atrophied, in Stratum VIIA.

Figure 2. Corbeled "tomb" at Megiddo

Ongoing Megiddo excavations, under the aegis of Tel Aviv University since 1992, shed light on the transition from Late Bronze to Iron I culture on the tell. Our Area M occupies the center of the tell. Its lower part sits in the trench identified by Schumacher as his *Mittelburg* (Schumacher 1908:75–77). Since 1998, it has not been clear whether the "corbeled" or

[3] Chicago attributed this temple to Stratum VIII; Kempinski (1989) to Stratum X. However, it seems prudent to associate the temple's origins to the first, and not a secondary, stage of Megiddo's elevation, under Egyptian auspices, to be the crown jewel of the Empire in Canaan. As Amihai Mazar has observed, the latest pottery on the floor of the temple stems from Stratum VI (Mazar 1985; 2002; Kempinski 1989:83, 185; Ussishkin 1995; Harrison 2004: 4, 10, 19). Still, Chicago found no substantial architectural evidence of the temple's existence at that time; if there is a similar structure in Stratum V, it is much smaller, and located to the northeast. It is possible, thus, that the sacred precinct continued in use in Strata VI and V, but that the building itself no longer stood; or, that, as Mazar suggests, the building continued in use, whether or not for sacral purposes, and that elements on site in Stratum VI continued traditional forms of worship. As to the glacis, our excavations in Area F found no evidence of anything other than LB I buried into its top, which could stem from later in the period; and, below it was MB IIC (see Franklin 2006a). Finally, while the Canaanite kings clearly chose Megiddo as their base in the battle against Thutmosis III, it is in this period that the construction of the IX palace could have been begun, with its more elaborate fittings coming later in the layer. See further Halpern 2000:542 and n. 9.

"Mycenean tomb" was built in the Late Bronze or Iron I, not least because the tomb was found empty, except for some open vessel fragments found by Schumacher, who dug two meters past the floor (1908:taf. 20), and because it was subterranean—witness the provisions, detected in 1998, against the seepage of water into the structure in the form of plastering of the outer sides of the tomb (see, generally, Finkelstein, Ussishkin, and Deutsch 2006:76; note also Schumacher 1908:75–76 on the interior mortar). Moreover, no provisions for drainage were made despite its low position (on drainage, cf. Isa. 28:15, 18).

Between the corbeled tomb and Schumacher's *Nordburg*, a foundation trench for the tomb cut through a Late Bronze II floor on the eastern balk. Were the tomb coeval with the LB *Nordburg*, in our LB II M-6, one would expect the mudbrick collapse of the LB area to reach it to a reasonable height. If later, the tomb was, however, tailored to remains of the *Nordburg* by the builders of M-4 or M-5, who constructed a villa above on the remains of M-6. Some maintain that the original tomb was only partly subterranean, but its recent history suggests the opposite—it is collapsing from people crossing it on foot, and from rainwater. And this in the course of just six years.[4]

Just to the south of the corbeled tomb stood tombs with MB and LB materials. To the northeast stood the Migdol temple of the Late Bronze, the successor to the one surviving EB (or, in Ussishkin's view, IB) megaron, 4040. Rachel Hallote (1994:69–92) argues that the original Migdol temple, surrounded by graves, succeeded a mortuary cult, which flourished and exhibited an increase in the insignia of rulership versus the insignia of warfare associated with burials of the EB. The insertion of the corbeled tomb in VI would represent a return to Middle Bronze tradition (and, further below), the more so if the Temple 2048's last floor is VIA (Kempinski 1989:83, 185; Mazar 2002). Notionally, the Migdol is the only public structure to survive from Stratum VII into VI, when stone is rejected, at least in VIA, in favor of mudbrick, possibly for sumptuary reasons, or possibly because extreme heat baked the bricks into stone and thus preserved them. Still, it is possible that beneath the VIA connections to the corbeled tomb lies a VIIA predecessor. The principal argument for it is the existence of structures similar to this tomb in the LB, and Mycenean archetypes. The principal argument against it is that a structure that would have been terrestrial in the LB had then to be buried in the Iron I under a massive fill with a complex and crowded set of retaining walls.

Subterranean chambers are subterranean, even in the case of Mycenean tomb types, and, comparatively, of painted banquet chambers in later, archaizing, Etruscan tombs. So the hypothesis of a partially terrestrial VIIA antecedent to the structure is unlikely on this score as well—not just because the population of VI would have had to have buried the area.

The tomb-complex is probably VIA, with no LB antecedent except the Migdol royal temple. This latter can of course have continued in use, into Iron I, whether architecturally complete or not. Earlier, the MB burials in the sacral area conform more or less to the church and cemetery model for the use of the space (see Hallote 1994).

There *is* bricky collapse in the Stratum VII Area M-6 (LB II), as Finkelstein points out. M-6 contained remnants of buildings from Schumacher's *Nordburg*. There remains a foundation trench north of the tomb, down to a large basin.[5] The tomb is on this view VIA on VIIA walls.[6] In a sense, this is the opposite of the eastern exposure of the Solomonic gate, since larger stones are piled on smaller, which is either a stratigraphic or a hydrodynamic indication. The possibility of M-5 tomb construction thus remains.

Figure 3. Bronze cymbals from Stratum VIA

Photograph courtesy of the Megiddo Expedition of Tel Aviv University

[4] Efforts were made in 2002 to reinforce and preserve the failing structure.

[5] I imagine there was also one from the south, now invisible except perhaps at the very bottom, where further excavation might destabilize the structure anew.

[6] The architect who supervised the conservation suggested that the lower part is very different from the upper, although he nevertheless sees a unified structure here. If one dates the original structure to the LB II, one would do best to place it later, rather than earlier, in this period, and under a deliberate platform fill, and then to conclude that any architecture to which it was originally connected was cleared in the construction of Stratum VIA.

In 2000, we connected Stratum VIA to the tomb. In that level, at the entrance from a VIA structure to the tomb, we found a pair of bronze cymbals, with clips for handles set through their center (figure 3). We also found a number of large storage vessels. Norma Franklin, then supervising Area M, reports that excavations in 2004 yielded what was possibly a flute, along with further storage vessels. The combination of storage jars, musical instruments, and an empty tomb, with the exception of a few open vessel fragments, suggests that the corbeled tomb was actually a cultic structure, and specifically a *marzēăḥ*, or point of assembly for a funerary society, or of an association identified with piety toward the dead.

There are other subterranean rooms. An example is Jerusalem Cave 1 in the seventh century, where numerous figurines appear, in association, as at Megiddo, to a terrestrial building (Franken and Steiner 1990:30–50, with comparison to Samaria shrine E 207). Another subterranean room was found below a house in Late Bronze Shechem (Campbell 2002:188, 192, 201, 205–8, interpreted as a storage area). Other sites probably also contain such rooms, and some tombs at Ugarit may not only be tombs—note those with breathing tubes (compare with the central hole in the roof of the corbeled tomb) may have been *marzēăḥ*s. These sites may represent holdovers of the family mortuary cult of the MB into the period of public/royal worship in the LB (so the implication of Hallote 1994).

Attestations of the *marzēăḥ* come from Ugarit (see Miller 1971, with bibliography; Friedman 1979–1980; Halpern 1979; on tombs, Lewis 1989; Schmidt 1996), Israel (Amos 6:3–7; Isa. 28:14–15, 18–21 [Halpern 1986], indirectly, indicating celebration underground, Jer. 16:5–9, also with an implication of performance), Phoenician texts (Sakkunyaton on child sacrifice, but more directly the Marseille Tariff [KAI 69]), Palmyra (extensively: Hillers and Cussini 1996:386–87), Elephantine, the Mishnah (Porten 1968:179–86), Greece (*homotaphoi*), and Rome (*collegia funeraria*). The Greek and Roman versions, probably themselves under eastern influence, were sometimes outlawed along with other cross-cutting groups, such as trade unions (see Ward 1910:1.127, 278; 342, 548; 2.168, 199, 253, 268, 295–96, 348–50). Latterly, suggestions for identifying other physical structures with the *marzēăḥ* have been submitted: citing some of these parallels, Bietak and Stager have plausibly proposed the association of extramural MB structures with its antecedents (Bietak 2003, with additional bibliography; Stager 2006, adverting to the Ugaritic and Israelite evidence in particular for the identification of its banquet and mercantile character, as in Greece and Rome).

The Ugaritic and Palmyrene evidence makes it clear that storage was characteristic of these societies. The Israelite evidence makes it clear that music and banqueting were integral as well. This again comports with evidence in the area and in epigraphs, and with the transformation, in the ninth or eighth century, of Etruscan burial customs and with the paintings involving not just banqueting but accompanying music in the tombs.

Such funerary societies had multiple functions. They were, of course, the antecedents of the Greek symposium (Burkert 1992:19 with bibliography) and the familial Roman banquet. In addition, they functioned as orders, to which members united by real or fictive kinship belonged, and in which they shared a common interest, particularly in the protection of landholdings. Most of all, they represented holdovers of the mortuary orientation that characterized most of the Middle Bronze Age (Hallote 1994:69–86), with some exceptions in MB IIC (Hallote 1994:98).

To the east of and above the corbeled tomb was a large mudbrick mansion (figure 4), destroyed in the fierce conflagration at the end of Stratum VIA—Schumacher's "burnt layer" (1908:75–90; Finkelstein, Ussishkin, and Deutsch 2006). This compound was probably a courtyard structure surrounded by dwelling and storage rooms. It included a dromos entrance into the corbeled tomb. So, in the center of the tell in Iron IA, we have a patrician residence with a cult focused on the underworld and perhaps collective ancestors—but collective patrician ancestors of this and perhaps other compounds (the *rapiʾu* of Stager 2006), not necessarily those of earlier kings of the site.

Figure 4. Stratum VIA courtyard structure located east of and above the corbeled tomb

Photograph by B. Halpern

Another large estate occupies the southeastern corner of the tell. In 2000, we broke through to the floors of the massive VIA destruction in Area K, Level 4. This was a courtyard house characterized by heavy and varied domestic industry, from flint retouching—represented by hundreds of retouched flints and pieces of debitage—to brick manufacture and stockpiling to oil stockpiling (and therefore marketing) to the import of Nile perch. The oil and perch probably belong together, suggesting the manufacture of fish oil and/or fish sauce in the area; and the perch, which appeared in large chunks represented by articulated spinal sections, is an oily fish (up to 20% oil content) not readily dried. The large chunks, represented by articulated spinal sections reflecting pieces up to 17.5 kg in size (Lernau 2000), must have been shipped in oil or water (Halpern 2000:554). The presence of the Nile perch indicates direct or mediated trade between K and Egypt. There was also a collection of fine vessels (figure 5). We are talking of considerable wealth.

Figure 5. Vessels from Stratum VIA, Area K-4

Photograph courtesy of the Megiddo Expedition of Tel Aviv University

The K-4 level was destroyed with Stratum VIA, in a fire exacerbated by the oil stocks. Below, K-5 was patchy. But the stone walls of K-6, on which those of K-4 were almost entirely built, met a flagstone floor, on which some centimeters of dirt had accumulated by the time of K-4. The industry differs from that in K-4, but includes, for example, an olive press (another of which must have been present nearby in K-4). K-6 remains in the Iron I pottery tradition.

K-5, thus, is only a group of isolated changes made over time in the architecture. The transition from K-6 to K-4 remains within Stratum VI. Since most walls of K-4 are directly atop or abutting walls of K-6, we are speaking about continuity from VIB, or at least an earlier phase of Stratum VI, to VIA, the final Iron I phase of occupation on the site.

But, as at ᶜEin Zippori (Dessel 1999), the continuity runs deeper (see already Finkelstein 2000; 2003). There is a patchy K-7. Again, the alterations suggest a series of independent improvements to the earlier plan. In 2004, we exposed the LB IIB level K-8.[7] Most of its walls, too, directly underlie those of K-6 and K-4 (for further continuity from VIIA to VI, except in the area of the northern palace, AA, see Harrison 2004:10). The difference in K-8 is the presence, on the edge of the tell, of small square rooms, possibly for grain storage, in which, incidentally, a scarab ring with the image of Amun was found. The bottom of a Mycenean figurine of the "zebra signaling a touchdown" was found as well, in the middle square in the south. Gottlieb Schumacher associated another Mycenean-style sherd with Stratum VI (1908:taf. 24), along with numerous scarabs and seals, bronze and iron objects, lion figurines, and statuettes of baboons (1908:taf. 25–28).

What we see here is the development of a patrimonial estate (for which concept see Schloen 2001, although the economic model omits the issue of positive externalities, and Stager 2003). The estates developed through the accumulation of capital earned through intensive and extensive agriculture, through industry—mainly the processing of agricultural products and imported goods—through the diversification of activities, and especially through mediation of trade among partners north and south. Over time this led to the vast wealth exhibited in VIA in K-4 and M-4, including massive wooden beams in various areas of the site (our K-4 and see Harrison 2004:19 and n. 8). Indeed, the Ramses VI statue base "under" a wall of VII in CC may really be from one of several such estates in the southern part of the mound, with the statue removed at a later date, and the base being left, as at Twenty-first Dynasty Dabᶜa.[8] In this area, too, Chicago's excavation produced considerable evidence of continuity from VIIA directly to VIA (Harrison 2004:19). A large number of Aegean-, Cypriot-, or Philistine-style loomweights (Stager 1991:15) appeared in Area CC, along with its "bathtubs" (and Area AA, where the four "bathtubs" may have been associated with textile or with wine production: compare Harrison 2004:17–20), and a number of bronzes.

[7] This will not be published until *Megiddo 5* is assembled and issued (probably in 2010 or so).

[8] One scenario might be that either the proprietor of the VIIA palace or that of some other, patrimonial, estate, forcibly removed the statue itself to his own establishment. A relocation of the Twenty-first Dynasty to Tanis may have been roughly contemporary with this development. On the other hand, the statue may have reached the site only in VIB. See below.

The wealth of VIA was not focused on a palace near the gate of the mound. Rather, exotic objects such as offering stands, theriomorphic containers for precious liquids, seals, a model shrine, scarabs, amulets, and other imports such as Aegean-style sconces are distributed around the site (Paice 2004; Halpern 2000: 553–54).

K-6, assuming that Stratum VI evolved at differential rates in different parts of the tell, represents the earliest phase of Stratum VI in Area K. It divulged two unexpected zoological finds. Two butchered dogs—one a puppy in a pot—have parallels in the Mycenean IIIC1:b phases of Ashkelon, Tel Miqne (Ekron), and Tel Batash (Timnah), though the butchered adult dog is so far paralleled only at Ashkelon.[9] Pig is present as well, and it is attested in elevated quantity at Mycenean IIIC1:b and perhaps early bichrome levels at Ashkelon, Miqneh and Batashi (e.g., Hesse 1986; 1990). This and the Mycenean figurine, and some late sub-Mycenean ware, more amply represented in the Chicago excavations of the stratum, attest relations with Philistia, or one of its congeners, in a private estate rather than in the palace, as do ceramic pieces, such as the sconces, in AA and CC with Cypriote or Aegean connections. (Some scholars have suggested a Philistine presence in AA Building 2072, as Kempinski 1989:83.) In addition, the Amun scarab ring in Area K attests an Egyptian relation, as does the Ramses VI statue base in CC Room 1832. Although K-6 postdates the destruction of the VIIA palace, the presence of such ambassadors there, in a villa, mirrors the distribution of wealth in the rest of VIA. Relations with foreign ambassadors were now separated from the palace economy of the LB. By contrast, the Phoenician bichrome in VIA probably reflects ordinary local trade.

A possible parallel is to the history of British involvement in India. Originally, the East India Company sent agents to negotiate and manage trade. But their trade embassies rapidly became embroiled in local conflicts and wound up taking sides with local factions; the rival factions were in turn supported by competing external groups, primarily French but also Portuguese. The same model applies to British involvement in southern Africa. This is probably the history of competing East Greek and Anatolian trade sponsors in Philistia as well (and note Barako 2000). Here, we should be seeking clear demarcation of the outsiders' political and cultural differences, and regard them as competing with one another. (Imagine speaking of the "European" conquest of India in the eighteenth century, rather than the "British".) Instead, it has been scholars' tendency to lump the intruders together as "Sea Peoples" on the model of Ramesses III, or as "Philistines," on the model of biblical texts starting perhaps in the late twelfth or eleventh century (Exodus 15); this model was certainly regnant by the tenth century (2 Samuel). But it may instead reflect eventual Philistine domination of other groups in the Pentapolis.[10] The eleventh-century Onomasticon of Amenope, after all, lists Sherden, Tjekker, and Philistines separately, after three names separating them from an enumeration of the towns our texts associate with "Philistia" (Gardiner 1948:nos. 262–70 [261 may be Ekron]).

In other words, had we an archive comparable to that of Amarna for the twelfth and eleventh centuries, we should likely be hearing a great deal about competition and conflict even among the "Philistine" cities. Still, at Megiddo, there is no real sign, in the sense that we encounter in Philistia and at Dor, of exogenous colonization after VIIA, the last Late Bronze city there. Indeed, Finkelstein (2003:77) speaks of a "New Canaan" on the Iron I horizon, in which he includes not just Megiddo VIA but corresponding phases at Kinneret, Rehov, Dor, and possibly Tell Keisan, as well as numerous village sites (see esp. Ilan 1999:162–71; Faust 2000). Mazar (2003:93) adds Yoqneam to the list. The social developments hypothesized here at Megiddo may have been relatively widespread in the wealthier areas of the north.

The K estate hosted foreign visitors. The *marzēăḥ* in Area M is away from the palatial area, AA (if, indeed, Building 2072 there *was* a palace), by the northern gate. In AA, Building 2072 exhibits contacts with Philistia and with Cyprus, as well as with Phoenicia. These Stratum VI estates had lands in the Jezreel and probably the hills along the Wadi ᶜAra, otherwise almost devoid of LB occupation (Gadot 1999: 133–35).[11] Those living on the tell were the elite,

---

[9] Brian Hesse, who identified the bones, in conversation; Hesse reports that the phenomenon occurs in late second millennium Spain in quantity, citing a conference paper that was unfortunately never published.

[10] One theory might be that the group who first developed Philistine bichrome dominated the others, whether by diplomacy (Ekron) or by warfare (Ashdod).

[11] There is no indication that the VIB/VIA distinction is a chronological indicator for more than local architecture. But for the distribution of objects in these layers, and particularly in the destruction of VIA, see Halpern 2000:553–54. The flint knapping in K-4 indicates an agricultural hinterland for the site, as does the massive quantity of olives and of oil there, not to mention the K-6 oil press. The textile industry in Area CC suggests either local or contracted

probably housing dependent populations, to judge at least from the skeletons found in Area K, and the larger number found by the University of Chicago expedition in Area CC (Harrison 2004:3–4, 8–9), some partly buried, others not. This fits, too, with the presence of the Ramses VI statue base. Both K and Area CC yielded a number of collar-rim storejars as well (Mazar 2002 versus Finkelstein, Zimhoni, and Kafri 2000:254 on the association of the type with VIA): this suggests that highland populations were at least trade partners, mixing like the Egyptians and Philistines into local politics, and possibly were even involved in connubium (see Esse 1992).

On this scenario, the VIIA palace, and even the VIIB palace, may have been destroyed by wealthy kin-groups, proprietors of these estates, as once suggested by Albrecht Alt (1953c). In Alt's view, the "aristocracy" was in league with the Tjekker at Dor and especially with the Philistines. But the indications are rather that its various factions were in league with and especially trading, already in VIIA, with various foreign powers, possibly including competing groups among the Philistines, Phoenicians, and Cypriots, as well as the Tjekker and Egypt. The grievances of the local elites will have related to the resumption of trade toward the middle of Iron IA, at a regional level, partly because of Sea-People colonization and the *cordon sanitaire* erected around the colonies by Egypt (see Stager 1995; compare with the response of Finkelstein and Singer-Avitz 2001; Finkelstein 2005:33). While the economic stakes in such regional trade were probably small, the issue of social prestige loomed large, at least among the prosperous. In this view, the fall of the palace and the transformation of the site into the mudbrick town of Stratum VI, was partly a result of the introduction of Sea-People, Egyptian, Syrian, Canaanite, and Israelite elements as allies of some of the aristocracy on the site against the king. A picture of competing alliances, among the Sea Peoples themselves and with other local populations, emerges. Where Egypt stood after Ramesses III is an issue.

To review, after the Asiatic campaigns of Thutmosis I had established Egyptian claims to an extensive empire, Thutmosis III made Megiddo IX the forward staging point for abiding administrative expansion in Asia. Under Amenhotep II, witnessed among other things by the organization of an expedition leaving from Megiddo in the Taanach Letters, it retained this status (Halpern 2000:543–45). The palace in Stratum IX did not just expand, but featured imports, such as seashell floors and Golan basalt, and exhibited some walls serviceable as fortifications (a similar thickness of walls is found in a massive Stratum VIII structure on the lower tell in the north). Meanwhile, the erection of Migdol Temple 2048 restored a royal cult to the sacral area in BB, replacing the familial cult located there during the Middle Bronze.

In Stratum VIII, the royal establishment continued waxing with support from the Egyptian state and army, and perhaps by mobilizing local and even regional resources based on that support. The palace, though larger, no longer exhibits the massive walls of Stratum IX. We now find large basalt tables both in the palace and in Schumacher's *Nordburg*. Although the palace of VIIB was destroyed, signaling the weakening of royal authority on site, the palace of VIIA was wealthier still, including the Megiddo ivories. Even though the durables in this stratum could be heirlooms, they attest the accumulation and concentration of wealth specifically in the palace. Independence was unimaginable until later; but the statue of Ramesses VI could well be an artifact of the transition to Stratum VI, some of whose early phases exhibited stone foundations and even structural stone wainscoting that might be mistaken for construction of an earlier stratum. It is a possibility that the statue base was anchored in a secondary location by a Stratum VI foundation structure, although it must have reached the site originally in VIIA (compare with Harrison 2004:11).

The later stages of the LB are represented in new excavation, thus far, primarily in our K-8. On that temporal horizon, the palace, whose defenses had earlier diminished, declined and fell. Further analysis is necessary to isolate insulae in VIIB–A architecture around the site, to complement the case of K-8; there may be several in CC (covered admirably in Harrison 2004). The object would be to identify further patrimonial compounds in this layer, and, later, in Stratum VI architecture in the southern end, where the Ramses VI base appears in Area CC. But certainly the Ramses VI statue should have been in the northern, palatial sector of the VIIA site were powerful forces not at work elsewhere at Megiddo in securing contacts—and this possibly already after the demise of the VIIB palace—recalling again the shrinking of the royal temple, 2048 in VIIA. Notably, the basalt basins of the VIII (DD) palace enjoy parallels only in M, and we have olive presses in K-6 and M-6. Note also the growth of insulae compounds from VIIB to VIA. The shift in VB could not, in any sense, be more clear—VB represents the first serious break since IX. But, again, outside the area of the northwest

pastoralism, more likely the former, and indications of local wine production suggest engagement in viticulture as well.

palace, there is considerable continuity from Stratum VIIA to Stratum VI.

But the key point is that the changes in the Canaanite city-states, either in the eleventh or indeed in the twelfth centuries, do not reflect "peasant revolt" or even "flight." At Amarna, the situation is similar (Halpern 1983:88). For example, it is a regular complaint that captors ransom captives back to their original, mostly coastal, towns for certain sums (as Knudtzon 1915:55:48–52; 116:42–44; 245:24–35; 292:48–51; and, probably, 89:39–50; the issue is related to demands from Egyptian officials). Why? Because in the LB, cash-crop agriculture in the hills was a rarity. Rather, as in the accounts of the Peloponnesian War, much of the conflict was among elite groups, some of whom allied, say, with Amurru, and some of whom allied with forces to the south—this is why Rib-Addi's successor in Byblos was in fact his brother (Knudtzon 1915:136–38; 142; 162:7–21). There was probably precious little authentic versus convenient loyalty to Egypt.

The palace of the Canaanite city-state in the twelfth–eleventh centuries depended heavily on the support of landed classes, of clients, who had accumulated land, capital, and power over the course of the LB II. Some of them allied with elements—as Rib-Addi's brother and his faction did—that opposed the policies and network of alliances of their predecessors. But this was inevitably the nature of politics within the hierarchy. What is interesting at Megiddo is that there is little evidence of much destruction outside of the LB palaces. This suggests that, in the instance, it was the local elites who, probably in the absence of a real Egyptian garrison, and thus after about 1160, turned on the king. In line with authentic Marxian ideas, the revolt was not proletarian, but *haut bourgeois*.

One can imagine that processes, different but not dissimilar, characterized other lowland sites in the aftermath of Egypt's effective withdrawal. But the simple opposition of palace to commons is not reflected at Megiddo. Such a theory would underestimate the complexity of political alliance, among differential parts of the palace, the elite and the commons, as well as with foreign agents, that no doubt was more than less characteristic of city-state reality. Even for Amarna, with its rich documentation, no adequately diachronic and complex political analysis along such lines has been done.

How the lowland sites were integrated into the United Monarchy of Israel remains a mystery. David did not conquer them—certainly, no such claim is lodged in Samuel, and Judges 1 simply reinforces this impression. Yet Dor and the Jezreel fortresses were integrated into Solomon's kingdom. There are only two possibilities, disallowing conquest. The first is that locals who hoped to control sites such as Dor and Megiddo made common cause with the Israelite United Monarchy against factions of the Philistines; the latter, after all, were projecting their influence up the coast and across the Jezreel Valley (1 Samuel 27–2 Samuel 1).

The second possibility is that local "aristocracies" engaged in warfare against one another on all sides of the conflicts of the time—between Saul and the "Philistines," between David and Absalom, and in circumstances of which we are not informed—some of them on the assumption that David would permit autonomy in local governance, although demanding remissions from them. The installation of regional governors under Solomon (1 Kings 4:7–19), all with primary loyalty to the national state in Jerusalem (Mettinger 1971:120–121; Halpern 1974), and the dedication of former city-states such as Megiddo and Hazor to administrative populations, only put paid to that arrangement in some cases, suggesting that these towns were resistant to the new order (versus, say, Rehov or Taanach). Still, the wholesale incorporation of the Jezreel and coast into Solomon's kingdom does suggest—as does the archaeology—that the Israelite state, under Saul, David (perhaps most likely), or Solomon picked up the pieces of a system of political and economic relations that had fallen apart. Whether the origin of the change was Saulide, or came in the context of the Absalom revolt, is not yet clear.

What *is* clear from the evidence at hand is that we should be placing a premium on two aspects of scholarship. One is the political economy reflected in biblical texts about the early monarchic period, including patterns of settlement and the development of administrative structures (on this last, see Niemann 1993). The other is the archaeology of social organization, and economic and mercantile relations, and their symbolic as well as practical expression, a subject to which Larry Stager has been a consistently innovative contributor. It is a pleasure and an honor to dedicate this article to him.

Bibliography

Alt, A.

1953a Die Landnahme der Israeliten in Palästina. In *Kleine Schriften zur Geschichte des Volkes Israels*, by A. Alt, 1:89–125. Munich: C. H. Beck.

1953b Erwägungen über die Landnahme der Israeliten in Palästina. In *Kleine Schriften zur Geschichte des Volkes Israels*, by A. Alt, 1:126–75. Munich: C. H. Beck.

1953c Megiddo im Übergang vom Kanaanäischen zum Israelitischen Zeitalter. In vol. 1 of *Kleine Schriften zur Geschichte des Volkes Israels*, by A. Alt, 1:256–73. Munich: C. H. Beck.

Barako, T. J.

2000 The Philistine Settlement as Mercantile Phenomenon? *AJA* 104:513–30.

Ben-Tor, A., and D. Ben-Ami

1998 Hazor and the Archaeology of the Tenth Century B.C.E. *IEJ* 48:1–37.

Bietak, M.

2003 Temple or "Bêt Marzeaḥ"? In *Symbiosis, Symbolism, and the Power of the Past: Canaan, Ancient Israel, and Their Neighbors from the Late Bronze Age through Roman Palaestina*, ed. W. G. Dever and S. Gitin, 155–68. Winona Lake, Ind.: Eisenbrauns.

Breasted, J. H.

1948 Bronze Base of a Statue of Ramses VI Discovered at Megiddo. In *Megiddo*, vol. 2, *Seasons of 1935–39 (Text)*, ed. G. Loud, 135–38. OIP 62. Chicago: Oriental Institute, University of Chicago.

Burkert, W.

1992 *The Orientalizing Revolution: Near Eastern Influence on Greek Culture in the Early Archaic Age*. Cambridge, Mass.: Harvard University Press.

Coote, R. B.

1990 *Early Israel: A New Horizon*. Philadelphia: Fortress.

Dessel, J. P.

1999 Tell ᶜEin Zippori and the Lower Galilee in the Late Bronze and Iron Ages: A Village Perspective. In *Galilee through the Centuries: Confluence of Cultures*, ed. E. M. Meyers, 1–32. Duke Judaic Studies 1. Winona Lake, Ind.: Eisenbrauns.

Dever, W. G.

1987 The Contribution of Archaeology to the Study of Canaanite and Early Israelite Religion. In *Ancient Israelite Religion: Essays in Honor of Frank Moore Cross*, ed. P. D. Miller, P. D. Hanson, and S. D. McBride, 209–47. Philadelphia: Fortress.

1990 Archaeology and Israelite Origins: Review Article. *BASOR* 279:89–95.

1993 Cultural Continuity: Ethnicity in the Archaeological Record and the Question of Israelite Origins. *EI* 24:21*–33*.

1995 Ceramics, Ethnicity, and the Question of Israel's Origins. *BA* 58:200–13.

Dothan, T., and A. Zukerman

2004 A Preliminary Study of the Mycenaean IIIC:1 Pottery Assemblages from Tel Miqne-Ekron and Ashdod. *BASOR* 333:1–54.

Epstein, C.

1965 An Interpretation of the Megiddo Sacred Area during the Middle Bronze II. *IEJ* 15:204–21.

Esse, D. L.

1992 The Collared Pithos at Megiddo: Ceramic Distribution and Ethnicity. *JNES* 51:81–103.

Faust, A.

2000 Ethnic Complexity in Northern Israel during the Iron Age II. *PEQ* 132:2–27.

Finkelstein, I.

1988 *The Archaeology of the Israelite Settlement*. Jerusalem: Israel Exploration Society.

1995 The Date of the Settlement of the Philistines in Canaan. *Tel Aviv* 22:213–39.

1996 The Stratigraphy and Chronology of Megiddo and Beth-Shan in the Twelfth–Eleventh Centuries B.C.E. *Tel Aviv* 23:170–84.

2000 Hazor XII–XI with an Addendum on Ben-Tor's Dating of Hazor X–VII. *Tel Aviv* 27:231–47.

2003 City-States to States: Polity Dynamics in the Tenth–Ninth Centuries B.C.E. In *Symbiosis, Symbolism, and the Power of the Past: Canaan, Ancient Israel, and Their Neighbors from the Late Bronze Age through Roman Palaestina*, ed. W. G. Dever and S. Gitin, 75–83. Winona Lake, Ind.: Eisenbrauns.

2005 A Low Chronology Update: Archaeology, History and Bible. In *The Bible and Radiocarbon Dating: Archaeology, Text and Science*, ed. T. E. Levy and T. Higham, 31–42. London: Equinox.

Finkelstein, I., D. Ussishkin, and B. Halpern, eds.

2000 *Megiddo*. Vol. 3, *The 1992–1996 Seasons*. 2 vols. Tel Aviv: Institute of Archaeology, Tel Aviv University.

Finkelstein, I., D. Ussishkin, and R. Deutsch

2006 Western Area M (The 1998–2000 Seasons). In *Megiddo*, vol. 4/1, *The 1998–2002 Seasons*, ed. I. Finkelstein, D. Ussishkin, and B. Halpern, 66–80. Tel Aviv: Institute of Archaeology, Tel Aviv University.

Finkelstein, I., O. Zimhoni, and A. Kafri
2000 The Iron Age Pottery Assemblages from Areas F, K and H and Their Stratigraphic and Chronological Implications. In *Megiddo*, vol. 3/1, *The 1992–1996 Seasons*, ed. I. Finkelstein, D. Ussishkin, and B. Halpern, 244–324. Tel Aviv: Institute of Archaeology, Tel Aviv University.

Finkelstein, I., and L. Singer-Avitz
2001 Ashdod Revisited. *Tel Aviv* 28:231–59.

Finkelstein, I., D. Ussishkin, and B. Halpern, eds.
2006 *Megiddo*. Vol. 4, *The 1998–2002 Seasons*. 2 vols. Tel Aviv: Institute of Archaeology, Tel Aviv University.

Franken, H. J., and M. L. Steiner
1990 *Excavations in Jerusalem, 1961–1967*. Vol. 2, *The Iron Age Extramural Quarter on the South-East Hill*. British Academy Monographs in Archaeology 2. Oxford: Oxford University Press.

Franklin, N.
2006 Area F. In *Megiddo*, vol. 4/1, *The 1998–2002 Seasons*, ed. I. Finkelstein, D. Ussishkin, and B. Halpern, 54–65. Tel Aviv: Institute of Archaeology, Tel Aviv University.

Friedman, R. E.
1979–1980 The MRZḤ Tablet from Ugarit. *Maarav* 2/2:187–205.

Fritz, V.
1987 Conquest or Settlement? The Early Iron Age in Palestine. *BA* 50:84–100.
1990 Die Landnahme der israelitischen Stämme in Kanaan. *ZDPV* 106:63–77.
1994 *Das Buch Josua*. Handbuch zum Alten Testament 1/7. Tübingen: J. C. B. Mohr.

Gadot, Y.
1999 The Wadi ᶜAra Pass As an International Highway during the Bronze Age, Iron Age and the Persian Period, in the Light of the Settlement Pattern [in Hebrew]. M.A. thesis, Tel Aviv University.

Gardiner, A. H.
1947 *Ancient Egyptian Onomastica*. 3 vols. London: Oxford University Press.

Gottwald, N. K.
1979 *The Tribes of Yahweh*: *A Sociology of the Religion of Liberated Israel, 1250–1050 B.C.E.* New York: Orbis.

Hallote, R. S.
1994 Mortuary Practices and Their Implications for Social Organization in the Middle Bronze Southern Levant. Ph.D. diss., University of Chicago.

Halpern, B.
1974 Sectionalism and the Schism. *JBL* 93:519–32.
1979 A Landlord-Tenant Dispute at Ugarit? *Maarav* 2/1:121–38.
1983 *The Emergence of Israel in Canaan*. Society of Biblical Literature Monograph Series 25. Chico, Calif.: Scholars.
1986 "The Excremental Vision": The Doomed Priests of Doom in Isaiah 28. *Hebrew Annual Review* 10: 109–21.
1992 Settlement of Canaan. In *The Anchor Bible Dictionary*, ed. D. N. Freedman, 5:1120–43. New York: Doubleday.
2000 Centre and Sentry: Megiddo's Role in Transit, Administration and Trade. In *Megiddo*, vol. 3, *The 1992–1996 Seasons*, ed. I. Finkelstein, D. Ussishkin, and B. Halpern, 535–75. Tel Aviv: Institute of Archaeology, Tel Aviv University.
2001 *David's Secret Demons: Messiah, Murderer, Traitor, King*. Grand Rapids, Mich.: Eerdmans.

Harrison, T. P.
2004 *Megiddo*. Vol. 3, *Final Report on the Stratum VI Excavations*. OIP 127. Chicago: Oriental Institute, University of Chicago.

Hesse, B. C.
1986 Animal Use at Tel Miqne-Ekron in the Bronze and Iron Age. *BASOR* 264:17–28.
1990 Pig Lovers and Pig Haters: Patterns of Palestinian Pork Production. *Journal of Ethnobiology* 10: 195–225.

Hillers, D. R., and E. Cussini
1996 *Palmyrene Aramaic Texts*. Baltimore: Johns Hopkins University Press.

Ilan, D.
1999 Northeastern Israel in the Iron Age I: Cultural, Socioeconomic and Political Perspectives. Ph.D. diss., Tel Aviv University.

Ilan, D., N. Franklin, and R. S. Hallote
2000 Area F. In *Megiddo*, vol. 3, *The 1992–1996 Seasons*, ed. I. Finkelstein, D. Ussishkin, and B. Halpern, 75–103. Tel Aviv: Institute of Archaeology, Tel Aviv University.

Kempinski, A.
1989 *Megiddo: A City-State and Royal Centre in North Israel*. Materialen zur allgemeinen und vergleichenden Archäologie 40. Munich: C. H. Beck.

Kenyon, K.
1969 The Middle and Late Bronze Age Strata at Megiddo. *Levant* 1:25–60.

Knudtzon, J. A.
1915 *Die El-Amarna-Tafeln*. Vorderasiatische Bibliothek. 2 vols. Leipzig: J. C. Hinrichs.

Lernau, O.
2000 Fish Bones. In *Megiddo*, vol. 3, *The 1992–1996 Seasons*, ed. I. Finkelstein, D. Ussishkin, and B.

Halpern, 463–77. Tel Aviv: Institute of Archaeology, Tel Aviv University.

Lewis, T.
1989 *Cults of the Dead in Ancient Israel and Ugarit*. HSM 39. Atlanta: Scholars.

Loretz, O.
1984 *Habiru-Hebräer: Eine sozio-linguistische Studie über die Herkunft des Gentiliziums* ᶜibrî *vom Appellativum* ḫabiru. BZAW 160. Berlin: Walter de Gruyter.

Loud, G.
1948 *Megiddo*. Vol. 2, *Seasons of 1935–39*. OIP 62. Chicago: Oriental Institute, University of Chicago.

Marx, K.
2003 [1851] *The Eighteenth Brumaire of Louis Bonaparte*. U.S.: IndyPublish.com.

Mazar, A.
1985 The Emergence of the Philistine Material Culture. *IEJ* 35:95–107.
1997 Iron Age Chronology: A Reply to I. Finkelstein. *Levant* 29:157–67.
2002 Megiddo in the Thirteenth–Eleventh Centuries B.C.E.: A Review of Some Recent Studies. In *Aharon Kempinski Memorial Volume: Studies in Archaeology and Related Disciplines*, ed. E. Oren and S. Aḥituv, 265–82. Beer-Sheva Studies by the Department of Bible and Ancient Near East 15. Beer-Sheva, Israel: Ben-Gurion University of the Negev.
2003 Remarks on Biblical Traditions and Archaeological Evidence concerning Early Israel. In *Symbiosis, Symbolism, and the Power of the Past: Canaan, Ancient Israel, and Their Neighbors from the Late Bronze Age through Roman Palaestina*, ed. W. G. Dever and S. Gitin, 85–98. Winona Lake, Ind.: Eisenbrauns.

Mendenhall, G. E.
1962 The Hebrew Conquest of Palestine. *BA* 25:66–87.

Mettinger, T. N. D.
1971 *Solomonic State Officials: A Study of the Civil Government Officials of the Israelite Monarchy*. Coniectanea Biblica Old Testament Series. Lund: Gleerups.

Miller, P. D.
1971 The MRZḤ Text. In *The Claremont Ras Shamra Tablets*, ed. L. R. Fisher, 37–49. AnOr 48. Rome: Pontifical Biblical Institute.

Mills, C. W.
1959 *The Sociological Imagination*. New York: Oxford University Press.

Moran, W. L.
1987 Join the ᶜApiru or Become One. In *"Working with No Data": Semitic and Egyptian Studies Presented to Thomas O. Lambdin*, ed. D. M. Golomb, 209–12. Winona Lake, Ind.: Eisenbrauns.

Müller, K. O.
1970 [1825] *Prolegomena zu einer wissenschaftlichen Mythologie*. Darmstadt: Wissenschaftlicher.

Neumann, J., and S. Parpola
1987 Climatic Change and the Eleventh–Tenth-Century Eclipse of Assyria and Babylonia. *JNES* 46:161–82.

Niebuhr, B. G.
1811–1812 *Römische Geschichte*. 2 vols. Berlin: G. A. Reimer.

Niemann, H. M.
1993 *Herrschaft, Königtum und Staat: Skizzen zur soziokulturellen Entwicklung im monarchischen Israel*. Forschungen zum Alten Testament 6. Tübingen: J. C. B. Mohr.

Paice, P.
2004 The Small Finds. In *Megiddo*, vol. 3, *Final Report on the Stratum VI Excavations*, ed. T. P. Harrison, 59–103. OIP 127. Chicago: Oriental Institute, University of Chicago.

Porten, B.
1968 *Archives from Elephantine: The Life of an Ancient Jewish Military Colony*. Berkeley, Calif.: University of California Press.

Schloen, J. D.
2001 *The House of the Father as Fact and Symbol: Patrimonialism in Ugarit and the Ancient Near East*. SAHL 2. Winona Lake, Ind.: Eisenbrauns.

Schmidt, B. B.
1996 *Israel's Beneficent Dead: Ancestor Cult and Necromancy in Ancient Israelite Religion and Tradition*. Winona Lake, Ind.: Eisenbrauns.

Schumacher, G.
1908 *Tell el-Mutesellim: Bericht über die 1903 bis 1905 mit Unterstützung Sr. Majestät des Deutschen Kaisers und der Deutschen Orient-Gesellschaft vom Deutschen Verein zur Erforschung Palästina veranstalteten Ausgrabungen I: Fundbericht*. 2 vols. Leipzig: Rudolf Haupt.

Stager, L. E.
1991 *Ashkelon Discovered: From Canaanites and Philistines to Romans and Moslems*. Washington, D.C.: Biblical Archaeological Society.
1995 The Impact of the Sea Peoples in Canaan (1185–1050 B.C.E.). In *The Archaeology of Society in the Holy Land*, ed. T. E. Levy, 332–48. London: Leicester University Press.

2003 The Patrimonial Kingdom of Solomon. In *Symbiosis, Symbolism, and the Power of the Past: Canaan, Ancient Israel and Their Neighbors from the Late Bronze Age through Roman Palaestina*, ed. W. G. Dever and S. Gitin, 63–74. Winona Lake, Ind.: Eisenbrauns.

2006 The House of the Silver Calf of Ashkelon. In *Timelines: Studies in Honour of Manfred Bietak*, ed. E. Czerny, I. Hein, H. Hunger, D. Melman, and A. Schwab, 403–10. OLA 149. Leuven: Peeters.

Stiebing, W. H.

1989 *Out of the Desert? Archaeology and the Exodus/Conquest Narratives*. Buffalo, N.Y.: Prometheus.

Ussishkin, D.

1995 The Destruction of Megiddo at the End of the Late Bronze Age and Its Historical Significance. *Tel Aviv* 22:240–67.

Ward, C. O.

1910 *The Ancient Lowly: A History of the Ancient Working People from the Earliest Known Period to the Adoption of Christianity by Constantine*. 2 vols. Chicago: C. H. Kerr.

Zarzecki-Poleg, A.

1997 Hazor, Jokneam and Megiddo in the Tenth Century B.C.E. *Tel Aviv* 24:258–88.

18. Compositional Techniques in the Book of Haggai

by Paul D. Hanson

THE sociopolitical and religious conditions of the early Second Temple Period are as interesting as they are complex.[1] The Babylonian conquest and the exile had fractured all of the institutions of Judah and had threatened the very existence of Jewish culture and religion. The fact that foreign armies, and by implication, pagan deities, were able to ravage Jerusalem and the temple gave rise to questions concerning the viability of Jewish religion and the validity of the theological assumptions upon which it was built. The crisis was such as to lead some to cast their fortunes with deities from a variety of foreign cults rather than to risk further calamity under Yahweh (Jer. 44:15–19; Isa. 57:4–10 and 65:3–7; Ezek. 8:7–15).

Debunking the values of the old order, however, was not a promising course of action for the leaders of a nation faced with rebuilding social structures and institutions after the Edict of Cyrus in 538 had allowed a sizable number of the exiles to return to a decimated homeland. Their concern revolved around the search for traditions capable of consolidating widespread support within the Jewish community and providing the ingredients necessary for reconstituting a national myth or epic.

From the literature of the time we know that a wide range of Israel's traditions presented themselves for consideration: the Torah of Moses, the story of the Exodus, the hymns celebrating temple and king, as well as sapiental reflections. We shall focus on one writing from the period of the restoration, the Book of Haggai, as an example of how antecedent tradition was enlisted in the task of rebuilding the Jewish community. We shall note how the tradition of the temple occupies center stage in the thought of this prophet and observe the extent of its influence, ranging from the ritual and economic policies he seeks to establish to the literary structure of his compositions themselves.

[1] It is a distinct honor to be included in a Festschrift dedicated to my colleague and friend Larry Stager. Not only has he sustained a personal interest in archaeology tracing back three decades to my participation in the Gezer excavations, but he has amazed me in subsequent years by offering thoughtful responses to my biblical scholarship, a sure mark of the broad humanistic perspective that he brings to his field.

The Temple-centered Symbolic Universe of Haggai

Recognition of the determinative force of temple tradition in Haggai's thought depends on awareness of the symbolic significance of temple in ancient Near Eastern national cults in general. Unless one brings to the Book of Haggai such comparative breadth, one runs the risk of treating temple strictly in terms of worship and piety. In Mesopotamia, Egypt, and Canaan, temple was a much more inclusive concept. By giving earthly representation to the sphere of the gods, it both symbolized the cosmic order established and maintained by the gods and provided the setting within which humans could influence cosmic forces in directions favorable to their personal and corporate interests. If one wished to speak of an ancient Near Eastern cosmogonic "orthodoxy," it would have to be in reference to the concept of divine governance and human participation centered in the temple. The temple linked human society with its vital source in the divine realm. Of central importance in this schema was the king, the human representative of a nation's patron deity (compare Anderson 1987).

The comprehensive symbolization of the world provided by the cosmology of temple and monarchy did not exist in preexilic Israel without qualification, for its protagonists were exposed to the persistent scrutiny of prophetic critics. David was obliged to respond to Nathan, Jeroboam I to the "Man of God," Ahab to Elijah, Jeroboam II to Amos. Drawing on a tenacious aniconic tradition, the prophet Jeremiah, on the threshold of the Babylonian invasion, warned the people against placing unqualified trust in the temple as guarantor of the nation's security (Jeremiah 7 and 26). Only by conforming their lives to the commandments of Yahweh could they hope for divine protection.

Even Jeremiah's anti-temple polemic, however, provides indirect evidence for the persistence of a well-established temple theology. Those deriving comfort from the *mantra* "the temple of the Lord" were able to appeal to a tradition associated with the prophet Isaiah, who during the earlier crisis of the Assyrian invasion in 701 B.C.E. drew attention to the mysterious tenacity of the Ariel even in the face of the devastating force of the enemy (Isa. 29:1–10; compare with 37:33–35).

The so-called "royal psalms" give ample evidence that symbols and themes associated with king and temple in major cult centers in both Egypt and Mesopotamia had become a part of Judean religious thought in the preexilic period:

> Awesome is God in his sanctuary,
> the God of Israel;
> he gives power and strength to his people.
> (Ps. 68:36 [Eng. 35]).[2]

Though the indigenous aniconic tradition restrained what otherwise would have been a natural move to visible representation of the deity in the temple, the poetic depiction of God as Divine Warrior defeating primordial chaos and installing his chosen king for the purpose of maintaining order on earth evaded censorship, and resonance with the mythologoumenon of the Babylonian *akītu* festival or the Baᶜl myth from Ugarit in Psalm 89 is striking:

> You rule the raging of the sea;
> when its waves rise, you still them.
> You crushed Rahab like a carcass;
> you scattered your enemies with your mighty arm.
> (Ps. 89:10–11 [Eng. 9–10]).

> I will set his hand on the sea
> and his right hand on the rivers.
> (Ps. 89:26 [Eng. 25]).

Within the context of Israelite religion, and against the background of the stringent conditions of the Mosaic covenant, the predication of the permanence of the bond between God and king on a divine oath is extraordinary. But seen from the perspective of the *Realpolitik* of the royal court in Jerusalem with its need to establish the unchallenged authority of the king over his subjects, it becomes quite plausible, though no less Machiavellian:

> I have made a covenant with my chosen one,
> I have sworn to my servant David:
> I will establish your descendants forever,
> and build your throne for all generations.
> (Ps. 89:4–5 [Eng. 3–4]).

Reflected in Psalm 89 and other royal psalms is thus the ancient view holding that the vitality of a nation is dependent on a divinely appointed king who in turn sponsors an elaborate temple structure administered by an official priesthood. For some, the fact that this close tie between deity and king failed to secure the nation from defeat and destruction (including the patron deity's temple) discredited the royal theology and created an openness to a different construal of the relation between God and people (e.g., Isa. 55:3). Others managed to overlook the historical contradiction and reaffirmed the ancient mythologoumenon of deity, temple, and king as the foundation for restoration of the nation from the rubble left by the Babylonian destruction in 587–586 B.C.E.

The attractiveness of this mythologoumenon during a time of crisis such as that encountered by the returnees from exile in the years 538–520 B.C.E. is not difficult to understand. We turn now to explain why, with reference specifically to the book of Haggai.[3]

The Book of Haggai is a slender book. Yet the evidence it gives for the socioeconomic situation it addresses and the tradition to which it appeals is remarkably clear. The situation is one of drought, rampant inflation, and low consumer confidence. The nation's leadership has failed to act with a clear program for recovery. Their attention is preoccupied with self-gain. The tradition to which Haggai appeals as the basis for his call to decisive action is the tradition that recognizes the temple as the vital heart of the entire socioeconomic order: "Go up to the hills and bring wood and build the house, so that I may take pleasure in it and be honored" (1:8), "and in this place I will give prosperity, says the Lord of hosts" (2:9).

The lines of connection between Haggai's world view and the temple ideology that recurs with local adaptations throughout the ancient Near East are striking. According to this prophet, the rebuilding of the temple (explicitly) and reinstitution of its priesthood and sacrificial ritual (by clear implication) were indispensable to the restoration of order and prosperity in Jerusalem and Judah. To be sure, the temple tradition upon which Haggai drew had been thoroughly adapted to Jewish concepts. Connections with the rebuilding program of Ezekiel 40–48 and to the *kābôd* theology of the Priestly Writing are obvious. And although subtle differences can be detected between the Book of Haggai and Zechariah 1–8, both clearly develop facets of the same Jewish temple tradition.

Also evident in Haggai is the degree to which temple ideology has been adapted to Israelite covenantal notions, clear evidence of the triumph of the Deuteronomistic theological synthesis. To build and maintain the temple no longer stands in tension with Mosaic Torah, but has become one of the solemn

2. All biblical citations are according to the New Revised Standard Version.

3. We shall not treat the closely related message in Zechariah 1–8; however, compare with Marinkovic 1996.

commands set forth by God as conditions for the covenant relationship. Obedience on the part of the people would be followed by blessing, disobedience by curse. Even the specific curses included in the Book of Haggai are the standard ones found in Deuteronomy (e.g., Deut. 28:38), though here too lines of connection with a broader ancient Near Eastern treaty tradition are evident. Involved, however, is more than the borrowing of conventional treaty language, for on the proper functioning of the temple cult with its system of tithes and sacrifices hinged the prosperity of all aspects of the national life. For example, in the realm of commerce, nothing less was at stake than the efficient collection and redistribution of the nation's produce. In Haggai, traditional treaty stipulations and conventional temple terminology are restored to their archaic setting, a mythologoumenon in which the temple is the center of cosmic order and in which humans participate through the contribution of their productivity and devotion.

The Imprint of Haggai's Symbolic Universe on the Literary Structure of His Message

It is now our aim to move the discussion a step beyond the description of the temple-centered symbolic universe of Haggai and the accompanying institutional structures for which it provided divine warrant to a literary question: Does that symbolic universe also influence the literary structure of Haggai's prophecy? That it has an impact on the substance of the prophet's message is clear. All attempts to reconstruct the world view of Haggai depend on that connection. But does influence go beyond the contents of Haggai's message to the form that it assumes?

Rolf Knierim opened a new dimension for biblical form-criticism when he asked whether the usual definition of *Sitz im Leben*, involving a search for a social practice or institution as the generative matrix of a given unit of tradition, was adequate in relation to late prophetic texts (Knierim 1973). In the case of Second Isaiah, he averred that the creative imagination (*Geistesbeschäftigung*) of the prophet was at least as important as any institutional point of reference in the shaping of the specific form of a prophetic message. Knierim cited a study of Zechariah 9 that I had published in the *Journal of Biblical Literature* as illustrative of this phenomenon (Hanson 1973). In a Festschrift in honor of Marvin Pope, I further developed the argument by pointing to the structure of the seven-vision cycle in Zechariah 1–6 as substantiating Knierim's point: It reflects not so much a received convention as the world view of that prophet (Hanson 1987a).

Let us expand the inquiry: Is it profitable to pursue this approach in consideration of the Book of Haggai? We shall broach this question by examining the first prophetic unit in Haggai, verses 1–15 of chapter 1. It should be a fair assumption that a unit of tradition, whether oral or written in origin, will incorporate certain structuring devices, that is to say, stylistic and architectural features that give coherence to that unit and set it apart from those that precede and follow. In early Hebrew poetry, parallelism within bi- and tricola and a certain degree of regularity in meter tends to bind verses together into larger units. Scholars have also sought to recognize the recurrent structural traits associated with literary genres both as a reflection of their social or institutional settings and as a device for ordering the contents of a message unit.

Canons and patterns that can be discerned in earlier biblical materials, however, are of diminishing value as one moves into the late prophetic period. In the case of a unit such as Haggai chapter 1, one either concludes that the author followed no principles of composition at all, or one seeks to determine whether new canons may have come into play.

In relation to the standard distinctions between prose and poetry, Haggai 1 runs the gamut from normal prose syntax to elevated prose to lists based on syntactic and thematic repetition to fairly regular poetic meter. In other words, the first blush impression given is one of disorder rather than regularity. But is there order of another sort that accounts for our impression, after reading these fifteen verses, that we are dealing after all with a discrete unit?

We can best approach this question by focusing first on the seven lines comprising verses 6 and 9a that do give the impression of a degree of metric regularity and thematic unity. They conform to what Delbert Hillers has identified—on the basis of parallels between materials in Leviticus, Deuteronomy, the prophetic books, and lists in Sefire I and Ashurbanipal's annals—as "futility" curses. Of these he concluded:

> both in Israel and elsewhere there were living and primarily oral traditions of curses on which writers and speakers might draw for various purposes, either leaving the material as they found it or recasting it into their own style. [Hillers 1964:42]

Within the Hebrew Bible, curses such as we find in Haggai 1:6 and 9a form part of the conceptual world of the Israelite notion of covenant between Yahweh and Israel, that is to say, they describe the consequences of disobedience to the stipulations of the covenant. Of course, the particular divine command or commands that are stressed in a given context shed light on the intentions of the author in question. In the case of this unit in Haggai, there is no uncertainty of the command that occupies the center of the author's concern. This is shown dramatically by a peculiar structural feature, to which we now turn.

On first reading, verses 7 and 8 strike one as awkwardly intrusive. They break what is in all other respects the smooth flow of a list of futility curses. The disruptiveness of this intrusion is evident in the syntax. Verse 6 begins with a curse introduced by a finite verb (perfect), followed by three curses introduced by infinitive absolutes and one by a participle. After the intrusion of verses 7 and 8, verse 9a begins with a curse introduced by another infinitive absolute and concludes with one patterned after the verbal construction (with the perfect) found at the beginning of the list. This envelope structure, combined with the metric and syntactic regularity of the curse list, creates a nice sense of symmetry.

But how can one account for the intrusion of verses 7 and 8 into this tightly structured list of curses? These verses give expression to a tersely formulated divine commandment: "Go up to the heights and bring wood; build the house that I may take pleasure in it and that I may be glorified." Piercing into the list of futility curses and thus taking a position at the center of the unit is a command to build the temple. Though this break in the flow of the list of curses is so abrupt as to lead one to ask whether the intrusion might be secondary, the ubiquity of the temple theme in Haggai commends another conclusion: the composer was prompted by his symbolic universe with the temple at its center to create a specific image with this unusual structure. On the one hand, it gives a picture of the life-promising powers of the temple being held hostage by the curses weighing upon the land and the people. At the same time it hints at the power of the temple and the God who desired to be glorified by being present there to break the curse that weighed upon the land and its inhabitants and to restore order and prosperity.

As the perfect verbs formed an envelope around the list of curses, the two segments of the curses in turn envelop the command. This envelope structure proceeds out further from the temple center. Verses 3–4 contain a divine query delivered to the people by Haggai: "Is it a time for you yourselves to dwell in your paneled houses while this house lies in ruins?" At the opposite end of the curse list, another divine word explains the plight of the land: "because of my house that lies in ruins, while you busy yourselves each with his own house." The structure again seems to arise from the prophet's temple-centered world view; the curse list with the temple held hostage at its center is enveloped by the root cause of this tragic situation: The people live in their paneled houses, Yahweh's house lies in ruins (v. 4), Yahweh's house lies in ruins, the people all hurry off to their own houses (v. 9). Note that this envelope itself incorporates the *abba* pattern characteristic of the device of inclusio.

Verses 10–11 pick up the concept of the temple lying in ruins and turn it into an amplification of the curse by playing on two meanings of the root *ḥrb*: Because the temple lies in ruins (*ḥārēb*), Yahweh has called a drought (*ḥōreb*) upon the land.

The next envelope is formed by verses 1b to 2 and 12 to 14. The former half of the envelope records Yahweh's indictment of the people delivered to Zerubbabel and Joshua by Haggai: "This people say the time has not yet come to rebuild the house of the Lord." The latter half reports that Zerubbabel, Joshua, and the people responded positively to the divine command, and went to work on Yahweh's house. Though the repetition of the names and titles of Zerubbabel and Joshua, as well as the resumption of the theme of temple construction, create the inclusio effect that we found in the other envelopes, in the case of this one we see that the impasse created by the curse shows signs of breaking; no longer are the people asserting that the time has not come to rebuild the temple; they have set out to do the work.

The final envelope consists of chronological notes, constructed again with a chiastic pattern creating envelopes within the envelope, that is, *abccba*: "In the second year of Darius the king, in the sixth month, on the first day of the month" (v. 1) // "on the twenty-fourth day of the month, in the sixth month, in the second year of Darius the king"(v. 15). This is an echo with a subtle variation. While year and month remain the same, we move from the first day to the twenty-fourth, thereby adding a chronological movement to the thematic progression from inaction to action seen in the previous envelope.

While the dominant pattern in the unit is thus spatial, determined by the temple at the center, and moving out in both directions through the curse, to the cause of the curse in the contrast between attention to personal houses and neglect of Yahweh's house, to the role of Zerubbabel, Joshua, and the remnant of the people, to the chronological framework, there is a second pattern that is linear in nature, moving from the first day of the month to the twenty-fourth and from refusal to rebuild to the onset of building activity, and thus by implication, from the captivity of temple and land within the curse to a renewal of

Yahweh's habitation in the temple and the consequent restoration of *šālôm* in the land.

Though we have confined our examination to the first unit, the subsequent units of Haggai betray a similar juxtaposition of a temple-centered spatial pattern and a linear movement, which is to say, the tension between an epic and a mythical view of reality that is one of the cardinal marks of late prophecy and early apocalyptic (Hanson 1987b). And when one takes the other units and chronological notes in the Book of Haggai into consideration, one sees a completion of the movement from inactivity in relation to the temple to rebuilding of Yahweh's house and the consequent transformation from a condition of chaos imposed by covenant curses to universal *šālôm* established by fidelity to divine command.

My earlier study of Zechariah 1–6 uncovered a similar juxtaposition in the seven-vision cycle of that prophet (1987a). Spatially, the center was formed by the temple vision, and from that center the visions moved in both directions through the land of Judah, to the nations, to the threshold between earth and heaven. But at the same time, a linear progression was evident from the questioning of the first vision—"How long?"—to the announcement of final rest in the seventh vision.

Though the questions of how world views affect literary structures and how patterns of the mind influence patterns of composition, and the related question of whether such influence is more likely on an oral than a literary level, remain elusive ones, our study at least adds weight to the suggestion that there is more to the phenomenon of *Sitz im Leben* than social structures and institutions in the exterior world of the author. The interior world of the author, though elusive, is also deserving of close scrutiny.

Bibliography

Anderson, G. A.
1987 *Sacrifices and Offerings in Ancient Israel: Studies in their Social and Political Importance*. HSM 41. Atlanta: Scholars.

Hanson, P. D.
1973 Zechariah 9 and the Recapitulation of an Ancient Ritual Pattern. *JBL* 92:37–59.
1987a In Defiance of Death: Zechariah's Symbolic Universe. In *Love and Death in the Ancient Near East: Essays in Honor of Marvin H. Pope*, ed. J. H. Marks and R. M. Good, 173–79. New Haven, Conn.: Four Quarters.
1987b Israelite Religion in the Early Postexilic Period. In *Ancient Israelite Religion: Essays in Honor of Frank Moore Cross*, ed. P. D. Miller, P. D. Hanson, and S. D. McBride, 485–508. Philadelphia: Fortress.

Hillers, D. R.
1964 *Treaty-curses and the Old Testament Prophets*. Rome: Pontifical Biblical Institute.

Knierim, R.
1973 Old Testament Form Criticism Reconsidered. *Interpretation* 27:435–68.

Marinkovic, P.
1996 *Stadt ohne Mauer: Die Neukonstitution Jerusalems nach Sacharja 1–8*. Munich.

19. Lifting the Veil on a "Dark Age": Ta^c^yinat and the North Orontes Valley during the Early Iron Age

by Timothy P. Harrison

It has become axiomatic that the collapse of the Egyptian and Hittite empires at the end of the thirteenth century B.C.E., and with them the collapse of the widely integrated economic and political networks that characterized the terminal phase of Bronze Age civilization in the eastern Mediterranean, ushered in a prolonged "Dark Age" in the region. Coinciding with reports of widespread famine and political conflict, largely precipitated (according to the conventional view) by the migratory incursions of the "Sea Peoples"—often portrayed as the "Vikings" of the ancient world—these events brought to an end the centralized state bureaucracies that had long held sway in the region, ending the rich literary traditions (and archives) they had created. The ensuing Dark Age, correspondingly, devolved into an era of political fragmentation and turbulence marked by chronic ethnic strife, yet out of which eventually emerged the small territorial "nation-states" of biblical fame in the early centuries of the first millennium B.C.E.

Increasingly, however, the results of ongoing archaeological investigations, and a growing corpus of epigraphic discoveries, have begun to challenge this established historical view. The emerging picture is of a considerably more complex political landscape marked by both continuity and change. The pace of discovery has been particularly significant in the Hittite realm, including the recovery (or reinterpretation) of important epigraphic finds that have begun to force a rethinking of the Hittite Empire's political fortunes during its final stages, and in the aftermath of its collapse. While scholars have long assumed that the Neo-Hittite states of the first millennium B.C.E. were linked culturally and linguistically to their Bronze Age Anatolian forebears, thus far only the "Great Kings" of Karkamiš have produced a dynastic line that actually bridges the intervening era, while the archaeological record remains largely devoid of well-excavated cultural sequences for this period. But a Luwian hieroglyphic inscription recently discovered on the Aleppo Citadel has now raised the prospect of tracing the historical development of another such state, associated with the "Land of Palastin," as recently proposed by J. D. Hawkins (2008).

Drawing on the results of the renewed excavations at Tell Ta^c^yinat, the site of ancient Kunulua, capital of the historically attested ninth- and eighth-century Kingdom of Patina/Unqi, this paper will review the archaeological and epigraphic evidence for the foundation of a Neo-Hittite kingdom centered in the Amuq plain during this formative early Iron Age (ca. 1200–900 B.C.E.) period. The existing evidence points to the emergence of a powerful regional kingdom, essentially a "rump" state, and possibly an appanage kingdom, which survived the demise of the ruling Hittite dynasty in Hattuša, reasserting political control over the region following a brief interlude dominated by the presence of settlers with strong Aegean cultural associations. Though admittedly fragmentary and incomplete, this evidence is presented here with the aim of sketching a historical outline for a region of gathering research focus during this period of longstanding interest to Professor Stager.

Historical Context

The evidence for Hittite political and cultural continuity in northwest Syria during the Late Bronze–Iron Age transition must be understood within the context of the Hittite imperial expansion that occurred in the later stages of the Late Bronze Age. Hittite imperial ambitions took a decisive turn in the mid-fourteenth century with Šuppiluliuma I's seizure of the throne following the troubled reign of his father Tudhaliya III.[1] After consolidating the Hittite heartland, Šuppiluliuma launched a series of devastating attacks against the powerful kingdom of Mitanni, eventually sacking its royal capital Waššukanni and installing a client ruler over a considerably diminished realm. With Mitanni eliminated as a regional rival, Šuppiluliuma turned his attention to the smaller, dependent states of western Syria, quickly disposing of any remaining opposition from those who had maintained loyalty to Mitanni, including the kingdoms of Aleppo (Halab), Mukiš (Alalakh), Niya and Nuhašše. It took a subsequent campaign to subdue the Mitannian stronghold entrenched at Karkamiš, and a formal treaty with Niqmaddu II, consummated during a meeting between the two rulers at Alalakh, to secure Ugarit as a vassal (Bryce 1998:175–79; Kuhrt 1995:306–8).

---

[1] For more thorough surveys of this political history, see Kuhrt (1995:250–66), Bryce (1998:158–205), and Klengel (1992:106–120; 1999).

With the opposition neutralized, Šuppiluliuma moved to consolidate his Syrian conquests, imposing a series of binding treaties on the newly conquered kingdoms that resulted in a network of Hittite vassal states. However, Šuppiluliuma also took the unprecedented further step of placing the region under direct Hittite control, which he accomplished by installing two of his sons as viceroys at the strategically important centers of Aleppo and Karkamiš. Telipinu, the elder of the two brothers, was enthroned as "king" (lit. LUGAL) of "the lands of Aleppo," and also assigned the position of "Great (or Chief) Priest" for this important cult center, while his younger brother, Piyassili, was appointed ruler of "the lands of Karkamiš," assuming the Hurrian throne name Šarri-Kušuh (Bryce 1992; 1998:203–4). Šuppiluliuma's actions clearly were designed to counter the growing threat of Egypt and Assyria and to manage the fluctuating loyalties and chronic instability of these local Syrian kingdoms. Since Aleppo and Karkamiš appear to have been the only kingdoms not to have had local rulers installed (compare Naʾaman 1980:38), their appointments also suggest a calculated attempt to integrate the region into an expanding empire and achieve a lasting *pax Hethitica* (Bryce 1998:195).

As Bryce has noted (1992:18; 1998:203–4), their vice-regal duties appear to have been coordinated, with political and military authority concentrated in the hands of the Karkamiš viceroys, and religious and judicial responsibilities handled by the viceroys in Aleppo, effectively replicating the primary duties of the "Great King of Hatti" himself. Although ultimate authority remained with the Great King throughout the Empire period, it is also clear that these viceroys enjoyed increasing autonomy and power, particularly the Karkamiš dynasty. Even before the end of Šuppiluliuma's reign, Šarri-Kušuh had emerged as the principal power broker in the region, as evidenced by his prominent role in securing the Hittite treaty with Šattiwaza (Bryce 1998:200–1).

Although Hittite control of northwest Syria was challenged periodically during the subsequent Empire period, the basic administrative structure created by Šuppiluliuma remained intact, including the dynastic lines established at Aleppo and Karkamiš. A century later, for example, texts dating to the reign of Tudhaliya IV describe the role played by Šarri-Kušuh's grandson Ini-Tešub as viceroy at Karkamiš and the ruler responsible for north Syria, in the delicate arbitration of a difficult divorce between members of the ruling families of Amurru and Ugarit (Kuhrt 1995: 310–13). By simply adding an administrative tier, therefore, while leaving much of the existing political structure in place, Šuppiluliuma successfully integrated the region into an expanding Hittite imperial realm.

The final years of the Hittite Empire have become the focus of renewed scholarly attention in recent years, prompted in large part by a growing body of archaeological and epigraphic evidence that are forcing reconsideration of prevailing understandings of the Empire's demise.[2] While a synthesis may be premature, it nevertheless has become increasingly clear that a complex set of interrelated factors contributed to its collapse, and that this collapse was not precipitated by a single, decisive event. Nor was it perhaps quite as terminal as once thought. Indeed, the most striking development has been the growing evidence for political and cultural continuity in the post-Empire period.[3]

By the end of the thirteenth century, the imperial administrative structure installed by Šuppiluliuma more than a century before had begun to fragment. In particular, the appanage kingdoms he and his successors had established had become increasingly independent, exercising their autonomy to leverage political concessions (and of course power) from a steadily weakening center. Most notable of these were the kingdoms of Tarhuntašša (see Singer 1996; Dinçol et al. 2000) and Karkamiš. In the case of Karkamiš, as we have seen, considerable power had already been transferred during Šuppiluliuma's reign, when his vice-regal son Šarri-Kušuh was given responsibility for virtually all of Hittite-controlled territory in Syria. Šarri-Kušuh was succeeded by a line of progressively more powerful and independent viceroys, with Ini-Tešub apparently one of the more active, and they eventually grew to rival their cousins on the throne at Hattuša.

In 1985, two seal impressions bearing the name of Kuzi-Tešub were discovered at Lidar Höyük. The impressions identified him as a king of Karkamiš and the son of Talmi-Tešub, the third viceroy to follow Šarri-Kušuh and a cousin and contemporary of Šuppiluliuma II, the final ruler of Hattuša, thus extending the line of viceroys at Karkamiš to a fifth generation (Sürenhagen 1986; see also Güterbock 1992; Bryce 1998:384). Shortly thereafter, additional references to the same Kuzi-Tešub were recognized in the gene-

---

[2] For diverging views on this subject, see Hoffner 1992, Muhly 1992, Drews 1993, Yakar 1993, Singer 2000, and Hawkins 2002.

[3] Although beyond the focus of this paper, the results of recent investigations at Boğazköy, for example, have begun to cast doubt on the longstanding view that the final LB settlement at Hattuša was violently destroyed ca. 1200 B.C.E. See further in Seeher 1998; 2001; and Genz 2003; 2004.

alogies of two kings of Malatya (ancient Melid). The Malatya inscriptions identified Kuzi-Tešub as "Great King" and "Hero of Karkamiš" and linked him to a dynasty that ruled at Karkamiš during the later part of the early Iron Age (Hawkins 1988:99–102). Since Kuzi-Tešub appears to have been the first ruler at Karkamiš to claim the title of "Great King," until then a privilege reserved only for the royal line at Hattuša, use of this epithet implies that his reign also coincided with the fall of Hattuša and the elevation of Karkamiš to full independence (Hawkins 1988; 2002: 147–48). These epigraphic discoveries have thus provided the first concrete link bridging the historical gap between the fall of the Hittite Empire, and with it the end of the scribal tradition responsible for the cuneiform tablets preserved in the Hittite archives at Hattuša, and the emergence of the Neo-Hittite states of northwest Syria in the early centuries of the first millennium B.C.E.

However, the Malatya inscriptions also attest to the existence of other, apparently secondary, ruling dynasties that were related to the dynasty at Karkamiš through marriage. Thus, as Hawkins has noted (1995; 2002:148), another important implication of these inscriptions is their confirmation that a direct ancestral link existed between the royal dynasty at Hattuša and an as yet undetermined number of regional dynasties that emerged during this post-Empire period. In the case of the Melid dynasty, not all of the named rulers were identified as kings, and only one is referred to as a "Hero." However, all bore the title "Country-Lord of the city of Malatya," which during the preceding Empire period appears to have been reserved for provincial governors or local magnates (Hawkins 1995:74–76). As descendants of Kuzi-Tešub, therefore, it is reasonable to infer that the Malatya line was initially subordinate to Karkamiš, but there is nothing in the epigraphic evidence that indicates it necessarily remained so, which in any case seems unlikely, because later dynasts at Karkamiš also bore the same title (Hawkins 1995: 78–84).

The recent discovery of a temple dedicated to Tešub, the Hittite Storm God, on the Aleppo Citadel has now raised the prospect of delineating the political fortunes of another such early Iron Age kingdom. Given Aleppo's prominence as a religious center, and its close association with the Storm God in particular, this important discovery should perhaps have come as no surprise. Indeed, there had been prior hints that such an edifice existed. For example, a fragmentary Luwian inscription, first reported in the late nineteenth century and still visible in the wall of an Aleppo mosque (see Gonnella et al. 2005:Abb. 8), commemorates the construction of a temple to Hebat and Šarruma by Talmi-Šarruma, Telipinu's son and successor as king of Aleppo (Laroche 1956; Hawkins 2000:388). Additionally, in a brief article published in 1995, M. van Loon drew attention to two orthostats found reused in the walls of the medieval citadel that bore a striking stylistic resemblance to orthostats from the early Iron Age temple at ᶜAin Dara, and proposed (rather perceptively, as it turned out) that they might in fact have come from the elusive temple (1995:184). The Aleppo Citadel excavations have since provided confirmation, uncovering the walls of a temple lined with similarly carved orthostats, which very likely is contemporary to the ᶜAin Dara temple (see Orthmann 2002), and, in 2003, an intact Luwian inscription dedicating the building to Tešub (for the preliminary reports, see Kohlmeyer 2000 and Gonnella et al. 2005:73–113).

Although a full publication of the Aleppo inscription has yet to appear (a photograph is provided in Gonnella et al. 2005:Abb. 126), a number of observations with potentially significant historical implications have been made recently by J. D. Hawkins, who has undertaken its translation and publication.[4] In particular, Hawkins has dated the inscription to ca. 1100–1000 B.C.E., based on the paleography of the script and the iconography of the associated reliefs,[5] and he has drawn attention to the similarity between the name and title of its author, a certain Taitas, "Hero and King of the land of Palastin," and three previously known fragmentary Luwian inscriptions (Hawkins 2004; 2008; Gonnella et al. 2005:92). Two of these inscriptions were found on stelae discovered out of context in the villages of Meharde and Sheizar, located near Qalᶜat al-Mudiq, northwest of Hama (for translations and commentary, see Hawkins 1979; 2000:415–19), and concern a Queen Kupapiyas, "wife of Taitas." Both inscriptions refer to Taitas as

[4] His preliminary observations about the inscription first appeared in a post-publication insert to his 2002 article, and were then presented in papers delivered at the Fourth International Congress on the Archaeology of the Ancient Near East (ICAANE) in Berlin in 2004, and at a symposium celebrating the opening of the Syro-Anatolian Gallery at the Oriental Institute Museum in Chicago in 2005. Most recently, at the Sixth ICAANE meetings in Rome, held May 5–10, 2008, Hawkins announced the discovery of a fragmentary second inscription, and proposed that the territorial reference made in the Aleppo inscriptions be read "Palastin" and linked to the Peleset of Sea Peoples fame.

[5] However, it should be noted that the inscription encroaches onto the adjacent relief (see photograph in Gonnella et al. 2005:Abb. 126), and therefore conceivably might have been applied at a later date.

"Hero" but identify his kingdom as "Walastin," rather than Palastin, as in the Aleppo inscription.

The third inscription was recovered during the excavations of the Syro-Hittite Expedition at Tell Taᶜyinat (specifically Tell Taᶜyinat Inscription 1; see Hawkins 2000:365–67) in the Plain of Antioch in the North Orontes Valley. However, the surviving hieroglyphic fragments do not actually mention Taitas, but instead refer to a second individual named Halparuntiyas, who also appears to have ruled "the land of Walastin." Hawkins, following Gelb (see 1939:39), has noted the similarity to Qalparunda, and has raised the possibility that he may be the same Patinean ruler said to have paid tribute to Shalmaneser III in 857 and 853 B.C.E. (Hawkins 2000:365–66; see further historical discussion in Harrison 2001:117–19).

Unfortunately, confusion regarding the precise stratigraphic context(s) of the six hieroglyphic fragments that comprise this inscription, as well as the more than 80 other Luwian hieroglyphic fragments recovered by the Syro-Hittite Expedition, has clouded discussion of their broader historical significance. Contrary to the assumption that the fragments of Taᶜyinat Inscription 1 formed part of a colossal seated figure destroyed during the 738 B.C.E. campaign of Tiglath-pileser III (first proposed by Gelb [1939:39]; but see in particular, Hawkins 2000:366), the Expedition's field records clearly indicate that these epigraphic remains were recovered in fragmentary condition from a wide range of secondary and tertiary contexts associated with the Second Building Period, including construction fill (Harrison 2001: 127–28).[6] The production of these inscriptions as part of intact monuments, in other words, predates at least the terminal phase of the Second Building Period, and probably should be assigned to the preceding First Building Period, described further below.

Regardless of their precise date, however, as Hawkins has observed (2004; 2008; see also Gonnella et al. 2005:92), the new Aleppo inscriptions, when taken together with the Meharde, Sheizar, and Taᶜyinat inscriptions, imply the existence of an early Iron Age kingdom known variously as Palastin or Walastin, with its capital possibly located at Tell Taᶜyinat in the North Orontes Valley. Moreover, the wide area encompassed by these inscriptions suggests a kingdom of considerable power and influence, extending east to include Aleppo and south at least as far as the Middle Orontes Valley region west of Hama. If we accept a twelfth-century date for the Storm God Temple at Aleppo, this would render Taitas's kingdom more or less contemporary with the post-Empire Hittite dynasties based at Karkamiš and Melid, and raise the possibility that a third local dynasty survived the Hittite Empire's collapse.

As further support for this possibility, it is intriguing to note the striking similarity between the apparent territorial extent of the Land of Palastin/Walastin and the combined territories of the Late Bronze Age vassal kingdoms of Mukiš, Niya and Nuhašše (or Astour's "confederation"; see Astour 1969), together with Aleppo, and it is tempting to propose that this area also corresponded roughly to the territory assigned by Šuppiluliuma to the kingdom of Aleppo during his administrative reorganization in the late fourteenth century. Such a reconstruction, however, would also imply that a significant power shift had occurred at some point in the twelfth century, with a ruling dynasty based in the Amuq plain emerging and then eclipsing Aleppo as the dominant power in the region. Later historical developments do support this possibility. Although its political fortunes are obscured by a lack of direct historical evidence, Aleppo undoubtedly had lost its regional prominence well before the ninth century B.C.E., when the Aramean kingdom of Bit-Agusi, with its capital at nearby Arpad (Tell Rifaᶜat), 35 km north of Aleppo, emerged as the most powerful presence in the region (Hawkins 1975). In contrast to Aleppo, a variety of historical sources confirm that Palastin, or more properly, the kingdom of Patina/Unqi,[7] and its royal city Kunulua (almost certainly to be identified with Tell Taᶜyinat), survived as an independent Neo-Hittite state until at least the latter part of the ninth century, and very possibly until the reign of Tiglath-pileser III in the eighth century, although it did so within considerably diminished borders (see further in Harrison 2001).

Though fragmentary, the growing corpus of inscriptions that date to this formative "Dark Age" period thus point to a historical process marked by considerably greater political continuity than previously thought. In the aftermath of the collapse of the imperial center at Hattuša, the viceroys installed at Karkamiš were left holding a much reduced "rump" state that extended from Malatya southeast to the great bend of the Euphrates. In time, this entity appears to have fragmented further into the smaller

[6] It should also be pointed out that only Fragments 3, 4, and 5 of the inscription preserve actual joins. The "Walastin" reference occurs in Fragment 3, while Halparuntiyas is named in Fragment 6.

[7] The etymological similarity between Wadasatini (as originally read) and Patina (p>b>w, with a dropping of the intervocalic *–ds/ts*) was first noted by Yamada (2000:96, n. 71), and further strengthens the historical link between the two kingdoms.

kingdoms of Karkamiš, Melid, and Kummuh, and to the west, Gurgum, and now also Palastin. Still farther west, in southern Anatolia, early Iron Age polities also appear to have survived Tarhuntašša, which became known as Hilakku, and in the Cilician plain, where Kizzuwatna was supplanted by Hiyawa, while new polities appear to have been formed to the north in the Konya plain region, which became known as Tuwana, and in the region of Kayseri and Nevşehir, known in later times as Tabal (Hawkins 2002:148). The result was a mosaic of small regional kingdoms out of which would eventually emerge the better known Neo-Hittite states of the later Iron Age (see figure 1).

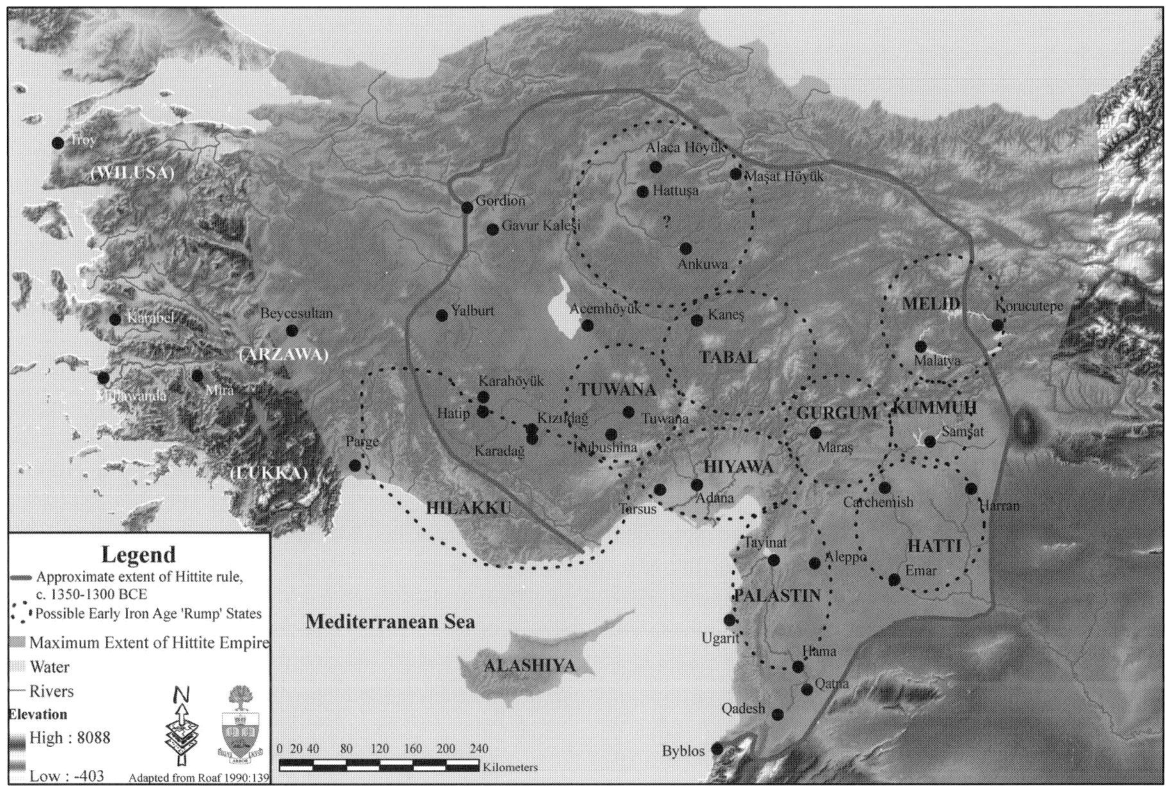

Figure 1. Map showing the extent of the Hittite Empire, with the approximate territorial boundaries of the early Iron Age "rump" states that survived its collapse

Created by S. Batiuk (adapted from Roaf 1990:139)

Settlement Trends in the North Orontes Valley

Survey data for the North Orontes Valley region indicate a relative decline in settlement during the Late Bronze Age that mirrors a general decline throughout the ancient Near East during this period (McClellan 1992; Yener et al. 2000:187–89). This trend was reversed during the Iron Age, when the number of sites in the region almost doubled. Closer examination of this survey data, however, elicits a number of more revealing patterns (for a more thorough treatment, see Harrison 2001:122–24). First, of the 30 LB (or Amuq Phase M) sites that have been identified by surface survey, 17 also preserved evidence of early Iron Age (Amuq Phase N) occupation, or almost two-thirds of the LB sites, suggesting significant settlement continuity between the two periods. However, these 17 sites also account for only about one-third of the total number of recorded Amuq N sites. Fully 74 percent, or 30 of the 47 known Amuq N sites, were new settlements. Moreover, of these 17 sites, 14 were occupied during all three periods, and represented multiperiod mounds with long occupational sequences. In contrast, the evidence for settlement continuity between the Iron I (Amuq N) and the later Iron II (Phase O) is very strong. 35 of the 47 known Amuq N sites, or a remarkable 75 percent, were also occupied in Phase O.[8]

[8] For a similar assessment of the settlement trends in the Amuq, although based on slightly different survey data, see Pruss 2002:162–4.

Site-size data clarify further the apparent shift toward settlement intensification evident in the overall site totals. While aggregate settled area also increased, more revealing is the average size of the sites, which actually decreased from 4.76 ha in the LB (or Phase M) to 3.61 in Phase N and 3.63 ha in Phase O. As Casana and Wilkinson have noted (2005:39–40), the Amuq survey data document a decisive settlement shift, or more specifically, a "dispersal" of the population into small, rural settlements during the Iron Age. While site-size distributions remained relatively stable throughout the latter half of the second millennium (Phases M and N), with approximately one-third of the sites falling into the medium size category (5–15 ha) and two-thirds into the small size category (<5 ha), in Phase O, more than eighty percent of the sites (n=26) qualify as small settlements.

What these survey data fail to reveal, however, is the emergence of Tell Taᶜyinat as the dominant settlement in the region. By the Iron II period (or Phase O), at 35 ha in size Tell Taᶜyinat had grown to account for fully 30 percent of the known settled area, and was more than three times larger than Çatal Höyük (AS 167), the next largest settlement in the regional site-size hierarchy. The dominance of Tell Taᶜyinat is also reflected in the spatial distribution of Phase O sites, which shows a heavy concentration of settlements in its vicinity along the southern edge of the plain. Thus, while the survey data indicate significant settlement continuity during the transition from the Late Bronze to the early Iron Age, equally revealing is the evidence that this early Iron Age settlement network subsequently developed into an integrated, urbanized regional entity, with Tell Taᶜyinat at its center.

The Syro-Hittite Expedition Excavations

Today, Tell Taᶜyinat forms a large, low-lying mound 1.5 km east of the town of Demirköprü on the northern bend of the Orontes River, at the point where the river turns west and winds along the southwestern edge of the Amuq plain. The site consists of an upper and lower mound, with the upper mound visible just north of the modern Antakya–Reyhanlı road and the lower mound now hidden by alluvial accumulation from the annual flooding of the Orontes River. The combined surface area of the two mounds measures approximately 500 m (E–W) × 700 m (N–S).

Large-scale excavations were conducted by the University of Chicago's Oriental Institute over the course of four field seasons between 1935 and 1938 as part of the "Syro-Hittite Expedition." The excavations focused primarily on the West Central Area of the upper mound, although excavation areas were also opened on the eastern and southern edges of the upper mound and in the lower settlement (for a more thorough description of the topography and archaeological history of the site, see Batiuk et al. 2005). In all, the Chicago expedition achieved large horizontal exposures of five distinct architectural phases, or Building Periods, which were assigned to the Iron II and III periods (Amuq Phase O), ca. 900–550 B.C.E. (Haines 1971:64–66). A series of isolated soundings below the earliest Phase O floors encountered remains that were dated primarily to the third millennium B.C.E. (specifically Amuq Phases H, I, and J; Braidwood and Braidwood 1960:13–14), suggesting a lengthy period of abandonment between the final Early Bronze Age settlement and the first Iron II settlement.

In a preliminary study of the second and first millennium B.C.E. Amuq pottery sequence (Phases K through O), completed as part of a doctoral dissertation by Gustavus Swift, the Phase O sequence was further divided into four subphases labeled Stages Oa–Od, with ceramic imports and key historical events providing a chronological framework (Swift 1958). Each stage also coincided with changes in the surface treatment of Red-Slipped Burnished Ware (RSBW), the dominant local fabric tradition during this period. Of particular significance, Swift (1958: 154–55) assigned sherds of imported Attic Geometric pottery to his Stage Oc (ca. 800–725 B.C.E.), and fragments of Corinthian, Attic Black Figure, and Assyrian Glazed and Palace wares to his Stage Od (ca. 725–550 B.C.E.).

According to the Chicago excavators, Building I, the most famous of Taᶜyinat's *bīt ḫilani* palaces, and the adjacent *megaron*-style temple (Building II) were constructed during the Second Building Period, the beginning of which they dated to the end of the ninth century B.C.E., based largely on the presence of the numerous Luwian hieroglyphic fragments that were found on or below their floors (Haines 1971:66). Renovations to these buildings accounted for most of the activity assigned to the Third and Fourth Building Periods, which were dated to the latter part of the eighth and the seventh centuries B.C.E. Although the links to the artifactual sequence remain tenuous, it is clear that these later architectural phases correspond loosely to Swift's Stage Od (for more on this phase of the site's settlement history, see Harrison 2005). In addition to Buildings I and II, the Second Building Period also included Building IV (a second *bīt ḫilani*) and Building VI, and altogether formed part of a large complex arranged around a paved central courtyard (Courtyard VIII). The Second Building Period complex was the most extensive and best preserved architectural phase uncovered by the Chicago expedition in the West Central Area. It also exhibited clear stratigraphic separation from the earlier, more fragmentary architectural remains encountered by the Chicago team and assigned to their First Building Period.

Limited exposures of two large structures, identified as Buildings XIII and XIV by the Chicago expedition, were achieved beneath the floors and walls of the buildings assigned to the Second Building Period complex. The east part of Building XIII extended under Building IV, while Building XIV was sealed by Buildings I and VI, and the southern portion of IV. Since they represented the earliest Iron Age architectural levels reached in the West Central Area, both buildings were assigned to the First Building Period (Haines 1971:64). As with the Second Building Period, both structures appeared to form part of a complex centered around a courtyard. A few fragmentary remains uncovered below Second Building Period levels elsewhere on the upper mound were also tentatively assigned to the First Building Period.

Building XIII was excavated during the 1937 season. Unfortunately, except for a few wall fragments along its east side, only the subfloor structural foundations of the building were found intact. Nevertheless, the general outline of Building XIII was reasonably clear, betraying the unmistakable characteristics of a *bīt ḫilani* (for the floor plan, see Haines 1971:pl. 94). The building was roughly rectangular in shape, measuring approximately 28 m (E–W) × 35 m (N–S), and was entered from the south through what appears to have been a porticoed entrance, with a series of side rooms arranged around a long, rectangular central room, presumably the main reception hall (Haines 1971:38–39). The building's foundations were formed by deeply cut, vertically-faced trenches filled with unbaked brick, a distinctive construction technique also used in many of the other monumental buildings of the West Central Area (Braidwood and Braidwood 1960:13).

Though poorly preserved, and only partially excavated, Building XIV appears to have been considerably larger than Building XIII. As with Building XIII, very little of its superstructure was found intact, and the excavators therefore were unable to reconstruct a coherent plan of the complex or determine its function (Haines 1971:39–40). However, they did succeed in piecing together a fragmentary plan that gives some indication of its truly enormous size (see Haines 1971:pl. 95), which the excavators estimated to have been at least 49 m (E–W) × 95 m (N–S).

Miscellaneous Architectural Finds

In addition to the Luwian hieroglyphic fragments, a number of isolated architectural finds appear also to belong to the First Building Period and add to the sense of scale and grandeur of this early phase. In particular, as many as two similarly carved basalt column bases, ranging between 1.3 and 1.4 m in diameter, were recovered from contexts that suggest they originally had come from either Building XIII or XIV. One was found on the surface of the mound (see Haines 1971:37, pls. 68d and 116b), while the second was found (apparently in reuse) in the paving of Courtyard VIII, directly above the vicinity of the porch entrance to Building XIII (Haines 1971:39; see depiction in the northeast corner of Square F-17 in pl. 99). A possible third (and fourth) column base was uncovered in a sounding (T 9) excavated beneath the pavement of Courtyard VIII in the area of Squares H-J 17–18 (see Haines 1971:41, pl. 89a and 98b). However, it is unclear whether the larger of these two column bases is different from the one described earlier by Haines as a surface find. In any case, the latter piece was found resting, out of position, on top of a wall attributed to Building XIV (see Haines 1971:pl. 95). Although of uncertain provenance, these column bases undoubtedly predate the Second (or Third) Building Period structures they were recovered from, while their simple architectural style anticipates the smaller, more elaborately rendered column bases found *in situ* in the entrance to Building I (compare with Haines 1971:pls. 78c–d, 103, and 116a).

Two carved lion-headed orthostats were also recovered during the Chicago excavations.[9] The first (T-3269) was found in secondary reuse in the north wall of Building IV (Haines 1971:42, pls. 71b and 97), in a context associated with the building's second phase of occupation (specifically Floor 1, or the Third Building Period, according to the Haines phasing sequence; see 1971:65). The principal features of the lion's head are clearly depicted, including its eyes, nose, slightly opened mouth with teeth, and five whiskers. Its head is turned 90 degrees to the right, indicating that the figure probably once guarded the left side of an entranceway. The second lion-headed orthostat (T-3270) was also found out of context on Floor 3 in Room A, the stairwell for Building I, a context dated by the excavators to the Second Building Period (see Haines 1971:65). This second lion figure exhibits stylistic features strikingly similar to

[9] My discussion of the Taʿyinat orthostats has benefited from a study conducted by Brian Janeway as part of a graduate seminar paper.

the first, but also differs slightly with its forward-looking stance, and roughly carved paws for a base (see figure 2). Both figures display characteristics typical of early Neo-Hittite sculpture, and almost certainly should be assigned to the First Building Period.[10]

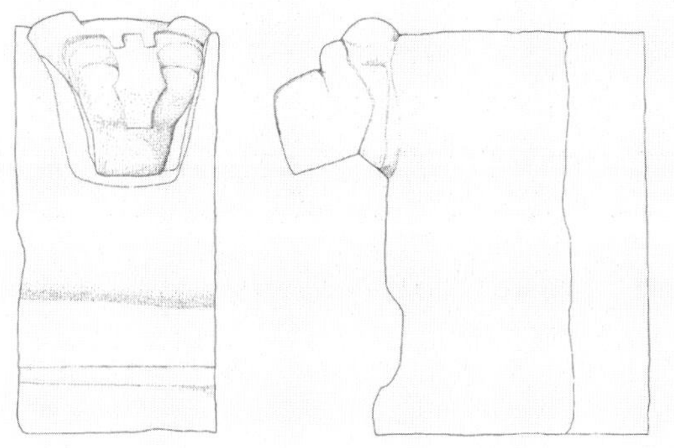

Figure 2. Lion-headed orthostat (T-3270) found reused in Building I at Tell Taᶜyinat
Drawing by F. Haughey

A final architectural piece should perhaps also be considered, though its association with Tell Taᶜyinat is not certain. The piece in question, a carved basalt orthostat depicting two charioteers driving over a defeated enemy, rendered larger than life size, was first reported in 1896, and is said to have come from Tell Taᶜyinat (Braidwood 1937:33, fig. 7). Although usually dated to the eighth century by art historians (compare with Vieyra 1955:46–47; Madhloom 1970:31; Orthmann 1971:83, 158–59), the carved chariot scene does resemble similar reliefs found at Karkamiš (Orthmann 1971:pl. 24) and Zincirli (Orthmann 1971:pl. 57a) that are generally dated to the tenth or ninth centuries B.C.E., and it contains specific features commonly associated with the ninth century or earlier, including the coiffure of the riders (pothook curls, hair bunched at the nape of the neck, and clean-shaven face), the presence of crossing arrow quivers on the side of the chariot, and the richly ornamented bar connecting the chariot to the horse. The eight-spoked wheel of the Taᶜyinat chariot, while generally considered typical of the eighth century B.C.E., does occur in ninth-century contexts (compare with Ussishkin 1969:128; Madhloom 1970:14, pl. I.3). Perhaps more significantly, if this orthostat is assigned to the Second (or Third) Building Period, in other words, to the eighth century B.C.E. or later, it would be the only carved basalt orthostat recovered from these levels, in contrast to the numerous plain orthostats that were uncovered *in situ* by the Chicago excavations.

The Taᶜyinat Archaeological Project Investigations

The Taᶜyinat Archaeological Project (TAP) was conceived within the framework of the Amuq Valley Regional Project (AVRP), which has been systematically documenting the archaeology of the Amuq plain in southeastern Turkey since 1995. Within this broader regional research framework, TAP was initiated as a long-term field project, designed to document fully and systematically the archaeological record preserved at the site, clearly identified by the Syro-Hittite Expedition as one of the principal Bronze and Iron Age settlements in the plain. Following preliminary field seasons devoted to surveying and mapping the site (see Batiuk et al. 2005), targeted excavations were resumed at Tell Taᶜyinat in 2004 and have continued on an annual basis since then.

With the commencement of excavations in 2004, an exploratory probe was initiated along the southern edge of the West Central Area to test, or "ground truth," remote-sensing data gathered during the surface survey. These excavations, limited to a 3 × 20-m trench, uncovered the northern wall and portions of the central room of Building II, the *megaron*-style temple first excavated by the Syro-Hittite Expedition. Building II, in turn, sealed a remarkably well-preserved sequence of early Iron Age remains, including a wealth of pottery and other material culture exhibiting strong Aegean connections.[11] During the following 2005 season, the 2004 probe was extended laterally to the south, expanding the excavated area to four 10 × 10-m squares, or a total area of 400 square meters. In all, the 2004 and 2005 excavations in this area, specifically Field I, succeeded in delineating seven superimposed architectural phases, or Field Phases (FP), with the primary sequence (FP 3–6) dating to the twelfth century B.C.E. or early Iron I.

The 2005 season also saw the opening of a new area, Field II, to the north of Field I in the vicinity of Building I, the principal *bīt ḫilani* palace uncovered during the Chicago excavations. The primary objectives of the excavations in this area were to determine

[10] Indeed, Mazzoni has used the second lion figure (T-3270) to argue for an eleventh–tenth-century B.C.E. date for the foundation of the Iron Age city (Mazzoni 1994:322, n. 20; 1995:188, n. 45).

[11] The evidence of an intrusive cultural presence with strong Aegean overtones during the early Iron Age certainly also has important historical implications and is the focus of another paper (see Janeway 2006–7).

what remained of Building I and then excavate below it into Building XIV to establish better the stratigraphic relationship between these two structures. The 2005 excavations, limited to a 10 × 10-m area, proceeded to uncover a series of large mudbrick walls immediately below the modern plow zone. The walls, which averaged more than 3 m in width, formed a tight grid pattern, resulting in two small rooms, neither of which was furnished with a doorway (see figure 3). The westernmost of the two rooms was also equipped with a circular bin-like installation. A probe in the southwestern corner of this room reached a depth of more than 3 m before encountering the bottom of the walls. Clearly the remains of an enormous structure, our excavations suggest that these walls very probably formed part of the foundations of Building XIV. Preliminary assessment of the pottery and associated material culture points to a late Iron I/early Iron II date (ca. tenth–early ninth centuries B.C.E.) for the complex. The renewed TAP investigations have also begun to shed more light on the depositional history of the numerous Luwian hieroglyphic fragments recovered during the course of the Chicago excavations, in part due to the discovery of additional fragments with the resumption of excavations. These fragments, and almost certainly most, if not all, of the Chicago fragments reported from this area, appear to have eroded, or "bled," from the unexcavated part of the mound immediately to the north of Building II; in other words, from the cultural stratum that has now begun to reveal the remains of Building XIV. To localize further the spatial distribution of these fragments, we have tried to plot their distribution across the site. If the fragments from Taᶜyinat Inscription 1 are reassigned to the Courtyard VIII area rather than to the colossal seated figure they were incorrectly attributed to in Gateway VII, all but two out of a total of 88 reported fragments were found in the West Central Area. Moreover, as illustrated in figure 4, the scatter plots created by their spatial distribution cluster tightly around Building XIV (outlined in light gray in the plan).

Figure 3. Plan of the early Iron Age walls in Field II at Tell Taᶜyinat
Created by S. Batiuk

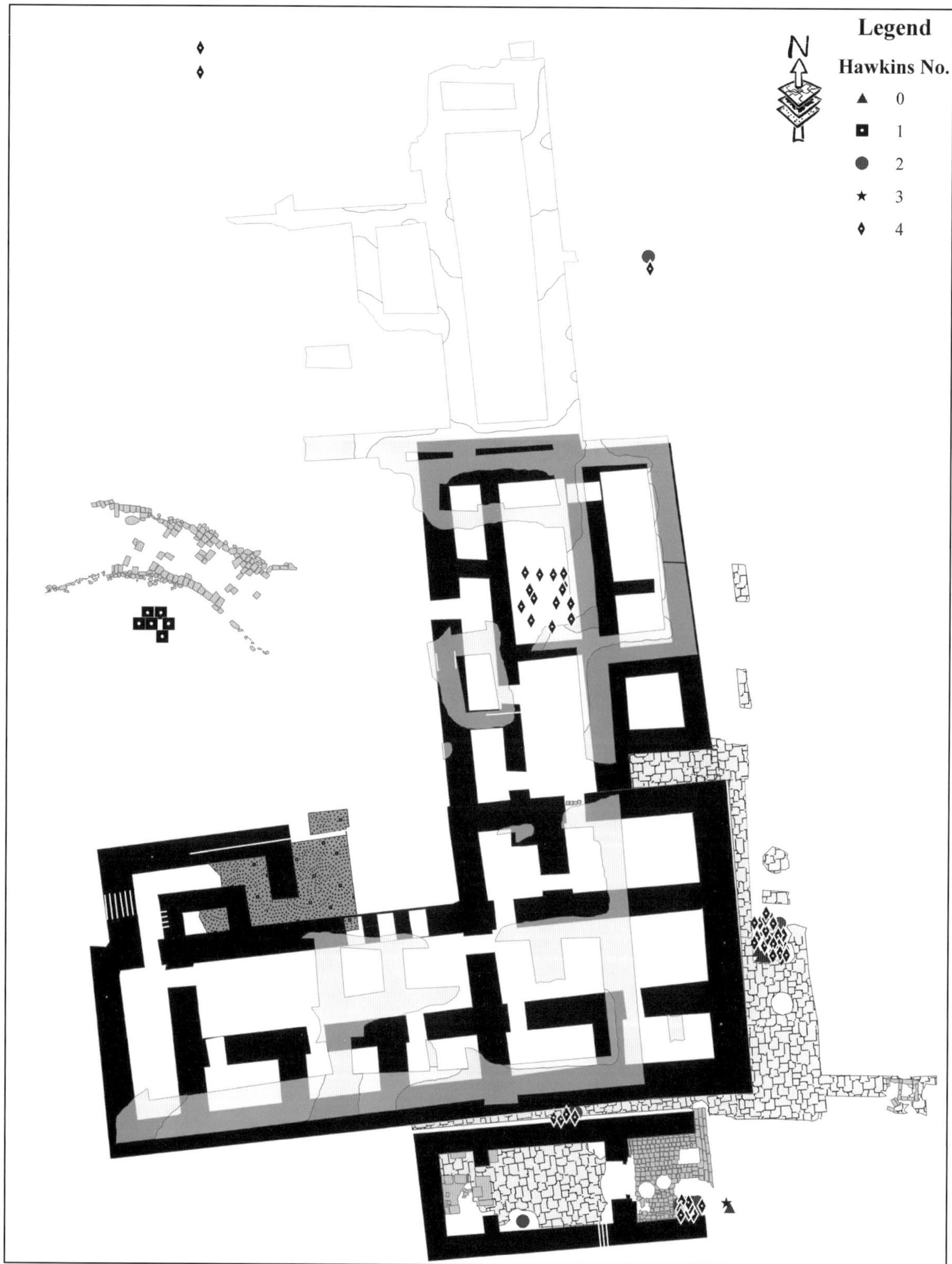

Figure 4. Plan of the spatial distribution of Luwian hieroglyphic fragments in the West Central Area
Created by S. Batiuk

The extraordinary size of the walls in Field II and the rich epigraphic record associated with it certainly mark Building XIV as an important structure. Its apparent date and relative stratigraphic position within the early Iron Age sequence at Tell Taᶜyinat also raises the possibility that it might have been the palatial residence of the kings of Palastin/Walastin. Further work must be done, however, before more definitive conclusions can be drawn about the historical role and function of this remarkable complex.

Summary Observations

While it is clear that the collapse of the Hittite Empire at the end of the Late Bronze Age created a political vacuum that fostered an era of prolonged regional instability, as we have seen, there is also growing evidence of cultural and political continuity. Indeed, at key centers of Hittite power, such as Karkamiš, Hittite imperial control appears to have survived in the form of diminished "rump" states ruled by dynastic lines with direct ancestral links to the royal family in Hattuša. However, interspersed between these reduced enclaves of Hittite influence, rival political centers, perhaps most importantly at Zincirli (ancient Samᵓal) and Tell Rifaᶜat (ancient Arpad), also began to materialize, reflecting their own newly emergent cultural (and linguistic) traditions. The result was a highly fragmented or "balkanized" political landscape upon which a diverse cultural (and ethnic) milieu was able to develop and flourish. Out of this cultural and political ferment emerged the small vibrant nation-states that would come to define Iron Age civilization in this region.

In the North Orontes Valley, the existing archaeological evidence supports this view of continuity and change. Despite the evidence for settlement continuity reflected in the survey data, there is also evidence of change, attested perhaps most revealingly in the shift of the primary settlement in the valley from Tell Atchana (ancient Alalakh) to nearby Tell Taᶜyinat. Whether the terminal LB settlement at Alalakh was destroyed or abandoned remains unclear, but the renewed excavations at Tell Taᶜyinat have now demonstrated conclusively that the site was resettled in the early Iron I (early twelfth century B.C.E.) after an eight-century hiatus corresponding to the period of Alalakh's ascendancy. Somewhat unexpectedly, however, the early Iron I levels at Taᶜyinat have also revealed a material cultural signature that betrays an intrusive Aegean influence, if not direct evidence of the presence of foreign settlers. Superimposed over these distinctive remains, in turn, are the monumental structures of the First Building Period, with their Hittite stylistic features and rich Luwian epigraphic record, followed by the late ninth–eighth-century *bīt ḫilani* complex of the Second Building Period.

Thus, although the specific historical circumstances remain elusive, the emerging archaeological picture, informed by an admittedly small but growing textual record, has begun to lift the obscuring veil of this Dark Age. In the North Orontes Valley, the evidence points to the emergence of a powerful regional kingdom, the Land of Palastin/Walastin, ruled in the aftermath of the Hittite Empire's collapse by a line of kings with Hittite names, and very possibly with direct ancestral links to the royal dynasty. This early Iron Age polity also exhibits strong Aegean cultural associations, both in its material culture, and now also epigraphically. Its rulers appear to have succeeded in asserting political control for a time over an area that encompassed much of northwest Syria, extending east to Aleppo and south as far as Hama. Centered at Tell Taᶜyinat, the wealth of this hypothesized early Iron Age kingdom are reflected in the impressive buildings and standing monuments of the First Building Period.

Acknowledgments:

Funding for the Taᶜyinat Archaeological Project (TAP) excavations has been provided by research grants from the Social Sciences and Humanities Research Council of Canada (SSHRCC) and by the Institute for Aegean Prehistory (INSTAP). I wish also to thank the Directorate of Cultural Heritage and Museums of Turkey, which awarded the research permits necessary to conduct these excavations, as well as the project staff, whose dedicated efforts have ensured the success of each field season.

Bibliography

Astour, M. C.
1969 The Partition of the Confederacy of Mukiš–Nuhašše–Nii by Šuppiluliuma: A Study in the Political Geography of the Amarna Age. *Orientalia* N.S. 38:381–414.

Batiuk, S., T. P. Harrison, and L. Pavlish
2005 The Ta^{c}yinat Survey, 1999–2002. In *The Amuq Valley Regional Projects*, vol. 1, *Surveys in the Plain of Antioch and Orontes Delta, Turkey, 1995–2002*, ed. K. A. Yener, 171–92. OIP 131. Chicago: Oriental Institute, University of Chicago.

Braidwood, R. J.
1937 *Mounds in the Plain of Antioch: An Archaeological Survey*. OIP 48. Chicago: University of Chicago Press.

Braidwood, R. J., and L. S. Braidwood
1960 *Excavations in the Plain of Antioch*. Vol. 1, *The Earlier Assemblages; Phases A–J*. OIP 61. Chicago: University of Chicago Press.

Bryce, T. R.
1992 The Role of Telipinu, the Priest, in the Hittite Kingdom. *Hethitica* 11:5–18.
1998 *The Kingdom of the Hittites*. Oxford: Oxford University Press.

Casana, J. J., and T. J. Wilkinson
2005 Settlement and Lanscapes in the Amuq Region. In *The Amuq Valley Regional Projects*, vol. 1, *Surveys in the Plain of Antioch and Orontes Delta, Turkey, 1995–2002*, ed. K. A. Yener, 25–65. OIP 131. Chicago: Oriental Institute, University of Chicago.

Dinçol, A., J. Yakar, B. Dinçol, and A. Taffet
2000 The Borders of the Appanage Kingdom of *Tarhuntašša*: A Geographical and Archaeological Assessment. *Anatolica* 26:1–29.

Drews, R.
1993 *The End of the Bronze Age: Changes in Warfare and the Catastrophe ca. 1200 B.C.* Princeton: Princeton University Press.

Gelb, I. J.
1939 *Hittite Hieroglyphic Monuments*. OIP 45. Chicago: University of Chicago Press.

Genz, H.
2003 The Early Iron Age in Central Anatolia. In *Identifying Changes: The Transition from Bronze to Iron Ages in Anatolia and Its Neighbouring Regions*, ed. B. Fischer, H. Genz, E. Jean, and K. Köroğlu, 179–91. Istanbul: Türk Eskiçağ Bilimleri Enstitüsü.
2004 *Büyükkaya*. Vol. 1, *Die Keramik der Eisenzeit*. Boğazköy-Ḫattuša 21. Mainz am Rhein: Philipp von Zabern.

Gonnella, J., W. Khayyata, and K. Kohlmeyer
2005 *Die Zitadelle von Aleppo und der Tempel des Wettergottes*. Münster: Rhema.

Güterbock, H. G.
1992 Survival of the Hittite Dynasty. In *The Crisis Years: The Twelfth Century B.C.*, ed. W. A. Ward and M. S. Joukowsky, 53–55. Dubuque, Iowa: Kendall/Hunt.

Haines, R. C.
1971 *Excavations in the Plain of Antioch*. Vol. 2, *The Structural Remains of the Later Phases: Chatal Höyük, Tell al-Judaidah, and Tell Ta^{c}yinat*. OIP 92. Chicago: University of Chicago Press.

Harrison, T. P.
2001 Tell Ta^{c}yinat and the Kingdom of Unqi. In *The World of the Aramaeans*, vol. 2, *Studies in History and Archaeology in Honour of Paul-Eugène Dion*, ed.P. M. M. Daviau, J. W. Wevers, and M. Weigl, 115–32. JSOTSup 325. Sheffield, England: Sheffield Academic Press.
2005 The Neo-Assyrian Governor's Residence at Tell Ta^{c}yinat. *Bulletin of the Canadian Society for Mesopotamian Studies* 40:23–32.

Hawkins, J. D.
1975 Halab: The First Millennium. In *Reallexikon der Assyriologie und vorderasiatischen Archäologie*, ed. E. Ebeling and B. Meissner, 4:53. Berlin: Walter de Gruyter.
1979 The Hieroglyphic Luwian Stelae of Meharde-Sheizar. In *Florilegium Anatolicum: Mélanges offerts à Emmanuel Laroche*, 145–56. Paris: Boccard.
1988 Kuzi-Tešub and the "Great Kings" of Karkamiš. *Anatolian Studies* 38:99–108.
1995 "Great Kings" and "Country-Lords" at Malatya and Karkamiš. In *Studio Historiae Ardens: Ancient Near Eastern Studies Presented to Philo H. J. Houwink ten Cate on the Occasion of his 65th Birthday*, ed. T. van den Hout and J. de Roos, 73–85. Istanbul: Nederlands Historisch-Archaeologisch Instituut.
2000 Inscriptions of the Iron Age: Texts. In *Corpus of Hieroglyphic Luwian Inscriptions*, vol. 1/2, by J. D. Hawkins. Berlin: Walter de Gruyter.
2002 Anatolia: The End of the Hittite Empire and After. In *Die nahöstlichen Kulturen und Griechenland an der Wende vom 2. zum 1. Jahrtausend v. Chr.: Kontinuität und Wandel von Strukturen und Mechanismen kultureller Interaktion*, ed. E. A. Braun-Holzinger and H. Matthäus, 143–51. Möhnesee: Bibliopolis.

2004 The Hieroglyphic Luwian Inscription Aleppo 3. Paper presented at the Fourth International Congress on the Archaeology of the Ancient Near East (ICAANE), Berlin, Germany.

2008 Cilicia, Aleppo and the Amuq: New Evidence on the Late Bronze–Iron Age Transition. Paper presented at the Sixth International Congress on the Archaeology of the Ancient Near East (ICAANE), Rome, Italy.

Hoffner, H. A.

1992 The Last Days of Khattusha. In *The Crisis Years: The Twelfth Century B.C.*, ed. W. A. Ward and M. S. Joukowsky, 46–52. Dubuque, Iowa: Kendall/Hunt.

Janeway, B.

2006–7 The Nature and Extent of Aegean Contact at Tell Taᶜyinat and Vicinity in the Early Iron Age: Evidence of the Sea Peoples? *Scripta Mediterranea* 27–28:123–46.

Klengel, H.

1992 *Syria, 3000 to 300 B.C.: A Handbook of Political History*. Berlin: Akademie.

1999 *Geschichte des hethitischen Reiches*. Leiden: Brill.

Kohlmeyer, K.

2000 *Der Tempel des Wettergottes von Aleppo*. Münster: Rhema.

Kuhrt, A.

1995 *The Ancient Near East, c. 3000–330 BC*. Vol. 1. London: Routledge.

Laroche, E.

1956 L'Inscription hittite d'Alep. *Syria* 33:131–41.

Madhloom, T. A.

1970 *The Chronology of Neo-Assyrian Art*. London: Athlone.

Mazzoni, S.

1994 Aramaean and Luwian New Foundations. In *Nuove fondazioni nel Vicino Oriente antico: realta e ideologia*, ed. S. Mazzoni, 319–40. Pisa: Giardini Editori e Stampatori.

1995 Settlement Pattern and New Urbanization in Syria at the Time of the Assyrian Conquest. In *Neo-Assyrian Geography*, ed. M. Liverani, 181–91. Quaderni di Geografia Storica 5. Rome: University of Rome.

McClellan, T. L.

1992 Twelfth Century B.C. Syria: Comments on H. Sader's Paper. In *The Crisis Years: The Twelfth Century B.C.*, ed. W. A. Ward and M. S. Joukowsky, 164–73. Dubuque, Iowa: Kendall/Hunt.

Muhly, J. D.

1992 The Crisis Years in the Mediterranean World: Transition or Cultural Disintegration? In *The Crisis Years: The Twelfth Century B.C.*, ed. W. A. Ward and M. S. Joukowsky, 10–26. Dubuque, Iowa: Kendall/Hunt.

Naᵓaman, N.

1980 The Historical Introduction of the Aleppo Treaty Reconsidered. *JCS* 32:34–42.

Orthmann, W.

1971 *Untersuchungen zur späthethitischen Kunst*. Saarbrucker Beitrage zur Altertumskunde 8. Bonn: Rudolf Habelt.

2002 Die Bildkunst im Übergang von der Groβreichszeit zur späthethitischen Periode. In *Die nahöstlichen Kulturen und Griechenland an der Wende vom 2. zum 1. Jahrtausend v. Chr.: Kontinuität und Wandel von Strukturen und Mechanismen kultureller Interaktion*, E. A. Braun-Holzinger and H. Matthäus, 153–59. Möhnesee: Bibliopolis.

Pruss, A.

2002 Ein Licht in der Nacht? Die Amuq-Ebene während der Dark Ages. In *Die nahöstlichen Kulturen und Griechenland an der Wende vom 2. zum 1. Jahrtausend v. Chr.: Kontinuität und Wandel von Strukturen und Mechanismen kultureller Interaktion*, ed. E. A. Braun-Holzinger and H. Matthäus, 161–76. Möhnesee: Bibliopolis.

Roaf, M.

1990 *Cultural Atlas of Mesopotamia and the Ancient Near East*. New York: Facts On File.

Seeher, J.

1998 Neue Befunde zur Endzeit von Hattuša: Ausgrabungen auf Büyükkaya in Boğazköy. In *Acts of the Third International Congress of Hittitology, Çorum, September 16–22, 1996*, ed. S. Alp and A. Süel, 515–23. Ankara.

2001 Die Zerstörung der Stadt Hattuša. In *Akten des IV. Internationalen Kongresses für Hethitologie, 4–8. Oktober 1999*, ed. G. Wilhelm, 623–34. Studien zu den Boğazköy-Texten 45. Wiesbaden: Harrassowitz.

Singer, I.

1996 Great Kings of Tarhuntašša. *SMEA* 38:63–71.

2000 New Evidence on the End of the Hittite Empire. In *The Sea Peoples and Their World: A Reassessment*, ed. E. D. Oren, 21–34. University Museum Monographs 108. Philadelphia: University Museum, University of Pennsylvania.

Sürenhagen, D.

1986 Ein Königssiegel aus Kargamis. *MDOG* 118: 183–90.

Swift, G. F.
1958 The Pottery of the ᶜAmuq, Phases K to O, and Its Historical Relationships. Ph. D. diss., University of Chicago.

Ussishkin, D.
1969 The Date of the Neo-Hittite Enclosure in Karatepe. *Anatolian Studies* 19:121–37.

Van Loon, M.
1995 A Neo-Hittite Relief in Aleppo. In *Studio Historiae Ardens: Ancient Near Eastern Studies Presented to Philo H. J. Houwink ten Cate on the Occasion of his 65th Birthday*, ed. T. van den Hout and J. de Roos, 181–86. Istanbul: Nederlands Historisch-Archaeologisch Instituut.

Vieyra, M.
1955 *Hittite Art: 2300–750 B.C.* London: Alec Tiranti.

Yakar, J.
1993 Anatolian Civilization Following the Disintegration of the Hittite Empire: An Archaeological Appraisal. *Tel Aviv* 20:3–28.

Yamada, S.
2000 *The Construction of the Assyrian Empire: A Historical Study of the Inscriptions of Shalmanesar III (859–824 B.C.) Relating to His Campaigns to the West.* Leiden: Brill.

Yener, A., C. Edens, T. P. Harrison, J. Verstraete, and T. J. Wilkinson
2000 The Amuq Valley Regional Project, 1995–1998. *AJA* 104:163–220.

20. Other Edens

by Ronald Hendel

> *We were created to live in paradise, and paradise was destined to serve us. Our destiny has been altered; that this also happened with the destiny of paradise is not told.*
>
> Franz Kafka

In his article "Jerusalem and the Garden of Eden," Lawrence Stager marshals a variety of textual and archaeological evidence to explore the symbolic significance of the Jerusalem Temple and to argue that the J writer "was already identifying the Garden of Eden (meaning 'abundant, luxuriant, fertile') with the Garden of God in Jerusalem" (Stager 1999:189). He rightly observes:

> Celestial archetypes were embodied in architecture, iconography, cultic vessels and religious paraphernalia on the Temple Mount and in the surrounding areas. Jerusalem, the regal-ritual city par excellence, became a miniature cosmion, the source of "living waters" that flow forth from Zion. [ibid.]

While others have noted various symbolic analogies between the Temple, Jerusalem, and the Garden of Eden (Wenham 1994; Levenson 1985:128–32), Stager's argument is both more substantial and more precise, for he has reconstructed the landscape of Jerusalem both within and outside the Temple compound that embodies this symbolic geography. In addition to the shared iconography of sacred trees, cherubim, and the eastern orientation, he notes that "the whole [Kidron] valley was a cascade of terraced gardens and parks," which, like other royal and temple gardens, had a cosmic-mythic significance. As celestial archetypes, these gardens were in some respect the gardens of God. Stager notes, "It would not have taken much effort for Yahweh to rise from his throne in the Holy of Holies and stroll down into the nearby gardens of the Kidron valley" (1999:189). The Garden of God, filled with exotic and lush trees, was an emblem of paradise, both in the cityscape and in the myth.

In the following, I wish to extend and complicate Stager's analysis of the relationship between the regal-ritual city of Jerusalem and the mythic text of the Garden of Eden. Granting his thesis that the text and the city participate in a shared symbolic system, I wish to point out some of the frictions that exist in relationship between the two. In some important senses, the myth takes away that which the ritual city provides—the possibility of a return to paradise. In this respect the mythic text and the sacred place contradict each other. But if there is an implicit allusion to the cultic topography in the myth, then there may be a kind of compromise at a different level, or at least a kind of oscillation between the impossibility and the availability of a return to paradise. In this respect, the myth and the ritual may be both contradictory and complementary, in an unsystematic way that defies easy explanation.

My approach accepts the premise that mythic and religious thought tend to operate by what Pierre Bourdieu calls a logic of practice, a pragmatic and unsystematic logic, where contradictions and inconcinnities are natural and expected. Bourdieu argues that

> symbolic systems [have] practical coherence—that is, on the one hand, their unity and their regularities, and on the other, their "fuzziness" and their irregularities and even incoherences, which are both equally necessary, being inscribed in the logic of their genesis and functioning. [Bourdieu 1990:86]

That is, a symbolic system must have some internal coherence, but must also function in the world of lived experience, which is a complicated and confusing place. Religious concepts and habits are therefore both consistent and incoherent in turns, since they respond to a variety of problems and circumstances, which are not in themselves orderly or coherent. In order to be adequate, a symbolic system "performs an uncertain abstraction which brings the same symbol into different relationships by apprehending it through different aspects" (ibid., p. 87), thus allowing for its continued resilience and resonance across the different facets of human life. A symbolic form, like the garden of God, and a real-life circumstance, like death or suffering, will interrelate in various ways, and the symbol will be vested with varying and inconsistent meanings.

My larger claim, which is implied in Stager's study, is that myth, cult, and culture should be held together in our investigations of the Hebrew Bible. What is required is a cultural poetics that attends to the complex circulation of meanings among texts, material culture, political institutions, and conceptual forms (see Greenblatt 1990). The Garden of Eden story and the Temple cult belong to different levels of Israelite culture, but their complex meanings are nonetheless part of a whole, even if the whole is riven with contradictions.

Out of Eden

Let us begin with some statements and implications of the text of Gen. 2:4–3:24. The first human, called האדם, "the (hu)man," is portrayed as both a historical ancestor and a symbolic archetype of all humans. He is a character and a symbol. As such, his deeds—and the deeds of his counterpart, אשה, "woman"—and their consequences affect us all, and in some sense all humans recapitulate the story in our individual lives. Idyllic memories of childhood, of subsequent willfulness and disobedience, the adolescent awakening of knowledge—including sexual knowledge—are all inscribed in the story and in our lives. The burden of death is faced by all humans. The harsh realities of life in ancient Israel, including subsistence agriculture and the dangers of childbirth, are given universal scope, as Gunkel vividly describes:

> It portrays the man as a farmer—it knows no other profession—the woman as childbearer. Now the myth considers the heavy toil of both: the toil of the childbearer, the toil of the farmer. . . . It describes the fate of humanity in the disturbing words of the curse: it is distress and suffering and finally death. This destiny is without hope: as long as there are people, women will bear in pain and men will eat from the sweat of their brow. [Gunkel 1997:29]

As Gunkel further notes, this painful outcome is mingled with resignation:

> Along with pain, resignation sounds clearly. A kind of resigned comfort is added to the announcement of death: "For you are dust and to dust you return." Nothing unusual happens to man when he dies. . . . Eternal life is a good which God has reserved for himself. Do not desire the impossible! [ibid., 31–32]

The Eden story describes the sorrows and the advantages ("knowledge like the gods," the joy of becoming "one flesh") of life outside of Eden with a note of finality, grounding these conditions in the most distant past. It is impossible to return to the Garden of Eden for two reasons:

1. The geographical location of Eden is impossible to locate. According to the mythic topography of Gen. 2:10–14, Eden is the source of four rivers, the Pishon, the Gihon, the Tigris, and the Euphrates. The sources of the latter two are in eastern Anatolia—perhaps near ʾEl's home in Canaanite myth and the mythic Cedar Forest in the standard version of the Gilgamesh epic (Wallace 1985:70–88; on the Cedar Forest and Cedar Mountain, see George 2003:93–94). But the Pishon, in Arabia, is unknown and in any case does not intersect with the headwaters of the Tigris or Euphrates. The Gihon, whose location is specified as the land of Cush (which usually means Upper Egypt or Sudan, and in Gen. 10:8 may refer to Kassite Mesopotamia), is only known elsewhere as the river of Jerusalem. This allusion or analogy to the river that waters the Temple city is a gesture that both hints at and precludes identification of Eden with Jerusalem (since Jerusalem's Gihon does not flow to Cush). The location of Eden cannot be found on any map because its geographical coordinates are contradictory and fantastic.

2. Even if one could locate the Garden, one would not be able to enter, for it is guarded by "the cherubim and the flame of the whirling sword" (Gen. 3:24). This is another fantastic and barely fathomable scene. The cherubim are mixed creatures, fierce of visage, who guard the threshold to the divine garden—liminal beings guarding a liminal threshold. The mysterious "flame of the whirling sword" seems to be either an animated fiery sword or a fiery creature wielding a sword. In either case it is fierce and ambiguous—another liminal phenomenon guarding the threshold. If one tried to enter the Garden in search of the Tree of Life, one would be cut down by its strange guardians. Death would be the consequence of attempting to return to paradise.

This is a story of the human condition: how it became what it is, and why we cannot return to paradise. It makes major aspects of human experience thinkable: its pain, suffering, and death, and its countervailing joy of marriage, sex, and knowledge. It offers insight and resignation to a world that we can recognize as the world of ancient Israel (for example, in its economy and gender roles) and in many respects to the *longue durée* of human existence.

The Temple/Eden Analogy

As a celestial archetype, the Temple and its sacred geography provide a link between heaven and earth, between the ideal and the real. Jon Levenson has elegantly explored this symbolic relation:

> In the Hebrew Bible, it is clear that the Temple precincts are perceived as radically and qualitatively dif-

ferent from the rest of the world. Between the Temple and ordinary reality lies a barrier of holiness, a palpable energy or force which resists the intermingling of the two modes of reality. . . . The sanctuary, then, is a place in which reality is perceived as a whole, as fresh and untarnished, where the costs exacted by the harshness of normal life are not paid . . . the sanctuary is an enclave of ideal reality within the world of profanity. [Levenson 1985:127–28]

As seen most profusely in the language of the psalms, the Temple is a place where suffering has no hold, where God is a gracious and protective host, where life is perfect. The second half of Psalm 23 is the most famous portrayal of this idyllic experience of the Temple:

> You spread a table before me
> in the sight of my adversaries;
> You anoint my head with oil,
> my cup overflows.
> Only goodness and lovingkindness shall pursue me
> all the days of my life;
> and I shall dwell in the House of God (the Temple)
> for an abundance of days.

Although the adversaries are in plain sight, they cannot harm the worshiper who is under God's protection. The boundary between sacred and the profane is inviolable. The enemies, who recall the "evil" and the "shadow of death" of v. 4, cannot "pursue me" in this place; rather, only ideal qualities may do so: "only goodness and lovingkindness shall pursue me all the days of my life." The meal—alluding to the sacrificial meal—is abundant and sensual, accompanied by dripping oil and brimming wine. This is a ritual meal in paradise, where life itself is full and good. The last lines reveal that this paradisiacal place is none other than the Temple, where the speaker longs to dwell for "all the days of my life / for an abundance of days." In the sacred place, life is perfect.

Many psalms, particularly those of thanksgiving and pilgrimage, describe the ideal quality of life in the Temple precincts. As Levenson explains: "It is, in a sense, the gateway to life as it was meant to be, unlimited by death, eternal life, life *in illo tempore*, sacred time, always new, always just created" (1985: 133). But this suspension of the real and the return to paradise contradicts the plain import of the Garden of Eden story, in which the world of human finitude is our only world and paradise is sealed off from us. The ritual experience bypasses the text, in which fierce creatures and incomprehensible geography bar the way to paradise. If, as Stager and others maintain, the J writer "was already identifying the Garden of Eden . . . with the Garden of God in Jerusalem," this cannot be a straightforward equivalence, for the two are contradictory and in many ways incommensurate.

The Senses of Paradise

The myth and the regal-ritual city are alike and contradictory simultaneously. There is a larger symbolic system—an unsystematic one—that both participate in and that operates by a necessarily fuzzy logic. Human life is imperfect, even as we long for paradise. The realism of the myth is effaced by the idealism of the ritual. As Jonathan Z. Smith and others have emphasized, ritual offers an ideal alternative to the real world, which serves to focus and enrich ordinary life:

> Ritual is a means of performing the way things ought to be in conscious tension to the way things are in such a way that this ritualized perfection is recollected in the ordinary, uncontrolled course of things. [Smith 1982:63]

The memory of the Temple ("this ritualized perfection") in the course of ordinary life animates the desire for refuge, transcendence, and God's protective care. The Garden of Eden narrative is the other side of this tension, for it portrays the world in which humans are exiled from paradise, resigned to a world of toil and death, which is leavened with domestic joy. In this respect, the myth portrays the way things are rather than the way things ought to be. That is, the text is animated by realism, whereas the cult offers a return to paradise, a taste of the ideal life. Arguably, human life requires both—insight and resignation in relation to the real, and the hope and self-transcendence offered by the ideal.

The myth and the ritual are in tension. Suspended within this tension is the lived experience of the ancient Israelites—men and women, peasants, scribes, kings, and others. We should not overlook the royal interests in the Jerusalem rites: the idyllic symbolism of Jerusalem has a political function, expressing the magnificence of the king and the divine authority of his rule. The myth lacks this political subtext, for in the J text there is no human king in paradise, but Yahweh alone. But this is not a critique of human kingship because it portrays a prepolitical era. In this respect, the ritual anchors the political reality, while the myth is oblivious to it.

The diverging senses of the myth and the regal-ritual city are part of the symbolic capital of Israelite culture and religion. They participate in a polyphony, both discordant and compensatory, which melds the ideal and the real into a rough system that accommodates the complexities of experience. The synthesis is at the level of practice, where the jangled habits, burdens, and joys of life exist together.

Afterward: In the Cave

Another layer in this nexus of myth, ritual, and reality may be seen in the Ketef Hinnom inscriptions (Barkay et al. 2004), in which the ideal language of the Temple is transposed into the context of death and the practice of family religion. Two silver amulets, dating to the late seventh–early sixth century B.C.E, were discovered in a burial cave outside Jerusalem. The texts are protective incantations, appealing to Yahweh's blessing and care in the transition to the grave and Sheol. The amulets "offer God's protection from Evil through the invocation of his holy name and the text of his most solemn of protective blessings" (ibid., p. 68), that is, the Priestly Benediction:

> Yahw[eh] . . . grea[t]. . . the covenant, and graciousness to those who love [him] and those who keep . . . [the] blessing more than any [sna]re and more than Evil. For redemption is in him. For Yahweh is our restorer [and] rock. May Yahweh bless you [and] keep you. May Yahweh make [his] face [sh]ine . . .
>
> (Ketef Hinnom I; translation adapted from Barkay et al. 2004:61)

> May [X] be blessed by Yahwe[h], the helper and the rebuker of [e]vil. May Yahweh bless you and keep you. May Yah[w]eh make his face shine [upo]n you and grant you p[ea]ce.
>
> (Ketef Hinnom II; translation adapted from Barkay et al. 2004:68)

In these inscriptions we see the language of the ideal in the context of sorrow and finitude, when one "returns to the earth, for from it you were taken, for dust you are and to dust you shall return" (Gen. 3:19). In this burial context, the harsh reality is ameliorated by ritual—mortuary ritual—and the language is adapted from the Temple cult. Death is an end, but Yahweh's protection and blessing extends over it. The ideal experience of the Temple described in the Priestly Benediction—the transcendent face of God, divine protection from evil, a life of blessing—transitions the worshiper (and his survivors) into death.

The sense of the ideal in this ritual invocation does not mean that death brings a return to paradise. It is optative in mood, corresponding to Smith's (1982:63) definition of ritual as "performing the way things ought to be in conscious tension to the way things are." The real expectation of paradise in death will come later, in apocalyptic eschatology, where the language of Eden and the Temple are fused in a portrait of the eschatological paradise:

> Then [the tree] will be given to the righteous and
> the pious,
> and its fruit will be as food for the chosen.
> And it will be transplanted to the holy place,
> by the House of God, the King of eternity.
> Then they will rejoice greatly and be glad,
> and they will enter into the sanctuary.
> (Enoch 25:3–6; trans. Nickelsberg 2001:312)

At Ketef Hinnom we see an earlier phase of this rhetorical and conceptual move, where the language of the Temple is brought to death, and peace is cast over suffering and loss.

BIBLIOGRAPHY

Barkay, G., M. J. Lundberg, A. G. Vaughn, and B. Zuckerman
2004 The Amulets from Ketef Hinnom: A New Edition and Evaluation. *BASOR* 334:41–71.

Bourdieu, P.
1990 *The Logic of Practice*. Translated by Richard Nice. Stanford: Stanford University Press.

George, A. R.
2003 *The Babylonian Gilgamesh Epic: Introduction, Critical Edition and Cuneiform Texts*. 2 vols. Oxford: Oxford University Press.

Greenblatt, S. J.
1990 Towards a Poetics of Culture. In *Learning to Curse: Essays in Early Modern Culture*, ed. S. J. Greenblatt, 146–60. New York: Routledge.

Gunkel, H.
1997 *Genesis*. Translated by M. E. Biddle. Macon, Ga.: Mercer University Press.

Levenson, J. D.
1985 *Sinai and Zion: An Entry into the Jewish Bible*. Minneapolis: Winston.

Nickelsburg, G. W. E.
2001 *1 Enoch 1: A Commentary on the Book of 1 Enoch, Chapters 1–36; 81–108*. Hermeneia 53E6. Minneapolis: Fortress.

Smith, J. Z.
1982 *Imagining Religion: From Babylon to Jonestown*. Chicago: University of Chicago Press.

Stager, L. E.
1999 Jerusalem and the Garden of Eden. *EI* 26:183*–94*.

Wallace, H. N.
1985 *The Eden Narrative*. HSM 32. Atlanta: Scholars.

Wenham, G. J.
1994 Sanctuary Symbolism in the Garden of Eden Story. In *I Studied Inscriptions from Before the Flood: Ancient Near Eastern, Literary, and Linguistic Approaches to Genesis 1–11*, ed. R. S. Hess and D. T. Tsumura, 399–404. Sources for Biblical and Theological Study 4. Winona Lake, Ind.: Eisenbrauns.

21. The House of the Father at Iron I Tall al-ᶜUmayri, Jordan

by Larry G. Herr

From my first days in graduate school at Harvard in 1971, when I attended a seminar on the Early Bronze Age conducted by a Teaching Fellow named Larry Stager, his influence has helped mold my thinking. Later, as I helped him set up one season of excavation at Carthage in 1976 and then dug in the Tophet under his direction, I saw his human and archaeological interests combine to make a dig genuinely fun. Since then, it has been a pleasure to follow the directions his probing curiosity, sense of humor, and expansive intellect have taken him. Because his influence on me carries to this day through the strength and eloquence of his arguments and the synthetic and seminal nature of his publications, it is a pleasure to add my small voice to this volume in Larry's honor.

The Early Iron I Remains at Tall al-ᶜUmayri

Although those of us who began the Madaba Plains Project in 1984 knew there were Iron I remains at Tall al-ᶜUmayri when we began digging, we had no idea the site would produce such extensive and well-preserved discoveries. This paper examines these finds in light of one of Larry's most influential interests, that of the archaeology of the family, more specifically, the "house of the father" (Stager 1985). I will attempt to describe aspects of our finds that relate to that idea but will not discuss the more theoretical implications in this short contribution.

The two private dwellings discussed here were first encountered in the 1989 season of excavation, but because of their excellent preservation and the huge accumulation of debris that had to be removed from the rooms, we needed five more seasons to excavate both buildings. The remains were discovered in two different fields of excavation (figure 1). The whole of House B and the northern portion of House A lay within Field B and the southern part of House A was located within the area of Field A. Moreover, the discoveries in Field B (in 1989, 1992, 1994, and 1996) occurred prior to those in Field A (in 2000). Thus, for a detailed description of the remains, researchers must locate the discussions of the appropriate phase within the relevant reports of both fields for the seasons the excavation took place. Although I do not present the details here, I present a summary of the finds. All the details may be found in our seasonal reports for the first three seasons in Field B (1989 [Clark 1997]; 1992 [Clark 2000]; and 1994 [Clark 2002]); the fourth season of 1996 is in press (Clark, in press); and the fifth season (Field A) has appeared only in preliminary reports (Lawlor in Herr, Clark, and Trenchard 2001 and 2002), but the seasonal report is in preparation.

Both houses abutted the perimeter wall of the site and, indeed, used it as the western wall of their structures. The houses were very well preserved, some of the walls standing almost two meters high when we found them, protected by the deep destruction debris, which included (bottom to top) burned wooden beams, loamy roofing material, a colorful jumble of burned mud bricks, and a few stones from the top courses of the stone walls that we found *in situ*. Some of the bricks in the destruction were still stacked in clumps where they had fallen. We encountered the best preservation near the perimeter wall in the west. The massive amounts of bricks suggest strongly that at least the western portion of House A and all the rooms of House B were two stories high. Signs of fire were everywhere from the burned bricks and beams, carbonized seeds, burned human bones that fell from the upper story or the roof of House B, and charred stones in the wall, some of which were burned to lime. The underground fire was so hot that the grains in a mound of burned barley were difficult to crush in the fingers. The destruction was probably caused by a military attack, as several lance or spear points along with arrowheads and ballistic missiles in the destruction debris attest (Clark 2002:99).

House B (figure 2), the four-room house, has already been well described (Clark 1996; Herr 1998; 2000), and Rhonda Root's painting is by now very familiar (figure 3). The entrance to the house compound was in the southeast. Another entrance in the north is visible in figure 2 but was added later when the southeastern door was blocked. After going through the original entrance and passing south of a paved courtyard with a small enclosure limited by post bases, one entered the three long rooms of the house via the two northern long rooms. No eastern house wall beyond the southern long room was apparently built, suggesting the use of hanging carpets or blankets that could protect from the elements as well as provide air currents to remove smoke from the hearth inside the northern long room, while yet providing warmth for the house. The long rooms were separated by wooden posts for which we discovered the stone bases. The southern room was paved with two phases of flagstones, but the floors of the other rooms were laminated layers of beaten earth. There is no suggestion whatsoever that the central room was open or used as a courtyard. Indeed, the presence of a hearth in the northern room, the existence of a courtyard immediately outside the house to the east, and the vast accumulation of destruction debris everywhere within the house indicate very strongly that the whole house was roofed. The entrance into the broad room at the back was from the northern long room. The house plan, therefore, did not facilitate entrance to the broad room. It was apparently a protected area.

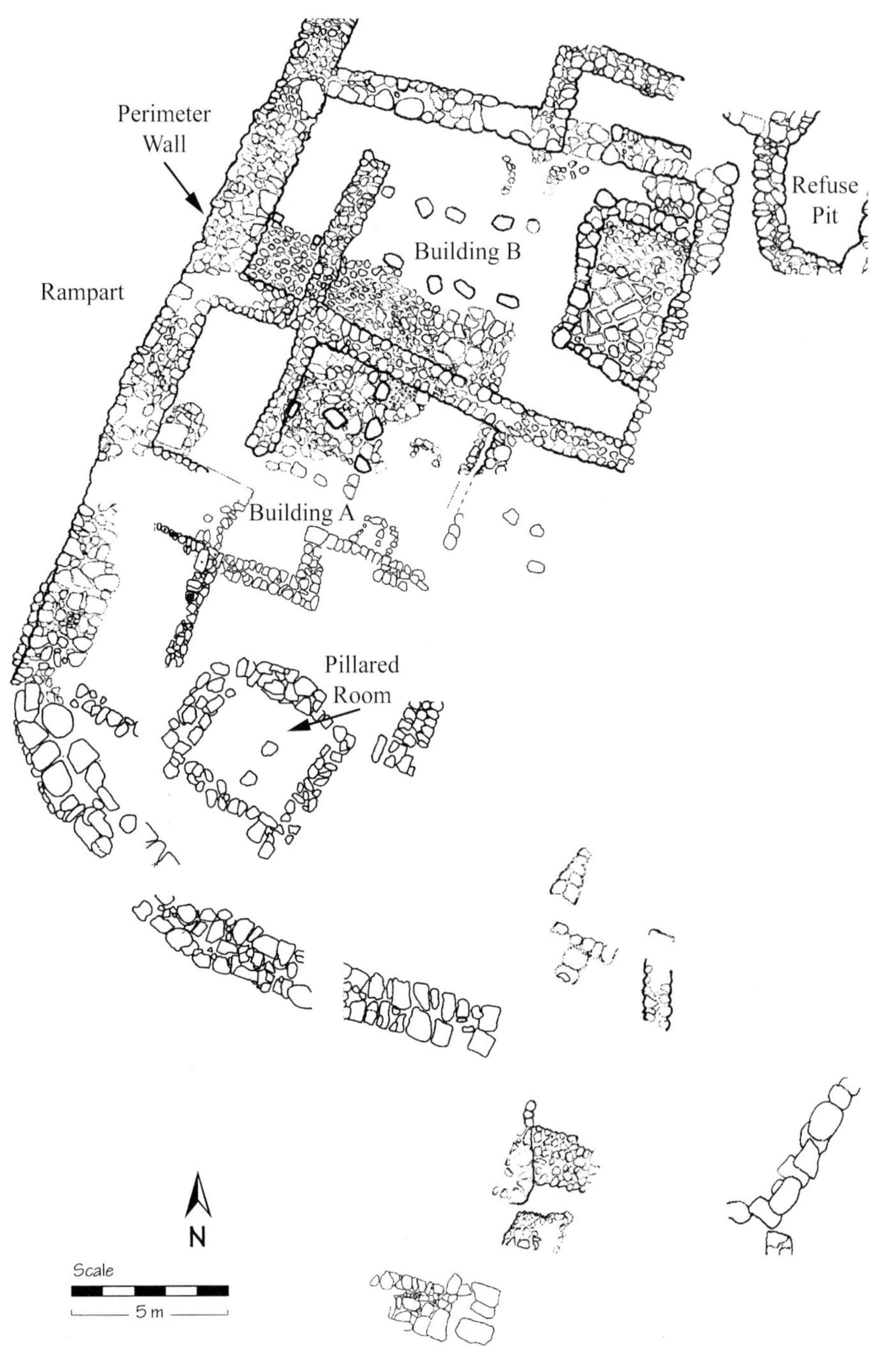

Figure 1. Plan of Houses A and B at Tall al-ᶜUmayri and associated refuse pit with the perimeter wall and finds from later Iron I phases between.

Figure 2. Photograph of House B (viewed from the east)

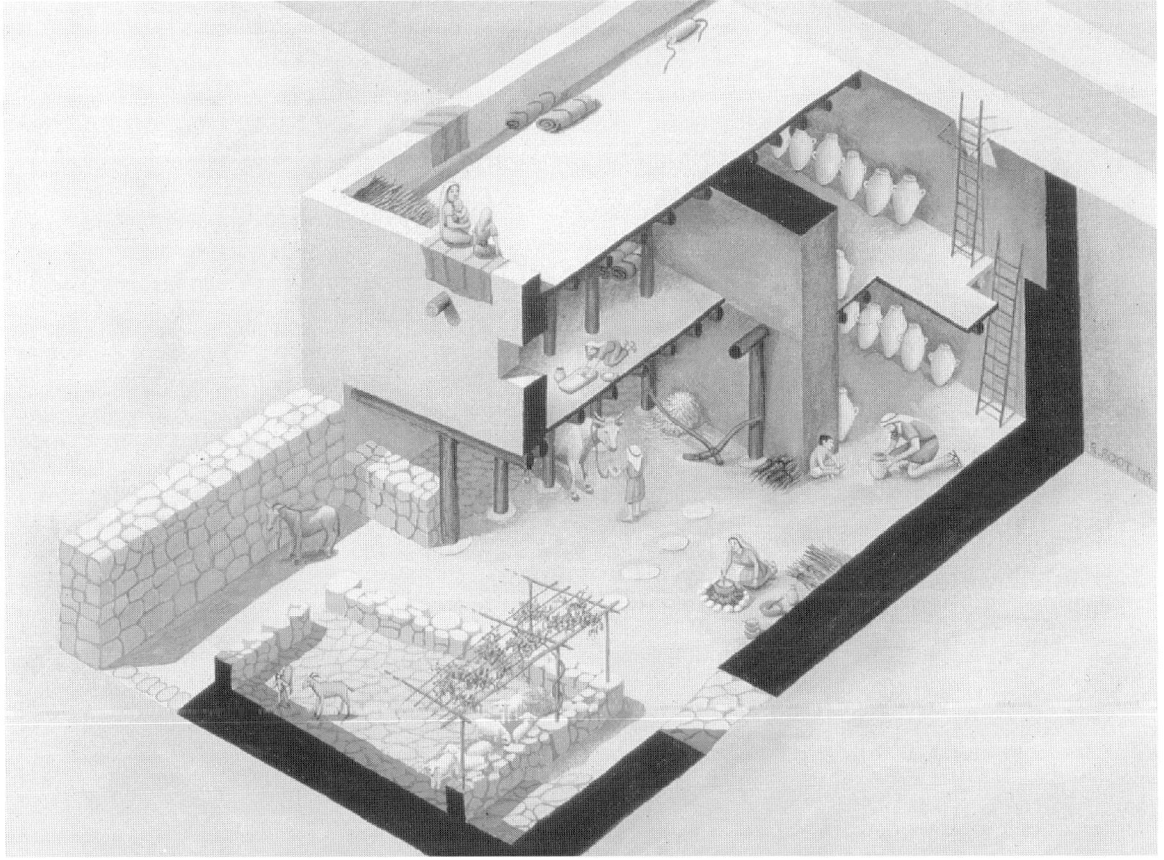

Figure 3. Artist's rendering of House B (painting by Rhonda Root)

The destruction sealed the remains in the house. Most of the items depicted in the painting (figure 3) were found by us. Only the ladders, blankets, and grapevine in the courtyard were added. We found the roof roller, more than 70 pithoi from the broadrooms of both floors (more than are in the painting), the large lower millstone (it was 60 cm above the floor, within the destruction debris, and must have come from the second story), the hearth inside the house, bones from the donkey (an equid, at least) and the cattle, burned bones from the people (though we do not intend to suggest that the bones represent necessarily the inhabitants; they could have been defenders of the town, as well), and smaller finds that could not be pictured in the painting.

For the purposes of this paper, House A may be the more important building, even though it was smaller and has not been as well described in previous publications (but see Herr 2006). It shares a common wall with House B to the north and, although its eastern limit is not yet clear, the building was most likely approximately the same length as House B. Composed of five isolatable spaces (or "rooms") in a somewhat linear plan, the destruction debris was much deeper in the west than the east, suggesting that a second story may have existed only in the western part of the house (figure 4).

Figure 4. Photograph of House A (from the east)

The wall near the eastern limit of the house is from a later phase. Immediately in the foreground is the courtyard of the house.

As in House B, the ancient inhabitants of House A most likely entered from the east into a courtyard with a possible animal pen or other structure in the southeast corner, where at least three surviving bases suggest the presence of posts (figures 1 and 4). But, unlike House B, there were no paving stones contained by the post bases. The eastern wall of the house itself is only weakly attested (the wall in figure 4 is a later wall), but fragmentary remains suggest a thin wall (figures 1 and 5) used much like the eastern house wall in House B. The relatively thick beaten-earth surface (or surfaces—there were at least two phases) was hard, with high clay content.

The eastern room of the house (west of the courtyard) contained domestic finds (figure 5), including two bins, a hearth, grinding implements, and a layer of smashed domestic pottery (Herr 2006). One bin, partially circular in plan, was located in the northwest corner and paved with pebbles, while the second, located along the south wall, had a square plan and was divided into two parts. Southeast of the first bin were the fragmentary remains of the hearth near which a grinding stone was found (by the time the photos in figures 4 and 5 were taken, after ten years of exposure, the stones of the hearth had disappeared). A concentration of smashed pottery lay on the surface between the hearth and the square bin.

This work room was separated from the next, central room by three post bases sitting on top of the eastern edge of a flagstone pavement (figure 5). The

Figure 5. Photo of House A (from the south) without the courtyard

most remarkable feature of this room was the standing stone leaning against the western wall. It was a tall (ca. 1 m high), almost perfectly rectangular natural stone of hard limestone coated with a veneer of calcrete, apparently placed in a position of veneration. Such standing stones are normally associated with divinities and are often placed near gates, such as the Iron II stones at Dan (Biran 1994:244; Zevit 2001:191–96; Dever 2005, and references there) and Bethsaida (Arav et al. 2000:49–50; Zevit 2001:149–53, and references there), among others. In front of the standing stone was another, similar stone, but irregularly oval in shape. It was also completely covered with a veneer of calcrete and lay flat immediately in front of the standing stone, as if it were intended as a presentation or votive altar. Unfortunately, no other cultic remains were found on the flagstone floor. However, we discovered a pile of carbonized barley immediately south of the standing stone and two or three chalice fragments came from the destruction debris in the room. South of this paved shrine was an open area that may have been intended to provide access, like a hallway, beyond the shrine to the inner broad room at the back. In the "hallway" the floor was made of beaten earth.

A small alcove protruded to the south of the shrine room (figure 5). Separating it from the beaten-earth surface of the "hallway" was an east-west line of stones laid too haphazardly to constitute a wall, yet too much in line to be part of the destruction. Future excavation will be needed to determine what happened to the surface at this point. Behind this line of stones was a group of seven flat-lying, rectangular stones similar to, but smaller than and slightly more amorphously shaped than, the standing stone in the shrine room. Another stone was found leaning against the south wall of the alcove. Were these stones once a series of standing stones, later dismantled? Or were they stored in the alcove awaiting use? Were they simply paving stones in the alcove? If so, they are unlike any other paving stones at ᶜUmayri from this, or any other, period. I suspect they were intended for use (active or dormant) in some way in the religious activities of the house. This would connect the function of the alcove with that of the paved shrine area to the north on the other side of the "hallway."

Like House B, the western room of House A used the perimeter wall for its western boundary. One entered it at its southeast corner. Immediately opposite the entrance was a plastered stone platform with a small, narrow series of three stone steps on the north side (this is best visible in Clark 1994:143, photo 11, but slightly visible in figure 5 above). Although other interpretations are possible, it may have been a small altar associated with the shrine in the neighboring room. But there were no signs of burning on the hard plaster that topped the stones. Moreover, the room must have been roofed and, being an inner room, would not have allowed smoke to exit easily. The northern part of the room was used for storage immediately prior to the destruction. Two well-preserved collared pithoi stood against the northern wall with four or five others smashed in front of them (Clark 1994:144, photo 13).

The overall plan of this house does not belong to the usual four-room type. Although it appears to comprise four rooms, those rooms consist of three broad rooms in a line, one behind the other, with a small alcove projecting to the side. The obvious shrine activity took place in the central room. It could be argued that the alcove was an architectural focus of the building, even though a "hallway" connecting the two domestic rooms of the house cut the central shrine room from the alcove. If that was not a problem for the cultic use of both spaces, the alcove may actually have been the more important room, especially if the stones found there were somehow considered to be in use, though not placed upright. More excavation may provide a clearer picture.

The destruction debris in the house was deepest in the two western rooms and the alcove, where it totaled 1.3–1.5 m in depth and included clear examples of stacked bricks fallen at various angles from the upper-story walls above the stones of the first story. The depth of the destruction sloped down toward the east (and somewhat to the south) until, in the courtyard, it was only 40–50 cm deep, suggesting that, while there were probably two stories for the western rooms, only one existed for the eastern parts of the house.

Both houses seem to have used a huge contemporary "refuse pit" to the northeast. This pit, only partially illustrated in figure 1 (where only the southern portion is visible), measured at least 7 m north-south by 2–3 m east-west by 3 m deep. The ancient inhabitants dug down into Late Bronze and Middle Bronze Age levels, leaving earlier walls on all sides as the edges of the pit. Any intervening spaces they filled in with their own small constructions. The fill in the pit consisted of domestic debris, including approximately 25,000 meat-bearing bones and a heavy concentration of cooking pot fragments discolored by burning, and a few other common artifacts (see Peters, Pöllath, and von den Driesch 2002 for the zooarchaeology of the pit contents). Although we found no evidence for micro-layers in the fill of the pit, it could have been used as a compost pit by the original inhabitants, as was the case at Ugarit (Schloen 2001: 340–42). Throughout the floors of the houses, the destruction layer, and the refuse pit, the pottery belonged uniformly to the earliest Iron I horizon, roughly the very late thirteenth to early twelfth centuries B.C.E. (Herr 2006).

The House of the Father

After Stager's seminal article on the Israelite family (1985), he and his students and others have done considerable work giving flesh to the idea of the patriarchal household (Hebrew *bêt ʾāb*) and providing a philosophical underpinning (most notably Bendor 1996 and Schloen 2001; see also Lehmann 2004). All have pointed out various archaeological sites and features that could relate to the idea on the ground. Most other authors writing about social aspects of the Iron Age or daily life also mention it (e.g., King and Stager 2001; Dever 2005). In this volume honoring Larry, I would like to jump on the bandwagon and suggest in the most general terms that the two houses at ᶜUmayri, along with the refuse pit and perhaps other houses still to be discovered to their immediate south, constitute an excellent archaeological realization of the "house of the father" concept.

Although estimates of the social extent and size of this social unit vary from author to author, from constituting one house to a small village of 3–10 houses, a certain looseness should be allowed, because patriarchal families grow (by birth and marriage) and decrease (by death and subdivision) in time and space. That our Houses A and B share a common wall and refuse pit seems to suggest a certain sense of commonality. Furthermore, if the refuse pit was used as a compost pit for use in family agricultural fields (Schloen 2001:340), the likelihood that several individual households used the same compost pit suggests purposive pooling of agricultural economic resources, which is behavior typical of closely related social units.

House B contained huge storage facilities. From the broad room alone, where access was somewhat restricted, over 70 collared pithoi were excavated and are now being reconstructed at Walla Walla University in a former chemistry lab in what must be the world's largest puzzle. Some came from the floor of the room and others were found splayed out in the destruction debris above. They were thus most likely present on both the first and second stories (perhaps even the roof?). A large amount of food supplies could be stored in them to help the family eke out its existence through the year. Although massive storage capability suggests a large family, it is possible that the supplies could be shared with other inhabitants of the patrimony. House A, which also contained five to ten collared pithoi, would imply a much smaller number of inhabitants or that they shared in the storage facilities of House B.

In any case, House A very likely held fewer people than House B and those people may have been logistically dependent on the inhabitants of House B. The evidence for fewer inhabitants comes from the lack of deep destruction debris in the eastern parts of the house, implying there was no second story there. Living space was thus reduced. Moreover, when one includes the two spaces on the ground floor apparently given over to religious activities, room for inhabitants to live is further reduced. Although six or seven pithoi were discovered in the broad room (and nowhere else), this seems like insufficient storage capacity for even two people. I have therefore suggested a dependency on the storage facilities of House B for the inhabitants of House A. If so, such dependency is a further indication for the close ties of a patriarchal household.

Although House A produced definite and frequent signs of domestic activities, it also dedicated considerable space to cultic activities, as the standing stone and perhaps the alcove attest (Dever 2005:118, among many others). Stories in the Hebrew Bible reflect the common idea that the head of the patriarchal family was the religious leader of that social unit. The story of Micah in Judges 17 even describes how a family shrine could be built and used. House A was probably the dwelling of an individual who was the religious leader of the family unit, most likely the patriarch himself. Was House A the dwelling of the patriarch and possibly a spouse? Does its limited domestic space imply the inhabitants were limited to him/them? Of course, a patriarchal household could have many variations on the ground. If the patriarch is vigorous and healthy, he need not move in with his children, who had perhaps constructed their own house. However, he may not have worked in the fields very much and would have been dependent on his children at the same time.

Although I do not wish to speculate here on the ethnicity of the people living in our houses, and although we tend to use biblical descriptions as our primary textual source to understand the patriarchal household, we must understand those biblical descriptions to reflect a wider social world than the Israelites. Certainly, the basic social values reflected in the Bible were also held by other, similar people groups of the region.

In coming seasons we will excavate other remains from the same period immediately to the south of

Houses A and B. Although the perimeter wall curves into the town farther to the south (figure 1), perhaps as part of a gateway, there is room for one or two houses between House A and the curve of the perimeter wall (please note that the remains illustrated in figure 1 in that area are from later Iron I phases). This area could also belong to the same patriarchal family unit.

The overall site is much larger than a small agricultural village and is protected by a very significant fortification system (Herr 2000). It probably, therefore, contained several households that cooperated in large-scale endeavors. The perimeter wall, constructed in different techniques in different locations, suggests various groups working on it for the common good at the same time. Such activity implies the cooperative labor of several patriarchal units in the town and illustrates the second level of social activity above the "house of the father."

In summary, these two houses illustrate very clearly the multifunctional activities and interdependence that we would expect of a *bêt ᵓāb*.

Bibliography

Arav, R., R. A. Freund, and J. F. Shroder
2000 Bethsaida Rediscovered. *BAR* 26/1:44–56.

Bendor, S.
1996 *The Social Structure of Ancient Israel: The Institution of the Family (Beit ᵓab) from the Settlement to the End of the Monarchy*. Jerusalem: Simor.

Biran, A.
1994 *Biblical Dan*. Jerusalem: Israel Exploration Society.

Clark, D. R.
1994 The Iron I Western Defense System at Tell el-ᶜUmeiri, Jordan. *BA* 57:138–48.
1996 Early Iron I Pillared Building at Tall al-ᶜUmayri. *BA* 59:241.
1997 Field B: The Western Defensive System. In *Madaba Plains Project*, vol. 3, *The 1989 Season at Tell el-ᶜUmeiri and Vicinity and Subsequent Studies*, ed. L. G. Herr, L. T. Geraty, Ø. S. LaBianca, R. W. Younker, and D. R. Clark, 53–98. Berrien Springs, Mich.: Andrews University.
2000 Field B: The Western Defense System. In *Madaba Plains Project*, vol. 4, *The 1992 Season at Tall al-ᶜUmayri and Subsequent Studies*, ed. L. G. Herr, D. R. Clark, L. T. Geraty, R. W. Younker, and Ø. S. LaBianca, 59–94. Berrien Springs, Mich.: Andrews University.
2002 Field B: The Western Defense System. In *Madaba Plains Project*, vol. 5, *The 1994 Season at Tall al-ᶜUmayri and Subsequent Studies*, ed. L. G. Herr, D. R. Clark, L. T. Geraty, R. W. Younker, and Ø. S. LaBianca, 48–116. Berrien Springs, Mich.: Andrews University.
in press Field B: The Western Defense System and Northwestern Domestic Area. In *Madaba Plains Project*, vol. 6, *The 1996–1998 Seasons at Tall al-ᶜUmayri and Subsequent Studies*, ed. L. G. Herr, D. R. Clark, L. T. Geraty, R. W. Younker, and Ø. S. LaBianca. Berrien Springs, Mich.: Andrews University.

Dever, W. G.
2005 *Did God Have a Wife?: Archaeology and Folk Religion in Ancient Israel*. Grand Rapids, Mich.: Eerdmans.

Herr, L. G.
1998 Tell el-ᶜUmayri and the Madaba Plains Region during the Late Bronze–Iron Age I Transition. In *Mediterranean Peoples in Transition: Thirteenth to Early Tenth Centuries* B.C.E., ed. S. Gitin, A. Mazar, and E. Stern, 251–64. Jerusalem: Israel Exploration Society.
2000 The Settlement and Fortification of Tell al-ᶜUmayri in Jordan during the LB/Iron I Transition. In *The Archaeology of Jordan and Beyond: Essays in Honor of James A. Sauer*, ed. L. E. Stager, J. A. Greene, and M. D. Coogan, 167–79. SAHL 1. Winona Lake, Ind.: Eisenbrauns.
2006 An Early Iron Age I House with a Cultic Corner at Tall al-ᶜUmayri, Jordan. In *Confronting the Past: Archaeological and Historical Essays on Ancient Israel in Honor of William G. Dever*, ed. S. Gitin, J. E. Wright, and J. P. Dessel, 61–73. Winona Lake, Ind.: Eisenbrauns.

Herr, L. G., D. R. Clark, and W. C. Trenchard
2001 Madaba Plains Project: Excavations at Tall al-ᶜUmayri, 2000. *ADAJ* 45:237–52.
2002 Madaba Plains Project: Excavations at Tall al-ᶜUmayri, 2000. *Andrews University Seminary Studies* 40:105–23.

King, P. J., and L. E. Stager
2001 *Life In Biblical Israel*. Louisville, Ky.: Westminster John Knox.

Lehmann, G.
2004 Reconstructing the Social Landscape of Early Israel: Rural Marriage Alliances in the Central Hill Country. *Tel Aviv* 31:141–93.

Peters, J., N. Pöllath, and A. von den Driesch
2002 Early and Late Bronze Age Transitional Subsistence at Tall al-ᶜUmayri. In *Madaba Plains Project*, vol. 5, *The 1994 Season at Tall al-ᶜUmayri and Subsequent Studies*, ed. L. G. Herr, D. R. Clark, L. T. Geraty, R. W. Younker, and Ø. S. LaBianca, 305–47. Berrien Springs, Mich.: Andrews University.

Schloen, J. D.
2001 *The House of the Father as Fact and Symbol: Patrimonialism in Ugarit and the Ancient Near East*. SAHL 2. Winona Lake, Ind.: Eisenbrauns.

Stager, L. E.
1985 The Archaeology of the Family in Ancient Israel. *BASOR* 260:1–35.

Zevit, Z.
2001 *The Religions of Ancient Israel: A Synthesis of Parallactic Approaches*. New York: Continuum.

22. Israel's Ancestors Were Not Nomads

by Theodore Hiebert

One of the oldest and most enduring images of Israel's ancestors in scholarly and popular literature is the conception of them as pastoral nomads. Roland de Vaux, in his study of Israel's life and institutions, described this viewpoint in classic form:

> At the beginning of their history the Israelites, like their ancestors before them, lived as nomads or seminomads, and when they came to settle down as a nation, they still retained some characteristics of that earlier way of life. Consequently any study of Old Testament institutions must begin with an investigation into nomadism. . . . Naturally, such a life entails a distinct pattern of society, and enjoins a code of behavior all its own. [de Vaux 1961:3–4]

In the earliest version of this viewpoint, reflected in such influential works as Albrecht Alt's reconstructions of the origins of Israelite religion (1925; 1929; 1934) and H. and H. A. Frankfort's *Before Philosophy: The Intellectual Adventure of Ancient Man* (1949), Israel's ancestors were characterized as pure desert nomads who brought with them a distinctive set of beliefs and practices when they settled among Canaanite farmers.

When the new archaeological and anthropological scholarship in the second half of the twentieth century showed that such autonomous desert pastoralism did not exist until the end of the second and beginning of the first millennium B.C.E, and that even then it was integrated into sedentary societies, scholars adopted a new model for the nomadism of early Israel and its ancestors. According to this model, which remains the dominant conception among scholars today, Israel's ancestors were seminomadic or transhumant pastoralists, shepherds who possessed a sedentary base in the semiarid zones contiguous with the arable land of the Canaanite hill country and moved their herds in rather confined and regular patterns to exploit seasonal pasturage (Luke 1965; Rowton 1974; 1977; Matthews 1978; 1981; 1986). Israel Finkelstein (1988) has provided a contemporary archaeological argument for this viewpoint by interpreting aspects of the earliest "Israelite" settlements as vestiges of a previous nomadic existence which preceded sedentarization.

One important reason for the view that ancient Israel evolved from a nomadic to a sedentary culture was the nineteenth-century anthropological theory that human society developed naturally through three stages: from hunting and gathering to herding to cultivation. Based on newer information, for example the discovery that plants were domesticated before animals, such a unilinear view of cultural development has been abandoned (Khazanov 1984; Bar-Yosef and Khazanov 1992), but it exerted a powerful influence on biblical scholarship. Another reason for these scholarly reconstructions of Israel's nomadic origins was the biblical narrative itself. In the origin stories of Genesis and Exodus, Israel's ancestors are described as owners of large herds of sheep and goats and they are pictured moving from place to place throughout the Canaanite hill country and beyond. When they travel to Egypt because of the Canaanite famine, they put themselves at Pharaoh's disposal by volunteering to care for his herds. Upon leaving Egypt, they spend years traversing the desert with their flocks before eventually settling down in the highlands of Canaan. All of this data fit together and seemed to make perfectly obvious de Vaux's claims that the origins of Israelite life and thought ought to be traced back to nomadic culture.

The archaeological work of Lawrence Stager, to whom this volume is dedicated, raises serious questions about this popular and still powerful reconstruction of Israel's origins, and I would like to take this opportunity to discuss some of the consequences of Stager's scholarship for our understanding of the origins of Israelite life and thought. In his study of "The Archaeology of the Family in Ancient Israel" (Stager 1985a) and in his other work (Stager 1985b; King and Stager 2001:8–68, 85–122), Stager has shown that in the earliest Iron I villages that we may reasonably consider "Israelite," the economy of the inhabitants was the mixed agricultural economy typical of the Canaanite highlands, combining the cultivation of grains and fruits with the herding of sheep and goats. In such villages, pillared houses with their stables and pottery repertoire, multiple family compounds, and slope-terracing technology all point to a successful adaptation to farm life in the hill country by local agriculturalists, not to the vestiges of nomadic people settling down. While Stager himself recognizes that some elements of early Israel may have practiced a form of specialized pastoralism—the tribe of Reuben as represented in Judges 5 for example (Stager 1988)—he has nevertheless provided one of the most complete pictures of the agricultural character of Israelite origins in the biblical hill country.

Stager's reconstruction of the earliest stages of Israel's agrarian culture and the challenges it raises for the traditional notion of nomadic origins was the context within which I began my study of the Yahwist's landscape some years ago, in which I aimed to reevaluate the actual environmental context for the oldest Pentateuchal traditions and the values toward that environment embedded in those traditions (Hiebert 1996). What I discovered was that Israel's own traditions of its origins, in the narratives in Genesis and Exodus, show that Israel understood itself, from the beginning, as an agricultural society of the very kind described in Stager's archaeological investigations of the earliest Israelite villages. Thus Stager's view of Israelite agrarian origins can be confirmed not only from Israel's earliest material remains but from Israel's own self-understanding in biblical texts. Here I would like to pull together the key data in Israel's origin traditions to make the point that all of our data, archaeological and textual, are consistent in locating Israel's origins in the typical agricultural economy of the Canaanite highlands and that it was this context, rather than nomadism, that gave birth to Israel's practices and beliefs.

Creation Traditions

Israel's oldest creation traditions, found in the Garden of Eden narrative attributed to the Yahwist (Gen. 2:4b–3:24), claim that Israel's first ancestor, the archetypal man, was a farmer (Hiebert 1996:32–38, 51–62). In these traditions, the first man, *ʾādām*, is made from *ʾădāmâ*, the Yahwist's technical term for arable land, the sector of his landscape suitable for cultivation (Gen. 2:7; Hiebert 1996:32–38, 51–62). Having been made from arable land, this first man is immediately given the task of cultivating it (Gen. 2:15). This primal link between humanity and arable soil—made from it and made to farm it—is, of course captured in the Yahwist's play on words, *ʾādām* from *ʾădāmâ*. Rendered by some as "earthling" from "earth," or "human" from "humus," this wordplay is more precisely translated, given the Yahwist's technical use of *ʾădāmâ*, "farmer" from "farmland." In its very name, *ʾādām*, the Yahwist thus sees humanity's agricultural identity. And this identity is to be humanity's destiny not just inside the Garden of Eden but outside of it as well (3:23).

The details of the Eden narrative all reflect the local agricultural environment of biblical Israel. Though the story contains elements impossible to connect with ordinary reality—the trees of life and the knowledge of good and evil, the identities and locations of some of the rivers—its concrete details are drawn from the Yahwist's own agricultural landscape. References at the beginning and end of the story to *ʿēśeb haśśādeh*, "field grains" (Gen. 2:5; 3:18–19), as essential for human life reflect Israel's grain-based farming, supplemented with fruits, such as figs (3:7). The lack of rain at the story's outset refers to the dry-farming necessary in the Canaanite highlands (2:5), while the garden's spring is one example of the myriad springs that dotted the hill country and its environs. The creation of the first woman from the first man brings into being the nuclear family unit at the heart of the agricultural village, with the male tending the arable land from which he was made (3:17–19) and the female raising the children (3:16). Thus the culture created in these traditions is the agricultural economy which typified biblical Israel itself.

Israel's other great creation tradition, the account of the world's creation in six days followed by God's institution of the Sabbath, is designed by its Priestly author above all to ground Israel's cultic practices in the structures and rhythms of the cosmos. In this tradition, the human being is fashioned not as a farmer but as a kind of priestly mediator of God's sovereignty in the world (Gen. 1:26–28), and the world itself is described with broader, more cosmic dimensions. Yet the details of the Priestly account of origins reflect the same local Israelite agricultural economy present in the Yahwist's traditions. The earth's vegetation, for example, is described in the categories of the two kinds of crops cultivated by Israelite farmers (1:11–12). The vegetation (*dešeʾ*) the earth brings forth is divided into two types: grain (*ʿēśeb*) which bears seed (*mazrîaʿ zeraʿ*), that is, which bears seed that is clearly visible, and fruit (*ʿēṣ pĕrî*) whose seed is enclosed within the fruit itself (*zarʿô bô*). In spite of the cosmic sweep of this creation account, the Priestly writer has not provided a comprehensive catalogue of the earth's vegetation but a precise inventory of Israel's own agricultural regime: the cereals planted annually and the fruits that supplemented cereal production.

Creation traditions are particularly important for investigating a society's understanding of its origins and identity, for they serve to ground a society's own core realities in the very orders of creation: we are this way because God made us this way. In Israel's oldest traditions, the human is a farmer—by derivation, by vocation, by name—and the landscape brought into existence in these traditions is the agrarian environment of the biblical hill country. The archetypal human is not the nomadic pastoralist, nor is the environment in these creation traditions the desert or the desert fringes inhabited by nomads or seminomads. Israel's creation traditions make the claim that God created into the fabric of the world and of human existence the mixed agrarian economy which it itself practiced.

Primeval Traditions

Israel's primeval traditions build on its creation traditions, reflecting the same agrarian environment brought into being at creation. The narrative traditions here are primarily the Yahwist's, and they depict a world in which the primary line of Israel's (and the world's) earliest ancestors, just as the first archetypal ancestor in Eden, were typical Mediterranean farmers. Cain, the firstborn who cultivates his family's arable land; Lamech, who looks for his son Noah to lift the curse on arable land; and Noah himself, who reestablishes an agricultural economy after the flood, are all agriculturalists (Hiebert 1996:38–51).

J's first primeval tradition, the story of Cain and Abel, is set within the simple agrarian family brought into being in J's Eden narrative, but this has been overlooked because of the strong scholarly interest in nomadism. Nomadism has been prominent in the history of the interpretation of this story, which has been regarded variously as: (1) an etiology of the desert nomads south of Israel, the Kenites (Wellhausen 1885); (2) an account of the archetypal division in early human culture between sedentary farmers and nomadic shepherds (Westermann 1984:292–96, 317–18); and (3) an allegory of the conflict between the nomadic Israelite pastoralists (Abel) and the sedentary Canaanite farmers (Cain) among whom they settled (Ellis 1968:167, 199). Cain and Abel are, in fact, brothers on a typical Israelite family farm, where the older, who will inherit the primary share of the family estate, is cultivating the family's arable land (*ʾădāmâ*, Gen. 4:2, 3, 10, 11, 12, 13, 14), while the younger, as is customary, is assigned the care of the family's flocks (4:2, 4). This is the picture of the typical Israelite family practicing the mixed agricultural economy of the Mediterranean highlands, in which the cultivation of crops is combined with the herding of sheep and goats, to exploit both the arable and grazing lands of the hills and to provide the necessary products for subsistence farming.

The agony of Cain's banishment to wander in the desert shows just how much of a farmer he actually is and how deeply this agrarian perspective informs the story (4:11–16). Though scholars have identified Cain's descendents with desert nomads (Gunkel 1910:51) or with city dwellers (Wallis 1966:133–35; Frick 1977:205–6), it is this agrarian orientation that determines the profile of Cain's primary descendent, Lamech, who sees in his son Noah's birth the end of the curse on arable land with which he and his predecessors have been struggling: "This one will give us relief from our work, from the painful labor of our hands, from the arable soil (*ʾădāmâ*) which Yahweh has cursed" (Gen. 5:29). In this speech, Lamech identifies not only his own vocation as a farmer, but he also describes the flood hero Noah's mission in agricultural terms: Noah is born to free arable land from its primeval curse.

Before we turn to Noah's career as a farmer, we must examine the one true reference to pastoral nomadism in the primeval traditions, the notice that it originated with one of Lamech's son's, Jabal: "he is the ancestor of those who live with tents and herds" (Gen. 4:20). The traditions about Lamech's sons describe some of the key specializations with which a typical Mediterranean agrarian society would have been familiar: the village blacksmiths descended from Tubal-Cain, "the blacksmith for all who plow with bronze and iron" (4:22); the epic singers descended from Jubal, "the ancestor of all who play the lyre and flute" (4:21); and the specialized seminomadic pastoralists descended from Jabal. Such pastoralists, such as the modern Bedouin, have been a constant feature of the Middle Eastern landscape, exploiting the semiarid terrain contiguous with the more humid agricultural zones. Their close relationship to sedentary agricultural society and their status as a specialized, peripheral minority are reflected accurately in their position as descendents of one of Lamech's less important sons. The nomadic pastoralist is thus viewed as an offshoot of the dominant agricultural society represented by the Yahwist's main characters, Adam, Cain, Lamech, and Noah.

Ancestral Traditions

While scholars have customarily located Noah in Israel's primeval traditions, he is actually a transitional figure, who lives through the end of the primeval age but who also inaugurates a new age of human history and culture (Hiebert 1996:80–82). If we want to examine Israel's understanding of its nearer ancestors, we must begin with the ancestor who founded the age in which they lived, the post-flood era, the era of Israel's most well-known ancestors and the era in which Israel's origin traditions themselves came into being. As the prototypical ancestor of this new age, Noah reestablishes for his heirs the same agricultural regime initiated at the beginning of time by his ancestor Adam. The Yahwist refers to Noah as "the man of arable soil" (*ʾîš hāʾădāmâ*), the farmer, so to speak.

Noah's identity as the flood hero, especially in the Yahwist's traditions, is largely bound up with his role in establishing a stable agricultural economy in the period following the flood. His birth announcement identifies Noah's primary role as providing relief from the arable land's curse which had afflicted agriculture in the primeval age (Gen. 3:17; 4:11–12; 5:29). And this is exactly the role he undertakes when he exits the ark. Noah's first act after the flood is to build an altar and make offerings to God (8:20), as the result of which God promises to lift the curse on arable land (8:21) and to establish the regular occurrence of the seasonal cycle on which highland agriculture depends for success (8:22). Indeed, the description of the seasonal cycle in 8:22 lists the major occasions of the agricultural year in the Israelite hill country: the planting of grain in the fall (*zeraᶜ*), the harvesting of grain in the spring (*qāṣîr*), the harvest of summer fruit, including primarily grapes and figs (*qayiṣ*), and the autumn harvest of olives (*ḥōrep*). Upon receiving God's promise of a reliable agricultural world in the new age, Noah's immediate response (in J's traditions) is to plant the first vineyard in the new age (9:20), mirroring the garden with which the primeval age began. Thus the Yahwist has established his own agricultural economy as the economy of his ancestors in the post-flood age, just as it had been established as the economy of his first ancestors in the primeval age.

While scholars have recognized some of the agricultural aspects of these early narratives in Genesis, they have been universally convinced that the economy of Noah's descendents, Abraham, Isaac, and Jacob, in the following stories in Genesis was pastoral nomadism. The most thorough defense of this viewpoint has been undertaken by J. T. Luke (1965), M. B. Rowton (1974), and V. H. Matthews (1978), who saw in the seminomadic pastoralists at Mari in the beginning of the second millennium B.C.E. a model for the economy of Israel's ancestors in Genesis. This view is more or less assumed in commentaries on Genesis today (e.g., Westermann 1985:74–79; Sarna 1989:90–91). Among the few scholars who have challenged this viewpoint are George Mendenhall (1962:66–87) and Norman Gottwald (1979:435–63), who wished to support their theory that Israel began as a peasant revolt by indigenous peoples rather than through the settlement of outside pastoralists.

Israel's portraits of its ancestors Abraham, Isaac, and Jacob in Genesis contain numerous details which identify them directly with the sedentary agriculture established by Noah after the flood rather than with the specialized pastoralism with which they have customarily been associated (Hiebert 1996:85–97). Biblical traditions link them not to the semiarid zones inhabited by nomadic pastoralists but to the agricultural heartland of biblical Israel. This is obvious in the divine promises which cede to them and their descendents the arable land in the northern (12:6–7), central (13:14–15; 28:13–16), and southern (13:8; 15:7–21; 26:2–5, 23–25, 32–33) parts of the biblical hill country. It is only the members of the secondary lines of Israel's genealogy, Ishmael for example, who inhabit the arid and semiarid zones contiguous with these ancestral lands (16:7–12).

The link between Israel's ancestors and their agricultural heartland is further strengthened by the Yahwist's conscious use of vocabulary to identify them as residents at home in it. When J describes his ancestors residing in the lands they have been granted by God, he uses the verb *yāšab*, "live, dwell" (e.g., Gen. 13:7, 18; 22:9; 24:3; 34:10). The expression J consistently avoids for Israel's ancestors as residents of the arable lands of the hill country is *gēr*, "resident alien," an individual residing outside of his own landed property and outside the protection of his own kinship structures (Stager 1988:229–32). J uses *gēr* for the ancestors only when they travel outside the hill country and take up temporary residence away from home in Egypt (12:10; 15:13; 47:4), Philistia (21:34; 26:3), or Syria (32:5). The Yahwist thus regards his ancestors as residents of the agricultural zones of the biblical hill country, not as transient pastoralists at its edges.

On this point of vocabulary, the Priestly Writer differs from the Yahwist, since he employs the root *gûr* regularly for the ancestors, especially in his frequent reference to the biblical hill country as the *ʾereṣ mĕgūrêhem*, "the land of their sojourning/alien residence" (Gen. 17:8; 28:4; 36:7; 37:1; Exod. 6:4; compare 23:4; 35:27). But it is unlikely that P uses this phrase to identify his ancestors as nomadic pastoralists. It is much more likely that, given P's aim to divide Israelite history into distinct periods, P uses the phrase to distinguish the ancestral age from the age of Israel as a nation, or that P uses it to reflect Israel's current status as a nation in exile (Westermann 1985:263). Indeed, P describes Abraham's actual purchase of an estate in or near Hebron to bury Sarah, and given the close association between family patrimony and burial, this act associates Abraham with the biblical hill country rather than its desert fringes (King and Stager 2001:364–65).

This portrait of the ancestors as residents of the agricultural heartland is further amplified by references in these traditions to the ancestors' cultivation of the arable lands they inhabit. The Yahwist describes Isaac sowing grain and reaping an abundant harvest (Gen. 26:12). The Elohist describes Reuben returning from the wheat harvest (*qĕṣîr ḥiṭṭîm*; 30:14) and describes Joseph and his brothers binding sheaves in the field at harvest time (37:5–8). When the ancestors' dry-farming is threatened by the lack of rain, they are forced to buy grain from Egypt to supplement their own harvests (43:1–2; 44:1–2). The agricultural perspective of these ancestral traditions is nowhere better described than in Isaac's blessing on Jacob: "May God grant to you the dew of the skies and the plenty of the earth, an abundance of grain and wine" (27:28).

Perhaps the most important evidence from these stories for the traditional notion that Israel's ancestors were nomadic pastoralists are the impressive lists of animals that they own (e.g., Gen. 12:16; 24:35; 32:6). However, when these lists are examined carefully, they fit perfectly into the mixed agrarian economy typical of Mediterranean highland farmers, in which raising animals was one aspect of sedentary village agriculture. The animals owned by Israel's ancestors—sheep and goats (*ṣōʾn*), cattle (*bāqār*), donkeys (*ḥămôrîm/ʾătōnōt*), and camels (*gĕmallîm*)—are the same domestic species typical of sedentary agricultural sites from the biblical period from which archaeologists have analyzed faunal remains. Moreover, the order in which these animals are listed in Genesis, as noted above, corresponds precisely to the population pattern of livestock in these agricultural sites. At Iron Age hill country sites, based on the number of bones found, sheep and goats made up about two-thirds of the animal population, cattle somewhat less than a third, and donkeys and camels much smaller percentages (Hellwing and Adjeman 1986:141–52; Zeder 1990:24–29). Of particular note in this list is cattle (*bāqār*), since they are directly related to sedentary agriculture, being employed as draft animals for cultivation. The size of the ancestors' flocks and herds is not direct evidence for specialized pastoralism; it simply communicates the economic status of their owners (King and Stager 2001:113, 119).

The other important evidence from these stories for the customary idea that Israel's ancestors were pastoral nomads is in the frequent narratives of their movement from place to place. Looked at closely, however, the ancestors' movements are not the movements of seminomadic pastoralists in the semiarid zones of the hill country where we would expect them. Rather, the ancestors' travels serve two other distinct purposes. At one level, they are simply migrations, relocations of residence for a variety of reasons. Abraham moves from Ur to Haran, and then from Haran to Shechem at God's command (Gen. 11:31–12:6). Jacob moves to Haran to escape Esau's anger (J: 27:41–45) or to marry endogamously (P: 27:46–28:4). Jacob moves his family to Egypt because of a drought in the hill country where he resides (42:1–5).

At a deeper and more significant level, the ancestors' movements are etiological. They are movements designed to explain and legitimate Israel's relationship to its land and to its neighbors. Regarding the ancestors' travels within Canaan itself, Wellhausen understood this clearly: "The patriarchal journeys up and down in JE are not designed to represent them as wandering nomads, but to serve to bring them in contact with all the sacred places with which they had special associations" (1957:334). Such is precisely the aim of Abraham's stops at Shechem, Bethel, and Hebron, where Abraham and his descendents are granted the agricultural heartland of biblical Israel, and where Abraham builds altars founding and legitimating the Yahwistic cult centers in the hill country's major urban centers (12:6–7; 13:3, 14–17; 13:18). When the ancestors travel outside the hill country into the territories of other peoples, the goal of these travelogues is not transhumance pastoralism but rather to define and legitimate the relationships, balances of power, and boundaries between Israel and its neighbors. Jacob's trip to Haran, for example, provides the historical justification for features of the Aramean-Israelite relationship during the monarchy, including the political alliances and boundaries between them (31:43–54).

Exodus Traditions

The biblical narratives of Israel's ancestors' travels into and out of Egypt are told from the same agricultural orientation that shaped the primeval and ancestral traditions. This can be seen first of all in the settlement of Jacob's family in the land of Goshen, some of the prime agricultural land in Egypt (Gen. 45:10–11, 18; 47:5–6, 11). There they cultivate grain and raise livestock (Exod. 9:1–6, 22–26). One of these narratives, on the surface, appears to identify Jacob's family as specialized pastoralists, since in it they present themselves to Pharaoh as shepherds (*rōʿēh ṣōʾn*) and volunteer to care for his livestock (46:31–47:6; Westermann 1986:167–70). Yet the point of the narrative is just the opposite. The fact that Joseph has to instruct his family to identify themselves as shepherds signifies that this would not have been their natural response to Pharaoh (46:31–

34). Further, Joseph's logic makes it clear that taking on such an identity is simply a strategy to ingratiate themselves to Pharaoh in order to relocate in Egyptian territory (46:34; 47:4–6).

Just as Egypt's prime agricultural land in the Delta is described as a natural home for Israel's ancestors, so the desert at its fringes is described as a foreign, inhospitable landscape. When the Israelites finally enter the desert in order to escape from Egyptian slavery, they are in constant peril, either because of the lack of water (Exod. 15:22–25) or because of the lack of food (Exod. 16:1–3). In fact, the Israelites complain incessantly, comparing the desert constantly and unfavorably to cultivable land and its agricultural produce, either in the Nile Valley which they had left (Num. 11:5, 18) or in the Canaanite hill country to which they were headed (Num. 16:12–14). Indeed, in the desert the people's greatest fear is death (Exod. 16:3; 17:3), a fear not unlike that of their primeval ancestor, the farmer Cain, when he was banished from arable land (Gen. 4:13–14). To traverse the desert safely, the Israelites must rely not on their own experience but on that of the Midianite, Hobab, who is in fact at home in the wilderness (Num. 10:29–32). The image of the desert found in these details of the Exodus traditions is not an image held by the desert pastoralist native to it, but the image of the agriculturalist for whom the desert is a place of danger and death.

Just as the narratives of Egypt and the desert identify Israel's ancestors as an agrarian people, so the legal materials which are embedded within these narratives and associated with the sacred desert mountain, Mount Sinai, reflect a sedentary agricultural society rather than the culture of desert pastoralists. One cogent example of this is the ritual calendar found among the ancient laws in the covenant code (Exod. 23:14–19, compare Exod. 34:18–26, Lev. 23:1–44, Deut. 16:1–17). This sacral calendar is entirely shaped by the agricultural year. Its three primary festivals celebrate the major harvests of Mediterranean farmers: (1) *ḥag hammaṣṣôt*, the feast of unleavened bread held in the month of *ʾābîb*, the time of the barley harvest (Exod. 23:15); (2) *ḥag haqqāṣîr*, the feast of the grain harvest held when the major grain crop, wheat, was harvested (23:16, compare 34:22); and (3) *ḥag hāʾāsîp*, the feast of the ingathering, held when fruit crops were harvested in the late summer and fall (23:16). The central ritual at each of these feasts was offering to God in gratitude for the divine gift of fertility the first grains or fruits harvested from the arable soil (*ʾădāmâ*), the center of the agricultural landscape (23:19). The rhythm of sacred time for biblical Israel found in its most ancient cultic traditions is not the rhythm of the transhumant pastoralist but the seasonal cycle of the sedentary farmer in the biblical hill country.

The entire sweep of Israel's origin traditions in the Pentateuch, from the creation of the world to the promulgation of law at Mount Sinai, describe Israel's beginnings in terms of sedentary agriculture rather than nomadic pastoralism. According to Israel's own self-understanding reflected in its origin stories, Israel's ancestors practiced the kind of mixed agricultural economy, combining the cultivation of grains and fruits with the herding of sheep and goats, typical of the early Israelite highland villages in the heartland of biblical Israel, whose material remains Stager has investigated and analyzed. Thus our material and textual witnesses for the origins of Israel support and illuminate one another. They tell us that we must look for the origins of Israelite life and thought not in nomadism, as de Vaux argued, but in the realities of the ordinary farmer in the Mediterranean highlands.

Bibliography

Alt, A.
1925 *Die Landnahme der Israeliten in Palästina; Territorialgeschichtliche Studien.* Leipzig: Werkgemeinschaft.
1929 *Der Gott der Väter: Ein Beitrag zur Vorgeschichte der israelitischen Religion.* Stuttgart: Kohlhammer.
1934 *Die Ursprünge des israelitischen Rechts.* Leipzig: Hirzel.

Bar-Yosef, O., and A. M. Khazanov, eds.
1992 *Pastoralism in the Levant: Archaeological Materials in Anthropological Perspective.* Madison, Wis.: Prehistory Press.

Ellis, P.
1968 *The Yahwist: The Bible's First Theologian.* Collegeville, Minn.: Liturgical Press.

Finkelstein, I.
1988 *The Archaeology of the Israelite Settlement.* Jerusalem: Israel Exploration Society.

Frankfort, H., and H. A. Groenewegen-Frankfort, eds.
1949 *Before Philosophy: The Intellectual Adventure of Ancient Man; An Essay on Speculative Thought in the Ancient Near East.* New York: Penguin.

Frick, F. S.
1977 *The City in Ancient Israel.* Missoula, Mont.: Scholars.

Gunkel, H.
1910 *Genesis.* Göttingen: Vandenhoeck and Ruprecht.

Gottwald, N. K.
1979 *The Tribes of Yahweh: A Sociology of the Religion of Liberated Israel, 1250–1050 B.C.E.* Maryknoll, N.Y.: Orbis.

Hellwing, S., and Y. Adjeman
1986 Animal Bones. In *ᶜIzbet Ṣarṭah: An Early Iron Age Site Near Rosh Haᶜayin*, ed. I. Finkelstein, 141–52. Oxford: British Archaeological Reports.

Hiebert, T.
1996 *The Yahwist's Landscape: Nature and Religion in Early Israel.* New York: Oxford University Press.

Khazanov, A. M.
1984 *Nomads and the Outside World.* Translated by J. Crookenden. Cambridge: Cambridge University Press.

King, P. J., and L. E. Stager
2001 *Life in Biblical Israel.* Louisville, Ky.: Westminster John Knox.

Luke, J. T.
1965 Pastoralism and Politics at Mari in the Mari Period. Ph.D. diss., University of Michigan.

Matthews, V. H.
1978 *Pastoral Nomadism in the Mari Kingdom, ca. 1830–1760 B.C.* Cambridge, Mass.: American Schools of Oriental Research.
1981 Pastoralists and Patriarchs. *BA* 44:215–18.
1986 The Wells of Gerar. *BA* 49:118–26.

Mendenhall, G. E.
1962 The Hebrew Conquest of Palestine. *BA* 25:65–87.

Rowton, M. B.
1974 Enclosed Nomadism. *JESHO* 17:1–30.
1977 Dimorphic Structure and the Parasocial Element. *JNES* 36:181–98.

Sarna, N.
1989 *Genesis: The Traditional Hebrew Text with JPS Translation.* JPS Torah Commentary. Philadelphia: Jewish Publication Society.

Stager, L. E.
1985a The Archaeology of the Family in Ancient Israel. *BASOR* 260:1–35.
1985b Merenptah, Israel, and Sea Peoples: New Light on an Old Relief. *EI* 18:56–64.
1988 Archaeology, Ecology, and Social History: Background Themes to the Song of Deborah. In *Congress Volume: Jerusalem, 1986*, ed. J. A. Emerton, 221–34. VTSup 40. Leiden: Brill.

Vaux, R. de
1961 *Ancient Israel: Its Life and Institutions.* Translated by J. McHugh. New York: McGraw-Hill.

Wallis, G.
1966 Die Stadt in den Überlieferungen der Genesis. *ZAW* 78:133–48.

Wellhausen, J.
1885 *Die Composition des Hexateuchs und der historischen Bücher des alten Testaments.* [Reprint: Berlin: Walter de Gruyter, 1963.]
1957 *Prolegomena to the History of Ancient Israel.* New York: Meridian Books.

Westermann, C.
1984 *Genesis 1–11: A Commentary.* Minneapolis: Augsburg.
1985 *Genesis 12–36: A Commentary.* Minneapolis: Augsburg.

Zeder, M.
1990 Animal Exploitation at Tell Halif. In *Preliminary Reports of ASOR-Sponsored Excavations, 1983–87*, ed. W. E. Rast, 24–32. Baltimore: Johns Hopkins University.

23. How Much Is That in . . . ? Monetization, Money, Royal States, and Empires

by John S. Holladay

Most of us are familiar with a nested series of paradigms governing studies of the Hebrew Bible. "Israel" was one or two small, insignificant, agricultural countries at the wrong end of the Levantine coastal strip. Aside from reasonably good dry-farming capabilities and a landscape suited to a wide variety of agricultural, horticultural, and pastoral pursuits (Stager 1985; Hopkins 1985), there were few natural resources beyond hard-working peasant populations governed by a frequently oppressive ruling elite, against which their only human defense was an ill-understood spontaneous movement of charismatic "prophets." National income, when considered at all, is assumed on recent historical models to have come from taxes and tithes on this peasantry and, possibly, upon the ruling elite as well, or, early in the country's existence, bloody raids upon even more poverty-stricken tribal peoples to the east. In the absence of either a monetary system or markets (Dalton 1971; 1975; cf. Hopkins 1996; Schloen 2001:76–89), taxes and tithes were paid in kind and goods were exchanged in kind as "gifts" or "barter" to a richer and more powerful neighbor to the north—a single Phoenician city—as is known from one celebrated case at each extreme of these states' existence (1 Kings 5: 10–11; Ezek. 27: 17). In exchange, the Israelite kings received "gifts" (although the text, 1 Kings 5:6, reads "I will pay you for your servants such wages as you set"), together with timber and the stone-cutters' expertise required to build not only defensive fortifications,[1] but also the centralized religious system and the governmental palaces, together with "gifts" of horses and chariots,[2] fine clothes, and jewelry for the nation's elites, and inordinate riches for the kings and their clientele, so that Israel and Judah could be more "like the nations" who worship other gods.

Our only really dependable resources in pursuit of understanding these highly compromised materials are our literary skills and creative ingenuity, constantly upgraded or overturned by the latest philosophical revolution and a dependent obscurity called Hermeneutics. On the genuinely "historical" side, these powerful tools are only marginally controlled by ancient textual materials, although the opposite is true with respect to linguistics and lexicography. Mostly, however, those contemporary resources are written in languages uncontrolled by the majority of scholars, and, in any case, most materials are seen as largely inapplicable to either Israel or Judah, and attempted applications are invariably open to criticism or debate. Archaeology is recognized as somehow "relevant," but seldom a tie-breaker. As is frequently noted, rather than being a "science", archaeology seems highly dependent upon hugely debatable assumptions and discords among school-based "practitioners," and, except for the odd case, may safely be ignored (the occasion for Dever 2001).

Obviously, I would not have written the above if I thought *any* of the paradigms described were legitimate or even "close"! Yet I think they remain operative for a great majority of scholars. What would I put in their place? And why?

The Overall Economy

The overall economy is an obvious starting point. Contrary to expectation, huge amounts of "banked" silver and gold were available to the three inland states, Aram-Damascus, Israel, and Judah, together with three (and surely all) of the coastal trading powers: Tyre, Arpad, and Tabal, as shown by recent analysis of tribute payments to Neo-Assyrian kings of the late ninth and eighth centuries B.C.E. Individual rulers were capable of paying enormous quantities of tribute in treasured gold and silver bullion, quite apart from base-metal bullion, in most cases, and expensive palace goods, in all cases (Holladay 2006; see table 1 below).

Inexplicably, as far as I am aware, the explanatory power of this fully quantified, objective body of information appears to have been unrecognized to date. These data afford us a wholly new perspective on the nature and *relative scale* of the hitherto unrecognized central pillar of ancient Levantine economies: their bullion resources; and in some cases they also offer us a certain amount of control over the *recovery rates*

[1] E.g., the Outer Gateway at Gezer (Dever 1986:figs. 11, 12, 13, 14); the original three-entryway gate at Megiddo; (Holladay, *Gezer Field III: Excavations in the Solomonic Gateway*, in preparation); the walls of Samaria (conveniently, Pritchard 1969b:fig. 718, with refs.; Dever 2001: 149—the caption is misleading).

[2] In fairness, the text makes it clear that the writer thought these military essentials were "bought," even to the point of stating prices (1 Kings 10:28–29).

Table 1. Major Tributes and Exactions during the Reigns of Adad-nārāri III[+] (810–783 B.C.E.), Tiglath-pileser III[++] (744–727 B.C.E.), and Sennacherib[+++] (704–681 B.C.E.)

Name	*Usurper?*	*Tribute*	*Gold*	*Silver*	*Assyrian Value (U.S $)*
"Marʾī" of Damascus (Bir-Hadad III?)	no	spot palace tribute	20 talents (0.6 tonnes)	2,300 talents (69 tonnes)	$135,496,741
Metenna[++] of Tyre** unparalleled "tribute"	yes	usurper's palace tribute	50 talents (1.5 tonnes)	2,000 talents (60 tonnes)	$130,114,672
Matiʾil[++] of Arpad** unparalleled "tribute"	no	complete sack; Arpad annexed	30 talents (0.9 tonnes)	2,000 talents (60 tonnes)	$122,575,929
Hulli[++] of Tabal	yes	usurper's palace tribute	10 talents (0.3 tonnes)	1,000 talents (30 tonnes)	$ 89,558,251
Hoshea[++]	yes	usurper's palace tribute	10 talents (0.3 tonnes)	1,000 talents (30 tonnes)	$ 89,558,251
Menahem[++]	yes	usurper's palace tribute	*nil*	1,000 talents (30 tonnes)	$ 55,633,912
Hezekiah[+++]	no	spot palace tribute	30 talents (0.9 tonnes)	800 talents (24 tonnes)	$ 49,000,087
Ahaz[++]	no	bribe (*šoḥad*)	*no data—presumably in the above range*		

For "Marʾī" of Damascus, see Holladay 2006:322–25, with references. The dollar valuation of gold and silver is based on New York closing prices on April 21, 2004: $390.80 (U.S.) per troy ounce of gold; $7.21 (U.S.) per troy ounce of silver. Since silver was more valued in ancient Mesopotamia (ratio of 8 silver to 1 gold, or 8:1) than it is today (ratio of 54.2:1), the silver component in the "Assyrian Value" column in the table has been adjusted to reflect the Assyrian worth of the silver, as opposed to the New York value on April 21, 2004.

of depleted bullion resources, thus giving us a rough vernier or proportional measure of national income; and, finally, they give us a secure insight into the *directionality of flows* of gold and silver, key commodities that can be regarded as "treasure" and "money."

Gold ("treasure") is the primary key. Aside from Egypt, which was extraordinarily possessive of its gold hoard, there were few other sources of gold available within the Levant or the Mediterranean world in general, apart from the South Arabian trade, which could independently tap the resources of eastern Africa and even India. Thus, gold in quantity seems to be an excellent surrogate measure of the activity of this traffic.[3]

Silver ("money"), on the other hand, which can be sourced by lead-isotope analysis, was readily available to the merchants of the coastal ports, primarily from greater Greece and Sardinia, and via both maritime and overland routes from Anatolia (and, likely, points north) to more northerly Levantine ports and Neo-Hittite inland centers such as Carchemish and Patina. As with the gold holdings, the large quantities of silver inland in the southern Levant, and less certainly in Mesopotamia as well (note the title of G. van Driel's [2002] study: "Elusive Silver"), may be taken as a surrogate measure of trade with—or, in the Mesopotamian case, both trade with and tribute from—these coastal and northern entities.

The only direct routes by which the South Arabian caravan trade, carried by camels since the late Late Bronze II period (Wapnish 1997),[4] could reach the Mediterranean coast and the markets of the Mediterranean world passed through Syria-Palestine. Thus, these large, vulnerable caravans[5]

[3] Concerning the role of gold in Ur III Umma, G. van Driel (2002:19) writes: "In considering the facts available . . . [regarding] the changing of agricultural bulk products into silver . . . some attention must be paid to the additional role of gold in these accounts, as the buying of gold seems to absorb notable amounts of silver. Not that gold should be considered as a type of currency, as silver was, but it deserves some special attention. In general it will have disappeared into the various treasuries in the shape of valuable objects, or it was used for gilding in a cultic or ceremonial context." The same would appear to be true of first-millennium B.C.E. Judah and Israel. I owe the reference to P.-A. Beaulieu.

[4] It is certain that there were earlier *donkey* caravans, but these were, as in the Old Assyrian trading system, far less capable and at a much smaller scale (Holladay 1997:203–4; 2001:174–77).

[5] The only one on which we have direct information had at least 200 camels and 100 persons, but in fact it very

had to pass through at least one of the states of Israel (later Judah and Israel) or Aram-Damascus.[6] Returning caravans, laden with the goods of the Phoenician and Philistine coast, had to go back the same way. Naturally, as with the Old Assyrian trade and all other known parallels, tolls, palace gifts, and service fees applied. In return, the caravaneers were assured security, lodging(?), water, food, and fodder for their animals, as well as veterinary and other services. These fees probably were in the range of 20–25 percent of the cargo's net worth, each way (Holladay 2006 *passim*, esp. pp. 327–28), and it is extremely likely that David's Transjordanian wars were expressly focused on "pacifying" that frontier so as to assure the security of the caravans.

Table 1 lists the seven highest Neo-Assyrian tributes recorded, together with the (amount unspecified) bribe (*šoḥad*) of Ahaz of Judah (2 Kings 16:7–9) in the same general time period.[7] In Hezekiah's case, a massive outlay had obviously already been paid out as a bribe to Egypt for intervention in the event of the Assyrian invasion. In each case, these tributes reflect gold and silver bullion reserves over and above the costs of governance; that is, over and above the costs of public officials, including professional military commanders (see "Redistribution" below); public construction, including building palaces and caravan-cities (e.g. Beersheba); fortresses; fortifying major towns and cities;[8] continuing outlays for extremely expensive horses and chariots and ready-made military equipment (see Sennacherib's listing of weaponry in his account of Hezekiah's tribute in Holladay 2006); together with, in all likelihood (though for the most part they would not have engaged the attention of the biblical writers and tradents) full-time soldiers and high-priced foreign mercenaries ranging from charioteers and masters of horse to warriors such as David's *Kērētîm* and *Pēlētîm*, Hittites (Uriah and Ahimelech), and the *Kittiyîm* of the Arad Letters (Aharoni 1981:22).[9] Nor were the massive bullion tributes of the late eighth century outlined in Table 1 unique to the Neo-Assyrians, as the turbulent histories of Judah and Israel, outlined in Table 2 below, demonstrate.

How the Israelite Economy Worked

Apart from the "Neo-Hittite" continuities in northwestern Levant, which occasionally trickled southward, there is practically no carryover between the Late Bronze II civilization(s) of the Levant and what happens during the Iron II period. What were the triggers that brought about such sweeping changes? Although there are many different factors, including large-scale population movements (e.g., Pitard 1987:81–89; Frayne forthcoming), in this study we can only seek to understand the basic economics.

The problem we are addressing in this paper actually begins with a trio of articles by Kenneth Kitchen and Alan Millard (Kitchen 1989a; 1989b; Millard 1989), in which they describe an astonishingly large series of gifts over a period of four years by Osorkon I, summarized by Kitchen as "at least 383 tons" of gold and silver (Kitchen 1989: 30), to temples and foundations in Egypt immediately following the death of Sheshonq I, the biblical "Shishak." As Kitchen emphasizes, this huge series of gifts immediately followed Sheshonq's campaign of pillage and destruction throughout Israel and, most probably, southern Phoenicia as well, when "he [Shishak] carried off the treasures of the Temple of the Lord and the treasures of the royal palace. He took everything, including all the gold shields Solomon had made" (1 Kings 14:26).

probably had, say, another 50 camels standing well off in the desert carrying high-value cargos and being guarded by another 100 well-armed security guards. Despite what the self-congratulating governor of the land of Sūḫu and Mari thought, these long-distance caravaneers were not naïve "innocents" (Holladay 2006: 320–21).

6 That this requirement should have led David and Solomon to imperialistic expansion, or Damascus to cutting off portions of Israel (the Dan Inscription), or even seeking to control all of Israel and Judah, or, for that matter, Israel seeking to dominate, diminish, or completely conquer Judah, should come as no surprise.

7 Cogan 2001:400 rejects the term *šoḥad* both here and in the case of Ahaz (2 Kings 16:8; cf. Cogan and Tadmor 1988:188) as "one inserted by Dtr in order to taint Asa's act," while simultaneously accepting "the sending of a rich offering . . . [in connection with] asking Ben-Hadad to break an existing alliance and turn against a treaty-brother." To my mind, this is a distinction without a difference, but, in any case, the act itself is not what is being rejected, but the semantically challenged word used, possibly by a later editor, to define it.

8 For the southern corridor, within which Tell Arad, Tell ʿIra, Tell Malhata, Tel Masos, and Beer-sheba played varying roles at varying times, see Holladay 1995:383–86.

9 Although generally considered Egyptian mercenaries (Niemeier 2002, with references) given the nature of their provisions—for the feast of the New Moon (Naʾaman 2006)—these *Kittiyîm* are perhaps better regarded as "Judean" mercenaries. For their origins, see Dion 1992.

Table 2. Israelite and Judean "Tributes," 925–597 B.C.E.

Donor	*Recipient*	*Reference*	*Type*	*Booty*
Rehoboam of Judah 928–911 B.C.E. (and, surely, others)	Sheshonq I of Egypt	1 Kings14:25–26	wholesale sack (major campaign throughout Palestine)	"everything" Solomon had accumulated
Asa of Judah 908–867 B.C.E.	Ben-hadad I of Damascus	1 Kings 15:18–21	bribe (*šoḥad*) to break his alliance with Baasha of Israel and attack Israel	all temple and palace gold and silver
Jehu of Israel 842–814 B.C.E.	Shalmaneser III	"Black Obelisk" of Shalmaneser III	bribe to attack Hazael of Damascus, and usurper's palace tribute(?)	presumably all palace and temple holdings
Joash of Judah 836–798 B.C.E.	Hazael of Damascus	2 Kings 12:17–18	tribute, presumably "palace tribute"	presumably all palace and temple holdings
Joash of Israel	Ben-Hadad II's demand upon Israel	1 Kings 20:1–6	palace sack, escalated to a wholesale sack	unsuccessful
Amaziah of Judah 798–769 B.C.E.	Joash of Israel	2 Kings 14:13–14	wholesale looting of Jerusalem	hostages (for ransom) and all palace and temple holdings
Menahem of Israel 747–737 B.C.E.	Tiglath-pileser III	2 Kings 15:19–20	usurper's palace tribute	1,000 talents of silver (50 shekels per man levy upon Menahem's "Mighty Men")
Ahaz of Judah 743–727 B.C.E.	Tiglath-pileser III	2 Kings 16:5–10	bribe (*šoḥad*) to attack Rezin of Damascus and Pekah of Israel	the temple's silver and gold and the palace treasures
Hoshea of Israel 732–724 B.C.E.	Tiglath-pileser III	Tadmor 1994:140, n. 18, III R 10, 2.	usurper's tribute, apparently from palace and treasury resources alone	10 talents of gold and probably 1,000 talents of silver
Hoshea of Israel 732–724 B.C.E.	Shalmaneser V	2 Kings 17:3	tribute	unknown, but prob. not insignificant
Hoshea of Israel 732–724 B.C.E.	Tefnakht of Sais[a] ("So, king of Egypt")	2 Kings 17:4	bribe, possibly never delivered	unknown, but if delivered probably not insignificant
Hezekiah of Judah 727–698 B.C.E.	Tirhaka, "king of Ethiopia"[b]	2 Kings 19:8–9	bribe	Tirhakah appeared and fought at Libnah, so presumably the bribe was received
Hezekiah of Judah 727–698 B.C.E.	Sennacherib	2 Kings 18:13–16[c]	belated "spot palace tribute"	30 talents of gold, 800 talents of silver, plus palace treasures and personnel
Jehoahaz of Judah 609 B.C.E.	Necho I of Egypt	2 Kings 23:32–35	tribute	one(?)[d] talent of gold, 100 talents of silver
Jehoiachin of Judah 597 B.C.E.	Nebuchadnezzar of Babylon	2 Kings 24:10–16	palace and temple sack	no figures given; all converted to bullion

[a] Goedicke 1963:64–66; Albright 1963:66; cf. Cogan and Tadmor 1988:196.

[b] At this point, Tirhaka was possibly a field commander and not yet king (Cogan and Tadmor 1988:234, note to v. 9).

[c] For a more complete and accurate record of the event, see Sennacherib's account on the Rassam Cylinder (Pritchard 1969: 288; Cogan 2000:303).

[d] See Cogan and Tadmor 1988:304. LXX gives "one hundred" talents of gold. The Lucianic recension has "ten talents." Cogan and Tadmor suggest "a talent of gold" as more nearly approximating normal ratios of gold and silver in tribute lists. This seems more reasonable than either of the Septuagintal figures.

Given the skepticism of many present-day biblical scholars concerning the "historical Solomon," these data may perhaps be disregarded. What cannot be disregarded, however, is the greatly neglected direct historical record of Hezekiah's belated "peace gift" to Sennacherib following the breaking off of his Palestinian campaign in 701 and his return home to Nineveh. In Sennacherib's (or his scribe's) own words:

> Hezekiah . . . sent me after my departure to Nineveh, my royal city, his elite troops (and) his best soldiers, which he had brought in as reinforcements to strengthen Jerusalem, with 30 talents of gold, 800 talents of silver,[10] choice antimony, large blocks of carnelian, beds (inlaid) with ivory, armchairs (inlaid) with ivory, elephant hides, ivory, ebony-wood, boxwood, multicolored garments, garments of linen, wool (dyed) red-purple and blue-purple, vessels of copper, iron, bronze and tin, chariots, siege shields, lances, armor, daggers for the belt, bows and arrows, countless trappings and implements of war, together with his daughters, his palace women, his male and female singers. He (also) dispatched his messenger to deliver the tribute and to do obeisance.
>
> [Cogan's translation of the "Rassam Cylinder" or "Oriental Institute Prism of Sennacherib," in Hallo and Younger 2000:303b; cf. Pritchard 1969:288]

This works out, for "poor little Judah," to a staggering 900 kg or 0.9 metric tonnes of gold and 24 tonnes of silver capable of simply being stripped out of the temple and palace holdings and shipped off to Nineveh. But how does it compare across the board? Table 1 above, a slightly modified version of Table 2 in my Dever Festschrift paper (Holladay 2006), lists the six other highest preserved/recorded tributes of the Neo-Assyrian period, amounting to 4.96 metric tonnes of gold and 303 metric tonnes of silver in all. This misses Kitchen's total of 383 (short) tons by only about 44 tons, or 11.4 percent. Assuming fairly long, healthy reigns for Solomon and his coastal seaport contemporaries, and assuming access to precious metals similar to that of eighth-century monarchs and rulers of port cities (Holladay 2006 and below), and further assuming that at least four or five other silver-rich seaport entities must have suffered along with Solomon and Israel (Gaza, Ashkelon, Ashdod, Tell Qasile, and Dor), Kitchen's figures look amazingly correct.

Nor were Solomon, Ahaz, Menahem, Hoshea, and Hezekiah the only Judean or Israelite kings to access their bullion stores to bribe assistance in times of peril, or to give over all their bullion and palace treasures—standard operating procedure in the Neo-Assyrian period—to save their necks from an aggressor (including their own kinsmen). This can be seen from the data in Table 2 above, which is surely incomplete. More broadly and more significantly, with respect to bribes, see my colleague Paul Dion's definitive study (2006), which he graciously brought to my attention.[11] All the above, coupled with the fact that Menahem's tribute was made up of 50-shekel contributions by every "capable" (probably combat-ready, *not* "rich"—there should be so many!) man, is sufficient proof that ancient Israel did not live by bread, olives, and wine alone.

According to Magen Broshi and Israel Finkelstein (1992:54), "the kingdom's population could have reached about 350,000." Reckoning one capable (fighting) man per nuclear family yields a mean nuclear-family size of 5.83 individuals,[12] slightly higher than David Schloen's "5 persons on average, including servants and relatives" (2001:136). It would be well within Lawrence Stager's median figures of 5.0–6.2 (Stager 1985:21, table 4), and it would be considerably above the average of all estimates with mean living space at 10 m^2 per person (ibid., table 3). My option in all this would be to take Schloen's carefully worked-out Tell Beit Mirsim Stratum A data in his Table 6 (2001:174), select the only operable assumption (that "100% of [the] "courtyard" [was] covered") and, utilizing Schloen's slightly inflated version (8 m^2) of Patty Jo Watson's "Hasanabad" "average of 7.3 m^2 per person" figure, arrive at an average of 6.2 persons/house. All of which is to say that a mean nuclear family size of 5.83 individuals is an eminently respectable approximation.

In other words, halfway through the eighth century, not only could the average Israelite family be

---

[10] 2 Kings 18:14 has "three hundred talents of silver and thirty talents of gold."

[11] Further to my opening remarks on the general parameters of Old Testament studies, Miller and Hayes spend nearly a page (2006:398) listing reasons why the account of Ahaz's bribe to Tiglath-pileser III is improbable (e.g., "The Assyrian monarch was no international mercenary waiting to pick up a few shekels as payment for rescuing beleaguered states"). But we are talking about something like 3,000,000 shekels, the amounts of Menahem's tribute in silver and Hoshea's probable silver offerings alone (see Table 1 above). Simon Parker's (1997) well-made argument that bribes actually were operational (and operative) "under certain circumstances" (Miller and Hayes's term) is reduced to a four-line "for an alternative view" footnote. Definitively now, with special reference to Ahaz, see Dion 2006.

[12] A total population of 350,000 divided by 60,000 "capable men" yields 5.83 persons per family. Thus, the contributing group *must* have been the nuclear family, as opposed to any larger or smaller cohort.

assessed 50 shekels of silver, but, one way or another, almost every family in Israel met that threshold, whether by begging, borrowing, or stealing. Undoubtedly, the extended family (*mišpāḥâ*) fulfilled its obligations toward its weaker members. But the point remains: one Mesopotamian mina of silver was available to every family in Israel. When one ponders that fact, one is forced to two further conclusions. Lacking coinage, there must have been some commonly employed means in every city, town, and village of accurately weighing out specific small amounts of silver. And secondly, there must already have been some established fail-safe system for gathering up and forwarding large quantities of wealth reliably to Samaria. Everything had to happen in a very short time, all the silver totaled up and the tribute delivered to Tiglath-pileser III while the royal patience held.

None of the above would have been possible on short notice without two long-established institutions. The first institutional necessity was a smoothly-running, all-pervasive, silver-based "market system." That is, there must have been a long-established routine system involving a large, all-pervasive quantity of high-value metal (i.e., silver) in the form of *Hacksilber* or silver plate or small silver ingots and silver jewelry (which are well, if sketchily, attested) throughout the entire country. And this must have been combined with a multitude of locally trusted traders, all with standardized (i.e., publicly accepted) "honest" weights, which were routinely and familiarly used in trafficking in goods and materials valuated in and sold for silver.

But this was nothing new within the Levant and Mesopotamia. Within the limitations imposed by the paucity of data, it can be argued that such a system, including public markets and a silver-based economy, had existed in Mesopotamia since at least the Ur III period (Powell 1999:5–18). Unquestionably, a full market economy undergirded all the operations of the Old Assyrian trade (Veenhof 1995; 1999; Yoffee 1981), which of course operated alongside other "economies," something still true of our own market-based economy. And the story of Wen-Amun gives a wonderful insight into the mind of a low-ranking Egyptian temple official encountering, for the first time, a completely market-dominated Phoenician culture (Pritchard 1969:25–29).

To put it in the strongest terms, already by the time of Israelite state formation, the entire Levant would appear to have either been on a silver economy, with gold as the highest governmental monetary reserve or a more directly monetary choice for people with more gold than silver (e.g., the westbound South Arabian traders), or it was heading in that direction. Obviously, there were other economies, as there still are within our overwhelmingly capitalistic market-driven economy: the household or domestic economy, which was probably coextensive with the extended family and, as a barter economy, throughout entire neighborhoods and even with neighboring towns; redistributive mechanisms such as feasts and communal sacrifices; a well-entrenched temple economy (priests and Levites), which existed on taxes (tithes) and gifts, either in kind or in silver equivalent (see below); and a certain amount of gift-giving, seen not only internally, but externally utilized as an instrument of state by, for example, Philistine, Phoenician, and Cypriot cities. These "gifts" were self-servingly perceived as "tribute" by imperial Assyria and Egypt.

This must have had decisive effects upon every aspect of Israelite economic life. It is highly probable, moreover, that this "monetary" status of silver and gold was already operative in the Middle Bronze Age, as it had been in Mesopotamia since the Ur III Period (Powell 1999:14–18, with references). Thus, gold and silver served not only the needs of the earlier east-west South Arabian donkey caravan traffic, the likely source of the anomalous MB IIA–B gold holdings discussed by Abraham Malamat (2006:352–53), but also as the fiscal basis, the motor and the lubricant (to use Veenhof's [1999:55] description of the role of silver in the Old Assyrian trade), of the massive, wide-ranging long-distance trade of Hyksos Avaris (Holladay 1997), and of the long-distance Syro-Palestinian overland trade diasporas, at least one (and probably several) with deep Anatolian roots, highlighted in Holladay 2001. In the most basic sense, deals simply could not be struck and easily negotiated profits taken if items and cargoes could not be compared in terms of stated metal equivalents and, eventually, purchased and sold on the same basis.[13] As in Mesopotamia and Egypt, the "low-value money" would have been the dominant food-grain, generally wheat or barley, or, in Mesopotamia during the later periods, dates, depending on the basic food crop in the region (Powell 1999:14–16). In Egypt, it was "silver and copper/bronze," "grain," and "sesame oil" (and "fat"), although copper and grain seem to have predominated ("a jar of fat worth 30 *deben*" [of copper]). Valuations and totals were normally reckoned in *deben* of copper, for example, "10 *hin* of vegetable oil worth 5 *deben*" [copper understood]

[13] See Barry Kemp's model discussion of village trade in New Kingdom Egypt, where copper was the standard "high value money" (1989:248–52, with refs.), with silver and gold as progressively yet higher "monies."

(Kemp 1989:248). Due to high transport costs, low-value money was useless for any but local transactions, although this would not be the case if water transport were easily available and quantities sufficient to warrant shipping.

The second institution, which involves the hypothesized long-established fail-safe system for gathering up and forwarding large quantities of wealth reliably to Samaria, must have been a highly efficient bursary system, possibly based only in larger towns and "central places," not only capable, in this situation, of collecting, assessing, guarding, and forwarding a huge quantity of wealth to one central location, but more normally operating (since this was a singular, hopefully "once only" event) as a centrally-directed system of routine silver-based redistribution. Presumably, this would have been based in a fairly secure building such as the local "palace," which could have been as humble a structure as the "North-west Tower" at Tell Beit Mirsim.

Redistribution

This may require some explication. All organizations reward their workers by issuing to them ("redistributing") some portion of the organization's income. The general concept of redistribution within ancient Near Eastern palace- and temple-based farming and manufacturing enterprises is, perhaps, excessively familiar to every student, particularly for Mesopotamia and Egypt, but also, by association, for other parts of the ancient Near East, particularly during the Middle and Late Bronze Ages and, by extension, to the great mass of the population during the Iron Age as well. Any city-state or nation-state had (and still has) the obligation to support its officials and servitors, which, in Egypt, included such diverse entities as pyramid cities/workmens' villages, mortuary cults, vast temple-based agricultural estates, and far-flung trading enterprises. In Mesopotamia, we have temples with vast agricultural holdings, particularly in the irrigated bottomlands of the Tigris and Euphrates rivers, as well as a wide variety of manufacturing interests, from metalworking to weaving. In both Egypt and Mesopotamia, the palaces also had their own manufacturing, processing, and trading operations. Local government was on the shoulders of the provincial administrations, which, in Mesopotamia, oversaw the *ilku*-system, under which "various grades of soldier[s and] . . . suppliers of labour for royal building schemes and produc[ers of] certain items for the palace . . . were given landholdings which carried with them the obligation to fulfill certain duties required by the government. . . . Anyone who acquired such a land-parcel, but had not been the original grantee, was required to take over the duties incumbent on the land" (Kuhrt 1995:110).

We are not so well informed about Israel because, significantly, there was no parallel to this deeded land-tenure system for public service in ancient Israel, where landholdings were tribal and familial. Yet public service had to be supported. In our own times, we have a vast array of national, state, county, city, town, and village officials dependent upon the public purse. In most contemporary societies, that redistributive purse overwhelmingly comes from taxes, but this is not necessarily the case in all instances.

National Income

Consider two different models. In an ideal world of our own time, picture a small forlorn country without wealth or prospects subsisting, for a time, on international grants, which it (being honest) redistributes to its citizens and uses to build up national economic resources to the point where it can stand on its own feet and pay its own way through a socially responsible system of taxation. Alternatively, in our less-than-ideal world, some oil-rich countries redistribute the income from that resource to the extent that some of the royal house are extremely rich indeed, but even the poorest citizen (not necessarily the "guest-worker") has more than enough on which to subsist.

Now, further consider a possible historical entity, such as Solomon's empire, or a set of entities, such as the kingdoms of Judah, Israel, and Aram-Damascus, which suddenly discover that they are sitting on a vast and potentially inexhaustible resource—the land bridge between great wealth to the east and talented entrepreneurs to the west—which allows them to offer a "pipeline" to South Arabian possessors of wealth that is of little earthly good to themselves, thereby allowing them safely and easily to carry their surplus high-priced goods and deliver them to commercially minded third parties (the Philistines and Phoenicians), who, for their own part, have things to offer the "easterners" that they, in turn, can make use of back home and in their own sphere of long-distance trading influence (the Red Sea coast, East Africa, the Persian Gulf, India, and the Far East, possibly including the Spice Islands). A modern analogy is that of a country eager, on the one hand, to sell products such as oil, diamonds, or even palm-oil that are in excess to its own needs to other countries eager to buy rare goods and needed materials.[14]

---

[14] For a brilliant discussion of the Phoenicians' widely-varying and critical roles with respect to "world trade" and

Doing everything necessary to ensure the safety and integrity of the South Arabian camel caravans (David's Transjordanian wars and various Syro-Ephraimite and Israelite-Judaean wars?) and allowing the caravans to pass through the land (symbolized by the Queen of Sheba's visit to Solomon) would have provided sufficient income—probably 20–25 percent of the value of the total cargo, each way—for the country to feed itself and care for its own territorial integrity without much taxation of its own citizens, perhaps only a token head tax and/or some form of tithing to help ensure the participation of every citizen in the national cult.

Redistribution in a Monetized Economy

Arguably, that 20–25 percent could fund the entire range of governmental, religious, and military services, including the essential build-up of the nation's bullion reserve (Holladay 2006). But how was income from that source redistributed to feed and care for the state's institutional "employees"?[15] Since Table 1 above deals entirely in "money" (apart from the palace goods that generally accompanied forced tribute, which may be taken as harsh personal punishment of the guilty king or city ruler), it follows that redistribution should also have been in "money." This solves what has been a longstanding, though generally overlooked, problem for Palestinian archaeologists and historians. Whereas Egypt and Mesopotamia had their granaries and storehouses, herds, and palace and temple workshops, more than a hundred years of excavation in Palestine have produced nothing approaching the needed facilities. Prior to the Persian period, virtually all the granaries and storehouses were either part of palace complexes (Samaria, Hazor, Tell Beit-Mirsim) or stable complexes (Megiddo, Hazor, Tel Masos, Beersheba(?), Tel Hadar [Kochavi 1989; 1991]). Especially when one considers the costs of widespread warehousing and distribution of low-value commodities over long distances to meet the government's redistributive needs, the attractions of transporting and redistributing silver, with which recipients can buy their own low-value and often perishable needs from local sources "in the gate" or at marketplaces and shops (Stager 2001:191; Holladay in process), become obvious.

This takes us back to the point stated above, that there must have been a highly efficient bursary system, possibly based only in "central places," that was not only capable of collecting, assessing, guarding, and forwarding a huge quantity of wealth to one central location (a singular, hopefully "once only" event), but was capable of more normally operating as a centrally directed system of routine silver-based redistribution.

Neither Israel nor Judah, nor, for that matter, probably Damascus as well, had huge temple economies or landholdings. Their environments and local economies simply were unsuited to centralized management (Hopkins 1985). Given the multitudinous and multifarious tasks of redistribution within the large and complex structures of the palace establishment, its regional governors, and the military, each of which had elements stretching across the entire country and beyond, it is obvious that given the necessary resources—namely, a reasonable supply of "money"—a "payroll" system would far outperform a distributed (let alone centralized) system of stores (e.g., of grain) and of services such as milling, baking, brewing/vinting, and distribution on a daily basis. It was far simpler to distribute a fixed amount of silver to each "ranking," with additional funding available for extended or special duty. Isolated forts and duty stations (e.g., Tel Arad) would, of course, have had their own facilities, but, given the costs of transport, even they would have purchased their provisions as locally as possible. In short, some modification of the "benign neglect" management system

the various ancient Near Eastern and world power centers, see Susan Frankenstein's "The Phoenicians in the Far West: A Function of Neo-Assyrian Imperialism" (1979).

[15] In his model 1979 article on "The Economic Structure of the Assyrian Empire," Nicholas Postgate suggests that, within the "Assyrian Empire, which always seems to have made an effort to reduce the number of administrative procedures needed to route a given item from its origin to where it was to be used, . . . all available evidence indicates that the government would determine a man's *ilku* obligation and then leave it to the individual to make the relevant payment direct to its eventual recipient. Quite apart from the reduced administration, this system relieved the government of the physical burden of collecting and distributing the items, and enabled it, in theory at least, to calculate exactly how many soldiers and animals could be supported, without ever handling the relevant materials themselves. A similar policy is reflected in a practice attested at Assur, whereby cavalrymen from certain villages took their animals home with them for the winter, and fed them, although we do not know who actually bore the responsibility for the fodder" (Postgate 1979:203–4). "The *iškāru* system, . . . designed to convert raw materials under the direct control of the government into the finished products needed by it [operated similarly]. . . . Quantities of raw materials . . . were allocate[d] . . . to the craftsmen [who were then obligated] . . .to supply the finished products with a commercial-style debt-note. . . . It is clear that supervision was minimal and . . . that the system worked more on the principle of . . . fiscal obligations (Postgate 1979:203–5).

suggested by Postgate for the Assyrian Empire (see note 15 above), coupled with a streamlined busary system, seems to be the most reasonable process for achieving reasonable outcomes with a minimum of bureaucratic overhead. We discuss a smaller-scale variant of this process below.

An End-run around Bureaucratic Self-enrichment

Jehoash's repairs to the temple in ca. 814 B.C.E. serve as a delightful model of "minimalist bureaucratic efficiency." After twenty-three years of his reign, the priests had accomplished exactly nothing except self-enrichment with respect to repairs of the temple in response to the king's initial command upon assuming his throne: "Let the priests take for themselves, each from his acquaintance, and they shall repair the House wherever damage may be found" (2 Kings 12:5). So a new order went out:

> "Now, do not keep silver from your acquaintances, but donate it for the repair of the House." The priests agreed not to take silver from the people, nor [themselves] to make repairs on the temple. Then Jehoiada the priest took a chest and bored a hole in its side, and he set it near the altar, on the right as one enters the House of YHWH; and the priests, keepers of the threshold, would put there all the silver brought to the House of YHWH. Whenever they saw that there was much silver in the chest, the king's scribe and the high priest would come and *tie (it) up and count* [i.e., "weigh"] the silver found in the House of YHWH. They would give the silver that was weighed over to the workmen in charge of the House of YHWH; they used it to pay the carpenters and builders working in the House of YHWH, and the masons and stone cutters, to buy timber and quarry stone to repair the House of YHWH, and for all other expenditures needed to repair the House. However, no silver basins, snuffers, sprinkling bowls, or trumpets—vessels of gold and silver of any kind—were made for the House of YHWH from the silver brought into the House of YHWH. But they paid it to the workmen who repaired the House of YHWH. Furthermore, no accounting was made with the men to whom the silver was given to pay the workmen, for they dealt honestly. Silver from guilt offerings and from sin offerings was not given over to the House of YHWH; it belonged to the priests.
>
> [2 Kings 12:8b–17, as translated in Cogan and Tadmor 1988:135–36 (emphasis added)]

Here, the *people's* tithes and free-will offerings *in silver* are kept from the priests' acquisitive hands and used to pay the contractors and foremen, skilled carpenters, builders, masons and stone-cutters (Tyrians?), "and . . . all other expenditures needed to repair the House." They were paid with preweighed tied-up bags of silver, the same kinds of sealed bags occasionally found in archaeological contexts, which contained one mina of silver (Thompson 2003:78–83; King and Stager 2001:174–76; each includes a photograph of a bag containing one mina of *Hacksilber*)[16]. If we follow the general indications present in the observed finds, it is not impossible that the temple workmen's standard wages came in one-mina increments.

This bears reflection. It is entirely likely that *local* tithes in kind were delivered to the temple, and that those tithes went toward the upkeep of the priests. But what about people living farther than, say, a half-day's journey to the temple (and less than that for most commodities)? Obviously, those people, whether agriculturalists or pastoralists or laborers, various professionals and government workers, including the standing forces, paid their tithes in weighed-out silver whenever they made their pilgrimages to the temple. Of course, this meant that they must have had some way, which can hardly have been anything other than local "market prices," of determining the silver equivalent of the tithed produce. Professionals paid in silver, which would have included all the governmental officials and workers, thousands of soldiers, charioteers, stable-masters and handlers all the way down to stable-boys, obviously tithed a fixed proportion of their income, and may have given free-will gifts over and above that, all in silver. None of this is "barter" or is any different from the later "temple tax" paid in specially struck coinage (except that the moneyers kept their portion of the silver). Simply and purely, they were not only paid their "wages" in silver but they also paid their tithes and other taxes in silver "money," exactly as did people of the same standing in Neo-Assyrian society (Postgate 1979:203–13). But unless they were

[16] A mina is 1/60th of a talent and there is a certain amount of controversy as to whether a "western" mina was made up of 50 or 60 shekels (probably the former). Exactitude in this is difficult (see Powell 1992:905–97). Quite apart from the inherent variability of the standard limestone weights, other variables would include the question of which shekel was employed (was the bag Ashkelonite or Judean or Phoenician?) and the percentage of the present weight made up of corrosion products. Thompson suggests that the 17 Dor bundles "were based on the 8.3–8.6-g shekel (thus 60-unit minas of about 500 g): 17 × 500 g = 8.5 kg." This, then, would, equal the biblical *pym*, which "probably denotes the 'shekel' of Ashdod [and, therefore, probably Dor and Ashkelon as well—JSH]. In the LB Age this 'shekel' seems to have weighed about 80 percent of the Ugaritic shekel . . . this suggests that the *pym* should be in the 7.2–8-g range" (Powell 1992:906).

part of a landowning family, or at least a member in good standing of a local *mišpāḥâ*, they would have had to buy their own foodstuffs and other provisions, again, for money (silver), and at some fixed place such as a "market," whether this was held on certain days in or near the city gate, or on some "bazaar" street, or in some extramural marketplace unexcavated to date simply because none of us spends much time excavating *outside* of city walls—or in all three.

Money in the Bible and the Biblical World

Our recourse to "money" as a way of explaining social processes in ancient Israel and Judah is, of course, fully in line with the biblical text throughout. Quite apart from the plain fact that almost every reference to buying or selling goods or property, including tombs (Gen. 23:16–20), threshing floors (2 Sam. 24:24), sites for future capital cities (1 Kings 16:23–24; see Stager 1990), slaves (Hos. 3:1–2, an excellent example of the use of both "high value" [silver] and "low-value" [barley] money), and famine and post-famine prices (2 Kings 6:24–7:20), gives the price in shekels of silver and, in Hosea's case, both silver and measures of barley (Powell 1992:904–7; 1999, esp. pp. 14–18), we also have, hardly coincidentally, actual inscribed Judean weights in great numbers. As of 1998, there are 434 examples, 211 of which were found in excavations and surveys (Kletter 1998:17, 91), with other uninscribed weights of similar size (Kletter 1998:132–37) and even smaller ones of greater sophistication (gold weights?) going back to the Late Bronze Age and earlier. Needless to say, despite these numbers, we have only the barest fraction of all the weights that originally existed in Judah and Israel.[17]

Obviously, the coastal ports could not have existed apart from the silver standard, nor, for that matter, could the Neo-Assyrian and Neo-Babylonian monarchs have carried off their enormous building programs without all the "money" their campaigns and terror tactics brought in. Bullion has its uses, as the Ishtar Gate in Babylon attests. Nor did the later introduction of coinage change much for, say, the Phoenician merchants, since, as is well-known, they treated silver money exactly as they would have treated small silver ingots or larger pieces of plate or *Hacksilber* (Thompson 2003:69). They chiseled it to determine its quality, they weighed it to determine its "worth," and they hacked it up to make small change—early forerunners of "quarters" and "pieces-of-eight" (ibid.).

Householding and Reciprocity in a Monetized Economy

Large sectors of the economy, while not unaffected by the widespread existence of a wide-reaching and dominant silver-based monetary system, as seen above with respect to Menahem's massive levy, must also have operated on a completely different plane, that of the household, involving (1) the *bêt ʾāb*, or "house of the father," where, apart from outside labor or government employment of various members of the family, the head of the house likely had absolute authority, and (2) the *mišpāḥâ*, the "clan" or extended family, although, even there, silver, and, for small change, barley, almost certainly were used as the measure of valuation of goods transferred between household and intraclan entities—thus Cousin Eli's raisins and dried figs would add up to a reasonable exchange for only so many measures of Father's new wheat.[18] It is not at all unreasonable that similar transactions could occur in a market setting between

[17] Kletter almost grudgingly admits the inscribed weight system into the late eighth century, with the greatest bulk appearing in seventh century contexts (1998:138). The interesting point, seldom mentioned, is that we have few well-defined, published, Judean strata between the massive "burnished red-slip" layers (e.g., for Israel, Megiddo VA/IVB) and the putatively 701 B.C.E. Sennacherib destruction layers (e.g., Khirbet el-Qom with its 11 weights, Dever 1970:169–87), and finding scarce weights in very limited sub-701 exposures would be a matter of pure luck. Thus, while we are certain (from the paleography, if nothing else) that these inscribed weights are relatively late, much work remains to be done on earlier stratigraphy and dealing with the uninscribed weight series.

[18] Barry Kemp's explanation of "barter" (a term I find inapplicable, since "gain" obviously entered into the transaction) in New Kingdom Egypt applies perhaps better to this "familial" type of transaction than to others: "Everything had a value, expressed in various units which coincided with quantities of certain commodities: weights of silver and copper/bronze, and units of capacity of grain and sesame-oil. . . . Metals were themselves used in exchanges but not as coinage. The nearest step on the road to money is to be found in the stone weights which, when used in the pans of scale balances, checked the weights and thus the values of metals, precious and otherwise. . . . In a typical transaction a policeman buys an ox from a workman, and pays for it with a jar of fat worth 30 *deben*, 2 tunics worth 10 *deben*, scraps of copper/bronze weighing (and thus worth) 5 *deben*, and 10 *hin* of vegetable oil worth 5 *deben*. The total is 50 *deben* (of copper), and the little receipt calls the total 'silver,' which word was used colloquially to mean something very close to the modern word 'money.' This system of values also covered the price of labour and of raw materials" (Kemp 1989:249–50).

active participants, but if the wheat were to go to a middleman for transport to another market, it would seem unwise, unless there were strong personal relations, that mere verbal promises would have been accepted without formally witnessed debt chits, which seem to be rare on the ground.[19] On the other hand, we have a goodly number of "delivery chits" for transported goods to be credited to certain individual's accounts: the Samaria Ostraca (Kaufman, 1982:229; 1992), Aramaic grain-delivery chits for the Persian store-facilities at Beersheba (Naveh 1973: 79–82) and Tell el-Hesi (Bennett and Blakeley 1989: 67 [no chits to date, though they must have once existed]),[20] and ration requests (Aharoni 1967:325–6).

Reassessing Solomon's Reign

Despite what I said in my contribution to the Dever Festschrift (Holladay 2006:325), there is nothing in the history of the united Israel or the Divided Monarchies to argue that they suddenly "came into money" in the later eighth century. Indeed, the opposite can now be argued, given the combined force of Table 1, where quantified surrogate measures of Levantine net worth appear in the form of amounts of tribute exacted, and Table 2, where the standing patterns of tribute exaction involving Israel and Judah are listed. Thus, were we to credit the Solomonic history, including what we now know of at least some of its constructional activities at Gezer, Megiddo, Hazor, and the confirmatory archaeologically attested beauty and costliness of construction and material wealth exhibited by Omri and Ahab's Samaria, it would seem more reasonable to argue for at least as a rich a past as that witnessed in the late eighth century. From this perspective, it makes sense to see Kitchen's (1989a; 1989b) Egyptian evidence (see above), which is totally outside the stream of biblical transmission, as telling us almost everything we need to know about the Levantine wealth already in existence in 925 B.C.E., which is roughly as much wealth as later.

Since most of Osorkon's largesse to the gods was silver, and the Levant does not produce silver, all of that silver must have come from market trade involving large quantities of expensive commodities. The gold, avariciously sought by Egypt (and therefore certainly not the result of inordinate Egyptian "royal gifts" to northern barbarians), could only have come from either Africa or India, almost surely the former. Thus, reckoning thirty to forty years of mostly uncontested rule to Solomon, it seems possible, or even probable,[21] that Solomon's net worth could easily have been greater than the later tribute paid by "Marʾī of Damascus" (Bir-Hadad III) to Adad-nārāri III (810–783 B.C.E.), namely, 20 talents of gold and 2,300 talents of silver (Holladay 2006:324–25, with references). Further to the Solomonic accounts, Millard (1989) illustrates a wide range of golden items, biblical parallels, furniture, etc., including provisions for gold-plating columns, supporting his contention that the account and description of King Solomon's wealth is not only not fanciful, but fully in line with archaeologically attested ancient realities.

Viewed in this light, and assuming that the South Arabian camel traffic may have been conducted on a more or less constant level, consistent with its own resources, over a very long period,[22] it becomes important to consider more exactly just what we do know about the extent of David and Solomon's empire—if it, or Solomon, existed at all (Soggin 1993: 32; Finkelstein and Silberman 2001:123–45 *et passim*). The basic question is: How large a territory did Solomon control? The two major options are: (1) some approximation of later Israel, Judah, Moab, and Ammon; or (2) most of the inland Levant including the Transjordan, and Damascus (1 Kings 5:1 [Eng. 4:21], cf. 11:23–25). The more interesting operative question is: Did Solomon actually control most of the possible trade routes, or were the northern routes, which contributed so much to Damascus's wealth (Table 1 above) already in Aramean hands?

The best treatment I know of this issue is Wayne Pitard's *Ancient Damascus* (1987:81–97). Beginning with Tiglath-pileser I (ca. 1116–1076) of Assyria's first and continually recurring encounters (28 in all) with the "Aramean Aḫlamu" starting "from the land of Sūḫu [on the middle Euphrates] to the city of Carchemish of the land of Ḫatti," Pitard carefully threads

[19] At the risk of sounding like previsitation Scrooge in Charles Dickens's *A Christmas Carol*, it seems to me possible that the unhappy supplicant writing or dictating the Meṣad Ḥashavyahu Ostracon may have been paid in advance for his work, with the "garment" in question being taken in surety when he left before the full completion of his contract, a situation which, banking on the letter of the law instead of its intent, he may conveniently have left out of his complaint.

[20] Bennett and Blakeley 1989 (summary statement on p. 67): "During [the] . . . latest period of Stratum V, the acropolis served as a granary designed for the long-term storage of cereal grains . . . in well-prepared pits [or silos, many with mudbrick linings]."

[21] We can infer the density of the old South Arabian trade in any one period only from its effect upon the relative wealth of tributes documented in preceding or succeeding records, of which we possess only a fraction.

[22] Reconstruction of the earlier donkey caravan trade should be possible, but I will leave that to others.

his way through the Hebrew Bible, the Septuagint, the cuneiform literature, and well-informed technical biblical scholarship to a conclusion:

> The severe shrinkage of the empire must have occurred fairly late in Solomon's reign . . . considering the reports of Solomon's power and wealth in 1 Kings 4–11. . . . Rezon's capture of Damascus cannot be precisely dated. Many place this event quite early in Solomon's reign and suggest that Solomon was able to maintain his northern trade connections by diverting the caravan route through the Biqāᶜ and bypassing Damascus. The notice in 1 Kings 11:23–24 also suggests that the capture took place fairly early in Solomon's reign, since vs. 52 says that Rezon "was an adversary of Israel all the days of Solomon." On the other hand, the language of this passage should not be pressed too far; it is more likely that the revolt of Damascus took place well along in Solomon's reign, as the entire empire began to weaken. [Pitard 1987:97]

This sober assessment, which should be read in its entirety, is as far removed from Finkelstein and Silberman's (2001) rambling, occasionally factually erroneous, and certainly dismissive, discourse as can be. Obviously, later Damascene policy toward Israel and Judah, and Israelite policy toward both Damascus and Judah, can better be explained as battles over the control of wealth-creating trade routes than as mere expansionistic hubris.

The present "middle of the road" approach may well be that of J. Maxwell Miller and John Hayes (2006:206–9, map 17). After a lengthy but selective review of the standard biblical literature, some of which I have perhaps caricatured in my introduction, they grant Solomon territory up to Lake Huleh, slightly north of Hazor; plus the Judean heartland, all the coast from Gezer to Akko, a narrow strip extending down the western Arabah to Ezion-Geber/Elath on the Red Sea, and the Transjordanian territories of Moab and Ammon. The only trade corridors mentioned are the "Way of the Sea" and the Transjordanian "Way of the Kings," both of which were north-south land-transit routes better suited to army movements and local traffic than long-distance trafficking, although, as more efficient modes of transport requiring a level path, camel caravans in the northern branches of the South Arabian trade must have followed the "Way of the Kings" for part of their route to Tyre and Damascus. Something of the tenor (not to say *Tendenz)* of Miller and Hayes's treatment may be judged from the following quote:

> There would have been ways for Solomon to derive profit from commercial traffic through his realm without undertaking commercial ventures of his own, by imposing customs duties, for example, and by taxing transit traffic. One is tempted to read this sort of thing between the lines of 1 Kings 10:14–15, which states literally: "The weight of gold that came to Solomon in one year was six hundred sixty-six talents [about 20 tons] of gold,[23] besides that which came from the traders and from the business of merchants, and from the kings of Arabia and the governors of the land." Typical of the sweeping and generalized editorial statements of this Solomon section of Genesis–2 Kings, the terminology is vague and the description based on later fantasies about Jerusalem's "golden age." Who were "the traders and merchants" or "the kings of Arabia"? The expression translated "governors of the land" (*pachoth ha*ᵓ*arets*) derives from the later political vocabulary of the period of Assyrian domination. [Miller and Hayes 2006:210].

In other words, one would be foolish to try to make any sense of this at all—unless one actually did take seriously the details in the text and try to understand how the queen of Sheba and her camels and spices and "the traders" and the "business of merchants" ever got into the tradition. Baldly stated, while we do know a great deal about Arabian rulers, camels and all, from Assyrian sources starting with the "1,000 camels (ANŠE *gam-ma-lu*) of Gindibuᵓ of Arabia" on Shalmaneser III's Kurkh Monolith, which recounts his version of the Battle of Qarqar in 853 B.C.E. (Hallo and Younger 2000:264), it would appear that in earlier times the Assyrians simply did not know anything about them. But we should not believe that Neo-Assyrian spies or even the general populace actually knew nothing about them. That cannot have been true. The issues are twofold. First, given the nature of our sources dealing with the opening centuries of the Neo-Assyrian period, which focus upon royal campaigns, triumphs, and booty, it would appear that they never encountered either the South Arabian traders or any of their North Arabian collaborators until Assyrian forces penetrated into the region of Damascus. Secondly, we have not seriously dealt with "curious facts and discrepancies" in what we do know.

---

[23] This figure seems to be an editorial conflation and mythic upgrading (from 540, below, to 666 talents) of the preceding "four hundred and twenty talents" of gold from Hiram and Solomon's joint Ezion-geber venture to "Ophir" with the queen of Sheba's (unmentioned by Miller and Hayes) "hundred and twenty talents of gold [the two sums would equal 540 talents of gold] and a very great quantity of spices, and precious stones; never again came such an abundance of spices as these which the queen of Sheba gave to King Solomon."

While the Kurkh Monolith has the first attested mention of "Arabs" and the first use of ANŠE *gam-ma-lu* in Akkadian literature, there is one temporally and regionally restricted group of significantly earlier mentions of camels and South Arabian trade goods.[24] Following the Battle of Qarqar in 853, there is silence until the time of Tiglath-pileser III (744–727), at which time the Neo-Assyrian records are full of difficult Arabs, both kings and queens. Turning to Israel Ephᶜal's masterful *The Ancient Arabs* (1982), we learn that the first Arab queen known to objective history is Zabibē, queen of the Qedarites, who paid tribute to Tiglath-pileser III in 738 in connection with "the Arabian trade in the Syro-Arabian desert, in which nomad leaders took significant part" (Ephᶜal 1982:23, 82–83). By this time we are in the full, if somewhat fractured, light of history, and know a great deal from contemporary sources. Ephᶜal goes on to note that:

> [The northern part of] this trade was conducted primarily along the King's Highway, whose principal outlets were Damascus and Tyre (the western bifurcation which branched off to Tyre from the King's Highway passed through the territory of the kingdom of Israel). Consequently, when the rulers of these two trade centers became subordinate to the Assyrian king (even Menahem king of Israel paid tribute), Zabibē too was obliged to join the tributaries to avert a possible disruption of the Arabian trade and her income from it. [Ephᶜal 1982:83]

Only slightly later we encounter the redoubtable Samsi, queen of the Arabs, who seems to have paid tribute to Tiglath-pileser in 734(?) but then "violated her oath," apparently in company with "the extensive anti-Assyrian activity of the kings of Damascus, Israel and Tyre throughout the area" (Ephᶜal 1982:84). Defeated in an epic battle in 733–32, "Samsi fled for her life 'like a wild she-ass' to the desert," but then surrendered and paid a heavy (but ill-preserved) tribute, following which an Assyrian overseer was appointed (see Ephᶜal 1982:85–92, which bears serious reading with reference to the Arabian trade, but cannot be further treated here). In a running summary comment, Ephᶜal says:

> [Their] tribute included gold, silver and spices, indicating that [Samsi's] border nomads lived along the Arabian trade routes and profited thereby. Since Arabian trade was confined to established routes, it would have been sufficient for Tiglath-pileser to control the northern termini in order to affect their use as commercial arteries even in the remotest sections. No wonder that even far-away Arabs, remote from the scene of Tiglath-pileser's activity, paid to protect their interests in the regular conduct of the Arabian trade within their territory. [Ephᶜal 1982:91]

Regarding the Queen of Sheba herself, Ephᶜal writes:

> I Kings 10:1–10, 13 (= II Chron. 9:1–9, 12) . . . is part of the Wisdom Literature devoted to Solomon and his wisdom that surpassed that of all other peoples. Most scholars, assuming that this account has a kernel of authenticity, locate the homeland of Solomon's royal visitor in northern Arabia, and connect her with the Sabaeans known from the inscriptions of Tiglath-pileser III and from Job 1:15. However, recent archaeological research has uncovered evidence of sedentary populations organized as kingdoms in southern Arabia at the beginning of the first millennium B.C., suggesting that the spice trade operated from there at that time. It is therefore highly probable that the queen mentioned in I Kings chap. 10 came to Jerusalem from Sheba in southern Arabia to settle questions of the spice trade with king Solomon, who dominated all the Palestinian trade routes from the Mediterranean and the Gulf of Elath to the desert border regions [Albright 1958:1*-9*; see also Psalm 72:10]. Although dozens of rulers are known from the Sabaean inscriptions, not one is a woman, but it should be remembered that these inscriptions do not antedate the 8th century B.C. . . . and that, actually, we know nothing about the earlier leaders of the South-Arabian kingdoms. [Ephᶜal 1982:63–64]

Summing up, were we to accept the applicability of the entire range of authentic ancient Near Eastern records to the scholarly study, on the one hand, of the Hebrew scriptures, and on the other, of Middle Eastern economics in the Iron Age (and presumably earlier), particularly in the sense of providing quantified "forensic evidence for following the money trail," it seems painfully apparent that current "scholarly" reconstructions of both premodern economics and the historical books of the Hebrew Bible, while perhaps in tune with our times, simply fail to do justice either to ancient economics as they played out in daily life and the life of nations, or to the quality of documentation and preservation of Israel's historical records and traditions under the monarchy and, almost certainly, into the Babylonian Captivity.

---

[24] In preparation for publication elsewhere, this singular event—better, missed opportunity—speaks volumes with respect to the early Neo-Assyrian monarchy's predatory mindset and hide-bound perspectives, paralleled only by the mindless arrogance, in a similar situation, of the later governor of the land of Sūḫu and Mari (see n. 5 above).

Bibliography

Aharoni, Y., ed.
1973 *Beer-Sheba.* Vol. 1, *Excavations at Tel Beer-Sheba, 1969-1971 Seasons.* Tel Aviv: Institute of Archaeology, Tel Aviv University.

Aharoni, Y.
1981 *The Arad Inscriptions.* Jerusalem: Israel Exploration Society.

Albright, W.F.
1958 Was the Age of Solomon without Monumental Art? *EI* 5:1*–9*.
1963 The Elimination of King "So." *BASOR* 171:64–66.

Balmuth, M. S., ed.
2001 *Hacksilber to Coinage: New Insights into the Monetary History of the Near East and Greece.* Numismatic Studies 24. New York: American Numismatic Society.

Bennett, W. J., and J. A. Blakeley, eds.
1989 *Tell el-Hesi.* Vol. 3, *The Persian Period (Stratum V).* Winona Lake, Ind.: Eisenbrauns.

Cavigneaux, A., and B. Kh. Ismail
1990 Die Statthalter von Suḫu und Mari im 8. Jh. v. Chr. *Baghdader Mitteilungen* 21:321–456.

Cogan, M.
2001 *I Kings: A New Translation with Introduction and Commentary.* New York: Doubleday.

Cogan, M., and H. Tadmor
1988 *II Kings: A New Translation with Introduction and Commentary.* New York: Doubleday.

Dalton, G., ed.
1971 *Primitive, Archaic and Modern Economics.* Boston: Beacon.
1975 Karl Polanyi's Analysis of Long-Distance Trade and His Wider Paradigm. In *Ancient Civilization and Trade*, ed. J. A. Sabloff and C. C. Lamberg-Karlovsky, 63–132. Albuquerque, N.M.: University of New Mexico Press.

Dercksen, J. G., ed.
1999 *Trade and Finance in Ancient Mesopotamia.* Uitgaven van het Nederlands Historisch-Archaeologisch Instituut te İstanbul 84. Leiden: Nederlands Instituut voor het Nabije Oosten.

Dever, W. G.
1970 Iron Age Epigraphic Material from the Area of Khirbet el-Kōm. *HUCA* 40–41:139–204.
1986 Late Bronze Age and Solomonic Defenses at Gezer: New Evidence. *BASOR* 262:9–34.
2001a *What Did the Biblical Writers Know, and When Did They Know It? What Archaeology Can Tell Us about the Reality of Ancient Israel.* Grand Rapids, Mich.: Eerdmans.
2001b The Silver Trail: Response to the Papers of Ephraim Stern and Seymour Gitin. In *Hacksilber to Coinage: New Insights into the Monetary History of the Near East and Greece*, ed. M. S. Balmuth, 13–15. Numismatic Studies 24. New York: American Numismatic Society.

Dion, P.-E.
1992 Les KTYM de Tel Arad: Grecs ou Phèniciens? *RB* 99:70–97.
1995 Aramean Tribes and Nations of First-Millennium Western Asia. In *Civilizations of the Ancient Near East*, ed. J. M. Sasson, 2:1281–94. New York: Scribners.
2006 Ahaz and Other Willing Servants of Assyria. In *From Babel to Babylon: Essays on Biblical History and Literature in Honour of Brian Peckham*, ed. J. R. Wood, J. E. Harvey, and M. Leuchter, 133–45. Library of Hebrew Bible/Old Testament Studes 455. London: T. and T. Clark.

Driel, G. van, ed.
2002 *Elusive Silver: In Search of a Role for a Market in an Agrarian Environment.* Uitgaven van het Nederlands Instituut voor het Nabije Oosten te Leiden 95. Leiden: Nederlands Instituut voor het Nabije Oosten.

Ephᶜal, I.
1982 *The Ancient Arabs: Nomads on the Borders of the Fertile Crescent, 9th–5th Centuries B.C.* Jerusalem: Magnes.

Finkelstein, I., ed.
1986 *ᶜIzbet Ṣarṭah: An Early Iron Age Site near Rosh Haᶜayin, Israel.* BARIS 299. Oxford: British Archaeological Reports.

Finkelstein, I., and N.A. Silberman
2001 *The Bible Unearthed: Archaeology's New Vision of Ancient Israel and the Origin of Its Sacred Texts.* New York: Simon and Schuster.

Frankenstein, S.
1979 The Phoenicians in the Far West: A Function of Neo-Assyrian Imperialism. In *Power and Propaganda: A Symposium on Ancient Empires*, ed. M. T. Larsen, 263–94. Mesopotamia 7. Copenhagen: Akademisk.

Goedicke, H.
1963 The End of "So, King of Egypt." *BASOR* 171:64–66.

Hallo, W. W., and K. L. Younger, eds.
2000 *The Context of Scripture.* Vol. 2, *Monumental Inscriptions from the Biblical World.* Leiden: Brill.

Holladay, J. S., Jr.
1995 The Kingdoms of Israel and Judah: Political and Economic Centralization in the Iron IIA–B (ca. 1000–750 B.C.E.). In *The Archaeology of Society in the Holy Land*, ed. T. E. Levy, 368–98. New York: Facts on File.
1997 The Eastern Nile Delta during the Hyksos and Pre-Hyksos Periods: Toward a Systemic/Socioeconomic Understanding. In *The Hyksos: New Historical and Archaeological Perspectives*, ed. E. D. Oren, 183–226. University Museum Monograph 96. Philadelphia: University Museum, University of Pennsylvania.
2001 Toward a New Paradigmatic Understanding of Long-Distance Trade in the Ancient Near East: From the Middle Bronze II to Early Iron II—A Sketch. In *The World of the Aramaeans: Studies in History and Archaeology in Honour of Paul-Eugène Dion*, ed. P. M. M. Daviau, J. W. Wevers, and M. Weigl, 2:136–98. JSOTSup 325. Sheffield, England: Sheffield Academic Press.
2006 Hezekiah's Tribute, Long-Distance Trade, and the Wealth of Nations ca. 1000–600 B.C. In *Confronting the Past: Archaeological and Historical Essays on Ancient Israel in Honor of William G. Dever*, ed. S. Gitin, J. E. Wright, and J. P. Dessel, 309–31. Winona Lake, Ind.: Eisenbrauns.
in prep. The Phoenician Wine-Houses of Hazor.
in prep. Assyria in the Shade: Levantine Wealth vs. the Neo-Assyrian Ambit and What Assyria Did About It prior to the Battle of Qarqar (853 B.C.E.).

Hopkins, D. C.
1985 *The Highlands of Canaan: Agricultural Life in the Early Iron Age.* Sheffield, England: Almond.
1996 Bare Bones: Putting Flesh on the Economics of Ancient Israel. In *The Origins of the Ancient Israelite States*, ed. V. Fritz, 121–39. Sheffield, England: Sheffield Academic Press.

Kaufman, I. T.
1982 The Samaria Ostraca: An Early Witness to Hebrew Writing. *BA* 45:229–39.
1992 Samaria (Ostraca). In *The Anchor Bible Dictionary*, ed. D. N. Freedman, 5:921–26. New York: Doubleday.

Kemp, B.
1989 *Ancient Egypt: Anatomy of a Civilization.* London: Routledge.

King, P. J., and L. E. Stager
2001 *Life in Biblical Israel.* Louisville, Ky.: Westminster John Knox.

Kitchen, K. A.
1989a Where Did King Solomon's Gold Go? *BAR* 15/3: 30.
1989b Shishak's Military Campaign in Israel Confirmed. *BAR* 15/3:32–33.

Kletter, R.
1991 The Inscribed Weights of the Kingdom of Judah. *Tel Aviv* 18:121–63.
1998 *The Weight System of the Kingdom of Judah.* JSOTSup 276. Sheffield, England: Sheffield Academic Press.

Kochavi, M.
1989 The Land of Geshur Project: Regional Archaeology of the Southern Golan, 1987–1988 Seasons. *IEJ* 39:1–17.
1991 The Land of Geshur Regional Project, 1989–1990: Tel Hadar. *IEJ* 41:181–82.
1993 The Land of Geshur Regional Project: Attempting a New Approach in Biblical Archaeology. In *Biblical Archaeology Today, 1990: Proceedings of the Second International Congress on Biblical Archaeology, Jerusalem, June–July 1990*, ed. A. Biran and J. Aviram, 725–37. Jerusalem: Israel Academy of Sciences and Humanities.

Kuhrt, A.
1995 *The Ancient Near East c. 3000–330 B.C.* 2 vols. London: Routledge.

Larsen, M. T., ed.
1976 *The Old Assyrian City-State and Its Colonies.* Mesopotamia 4. Copenhagen: Akademisk.
1979 *Power and Propaganda: A Symposium on Ancient Empires.* Mesopotamia 7. Copenhagen: Akademisk.

Larsen, M. T.
1967 *Old Assyrian Caravan Procedures.* Uitgaven van het Nederlands Historisch-Archaeologisch Instituut te İstanbul 22. Leiden: Nederlands Instituut voor het Nabije Oosten.

Leemans, W. F.
1960 *Foreign Trade in the Old Babylonian Period As Revealed by Texts from Southern Mesopotamia.* Studia et Documenta ad Iura Orientis Antiqui Pertinentia 6. Leiden: Brill.

Millard, A. R.
1988 King Solomon's Gold: Biblical Records in the Light of Antiquity. *Bulletin of the Society for Mesopotamian Studies* 15:5–11.
1989 Does the Bible Exaggerate King Solomon's Golden Wealth? *BAR* 15/3:20–34.

Miller, J. M., and J. H. Hayes
2006 *A History of Ancient Israel and Judah.* 2d ed. Louisville, Ky.: Westminster John Knox.

Parker, S. B.
1997 *Stories in Scripture and Tradition: Comparative Studies in Northwest Semitic Inscriptions and the Hebrew Bible.* Oxford: Oxford University Press.

Pitard, W. T.
1987 *Ancient Damascus: A Historical Study of the Syrian City-State from Earliest Times until Its Fall to the Assyrians in 732 B.C.E.* Winona Lake, Ind.: Eisenbrauns.

Postgate, J. N.
1979 The Economic Structure of the Assyrian Empire. In *Power and Propaganda: A Symposium on Ancient* Empires, ed. M. T. Larsen, 193–221. Mesopotamia 7. Copenhagen: Akademisk.

Potts, D. T.
1990 *The Arabian Gulf in Antiquity.* Vol. 1, *From Prehistory to the Fall of the Achaemenid Empire.* Oxford: Clarendon Press.

Powell, M. A.
1979 Ancient Mesopotamian Weight Metrology: Methods, Problems and Perspectives. In *Studies in Honor of Tom B. Jones*, 71–109. AOAT 203. Kevelaer/Neukirchen-Vluyn.
1989–90 Masse und Gewichte. *RLA* 7:457–530.
1990 Identification and Interpretation of Long-term Price Fluctuations in Babylonia: More on the History of Money in Mesopotamia. *AoF* 17:76–99.
1996 Money in Mesopotamia. *JESHO* 39:224–42.
1999 "Wir müssen unsere Nische nutzen": Monies, Motives and Methods in Babylonian Economics. In *Trade and Finance in Ancient Mesopotamia*, ed. J. G. Dercksen, 5–24. Uitgaven van het Nederlands Historisch-Archaeologisch Instituut te İstanbul 84. Leiden: Nederlands Instituut voor het Nabije Oosten.

Pritchard, J. B.
1969 *Ancient Near Eastern Texts Relating to the Old Testament.* 3d ed. Princeton: Princeton University Press.

Schloen, J. D.
2001 *The House of the Father As Fact and Symbol: Patrimonialism in Ugarit and the Ancient Near East.* SAHL 2. Winona Lake, Ind.: Eisenbrauns.

Soggin, J. A.
1993 *An Introduction to the History of Israel and Judah.* 2d ed. Valley Forge, Pa.: Trinity Press International.

Stager, L. E.
1985 The Archaeology of the Family in Ancient Israel. *BASOR* 260:1–35.
1990 Shemer's Estate. *BASOR* 277/278:93–107.
2001 Port Power in the Early and Middle Bronze Age: The Organization of Maritime Trade and Hinterland Production. In *Studies in the Archaeology of Israel and Neighboring Lands in Memory of Douglas L. Esse*, ed. S. R. Wolff, 625–38. SAOC 59. Chicago: Oriental Institute, University of Chicago.

Tadmor, H.
1975 Assyria and the West: The Ninth Century and Its Aftermath. In *Unity and Diversity: Essays in the History, Literature, and Religion of the Ancient Near East*, ed. H. Goedicke and J. J. M. Roberts, 36–48. Baltimore: Johns Hopkins University Press.
1994 *The Inscriptions of Tiglath-pileser III, King of Assyria: Critical Edition with Introduction, Translations and Commentary.* Jerusalem: Israel Academy of Sciences and Humanities.

Thompson, C. M.
2003 Sealed Silver in Iron Age Cisjordan and the "Invention" of Coinage. *Oxford Journal of Archaeology 22*:67–107.

Veenhof, K. R.
1995 Kanesh: An Assyrian Colony in Anatolia. In *Civilizations of the Ancient Near East*, ed. J. M. Sasson, 1:859–71. New York: Scribners.
1999 Silver and Credit in Old Assyrian Trade. In *Trade and Finance in Ancient Mesopotamia*, ed. J. G. Dercksen, 55–84. Uitgaven van het Nederlands Historisch-Archaeologisch Instituut te İstanbul 84. Leiden: Nederlands Instituut voor het Nabije Oosten.

Wapnish, P.
1997 Camels. In *The Oxford Encyclopedia of Archaeology in the Near East*, ed. E. M. Meyers, 1:407–8. New York: Oxford University Press.

Yoffee, N.,
1981 *Explaining Trade in Ancient Western Asia.* Monographs on the Ancient Near East 2/2. Malibu, Calif.: Undena.

24. The Levitical Diaspora (I): A Sociological Comparison with Morocco's Ahansal

by Jeremy M. Hutton

Scholars have repeatedly been stymied in their attempts to understand the peculiar distribution of the Levitical cities across the southern Levant. Lawrence Stager has suggested a model based on the Ahansal tribe of northern Africa that may help us comprehend the reasons for the "Levitical diaspora."[1] Upon inspection, this model proves useful in explaining the distribution of the Levitical cities. The purpose of the present article is to provide a fuller account of the parallels in familial structure and social function between ancient Israel's Levites and the Ahansal, and thereby to adduce possible topographical, ecological, and sociological reasons for the correspondence between many of the town names in the list of Levitical cities (Josh. 21:10–40; 1 Chr. 6:39–66 [Eng. Vv. 54–81]) and in the boundary descriptions (Josh. 13:15–19:51).

The Complexity of the Levitical City System

It has long been recognized that the system of Levitical cities presented in Joshua 21 and 1 Chronicles 6 is a somewhat idealized construct that the biblical writers employed to arrange Israelite social life meaningfully (see, e.g., Wellhausen 1885:161–63; Kaufmann 1953:42–44; Haran 1961b:157–59 [but cf. Milgrom 1983]; Kallai 1986:463, 468). But the exact degree of artificiality in the system presented in Numbers 35:1–8, Joshua 21, and 1 Chronicles 6 remains uncertain. Some argue that the roughly 48 cities of the two lists never existed as religious centers as such (Kaufmann 1953:46), or that the lists were a relatively late concoction (Wellhausen 1885:161–62; also Noth 1953: 131–32 and Spencer 1980:244–51), while others hold that an authentically historical system of holy sites underlies the two lists. This authenticity can be sustained regardless of whether all the cities held the distinction of being "Levitical" cities concurrently (e.g., Boling 1985:31), or whether all the cities belonged exclusively to Levites (Albright 1945:55–58; Mazar 1960:195; de Vaux 1961:366; Haran 1961b: 160, 164–65; 1978:130–31; Peterson 1977:723). Among those who believe in a historical background for the lists, the date of that background is still under discussion, with suggestions ranging from the time of the conquest (Kaufmann 1953:40–46), to the United Monarchy under David and Solomon (Albright 1942:121–25; 1945:50–58; Mazar 1960; Mettinger 1971:98–99; Aharoni 1979: 301–5; Hauer 1982; Kallai 1986:447–76, esp. 457–58; J. M. Miller 1987: 282), to the divided kingdoms (de Vaux 1961:366–67; 8th cent.: Peterson 1977:698–724, esp. 701–3; Boling 1985:29–31; or 7th cent: Alt 1951:199–206; 1952:313–15; Naʾaman 1986:229–30), or—if the account is historical at all—to the postmonarchic period (Noth 1953:131–32; Gunneweg 1965:64–65; Auld 1979; Spencer 1992; Ben Zvi 1992:100).[2] Most likely, the middle road should be taken and the historicity of the lists separated from the present form of the lists themselves. The latter is almost certainly relatively late, while the historical Levitical cities predate the lists' final form by two centuries or more (Cody 1969:161–65; Haran 1978:112–31 and esp. 148).

The best argument against the fundamental historicity and relative antiquity of the lists is adduced by those who deduce the utopian and ideal nature of the lists of Levitical cities based on their apparent dependence on the list and accounts of the cites of refuge (Num. 35:9–15; Deut. 4:41–43, 19:1–9; Joshua 20) and on the boundary descriptions of the Israelite inheritances in Josh. 13:15–19:51 (e.g., Noth 1953:127; Spencer 1980:250; Naʾaman 1986: 216–19 [based on Auld 1979]; Ben Zvi 1992:89–90, 101–2).

---

[1] This paper is based on a topic raised by Professor Lawrence E. Stager during personal communication. It is with his permission for publication (although I did my best to conceal from him the venue) that I have taken up this topic for presentation in a collection of essays with common purpose: to testify to the intellectual legacy of Lawrence Stager in the fields of biblical archaeology and Near Eastern social history. I hope only that I have been able to write on the topic as eloquently, doing it as much justice, as he surely would have himself. I would like to thank him for the opportunity to continue one small facet of his work, as well as for his many years of guidance and friendship during my time as a graduate student at Harvard University. My colleague Shane Berg kindly read an earlier draft of this study and commented on it productively. Thanks are due also to my research assistant Raymond Bonwell, and to T. Wangyal Shawa of the Geosciences and Map Library at Princeton University for their kind assistance in making figure 1.

[2] For more in-depth discussions of the history of scholarship, see Haran 1961a:45–48; Auld 1979:201–6; and Ben Zvi 1992.

While this apparent dependence on the purportedly earlier boundary descriptions is clearly problematic, Stager has suggested a possible ethnohistorical analogy to the Levites that expains the correspondence between the various lists. At the end of his seminal article on family life in ancient Israel, Stager makes reference to the odd distribution of Levites across the land of Israel: "In the absence of a centralized priesthood, a 'Levitical diaspora' was necessary for these holy men to find individual or corporate patrons among the lay tribes (cf. Gellner 1969)" (Stager 1985a:27; cf. previously Noth 1953:131). Stager cites Gellner's ethnographic study of the Ahansal tribe of Morocco's High Atlas Mountains without elaboration and he makes no explicit mention of the Levitical cities; however, in the present article and four planned companion studies (Hutton forthcoming a, b, c, and d), I argue that several socially defined commonalities emerge between Morocco's Ahansal tribe and the Levites, thus generating a reasonable heuristic model of Levitical social function and familial life through which to study the Levites;[3] and I argue further that an investigation of the position of the Levitical cities as constrained by ecology and topography will elucidate the explanatory (although not necessarily the predictive) power of the model. Moreover, although this concern is side-stepped in the remainder of the present study, this model can help to determine the approximate date of the historical Levitical cities and their lists.

Social Function: Intergroup Mediation

The Ahansal are a tribe of Berber origin who remain separated genealogically from the other Berber tribes of the Moroccan uplands. Although they are not the only brotherhood of marabouts operating in northern Africa (see Hammoudi 1980; Abitbol 1988; Bowen 1988; El-Mansour 1991; Joffé 1991), the Ahansal comprise the most complete social system for study because of the thoroughness with which Gellner's analysis was performed. While the material culture of the Ahansal is essentially Berber, their claim to *shurfa* status (i.e., status as Muslim holy men by virtue of direct genealogical descent from Muhammad; but cf. Hammoudi 1980:621; Hart 2001b) through their common ancestor Sidi Said Ahansal sets them apart functionally from the surrounding Berber tribes. The members of several prominent Ahansal sublineages play an important role in the highland culture and ecology of the High Atlas, functioning as inter- and intratribal arbitrators for other tribes, and as mendicant holy men—thus, Gellner's locution "Saints of the Atlas." The mediational function of the Ahansal can take numerous different forms, but is displayed most effectively in two circumstances.

Intratribal Referees

First, the Ahansal serve as the "referees" at tribal election ceremonies (Gellner 1969:81–104; 1972: 64–65; de Hen 1964:298; Kraus 1998:6–7). Because Berber leadership within a tribe tends to be a responsibility that rotates from clan to clan, the various clans of a tribe ask outsiders—the Ahansal—to oversee the leadership selection process and to arbitrate between the various competing agnatic groups.[4] Because of their status outside the normal power structure of the Berber tribes, the Ahansal are able to maintain an apparently neutral and noncombative stance in the view of all those concerned. Commonly, Berber tribes in need of intersegmental arbitration will rely on an Ahansal patron saint or family of saints with whom they have established a longstanding relationship. The continuing ability of any single Ahansal *agurram* ("marabout" or "saint"; pl. *igurramen*) to command fees for this service (generally

[3] The usefulness of ethnographic comparison in providing an eventual solution to the problems of the historical basis and date of the Levitical city system cannot be overstated. Although Talmon (1978) has challenged the validity of ethnographic comparison, see the recent treatment of R. Miller (2005:4–5 and bibliography there) for a defense of the method.

[4] Several commentators have disputed Gellner's analysis of Berber culture based on Evans-Pritchard's analysis of segmentary society, in which the balanced and complementary opposition of segmentary descent is stressed (e.g., Munson 1991; 1993; Roberts 2002), but note the generally supportive stance of Fernea (1971) and Hart (1972:28–31; 1999a; cf. 2001a), as well as the dialogue between Gellner and Munson (1995). Shankland (1999:143–44) has recently written in support of the applicability of some aspects of Gellner's model to modern Turkey, and Kraus (1998) has clarified the value of Gellner's ideal model. Much of the debate is centered on the saints' relationship to the central political authority (the *makhzen*; see in this regard Hammoudi 1980 and Temsamani 1991), a problem equally at home in a study of the Levitical cities. Did the Levitical cities function as outposts of monarchic administration (with Mazar 1960:200–1 and Polk 1979:17–18)? Or were they perhaps "Yahweh teaching centers" whose relationship to the monarchy remains ambiguous (Peterson 1977: 718)? Or could they conceivably have arisen as centers of arbitration independent of a central authority? For example, de Vaux (1961:367; 1978:530) argued that Levitical presence in the cities preceded the late tenth-century period of the original list's composition. Unfortunately, a solution to this problem must be left for future investigations.

couched in the language of "accepting donations") is directly correlated to his perceived *baraka*, the divine mediation that enables the mendicant saints to act fairly and appropriately in a given situation (Gellner 1969:79; 1972:60–61). The greater the saint's perceived *baraka*, the more likely he is to be asked to mediate such intratribal ceremonies and conflicts. In practice, *baraka* tends to be manifested by wealth and power among the Ahansal; thus, those Ahansal who are wealthiest to begin with have a disproportionate advantage over their brethren when it comes to securing work and donations (Gellner 1969:74–77; 1972: 61; see further below).[5]

The Ahansal have insufficient numbers to enforce any decisions arising from their arbitrations; however, individual tribal segments that refuse to abide by the arbitration of the saints are often subject to "anathemization." The reverence for the saints throughout the remaining segments of the tribe underpins the saints' authority and effectiveness. Those segments that respect the decision arrived at by the Ahansal mediator act as the guarantors of the arrangement (Gellner 1969:134–35; 1972: 61–66).

Mediation between Transhumant Pastoralists and Sedentarists

The marabouts' social status, which is derived from—and which fuels—the other tribes' attribution of *baraka* to the Ahansal, helps to support the second major function of the tribe, a function embedded in the ecological and sociological forces at work in the High Atlas. While Gellner's model of the transhumant/sedentarist dichotomy in the Atlas highlands is undoubtedly somewhat reductionistic (but see the study of Bourbouze 1986), it provides a suitable starting point from which to venture a few observations concerning the function of the Ahansal.

The Atlas highlands separate the warm and arid, but relatively fruitful, Moroccan plain from the much more inhospitable northern reaches of the Sahara Desert. The rivers formed by the winter and spring run-off from the mountains provide some sustenance for the flocks and herds of transhumant groups, such as the Ait ᶜAtta, who live on the southern side of the mountain range.[6] However, as the weather warms and the snows dwindle in the Atlas highlands, the lowland pasturages of the southern slopes of the Atlas bear less and less usable herbage, forcing the pastoralists to move their livestock uphill into the mountains. These transhumant pastoralists cross the mountain passes after the snows from the winter before have melted sufficiently to allow passage. This crossing occurs earlier in dry years than in years with normal amounts of precipitation. Once the herdsmen have made this journey, usually in May, they find themselves on the northern slope of the Atlas watershed with a veritable paradise of greenery (Gellner 1969:31–34, 169–72; Bourbouze 1986:66; and Gellner and Munson 1995:821–22). But often, the Berber tribes who occupy the northern slopes of the Atlas year-round (for example, the Ait Mhand and Ait Isha) have already laid claim to this lush territory. What is alluringly verdant pastureland to the incoming pastoralists is equally prime farmland (both crop fields and pasturage) to the indigenous northern tribes. Inevitably, conflicts ensue between the indigenous northern tribes and the incoming pastoralists.

To complicate matters, the Ait Bu Iknifen segment of the Ait ᶜAtta remain permanently settled to the north of the watershed. In theory, they act as a vanguard for their incoming relatives, preserving the Ait ᶜAtta rights of pasturage in the highland *agdal* ("communal pasturage"; pl. *iguldan*) around Talmest.[7] However, in practice, their sedentarist agropastoralist lifestyle dictates its own concerns for arable cropland, thus drawing them into conflict with the incoming pastoralists as well (Gellner 1969:177; Hart 1999b:197–98, 202). All parties involved view the highland fields as necessary to their survival, not to mention theirs by virtue of past claim to the land (Gellner 1969:174–78; Morsy 1986:307; Hart 1993: 28–31; 1999b:197–98, 202; 2001a:20–22). Therefore, these conflicts could prove disastrous, were it not for the arbitration of the respected lineages of the Saints of the Atlas.

---

[5] For various views of *baraka*, see Westermarck 1926:35–261; Hammoudi 1980:619–20; El-Mansour 1991:73–77.

[6] While the Ait ᶜAtta are often portrayed as primarily transhumant pastoralists, Hart (2001a:19) notes that "[a]lthough most Ait ᶜAtta today are sedentary, with transhumants only a minority . . . the two moves per year involved in this mode of life . . . are highly characteristic." For more detailed discussions of transhumance, see Gottwald 1979: 444–48 and Hart 1993:28. This idealized (self-)conception of the tribe as pastoralist despite its primary reliance on sedentary agriculture is not uncommon among tribal societies that practice both systems of production (Marx 1977: 344).

[7] The Berber system of *agdal* is much more complex than presented by Gellner and in this schematic discussion. The "communal pasturage" is held in common among various agnatic groups who sometimes live in different areas. The pasturage is divided at different levels of segmentation, so that some land is tribally owned while other land belongs only to specific segments of the tribe (Hart 1993:28–29; Ilahiane 1999).

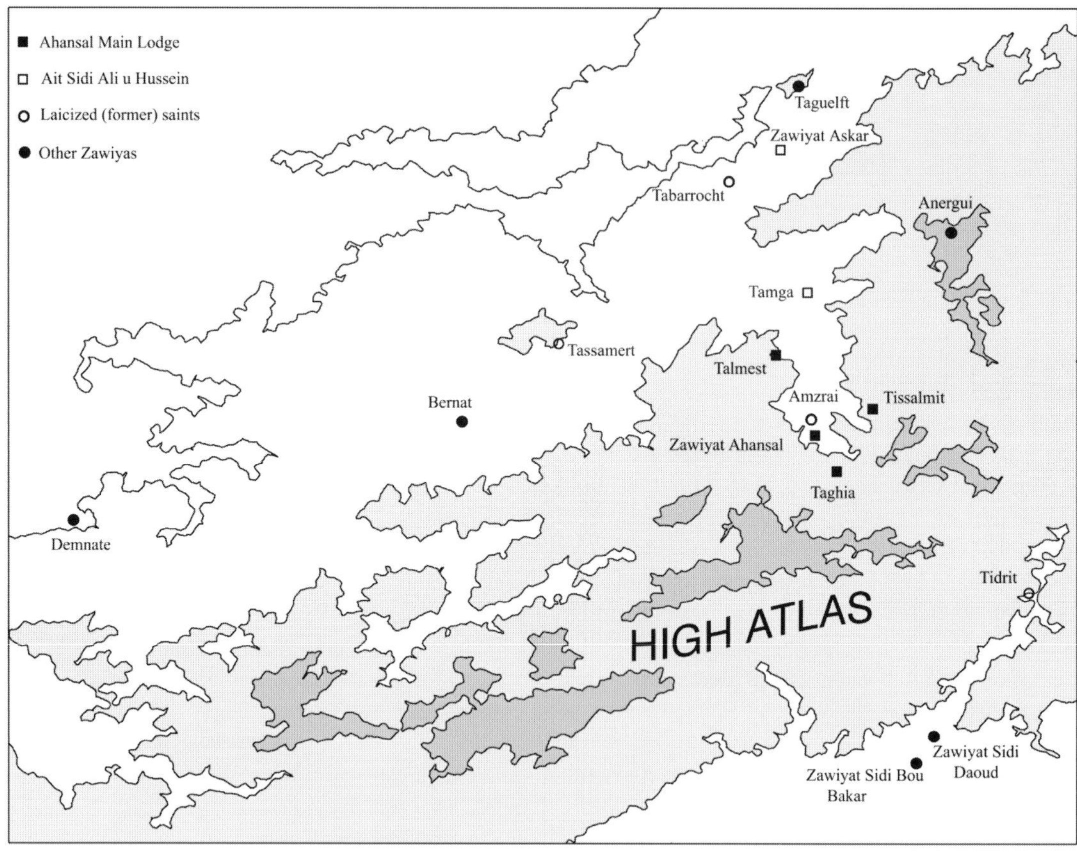

Figure 1. Locations of selected Ahansal and non-Ahansal *zawiya*s in the Central High Atlas
Contour interval is 1,000 m with areas above 2,000 m shaded.

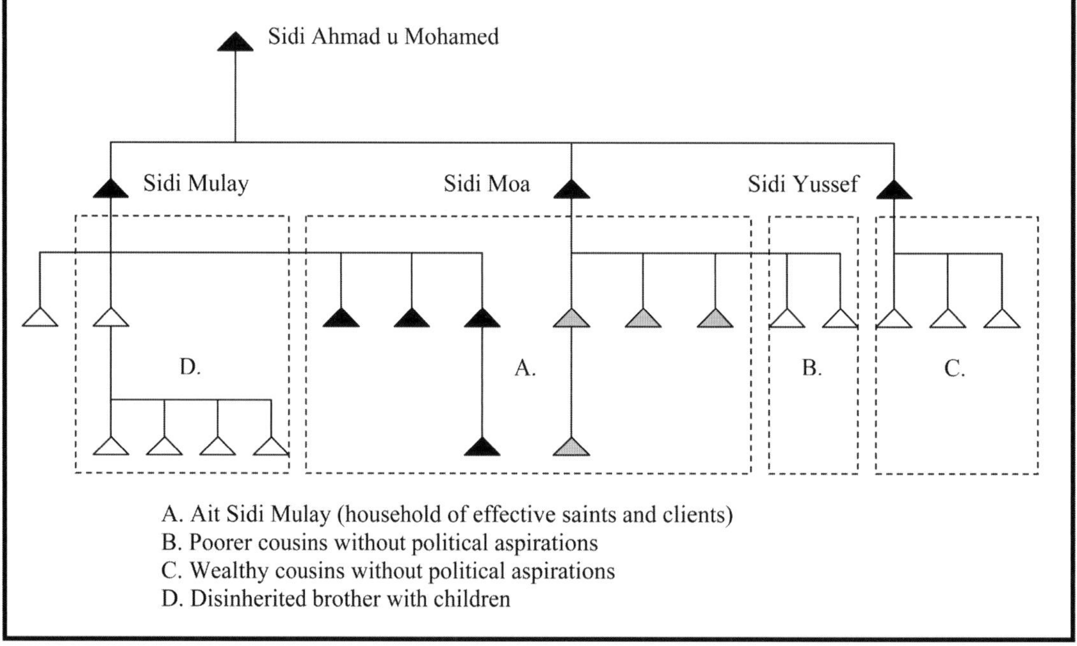

Figure 2. Male members of the Ait Ahmad u Mohamed with effective saints blackened, and lesser clients shaded (after Gellner 1969:180, diagram 3)

The Ahansal *igurramen*, who themselves have a stake in the territorial disputes of the region because of their families' dependence on agricultural systems of production, play the role of mediators in this yearly conflict (Gellner 1969:168–72; Morsy 1986: 307). They arbitrate between the various represented groups and are often able to guarantee the geographical and temporal boundaries that divide the open communal pastures from seasonally closed pastures and from sown agricultural plots in the highlands. The Ahansal also settle disputes over the fields that remain covered in snow until the very end of the summer, reserving these most well-watered areas until the point at which it becomes absolutely necessary to rely on them. The possibility of conflict between the indigenous sedentarists and their transhumant visitors persists until the latter return to their southern homeland in September or October (Bourbouze 1986:66; de Hen 1964:307). The social function of the Ahansal as intertribal arbitrators derives precisely from the peculiarities of the topography and ecology of the Atlas highlands, as well as from the systems of production most commonly practiced by the highland Berber tribes, sedentary agriculture and transhumant pastoralism (de Hen 1964:289–90; Bourbouze 1986:64–67). The same social function serves as an important factor in determining the concentration of effective saints in any given region, as well as the power structures of individual households.

Geographical Separation and Household Dynamics

The same conditions that ensure the continued social authority of the Ahansal also guarantee the persistence of competition and division among the Ahansal tribe. The attribution of greater *baraka* to certain Ahansal lineages provides those lineages with greater authority during the yearly disputes over territory. For instance, at Zawiyat Ahansal, the primary *zawiya* ("lodge" or holy center) of the Ahansal tribe, there are two competing families that vie for the prestige (and wealth) attendant to being selected as the arbitrator in any given dispute. The more *baraka* any given family possesses, the more likely it is that family will continue to be selected by their client litigants to mediate the dispute, and the more likely it is that the family's capital, both monetary and symbolic, will increase, so long as the matter is resolved satisfactorily to the parties involved (see Bourdieu 1977: 171–83).

A second factor determining the amount of *baraka* attributed to a given family is the presence or absence of an ancestral shrine at the lodge of the family in question. For example, at Zawiyat Ahansal can be found the shrine of the genealogical ancestor common to all Ahansal—Sidi Said Ahansal (Gellner 1969:160). Similarly, several Ahansal settlements can boast the presence of a shrine marking the grave of the ancestor common to the saints in practice at that site (Gellner 1969:157, 163–64).

These factors determine how much *baraka* a given family is credited relative to other Ahansal families. But because the supply of potential saints well outstrips the lay tribes' demand for arbitrators, Ahansal lineages experience two related phenomena, which fall under the rubrics "fission" and "fusion."

Fission

The competition over what is, at least in practice, a limited supply of "saintly function" is a primary cause of geographic division among the Ahansal (Gellner 1969:140–45; 1972:59, 61; 1990:118). Because the natural boundary of the Atlas watershed stretches for several hundred miles, separating the northern Berber tribes from the southern pastoralists, and because the Berber tribes located further from the main lodge remain similarly in need of neutral mediators, opportunities are ripe for Ahansal *igurramen* who are willing to leave the main lodge and establish themselves at lesser sites. The decision to make this departure is generally based on perceived relative *baraka* within the family: while an *agurram* may possess little *baraka* in the context of the main lodge, his familial ties and Ahansal lineage nonetheless provide him with the necessary credentials to support himself with his arbitrational work in an area away from the main lodge, where his *baraka* appears to be the greatest. For this reason, those saints who have aspirations of maintaining their sainthood but who do not possess the requisite charismatic virtues to command the establishment of a continuous contract with any given Berber tribe over against the most well-respected *igurramen* of the main lodge will generally depart the main lodge (or other such main Ahansal town) and establish themselves somewhere along a major border. Gellner recognizes several Ahansal towns as offshoots of the main lodge;[8] of the main lodge's primary competitors, the Ait Sidi Ali u Hussein;[9] or of other, smaller families.[10]

---

[8] For example, Taghia, Talmest, Igli, and U'Tarra, many of which are now laicized (Gellner 1969:214–16, 239–41, 259).

[9] For example, Temga, Zawiya Asker, and Zawiya Sidi Aziz (Gellner 1969:241–56).

The limited supply of *baraka* among the Ahansal contributes to attrition among the saints as well. It is common for the *igurramen* with the lowest attributed charisma to drop out of sainthood entirely. That is to say, they give up on the attempt to survive by serving as mediators in disputes, and return to the tried-and-true subsistence farming that has sustained the Ahansal tribe for generations. In short, they give up their *agurram* status (Gellner 1969:145–50). Gellner's survey of Ahansal towns noted a few towns that had once functioned as active centers of Ahansal *igurramen* but had subsequently fallen out of sainthood.[11]

The movement from a dependence on the saintly lifestyle to "ordinary modes of livelihood" can be quite difficult (Gellner 1969:153). Still, the claim to Ahansal genealogy remains marketable and it is not unheard of for an Ahansal tribesman to attempt to capitalize on his heritage by reviving his potential *agurram* status. While in practice this may be difficult (or impossible) to do, it remains a theoretical possibility because of the essentially hereditary nature of the sainthood. Gellner documented the attempts of an Ahansal family in the town of Tidrit to reenter the sainthood (Gellner 1969: 230–36; see also Vinogradov 1972:78). *Agurram* status should therefore not be considered a fixed sodality; the membership of that brotherhood, while limited in practice to men of Ahansal lineage, remains constantly in flux.

Fusion

Within the main lodge, the competition for prestige influences the dynamics of familial households as well. Gellner describes the case of the preeminent family in Zawiyat Ahansal during his period of study there (the Ait Ahmad u Mohamed), in which the descendents of three brothers (Sidi Mulay, Sidi Moa, and Sidi Yussif) had split the effective saintly power of the family among themselves (figure 2). Three sons of Sidi Mulay held the bulk of the family's saintly power (A). Several family members had fallen out of the sainthood despite their close genetic ties to the holders of *baraka*. The sons of Sidi Yussif and two sons of Sidi Moa who did not aspire to sainthood had managed to secure some degree of wealth, but did not compete with their cousins for political authority (B and C). As a poignant illustration that sainthood is not conveyed solely by genealogy, the oldest living brother of the Ait Sidi Mulay saints had been effectively disinherited (D). As a result, he was impoverished, dependent upon his brothers, and at the same time seeking to compete with them (Gellner 1969:193–94). In opposition, three sons of Sidi Moa had attached themselves as clients to the household of effective saints, the Ait Sidi Mulay. These sons of Sidi Moa, by virtue of their deference to the higher authority of the cousins to whom they had attached themselves, were able to participate in that household's enterprises with a high degree of saintly effectiveness (Gellner 1969:186). This arrangement displays the fluidity of genealogical ties among the Ahansal and the theoretical possibility of attaching oneself to a (more) saintly household.[12]

Levitical Parallels

From this relatively brief treatment of Ahansal genealogies, social function, and intra- and intertribal power dynamics, four elements of saintly familial and social life emerge as parallel to Levitical exemplars.

First, the Ahansal *igurramen* function as mediators and arbitrators in disputes between practitioners of the two major systems of highland production and between various levels of Berber agnatic groups in general. This function is intimately intertwined with Gellner's model of opposed and complementary systems of Berber moieties, which—despite arguments to the contrary—seems to me to explain adequately much of the data. This function of the Ahansal may be compared to the Levites' various functions as scholars and teachers of the law (von Rad 1953:66–68; Peterson 1977:718); judges in the gates who provide a local presence of the monarchic juridical procedure (Mazar 1960:200–201; J. M. Miller 1987: 282–83; Leuchter 2007); intertribal mediators and administrators of the Israelite confederation (Joshua 22; Judges 19–20; Gunneweg 1965:23–26; Robinson 1978); and cultic personnel at peripheral altars (Emerton 1962). Through ethnographic comparison, we might tentatively hypothesize a further function of the Levites: like the Ahansal, they served as arbitra-

[10] For example, Taguelft, Anergui, Bernat, and Demnate (Gellner 1969:245–46, 259; see also Hammoudi 1980: 629–34).

[11] For example, Amzrai, Tighinimin, Tassamert, Tabarrocht, Akka n'Ahansal, and Aganan (Gellner 1969:217–30, 257–59).

[12] If the segmentary lineages of the Ahansal were indeed understood by Gellner to have been immutable (cf. note 4), such movement between saintly houses should theoretically have gone unnoticed or been explained away in Gellner's study. See also Hammoudi's discussion (1980:623–26) of the importance of marital ties in the transference of power between lineages in Tamgrout, a non-Ahansal *zawiya* south of the Atlas.

tors between practitioners of the two major Levantine systems of highland production: pastoralism and agriculture (Marfoe 1979; Stager 1985b; van der Steen 1995:146–47; Palmer 2001). While there is no textual attestation for this proposed social function, the distribution of the Levitical cities may plausibly be linked to a similar Levitical authority (see Hutton forthcoming c).

Secondly, the hereditary qualification for *agurram* status, namely, descent traceable from the eponymous common ancestor of all the Ahansal, Sidi Said Ahansal himself, is necessary but insufficient to ensure the authority of any given individual. Individuals and whole families may fall out of sainthood and then may attempt to reenter sainthood. One of the methods used in such an attempt, particularly at the level of the nuclear family, may be to attach oneself to a particularly effective *agurram*'s household. This model may therefore help to solve the longstanding problem of Levite hereditary authority. While some biblical texts (e.g., Judges 17–19; 1 Samuel 1–2; 1 Sam. 7:1; 2 Sam. 6:3; and 1 Sam. 22:11, 20–23) suggest that the priesthood in Israel was hereditary in its earliest days (Wellhausen 1885:121–51; de Vaux 1961:359–60), other passages (for example, Judg. 17:7; 1 Sam. 1:1; 2:18–21; and 3:1 in juxtaposition to 1 Chr. 6:18–23 [Eng. vv. 33–38]; 2 Sam. 6:11–12 and 1 Chr. 13:13–14 in comparison with 1 Chr. 15:16–24) indicate the fluidity of genealogical ties, suggesting that the Levitical priesthood was instead a "cross-cutting association"[13] to which clients could attach themselves and non-Levites could aspire to join (Möhlinbrink 1934:191–97; Albright 1942:109–10; de Vaux 1961:362, 371; Gunneweg 1965:32–34; J. M. Miller 1970:65–68; Robinson 1978; Haran 1978:76–83; Gottwald 1979:320; Polk 1979; Stager 1985a:27–28).

Over against this situation of relative fluidity found during the early monarchy, there seems to have been some formalization of the genealogical requirements for priesthood by the time Deuteronomy was composed. In 1954, G. E. Wright suggested that the two terms used in Deuteronomy, "the Levitical priests" and "the whole family of Levi" (Deut. 18:1), identified two different groups: (1) "the Levitical priests" designated only those Levites who served at the peripheral altars before Josiah's centralization of the cult, and were therefore the only Levites capable of serving as altar personnel once established at the central Jerusalem sanctuary; and (2) "the whole family of Levi" designated the remaining Levites, all of whom were qualified to serve as teachers and as judges (Wright 1954; see also von Rad 1953; Peterson 1977:718; Spencer 1980:246–48). In opposition to Wright, J. A. Emerton argued that Deuteronomy makes no explicit differentiation between the two terms, and that we should take "the Levitical priests, the whole family of Levi" as two synonymous terms in apposition (Emerton 1962, esp. 133–34; cf. Abba 1977; Duke 1987). On this understanding, *all* Levites were eligible to serve at the Jerusalem altar, according to Deuteronomy (de Vaux 1961:362–63).

The ethnographic model provided by the Ahansal may bring us a step closer to solving the problem posed by the juxtaposition of these two terms. We might argue (with Emerton) that Deut. 18:1–8 provided for the hereditary authority of *all* Levites to serve in the central sanctuary, but (with Wright) that before Josiah's consolidation of the cult, two offices of Levites had developed *de facto*: a small minority possessed the prerequisite *baraka* to serve as effective *igurramen* (i.e., as altar personnel) at already established *zawiyas* (for example, Eli and Samuel at Shiloh), and some were able to establish new *zawiyas* in productive locations (Judges 17–18), but the vast majority of Levites were left reliant upon the charity of the Israelites within whose cities they lived, or as clients in the households of their more successful agnatic relatives (for example, the brothers of Ahimelek; 1 Sam. 22:11, 18). Only through the democratizing tendencies of Deuteronomy were these previously disenfranchised Levites capable of actualizing their aspirations to "effective sainthood" (although compare Haran 1978:61–63).

Thirdly, and corollary to the preceding observation, *baraka* is perceived both as the resultant sign of, and as the prerequisite for, capable political mediation. *Baraka* is a function of many factors including familial relations and direct descent from notable forebears; an individual and familial history of effective and efficient services; the presence of a recognized shrine to which the individual is somehow attached; and, not insignificantly, public perception. Competition between Ahansal lineages appears as a function of varying concentrations of *baraka*. Similarly, tension between various Levitical lineages is evidenced in biblical accounts (Cross 1973:195–215; Halpern 1976; Spencer 1995). Furthermore, the loss of prominent status may be occasioned through the perceived loss of saintly integrity (e.g., 1 Sam. 2:27–36; but cf. R. Miller 2005:121–24) or political altercation with the central authority (1 Kings 2:26–27; Halpern 1974).

Fourthly, several environmental and social constraints condition the number and location of possible effective Ahansal lodges. The constraints include the

[13] For a fuller discussion of this term's meaning and referents, see Gottwald 1979:318–21.

ecological and topographical factors that also condition and fuel the conflicts surrounding various systems of production in the Atlas highlands; the intertribal relations based on these conflicts; and the distances separating the lodges, as well as the perceived effectiveness of each. As summarized by Gellner:

> [s]egmentary tribes are almost infinitely rich in frontiers. There is always a further line of division in any group, until individual males are reached. So, there is a vast number of frontiers, on which holy men about to be pushed out of holiness or desiring to re-activate it could settle. Of course, most of these frontiers . . . between very small groups, are not very lucrative. A profitable frontier is [one that occurs] . . . between very large groups. The main lodge is not merely at a crucial frontier, indeed near a number of frontiers—*it is at a place destined by ecology to be a frontier*... Opportunities for settlement along such frontiers are very likely to arise: the land there is unsafe for settlement for either of the two sides. Holy men are sooner or later invited to settle along it, the place being not much use to anyone else. A frontier guarantor, who is at the same time a bridge for trade, is welcome. Thus saints are pushed both into proliferation and dispersal. [Gellner 1969:273; my italics]

This suggests that the distribution of the Levitical cities at the extremities of Israel, already noted by several scholars (e.g., Alt 1951:199–202; 1952:311–15; Noth 1953:129; Peterson 1977:717–18; Aharoni 1979:301, 305; Kallai 1986:475–76; Naʾaman 1986: 216–27), might be correlated to the Levites' function as intertribal arbitrators distributing justice in the gates (Peterson 1977:718; Wright 1954).

Furthermore, if one accepts the suggestion offered above that the Levites were functionally akin to the Ahansal in that they mediated yearly or seasonal disputes between the sedentary population of Israel and the transhumant pastoralist population, then several correlations between the sites of Levitical cities and environmental factors, both topographic and ecological, should be expected. Kallai long ago pointed out that "all the Levitic cities in Reuben's allotment were located at the eastern extremity of the settled area, on the edge of the wilderness" (1986:475). The proposal suggested in this paper gives an account of at least some of the reasons why such a distribution obtained. In the heuristic model suggested here, the area at the eastern edge of permanent settlement in Reuben's tribal allotment was, in the words of Gellner, "a place destined by ecology to be a frontier." More specifically, every one of the Levitical cities of Reuben falls within the zone in which the pastoralist and sedentarist agricultural systems coincide and often come into conflict—M. B. Rowton's "dimorphic zone" (1976:19–23), located between the 400 mm and 200 mm isohyets (for a map displaying rainfall zones, see *Tübinger Atlas des Vorderen Orients* B IV 6). While opinions differ on the respective locations of the Levitical cities (cf. Boling 1985; Dearman 1989), this observation applies to all the sites suggested. If the model laid out in this paper is at all representative of the social function of the Levites and of Levitical familial dynamics, similar topographic and economic constraints should be demonstrable for all the cities of Gad and Reuben (Hutton forthcoming c).

Conclusion and Directions for Further Research

To summarize, an ethnographic comparison with the Ahansal tribe of Morocco provides a heuristic model through which several aspects of Levitical function, distribution, and familial dynamics can be studied. I have laid out here the basic contours of the model, all centered on the role potentially played in the distribution of the Levites by social function and topographic and ecological constraints. Over the course of this paper, it has become clear that Stager's enigmatic reference to Gellner 1969 is not without merit, and indeed requires much further study.

Although the present paper can only be considered a sketch of the total project, it is my intention that several common questions concerning the Levites and the Levitical cities that were sidestepped in this study will be addressed in future papers: the relationship between the Levitical cities and the central authority (Hutton forthcoming a); a more detailed comparison and contrast of Ahansal and Levitical function and familial dynamics (Hutton forthcoming b); a more precise elaboration of the constraints formed by topography and ecology, as exemplified in the tribal regions of Gad and Reuben (Hutton forthcoming c); and finally, the date of the Levitical cities and the Levitical cities lists, as well as the relationship of the list of the cities of refuge to the Levitical cities lists (Hutton forthcoming d).

Bibliography

Abba, R.
1977 Priests and Levites in Deuteronomy. *VT* 27: 257–67.

Abitbol, M.
1988 Maraboutism and State Formation in Southern Morocco. In *The Early State in African Perspective: Culture, Power and Division of Labor*, ed. S. N. Eisenstadt, M. Abitbol, and N. Chazen, 134–47. Leiden: Brill.

Aharoni, Y.
1979 *The Land of the Bible: A Historical Geography*. 2d ed. Philadelphia: Westminster.

Albright, W. F.
1942 *Archaeology and the Religion of Israel*. Baltimore: Johns Hopkins University Press.
1945 The List of Levitic Cities. In *Louis Ginzberg Jubilee Volume*, 49–73. New York: American Academy for Jewish Research.

Alt, A.
1951 Bemerkungen zu einigen judäischen Ortslisten des alten Testaments. *Beiträge zur biblischen Landes- und Altertumskunde* [=*ZDPV*] 68: 193–210.
1952 Festungen und Levitenorte im Lande Juda. In *Kleine Schriften zur Geschichte des Volkes Israels* by A. Alt, 2:306–15. Munich: Beck.

Auld, A. G.
1979 The "Levitical Cities": Texts and History. *ZAW* 91:194–206.

Ben Zvi, E.
1992 The List of the Levitical Cities. *JSOT* 54:77–106.

Boling, R. G.
1985 Levitical Cities: Archaeology and Texts. In *Biblical and Related Studies Presented to Samuel Iwry*, ed. A. Kort and S. Morschauser, 23–32. Winona Lake, Ind.: Eisenbrauns.

Bourbouze, A.
1986 Adaptation à differents milieux des systèmes de production de paysans du Haut-Atlas. In *De L'Himalaya au Haut Atlas, de l'Asir aux Andes*, 59–91. Techniques et culture 7. Paris: Éditions de la Maison des sciences de l'homme.

Bourdieu, P.
1977 *Outline of a Theory of Practice*. Cambridge Studies in Social and Cultural Anthropology 16. Cambridge: Cambridge University Press.

Bowen, D. L.
1988 Congruent Spheres of Religious Authority: National and Local Levels of Charismatic Leadership. *Maghreb Review* 13/1–2:32–41.

Cody, A.
1969 *A History of Old Testament Priesthood*. Analecta Biblica 35. Rome: Pontifical Biblical Institute.

Cross, F. M.
1973 *Canaanite Myth and Hebrew Epic: Essays in the History of the Religion of Israel*. Cambridge, Mass.: Harvard University Press.

Dearman, J. A.
1989 The Levitical Cities of Reuben and Moabite Toponymy. *BASOR* 276:55–66.

Duke, R. K.
1987 The Portion of the Levite: Another Reading of Deuteronomy 18:6–8. *JBL* 106:193–201.

El-Mansour, M.
1991 Sharifian Sufism: The Religious and Social Practice of the Wazzani Zawiya. In *Tribe and State: Essays in Honour of David Montgomery Hart*, ed. E. G. H. Joffé and C. R. Pennell, 69–83. Cambridgeshire: Middle East and North African Studies Press.

Emerton, J. A.
1962 Priests and Levites in Deuteronomy: An Examination of Dr. G. E. Wright's Theory. *VT* 12:129–38.

Fernea, R.
1971 Review of *Saints of the Atlas* by Ernest Gellner. *American Anthropologist* N.S. 73:357–59.

Gellner, E.
1969 *Saints of the Atlas*. London: Weidenfeld and Nicolson.
1972 Political and Religious Organization of the Berbers of the Central High Atlas. In *Arabs and Berbers: From Tribe to Nation in North Africa*, ed. E. Gellner and C. Micaud, 59–66. London: Duckworth.
1990 Tribalism and the State in the Middle East. In *Tribes and State Formation in the Middle East*, ed. P. S. Khoury and J. Kostiner, 109–26. Berkeley and Los Angeles: University of California Press.

Gellner, E., and H. Munson
1995 Segmentation: Reality or Myth? *Journal of the Royal Anthropological Institute* 1:821–32.

Gottwald, N. K.
1979 *The Tribes of Yahweh: A Sociology of the Religion of Liberated Israel, 1250–1050 B.C.E.* Maryknoll, N.Y.: Orbis.

Gunneweg, A. H. J.
1965 *Leviten und Priester: Hauptlinien der Traditionsbildung und Geschichte des israelitisch-jüdischen Kultpersonals.* FRLANT 89. Göttingen: Vandenhoeck & Ruprecht.

Halpern, B.
1974 Sectionalism and the Schism. *JBL* 93:519–32.
1976 Levitic Participation in the Reform Cult of Jeroboam I. *JBL* 95:31–42.

Hammoudi, A.
1980 Sainteté, pouvoir et société: Tamgrout aux XVIIe et XVIIIe siècles. *Annales: Économies Sociétés Civilisations* 35:615–41.

Haran, M.
1961a Studies in the Account of the Levitical Cities: Preliminary Considerations. *JBL* 80:45–54.
1961b Studies in the Account of the Levitical Cities: Utopia and Historical Reality. *JBL* 80:156–65.
1978 *Temples and Temple Service in Ancient Israel: An Inquiry into Biblical Cult Phenomena and the Historical Setting of the Priestly School.* Oxford: Clarendon.

Hart, D. M.
1972 The Tribe in Modern Morocco: Two Case Studies. In *Arabs and Berbers: From Tribe to Nation in North Africa*, ed. E. Gellner and C. Micaud, 25–58. London: Duckworth.
1993 Four Centuries of History on the Hoof: The Northwest Passage of Berber Sheep Transhumants across the Moroccan Atlas, 1550–1912. *Morocco: The Journal of the Society for Moroccan Studies* 3:21–55.
1999a Scission, Discontinuity and Reduplication of Agnatic Descent Groups in Precolonial Berber Societies in Morocco. *Journal of North African Studies* 4:27–36.
1999b Comparative Land Tenure and Division of Irrigation Water in Two Moroccan Berber Societies: The Ait Waryaghar of the Rif and the Ait ᶜAtta of the Saghru and South-Central Atlas. *Journal of North African Studies* 4:172–218.
2001a Making Sense of Moroccan Tribal Society and History. *Journal of North African Studies* 6: 11–28.
2001b An Awkward Chronology and a Questionable Genealogy: History and Legend in a Saintly Lineage in the Moroccan Central Atlas, 1397–1702. *Journal of North African Studies* 6:95–116.

Hauer, C.
1982 David and the Levites. *JSOT* 23:33–54.

Hen, F. J. de
1964 Quelques Notes Ethnographiques sur les Ihansalen. *Jahrbuch des Museums für Volkerkunde zu Leipzig* 20:282–318.

Hutton, J. M.
forthc. a The Levitical Diaspora (II): A Review of Opinions.
forthc. b The Levitical Diaspora (III): Ahansal and Levite Social Function
forthc. c The Levitical Diaspora (IV): The Distribution of the Gadite and Reubenite Cities as a Function of Topography and Ecology.
forthc. d The Levitical Diaspora (V): Levite Function and Ahansal Protection.

Ilahiane, H.
1999 The Berber *agdal* Institution: Indigenous Range Management in the Atlas Mountains. *Ethnology* 38:21–45.

Joffé, G.
1991 The Zawiya of Wazzan: Relations between Shurafa and Tribe up to 1860. In *Tribe and State: Essays in Honour of David Montgomery Hart*, ed. E. G. H. Joffé and C. R. Pennell, 84–118. Cambridgeshire: Middle East and North African Studies Press.

Kallai, Z.
1986 *Historical Geography of the Bible: The Tribal Territories of Israel.* Jerusalem: Magnes.

Kaufmann, Y.
1953 *The Biblical Account of the Conquest of Palestine.* Jerusalem: Magnes.

Kraus, W.
1998 Contestable Identities: Structures in the Moroccan High Atlas. *Journal of the Royal Anthropological Institute* 4:1–22.

Leuchter, M.
2007 "The Levite in Your Gates": The Deuteronomic Redefinition of Levitical Authority. *JBL* 126:417–36.

Marfoe, L.
1979 The Integrative Transformation: Patterns of Sociopolitical Organization in Southern Syria. *BASOR* 234:1–42.

Marx, E.
1977 The Tribe As a Unit of Subsistence: Nomadic Pastoralism in the Middle East. *American Anthropologist* N.S. 79:343–63.

Mazar, B.
1960 The Cities of the Priests and the Levites. In *Congress Volume: Oxford, 1959*, 193–205. VTSup 7. Leiden: Brill.

Mettinger, T. N. D.
1971 *Solomonic State Officials: A Study of the Civil Government Officials of the Israelite Monarchy*. Coniectanea Biblica, Old Testament Series 5. Lund: Gleerup.

Milgrom, J.
1983 The Levitic Town: An Exercise in Realistic Planning. In *Essays in Honour of Yigael Yadin*, ed. G. Vermes and J. Neusner, 185–88. Totowa, N.J.: Allanheld and Osmun.

Miller, J. M.
1970 The Korahites of Southern Judah. *CBQ* 32: 58–68.
1987 Rehoboam's Cities of Defense and the Levitical City List. In *Archaeology and Biblical Interpretation: Essays in Memory of D. Glenn Rose*, ed. L. G. Perdue, L. E. Toombs, and G. L. Johnson, 273–86. Atlanta: John Knox.

Miller, R. D.
2005 *Chieftains of the Highland Clans: A History of Israel in the Twelfth and Eleventh Centuries* B.C. Grand Rapids, Mich.: Eerdmans.

Möhlinbrink, K.
1934 Die levitischen Überlieferungen des Alten Testaments. *ZAW* 11:184–231.

Morsy, M.
1986 Aḥanṣal. *Encyclopédie berbère* 3:307–11.

Munson, H.
1991 The Segmentary Lineage Model in the Jbalan Highlands of Morocco. In *Tribe and State: Essays in Honour of David Montgomery Hart*, ed. E. G. H. Joffé and C. R. Pennell, 48–68. Cambridgeshire: Middle East and North African Studies Press.
1993 Rethinking Gellner's Segmentary Analysis of Morocco's Ait ᶜAtta. *Man* N.S. 28:267–80.

Naᵓaman, N.
1986 *Borders and Districts in Biblical Historiography*. Jerusalem Biblical Studies 4. Jerusalem: Simor.

Noth, M.
1953 *Das Buch Josua*. 2d ed. Tübingen: Mohr-Siebeck.

Palmer, C.
2001 Traditional Agriculture. In *The Archaeology of Jordan*, ed. B. MacDonald, R. Adams, and P. Bienkowski, 621–29. Sheffield, England: Sheffield Academic Press.

Peterson, J. L.
1977 A Topographical Surface Survey of the Levitical "Cities" of Joshua 21 and I Chronicles 6: Studies on the Levites in Israelite Life and Religion. Ph.D. diss., Seabury-Western Theological Seminary.

Polk, T.
1979 The Levites in the Davidic-Solomonic Empire. *Studia Biblica et Theologica* 9/1:3–22.

Rad, G. von
1953 *Studies in Deuteronomy*. London: SCM.

Roberts, H.
2002 Perspectives on Berber Politics: On Gellner and Masqueray, or Durkheim's Mistake. *Journal of the Royal Anthropological Institute* 8:107–26.

Robinson, R. B.
1978 The Levites in the Pre-Monarchic Period. *Studia Biblica et Theologica* 8/2:3–24.

Rowton, M. B.
1976 Dimorphic Structure and Typology. *Oriens Antiquus* 15:17–31.

Shankland, D.
1999 Integrating the Rural: Gellner and the Study of Anatolia. *Middle Eastern Studies* 35:132–50.

Spencer, J. R.
1980 The Levitical Cities: A Study of the Role and Function of the Levites in the History of Israel. Ph.D. diss., University of Chicago.
1992 Levitical Cities. In *The Anchor Bible Dictionary*, ed. D. N. Freedman, 4:310–11. New York: Doubleday.
1995 Priestly Families (or Factions) in Samuel and Kings. In *The Pitcher Is Broken: Memorial Essays for Gösta W. Ahlström*, ed. S. W. Holloway and L. K. Handy, 387–400. JSOTSup 190. Sheffield, England: Sheffield Academic Press.

Stager, L. E.
1985a The Archaeology of the Family in Ancient Israel. *BASOR* 260:1–35.
1985b Response. In *Biblical Archaeology Today: Proceedings of the International Congress on Biblical Archaeology, Jerusalem, April 1984*, 83–87. Jerusalem: Israel Exploration Society.

van der Steen, E.
1995 Aspects of Nomadism and Settlement in the Central Jordan Valley. *PEQ* 127:141–58.

Talmon, S.
1978 The "Comparative Method" in Biblical Interpretation—Principles and Problems. In *Congress Volume: Göttingen, 1977*, 320–56. VTSup 29. Leiden: Brill.

Temsamani, A. K.
1991 The Jabala Region: Makhzan, Bandits and Saints. In *Tribe and State: Essays in Honour of David Montgomery Hart*, ed. E. G. H. Joffé and C. R. Pennell, 14–47. Cambridgeshire: Middle East and North African Studies Press.

de Vaux, R.
1961 *Ancient Israel: Its Life and Institutions*. London: Darton, Longman and Todd.
1978 *The Early History of Israel: To the Period of Judges*. London: Darton, Longman and Todd.

Vinogradav, A. R.
1972 The Socio-political Organization of a Berber "Taraf" Tribe: Pre-Protectorate Morocco. In *Arabs and Berbers: From Tribe to Nation in North Africa*, ed. E. Gellner and C. Micaud, 67–83. London: Duckworth.

Wellhausen, J.
1885 *Prolegomena to the History of Israel*. [Reprint, Atlanta: Scholars Press, 1994.]

Westermarck, E.
1926 *Ritual and Belief in Morocco*. Vol. 1. London: Macmillan.

Wright, G. E.
1954 The Levites in Deuteronomy. *VT* 4:325–30.

25. A Cypriot Workshop of Middle Bronze Age Askoi

by Vassos Karageorghis

Cypriot potters have always been fond of imaginative pottery shapes—in response, no doubt, to the taste of their clientele. Anthropomorphic and zoomorphic vases are known as early as the Chalcolithic period, particularly in the area of Palaepaphos. One such askos is exhibited in the Kouklia Museum at Palaepaphos (Karageorghis 1991:18, pl. 6.22).

Bird-shaped vases are predominant during the Early and Middle Bronze Ages (in Red Polished Ware) because the body of a bird is easier to reproduce in clay. But there are also vases in the shape of quadrupeds (bulls, stags, and other animals). These are all hollow and should be distinguished from similar examples in solid clay, which are terracottas and not vases. The hollow vases are all handmade, like the other vases of the same period. In most cases, details of the body such as the facial features and the legs are rendered in solid clay. The vases have a handle (basket handle) and legs (usually three or four) to allow them to stand upright. They also have a tubular spout so that liquid may be poured out of them. Yon has defined askoi as

> vases fermés de formes diverses, assez souvent figuratives, qui s'organisent de part et d'autre d'un plan de symétrie et non d'un axe: c'est-à-dire que l'ouverture principale qui sert au remplissage, qu'elle soit verticale ou oblique, n'est pas dans le prolongement d'un axe du reste du vase, en admettant que le corps soit un solide de révolution.
>
> Certains de ces vases ont une ouverture unique, qui sert à la fois à remplir et à verser: le prototype en est le vase en forme de "sac" ou d'"outre," désigné pour cette raison sous le nom d'"askos", et dont on a le témoignage depuis le Chyp. Anc. Il en est d'autres qui, en plus de leur ouverture principale, désaxée par rapport au reste du vase, ont un bec ou une ouverture secondaire qui sert à "verser," ce qui leur a fait donner le nom de "rhyton." [Yon 1976:169–70]

Caubet and Merrillees (1997) studied the technique of such vases in detail. They called them askoi, whereas Stewart calls them askoïdes (1992:36, class III), a term which is perhaps more appropriate. The predominant term is, however, askoi and it will be employed here. This note concerns not the technique but the conclusions that may be drawn from the painted decoration of these vases.

Although a particular class of askoi in Red Polished III Ware (the so-called "duck-askoi") may have been influenced by Aegean prototypes (Merrillees 1979; Graziadio 2005), the Cypriot askos, which appears as early as the Chalcolithic period, is an indigenous ceramic form and had a long life in the ceramics of the island. It developed particularly during the Early and Middle Cypriot periods (Morris 1985:184–232; Misch 1992).

In the present note, I will try to isolate a group of Middle Cypriot askoi which may have been made in the same workshop. This exercise, which is current in the study of Mycenean and Greek vases, has rarely been attempted in the case of Early and Middle Cypriot pottery. The idea of grouping prehistoric ceramics in Cyprus and attributing them to individual workshops or even individual potters started with Basil Hennessy in 1973, when he attempted to distinguish the hand of several potters of Red Polished vases (Hennessy 1973; see also Caubet and Merrillees 1997:20); I followed him in 2001, by attributing two Red Polished anthropomorphic vases to the hand of another potter (Karageorghis 2001a).

The White Painted technique of Middle Bronze Age Cypriot pottery offered many opportunities for the Cypriot potter to exercise his/her ingenuity both as a coroplast and as a vase-painter. The appearance of Middle Bronze Age White Painted Ware zoomorphic askoi is more naturalistic than that of the askoi in Red Polished Ware. The facial and body details could be rendered more accurately with paint than with incised lines and the painted decoration of almost the whole surface of the askos (occasionally with the addition of purple paint) enhanced the decorative qualities of these vases. The White Painted technique is predominant, but there are occasionally askoi in other fabrics, for instance in Red-on-Black Ware and Black Slip III Ware (see Karageorghis 1976: 125, fig. 93, and 155, fig. 111).

The bull and the ram were particularly favored by the makers of askoi. Whether this preference may be related to the qualities of these two animals as symbols of male fertility is difficult to say (see Caubet and Merrillees 1997:23). These askoi are usually found as gifts in tombs. As is the case with other vases of the same period with anthropomorphic features, they may simply represent the imaginative spirit of the potter, whose ability to combine anthropomorphic and zoomorphic features on vases, to make them more "lively," was quite developed.

The askoi grouped together in this note are decorated in the White Painted V–VI or Bichrome Handmade technique and may be dated to the end of the Middle Cypriot III and the very beginning of the Late Cypriot IA period (ca. 1600 B.C.E.). They were particularly favored in the northwestern part of Cyprus (see Merrillees 1968). The potters of this region also favored the decoration of vases with human and animal plastic decoration (Vermeule and Wolsky 1990).

The number of zoomorphic vases and askoi of White Painted V–VI Ware has increased since Åström's list in 1972 (P. Åström 1972:76–77), with discoveries from the necropolis of Ayia Irini (Pecorella 1977:230; Quilici 1990:111–12, n. 138, with references to other vases of similar type) and Kazaphani (Courtois in Nicolaou and Nicolaou 1989:80 no. 131, 92 nos. 34, 125). Several other askoi have been published by Morris; they formed part of his private collection (Morris 1985:197–99, pls. 224–28). It is interesting that many of these vases are ram-shaped askoi.

While studying a zoomorphic vase at the Institute of Archaeology in Bucharest, I was struck by the fact that the shape and decoration of this vase were strikingly similar to the shape and decoration of other zoomorphic vases of the same period, some of them of known provenance, hence the idea of grouping them together and suggesting that they may have been made in the same workshop.

The following zoomorphic vases may be grouped together, perhaps having been made in the same workshop:

1. Ram-shaped askos of White Painted V Ware in the collection of the Institute of Archaeology, Bucharest, inv. no. 06922 (figure 1). Provenance unknown. Height: 15.5cm; length: 21cm. Hollow, cylindrical, handmade body, supported on three short legs, triangular in section. At one end of the body a ram's head with coiled horns; at the other end an obliquely arranged tubular spout, rim damaged. Between the spout and the animal's head a flat basket handle. The breast and hind part of the animal are decorated with two horizontal panels filled with lattice pattern and flanked by horizontal parallel lines, in matte red and black paint. The sides of the body are decorated with three similar vertical bands.

   Reference: Corpus Vasorum Antiquorum Bucharest 1, pl. 5, nos 1–2.

   I have identified the decoration of this vase as White Painted V, although it is in fact Bichrome Handmade, following Åström's standard terminology for the Middle Bronze Age pottery of Cyprus, as used in the *Swedish Cyprus Expedition*. The Bichrome technique is quite rare in early Late Cypriot I vase-painting (see Courtois in Nicolaou and Nicolaou 1989:92, Vase 522 and n. 123, with references to other Bichrome Handmade vases from Akaki, Myrtou-Stephania and Kalopsidha; see also Pieridou and Karageorghis 1963:32, pl. 6.5 and Spiteris 1970:61; also Johnson 1980:28, Tomb 24, nos. 191–92, pl. 38.191 from Maroni). It is not certain whether this technique was influenced by the contemporary Bichrome Wheelmade vases (Karageoghis 2001b: 148–53; in this respect I should mention the Bichrome Wheelmade askos from Akhera, Karageorghis 1964:89, fig. 26.1).

2. Fragmentary ram-shaped askos of White Painted V Ware, much restored, legs triangular in section (figure 2). From Kazaphani, Tomb 2A, no. 171. Cyprus Museum, Nicosia. Preserved height: 15.8 cm.; preserved length: 10.7cm. Decoration in matte black paint.

   Reference: Nicolaou and Nicolaou 1989:16–17, no. 171, pl. 2.

   The tomb in which this vase was found was originally used in the Middle Cypriot III/Late Cypriot IA period (between 1600–1575 B.C.E.) and was continuously used until the end of the Late Cypriot IIC period (Nicolaou and Nicolaou 1989:36).

3. Bull-shaped askos of White Painted V(?) Ware, legs triangular in section (figure 3). From Kazaphani, Tomb 2B, no. 34. Cyprus Museum, Nicosia. Height: 17.5 cm. Decoration in matte black paint.

   Reference: Nicolaou and Nicolaou 1989:38, no. 34, fig. 10, pl. 17.

4. Ram-shaped askos of White Painted V Ware (figure 4). Museum of Fine Arts, Boston, inv. no. 72.132. Provenance unknown. Height: 16.1 cm; length: 20.3 cm.

   Reference: Vermeule 1972, fig. 6; Morris 1985: 216, fig. 353.

The four vases described above are assigned with a high degree of certainty to the same workshop or even to the hand of the same potter. There are others, however, which I would consider as belonging to the same workshop, but with less certainty. It might also be suggested that they were the products of a workshop that followed stylistic tendencies similar to the workshop in which the above vases were made.

5. Bull-shaped askos of White Painted V–VI Ware, from Ayia Irini, Tomb 3, no. 14 (figure 5). Cyprus Museum, Nicosia. Height: 13.9 cm; length: 18 cm.

   Reference: Pecorella 1977:20–21, fig. 28a–b, 47, no. 14. The decoration of the body is very similar to that of the askoi mentioned above.

6. Goat-shaped askos of White Painted V Ware, from Ayia Irini, tomb excavated in the settlement area, no. 402 (figure 6). Cyprus Museum, Nicosia. Height: 16 cm; length: 22 cm. Unlike the other askoi described above, this one has a small animal's head and a long neck.

   Reference: Quilici 1990:111–12, fig. 309, 117, fig. 317a, no. 402.

7. Goat-shaped rhyton of Bichrome Handmade Ware (with a tubular spout at one end and a hole through the animal's muzzle at the other end) in the Cyprus Museum, Nicosia, inv. no. 1963/IV-20/43 (figure 7). Height: 14 cm; length: 22 cm. Provenance unknown, formerly in the Hubbard Collection, Kyrenia. The sides of the body are decorated with two vertical latticed bands and a large latticed diamond in the middle. In many ways the form of the rhyton recalls that of askos no. 6.

8. Zoomorphic askos of White Painted V Ware, with tubular spout at one end and upright animal protome at the opposite end (figure 8). Provenance unknown. Cyprus Museum, Nicosia, inv. no. A924. Height: 13 cm; length: 15.5 cm. Decoration similar to the askoi described above.

   Reference: Buchholz and Karageorghis 1973:421, no. 1553.

Askoi and rhyta were characteristic of the Early and Middle Bronze Ages and reached their zenith at the very beginning of the Late Cypriot IA. During the Late Cypriot II period, they started to decline and were replaced mainly by Base-ring Ware rhyta (L. Åström 1972:514–15) and hollow terracottas of Plain Ware or by painted hollow or solid terracottas (Karageorghis 1993:19–21, 35–43). The variety of types of zoomorphic askoi of the Early Cypriot III–Late Cypriot IA was then replaced by rather repetitive types with only some exceptions during the eleventh century B.C.E. and the early Iron Age (Karageorghis 1993:45–53; 1975:54–56). The askoi and rhyta gradually died out except for some animal-shaped askoi of the Cypro-Geometric and Cypro-Archaic I periods (e.g., Gjerstad 1948:figs. 7.3–7, 13–15, 15.6–7, 24.5–7, 36.10–12).

The imaginative spirit of the Early Cypriot III Late Cypriot IA Cypriot potters, as shown by the askoi, is indicative of the high cultural development attained in the northern part of Cyprus during these periods, before the shifting of importance to the south and east coasts of the island. Apart from the askoi and rhyta, this part of Cyprus has also yielded other imaginative forms of vases decorated with plastic attachments of human and animal form, for instance at Pendayia, Morphou, Akhera, and Ayia Irini (see, e.g., Vermeule and Wolsky 1990:figs. 137–39).

The identification of prehistoric Cypriot ceramics probably made in the same workshop, perhaps even by the same potter, is a promising field of research to which much further attention should be paid. Such studies should lead to a better understanding of Bronze Age Cypriot ceramic art, and they will also assist in the resolution of chronological problems.

Figure 1. Ram-shaped askos of White Painted V (Bichrome Handmade) Ware
Institute of Archaeology, Bucharest, inv. no. 06922
Photographs courtesy of the Institute of Archaeology; drawn by Christina Georgescu.

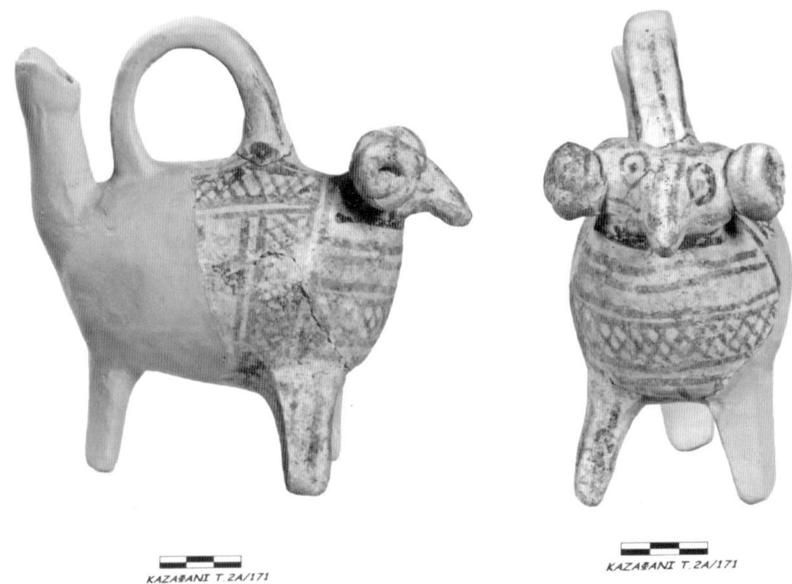

Figure 2. Fragmentary ram-shaped askos of White Painted V Ware
Kazaphani, Tomb 2A, no. 171; Cyprus Museum, Nicosia
Photographs courtesy of the Museum.

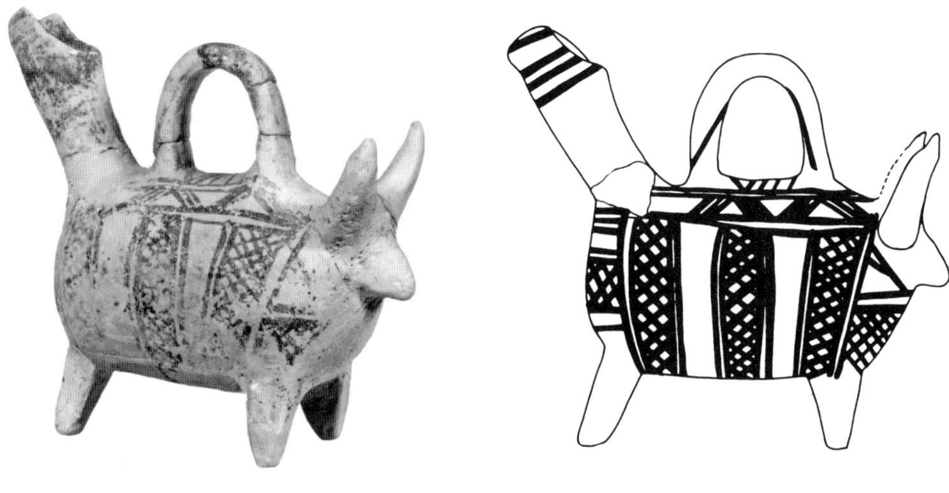

KAZAΦANI T.2B/34

Figure 3. Bull-shaped askos of White Painted V(?) Ware
Kazaphani, Tomb 2B, no. 34; Cyprus Museum, Nicosia
Photograph courtesy of the Museum; drawing after Nicolaou and Nicolaou 1989:fig. 10.

Figure 4. Ram-shaped askos of White Painted V Ware
Museum of Fine Arts, Boston, inv. no. 72.132
Drawing after Morris 1985:fig. 353.

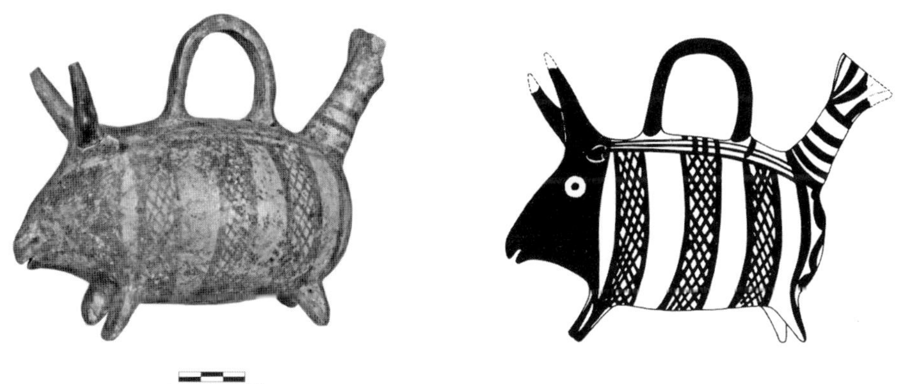

ΑΓΙΑ ΕΙΡΗΝΗ 1970
T.3/14

Figure 5. Bull-shaped askos of White Painted V–VI Ware
Ayia Irini, Tomb 3, no. 14; Cyprus Museum, Nicosia
Photograph courtesy of the Museum; drawing after Pecorella 1977:fig. 47.

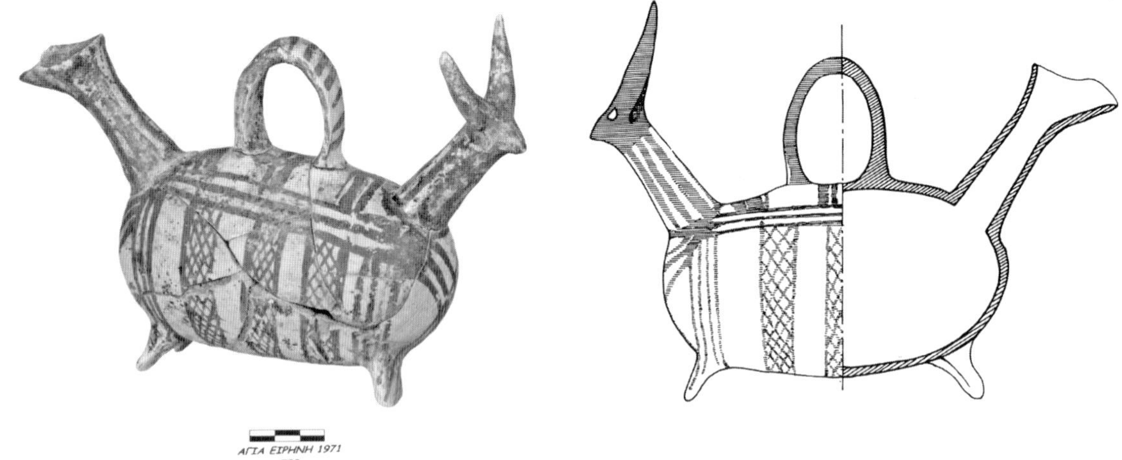

Figure 6. Goat-shaped askos of White Painted V Ware
Ayia Irini, Tomb no. 402, excavated by Quilici in 1971; Cyprus Museum, Nicosia
Photograph courtesy of the Museum; drawing after Quilici 1990:fig. 317a.

Figure 7. Goat-shaped rhyton of White Painted V (Bichrome Handmade) Ware
Cyprus Museum, Nicosia, inv. no. 1963/IV-20/43
Photograph courtesy of the Museum.

Figure 8. Zoomorphic askos of White Painted V Ware
Cyprus Museum, Nicosia, inv. no. A924
Photographs courtesy of the Museum.

Bibliography

Åström, L.
1972 Other Arts and Crafts. In *The Swedish Cyprus Expedition*, vol. 4/1d, *The Late Cypriote Bronze Age*, ed. L. Åström and P. Åström, 473–557. Lund: Swedish Cyprus Expedition.

Åström, P.
1972 *The Swedish Cyprus Expedition*. Vol. 4/1b, *The Middle Cypriote Bronze Age*. Lund: Swedish Cyprus Expedition.

Buchholz, H.-G., and V. Karageorghis
1973 *Prehistoric Greece and Cyprus: An Archaeological Handbook*. Translated by F. Garvie. London: Phaidon.

Caubet, A., and R. S. Merrillees
1997 Les askoi anthropomorphes et zoomorphes aux périodes CA et CM. In *Four Thousand Years of Images on Cypriote Pottery: Proceedings of the Third International Conference of Cypriote Studies, Nicosia 3–4 May, 1996*, ed. V. Karageorghis, R. Laffineur, and F. Vandenabeele, 15–24. Brussels-Liège-Nicosia: A. G. Leventis Foundation.

Gjerstad, E.
1948 *The Swedish Cyprus Expedition*. Vol. 4/2, *The Cypro-Geometric, Cypro-Archaic and Cypro-Classical Periods*. Stockholm: Swedish Cyprus Expedition.

Graziadio, G.
2005 *I "duck askoi" ciprioti. ΑΓΩΓΗ* 2:7–18.

Hennessy, J. B.
1973 Cypriot Artists of the Early and Middle Bronze Ages. In *The Cypriot Bronze Age: Some Recent Australian Contributions to the Prehistory of Cyprus*, ed. J. M. Birmingham, 10–22. Australian Studies in Archaeology 1. Sydney: University of Sydney.

Johnson, J.
1980 *Maroni de Chypre*. SIMA 59. Göteborg: Paul Åströms.

Karageorghis, V.
1964 *Nouveaux documents pour l'étude du Bronze Récent à Chypre: Recueil critique et commenté*. Études Chypriotes 3. Paris: Boccard.
1975 *Alaas: A Protogeometric Necropolis in Cyprus*. Nicosia: Department of Antiquities of Cyprus.
1976 *The Civilization of Prehistoric Cyprus*. Athens. Ekdotike Athenon S.A.
1991 *The Coroplastic Art of Ancient Cyprus*. Vol. 1, *Chalcolithic–Late Cypriote I*. Nicosia: A. G. Leventis Foundation.
1993 *The Coroplastic Art of Ancient Cyprus*. Vol. 2, *Late Cypriote II–Cypro-Geometric III*. Nicosia: A. G. Leventis Foundation.
2001a Two Anthropomorphic Vases of the Early Cypriote Bronze Age. *Report of the Department of Antiquities, Cyprus* 2001:45–48.
2001b Bichrome Wheel-made Ware: Still a Problem? In *The Chronology of Base-ring Ware and Bichrome Wheel-made (Proceedings of a Colloquium held in the Royal Academy of Letters, History and Antiquities, Stockholm, May 18–19, 2000)*, ed. P. Åström, 143–55. Stockholm: Royal Academy of Letters, History and Antiquities.

Merrillees, R. S.
1968 Two Late Cypriote Vases. *Opuscula Atheniensia* 8:1–10.
1979 Cyprus, the Cyclades and Crete in the Early to Middle Bronze Ages. In *Acts of the International Archaeological Symposium "The Relations between Cyprus and Crete, ca. 2000–500 B.C.,"* ed. V. Karageorghis, 8–40. Nicosia: Department of Antiquities.

Misch, P.
1992 *Die Askoi in der Bronzezeit: Eine typologische Studie zur Entwicklung askoider Gefässformen in der Bronze- und Eisenzeit Griechenlands und angrenzender Gebiete*. Studies in Mediterranean Archaeology Pocket-Book 100. Jonsered: Paul Åströms.

Morris, D.
1985 *The Art of Ancient Cyprus*. Oxford: Phaidon.

Nicolaou, I., and K. Nicolaou
1989 *Kazaphani: A Middle/Late Cypriot Tomb at Kazaphani–Ayios Andronikos: T. 2A, B*. Nicosia: Department of Antiquities of Cyprus.

Pecorella, P. E.
1977 *Le tombe dell'età del Bronzo Tardo della necropolis a mare di Ayia Irini Paleokastro*. Biblioteca di antichitá cipriote 4/1. Rome: Consiglio Nazionale delle Ricerche, Istituto per gli Studi Micenei ed Egeo-Anatolici.

Pieridou, A., and V. Karageorghis
1963 Recent Acquisitions by the Cyprus Museum. *Report of the Department of Antiquities, Cyprus* 1963:29–32.

Quilici, L.
1990 *La tomba dell'età del Bronzo Tardo dell'abitato di Paleokastro presso Ayia Irini*. Biblioteca di antichitá cipriote 6. Rome: Consiglio Nazionale delle Ricerche, Istituto per gli Studi Micenei ed Egeo-Anatolici.

Spiteris, T.
1970 *The Art of Cyprus*. Paris: Reynal

Stewart, J. R.
1992 *Corpus of Cypriot Artefacts of the Early Bronze Age II*. SIMA 3/2. Jonsered: Paul Åströms.

Vermeule, C. C.
1972 *Art of Ancient Cyprus*. Boston: Museum of Fine Arts.

Vermeule, E. D. T., and F. Z. Wolsky
1990 *Toumba tou Skourou: A Bronze Age Potters' Quarter on Morphou Bay in Cyprus*. Cambridge, Mass.: Harvard University Museum of Fine Arts.

Yon, M.
1976 *Manuel de céramique Chypriote*. Vol. 1, *Problèmes historiques, vocabulaire, méthode*. Lyon: Maison de l'Orient Méditerranéen Ancien.

26. Slavery in Antiquity

by Philip J. King

When Lawrence Stager and I coauthored *Life in Biblical Israel* (2001), we were gratified by the positive reviews and awards it received; however, one observant reviewer was disappointed that we had not included the institution of slavery. Naturally, it is almost impossible to do justice to all the topics that *Life in Biblical Israel* encompasses, but the criticism was quite justified. To remedy the deficiency, I thought that the institution of slavery would be an appropriate subject for a festschrift honoring Professor Stager. I only wish I had his help in crafting this essay, but that would have violated protocol. His personal contributions to *Life in Biblical Israel* were invaluable and also responsible for converting what may have been a good book into a better book. In the process of our research and writing, I learned much from him, as I did when we excavated together at several sites. This essay is my attempt to repay my indebtedness to this preeminent archaeologist.

Introduction

The literature on slavery is so extensive and the institution of slavery so wide-ranging that, of necessity, this essay will be limited to the ancient Near East *in genere* and to the biblical world *in specie*. The subtitle of Isaac Mendelsohn's (1978:iii) *Slavery in the Ancient Near East* summarizes the situation: "A Comparative Study of Slavery in Babylonia, Assyria, Syria, and Palestine from the Middle of the Third Millennium to the End of the First Millennium." Finley's (1998:77) comment: "Although slaves have been exploited in most societies as far back as any records exist, there have been only five genuine slave societies, two of them in antiquity: classical Greece and classical Italy."

Slavery is the institution of involuntary servitude whereby one person exerts ownership rights over another. As property of the master, the slave is considered mere chattel. Emphasis was placed on the relationship between slave and master. Slavery took on many different forms throughout the ancient world. It existed throughout the ancient Near East, but only the extant Mesopotamian and Hittite texts provide insights into its functioning. "Slavery had a profound influence on the social structure, ideology, law, and social psychology of the ancient Near Eastern cultures" (Dandamayev 1992:65). Mendelsohn (1978:vi) points out that since slavery was a "labor institution," it should be of great interest to the historian, economist, and sociologist. It played an enormous role in the social and economic life of the ancient Near East.

To equate slavery in antiquity with New World slavery as experienced in the West during the seventeenth to nineteenth centuries would be very misleading. Slavery of earlier times (especially the first century C.E.), unlike in the New World, was not based on racial factors or skin colors. Many erroneous impressions have emerged from this too-facile equation. Change in the character of slavery was brought about by the change from subsistence to market economy when large landed estates (*latifundia*) came into the hands of a small number of affluent landowners. At the same time, the slaves' social status differed from nation to nation; consequently, superficial analogies can be very misleading. In the ancient Near East, in the classical world, in the biblical world, and elsewhere, the words for "slave" are often ambiguous.

Mendelsohn (1978:1–6) cites four principal causes of slavery in the ancient Near East: prisoners of war (the earliest source of slaves in antiquity), sale of children by impoverished parents, self-sale by indigents, and insolvency of debtors. Important sources of slavery in the ancient Near East were warfare, piracy, and kidnapping. The Torah (Pentateuch) enumerates four quite similar legal means of acquiring slaves: purchase (Lev. 25:44–46), prisoners of war (Num. 31:32–35; Deut. 21:10–14), punishment for larceny (Exod. 22:1–3), and debt slavery (Lev. 25:39; Exod. 21:7).

Slave traffic was compatible with the *Weltanschauung* of the ancient Near East. Condoned, and not condemned, slavery was widespread in antiquity. The Israelites adopted the practice from foreign peoples, and the slaves would have labored in the sanctuaries, in the palaces, and in public works.

Slavery in the Hebrew Bible

"We have in the Bible the first appeals in world literature to treat slaves as human beings for their own sake " (Dandamayev 1992:65). Sirach 33:32 admonished: "If you have but one slave, treat him like a brother, for you will need him as you need your life." Two types of servitude existed in the biblical world: permanent and indentured (for a specific period); most of the biblical ordinances relate to the latter.

Debt-slavery was the principal means of restoring the slave population. A widow (an insolvent debtor) called out to Elisha, "a money-lender has come to take away my two children as slaves [in payment of debt]." The prophet intervened miraculously, and the children were spared (2 Kings 4:1–7). The prophet Amos indicted the wealthy of Israel for exploiting the poor: "they sell the righteous for silver, and the needy for a pair of sandals" (Amos 2:6). Amos indicts slave traffic, in general throughout the ancient Near East, specifically in Gaza and Tyre where the inhabitants dealt in prisoners: "they [inhabitants of Gaza] carried into exile entire communities, to hand them over to Edom" (Amos 1:6); "they [inhabitants of Tyre] delivered entire communities over to Edom" (Amos 1:9).

Although the Israelites adopted the institution of slavery from their neighbors, the differences were many and varied. As noted, it was also quite different from slavery of later times practiced in North America; slavery in the Bible was not based on ethnicity or skin color. These dissimilarities will become apparent in the ensuing exegesis of selected texts from both the Old and New Testaments.

Generally, slaves in Bible times were treated well. They enjoyed certain human rights; for example, they could acquire property. Also, they could participate in religious celebrations after having been circumcised (Gen. 17:12–14) because then they were members of the slaveowner's family. "Any slave who has been purchased may eat it [passover] after he has been circumcised" (Exod. 12:44). "The Old Testament did [*sic*] a definite attempt to raise the position of Israelite slaves; if possible, it would have abolished slavery among the Israelites themselves" (van der Ploeg 1972:87). However, history attests that the authors of both Old and New Testament accepted slavery as a normative social institution.

The usual term for "slave" in Akkadian is *wardum*; it corresponds to Hebrew *ᶜebed* and Greek *doulos*. Several Hebrew words are used in the context of slavery. *ᶜebed* is the most common word for "slave," in reference to chattel slave, but it is ambiguous; it may also mean "servant." In the LXX *doulos* always translates the Hebrew *ᶜebed*. "The innumerable biblical references in the original Hebrew and Greek languages are all softened to 'servant' and the like in the King James Bible" (Michell 1957:149). There is no feminine form of *ᶜebed*; instead, in the Bible, both *ʾāmāh* and *šipḥā* denote a female slave. *naᶜar* (fem. *naᶜarâ*), literally a "youth," denotes, sometimes but not always, a "(young) slave" or a personal retainer. *ᶜebed* designates the actual slave, and also one who occupies a subservient position vis-à-vis the king or other royal officials. In the context of the court (*der Hof*), *ᶜebed* may be rendered "servant"; for example, "servant of the king" (*ᶜebed hammelek*), which was a prominent position. Jonas Greenfield (1967:117–19) demonstrated that in both Hebrew and Ugaritic *ᶜebed* has a technical meaning of "vassal"; for example, "I [Achish, king of Gath] shall have him [David] as my vassal (*ᶜebed*) forever" (1 Sam. 27:12). *ᶜebed* is clearly distinguished from *śākîr/śekîrâ* "wage earner." The Piel of *šārat* (*šērēt* "to serve"), in contrast to *ᶜabad* "to serve," is usually used with reference to service of Yahweh in the temple.

In Israel *ʾādôn* "lord, master," frequently a noble title or a courteous form of address, denotes the slave master in contrast to *baᶜal* "owner." Hosea, enlisting the metaphor of marriage, helps to shed light on *baᶜal* as distinct from *ʾādôn*. "On that day, says Yahweh, she shall call me 'My husband (*ʾîšî*),' and never again 'My baal (*baᶜali*)'" (2:18 [16]). "Husband" is a term of endearment whereas "baal" is a contemptible epithet.

Exodus 21:1–11

The first section on slavery in the Hebrew Bible is introduced by the superscription of the Book of the Covenant (Covenant Code, Exod. 20:22–23:19). The earliest of the biblical "legal" collection, the Covenant Code reflects a tribal society, whereas the comparable passage in Lev. 25:39–55 is concerned with the family. The key word is *mišpāṭîm* "ordinances," consisting of casuistic laws in contrast to unconditional laws. These case laws bear a close resemblance to other legal codes of the ancient Near East, especially the Code of Hammurabi, consisting of some 282 case laws. Exod. 21:2–11 deals with the rights of slaves (vv. 2–6: male debt-slaves; vv. 7–11: female debt-slaves).

ᶜebed ᶜibrî "Hebrew slave" (v. 2) is the source of disagreement among commentators; contrary to Edward Lipinski (1976:120–24) and others, a scholarly consensus, including Martin Noth (1962:177), Niels Lemche (1975:136, 138), Bernard Jackson (1988:92), Brevard Childs (1974:468) and others, understand *ᶜibrî* as an appellative, not a gentilic. "The term does not designate an ethnic group, but tends to be a pejorative designation of a legal or social status within the ancient Near Eastern society of the second millennium" (Childs 1974:468). Lipinski interpreted *ᶜebed ᶜibrî* as a designation of an Israelite of inferior social status who had become a slave (1976:120–24). *Ḥōpšî* "freed" is a technical term designating one who has been liberated from slavery but has yet to attain the full rights of the free citizen (Noth), thereby ranking somewhere between a freedman and a slave.

A male (but not a female) debt-slave can be kept in servitude for a maximum of six years. Despite the fact that the biblical laws are characterized by greater benevolence than laws of the neighboring peoples, the Code of Hammurabi 117 legislates that a slave may go free after only three years. Exodus 21 includes some qualifications: (1) concerning marital status; (2) a spouse and children born in slavery are not liberated with the slave; (3) at the end of six years the slave may opt to remain in perpetual servitude (*ᶜabādô le ᶜolām* "he shall serve him for life") out of love (*ʾāhab*) for his master, spouse, and children.

Verse 6 (also Deut. 15:16–17) describes the ceremony for remaining voluntarily in servitude. His master will bring him "before God," (*ʾel hāʾelohîm*) that is, to the local sanctuary, and pierce his ear with an awl as a symbol of perpetual servitude. An analogy exists in Isaiah 44:5 and 49:16, alluding to the Babylonian custom of tattooing the master's name on the hand of the slave. "This one shall write on his hand, '[I am] the Lord's'" (Isa. 44:5). "See, upon the palms of my hands I have inscribed you [your name]" (Isa. 49:16). These texts signify that the recipient belongs to Yahweh. Mendelsohn (1978:49) suggested that the hole was made in the ear to accommodate a ring or cord, "on which was fastened a tag made of clay or metal." According to Deut. 15:16–17, the ceremony did not take place in the sanctuary, since local sanctuaries had been abolished by that time; hence this practice was no longer sacral, but secular. As the organ of hearing, the "ear" may suggest "obedience," as the psalmist comments: "Sacrifice or oblation you wished not, but ears open to obedience you gave me" (Ps. 40:7 [6]). *Shema* (*šemaᶜ* [imperative] "hear"), the first word of the great profession of faith in Judaism (Deut. 6:4–5), is the customary term denoting "to obey." "If a male slave has said to his master, 'You are not my master,' his master shall prove him to be his slave and cut off his ear" (Code of Hammurabi 282).

The situation of *ʾāmāh* "female slave," in v. 7 is quite different; as the concubine of her master, she is not liberated after six years. This distinction, later abrogated by the Deuteronomic law (Deut. 15:12–18), "may rest on the view that only the man is a person, while the woman on the other hand is a possession" (Noth 1962:177). However, if the female slave is given in marriage, specific regulations are to be observed (vv. 8–11). As Noth (1962:179) remarks, she is no longer considered a "thing," but now has limited rights as a spouse. If the master grows tired of her, he may not simply return her to the status of slave but may allow another Israelite to marry her, that is, "he shall let her be redeemed" (*hepdah,* v. 8).

Deuteronomy 15:12–18

The Deuteronomic Code encompasses chapters 12–26. The present text from Deuteronomy appears to be a more humane version of the slave laws of Exodus 21:1–12, characterized by generosity and compassion; for example, by supplying provisions to manumitted slaves. Moshe Weinfeld (1972:291) remarks that "the book of Deuteronomy shows a particularly humanistic attitude toward women." The principal concern of the Deuteronomic author is not the law itself, but its inherent "religio-moral force" (Weinfeld 1972:3). Many of the ethical laws in Deuteronomy have no parallels in the remainder of the Pentateuch. Where they do exist, the implications of Deuteronomic law are more humanistic (Weinfeld 1972:282–97). The contrasts between Exod. 21:1–11 and Deut. 15:12–18 are a relevant example. In his chapter, "Slavery and Humanity," Finley insists "on a sharp distinction between more or less humane treatment of individual slaves by individual masters and the inhumanity of slavery as an institution" (1998:190).

Verse 12—The equality of the Hebrew man (*hāᶜibrî*) and the Hebrew woman (*hāᶜibrîyâ*), both included under *ʾāḥ* "brother" in a general sense, is evident in this verse. *ʾāḥ* signifies a member of the community; *ᶜibrî* "Hebrew" refers to a fellow Israelite, as the parallel *ʾāḥîkā* "your brother" illustrates. "The slave of Deuteronomy is regarded as a citizen, a brother (*ʾāḥ*) who only sells his service, but not his person, to the master" (Weinfeld 1972:282). *ʾādôn* "master" does not appear in the Deuteronomic slave law since the slave is considered the "brother" of the slave owner. The duration of service in Deuteronomy, unlike Exodus, applies to both a male and a female debt-slave and is specified as six years; afterwards "let him go free (*ḥopšî*)." The human quality of the Deuteronomist is demonstrated by the choice of the verb *šlḥ*, suggesting that manumission is obligatory on the part of the master, whereas *yēṣēʾ* in Exod. 21:2 implies the slave's right to manumission (Weinfeld 1972:282).

Verse 13—The Deuteronomic law adds "don't send him away empty-handed (*rêqām*)." This ordinance is an innovation and, at the same time, an indication of the generous spirit of Deuteronomy. Its purpose was to smooth the transition from slavery to freedom. There is, of course, a precedent: "I [Yahweh] will even make the Egyptians so well-disposed toward this people that, when you leave, you will not go empty-handed (*rêqām*). Every woman shall ask her neighbor and her house guest for silver and gold articles for clothing to put on your sons and daughters" (Exod. 3:21–22).

Verse 14—"bounteous gifts," derived from *ʿānaq* "to furnish liberally," is related to *ʿanāq* "necklace," whence the verb form "to surround as a necklace," as the psalmist reproaches: "So pride surrounds them as a necklace (*ʿanāq*)" (Ps. 73:6).

Verse 15—The Deuteronomist appeals to the age-old belief: "Remember you too were slaves in Egypt, and Yahweh, your God, ransomed (*pādâ*) you." This is the motivation for the provisions in vv. 12–15.

Verses 16–17—If the slave prefers to remain in the service of the master for life (*ʿebed ʿōlām*) because he loves (*ʾāhab*) him, then he will thrust an awl through his ear into the door, "and he shall then be your slave forever" (v. 17). This ritual bears close resemblance to that in Exod. 21:6, except (as noted) Deut. 15:17 makes no reference to the ratification ritual being performed before God (*hāʾelohîm*), that is, in the local sanctuary (since there was none) close by the door or the doorpost.

Verse 18—The six-year service of the slave was the equivalent to twice (*mišne*) the hired laborer's salary, that is, the slave works twice as hard as the hired laborer. Commentators have offered a variety of opinions about *mišne*, but the most convincing, based on his research, is that of James Lindenberger who settles for "double" (1991:479–82). The sense of the verse is: "It shall not seem hard to you . . . for he has served you six years, and has been worth *twice as much* to you as a hired servant."

Leviticus 25:39–55

The Holiness Code, which is utopian in its vision, consists of Leviticus 17–26.

Verses 39–43—Scholars comment on the "anti-slavery ideal" of Leviticus. The law forbade the enslavement of one Israelite to another. The reason is stated parenthetically in vv. 42 and 55: "Since those whom I brought out of the land of Egypt are my slaves (*ʿabāday*), and they shall not be sold as slaves to anyone." If poverty drives a "brother" (*ʾāḥ*, a member of the Israelite community) into slavery, "do not make him work as a slave (*ʿavodat ʿebed*)" (v. 39), but as a "wage earner" (*śākîr*), or an "economic dependent" (*tôšāb*) until the Jubilee Year (derived from the *yōbēl* "ram's horn" blown at the beginning of the Jubilee Year). The Law of Jubilee, a part of the Holiness Code, occurring every fifty years, espouses the ideals of social justice. Roland de Vaux described it as a "Utopian law" (1997:177) that may never have been implemented, and many scholars agree with his observation.

Verses 44–46—Israelites, male and female, were permitted to possess slaves provided they were acquired from foreign nations. These slaves were obligated to slavery for life. Israelite slaves were to be accorded better treatment than the slaves of neighboring people.

Verses 47–55—Israelites who sold themselves to resident foreigners still possessed the right of redemption (*geʾūllâ*) by relatives or friends, or they may redeem themselves. The foreign master is to treat each as a *śākîr*, and never harshly.

Jeremiah 34:8–22

This pericope was largely influenced by Deut. 15:12–18; the stylistic parallels are compelling. Direct dependence of Jer. 34:8–22 on Exod. 2:1–11 is out of the question. Several times the Israelite slave is denominated *ʾāḥ* "brother" in Jer. 34:9, 14, 17, corresponding precisely to the dictum in Deut. 15:12.

Zedekiah (Mattaniah), the last king of Judah (597–586 B.C.E.), ruled as a Babylonian puppet during the final decade of Judah's existence. In 594 B.C.E he convoked in Jerusalem an anti-Babylonian conference of neighboring states. Egypt may have been responsible for fomenting anti-Babylonian feelings in Zedekiah. Concluding a treaty with the ineffectual Pharaoh Hophra (Apries) of the Twenty-sixth Dynasty, Zedekiah rebelled against Babylon. Invading Judah in 589 B.C.E., Hophra temporarily supported the southern kingdom, but then retreated. In his early reign, Nebuchadrezzar II made annual incursions into Judah. Having besieged Jerusalem in 597 B.C.E., he departed Jerusalem to check the Egyptian invasion. Afterward (589 B.C.E.), Nebuchadrezzar II laid siege to Jerusalem a second time, but the city was able to withstand the assault for a year and a half. Subsequently, Nebuchadrezzar II, a capable but cruel ruler, suppressed the rebellion, and only the fortified cities of Lachish, Azekah, and Jerusalem remained standing (Jer. 34:7). In 586 B.C.E. Nebuchadrezzar destroyed and decimated Jerusalem.[1]

Towards the end of 588 B.C.E., Zedekiah declared "a proclamation of liberty" (*liqroʾ derôr*), a general manumission of (his) male slave(s) (*ʿabdô*) and (his) female slave(s) (*šipḥātô*), formalized in a ceremony before Yahweh (Jer. 34:15), during Nebuchadrezzar II's siege of Jerusalem. Among the reasons for this emancipation, scholars suggest the following: the rigors of the siege; inability or unwillingness to provide sustenance for the slaves; the Egyptian army had

[1] Ziony Zevit (1969:74–77), expanding on the research of Jonas Greenfield concerning *ʿebed* as a technical term for "vassal," proposes to render the phrase *melek bābel ʿabdî* in Jer. 25:9 as "the king of Babylon, my *vassal*."

weakened the Babylonian siege temporarily; and/or to augment the number of combatants.

Both Jer. 34:13 and Deut. 15:15 relate the manumission of the slaves to the redemption of the ancestors from Egyptian captivity. Jer. 34:14, a paraphrase of Deut. 15:1, 12, alludes to the conditions of Yahweh's covenant (*berît*) about freeing Israelite slaves after six years, as delineated in Deut. 15:12–18. The ancestors had reneged on this agreement, but Jeremiah's contemporaries were adhering to it. However, when the danger appeared to have passed, they reinstated slavery. Yahweh, through Jeremiah, delivered a menacing judgment by alluding to an ancient rite of ratifying a covenant, as described in Gen. 15:10–17. The Hebrew idiom is *kārat berît*, "to cut a covenant." Abram (Abraham) cut in two a heifer, a goat, and a ram. Afterward a smoking fire-pot and a flaming torch, both representing the Deity, passed between the pieces. Violators of the covenant would incur the same fate as the bisected animals (Jer. 34:18). Parallels to this covenant rite appear among the Amorites, who slew donkeys, goats, and puppies.

Jer. 34:20 is taken directly from Deut. 28:26; the corpses of those who violated the covenant will remain unburied, and "their corpses shall become food for the birds of the air and the wild animals of the earth" (Jer. 34:20).

Slavery in the New Testament

The society of the Greco-Roman world was in general a slave economy. "Greco-Roman society had come to depend on persons in slavery as the basic labor force, as essential components of the imperial economy" (Bartchy 1992:69). Slavery was integral to the society of the Roman Empire, so the New Testament authors did not challenge it. "In all Greek or Roman establishments larger than the family unit . . . the *permanent* work force was composed of slaves" (Finley 1998:149).

Raymond Collins observes that the institution of slavery in the Hellenistic world "was an accepted part of the social and economic fabric of the times" (Collins 1999:278). Florentinus, a second-century lawyer, summarized the doctrine of the Roman law concerning slavery as "an institution of the *ius gentium* (law of nations), whereby a man is, contrary to nature, subjected to the ownership of another" (de Vaux 1980:856). In the Greek tradition, slaves were considered inferior by nature, and this conviction is clear in Herodotus, Plato, and Aristotle.

In the New Testament, as in the Hebrew Bible, nowhere is there a sign of disapproval for the institution of slavery. "Paul, in the final analysis, does not present a polemical argument against slavery as an ideology or institution in the Roman world" (Harrill 2006:30). In interpreting literature (especially the Bible), it is imperative to bear in mind the worldview of the biblical authors; it was far removed from present-day political, economic, civil, and social values. The enslavement of debtors was a wide-scale phenomenon in Palestine, well illustrated in the parable of the unforgiving servant (Matt. 18:23–34). Some English-language translators of the Bible tendentiously use "servants" in place of "slaves," despite its inaccuracy, as their way of "softening" the concept.

The common Greek verbs for slavery are *douleuō*, "to serve as a slave," and *diakoneō*, "to render service to others." *Douleuō* in the New Testament concentrates on the Christian's submission to Jesus as Lord. Slaves, although not their own persons, fared quite well, nor was slavery in antiquity very oppressive, despite the horror stories to the contrary as portrayed in the modern media. In the Roman society, in contrast to the Greek world, slaves awaited manumission in the course of ten to twenty years. The masters provided food, clothing, and housing; just as in Old Testament times, so too in New Testament times, slaves were looked upon as members of the household and shared in religious festivals. Christian slaves were called to serve their owners faithfully, just as their masters were expected to treat them well. "Slaves, obey your human masters with the reverence, the awe, and the sincerity you owe to Christ. . . . Masters, act in a similar way toward your slaves" (Eph. 6:5–9; also, Col. 3:22; 1 Tim. 6:1–2). For the most part, slavery was domestic, focusing on the household, not on the plantation. Most of the slaves were laborers; among them were artisans, educators, and physicians.

Epictetus was born into Roman slavery about 55 C.E.; after his release he settled in Rome. He laments that the lot of the *eleutheros* ("freed person") was worse than the state of the slave: "Someone else kept me in clothes, and shoes, and supplied me with food, and nursed me when I was sick; I served him in only a few matters. But now, miserable man that I am, what suffering is mine, who am a slave to several instead of one" (*Discourses* 4.1.37).

1 Corinthians 7:21–24

This pericope, a rhetorical digression, is the earliest Christian text pertaining to slavery, and also Paul's most direct discussion of the slave status. However, "the correct translation of 1 Cor. 7:21 remains to this day an open question." (Harrill 1995: 108). John Chrysostom (ca. 354–407 C.E.) was the first exegete to consider the meaning of this text in terms of slavery. Before the modern period, most commentators adopted Chrysostom's preference for "use slavery" (below). Verse 21b is a famous *crux interpretum* in the New Testament. Harrill comments that when the translators of the NRSV changed the Revised Standard Version's rendition of 1 Cor. 7:21, this was but another example of the "continuing lack of scholarly consensus" (Harrill 1995:108). The NRSV translates "use slavery" in the text and places the alternative "use freedom" in a footnote; whereas the RSV had translated "use freedom" in the text and the alternative "use slavery" in a footnote. The apodosis *mallon chrēsai* (lit. "use all the more") is elliptical; the verb lacks a direct object. It is this ellipsis in 1 Cor. 7:21 that has been the source of the constant confusion. What is the logical completion of the "rather use . . ." (*mallon chrēsai* . . .)? The Greek text itself does not present difficulties; but it is the "absence of the words needed to complete the verse's final phrase, *mallon chrēsai*" (Bartchy 1985:7ff.). The adverb *mallon* means "all the more"; the usual meaning of *chrēsai* is "to make use of." Harrill (1995:108) summarizes the meanings of *mallon chrēsai* (aorist imperative of *chraomai*) proposed by the commentators: (1) "rather use freedom," (2) "indeed use slavery," and (3) "by all means (as a freedman/woman) live according to (God's calling)." In my opinion, *eleutheria* ("freedom") is the implied antecedent.

Bartchy's conclusion regarding 1 Cor. 7:21: "Were you a slave when you were called? Don't worry about it. But if, indeed, your owner should manumit you, by all means (now as a freedman) live according to God's call" (Bartchy 1985:159). Collins translates 1 Cor. 7:21: "But if you really are able to be free, take advantage." S. R. Llewelyn, and other modern commentators, argue in favor of "use freedom," while there are several who espouse "use slavery," concurring with John Chrysostom "whose view prevailed nearly universally up to the reformation" (Harrill 1995:104). Llewelyn (1992:69), after analyzing the *crux*, concludes: "It is apparent that the use of ellipsis at 1 Cor. 7:21 must imply the pleonastic reading *mallon chrēsai tē eleutheria* . . . Accordingly, Paul advised the believing slave, when presented with the opportunity to acquire freedom, to avail himself of it." Briefly, "In 1 Cor. 7:21, the Apostle exhorts slaves who are offered manumission *indeed* to avail themselves of the opportunity and to *use freedom*" (Harrill 1995:127).

The literary device of *inclusio* or envelope construction demarcates 1 Cor. 7:17–24, a discrete literary unit, from the remaining text of 1 Corinthians. The following three elements—*ho theos* "God," *kaleō* "call," and *hekastos* "each"—appear in both 7:17 and 7:24 (Collins 1999:274). In sum, *God's call* is directed to *each* Christian individually.

At the time of one's "call," circumcised or uncircumcised, he should retain his particular condition. *Peritetmēmenos tis eklēthē, mē epispasthō.* "Was someone called after he had been circumcised? He should not try to hide his circumcision" (1 Cor. 7:18). In Greco-Roman culture, circumcision was looked upon as abhorrent. Participants in Greek gymnasia and Roman baths exercised naked, where Jews, with their exposed glans, would be ridiculed. To participate in the games in the Greek gymnasia, some Jews simulated a foreskin by practicing epispasm (Gr. *epispasmos* from *epispaomai*, lit. "draw to oneself" (Heb. *mešikat* ᶜ*orlâ*, "drawing down the foreskin"). This is the opposite of circumcision. It involves the painful stretching of the vestigial prepuce to form a fabricated foreskin (King 2006:53–55). In the Bible, "Philistines" and "Gentiles" are synonymous terms for "uncircumcised."

Letter to Philemon

Scholarly opinion is not unanimous about many details surrounding the Letter to Philemon, among them its date and place of composition. The letter emanated from prison, but where was Paul imprisoned at the time? Speculations encompass Rome, Caesarea Maritima, and Ephesus, the latter being the more plausible, considering the distance of Ephesus from Colossae where Philemon resided, and with him Onesimus, a slave of the household (Fitzmyer 2000: 10–11). Apparently Paul had converted Philemon, an affluent young man and slave owner who had met Paul in his travels.

After evaluating several possible explanations about the occasion of the Letter to Philemon, Joseph Fitzmyer (2000:17–18) adopts the view that Onesimus, Paul's convert to Christianity (v. 10), who had been in "domestic trouble" (no mention of flight) with Philemon, approached Paul to intervene on his behalf, so that he might return to service in the slave master's household and there reside once again in peace and harmony. In the Letter to Philemon, Paul intercedes for Onesimus, entreating that he be restored as a member of Philemon's household, "no longer as a slave but . . . as a beloved brother (*adelphos agapētos*) (v. 16), without recrimination. Paul would have preferred to retain Onesimus as his coworker in evangelization, but at the same time he acknowledged Philemon's prior right to the services of his slave Onesimus (vv. 13–14). "Nowhere in any of his letters does Paul try to change the existing social structure, which reckoned with slavery, perhaps because he realized the futility of attempting to change the system, which was so much part of the world in which he lived" (Fitzmyer 2000:35).

In conclusion, it is my hope that this eclectic treatment of a vastly complex subject may encourage others to continue the much-needed research on one or several components of slavery as an institution. For my part, in the words of the eminent biblical scholar Hermann Gunkel: "Ich bin zu Ende, beginne ich."

Bibliography

Bartchy, S. S.
1985 *Mallon chrēsai: First-Century Slavery and the Interpretation of 1 Corinthians 7:21*. Atlanta: Scholars.
1992 Slavery (Greco-Roman). In *The Anchor Bible Dictionary*, ed. D. N. Freedman, 6:65–73. New York: Doubleday.

Childs, B.
1974 *The Book of Exodus: A Critical, Theological Commentary*. Old Testament Library. Philadelphia: Westminster.

Dandamayev, M.
1992 Slavery (Old Testament). In *The Anchor Bible Dictionary*, ed. D. N. Freedman, 6:62–65. New York: Doubleday.

de Vaux, R.
1997 *Ancient Israel: Its Life and Institutions*. Grand Rapids, Mich.: Eerdmans.
1980 Slavery. *Encyclopaedia Britannica* (15th ed.) 16: 853–57.

Finley, M.
1998 *Ancient Slavery and Modern Ideology*. Princeton, N.J.: Markus Wiener.

Fitzmyer, J.
2000 *The Letter to Philemon: A New Translation with Introduction and Commentary*. Anchor Bible 34C. New York: Doubleday.

Greenfield, J.
1967 Some Aspects of Treaty Terminology in the Bible. In *The Fourth World Congress of Jewish Studies: Papers*, 2:117–19. Jerusalem: World Union of Jewish Studies.

Harrill, J. A.
1995 *The Manumission of Slaves in Early Christianity*. Tubingen: J. C. B. Mohr.
2006 *Slaves in the New Testament: Literary, Social, and Moral Dimensions*. Philadelphia: Fortress.

Jackson, B.
1988 Biblical Laws of Slavery: A Comparative Approach. In *Slavery and Other Forms of Unfree Labour*, ed. L. J. Archer, 86–101. London: Routledge.

King, P.
2006 Circumcision—Who Did It, Who Didn't and Why. *BAR* 32/4:48–55.

Lemche, N.
1975 The "Hebrew Slave": Comments on the Slave Law Ex xxi 2–11. *VT* 25:129–44.

Lindenberger, J.
1991 How Much for a Hebrew Slave? The Meaning of *mišneh* in Deut. 15:18. *JBL* 110:479–82.

Lipinski, E.
1976 L'"Esclave Hébreu." *VT* 26:120–24.

Llewelyn, S. R.
1992 "If You Can Gain Your Freedom": Manumission and 1 Cor. 7:21. In *New Documents Illustrating Early Christianity*, ed. S. R. Llewelyn et al., 6:63–70. Sydney, Australia: The Ancient History Documentary Research Centre, Macquarie University.

Mendelsohn, I.
1978 *Slavery in the Ancient Near East: A Comparative Study of Slavery in Babylonia, Assyria, Syria, and Palestine from Middle of the Third Millennium to the End of the First Millennium*. Westport, Conn.: Greenwood.

Michell, H.
1957 *The Economics of Ancient Greece*. 2d ed. Cambridge: Heffer.

Noth, Martin
1962 *Exodus: A Commentary*. Translated by J. S. Bowden. Old Testament Library. Philadelphia: Westminster.

Ploeg, J. P. M. van der
1972 Slavery in the Old Testament. VTSup 22:72–87. Leiden: Brill.

Weinfeld, M.
1972 *Deuteronomy and the Deuteronomic School*. Oxford: Clarendon.

Zevit, Z.
1969 The Use of עֶבֶד as a Diplomatic Term in Jeremiah. *JBL* 88:74–77.

27. Ethnic Identity in Biblical Edom, Israel, and Midian: Some Insights from Mortuary Contexts in the Lowlands of Edom

by Thomas E. Levy

Conflict with and resistance to other ethnic groups can be one of the primary catalysts for the formation and maintenance of ethnic identity. In this short contribution, it is suggested that the crystallization of Edomite identity occurred in the crucible of conflict with neighboring tribal groups, such as the Israelites and Midianites. The data for testing this hypothesis come from the recent excavations of a tenth-century B.C.E. Iron Age cemetery in the region known historically as the lowlands of Edom in southern Jordan.

Introduction

In beginning this discussion of Edomite ethnogenesis, it is important to try to identify when in the Near Eastern historical sources it is possible to identify a geographical region known as Edom, and Edomites as the name of a people. It will then be possible to suggest a number of hypotheses that link our recent excavation of a tenth-century B.C.E. cemetery in southern Jordan with some suggestions concerning Edomite ethnogenesis. However, as we are especially interested in understanding the processes that led to ethnogenesis, we must look deeper in time, earlier than the sixth–seventh centuries B.C.E., when we know that an Edomite state, with its own script, palace architecture, and other accoutrements of the state were in place (Bienkowski 2002; Crowell 2004; Porter 2004).

The earliest reference to Edom comes from Egyptian sources dating to the late thirteenth century B.C.E., in particular, in Papyrus Anastasi VI. This document contains a report from an Egyptian frontier official who served during the reign of Pharaoh Merneptah (ca. 1224–1214 B.C.E.)—the same Merneptah whose stele discovered at Thebes by Sir Flinders Petrie in 1896 preserves the earliest mention of the ancient ethnic group known as "Israel" (Shanks et al. 1992). With regard to the region of Edom, Papyrus Anastasi VI states: "We have finished letting the Bedouin tribes of Edom pass the Fortress [of] Merne-Ptah Hotep-hir-Maat—life, prosperity, health—which is (in) Tjeku, to the pools of Per-Atum . . . to keep them alive and to keep their cattle alive."

There are other fourteenth- to twelfth-century B.C.E. Egyptian sources that mention Edom, and also Seir—another, perhaps earlier, name for Edom. For example, in one of the Late Bronze Age Amarna letters (mid-fourteenth century), King Abdi-heba of Jerusalem wrote to the Egyptian Pharaoh Amenhotep III: "The land of the king is lost: there is war against us, as far as the lands of Seir (and) as far as Gath-Carmel!" (EA 288; see Pritchard 1969:488).

Recently, Yuval Goren, Israel Finkelstein, and Nadav Naʾaman (Goren et al. 2004:267) carried out a petrographic analysis of this Amarna tablet and demonstrated that it was a Jerusalem-made tablet from the central hill country. This early fourteenth-century B.C.E. reference to Seir provides extrabiblical textual confirmation that the name Seir was in use in the eastern Mediterranean region even before the biblical sources.

During the mid-twelfth century B.C.E., there is additional proof that Seir remained a geographical location well known to the ancient Egyptians. For example, in Papyrus Harris I, Ramesses III (1193–1162 B.C.E.) claims: "I have destroyed the people of Seir among the Shosu tribes. I have laid waste their tents, with their people, their belongings, and likewise their cattle without number" (see Albright 1944: 229; Giveon 1971:134–37).

While these early Egyptian historical sources tell us that the inhabitants of Seir/Edom were "Shosu/ Shasu," a nomadic people, they do not tell us what the people of Seir/Edom actually called themselves. According to Ward (1972:56–59), "Shasu" probably derives either from a Northwest Semitic root meaning "plunderers" or an Egyptian word meaning "wanderers." The term appears only in Egyptian sources dating to the period 1500–1100 B.C.E. It refers to both a people and a territory and thus did not designate an ethnic group but rather a social class (Ward 1992: 1165). Thus, Shasu is similar to the generic Arabic term Bedouin or "pastoral nomad." However, these Egyptian documents offer a rich contribution to historical reconstruction because they confirm that the Northwest Semitic term "Edom" (Avishur 1996) was already in use in the region during the late thirteenth century B.C.E. and that the social-subsistence base of the inhabitants of this desert region was rooted in pastoral nomadism. But the problem remains—when do the people, the Edomites, appear in the historical records?

Background: The Hebrew Bible and Early Edom

Unlike neighboring Moab, which produced at least one historical source, the Moabite Stone (Harrison and Barlow 2005; Routledge 2004), there are no extant historical records from ancient Edom. Thus, without historical sources of their own, the Edomites, as a separate ethnic group, appear earliest in the Hebrew Bible. As Bartlett (1992:288) points out, some information may be gleaned from Genesis 36 concerning the early inhabitants of Edom, but in its current form the information comes from a rather late Israelite editor of the sixth century B.C.E. In the Biblical accounts about the eponym "Esau who is Edom" (Gen. 36:1), the Edomites are related to the Hebrews because Esau was the grandson of Abraham the Hebrew and was the son of Isaac. As the twin brother of Jacob-Israel, the relationship between the two peoples was close but antagonistic. According to Avishur (1996:370) it is possible to distinguish earlier and later elements in the ethnic composition of Edom. Thus, in the Deuteronomic tradition about the ancient settlers of Edom before the advent of the Hebrews, it is asserted: "Seir was formerly inhabited by the Horites; but the descendants of Esau dispossessed them, wiping them out and settling in their place" (Deut. 2:12).

According to E. A. Knauf (1992:288), this so-called displacement of the local Horite population by the Edomites mirrors the Israelite displacement or conquest of the Canaanites presented by the Deuteronomistic school in the Book of Joshua. Gen. 14:6 assumes that there is no difference between the regions of Edom and Seir, something that Knauf disagrees with. Knauf argues that it is important to distinguish "Edom" and "Seir" as separate areas in southern Transjordan, with the "sons of Esau" inhabiting Edom, which he locates on the agricultural land of the Transjordanian plateau, and the Horites occupying the wooded mountain slopes. By taking this position, however, Knauf ignores the possibility of multiple models of "Edomite settlement," just as there is a range of models that can be used to explain "Israelite settlement" (Shanks et al. 1992) based on the different narratives of Israel's relations with the Canaanites as portrayed in Joshua and Judges. However, as the extrabiblical Egyptian sources noted earlier stress, Seir and Edom are indeed terms for the same general region of southern Transjordan and occasionally, parts of the Negev (Kitchen 1992). Thus, Knauf's idea that "Edom" and "Seir" were different "microzones" in southern Jordan loses credence. In addition, by locating Seir on the "wooded slope" of the Edomite plateau, the lowlands of Edom—the copper-rich Faynan district—are left out of Knauf's model.

According to Avishur (1996:372), Genesis 36 indicates that prior to Edom's conquest by David, two periods can be distinguished: the "period of the chiefs" and the "period of the kings." This parallels the division of Israelite history into the "period of the judges" and the "period of the monarchy." If we focus on the "period of the chiefs" (Heb. *ʾallufim*), the tribal structure of Edom also parallels that of Israel during the "period of the judges," as well as nomadic pastoral chiefdoms in general (Sahlins 1968). While Genesis 36 mentions only 11 chiefs of Edom, Avishur (ibid.) points out that a twelfth name is found in the Septuagint, but left out of the Masoretic text. Marshall Sahlins (ibid, p. 24), a noted cultural anthropologist, has used the conical clan model, based on the Polynesian type of complex chiefdom, to describe a wide range of complex chiefdom-level societies, including the ancient Israelites, societies in Central Asia and parts of Africa, as well as the Celtic peoples. The twelve-fold chiefdom organization of conical clans is characteristic of a number of ethnic groups known from the Hebrew Bible, namely, the Nahorites (Gen. 22:20–24), the Ishmaelites (Gen. 25:13–15), the Israelites, and the Edomites. This conical clan social organization is typical of Near Eastern nomadic societies both in the ethnographic (Barfield 1993; Musil 1927) and historical record (Faust 2006; Levy and Holl 2002), and provided it the primary crucible in which Edomite and Israelite ethnogenesis crystallized.

Anthropology and Ethnic Identity

Now that we have outlined the tribal nature of Late Bronze Age and early Iron Age social organization in northwestern Arabia and southern Jordan, it is necessary to define what is meant by ethnic identity. For anthropologist George De Vos (1995), ethnicity refers to the "self-perceived inclusion of those who hold in common a set of traditions not shared by others with whom they are in contact." Some of these traditions include: "folk" religious beliefs and practices, language, aesthetic cultural patterns (such as tastes in food, dance tradition, styles of clothing, and definitions of physical beauty), a shared sense of historical continuity, common ancestry or place of origin, territoriality, and economic specialization. Many of these variables have an archaeological signature and will be touched on in relation to the Iron Age cemetery at Wadi Fidan 40 in southern Jordan.

Operating with this understanding of ethnicity, we can now look at ethnogenesis, the process by which ethnic groups are formed. According to the *Macmillan Dictionary of Anthropology* (Seymour-Smith 1986), ethnogenesis refers to "the construction of group identity and resuscitation or persistence of cultural features of a people undergoing rapid and radical change. It may also be used to refer to a new ethnic system emerging out of an amalgamation of other groups." Underlying this concept of ethnic formation in the context of rapid cultural change is the notion of resistance to "the other"—whatever the level of social organization (band, tribe, chiefdom, state). One of the most recent examples of ethnogensis may be the crystallization of Palestinian ethnic identity in the early 1960s following their resistance to Zionism. When the Zionist project began in Palestine during the late nineteenth century, the local Arab inhabitants viewed themselves as "Arabs" and as part of the greater Arab people. It took over sixty years of resistance to and conflict with the neighboring Jewish population before the local Arab population defined themselves as a separate ethnic group. Thus, as shown in A. Faust's (2006) study of ancient Israelite ethnogenesis, resistance is indeed a key factor that promotes ethnogenesis.

Ethnic Diversity in the Iron Age Southern Levant

As indicated above, during the Late Bronze to early Iron Age, the Hebrew Bible and other ancient texts refer to a wide range of ethnic groups in the southern Levant. These include Canaanites, Amorites, Hittities, Egyptians, Perizzites, Hivites, Horites, Israelites, Jebusites, Amalekites, Midianites, Philistines, and Shasu. By the tenth–eighth centuries B.C.E., many of these ethnic groups evolved into secondary "ethnic" mini-states such as Aram, Phoenicia, Philistia, Judah, Israel, Ammon, Moab, and Edom. The timing and processes that led to the emergence of each of these mini-states are contentious issues (Joffe 2002; Levy and Higham 2005; Routledge 2004) that are beyond the scope of this paper. However, as noted above, we must look deeper in time, earlier than the sixth and seventh centuries B.C.E. when we know that an Edomite state, with its own script, palace architecture, and other accoutrements of the state were in place.

There are a number of reasons why the best place to begin investigating Edomite ethnogenesis is the Iron Age cemetery at Wadi Fidan 40 (WFD 40). First, the closest that archaeologists, historians, bioanthropologists, and molecular scientists can get to the actual people who lived in a historic region are the human skeletal remains found in mortuary contexts (Pearson 2000). Following the 2004 excavations in this cemetery, 235 individuals were recovered from 172 distinct burial contexts (Levy, Najjar, Muniz et al. 2005:473). Second, a new suite of radiocarbon dates from the WFD 40 cemetery securely place it in the tenth century B.C.E., close in time to some of the Egyptian references to Edom/Seir (Kitchen 1992), as well as the earliest poems in the Hebrew Bible (Freedman 1980) that relate to this region such as the "Song of the Sea" (Exodus 15) and the "Song of Deborah" (Judges 5). Third, as the anthropological record indicates that the notion of "territoriality" among social groups is marked by their establishment of separate cemeteries in the landscape (Chapman et al. 1981), the large Iron Age cemetery at WFD 40 provides an ideal locale to investigate the growth of the buried population's control of this part of Edom. And, fourth, any grave offerings found in the WFD 40 cemetery can provide important clues about the socioreligious beliefs and identity of the buried population. Taken together, these factors indicate the great potential of this cemetery for investigating the nature of ethnogenesis in Iron Age Edom (although the present paper should be viewed as a prelude to a more in-depth study).[1]

Significance of the WFD 40 Cemetery Excavations

Among the most notable aspects of the Iron Age cemetery at Wadi Fidan 40 are the stylistic differences of this mortuary site (linked to pastoral nomads) and contemporary tombs in Judah, Ammon, and other neighboring regions (Bloch-Smith 1992; Faust 2004; Tubb et al. 1997; Yassine 1983). Earlier studies explain in detail the archaeological correlates that connect this cemetery to a pastoral nomadic community and its probable links to the Shasu nomads (Levy, Adams, and Muniz 2004; Levy, Adams, and Shafiq 1999). To date, WFD 40 may be the most comprehensively excavated Iron Age pastoral nomad cemetery in northwestern Arabia and southern Jordan. Thus, it provides a stepping stone for examining the formation of the pastoral nomadic population in this part of Jordan.

The WFD 40 cemetery was initially probed by R. B. Adams (1991), who linked the cemetery to the Early Bronze Age village of Wadi Fidan 4 located on the opposite bank of the Wadi Fidan (Adams and Genz 1995; Levy, Adams, and Najjar 1999). The first large-scale excavations at WFD 40 were carried out

[1] My student Marc Beherec is using the mortuary data from the UCSD–Department of Antiquities of Jordan Wadi Fidan 40 cemetery excavations for his doctoral research on this topic at the University of California, San Diego.

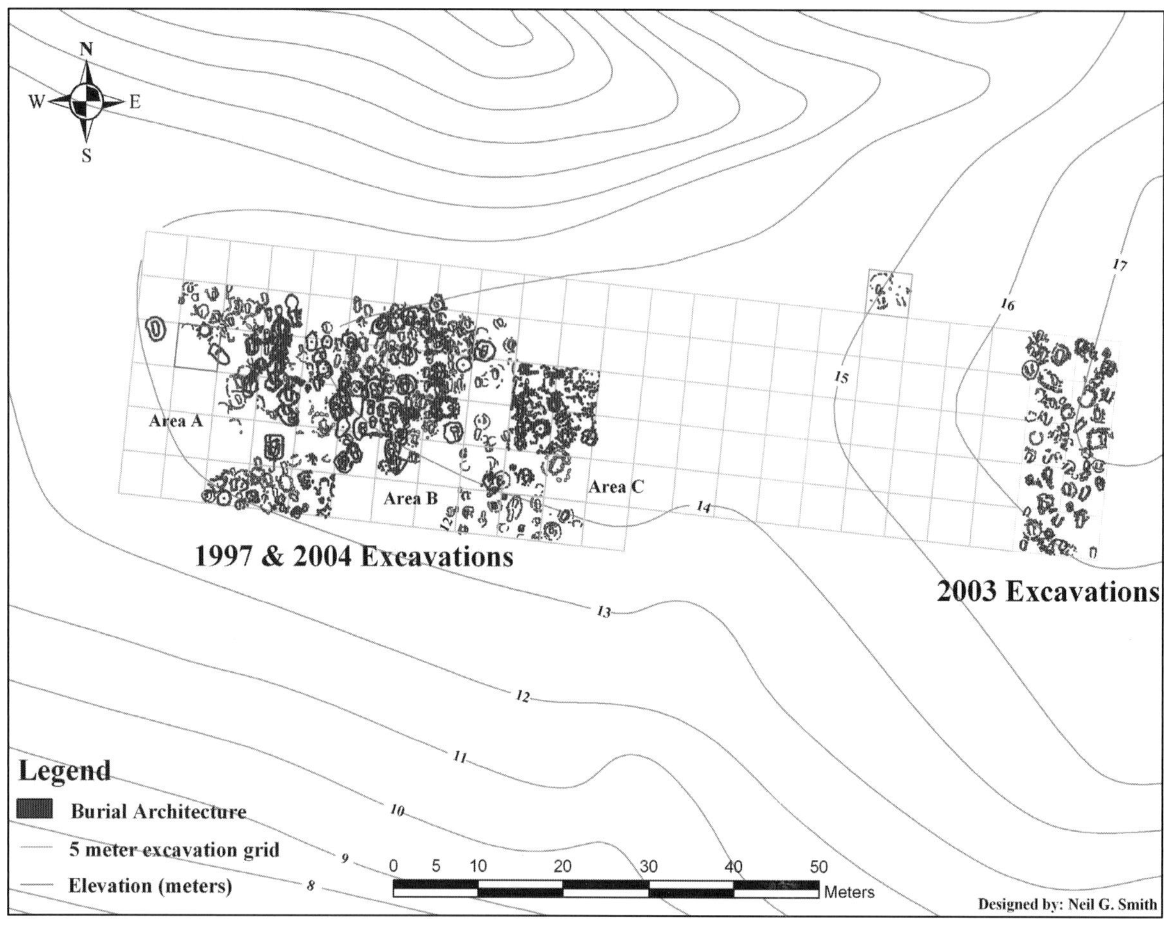

Figure 1. Plan of the excavated tombs in the Wadi Fidan 40 Iron Age cemetery

by T. E. Levy and Adams in 1997, when 62 circular tombs were excavated (Levy, Adams, and Shafiq 1999) and the site was subsequently dated to the Iron Age. Jewelry, other burial goods, and a single radiocarbon date taken from a pomegranate found buried in Tomb 92 (Beta-111366; 2800±70 B.P., 1 sigma cal. 1015–845 B.C.E.; 2 sigma cal. 1130–815 B.C.E.) placed the cemetery in the Iron Age. In 2003 and 2004, Levy and M. Najjar directed emergency excavations at the site under the auspices of the Department of Antiquities of Jordan that brought the total number of graves excavated in the cemetery to 287.

The tombs typically have a stone circle ca. 1.0–1.8 m in diameter situated ca. 0.80–1.0 m above a well-built stone-lined cist tomb large enough for an extended burial (figures 1 and 2). In many cases, elaborate mortuary structures were built on the site surface among the cemetery tombs, consisting of pavements, rectangular structures, concentric circles with standing stones (figure 5), and other structures. While the western sector of the cemetery and eastern extremity of the cemetery have been extensively sampled, a large portion of the eastern half remains to be investigated (figure 1). In order to date the cemetery more adequately, a series of eight additional high-precision radiocarbon dates were obtained from pomegranates found in tombs exposed in the 2004 excavations. Seven of these dates were from different pomegranate offerings found in a single tomb (no. 59) and at the 95.4% probability level produced an average date of 1010–920 B.C.E. (Levy, Najjar, Muniz, et al. 2005). While more radiocarbon dates are certainly needed, the fact that a corpus of radiocarbon dates was obtained from three different tombs spread over different parts of the cemetery—and all are from stylistically similar tombs characteristic of the entire cemetery sample—suggests that the main use-period of the cemetery was during the tenth century B.C.E. This was confirmed by an Egyptian stamp seal found as a grave offering in Tomb 91 in Area A. According to Stefan Munger (in Levy et al. 2005a:470–71), this type of seal is typical of the transition between Iron Age IB and Iron IIA. In Egyptian terms, this correlates primarily with Dynasty 21 (ca. 1075–945

B.C.E.), with examples found at Tell Abu Hawam, Gezer, Tell el Farᶜah (South), Megiddo, and other sites. The temporal correlation between the Tomb 91 seal and the radiocarbon dates from the cemetery is remarkable and indicates that the majority of burial activities took place during the late Iron I to Iron IIA periods. Extensive surveys within a 5 km radius of Wadi Fidan 40 failed to find any villages or habitation sites in the area and strengthen the interpretation that this cemetery was an important territorial marker for the nomadic inhabitants of the lowlands of Edom.

Summary and Interpretations

The present paper should be viewed as a work in progress because archaeological research on Iron Age Edom is still in its infancy. However, what is becoming increasingly clear from our work in the lowlands of Edom is the importance of conceptualizing the Edomites as one of a number of tribal peoples who emerged out of the ethnic melting pot of northwestern Arabia and southern Jordan toward the end of the Late Bronze Age. This certainly included the Israelites, Edomites, and Midianites. As noted above, the close links between "Esau who is Edom" (Gen. 36:1) and his twin brother Jacob/Israel are well known. The links between the Late Bronze Age and early Iron Age Israelites and the Midianites, whose core territory was situated in the northern Hijaz (Bawden 1983; Parr 1982; Rothenberg 1998; Rothenberg and Glass 1983), were both consanguineous and acrimonious, as were the links between the Israelites and Edomites (Halpern 2001; 2005). In Frank Moore Cross's (1988:55) article "Reuben, First-Born of Jacob," a case is made for close relations between the Israelites and Midianites based on the tradition that Moses married a Midianite woman and tended the flocks of the priest of Midian (Exod. 2:21; 3:13–15), and based on the central role played by the Midianites at Mount Sinai, where the priest of Midian offered sacrifices to Yahweh and instituted a juridical system (Exodus 18). For a variety of reasons, including the fact that the distinctively decorated "Midianite" pottery (also referred to as Hijaz or Qurayyah Ware) is not found in the Sinai Peninsula but is found radiating from the Midianite center at Qurayyah in

Figure 2. Overview of excavations in the Wadi Fidan 40 cemetery (view to north)
Photograph by T. E. Levy

Figure 3. Overview of Tomb 92 found during the 1997 excavations in the Wadi Fidan 40 cemetery

One of the pomegranates found in this tomb produced a radiocarbon date spanning the late eleventh–late ninth centuries B.C.E. (Beta-111366; 2800±70 B.P., 1 σ cal. 1015–845 B.C.E.; 2 σ cal. 1130–815 B.C.E.)

Photograph by T. E. Levy

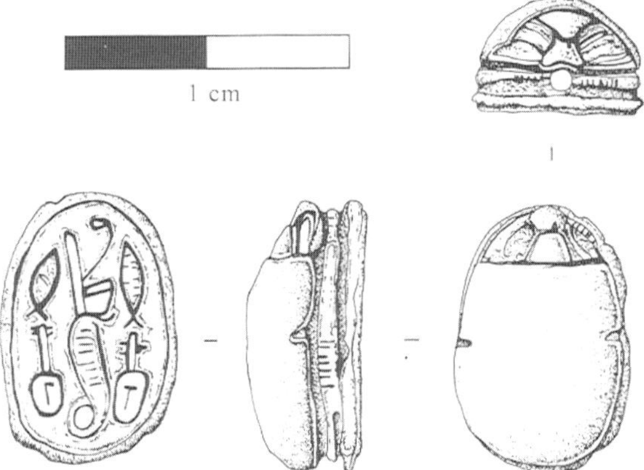

Figure 4. Scarab found in Grave 92, B. 2152 (from Levy, Adams, and Shafiq 1999)

Uraeus with red crown (MB IIB, ca. 1640–1500 B.C.E.). Parallels: Tell el-Ajjul, Lachish, Megiddo Tombs.

Figure 5. Stone circle burial monument with standing stone found in 2004 (Area C, Grave 712)

Photograph by T. E. Levy

Figure 6. Anthropomorphic standing stone found in 2004 (EDM no. 70337, Area A, Basket 3233)

Photograph courtesy of UCSD Levantine Archaeology Laboratory

Figure 7. Egyptian stamp seal with loop handle (Grave 91, Area A)
Photographs courtesy of the UCSD Levantine Archaeology Laboratory

northwestern Saudi Arabia, and throughout southern Jordan and at Timna in southern Israel, Cross argues that Mount Sinai (Horeb) must be sought in southern Edom or northern Midian, not in the Sinai Peninsula.

Our own excavations at Khirbat en-Nahas, some 50 km south of the Dead Sea, provide the northernmost evidence of "Midianite" pottery (figure 8) in the Wadi Araba region that separates modern Israel and Jordan (Levy, Adams, Najjar, et al. 2004). Bearing in mind the problems of linking pottery with distinct ethnic groups, if the known distribution of Midianite pottery is coupled with the biblical traditions associating Yahweh with Edom/Seir, as in the Song of Deborah (Judges 5:4), which proclaims that Yahweh marched from the region of Edom, the case for Mount Sinai being in Edom or the region of Midian makes sense. The idea that the Yahweh tradition is rooted in Edom can be supported by the Late Bronze Age Egyptian records that link the god *yhwꜣ* = *Yahweh* with the Shasu nomads of Edom (Giveon 1971; Levy, Adams, and Muniz 2004; Rainey 1995; Ward 1992). This is important for our study of Edomite ethnogenesis because it brings together some of the archaeological, biblical, and extrabiblical data which indicate that these three chiefdom-level societies—Israel, Edom, and Midian—interacted in meaningful and profound ways in the cauldron of northwestern Arabia and Jordan in the Late Bronze Age and early Iron Age. Thus, competition, conflict, and resistance between these three groups, for reasons not yet elucidated, led to the process of fission so typical of tribal societies, and sparked both Edomite and Israelite ethnogenesis. The Israelite section moved out of Jordan and northwestern Arabia into Canaan (Faust 2006; Shanks et al. 1992), while the Edomite section displaced the local populations (Horites?) of Seir and established their hold on the lowlands of Edom in the vicinity of the copper-rich Faynan district of southern Jordan.

The intensified use of the Iron Age cemetery of Wadi Fidan 40 in the lowlands of Edom during the tenth century B.C.E. can be seen as a major expression of territoriality among this nomadic population following the processes of fission that affected the tribal confederations of northwest Arabia and Jordan earlier in the Late Bronze and early Iron Age. The recent excavations and studies of the radiocarbon dates from

Figure 8. "Midianite" pottery from Khirbat en-Nahas, Jordan (from Levy et al. 2004:876)

the stratified Iron Age site of Khirbat en-Nahas, located some 5 km northeast of WFD 40, illustrate that there is a deep-time Iron Age history in Edom that spans at least the twelfth–ninth centuries B.C.E. (Higham et al. 2005; Levy, Najjar, van der Plicht et al. 2005). At Khirbat en-Nahas, the Qurayya or "Midianite" ware, scarabs, Cypro-Phoenician ceramics, and black burnished juglets may indicate oscillations in interaction throughout this period between Edomites, Phoenicians, Egyptians, Israelites, and Midianites.[2] Excavations in the WFD 40 Cemetery suggest that by the tenth century B.C.E. there was a large nomadic population in the lowlands with its own ethnic markers such as circular mortuary monuments, cist graves (figures 1–3), and burial practices. Some of these rituals included placement of the deceased in leather shrouds (Levy et al. 1999), special burial offerings using pomegranates, and the placement of highly abstract anthropomorphic standing stones (Heb. *maṣṣēbôt*) with stylized nose and ear features (figure 6). In the absence of clearly defined ranking of burial monuments or grave offerings (figure 1), the Wadi Fidan 40 cemetery seems to reflect the same type of segmentary social organization, perhaps according to a conical-clan level of social integration as implied in the "Song of the Sea," which states that chiefs ruled in Edom (Exod. 15:15) at the end of the Late Bronze Age—an organizational pattern that may have extended into the tenth century B.C.E. The Egyptian scarabs and stamp seal found at Khirbat en-Nahas and the Wadi Fidan 40 cemetery indicate that nomads had connections with Egypt from the late fifteenth century (see figure 4) to the tenth century B.C.E., providing archaeological evidence for the "tribes" or Shasu nomads known from Papyrus Harris, Papyrus Anastasi, and other extrabiblical sources alluded to above.

In conclusion, twelfth- to ninth-century B.C.E. Edomite identity was shaped by local peer-polity interaction and processes of resistance to neighboring related societies such as the Israelites and Midianites, and social groups linked together through blood and marriage ties. This relationship extended back in time to the period when the only name we can link to the inhabitants of Seir/Edom and northwest Arabia is the Egyptian term "Shasu." By the time the sixth-century B.C.E. biblical editors compiled the Hebrew Bible (Friedman 1988), the various competing northwest Arabian ethnic groups were known as Midianites, Edomites, Israelites and the relationships among them were understood in terms of kinship, marriage, history, and myth. Perhaps the latest development in Edomite ethnogenesis occurred during the seventh–sixth century B.C.E., when the Edomite script developed for use amongst elite groups in their society (DiVito 1993; Porter 2004). The new archaeological data from the lowlands of Edom briefly touched on here, coupled with the biblical and Egyptian texts, suggest that for most of their history, the Edomite social organization remained rooted in tribal social structure (LaBianca 1999; LaBianca and Younker 1995). Much more work needs to be done to clarify the nature of seventh–sixth century B.C.E. social organization in Edom, when monumental palatial architecture was established in the highlands at sites such as Busayra (Bienkowski 2002) and the region was subservient to the Assyrian core civilization. We do know that the tension and resistance between the two related societies, Israel and Edom, continued to be strong at this time and fueled the processes of Edomite and Israelite ethnogenesis.

Acknowledgments:

It is an honor to present this article in honor of my friend and inspirational colleague, Lawrence Stager. I would especially like to thank my colleague William Propp for his comments and insights. However, any factual or other errors are mine. Thanks also to my graduate student, Neil Smith, for preparing the GIS map used in this paper.

[2] The topic of "Midianite" and Qurayya ware during the early Iron Age is being investigated by my student Sarah Malena in her doctoral dissertation dealing with "Trade in the Biblical Texts and Levantine Societies" at the University of California, San Diego.

Bibliography

Adams, R. B.
1991 The Wadi Fidan Project, Jordan, 1989. *Levant* 23: 181–86.

Adams, R. B., and H. Genz
1995 Excavations at Wadi Fidan 4: A Copper Village Complex in the Copper Ore District of Feinan, Southern Jordan. *PEQ* 127:8–20.

Albright, W. F.
1944 The Oracles of Balaam. *JBL* 63:207–33.

Avishur, I.
1996 Edom. *Encyclopaedia Judaica* 6:369–77.

Barfield, T. J.
1993 *The Nomadic Alternative*. Englewood Cliffs, N.J.: Prentice Hall.

Bartlett, J. R.
1992 Edom. In *The Anchor Bible Dictionary*, ed. D. N. Freedman, 2:287–95. Doubleday: New York.

Bawden, G.
1983 Painted Pottery of Tayma and Problems of Cultural Chronology in Northwest Arabia. In *Midian, Moab and Edom: The History and Archaeology of Late Bronze and Iron Age Jordan and North-West Arabia*, ed. J. F. A. Sawyer and D. J. A. Clines, 37–52. JSOTSup 24. Sheffield, England: JSOT Press.

Bienkowski, P.
2002 *Busayra: Excavations by Crystal M. Bennett, 1971–1980*. British Academy Monographs in Archaeology 13. Oxford: Oxford University Press.

Bloch-Smith, E.
1992 *Judahite Burial Practices and Beliefs about the Dead*. Sheffield, England: JSOT Press.

Chapman, R., I. Kinnes, and K. Randsborg, eds.
1981 *The Archaeology of Death*. London: Cambridge University Press.

Cross, F. M.
1988 Reuben, First-Born of Jacob. *ZAW* 100:46–64.

Crowell, B. L.
2004 On the Margins of History: Social Change and Political Development in Iron Age Edom. Ph.D. diss., University of Michigan.

De Vos, G. A.
1995 Ethnic Pluralism: Conflict and Accommodation—The Role of Ethnicity in Social History. In *Ethnic Identity*, ed. L. Romanucci-Ross and G. A. De Vos, 15–47. 3d ed. Walnut Creek, Calif.: AltaMira.

DiVito, R. A.
1993 The Tell el-Kheleifeh Inscriptions. In *Nelson Glueck's 1938–1940 Excavations at Tell el-Kheleifeh: A Reappraisal*, ed. G. D. Pratico, 51–63. Atlanta: Scholars.

Faust, A.
2004 Mortuary Practices, Society and Ideology: The Lack of Iron I Burials in the Highlands in Context. *IEJ* 54:174–90.
2006 *Israel's Ethnogenesis: Settlement, Interaction, Expansion and Resistance*. Approaches to Anthropological Archaeology. London: Equinox.

Freedman, D. N.
1980 *Pottery, Poetry, and Prophecy: Studies in Early Hebrew Poetry*. Winona Lake, Ind.: Eisenbrauns.

Friedman, R. E.
1988 *Who Wrote the Bible?* London: Jonathan Cape.

Giveon, R.
1971 *Les Bédouins Shosou des documents Egyptiens*. Documenta et Monumenta Orientis Antiqui 22. Leiden: Brill.

Goren, Y., I. Finkelstein, and N. Naʾaman
2004 *Inscribed in Clay: Provenance Study of the Amarna Letters and Other Ancient Near Eastern Texts*. Tel Aviv: Institute of Archaeology, Tel Aviv University.

Halpern, B.
2001 *David's Secret Demons: Messiah, Murderer, Traitor, King*. Grand Rapids, Mich.: Eerdmans.
2005 David Did It, Others Did Not: The Creation of Ancient Israel. In *The Bible and Radiocarbon Dating: Archaeology, Text and Science*, ed. T. E. Levy and T. Higham, 422–38. London: Equinox.

Harrison, T. P., C. and Barlow
2005 Mesha, the Mishor, and the Chronology of Iron Age Madaba. In *The Bible and Radiocarbon Dating: Archaeology, Text and Science*, ed. T. E. Levy and T. Higham, 179–90. London: Equinox.

Higham, T., J. van der Plicht, C. Bronk Ramsey, H. J. Bruins, M. Robinson, and T. E. Levy
2005 Radiocarbon Dating of the Khirbat-en Nahas Site (Jordan) and Bayesian Modeling of the Results. In *The Bible and Radiocarbon Dating: Archaeology, Text and Science*, ed. T. E. Levy and T. Higham, 164–78. London: Equinox.

Joffe, A. H.
2002 The Rise of Secondary States in the Iron Age Levant. *JESHO* 45:425–67.

Kitchen, K. A.
1992 The Egyptian Evidence on Ancient Jordan. In *Early Edom and Moab: The Beginning of the Iron Age in Southern Jordan*, ed. P. Bienkowski, 21–34. Sheffield Archaeological Monographs 7. Sheffield, England: Collis.

Knauf, E. A.
1992 The Cultural Impact of Secondary State Formation: The Cases of the Edomites and the Moabites. In *Early Edom and Moab: The Beginning of the Iron Age in Southern Jordan*, ed. P. Bienkowski, 47–54. Sheffield Archaeological Monographs 7. Sheffield, England: Collis.

LaBianca, Ø. S.
1999 Salient Features of Iron Age Tribal Kingdoms. In *Ancient Ammon*, ed. B. MacDonald and R. W. Younker, 19–29. Studies in the History and Culture of the Ancient Near East 17. Leiden: Brill.

LaBianca, Ø. S., and R. W. Younker
1995 The Kingdoms of Ammon, Moab and Edom: The Archaeology of Society in Late Bronze/Iron Age Transjordan (ca. 1400–500 B.C.E.). In *The Archaeology of Society in the Holy Land*, ed. T. E. Levy, 399–415. London: Leicester University Press.

Levy, T. E., R. B. Adams, and A. Muniz
2004 Archaeology and the Shasu Nomads: Recent Excavations in the Jabal Hamrat Fidan, Jordan. In *Le-David Maskil: A Birthday Tribute for David Noel Freedman*, ed. W. Propp and R. E. Friedman, 63–89. Winona Lake, Ind.: Eisenbrauns.

Levy, T. E., R. B. Adams, and M. Najjar
1999 Early Metallurgy and Social Evolution: Jabal Hamrat Fidan. *American Center of Oriental Research Newsletter* 11/1:1–3.

Levy, T. E., R. B. Adams, M. Najjar, A. Hauptmann, J. Anderson, B. Brandl, M. A. Robinson, and T. Higham
2004 Reassessing the Chronology of Biblical Edom: New Excavations and 14C dates from Khirbat en-Nahas (Jordan). *Antiquity* 78:863–76.

Levy, T. E., R. B. Adams, and R. Shafiq
1999 The Jabal Hamrat Fidan Project: Excavations at the Wadi Fidan 40 Cemetery, Jordan (1997). *Levant* 31:293–308.

Levy, T. E., and T. Higham, eds.
2005 *The Bible and Radiocarbon Dating: Archaeology, Text and Science*. London: Equinox.

Levy, T. E., and A. F. C. Holl
2002 Migrations, Ethnogenesis, and Settlement Dynamics: Israelites in Iron Age Canaan and Shuwa-Arabs in the Chad Basin. *Journal of Anthropological Archaeology* 21:83–118.

Levy, T. E., M. Najjar, A. Muniz, S. Malena, E. Monroe, M. Beherec, N. G. Smith, T. Higham, S. Munger, and K. Maes
2005a Iron Age Burial in the Lowlands of Edom: The 2004 Excavations at Wadi Fidan 40, Jordan. *ADAJ* 49:443–87.

Levy, T. E., M. Najjar, J. van der Plicht, N. G. Smith, H. J. Bruins, and T. Higham
2005b Lowland Edom and the High and Low Chronologies: Edomite State Formation, the Bible and Recent Archaeological Research in Southern Jordan. In *The Bible and Radiocarbon Dating: Archaeology, Text and Science*, ed. T. E. Levy and T. Higham, 129–63. London: Equinox.

Musil, A.
1927 *Manners and Customs of the Rwala Bedouin*. New York: American Geographical Society.

Parr, P. J.
1982 Contacts between Northwest Arabia and Jordan in the Late Bronze and Iron Ages. In *Studies in the History and Archaeology of Jordan*, vol. 1, ed. A. Hadidi, 127–34. Amman: Department of Antiquities of Jordan.

Pearson, M. P.
2000 *The Archaeology of Death and Burial*. College Station, Tex.: Texas A&M University Press.

Porter, B. W.
2004 Authority, Polity, and Tenuous Elites in Iron Age Edom (Jordan). *Oxford Journal of Archaeology* 23:373–95.

Pritchard, J. B.
1969 *Ancient Near Eastern Texts Relating to the Old Testament*. 3d ed. Princeton, N.J.: Princeton University Press.

Rainey, A. F.
1995 Unruly Elements in Late Bronze Canaanite Society. In *Pomegranates and Golden Bells: Studies in Biblical, Jewish, and Near Eastern Ritual, Law, and Literature in Honor of Jacob Milgrom*, ed. D. P. Wright, D. N. Freedman, and A. Hurvitz, 481–96. Winona Lake, Ind.: Eisenbrauns.

Rothenberg, B.
1998 Who Were the "Midianite" Copper Miners of the Arabah? In *Metallurgica Antiqua: In Honour of Hans-Gert Bachmann and Robert Maddin*, 197–212. Bochum, Germany: Deutschen Bergbau-Museums.

Rothenberg, B., and J. Glass
1983 The Midianite Pottery. In *Midian, Moab and Edom*, ed. J. F. A. Sawyer and D. J. A. Clines,

65–124. JSOTSup 24. Sheffield, England: JSOT Press.

Routledge, B.
2004 *Moab in the Iron Age: Hegemony, Polity, Archaeology*. Philadelphia: University of Pennsylvania Press.

Sahlins, M.
1968 *Tribesmen*. Englewood Cliffs, N.J.: Prentice Hall.

Seymour-Smith, C.
1986 *Macmillan Dictionary of Anthropology*. London: Macmillan.

Shanks, H., W. G. Dever, B. Halpern, and P. K. McCarter
1992 *The Rise of Ancient Israel*. Washington, D.C.: Biblical Archaeology Society.

Tubb, J. N., P. G. Dorrell, and F. J. Cobbing
1997 Interim Report on the Ninth Season (1996) of Excavations at Tell Es-Saᶜidiyeh, Jordan. *PEQ* 129:54–77.

Ward, W. A.
1972 The Shasu "Bedouin": Notes on a Recent Publication. *JESHO* 15:35–60.
1992 Shasu. In *The Anchor Bible Dictionary*, ed. D. N. Freedman, 5:1165–67. New York: Doubleday.

Yassine, K. N.
1983 Social-religious Distinctions in Iron Age Burial Practice in Jordan. In *Midian, Moab, and Edom: The History and Archaeology of Late Bronze and Iron Age Jordan and Northwest Arabia*, ed. J. F. A. Sawyer and D. J. A. Clines, 29–36. Sheffield, England: JSOT Press.

28. A Reconstruction of Achaemenid-Period Ashkelon Based on the Faunal Evidence

by David Lipovitch

Recent excavations under the direction of Lawrence Stager at Ashkelon have uncovered substantial remains from the Achaemenid period.[1] The finds represent one of the largest collections from this period in Israel. They include more than half a million pieces of mammalian bone.

In identifying faunal bone, a specialist can recognize the species, sex, and age at death of the animal. The zooarchaeologist can reconstruct the ratios of males to females, culling patterns, the ratio of various species to each other, and recognize sudden changes in stockbreeding patterns. While zooarchaeological studies are often thought of as exercises in such dry statistical information, this data can then be used in historical context to provide important information about the history of a site (Wapnish 1993:440). For instance, changes in the zooarchaeological record can be reflections of external pressure such as political, climatic, or economic change. By examining the zooarchaeological data from Ashkelon in combination with what is known of Achaemenid-period history, it is possible to connect the material remains with the historical record to gain a better understanding of Achaemenid-period Ashkelon.

The Leon Levy Expedition to Ashkelon

Ashkelon has been excavated sporadically since the nineteenth century. The most extensive long-term excavations of the site were those sponsored by the Leon Levy Expedition and the Harvard Semitic Museum under the direction of Lawrence E. Stager (see Stager 1993; Stager, Schloen, and Master 2008). The material studied here was excavated between the summers of 1985 and 1992.

The Leon Levy Expedition used excavation techniques similar to those used in most places in the Levant for large-scale tell excavations. Due to the extremely large amount of material removed during excavations, much of which was sterile fill, screening of excavated material was not universally conducted. In features identified as living surfaces, flotation samples were taken and all other material excavated was dry-sifted through quarter-inch mesh. If a depositional unit was determined not to be a living surface, sifting occurred in a 1:5 ratio.

Stratigraphic Context

Achaemenid Ashkelon has a very complicated depositional history. As a result, it proved to be difficult, in many cases, to phase the units studied in this collection. Thus, the material from the Grid 50 excavation area that is studied here has been divided into three subcollections belonging to the early, middle and late Achaemenid periods.

The earliest Persian-period architectural phase consists of a single large building with narrow north-south oriented rooms (figure 1). It served as a large warehouse during the early Achaemenid period. The dates represented by the datable pottery span the sixth and fifth centuries B.C.E. The presence of numerous Chian amphora sherds that can be dated to ca. 475–450 B.C.E. means that the end of the early period cannot be before 475 B.C.E. (Charles Adelman, personal communication). Since, however, the matrix into which the later dog burials were cut also contains numerous Chian sherds, it is probable that the "dog cemetery" was in use during at least part of the mid-fifth century B.C.E., if we are to allow enough time for the accumulation of more than a meter of industrial debris and the interment of hundreds of dogs.

The middle Achaemenid period is represented by the use of the Grid 50 area as part of the so-called dog cemetery (Stager 1991; Wapnish and Hesse 1993). No architecture is associated with this phase; however, in addition to numerous dog burials, there is substantial evidence for the use of this area to dispose of large amounts of industrial debris and possibly as an open-air metalworking area. Virtually every layer excavated contained large amounts of slag and fragmentary metal artifacts. Also found were fragments of crucibles, fire-pits and sandpits that may have been used to hold molds. The ceramic material from this phase yields dates from the latter third of the sixth century to the early fourth century B.C.E.

[1] The research presented here represents the culmination of several years of my dissertation research at Harvard University under the direction of Lawrence Stager (my primary adviser), Brian Hesse, Peter Machinist, and Richard Meadow. For detailed acknowledgments, see my dissertation (Lipovitch 1999). A preliminary presentation of a much longer version of this paper was made at a conference in Professor Stager's honor at Wheaton College in November of 2002. My thanks go to all who helped in the process, but primarily to the following: the excavators of Grid 50 at Ashkelon; the late Leon Levy; Shelby White; and, of course, to Larry, who made this all possible. I would also like to thank Lynn Welton for her editorial assistance and suggestions.

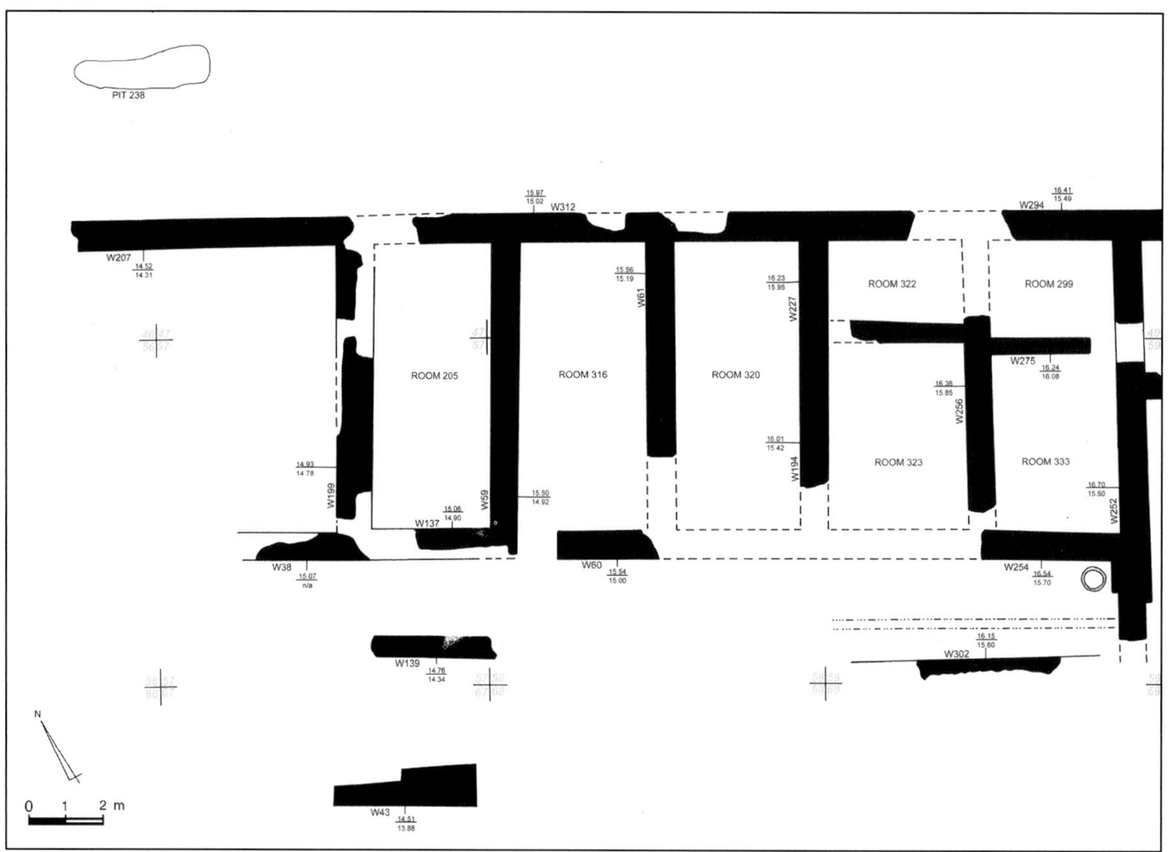

Figure 1. Early Achaemenid-period warehouse at Ashkelon (Grid 50 Phase 6)

The bulk of the datable pottery spans the period from 475 to 400 B.C.E. Several of the sherds recovered represent slightly later forms, dating to the period ca. 430 B.C.E.; thus it would seem that the "dog cemetery" was still in use in the last third of the fifth century. The presence of numerous fragments of Chian amphoras typical of the period between 475 and 425 (Charles Adelman, personal communication) suggests that the use of this area for dog burials did not begin before 475 B.C.E.

The late Achaemenid period is represented by material recovered from the large buildings built in Grid 50 during the latest stages of the Persian period. Since no buildings are associated with the period of the dog burials, all walls stratigraphically above them must be late Achaemenid or later. But since there is little evidence for any substantial architecture, aside from drains, later than the Persian period, one may assume that nearly all post-dog walls are late Achaemenid in date.

It is difficult to ascertain the function of the late Achaemenid buildings. They are large structures and are in general well constructed. They have distinctly different layouts from the earlier warehouse building and are composed of a mixture of large and small rooms. Based on their size and substantial walls, it is likely that they represent some sort of public buildings.

The handful of pieces of dated pottery recovered from units clearly associated with the earliest of the structures suggests a date in the latter third of the fifth century B.C.E. The remainder of the architectural remains can be associated with ceramic finds dated to the fourth century based on the presence of rouletted Attic Black Glaze Ware. However, it should be noted that the middle Achaemenid phase contains several sherds that may date slightly later than the final quarter of the fifth century, indicating that the beginning of the late Achaemenid period is probably closer to the end of the fifth century B.C.E.

Ashkelon and Its Historical and Archaeological Context

The statistical data that are the foundation of animal-bone archaeology are meaningless without context. By contextualizing the material, it is possible to make interpretive statements that address Ashkelon's role

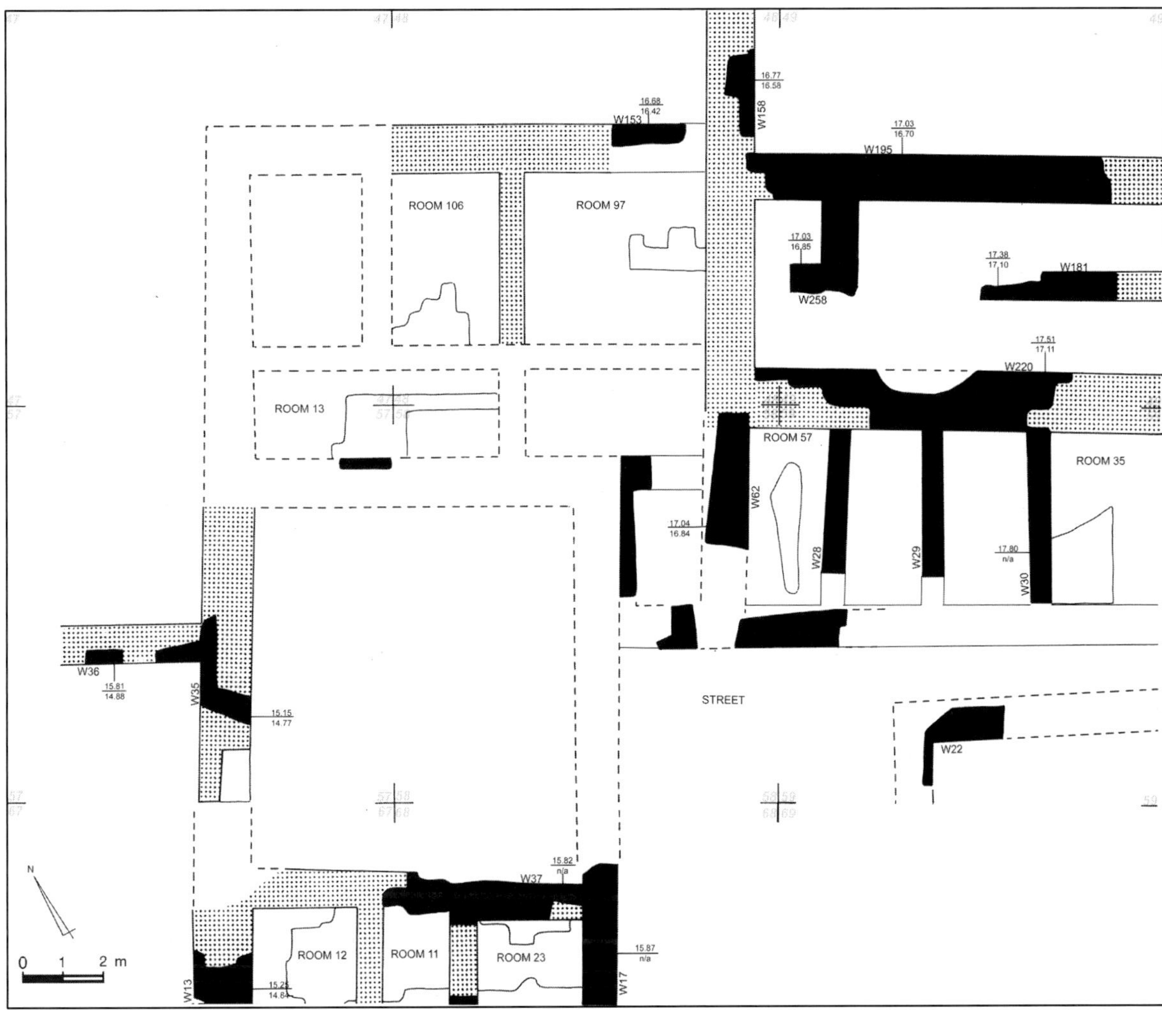

Figure 2. Late Achaemenid-period building at Ashkelon (Grid 50 Phase 4)

during the Achaemenid period and the state of the local economy during the various phases of imperial expansion, management, and collapse in the region.

In examining site locations in the Persian period, a number of patterns became evident. Sites tend to cluster around the various provincial capitals. The only notable exception here is Ashdod, which had only a handful of sites associated with it. Gaza, while not a provincial capital, was probably of the same scale of importance, functioning as a kind of Arab-controlled free city. While there are some small sites clustered around Ashkelon (Allen 2008), they do not exist in the numbers found around other major centers. All three of these sites were within the same province, so this may be a feature of the Ashdod province; that is, the Ashdod province was more urbanized than any other area of the Levant. It is also possible that in the case of Ashdod and Gaza, the lack of identified sites stems from incomplete survey, poor visibility, or poor preservation in the region.

While the Ashkelon region shows some evidence of nearby sites, they are few in number, small in size, and occur less frequently than in the late Iron Age. Most of these sites occur along the modern Tel Aviv–Gaza highway, along the eastern spur of a large *kurkar* ridge. They appear to have been located in such a way as to control access to communication routes (Allen 2008).

The distribution of sites follows a pattern that places them along the most important strategic supply routes. It would seem therefore, that during the Achaemenid period, the protection of supply routes for both trade and military purposes was of paramount importance.

At the end of the Iron Age, the Babylonians had virtually obliterated the city and it was not reoccupied until after a substantial hiatus. With much of Ashkelon's native population exiled by the Babylonians, and no historical evidence of their return from exile, we may surmise that the new Tyrian rulers of the site had no vested interest in it beyond its strategic location. Ashkelon was probably not rebuilt to the scale of its former glory. Although it was an urban center during the Achaemenid period, its importance must have been diminished in the wake of its destruction by Nebuchadrezzar and subsequent abandonment. Its most important function in the Achaemenid period was not as a population center but to control access to key transportation routes needed to maintain trade and supply the Persian army. The site therefore would have played host to large numbers of transient military personnel during military campaigns and to garrison troops during peacetime.

The Levant during the Achaemenid period formed part of the administrative unit known as the satrapy of Abar-Nahara or Ebir-Nari, which included Phoenicia, Syria-Palestine (Herodotus's Coele-Syria), and Cyprus (Herodotus 3.91). As part of this satrapy, the Levantine coast played an essential strategic role in Persian military planning. Their campaigns against both Egypt and Greece required control of the port cities and of the coastal road in order to guarantee supplies, thus the Persians would have considered maintenance of firm control over Syria, Phoenicia, and Philistia to be of primary importance (Ephᶜal 1988:139).

According to the Greek geographer Pseudo-Scylax, the Phoenician cities of Tyre and Sidon, as vassals of the Persians, ruled the Levantine coast from the Orontes River in Syria as far south as Ashkelon (Stern 1995:2). Crocodilonopolis and Ashkelon were ruled by the Tyrians (Ephᶜal 1988:150). Beyond this region, the coast from Gaza (Cadytis) to Ienysus (possibly Khan Yunis) formed an "Arab district" under the nominal control of the king of the Arabs at Dedan (Herodotus 3.5; Ephᶜal 1988:162; Wapnish 1984:179).

Expansion of Empire: The Early Achaemenid Period (539–ca. 450 B.C.E.)

While it is not possible definitively to correlate any of the architectural or depositional remains of Persian-period Ashkelon with specific events, it is likely that the early Achaemenid period was contemporary with all or part of a period of imperial expansion. Achaemenid expansion into the region began with the conquest of the Babylonian Empire by Cyrus II in 539 B.C.E. (Dandamaev 1989:47, 351). In the absence of any mention of campaigns in the ancient texts or of archaeological evidence for destruction at major Levantine sites, we can conclude that the Levant submitted willingly to the Persian yoke at this time (Dandamaev 1989:351). Unlike the Judahites, the Philistines did not return from exile. Instead, the Persians ceded control of the formerly Philistine coast to the Phoenician city-states of Sidon and Tyre in return for guarantees of loyalty, and most importantly, in return for the use of their merchant and naval fleets and ports.

The region remained largely calm and stable until after the death of Cyrus in 530 B.C.E. and the accession of Cambyses II to the Persian throne (Dandamaev 1989:66, 70, 351). At this time, Persia controlled most of the Near East with one very significant exception: Egypt. Cambyses, well aware of this serious threat to his empire's size and security, sets out to remedy this.

Cambyses II's decision to take Egypt would alter forever the significance of the Levant to the Achaemenid Empire. Previously, its main role had been economic. From this point forward, while trade would always play an important role in Persian policies in the region, the control of strategic lines of supply and communications along the Levantine coast and back through Syria to Mesopotamia would become of paramount importance.

In 525 B.C.E., Cambyses defeated the Egyptian armed forces at Pelusium and established himself as king of Egypt and founder of the Twenty-seventh dynasty (Dandamaev 1989:351; Herodotus 3.1, 7, 10; Katzenstein 1989:72). As a reward for their assistance, the Persians made various grants to the Phoenician city-states. Subsequent Persian control over Egypt was fragile, with revolts in 522, 486, and 460 B.C.E. and major Persian military campaigns in the region in 519, 483, and 456 B.C.E. (Bright 1981:374; Dandamaev 1989:83, 141, 188, 352; Herodotus 4.166–67, 200–203; 7:1, 4, 7; Rainey 1989:13).

Around 450, Megabyzus, the satrap of Syria, rebelled against his royal brother-in-law, and the emperor was forced to send a loyal Persian army to re-establish control over the region (Dandamaev 1989:239–40, 244). While unsuccessful, it is certain to have left its mark on the region (Ctesias *Persica* 37; Dandamaev 1989:353; Rainey 1989:13). Eventually, Megabyzus and Artaxerxes conclude a favorable peace (Dandamaev 1989:244). With the re-establishment of Persian control over the region ends the period of Achaemenid expansion in the west.

The Calm before the Storm: The Middle Achaemenid Period (ca. 450–404 B.C.E.)

The remains from this period at Ashkelon are tentatively dated, based on ceramic evidence, to the second half of the fifth century B.C.E. In 449 B.C.E., the Greeks and Persians negotiated the Peace of Callias

(Dandamaev 1989:252). With this change in policy *vis-à-vis* the Aegean world, Persia could now divert resources from military preparations against the Greeks to other more pressing issues, such as stabilizing their hold over their extant territory. Furthermore, shortly thereafter in 431, the Peloponnesian Wars begin in Greece. As a result, the Persians did not need to worry about threats from the Aegean. This probably resulted in a period of calm in the Levant corresponding to the general level of stability found throughout the Empire. But since the Levant was still of extraordinary strategic significance, it is likely that a substantial military presence was maintained in the region throughout this period.

This new period marked a change in Persian policy. No longer was the goal expansion, but rather maintenance. Furthermore, with peaceful relations with the Aegean world for the first time since 517, trade with the Greek world increased. Since the Phoenician cities were the middlemen in such transactions, this period was not only peaceful but also economically prosperous for the Levant.

The Waning of an Empire: The Late Achaemenid Period (404–332 B.C.E.)

The late Achaemenid period at Ashkelon encompassed a period of imperial weakness in the region, but it may also have included the later portion of the previous period of calm. With the end of the Peloponnesian Wars, the period of stability that had existed for the previous half-century came to an end. The reign of a weak king, Artaxerxes II, marked the beginning of a weakening of Persian hegemony in the Levant, and from 404 to 343 B.C.E., during his reign and part of his successor's, Egypt had a period of independence from Persia (Dandamaev 1989:272–73). With a weak Persian emperor and the Greek world at peace with itself, the Spartans were able to trouble the Persian Empire. They joined in an alliance against Persia with the Egyptians (Dandamaev 1989: 353) and Egypt made various attempts to regain its influence in the Levant.

Rebellions occurred in the region in 398, 362, and 346 B.C.E. The Persians put all of them down through military intervention that resulted in at least five campaigns through the region in 379, 360, 350, 345, and 342 B.C.E. Unlike the early Achaemenid period, however, the Persians never fully controlled the region and there were several times when much of the region, including Ashkelon, was under Egyptian hegemony, or under the control of independent Phoenician city-states (Dandamaev 1989:299, 307–9, 354; Diodorus 15.2:3, 8–9; Ephᶜal 1988:145–46; Katzenstein 1989:82; Landau 1904; Macalister 1912:313; Miller and Hayes 1986:453; Olmstead 1948:399; Rainey 1989:13–14; Stern 1982:281; 1995:273).

In 342 B.C.E., after subduing the Levant, Artaxerxes III turned his attention once more to Egypt and retook it. After a string of successes, Artaxerxes's luck came to a sudden end when an assassin took his life in 338 B.C.E. His death marked the beginning of the end for the Persian Empire. While the Persian heartland was tumultuous, the contemporary Levantine periphery was relatively calm. Achaemenid rule of the Levant came to a close in 332 B.C.E. with the conquest of Tyre by Alexander the Great and the beginning of the Hellenistic period (Dandamaev 1989:354).

The Non-Canid Mammalian Faunal Collection from the Grid 50 Excavation Area

Given the size of the faunal collection recovered from Ashkelon's Achaemenid period, it was decided to limit the scope of the project and implement a sampling strategy. Material was selected from living surfaces, pits, dumps, and occupational debris, under the assumption that these would best represent everyday life and could be more easily tied to the architectural phases of the site. This yielded a sample of some 40,000 fragments.

Sheep and Goats

In the late Iron Age at Ashkelon, before the Achaemenid periods under consideration in this paper, sheep and goats made up more than 83 percent of the identifiable specimens. Sheep- and goat-raising were clearly the most important aspects of the animal economy. Sheep were found to outnumber goats by a ratio of four to one. Age at death information for the late Iron Age is available in the form of mandibular tooth-wear data. The main slaughtering age was from 12 to 24 months.

Similarly, in the early Achaemenid period, ovicaprid remains comprised approximately 88 percent of the identifiable elements analyzed. Sheep appear to have outnumbered goats by at least 1.3 to 1. Examination of the ages at death of ovicaprid remains suggests that the main period of slaughter was around 6 to 12 months of age with 25 percent mortality reached during this period. Seventy-five percent mortality was reached by about 36 months of age. This would suggest that a large number of these animals were slaughtered before reaching maturity and that few survived to old age.

In the middle Achaemenid period, ovicaprid elements comprised nearly 87 percent of the identifiable specimens recovered. Examination of the data on aging suggests that the median age of death was sometime after approximately two years of age. The bulk of the remains belonged to animals in the prime ages of one to three years. This distribution most resembles the pattern seen in situations where the animals are raised for sale in the market (Brian Hesse, personal communication).

In the late Achaemenid period, ovicaprid remains comprise some 90 percent of the identifiable portion of the collection based on NISP. Collectively, sheep and goats outnumber the next most prevalent species, *Bos taurus*, by 12 or 13 to 1. The ratio of sheep to goats appears to have been around 6.3 to 1.

Unfortunately, the late Achaemenid sample is too small to do a proper analysis of ages at death for ovicaprines based on epiphysial fusion data. The bulk of animals (55 percent) appear to have died between the ages of one and three years. Twenty-five percent mortality was however reached before the first year. Mandibular tooth wear data yielded slightly better results, suggesting that most animals were killed during their prime market age rather than being killed at a young age or allowed to live until their ability to produce secondary products had waned.

Ovicaprines are the only taxa that show any sign of real stability over time during the Persian period. During all periods, they represent the most significant taxa in the economy. Looking at the data for the individual categories of *Capra hircus* and *Ovis aries* suggests that while the overall role of ovicaprines did not change, the ratio of sheep to goats may in fact have changed significantly over time. Examination of the statistics for both species suggests that the proportion of sheep fell while the proportion of goats rose in the early Achaemenid period. This may be reflective of a stress on the economy. Goats are often raised during times of economic hardship since they are better at foraging and need less care than do sheep. It may also have coincided with the increased needs of large military forces on their way to Egypt. Such troops would have needed immediate supplies that would require depleting local stock. Given the limits of food-preservation technology, it would have been most efficient for the sheep to be provided alive to the Persian troops so they could be slaughtered as needed elsewhere. This would of course remove evidence for them from the local economy.

Cattle

The percentage of the sample represented by cattle remains diminishes in the Persian period in comparison to the seventh century. *Bos taurus* constitutes roughly five percent of the total number of identified specimens in both the complete Persian period sample and the early Achaemenid subsample, while in the late Iron Age, it constitutes roughly eight percent of the sample. This would suggest that cattle played a less significant role at Ashkelon than at other Levantine sites.

Cattle are slightly more problematic than most of the other taxa. Cattle can be used for both traction and food, so it is difficult to say what role a given "archaeological animal" played. But since cattle seem to have played a statistically smaller role—comparable in number more to camels and equids than to sheep and goats—they are dealt with here primarily as traction animals.

Between the late Iron Age and the end of the middle Achaemenid period, there was a steady decrease in the cattle population at the site. With the introduction of camels for long-range transportation of heavy goods over land, there was probably a related decrease in the use of ox-carts. Thus cattle likely played a smaller role in transportation during this period and instead became primarily food-producing livestock. With the presence of transient troops in need of supply on their way to campaign in Egypt, meat may have been easier to supply as rations than dairy products. Some of the cattle may have left the site in the form of livestock on-the-hoof to be used as supplies for the troops. This would of course have removed them from the local zooarchaeological record. The local population would have likely then raised ovicaprines as the primary meat source on site. The remaining cattle bones found are likely reflective primarily of the small amount of cattle used by the native population as traction animals solely for local needs. While there appears to have been a subsequent rise in the late Achaemenid phases, this again may be more a factor of the small sample size rather than a reflection of the actual ancient economy.

Transport Animals

No camel remains were identified among the nearly ten thousand pieces of bone analyzed from the late Iron Age faunal collection from Ashkelon. Thus the very presence of camels in the early Achaemenid period is remarkable. Transport animal remains made up less than three percent of the elements identified from the early Achaemenid subsample. They consisted of camels and equids in a roughly two to one ratio. The appearance of camels in the early Achaemenid period probably reflects the presence of caravans associated with the various campaigns into Egypt and with interregional trade. While camels would be present in higher numbers than in late Iron Age urban centers, the transient nature of campaigning troops would mean that the numbers need not be very high. With the establishment of a certain amount of stability in the region, the camel population would likely increase due to the presence of garrisoned troops left at the site to maintain control over the vital coastal road. The less transient nature of these troops would mean the presence over the long term of more transport animals. In addition, an increase in peacetime trade involving Arab camel caravans would significantly contribute to these numbers.

Less than three percent of the identifiable elements from the middle Achaemenid period were either camel or equids. Camels outnumbered equids by as much as two to one during this period. The final slight drop on numbers probably reflects the turmoil within the Persian Empire in its final years. With the loss of control over the Levant that came with the various Egyptian and Phoenician revolts alongside problems in the heartland of the Empire, it is likely that for much of the later part of the period, Ashkelon did not have a Persian garrison. Without such a garrison, there would likely be a drop in the number of camels. The fact that the number does not drop dramatically is probably reflective of local trade with Egypt and others during this period.

There were very few equid remains at the site in the late Iron Age, but the number increased dramatically with the beginning of the Achaemenid period, only to drop again during the middle Achaemenid period. The absolute percentage of *Equus* fragments more than doubled in the Achaemenid period as a whole and nearly quadrupled in the transition from the Iron Age to the Persian period. This means there was a substantial increase in the number of transport animals at the site during the Achaemenid period in comparison to what was typical of the urban coastal economy in Iron Age Ashkelon. This pattern may be explained by the greater use of horses by assault troops than by a local garrison and by the presence of larger numbers of mules and donkeys needed to haul supplies for the various campaigns.

Game Animals

Game species increased dramatically during the Achaemenid period. The transition from late Iron Age to the early Achaemenid period saw an increase in the percentage of the sample represented by game animals of more than 500 percent. This drastic increase is small when compared to the overall value for the entire Persian period, where the increase is on the order of 800 percent. While some gazelle remains were identified in the Iron Age sample, none of the large game animals that were found during the later Persian period were identified in Iron Age contexts. Large game found at the site in the Persian period include: red deer (*Cervus elaphus*), fallow deer (*Dama dama mesopotamica*), and hartebeest (*Alcelaphus alcelaphus*). While they were present in relatively small numbers, their very presence is remarkable. These numbers increase in the transition from the early to middle Achaemenid periods. No large cervid remains were recovered from the late Achaemenid period.

Small game is represented at the site primarily by the remains of gazelles. The relative amount of gazelle and possible roe deer follows much the same pattern as was seen in the large cervid taxa. Very few gazelle remains were seen in the late Iron Age assemblage; there was a significant increase in the early Achaemenid period. A further increase in relative quantity is seen during the middle Achaemenid period.

Since the presence of game at an urban site is generally a marker of either military activity or some sort of severe economic or ecological crisis (Hesse and Wapnish 1985:16), the marked changes in relative abundance over time are highly significant. The early Achaemenid period is marked by the presence of transient Persian military personnel on campaign in Egypt. These troops probably hunted in the region as a way to supplement their rations and as a way to practice their martial skills. This would create a noticeable increase in large cervid remains at the site. With peacetime garrisoning of this important supply center, the amount of game remains would again increase. Not only would a garrison hunt for all the same reasons, but they would also be encouraged to vent their aggressive tendencies on the local fauna rather than the local populace. This would account for the increase seen in the middle Achaemenid period. The drop seen in the later Persian phases would correlate with the departure of the garrison coincident with the changes in the local situation. Alternatively, another possible source for such "exotic" animals is the presence at the site of a zoological game park maintained by the site's elite (Lawrence Stager, personal communication).

Game animal remains made up approximately three percent of the identified specimens in the early Achaemenid period. But a calculation of the minimum number of individuals (MNI) yielded a considerably larger proportion of game animals, on the order of thirteen percent of the subsample. Game animal remains included specimens of red deer (*Cervus elaphus)*, gazelle (*Gazella* sp.), and possibly roe deer (*Capreolus capreolus*). Game animal species, however, appear to have played a fairly significant role in the economy of the middle Achaemenid period. Game animal remains including elements of hartebeest, red deer, fallow deer, gazelle, and possibly roe deer, were recovered. The total amount of game bone represented more than five percent of the identifiable fragments from middle Achaemenid contexts.

Dogs

The remains of canids were found in the early Achaemenid period in very small numbers. The middle Achaemenid period, however, is most notable for the presence of the so-called "dog cemetery," which contained more than 970 dog burials in the excavated area, most of which were concentrated in the Grid 50 excavation area (Wapnish and Hesse 1993:57). According to Stager, these remains probably represent the burial of dogs from a healing cult most likely associated with the Phoenician deities Resheph-Mukol or Eshmun (Stager 1991:33, 36). But an examination of the remains by Wapnish and Hesse suggests that there is little archaeological evidence that the inhumations were cultic in nature (Wapnish and Hesse 1993:58, 74–76).

Each dog burial consisted of a single individual buried in an unlined pit. None of the interments was found to have any associated grave offerings, nor were any of the pits marked; in many cases, later burials cut earlier ones (Wapnish and Hesse 1993: 58). Most of the individuals were puppies; adult remains made up roughly one-third of the finds. At least one individual showed evidence of trauma consistent with physical abuse. Some of the dogs showed evidence of extreme tooth wear consistent with a diet composed largely of material scavenged from Ashkelon's beaches (ibid., p. 60). No evidence was found for selective breeding and the individual dogs appear to conform to the patterns seen in modern local pariah dogs (ibid., pp. 65, 67). Interestingly, no canid remains were identified in the late Achaemenid sample.

Pigs

Pig remains were scarce in the late Iron Age collection. This pattern continued through the Persian period. The pig (*Sus scrofa*) appears to have made up a very small proportion of the early Achaemenid economy (approximately one percent). Pig remains made up less than one-tenth of a percent of the identifiable elements analyzed from middle Achaemenid period. This would suggest that although pigs were present, they played an extraordinarily small role. By the late periods, no *Sus* remains were found at the site.

In many ways, the faunal collection from Ashkelon's Achaemenid period is typical of most sites in Israel after the establishment of the typical Mediterranean economy. Sheep and goats comprised the main species and provided milk, meat, wool and hair. Cattle, which were raised both as food (or food producers) and as traction animals, were the next most prevalent species. Where our collection differs from earlier assemblages is in the ratios of species, the presence of camels, and the higher visibility of game animals.

Conclusions

The relative proportions of the species at Ashkelon in the Persian period changed in conjunction with the state of the local economy and of the Persian Empire. As a result of its geographical location, Ashkelon played an essential strategic role in controlling communication and supply routes between the Persian heartland, Phoenicia, the Arab kingdoms, and—most importantly—Egypt.

During the earliest Achaemenid phase, the presence of large numbers of transient Persian military units used in Persia's initial campaigns against Egypt would have brought in many non-local people to feed. This would have placed a strain on the economy and would have caused changes in the quantities of animals associated with military populations.

As one of the southernmost Persian-controlled sites in the Levant with a harbor and with access to the main coastal road, Ashkelon would inevitably have become an essential military supply center. The increase seen in transport animals is reflective of the change from a standard urban economy to one heavily affected by the presence of transient military units. This is also supported by the dramatic increase in the quantity of game animal remains recovered in Grid 50 from the early Achaemenid period.

With the completion of imperial expansion, changes would have occurred in the local economy. No longer was the Persian military passing through on the way to Egypt or back to Persia. This, however, would not have meant an end to the Persian military presence in the region. On the contrary, a more permanent military presence would have been required in order to safeguard the strategic communications routes. Therefore, the region would have been marked by changes in the economy reflective of the addition of a garrisoned Persian military population.

Draft-animal remains decreased significantly with the change in function of Grid 50 from a storage facility to an area for the disposal of industrial waste and dog carcasses. Furthermore, there was a dramatic increase in game animals. With the relative calm seen in this period, the garrisoned Persian soldiers would have had a greater need to maintain martial skills by hunting local game animals, which was probably encouraged as a way both to keep the men sharp and to provide them with a means of healthy catharsis.

As always, the bulk of the animal-based economy was focused on sheep- and goat-herding. Interestingly, there was a dramatic increase in the proportion of goat remains and a corresponding decrease in the ratio of sheep to goats. This would seem to reflect a dramatic shift in the local economy and may reflect an economy under severe pressure. This probably stems from the burden placed on the local populace, who not only had to feed themselves but also had to supply the Persian troops garrisoned at the site.

In the later periods, as a result of the waning of the Persian Empire's control that occurred in its final years, the region gained more autonomy, and sometimes independence, from the Persians. This would have resulted in the departure of the Persian military troops garrisoned at the site and likely improvements in the local economy. During this transition, there was a dramatic rise in the proportion of draft animals, likely stemming from the return of this area to a role in storage and heavy industry. It may also reflect an increase in trade, likely with the Arabs. Game animals show a significant decrease in number corresponding with the probable absence of a Persian garrison.

Furthermore, pig remains were entirely absent in the late imperial period, suggesting that the population was now almost uniformly local in origin. Ovicaprid remains still formed the bulk of the collection, but during this transition there was a dramatic increase in the ratio of sheep to goats. This likely reflects an improved local economy that was no longer under stress. The economy may have improved as Tyre and her cities gained temporary independence from Persia in a period of localized stability coincident with a weakened Persian Empire.

Bibliography

Allen, M.
2008 Regional Archaeological Survey. In *Ashkelon*, vol. 1, *Introduction and Overview (1985–2006)*, ed. L. E. Stager, J. D. Schloen, and D. M. Master, 21–65. Winona Lake, Ind.: Eisenbrauns.

Bright, J.
1981 *A History of Israel*. 3d ed. Philadelphia: Westminster.

Dandamaev, M. A.
1989 *A Political History of the Achaemenid Empire*. Translated by W. J. Vogelsang. Leiden: Brill.

Eph^cal, I.
1988 Syria-Palestine under Achaemenid Rule. In *The Cambridge Ancient History*, ed. J. Boardman, N. G. L. Hammond, D. M. Lewis, and M. Ostwald, 4:139–64. 2d ed. Cambridge: Cambridge University Press.

Hesse, B., and P. Wapnish
1985 *Animal Bone Archeology: From Objectives to Analysis*. Washington, D.C.: Taraxacum.

Katzenstein, H. J.
1989 Gaza in the Persian Period. *Transeuphratène* 1: 67–86.

Landau, W. V.
1904 Die Inschrift von Achoris, König von Ägypten. *Mitteilungen der vorderasiatische Gesselschaft* 9: 342–47.

Lipovitch, D.
1999 Can These Bones Live Again? An Analysis of the Non-Canid, Mammalian Faunal Remains from the Achaemenid-Period Occupation of Tel Ashkelon, Israel. Ph.D. diss., Harvard University.

Miller, J. M., and J. H. Hayes
1986 *A History of Ancient Israel and Judah*. Philadelphia: Westminster.

Olmstead, A. T.
1948 *History of the Persian Empire*. Chicago: University of Chicago Press.

Stager, L. E.
1991 Why Were Hundreds of Dogs Buried at Ashkelon? In *Ashkelon Discovered: From Canaanites and Philistines to Romans and Moslems*, ed. L. E. Stager, 20–36. Washington, D.C.: Biblical Archaeological Society.
1993 Ashkelon. In *The New Encyclopedia of Archaeological Excavation in the Holy Land*, ed. E. Stern, 1:103–12. New York: Simon and Schuster.

Stager, L. E., J. D. Schloen, and D. M. Master, eds.
2008 *Ashkelon*. Vol. 1, *Introduction and Overview (1985–2006)*. Winona Lake, Ind.: Eisenbrauns.

Stern, E.
1982 *Material Culture of the Land of the Bible in the Persian Period, 538–332 B.C.* Warminster, England: Aris and Phillips.

1995 Historical Conclusions. In *Excavations at Dor: Final Report*, vol. 1a, *Areas A and C: Introduction and Stratigraphy*, ed. E. Stern, 271–84. Qedem Reports 1. Jerusalem: Institute of Archaeology, Hebrew University.

Stern, E., and Y. Magen
1984 A Pottery Group of the Persian Period from Qadum in Samaria. *BASOR* 253:9–27.

Wapnish, P.
1984 The Dromedary and Bactrian Camel in Levantine Historical Settings: The Evidence from Tell Jemmeh. In *Animals and Archaeology*, vol. 3, *Early Herders and Their Flocks*, ed. J. Clutton-Brock and C. Grigson, 171–200. BARIS 202. Oxford: British Archaeological Reports.
1993 Archaeozoology: The Integration of Faunal Data with Biblical Archaeology. In *Biblical Archaeology Today, 1990: Proceedings of the Second International Congress on Biblical Archaeology*, ed. A. Biran and J. Aviram, 426–42. Jerusalem: Israel Exploration Society.

Wapnish, P., and B. Hesse
1993 Pampered Pooches or Plain Pariahs? The Ashkelon Dog Burials. *BA* 56/2:55–80.

29. Hazael, Birhadad, and the *Ḥrṣ*

by Aren M. Maeir

Several years ago, the esteemed honoree, Lawrence Stager, in a joint study with Israel Ephᶜal (mentioned in Stager 1991:8; see now as well Stager et al. 2008:218–21), argued that a central consideration behind the construction of the massive earth ramparts around many Middle Bronze Age II sites in the Levant was the use of these ramparts to obstruct and delay offensive tunneling under the fortifications of the site.[1] Accordingly, they suggested that during the early part of the second millennium B.C.E. tunneling became a commonly used method of capturing fortified positions, and the massive ramparts were an answer to this threat. In addition, they noted that just at this time, in the Old Babylonian sources, there is mention of the term *pilšu*, which relates to just such tunneling attempts. With this argument, they attempted to strengthen the view that the various elements of Middle Bronze Age II fortifications had a distinctly functional (and, in fact, martial) origin, and not, as suggested by some, a primarily symbolic purpose (e.g., Bunimovitz 1992; Finkelstein 1992; Herzog 1997:132).[2] Subsequently, in his general study of siegecraft in the ancient Near East, Ephᶜal (1996:72–77) elaborated on the use of tunneling described in various ancient Near Eastern sources well into the Iron Age.

I do not intend in this study to discuss further either the function and/or the sources relating to the Middle Bronze Age II ramparts. I would, however, like to deal briefly with Ephᶜal's suggestion that the tactic of tunneling under a city wall is mentioned in the description of the siege of the city of Ḥazrak in the "Zakkur" Inscription from northern Syria. I will argue that this interpretation cannot be accepted, and that in fact, this text refers to the use of a "siege trench."

[1] It is with much pleasure that I dedicate this short study in Larry Stager's honor. Since our mutual interests in Middle Bronze Age II studies on the one hand, and Philistine studies on the other, have "crossed paths" on several occasions in the past, it is an honor to be able to present to him a study in which both aspects are involved.

[2] Personally, I agree with the functional/military interpretation of the Middle Bronze Age II ramparts, basing my view on, among others, the old adage (attributed to Groucho Marx): "If it walks like a duck and quacks like a duck—it's a duck!"

ḥrṣ *in the Zakkur Inscription*

The Zakkur Inscription was discovered by H. Pognon in 1903 at the north-Syrian site of Tell Afis and published soon after (Pognon 1907). In this well-known inscription, Zakkur, the king of the north-Syrian Aramaic kingdom of Laᶜash and Ḥamath, mentions how the deity Baᶜalshamin saved him from the siege that Birhadad, son of Hazael, king of Aram-Damascus, had placed on the city of Ḥazrak.[3] Although the exact date of this siege is not clear, in all likelihood it occurred during the first decade of the eighth century B.C.E.[4] In describing the siege itself, the following tactics are mentioned in line 10 of the inscription:

whrmw šr mn šr ḥzrk whᶜmqw ḥrṣ mn ḥr[*ṣh*]

Most translations (e.g., *KAI* 202; *ANET*[3], p. 655f.; *COS* 2.35; Gibson 1975:9, 15; Lipiński 1975:248; Delsman 1985:627) and scholarly discussions of this phrase (e.g., Pitard 1987:171; Kern 1999:54; Lipiński 2000:254–55) interpret the term *ḥrṣ* as a trench, excavation, or moat, and have thus suggested various nuances of the following interpretation: "And they built a wall higher than the wall of Ḥazrak, and they dug a moat deeper than [its] moa[t]." In other words, according to these interpretations, as part of Birhadad's siege against the city, his army built a siege wall that was taller than the city's wall and dug a siege trench that was deeper than the city's moat. This has been the standard interpretation of this verse since the original publication of the inscription, al-

[3] The identification of Ḥazrak has been extensively discussed over the years. Although its identification with Tell Afis is now commonly accepted (e.g., Matthiae 1978:2; Roth 1992:17; Dion 1997:139–43; Lipiński 2000:256; Mazzoni 2001), other identifications have been suggested (e.g., Dussaud 1927:237–38; Hawkins 1990:159–60). Although the inscription was found at Tell Afis, both Ḥazrak and a toponym ᵓApiš are mentioned in the inscription. Thus, some have suggested that since Tell Afis should be identified with the ᵓApiš in the inscription, Ḥazrak should be located elsewhere. Lipiński (2000:255) has suggested that the ᵓApiš in the inscription refers to part of the town of Ḥazrak (possibly the acropolis), so that both names could be identified with Tell Afis.

[4] For discussions on the date of this event (ranging from 805 to 772 B.C.E., although most likely in the first decade of the eighth century B.C.E.), see, e.g., Pitard 1987:173–74; Lipiński 2000:309–10.

though, to the best of my knowledge, there has been no in-depth discussion of the specific siege technique described.

In his overview of siege and its manifestations in the ancient Near East, Ephᶜal (1996) discussed the various tactics, methods, and means that were used to capture ancient cities, including, among others, the use of siege trenches to besiege a city (ibid., p. 41) and tunneling to get under, or destroy, the city wall (pp. 72–77). He mentions two instances from the ancient Near East in which a siege trench was used: (1) in Thutmosis III's siege of Megiddo, and (2) in a text from Old Babylonian Mari (p. 41). Despite this, in his discussion of the Zakkur text, he proposes (p. 77) to interpret line 10 in an alternative manner, namely, that this line refers to an attempt on the part of Birhadad's army to tunnel under the city wall of Ḥazrak. If one follows Ephᶜal's suggestion, this would be the earliest written reference to such a siege method, which became well known, and apparently often used, in later periods.

But this suggestion, despite its originality and despite the fact that tunneling doubtless did serve as an important method of overcoming a besieged city's defenses, cannot be accepted. I argue this based on two points:

1. Linguistically, the term *ḥrṣ* cannot refer to a tunnel; rather it always refers to a trench, channel, excavation, etc.

2. There is a clear-cut archaeological parallel to exactly just such a "siege trench" from a contemporary site, strengthening the original interpretation of the Zakkur Inscription's account of the siege of Ḥazrak.

ḥrṣ *in Aramaic and Cognate Semitic Languages*

The term *ḥrṣ* has several meanings in Aramaic and cognate Semitic languages (Akkadian, Hebrew, Syriac, etc.), but only one can be relevant to our discussion—a definition referring to a trench, moat, or channel (see *AHw*, *CAD* s.v. *ḫarāṣu*; *BDB*, *HALAT* s.v. *ḥrṣ* [*ḥāraṣ*]; Jean and Hoftijzer 1965:96; Hoftijzer and Jongeling 1995:406; Sokoloff 2002:484; compare Dan. 9:26). To the best of my knowledge, there are no examples in the various Semitic languages in which the term *ḥrṣ* is used to refer to a tunnel. On the other hand, there are terms for tunnel in Akkadian: the term *pilšu*, which was mentioned above (see *AHw*, *CAD* s.v.; Ephᶜal 1996:74), and possibly the term *niksu* (see *AHw*, *CAD* s.v.; Ephᶜal 1996:74, n. 124; Younger 2003:260). Thus, from a linguistic point of view, there is no reason to interpret *ḥrṣ* in the Zakkur Inscription as a tunnel.

Archaeological Evidence

As extensively discussed by Ephᶜal (1996), there is ample evidence of siege warfare from the ancient Near Eastern historical and epigraphic sources. Despite this, direct archaeological evidence of sieges is much less common. In fact, from the pre-Hellenistic Near East, Ephᶜal noted only two examples in which explicit archaeological evidence of a siege has been revealed (as opposed to the much more common evidence of destruction, which is often the result of a siege), namely, the archaeological evidence of the Assyrian siege of Lachish (Ephᶜal 1996:33–34; see, e.g., Ephᶜal 1984; Ussishkin 1990:2), and the archaeological evidence of the Persian siege of Alt-Paphos (Ephᶜal 1996:34–36; see Maier and Karageorghis 1984:186–203).

Various siege methods were employed in the ancient Near East (see Yadin 1963:16–24; Ephᶜal 1996; 1997; Kern 1999; Hasel 2005). One of the most important components of a siege was the physical blockade or "circumvallation" in which the besieging army enclosed the besieged city, preventing the defenders from escaping and from receiving supplies, and, most importantly, hindering the ability of the defender to make forays against the besieging forces.[5] The blockade could be implemented through a dispersal of troops around the city or by creating a physical barrier—either a wall or a "siege moat" or trench. Although, as mentioned above, there is epigraphic evidence for the use of siege trenches from the ancient Near East, this clearly was not a common practice; it is only mentioned in three sources. In much later periods (subsequent to the invention of gun powder) the use of siege trenches was a common phenomenon because of the need to protect the besieging army against the defenders' artillery fire.[6] Presumably, the great effort required to dig a trench around a city made this tactic unpopular and, apparently, quite impractical in earlier periods, which would explain its rarity.

The recent excavations at Tell eṣ-Ṣāfi (biblical Gath of the Philistines) have now provided excellent

[5] Among the best known examples of archaeologically attested circumvallations are to be found in the Roman sieges of Masada in Judea (Richmond 1962; Yadin 1966) and Alesia in Gaul (Harmand et al. 1967; Barral et al. 2001).

[6] For a brief discussion of late medieval/early modern siege techniques, see Parker 1995:106–17. For a modern-period (Napoleonic era) siege trench in Israel, see Berman 1997.

archaeological evidence for just this type of siege trench. As previously reported (Maeir 2003; 2004; 2008; Maeir et al. 2006; Ackermann et al. 2004; 2005) compelling evidence of a siege trench has been discovered surrounding the site of Tell eṣ-Ṣāfi. First identified in aerial photographs, over the last ten years it has been surveyed, excavated, and analyzed using a broad spectrum of analytic methods. Accordingly, the trench and related features can be dated to the Iron Age IIA (ca. ninth century B.C.E.). It has been demonstrated that the only viable explanation of this feature is as a siegework constructed by a military force that besieged Tell eṣ-Ṣāfi/Gath during the ninth century B.C.E. The siege trench and related earthen berm, towers, and other features, are components of a monumental engineering feat, clearly carried out by a very large and well-organized military force.[7]

As previously argued (Maeir 2004), this siege system can be related to the conquest of Gath of the Philistines by Hazael, king of Aram-Damascus, most probably in the second half of the ninth century B.C.E., as mentioned in 2 Kings 12:18 (MT; see, e.g., Pitard 1987:152; Ehrlich 1996:72–74; Dion 1997: 2000; Lipiński 2000:387).[8] In addition to the siege system, it has been suggested that extensive evidence of the conquest and destruction of Gath by Hazael has been revealed in the excavations (Stratum A3). The rich and well-preserved finds from this stratum are well-dated to the second half of the ninth century B.C.E. based on typological analysis of the finds, radiometric dating, and so on, and they fit in well with the suggested historical scenario (Hazael's conquest). The existence of both the late ninth century B.C.E. destruction level and the similarly dated siege system surrounding the site, present a cogent case for connecting both of these elements to the siege and conquest of the site by Hazael of Aram Damascus.

This being the case, it would appear that the siege system at Tell eṣ-Ṣāfi/Gath is an example of just the type of siege depicted in the accepted interpretation of line 10 in the Zakkur Inscription—a siege including the digging of a deep trench surrounding the site. In light of the suggested connection between Hazael and the siege at Tell eṣ-Ṣāfi/Gath, it strengthens the suggested interpretation of the methods used by Birhadad, *the son of Hazael*, during his siege of Ḥazrak, just a few years after the siege at Tell eṣ-Ṣāfi/Gath.[9] Perhaps the use of siege moats was a technique that should be seen as being typical of Aramean military practice.

Conclusions

It appears that the mainstream interpretation of the word *ḥrṣ* in line 10 of the Zakkur Inscription, according to which Birhadad is credited with besieging the city of Ḥazrak with the aid of a siege trench, is to be preferred. Ephᶜal's innovative suggestion to identify the word *ḥrṣ* as a reference to a tunneling tactic, al-

[7] The magnitude of the engineering work and logistics required for the construction of this system indicates that it could not have been made by any of the small-scale polities of the region during the Iron Age. The excavation of a siege trench such as the one at Tell eṣ-Ṣāfi/Gath would have undoubtedly taken several months of work. A rough estimate of ca. 60,000 cubic meters of excavated stone, as well as the related logistical and military activities, would have required thousands of men over a period of at least several months. Only a very large and well-organized military organization (and related polity) could have conducted such an operation. In the Levant during the ninth–eighth centuries B.C.E. there are only two candidates for this: the Assyrians, and in the second half of the ninth century (and possibly in the very early eighth century), the kingdom of Aram-Damascus. Assyrian involvement in this siege can be ruled out for several reasons: (1) there are no Assyrian-related finds in or near the siege system; (2) the siege system is dated to the second half of the ninth century, a period when there was little if any Assyrian activity in this region; (3) such a siege system runs counter to standard Assyrian siege tactics, which involved quick blitzkrieg methods for overcoming besieged cities. On this latter preference and the reasons behind it, see Ephᶜal 1983.

[8] Various suggestions have been proposed as to the date of this campaign, most falling within the last two decades of the ninth century B.C.E. (e.g., Mazar 1954:230; Hallo 1960:42; Ehrlich 1996:73; Lipiński 2000:387), and most recently, 797 B.C.E. (Rainey and Notley 2006:215. See, though, Cogan and Tadmor (1988:141, n. 4) and Ephᶜal and Naveh (1989:199, n. 36), who have questioned the validity of reconstructing the date of this campaign based on the available historical data. Radiometric dates from the relevant destruction level at Tell eṣ-Ṣāfi/Gath (Stratum A3) support a mid-ninth century date for this event (see Sharon et al. 2007:44).

[9] With the discovery of this unique feature at Tell eṣ-Ṣāfi/Gath, the logical consequence would be to see if a similar feature existed at Tell Afis (granted that its identification as Ḥazrak is correct). Although S. Mazzoni, the current director of excavations at Tell Afis was not aware of any similar feature in the vicinity of Tell Afis (personal communication), further scrutiny of this issue may be warranted. Due to the very different topographic and geomorphological surroundings of Tell Afis as compared to Tell eṣ-Ṣāfi/Gath, such a feature, if it indeed exists, may be buried below surface and would require remote-sensing techniques for its recovery. Nevertheless, a cursory look at the satellite imagery of Tell Afis and its surroundings (available on Google Earth [http://earth.google.com]) indicates several topographic features that might be related to a siege trench.

though intriguing, does not withstand scrutiny. The linguistic evidence of the accepted meaning of *ḥrṣ* in cognate Semitic languages ("trench," "moat," etc.), as well as the existence of other terms in Assyrian for tunneling (*pilšu*, *niksu*), argues against this suggestion. Finally, the recent discovery of archaeological evidence of a siege moat surrounding Tell eṣ-Ṣāfi/Gath, dated to the same period, and most probably constructed by the father of Birhadad, Hazael, leaves no doubt in my mind that Birhadad utilized just this method of siege in his failed attempt to capture the city of Ḥazrak.

Bibliography

Ackermann, O., A. Maeir, and H. Bruins
2004 Unique Human-made Catenary Changes and Their Effect on Soil and Vegetation in the Semiarid Mediterranean Zone: A Case Study on *Sarcopterium Spinosum* Distribution near Tell eṣ-Ṣāfi/Gath, Israel. *Catena* 57:309–30.

Ackermann, O., H. Bruins, and A. Maeir
2005 A Unique Human-Made Trench at Tell eṣ-Ṣâfi/Gath, Israel: Anthropogenic Impact and Landscape Response. *Geoarchaeology* 20:303–27.

Barral, P., M. Reddé, and S. von Schnurbein
2001 *Alésia: Fouilles et recherches Franco-Allemandes sur les travaux militaires Romains autour du Mont-Auxois (1991–1997)*. Memoires de l'Académie des inscriptions et belles-lettres N.S. 22. Paris: Boccard.

Berman, A.
1997 Excavation of the Courthouse Site at ᶜAkko: A Siege-Trench of Bonaparte's Army in Areas TB and TC. *ᶜAtiqot* 31:91–103.

Bunimovitz, S.
1992 The Middle Bronze Age Fortifications in Palestine As a Social Phenomenon. *Tel Aviv* 19:221–34.

Cogan, M., and H. Tadmor
1988 *II Kings: A New Translation with Introduction and Commentary*. Garden City, N.Y.: Doubleday.

Delsman, W. C.
1985 Die Inschrift des Königs Zakkur von Hamath. In *Texte aus der Umwelt des Alten Testaments*, vol. 1, *Rechts- und Wirtschaftsurkunden, historisch-chronologische Texte, Lieferung* 6, pp. 626–28. Gutersloh: Mohn.

Dion, P.-E.
1997 *Les Araméens à l'âge du Fer: Histoire politique et structures sociales*. Études Bibliques, Nouvelle série 34. Paris: Gabalda.

Dussaud, R.
1927 *Topographie historique de la Syrie antique et médiévale*. BAH 4. Paris: Geuthner.

Ehrlich, C.
1996 *The Philistines in Transition: A History from ca. 1000–730 B.C.E.* SHCANE 10. Leiden: Brill.

Ephᶜal, I.
1983 On Warfare and Military Control in the Ancient Near Eastern Empires: A Research Outline. In *History, Historiography and Interpretation*, ed. H. Tadmor and M. Weinfeld, 88–106. Jerusalem: Magnes.
1984 The Assyrian Siege Ramp at Lachish: Military and Lexical Aspects. *Tel Aviv* 11:60–70.
1996 *Siege and Its Ancient Near Eastern Manifestations* [in Hebrew]. Jerusalem: Magnes.
1997 Ways and Means to Conquer a City, Based on Assyrian Queries to the Sungod. In *Assyria 1995: Proceedings of the Tenth Anniversary Symposium of the Neo-Assyrian Text Corpus Project, Helsinki, September 7–11, 1995*, ed. S. Parpola and R. Whiting, 49–53. Helsinki: Neo-Assyrian Text Corpus Project.

Ephᶜal, I., and J. Naveh
1989 Hazael's Booty Inscriptions. *IEJ* 39:192–200.

Finkelstein, I.
1992 Middle Bronze Age "Fortifications": A Reflection of Social Organization and Political Formations. *Tel Aviv* 19:201–20.

Gibson, J. C.
1975 *Textbook of Syrian Semitic Inscriptions*. Vol. 2, *Aramaic Inscriptions including Inscriptions in the Dialect of Zenjirli*. Oxford: Clarendon.

Hallo, W. W.
1960 From Qarqar to Carchemish: Assyria and Israel in the Light of New Discoveries. *BA* 23:33–61.

Harmand, J.
1967 *Alésia: Une campagne Césarienne.* Paris: Picard.

Hasel, M.
2005 *Military Practice and Polemic: Israel's Laws of Warfare in Near Eastern Perspective*. Berrien Springs, Mich.: Andrews University Press.

Hawkins, J. D.
1990 Luḫuti. *RLA* 7:159–61.

Herzog, Z.
1997 *Archaeology of the City: Urban Planning in Ancient Israel and Its Social Implications*. Tel Aviv: Institute of Archaeology, Tel Aviv University.

Hoftijzer, J., and K. Jongeling
1995 *Dictionary of North-West Semitic Inscription*. Vol. 1. Handbuch der Orientalistik. Leiden: Brill.

Jean, C., and J. Hoftijzer
1965 *Dictionnaire des inscriptions sémitiques de l'ouest*. Leiden: Brill.

Kern, P.
1999 *Ancient Siege Warfare*. Bloomington, Ind.: Indiana University Press.

Linpiński, E.
1975 Die Zakkur-Inschrift. In *Religionsgeschichtliches Textbuch zum Alten Testament*, ed. W. Beyerlin, 247–50. Göttingen: Vandenhoeck and Ruprecht.
2000 *The Aramaeans: Their Ancient History, Culture, Religion*. OLA 100. Leuven: Peeters.

Maeir, A. M.
2003 Notes and News: Tell eṣ-Ṣafi/Gath. *IEJ* 53:237–46.
2004 The Historical Background and Dating of Amos vi 2: An Archaeological Perspective from Tell eṣ-Ṣâfī/Gath. *VT* 54:319–34.
2008 Zafit, Tel. In *The New Encyclopedia of Archaeological Excavations in the Holy Land*, vol. 5, *Supplementary Volume*, ed. E. Stern, 2079–81. Jerusalem: Israel Exploration Society.

Maeir, A. M., O. Ackermann, and H. Bruins
2006 The Ecological Consequences of a Siege: A Marginal Note on Deuteronomy 20:19–20. In *Confronting the Past: Archaeological and Historical Essays on Ancient Israel in Honor of William G. Dever*, ed. S. Gitin, J. E. Wright and J. P. Dessel, 239–44. Winona Lake, Ind.: Eisenbrauns.

Maier, F., and V. Karageorghis
1984 *Paphos: History and Archaeology*. Nicosia: Leventis Foundation.

Matthiae, P.
1979 Sondages à Tell Afis (Syrie), 1978. *Akkadica* 14:2–5.

Mazar, B.
1954 Gath and Gittaim. *IEJ* 4:227–35.

Mazzoni, S.
2001 Tell Afis and the Luʿash in the Aramaean Period. In *The World of the Aramaeans: Biblical Studies in Honour of Paul-Eugène Dion*, ed. P. M. M. Daviau, J. W. Wevers, and M. Weigl, 2:99–114. JSOTSup 325. Sheffield, England: Sheffield Academic Press.

Parker, G.
1995 The Gunpowder Revolution 1300–1500. In *The Cambridge Illustrated History of Warfare: The Triumph of the West*, 106–17. Cambridge: Cambridge University Press.

Pitard, W. T.
1987 *Ancient Damascus: A Historical Study of the Syrian City-State from Earliest Times until Its Fall to the Assyrians in 732 B.C.E.* Winona Lake Ind.: Eisenbrauns.

Pognon, H.
1907 *Inscriptions sémitiques de la Syrie, de la Mésopotamie, et de la région de Mossoul*. Paris: Imprimerie nationale.

Rainey, A., and R. S. Notley
2006 *The Sacred Bridge: Carta's Atlas of the Biblical World*. Jerusalem: Carta.

Richmond, I.
1962 The Roman Siege-Works of Masada, Israel. *Journal of Roman Studies* 52:142–55.

Roth, R.
1992 Hadrach. In *The Anchor Bible Dictionary*, ed. D. N. Freedman, 3:17. New York: Doubleday.

Sharon, I., A. Gilboa, T. Jull, and E. Boaretto
2007 Report on the First Stage of the Iron Age Dating Project in Israel: Supporting the Low Chronology. *Radiocarbon* 49:1–46.

Sokoloff, M.
2002 *A Dictionary of Jewish Babylonian Aramaic of the Talmudic and Geonic Periods*. Ramat-Gan, Israel: Bar-Ilan University Press.

Stager, L. E.
1991 *Ashkelon Discovered: From Canaanites to Philistines to Romans and Moslems*. Washington, D.C.: Biblical Archaeology Society.

Stager, L. E., J. D. Schloen, D. M. Master, M. Press, and A. Aja
2008 Part Four: Stratigraphic Overview. In *Ashkelon*, vol. 1, *Introduction and Overview (1985–2006)*, ed. L. E. Stager, J. D. Schloen, and D. M. Master, 212–323. Winona Lake, Ind.: Eisenbrauns.

Ussishkin, D.
1990 The Assyrian Attack on Lachish: The Archaeological Evidence from the Southwest Corner of the Site. *Tel Aviv* 17:53–86.

Yadin, Y.
1963 *The Art of Warfare in Biblical Lands in the Light of Archaeological Study*. Jerusalem: International.
1966 *Masada: Herod's Fortress and the Zealots' Last Stand*. London: Weidenfeld and Nicolson.

Younger, K. L.
2003 Assyrian Involvement in the Southern Levant at the End of the Eighth Century B.C.E. In *Jerusalem in Bible and Archaeology : The First Temple Period*, ed. A. Vaughn and A. Killebrew, 235–63. Society of Biblical Literature Symposium Series 18. Atlanta: Society of Biblical Literature.

30. Divination at Ebla during the Old Syrian Period: The Archaeological Evidence

by Nicolò Marchetti

During the excavation campaigns of 1976, 1985, and 1988 at Ebla, a small chapel (called G3) and its surroundings were exposed in the Middle Bronze Age sacred area on the western acropolis, bringing to light important material evidence for the practice of divination.[1] Archaeological data about divination from other Middle Bronze Age sites are limited and relevant contextual information is almost lacking; the material from Ebla thus represents a significant addition and allows us to draw conclusions about the function and use of clay models, and to begin to evaluate the significance of divination in Old Syrian society.

On the western flanks of the acropolis, namely in Areas D and G, the ruins of Royal Palace G dating from EB IVA were leveled at the beginning of the Middle Bronze Age and a sloping open area was created in which a monumental stairway led to Temple D on the summit.[2]

Temple D is a temple *in antis*, 30 m long, founded in MB I on an earlier building, likewise sacred. The plan is tripartite, with porch, antecella, and cella, in the back wall of which there is a deep niche. Outside Temple D, there was a large round limestone basin and two round plastered bases, which likely were used in ritual activities. In front of the temple there was a square, to the south of which was located the Great Stairway, representing the monumental access to the sacred area. Further to the southwest, the sloping terrain of the acropolis was terraced with large retaining walls, directly built over the earlier structures of Royal Palace G. Rainwater was collected in a long and well-built drain. At the foot of the acropolis there was a stone fortification wall. The southern limit of the area was actually delimited by an upslope continuation of the latter wall, with buttresses. On the slope were built some small bipartite buildings, the plan of which differs from domestic architecture: they may be called subsidiary rooms. Halfway uphill, just to the east of the Great Stairway, there is the small Chapel G3 (figure 1).

Three phases were distinguished within this shrine, the first one dated to MB IB and the other two to MB II (see table 1 for the chronological terminology employed here).[3] An LB I reconstruction was shifted slightly to the east and had a different layout (Mazzoni 2002:131).

In the plan of the final MB phase, which ended with the destruction of the town, two antae were located by the entrance; against the southern one there was the base of a stele, set there during the second phase.[4] The axial niche was placed in the thickness of the back wall. The temple has a slightly latitudinal plan. The small scale and the topographical position of Chapel G3, on a side of the Great Stairway leading to Temple D, confirm that its function was a secondary one within the organization of the sacred area.

During the second phase, an annex (L.3816) was added to the south of the shrine, which is a unique feature in Eblaite temples. The presence of benches in that annex and the absence of a directional axis and of installations indicate that its function must have been ritual rather than cultic. It is in and around this room that the clay models for divination activities were retrieved (figure 2).

---

[1] I wish to thank Paolo Matthiae, director of the Ebla excavations by the University of Rome "La Sapienza," for permission to publish the material presented here. A paper on this subject was presented during the forty-third "Rencontre Assyriologique Internationale" in 1996 in Prague (Marchetti 1996). The figurines studied here have been drawn by Khalid Hsin, inked by Simona Pellegrini, and photographed by Paolo Matthiae and Maurizio Necci; Leonarda De Ninno inked the plan reproduced in figure 1; Avi Winitzer offered some comments on the final draft of the manuscript. I express my sincere gratitude to all of them

[2] See in general, on Areas D, F, and G, Matthiae 1985: pls. 52–53; Matthiae 1989:155–59, fig. 32, pls. 72, 101–2; Marchetti 2001:11–12 n. 14, 14 n. 27, pl. 304. Later superimpositions are particularly thick near the top of the acropolis due to the remains of villages from the Iron Age and later periods, elsewhere scantily represented at Ebla (Matthiae 1989:56–57).

[3] On Chapel G3, see Matthiae 1987a:148–49, fig. 8; Matthiae 1987b:447–50, figs. 1–2; Matthiae 1989:159–60, pl. 100; Matthiae 2006:221–25, figs. 1–3.

[4] That context seems already a secondary one, since two sides were not visible in such position: for the stele, see Matthiae 1987a:149–50, fig. 9; Matthiae 1987b:451–64, figs. 3–21; Matthiae 1989:196–97, pls. 118–25; Matthiae et al. 1995:390–91 no. 236. Two fragments of a standing male statue were found inside the cella L.3939 and just north of it (Matthiae 1987b:450 n. 8; Matthiae 2006:223 n. 39): TM.75.G.728 in square EbV6iii (for which see Matthiae 1980:61 n. 35, fig. 13, where wall M.2845 corresponds to M.3899 of the final plan; Marchetti 2001:pl. 308.3) and TM.75.G.6051 from L.2840 in square EbV6iv, respectively.

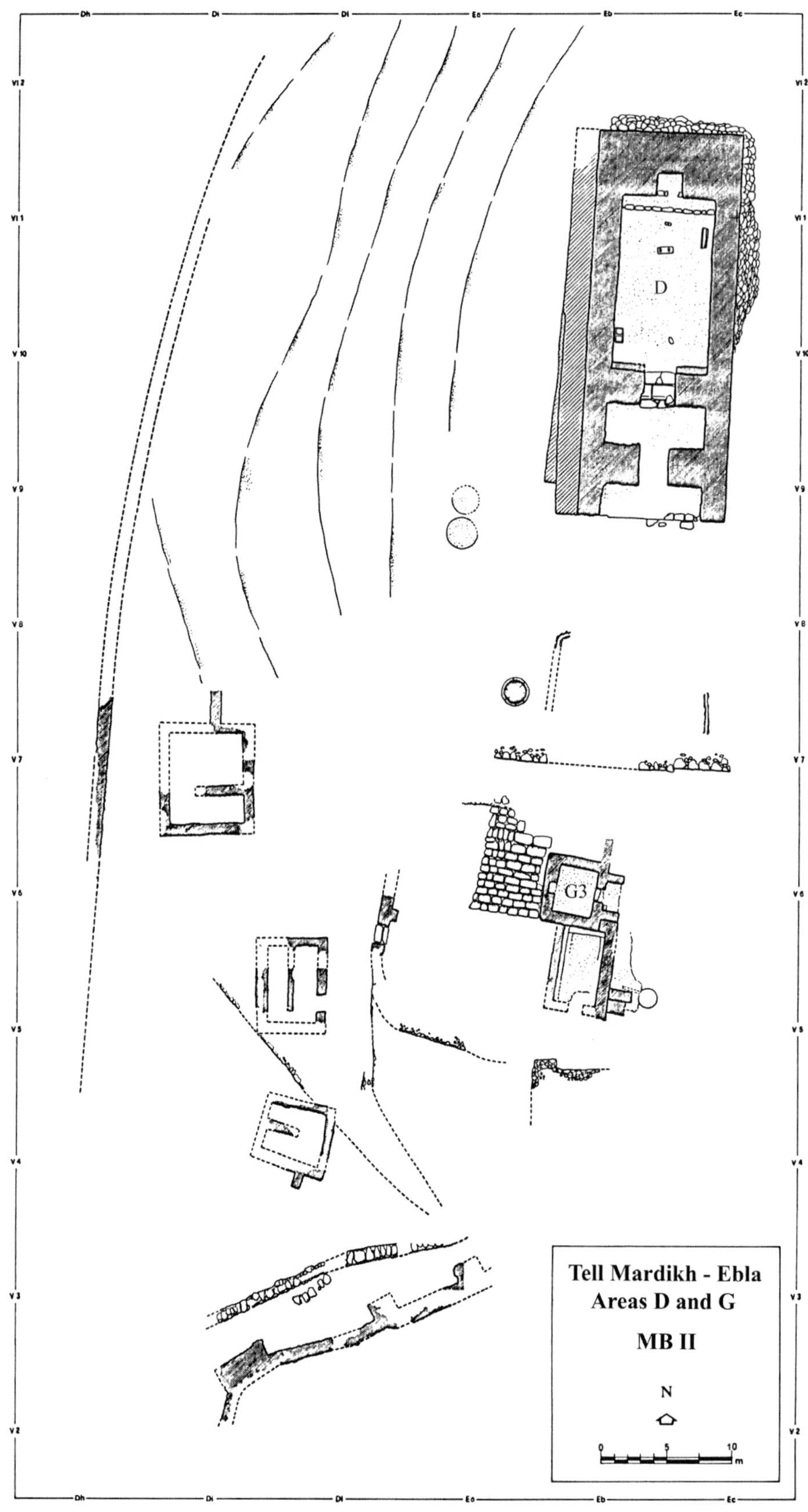

Figure 1. Schematic plan of Areas D and G at Ebla, MB II

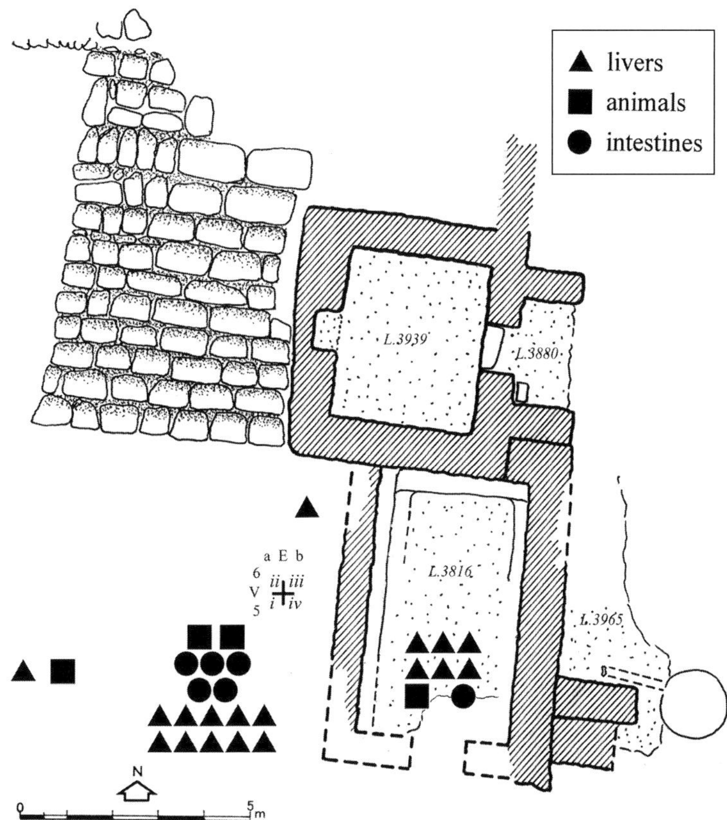

Figure 2. Schematic plan of Chapel G3 at Ebla, MB II, showing the findspots of clay figurines for divination

The Practice of Divination in Chapel G3

Annex L.3816 was entered from the south, so this room did not open on the same side as Chapel G3 but in front of the area at the foot of the Great Stairway. To the east of the annex was a small pipe draining into a pit: it is possible that it was in some way connected to the activities carried on in the nearby room.

In the annex itself, six clay models of livers were found, one model of an intestine, and one malformed animal figurine, while many other models lay just to the west of the annex (figure 2). In total, eighteen liver models, whole or fragmentary, six fragments of intestines, and four malformed animal figurines were found (figure 3; see the catalogue below).[5] From their distribution it seems possible to deduce that they had been scattered at the moment of the destruction and were thus probably all originally kept inside the annex. The models are all uninscribed and are covered with a thin coating of red paint, perhaps in order to imitate the color of entrails.[6] Their paste, yellowish and highly fired, is especially characteristic of the MB IIB period.[7] Although typologically different from contemporary productions,[8] the figurines from Chapel G3 should thus be dated no earlier than mid-MB II based on their technical characteristics and also based on their retrieval context.

[5] For a typological subdivision, see Marchetti 2001:134–35. The livers studied here all belong to type D20F1 (it is doubtful whether no. 9 actually belongs to D20F2, since it is insufficiently preserved), intestines belong to type D20I1, and malformed four-legged animals to type D20A1.

[6] The red paint in some pieces is actually pinkish. Its thickness varies greatly (it can look like a slip in certain cases) and in some liver models the bottom is unpainted. Only two liver model fragments are apparently unpainted (nos. 8 and 9). Malformed animal figurines are also lightly burnished.

[7] All of them are made in paste C1, except two pieces (nos. 2 and 5) in C3 and two (nos. 3 and 9) in E, while the last-three (nos. 32–34) are made in pastes C2, E, and A2, respectively. For a description and classification of the pastes during the Middle Bronze Age, see Marchetti 2001:17–23, table 2.3.

[8] MB IIB figurines were mass produced and are in fact more schematic than the animal specimens from Chapel G3, a trend common to all late Old Syrian choroplastic (Marchetti 2001:113–14, 316–17).

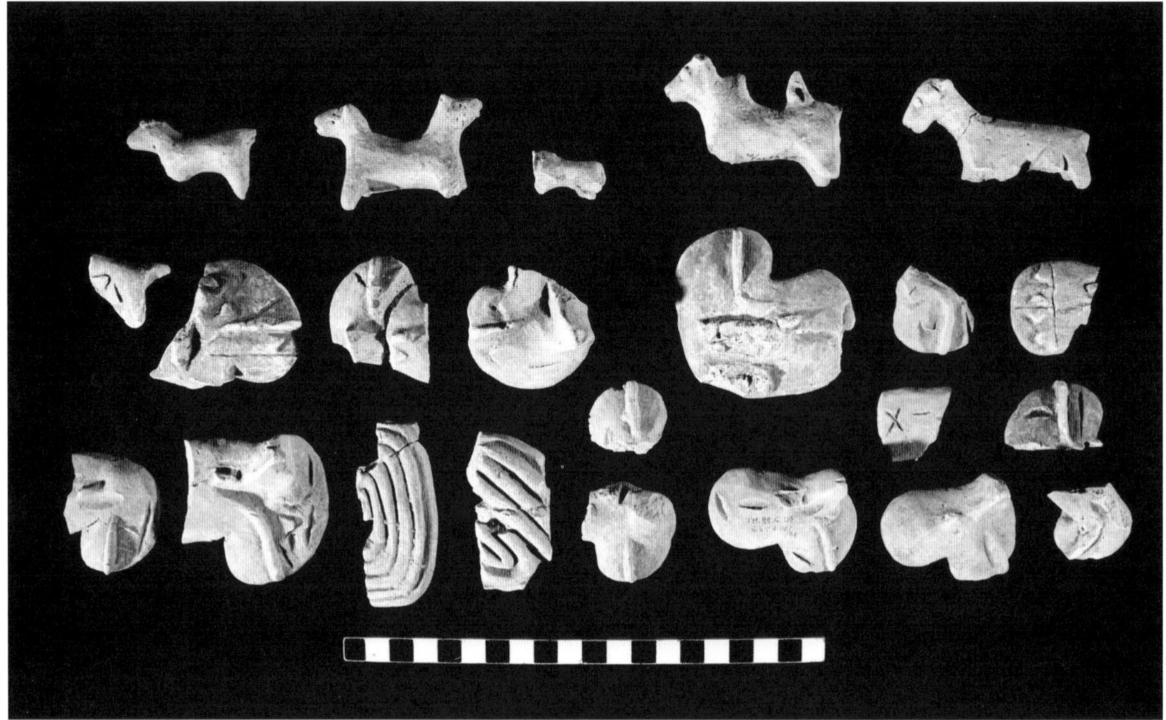

Figure 3. Some of the late Old Syrian clay figurines for divination from Chapel G3 at Ebla

All the livers are marked with incisions in various spots, although never on their bottom side. These marks presumably refer to anomalies in the livers of sacrificial sheep.[9] A few marks on some of the livers are more complex. The livers are of two sizes: smaller, that is ca. 5–6 cm long, and larger, ca. 8–9 cm long, which, incidentally, are close in size to actual sheep livers.

The intestines found are all fragmentary. They have an elongated rounded shape and represent coils in relief (catalogue nos. 21–26). The best preserved fragments (nos. 21 and 22) seem to represent intestines with twelve coils.[10]

Four figurines of quadrupeds are of great interest because they represent animals with clear deformities. It is interesting that they are also painted red: this might be explained as depending on a traditional technique in producing figurines for the diviner's use. One piece presents eight legs (catalogue no. 27), another figurine has two heads and one body (no. 28) and a third one presents only two legs (no. 31).[11] These three figurines seem to represent sheep, while a fourth piece looks like a malformed calf, with two humps on the back, one of which is perforated (no. 29).[12] A fifth specimen, although much smaller than the others, is also painted red and thus belongs to this class (no. 30); at the base of the neck there is a shallow hump which must refer to a deformity.

This evidence indicates that extispicy included three kinds of operations at Ebla, as the different types of models suggest: hepatoscopy, inspection of intestines, and teratological observations. Since the "canonical" Old Babylonian inspection of the entrails goes from head to tail of the animal, with liver, lungs, heart, and intestine examined usually in that order (Goetze 1947:8–9; Starr 1983:69–77; see also Goezte 1957:nos. 1–15, 23 for some order variants or omissions), it is likely that liver and intestine models were used together within a single divinatory operation. On the other hand, clay models of malformed animals

[9] In the case of the liver no. 6, for example, Meyer (1987: 247) thinks that it represents a positive omen, because the negative marks—the three side indentations and the incision—appear on the *pars hostilis*, the left side (the tip, in fact, was oriented downwards normally), thus giving a positive result.

[10] The number of coils of the colon recorded normally varied between 10 and 14 (see Starr 1983:95; Koch 2002; Richardson 2002). The Old Babylonian models illustrated in Goezte 1947:15, nos. 64–66, pl. 133 also present this number of coils.

[11] The two legs along the left side in fact are not broken away but have been smoothed and are also covered by the red paint, so it is sure that they were intended to be lacking.

[12] These animal figurines bear no resemblance to contemporary, late MB II choroplastic productions (see n. 9 above) and are thus of difficult identification.

have been found for the first time and moreover in a well-defined context.[13] Actually, this association of monstrous animal figurines with liver and intestine models provides very instructive evidence for reconstructing the practice of divination in light of the archaeological context.

Two other specimens of figurines for divination activities from secondary contexts in nearby areas on the acropolis may be mentioned here (see catalogue nos. 32–33), since they possibly also originate from Chapel G3.[14] They are a fragment of an intestine found east of Temple D (no. 32), also painted red; and a water turtle from the southern slope of the acropolis (no. 33). The latter specimen has a very elaborate pattern of incised marks on the carapace which are filled with red paint, recalling an almost identical specimen from a MB II house at Tell Tuqan, 15 km to the east, where, however, the marks are not incised but are painted in red and white (no. 34). These two interesting pieces suggest the existence of a divination practice perhaps based on the interpretation of the pattern of cracks which appeared on the surface of the carapace after heating it, as was the case with Chinese oracular bones and carapaces dating from the Shang Dynasty in the mid-second millennium B.C.E. (see Keightley 1978). The marks on these two Old Syrian turtle models do not seem to accord with the system unraveled for the livers by Meyer (1984; 1987).[15]

Contemporary Evidence for Divination from Other Sites

Although the main purpose of the present paper is to present a group of stratified material for divination activities in its context, it is also necessary to set this material—however briefly—within a wider framework. Comparative evidence from other MB II contexts will thus be reviewed here, as well as contemporary textual references.[16]

Clay liver models find their most elaborate discussion in Meyer's work, while other types of figurines for divination have not yet been systematically studied.[17] The bulk of that material comes from Syria-Palestine and dates from the Late Bronze Age, while Middle Bronze Age models are a minority. One should also note that specimens from the east were found in secular contexts, while those from the west come mainly, but not only, from sacred areas (as is the case at Ebla). It seems likely that in the west partly autonomous lines of enquiry were developed; uninscribed liver models probably represent a regional feature and must have been read by diviners in a binary way, as giving a positive or negative omen.[18]

Provenanced Middle Bronze Age inscribed liver models come from the scribal-school building and private houses at Tell al-Seib in the Hamrin,[19] dating from the classic Old Baylonian period, and from a

---

[13] Only very rare figurines in museum colletions may be recalled, such as one from the AUB Museum in Beirut (Marchetti 2001:272, table 3:30 *sub* 64.23), and they lack the most characteristic features of the small Eblaite series.

[14] The single clay liver model found in the southern lower town at Ebla (Meyer 1987:34, pl. 25 bottom left; S. Mazzoni in Matthiae et al. 1995:420, no. 288; Marchetti 2001: 437 no. 2212), between Temple B1 and Chapel B2, which were possibly dedicated to the cult of Rašap and of royal ancestors, respectively (Matthiae 1989:153–54; Matthiae 2006:219), perhaps belongs, however, to overlying LB I layers ("level 2"; see Marchetti 2001:136). Another liver, also unpainted but of a different, more squared type comes from a MB II layer in Fort V (Marchetti 2000:848–49, fig. 24; Marchetti 2001:134, fig. 69; note that the piece comes from room L.6528, not far from the chapel in L.7113, on which see Matthiae 2006:fig. 7).

[15] The incisions on a clay model of a lung from Alalakh, also defying interpretation, can be recalled: see C. J. Gadd in Woolley 1955:250–57, pl. 59. The precise findspot of this object is not given in the publication: in the list of plates (ibid., p. vii *sub* LIX) it is said to come from Level VI, dated to early LB I; on the other hand, the latter is almost completely lost (ibid., p. 66) and so the relevant stratigraphy cannot be considered reliable. One can note that the excavation number of the lung model (AT/47/75) is very close to the series of the objects from the temple area of level VII (ibid., p. 64).

[16] The early history of divination in Mesopotamia falls outside the scope of this paper; see in general Koch-Westenholz 2000:13–19, which must be integrated with the evidence from classic Early Syrian (i.e., Early Dynastic IIIb) Ebla, for which see Fronzaroli 1997; Catagnoti and Bonechi 1998; Biga 1999; Coser 2000.

[17] For liver models, see Meyer 1987. For a list of intestines and lung models see, e.g., Nougayrol 1968:32, to which one can add Meyer 1993, a spleen model. While models of malformed newborn animals and of water turtles were not previously attested, one should also note here that intestines are much rarer than livers and contextual information was until now completely lacking for the former ones.

[18] Oppenheim (1977:372 n. 46) opposes the "scholarly approach" of southern Mesopotamia to "folklore divination," as practiced at Mari (but compare Leichty 1966:133 and, from another perspective, Koch-Westenholz 2000:12). Durand (2000:92) speaks of "une tradition mariote." See also the comments by Durand 1997:274 about the practice of divination using birds at Mari.

[19] For the specimen from the school building see Hanoun 1979:fig. 6 and Meyer 1987:46–47, while for that from the house, see al-Rawi 1994:38–40, figs. 7–8 (the model has the marks of the liver incised on its top part and the written description of belly, heart, intestines, and breastbone on the bottom one). See also ibid., p. 41, figs. 9–19 for an inscribed model liver fragment from nearby Tell Haddad.

contemporary secondary archive (Room 108) in the royal palace at Mari.[20] These two contexts speak for a documentary function within the scribal milieu, that is, of instruction models kept as reference records for the palace chancery or for teaching and study purposes. The Eblaite uninscribed material adds new evidence for the use of models during this early period. They come from a sacred area and thus connect the various types of models with a system of examining entrails (livers and intestines) and newborn malformed animals.

Clay liver models from the Late Bronze Age, not discussed here, continue the Ebla tradition. As far as their retrieval context is concerned, the most interesting case is perhaps the one at Tell Munbaqat on the Euphrates, where thirteen models were found in the vicinity of the "Steingebäude," an annex of the tripartite temple *in antis* "Steinbau 1" (Orthmann 1976:28–29, 41, figs. 1, 10).[21] The layout of this area closely resembles that of Temple D and Chapel G3 at Ebla.

While the evidence for the relationships between written diviner's manuals and clay liver models has been extensively discussed (see Meyer 1987:55–79; Koch-Westenholz 2000:38–70), it is interesting to note here the correspondence of malformed animal figurines from Ebla with some of the records preserved in the most complete late Old Babylonian specimen of the *šumma izbu* series.[22] Among the cases listed by this approximately contemporary text, one passage may be quoted for no. 27: "if an anomaly has one head, two spines, two tails, eight feet—the king will conquer a land which is not his own."[23] With regard to no. 28, with two heads, one may recall: "if an anomaly has two heads—a person with no right to the throne will seize it" (Leichty 1970:204, no. 23); while our no. 31, with only the two left legs, seems related to "if an anomaly's right shoulder is already torn out—an enemy will seize your border city" (Leichty 1970:202, no. 5).

Specific reports on malformed newborns were addressed to priests (Leichty 1970:7–8) or to the king.[24] Divination was presumably not specifically connected with kingship during the classic and late Old Babylonian period, as far as we can judge.[25] But since it was a direct means of communication between the heavenly and earthly spheres and since the palace administration was obviously the main patron, it seems natural that the extant documentation focuses on the king and on matters potentially affecting the whole country. At Ebla, the practice of divination took place in an annex adjoining a chapel: since Chapel G3 was part of the sacred area of Temple D on the acropolis, dedicated to Ištar as dynastic goddess (as opposed to her sacred area in the lower town, where somewhat different rites were carried out), it is likely that divination was done there in close relationship with the role of kingship in ritual activities.[26]

---

[20] Meyer 1987:44–46, pls. 14:4–9, 17:1–6. The Mari specimens were deemed older than the associated tablets by Rutten (1938:36), but Durand (1982) says they are "d'époques mêlées." See also Michalowski 2006:249 for the "didactic purpose" of the omen exemplars on the Mari livers and for an evaluation of the role of extispicy texts in general in school milieus.

[21] Interestingly enough, a model was embedded in the stairway of Steinbau 2, possibly representing a positive omen for the temple construction (Meyer 1987:37).

[22] For the textual history of this collection, see Leichty 1966; Leichty 1970:23–24. One can now add materials such as Salvini 1996:117–22.

[23] Leichty 1970:206, no. 45. Malformations are especially typical in flocks for three main reasons: these animals are strictly consanguineous; they may eat—by reaching new grazing areas—plants containing alkaloids, which are teratogenous; and, finally, the lack of proteins during the final stage of pregnancy is sufficient cause for a malformation (see Leipold et al. 1972). I wish to thank Sergio Biavati (curator of the Museum of Veterinary Pathology and Teratology at the Alma Mater Studiorum—University of Bologna) for providing me with this information.

[24] For example, a letter from the royal archives of Mari says: "un agneau-*izbum* est né à Zarrum Rabbum. . . . Il n'a qu'un tête; sa face est est celle d'un ovin mâle; il n'a qu'une poitrine, (qu'un) coeur, (qu'un seul) ensemble de viscères; (mais) depuis son nombril jusqu'à sa hanche, (il a) deux corps. . . . Maintenant, je (l')ai fait porter à mon Seigneur afin que mon Seigneur le voie" (Durand 1988:497, no. 241). Ominous births and entrails were thus physically sent to the palace, presumably for direct examination by specialists (Durand 1988:52–53; Guichard 1997:308; Durand 2000:94; that models were actually done on purpose seems unlikely, *contra* Oppenheim 1954:143–44), at a time when, according to Durand (1988:488), written compendia were not yet available.

[25] In fact a tablet, dating from the late Old Babylonian period and belonging to the *šumma ālum* series, comes from a Level 3A private house at Haradum on the Euphrates (Joannès 1994). The case discussed by Guichard 1997:309 does not seem to justify the question whether "une naissance prodigieuse était à cette époque exclusivement de caractère royal." Pongratz-Leisten (1999:133) offers a balanced approach to this matter. See the arguments by Starr (1983:12–14) on the early passage from an empirical to a theoretical stage with "stock"-apodoses; cf. also Koch-Westenholz 2002:140–45 on private versus public (at Mari) divinatory enquiries, whereas the king and the administration are called "the most important client" (ibid., p. 141).

[26] It remains hypothetical, though fascinating, that "das Gebäude G3 ist als eigener Bereich des *bārû* zu interpretieren" (Pongratz-Leisten 1999:133). See also Richardson 2002 on the life of the diviner. On the sacred area P in the lower town at Ebla, see Marchetti and Nigro 1997.

The greatest part of the archaeological and epigraphic evidence about divination during the Old Babylonian and Old Syrian periods dates from the second half of the period (MB II). Clay models of livers were either kept for instruction and recording purposes, as at Tell as-Seib and Mari, or were used in direct connection with the practice of divination. At Ebla, divination was carried out in a secondary sector of the main sacred area of the town. It included extispicy and also the interpretation of monstrous animal births, as is demonstrated by the discovery of figurines of malformed animals, the only ones of this kind found thus far. If we are to foster our understanding of ancient intellectual processes, it seems necessary to study separately the archaeological and epigraphic evidence before comparing and elaborating the respective results. An archaeological approach in historical perspective, through its specific methods and aims, may supply independent answers concerning how the ancients shaped their religious thought and consequently represented it in artistic media and in material culture.

Table 1. Relative Chronology of Syria, Palestine, and Mesopotamia during the Middle Bronze Age

<table>
<tr><th>Syria (archaeological)</th><th>Syria (art historical)</th><th>Ebla</th><th>Alalakh</th><th>ʿAmuq</th><th>Palestine</th><th>Mesopotamia</th></tr>
<tr><td rowspan="2">MB IA</td><td rowspan="3">early
Old Syrian</td><td rowspan="2">IIIA1</td><td rowspan="2">XVI
XIV</td><td rowspan="3">K</td><td rowspan="3">MB I
MB IIA</td><td>↓
Ur III</td></tr>
<tr><td rowspan="2">early
Old Babylonian
Isin-Larsa</td></tr>
<tr><td>MB IB</td><td>IIIA2</td><td>XIII
X</td></tr>
<tr><td>MB IIA</td><td>frühklassisch
initial
classic
Old Syrian
hochklassisch
full
spätklassisch</td><td>IIIB1</td><td>IX
VIII</td><td rowspan="2">L</td><td>MB II
MB IIB</td><td>classic
Old Babylonian</td></tr>
<tr><td>MB IIB</td><td>late
Old Syrian
nachklassisch</td><td>IIIB2</td><td>VII</td><td>MB III
MB IIC</td><td>late
Old Babylonian</td></tr>
<tr><td>LB I</td><td>early
Middle Syrian</td><td>IVA</td><td>VI
V</td><td>M</td><td>LB I</td><td>early Middle
Babylonian
early Kassite</td></tr>
</table>

N.B. Alternative terminologies are in italics.

Catalogue of MB II Figurines for Divination Activities from Chapel G3 at Ebla

Measurements are in centimeters. For a detailed explanation of the recording system for the various findspots, see Marchetti 2001:335–37. The scale of the drawings is 1:2.

Livers

1. TM.76.G.397

Paste: C1
Square: EaV5i; Level: 3
Degrees: 265° EaV5i
Distance: 190 EaV5i
Elevation: -132 EaV5i
Pottery bucket: 428
Height: 5.3
Length: 4.3
Thickness: 1.7
Museum: Idlib, deposit
Bibliography: Marchetti 2001:134, 436 no. 2203, pl. 228

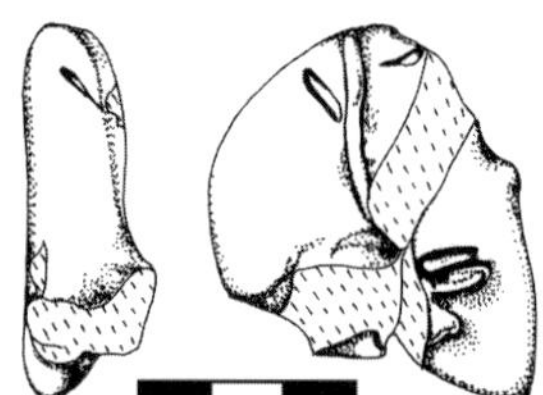

2. TM.76.G.398

Paste: C3
Square: EaV5i
Level: 3
Degrees: 265° EaV5i
Distance: 190 EaV5i
Elevation: -132 EaV5i
Pottery bucket: 428
Height: 2.8
Length: 3
Thickness: 1.1
Museum: Idlib, deposit
Bibliography: Marchetti 2001:134, 436 no. 2204

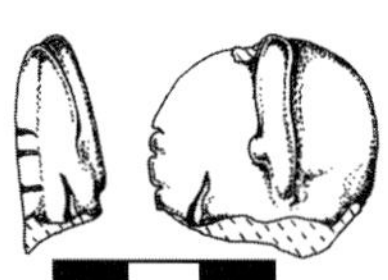

3. TM.76.G.399

Paste: E
Square: EaV5i
Level: 3
Degrees: 265° EaV5i
Distance: 190 EaV5i
Elevation: -132 EaV5i
Pottery bucket: 428
Height: 3.9
Length: 4.5
Thickness: 1
Museum: Idlib, deposit
Bibliography: Marchetti 2001:134, 436 no. 2205

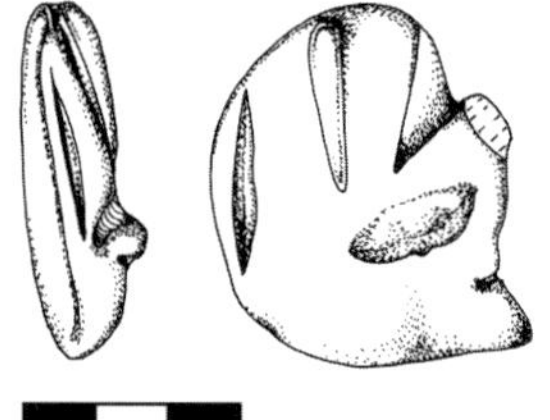

4. TM.76.G.400+406

Paste: C1
Square: EaV5i
Level: 3
Degrees: 265° EaV5i
Distance: 190 EaV5i
Elevation: -132 EaV5i
Pottery bucket: 428
Height: 6.5
Length: 5.5
Thickness: 2.5
Museum: Idlib, deposit
Bibliography: Marchetti 2001:134, 437 no. 2206

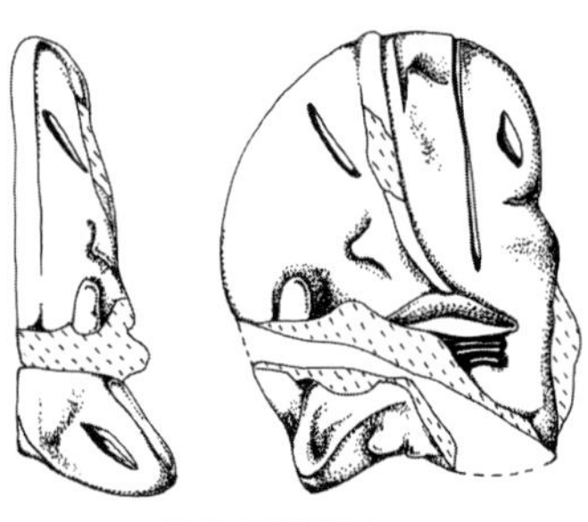

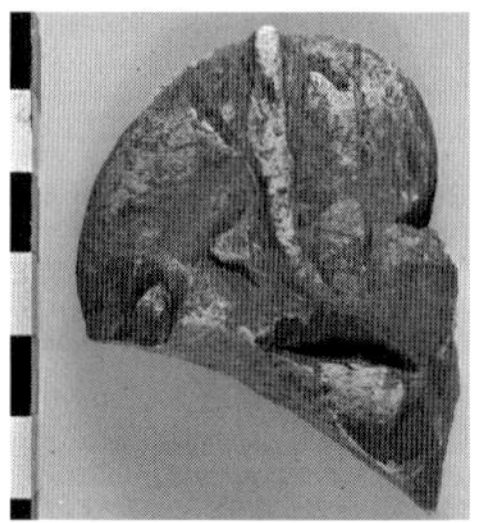

5. TM.76.G.402

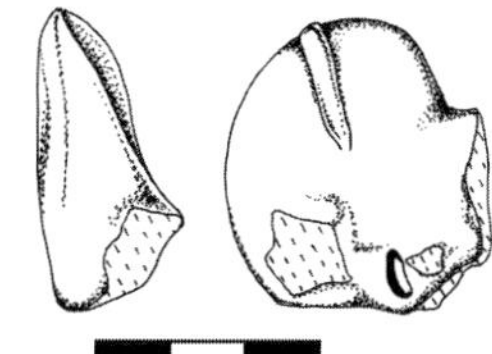
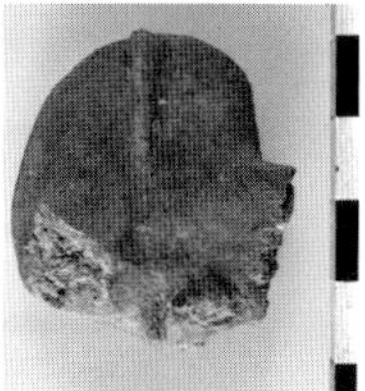

Paste:	C3
Square:	EaV5i
Level:	3
Degrees:	265° EaV5i
Distance:	190 EaV5i
Elevation:	-132 EaV5i
Pottery bucket:	428
Height:	3.6
Length:	3.7
Thickness:	1.8
Museum:	Idlib, deposit
Bibliography:	Marchetti 2001:134, 437 no. 2207

6. TM.76.G.403

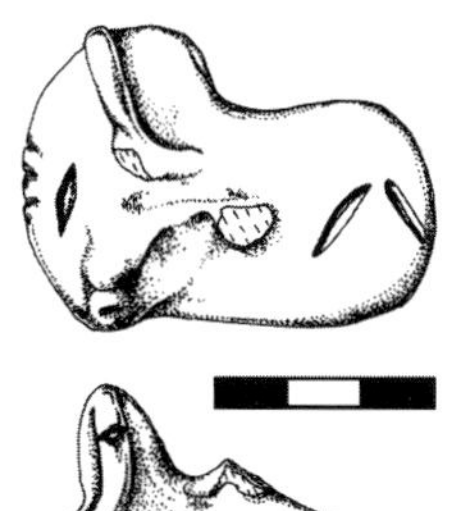

Paste:	C1
Square:	EaV5i
Level:	3
Degrees:	265° EaV5i
Distance:	190 EaV5i
Elevation:	-132 EaV5i
Pottery bucket:	428
Height:	5.7
Length:	4
Thickness:	2.3
Museum:	Idlib, showcase
Bibliography:	Marchetti 2001:134, 437 no. 2208, pl 92; Meyer 1987:35, 247, pl. 25 bottom right

7. TM.76.G.404

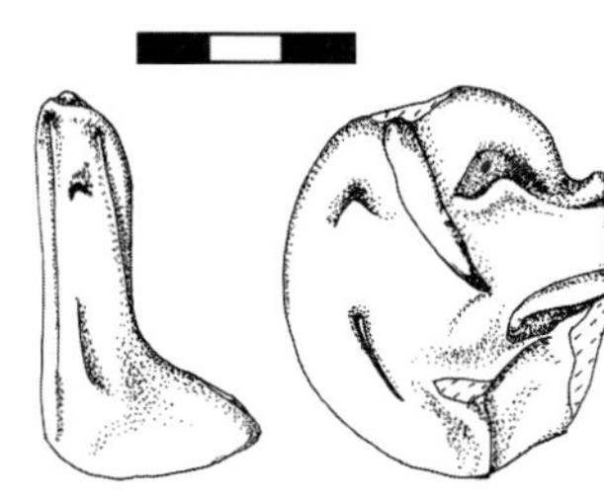

Paste:	C1
Square:	EaV5i
Level:	3
Degrees:	265° EaV5i
Distance:	190 EaV5i
Elevation:	-132 EaV5i
Pottery bucket:	428
Height:	4.5
Length:	5
Thickness:	2.8
Museum:	Idlib, deposit
Bibliography:	Marchetti 2001:134, 437 no. 2209

8. TM.76.G.405

Paste:	C1
Square:	EaV5i
Level:	3
Degrees:	265° EaV5i
Distance:	190 EaV5i
Elevation:	-132 EaV5i
Pottery bucket:	428
Height:	2.5
Length:	2.3
Thickness:	1.8
Museum:	Idlib, deposit
Bibliography:	Marchetti 2001:134, 437 no. 2210

9. TM.76.G.407

Paste:	E
Square:	EaV5i
Level:	3
Degrees:	265° EaV5i
Distance:	190 EaV5i
Elevation:	-132 EaV5i
Pottery bucket:	428
Height:	3
Length:	2.5
Thickness:	1
Museum:	Idlib, deposit
Bibliography:	Marchetti 2001:134, 437 no. 2213

10. TM.76.G.408

Paste:	C1
Square:	EaV5i
Level:	3
Degrees:	265° EaV5i
Distance:	190 EaV5i
Elevation:	-132 EaV5i
Pottery bucket:	428
Height:	1.7
Length:	1.8
Thickness:	1.3
Museum:	Idlib, deposit
Bibliography:	Marchetti 2001:134, 437 no. 2211

11. TM.85.G.46

Paste:	C1
Square:	EbV5iv
Level:	4
Pottery bucket:	470
Height:	3.7
Length:	3
Thickness:	1.4

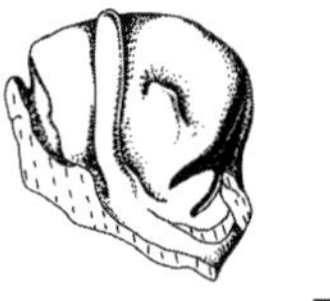
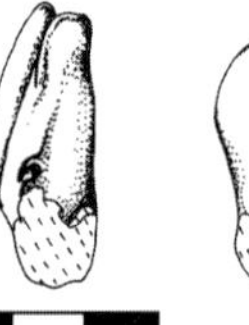

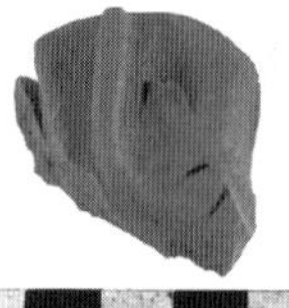

12. TM.85.G.50

Paste:	C1
Square:	EbV5iv
Level:	4
Elevation:	-160 from top of M.3803
Pottery bucket:	71
Height:	5.6
Length:	4.5
Thickness:	2.8

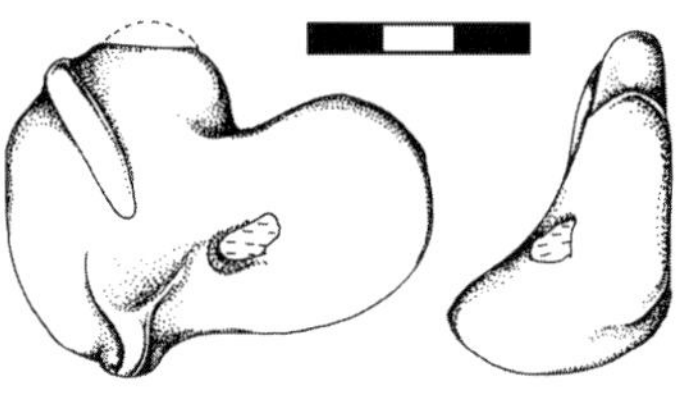

13. TM.85.G.51

Paste:	C1
Square:	EbV5iv
Level:	4
Elevation:	-160 from the top of M.3803
Pottery bucket:	71
Height:	4.3
Length:	3
Thickness:	1.3

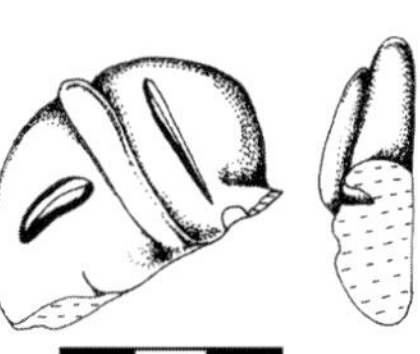
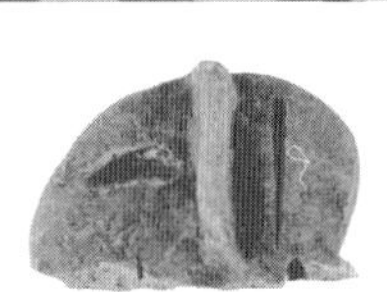

14. TM.85.G.52

Paste:	C1
Square:	EbV5iv
Level:	4
Elevation:	-160 from the top of M.3803
Pottery bucket:	71
Height:	3.8
Length:	3.3
Thickness:	1.4

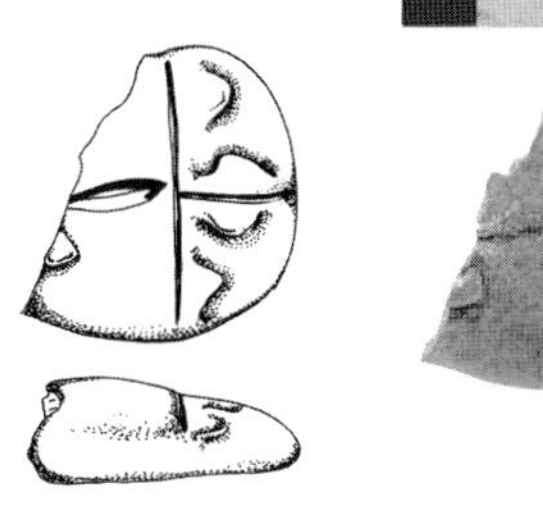

15. TM.85.G.53

Paste:	C1
Square:	EbV5iv
Level:	4
Elevation:	-160 from the top of M.3803
Pottery bucket:	71
Height:	3.3
Length:	3.5
Thickness:	1.3

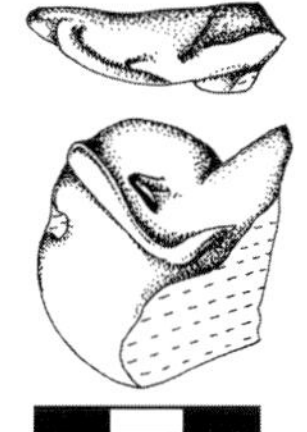

16. TM.85.G.54

Paste:	C1
Square:	EbV5iv
Level:	4
Elevation:	-160 from the top of M.3803
Pottery bucket:	71
Height:	3.1
Length:	0.7
Thickness:	1

17. TM.85.G.122

Paste:	C1
Square:	EbV5iv; L.3816
Level:	4
Elevation abs.:	422.64
Pottery bucket:	95
Height:	6.2
Length:	4.2
Thickness:	2.2

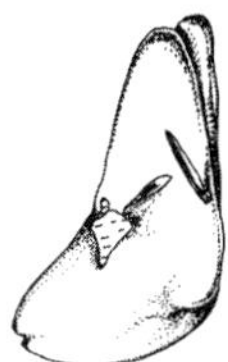

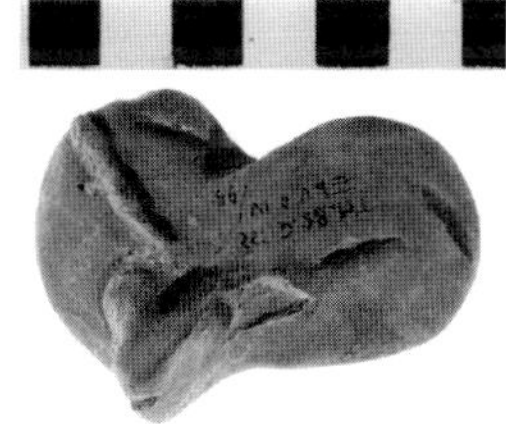

18. TM.85.G.229

Paste:	C1
Square:	EbV8iii+EbV7iv
Height:	3
Length:	2.8
Thickness:	1

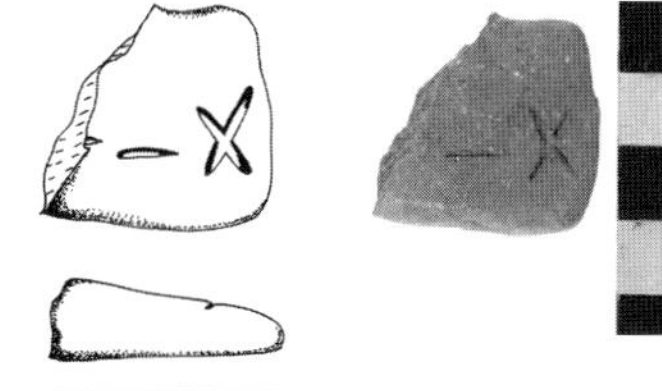

19. TM.85.G.280

Paste:	C1
Square:	EbV6ii; west of M.3817
Level:	5
Pottery bucket:	531
Height:	7.8
Length:	6.2
Thickness:	1.5

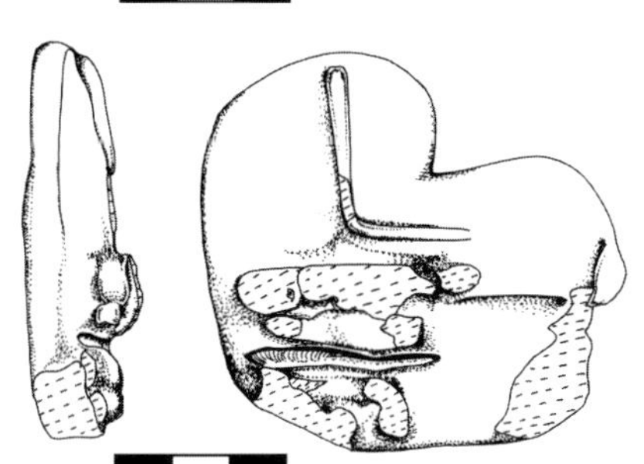

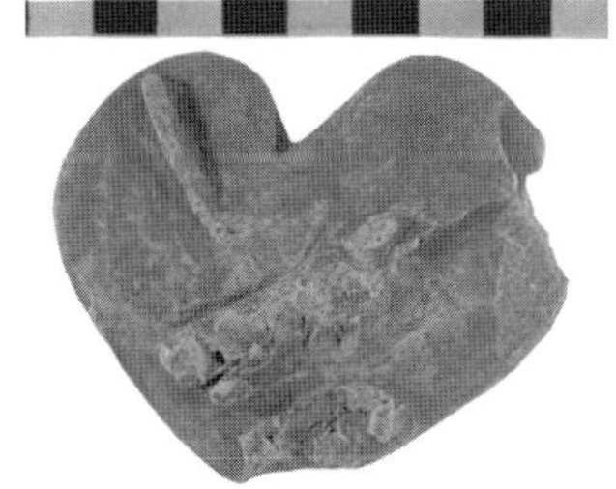

20. TM.88.G.432

Paste:	C1
Square:	EaV5i; L.2890
Height:	5.7
Length:	5.8
Thickness:	2.9

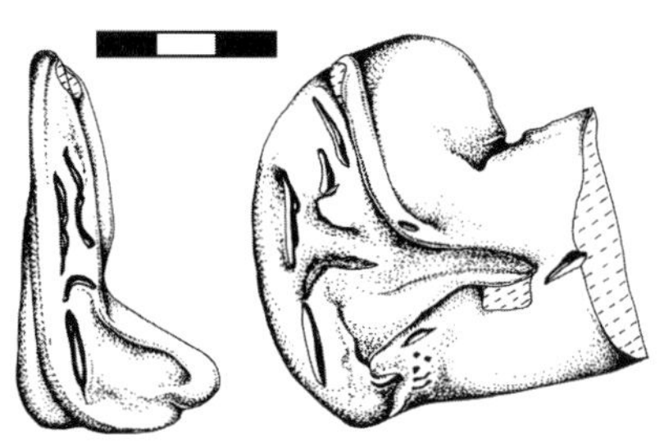

Intestines

21. TM.76.G.395+396f

Paste:	C1
Square:	EaV5i
Level:	3
Degrees:	265° EaV5i
Distance:	190 EaV5i
Elevation:	-132 EaV5i
Pottery bucket:	428
Height:	7.5
Length:	3.3
Thickness:	1
Museum:	Idlib, deposit
Bibliography:	Marchetti 2001:135, 437 no. 2215, pl. 92

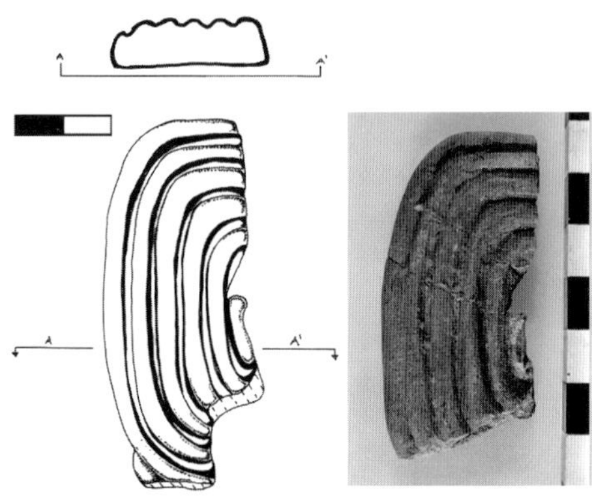

See also (f) in photograph for no. 23.

22. TM.76.G.396a

Paste:	C1
Square:	EaV5i
Level:	3
Degrees:	265° EaV5i
Distance:	190 EaV5i
Elevation:	-132 EaV5i
Pottery bucket:	428
Height:	4.2
Length:	4.3
Thickness:	1
Museum:	Idlib, deposit
Bibliography:	Marchetti 2001:135, 437 no. 2216

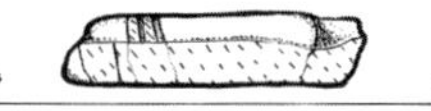

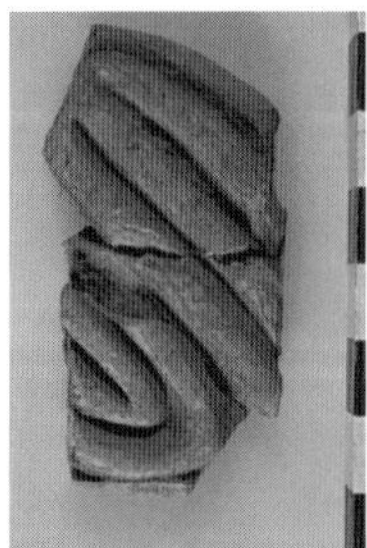

23. TM.76.G.396b *See b in photograph.*

Paste:	C1
Square:	EaV5i
Level:	3
Degrees:	265° EaV5i
Distance:	190 EaV5i
Elevation:	-132 EaV5i
Pottery bucket:	428
Height:	4.3
Length:	2.7
Thickness:	1
Bibliography:	Marchetti 2001:135, 437 no. 2217

24. TM.76.G.396c *See c in photograph for no. 23 above.*

Paste:	C1
Square:	EaV5i
Level:	3
Degrees:	265° EaV5i
Distance:	190 EaV5i
Elevation:	-132 EaV5i
Pottery bucket:	428
Height:	2.5
Length:	2
Thickness:	1
Museum:	Idlib, deposit
Bibliography:	Marchetti 2001:135, 437 no. 2218

25. TM.76.G.396d *See d in photograph for no. 23 above.*

Paste:	C1
Square:	EaV5i
Level:	3
Degrees:	265° EaV5i
Distance:	190 EaV5i
Elevation:	-132 EaV5i
Pottery bucket:	428
Height:	2.8
Length:	2.2
Thickness:	0.7
Museum:	Idlib, deposit
Bibliography:	Marchetti 2001:135, 437 no. 2219

26. TM.76.G.396e *See e in photograph for no. 23 above.*

Paste:	C1
Square:	EaV5i
Level:	3
Degrees:	265° EaV5i
Distance:	190 EaV5i
Elevation:	-132 EaV5i
Pottery bucket:	428
Height:	2.7
Length:	1.5
Thickness:	1.1
Museum:	Idlib, deposit
Bibliography:	Marchetti 2001:135, 437 no. 2220

Malformed Animals

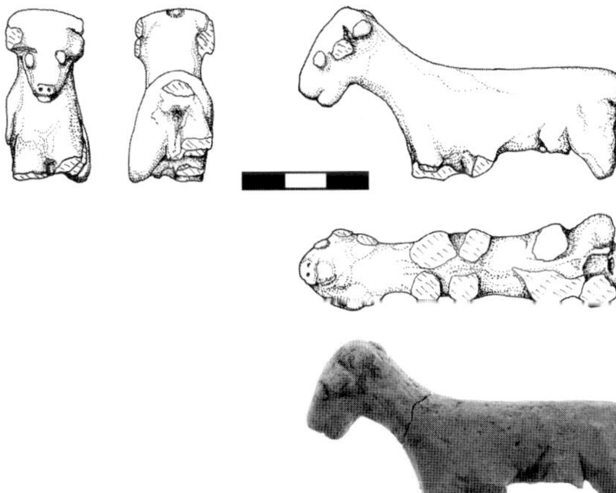

27. TM.76.G.385

Paste:	C1
Square:	EaV5i
Level:	3
Degrees:	250° EaV5i
Distance:	270 EaV5i
Elevation:	-114 EaV5i
Pottery bucket:	428
Height:	3.7
Length:	7.6
Thickness:	1.8
Museum:	Idlib, storeroom
Bibliography:	Marchetti 2001:135, 437 no. 2221, pl. 92

28. TM.76.G.401

Paste:	C1
Square:	EaV5i
Level:	3
Degrees:	265° EaV5i
Distance:	190 EaV5i
Elevation:	-132 EaV5i
Pottery bucket:	428
Height:	4.1
Length:	6.7
Thickness:	2.1
Museum:	Idlib, deposit
Bibliography:	Marchetti 2001:135, 437 no. 2222

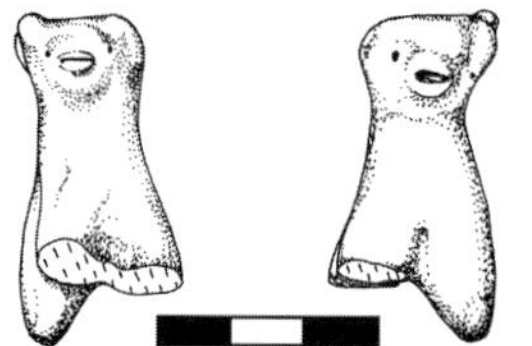
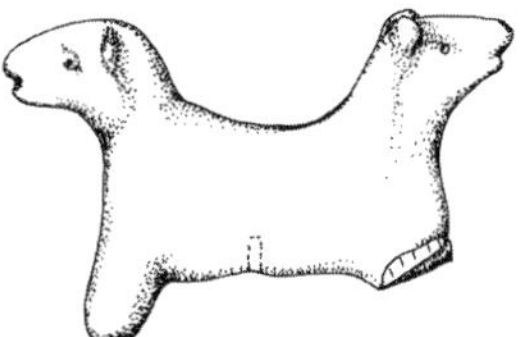

29. TM.85.G.49

Paste:	C1
Square:	EbV5iv; Level: 4
Elevation:	-160 from top of M.3803
Pottery bucket:	71
Height:	4.5
Length:	7
Thickness:	3.1

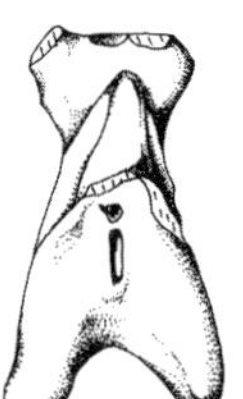
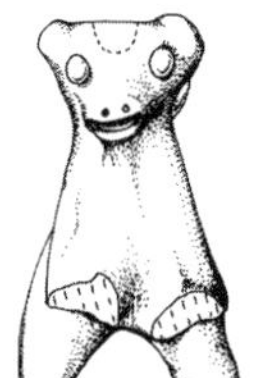
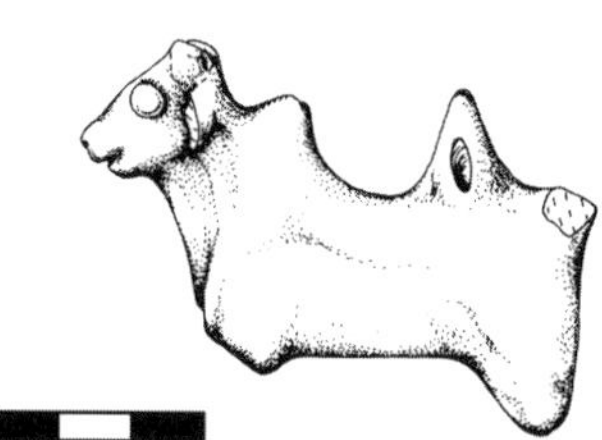
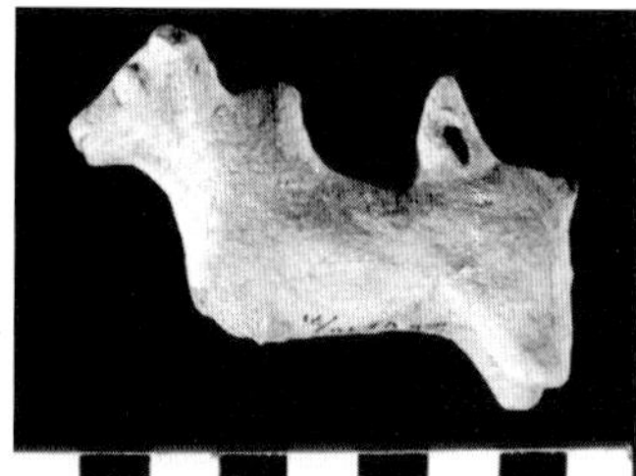

30. TM.85.G.55

Paste:	C1
Square:	EbV5iv
Level:	4
Elevation:	-160 from top of M.3803
Pottery bucket:	71
Height:	1.5
Length:	3.1
Thickness:	1.3

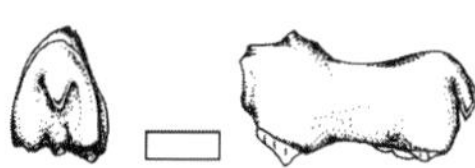

31. TM.88.G.439

Paste:	C1
Square:	EaV5i; L.2890
Height:	4
Length:	1.7
Thickness:	5.2

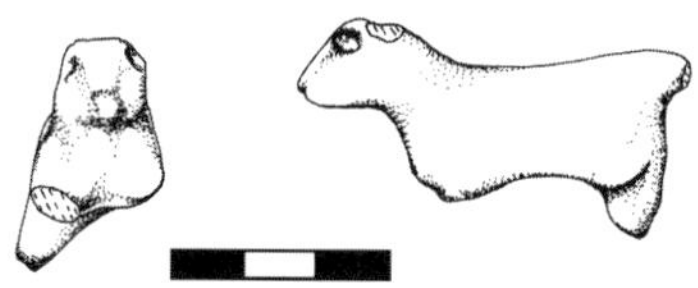

OTHER MB II FIGURINES FOR DIVINATION ACTIVITIES FROM EBLA AND TELL TUQAN

Intestine

32. TM.67.F.657

Paste:	C2
Pottery bucket:	78
Height:	4.2
Length:	3.2
Thickness:	0.8
Museum:	Idlib, deposit
Bibliography:	Marchetti 2001:135, 437 no. 2214

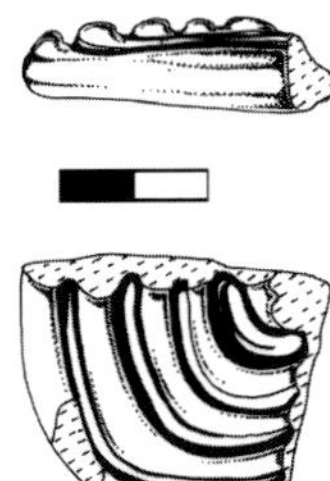

Water Turtles

33. TM.83.G.311

Paste:	E
Square:	EfIV10iv, level 10, from a pit (against wall M.3467)
Pottery bucket:	446
Height:	3.7
Length:	8.1
Thickness:	7
Museum:	Idlib, deposit
Bibliography:	Marchetti 2001:135 n. 244

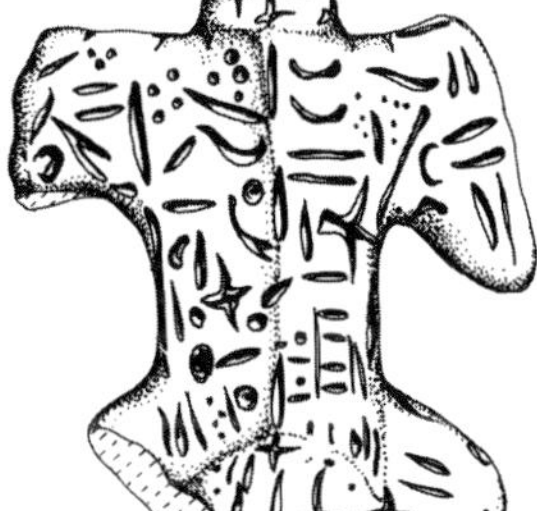

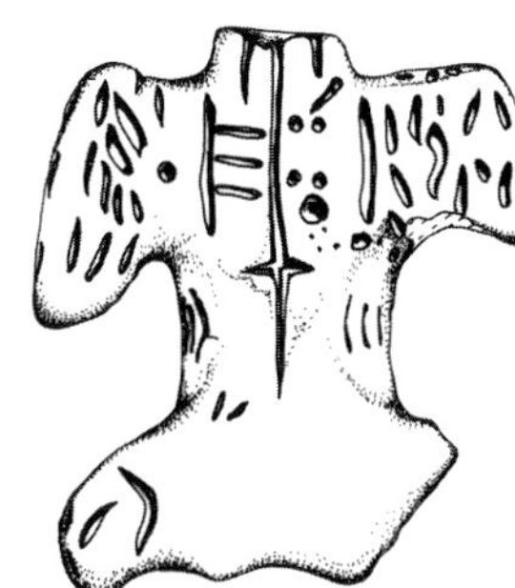

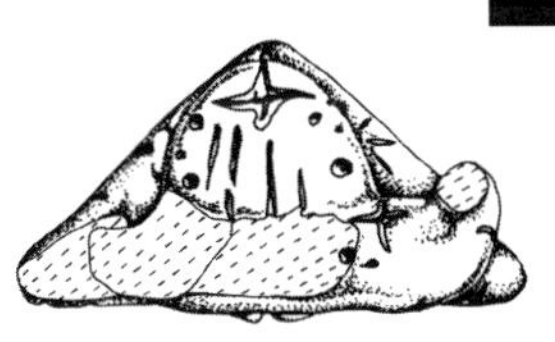

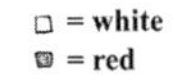

□ = white
▣ = red

34. TT.86.H.50

Paste:	A2
Square:	DeVI13; L.348
Pottery bucket:	146
Height:	3.7
Length:	8.1
Thickness:	7
Museum:	Idlib, showcase (Idlib inv. 2368)
Bibliography:	Marchetti 2001:135 n. 244; R. Fiorentino in Baffi 2006: 121, 125, fig. 50d

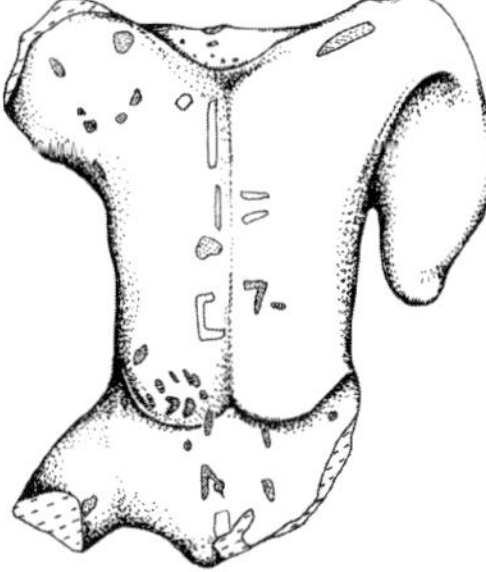

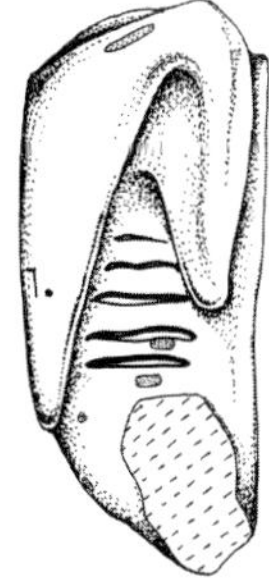

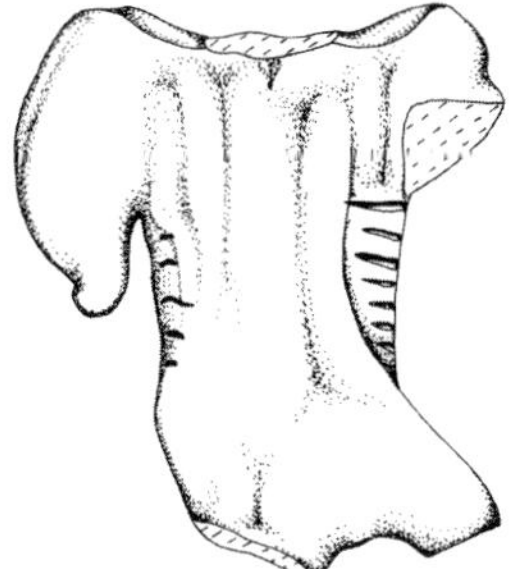

Bibliography

Baffi, F., ed.
2006 *Tell Tuqan: Ricerche archeologiche italiane nella regione del Maath (Siria).* Galatina: Congedo.

Biga, M. G.
1999 Omens and Divination at Ebla. *NABU* 1999:109.

Catagnoti, A., and M. Bonechi
1998 Magic and Divination at IIIrd Millennium Ebla, I. *SEL* 15:17–39.

Coser, M.
2000 An Extispicy Report in III Millennium Ebla. *UF* 32:169–76.

Durand, J.-M.
1982 A propos de foies de Mari. *MARI* 2:218.
1988 *Archives épistolaires de Mari.* Vol. 1/1. ARM 26. Paris: Éditions Recherche sur les Civilisations.
1997 La divination par les oiseaux. *MARI* 8:273–82.
2000 *Les documents épistolaires du palais de Mari.* Vol. 3. LAPO 18. Paris: Éditions du Cerf.

Fronzaroli, P.
1997 Divinazione a Ebla (TM.76.G.86). In *Miscellanea Eblaitica,* vol. 4, ed. P. Fronzaroli, 1–22. Florence: University of Florence.

Goetze, A.
1947 *Old Babylonian Omen Texts.* Yale Oriental Studies—Babylonian Texts 10. New Haven, Conn.: Yale University Press.
1957 Reports on Acts of Extispicy from Old Babylonian and Kassite Times: *JCS* 11:89–105.

Guichard, M.
1997 Présages fortuits à Mari (copies et ajouts à *ARMT* XXVI/1). *MARI* 8:305–28.

Hanoun, N.
1979 Himrin Basin—Tell al-Seib. *Sumer* 35:436–39.

Joannès, F.
1994 Un précurseur paléo-babylonien de la série *Šumma ālu.* In *Cinquante-deux reflexions sur le Proche-Orient ancien offertes en hommage à Léon De Meyer,* ed. H. Gasche et al., 305–12. Mesopotamian History and Environment Occasional Publications 2. Leuven: Peeters.

Keightley, D. N.
1978 *Sources of Shang History: The Oracle-Bone Inscriptions of Bronze Age China.* Berkeley and Los Angeles: University of California Press.

Koch-Westenholz, U.
2000 *Babylonian Liver Omens: The Chapters Manzāzu, Padānu and Pān Tākalti of the Babylonian Extispicy Series mainly from Aššurbanipal's Library.* Copenhagen: Carsten Niebuhr Institute, University of Copenhagen.
2002 Old Babylonian Extispicy Reports. In *Mining the Archives: Festschrift for Christopher Walker on the Occasion of His 60th Birthday, 4 October 2002,* ed. C. Wunsch, 131–45. Babylonische Archive 1. Dresden: ISLET.

Leichty, E.
1966 Teratological Omens. In *La Divination en Mésopotamie ancienne et dans les régions voisines: 14e Rencontre assyriologique internationale, Strasbourg, 2–6 juillet 1965,* 131–39. Paris: Presses universitaires de France.
1970 *The Omen Series Šumma Izbu.* Locust Valley, N.Y.: Augustin.

Leipold, H. W., S. M. Dennis, and K. Huston
1972 Congenital Defects of Cattle: Nature, Cause, and Effect. *Advances in Veterinary Science and Comparative Medicine* 16:103–50.

Marchetti, N.
1996 About Sheep and Livers: The Sanctuary G3 and the Practice of Divination at Ebla during the Old Syrian Period. In *Intellectual Life of the Ancient Near East: 43^e^ Rencontre Assyriologique Internationale, Prague, July 1–5, 1996—Summaries of Papers,* ed. P. Vavroušek, B. Hruška, and P. Zemánek, 19. Prague.
2000 Clay Figurines of the Middle Bronze Age from Northern Inner Syria: Chronology, Symbolic Meaning and Historical Relations. In *Proceedings of the First International Congress on the Archaeology of the Ancient Near East, Rome, May 18–23, 1998,* ed. P. Matthiae et al., 839–67. Rome: Università di Roma "La Sapienza."
2001 *La coroplastica eblaita e siriana nel Bronzo Medio: Campagne 1964–1980.* Materiali e Studi Archeologici di Ebla 5. Rome: Università di Roma "La Sapienza."

Marchetti, N., and L. Nigro
1997 Cultic Activities in the Sacred Area of Ishtar at Ebla during the Old Syrian Period: The *Favissae* F.5327 and F.5238. *JCS* 49:1–44.

Matthiae, P.
1980 Sulle asce fenestrate del "Signore dei Capridi." *Studi eblaiti* 3:53–62.
1985 *I tesori di Ebla.* 2d ed. Rome: Laterza.
1986 Sull'identità degli dèi titolari dei templi paleosiriani di Ebla. *Contributi e Materiali di Archeologia Orientale* 1:335–62.
1987a Les dernières découvertes d'Ebla en 1983–1986. *CRAIBL* 1987:135–61.
1987b Una stele paleosiriana arcaica da Ebla e la cultura figurativa della Siria attorno al 1800 a.C. *Scienze dell'Antichità* 1:447–95.
1989 *Ebla: Un impero ritrovato.* 2d ed. Turin: Einaudi.

2006 Middle Bronze Age II Minor Cult Places at Ebla? In *"I will Speak the Riddles of Ancient Times": Archaeological and Historical Studies in Honor of Amihai Mazar on the Occasion of His Sixtieth Birthday*, ed. A. Maeir and P. de Miroschedji, 217–33. Winona Lake, Ind.: Eisenbrauns.

Matthiae, P. , F. Pinnock, and G. Scandone Matthiae, eds.
1995 *Ebla: Alle origini della civiltà urbana; Trenta anni di scavi in Siria dell'Università di Roma "La Sapienza."* Milan: Electa.

Mazzoni, S.
2002 Late Bronze Age Pottery Production in Northwestern Central Syria. In *La Céramique de l'âge du bronze en Syrie,* vol. 1, ed. M. Al-Maqdissi et al., 129–51. BAH 161. Beirut: Institut français d'archéologie du Proche-Orient.

Meyer, J.-W.
1984 Einige Aspekte zur Bearbeitung unbeschrifeteter Tonlebermodelle. *MDOG* 116:119–30.
1987 *Untersuchungen zu den tonlebermodellen aus dem Alten Orient*. AOAT 39. Neukirchen-Vluyn: Butzon and Bercker.
1993 Ein Milzmodell aus Mari (AO 27906). *MARI* 7: 349–54.

Michalowski, P.
2006 How to Read the Liver—in Sumerian. In *If a Man Builds a Joyful House: Assyriological Studies in Honor of Erle Verdun Leichty*, ed. A. K. Guinan et al., 247–57. Leiden: Brill.

Nougayrol, J.
1968 Le foie "d'orientation" BM 50494. *RA* 62:31–50.

Oppenheim, A. L.
1954 *The Archives of the Palace of Mari II:* A Review Article. *JNES* 13:141–48.
1977 *Ancient Mesopotamia: Portrait of a Dead Civilization*. 2d ed. Chicago: University of Chicago Press.

Orthmann, W.
1976 Mumbaqat 1974: Vorläufiger Bericht über die von der Deutschen Orient-Gesellschaft mit Mitteln der Stiftung VolkswagenWerk unternommenen Ausgrabungen. *MDOG* 108:25–44.

Pongratz-Leisten, B.
1999 *Herrschaftswissen in Mesopotamien: Formen der Kommunikation zwischen Gott und König in 2. und 1. Jahrtausend v.Chr.* State Archives of Assyria Studies 10. Helsinki: Neo-Assyrian Text Corpus Project.

al-Rawi, F. N. H.
1994 Texts from Tell Haddad and Elsewhere. *Iraq* 56: 35–43.

Richardson, S.
2002 Ewe Should Be So Lucky: Extispicy Reports and Everyday Life. In *Mining the Archives: Festschrift for Christopher Walker on the Occasion of His 60th Birthday, 4 October 2002*, ed. C. Wunsch, 229–44. Babylonische Archive 1. Dresden: ISLET.

Rutten, M.
1938 Trente-deux modèles de foies en argile inscrits provenant de Tell-Hariri (Mari). *RA* 35:36–70.

Salvini, M.
1996 *The Habiru Prism of King Tunip-Teššup of Tikunani*. Documenta Asiana 3. Rome: Istituti Editoriali e Poligrafici Internazionali.

Starr, I. S.
1983 *Rituals of the Diviner*. Bibliotheca Mesopotamica 12. Malibu, Calif.: Undena.

Woolley, C. L.
1955 *Alalakh: An Account of the Excavations at Tell Atchana in the Hatay, 1937–1949*. London: Society of Antiquaries.

31. Egyptian Fingerprints at Late Bronze Age Ashkelon: Egyptian-style Beer Jars

by Mario A. S. Martin

"At Ashkelon you find anything you want," I was convinced when I started to understand the abundance of finds on this tell in any given period. But while studying Egyptian influence in Canaan in the Ramesside period, I was puzzled by one question about Ashkelon: since Egypt's interest in this impressive urban center is evident for this period (Stager 1993:103), would it not be likely that an Egyptian garrison was stationed at this important harbor town so close to Gaza, only 16 km south? Soon after, however, the Leon Levy Expedition directed by Larry Stager discovered the foundations of an "Egyptian fortress," a massive mudbrick wall of clearly Egyptian character (Stager, Schloen, and Master 2008:256; Master 2005:337–40), and a nice assemblage of imported Egyptian and, mainly, locally produced Egyptian-style pottery, of the kind we know from Egyptian garrison sites such as Beth Shean, Tel Mor, Tel Sera^c (Martin 2005), and Deir el-Balaḥ (figure 1; Gould forthcoming).[1] The most distinctive form in this assemblage, the Egyptian-style beer jar, is the focus of this paper. While clearly a matter of utmost seriousness, discussions between Larry and me about this type—inexplicably enough—always ended in untamed laughter. That should be enough reason to dedicate this article to this interesting form.

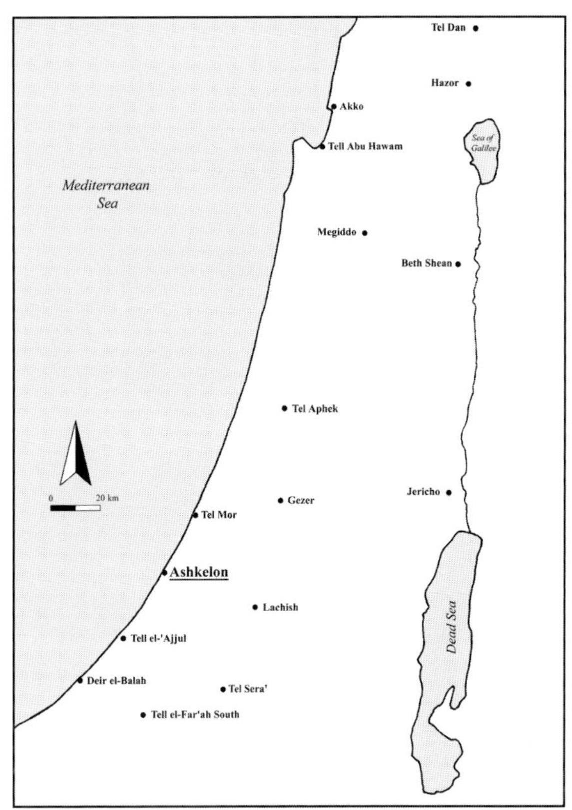

Figure 1. Late Bronze Age sites in Canaan

The Egyptian Assemblage

The Egyptian assemblage retrieved so far is very fragmentary in nature. The material originates from LB IIB levels in two areas on the tell: Phase 21 in Grid 38, in the central part of the tell, in contexts associated with the above-mentioned mudbrick foundation; and Phase 10 in Grid 50, about 200 meters southwest of Grid 38 along the seashore. Directly above both of these phases, without any signs of destruction, the first Philistine settlement was established, characterized by locally produced Mycenean IIIC wares that appear for the first time in the post-LB IIB layers (Phase 20 in Grid 38 and Phase 9 in Grid 50).

Egyptian forms mostly comprise locally produced wares. These are the characteristic Egyptian household wares. Apart from their shape, their utilitarian character is also indicated by their somewhat careless manufacture, indicating mass production. Simple bowls form the vast majority of the assemblage (98 percent). They are typically medium-sized, rounded- to straight-sided, flat-based bowls with plain or flaring rims. Occasionally, very shallow variants occur, which are best referred to as plates. Simple bowls and plates functioned as serving vessels of all kinds for eating and drinking. Among the Egyptian-style closed vessels, the tell-tale beer jars are most prominent.

In addition to the local Egyptian-style assemblage, a nice collection of Egyptian imports was retrieved, in which two-handled storage jars were the predominant type. Such amphoras can be interpreted as transport containers that arrived at Ashkelon by sea (Martin 2005:314–19). The share of Egyptian forms

[1] "Egyptian-style" is the most common designation for the locally produced Egyptian forms. These locally made types constitute the bulk of this material at all the sites mentioned above, while actual Egyptian imports are rather rare.

within the entire LB IIB assemblage at Ashkelon amounts to as much as 30 percent.[2]

Local Egyptian types are not only Egyptian in their form; technological traits such as manufacturing techniques and fabric properties relate them to the Egyptian pottery tradition. It has previously been argued that locally produced Egyptian-style household assemblages, which were mass-produced and in a variety of types, indicate physical Egyptian presence and probably even craftsmanship by resident Egyptian potters (James and McGovern 1993:244–45; Cohen-Weinberger 1998:411; Killebrew 1998: 275; Martin 2004:279–80). Arguments in favor of this conclusion are based on observations of the geographical and chronological distribution of the Egyptian-style vessels, their function and character, and their manufacture and fabric. On the strength of the Egyptian-style architecture (the "Egyptian fortress") and the Egyptian-style ceramic assemblage in LB IIB Ashkelon, the physical presence of Egyptians can now also be posited for that site.

The Beer Jars

In the assemblage under review, beer jars or "beer bottles," as they were first called by Holthoer (1977: 86–87), are represented by a number of rim and base fragments (figures 3 and 4).[3] They can be described as medium-sized, tall jars with a short neck and a flat base that is generally rather heavy (figure 2). Rims can be inward-sloping (figure 4:1), straight (figure 4:3), or slightly outward-sloping (figure 4:2). The major characteristic of these jars is their crude manufacture and their careless finish. This is most evident on the exterior of their bases, on which superfluous lumps of clay (figure 4:5) and fingerprints (figure 4:4, 6) often remain. These fingerprints were evidently created when the vessel was removed from the wheel with the hands during the manufacturing process (Bourriau and Aston 1985:34–35), and no attempt was made to eradicate them at a later stage. Furthermore, all the beer-jar bases at Ashkelon were perforated at the bottom, mostly in a crude way. The sidewalls of beer jars generally exhibit heavy ribs on the outside and inside. The surface is almost exclusively left undecorated, as in all the Ashkelon examples.

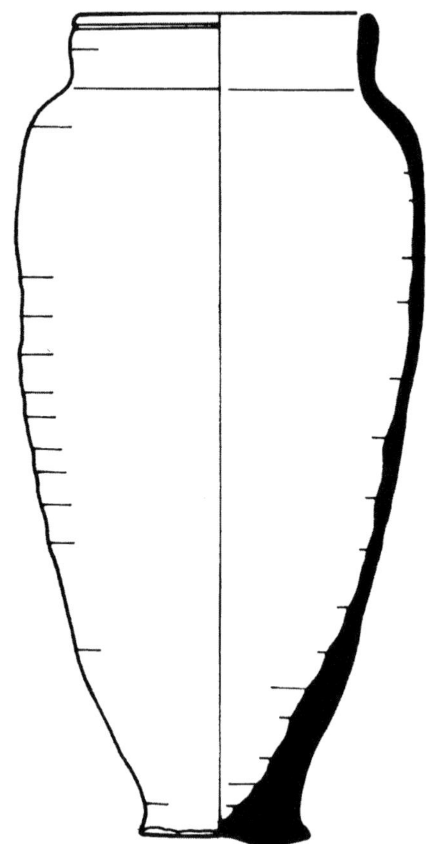

Figure 2. Complete profile of Egyptian-style beer jar
*From Tel Sera*ᶜ *Stratum IX; Oren 1984:fig. 7:1 (scale 2:5)*

These jars are found throughout Egypt in massive amounts and have been retrieved from virtually every site that has produced New Kingdom pottery (for discussions, see Aston 1996:12–13, 69; Aston and Pusch 1999:42; Aston 2001:169–71). In Canaan, beer jars appear almost exclusively at the most strongly Egyptian-influenced sites of the Ramesside period: Beth Shean, Tell es-Saᶜidiyeh, Tel Mor, Tel Seraᶜ, Deir el-Balaḥ, and now Ashkelon (for occurrences at the various sites, see Martin 2005, Type BB10). They seem to be strongly connected to physical Egyptian presence. Their distribution, technological properties, and distinctive appearance make them one of the hall-

2 This is the result of a statistical analysis of the Phase 21 material conducted by the author.

3 In their earliest form (early to mid-Eighteenth Dynasty), these vessels had a slender body and tall neck, hence their designation as bottles. By the late Eighteenth and Nineteenth Dynasties, they developed their typical jar shape. Holthoer divided his beer bottles into four subtypes, BB 1–BB 4 (1977:pl. 18). BB 1 he defined as "cylindrical," BB 2 as "transitional," BB 3 as "simple," and BB 4 as the "ordinary" beer bottle. For Canaanite assemblages, only his type BB 4 is of relevance. This is due to the fact that the other three subtypes are restricted to the early to mid-Eighteenth Dynasty, which is prior to the appearance of large amounts of Egyptian-style pottery in Canaan. Type BB 4 first appears in the early Eighteenth Dynasty, but becomes popular only in the Nineteenth Dynasty, and continues with slight modifications well into the Third Intermediate Period (Aston 1998:182).

Figure 3. Selection of Egyptian-style beer-jar bases found at Ashkelon (from Grids 38 and 50)

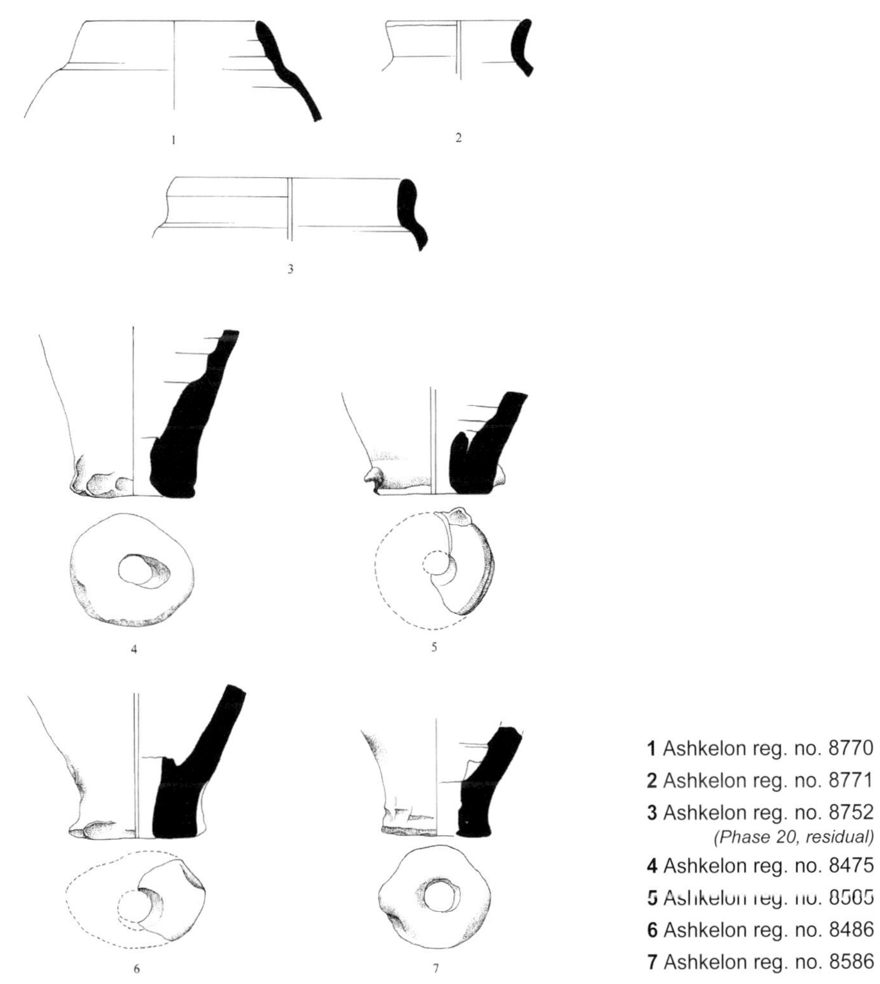

Figure 4. Selection of beer-jar rims (nos. 1–3) and bases (nos. 4–7) from the last Late Bronze Age level at Ashkelon (Grid 38, Phase 21; scale 1:4)

marks of Egyptian-style material culture in Ramesside Canaan and one of the strongest ethnic markers for the physical presence of Egyptians.

In Egypt, beer jars were made exclusively of Nile silt, while in Canaan they were always locally produced and were commonly tempered with large amounts of chopped straw, as at Ashkelon. The admixture of chopped straw has been noted in Egyptian-style vessels in general and has an Egyptian technological background.[4] In accordance with Egyptian examples, beer-jar rims at Ashkelon vary between 8 and 14 cm in diameter and bases between 5.5 and 7.8 cm (see below for the chronological implications).

Then there is the matter of perforations. All beer jars at Ashkelon were pierced through the bottom. In all cases, this perforation was executed prior to firing, evidently not long after the vessel was removed from the wheel, while the clay was still in a wet and soft condition. Perforated beer jars are well attested at other sites in Canaan that produced Egyptian-style assemblages (almost all examined examples exhibit prefiring perforations). At Beth Shean almost half of the beer-jar bases were pierced (Martin forthcoming a), a proportion that concurs with the evidence at Tel Mor (Martin and Barako 2007:149). Of only two beer-jar bases retrieved in the excavations at Tel Seraᶜ, one was perforated (Martin forthcoming b). The answer to why, in contrast to the other sites, all beer jars at Ashkelon were pierced probably lies in the correct interpretation of the (arguably different) functions of perforated and unperforated beer jars; but unfortunately this is still a matter of mere guesswork (see below). Beer jars with pierced bottoms are also known from Egypt itself.[5]

When examining the Ashkelon beer jars, it is apparent that the holes in their bottoms were in most cases poked through with a finger, obviously from the exterior towards the interior of the vessel.[6] Most likely, one would hold the vessel on its base with one hand and pierce the base with one finger of the other, probably the index or little finger. Although shrinkage during drying and firing must be taken into consideration, the size of most of the perforations fits well the average size of human fingers (index finger ca. 1.65 × 1.35 cm, little finger ca. 1.35 × 1.10 cm). After poking the hole, superfluous clay remained on the interior bottom of the vessel, commonly and most characteristically in form of a tongue smeared against the interior sidewall with the finger—best visible in figure 4:5 and figure 3 (front center and front left).[7] On some vessels, the interior bottom was smoothed to remove the remains of the perforation process.

What is puzzling is the function of these jars, perforated or not. While their designation as "beer jars" seems to say it all, the truth is that in the absence of conclusive data—for instance, residue analysis or *in situ* evidence—we are still groping in the dark.[8] Unperforated jars might well have been used to hold beer (note that beer jars were mass-produced and beer was a staple food item in ancient Egypt; Martin 2005:114), but they might also have contained any other liquid or nonliquid commodity. In this respect, perforated examples might be more illuminating. Although the hole in the base eliminates the possibility that they contained liquids, a function in a food-production process seems an appealing alternative.[9]

The first to connect these vessels with beer was R. Holthoer (1977:83). He based his theory on their occasional contextual association with deep, conical bowls, so-called flower pots, which seem to be closely related to our beer jars in their overall appearance—ribbed sidewalls, fingerprints and, commonly, perforated bottoms. Based on the similarity of these bowls to Old Kingdom bread molds (see, e.g., Steindorff 1913:pl. 84, Tomb of Ti), Holthoer (1977:fig. 61) interpreted the flower pots as bread molds, with perforated and unperforated specimens used in an

[4] Egyptian Nile clays are typically straw- or dung-tempered (for a discussion of ware fabrics of Egyptian-style ceramics see, e.g., Martin 2004:274–77).

[5] The author encountered them at Tell el-Dabᶜa. Interestingly enough, they are rare in the published record. Whether this is pure coincidence or fuel for an argument that perforated beer jars played a less important role in Egypt proper than in Canaan (and here again the vessels' function is decisive) is a matter for further research. For a perforated example with completely preserved profile, see Stratum Ba in Sector Q-IV at Qantir (Aston and Pusch 1999:no. 2; hole pierced post-firing).

[6] This seems to have been the prevalent method also at the other sites mentioned above. Instead of a finger, a pointed tool may have been used. Another method, which is encountered occasionally, was to create the perforation in an earlier stage, namely, by cutting the vessel off the wheel slightly too high, leaving a baseless center at the bottom of the jar.

[7] While lumps of superfluous clay on the interior bottom were also encountered at other sites, the tongues described above are a distinctive feature of the Ashkelon beer jars.

[8] Unfortunately, spot-testing for calcium oxalate ("beerstone") carried out by Margie Burton at the Scripps Institution of Oceanography at the University of California on a beer jar from Tel Mor produced negative results (Martin and Barako 2007:165 n. 30).

[9] An interpretation as drainpipes (perforated beer jars stuck into each other) goes in a completely different direction (Homan 2004:88) but, until now, lacks any actual support in the archaeological record.

ensemble of two.[10] He noted a weak point in his theory, admitting that there is very little evidence that flower pots were subjected to secondary exposure to heat. To bypass this problem, he concluded that some vessels might have functioned as mere votive symbols for bread. The same votive function he assigned to beer bottles. He further assumed that, when the flower pot and beer jar are found together they represent the Egyptian bread- and beer-offering typical of the Egyptian *ḥtp dj nsw* offering formulae (Holthoer 1977:86; for bread and beer in the offering formulae see, e.g., Barta 1968). In short, in Holthoer's interpretation, the association of our jars with beer is entirely built upon the similarity of flower pots with Old Kingdom bread molds. But not only is this association already quite weak, it further founders on the fact that flower pots are restricted to the Eighteenth Dynasty (Williams 1992:34–35) while beer jars are most common in the Nineteenth and Twentieth Dynasties.

A more promising line of evidence starts with an observation of W. M. F. Petrie, referring to a specimen of a "large conical bowl with a hole in the bottom"—clearly referring to a flower pot—that contained a pressed cake of barley mash and grains (Petrie 1907:23). Petrie then suggests that vessels of this type "were used to squeeze out the fermented beer from the grain, the cake being sufficiently tenacious not to break through at the hole" (1907). In short, Petrie's flower pot may have served as filtration container to strain liquid from the beer mash. Gould (forthcoming) has suggested expanding this function also to our beer jars. Viewing our perforated jars in this light, we may recall the description of how beer drips out of perforated fermentation containers in Mesopotamian texts (see Homan 2004:89 for a recent summary of the evidence). With the opening of the container sealed and the hole stopped up with a cloth, the beer would slowly drip out under the increased pressure caused by the fermentation (Homan 2004).

Another interpretation attempts to explain perforated beer jars as molds to bake barley bread (which, to produce beer, was then soaked in water in a further stage). "The brewer would expel the baked bread by placing a finger inside the perforation, thus pushing the bread out through the mouth" (Homan 2004:89). I believe that this interpretation should be rejected for three main reasons. (1) While such a practice might be feasible for flower pots, beer jars have a slightly restricted upper part (a shoulder and, commonly, an in-slanting rim), which would make it hard to push baked bread out through the mouth. (2) Beer jars generally show no evidence of secondary fire influence (compare with the flower pots). (3) Bread molds in ancient Egypt tended to be made with strongly sand-tempered clays (M. Bietak, personal communication), while beer jars were not.[11]

Although beer jars leave us puzzled as to their function, their value as a dating tool is unquestionable. As shown by D. Aston, Egyptian beer jars undergo a morphological development (1996:68 and 89; 1999:26–27), which is most evident between Phase 3 (late Eighteenth to late Nineteenth Dynasties or Amenophis III to Merneptah) and Phase 4 (late Nineteenth to Twentieth Dynasties, that is post-Merneptah) of the Egyptian ceramic sequence.[12] As opposed to earlier examples, Phase 4 beer jars tend to have a narrower base in relation to the vessel height, which is often restricted to form what resembles a stump, and to have a more slender body, which is commonly more heavily ribbed. In Phase 4, the base diameter commonly ranges around 6 cm or even less, while in Phase 3, examples with a diameter of 7–9 cm prevail.[13]

[10] That at least some of these conical bowls served as actual flower pots is indicated by *in situ* evidence at Tell el-Dabᶜa, where a group of perforated examples was discovered in a garden complex (Jánosi 1994:30–31 and fig. 8; Hein 1994: 39–40 and fig. 11a).

[11] It is worth noting two perforated stump bases found at Ashkelon, which originally belonged to two-handled Canaanite storage jars. One comes from a Late Bronze Age context in Grid 50 (Square 59, Layer 563, Bucket 12); another one comes from an Iron Age context in Grid 38 and may well be residual (Square 74, Layer 1000, Bucket 141, reg no. 1704; Phase 18). In both cases, the perforation was made before firing. It is possible that there was a functional similarity with our beer jars.

[12] The pottery corpus of New Kingdom Egypt was divided into four major chronological phases by Bourriau (1981: 72–73; 1990:19*). While Phase 3 was dated from the reigns of Amenophis III to Ramesses II by Bourriau (1990:19*), it was extended to the reign of Merneptah by Aston, Aston, and Brock (1998:145) in light of the material from the tomb of Merneptah (KV 8). The transition to Phase 4 clearly occurred after Merneptah (1213–1203) and before Ramesses III (1184–1153) (dates after Kitchen 2000). The changeover had probably already taken place in the reign of Sethnakhte (1186–1184), and therefore seemingly evolved during the late Nineteenth Dynasty in the reigns of Seti II (1200–1194), Siptah (1194–1188), and Twosret (1188–1186) (Aston 1996:20; Aston and Pusch 1999:41).

[13] The author conducted a survey of around 30 Nineteenth and Twentieth Dynasty beer jars from the published Egyptian record. First, the average base diameter clearly decreases in the late Nineteenth–Twentieth Dynasties. Secondly, while the proportion between base and height approximates 1:3 in the Nineteenth Dynasty jars until

At Ashkelon more than a dozen beer jar bases come from the last Late Bronze Age levels in Grid 38 and Grid 50, respectively. A few more bases come from later contexts and were probably residual. Bases from the last pre-Philistine horizon range around 6 cm in diameter, with an average of 6.2–6.5 cm (considering minimum and maximum width of deformed examples). They therefore clearly indicate a Phase 4 date in the Egyptian sequence. Two beer jars from twelfth-century contexts at Tel Sera^{c} (Stratum IX) have bases with a diameter of 5 and 6 cm respectively (Martin forthcoming b). In contrast, beer-jar bases at Tel Mor have an average width of 8.8 cm (Martin and Barako 2007:148), which accords well with the fact that the bulk of the material originates from fourteenth- and thirteenth-century contexts (Phase 3). In Twentieth Dynasty levels at Beth Shean, beer-jar bases with a diameter around 6 cm appear, but also larger variants (7–8 cm) are common, which is slightly anomalous (Martin forthcoming a).[14] Apart from their narrow base, some of the Ashkelon beer jars show a prominent restriction several centimeters above their bottom, creating a stump-like lower part of the vessel (most developed on figure 4:6–7). Such a stump is known on Phase 4 beer jars in Egypt but is not characteristic of Phase 3 beer jars. In summary, it can be said that the narrow base diameter and restricted lower part on beer-jar bases at Ashkelon clearly argue for a date at the very end of the Nineteenth or in the Twentieth Dynasty (i.e., not earlier than ca. 1200 B.C.E.). The best parallels from Egypt are from Elephantine (Aston 1999: nos. 57–60).

Finally, there is the question of the chronological value of rim stances. Aston argues that inward-sloping rims prevail in the Eighteenth and Nineteenth Dynasties, while they are outnumbered by straight or slightly outwardly slanted rims in the Twentieth Dynasty (1996:89). This observation creates a certain discrepancy with the evidence at Ashkelon, where beer-jar rims are mainly inwardly slanting in the last Late Bronze Age levels, which would place them in the Nineteenth Dynasty.[15] However, upon closer examination, Aston's guideline seems to be problematic at various sites in Egypt itself. Looking through published Nineteenth Dynasty material from Qantir (Aston 1998:Stratum B3/2) and Elephantine (Aston 1999:Phase 1), for instance, no prevalence of inwardly slanted beer jar rims could be fathomed at all (only 25 percent of 38 examples at Qantir and 10 percent of 10 examples at Elephantine). Thus, I would argue that the stance of beer jar rims cannot be used as chronological marker. Base diameter and base restriction are clearly the stronger indicators and the Phase 4 affiliation of the Ashkelon beer jars seems beyond doubt.

The Egyptian Interlude and the Philistine Settlement: Chronological Issues

The end of the Late Bronze Age and beginning of the Iron Age at Ashkelon are part of the Philistine debate raging among scholars in the last decade (for an overview see, e.g., Finkelstein 1995). The main chronological anchor for the arrival of the Philistines in Canaan was sought in the inscription at Medinet Habu from the eighth year of Ramesses III, which records land and sea battles between Egyptians and Sea Peoples. Whether the Philistines settled in the area of the later Philistine Pentapolis shortly thereafter (Bietak 1993; Stager 1995) or only a generation later (Finkelstein 1995) is one of the main issues of the Philistine debate.

Among the earliest Philistine material in Grid 38 was found a scarab of Ramesses III, which provides us with a *terminus post quem* for the first Philistine settlement of Phase 20 (Master 2005:344 and fig. 20.6). Another chronological hint may now be found in the Egyptian-style beer jars. The narrow-based variants in the last LB layers at Ashkelon date this horizon to the very end of the Nineteenth Dynasty, around 1200 B.C.E. at the earliest, and provide an upper peg for the last LB horizon at Ashkelon. The lack of evidence for twelfth-century Egyptian amphoras (of the wide-bodied and round-based type; Martin 2004:273–74) may provide us with a lower chronological peg very close to the upper one.

It is tempting to ascribe the erection of the "Egyptian fortress" at Ashkelon to a short Egyptian interlude sometime in the very late Nineteenth or early Twentieth Dynasty following the assumed capture of Canaanite Ashkelon by Merneptah in the fifth year of his reign (1209 B.C.E.), as indicated by the famous "Israel Stele," and preceding the settlement of the Philistines. The lack of much mudbrick detritus suggests that the Egyptian building was abandoned before it was completed. But whether there was only a short-lived Egyptian interlude before the arrival of

Merneptah, it decreases to 1:4 in the later examples (ca. 20 examples with complete profiles were included).

[14] The average base width in Strata S-5 to S-3 in Area S at Beth Shean is 7 cm, which is still much less than at Tel Mor (the bulk of the material dates to the Twentieth Dynasty).

[15] Nine inslanting rims, two straight, and one outslanting rim in the combined material of Grid 38 and Grid 50; another three inwardly sloping rims and one straight rim come from Phase 20 in Grid 38 and are probably residual.

the Philistines or whether the Egyptian presence can be pushed back further into the thirteenth century is a question that cannot be answered without further excavation and research.

Moreover, while the beer jars provide us with a clear *terminus post quem*, the fact that only three Egyptian amphoras (two of them fragmentary) were retrieved from the Ashkelon assemblage hardly confirms the absence of the twelfth-century type. The beer jars in the pre-Philistine level at Ashkelon tell us how early the Philistines could have come to the site, but the amphoras (or their lack) do not reveal how late they could have come. Interestingly enough, in the areas excavated by the Leon Levy Expedition (Grids 38 and 50), there is no evidence of destruction at the end of the Late Bronze Age, which strongly calls into question Mackenzie's (1913:pl. 1) and Phythian-Adams's (1923:figs. 3–4) claims of a massive destruction. After the Egyptian retreat, the Philistines settled at Ashkelon. In clean Philistine contexts, Egyptian material decreases to less than 5 percent of the pottery assemblage and should be regarded as residual. That Egyptian forms ceased to be produced after the Egyptian retreat can be regarded as evidence of the close connection of the Egyptian-style pottery with the physical presence of Egyptians in Ashkelon.

Bibliography

Aston, D. A.

1996 *Egyptian Pottery of the Late New Kingdom and Third Intermediate Period (Twelfth–Seventh Centuries B.C.): Tentative Footsteps in a Forbidding Terrain.* Studien zur Archäologie und Geschichte Altägyptens 13. Heidelberg: Heidelberg Orientverlag.

1998 *Die Keramik des Grabungsplatzes Q I.* Part, 1 *Corpus of Fabrics, Wares and Shapes.* Die Grabungen des Pelizaeus Museums Hildesheim in Qantir–Pi-Ramesse 1. Mainz: Zabern.

1999 *Pottery from the Late New Kingdom to the Early Ptolemaic Period.* Elephantine 19. Archäologische Veröffentlichungen 95. Mainz: Zabern.

2001 The Pottery from H/VI Süd Strata a and b: Preliminary Report. *Ägypten und Levante* 11:167–96.

Aston, D. A., and E. B. Pusch

1999 The Pottery from the Royal Horse Stud and its Stratigraphy: The Pelizaeus Museum Excavation at Qantir/Per-Ramesses, Sector Q IV. *Ägypten und Levante* 9:39–75.

Aston, D. A., B. Aston, and E. Brock

1998 Pottery from the Valley of the Kings—Tombs of Merneptah, Ramesses III, Ramesses IV, Ramesses VI and Ramesses VII. *Ägypten und Levante* 8:137–214.

Barta, W.

1968 *Aufbau und Bedeutung der altägyptischen Opferformel.* Ägyptologische Forschungen 24. Glückstadt: Augustin.

Bietak, M.

1993 The Sea Peoples and the End of the Egyptian Administration in Canaan. In *Biblical Archaeology Today, 1990: Proceedings of the Second International Congress on Biblical Archaeology*, ed. A. Biran and J. Aviram, 292–306. Jerusalem: Israel Exploration Society and Israel Academy of Sciences and Humanities.

Bourriau, J.

1981 *Umm el-Gaʾab:Pottery from the Nile Valley before the Arab Conquest.* Cambridge: Cambridge University Press.

1990 Canaanite Jars from New Kingdom Deposits at Memphis, Kôm Rabiʿa. *EI* 21:18*–26*.

Bourriau, J., and D. A. Aston

1985 The Pottery. In *The Tomb-Chapels of Paser and Raʿia at Saqqâra*, ed. G. T. Martin, 32–55. Egypt Exploration Society Excavation Memoir 52. London: Egypt Exploration Society.

Cohen-Weinberger, A.

1998 Petrographic Analysis of the Egyptian Forms from Stratum VI at Tel Beth-Shean. In *Mediterranean Peoples in Transition: Thirteenth to Early Tenth Centuries B.C.E.*, ed. S. Gitin, A. Mazar, and E. Stern, 406–12. Jerusalem: Israel Exploration Society.

Finkelstein, I.

1995 The Date of the Settlement of the Philistines in Canaan. *Tel Aviv* 22:213–39.

Gould, B.

forthc. Egyptian Pottery. In *Deir el-Balaḥ*, vol. 2, *The Settlement*. ed. T. Dothan. Qedem. Jerusalem.

Hein, I.

1994 Erste Beobachtungen zur Keramik aus ʿEzbet Helmi. In *Neue Grabungsergebnisse aus Tell el-Dabʿa und ʿEzbet Helmi im östlichen Nildelta (1989–1991)*, ed. M. Bietak, J. Dorner, I. Hein, and P. Jánosi. *Ägypten und Levante* 4:39–43.

Holthoer, R.

1977 *New Kingdom Pharaonic Sites: The Pottery.* The Scandinavian Joint Expedition to Sudanese Nubia 5/1. Stockholm.

Homan, M.

2004 Beer and Its Drinkers: An Ancient Near Eastern Love Story. *NEA* 67/2:84–95.

James, F. W., and P. E. McGovern, eds.
1993 *The Late Bronze Egyptian Garrison at Beth Shan: A Study of Levels VII and VIII.* 2 vols. University Museum Monograph 85. Philadelphia: University Museum, University of Pennsylvania.

Jánosi, P.
1994 Tell el-Dabᶜa–ᶜEzbet Helmi: Vorbericht über den Grabungsplatz H/I (1989–1992). In *Neue Grabungsergebnisse aus Tell el-Dabᶜa und ᶜEzbet Helmi im östlichen Nildelta (1989–1991)*, ed. M. Bietak, J. Dorner, I. Hein, and P. Jánosi. *Ägypten und Levante* 4:20–38.

Killebrew, A.
1998 Ceramic Craft and Technology during the Late Bronze and Early Iron Ages: The Relationship between Pottery Technology, Style, and Cultural Diversity. Ph.D. diss., Hebrew University of Jerusalem.

Kitchen, K. A.
2000 Regnal and Genealogical Data of Ancient Egypt (Absolute Chronology I): The Historical Chronology of Ancient Egypt, a Current Assessment. In *The Synchronization of Civilizations in the Eastern Mediterranean in the Second Millennium* B.C., ed. M. Bietak, 39–52. Vienna: Österreichischen Akademie der Wissenschaften.

Mackenzie, D.
1913 The Philistine City of Ashkelon. *PEQ* 45:8–23.

Martin, M. A. S.
2004 Egyptian and Egyptianized Pottery in Late Bronze Age Canaan: Typology, Chronology, Ware Fabrics and Manufacture Techniques. Pots and People? *Ägypten und Levante* 14:265–84.
2005 The Egyptian and Egyptian-style Pottery: Aspects of the Egyptian Involvement in Late Bronze and Early Iron Age Canaan. A Case Study. Ph.D. diss., University of Vienna.
forthc. a The Egyptian-style Pottery from Areas S and N. In *Excavations at Tel Beth Shean*, vol. 3, ed. A. Mazar. Qedem. Jerusalem.
forthc. b The Egyptian and Egyptian-style Pottery at Tel Seraᶜ. In *Excavations at Tel Seraᶜ*, ed. E. Oren.

Martin, M. A. S., and T. J. Barako
2007 Egyptian and Egyptianized Pottery. In *Tel Mor: The Moshe Dothan Excavations, 1959–1960.* Israel Antiquities Authority Reports 32. Jerusalem: Israel Antiquities Authority.

Master, D. M.
2005 Iron I Chronology at Ashkelon: Preliminary Results of the Leon Levy Expedition. In *The Bible and Radiocarbon Dating: Archaeoloy, Text and Science*, ed. T. E. Levy and T. Higham, 337–48. London: Equinox.

Oren, E. D.
1984 "Governors' Residencies" in Canaan under the New Kingdom: A Case Study of Egyptian Administration. *JSSEA* 14:37–56.

Petrie, W. M. F.
1907 *Gizeh and Rifeh.* British School of Archaeology in Egypt 13. London: School of Archaeology.

Phythian-Adams, W. J.
1923 Report on the Stratification of Askalon. *PEQ* 55: 60–84.

Stager, L. E.
1993 Ashkelon. In *The New Encyclopedia of Archaeological Excavations in the Holy Land*, ed. E. Stern, 1:103–12. New York: Simon and Schuster.
1995 The Impact of the Sea Peoples in Canaan (1185–1050 B.C.E.). In *The Archaeology of Society in the Holy Land*, ed. T. E. Levy, 332–48. London: Leicester University Press.

Stager, L. E., J. D. Schloen, and D. M. Master, eds.
2008 *Ashkelon.* Vol. 1, *Introduction and Overview (1985–2006).* Winona Lake, Ind.: Eisenbrauns.

Steindorff, G.
1913 *Das Grab des Ti.* Leipzig: Hinrichs.

Williams, B.
1992 *New Kingdom Remains from Cemeteries R, V, S and W at Qustol and Cemetery K at Adindan.* Chicago: Oriental Institute, University of Chicago.

32. From the Buqê^{c}ah to Ashkelon

by Daniel M. Master

THE violent campaign of Sennacherib in the late eighth century B.C.E. changed the southern Levant. If Assyria's previous conquests had failed to dispel Judah's illusion that Egypt remained a dominant international power, Sennacherib's fury against both Egypt and Judah left little doubt as to the identity of the new hegemon.[1] Towns "without number" in Judah were destroyed and plundered. The accumulated wealth of Jerusalem, held as decoration in the central sanctuary, was stripped in a futile attempt to end the devastation (Cogan 2003:303).

But even more revolutionary, according to some, was that Sennacherib's success opened the eyes of Judah to a new type of world empire: a sweeping military, cultural, and commercial force that oversaw the disenchantment of the old order and the birth of a new way of conceiving of history. With Assyria triumphant, Gitin (1997) has described a *pax Assyriaca* that opened the southern Levant to an Assyrian periphery extending across the Mediterranean. According to many scholars, the new markets spurred massive centralization, from the cosmopolitan port of Ashkelon all the way into the deep recesses of the monastic Judean desert. Household economies gave way to mass production of olive oil at Ekron (1997: 84), of wine at Gibeon (Halpern 1991:62) and Ashkelon (Faust and Weiss 2005), and of grain in the Beersheba Valley (Finkelstein 1994) and Judean Desert (Gitin 1997:83; Faust and Weiss 2005:74). The dislocation caused by Sennacherib's campaigns did not just cut off part of the Judahite kingdom; it forced the comprehensive reorganization of the entire social and economic world. In this reconstruction, the emergent seventh-century economy was made up of highly specialized cities organized to serve efficiently the Phoenician commercial world (Faust and Weiss 2005). Or, in another formulation, when the Assyrians destroyed all towns but Jerusalem, the traditional balance in Judah between the urban elites and the rural population was shattered and Hezekiah's successors were free to impose their literalistic "counter-religion" (Halpern 1991; Assmann 1997).

It is also possible, however, to see the seventh-century economy as merely a continuation of typical Iron Age patterns. Labianca (1997) has persuasively argued that the underlying "local small-scale economy" (cf. Stager 1989:62) of the highlands of the southern Levant was extremely resilient. Despite deep military, economic, or political shocks, survivors showed an amazing tendency to follow the same economic patterns as their predecessors. Kin networks were quickly reformed, agricultural and pastoral production was rebalanced, and life continued on much as it had before. Close links to local subsistence and a lack of regional specialization were important risk-spreading mechanisms in the Iron Age and beyond.

Fortunately, the last forty years of excavation, from the insular Buqê^{c}ah Valley to the cosmopolitan port of Ashkelon, have provided data with which to test these models. These excavations have not only uncovered new sites; they have described entirely new datasets which are critical for determining ancient patterns of subsistence and regional integration. Stager's (1975) synthetic summaries of Khirbet Abū Ṭabaq, Khirbet es-Samrah, and Khirbet el-Maqârī in the Buqê^{c}ah Valley serve as an apt starting point from which to examine the economy of the southern Levant in the wake of Sennacherib's attacks.

The Buqê^{c}ah Valley

When Edward Robinson traveled from En-Gedi to Jericho in the mid-nineteenth century, he was obliged to climb onto the dry plateau west of Dead Sea because of the impassibility of the western shore. After crossing several wadis, Robinson came through the Buqê^{c}ah Valley to Ras el-Feshkhah. Robinson described his various journeys through the wilderness as following tracks by which desert groups could move quickly without having to encounter resistance from the settled groups to the west. In particular, he described a raid on Mar Saba in which the perpetrators came undetected from Transjordan (Robinson and Smith 1856:524–34). Somewhat later, Masterman traveled through the Buqê^{c}ah on his way from Jerusalem to Mar Saba to the Dead Sea. Both explorers viewed the Buqê^{c}ah Valley as a place that one traveled through rather than settled in. In Robinson's case, the valley allowed undetected movement from as far away as the southern Transjordan, and for Masterman it provided convenient access to the northern reaches of the Dead Sea (Masterman 1903).

[1] It is a pleasure to honor Lawrence E. Stager and to acknowledge the debt that I owe to my *Doctorvater*. The opportunity to work for him at the Leon Levy Expedition to Ashkelon continues to be a most exciting intellectual adventure. Thanks are also due to Avi Faust for his input into a draft of this paper. Any errors are my own.

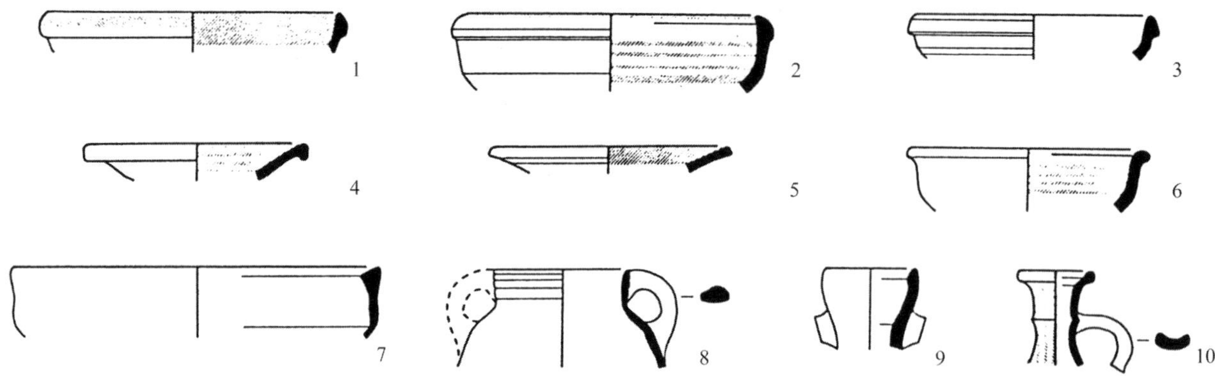

Figure 1. Buqê[c]ah pottery made with local clays

1 Abū Tabaq, Area 3
2 el-Maqârī, Trench B
3 el-Maqârī, Trench B
4 el-Maqârī, Trench B
5 Abū Tabaq, Area B
6 es-Samrah, Area B, Reg. 518
7 Abū Tabaq, Area 5
8 el-Maqârī, Trench A
9 el-Maqârī, Trench B
10 el-Maqârī, Trench B

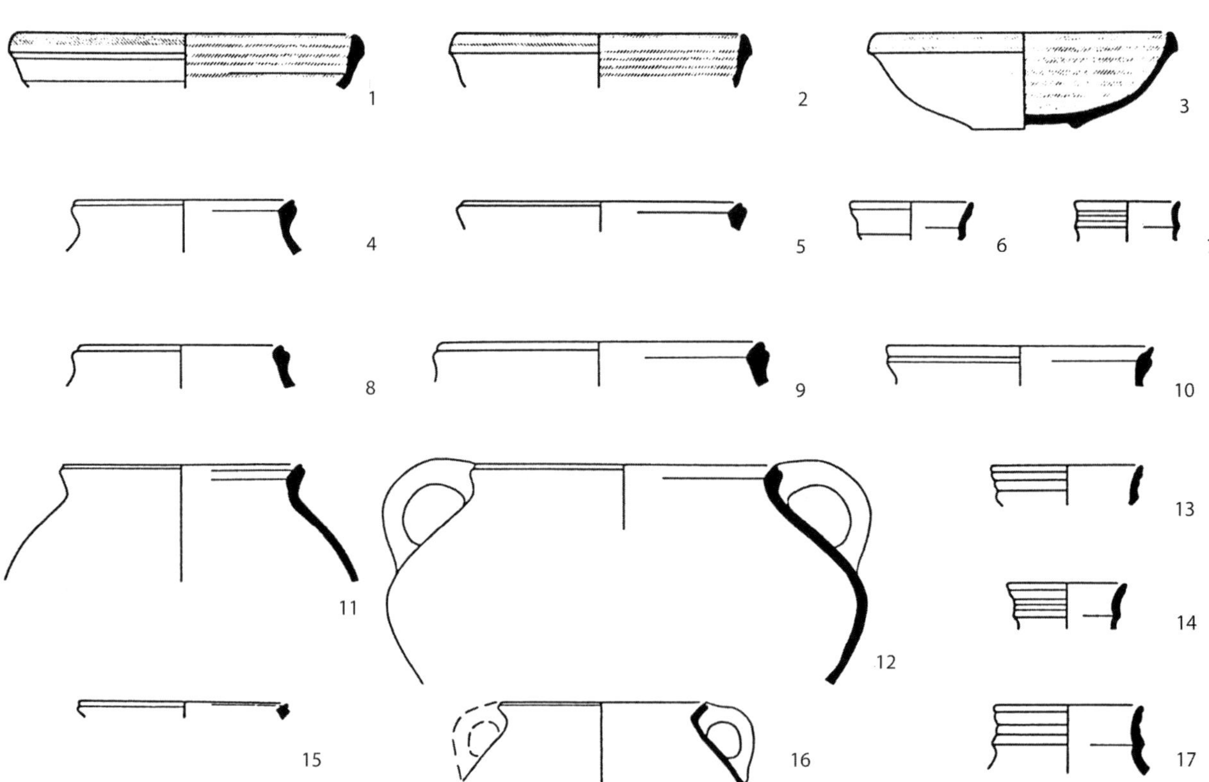

Figure 2. Buqê[c]ah pottery made with wadi clays

1 es-Samrah, Area 8, Reg. 2674
2 es-Samrah, Area 8, Reg. 2696
3 Abū Tabaq, Area 4, Reg. 5222
4 es-Samrah, Area 9, Reg. 1709
5 es-Samrah, Area 9, Reg. 446
6 es-Samrah, Area B, Reg. 889
7 Abū Tabaq, Area 5
8 el-Maqârī, Trench B
9 Abū Tabaq, Area 4, Reg. 1251
10 Abū Tabaq, Area 4, Reg. 2015
11 el-Maqârī, Trench B
12 el-Maqârī, Trench A
13 es-Samrah, Area B, Reg. 640
14 Abū Tabaq, Area 4
15 Abū Tabaq, Area 5
16 el-Maqârī, Trench A
17 Abū Tabaq, Area 3

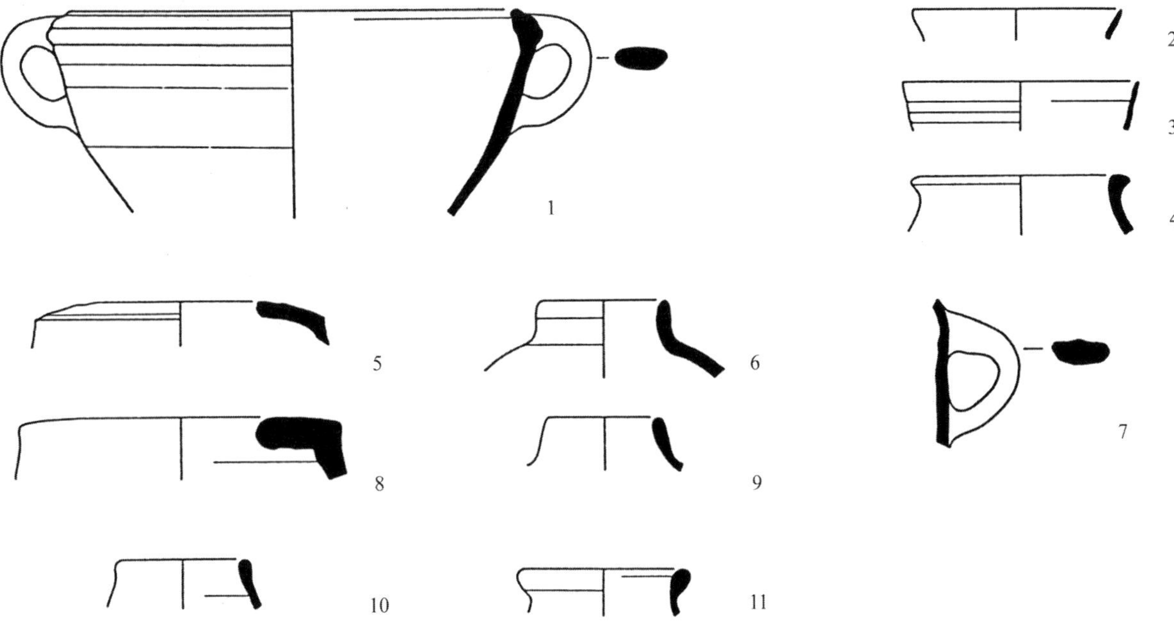

Figure 3. Imports to the Buqê[c]ah from the west

1 el-Maqârī, Trench B (Moza clay)
2 Abū Tabaq, Area 4, Reg. 1411 (Moza clay)
3 el-Maqârī, Trench B (Moza clay)
4 Abū Tabaq, Area 4, Reg. 2579 (Moza clay)
5 el-Maqârī, Trench B (Moza clay)
6 es-Samrah, Area 8, Reg. 183 (Moza clay)
7 es-Samrah, Area 9, Reg. 341 (Moza clay)
8 el-Maqârī, Trench B (Moza clay)
9 Abū Tabaq, Area 4, Reg. 4607 (Moza clay)
10 Abū Tabaq, Area 3, Reg. 3375 (loess with *narī*)
11 es-Samrah, Area B, Reg. 522 (loess with *narī*)

The records of these early travelers were not forgotten by Stager in his synthesis of the Buqê[c]ah evidence. At the outset, he saw that the small farmstead fortresses served the purpose of guaranteeing "travelers and merchants safe passage" (Stager 1976:145). In the Iron Age, it is likely that the Dead Sea coastline was exploited for sulfur, salt, bitumen, and date palms, at the very least (Stager 1975:225–26), and so the connection to Jerusalem, noted already by Masterman, was well worth protecting. In addition, the presence of antagonistic Transjordanian kingdoms nearby might have necessitated, as in Robinson's day, some early warning systems to protect the Judahite heartland.

But the oddity of the Buqê[c]ah was that the settlements in the late Iron Age were farmsteads. The Buqê[c]ah usually lies outside the 200 mm isohyet necessary for rainfall agriculture, but a series of seventh-century agricultural features manipulated the occasional runoff water that flowed through the wadis of this desert region. As many have shown (see summaries in Finkelstein 1995 and Bruins 1986), the manipulation of runoff water can radically alter the productive capacities of the desert, allowing yields that approach those of the well-watered Judahite highlands.

In this case, Stager's report (1975) was ahead of its time for the way in which it integrated new datasets in order better to understand ancient subsistence and economy. Stager's use of botanical analysis showed a range of goods that the inhabitants were consuming: wheat, barley, legumes, olives, and grapes. It seems likely that cereals and legumes, at least, were being produced on site (Stager 1976:146) although the local production of grapes cannot be ruled out (Stager 1975:196–200). Micromorphological profiles of some of the excavated rooms also revealed sedimentary accumulations typical of sheep- or goat-herding (Stager 1975:87). Taken together, Stager's work outlined a diverse set of subsistence strategies used to spread the risk of living on such marginal land.

In Stager's (1975:190) rough estimation, based on the roofed space all of the farmsteads, 60 to 100 people lived in the Buqê[c]ah. He also estimated that approximately 12 hectares were farmed intensively, using the irrigation strategies necessary for substantial production. Using Bruins's (1986:89–92) estimates of desert farming under runoff conditions, such farms might have produced "646 kg" of wheat per sown hectare. In the case of the Buqê^c^ah farms, the total yield of under 8,000 kilograms of wheat would support about forty people (Finkelstein 1995:56). This is, of course, a rough calculation, with substantive debate possible concerning every estimate. Still, once the growing of legumes or perhaps even grapes on some of this prime agricultural land is accounted for, the carrying capacity of this farmland might have been somewhat lower. Even allowing for widespread pastoralism to supplement subsistence, and even if Stager's original survey was not comprehensive, the valley's production capacity still would have struggled to meet the subsistence needs of the population.

The ceramic assemblage in the Buqê^c^ah points to a largely self-sufficient community that received some support from the Judahite highlands. Chronologically, this assemblage is a mix of eighth- and seventh-century B.C.E. forms. The chronologically distinctive forms such as *LMLK* jar handles and eighth-century cooking pots (figure 2:12, 17) were found together with seventh-century cooking pots (figure 2:6–7, 11, 14, 15). Most of the other forms could fit in equally well in either the eighth or seventh century. While the original seventh-century date for this assemblage was based on an incorrect understand of the chronology of Lachish, the excavators have since modified their opinion to allow for wider chronological options (see Cross 1993:269).

My petrographic study of the Buqê^c^ah pottery uncovered definite patterns that aid in understanding the function of the Buqê^c^ah farmsteads. A surprising amount of the domestic pottery was made locally (figure 1). It might seem strange to have local pottery production in a fuel- and water-poor region (Arnold 1985:96–97; Rice 1987:177–80), but the dominant inclusions in these vessels were biomicritic chalks typical of the Ghareb formation (Sneh, Bartov, and Rosensaft 1998; Rosenthal et al. 2000). Because clays filled with the local chalk of the Buqê^c^ah Valley would have been unsuitable for cooking vessels (Rice 1987:97–98), potters of this region exploited the clays of the wadis within the Judean Desert (Michniewicz and Krzysko 2003:65). The wadi clay fabrics (figure 2) found in the Buqê^c^ah had been frequently levigated to remove chalk sand and, in several cases, tempered to include rounded-quartz sand.

The nonlocal pottery (figure 3) was made up of the clays of the Moza formation of the highlands (Goren 1995:300) or of clays containing *nari* chalks typical of the southern Shephelah (Goren, Finkelstein, and Na^ɔ^aman 2004:287–90). All of the storage vessels in this study fell within these nonlocal groups. The *LMLK* handles found at Khirbet es-Samrah were not tested, but these vessels are well known to have been made from clays originating in the Shephelah (Mommsen, Perlman, and Yellin 1984). While several explanations might account for the lack of locally produced storage vessels, their appearance in storage magazines (Stager 1975:147) may highlight the way in which these peripheral fortress/farmsteads had their subsistence supplemented by goods from central Judah.[2]

The Beersheba Valley

The Beersheba Valley contained a larger, far more complex set of settlements, but, like the Buqê^c^ah, it also saw expanded settlement in the seventh century. As in the Buqê^c^ah, the chronology here is not entirely certain (Vaughn 1999:50–58), and population growth may have started already in the late eighth century. Still, the trajectory is clear. The total settled area expanded by almost 250 percent from that of the mid-eighth century (Finkelstein 1994:176), and the seventh century population likely consisted of some three thousand people at its height (Lipschits 2005: 270).

The rationale for this population expansion has long been thought to have been related to the Arabian spice trade (van Beek 1960; Ephal 1984; Bienkowski and van der Steen 2001; Holladay 2006), even if the mechanisms of that trade have been disputed. The spice routes originating in southern Arabia entered the valley either from the south via the *ma^c^ălēh aqrabîm* (Numbers 34; Joshua 15) and Aroer, or from the east via the *derek ĕdôm* (2 Kings 3:20) and Arad. In the eighth century, both of these routes then ran past Tel Sheva, which served as a "gateway community in southern Arabian long-distance trade" (Singer-Avitz 1999).

This longstanding concept has recently been challenged because so little material evidence of trade has been discovered at these sites. Goren's petrographic work on the Beersheba pottery has demonstrated that the "Edomite" pottery was actually made locally or in Judah. A supposedly "South Arabian" stamp was carved in local stone. At Tel Sheva, with the exception of one Red Sea shell, no material remains have their geological origin to the south or east (Singer-Avitz 1999). The absence of evidence for long-

[2] One can compare the seventh-century fortress/farmsteads with the settlement at Khirbet Mird. This site was a far superior observer and guardian of the Buqê^c^ah Valley and sat at the end of a ridge route running directly to Jerusalem, but its advantages came at the expense of any agricultural self-sufficiency. With Khirbet Mird, the idea of a specialized settlement finally came to the Buqê^c^ah.

distance trade has given rise to the alternative explanation that the Beersheba Valley was settled because of seventh-century Judah's need for grain, a need that could be supplied by expanded settlement in the valley. Herzog hypothesized that if "optimal" conditions existed in which the valley received an evenly spread 250 mm of rain in a year and the inhabitants were able to cultivate 300 square kilometers of the valley, then a massive grain surplus would result (Herzog 1994:126–27).[3] Finkelstein (1994) argued that the central government was aware that a massive grain surplus was possible in the Beersheba Valley and promoted settlement expansion there as a way to offset the loss of Judahite towns destroyed in Sennacherib's onslaught. Faust and Weiss (2005:74–75) built on Finkelstein's conclusions and saw this grain specialization as an important indication of an integrated, regionally specialized seventh-century economy.

Unfortunately, this alternative explanation rests on a misreading of Herzog's estimates of the productive capacities of the Beersheba Valley itself. As Herzog rightly recognized in his original presentation, these "optimal" conditions may never have existed. The average measured rainfall over a modern thirty-year period was only 204 mm of rain per year (Herzog 1994:125–26), and such conditions make permanent settlement linked to dry farming a risky proposition, even in terms of bare subsistence, let alone surplus production. Even an average of 250 mm per year would have had to allow for frequent crop failures during below-average years in which the rainfall dipped below 200 mm (Russell 1988:110; Finkelstein 1995:53; Marx 1977:345–47). Furthermore, even assuming that rainfall met the 250 mm target annually, it is not clear that the three thousand valley inhabitants could have farmed the entirety of the valley. Using Gallant's estimates for ancient Greece, families of four struggled to produce the labor to work anything larger than a six-hectare farm (Gallant 1991: 92; for family size, see Stager 1985:18–20).[4] Using such estimates, the inhabitants of the Beersheba Valley would have exploited fewer than 40 square kilometers of farmland and would have produced only a small surplus (enough to feed an additional thousand people). Such a small surplus, if it existed, would have been wiped out if any of these hypothetical conditions changed; that is, if some of the population engaged in other forms of industry or if rainfall did not meet optimal (250 mm) expectations. It is hard to imagine any central authority promoting the Beersheba Valley as a breadbasket under these conditions.

The direct archaeological evidence at these sites indicates that life in the more populous (as of the seventh century) Beersheba Valley looked much like it had in earlier periods. While Herzog (1994) noted originally that even the optimal conditions he proposed were not sufficiently propitious for dry farming to be the "main basis" of the economy, direct evidence shows that wheat fields were at least one component of local subsistence. Baron describes terraces from Tel ᶜIra that diverted rainwater runoff to ensure better grain yields. Pollen analysis demonstrates that cereals were grown in these plots, perhaps protected by cypress planted as a windbreak (Horowitz 1999: 114; Baron 1999:110–13). Wheat (*Triticum*) was also found in Iron Age deposits within the city (Liphschitz 1999:479). Instead of relying on rainfed agriculture to grow industrial tracts of grain for a far-off population, the inhabitants intensively cultivated small plots close to the cities, using some runoff agricultural techniques to grow small stands of wheat for local consumption. In addition to wheat, olive pollen was present in the fields (Horowitz 1999:114) and olive stones (*Olea europaea*) and grape pips (*Vitis vinifera*) were found within the city (Liphshitz 1999). It is likely that most olives and grapes were imported from Judah, but Finkelstein's (1995:59) and Wilkinson's (2003:159–60) descriptions of irrigated desert fruit trees caution us against assuming that the local economy did not include some household horticulture.

Herzog contended that extensive pastoralism formed another important avenue for economic survival and even subsistence (see also Marx 1977:346–47). It appears from the studies of caprine exploitation conducted at Tel ᶜIra that "large herds of caprines" (including *Ovis aries* and *Capra hircus*) were exploited first for milk, wool, and hair, and only at a later stage of life were culled for meat (Dayan 1991: 486; Horwitz 1999:490). Similarly, cattle, which may actually have made up a larger portion of the diet (Hellwig 1984:114), were not slaughtered until after they had been used for their secondary products. This is what Horwitz describes as the "traditional Middle

[3] Even the return is described by Russell as "marginal" in his cross-cultural assessment of farming strategies (1988: 109–33).

[4] Gallant's estimates are based upon Chayanov's studies of peasant farming (Chayanov 1986:222–23). Chayanov's studies are helpful because of their articulation of the family cycle and its effects on labor, but they do not provide an easily applied cross-cultural norm. If, for instance, farmers were to be motivated by factors other than family subsistence (religious fervor, nationalism, a Weberian "work ethic"), their labor output might have reason to increase beyond the peasant output that Chayanov observed. Gallant is able to overcome this hurdle by frequent reference to ancient texts and additional ethnographic analogies.

Eastern subsistence pattern" (Horwitz 1999:486; Horwitz, Tchernov, and Dar 1990:297–303).

The pastoral component of the Beersheba Valley sites was not only robust, it was regional. While the age of the animals killed for food does not vary across the valley, the percentage of cattle relative to sheep and goats varies from site to site (Horwitz 1999:491). It seems straightforward to note that the better watered sites farther to the west (Tel ᶜIra and Tel Masos) had more cattle than the drier sites to the east (Arad and Horvat Uza). The production differences between the sites in the eastern Negev and those in the western Negev were closely mirrored by consumption differences. Given the close relationship between the underlying ecology of the sites and this consumption pattern, it seems likely that it reflects the local consumption of locally raised animals. Thus even within the Beersheba Valley, regional markets were not so developed that consumption patterns were an amalgamation of larger units, even for something as mobile as animal herds.

In his reconstruction of Beersheba Valley farming, Finkelstein (1994:177) cites the Arad Ostraca as indications of the control of, or even sophisticated central planning of, the seventh-century settlement expansion. The Arad Ostraca, for the most part, record small transactions of ready-to-eat foodstuffs that were perhaps directed by the central administration (Aharoni 1981). Bread or flour was commonly accompanied by products such as oil or wine that were quite likely imported from central Judah. In one of the few texts that speaks of larger amounts of grain (Arad Inscription 25), the record indicates that even grain was imported from the Judahite highlands (Aharoni 1981:50–51; Rainey and Notley 2006:265). While the Arad Ostraca do show administrative control being exercised from central Judah, they also show that the central administration was a supplier of foodstuffs to the peripheral Beersheba Valley.

Studies of the seventh-century pottery reinforce the picture of border settlements practicing subsistence agriculture with some support from the highlands of Judah. Tel ᶜIra was characterized by extensive storage facilities and silos (Finkelstein and Beit-Arieh 1999:87; Neidinger 1999:65–66; for the idea of grain storage, see Lipschits 2005:n. 163), and Kletter's study of the pithoi found in the Area E storehouse showed that they were made from clays originating in the Moza formation of the Judahite hills. Certainly, ceramic production took place at most of the Beersheba Valley sites in the seventh century—likely a continuation of the mix of imports and local forms outlined in Goren's analysis of the eighth-century assemblage from Tel Sheva (Singer-Avitz 1999). But, as in the Buqêᶜah farmsteads, the storage areas were full of imported Judahite jars.

All of the available evidence supports the traditional picture. As Rosen states: "Subsistence is more difficult in the desert, and therefore the *raison d'etre* of permanent settlement in the Negev has always been its integration with some other core region" (Rosen 2000:57). The Beersheba Valley was no doubt integrated with Judah, but not as a grain-surplus producer. In the ancient Near East, way-stations were often supported by local agriculture to whatever extent was possible. Through the manipulation of runoff water, pastoralism, and other strategies, risk was reduced and long-term settlement was made possible in otherwise marginal landscapes (Wilkinson 2003:165–72). This is exactly the picture we find in the Beersheba Valley in the seventh century B.C.E. Small fortresses and towns emerged that were created or expanded because of the Judahite desire to protect the kingdom's southern frontier and to be involved in trade in the Negev (Holladay 2006). That these sites engaged in marginal farming, pastoralism, and perhaps even occasional horticulture should not obscure the well-founded conclusion that their primary purpose was to promote and protect lucrative long-distance trade on Judah's periphery.

Jerusalem

If the Buqêᶜah and Beersheba valleys were on the periphery, certainly Jerusalem was at the very center of Iron Age Judah. Faust and Weiss nicely summarize recent studies of Jerusalem that show its international connections (Faust and Weiss 2005). What is less apparent from their presentation, however, is that the seventh-century regional and international connections at Jerusalem were not new. Fish and shells show connections with the Red Sea and Mediterranean as clearly in the eighth century as they do in the seventh (Lernau and Lernau 1992:135–36; Meinis 1992:128). Horwitz's extensive study of the animal bones shows no marked change in exploitation strategy throughout the entire Iron Age. Only in the early Roman period did animal exploitation shift to what Horwitz calls a "consumption oriented economy," perhaps related to a "market system" (Horwitz 1996: 314).

As Monson has argued, one can find substantial north Syrian architectural connections as early as the tenth century B.C.E. (Monson 1999:12–22). Throughout much of the Iron Age II, Jerusalem was the capital of a highland kingdom, it was familiar with the international scene, and it probably had substantial access to rare luxury items from around the known world.[5] From the excavated material recovered thus far, Jerusalem seems to have functioned in the seventh century much as it had in the eighth century and earlier.

Gibeon

Halpern (1991) has referred to Pritchard's discoveries at el-Jib, ancient Gibeon, as evidence of an enormous wine industry that shows the mass production characteristic of the seventh century. Pritchard's key find was a series of shallow bell-shaped caves that he thought were linked to the fermentation of wine. The problem, however, which Pritchard (1964:13–16) himself noted, is the difficulty in dating the use of these caves as wine cellars. Seventh- and sixth-century ceramics mark the point at which the caves went out of use. It is possible that the caves were used as early as the late eighth century: in other areas, Pritchard's team found abundant *LMLK* jar sealings, which point to Gibeon's substantial involvement in the regional economy of the late eighth century (Pritchard 1959). While the role of *LMLK* jars in the economy of Judah is a complex issue, Rainey's convincing linkage of royal wine production and the *LMLK* jars (most recently Rainey and Notley 2006: 251–52) certainly enhances the possibility that Gibeon's wine production was not limited to the seventh century. In any case, whether in eighth-century *LMLK* jars, seventh-century rosette-style jars (Pritchard 1964:fig. 32:11), or as described in sixth-century records (Ezek. 27:17), Judahite wine never made it to Mediterranean markets (also Holladay 2006:323). It was likely a local affair conducted "for the king."

Ekron

The dramatic changes at Ekron in the seventh century are well known. The site expanded immensely and became the preeminent producer of olive oil in the Levant. Despite assertions to the contrary (Naʾaman 2003; Stager 1996), the dedicatory inscription found in the Ekron temple, which sits on some of the best land in the lower city, is strong evidence in favor of dating the foundation of the lower city to the early seventh century (Gitin, Dothan, and Naveh 1997). It is also well-established that Ekron's rise should be linked to the pro-Assyrian stand of its ruler in the late eighth century. This political choice, at the very least, allowed Ekron to gain more territory at the expense of its Judahite neighbors (Cogan 2003:303).

Finkelstein and Naʾaman (2004) have recently doubted the uniqueness of Ekron by noting the similarity of the olive-press installations at earlier eighth-century sites.[6] In comments on Tell Beit Mirsim, they describe this industry as "intensive, and state sponsored" (p. 74). While they do not articulate any reason why olive presses in houses point to "state sponsorship," their point reiterates Schloen's earlier suggestion that the presses at Tell Beit Mirsim and Ekron were not different in kind, only in quantity (2001:141–47). By quantity, however, Schloen did not assume that olive oil production dramatically increased. Instead, with the breakdown in clan groups following Sennacherib, he argued that the newly settled families at Ekron might have duplicated all of the economic apparatus of extended family groups within each living unit, resulting in more presses but with fewer people using each press. Speculations about the efficiency of the Ekron presses are difficult to support, but it is straightforward to observe that the presses themselves were quite similar to earlier eighth-century presses.

Thanks to Gitin's (1989) detailed preliminary publication, the pottery at Ekron found alongside olive presses can be employed in the reconstruction of Ekron's economy. Mazar has argued that this assemblage's quantitative profile is most similar to oil-pressing rooms at contemporary Tel Batash (Mazar and Panitz-Cohen 2001:176). Tel Batash Stratum II would be considered a "miniature version of Ekron" were it not for the extensive Judahite connections found at Batash (Mazar and Panitz-Cohen 2001:281–82). Schloen (2001:143–45) argues that Ekron's assemblage might be described as domestic, noting that

[5] Whether the product was fish, cedar planks (Liphschitz and Biger 1991), or basalt grinding stones, trade in specialty items was a feature of the Iron Age that does not necessarily imply a specialization and regional integration of the economy (Sherratt and Sherratt 1991:358). Still, even such occasional trade could still be conducted according to "market" principles (Hodder 1971).

[6] The relationship between Tell Beit Mirsim (3 ha) and Ekron (34 ha) described by Finkelstein and Naʾaman is warped by some odd statistics. While only six presses were discovered at Tel Beit Mirsim, Finkelstein and Naʾaman follow Albright's estimate that as many as 30 could have been there. They then argue that this estimate results in a ratio of 10 oil presses per hectare. In calculating the same presses per hectare statistic for Tel Miqne, they use only the number of presses actually viewed in excavations and surveys (115) to argue that Tell Beit Mirsim had an even more intensive production capacity than did Ekron. Any use of commensurable statistics (total estimated number of presses at both sites, total excavated presses at both sites, presses per household at both sites) shows this conclusion to be fallacious.

it could have supplied the food storage capacity necessary for a family of five.

The petrographic profile of Ekron's ceramics provides further nuance. Gitin reported neutron activation analysis (NAA) results which showed that up to "30 percent of the storejars" were imported from Ashdod (1997:84), but two recently conducted petrographic studies, one by the present author and one by Yuval Goren, independently concluded that all tested examples of the most common storejar form (Gitin 1997:fig. 14:4), and a large percentage of the other forms, were made of local clays.[7] The petrographic results are not surprising given the typically local nature of Bronze and Iron Age pottery production, and, if they hold up in further analysis and dialogue with NAA results, they would stand as another indication that some of Ekron's production retained its traditional local form of expression and was not subject to regional integration and specialization.

The bigger issue is whether the changes in Ekron show a new economy and a new level of integration with the Mediterranean world or the Assyrian Empire. Certainly, at least in terms of scale and probably in terms of organization, Ekron changed dramatically. Gitin argues that Ekron was "targeted for growth" and that the cities of Philistia were organized by the "broad economic policy of Assyria" into cities of specialized "mass production" in the service of the empire (Gitin 1997:84). The "cottage industry" of earlier periods gave way to "olive-oil factories" located in specialized zones throughout the city (Gitin 2003:63–64).[8] We might soften Gitin's loaded terminology here, but Ekron certainly grew on the shoulders of a substantial population change in the Shephelah that accompanied the campaigns of Sennacherib, and Halpern correctly stresses the deep trauma that such events would have had on the kinship networks (particularly on the clan sector), so important in diffusing risks and protecting regional interests (Halpern 1991:74–75).

However, these changes were not likely the result of Assyrian economic policy (Master 2003; Faust and Weiss 2005). It is difficult to find a contemporary site that was transformed in the same way and on the same scale as Ekron anywhere else in the Assyrian Empire. Assyrian interests seem to have focused on supply depots for the army and fortresses to protect routes of travel. Instead, it is probably more helpful to look at other sites in the Shephelah that went through similar transformations in later periods. Hellenistic-period Mareshah, for example, shows the effects of the oscillation between a coastal economy and an inland economy. When it was connected to Ashkelon via Idumean interests, Mareshah contained silver hoards, large-scale production of olive oil, and a substantial population. When it reverted to Hasmonean control in the late second century, the population diminished, production declined, and even the Hippodamian plan of the site was rejected in favor of insular highland alleyways (Avi-Yonah 1993; Kloner 1993b; 2008). The growth of Eleutheropolis (Kloner 1993a) in the Roman period might also serve to place Ekron's growth in perspective. Rather than an exceptional shift due to Assyrian patronage, the growth of Ekron seems to represent a typical oscillation in the Shephelah as opportunities in the international world of Mediterranean commerce gained the upper hand over connections to the more insular highlands.

Ashkelon

On the coast, Lawrence Stager discovered a marketplace with direct evidence of regular exchanges of basic commodities gathered from the entire Mediterranean world. In microcosm, this is the depersonalized, specialized, and integrated world that is supposed to characterize the new economy of the seventh century. The date of this market is secure because fills beneath it contain East Greek Wild Goat II pottery, creating a *terminus post quem* for the foundation of the market of at least 625 B.C.E. Moreover, the end of the Ashkelon market is marked by the comprehensive destruction wrought by Nebuchadnezzar in 604 B.C.E. Within the marketplace, trade in wine, meat, grain, and exotic Mediterranean imports was facilitated by the use of weights and

---

[7] I would like to thank Seymour Gitin and the Tel Miqne/Ekron project for permission to cite these results. For my study, definitions of "local" clays surrounding Ekron were taken from Killebrew's (1998) descriptions. The references for Ashdod clays were taken from petrographic samples of published pottery from kiln loci (described in Master 2001: 200–1).

[8] Recently, Gitin and Golani (2001; 2004) and Kletter (2003) have discussed Ekron's silver hoards as an indication of economic changes in the seventh century. Gitin and Golani relate these hoards to a new Assyrian economic system that revolved around the use of silver. Of these hoards, however, five were found in contexts which date to the very end of the seventh century, after the time of Assyrian hegemony. While Kletter is probably incorrect to assert that only coinage marks the beginning of a "monetary economy," he is likely correct that Ekron hoards are part of a series of similar hoards throughout the Iron Age. The use of a precious-metal monetary economy can be traced throughout the Bronze and Iron Ages, not only by the infrequent finds of silver hoards, but by the more common associated finds of scales and weights (Barkay 2004:2086). The seventh century did not mark a decisive moment in this long-term development (see Temin 2003).

balances to measure payment in *Hacksilber* (Stager et al. 2008:309–12; Cross 2008:334–49). While the red wine (*ynʾdm*), date-palm wine (*šēkār*), and meat may have been local (Stager 1996), Chian, Samian, and Phoenician amphoras highlighted the products of the Mediterranean (Master 2003). Recently, Weiss and Kislev have demonstrated that the grain found in the market was a product of Judah's fields (Weiss and Kislev 2004). While much of the produce of the market was consumed locally, Egypt was another customer for goods transshipped through Ashkelon, and, from the ceramic record, the Phoenicians seem to have been a robust trading partner as well (Master 2003).

While it is true that Ashkelon was a highly specialized city in the seventh century, it was not much more specialized than it had been in other periods (Stager and Schloen 2008:7–8). As Stager (1992:40; 2001:616) has demonstrated, the association between "Ashkelon" and commerce has always been a tautology. Both in the Early and Middle Bronze Age, Ashkelon's commercial markets purchased so much of the surplus agricultural produce of the inland cities that cash crops for export became a regular part of the life in the Shephelah. The physical marketplace uncovered by Stager at Ashkelon dates to the seventh century, but even it has precursors in the famed *ḥûṣôt* described in Hebrew poetry (Cross 1973:121–23; McCarter 1984:78–79). While Ashkelon may represent a depersonalized, integrated, and specialized economy, Stager's extensive excavations under the aegis of the Leon Levy Expedition show that these economic patterns were not chronologically limited to the seventh century, but were a characteristic of maritime ports for millennia (Stager et al. 2008:218–318).

Summary

In an essay some years ago on the future of biblical archaeology, Stager (1993:751) highlighted several types of change. The most radical was the "catastrophe" in which a way of life disintegrates and those things that come after are of a different order. For Halpern, Sennacherib's conquest was just such an event which led to "literalization," "elite alienation," and "individuation." Judah was transformed from an "agrarian" to an "industrial" society (1991:91). In their own ways, Gitin (1997; 2003:63–69) and Finkelstein and Naʾaman (2004) have continued in this vein, with talk of an "imperial ideology of aggressive commercial exploitation," or "intensive, state-sponsored production." Sweeping changes that upended the normal geographical divisions of the southern Levant are conceivable (Isa. 40:3–5), but they were also quite rare, and the unlikely persistence of the House of David in the face of an Assyrian assault highlights the limited consequences of this raid and should give one pause in considering some of the more dramatic economic reconstructions above.

Judah's economy was shocked and diminished by Sennacherib's campaigns, but it was not radically altered. After a few years, the economy returned to its normal Iron Age patterns (Isa. 37:30). Throughout the seventh century, highland Judah remained a net exporter of grain to its immediate hinterland (2 Kings 19:29–31). Judah expanded its date palm and terebinth groves along the Dead Sea and protected the access routes to the sources of *dĕbaš* (King and Stager 2001:103–4) and *ṣŏrî* (King 1993:153). Strikingly, according to Ezekiel 27 (also Jer. 41:8), even olive oil was still part of the Judahite basket of goods in the early sixth century (Diakonoff 1992:185). All in all, Judah continued as it had for centuries. Its sole concession to its weakened state seems to have been a strengthening of the eastern and southern frontiers in order to keep alive the lifeline of trade that supported the center (Holladay 2006). The durable socioeconomic structure typical of the Bronze and Iron Age highland polities was up to the challenge of Sennacherib (Labianca 1997).

Meanwhile, those cities on the coast which survived Sennacherib's purge prospered without Judahite meddling. As always, the Shephelah was "debatable ground," shifting in its allegiances between the markets of the coast and the fortresses of the highlands (Smith 1966:143). Even in the eighth century, it began to feel the pressures of the Mediterranean market, pressuring producers to promote efficiency at the expense of social cohesion (Micah 2:1–5). Ekron was the only viable Shephelah city that survived the Assyrians, and its inhabitants were now able to turn their attention toward economic opportunities to the west. The lowlands came alive with production for international commerce once again, just as they had in the Early Bronze II–III, the Middle Bronze II, and the Late Bronze II. On the coast, the inhabitants of Ashkelon continued to look to the promise of a burgeoning maritime economy. Just as it had for millennia, Ashkelon was able to unite the productive capacities of the southern Levant with the markets of the Mediterranean.

In some ways, for both highland Judah and the coastal Philistine cities, it was the lessons forgotten after Sennacherib that were more significant. Whether through the continued Judahite reliance on the inviolability of Yahweh's temple (Jer. 7:1–4) or a renewed belief in the power of Egypt (Porten 1981; Jer. 37:6–11), the devastating events of the late seventh and early sixth centuries showcased a failure to remember the mistakes of the eighth century. This time however, Ekron and Ashkelon were not so fortunate and Judah had no lowland cities to buffer the blow. The eighth-century destructions were merely a prelude to the devastation to come, and the seventh-century economy was merely a continuation of what had gone before.

Bibliography

Aharoni, Y.
1981 *Arad Inscriptions*. Translated by J. Ben-Or. Jerusalem: Israel Exploration Society.

Arnold, D. E.
1985 *Ceramic Theory and Cultural Process*. Cambridge: Cambridge University Press.

Assmann, J.
1997 *Moses the Egyptian: The Memory of Egypt in Western Monotheism*. Cambridge, Mass.: Harvard University Press.

Avi-Yonah, M.
1993 Mareshah (Marisa). In *The New Encyclopedia of Archaeological Excavations in the Holy Land*, ed. E. Stern, 3:948–51. New York: Simon and Schuster.

Barkay, G.
2004 Section C: A Balance Beam. In *The Renewed Archaeological Excavations at Lachish (1973–1994)*, ed. D. Ussishkin, 4:2084–87. Tel Aviv: Institute of Archaeology, Tel Aviv University.

Baron, A. G.
1999 Area K—The Agricultural Terraces. In *Tel ᶜIra: A Stronghold in the Biblical Negev*, ed. I. Beit-Arieh, 110–13. Tel Aviv: Institute of Archaeology, Tel Aviv University.

Bienkowski, P., and E. van der Steen
2001 Tribes, Trade, and Towns: A New Framework for the Late Iron Age in Southern Jordan and the Negev. *BASOR* 323:21–47.

Bruins, H. J.
1986 *Desert Environment and Agriculture in the Central Negev and Kadesh-Barnea during Historical Times*. Nijkerk: Midbar Foundation.

Chayanov, A. V.
1986 *The Theory of Peasant Economy* [orig. Russian 1925]. Translated by R. Smith. Madison, Wis.: University of Wisconsin Press.

Cogan, M.
2003 Sennacherib's Siege of Jerusalem. In *The Context of Scripture*, ed. W. W. Hallo and K. L. Younger, 2:302–3. Leiden: Brill.

Cross, F. M.
1973 *Canaanite Myth and Hebrew Epic: Essays in the History of the Religion of Israel*. Cambridge, Mass.: Harvard University Press.
1993 Buqeiᶜa, el-. In *The New Encyclopedia of Archaeological Excavations in the Holy Land*, ed. E. Stern, 1:267–69. New York: Simon and Schuster.
2008 Inscriptions in Phoenician and Other Scripts. In *Ashkelon*, vol. 1, *Introduction and Overview (1985–2006)*, ed. L. E. Stager, J. D. Schloen, and D. M. Master, 333–72. Winona Lake, Ind.: Eisenbrauns.

Dayan, T.
1999 Faunal Remains: Areas A–G. In *Tel ᶜIra: A Stronghold in the Biblical Negev*, ed. I. Beit-Arieh, 480–87. Tel Aviv: Institute of Archaeology, Tel Aviv University.

Diakonoff, I. M.
1992 The Naval Power and Trade of Tyre. *IEJ* 42: 168–93.

Ephᶜal, I.
1984 *The Ancient Arabs: Nomads on the Borders of the Fertile Crescent 9th–5th Centuries* B.C. Jerusalem: Magnes.

Faust, A., and E. Weiss
2005 Judah, Philistia, and the Mediterranean World: Reconstructing the Economic System of the Seventh Century B.C.E. *BASOR* 338:71–92.

Finkelstein, I.
1994 The Archaeology of the Days of Manasseh. In *Scripture and Other Artifacts: Essays on the Bible and Archaeology in Honor of Philip J. King*, ed. M. D. Coogan, J. C. Exum, and L. E. Stager, 169–87. Louisville, Ky.: Westminster John Knox.
1995 *Living on the Fringe: The Archaeology and History of the Negev, Sinai and Neighbouring Regions in the Bronze and Iron Ages*. Monographs in Mediterranean Archaeology 6. Sheffield, England: Sheffield Academic Press.

Finkelstein, I., and I. Beit-Arieh
1999 Area E. In *Tel ᶜIra: A Stronghold in the Biblical Negev*, ed. I. Beit-Arieh, 67–96. Tel Aviv: Institute of Archaeology, Tel Aviv University.

Finkelstein, I., and N. Naʾaman
2004 The Judahite Shephelah in the Late Eighth and Early Seventh Centuries B.C.E. *Tel Aviv* 31:60–79.

Gallant, T. W.
1991 *Risk and Survival in Ancient Greece: Reconstructing the Rural Domestic Economy*. Stanford, Calif.: Stanford University Press.

Gitin, S.
1989 Tel Miqne-Ekron: A Type-Site for the Inner Coastal Plain in the Iron Age II Period. In *Recent Excavations in Israel: Studies in Iron Age Archaeology*, ed. S. Gitin and W. G. Dever, 23–58. AASOR 49. Winona Lake, Ind.: Eisenbrauns.
1997 The Neo-Assyrian Empire and Its Western Periphery: The Levant, with a Focus on Philistine Ekron. In *Assyria 1995: Proceedings of the Tenth Anniversary Symposium of the Neo-Assyrian Text Corpus Project, Helsinki, September 7–11, 1995*, ed. S. Parpola and R. M. Whiting, 77–103. Helsinki: Neo-Assyrian Text Corpus Project.
2003 The Philistines: Neighbors of the Canaanites, Phoenicians and Israelites. In *One Hundred Years of American Archaeology in the Middle East*, ed. D. R. Clark and V. H. Matthews, 57–86. Boston: American Schools of Oriental Research.

Gitin, S., T. Dothan, and J. Naveh
1997 A Royal Dedicatory Inscription from Ekron. *IEJ* 47:1–16.

Gitin, S., and A. Golani
2001 The Tel Miqne-Ekron Silver Hoards: The Assyrian and Phoenician Connections. In *Hacksilber to Coinage: New Insights into the Monetary History of the Near East and Greece*, ed. M. S. Balmuth, 27–48. Numismatic Studies 24. New York: American Numismatic Society.
2003 A Silver-Based Monetary Economy in the Seventh Century B.C.E.: A Response to Raz Kletter. *Levant* 36:203–5.

Goren, Y.
1995 Shrines and Ceramics in Chalcolithic Israel: The View through the Petrographic Microscope. *Archaeometry* 37:287–305.

Goren, Y., I. Finkelstein, and N. Naᵓaman
2004 *Inscribed in Clay: Provenance Study of the Amarna Tablets and Other Ancient Near Eastern Texts*. Tel Aviv: Institute of Archaeology, Tel Aviv University.

Halpern, B.
1991 Jerusalem and the Lineages in the Seventh Century B.C.E.: Kingship and the Rise of Individual Moral Liability. In *Law and Ideology in Monarchic Israel*, ed. B. Halpern and D. W. Hobson, 11–107. JSOTSup 124. Sheffield, England: Sheffield Academic Press.

Hellwing, S.
1984 Human Exploitation of Animal Resources in the Early Iron Age Strata at Tel Beer-sheba. In *Beer-Sheba*, vol. 2, *The Early Iron Age Settlements*, ed. Z. Herzog, 105–15. Tel Aviv: Institute of Archaeology, Tel Aviv University.

Herzog, Z.
1994 The Beer-Sheba Valley: From Nomadism to Monarchy. In *From Nomadism to Monarchy: Archaeological and Historical Aspects of Early Israel*, ed. I. Finkelstein and N. Naᵓaman, 122–49. Jerusalem: Israel Exploration Society.

Hodder, B.
1971 Periodic and Daily Markets in West Africa. In *The Development of Indigenous Trade and Markets in West Africa*, ed. C. Meillassoux, 347–58. Oxford: Oxford University Press.

Holladay, J. S.
2006 Hezekiah's Tribute, Long-Distance Trade, and the Wealth of Nations ca. 1000–600 B.C.: A New Perspective. In *Confronting the Past: Archaeological and Historical Essays on Ancient Israel in Honor of William G. Dever*, ed. S. Gitin, J. E. Wright, and J. P. Dessel, 309–32. Winona Lake, Ind.: Eisenbrauns.

Horowitz, A.
1999 Appendix: Pollen Analyses. In *Tel ᶜIra: A Stronghold in the Biblical Negev*, ed. I. Beit-Arieh, 114. Tel Aviv: Institute of Archaeology, Tel Aviv University.

Horwitz, L. K.
1996 Faunal Remains from Areas A, B, D, H and K. In *Excavations of the City of David, 1978–1985*, vol. 4, *Various Reports*, ed. D. T. Ariel and A. DeGroot, 302–15. Qedem 35. Jerusalem: Institute of Archaeology, Hebrew University.
1999 Faunal Remains: Areas L and M. In *Tel ᶜIra: A Stronghold in the Biblical Negev*, ed. I. Beit-Arieh, 488–94. Tel Aviv: Institute of Archaeology, Tel Aviv University.

Horwitz, L. K., E. Tchernov, and S. Dar
1990 Subsistence and Environment on Mount Carmel in the Roman–Byzantine and Mediaeval Periods: The Evidence from Kh. Sumaqa. *IEJ* 40:287–304.

Killebrew, A. E.
1998 Ceramic Craft and Technology during the Late Bronze and Early Iron Ages: The Relationship Between Pottery Technology, Style and Cultural Diversity. Ph.D. diss., Hebrew University of Jerusalem.

King, P. J.
1993 *Jeremiah: An Archaeological Companion*. Louisville, Ky.: Westminster John Knox.

King, P. J., and L. E. Stager
2001 *Life in Biblical Israel*. Louisville, Ky.: Westminster John Knox.

Kletter, R.
1999 Late Iron Age Pithoi with Potter's Marks. In *Tel ᶜIra: A Stronghold in the Biblical Negev*, ed. I. Beit-Arieh, 350–59. Tel Aviv: Institute of Archaeology, Tel Aviv University.
2003 Iron Age Hoards of Precious Metals in Palestine—An "Underground Economy"? *Levant* 35: 139–52.

Kloner, A.
1993a Beth Guvrin. In *The New Encyclopedia of Archaeological Excavations in the Holy Land*, ed. E. Stern, 1:195–201. New York: Simon and Schuster.
1993b Mareshah (Marisa). In *The New Encyclopedia of Archaeological Excavations in the Holy Land*, ed. E. Stern, 3:951–57. New York: Simon and Schuster.
2007 Mareshah (Marisa). In *The New Encyclopedia of Archaeological Excavations in the Holy Land*, ed. E. Stern, 5:1919–25. Jerusalem: Israel Exploration Society.

Labianca, Ø.
1997 Indigenous Hardiness Structures and State Formation in Jordan: Towards a History of Jordan's Resident Arab Population. In *Ethnic Encounter and Culture Change*, ed. M. Sabour and K. Vikør, 143–57. Nordic Research on the Middle East 3. Bergen: Nordic Society for Middle Eastern Studies.

Lernau, H., and O. Lernau
1992 Fish Remains. In *Excavations in the City of David, 1978–1985*, vol. 3, *Stratigraphical, Environmental, and Other Reports,* ed. D. T. Ariel and A. DeGroot, 131–48. Qedem 33. Jerusalem: Institute of Archaeology, Hebrew University.

Liphschitz, N.
1999 Botanical Remains. In *Tel ᶜIra: A Stronghold in the Biblical Negev*, ed. I. Beit-Arieh, 476–79. Tel Aviv: Institute of Archaeology, Tel Aviv University.

Liphschitz, N., and G. Biger
1991 Cedar of Lebanon (*Cedrus libani*) in Israel during Antiquity. *IEJ* 41:167–75.

Lipschits, O.
2005 *The Fall and Rise of Jerusalem: Judah under Babylonian Rule*. Winona Lake, Ind.: Eisenbrauns.

Marx, E.
1977 The Tribe as a Unit of Subsistence: Nomadic Pastoralism in the Middle East. *AA* 79:343–63.

Master, D. M.
2001 The Seaport of Ashkelon in the Seventh Century B.C.E.: A Petrographic Study. Ph.D. diss., Harvard University.
2003 Trade and Politics: Ashkelon's Balancing Act in the Seventh Century B.C.E. *BASOR* 330:47–64.

Masterman, E. W. G.
1903 Notes on some Ruins and a Rock-cut Aqueduct in the Wâdy Ḳumrân. *PEFQS* 1903:264–67.

Mazar, A., and N. Panitz-Cohen
2001 *Timnah (Tel Batash).* Vol. 2, *The Finds for the First Millennium B.C.E.* 2 vols. Qedem 42. Jerusalem: Institute of Archaeology, Hebrew University.

McCarter, P. K.
1984 *II Samuel: A New Translation with Introduction, Notes, and Commentary.* Anchor Bible 9. Garden City, N.Y.: Doubleday.

Michniewicz, J., and M. Krzyśko
2003 The Provenance of Scroll Jars in the Light of Archaeometric Investigations. In *Fouilles de Khirbet Qumrân et ᶜAïn Feshkha*, vol. 2, ed. J.-B. Humbert and J. Gunneweg, 59–99. Fribourg, Switzerland: Éditions Universitaires.

Mienes, H.
1992 Molluscs. In *Excavations of the City of David, 1978–1985*, vol. 3, *Stratigraphical, Environmental, and Other Reports,* ed. D. T. Ariel and A. DeGroot, 122–30. Qedem 33. Jerusalem: Institute of Archaeology, Hebrew University.

Mommsen, H., I. Perlman, and J. Yellin
1984 The Provenience of the LMLK Jars. *IEJ* 34:89–113.

Monson, J.
1999 The Temple of Solomon: Heart of Jerusalem. In *Zion, City of Our God*, ed. R. Hess and G. Wenham, 1–22. Grand Rapids, Mich.: Eerdmans.

Naᵓaman, N.
2003 Ekron under the Assyrian and Egyptian Empires. *BASOR* 332:81–91.

Neidinger, W.
1999 Area D. In *Tel ᶜIra: A Stronghold in the Biblical Negev*, ed. I. Beit-Arieh, 60–66. Tel Aviv: Institute of Archaeology, Tel Aviv University.

Porten, B.
1981 The Identity of King Adon. *BA* 44:36–52.

Pritchard, J. B.
1959 *Hebrew Inscriptions and Stamps from Gibeon.* Philadelphia: University Museum, University of Pennsylvania.
1964 *Winery, Defenses, and Soundings at Gibeon.* Philadelphia: University Museum, University of Pennsylvania.

Rainey, A., and S. Notley
2006 *The Sacred Bridge: Carta's Atlas of the Biblical World*. Jerusalem: Carta.

Rice, P.
1987 *Pottery Analysis: A Sourcebook*. Chicago: University of Chicago Press.

Robinson, E., and E. Smith
1856 *Biblical Researches in Palestine, and in the Adjacent Regions: A Journal of Travels in the Year 1838*. Boston: Crocker and Brewster.

Rosen, S. A.
2000 The Decline of Desert Agriculture: A View from the Classical Period Negev. In *The Archaeology of Drylands: Living at the Margin*, ed. G. Barker and D. Gilbertson, 45–62. London: Routledge.

Rosenthal, E., G. Weinberger, A. Almogi-Labin, and A. Flexer
2000 Late Cretaceous–Early Tertiary Development of Depositional Basins in Samaria as a Reflection of Eastern Mediterranean Tectonic Development. *American Association of Petroleum Geologists Bulletin* 84/7:997–1014.

Russell, K. W.
1988 *After Eden: The Behavioral Ecology of Early Food Production in the Near East and North Africa*. BARIS 391. Oxford: British Archaeological Reports.

Schloen, J. D.
2001 *The House of the Father as Fact and Symbol: Patrimonialism in Ugarit and the Ancient Near East*. SAHL 2. Winona Lake, Ind.: Eisenbrauns.

Singer-Avitz, L.
1999 Beersheba—A Gateway Community in Southern Arabian Long-Distance Trade in the Eighth Century B.C.E. *Tel Aviv* 26:3–74.

Smith, G. A.
1966 *The Historical Geography of the Holy Land*. New York: Harper and Row.

Sneh, A., Y. Bartov, and M. Rosensaft
1998 *Geological Map of Israel 1:200,000*. Jerusalem: Geological Survey of Israel.

Stager, L. E.
1975 Ancient Agriculture in the Judaean Desert: A Case Study of the Buqê^c^ah Valley in the Iron Age. Ph.D. diss., Harvard University.
1976 Farming in the Judean Desert during the Iron Age. *BASOR* 221:145–58.
1985 The Archaeology of the Family in Ancient Israel. *BASOR* 260:1–35.
1989 The Song of Deborah: Why Some Tribes Answered the Call and Others Did Not. *BAR* 15/1: 51–64.
1992 The Periodization of Palestine from Neolithic through Early Bronze Times. In *Chronologies in Old World Archaeology*, ed. R. W. Ehrich, 1:22–41. 3d ed. Chicago: University of Chicago Press.
1993 Toward the Future: It's Just a Matter of Time. In *Biblical Archaeology Today, 1990*, ed. A. Biran and J. Aviram, 746–55. Jerusalem: Israel Exploration Society and Israel Academy of Sciences and Humanities.
1996 Ashkelon and the Archaeology of Destruction: Kislev 604 B.C.E. *EI* 25:61*–74*
2001 Port Power in the Early and the Middle Bronze Age: The Organization of Maritime Trade and Hinterland Production. In *Studies in the Archaeology of Israel and Neighboring Lands in Memory of Douglas L. Esse*, ed. S. R. Wolff, 625–38. SAOC 59. Chicago: Oriental Institute, University of Chicago.

Stager, L. E., and J. D. Schloen
2008 Introduction: Ashkelon and Its Inhabitants. In *Ashkelon*, vol. 1, *Introduction and Overview (1985–2006)*, ed. L. E. Stager, J. D. Schloen, and D. M. Master, 3–10. Winona Lake, Ind.: Eisenbrauns.

Stager, L. E., et al.
2008 Stratigraphic Overview. In *Ashkelon*, vol. 1, *Introduction and Overview (1985–2006)*, ed. L. E. Stager, J. D. Schloen, and D. M. Master, 215–326. Winona Lake, Ind.: Eisenbrauns.

Temin, P.
2003 Mediterranean Trade in Biblical Times. *Massachusetts Institute of Technology Department of Economics Working Paper Series* 03–12, March 2003.

Van Beek, G. W.
1960 Frankincense and Myrrh. *BA* 23:69–95.

Vaughn, A.
1999 *Theology, History, and Archaeology in the Chronicler's Account of Hezekiah*. Atlanta: Scholars.

Weiss, E., and M. E. Kislev
2004 Plant Remains as Indicators of Economic Activity: A Case Study from Iron Age Ashkelon. *JAS* 31:1–13.

Wilkinson, T. J.
2003 *Archaeological Landscapes of the Ancient Near East*. Tucson, Ariz.: University of Arizona Press.

33. The Iron Age Dwellings at Tell Qasile

by Amihai Mazar

One of Larry Stager's main fields of interest has been Iron Age dwellings and daily life. It is thus appropriate to discuss an important group of Iron Age I–IIA dwellings at Tell Qasile in a volume in honor of Larry. Most of these buildings were excavated under the direction of the late Benjamin Mazar, with whom Larry had a close friendship and many common subjects of interest. This paper is thus also a small token to this friendship.

Tell Qasile is a 1.3-hectare site located on the western slope of a sandstone (*kurkar*) ridge overlooking the Mediterranean Sea and the Yarkon River (figure 1). The ancient name of the site is unknown. Four excavation seasons directed by Benjamin Mazar in 1949–1951 and 1956 revealed in the southern part of the site (Area A) part of an Iron Age town with nine buildings arranged on both sides of an east-west street (Maisler [Mazar] 1950–1951; Dothan and Dunayevsky 1993; Mazar 1980:9–12, 74–77). Seven of these buildings can be defined as dwellings of various sorts. Between the years 1972 and 1989, I excavated Area C, to the north of Area A, where a series of temples and four additional buildings, probably dwellings, were fully or partly excavated.

Altogether, eleven dwellings were excavated in Strata XII–X, comprising the largest sample of Iron Age I dwellings outside of Tel Masos. Following a severe destruction at the end of Stratum X, four of these houses were renovated during the Iron IIA period (tenth–ninth centuries B.C.E.).

The houses mentioned in this paper are arranged in table 1 by area and in order of stratigraphic sequence. Buildings other than dwellings are also shown in this table, but these will not be discussed in this paper. Although a final report on the first seasons of excavation at Tell Qasile was not completed, the high quality of the documentation enables reliable analysis of the architecture and of the distribution of finds.

The analysis and overall reconstruction of the stratigraphy at Tell Qasile was not an easy task because some of the mudbrick structures were in use for a long time and passed through several construction phases, while others were in use for only a short time. A clear stratigraphic marker was the severe destruction by fire of Stratum X, which created a thick layer of reddish burned-brick debris throughout the site. The schematic plans presented in this paper (figures 2–5) are based on Dunayevsky's last version of the plans and on my own understanding of the stratigraphy, which differs from that of Dunayevsky's mainly in relation to the stratigraphic attribution of Building L and several details relating to Buildings K and J.

The first part of this paper is more descriptive, while in the second part of the paper I will analyze several issues relating to the plan of the town, its houses, and its population.

Table 1. Architectural Units Excavated at Tell Qasile, Areas A and C

Stratum	***Area A***		***Area C***	
	Dwellings	*Other Buildings*	*Dwellings*	*Other Buildings*
XII	—	—	335 ("hearth building")	Temple 319
XI	J? U?	Q (industrial) Z (early phase?)	341 (= 201), 147?	Temple 200 Shrine 300
X	K, J, W, O, M, R, Q	L (commercial/administrative) Z (tripartite pillared store building) Q1 (shop/workshop)	225, 495, 326?	Temple 131
IX	K, J, W, O	L?	—	Temple(?) 118
VIII	K, J, W, O	L?	—	—

Note that Stratum VII is missing from this table. In my view, its very definition was based on a misunderstanding of the history of Building L. If this building is assigned to Stratum X, as I suggest, no remains justify the existence of Stratum VII as an independent stratum. After the 1972–1974 seasons, I assigned the label "Stratum VII" to a wash layer found above Strata XI–VIII remains. This layer contained eighth–seventh-century pottery (Mazar 1985:109–10). This period was not represented in Area A.

Structural Remains of Strata XII–XI (figure 2)[1]

In Area A, Strata XII–XI are known only from probes excavated in random places below Stratum X buildings. The sandstone (*kurkar*) bedrock was reached about 0.25–0.5 m below the floors of Stratum X structures. Beaten-earth and cobblestone floors were detected, as well as occupation debris with ash layers and various installations, including ovens, a few pits cut into the bedrock, and small silos. Yet the architectural remains were very few and fragmentary. Building remains of Stratum XI were found below Buildings L, J, Q, R, and Z of Stratum X.[2] However, in many cases it was difficult to distinguish between Strata XII and XI and in only a few places were elements of these two strata found superimposed. Thus the correlation between the various floor surfaces and fragmentary structural remains remained uncertain in many cases.[3] The architectural fragments from these strata cannot be classified as defined architectural units. The eastern wall of building J and several walls to its north which appear on the plan of Stratum X appear also on the plans of Stratum XI, yet it remains uncertain whether the buildings to which these walls belonged in Stratum X were indeed founded in Stratum XI. It may be conjectured that parts of Building J, or perhaps the entire building, were founded in Stratum XI, yet it is impossible to determine the plan of the structure during this phase. Probes below Building W of Stratum X recovered clear separation between oven and floor surfaces of Strata XII and XI, and both were earlier than the foundation of Building W in Stratum X. This is one of the few places where a clear differentiation between Strata XII and XI could be made.[4] The few fragmentary walls found below Street A of Stratum X indicate that the street did not yet exist in Strata XII–XI. In the southern part of space Q8, a metal workshop contained two melting furnaces and two ceramic crucibles.[5]

It thus appears that in the initial occupational phase in Stratum XII, Area A included large open spaces utilized for various functions; the only structure was Building Q, which served as a metal workshop. In Stratum XI, additional scattered buildings were founded, yet these are poorly known and there is no coherent plan.

In contrast to Area A, the structural remains from Strata XII–XI in Area C were more substantial. In Stratum XII, there was a small temple (Building 319) with a spacious courtyard (Mazar 1980:13–20), and the "hearth building" to the southeast of the temple (see below). This difference may be explained by the peripheral location of Area A as opposed to the more central location of Area C, indicating a process of settlement expansion from the center to the periphery.

The only residential building of Stratum XII in Area C was the partially preserved Building 335 (the "hearth building"; Mazar 1986:3–6). It was founded on bedrock at the highest topographical point of the mound and included a large hall (7.2 m in length) with an additional large room to its east; the southern part of this building was not preserved. Benches were situated along the walls of the hall and a "keyhole-shaped" hearth stood at its center. This must have been an assembly hall or main hall of a large residence of Stratum XII. Its architecture appears to retain Aegean traditions brought by the founders of the site (for Aegean and Cypriot hearth buildings, see Karageorghis 1998). This building is strong evidence in favor of the ethnic identification of the founders of Tell Qasile as Philistines. Building 341 to the west of the "hearth building" was probably founded in Stratum XI and is only partially known (Mazar 1986: 6–7). It seems to include a central small chamber surrounded by large rooms on all sides. This plan, if correctly reconstructed, does not recall any other known buildings of the period. These two buildings

[1] The topography of the site caused some difficulties in stratigraphic attribution because the settlement was built on the western slope of a ridge, the summit of which was at the eastern end of Areas A and C. This fact was not clarified during the first seasons because Byzantine and medieval structures and erosion had changed the topography of the hill, creating an artificial summit about 20 m west of the natural summit. This misled the excavators in the case of Building L, which in my view should be attributed to Stratum X rather than to Strata IX–VIII. In our excavations in Area C, building remains of Stratum XII were found just below topsoil in the eastern part of the area, while the same stratum was reached about 2.5 m below topsoil in the western part of the area, 25 m away.

[2] The excavators attributed the remains below Building L to Stratum X because they believed that the building belonged to Stratum IX or VIII. Yet the reassignment of Building L to Stratum X enables us to attribute the earlier remains to Strata XII and XI.

[3] This is evident in the fact that Dunayevsky prepared several versions of plans for Strata XII and XI but never finalized any of them.

[4] Probes carried out in 1950 and in 1962 by Dunayevsky in the area of Building J did not reveal any stratigraphic elements earlier than the Stratum X floor.

[5] The reconstruction of the furnace as published by Mazar (1950–1951:74, fig. 3) is imaginary (Rothenberg 1967:57–58). There is no evidence for the reconstructed chimney and only traces of the air channel were discovered. The V shape of the crucibles is correct.

Figure 1. Topographic map of Tell Qasile showing the main structural remains of Stratum X

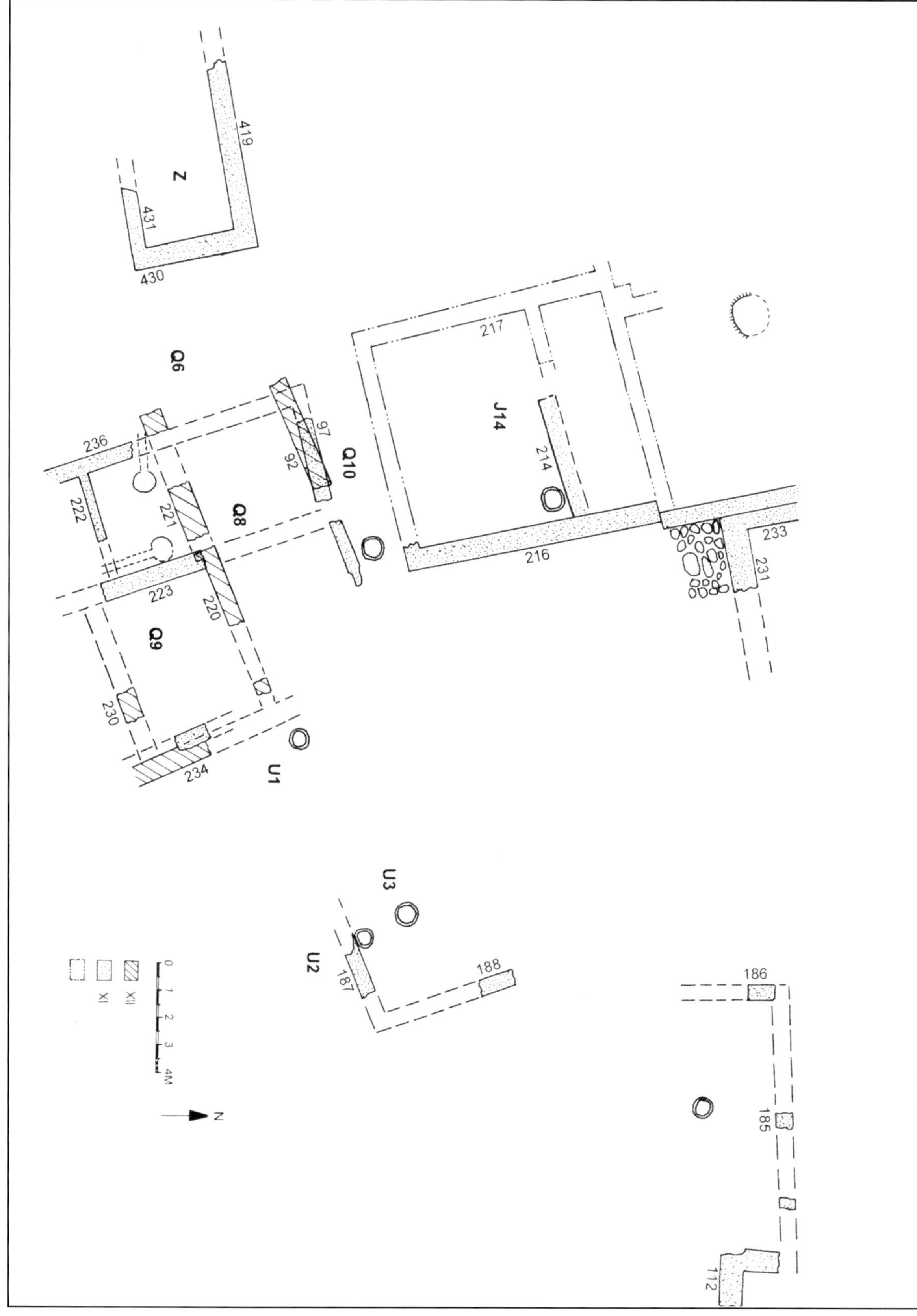

Figure 2. Tell Qasile, schematic plan of Area A, Strata XII–XI

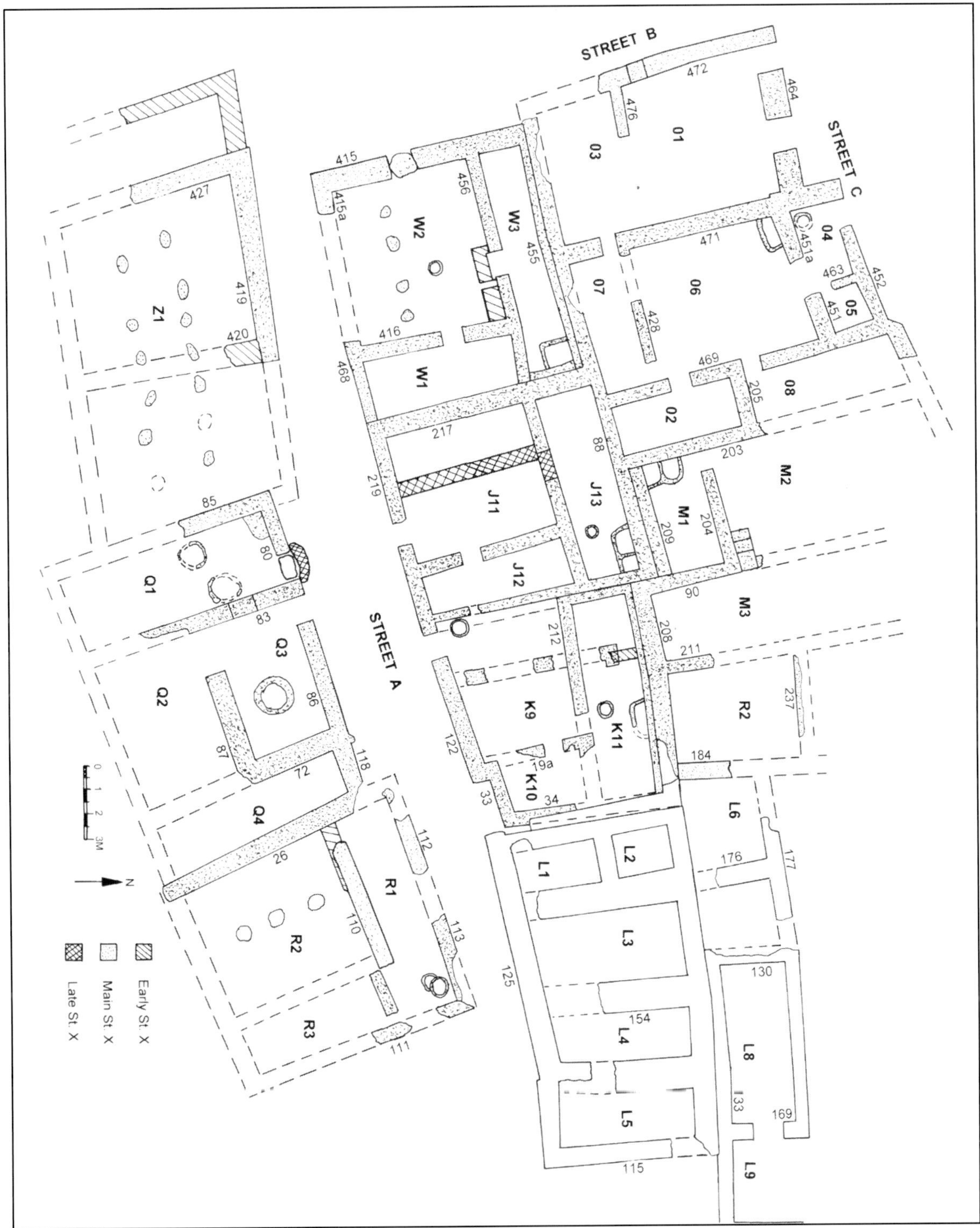

Figure 3. Tell Qasile, schematic plan of Area A, Stratum X

of Strata XII–XI differ in all respects from those of Stratum X.

Stratum X (figures 1 and 3)

Stratum X is the best preserved at Tell Qasile due to its wide exposure (about 0.23 hectares were exposed) and distinct destruction debris in each of the buildings. An exceptionally well-planned quarter was excavated in Area A, with two blocks of buildings separated by Street A and bounded by Streets B and C on the west and north (Maisler [Mazar] 1950–1951; Dothan and Dunayevsky 1993; Mazar 1980:74–77). South of Street A, erosion removed the southern ends of Stratum X buildings, and thus the plans of these buildings in figure 3 are reconstructed. The streets are parallel or perpendicular to each other as well as to the streets in Area C, and the buildings are attached to one another with no wasted spaces. This is a unique example of a coherent, orthogonal urban plan in the late Iron Age I. The Stratum X structures and streets were founded in that stratum and were preceded in several cases by structures on a different plan.[6] It thus appears that the residential and commercial quarter in Area A Stratum X was a planned project constructed during a rather short time in the town's life to fit the needs of a densely built town.

Nine complete or partly excavated structures are known in Area A (tables 1 and 2). Buildings K, J, W and R are typical four-room houses; Building Q is a dwelling and a workshop; Buildings O and M (the latter only party excavated) comprise large complexes that appear to have had mixed residential and commercial functions. Building Z is one of the earliest examples of a public structure of the "tripartite pillared building" type and Building L is an administrative building of public nature.

The houses were built of mudbrick walls 0.8–0.9 m wide constructed on poor local sandstone (*kurkar*) foundations, two to three courses high; a few of the outer walls facing streets were built of stone up to 1 m high. Adjoining buildings shared in many cases the same wall; in certain cases, the adjoining walls were constructed as separate narrow walls that were attached to one another (thus between Building J and K and between W and O). The only exception is a double wall (1.15 m wide) which separates Building J and Building M (in Room M1). Entrances either had no special features or had stone slabs or smaller stones as thresholds (in Buildings Q-west, W, and O-east). Pillar bases were made of flat *kurkar* slabs intended to carry wooden posts. Floors were usually made of beaten earth; stone floors were rarely found, yet in two cases (the southern space of Buildings W and the western space of Building 491 in Area C) there was a fine flagstone floor with slabs up to 1.4 m long. Since the houses were built on a slope descending to the northwest, the levels of wall foundations and floors in adjacent buildings differed considerably in order to fit the slope.

Pillared Houses

I use the term "pillared house" to designate houses with at least one row of pillars. The much discussed "four-room house" is one subtype of this more general type, which includes many variations incorporating three rooms, five rooms, and several other variants. At Tell Qasile Stratum X, six houses can be defined as pillared houses, four of them (K, J, W, and R) answer to the definition of the four-room house. The latter have similar dimensions and a similar general plan: a square house consisting of a square space with two narrow rectangular spaces perpendicular to one another (table 2 presents sizes and floor areas). The main square space was further divided in various ways: in Buildings R and W the division was made by a row of three or four wooden pillars on stone foundations; in Building K by two segments of mudbrick walls, which may have belonged to one wall;[7] in Building J by a brick wall partition.[8] It appears that Buildings K and J were initially three-room buildings with a large undivided square space and two perpendicular rectangular rooms; in a later phase of Stratum X, the square space was divided into two rectangular spaces by walls (with no use of pillars), thus turning them into true four-room houses. In contrast, Buildings R and W were typical four-room houses right from the beginning, with a row of pillars separating the square space into two subspaces.

[6] An exception is the eastern wall of Building J and the walls to its north, but as mentioned above, their attribution to Stratum XI is questionable.

[7] In the final plans, Dunyevsky attributed these two segments as well as a stone pavement slab at the southeastern corner of K9 to an early phase of Stratum IX, which he denoted IX2. Yet, in my view, there is no reason not to attribute these elements to Stratum X. The very existence of an early phase of Stratum IX is in doubt, and I exclude it from the stratigraphic development as represented here.

[8] The final plans prepared by Dunayevsky show this partition wall in Stratum IX2. In my view, it was constructed in a later phase of Stratum X against a blocked entrance into Room J13. As far as can be judged, the final destruction of Stratum X postdates the construction of this wall. Note that in the previously published schematic plan, the divisions of the square space are not shown (Mazar 1980:74, fig. 16).

Table 2. Pillared Dwellings at Tell Qasile

Building	***Outer Dimensions*** (m)	***Building Area***[a] (m^2)	***Floor Area of Main Space***[b] (m^2)	***Floor Area of Side Rooms*** (m^2)	***Total Floor Area*** (m^2)
K	9.1 × 9.1	83	K9: 25.9	K10: 6.5 K11: 18.45	50.85
J	8.8 × 10.1	89	J11[c]: 30.7	J12: 11.3 J13: 18.33	60.33
W	9.1 × 10.4[d]		W2: 39.1	W1: 21.4 W3: 16.32	76.82
R	10.4 × 9.9	103	R2[e]: 34	R1: 18.3 R3[f]: 11.7	64
Average					64
225	8.5 × 13.5	114.7	Spaces 225+193: 53	168: 14 141: 10.3	77.3
491	10.7× 13.4	143	495+770: 54 C448: 33	438: 5 406 (courtyard?)	92

[a] "Building Area" includes the walls (rounded to the nearest square meter).
[b] "Floor Area of Main Space" includes the area behind the pillar bases (net).
[c] J11 was probably divided into two chambers later in Stratum X.
[d] When buildings have joint walls, the area of the joint wall was calculated as part of only one of the adjoining buildings; thus in Building W, the eastern wall is not included.
[e] R2 is reconstructed, including the pillars.
[f] R3 is reconstructed.

Table 3. Other (nonpillared) Residential and Administrative Buildings in Stratum X

Building	***Outer Dimensions*** (m)	***Building Area***[a] (m^2)	***Floor Area of Main Space***[b] (m^2)	***Floor Area of Side Rooms*** (m^2)	***Total Floor Area*** (m^2)
Q	8.3 × 13 (reconstructed)	79	Q3: 22	Q2: 12.7 Q4: 13 (reconstructed) Q1: 21?	68.7
Z (upper phase)	9.8 × 13.8 (reconstructed)	135	ca. 100 (entire building)		ca. 100
L	12 or 8.2 × 14	168 (or 115 if only southern part)		L1: 6.75 L2: 4.2 L3: 18.25 L4: 12 L5: 12 L6*: 12 L7*: 8.25 L8: 16.6	90 (or 53.2 if only southern part)
O	12.5 × 12.9	161		O1: 35 O2: 17.3 O3: 18.1 O4: 5 O5: 2.9 O6: 36.3 O7: 12.3 O8: 12.3	139
M	unknown	unknown		M1: 10.7	unknown

* The attribution of these rooms to the building is not secure.

In Buildings J and W the entrance led into the central space, yet in Building K the entrance led into a side chamber (compare such a corner entrance in House 109b at ᶜIzbet Ṣarṭah; Finkelstein 1986:15, fig. 4). Building R is exceptional in that the rectangular broad space was constructed along Street A and the entrance from the street must have led directly into this room (though the entrance was not preserved). In Building W, two features should be noted: the massive flagstone of the southern space mentioned above, and the unusual dimensions of the northern room: 1.75 × 9.60 m; the walls of this room were plastered with white plaster and it contained about fifty pottery vessels, mainly storage jars.

The inner equipment of the houses included various installations. In each there was a single oven (*tabun*) inside the building and its location varied: near the entrance in Building K, at the central space in Building W, in the inner space in Building J, and in the front broad room in Building R. It thus appears that the location of cooking and baking activities in such houses was not consistent and was probably done in roofed spaces. Several industrial installations in these houses could be used for processing of agricultural products. Thus an installation in Building J, 0.8 × 1.8 m in size, included two connected plastered basins; it could be used as a simple wine press. Additional installations are storage bins in Buildings K and W. Heaps of several dozen doughnut-shaped clay loom weights found in almost every building are evidence for the use of vertical looms. It should be noted that the use of such looms with weights had been forgotten since the Middle Bronze Age, except in Iron Age I Philistia, where Aegean-type "spool" weights were found, and their revival in late Iron Age I sites is a novelty of this period.[9]

Two additional pillared houses were excavated in Area C: Buildings 225 and 495. Both are larger than the houses in Area A and differ in plan from one another and from those in Area A (table 2 and figure 6). Building 225, located south of and attached to the temple of Stratum X (Mazar 1980:43–45 and fig. 50), has a rectangular shape; its main rectangular space was divided into two narrower spaces by a row of five pillars. Its eastern side consisted of two adjacent square rooms; the inner could be entered only from the outer room. This outer room was used for storage (more than eighty jars were found there as well as a bin) while the inner room served as the main dwelling room (it contained several Philistine Bichrome stirrup jars). No oven was found in this house.

Building 495, on the other side of a street separating it from Building 225 (Mazar and Harpazi 1994:9–14), is the largest and most massive of the residential buildings of Stratum X. Its stone walls, up to 1.4 m wide, were constructed of large *kurkar* stones, partly worked to rectangular shapes, almost like ashlars. Its main space was bounded on the west by a row of four pillar bases of exceptional size; the area to the west of the pillars was paved with large *kurkar* slabs. An additional inner room was created (probably in a later phase of the building) by a division wall in the main central space. A baking chamber stood at the front of the building next to its entrance with a doorway leading from the street; its location and the unusual large oven found in it indicate public baking activity here. An opening in the southeast corner of the building led to a spacious courtyard to the east that was bounded by a massive wall. This open space seems to have been part of this unusual building.

The appearance of six pillared houses at Tell Qasile Stratum X raises questions as to the function and possible reconstruction of such houses, their history, and their ethnic and socioeconomic significance. These issues will be addressed below.

Other Buildings of Stratum X

In addition to the six pillared buildings, several additional buildings in Stratum X can be analyzed in terms of their architecture and function.

In Area A, five such buildings were revealed. Two of them (Buildings L and Z) can be defined as public structures; both were probably used for storage and redistribution of goods, perhaps in trade activity controlled by some central authority. As such, they are excluded from the following discussion. The other three are residential buildings (table 3).

Building Q: This building was preceded by the earlier Building Q of Stratum XI, which contained a metal-smelting workshop. In the new plan, the building faced Street A, which was established in Stratum X. The building contained a front space (Q3), an inner room (Q2), and a side room (note that its entire southern part is reconstructed). In the front space, there was a circular stone-built silo with a capacity of at least 1.75 m^3. To the west of this unit, space Q1 is a large rectangular space which probably served as a copper-smelting workshop, thus continuing the function of this area from Stratum XI. The evidence for this are two round stone-built installations, probably foundations of metal-casting furnaces, the western one located directly above the furnace of Stratum XI. This metal workshop faced the street but was probably connected also to the main part of Building Q,

[9] This issue is discussed by N. Yahalom and A. Yasur-Landau in Mazar and Mullins (eds.) 2007:666–71.

which perhaps was the residence of the metalsmith. During a later phase of Stratum X, the opening from the street to the workshop was blocked and the room became integral part of Building Q, which now had an almost symmetrical plan with two elongated spaces on two sides of a central unit divided into two spaces. The continuity between Strata XI and X in the function of the building, despite the far-reaching changes in the town plan, recalls the similar continuity in the temple structure between these two strata (Mazar 1980:21–24).

***Building O*:** This complex includes two wings: an eastern and a western, each having its own entrance from Street C, yet they are connected by an opening in the southern part of the building. The eastern unit is composed of an entrance room with an oven (O4), a small side chamber (O5), a main large space (O6), two rectangular side chambers (O2 and O8), and a back room (O7). The main space (O6) must have been an open courtyard due to its inner width of 5.5 m,[10] thus the building may be defined as a "courtyard house" with an entrance chamber, a well-known type of house in Canaanite architecture. In the northwestern corner of the courtyard was a stone-lined silo on a stone pavement. Room O2 served as a storeroom, containing numerous vessels (mostly storage jars). The western wing of Building O had a thick front wall with two openings leading into a large space (O1+O3), probably an unroofed courtyard (6 × 9.5 m) with a short partition wall dividing this space into two smaller units.

It seems that this unusual complex was a combination of a dwelling area (the eastern wing) and a commercial area (the western wing); the latter was approached both from the street and from the dwelling wing to its east. Perhaps it was owned by a single family that used it for both dwelling and business, recalling the division observed in Building Q.

Building M: The full plan of Building M cannot be determined; only its southern part was excavated, including one complete room (M1) and parts of two additional rooms (M2, M3), which are poorly known. In Room M1 there was a two-compartment installation similar to the one in Building J.

The Iron Age IIA: Strata IX–VIII

Following the destruction by fire of Stratum X, the town was rehabilitated to some extent, but it shrank in area. Street A and the buildings south of it went out of use, the southern entrances to Buildings K and J were blocked, and new entrances led to these houses from the north, where Building M and the eastern wing of Building O went out of use. Similarly, in Area C, none of the Stratum X houses continued to be in use in Strata IX–VIII and the temple was probably left as an unroofed ruin. This is substantial evidence for the decline of the town during the Iron IIA period. Yet Buildings K, J, W, and part of Building O continued to be in use and passed through several changes in Strata IX and VIII (figures 4 and 5).[11]

Building K: In Stratum IX the southern entrance of the previous phase was blocked and the new entrance was probably from the north, yet it was not preserved or discovered. The inner division walls of the main space (K3) were canceled and it was now divided by a line of four pillar bases preserved as postholes surrounded by small stones. A new floor and installations were constructed, including an oven, benches along the eastern wall, and a small winepress(?). The eastern room (K4) was now the only room in this building and it included a storage installation composed of four compartments. In Stratum VIII, the main space remained undivided by pillars and must have been an unroofed courtyard with a higher floor, a new oven, and a storage installation in its corner. The eastern room continued to be in use.

Building J: Here, too, the previous division wall of the main space was replaced in Stratum IX by a row of four pillar bases made of flat stones. A new floor was laid down and two installations were attached to the eastern wall of the central space. These could have been used for some home industry such as oil extraction. The northern and eastern rooms remained as in the previous stratum, yet with higher floors. The main entrance led to the northern room. In Stratum VIII, Building J passed through additional changes, including the rebuilding in stone of some of its walls and the creation of new floor surfaces; however, much of the building in this level was not preserved. No evidence for a division of the main space was found.

---

[10] A line of stones that appears in the pencil drawings of the plans along this space may hint that this large space was divided into two elongated spaces; this question remains unclear.

[11] B. Mazar and I. Dunayevsky divided Stratum IX into two phases: IX2 and IX1. Yet the only elements they attributed to IX2 which differ from IX1 are the division walls of the main spaces of Buildings K and J that create two elongated spaces. My analysis led me to attribute these divisions to Stratum X (as shown in figure 3) and thus phase IX2 should be canceled. As for Building L, the excavators attributed it to Strata IX and VIII alone, yet as mentioned above, it should be attributed to Stratum X, and there is only slight indication of its continued use in Strata IX–VIII.

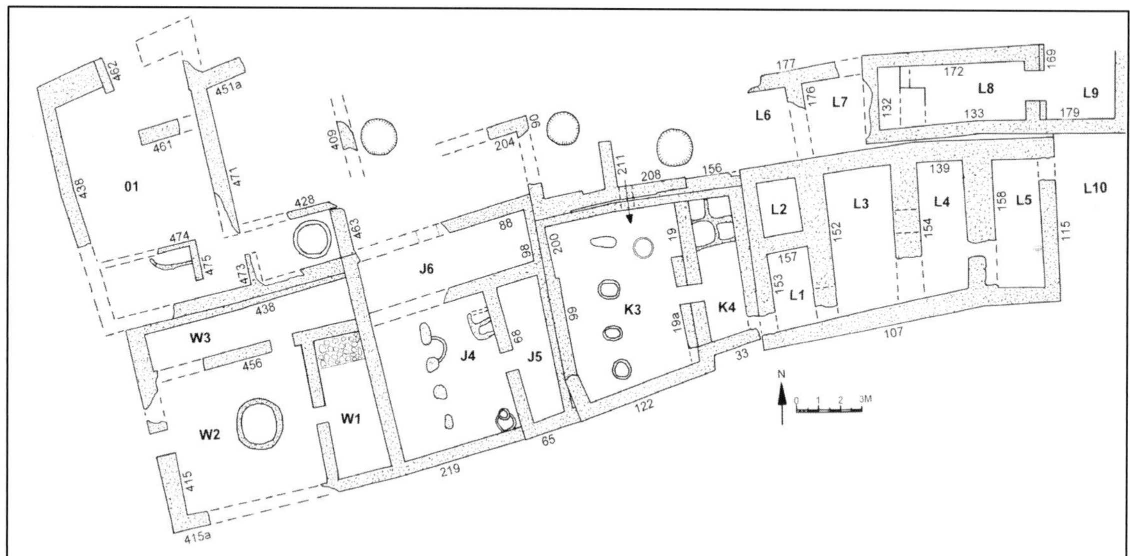

Figure 4. Tell Qasile, schematic plan of Area A, Stratum IX

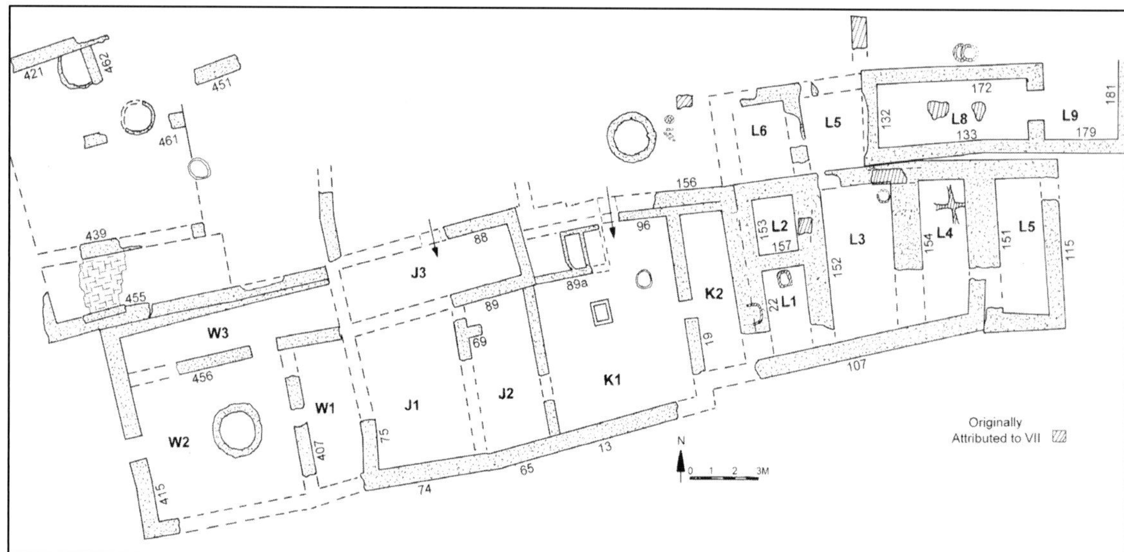

Figure 5. Tell Qasile, schematic plan of Area A, Stratum VIII

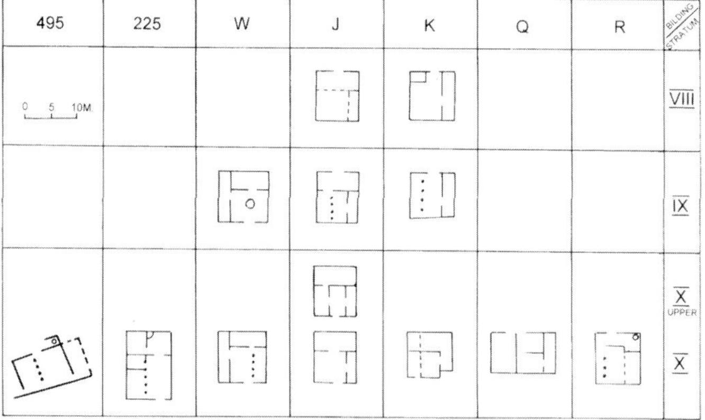

Figure 6. Schematic plans indicating the development of houses at Tell Qasile in Strata X–VIII

Building W: One construction phase subsequent to Stratum X is attributed to Strata IX–VIII. It includes the rebuilding in stone of two of the eastern walls, the cancellation of the pillars or any other division of the main space, and the construction of a circular stone-lined silo at the center of the main space, a feature unknown in other Iron Age houses.

Building O: One phase subsequent to that of Stratum X was observed, and even this only in the western wing of complex O. Walls were rebuilt with stones, some changes to the plan occurred, and the floor level was raised, yet the overall design appears to be the same as in Stratum X. Of the eastern wing of Building O almost no remains were preserved.

Building M of Stratum X went out of use and in its area a circular stone silo was constructed. A similar silo was found in Area C, in the area of a previous street of Stratum X.

This evidence is sufficient to indicate a general decline of the town in the Iron Age IIA. Many of the previous buildings of Stratum X went out of use and became open spaces, and others went through one or two construction phases. The idea of pillared houses, with an internal division that recalls four-room houses, was retained only in the cases of Buildings K and J. A prominent feature of this period is the construction of stone-lined circular silos.

Thus the story of Tell Qasile is that of a small town that passed through a period of foundation on bedrock and slow growth in Strata XII–XI, flourishing as a well-planned and rich town in Stratum X, and ending in a heavy destruction that marks the end of the Iron Age I, followed by a period of decline and partial rebuilding of several residences in Strata IX–VIII of the Iron Age IIA.

Chronology and Material Culture

Table 4 shows the dates assigned by B. Mazar (1950–1951) to each of the Tell Qasile strata and the alternative dates suggested by me for Strata IX–VII (Mazar 1980:125–28, updated here). The temporal development of the material culture at Tell Qasile was discussed in detail in past studies (Mazar 1985) and can be summarized in the following points:

1. Strata XII and XI contain typical Iron Age I pottery of local, Canaanite-coastal tradition, mixed with a substantial quantity of Philistine Bichrome Ware, probably produced locally.[12] Red slip without burnish started to appear in Stratum XI.

Table 4. Suggested Dates of the Iron Age Strata at Tell Qasile

Stratum	*B. Mazar 1950–51*	*A. Mazar 1985*
VII1	8th cent. B.C.E. until 732	Orig. Stratum VII canceled; "Stratum VII" in Area C is a later Iron II debris layer with no architectural remains (mainly 7th cent. B.C.E.).
VII2		
VIII	9th cent. B.C.E.	Iron IIA, 10th–mid-9th cent.
IX1	10th cent. B.C.E.	
IX2		
X	end of 11th and beginning of 10th cent. B.C.E.	same
XI	end of 12th and 11th centuries	same
XII		

2. Stratum X is characterized by the continuation of Iron I local pottery, an increase in red slip, the beginning of hand-burnish, the appearance of Phoenician Bichrome imported pottery, the appearance of a few sherds of Cypriot White Painted I pottery, and the appearance of a local style of depleted Philistine pottery (red-slipped kraters with black, disconnected spirals). It should be noted that Bichrome Philistine pottery was missing from Stratum X houses in Area A as well as from House 495 in Area C, and this led B. Mazar to define Stratum X as a "post-Philistine" town (1950–1951: 128). However, eight complete painted Bichrome Philistine vessels were found in Building 225 (Mazar 1985:pls. 46–51) as well as in Temple 131 and its courtyards. This phenomenon raises several questions: Were the Philistine Bichrome vessels in Area C heirlooms from the previous stratum? Had they been used for a long time in the temple due to the sanctity and special function of this building? If this is the case, why do we find such vessels in the adjacent residential building 225? An alternative explanation—that there was a social or ethnic difference between the inhabitants of the two areas—will be considered below.

[12] The following is a list of Philistine Bichrome pottery vessels from Strata XII and X in Area A published by Dothan (1982:58–69). *Stratum XII:* p. 107, fig. 9:1; p. 108, fig. 10:1; p. 204, fig. 61–62:31. *Stratum XI:* p. 99, fig. 1:1, 6; fig. 2:6, 12; p. 126, fig. 18:2, 6; Motifs: p. 206, fig. 66:13–14. Undefined: p. 156, fig. 32:2. *Stratum X:* p. 158, fig. 33:6; p. 162, fig. 35:3 (both unpainted). Depleted style: p. 195, fig. 60:1, 3, 4, 5. Many additional Philistine painted sherds from these strata were catalogued.

B. Mazar suggested that the dramatic destruction of Stratum X occurred as a result of the supposed conquest by David of the Jaffa and Yarkon region (Maisler [Mazar] 1951:23; B. Mazar 1986:71 [first published in 1964]). Kempinski (1989:89–90) suggested a destruction by earthquake and I considered both suggestions as legitimate possibilities (Mazar 1985:127). The current skepticism concerning the potential military achievements of David may cast doubt on the link between David's conquests and Stratum X destruction, yet there is no other known historical event to relate to this destruction. The earthquake alternative remains possible, especially because of the strong evidence that Megiddo VIA, which was contemporary with Qasile X and similarly heavily burned, was destroyed by an earthquake (Kempinski 1989:89; Mazar 2007).[13]

Six samples of charred seeds from sealed contexts in the destruction layer of Stratum X at Tell Qasile were analyzed, some with several replications, providing twenty measurements altogether (table 5). Samples 3931 and 3932 and GrN27719 are of *lathyrus* seeds found in a small bin in Room 168 of Stratum X (Mazar 1980:43–44, fig. 50). Sample 3853 is a sample of charred grain found in the small bin C653 from Stratum X (Mazar and Harpazi-Ofer 1994). Sample 3933 is of seeds found on the floor of Temple 131 of Stratum X (Mazar 1980:33–40). All the samples except one were analyzed in the framework of the "Early Iron Age Dating Project" directed by A. Gilboa, E. Boaretto, T. Jull, and I. Sharon at the Rehovot, Tucson, and Groningen radiocarbon laboratories using different measurement techniques (Boaretto et al. 2005; Sharon et al. 2007). GrN27719 was measured at Groningen independently of the above-mentioned project. In a study of the issue (Mazar and Bronk-Ramsey 2008), we retained the division into groups according to the method of dating, as was originally published by Boaretto et al. A problem was raised by the six measurements of Sample 3932 due to an internal discrepancy in the results. The individual dates of this sample are as follows:

RTT3932.3: 2745±45
RTT3932.4: 2765±75
RTT3932.5: 2685±50
RTT3932.6: 2650±40
RTT3932a: 2780±35
RTT3932aa: 2862±40

The internal discrepancy in this particular sample has been discussed elsewhere (Sharon et al. 2005:85–89; Sharon et al. 2007:8–9; Mazar and Bronk-Ramsey 2008:172–74). Our evaluation and choice of outliers in this group differs from that of Sharon et al. and leads to a date range of 1039–979 B.C.E. (with 68.2 percent probability) or 1051–938 B.C.E. (with 95.4 percent probability) for the destruction of Tell Qasile Stratum X. Similar dates were obtained for the destruction of Megiddo VIA, Yoqneam XVII, and Tel Hadar IV, all in the same pottery horizon (for a detailed discussion, see Mazar and Bronk-Ramsey 2008:176–97). The radiocarbon dates we have calculated fit the conventional date for the destruction of Qasile X and these other sites (i.e., ca. 1000/980 B.C.E.).

Table 5. Radiocarbon Dates from Tell Qasile X

Lab No. *(Boaretto et al. 2005)*	***Sample No.*** *(Sharon et al. 2007)*	***^{14}C B.P. Date*** *(or average of several dates)*
T18161a, aa	3932a, aa*	2818±26
RTT3932.3-6	3932.3-6*	2692±24
RTT3931.3-5	3931.3-5	2911±26
LSC3931.1	3931.1	2853±25
	GrN27719	2895±25
RTT and T	3853.1,3,4	2753±22
T	3930	2800±25
T	3933a, aa	2882±28
GrA25535	same as 3931	2864±40
GrA25710	same as 3931	2818±38
Gr A25768	same as 3931	2897±44

The sample numbers in the second column are taken from Sharon et al. 2007; the samples are identical to those in the first column. The division of samples 3932 and 3931 into several lines follows the original publication by Boaretto et al. (2005). GrN27719 was measured at Groningen University. Averages cited from Sharon et al. 2007.

Abbreviations:

GrN: Samples measured at Groningen University using proportional gas counting.
GrA: Samples measured at Groningen University using the AMS method.
LSC: Samples prepared and measured at the Weizmann Insitute in Rehovot using liquid scentillation counters, followed by the sample number of the Iron Age Dating Project.
RTT: Samples prepared at the Weizmann Institute in Rehovot and measured in Tucson by the AMS method, followed by the sample number of the Iron Age Dating Project.
T: Samples prepared and measured in Tucson by the AMS method, followed by the Tucson laboratory number.

[13] According to Finkelstein's low chronology, Megiddo VIA was destroyed by Shishak. The unfeasibility of this date was discussed by me elsewhere (Mazar 2005; 2007). Indeed, Finkelstein (2006:18–182) recently gave up this idea and now dates the destruction of Stratum VIA earlier in the tenth century B.C.E.

Stratum IX was dated by B. Mazar to the tenth century B.C.E. and Stratum VIII to the ninth century (B. Mazar 1950–1951:195). In the publication of Tell Qasile, I suggested to condense both these strata to the tenth century B.C.E. in accordance with the conventional chronology (Mazar 1980:127–28). Since 1997, however, I have become aware that the Iron Age IIA period to which these two strata belong continued well into the ninth century (for a recent summary, see Mazar 2005), and thus B. Mazar's original dating might have been correct. And yet the evidence for the independent existence of Stratum VIII is very slim and it appears that neither Stratum IX nor Stratum VIII lasted very long, most probably during the tenth century B.C.E. alone.

The Town's Economy

The *raison d'être* of the foundation and duration of the settlement at Tell Qasile was probably its role as a mercantile town participating in maritime trade along the eastern Mediterranean coast. The nearby Yarkon River estuary would have served as a convenient harbor for the small merchant ships of the time, which perhaps sailed between Egypt, the Philistine and Phoenician towns, and Cyprus. This function may explain the dense urban planning of the eleventh century B.C.E. town of Stratum X. The rich finds from that stratum hint at dynamic trade with Egypt, Philistia, Phoenicia, Cyprus, and the hill country hinterland (via the Yarkon River and Aphek).

In several houses, one of the side rooms contained concentrations of dozens of storage jars, each with a capacity of 20–22 liters of liquid. In Building 225, more than eighty such jars were found in one single room, with a total capacity of about 1,800 liters (compare the calculation of capacities with similar results at seventh-century Ekron in Schloen 2001: 144). It appears that such a quantity of jars was beyond the needs of local domestic consumption and was intended for trade in olive oil or wine. The small domestic industrial installations, however, indicate that some processing of agricultural products (wine? olive oil?) took place in the central spaces of the houses.

Trade activity and administration are manifested in public buildings such as Z and L, which probably served in the organization of the trade by some central authority in the town. Complexes like Q and O were probably used for a combination of living space and craft or trade activity, and the local temples and rich cult objects indicate a local priesthood and cultic activity that was perhaps related to and supported by the economic activity.

Summary of the Town's Development

The stratigraphic and architectural data from Tell Qasile presented above provide an unusual picture of the rise and decline of an Iron Age I–IIA town. As we have seen, in the initial occupation phases (Strata XII–XI), Area C was a planned built-up area, while Area A remained mainly an open area with scattered buildings and no urban planning. The architecture included, in addition to the temples, the "hearth building" and few architectural fragments that cannot be well defined. No evidence for pillared buildings was found in these strata.

In Stratum X an extreme change in the town plan took place: a new street system was laid out separating well-planned and densely-built blocks of buildings, including dwellings, commercial-administrative, and cultic buildings. Based on the total excavated area in Stratum X—1,370 m^2 in Area A and 625 m^2 in Area C (not including the temple and its courtyards)—and the data in table 1, we can calculate an average density of 65 buildings per hectare in Area A and a much lower average of 40 buildings per hectare in Area C (compare Zorn 1994:37, who calculates 166 buildings per hectare in the much denser town of Tell en-Naṣbeh). This indicates that Area C was much more spacious than Area A, probably due to the higher socioeconomic status of its inhabitants. Assuming that the rest of the town was similar to Area A, we may calculate a total of 80–85 houses in the entire 1.3-hectare town (taking into account the spacious Area C with its temple area).

With an average family size of 6–8 persons, we may calculate the population of Stratum X as being 480–680 people. This town appears to have been under some sort of central administration, though we have no idea of the nature of that administration or to which geopolitical entity it belonged.

Following the severe destruction of Stratum X, the town passed through two construction phases in the Iron Age IIA (Strata IX–VIII), yet it was declining: large parts went out of use and became open spaces, and only a few of the dwellings were rebuilt, retaining their former outline while their inner plans were changed. We may estimate that the number of houses and the population in the Iron IIA declined to less than half of that of Stratum X.

Interpreting Pillared Houses

Pillared houses, and four-room houses as a specific subtype, have been widely discussed (e.g., Shiloh 1970; Braemer 1982; Stager 1985; Holladay 1992; Netzer 1992; Schloen 2001:135–85; King and Stager

2001:28–35; Bunimovitz and Faust 2002; Faust 2005:237–55). The definition of such houses is somewhat complex, since on the one hand there are four-room houses without pillars (like Building 28636 at Beth-Shean; Mazar 2006:269–77 and parallels on p. 271), and on the other hand, there are many variants of Iron Age dwellings with rows of pillars. In fact, most of these are not the typical four-room house but rather display many variations. Among houses with elongated spaces and rows of pillars, "three-room" houses are the most abundant. Yet there are certain common features which identify this group.

The appearance of six pillared houses in Tell Qasile Stratum X, four of them of the four-room house plan, raises several questions regarding their origin, distribution, social meaning, and ethnic affiliation. This vast subject is beyond the scope of the present discussion, but I will comment on the origin of this architectural type. The Late Bronze Age dwellings with rows of wooden pillars on stone bases found at Tel Batash, Lachish, and Tel Harasim can be seen as prototypes for the Iron Age pillared buildings (Mazar 1997:252–54; Givon 1999). All the known examples are in the Shephelah, and yet Iron I examples are rare or nonexistent in this region![14] This appears to be contradictory evidence for the development of such houses, but it may be due to the lack of sufficient excavation of Iron Age I sites in the Shephelah.

The pillared houses at Tell Qasile were built in dense blocks, with common walls and no place for courtyards in front of the houses or between them. Ovens and other household installations were inside the houses. Were there open courtyards inside these houses? It was common in the past to interpret the central space in four-room houses as an unroofed courtyard, yet this interpretation was challenged by Stager, Holladay, and Netzer, and I now tend to accept their view (in contrast to my earlier view: Mazar 1990:485–89). As for a second floor, there is no hint of this at Tell Qasile, where no staircases were found and the walls appear to have been too thin to carry a second story. Yet even if there was no fully constructed second floor, the roof space could have been used for household work and for sleeping quarters built of light construction materials that perhaps occupied part of the roof space. If indeed the ground floor was fully roofed, it must have been quite dark inside due to the dense urban setting: only one wall (or two walls in the case of corner houses like Building W) in each house could contain windows to provide light and fresh air.

In terms of floor space and size, table 2 shows that the four-room houses in Area A have an average net floor area of 64 m^2 on the ground floor while the two houses in Area C are somewhat larger (77.3 and 92 m^2). The lower number is in accord with the average floor area at several Iron Age II sites where such calculations are available, although at these sites there are great deviations from the mean size. Schloen (2001:170–18) calculated for Tell Beit Mirsim Stratum A a mean of ca. 61.5 m^2 of floor area with a standard deviation of 20.3 m^2; for Tell en-Naṣbeh, a mean of 59.1 m^2 with standard deviation of 24.6 m^2; and for Tel Farᶜah (N) Stratum VIIb, a mean of 76.8 m^2 with standard deviation of 19.2 m^2.[15] However, for a sample area at Tel en-Nasbeh, Zorn (1994:39) calculated a much lower mean value of 59.8 m^2, including walls, and 36.5 m^2 of floor area with standard deviation of 12.7 m^2. If Schloen's numbers are correct, it would indicate that most of the houses at Tell Qasile were similar in size to most regular houses in the Israelite towns of the tenth–eighth centuries B.C.E. (for larger Israelite houses, see Mazar 2006:272). It should be noted that at the remote fortified site of Khirbat al-Mudayna al-ᶜAliya in Moab (contemporary with Tell Qasile X), the seven measured houses are somewhat larger than the regular houses of Tell Qasile, with floor areas range from 66 to 111 m^2 (Routledge 2000:62).

Calculations of the number of persons per house differ from one study to the other (e.g., Zorn 1994; Schloen 2001:174–75). If we utilize Naroll's coefficient of 10 m^2 of floor space per person, the houses in Area A would have accommodated ca. 6 persons; a lower coefficient of ca. 8 m^2 per person (Zorn 1994; Schloen 2001) would result in ca. 8 persons per house in Area A and 9–11 persons in the houses of Area C. If correct, such houses could accommodate nuclear families or slightly extended patrilineal-joint families of two to three generations (see calculations by Schloen 2001 and comments by Routledge 2000:62–63; one has to take into consideration instability in family size and dynamic changes in this size due to the fact that the mortality rate of adults at rather young ages and especially of infants was high

[14] There is no hint of the existence of pillared houses in Iron Age I strata in sites like Tell Beit Mirsim, Tel Batash, Beth Shemesh, and Gezer.

[15] I cite Schloen's calculation of overall roofed area, including the central spaces, not including outer walls. He also presents the calculations for house areas with assumed central unroofed courtyard. The mean in that case is 43.8 m^2 per house at Tel Beit Mirsim, 43 m^2 at Tell en-Nasbeh and 52.5 m^2 at Tell el-Farᶜah (though he does not believe that there were unroofed courtyards in the houses).

in all early societies). Calculations based on floor space are problematic because we do not know to what extent the roof area was utilized for accommodation and what part of the ground floor was utilized for accommodation. Yet such calculations may provide some idea about the nature of the households and population size in such houses. It should be emphasized that in most Israelite Iron II houses there were more rooms created by dividing the rectangular spaces with partition walls, while at Tell Qasile such partition walls do not exist and the ground floor in most cases contained no more than two rooms, in addition to the main space, which was divided by pillars. Larger houses like the houses in Area C did not necessarily accommodate more people than the smaller houses—they may rather have belonged to richer or more prestigious families. There is no evidence at Tell Qasile for clusters of houses around common courtyards of the type that would justify an extended family compound (*bêt ʾāb*) as suggested by Stager (1985) for early Israel (for a similar situation at Khirbat al-Mudayna al-ʿAliya, see Routledge 2000:60). The houses rather appear to have served individual families, either nuclear families or slightly extended "joint" families.

The ethnic affiliation of pillared houses, and four-room houses in particular, as "Israelite" was accepted by many scholars such as Shiloh, Holladay, Finkelstein, Stager, and others (see the references above). Faust (2005) even attempted to explain their popularity as reflecting Israelite identity and values. Such an ethnic affiliation may be correct for the Iron Age II, when pillared houses (among them four-room houses) comprise the majority of houses in Israelite towns, villages, and farmsteads, while they were almost entirely absent from non-Israelite territories in both Cis- and Transjordan. Yet every rule has its exceptions: the Iron Age IIA city of Tel Rehov is located inside the political territory of the United Monarchy in the tenth century and of the northern kingdom of Israel in the ninth century, and yet the houses in this large city lacked pillars and belong to an entirely different architectural tradition (Mazar 2005:plans on pp. 217, 222, 236, 245). On the other hand, pillared buildings were the most common house type at seventh-century Tel Miqne-Ekron and Timnah-Tel Batash—the first of which was definitely, and the second probably, a non-Israelite, late Philistine town (Gitin 1989; Mazar 1997).

The ethnic affiliation is much less clear in the Iron Age I. During this period, pillared houses appear in a wide and varied spatial distribution and their ethnic attribution remains elusive (Routledge 2000:64–65). The earliest example is a surprisingly fully mature four-room house at Tell el-ʿUmayri that dates to ca. 1200 B.C.E. (Herr 1999; 2000). A contemporary house from Giloh is an uneven and immature pillared building (Mazar 1981). At Tel Masos, pillared houses are found in Stratum III of the twelfth century B.C.E. and at Taanach a fragment of such a house was dated to the same century (Rast 1978:268). Most of the other Iron I examples can generally be dated to the late twelfth and eleventh centuries B.C.E. These include in the central hills several houses at ʿAi and Khirbet Raddanah (all of the "three-room" type), several houses at Shiloh of unclear plan (Finkelstein et al. 1993), and a large four-room house in ʿIzbet Ṣarṭah Stratum II (Finkelstein 1986:24–27). In the north, variations of pillared buildings are known from Megiddo Stratum VIB (fragmentary plans) and Taanach (fragmentary plans in Rast 1978:figs. 266–67). In the northern Negev, in Tel Masos Stratum II (late eleventh/early tenth centuries B.C.E.), four-room houses and their variants were dominant in Area A, while in the southern part of the site a large courtyard house of Canaanite type was found. In the same region, fragmentary pillared houses are known at Tel Esdar (Kochavi 1969).[16] In Transjordan, Iron Age I variants of pillared houses are known mainly from Khirbat al-Mudayna al-ʿAliya in Moab (where a variant was defined as an "L-plan" house; Routledge 2000), and fragments of such buildings are known from nearby Khirbat al-Mudayna al-Muʿaraja and from Sahab in the region of Amman. A single mature four-room house resembling those of Tel Masos is known from Barqa el-Hetiye in the Feinan area (Fritz 1990). Tell Qasile and Tel Masos yielded the largest number and the most homogeneous groups of such houses in Iron Age I contexts. Such houses are missing in Iron Age I Philistia,[17] are rare in the Shephelah, and are not known anywhere north of the Jezreel Valley or in the Jordan Valley before the Iron Age II.

The meaning of this strange temporal and spatial distribution remains elusive. It is impossible to define all these varied sites as "Israelite." They rather belong to a variety of population groups: Israelite (or "proto-Israelite") hill-country settlers, the Canaanite population (at Megiddo), a mixed Philistine/Canaanite population (Tell Qasile and perhaps also ʿIzbet

[16] I exclude from this survey the Negev Highland sites, which should be dated to the tenth century B.C.E.

[17] Oren (1993: 1331) mentions "typical four room houses" at Tel Seraʿ Stratum VIII, which is supposed to be an Iron I Philistine town, yet he also mentions "Ashdod Ware" and red-burnished pottery from this stratum—which must date to the Iron Age II. Thus the foundation date of these four-room houses remains unclear.

Ṣarṭah),[18] the northern Negev tribal population (Tel Masos and Tel Esdar), and "proto" Edomites, Moabites, and Ammonites in Transjordan (though Herr would identify the settlers at Tell el-ᶜUmayri as "Reubenites" and Routledge avoids any ethnic designation in relation to Mudayna al-ᶜAliya). Thus a clear-cut ethnic attribution of this house type in the Iron Age I seems a complex and perhaps impossible task, except that the lack of such houses from the heartland of Philistia as well as from Upper Galilee is telling (on the theoretical framework of ethnic designation in relation to house types, see Routledge 2000: 63–65).

The appearance of such houses at Tell Qasile Stratum X may indicate the complex development and nature of the population and/or of the material culture at this site. As mentioned above, the town of Strata XII–XI appears to be a Philistine outpost, as evidenced by the "hearth building" and the considerable amount of Philistine Bichrome pottery sherds in addition to other local Iron I pottery. The foundation of the well-planned and dense town of Stratum X appears to have been a brief operation. It remains difficult to explain this development. Was it initiated by the local population, who were inspired by the building fashions of the day? Or should we see the new houses as an expression of a new population group that settled at Tell Qasile alongside the old Philistine population? B. Mazar dubbed Stratum X a "post-Philistine" town. If he meant that there was an amalgamation of the old Philistine population with local Canaanites, he may have been right. Bunimovitz (1990), based on the lack of Philistine pottery in Area A of Stratum X, assumed that the southern part of Tell Qasile was inhabited by a local Canaanite population while Philistines continued to occupy the temple zone. It is difficult to accept such a sharp definition, yet the material culture of Tell Qasile X certainly seems to be complex and varied. The pillared buildings, which are unknown in Philistia, are one component in this complex society.

Conclusions

The following points were emphasized in this paper. Tell Qasile exhibits an exceptional settlement history, having been founded as a Philistine outpost in Strata XII–XI, developing into a well-planned town in Stratum X, being destroyed by heavy fire, and then undergoing a period of decline in the Iron IIA period. It appears that we can observe a shift from a rather "pure" Philistine society in Strata XII–XI to a more varied and "cosmopolitan" society in Stratum X. The conventional chronology, dating the end of Stratum X to between 1000 and 980 B.C.E., should be maintained.

The domestic architecture of Tell Qasile in the first two strata is little known, yet it appears to differ considerably from that of Stratum X. The "hearth building" relates this architecture to Cypriot-Aegean origins. The appearance of pillared buildings, including several examples of four-room houses, in Stratum X raises several questions relating to the function, spatial distribution, and ethnic affiliation of such houses. Their appearance at Tell Qasile, as at other peripheral sites in the Negev and Transjordan, may illustrate the adoption of certain accepted modes of life that were exhibited in architectural form. In the Iron Age I, these should not be seen as ethnic markers but rather as the adoption of a certain "fashion of the day," perhaps related also to socioeconomic status.

Intrasite social differentiation in Stratum X may be suggested based on the variability in house size between Areas A and C. Area C, close to the temples, appears to contain houses of more highly ranked families. Area A contained three types of buildings: several pillared houses of more or less equal size; larger "courtyard houses" that were used both for dwelling and for craft or commercial activity; and two public buildings that could have been related to the administration and management of trade. The pillared buildings appear to be the residences of nuclear families or slightly larger family units. The wide exposure at Tell Qasile enables calculation of the density of houses and a population estimate.

The economy of the town was probably based on maritime trade conducted by ships that used the nearby Yarkon estuary as an anchorage. Most of the houses at Tell Qasile therefore probably belonged to merchants, shipowners, and seamen.

[18] The material culture at ᶜIzbet Ṣarṭah (pottery and other artifacts) is closer to that of Tell Qasile than to the material culture of the hill country, so in my view it should be seen as a peripheral site of the coastal plain (more specifically of the Yarkon basin) rather than being characterized by the "Israelite" material culture of the hill country.

Bibliography

Boaretto, E., T. Jull, A. Gilboa, and I. Sharon
2005 Dating the Iron Age I/II Transition in Israel: First Intercomparison Results. *Radiocarbon* 47:39–55.

Braemer, F.
1982 *L'Architecture domestique du Levant à l'Âge du Fer*. Paris: Éditions Recherche sur les civilizations.

Bunimovitz, S.
1990 Problems in the "Ethnic" Identification of the Philistine Culture. *Tel Aviv* 17:210–22.

Bunimovitz, S., and A. Faust
2002 Ideology in Stone: Understanding the Four-Room House. *BAR* 28/4:32–41.

Dothan, T., and I. Dunayevsky
1993 Qasile, Tell. In *The New Encyclopedia of Archaeological Excavations in the Holy Land*, ed. E. Stern, 4:1204–7. New York: Simon and Schuster.

Faust, A.
2005 *Israelite Society in the Period of the Monarchy* [in Hebrew]. Jerusalem: Yad Ben Zvi.

Finkelstein, I.
1986 *ᶜIzbet Ṣarṭah—An Early Iron Age Site Near Rosh Haᶜayin, Israel.* BARIS 299. Oxford: British Archaeological Reports.
2005 A Low Chronology Update: Archaeology, History and Bible. In *The Bible and Radiocarbon Dating: Archaeology, Text and Science*, ed. T. E. Levy and T. Higham, 31–42. London: Equinox.
2006 The Last Labayu: King Saul and the Expansion of the First North Israelite Territorial Entity. In *Essays on Ancient Israel in Its Near Eastern Context: A Tribute to Nadav Naᵓaman*, ed. Y. Amit, E. Ben-Zvi, I. Finkelstein, and O. Lipschits, 171–88. Winona Lake, Ind.: Eisenbrauns.

Finkelstein, I., S. Bunimovitz, and Z. Lederman
1993 *Shiloh: The Archaeology of a Biblical Site.* Tel Aviv: Institute of Archaeology, Tel Aviv University.

Fritz, V.
1994 Vorbericht über die Grabungen in Barqā el-Hetīye im Gebiet von Fēnān, Wādī el-ᶜAraba (Jordanien) 1990. *ZDPV* 110:125–50.

Fritz, V., and A. Kempinski
1983 *Ergebnisse der Ausgrabungen auf der Ḫirbet el-Msas (Tel Masos) 1972–1975.* 3 vols. Wiesbaden: Harrassowitz.

Gitin, S.
1989 Tel Miqne-Ekron: A Type-Site for the Inner Coastal Plain in the Iron Age II Period. In *Recent Excavations in Israel: Studies in Iron Age Archaeology*, ed. S. Gitin and W. G. Dever, 23–58. AASOR 49. Winona Lake, Ind.: Eisenbrauns.

Givon, S.
1999 The Three-roomed House from Tel Harassim, Israel. *Levant* 31:173–77.

Herr, L. G.
1999 Tell al-ᶜUmayri and the Reubenite Hypothesis. *EI* 26:64*–77*.
2000 The Settlement and Fortification of Tell al-ᶜUmayri in Jordan during the LB/Iron I Transition. In *The Archaeology of Jordan and Beyond: Essays in Honor of James A. Sauer*, ed. L. E. Stager, J. Greene, and M. D. Coogan, 167–79. SAHL 1. Winona Lake, Ind.: Eisenbrauns.

Holladay, J. S.
1992 House, Israelite. In *The Anchor Bible Dictionary*, ed. D. N. Freedman, 3:308–18. New York: Doubleday.

Karageorghis, V.
1998 Hearths and Bathtubs in Cyprus: A "Sea Peoples'" Innovation? In *Mediterranean Peoples in Transition*, ed. S. Gitin, A. Mazar, and E. Stern, 276–82. Jerusalem: Israel Exploration Society.

Kempinski, A.
1989 *Megiddo: A City State and a Royal Centre in North Israel.* Munich: Beck.

King, P. J., and L. E. Stager
2001 *Life in Biblical Israel.* Louisville, Ky.: Westminster John Knox Press.

Kochavi, M.
1969 Excavations at Tel Esdar [in Hebrew]. *ᶜAtiqot* 5:14–48.

Mazar, A.
1980 *Excavations at Tell Qasile.* Part 1, *The Philistine Sanctuary: Architecture and Cult Objects.* Qedem 12. Jerusalem: Institute of Archaeology, Hebrew University of Jerusalem.
1981 Giloh—An Early Israelite Site in the Vicinity of Jerusalem. *IEJ* 31:1–36.
1985 *Excavations at Tell Qasile.* Part 2, *Various Finds, The Pottery, Conclusions, Appendices.* Qedem 20. Jerusalem: Institute of Archaeology, Hebrew University of Jerusalem.
1986 The Excavations at Tell Qasile, 1982–1984, Preliminary Report. *IEJ* 36:1–15.
1990 *Archaeology of the Land of the Bible, 10,000–586* B.C.E. New York: Doubleday.
1997 *Timnah (Tel Batash).* Vol. 1, *Stratigraphy and Architecture.* 2 vols. Qedem 37. Jerusalem: Institute of Archaeology, Hebrew University of Jerusalem.

2005 The Debate over the Chronology of the Iron Age in the Southern Levant: Its History, the Current Situation and a Suggested Resolution. In *The Bible and Radiocarbon Dating: Archaeology, Text and Science*, ed. T. E. Levy and T. Higham, 15–30. London: Equinox.

2006 *Excavations at Tel Beth-Shean 1989–1996*. Vol. 1, *From the Late Bronze Age IIB to the Medieval Period.* Jerusalem: Israel Exploration Society and the Hebrew University of Jerusalem.

2007 Review of *Megiddo III: Final Report on the Stratum VI Excavations*, by T. Harrison. *BASOR* 345: 83–87.

Mazar, A., and C. Bronk-Ramsey

2008 ^{14}C Dates and the Iron Age Chronology of Israel: A Response. *Radiocarbon* 50:159–80.

Mazar, A., and S. Harpazi-Ofer

1994 The Excavations at Tell Qasile from 1988 to 1991. *Israel: People and Land 1990–1993 (Eretz Israel Museum Yearbook)* 7–8:9–34.

Mazar, A., and R. Mullins, eds.

2007 *Excavations at Tel Beth-Shean 1989–1996*. Vol. 2, *The Middle and Late Bronze Age I–IIA Periods.* Jerusalem: Israel Exploration Society and the Hebrew University of Jerusalem.

Maisler (Mazar), B.

1950–51 The Excavations at Tell Qasile. *IEJ* 1:61–76; 125–140; 194–218.

1951 The Stratification of Tell Abu Hawam on the Bay of Acre. *BASOR* 124:21–25.

1986 The Philistines and the Rise of Israel and Tyre. In *The Early Biblical Period: Historical Studies*, ed. S. Aḥituv and B. A. Levine, 63–82. Jerusalem: Israel Exploration Society.

Netzer, E.

1992 Domestic Architecture in the Iron Age. In *The Architecture of Ancient Israel: From the Prehistoric to the Persian Periods,* ed. A. Kempinski and R. Reich, 193–201. Jerusalem: Israel Exploration Society.

Oren, E. D.

1993 Seraᶜ, Tel. In *The New Encyclopedia of Archaeological Excavations in the Holy Land*, ed. E. Stern, 4:1329–35. New York: Simon and Schuster.

Rothenberg, B.

1967 Negev. *Tsfunot Negev*. Tel Aviv: Masada. [In Hebrew.]

Routledge, B.

2000 Seeing through Walls: Interpreting Iron Age I Architecture at Khirbet al-Mudayna al-ᶜAliya. *BASOR* 319:37–70.

Schloen, J. D.

2001 *The House of the Father as Fact and Symbol*: *Patrimonialism in Ugarit and the Ancient Near East*. SAHL 2. Winona Lake, Ind.: Eisenbrauns.

Sharon, I., A. Gilboa, E. Boaretto, and T. Jull

2005 The Early Iron Age Dating Project: Introduction, Methodology, Progress Report and an Update on the Tel Dor Radiometric Dates. In *The Bible and Radiocarbon Dating: Archaeology, Text and Science*, ed. T. E. Levy and T. Higham, 65–94. London: Equinox.

Sharon, I., A. Gilboa, T. Jull, and E. Boaretto

2007 Report on the First Stage of the Iron Age Dating Project in Israel: Supporting the Low Chronology. *Radiocarbon* 49:1–46.

Shiloh, Y.

1970 The Four-Room House: Its Situation and Function in the Israelite City. *IEJ* 20:180–90.

Stager, L. E.

1985 The Archaeology of the Family in Ancient Israel. *BASOR* 260:1–35.

Zorn, J. R.

1994 Estimating the Population Size of Ancient Settlements: Methods, Problems, Solutions, and a Case Study. *BASOR* 295:31–48.

34. The Armor of Goliath

by Alan Millard

The detailed description of Goliath's arms and armor in the account of David's confrontation with the giant (1 Sam. 17:4–7) has attracted two basic approaches. One treats the narrative as a factual, or mostly factual, report of an event that took place in the eleventh century B.C.E. The other views it as the creation of one or several Hebrew historians writing at least five hundred years later, and mostly, or wholly, fictional.

Larry Stager has followed the first approach in stating: "Goliath was armed like a Mycenaean warrior—bronze helmet (*kôbaᶜ* is non-Semitic), coat of mail (*širyôn*, non-Semitic), bronze greaves (*miṣḥâ*, non-Semitic), scimitar (*kîdôn*, curved sword with convex cutting edge), bronze javelin [spear] (*ḥănît*) with thong and ring for slinging" (King and Stager 2001:228). He was treading the path other archaeologists have taken, such as Yigael Yadin (1963:265, 354–55) and Moshe and Trude Dothan (1992:47–49), by adducing material remains from the Late Bronze Age and the start of the Iron Age to compose the picture. On the other hand, the Israeli archaeologist Israel Finkelstein has followed the second approach, aligning himself with the majority of Old Testament scholars, who date the composition of the books of Samuel towards the end of the seventh century B.C.E., or later, as part of the Deuteronomistic History (Finkelstein 2002).

This essay reconsiders aspects of the two positions in tribute to a distinguished archaeologist and esteemed friend, attempting to support his position.[1]

A Mycenean Warrior?

Material remains attest the presence of people with strong Aegean links in southwest Palestine at the start of the Iron Age, but it is from foreign written sources alone, Egyptian and Hebrew, that the existence of the Philistines and the area of their settlement are known, for the Philistines themselves have left no written documents. The Egyptian reliefs of the "Peoples of the Sea" in Ramesses III's mortuary temple at Medinet Habu are well known, depicting warriors, some with feathered headdresses, some with round caps, and others with horned helmets, wearing ribbed cuirasses, carrying long tapering swords and round shields, and, some of them, one or two spears. The Egyptian texts identify the men with feathered headdresses as Philistines, Tjekker, and Danuna; those with round caps as Tursha; and those with horned helmets as Sherden (Kitchen 1973:57, 69). These accoutrements are often compared with the paintings on the Warrior Vase found at Mycenae. On one side is a row of spear-carrying warriors wearing horned helmets and cuirasses; on the other side, a row wearing "bristle-crested" helmets (Immerwahr 1990:150). The men in both rows apparently wear greaves. Examples of Mycenean weapons and armor from sites in the Aegean can be set beside these ancient illustrations.

Do these discoveries allow us to describe Goliath as "armed like a Mycenaean warrior"? His helmet evidently did not cover the forehead and so was more like the horned helmets worn by the Sherden, or the round caps of the Tursha, in the Medinet Habu reliefs than the horned helmets on the Warrior Vase, which have nose-pieces. The feathered headdress of some Sea Peoples and the bristle-crested helmets of the Warrior Vase might also be considered; there is no indication of the material from which they were made; the apparently feathered band may have surrounded a metal cap.[2] The coat of mail was a shirt of scale armor, such as is well attested across the Near East in the Late Bronze Age. Examples of bronze scale armor were recovered at Nuzi (Starr 1930:475–80), among other sites, and are depicted in Egyptian paintings (see Yadin 1963:196–97) and mentioned in many documents.[3] The textual and material information, preeminently from Nuzi, suggests that suits of scale armor in the fifteenth century B.C.E. comprised 400 to 560 bronze scales, sometimes with as many smaller scales for the sleeves. The weights of scales found at Nuzi range from 9.4 g to about 52 g each, the heaviest probably being for horse armor. A suit of 500 large scales of 31 g each and 500 small ones of 12 g each would have had an approximate weight of 22 kg. When the weight of the leather shirt, about one

[1] Larry Stager's stimulating and jovial company illumined the time we were privileged to spend at the Institute of Advanced Studies in the Hebrew University together with Israel Finkelstein and other eminent scholars under the chairmanship of Yigael Yadin in 1984.

[2] For an extensive discussion of Late Bronze Age helmets in the Near East and Mycenae, see Kendall 1981.

[3] Deszö (2004:319–23) has listed all the bronze scales from the Late Bronze Age known when he wrote (pp. 320–21).

half of the bronze, is added, the total would be about 33 kg (information taken from Kendall 1981). Given that Goliath was a giant, "six cubits and a span" in height, about 9 feet 9 inches or 3 meters, his coat of mail would be very much heavier than usual, so, using the Nuzi figures, the weight given, five thousand shekels, about 125 pounds or 57 kg, is acceptable. (The LXX reading, "four cubits and a span"—6 feet 9 inches or 2+ m—reduces the stature so much that it hardly allows the great weight.) Scale armor was not common in Mycenean areas, but examples have been found at some places, most recently one scale bearing the cartouche of Ramesses II in a Mycenean palace on the island of Salamis (reported by the Associated Press, 30 March 2006). Scale armor is very different from the bronze bands making up the famous suit of armor from Dendra. It is also different from the corselets of the Sea Peoples, shown as chevrons, or inverted chevrons, on the Egyptian reliefs. Whether those were metal bands or some other form of hauberk cannot be determined.

Goliath's greaves deserve a little more attention because all of the ancient pictures of Late Bronze Age warriors in Egypt and the Near East show them bare-legged. Greaves were apparently not used there then, or in the Iron Age. They did, however, form part of the equipment of Mycenean warriors of the thirteenth century and later. The Warrior Vase depicts the spearman wearing greaves, whether of metal or leather is unclear (Finkelstein [2002:142] believes they were not made of metal), but bronze examples have been found in tombs in Greece (Dendra, Kallithea in Achaea) and at Enkomi on Cyprus (Verdelis 1977). Consequently, rather than considering the description of Goliath's equipment "late" and so anachronistic, one authority on Classical times wrote, "we may suspect that in his time and country he was an oddity who maintained a foreign style of a past age" (Bowra 1961:109), as he was living a century or more after the Mycenean era. Following this reasoning, the biblical description makes Goliath an anachronism—behind the times, not ahead of them! In fact, greaves are attested in Greece during the Geometric period, from 900 B.C.E. onwards, so their use may have continued uninterrupted among leading warriors in the Aegean region.

The weapon Goliath wore "between his shoulders" (*kîdôn*), it is now widely accepted,[4] was the curved "sickle-sword" known from representations and actual examples in the second millennium B.C.E. and visible hanging on the backs of deities as depicted on cylinder seals of the first millennium (Galling 1965: 165–66, 168). But this is not certain because the *kîdôn* might be the short tapering sword borne by Sea Peoples according to Ramesses III's sculptors. The precise form of Goliath's spear with its shaft "like a weaver's beam" is also uncertain. Yigael Yadin's proposal that the spear was a javelin with thongs for throwing, which the Hebrew writer compared to a weaver's beam, the heddle rod of a loom, retains its attraction, but needs further evidence (Yadin 1955).[5]

A Greek Hoplite?

When Kurt Galling examined Goliath's equipment in a standard essay over forty years ago (Galling 1965), he observed that, in the light of modern knowledge covering the whole of the Iron Age, the account of Goliath's equipment is eclectic, not presenting a uniform picture—not conforming to the pattern of any one group of people or class of warrior or to a single era. Nowhere in the Late Bronze or early Iron Age can this equipment find an exact counterpart. Israel Finkelstein, with others, accepts that conclusion and assumes that "in the days of the Deuteronomistic Historian . . . Iron I realities have already disappeared, even from the collective memory" (Finkelstein 2002:133). In this view, the Deuteronomistic Historian, working late in the seventh century B.C.E. or after, could only reflect the fashions and circumstances of his own age in his writing, retrojecting them to earlier times. Those presuppositions, coupled with recent theories about the late development of Jerusalem, the "state" of Judah, and its literary productions, led Finkelstein to seek comparisons for Goliath's armor in the seventh century or later. He found that the Greek hoplites offered the closest comparison because although metal armor and weapons occurred at all periods from the Mycenean onwards, they were not common, and "as an assemblage, the description perfectly fits the armament of Greek hoplites from the seventh to the fifth centuries B.C.E." (Finkelstein 2002:143). This comparison gained strength from the evidence that there were Greek mercenaries serving in the Near East and Egypt in the seventh century, as well as Greek colonies on the Levantine coast.

[4] The identification was made by G. Molin (1956) after the publication of the scroll of the "War of the Sons of Light" among the Dead Sea Scrolls.

[5] A spearman holding a spear that seems to have a rope twined around its foot, carved on a basalt basin from Tell Mardikh, is now securely dated to the Middle Bronze Age, not the ninth century B.C.E., as Galling (1965:161) thought; see Matthiae 1980:135–36.

Eclectic Equipment?

Yet, although Finkelstein (2002:143) asserts that "as an assemblage, the description perfectly fits the armament of Greek hoplites . . . Their equipment included a metal helmet, plate-armor, metal greaves, two spears, a sword, and a large shield," he has to admit that the hoplites did not wear scale armor. To overcome the difficulty, he supposes that Assyrian elements were mixed into the description, or that some hoplites adopted Near Eastern scale armor. Furthermore, as the descriptions and depictions of Greek hoplites never include shieldbearers, they, too, may be an Assyrian element, for they appear on some Assyrian reliefs (ibid., p. 146). This produces a combination that deserves Galling's characterization as "eclectic' as much as the previous attempts to understand Goliath's gear!

Both Galling and Finkelstein make the assumption that the Philistine champion's equipment has to conform to a standard pattern. But should the modern reader suppose that so much is known about ancient warriors at all periods that the apparently "eclectic" collection of arms and armor the giant bore is impossible? Nothing compels anyone to expect that a giant, who putatively lived in the mid-eleventh century B.C.E., should have the same equipment as the Sea Peoples carry on Ramesses III's reliefs carved a century earlier, or share the panoply used by Mycenean warriors. The Philistines on the Egyptian reliefs wear feathered headdresses and the Sherden wear horned caps. Nothing implies that the two groups were so separate from each other that a member of one might not wear the headdress of the other. Yet the fact that Goliath was a champion would indicate that he could have the best that could be supplied, which would not necessarily be the same as what ordinary soldiers bore. A champion surely had the power to choose whatever equipment he wanted.

The Sea Peoples, as the Egyptians represented them, carried small shields, for they were fighting in ships where shield-bearers would encumber them, and none was a "champion." Goliath was advancing from his battle-line, exposed to his enemy, so he had a shieldbearer to protect him as much as possible. Evidently, he expected his opponent to engage him at close quarters, so the cover given by the shieldbearer would allow him freedom to wield his spear with the advantage of his greater reach. There is no reason to suppose the shield was unusually large, like those protecting archers carved on Assyrian reliefs, which Finkelstein adduces as a possible source for Goliath's shield and shieldbearer. In fact, the famous inlaid dagger and two gold seals from Grave Circle A at Mycenae, dated to the beginning of the Late Bronze Age, each depict a warrior holding an oblong shield large enough to cover his whole body. In addition, a painted grave stele shows warriors with large circular shields. Although these illustrations belong to the early part of the Late Bronze Age and warriors of the later part carry smaller, round shields, there is no reason why the large body shields should not have continued in use in single combat (see Hiller 1999). Knowledge of the armor and weapons current in the Late Bronze and Iron Ages is haphazard, dependent upon the survival of various texts and metal objects. No one can claim that there is a complete inventory of the equipment in use throughout the area for any century, so the failure of every attempt to place Goliath's into one category or another is no reason for doubting its existence.

Single Combat: A Greek Prototype or a Near Eastern?

The contest between David and Goliath has often been compared with the heroic contests in the *Iliad*, and Finkelstein (2002:146) adopts the comparison, with the later study by A. Yadin (2004) taking the same route. Both assert that there are closer similarities between the Hebrew and the Greek accounts than between the Hebrew and other ancient Near Eastern texts, notably in the enumeration of the weapons and armor. However, the similarities with ancient Near Eastern accounts on that point should not be minimized. The Egyptian Sinuhe, about to face the champion of a hostile tribe, relates how he prepared himself, enumerating his weapons: "At night I strung my bow, sorted my arrows, practiced with my dagger, polished my weapons"; and, in the fight: "When he charged me, I shot him, my arrow sticking in his neck. He screamed; he fell on his nose; I slew him with his ax" (lines 137–40 in Lichtheim 1996:79). Another, poetic, account of single combat occurs in the Babylonian Creation Epic, *Enuma elish*. There the gods' champion, Marduk, setting out to meet the ocean monster Tiamat, readied his arms: "He made the bow, appointed it his weapon. He mounted the arrow, set it on the string. He took up the mace, held it in his right hand. Bow and quiver he slung on his arm. Thunderbolts he set before his face. With raging fire he covered his body" (lines 35–40 in Foster 1993:373). Most ancient Near Eastern narratives, whether poetry or prose, concern the exploits of gods or kings in which single combat rarely takes place, so reducing the amount of comparison possible with David and Goliath. The fact that there is a greater number of cases in the *Iliad* does not mean the Hebrew text has to be related to the Greek.

A noteworthy feature of 1 Samuel 17 is the prosaic listing of the weights of the scale armor and the spear point. That means the description is not meant to show simply how the adversary appeared to Israelite soldiers quaking by the Valley of Elah, but gives ground for their fear in anticipating the victory when the giant was stripped and his accoutrements evaluated. Verses 5–7 fall, therefore, into the same class of enumerative description as the note of the provisions Abigail brought to David in the desert of Maon (1 Sam. 25:18), or of the crown weighing a talent of gold captured in Rabbath Ammon (2 Sam. 12:30). They may be compared with the frequent lists of booty in Assyrian and Egyptian royal inscriptions from all periods. Accordingly, R. Alter's (1999: 101) comment, that the "'Homeric' enumeration of armor and weapons is quite untypical of the Hebrew Bible" (cited by A. Yadin 2004:392) is ill founded.[6]

Early Hebrew Writing

A major basis for Finkelstein's contention is a denial of the possibility that Hebrew scribes were writing literature and history in Jerusalem before Hezekiah's time. The small size of the city, as attested by excavations, and the conviction that "Judah did not become a full-blown state with advanced administration before that time" (Finkelstein 2002:132) are the grounds for that denial. It is true that the number of Hebrew inscriptions, ostraca, seals, and graffiti that have been discovered and can be dated earlier than the Assyrian conquest of Samaria is much smaller than the number known from the later period (see Renz and Röllig 1995–2003). Yet the creation in the ninth century of the historical narrative known as the Mesha Inscription (the Moabite Stone) in equally small and undeveloped Moab, and the creation of the Aramaic narrative text on the Tel Dan stele, and of the prophetic account presented in the Deir ᶜAlla plaster text, clearly contradicts that. It is unlikely that the first two were composed orally and engraved immediately upon the stones that bear them, and the third is almost certainly a reproduction of a column of a scroll.[7] Admittedly, none are Judean, but each one attests scribal activity at the level of the biblical texts in the ninth century B.C.E.; they are only shorter because of their purposes and their writing materials (Millard, forthcoming). The graffiti written on walls and jars at the remote southern caravanserai of Kuntillet ᶜAjrud early in the eighth century B.C.E. prove that some people were capable of writing Hebrew in a literary style at that time, far from the main towns (see Renz 1995:47–64). Defining Judah as a "state"—a term without an ancient Semitic equivalent—involves imposing modern theories about state formation on ancient society, which can also give a misleading impression. Those theories make requirements that are at odds with the situations ancient kingdoms present, while the archaeological data introduced to support them are too meager or incomplete to bear the weight placed on them.

The Possibility of Historical Memory

That the Goliath episode forms part of the Deuteronomistic History need not imply that it was an invention of the seventh century, so that it "should be read against the background of the time when the story was put into writing" and understood as a reflection of that time (Finkelstein 2002:143). Unless there is indubitable proof that the author(s) or composer(s) had no means of access to information about earlier times, the possibility that they did have it, as they claim for many passages,[8] cannot be discounted. How accurate the information was, or how accurately the Deuteronomist(s) relayed it, has to be examined in each case. Now, it is a well-established fact that wherever a statement in the Deuteronomistic History can be checked against adequate external sources, the two prove to be remarkably harmonious, as shown by extrabiblical references to kings like Ahab or Hezekiah, Mesha of Moab, or Hazael of Damascus (no monumental inscriptions of his own have been discovered so far), or Tiglath-pileser or Sennacherib of Assyria. The portrayal of the varying political situations from the time of David until the fall of Jerusalem also agrees with the testimony of extrabiblical sources.

In the literature of other ancient Near Eastern societies, there are texts similarly describing events that supposedly occurred long before the works were composed. Again, where there is adequate information to check them, those texts often appear to reflect the more remote times well, as demonstrated in the Babylonian tales of Sargon of Akkad and his grandson Naram-Sin, surviving in copies made up to five centuries after their time (see Millard 2002:103–10

[6] If the size of the giant were reduced, with the Septuagint, to four cubits and a span (see above), that, while still making him larger than normal, would not give him the same visual impact from a distance, nor, as noted, would it justify the weight of the armor.

[7] See my observation in Millard 1978 (esp. 24–25), accepted by A. Lemaire (1991:45).

[8] As in, for example, "the book of Jashar" (2 Sam. 1:18), "the books of the chronicles of the kings of Israel" and "of Judah" (1 Kings 14:19, 29, etc.), or "the book of the chronicles of Solomon" (1 Kings 11:14).

and compare the study by Hallo 2001:195–209). The recent history of the study of those tales is instructive. A leading historian set out arguments to show how the stories really reflected the period when the available copies were written, the Old Babylonian period (ca. 2000–1600 B.C.E.), their purpose being to justify political actions by rulers in that time as emulating the exploits of famous ancient kings. He adduced in particular the absence from the historical inscriptions of those kings of various events and titles reported in the tales. But the publication of new texts about the kings of Akkad, reliable copies of their own inscriptions, has undermined much of his case, because they have revealed that events and titles he thought belonged to the later time already had their place in the earlier age.[9]

This sounds a caution in the case of Goliath's armor. Finkelstein asserts that the description of Goliath's panoply "as an assemblage . . . perfectly fits the armament of Greek hoplites of the seventh to the fifth centuries B.C.E. Their equipment included a metal helmet, metal greaves, two spears, a sword . . . and a large shield." Although each of these pieces can be found at earlier times, they were "not the most common" of their kind (Finkelstein 2002:145). Yet, as noted above, the fit is not perfect, nor is there good reason to insist that Goliath was armed in "the most common" style. "There is no reason to deny the possibility that there was an ancient tale of a duel between David and a Philistine warrior," Finkelstein (2002:147) writes, proceeding to erect his case for the Deuteronomist drawing on Greek hoplite armor as part of his depiction of "a golden United Monarchy." But the possibility of historical memory could also imply that the account of the warrior's equipment was correctly handed down over several centuries.

The Contrast of Bronze and Iron

Most significantly, the material of Goliath's armor—helmet, hauberk, and greaves—and of his sword (*kîdôn*), namely, bronze, is an embarrassment for those who ascribe the passage to a late date, for, as Finkelstein admits, "in the seventh century B.C.E. the scales of the armor, the javelin and the spear-head . . . were already made, in most cases, of iron" (Finkelstein 2002:146, n. 25).[10] He is reduced to the following comment: "But the bronze appearance is aimed to impress and enhance the figure of Goliath." Yet the contrast between the two words "bronze" and "iron" in 1 Sam. 17:5–7 seems to point to an early origin for the passage, notwithstanding Galling's (1966:161) dismissal of its value. All of Goliath's armor—helmet, scale armor, greaves—and his javelin (or sword) were of bronze (Hebrew *nḥšt* covers both copper and bronze), but the head of his spear was iron. The difference of metals is notable, for a national champion would be expected to have the best, currently fashionable, armor, and, had the account been written later in the Iron Age, in the seventh century or after, that would have been made of iron, as Finkelstein admits. Discoveries in Assyria of iron scale armor, helmets, and weapons illustrate this, although many other examples show that bronze was still current.[11] As it is, only the head of Goliath's spear was made of iron, which, again, is appropriate for the period when iron was newly available, costly, and only gradually coming into use (Millard 1988). It is pertinent to note that the rare references to iron in the fourteenth to twelfth centuries B.C.E. particularly concern weapons, daggers, and arrowheads (see *CAD* P s.v. *parzillu*; also Moorey 1995).

It is justifiable, therefore, to allow the possibility that the account of Goliath's panoply in 1 Sam. 17:5–7 preserves much older details, as early, indeed, as the eleventh century B.C.E. The present writer's experience over many years spent examining ancient narratives and finding repeatedly that their reports of circumstances and events are reliable strengthens his predisposition to treat the biblical text favorably. With regard to the books of Samuel and Kings, wherever ancient records cover the same events, they show themselves to be harmonious with the Hebrew ones, a fact that weighs in favor of reading other passages in those books positively, of assessing their testimonies against the situations they imply, and only discounting them if the case against them is convincing and indisputable. Larry Stager's approach should be emulated!

[9] Carefully explained by T. Potts (2001).

[10] P. K. McCarter (1980:293) observed that bronze "continued to be used when extreme hardness was not required down into Roman times."

[11] Iron scale armor was found at Nimrud (see Mallowan 1966:409–11; Stronach 1958, esp. pp. 172–74). Of 45 scales unearthed at Lachish in the level associated with Sennacherib's attack, 14 were of copper or bronze and 31 of iron (Sass and Ussishkin 2004:1970–74). A tablet found at Nimrud records "an iron coat of mail, of Damascus" in the late eighth century B.C.E. (ND 7060; Dalley and Postgate 1984:135, no. 75). See also the list of bronze and iron scales from the first millennium B.C.E. in Deszö 2005: 323.

Bibliography

Alter, R.
1999 *The David Story: A Translation with Commentary of 1 and 2 Samuel*. New York: Norton.

Bowra, C. M.
1961 Euknemides Achaioi. *Mnemosyne* 14:97–110.

Dalley, S., and J. N. Postgate
1984 *The Tablets from Fort Shalmaneser.* Cuneiform Tablets from Nimrud 3. London: British School of Archaeology in Iraq.

Deszö, T.
2004 Panzer. *RLA* 10:319–23.

Dothan, T., and M. Dothan
1992 *People of the Sea: The Search for the Philistines*. New York: Macmillan.

Finkelstein, I.
2002 The Philistines in the Bible: A Late-Monarchic Perspective. *JSOT* 27:131–67.

Foster, B. R.
1993 Epic of Creation: Tablet IV. In *Before the Muses*, by B. R. Foster, 1:372–77. Bethesda, Md.: CDL.

Galling, K.
1966 Goliath und seine Rüstung. In *Volume de Congrès: Genève, 1965*, ed. P. A. H. de Boer, 150–69. VTSup 15. Leiden: Brill.

Hallo, W. W.
2001 Polymnia and Clio. In *Historiography in the Cuneiform World: Proceedings of the Forty-fifth Rencontre Assyriologique Internationale*, ed. T. Abusch et al., 195–209. Bethesda, Md.: CDL.

Hiller, S.
1999 Scenes of Warfare and Combat in the Arts of the Aegean Late Bronze Age: Reflections on Typology and Development. In *Polemos: Le contexte guerrier en Egée à l'Âge du Bronze*, ed. R. Laffineur, 319–30. Aegaeum 19. Liège: Université de Liège.

Immerwahr, S. A.
1990 *Aegean Painting in the Bronze Age*. Philadelphia: Pennsylvania State University Press.

Kendall, T.
1981 *gurpisu ša awēli*: The Helmets of the Warriors at Nuzi. In *Studies on the Civilization and Culture of Nuzi and the Hurrians in Honor of Ernest R. Lacheman*, ed. M. A. Morrison and D. I. Owen, 1:201–231. Winona Lake, Ind.: Eisenbrauns.

King, P. J., and L. E. Stager
2001 *Life in Biblical Israel*. Louisville, Ky.: Westminster John Knox.

Kitchen, K. A.
1973 The Philistines. In *Peoples of Old Testament Times*, ed. D. J. Wiseman, 53–78. Oxford: Clarendon.

Lemaire, A.
1991 Les Inscriptions sur Plâtre de Deir ᶜAlla et leur signification historique et culturelle. In *The Balaam Text from Deir ᶜAlla Re-evaluated*, ed. J. Hoftijzer and G. van der Kooij, 33–57. Leiden: Brill.

Lichtheim, M.
1996 Sinuhe. In *The Context of Scripture*, vol. 1, *Canonical Compositions from the Biblical World*, ed. W. W. Hallo and K. L. Younger, 1:77–82. Leiden: Brill.

Mallowan, M. E. L.
1966 *Nimrud and Its Remains*. London: Collins.

Matthiae, P.
1980 *Ebla: An Empire Rediscovered.* Translated by C. Holme. London: Hodder and Stoughton.

McCarter, P. K.
1980 *I Samuel: A New Translation.* Anchor Bible 8. Garden City, N.Y.: Doubleday.

Millard, A.
1978 Epigraphic Notes, Aramaic and Hebrew. *PEQ* 110:23–26.
1988 King Og's Bed and other Ancient Ironmongery. In *Ascribe to the Lord: Biblical and Other Studies in Memory of Peter C. Craigie*, ed. L. Eslinger and G. Taylor, 481–92. JSOTSup 67. Sheffield, England: Sheffield Academic Press.
2002 History and Legend in Early Babylonia. In *Windows into Old Testament History: Evidence, Argument, and the Crisis of "Biblical Israel"*, ed. V. P. Long, D. W. Baker, and G. J. Wenham, 103–10. Grand Rapids, Mich.: Eerdmans.
forthc. Books in Ancient Israel. In *Du Sapounou au saphon: Sur les routes des peuples du Levant*, ed. C. Roche. Paris.

Molin, G.
1956 What is a *Kidon*? *JSS* 1:334–37.

Moorey, P. R. S.
1995 The Craft of the Metalsmith in the Ancient Near East: The Origins of Ironworking. In *From Gulf to Delta and Beyond*, 53–68. Beer-Sheva 8. Beer-Sheva, Israel: Ben-Gurion University of the Negev Press.

Potts, T.
2001 Reading the Sargonic "Historical-Literary" Tradition: Is There a Middle Course? (Thoughts on the Great Revolt against Naram-Sin). In *Historiogra-*

phy in the Cuneiform World: Proceedings of the Forty-fifth Rencontre Assyriologique Internationale, ed. T. Abusch et al., 391–408. Bethesda, Md.: CDL.

Renz, J.
1995 *Handbuch der Althebräischen Epigraphik*. Vol. 1, *Die althebräischen Inschriften*, part 1. Darmstadt: Wissenschaftliche Buchgesellschaft.

Renz, J., and W. Röllig
1995–2003 *Handbuch der Althebräischen Epigraphik*. Darmstadt: Wissenschaftliche Buchgesellschaft.

Sass, B., and D. Ussishkin
2004 Spears, Armour Scales and Slingstones. In *The Renewed Excavations at Lachish (1973–1994)*, ed. D. Ussishkin, 4:1970–82. Tel Aviv: Institute of Archaeology, Tel Aviv University.

Starr, R. F. S.
1930 *Nuzi: Reports of the Excavations at Yorgan Tepe near Kirkuk, Iraq*. Cambridge, Mass.: Harvard University Press.

Stronach, D.
1958 Metal Objects from the 1957 Excavations at Nimrud. *Iraq* 20:169–81.

Ussishkin, D.
1982 *The Conquest of Lachish by Sennacherib*. Tel Aviv: Institute of Archaeology, Tel Aviv University.

Verdelis, N. M.
1977 The Metal Finds: 2. The Greave(s). In *The Cuirass Tomb and Other Finds at Dendra*, ed. P. Åström, 45–48. SIMA 4/2. Göteborg: Åströms.

Yadin, A.
2004 Goliath's Armor and Israelite Collective Memory. *VT* 54:373–95.

Yadin, Y.
1955 Goliath's Javelin and the מנור ארגים. *PEQ* 86: 58–69.
1963 *The Art of Warfare in Biblical Lands in Light of Archaeological Study*. London: Weidenfeld and Nicholson.

35. Facts or Factoids? Some Historical Observations on the Trophy Inscription from Kition (*KAI* 288)

by Paul G. Mosca

The aim of this paper is to explore the historical implications of a Phoenician inscription discovered by chance in the area of modern Larnaca (Cyprus) in 1990 and published the following year with exemplary speed by Marguerite Yon and Maurice Sznycer (1991). It is offered, with the greatest affection and esteem, to Lawrence E. Stager, whose archaeological skills and keen historical sense I have so much admired, and whose friendship of forty years I have valued even more.

The text, now known as the Kition Trophy Inscription (although the trophy proper has not survived), is inscribed on one of the shorter sides of a large block of imported marble (Yon 2004:199 and n. 14). The inscription commemorates the victory of Milkyaton, king of Kition and Idalion, in the first year of his reign (ca. 392/1 B.C.E.). This dating makes it potentially of great importance for the history of Kition and of Cyprus in the early fourth century B.C.E., since it was at this time that Evagoras of Salamis, while attempting to gain control of the entire island, met with armed resistance from Amathous, Soloi, and Kition.

The basic structure of the monumental text is that of a standard Cypriot Phoenician dedicatory inscription, but narrative expansions (marked by italics in the following translation) offer details usually absent from such dedications. The text is essentially that of Sznycer (1991:805), with only one correction required: the addition of a second *nun* in *lʾdnnm* (line 1). My translation, however, differs from Sznycer's at a number of crucial points. (For a detailed discussion of these differences, see Mosca 2006.)

Text:

1. *trpy ʾz ʾš yṭnʾ mlk mlkytn mlk kty wʾdyl bn bʿlrm wkl ʿm kty lʾḋṅnm lbʿl ʿz bmṣʾnm*
2. *ʾbn wʿzrnm hppẏm lʾgd ln mlḥmt ḃ[ym]ṁ [ ] lyrḥ zyb št 1 lmlky ʿl kty wʾdyl wyṣʾ*
3. *ʿlṅ[m mḥ]nt (?) ʾš kty lʾgd lm mlḥmt bmqm ʾż bym hʾ bnty wytn ly wlk̇l ʿm kty*
4. *ḃʿl ʿ[z ʿ]z wnṣḥt bkl ʾbn wbʿzrnm hppym wyṭnʾt ʾnk wkl ʿm kty ʾyt htrpyʾ*
5. *z lb*[ʿl] *ʿż ʾdny kšmʿ qlm ybṙkm*

Translation:

1. This trophy (is that) which King Milkyaton, king of Kition and Idalion, son of Baʿalrom, and all the people of Kition, erected for their Lord, for Baʿal ʿOz, in *the place where*
2. *our enemies and their allies the Paphians came forth to do battle against us,* on the [?] day of the month of ZYB, in the first year of his reign over Kition and Idalion.
3. *And the* [*ar*]*my of the men of Kition came forth to do battle against them in this place, on that very day.*
4. *And Baʿal ʿOz gave to me and to all the people of Kition po*[*wer*] *and victory over all our enemies and over their allies the Paphians. And I and all the people of Kition erected*
5. *this trophy to Ba*[*ʿal*] *ʿOz, my Lord,* because he heard their voice. May he bless them!

Josette Elayi has described this text as an "importante inscription royale . . . dont la portée historique reste encore à exploiter" (Elayi and Sapin 2000: 230–31). I shall argue, however, that the Trophy Inscription offers us relatively little help in clarifying the problems associated with the early years of Milkyaton's reign. Indeed, the misguided attempts to exploit the historical importance of the inscription have too often given rise to "factoids" rather than facts. It was Franz Georg Maier (1985) who first introduced the term "factoid" into the study of ancient Cypriot history. Defining factoids as "mere speculations or guesses which have been repeated so often that they are eventually taken for hard facts," Maier noted that, on a linguistic level, factoids are created when "words or particles indicating the hypothetical character of a statement are dropped one by one in a process of constant repetition. The subjunctive is exchanged for the indicative, and in the end the factoid is formulated as a straightforward factual sentence" (Maier 1985:32).

The process described by Maier can once again be observed at work in connection with the Trophy Inscription. To be sure, the *editio princeps* is free of the phenomenon, because in it Yon and Sznycer (1991) made liberal use of those "words and particles" that accurately reflected the tentative nature of their more speculative historical conclusions. Regrettably, however, such qualifiers all too often disappear in subsequent publications (both their own and those of others), and we mark the emergence of true factoids. Here I wish to consider three of these newborn factoids in the hope that their lives will prove to be relatively short and unproductive. The first factoid has to do with the nature of the trophy and the victory, the second with the "enemies" named in the text, and the third with Milkyaton's accession to the throne of Kition.

The Nature of the Victory

In the *editio princeps*, both authors concluded that the newly recovered monument celebrated Kition's victory at sea, that it was "un *trophée naval*" (Yon 1991: 801; italics in original), "un trophée maritime" (Sznycer 1991:816). In context, this conclusion constitutes a hypothesis, not a factoid, for the various pieces of circumstantial evidence used to buttress the conclusion are clearly laid out for us to evaluate: (1) Yon's reasoning that led her to associate the monument's original location with the Bamboula hill, near the site of the ancient harbor, the city's "port de guerre"(1991:793–94, 801); (2) her citation of Diodorus Siculus's description of the siege of Salamis (15.4.1), with the phrases "*victoire sur mer*"and "*par terre et par mer*" italicised for emphasis (1991:796); and (3) Sznycer's rendering of *bym hʾ bnty* in line 3 as "près de la mer(?), là où je l'ai construit" (1991: 805, with discussion 814–16).

Unfortunately, but perhaps not surprisingly, the hypothesis presented in the *editio princeps* was soon replaced by a true factoid. In the published version of a report originally given in 1991, Yon (1995:454) described the trophy as celebrating "une victoire navale," as if this were a fact, and went on to quote Sznycer's translation of line 3, omitting its question mark entirely (in contrast to Yon 2004:201, which reproduces the *editio princeps* verbatim). Karageorghis (1995:329) followed suit, speaking unreservedly of "a naval trophy after a victorious naval battle." And Sznycer himself eventually began to drop the question mark from his translation of the text (2000: 288; 2001:101). As for the original location of the stone at Bamboula overlooking the port, by 2000 he regarded it as "vraisemblable"; a year later it was "sans doute" that the trophy had been first erected in the area of the port (Sznycer 2000:286; 2001:99).

Thus, as Maier (1985) has warned us, are factoids created. In the end, however, the hypothesis that the trophy celebrated a victory at sea is no stronger than its supporting pieces of circumstantial evidence (epigraphical, textual, and topographical); and it must be noted that none of these is particularly strong.

To begin with, Sznycer's translation of *bym hʾ bnty* in line 3 as "près de la mer(?), là où je l'ai construit" is simply impossible. As noted by Xella (1993: 63 n. 7), the meaning assigned to the demonstrative *hʾ* is unparalleled in Phoenician-Punic—and, I might add, in any other Northwest Semitic language. Moreover, there is general agreement in recent studies of the inscription that *ym* here is to be understood as "day," not "sea" (Krahmalkov 2000:108–9, s.v. *BNT* I = *BT* III; Lipiński 2004:95; Mosca 2006:182). There is thus no support in the text itself for locating the battle at sea.

Secondly, Yon's appeal to Diodorus Siculus is of questionable relevance. The siege of Salamis described in 15.4.1 took place in 386 B.C.E., some five years after the battle celebrated in the Trophy Inscription. Moreover, the fleet of 386 B.C.E. is clearly presented as the result of Persian initiative (14.98.3; 15.2.1; 15.4.1), with Kition mentioned only as the base for the attack on Salamis (15.4.1). Nor is a specifically naval dimension present in Diodorus's earlier account of the successes of Evagoras through 391 B.C.E. and the armed resistance of Kition, Amathous, and Soloi (14.98.1–2).

Lastly, the hypothesis that the trophy was originally erected in the area of the Bamboula and was moved from there only in 1879, when the British administration assigned Lt. Sinclair of the Royal Engineers to fill in the malarial area of the ancient harbor (Bailey 1969–1970:37–40), must be judged implausible. According to the accession book of the Larnaca Archaeological Museum (no. 1513),[1] the Trophy base was in fact discovered in 1990 in the area of the old refinery of Larnaca (southeast of the village of Livadia), over 2 km north of the city wall of ancient Kition and almost 3 km north of the Bamboula and its adjacent port. Nor is it likely that Sinclair and his team would have overlooked so large an inscribed block of stone. Yon herself has acknowledged that two Phoenician inscriptions were "saved and sent to the British Museum" (1992:158). What she failed to mention is that these inscriptions (*CIS* I 86, 87) were written not on monumental stones, but on two small alabaster tablets measuring 11 × 15 ×

[1] I wish to thank Dr. Demos Christou, then Director of the Department of Antiquities of Cyprus, and Mr. Andreas Savva, then Director of the Archaeological Museum of Larnaca, for their kind assistance in gaining access to the stone in 1996, and also Dr. Pavlos Flourentzos, the present Director of the Department of Antiquities, for permission to study the stone in 2005.

ca. 1.3 centimeters (*CIS* I 86) and 14 × 16.8 × 2.2 centimeters (*CIS* I 87) (Guzzo Amadasi and Karageorghis 1977:104 and 126, respectively). The Trophy stone measures 1.23 × 1.01 × 0.48 meters. To claim that workmen who could recognize two small inked tablets managed to overlook a massive incised block of marble can hardly be called "vraisemblable," let alone categorized as "sans doute."

In sum, there is no evidence that the battle fought and won by Milkyaton and "all the people of Kition" was fought wholly or even partly at sea. To assert otherwise is to perpetuate a factoid, not a fact.

The Identity of "Our Enemies"

The second, and admittedly more significant, issue deserving detailed discussion centers on the attacking forces. The victory claimed by Kition's king and people was over "(all) our enemies and their allies" (lines 2, 4). The allies are explicitly marked as "Paphians," but the enemies are left unnamed. How are they to be identified? In seeking to answer this question, both Yon and Sznycer, in the *editio princeps* (1991:795 and 819–20), called our attention to Diodorus Siculus 14.98.1–2, a passage which describes how Evagoras of Salamis set out to gain control of all Cyprus, and which names Kition as one of three cities to offer armed resistance to Evagoras and to appeal for aid to Artaxerxes II. Given the chronological proximity of these two sources—the inscription dating to Milkyaton's "first year" (ca. 392/1) and Diodorus's account placing Kition's armed resistance in 391 or slightly earlier—it is admittedly very tempting to identify the army of Evagoras with "our enemies." Sznycer made this identification, but he did so "à titre d'hypothèse" (1991:820), for he rightly emphasized that the phrase "our enemies" is used "d'une manière assez mystérieuse" (1991:819) and "de manière inhabituelle" (1991:820).

Here, as in our first example, we find a hypothesis soon transformed into a factoid. Within two years Xella asserted that the identification of "our enemies" with Evagoras's army "s'impose sans réserves" (1993:62). For Pierre Briant, in his magisterial history of the Persian empire, "[i]l ne fait guère de doute que le terme générique d'«ennemis» désigne Évagoras et ses alliés—parmi lesquels seuls les Paphiens sont nommément cites" (1996:666; ET 2002:647). Lipiński (2004:94), too, accepts the identification without any qualification, as now apparently do both Sznycer (2001:104 and 107) and Yon (1996:445; 1997:13; 2004:201).

Despite these claims of certainty, however, reservations and doubts must inevitably remain, for, in this simple equation of "our enemies" with the forces of Evagoras, the vagueness of the inscription's phrasing, so "mystérieuse" and "inhabituelle," remains without a satisfactory explanation. To be sure, Yon (1991:799) had suggested that the name of the enemy was too well known at the time to require explicit mention, and her explanation was adopted by Xella (1993:62). Yet this justification for anonymity can hardly be considered compelling, when the allies, presumably equally well known at the time, are specifically identified as Paphian. While conceding that the Trophy Inscription is in some way linked to the activities of Evagoras described by Diodorus Siculus (14.98.1–2), I would suggest that other and more complex possibilities cannot be excluded.

Two such possibilities are suggested by the inscription's repeated emphasis on "all the people of Kition" (lines 1, 3, 4). Firstly, a hermeneutic of suspicion might focus on the repeated (and unparalleled) repetition of *kl* "all" and entertain the possibility that "our enemies" are actually internal, either rebels or rivals for the throne of Kition that has been claimed by Milkyaton. Both the vagueness of "our enemies" and the repeated insistence on "*all* the people" would then be intentional, designed to preserve an illusion of unanimity within Kition itself. Alternatively, a less suspicious interpretation might rather note that, while "all the people of *Kition*" are said to have fought under Milkyaton's command, no such claim is made for the citizenry of Idalion, despite Milkyaton's kingship over both cities (lines 1, 2). Did Idalion, having been controlled by kings of Kition since the middle of the fifth century B.C.E., hope to shake off the yoke of Kition and exchange it for a more favorable position under Evagoras? In either of these scenarios, Evagoras might well have been responsible for the presence of the Paphian allies, but not actually a participant in the battle, nor included among the "enemies" defeated therein.

I would obviously not insist on the historical accuracy of either of these hypotheses. I raise them simply to demonstrate the need to face up to uncertainty when it exists rather than seek solace in a factoid, however comforting it may be in the short term. We cannot exclude the possibility that Evagoras and his army were intended by the phrase "our enemies" (whatever the reason for its vagueness), but neither can we present it as fact.

The Accession of Milkyaton

The third and last factoid can be treated more briefly, since it is less widespread than the two preceding. In the *editio princeps*, Sznycer suggested that it was "pas impossible" that the victory recorded in our inscription played a role in Milkyaton's accession to the throne (Yon and Sznycer 1991:820). Briant transformed Sznycer's "not impossible" into a certainty, considering it "tout à fait notable que c'est à l'issue de cette victoire que Milkyatôn prit le titre royal" (1996:666; ET 2002:647). Briant's endorsement was apparently sufficient for Sznycer to abandon his original reticence and to declare unreservedly that Milkyaton's installation as king was a consequence of the military victory celebrated in the Trophy Inscription (2001:103 and 104). In fact, of course, we have no way of knowing whether Milkyaton's accession to the throne preceded (or even precipitated) the battle, or whether his victory in battle paved the way for his installation. The wording of the inscription precludes neither possibility.

Having examined three factoids that have arisen since the discovery and decipherment of the Trophy Inscription, we are in a better position to address a more fundamental concern, namely, the historical significance of the inscription. I would argue that, despite the sometimes extravagant claims made on its behalf, our inscription in fact is not only consistent with what we already knew (or suspected) from Milkyaton's other inscriptions and from the narrative of Diodorus, but also that it adds little that is both new and unambiguous to our knowledge of the political and military history of Cyprus in the early fourth century B.C.E.

To begin with, the details surrounding Milkyaton's accession to the throne remain as murky as ever. Milkyaton's predecessor seems to have been Baᶜalrom, a king known only from his coinage (Peckham 1968:18). (As has often been noted, he is not to be equated with Milkyaton's father, Baᶜalrom, since the latter is never identified as "king of Kition and Idalion.") King Baᶜalrom was and remains simply a name. We still know nothing of his reign or his fate. Did he die a natural death without an heir? Was he assassinated by a pro- or anti-Evagoran party, or for some unrelated reason? Was Milkyaton an assassin and usurper, or a distant kinsman of Baᶜalrom, or a general chosen to succeed him? Although it has long been clear that Milkyaton founded a new dynasty, the Trophy Inscription regrettably does nothing to relieve our ignorance regarding the circumstances of the transition.

As for the battle and victory, the inscription only confirms what could already have been intuited from Diodorus Siculus's account and from epigraphic evidence. We knew from Diodorus (14.98.2) that Kition, in or shortly before 391 B.C.E., offered armed resistance (ἀντέχοντες τῷ πολέμῳ) to Evagoras's attempt to gain mastery of Cyprus; and *CIS* I 90 (= *KAI* 38) already made mention of Milkyaton's second year as king of Kition and Idalion. The former implies that Milkyaton waged war against forces loyal to Evagoras; the latter implies that he was victorious and thus able to retain control of his kingdom. The Trophy Inscription thus serves to confirm both battle and victory, but it adds little new aside from the presence of the Paphian allies and, of course, the name of the month in which the battle took place.

If we turn from *l'histoire événementielle* to *la longue durée*, we learn a bit more about the religious and cultural history of Kition. On the religious side, we are introduced to Baᶜal ᶜOz, the "Master of Might," a new deity, or perhaps a new divine title for an already known deity (so Xella 1993:67: "une manifestation particulière de Rašap-MKL"). And on the cultural side, we find the Phoenicians of Kition adopting the Greek practice of erecting a trophy following victory in battle and borrowing the Greek term τρόπαιον to memorialize it. This latter information seems to me especially important, since it furnishes an additional piece of evidence in support of Maier's thesis that "policies in Cyprus were dictated by the material interests of the kingdoms rather than by ideological motives" (1985:39). Just as the ambitions of Evagoras were resisted by Phoenician Kition, Greek Soloi, and Eteocypriot Amathous, so, too, did the Cypro-Phoenicians of Kition celebrate their victory over Cypro-Greeks (and possibly other Cypro-Phoenicians) with a Greek trophy. The alliances and conflicts of early fourth-century Cyprus were determined by self-interest far more than by ethnic or linguistic loyalties.

All this is not to deny that the Trophy Inscription has contributed greatly to our knowledge, but these contributions lie primarily in the areas of epigraphy, grammar, and lexicography. In the historical sphere, and especially in the arena of political and military history, the lines of Robert Frost aptly summarize the inscription's value:

> It gives us strangely little aid,
> But does tell something in the end.

Bibliography

Bailey, D. M.
1969–70 The Village Priest's Tomb at Aradippou in Cyprus. *British Museum Quarterly* 34:36–58, pls. 15–19.

Briant, P.
1996 *Histoire de l'empire perse de Cyrus à Alexandre.* Paris: Fayard.
2002 *From Cyrus to Alexander: A History of the Persian Empire.* Translated by P. T. Daniels. Winona Lake, Ind.: Eisenbrauns.

Elayi, J., and J. Sapin
2000 *Quinze ans de recherche (1985–2000) sur la* Transeuphratène *à l'époque perse.* Supplément à Transeuphratène 8. Paris: Gabalda.

Guzzo Amadasi, M. G., and V. Karageorghis
1977 *Fouilles de Kition.* Vol. 3, *Inscriptions phéniciennes.* Nicosia: Department of Antiquities of Cyprus.

Karageorghis, V.
1995 Cyprus and the Phoenicians: Achievements and Perspectives. In *I Fenici: ieri oggi domani; Ricerche, scoperte, progetti (Roma 3–5 marzo 1994)*, 327–34. Rome: Accademia Nazionale dei Lincei and Consiglio Nazionale delle Ricerche.

Krahmalkov, C. R.
2000 *Phoenician-Punic Dictionary.* OLA 90. Studia Phoenicia 15. Leuven: Peeters.

Lipiński, E.
2004 *Itineraria Phoenicia.* OLA 127. Studia Phoenicia 18. Leuven: Peeters.

Maier, F. G.
1985 Factoids in Ancient History: The Case of Fifth-Century Cyprus. *JHS* 105:32–39.

Mosca, P. G.
2006 Some Grammatical and Structural Observations on the Trophy Inscription from Kition (Cyprus). *Maarav* 13:175–92.

Peckham, J. B.
1968 *The Development of the Late Phoenician Scripts.* HSS 20. Cambridge: Harvard University Press.

Sznycer, M.
2000 Nouvelles précisions et réflexions à propos de l'inscription phénicienne, récemment publiée, de Milkyatôn, roi de Kition et Idalion. In *Philokypros: Mélanges de philologie et d'antiquités grecques et proche-orientales dédiés à la mémoire d'Olivier Masson*, ed. L. Dubois and E. Masson, 285–92. Suplementos a Minos 16. Salamanca: Universidad de Salamanca.
2001 À propos du "trophée" dans l'inscription phénicienne de Milkyatôn, roi de Kition et d'Idalion. In *Punica—Libyca—Ptolemaica: Festschrift für Werner Huß zum 65. Geburtstag dargebracht von Schülern, Freunden und Kollegen*, ed. K. Geus and K. Zimmermann, 99–110. OLA 104. Studia Phoenicia 16. Leuven: Peeters.

Xella, P.
1993 Le dieu *Bᶜ L ᶜZ* dans une nouvelle inscription phénicienne de Kition (Chypre). *SEL* 10:61–69.

Yon, M.
1995 Le royaume maritime de Kition: Travaux 1988–1991. In *Actes du IIIᵉ Congrès International des études phéniciennes et puniques: Tunis, 11–16 novembre 1991*, ed. M. H. Fanṭar and Mansour Ghaki, 2:449–57. Tunis: Institut National du Patrimoine.
1996 Les derniers rois phéniciens de Kition: État des recherches. In *Alle soglie della classicità: Il Mediterraneo tra tradizione e innovazione; Studi in onore di Sabatino Moscati*, ed. E. Acquaro, 1:441–50. Pisa: Istituti Editoriali e Poligrafici Internazionali.
1997 Kition in the Tenth to Fourth Centuries B.C. Translated by W. A. P. Childs. *BASOR* 308:9–17.
2004 *Kition dans les textes:* Testimonia *littéraires et épigraphiques et* Corpus *des inscriptions.* Kition-Bamboula 5. Paris: Éditions Recherche sur les civilisations.

Yon, M., and M. Sznycer
1991 Une inscription phénicienne royale de Kition (Chypre). *CRAIBL* 1991:791–823.
1992 A Phoenician Victory Trophy at Kition. *Report of the Department of Antiquities of Cyprus* 1992: 157–66, pl. 51.

36. ASHKELON UNDER THE ASSYRIAN EMPIRE

by Nadav Na'aman

THERE were three city-states on the coast of Philistia in the first half of the first millennium B.C.E.: Ashdod, Ashkelon and Gaza. The boundaries that separated them followed natural geographical lines and may be delineated with relative certainty: Naḥal Evtaḥ (Wādi Ibtaḥ) separated the kingdom of Ashdod from Ashkelon, and Naḥal Shiqma (Wādi el-Ḥesi) divided the territory of Ashkelon from that of Gaza. The natural southern boundary of the kingdom of Gaza is Naḥal Besor (Wādi Ghazzeh), and that of the kingdom of Ashdod on the north is Naḥal Sorek (Nahr Rubin). Given this delineation, the coast of Ashdod would have stretched over some 23 km, that of Ashkelon over some 18 km, and that of Gaza over about 20 km.

On the east, the boundaries of the three kingdoms in the eleventh to ninth centuries B.C.E. reached the western borders of the kingdom of Gath (see the drawing of schematic boundaries in Finkelstein 1996: 230). Following Hazael's conquest of Gath (Tell eṣ-Ṣāfi) in the late ninth century (2 Kings 12:18), Ashdod expanded eastwards and annexed the city of Gath and part of its territory.[1] Ashkelon and Gaza also no doubt took advantage of the fall of Gath to expand eastwards, up to the western border of the kingdom of Judah. But where should we draw the boundary? Gophna (1981) conducted a survey along Naḥal Shiqma and noted that there is a gap of settlements west of Tell el-Ḥesi. He suggested that this gap represents the boundary separating Ashkelon and Gaza from Judah. However, it is unlikely that following the disintegration of the kingdom of Gath, only Ashdod expanded eastwards, east of Tell eṣ-Ṣāfi (Gath), while the boundaries of its southern neighbors remained unchanged. I therefore suggest that the gap of settlements noted by Gophna marks the former boundary between the kingdom of Gath and its western neighbours, Ashkelon and Gaza.

The detailed survey conducted by Dagan (2000: 200–17, 257–66; 2004:2680–84) in the Shephelah corroborates these conclusions. Dagan drew the western border of the kingdom of Judah along the Tell eṣ-Sāfi–Tel ᶜErani–Tell Umm el-Baqar line. In light of this, we may draw the eastern boundary of the kingdom of Ashkelon along the Tel Nagila–Tel Qeshet (Tell el-Quneitira)–Tel ᶜErani (Tell esh-Sheikh Ahmed el-ᶜAreini) line (compare the map in Blakely and Hardin 2002:15).[2] The attribution of sites located near the border to either Judah or Ashkelon remains uncertain. In view of this, the estimated area of the kingdom of Ashkelon in the eighth–seventh centuries is about 400–450 square kilometers.

In the Late Bronze Age, Jaffa was an Egyptian center that was destroyed after the Egyptian withdrawal from Canaan in the mid-twelfth century B.C.E. There is no textual evidence on the affiliation of the Yarkon–Ayyalon Basin, including the city of Jaffa, in Iron Age I, so its attribution can be tentatively based on the archaeological evidence (for detailed discussion, see recently Gadot 2006). Given the prominent place of Ekron in the northern Shephelah in Iron Age I, I tend to assign this whole area to it (for different interpretations, see Tadmor 1960:54; 1966:87 n. 2; Singer 1994:308; Finkelstein 1996:228–31). Following the destruction of Ekron in the mid-tenth century, the area of Jaffa passed either to Ashdod, its southern neighbor, or to Ashkelon. We know for certain that in the late eighth century the city and its hinterland were possessed by Ashkelon, and were conquered and destroyed by Sennacherib in his 701 B.C.E. campaign. It is evident that in the Late Bronze and Iron Ages, Jaffa and its hinterland changed hands many times and was never an independent city.

Larry Stager (1996a:62) estimated that about 10,000–12,000 people lived in the city of Ashkelon in the late seventh century. In view of the modest size of the kingdom of Ashkelon, the population growth and the prosperity of the city are explained by its involvement in local and international commerce during the eighth and seventh centuries. The evidence of Ashkelon's prosperity and its international commercial connections was recently discussed in detail and need not be repeated here (Stager 1996a; 1996b; 2006; Waldbaum 2002; Master 2003; Weiss and Kislev 2004; Faust and Weiss 2005). It remains to be

---

[1] In the late eighth century, Gath was a secondary town in the kingdom of Ashdod that was conquered and possibly destroyed by Sargon II in his 711 B.C.E. campaign. For textual references to Gath (Gimtu), see Fuchs 1994:134, lines 250–51; p. 220, lines 104–5.

[2] This line of "cone tells" that runs from Tel ᶜErani to Tel Qeshet and Tel Milḥa (Tell Muleiḥah) was already noted by Wright (1971:81–86). However, he suggested that it formed the line of defense of the city-state of Lachish in the Late Bronze Age, a suggestion that is not supported by the excavations and surveys of these sites.

seen whether the prominent place of Ashkelon in commerce and the wealth accumulated in its treasury find similar expression in the documentary evidence.

Ashkelon in the Neo-Assyrian Sources

From the second half of the eighth century, Ashkelon was mentioned as a royal Philistine city in several biblical prophecies, side by side with Gaza, Ashdod, and Ekron (Jer. 25:20; Amos 1:6–8; Zeph. 2:4; Zech. 9:5–6). But other than mentioning its name, biblical sources offer no concrete data about Ashkelon under the Assyrian empire. For its history and political position, we must analyze the Assyrian documents.

Tiglath-pileser III

Ashkelon is first mentioned in two badly broken passages of Tiglath-pileser III's royal annals (Ann. 18 and 24; see Tadmor 1994:80–83) and two broken passages in his summary inscriptions (Summ. 8 line 19 and Summ. 9 rev. line 12; see Tadmor 1994:178, note on line 19; 181). The latter passages appear either before the Gaza episode or immediately after it, and since no other western kingdom is missing from the kingdoms listed there, their attribution to Ashkelon is quite certain.

The preserved texts of the two summary inscriptions are identical and run as follows: "[.....] x+100 talents of silver I removed (*assuhamma*) and [carried/brought] to Assyria." The use of the verb *nasāhu* probably indicates that the broken booty list included people as well as silver (compare Summ. 8 lines 15–16).

In his drawings of the Nimrud reliefs, Layard (1851:pls. 72b+73a; also 29b) copied two annal slabs that mention Ashkelon. Tadmor published the slabs separately (1994:80–83, pls.15 and 23), each in its own right. The annal fragments 18 and 24, which describe the struggle with Samsi, queen of the Arabs, the campaign against Israel, and the submission of Ashkelon, refer to events that took place in 733 B.C.E. (Tadmor 1994:220–21, 235). Since I have already discussed the fragmented annals in detail (Naʾaman 1998:219–23), I offer here only the tentative translation of the combined texts of the two slabs:

> Mitinti of Ashkelon [broke] the loyalty oath [of the great gods], revo[lted] against me [and joined[?] with my enemy[?]. The defeat of Re]zin he saw and in an attack of [insanity . . . He was stricken] with panic, [. . . and died].
>
> Rukibtu, [his[?]] son, sat on his throne. To [the city of GN . . . in front of me] he wandered around and implored me. 500 [talents of silver he brought and kissed my feet. I restored[?] him to his place[?]] and he entered his city. Fifteen town[s located[?] in the ... I entrusted[???] in his[???] hands[???]].

The restorations, uncertain as they are, may help us understand the Ashkelon episode. Mitinti of Ashkelon joined the anti-Assyrian coalition headed by Rezin of Damascus, comprising at least Israel, Tyre, Samsi, and Gaza. We may safely assume that Egypt was actively involved in the negotiation, and that Rezin hoped for Egyptian military aid (Begrich 1929: 218; Alt 1953:157–61). The preparation for the revolt must have started ca. 736 (Begrich 1929; Naʾaman 1991:91–94, with earlier literature). The Assyrian campaign of 734 to the Brook of Egypt (*Nahal Muṣur* = Naḥal Besor), on the southern border of Gaza, meant to block the possible approach of an Egyptian taskforce to Philistia, took the coalition by surprise (Naʾaman 1991:92–93). Hanunu of Gaza fled to Egypt, only to return and become an Assyrian vassal (Tadmor 1994:222–25; Ehrlich 1996:94–98; Uehlinger 2002:92–125). Mitinti must have paid his tribute to Assyria at that time, as indicated by the list of tribute-bearers of the year 734 B.C.E. (for the date of the list in Summ. 7 rev. 7–13, see Tadmor 1994:268).

Shortly afterward, Mitinti was killed by a *coup d'état* initiated by Rukibtu, possibly his son. In order to justify Tiglath-pileser's recognition of the rebel as a legitimate king in Ashkelon, the author of the annals described the disloyalty of the former king (Mitinti) and how he died stricken by panic and madness. He further described how the new king (Rukibtu) wandered around, seeking to be recognized as an Assyrian vassal, and how the Assyrian king finally installed him on the throne of Ashkelon, but not before he paid a heavy tribute of 500 talents of silver (Ephʿal 1982:25). Tadmor (1994:276) has demonstrated that a series of newly-installed kings, among them Hoshea of Israel, paid Tiglath-pileser huge sums in exchange for recognizing their rule. Rukibtu is another example of a ruler who paid a heavy tribute in order to be officially recognized by his overlord.

The restoration of the end of the Ashkelon episode (lines 12–13) is guesswork (for criticism, see Wazana 2003:113–14). The basis for my restoration is the appearance of an Ashkelonite enclave east of Jaffa (namely, Jaffa, Beth-dagan, Bene-berak, and Azor), in the time of Sennacherib's campaign to Palestine (Luckenbill 1924:31 lines 68–72). No reasonable explanation has been offered for the status of the king of Ashkelon in the Jaffa area, so far north of his kingdom. The transfer of a territory to a king who rebelled against Assyria has an exact parallel in Sennacherib's campaign to Palestine, when the Assyrian king transferred parts of the territory of Judah to the rebellious kings of Philistia (Luckenbill 1924:33, lines 30b–34; p. 70, lines 29b–30a). If this highly tentative suggestion is correct, it could explain Rukibtu's loyalty to Assyria in the time of Sargon II, when all the other Philistine kingdoms rebelled against the empire.

Sargon II

Upon the accession of Sargon II to the Assyrian throne in 721 B.C.E., rebellions broke out in many parts of the empire. In the year 720 Sargon crushed the rebellion in the west and conquered the Philistine cities of Gaza and Ekron (El-Amin 1953:35–39, 214–28; Reade 1976:99–102; Fuchs 1994:90, lines 53–57; pp. 197–98, lines 25-26; Uehlinger 1998:744–71). In the following years, Philistia was firmly under the rule of Assyria.

Of all the western vassal kingdoms only the envoys of Ashkelon are not mentioned in texts from the reign of Sargon II that relate the arrival of envoys (*ṣīrāni*) bringing tribute to the Assyrian court. However, at least one text, and probably two, relates in detail the tribute and gifts delivered by the king of Ashkelon.

An Assyrian administrative document from Calah (ND 2672) describes the tribute sent by the ruler of Ashkelon. Here is a translation of the first part of the delivery (Postgate 1974:387–88, lines 1–16):

> 2 talents of silver, tribute; 40 minas of silver, instead of [ivory?]; 1 talent of silver, deficit of last year, in all, 3 talents 40 minas. 20 linen cloths, 50 multicoloured cloths, in all 70 . . . cloths; 8 male horses, 3 potful of iced fish; 1,000 fish in 20 containers. All this is tribute (*madattu*). 4 selected multicoloured cloths made to measure, 3? male 12 female horses, 1 one-year-old, in all 16 [horses]. (All this is) audience gift (*nāmurtu*).

The tribute was delivered to Adda-hati, governor of the province of Hamath, in the reign of Sargon II (Postgate 1974:382 n. 2).[3] In additions to horses, it included silver, fine cloth, and containers of special kinds of fish. The dispatch included 45 male and female horses. A small group of nine horses is described in detail ("1 bay mare, with ears intact; 2 bay mares . . . ears cut, nostrils intact; 1 black mare, her ears cut, her nostrils intact"); they were probably delivered to the Assyrian king and/or high officials. The horses must have been of the breed known in the Assyrian documents as *māt Kūsayu*, i.e., "Cushite" (Postgate 1974:11).

In a letter from Nineveh (ABL 568), Sennacherib, the crown prince, informs his father, Sargon II, about the contributions received from two cities and their distribution among dignitaries of the royal Assyrian court (Martin 1936:40–49; Postgate 1984:111, 283–84; Parpola 1987:35–36, no. 34). The list of contributions is closely related to that recorded in tablet ND 2672 (see above). In view of the many similarities between the two tablets, in particular the deliveries of fish, the latter contributions were also sent by two Philistine coastal cities, apparently Gaza and Ashkelon.

Rev. line 1 was first read [...] *ma-da-tú* *mA-zu-r*[*i* ...] ("[...] the tribute of Azur[i ...]"), and scholars have suggested that it was sent by Azuri, king of Ashdod. However, Parpola (1987:35, rev. line 1; 255), who collated the tablet, has demonstrated that the reading is erroneous. In the light of his collation, the line may tentatively be restored [PAP *an-ni*]-⸢*ú* *ma-da-tú*⸣ *mA-ta*-[....]; "[All thi]s (is) tribute. Ata[.... sent/received (it)]." Whether Ata[...] was the ruler of Gaza in the time of Sargon II or the official who received the dispatch remains unknown.

According to this analysis, two rich deliveries of tribute and gifts were sent from Ashkelon to the Assyrian king. Whether they were the annual tribute or tribute sent on a special occasion cannot be determined due to the fragmentary state of the documentation.

Elat (1978:30–32) has analyzed the artifacts mentioned in the two tablets and shown that some of them were brought from Egypt. He therefore concluded that the Philistine cities acted as mediators, transmitting Egyptian goods to Assyria. We may assume that the Philistine rulers were directed to buy certain objects and the amounts they paid for these objects were deducted from their tribute. Of particular importance to Assyria were the Cushite horses, which were big and capable of drawing chariots (Dalley 1985:43–48; Heidron 1997). Large numbers of them are mentioned in the Assyrian records and the Philistine kingdoms must have been an important channel through which the horses were brought to Assyria.

In view of the "Egyptian connection," it is impossible to draw any conclusion from the lists of tribute and gifts about the kind of products made in Ashkelon. Nevertheless, one interesting conclusion can be drawn: wine and oil are not mentioned in the tributes of Ashkelon, Ekron (see Naʾaman 2003), and Gaza (see Naʾaman 2004). This is remarkable, given the great emphasis laid by scholars on the production

[3] For references to his correspondence, see Parpola 1987: 233 s.v. Adda-hati.

of oil at Ekron (Gitin 1995; 1997) and wine at Ashkelon (Stager 1996a:64*–67*; Faust and Weiss 2005). Indeed, only a very small number of late eighth–seventh century Palestinian vessels have been discovered in northern Mesopotamia. In the present state of research, there is no evidence that jars of wine and jugs of oil were sent from Philistia to Assyria. Master (2003:56) noted that Ashkelon imported nothing from near or far Assyrian provinces, and concluded that "were it not the overwhelming textual evidence demonstrating the dominance of Assyrian military power, there would be little if any evidence that a Mesopotamian empire was in control of the region of Philistia." The markets for the vast quantities of oil and wine produced in Philistia and exported to foreign countries are yet to be discovered in the archaeological research (for current evidence, see Negueruela et al. 1995; Maeir 2002; Master 2003:57–60).

Ashkelon is also mentioned in an Assyrian account of the additions and losses of mules, donkeys, and oxen written in the year 707 B.C.E. (Postgate 1987: 376–78). In the section of losses appears "1 (ass?)—ᶜAbdi-El, 'third man on chariot' (*tašlīšu*) of Ashkelon, chief eunuch, a messenger" (line 20). All the persons mentioned in the list were citizens of Assyria. ᶜAbdi-El has a West Semitic name and was probably an Ashkelonite deportee who served as a "third man on chariot" under the chief eunuch (for the integration of western deportees in the Assyrian chariotry, see Dalley 1985:31–43).

According to the Nineveh Prism of Sargon, in the year 712 Ashdod rebelled and tried in vain to induce some Assyrian vassals (the kings of Philistia, Judah, Edom, and Moab) to join the rebellion (Oppenheim 1969:287; Fuchs 1998:46, lines 25–28). The designation "kings of Philistia" (*šarrāni māt Pilište*) refers to the three kingdoms of Gaza, Ashkelon, and Ekron, described in the prism as "payers of tribute and gifts to Ashur, my lord," that is, loyal Assyrian vassals. In the next year (711), Sargon conquered Ashdod and its cities, deported part of its population and turned the kingdom into an Assyrian province (Fuchs 1994:76, lines 11–13; pp. 134–35, lines 250–54; pp. 220–21, lines 104–9). A governor of Ashdod was nominated eponym (*līmu*) in the year 669 B.C.E., thereby proving that the kingdom was indeed annexed by Assyria (Millard 1994:52, 61; see Alt 1945:145–46).

Unequivocal evidence of the annexation of Ashdod was discovered in a salvage excavation conducted recently near Tel Ashdod (Kogan-Zehavi 2005). A large public building standing on a square mudbrick podium was unearthed, and its size, plan, architecture, and artifacts all indicate that this was the palace of the Assyrian governor established at Ashdod. The exact date of the building is yet to be determined, but it could well have been built in the time of Sargon. Other Assyrian centers were built at Tell el-Ḥesi (Engstrom 2004, with earlier literature) and Khirbet Hoga (Naʾaman 1979:81), near the border of Ashkelon. It is evident that Sargon's conquest and annexation of Ashdod and the building of Assyrian centers on its southern border seriously damaged Ashkelon's independence. The place of the kingdom of Ashdod was taken over by a terrifying major power, whose objectives on the border of Egypt and intentions *vis-à-vis* Ashkelon were unpredictable. This might well explain the rebellion of Ashkelon following Sargon's death on the battlefield in 705 B.C.E.

Sennacherib

Sennacherib's western campaign and the suppression of the rebellion of Ashkelon have been discussed innumerable times (Tadmor 1966:95–97; Barnett 1985; Gallagher 1999:113–28, with earlier literature; Uehlinger 2003:297–302), and will be examined briefly.

An analysis of the annals indicates that Sharru-lū-dāri, king of Ashkelon, was replaced before the Assyrian campaign by Ṣidqa, probably his brother. Sharru-lū-dāri was the son of Rukibtu (Marcus 1977: 27–30)—his name may indicate that he was brought to Assyria as a hostage in the time of Tiglath-pileser and upon his father's death was brought back and took his father's place. He must have opposed the rebellion and was replaced by Ṣidqa, who supported the rebels.

According to Sennacherib's annals, he first conquered the Ashkelonite enclave at Jaffa, which was surrounded by Assyrian territories on all sides except the west. Following his victory over the Egyptian task force at Eltekeh, Sennacherib took Ekron after a short siege. Ashkelon surrendered about the same time, thereby avoiding siege and destruction. Sennacherib deported the rebellious king (Ṣidqa), some members of his family, and "the gods of his father's house" (Oppenheim 1969:287b). Sharru-lū-dāri was restored to the throne of Ashkelon and paid Assyria the yearly tribute.

In the course of his campaign, Sennacherib refrained from destroying the rebellious cities of Philistia and was content to replace the rebel rulers by others loyal to Assyria, receiving their loyalty oaths and tribute. That is why, except for the Ashkelonite Jaffa enclave, other Philistine cities were not badly damaged by the Assyrian campaign. Sennacherib even transferred western districts of Judah to the four Philistine kingdoms. Thus he created a kind of border zone on the Assyrian-Egyptian frontier that was governed by rulers loyal to Assyria. Whether he actually had a tacit agreement with the Cushite kings remains unknown; the twenty years of peace on the southwestern front of the Assyrian empire indicate the success of his campaign and policy.

What happened to Jaffa after its conquest is not clear. In a previous article I suggested that, after suppressing the rebellion, Sennacherib transferred the area of Jaffa to Padi, king of Ekron (Naᵓaman 1998: 223–25). However, it is better to assume that most of the Jaffa enclave, which from the early years of Sargon was surrounded on three sides by Assyrian territories, was annexed to the province of Samaria, while the coast of Jaffa was transferred to the province of Dor. The annexation of Jaffa to Dor may explain the Persian king's handing over of the territories of Dor and Jaffa in the mid-fifth century to Eshmunazer, king of Sidon (see *KAI* 14:18).

Esarhaddon and Ashurbanipal

The conflict between Assyria and Egypt resumed in the early days of Esarhaddon (680–669). In 679, the new Assyrian ruler undertook a campaign to Philistia, in the course of which he plundered Arza, possibly Tell Jemmeh, located on Naḥal Besor (*Nahal Muṣur*) southeast of Gaza, and took captive its king, Asuhilli, with his officials.

What was the background of the campaign to Philistia in Esarhaddon's second year? Two queries to the sun-god Shamash are important for the discussion. Let me first cite the relevant passages from the two queries (Starr 1990:94, lines 1–4a, 10–14; p. 97, rev. lines 1b–9a):

1. [Shamash] great lord, [give me a firm positive answer] to what I [am asking you]!

   [From] this day, the second day [of this month, the month . . . of this year, to] the 21st day of Sivan [of this year, . . . days and nights, my stipulated term—within] this stipulated term, should the [subject] of this query, [Esarhaddon, king of Assyria .... take the road] and go to Trans-Euph]rates ([*ēbir-nā*]*ri*), to the city Ashkel[on? If he ta]kes the road and goes, will the subject of [this] q[uery], Esarhaddon, king of Assyria, rea[ch Trans-Euphrates] (and) the city Ashkelon in good health? Will he return alive [from the city of Ashkelon] and enter [his palace in Nineveh]?

2. [I ask you Shamash, great lord], whether Esarhad[don, king of] Assyria, [should plan, and] go [with] men, horses, and [an army as great as he wishes], to the city of Ashkelon, (whether) as long as [he stays] and sets up camp in the dis[trict of Ashkelon], [the Cushite?? troops], or the Egyptian troops, [or the . . . troops will come t]o wage war [against Esarhaddon, king of Assyria, and (whether) they will fight] against each other.

There is no agreement among scholars about the date of these queries. Hirschberg (1932:61–69) dated them to 671 B.C.E., before Esarhaddon's conquest of Egypt, and Spalinger (1974:301–2) arrived at the same date. Tadmor (1966:99–100; 1983:41–42) dated them to before Esarhaddon's ill-fated campaign to conquer Egypt in 674 B.C.E. Ephᶜal (1982:52–54; 1983:98–99) attributed the queries to the campaign against Arza. But he dismissed the date assigned to the Arza campaign in the Esarhaddon and Babylonian chronicles (in the king's second year), and on the basis of Esarhaddon's inscriptions, dated the campaign after the conquest of Sidon in 677 B.C.E. However, the order of the campaigns in Esarhaddon's inscriptions is geographical and is influenced by ideological considerations (see recently Tadmor 2004:270–72); the chronicles are much better sources for dating the campaigns. Indeed, Kahn (2004:110), who adopted Ephᶜal's arguments for assigning the queries to Esarhaddon's campaign against Arza, dated them to 679 B.C.E.

The 679 dating of the queries agrees well with all the available evidence. First, the "city/district of Ashkelon" is referred to in the two queries, whereas Egypt and probably Cush are mentioned only in the context of sending troops to support the rebellion. Of all the western campaigns of Esarhaddon, only the 679 campaign was directed to the Egyptian border zone; all the other campaigns were aimed either against Sidon or against Egypt. Second, a fragmented query mentions "[Sharru-lū-dāri s]on of Rukibtu." Sharru-lū-dāri was replaced by Mitinti, and the query should be dated to before his replacement. Mitinti is included among the unnamed "twenty-two kings of the land of Hatti (and) of the coast and the islands" summoned in the year 676 by Esarhaddon to perform work at Nineveh (Heidel 1956:28, iv 54–v 12). His participation in the work is proved by the mention of his name among the twenty-two kings enumerated in Esarhaddon's Nineveh Prism (Borger 1967:60, lines 54–72). It is evident that Mitinti replaced Sharru-lū-dāri no later than 676 B.C.E. The only known campaign to the area of Ashkelon prior to 676 is that of 679, and this is the most likely date for the two queries in which Ashkelon is mentioned.

What might have been the background of the campaign against Ashkelon that caused so much concern in the Assyrian court? The most reasonable explanation is a Cushite campaign to Philistia, following the murder of Sennacherib in 681 B.C.E. and the civil war that broke out between Esarhaddon and his brothers. From the time of Tiglath-pileser III, revolts broke out in some part of the empire after the death of each Assyrian king, and the revolt in 681 was no exception.

Various artifacts of Asiatic origin are mentioned in Taharqa's stelae of his eighth (683 B.C.E.) and tenth (681 B.C.E.) years, but these artifacts were probably brought by commerce rather than war (Kahn 2004: 110). Cushite messengers and/or troops probably arrived on the Philistine coast in 681/680, and Sharru-lū-dāri, king of Ashkelon, trusted the Cushite support and rebelled against Assyria. The Assyrian reaction was immediate. Soon after Esarhaddon was firmly on the throne, he conducted a campaign to the Egyptian border. The queries to the sun-god reflect his apprehension concerning a possible clash with Egyptian-Cushite troops, as happened in Sargon's campaign of 720 B.C.E. and Sennacherib's campaign of 701. But the Egyptian-Cushite troops probably did not arrive to help the rebels. Esarhaddon successfully quelled the rebellion and replaced Sharru-lū-dāri by Mitinti. The latter was the son of Ṣidqa, who was deported by Sennacherib to Assyria, and after he grew up in the Assyrian court, was brought back to Ashkelon and placed on its throne (Tadmor 1966:98–99; Avigad and Sass 1997:399–400). The policy of installing on thrones of vassal kingdoms princes who had been educated in Assyria could well have been implemented in many other cases, but in most cases our sources do not reveal it.

Vernus (1975:1–72) published an inscription of Taharqa in which the Cushite king piously addressed Amun, his god, about misfortunes that befell him in Egypt and elsewhere. Among these mishaps he mentions the loss of the tribute (*inw*) of the land of Kharu. Vernus (1975:45–46) dated the inscription to about 677/6–674/3, and Spalinger (1978:43) dated it to 675 B.C.E. However, Kahn (2004) recently demonstrated that the inscription was written after the Assyrian invasion of Egypt and the conquest of Memphis in 671 B.C.E. The tribute (*inw*) mentioned in the inscription was probably special gifts dispatched to Taharqa by Asiatic rulers, possibly after the Cushite victory over Assyrian troops in Esarhaddon's seventh year (674/3). Following his success in battle, Taharqa probably renewed his efforts to form an anti-Assyrian alliance in the Assyrian territories. His involvement in the affairs of Philistia in these years (681–673 B.C.E.) is possibly echoed in the anachronistic reference to his arrival to fight Sennacherib in 2 Kings 18:9a. However, it is an exaggeration to assume effective Cushite control in Philistia and the Phoenician coast or the formation of an anti-Assyrian alliance (Hirschberg 1932:61–72; Kahn 2004:110–12). Taharqa's partial hold in Asia was temporary and he did not succeed in forming an operative anti-Assyrian alliance. When Esarhaddon conducted his campaign to the west, he easily crushed the rebellions and regained control over the Assyrian territories.

In his Nahr el-Kalb stele, Esarhaddon relates his 671 B.C.E. victory over Taharqa, his entrance to Memphis, and the enormous booty that he seized and brought to Assyria (Borger 1967:101–2). After the list of captives, he mentions Ashkelon, Taharqa, and Tyre in a badly broken context (". . . Ashkelon [. . . .] which Taharqa [. . . .] to their fortresses [. . . .] Tyre [. . . .]"). This text might refer to events that took place shortly before the Egyptian campaign of 671, but in its present state it is too broken to allow us to draw conclusions.

Mitinti, king of Ashkelon, took part in Ashurbanipal's campaign to Egypt in 667 B.C.E. (Oppenheim 1969:294), and this is the latest reference to the city in the Assyrian sources. Neither Ashkelon nor the other Philistine kingdoms are mentioned in the latter years of Ashurbanipal. The only evidence that we have for Ashkelon in the late years of the Assyrian empire and the period of Egyptian control of Philistia comes from the archaeological excavations of the city. They indicate its great prosperity in the second half of the seventh century, on the eve of the destructive Babylonian campaign of 604 B.C.E.

I opened this paper by emphasizing the relatively small territory of Ashkelon. But territory is only one factor in the strength and economic power of kingdoms. Other factors, such as location, maritime and land routes and means of transportation, capital and internal organization, are no less important. Although its territorial extent was limited, Ashkelon took advantage of these elements and became one of the most important cities in Palestine in the first half of the first millennium B.C.E.

Bibliography

Alt, A.
1945 Neue assyrische Nachrichten über Palästina. *ZDPV* 67:128–59.
1953 Tiglathpilesers III. erster Feldzug nach Palästina. In *Kleine Schriften zur Geschichte des Volkes Israel*, by A. Alt, 2:150–62. Munich: Beck.

Avigad, N., and B. Sass
1997 *Corpus of West Semitic Stamp Seals*. Jerusalem: Israel Academy of Sciences and Humanities, Israel Exploration Society and Institute of Archaeology, Hebrew University of Jerusalem.

Barnett, R. D.
1985 Lachish, Ashkelon and the Camel: A Discussion of Its Use in Southern Palestine. In *Palestine in the Bronze and Iron Ages: Papers in Honour of Olga Tufnell*, ed. J. N. Tubb, 15–30. London: Institute of Archaeology, University of London.

Begrich, J.
1929 Der Syrisch-Ephraimitische Krieg und seine weltpolitischen Zusammenhänge. *ZDMG* 83: 213–37.

Blakely, J. A., and J. W. Hardin
2002 Southwestern Judah in the Late Eighth Century B.C.E. *BASOR* 326:11–64.

Borger, R.
1967 *Die Inschriften Asarhaddons, Königs von Assyrien*. Archiv für Orientforschung, Beiheft 9. Osnabrück: Biblio-Verlag.

Dagan, Y.
2000 The Settlement in the Judean Shephelah in the Second and First Millennium B.C.: A Test Case of Settlement Processes in a Geographical Region [in Hebrew]. Ph.D. diss., Tel Aviv University.
2004 Results of the Survey: Settlement Patterns in the Lachish Region. In *The Renewed Archaeological Excavations at Lachish (1973–1994)*, ed. D. Ussishkin, 5:2672–90. Tel Aviv: Institute of Archaeology, Tel Aviv University.

Dalley, S.
1985 Foreign Chariotry and Cavalry in the Armies of Tiglath-pileser III and Sargon II. *Iraq* 47:31–48.

Ehrlich, C. S.
1996 *The Philistines in Transition: A History from ca. 1000–730 B.C.E.* Leiden: Brill.

El-Amin, M.
1953 Die Reliefs mit Beischriften von Sargon II. in Dûr-Sharrukîn. *Sumer* 9:35–59, 214–228.

Elat, M.
1978 The Economic Relations of the Neo-Assyrian Empire with Egypt. *JAOS* 98:20–34.

Engstrom, C. M. A.
2004 The Neo-Assyrians at Tell el-Hesi: A Petrographic Study of Imitation Assyrian Palace Ware. *BASOR* 333:69–81.

Ephᶜal, I.
1982 *The Ancient Arabs: Nomads on the Borders of the Fertile Crescent 9th–5th Centuries B.C.* Jerusalem: Magnes.
1983 On Warfare and Military Control in the Ancient Near Eastern Empires: A Research Outline. In *History, Historiography and Iterpretation: Studies in Biblical and Cuneiform Literatures*, ed. H. Tadmor and M. Weinfeld, 88–106. Jerusalem: Magnes.

Faust, A., and E. Weiss
2005 Judah, Philistia, and the Mediterranean World: Reconstructing the Economic System of the Seventh Century B.C.E. *BASOR* 338:71–92.

Finkelstein, I.
1996 The Philistine Countryside. *IEJ* 46:225–42.

Fuchs, A.
1994 *Die Inschriften Sargons II. aus Khorsabad*. Göttingen: Cuvillier.
1998 *Die Annalen des Jahres 711 v. Chr. nach Prismenfragmenten aus Ninive und Assur*. State Archives of Assyria Studies 8. Helsinki: Neo-Assyrian Text Corpus Project.

Gadot, Y.
2006 Aphek in the Sharon and the Philistine Northern Frontier. *BASOR* 341:21–36.

Gallagher, W. R.
1999 *Sennacherib's Campaign to Judah—New Studies*. SHCANE 18. Leiden: Brill.

Gitin, S.
1995 Tel Miqne-Ekron in the Seventh Century B.C.E.: The Impact of Economic Innovation and Foreign Cultural Influences on a Neo-Assyrian Vassal City State. In *Recent Excavations in Israel: A View from the West*, ed. S. Gitin, 61–79. Archaeological Institute of America Colloquia and Conference Papers 1. Dubuque, Iowa: Kendall-Hunt.
1997 The Neo-Assyrian Empire and Its Western Periphery: The Levant, with a Focus on Philistine Ekron. In *Assyria 1995: Proceedings of the Tenth Anniversary Symposium of the Neo-Assyrian Text Corpus Project*, ed. S. Parpola and R. M. Whiting, 77–103. Helsinki: Neo-Assyrian Text Corpus Project.

Gophna, R.
1981 The Boundary between the Kingdoms of Judah, Ashkelon and Gaza in the Light of an Archaeo-

logical Survey in the Shiqma Valley [in Hebrew]. In *Proceedings of the Seventh World Congress of Jewish Studies: Studies in the Bible and the Ancient Near East*, 49–53. Jerusalem: Daf-Hen.

Heidron, L. A.
1997 The Horses of Kush. *JNES* 56:105–14.

Hirschberg, H.
1932 *Studien zur Geschichte Esarhaddons König von Assyrien (681–669)*. Ohlau in Schlesien: Hermann Eschenhagen.

Kahn, D.
2004 Taharqa, King of Kush and the Assyrians. *JSSEA* 31:109–28.

Kogan-Zehavi, E.
2005 An Assyrian Building South of Tel Ashdod [in Hebrew]. *Qadmoniot* 38:87–90.

Luckenbill, D. D.
1924 *The Annals of Sennacherib*. OIP 2. Chicago: University of Chicago Press.

Maeir, A. M.
2002 The Relations between Egypt and the Southern Levant during the Late Iron Age: The Material Evidence from Egypt. *Ägypten und Levant* 12: 235–46.

Marcus, D.
1977 Sharruludari, Son of Rukibtu, Their Former King: A Detail of Phoenician Chronology. *Journal of the Ancient Near Eastern Society of Columbia University* 9:27–30.

Martin, W. J.
1936 *Tribut und Tributleistungen bei den Assyrern*. Studia Orientalia 8/1. Helsinki: Societas Orientalis Fennica.

Master, D. M.
2003 Trade and Politics: Ashkelon's Balancing Act in the Seventh Century B.C.E. *BASOR* 330:47–64.

Millard, A.
1994 *The Eponyms of the Assyrian Empire 910–612 B.C.* State Archives of Assyria Studies 2. Helsinki: Neo-Assyrian Text Corpus Project.

Naʾaman, N.
1979 The Brook of Egypt and Assyrian Policy on the Border of Egypt. *Tel Aviv* 6:68–90.
1991 Forced Participation in Alliances in the Course of the Assyrian Campaigns to the West. In *Ah, Assyria...: Studies in Assyrian History and Ancient Near Eastern Historiography Presented to Hayim Tadmor*, ed. M. Cogan and I. Ephʿal, 80–98. Scripta Hierosolymitana 33. Jerusalem: Magnes.
1998 Two Notes on the History of Ashkelon and Ekron in the Late Eighth–Seventh Centuries B.C.E. *Tel Aviv* 25:19–27.
2003 Ekron under the Assyrian and Egyptian Empires. *BASOR* 332:81–91.
2004 The Boundary System and Political Status of Gaza under the Assyrian Empire. *ZDPV* 120:55–70.

Negueruela, I., J. Pinedo, M. Gómez, A. Miñano, I. Arellano, and J. S. Barba
1995 Seventh-century B.C. Phoenician Vessel Discovered at Playa de la Isa, Mazarron, Spain. *IJNA* 24:189–97.

Oppenheim, A. L.
1969 Babylonian and Assyrian Historical Texts. In *Ancient Near Eastern Texts Relating to the Old Testament* [3d ed.], ed. J. B. Pritchard, 265–317, 556–67. Princeton, N.J.: Princeton University Press.

Parpola, S., ed.
1987 *The Correspondence of Sargon II.* Part 1, *Letters from Assyria and the West*. State Archives of Assyria 1. Helsinki: Helsinki University Press.

Postgate, J. N.
1974 *Taxation and Conscription in the Assyrian Empire*. Studia Pohl, Series Maior 3. Rome: Pontifical Biblical Institute.

Reade, J. E.
1976 Sargon's Campaigns of 720, 716 and 715 B.C.: Evidence from the Sculptures. *JNES* 35:95–104.

Singer, I.
1994 Egyptians, Canaanites, and Philistines in the Period of the Emergence of Israel. In *From Nomadism to Monarchy: Archaeological Aspects of Early Israel*, ed. I. Finkelstein and N. Naʾaman, 282–338. Jerusalem: Israel Exploration Society.

Spalinger, A.
1974 Esarhaddon and Egypt: An Analysis of the First Invasion of Egypt. *Orientalia* 43:295–326.
1978 The Foreign Policy of Egypt Preceding the Assyrian Conquest. *Chronique d'Égypt* 53:22–47.

Stager, L. E.
1996a Ashkelon and the Archaeology of Destruction: Kislev 604 B.C.E. *EI* 25:61*–74*.
1996b The Fury of Babylon: Ashkelon and the Archaeology of Destruction. *BAR* 22/1:54–77.
2006 New Discoveries in the Excavations of Ashkelon in the Bronze and Iron Ages [in Hebrew]. *Qadmoniot* 39:2–19.

Starr, I., ed.
1990 *Queries to the Sungod: Divination and Politics in Sargonid Assyria*. State Archives of Assyria 4. Helsinki: Helsinki University Press.

Tadmor, H.
1960 Jaffa and Its District in Assyrian Documents. *IEJ* 10:46–55.
1966 Philistia under Assyrian Rule. *BA* 29:86–102.
1983 Autobiographical Apology in the Royal Assyrian Literature. In *History, Historiography and Interpretation: Studies in Biblical and Cuneiform Literature*, ed. H. Tadmor and M. Weinfeld, 36–57. Jerusalem: Magnes.
1994 *The Inscriptions of Tiglath-Pileser III King of Assyria: Critical Edition, with Introductions, Translations and Commentary*. Jerusalem: Israel Academy of Sciences and Humanities.
2004 An Assyrian Victory Chant and Related Matters. In *From the Upper Sea to the Lower Sea: Studies on the History of Assyria and Babylonia in Honour of A. Kirk Grayson*, ed. G. Frame, 269–76. PIHANS 101. Leiden: Brill.

Uehlinger, C.
1998 ". . . und wo sind die Götter von Samarien?" Die Wegführung syrisch-palästinischer Kultstatuen auf einem Relief Sargons II. in Ḫorsābād/Dūr-Šarrukīn. In *"Und Mose schreib dieses Lied auf": Studien zum Alten Testament und zum alten Orient; Festschrift für Oswald Loretz zur Vollendung seines 70. Lebensjahres*, ed. M. Dietrich and I. Kottsieper, 739–76. Münster: Ugarit-Verlag.
2002 Hanun von Gaza und seine Gottheiten auf Orthostatenreliefs Tiglatpilesers III. In *Kein Land für sich allein: Studien zum Kulturkontakt in Kanaan, Israel/Palästina und Ebirnâri für Manfred Weippert zum 65. Geburtstag*, ed. U. Hübner and E. A. Knauf, 92–125. OBO 186. Freiburg, Switzerland: Universitätsverlag.
2003 Clio in the World of Pictures—Another Look at the Lachish Reliefs from Sennacherib's Southern Palace in Nineveh. In *"Like a Bird in a Cage": The Invasion of Sennacherib in 701* B.C.E., ed. L. L. Grabbe, 221–305. JSOTSup 363. Sheffield, England: Sheffield Academic Press.

Vernus, P.
1975 Inscriptions de la troisième pèriode intermédiaire (I). *Bulletin de l'Institut français d'archéologie orientale* 75:1–72.

Waldbaum, J. C.
2002 Trade Items or Soldiers' Gear? Cooking Pots from Ashkelon, Israel. In *Autour de la mer Noire: Hommage à Otar Lordkipanidzé*, ed. D. Kacharava, M. Faudot, and E. Geny, 133–40. Besançon, France: Presses universitaires franc-comtoises.

Wazana, N.
2003 "I Removed the Boundaries of Nations" (Isa. 10: 13): Border Shifts As a Neo-Assyrian Tool of Political Control in Ḫattu [in Hebrew]. *EI* 27:110–21.

Weiss, E., and M. E. Kislev
2004 Plant Remains as Indicators for Economic Activity: A Case Study from Iron Age Ashkelon. *JAS* 31:1–13.

Wright, G. E.
1971 A Problem of Ancient Topography: Lachish and Eglon. *BA* 34:76–86.

37. The Built Tombs on the Spring Hill and the Palace of the Lords of Jericho (ᶜḎMR RḪᶜ) in the Middle Bronze Age

by Lorenzo Nigro

Recent excavations by the University of Rome "La Sapienza" and the Palestinian Department of Antiquities and Cultural Heritage at the site of Tell es-Sultan have produced new data on the urban organization and stratigraphy of Jericho in the Middle Bronze Age. These discoveries shed unexpected light on the results of previous excavations (Marchetti and Nigro 1998:103–97; 2000:165–281; in press). Interesting information was gathered on the Spring Hill (figure 1), the artificial mound beside ᶜAin es-Sultan—the perennial spring that provides Jericho with a constant supply of fresh water.[1] The discovery there of a built tomb (D.641) in Area G (figure 2), with a distinguished burial inside, not only supports the idea that the MB palace (Garstang's "Hyksos Palace"—Garstang 1933:41; 1934:100–1, pl. 15, nn. 80, 81; Garstang and Garstang 1948:99–101) was located on the summit of the Spring Hill, but also provides a possible hint of the Egyptian name of Jericho during the Middle Kingdom and the Egyptian title of its rulers.

Tomb D.641 and the Other Built Tombs on the Eastern Flank of the Spring Hill

In 1999, a built tomb (D.641) was excavated in Area G. It consists of a square chamber lined with mudbricks (figure 3), in which two individuals were buried: an adult and a girl 9–10 years old (figure 4).[2] They were lying on their left sides and were accompanied by funerary equipment apparently related to the younger person. The young girl was clearly the more prominent individual because she wore a distinctive set of personal ornaments (the only case known in Jericho, including the huge nearby necropolis excavated by K. M. Kenyon), and she had at her side distinctive pottery and animal bones, which presumably resulted from sacrifices.

The stratigraphic location of Tomb D.641 (figure 5) and its chronology (end of period Sultan IVa; MB IB; 1825–1800 B.C.E.) are clear, based upon the examination of its ceramic assemblage. But what is more important is the observation that this tomb was situated well within a major wall delimiting the top of the Spring Hill. This wall, excavated by the Italian-Palestinian Expedition (W.633; Nigro 2006a:25, 27), had already been brought to light by John Garstang, who convincingly interpreted it as the boundary wall of a major building occupying the summit of the Spring Hill (figures 6 and 9; Garstang 1934:pl. 15, nn. 80, 81; Garstang and Garstang 1948:86, fig. 4). An examination of the original plan of this building (figure 7), which had rectangular rooms along its perimeter that recall contemporary palatial buildings like the so-called Courtyard Temples of Tell el-Balaṭah/Shechem (Nigro 1995:71–89, 417–19, pls. 12–14), as well as the MB III "Palace I" of Tell el-ᶜAjjul (Nigro 1995:112–18, pl. 21) and Palace P at Tell ed-Duweir/biblical Lachish (Nigro 1995:107–11, pl. 20), not only reveals the layout of what was most likely the royal palace of Jericho in the Middle Bronze Age, but also shows two other features important for the comprehension of this strategic spot in the ancient city. A main terrace-wall supported the top of the Spring Hill on its eastern flank (Kenyon's Wall HBF+HBN[+HDR], labeled "intermediate

[1] On the archaeology of the Spring Hill, see Bienkowski 1986:112–20 and Marchetti 2003a. The plans published in Marchetti 2003a:figs. 3–4, 6–8, 10–13 offer a partial stratigraphic reconstruction of the EB and MB phases on the Spring Hill; however, for a more coherent reconstruction of the occupational sequence at this central point of the ancient city, the elevations of buildings and layers and the location of the spring and the roads (ancient and modern), as well as the structures detected by Garstang in between these two key urban elements, should have been indicated. In this respect, some aporias could have been solved, such as (1) the attribution of two distinct architectural phases to MB I in spite of the limited layers and related pottery ascribable to this period [Sultan IVa] in the tell as a whole; (2) the stratigraphic multiplication of the same structures between MB I and II (e.g., the tower excavated by Kenyon ascribed to a different phase than the wall to which it is connected, and the walls and one tower that delimit an intramoenia cemetery); (3) the room called "X" by Garstang, from which a well-known EB IV goblet comes, ascribed to EB III, and (4) the dating to EB II of the rooms from which came the well-known ivory bull-head, dated by Marchetti himself to the EB III; see Marchetti 2003a, 299–310, figs. 3–4, 6–8, 10). These aporias show the difficulty of correlating the archaeological data gathered by different archaeologists in this sector of the tell. The main architectural structures in the area therefore must be reconsidered in light of the original documentation of the previous excavations, i.e., Garstang's unpublished plans.

[2] Human remains were examined by E. Spagnoli (Marchetti 2003a:306), who also hypothesized that the adult was a female.

Figure 1. View of Tell es-Sultan and the Spring Hill (right) in 1930, seen from the south, with the road cutting its eastern flank just in front of ᶜAin es-Sultan spring
Courtesy of the Palestine Exploration Fund

terrace-wall" in figure 9; Kenyon 1981:350–62, pls. 328b–333), while at the bottom of the slope, a major structure, possibly representing a fortification wall related to the great Eastern Tower discovered by Garstang roughly 15 m to the south (figure 8),[3] retained the foot of the hill (figure 9).[4] Within these massive walls, at least five built chambers had been used as tombs—quite surprisingly, if one considers that from the beginning of the Middle Bronze Age, the main burial place at Jericho was the nearby necropolis, where rock-cut tombs had been used since the Early Bronze Age (some of these tombs were reused for the earliest burials of the Middle Bronze Age).

The western and uppermost of these built chambers was Tomb D.641, which actually was located within the compound of the palace. In the underlying middle terrace, in between the limit of the palace and the main terrace-wall, a labyrinthine structure was excavated by Garstang (figure 7) that was tentatively interpreted as a tomb or cenotaph.[5] Actually, no human remains are reported to have been found in it, even if a group of complete pottery vessels may be considered part of a collection of funerary equipment.[6]

In the same terrace, abutting the inner face of Wall HBF+HBN(+HDR), Kenyon excavated Tomb HAR (Square HII), which offers a clear example of this kind of funerary construction. The plan is roughly square with an entrance near a corner blocked by a limestone slab; the mudbrick work was partially preserved in elevation, indicating the existence of a corbeled vault in bricks (figures 10 and 11; Kenyon 1981:349–50, pls. 188–89, fig. 5). Six people were buried in Tomb HAR, indicating that it was reopened several times, but only the last two were in primary deposition with flexed legs. The previous burials had been grouped against the walls of the chamber, together with animal bones that may have belonged to food offerings. The pottery associated with the last two burials consisted of two jugs, one dipper, a small jar, and a carinated bowl (Kenyon and Holland 1983:fig. 162).

In the lower terrace, between Wall HBF+HBN and the main fortification wall at the foot of the slope, Kenyon discovered three more tombs. Although these were in a worse state of preservation, they apparently belong to the same type. Tomb 10,[7] located in Square

[3] The Eastern Tower was a monumental building possibly connected to an inner gate giving access to the Spring Hill, erected at the beginning of the Middle Bronze Age (Garstang 1932:15–16, pl. 9; 1934:pls. 13, 15; Garstang and Garstang 1948:85–86, fig. 4, where he finally dated the tower to the Early Bronze Age; Nigro 2006a:26, fig. 38; 2006b:365–66).

[4] Garstang discovered this wall protruding from the Eastern Tower (Garstang 1932:16; Garstang 1934:pl. 15; Garstang and Garstang 1948:86, fig. 4); it was reexcavated in its northern extension by Kenyon in Square HVI (Walls HCJ and HCP; Kenyon 1981:356–58, pls. 331, 339–40). The wall abutting the tower to the north was reexcavated by the Italian-Palestinian Expedition (W.7) in the area just south of Kenyon's Square HVI (Marchetti and Nigro 2000:165–70, figs. 3:1–3:7; Nigro 2006a:25–26). Moreover, at least two drains (figure 7) connected the summit of the hill with the area of the spring (Garstang 1934:pl. 15), thus providing a useful tool for the stratigraphic correlation of the structures erected on the eastern flank of the mound.

[5] Garstang's Area 60 (1934:101, pl. 15, loci 61–63; note that n. 60 refers to the whole area including Rooms 61–63).

[6] Later LB I vessels were found, but from an upper and probably reused level of the building (Garstang 1934:107, 118, pls. 24:1–11, 13–14; 29:10–17). The attribution of this labyrinth-like structure to the LB I is thus to be corrected (compare Garstang 1934:105, 107, pl. 15 with Marchetti 2003a:317, fig. 12).

[7] This tomb and the two others discussed below were not named by Kenyon and so were given new names by the Italian-Palestinian Expedition: Tombs 10, 11, and 12.

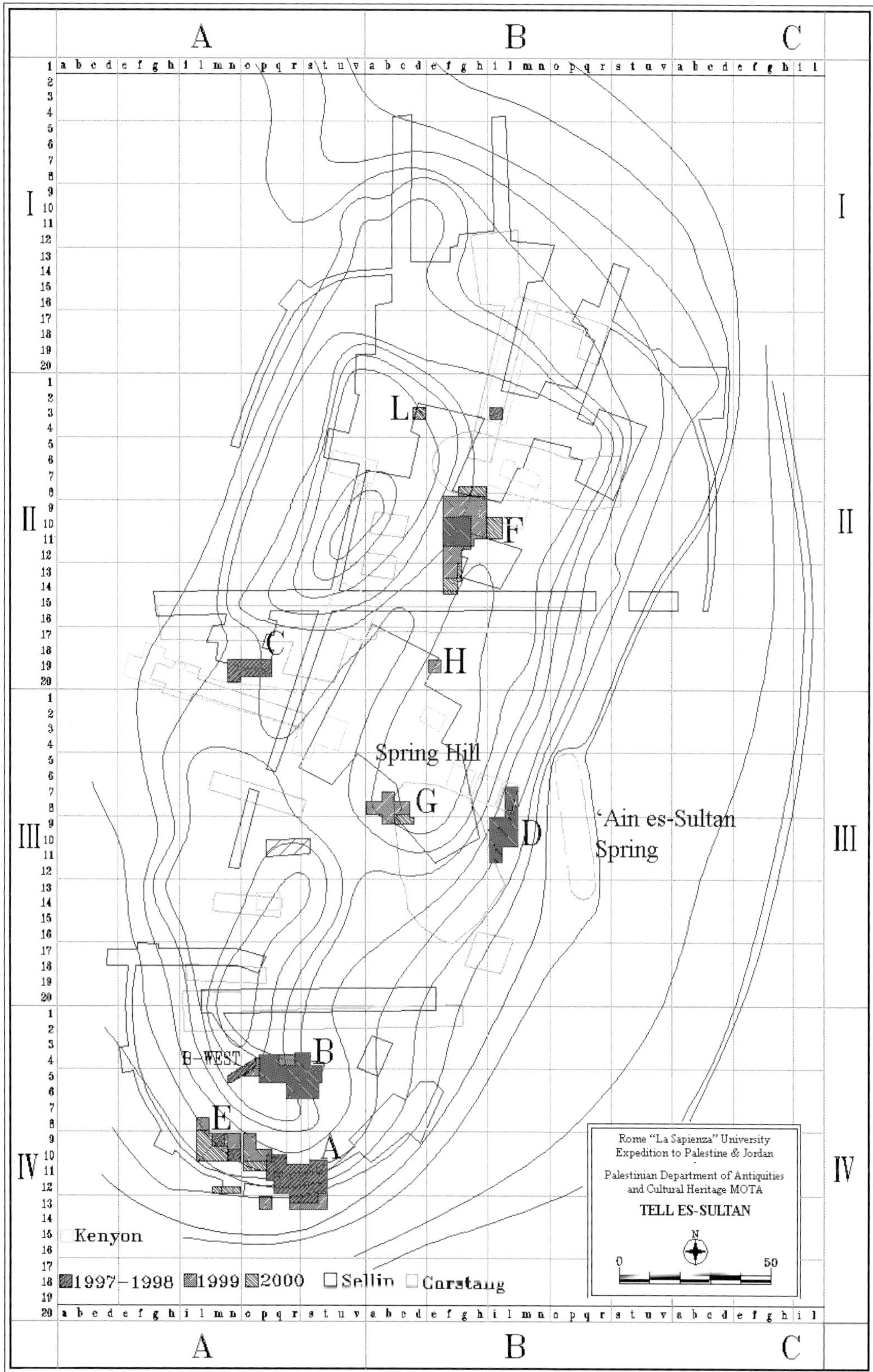

Figure 2. General plan of Tell es-Sultan with areas excavated by the Italian-Palestinian Expedition in 1997–2000 and the Spring Hill, and with the area of Kenyon's excavations in the 1950s (Squares HII, HIII, HVI); the location of the spring is also indicated.

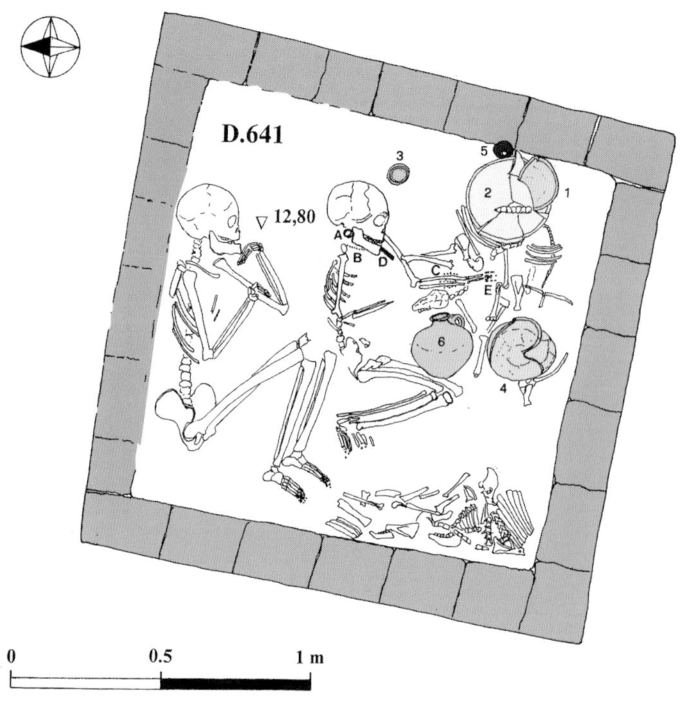

Figure 3. Plan of Tomb D.641

Figure 4. The two individuals buried in Tomb D.641 as they appeared during the excavation

Figure 5. The stratigraphic location of Tomb D.641 in Area G, just west of the eroded stone foundation of W.634 and over the destruction layers of the previous Sultan IIIc2 (EB IIIB) phase

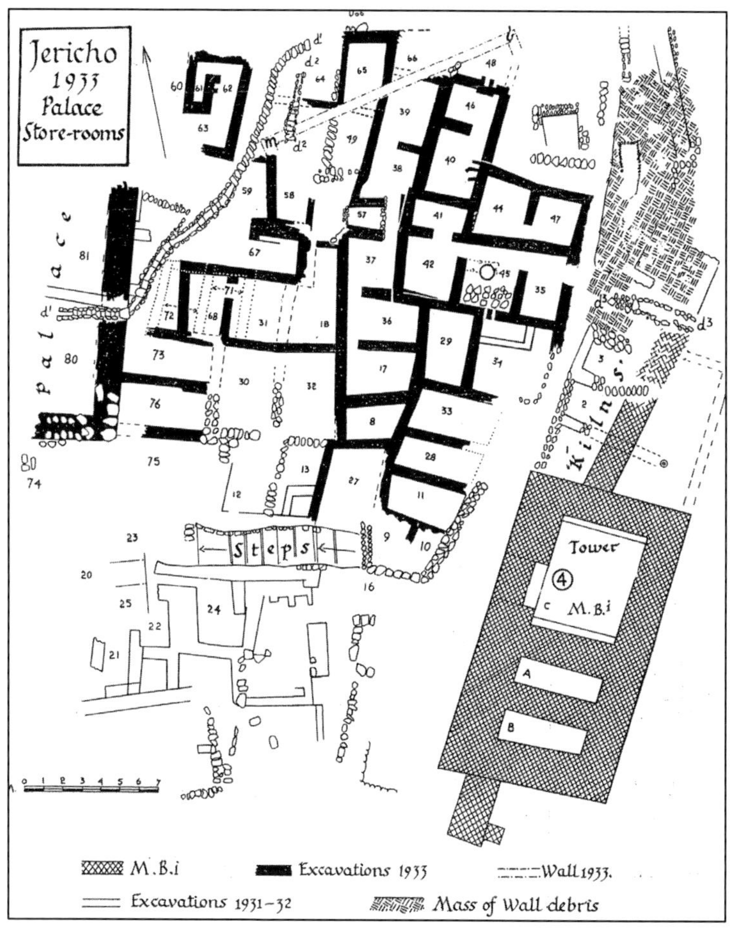

Figure 6. General plan of palace area excavated by Garstang in the 1930s on eastern flank of the Spring Hill; on left, the eastern boundary of the palace (nos. 80, 81); in middle, the labyrinth-like structure (Area 60) and so-called Palace Store-rooms; on right, the Eastern Tower and related walls (after Garstang 1934:pl. 15).

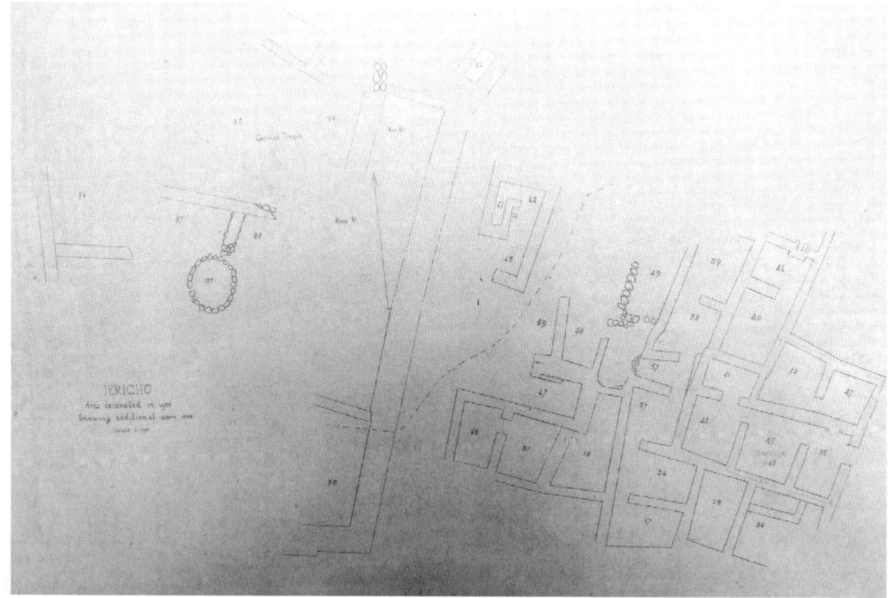

Figure 7. Unpublished plan of the structures of the palace area excavated by Garstang in the 1930s
Courtesy of the Palestine Exploration Fund

Figure 8. The Eastern Tower excavated by Garstang on the eastern flank of the Spring Hill
Courtesy of the Palestine Exploration Fund

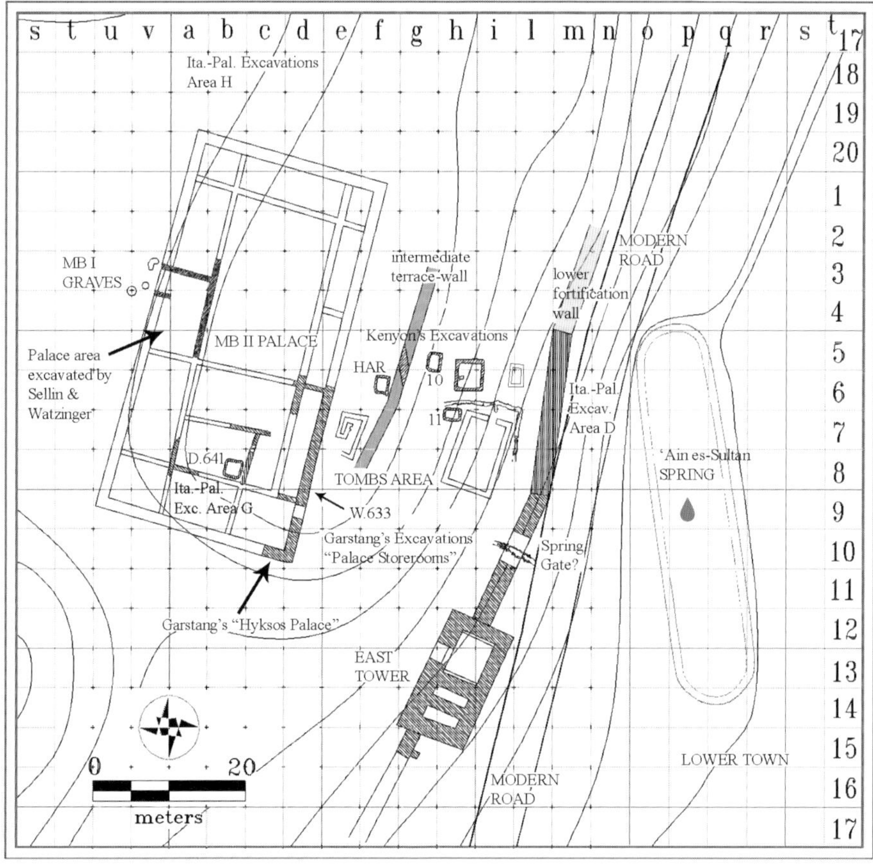

Figure 9. General plan of the MB II (Sultan IVb) palace and related structures excavated by the two British expeditions and the Italian-Palestinian Expedition on the eastern flank of the Spring Hill

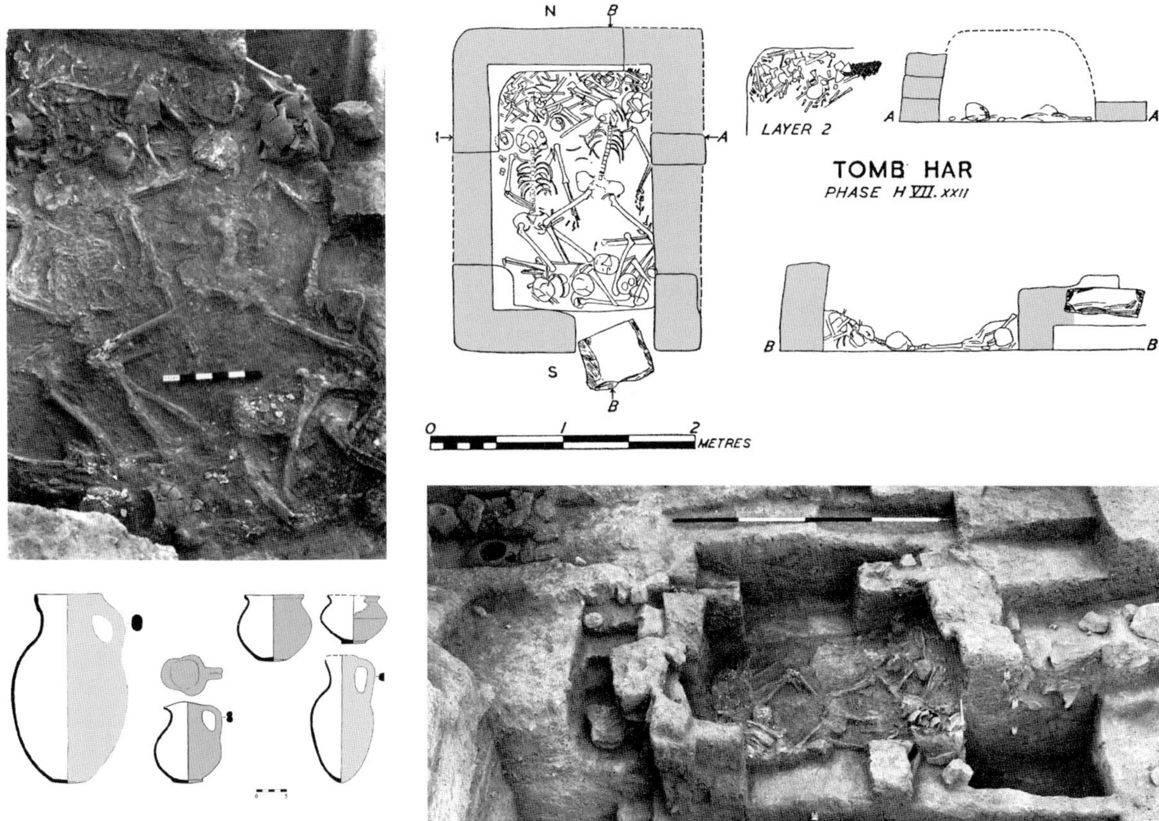

Figure 10. Plan, photographs, and pottery assemblage of Tomb HAR excavated by K. M. Kenyon in Square HII (after Kenyon 1981:pl. 188, fig. 5; Kenyon and Holland 1983:fig. 162)

HIII, contained two adults lying on their right sides with heads to the south and legs flexed. The border wall of this tomb was partly eroded and partly unexcavated, being buried in a balk (figures 11 and 12; Kenyon 1981:349, pls. 187b, 328a). The ceramic equipment, located beside the heads of the deceased, included three small jars and a jug, according to a standard funerary set known also from the contemporary necropolis (Kenyon and Holland 1983:fig. 161).[8] Noteworthy is the presence of animal bones near the heads of the deceased, which Kenyon interpreted as food offerings, but which, consisting mainly of goat *mandibulae* and *scapulae*, seem instead to be the remains of the sacrifice of a young goat.

Some meters further to the south was Tomb 11, another somewhat disturbed funerary structure, which contained a child burial (figure 13; Kenyon 1981:356; pl. 192b) with distinguished pottery equipment, including a carinated Gublite bowl, a small globular jar, a dish with a disc base, a trefoil-mouth juglet with squat body, and a piriform juglet of Black Burnished Ware (Kenyon and Holland 1983: fig. 174). The latter vessels, in particular, recall the ceramic equipment of Tomb D.641, which had a relatively wealthy assemblage that also included a Black Burnished Ware juglet and a dish. The peculiarity of that tomb is shown by the adoption of a funerary custom unusual for child burials, which in this period were typically placed in jars.[9]

The lowest burial, here called Tomb 12, was identified just inside the fortification wall HCP,[10] but was not related to the overlying structure consisting of Walls HBC+HBB+HBG, which was attributed to the following phase. Actually, it seems more likely that the latter structure contained the two burials, which belong to the same kind of built tombs. Finally, another mudbrick square structure (HAX+HBA) without any entrance that was exposed by Kenyon just to

[8] This kind of standard funerary set of pottery vessels is exemplarily shown in Tomb K3 (Kenyon 1965:203–6, figs. 92–93, pl. 11:1).

[9] Three child burials were also excavated by Garstang just to the west of the Eastern Tower (Garstang 1932:17; 1934: 119).

[10] The simple label "grave" indicates this burial in Kenyon 1981:pl. 328a, Square HVI.

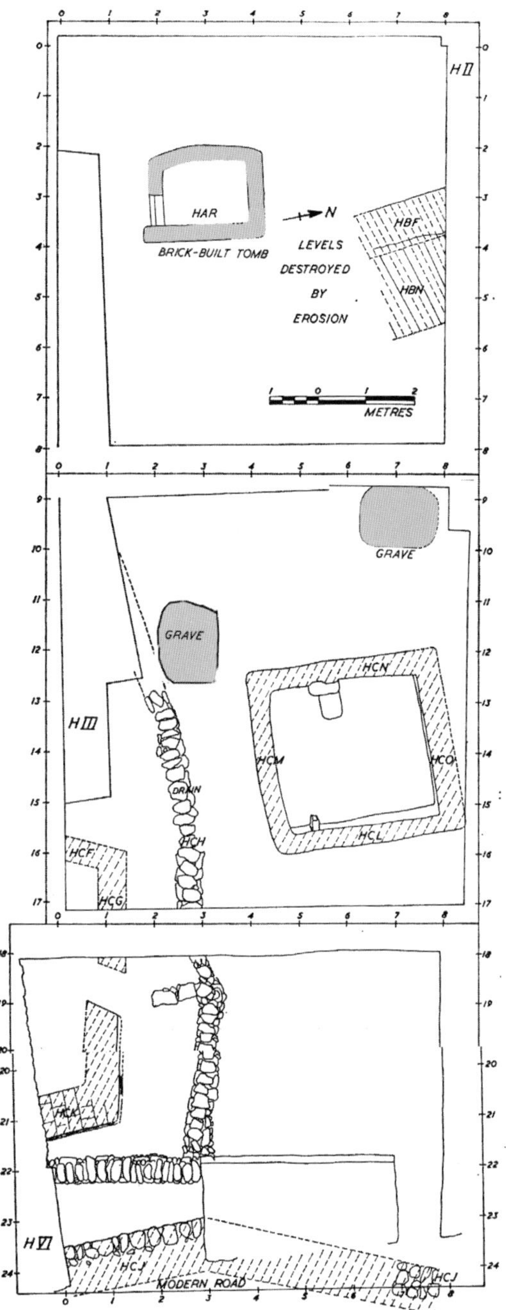

Figure 11. Plan of Kenyon's Squares HII, HIII, HVI (after Kenyon 1981:pls. 328a, 331a)

the side (Kenyon 1981:357–58, pls. 192a, 329b) was thought to be a cistern (the spring is at most 15 m away), but it may be interpreted as another tomb waiting to be used (figure 11).

The structural typology of the built tombs on the eastern flank of the Spring Hill finds very few parallels in the contemporary funerary architecture of Palestine, but it has a striking counterpart in the contemporary cemeteries of Tell ed-Dabᶜa (figure 14; Bietak 1991:figs. 16–17, 24–25, 30–32, 36, 43, 45, 47, 49, 53, 58, 75–77, 85, 87, 105, 113, 119, 122, 129, 131, 133, 139, 153, 155, 157, 172, 193, 199–200, 210, 219, 256). The funerary assemblages of the Jericho tombs are usually less wealthy and complex than those of the Egyptian city, except in the case of Tomb D.641.

The Earliest Burials and the Western Boundary Wall of the Middle Bronze Palace

A group of earlier burials of a very simple nature (pit burials) was also identified by the Austro-German Expedition on the opposite (western) side of the Spring Hill (figure 9). These burials were aligned along a north-south wall (Sellin and Watzinger 1913: 39, figs. 18–20), which possibly represents the western limit of the palace. Ceramic assemblages associated with these burials are very simple and date back to the very beginning of the Middle Bronze Age (Sultan IVa1; MB IA; 2000–1900 B.C.E.). They sometimes even include EB IV vestigial types, such as spouted bowls and small jars (figure 15; Sellin and Watzinger 1913:70–71, fig. 43).[11] The location of these burials along the perimeter of the palace, and the fact that they fall within a particular timespan, recalls a similar group of burials excavated by Schumacher along the western side of the *Nordburg* at Megiddo (Nigro 1994:20, n. 9), and suggests that they were cut at the beginning of the Middle Bronze period, when the Spring Hill was resettled. The Sultan IVa1 graves discovered on the Spring Hill show, on the one hand, that it was used as a burial place when the site was resettled at the beginning of the Middle Bronze Age, and offer, on the other hand, a clear *terminus post quem* for the erection of the palace, which took place in the second half of Sultan IV (IVa2; MB IB; 1900–1800 B.C.E.).

Tomb D.641 and the Lords of Jericho in the Middle Bronze Age

With the erection of the palace and the supporting walls on the eastern flank of the hill, the tradition of burying people in the area was preserved only for a select group of individuals who were buried in built tombs. The presence of chamber tombs is not unusual in a palatial area. Subterranean tombs have been discovered beneath the main palaces of the region, such as the *Nordburg* and *Mittelburg* at Megiddo (Schumacher 1906a; 1906b; 1908:13–21, figs. 9–10; Nigro 1994; Finkelstein, Ussishkin and Deutsch 2006), the

[11] Two more burials of this kind were excavated by Garstang in the area of the Eastern Tower.

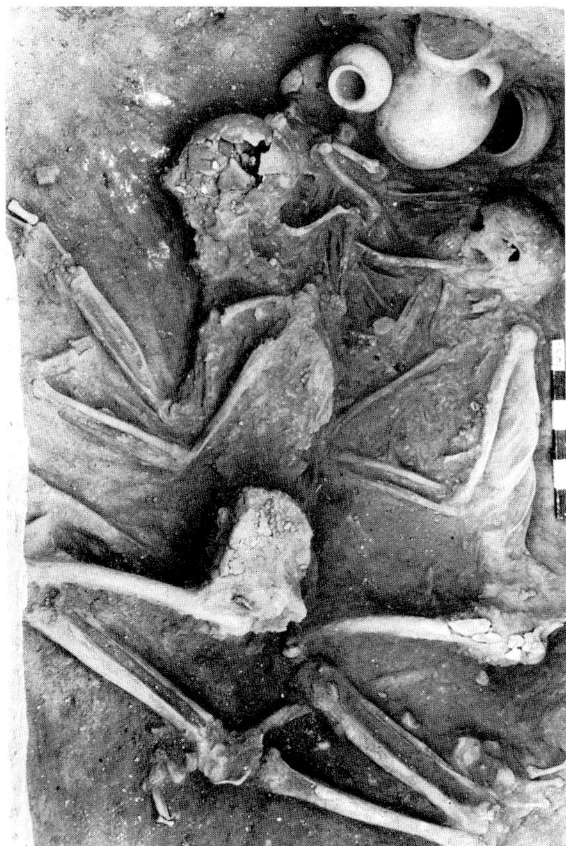

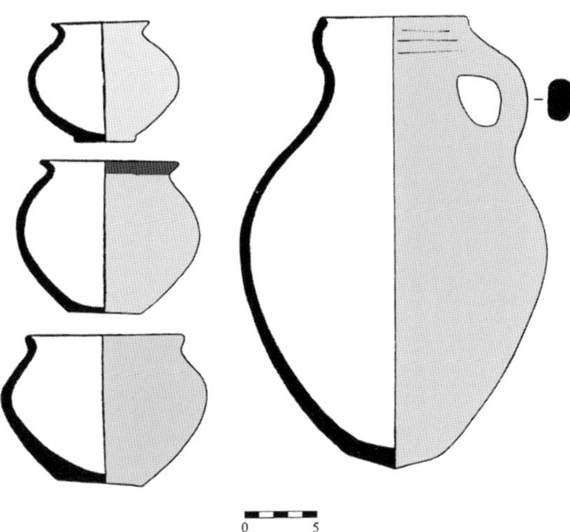

Figure 12. Burial of Tomb 10, excavated by Kenyon in Square HIII, with its pottery assemblage (after Kenyon 1981:pl. 187b; Kenyon and Holland 1983:fig. 161)

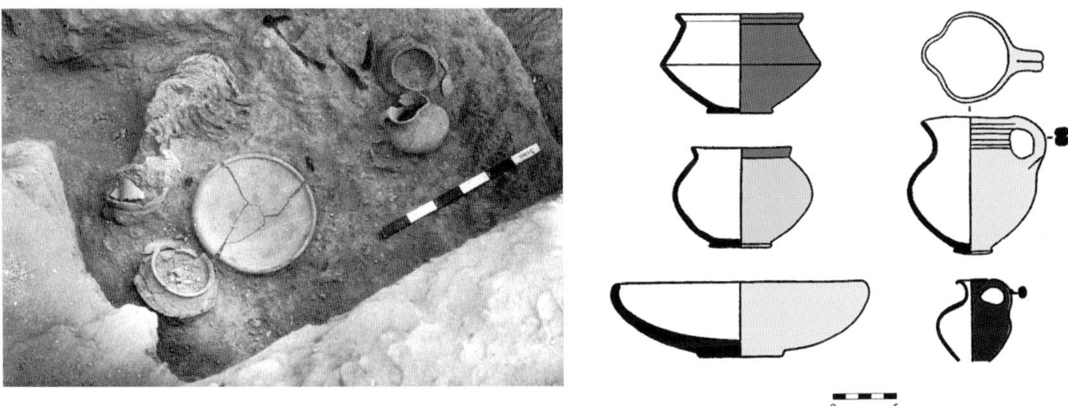

Figure 13. Burial of Tomb 11, excavated by Kenyon in Square HIII, with its pottery assemblage (after Kenyon 1981:pl. 192b; Kenyon and Holland 1983:fig.174)

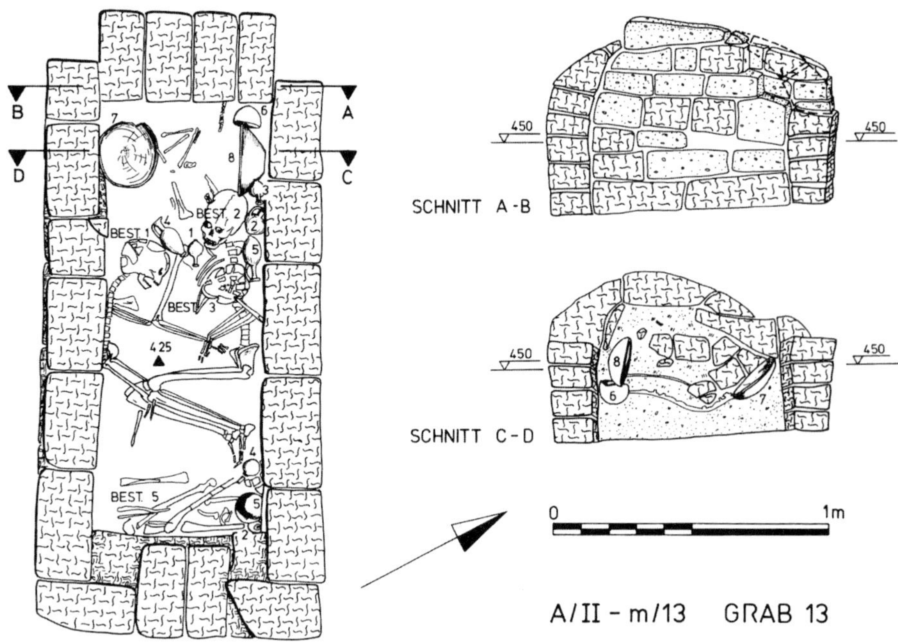

Figure 14. Plan of Tomb m/13–Nr. 13 at Tell ed-Dabᶜa (after Bietak 1991:fig. 45)

Figure 15. Ceramic assemblage associated with one of the burials excavated by the Austro-German Expedition on the western side of the Spring Hill (after Sellin and Watzinger 1913:fig. 43)

palace of Tell Taᶜannek (Sellin 1904:37–42, figs. 34–36, 38; 1906:32–34), and the palace of Kamid el-Loz (Hachmann 1982). These palatial tombs usually consist, however, of large hypogea with two or more chambers.[12] In the case of Jericho, only one tomb (Tomb D.641) lies directly under the palace itself, while the others were built in between the stepped substructure of the latter on the eastern flank of the Spring Hill. The architectural and structural relationship between the tombs and the palace thus remains somewhat difficult to determine (subsequently, the same terraced area was occupied by a subsidiary

[12] This feature is well known also at Alalakh, Ugarit, and of course at Byblos (where the palace was not surely identified but the description of Wenamun and topographic observation strongly supports the hypothesis that it was placed on top of the spur dominating the harbor where the royal necropolis is located).

building called by Garstang "Palace Store-rooms"; Garstang 1934:101, 118–30, pl. 15; Garstang and Garstang 1948:99–101). However, the location of Tomb D.641 beneath the palace bespeaks its special status. It is probably not by chance that it contained a special burial, indicated by the unusual personal ornament of the young girl buried in it (Nigro 2006a:27–28).

Figure 16. Funerary equipment of Tomb D.641

Figure 17. Burial and pottery assemblage of Tomb D.641 during the excavation

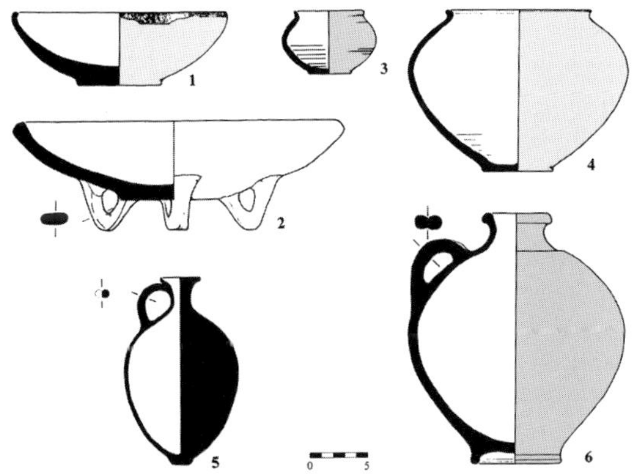

Figure 18. MB IB pottery assemblage from Tomb D.641 (end of Sultan IVa; 1825–1800 B.C.E.)

The funerary equipment of the tomb included a set of pottery vessels, some animal offerings, and the personal jewelry of the young lady (figure 16). The most interesting element in the ceramic assemblage (figures 17–18) is the Black Burnished Ware piriform juglet, which not only provides a chronological indication (last decades of the nineteenth century B.C.E.), but may be linked to a specifically female aspect: the juglet contained an ointment or a perfume. As for the personal ornaments, the lady was buried with a bronze pin on her right shoulder, which presumably had secured her vest (figure 19); a necklace with beads made of frit and a central pendant including a carnelian bead in between two beads of crystal (figure 20); two pairs of bronze earrings (figure 21);[13] a ring with a steatite scarab affixed to it (figure 22); and a second steatite scarab on her breast (figure 23).

Figure 19. Bronze pin from Tomb D.641

Figure 20. Necklace made of frit beads and pendant with a carnelian bead between two rock crystals from Tomb D.641

[13] See the bronze rings found by Garstang in Tomb 5 (Garstang 1933:fig. 10:5.b.9, 5.c, 5.d.6, 5.g) and the two pairs of earrings found in Tomb n/10–Nr. 4 at Tell el-Dabᶜa (Bietak 1991:147, fig. 106:2), which, however, are made of gold.

Figure 21. Two pairs of bronze earrings from Tomb D.641

Figure 22. Ring and steatite scarab TS.99.G.458 from Tomb D.641

Figure 23. The steatite scarab TS.99.G.500 from Tomb D.641 bearing the inscription *ᶜḏmr rḫᶜ* ("administrator of Jericho")

The scarab on the ring (TS.99.G.458)[14] belongs to a well-known Canaanite class with incised "Neferzeichen" formulae, as indicated by the hieroglyphs *sꜣ* "protection," *ᶜnḫ* "life," the head-rest *wrs* (Gardiner 1957:500, Q4), *wꜣḏ* "to be healthy" (Gardiner 1957:480, M13), and *nfr* "good." Since it was affixed on the ring on a small plaque and not hung as usual through the hole piercing the scarab, it was apparently no longer in use as a seal (it could not rotate). In any case, it is an early specimen of a type that would spread everywhere in the Sultan IVb period (MB II; Marchetti 2003b:11–14).

The latter scarab (TS.99.G.500) was retrieved on the breast of the young lady (figure 23).[15] The inscribed hieroglyphics allow a very interesting reading. A crouching lion is placed in the middle with two signs over it: the canal, which is read *mr*, and the "*bûri*-fish" (*Mugil cephalus*), which is read *ᶜḏ*, giving together the well-known Egyptian title *ᶜḏ-mr*, "administrator (of a province)," probably literally, "excavator of canal(s)" (Gardiner 1957:477, K3; Helck 1958:194–96, 199; Ward 1982). This title was in use since the Old Kingdom (Helck 1954:21, 79–80; Martin-Pardey 1976:13, 43–54) and its presence (which at Jericho perhaps acquires a special meaning, being a city-state extending its administration over a densely irrigated oasis)[16] suggests that we read the recumbent lion, *rw* (Gardiner 1957:460, E23), and the hieroglyphic below of the rising sun over a hill, *ḫᶜ* (Gardiner 1957:489, N28), as a personal name. But the name *rḫᶜ*[17] is not attested either as an Egyptian or as a Canaanite personal name in the available contemporary sources. In the large inventory of scarabs from Jericho (almost 400 specimens), only a few bear

[14] For a detailed description, see Marchetti 2003b:10–11, n. 5.

[15] For a detailed description, see Marchetti, ibid., (where, however, the hieroglyphic inscription on the scarab is not read).

[16] One may hypothesize for MB Palestine a use of this Egyptian administrative title similar to that attested in Syria at the time with Mesopotamian titles like, e.g., the renowned *šakkanakku* of Mari.

[17] In group-writing, the sign *rw* is conventionally read *r(e)*, the original vocalization being unknown.

Egyptian titles or royal names.[18] The interpretation of *rḫ*ᶜ as a personal name should therefore be ruled out. Another possibility does exist, however: that the hieroglyphic inscription reproduces the Egyptian transliteration of a West Semitic place name.[19] By comparison with the numerous biblical attestations of the ancient name of Tell es-Sultan (Elitzur 2004), we can suggest that *rḫ*ᶜ is the Egyptian writing of biblical "Jericho."[20] Ἱεριχώ, the Greek name of the site in antiquity, almost equal to modern Arabic *Ariḥa* (*ar-Riḥa*)—"scent, perfume," due to the flowers of the oasis—but also linkable to the Hebrew root of "vital spirit," seems, in fact, fully compatible with its transposition in hieroglyphic writing, as attested in scarab TS.99.G.500. Moreover, the Egyptian hieroglyphic writing *rw-ḫ*ᶜ of the West Semitic toponym Jericho adopts the same kind of transposition attested for the name Jerusalem in the Egyptian Middle Kingdom Execration Texts (*ANET*³, p. 228), where Jerusalem is transcribed *r()w-u-š()l-m-m* (Helck 1962:52, n. 12). In both instances, the initial semivowel is lost.[21] *Rḫ*ᶜ could thus be the name of Jericho, just as *Rushalimum* is Jerusalem.

If this is the case, did the young lady wear a scarab bearing the title of the local ruler? There is no proof, but the burial is a distinguished one, and it is located underneath the palace of the lords of Jericho.[22] Scarab TS.99.G.500 therefore may indicate the Egyptian name of the city during the Thirteenth Dynasty, and, equally noteworthy, the title of the local ruler, ᶜ*ḏmr*, which was presumably borrowed from older Egyptian administrative titles.

Figure 24. The scarab bearing the name of Pharaoh *ḥtp-ib-R*ᶜ found by Garstang in Tomb 30 (after Garstang 1934:fig. 4:7)

Does this mean that the city-state of Jericho was under Egyptian control? The evidence is too weak to support this interpretation. It seems more likely that only the title was borrowed, under a general cultural influence, without other political implications. The strong relationship of the "City of the Palms" with Egypt in the Second Intermediate Period is attested by other important finds, such as the scarab bearing the name of Pharaoh *ḥtp-ib-R*ᶜ (figure 24),[23] found by Garstang in Tomb 30,[24] which is one of very few attestations of this rather obscure royal personage, who undoubtedly established a special relationship between Egypt and Syria-Palestine.[25] Several mate-

[18] In the whole corpus of Jericho scarabs, there are four specimens showing a pharaonic name. Two bear a variant of the prenomen of Sesostris II, one (*ḫpr-R*ᶜ) found by Garstang in Tomb 31 (Garstang 1933:8–9, fig. 3:2) and the other (*ḫpr-ḫ*ᶜ*-R*ᶜ) found by Kenyon in Tomb J9 (Kenyon 1960:412–18; Kirkbride 1965:584, fig. 296:4); one, from Kenyon's Tomb B35, bears the prenomen of Sobekhotep V or VI, *ḫ*ᶜ*ḥ-ḥtp-R*ᶜ (Kenyon 1960:368–93; Kirkbride 1965:581–83, fig. 292:13); and one, from Garstang's Tomb 30, bears the prenomen of Hotepibra, *ḥtp-ib-R*ᶜ (figure 24; Garstang 1934:130–31, fig. 4.7). As for officials, there are three scarabs that mention Egyptian officers and six seal impressions on jars: two were found by Sellin and Watzinger (1913:156, pl. 42a) and four were found by Garstang (one in Room 17b and three in Room 44c of the Palace Store-rooms; Garstang 1934:122–24, 129, 131, fig. 3).

[19] In fact, the recumbent lion *rw* is scarcely attested in Egyptian and Canaanite scarabs and it thus seems strictly related to this specific writing. It has to be distinguished from the advancing or gradient lion, which is relatively common (see, e.g., Sellin and Watzinger 1913:156, pl. 42d¹; Kirkbride 1965:590; Keel 1995:195–98).

[20] It is very tentative to suggest a possible Egyptian writing for Jericho in the known hieroglyphic record. We might cite the so-far unidentified placename *rh*ᶜ*nu* (Ahituv 1984: 165, 167), or one of the three "Rehobs" (Ahituv 1984:163–65), the reading of which should be in several cases verified on the originals. On one hand, it seems quite strange to have a lack of cities in the lower Jordan Valley (Ahituv 1984:pl. 2, E-F/9-10); on the other hand, it must be stressed that in the Late Bronze Age, the period to which most of the available Egyptian sources refer, Jericho had fully lost its role of regional center.

[21] It should be recalled that Jerusalem in the Akkadian sources is referred to as URU *ú-ru-sa-lim* (EA 287, 289, 290, 335; Liverani 1998–99:87–94).

[22] The building was in use until the end of the Middle Bronze Age (around 1550 B.C.E.) and was rebuilt in a somewhat reduced layout, called the Middle Building by Garstang, in LB I (Garstang 1934:100–2, 105–6, 108–16, pls. 13–14, 31–37; Nigro 1996:52–55, fig. 8:2).

[23] Palestine Archaeological Museum (Rockefeller Museum, Jerusalem), inv. no. 33.1256 (Garstang 1934:130–31, fig. 4:7; Rowe 1936:5, pl. 1:18).

[24] Tomb 30 remained in use throughout the Middle Bronze Age, and its ceramic inventory, as recorded by Garstang in his files (currently in the Palestine Archaeological Museum, Jerusalem), mainly dates back to MB III (1650–1550 B.C.E.), including cylindrical juglets and large double-handled carinated bowls.

[25] The most striking find is the ceremonial mace retrieved at Ebla in the tomb of the "Lord of the Goats" (an Eblaite

rial-culture indicators corroborate this historical reconstruction by means of parallels at Tell ed-Dabᶜa, as shown by the burial customs of the Jericho elite, discussed above, and by distinctive artifacts, like the bronze belt retrieved by Kenyon in the warrior Tomb J3 (Kenyon 1960:311, fig. 117:1, 3–4, see also pl. 13: 2), which has a striking parallel in the capital of the eastern Delta (figure 25).[26]

In conclusion, it is not surprising that Jericho had durable and profound links with the Egypt of the Thirteenth Dynasty, and particularly with Tell ed-Dabᶜa, in the period of Jericho's maximum flourishing in MB II (Sultan IVb; 1800–1650 B.C.E.). We can reconstruct the political history of this central site of Palestine in relation to Egypt as follows. The city of Sultan IVa (MB I; 2000–1800 B.C.E.) was possibly destroyed by Sesostris III in his famous incursion into central Palestine, when he besieged and conquered Tell el-Balaṭah/Shechem. Jericho was subsequently rebuilt in monumental fashion at the end of the same period (Sultan IVa2; end of MB IB; 1850–1800 B.C.E.)—massive earthen ramparts were erected on its western, northern, and southern sides, while to the east, the side facing the spring, a complex terraced mudbrick structure was built supporting the palace of the local lords and concealing a group of built tombs used by the city's elite. One member of this aristocracy, a young lady, was buried here with her personal jewelry, including a scarab inscribed with the title of the local ruler: *ᶜḏmr rḫᶜ*, the "administrator of Jericho." The city and the palace grew further during the Sultan IVb period (MB II; 1800–1650 B.C.E.) and the following Sultan IVc (MB III; 1650–1550 B.C.E.), when the lords of Jericho established strong and durable relationships with the Egyptian pharaohs of the so-called Hyksos dynasties. And finally, perhaps due to this link with the Hyksos, they came to a violent end around 1550 B.C.E.

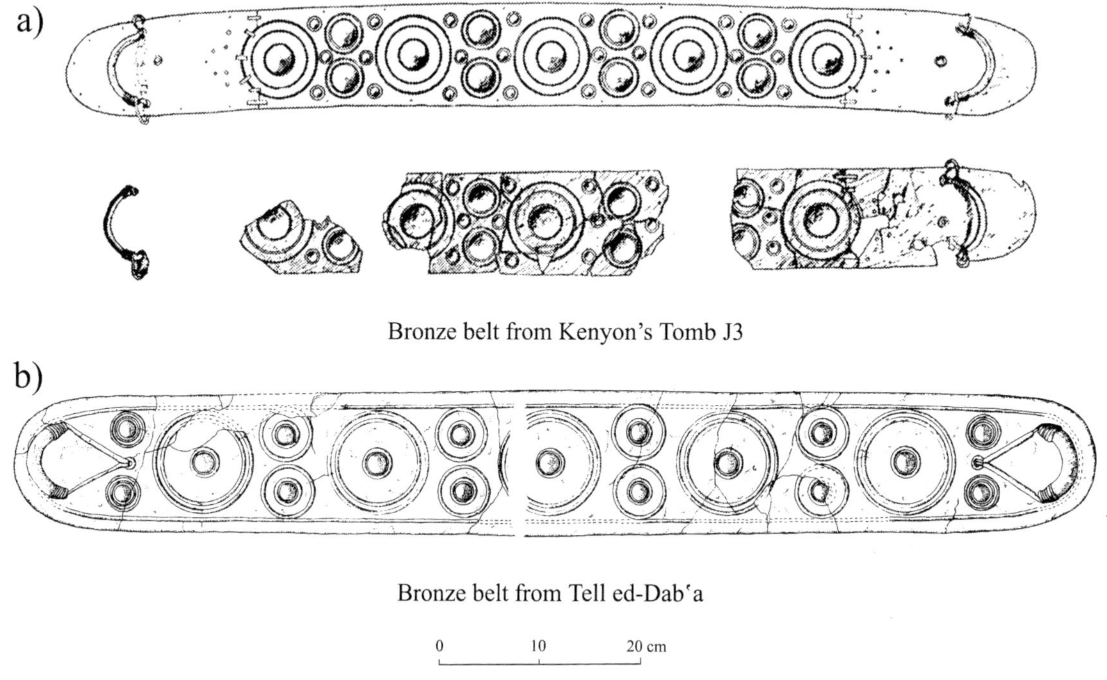

Figure 25. Bronze belt (a) from Kenyon's warrior Tomb J3 (after Kenyon 1960:fig. 117:3–4) and bronze belt (b) from Tomb F/I-o/19 Gr. 8 at Tell ed-Dabᶜa (after Philip 2006:fig. 38:2)

king of the eighteenth century B.C.E.); see Scandone-Matthiae 1987.

[26] The bronze belt found at Jericho in Tomb J3 shows exactly the same shape and decorative motifs as one found in Tomb F/I-o/19 Gr. 8 at Tell ed-Dabᶜa (Philip 2006:reg. no. 6140, 83–84, fig. 38:2), and one found in MB I Burial 42 at Sidon (Doumet-Serhal 2004:54, figs. 18–19).

Bibliography

Aḥituv, S.
1984 *Canaanite Toponyms in Ancient Egyptian Documents*. Leiden: Brill.

Bienkowski, P.
1986 *Jericho in the Late Bronze Age*. Warminster, England: Aris and Phillips.

Bietak, M.
1991 *Tell el-Dabᶜa*. Vol. 5, *Ein Friedhofsbezirk der Mittleren Bronzezeitkultur mit Totentempel und Siedlungsschichten*. Part 1. Vienna: Österreichische Akademie der Wissenschaften.

Bietak, M., and E. Czerny
2004 *Scarabs of the Second Millennium* B.C. *from Egypt, Nubia, Crete, and the Levant: Chronological and Historical Implications*. Vienna: Österreichische Akademie der Wissenschaften.

Doumet-Serhal, C.
2004 Sixth and Seventh Seasons of Excavation at Sidon: Preliminary Report. *Bulletin d'archéologie et d'architecture libanaises* 8:47–82.

Elitzur, Y.
2004 *Ancient Place Names in the Holy Land: Preservation and History*. Jerusalem: Magnes.

Finkelstein, I., D. Ussishkin, and R. Deutsch
2006 Western Area M (The 1998–2000 Seasons). In *Megiddo*, vol. 4, *The 1998–2002 Seasons*, ed. I. Finkelstein, D. Ussishkin, and B. Halpern, 66–80. Tel Aviv: Institute of Archaeology, Tel Aviv University.

Gardiner, A.
1957 *Egyptian Grammar, Being an Introduction to the Study of Hieroglyphs*. 3d ed. London: Oxford University Press.

Garstang, J.
1932 Jericho: City and Necropolis. *Liverpool Annals of Archaeology and Anthropology* 19:3–22, 35–54.
1933 Jericho: City and Necropolis. *Liverpool Annals of Archaeology and Anthropology* 20:3–42.
1934 Jericho: City and Necropolis; Fourth Report. *Liverpool Annals of Archaeology and Anthropology* 21:99–136.

Hachmann, R.
1982 Der Palast eines syrischen Kleinkönigs der späten Bronzezeit in Kāmid el-Lōz. In *Palast und Hütte. Bauen und Wohnen im Altertum*, ed. D. Papenfuss and V. M. Strocka, 21–41. Mainz am Rhein: Zabern.

Helck, W.
1954 *Untersuchungen zu den Beamtentiteln des Ägyptischen Alten Reiches*. Hamburg: Augustin.
1958 *Zur Verwaltung des Mittleren und Neuen Reichs*. Leiden: Brill.
1962 *Die Beziehungen Ägyptens zu Vorderasien im 3. und 2. Jahrtausend v. Chr.* Ägyptologisches Abhandlungen 5. Wiesbaden: Harrassowitz.

Keel, O.
1995 *Corpus der Stempelsiegel-Amulette aus Palästina/Israel: Von den Anfängen bis zur Perserzeit; Einleitung*. Orbis Biblicus et Orientalis, Series Archaeologica 10. Freiburg, Switzerland: Universitätsverlag Freiburg Schweiz.

Kenyon, K. M.
1960 *Excavations at Jericho*. Vol. 1, *The Tombs Excavated in 1952–1954*. London: British School of Archaeology in Jerusalem.
1965 *Excavations at Jericho*. Vol. 2, *The Tombs Excavated in 1955–1958*. London: British School of Archaeology in Jerusalem.
1981 *Excavations at Jericho*. Vol. 3, *The Architecture and Stratigraphy of the Tell*. 2 vols. London: British School of Archaeology in Jerusalem.

Kenyon, K. M., and T. A. Holland
1983 *Excavations at Jericho*. Vol. 4, *The Pottery Phases of the Tell and Other Finds*. London: British School of Archaeology in Jerusalem.

Kirkbride, D.
1965 Appendix E: Scarabs. In *Excavations at Jericho*, vol. 2, *The Tombs Excavated in 1955–1958*, ed. K. M. Kenyon, 580–655. London: British School of Archaeology in Jerusalem.

Liverani, M.
1998–99 *Le Lettere di el-Amarna*. Testi del Vicino Oriente antico 2; Letterature mesopotamiche 3. Brescia: Paideia.

Marchetti, N.
2003a A Century of Excavations on the Spring Hill at Tell es-Sultan, Ancient Jericho: A Reconstruction of Its Stratigraphy. In *The Synchronisation of Civilisations in the Eastern Mediterranean in the Second Millennium* B.C., vol. 2, ed. M. Bietak, 295–321. Vienna: Österreichische Akademie der Wissenschaften.
2003b Due scarabei in steatite del Bronzo Medio I finale da Tell es-Sultan, antica Gerico. *Ricerche di Egittologia e di Antichità Copte* 5:9–22.

Marchetti, N., and L. Nigro, eds.
1998 *Scavi a Gerico, 1997: Relazione preliminare sulla prima campagna di scavi e prospezioni archeologiche a Tell es-Sultan, Palestina*. Quaderni di Gerico 1. Rome: Università degli Studi di Roma "La Sapienza".
2000 *Excavations at Jericho, 1998: Preliminary Report on the Second Season of Excavations and*

Surveys at Tell es-Sultan, Palestine. Quaderni di Gerico 2. Rome: Università degli Studi di Roma "La Sapienza".

in press *Excavations at Jericho, 1999–2000: Preliminary Report on the Third and Fourth Seasons of Excavations and Surveys at Tell es-Sultan, Palestine*. Quaderni di Gerico 3. Rome: Università degli Studi di Roma "La Sapienza".

Martin-Pardey, E.
1976 *Untersuchungen zur ägyptischen Provinzialverwaltung bis zum Ende des Alten Reiches*. Hildesheimer Ägyptologische Beiträge 1. Hildesheim: Gerstenberg.

Nigro, L.
1994 The "Nordburg" of Megiddo: A New Reconstruction on the Basis of Schumacher's Plan. *BASOR* 293:15–29.
1995 *Ricerche sull'architettura palaziale della Palestina nelle Età del Bronzo e del Ferro. Contesto archeologico e sviluppo storico*. Contributi e Materiali di Archeologia Orientale 5 (1994). Rome: Università degli Studi di Roma "La Sapienza".
1996 Le residenze palestinesi del Bronzo Tardo—I modelli planimetrici e strutturali. *Contributi e materiali di archeologia orientale* 6:1–69.
2006a Results of the Italian-Palestinian Expedition to Tell es-Sultan: At the Dawn of Urbanization in Palestine. In *Tell es-Sultan/Jericho in the Context of the Jordan Valley: Site Management, Conservation and Sustainable Development*, ed. L. Nigro and H. Taha, 1–40. Rome "La Sapienza" Studies on the Archaeology of Palestine and Transjordan 2. Rome: "La Sapienza" Expedition to Palestine and Jordan.
2006b Sulle mura di Gerico: Le fortificazioni di Tell es-Sultan come indicatori della nascita e dello sviluppo della prima città di Gerico nel III millennio a.C. In *Ina Kibrāt Erbetti. Studi di Archeologi orientale dedicati a Paolo Matthiae*, ed. F. Baffi, R. Dolce, S. Mazzoni, and F. Pinnock, 349–97. Rome: Università degli Studi di Roma "La Sapienza."

Philip, G.
2006 *Tell el-Dabᶜa*. Vol. 15, *Metalwork and Metalworking Evidence of the Late Middle Kingdom and the Second Intermediate Period*. Vienna: Österreichische Akademie der Wissenschaften.

Rowe, A.
1936 *A Catalogue of Egyptian Scarabs, Scaraboids, Seals and Amulets in the Palestine Archaeological Museum*. Cairo: Institut français d'archéologie orientale.

Scandone-Matthiae, G.
1987 The Mace of Pharaoh Hotepibra and the Connections between Egypt and Syria-Palestine during the XIIIth Dynasty. In *Studies in the History and Archaeology of Palestine: Proceedings of the First International Symposium on Palestine Antiquities*, ed. S. Shaath, 2:49–58. Aleppo: Aleppo University Press.

Schumacher, G.
1906a Die Ausgrabungen auf dem Tell el-Mutesellim, IX: Die Ausgrabungen im Frühjahr 1905. *Mitteilungen und Nachrichten des Deutschen Palästina-Vereins* 12: 17–30.
1906b Die Ausgrabungen auf dem Tell el-Mutesellim, X: Die Ausgrabungen im Sommer und Herbst 1905. *Mitteilungen und Nachrichten des Deutschen Palästina-Vereins* 12:35–70.
1908 *Tell el-Mutesellim*. Vol. 1, *Fundbericht*. Leipzig: Haupt.

Sellin, E.
1904 *Tell Taᶜannek*. Denkschriften der kaiserlichen Akademie der Wissenschaften, Phil. Hist. Klasse 50/4. Vienna.
1906 *Eine Nachlese auf dem Tell Taᶜannek in Palästina*. Denkschriften der kaiserlichen Akademie der Wissenschaften, Phil. Hist. Klasse 52/3. Vienna.

Sellin, E., and C. Watzinger
1913 *Jericho: Die Ergebnisse der Ausgrabungen*. Wissenschaftliche Veröffentlichung der Deutschen Orient-Gesellschaft 22. Leipzig: Hinrichs.

Ward, W. A.
1982 *Index of Egyptian Administrative and Religious Titles of the Middle Kingdom with a Glossary of Words and Phrases Used*. Beirut: American University of Beirut.

38. A New Join of Fragments of the Baal Cycle

by Dennis Pardee

Though they have made the fame of Ugarit, the number of mythological texts from that Late Bronze Age site is actually quite small: in the first corpus of Ugaritic texts (Herdner 1963), only twenty-eight texts were so classified. In this collection, these texts were placed first and this ordering of the first twenty-five of these texts was maintained in subsequent collections when virtually everything else was changed (Dietrich, Loretz, and Sanmartín 1976; 1995; Cunchillos and Vita 1993). It is almost a shame to reduce the number even further, but collation of the eighth of these texts[1] has shown that it belonged to the same tablet as bears the third text of the Baal Cycle. It is a pleasure to offer this sacrifice of 1/28th of the original mythological corpus to my friend and one-time colleague at the Oriental Institute, Larry Stager.

Description

The fragment that bears the excavation number RS 3.364 is small, measuring only 66 mm in height by 41 mm in width (figure 1). It is a surface chip, the entire reverse having disappeared, and is only 10 mm thick. Its original position at either the upper or the lower edge of the tablet—obverse in the former case, reverse in the latter—is certain because part of the rounded edge is preserved above the first line of writing; not enough of that edge is preserved, however, to enable a certain decision between the two possibilities of positioning. The text consists of a narrow column of writing, well enough preserved to determine that it belongs to a literary composition similar to the poems of the Baal Cycle, with the vertical scoring visible on either side by which the columns of mythological texts were set off one from another. The editor identified this fragment as "la partie supérieure de la col. II d'une tablette à six colonnes" (Virolleaud 1932:158). Four considerations cast doubt on this description: (1) the preserved column is very narrow, about 4 cm wide (the uncertainty as to the precise width lies in the fact that the left side is preserved only near the bottom of the fragment, the right side only near the top), and the break to the right follows part of the vertical column divider while the break to the left runs just to the left of a vertical line, making it difficult to determine to which column on the original tablet this fragment belonged; (2) only one surface having been preserved, it is also difficult to determine the obverse/reverse orientation[2]; (3) a

[1] The identifying sigla of this fragment are: RS 3.364 (excavation number), M3353 (museum number in the Aleppo museum), AO 16.645 (Louvre museum number, still visible on the fragment from the time when it was kept in the Louvre before being sent back to Syria), *CTA* 8 (Herdner 1963), *UT* 51fg (i.e., a fragment identified as belonging to text 51 in Gordon 1965), *KTU/CAT* 1.8 (i.e., text 8 in section 1 in Dietrich, Loretz, and Sanmartín 1976; 1995). This fragment will be cited below as RS 3.364 and the other mythological texts discussed below will be identified by their *CTA* number. The text was published with hand copy but without complete translation by Virolleaud (1932:158). Though many scholars have applied the data of this text to the interpretation of *CTA* 4 vii 54–60, relatively few have dealt with this text per se. The publications of which I am aware that have dealt specifically with RS 3.364 are: Montgomery and Harris 1935:72 (transcription into square Hebrew characters); Bauer 1936:57 (transcription into Latin script); Ginsberg 1944:27–28 n. 13 (transliteration into Latin script of lines 6–12 with translation and notes) and Ginsberg 1950:131 (English translation); Gordon 1947:144 (and in subsequent editions; transcription into Latin script); Gordon 1949:38 (English translation) and 1977:102 (English translation); Driver 1956:118–21 (transliteration into Latin script with English translation); Fensham 1966:162–63 (transcription into Latin script of lines 6–12 with remarks); Herdner 1963:46–47 with plate 1 and figure 30 (transcription into Latin script with hand copy [reproduced from the *editio princeps*] and photograph); Dietrich, Loretz, and Sanmartín 1976:30–31 and 1995:30 (transcription into Latin script); Gibson 1978:132 (transcription into Latin script); Mullen 1980:67 (vocalized text of lines 1–5 with English translation); Lipiński 1981:385 (transcription into Latin script of lines 6–9 with French translation); del Olmo Lete 1981:501 (transcription into Latin script); Dijkstra 1983:28–29 (transcription into Latin script of lines 5–17 with hypothetical reconstructions and translation); Cunchillos and Vita 1993:45 (transcription into Latin script); Wiggins 1993:79 (transliteration into Latin script of lines 1–2 with English translation); Binger 1997:78 (transcription into Latin script of lines 1–5 with English translation); Smith 1997:197 (transliteration into Latin script with English translation); Merlo 1998:97 (transcription into Latin script of lines 1–7 with Italian translation); Wyatt 1998:152 (English translation); Mazzini 1999:82–83 (transliteration into Latin script of lines 5–11 with English translation of lines 7–9); Tropper 2000:584 (transcription into Latin script of lines 7–9 with German translation).

[2] Ginsberg (1948:142), followed by Herdner (1963:46), was the first to point out that the state of the fragment precludes identifying it with certainty as belonging to the obverse of the tablet.

small bit of the original surface is preserved to the left of the vertical line marking the left margin of the text, that is, at the bottom left of the fragment, and not only is there no trace visible there of a second line (internal column dividers on the mythological texts normally consist of a double vertical incision while the left margin of the first and last columns is often marked by a single vertical line), but that small bit of surface is slightly rounded, indicating proximity to the edge of the tablet itself; (4) the vertical lines do not intersect the upper edge of the tablet at right angles but acutely, at approximately 80 degrees, even more acutely than what the editor indicated on his copy (the angle he drew measures out at about 84 degrees). These observable features may be taken as indications that this fragment did not belong to one of the central columns of a multicolumned text,[3] but to the left-most column of such a text. The conclusion that the fragment comes from the left side of a tablet because of the single vertical line is borne out not only by the slight rounding of the surface on the left side of the fragment (see point 3 above), but also and especially by the acute angle of the vertical lines with respect to the upper edge: because the large tablets bearing the mythological texts tended to have concave edges (rather than forming a rectangle with perfectly straight sides—see any set of photographs of the better-preserved of these tablets), the writing of the left-hand columns tended to be placed at an angle to follow the curve of the tablet rather than being placed at perfect right angles to the theoretical rectangular form. The acute angle of the writing with respect to the upper edge that we observe on RS 3.364 is thus a strong indication of its once having belonged to the left column of a multicolumned text.

Only two tablets of the Baal Cycle, *CTA* 3 and 4, show a left-hand column narrow enough to permit the hypothesis that RS 3.364 may have once belonged to one or the other of these tablets: the width of columns i and viii of *CTA* 4 is slightly superior to that of RS 3.364 while the width of columns i and vi of *CTA* 3 is a touch narrower and very close to the width of the column fragment on RS 3.364. The only options available, then, are that RS 3.364 once belonged to one or the other of these tablets or to another tablet yet undiscovered.

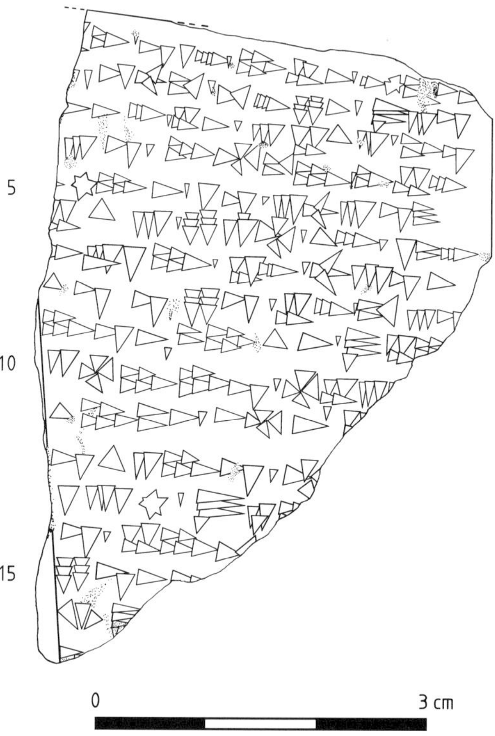

Figure 1. Ugaritic tablet fragment RS 3.364
Photograph courtesy of the Mission de Ras Shamra
Hand copy by D. Pardee

[3] All who have offered a description of this text either accept Virolleaud's view that the fragment comes from col. ii of a tablet bearing three columns on each side or Herdner's that the column in question could be the second on either the obverse or the reverse, i.e., col. ii or v.

Identification

The facts that the text is continuous, is laid out in column format, is expressed in vocabulary attested in the poetic texts, and with motifs characteristic of the Baal Cycle have left no doubt in anyone's mind that the text is mythological in nature. The question has been to determine whether it can be identified with one of the known texts and, if so, where it fits. Discovered in the House of the High Priest at the same "point topographique" as the major fragment of the third tablet of the Baal Cycle,[4] it was published by Virolleaud as helpful in restoring *CTA* 4 vii; but, in his brief presentation of the fragment (1932:158–59), he assumed that it belonged to another tablet (that is, he identified this fragment, as we have seen, as belonging to col. ii of a given tablet and as useful for restoring col. vii of *CTA* 4). He offered no proposal as to where this other tablet might fit in the Baal Cycle. Gordon (1947:144) ordered this text as a fragment of *CTA* 4, apparently on the basis of its place of publication, that is, inserted into the publication of *CTA* 4; however, in a footnote to his translation of the fragment, he remarks that that text actually "belongs to an entirely different episode" as compared with *CTA* 4 vii (1949:38) and a similar remark is found in his later translation (1977:102). In her corpus of the Ugaritic texts discovered between 1929 and 1939, Herdner placed this text in eighth position, after the six tablets of the Baal Cycle and a seventh text, fragmentary but written in a hand very different from that of ᵓIlîmilku, who inscribed texts 1–6. She describes it as belonging to the "Cycle de Baᶜal et ᶜAnat," observes that the fragment belongs in all probability to col. ii or col. v of a six-columned text, and remarks that the writing is "sensiblement plus grand" than what is found on the tablets signed by ᵓIlîmilku (Herdner 1963:46). We have already seen that the second point may not be maintained; the question of the size of the writing will be discussed now.

Doubt appears to be cast on any attempt to identify RS 3.364 as a fragment of one of the better-preserved tablets of the Baal Cycle by Herdner's description of the writing that has just been cited. Though I have great respect for Herdner's qualities as an epigrapher (see, e.g., Pardee 2000:602 n. 4), I fear that examination of RS 3.364 does not bear out her claim that the writing on this fragment is significantly larger than that of tablets signed by ᵓIlîmilku. Just to take two examples: the signs {mgn . rbt . ảṯrt} occupy about 33 mm in RS 3.364:1 and about 37 mm in *CTA* 4 i 21, while the signs {ṣḥrrm} occupy about 21 mm in RS 3.364:10, and the signs {ṣḥrrt} about 24 mm in *CTA* 4 viii 22. These variations show that the writing on RS 3.364 was in fact slightly smaller than the writing on *CTA* 4 i and viiii. There are no cases of identical or very similar wording between *CTA* 3 and 8 that occur in a single line of each text on which to base a similar comparison of those two texts. But we may count the number of signs in a comparable segment of text from the three texts: there are 77 signs in RS 3.364:1–7, 73 signs in *CTA* 4 i 21–27, i.e., the seven lines beginning with {mgn} in the two texts, and 69 signs in *CTA* 3 i 2–8. By the simple criterion of average number of signs per line when all the complete lines are taken into account, the script of *CTA* 8 would be the smallest of the three: the average is 11 per line in RS 3.364:1–7, 10.25 per line in *CTA* 3 i 2–25, and 9.9 per line in *CTA* 4 i 13–44. The proximity of the totals reflects a *ductus* in which the signs are formed, scaled, and distributed very similarly. Measuring individual signs gives the same kind of results: the {r} here is about 5 mm long and the {ǵ} about 3 mm, and the {l} is about 3 mm high and the {y} between 3 and 4 mm high—these signs on tablets bearing a colophon of ᵓIlîmilku average out at this size.

I am aware of only one proposal to attach RS 3.364 to a known tablet: Dijkstra (1980:201; 1982: 151; 1983:28–30) has suggested that the fragment once belonged to the upper part of the third tablet of the Baal Cycle (*CTA* 3), where it would be situated just before col. vi (". . . almost immediately precedes KTU 1.3.VI.1ff and hardly a line between both is missing" [1983:29]).[5] This proposal has been rejected by de Moor (1987:18 n. 96), who provided a literary argument and an epigraphic one for his decision. The latter, which interests us now, is expressed as follows: "There is no way to make the fragment KTU 1.8 match the traces of CTA, Pl. V" (this plate contains the photograph of the reverse of Text 3; according to Dijkstra's hypothesis, RS 3.364 would fit in the upper left corner, as viewed from the reverse,

[4] RS 3.363 = *CTA* 3 and RS 3.364 are the only two fragments identified in the inventory as having been discovered in the locus defined as "Tr[anchée] B 3, p[oint] t[opographique] 11 à 1,20[m]" (see Bordreuil and Pardee 1989: 32).

[5] Driver (1956:17), followed by Mullen (1980:67), suggested that this text "is clearly connected with Baal's request to Anat to approach Athirat on his behalf in the matter"; but he simply quotes Virolleaud's identification of the fragment as belonging to "the second column of a tablet which seems once to have been covered with six columns of text" and makes no concrete proposal for identifying RS 3.364 as belonging to an additional tablet or as attachable to one of the known tablets.

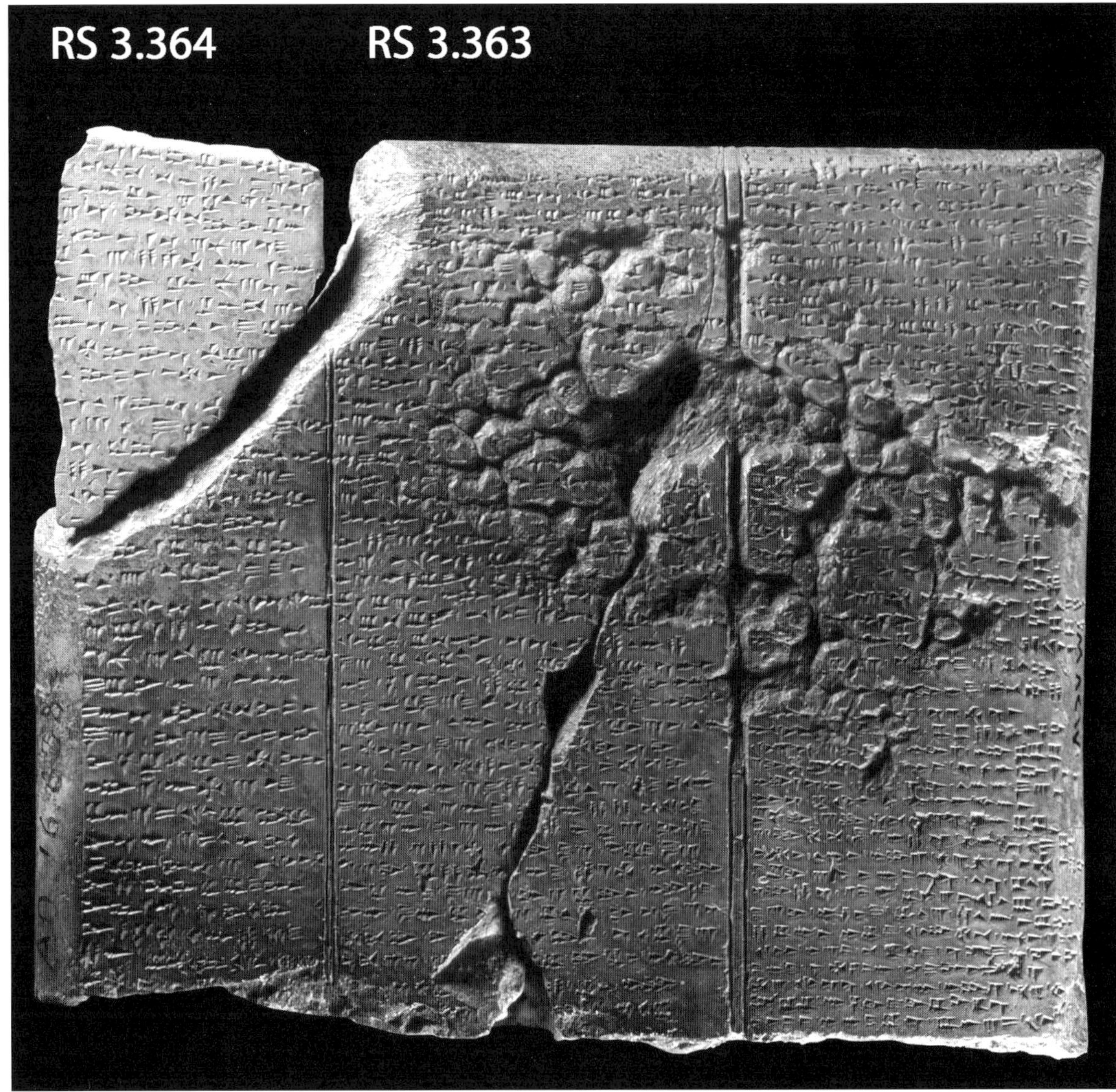

Figure 2. Join of tablet fragments RS 3.364 and RS 3.363 (*CTA* 3)

Courtesy of the Mission de Ras Shamra

where the corner of this tablet is broken away). The weight of de Moor's negative assessment and the implausibility of the text as reconstructed by Dijkstra have had the effect of essentially removing the proposal from the board.

At first, before testing this hypothesis against reality by collation, I preferred the option of attaching RS 3.364 to *CTA* 4. Ginsberg, taking at face value Virolleaud's description of the fragment as belonging to the second column of a multicolumned tablet (though, as we have seen, he allowed for the possibility of it belonging to the reverse rather than the obverse), proposed that the text of the fragment be placed literarily before *CTA* 4 and hence that it be identified as the only fragment discovered of another tablet that would have borne the narrative preceding the text of *CTA* 4.[6] The observation that the fragment belonged in all likelihood to one of the left-most columns of a multicolumned tablet would permit the acceptance of Ginsberg's literary analysis without the necessity of positing the existence of an additional tablet of which all other fragments would have disappeared: RS 3.364 would have belonged to the upper left corner of *CTA* 4 and would provide the text of the

[6] ". . . this tablet must have preceded II AB (UH 51), as should become clear to anyone upon comparing the former (note especially ll. 1–5) carefully with the latter (note especially 1:13–23 and 4–5:51–52); not improbably, it preceded it immediately" (Ginsberg 1948:142–43; cf. 1950:131).

beginning of col. i of that text.[7] As we have seen, the column width, which is atypically narrow, of the two texts matches reasonably well, the script is in all essential points identical, and, as Ginsberg pointed out, there is a plausible literary basis for positioning the fragment before the text of *CTA* 4. If, following the consensus of scholars since Dijkstra's proposal was made, *CTA* 3 is eliminated as a possibility, the only remaining ones are *CTA* 4 or another tablet of the Baal Cycle of which no other fragments were discovered. In this scenario, the plausibility of the identification of RS 3.364 as belonging to the same tablet as *CTA* 4 might be rated very good.

A very different type of explanation has become almost by default the reigning hypothesis for explaining the literary nature of RS 3.364: it would consist of "a collection of catchlines" (de Moor 1971:5).[8] This in spite of the fact that the proposal never corresponded well to what we know of the Ugaritic texts, for no such thing as a collection of catchlines has yet been convincingly identified, and where we do find texts that are in some sense derivative from the major mythological texts, these are all relatively brief texts inscribed in a single column on a single tablet in a *ductus* that differs considerably from that of ʾIlîmilku (see RS 24.245, RS 24.293, and RS 24.263, reedited, respectively, as chs. 3, 4, and 9 in Pardee 1988; see also there the summary statement on p. 265). This hypothetical collection of catchlines would, on the other hand, have belonged to a multi-columned tablet that was carefully inscribed in a hand identical to ʾIlîmilku's. Where the text is preserved, it is reasonably well understood, as the first generation of Ugaritic scholars saw; the last part has not been restorable because there were no direct literary parallels in the tablets as they are preserved, but, even before the join on which the present study is based, there was no serious literary reason to doubt that RS 3.364 consisted of a coherent and continuous text.[9]

That is where my view of the situation stood in June of 2006 when I was able to compare the three texts. As I knew before starting, there is no epigraphic criterion for certainly eliminating *CTA* 4 from the running because the gap between the missing upper left corner of this tablet and the beginning of col. i as preserved is significantly larger than the 66 mm of RS 3.364. If RS 3.364 were to be situated at the beginning of *CTA* 4 i, the calculation of the number of lines missing between the end of RS 3.364 and the first visible signs of *CTA* 4 i would depend, of course, on the original height of the tablet, with a minimum of approximately five and a maximum of approximately twenty lines.[10] On the other hand, I expected RS 3.364 not to fit into the space available at the upper left corner of *CTA* 3. The theoretical problem was as follows: Dijkstra proposed that RS 3.364:15–17 should line up with *CTA* 3 i 1–3. The first sign of RS 3.364:17, however, was not {t} as Dijkstra thought (following Dietrich, Loretz and Sanmartín 1976:31), but a sign consisting of multiple wedges, preferably {k,w}, though {m} cannot be excluded (see copy). Since Dijkstra's positioning of RS 3.364 hinges on this reading, the reconstruction presented in Dijkstra 1983:30 cannot be admitted. Moreover, it is impossible to accept that the same positioning of the fragment might be considered with

[7] From the purely epigraphic perspective, RS 3.364 could provide the end of *CTA* 4 viii, but that solution appears highly unlikely for literary reasons (cf. Pardee 1997:264–65, esp. nn. 201, 208).

[8] Scholars who have voiced similar views regarding RS 3.364 are: Gibson: "a summary in the form of a series of catch-verses" (1978:32); del Olmo Lete: "un índice" (1981: 498); Wiggins: "a summary of some of the main elements of the Palace of Baal episode" (1993:79); Dietrich, Loretz, and Sanmartín: "myth, scribal exercise?" (1995:30); Smith: "copies and/or variants of lines from the fourth tablet of the Baal Cycle" (1997:179); Wyatt: "Excerpts from *KTU* 1.4 ...Perhaps a scribal exercise?" (1998:152); Merlo: "un esercizio di scuola" (1998:97).

[9] Insufficient attention has perhaps been paid to the fact that de Moor had a literary ax to grind when he rejected Dijkstra's proposal to attach RS 3.364 to *CTA* 3. As we shall see below in discussing the literary implications of the attachment, the content of RS 3.364 makes the positioning of *CTA* 3 just before *CTA* 4 inescapable, but de Moor placed *CTA* 3 near the beginning of the Baal Cycle.

[10] The right side of *CTA* 4 is preserved to a greater height on the reverse, and one can calculate that col. 1 should have borne something like 22 to 25 lines in the broken space between the first visible sign there and the height corresponding to the top of col. iv/v as preserved (the measurement must be taken on the reverse, because the fragment that provides the end of col. v is a surface chip containing no remains of col. iv). The problem is that we cannot know how much of the tablet has disappeared above the fragment that provides the end of col. v. Herdner (1963:27 n. 6) once postulated that perhaps nothing has been lost, a hypothesis that is considered possible also by Dietrich, Loretz, and Sanmartín (1975:18 n. 3; 1995:19 n. 3). It must be remarked, however, that the break is irregular, preserving no trace of the upper edge of the tablet and no sign of curvature to that edge. Moreover, the center of the concave form of the right edge is situated roughly around line 40 of col. 5; thus, if the form of the tablet was symmetrical, as many as five to fifteen lines may be missing between col. v and col. vi (in the form of the tablet as presently reconstructed in the Aleppo museum, i.e., with a plaster cap approximating the restorer's idea of the original height of the tablet, presumably based on the form of the edge as preserved, about nine lines would be missing).

another set of restorations at this point of contact between the two texts, for the height of RS 3.364 is greater than the space available at the beginning of *CTA* 3 vi: if one places the fragment where Dijkstra proposes, the top of RS 3.364 extends roughly 10 mm above the edge of *CTA* 3 as preserved. Working from photographs, I also deemed it unlikely that it would be possible simply to slide RS 3.364 down so that the two upper edges match: I expected the bottom of RS 3.364 to meet the broken upper edge of the main tablet before it could be moved down far enough for the upper edges to match.

Reality, however, did not match expectations. Instead of the rough broken edge of the main fragment impeding the smaller fragment from sliding down far enough, the edge of the smaller fragment fitted perfectly into a set of corresponding notches on the larger fragment (figure 2). The association of the two fragments was not only plausible, there was a good physical join between the two: when the two fragments are properly aligned, one feels an actual click as they slide into place together. Because the join occurs below the surface level (i.e., the inscribed surface of the two fragments, especially that of *CTA* 3, is broken away along the line of the join), I was at first dubious about its validity. I have experienced other cases where what appears to be a subsurface join between fragments turns out to be illusory because of any one of several factors: the angle between the two fragments is wrong, the surface levels do not match, the texts do not match, etc. In the present case, however, there is a literary argument of the very first quality to substantiate the apparent physical join. It was always clear that RS 3.364:14 begins with the last sign of a word the first signs of which would have been inscribed at the end of the preceding line. The first thing I did after the two fragments had clicked into place together was to check to see whether this only possible positioning of RS 3.364 with respect to *CTA* 3 provided a plausible new text. The result left no doubt whatever: the last signs of *CTA* 3 i 13 were {rišk} with the tip of the {k} touching the column divider. This word is in parallel with {ʿnkm} in the following line and there can be no doubt that the {m} at the beginning of RS 3.364:14 belongs with {rišk} and that the parallel is {riškm} || {ʿnkm}, "your (du./pl.) heads"[11] || "your eyes." The scribe, almost certainly the well-known ʾIlîmilku, with no space available to place the last sign of the word *riškm* in line 13, decided, rather than to squeeze the sign in at an angle between lines 14 and 15 of col. v, to adopt his only other option, that of completing the writing of the word in the following line. Similar cases are found elsewhere in multicolumned tablets (cf. Dijkstra 1987), one just below in *CTA* 3 vi 19'–20' {tštḥ|wy}.

Text of RS 3.364

1) *[-]⸢-⸣k . mgn . rbt . ảṯrt*
2) *[y]⸢m⸣ . mǵẓ . qnyt . ỉlm*
3) *[-] ⸢t⸣tn . bt . l bʿl . km*
4) *[ỉ]lm . w ḥẓr . k bn*
5) *⸢ả⸣ṯrt . gm . l ǵlmh*
6) *⸢b⸣ʿl . yṣḥ . ʿn . gpn*
7) *⸢w⸣ ủgr . bn . ǵlmt*
8) *ʿmm ⸢.⸣ ym . bn . ẓlm[t]*[12]
9) *rmt . prʿt . ỉbr[. ⸢-⸣nt]*[13]
10) *ṣḥrrm . ḥbl⸢-⸣ [...]*
11) *ʿrpt . tḥt . ⸢-⸣ [...]*
12) *mʿṣrm . ḥ[...]*
13) *glṯ . ỉs⸢r⸣ [...]*
14) *m . brq[...]*
15) *ymt⸢m⸣ [...]*
16) *šỉ[...]*
17) ⸢-⸣[...]

[11] Singular in Ugaritic because each of the addressees would have had only one head.

[12] The first sign of the last word is certainly {ẓ}: Virolleaud copied it clearly as such but his transliteration of this sign as "s̱" (1932:159) was apparently mistaken by Driver (1956:119) for {ṣ} because that was his transliteration (cf. Clines 1974:24; refutation by Mazzini 1999:81–82), corrected by Gibson (1978:132). In the first full transliteration of the text into Latin script after the *editio princeps* (Bauer 1936:57), this sign, of which the value was still under dispute, was indicated by "x," but by the time Gordon published his transliteration (1947:144), the convention of using {ẓ} was established and he correctly transliterated the sign in this passage.

[13] The end of *CTA* 4 vii 56 is commonly read as {ỉbrmnt}, but, judging from an excellent digital photograph, the {m} is impossible. A word divider appears to have been placed right on the tip of the {r}, then there is either a very short wedge or else simply damage between the word divider and the clear vertical. The correct reading appears to be {ỉbr ⸢. g⸣nt} but {ỉbr ⸢. ṣ⸣nt} cannot be ruled out on the basis of this photograph (there appears also to be a word divider across the tail of the {t}, but that is of less importance). I have not yet collated this passage on the original, however, and am loath to propose a reading on the basis of the photograph alone.

Composite Text[14]

12) *mᶜṣrm . ḥ*[--]⸢-⸣[15] *CTA* 3 vi 1'
13) *gl*<u>*t*</u> *. i̇s*⸢*r*⸣ [.]⸢*r*⸣*i̇šk* *CTA* 3 vi 2'
14) *m . brq*[*m .*] ⸢*b*⸣*n ᶜnkm* *CTA* 3 vi 3'
15) *y mt*⸢*m*⸣ [--]⸢.⸣*ålp* *CTA* 3 vi 4'
16) *ši̇* [*r . b*] *ym . rbt* *CTA* 3 vi 5'
17) ⸢-⸣ [-- .]*b nhrm* *CTA* 3 vi 6'
18) [ᶜ]⸢*b*⸣*r . gbl . ᶜbr* *CTA* 3 vi 7'
19) *qᶜl . ᶜbr . i̇ht* *CTA* 3 vi 8'
20) *np* ⸢.⸣ *šmm . šmšr* *CTA* 3 vi 9'
21) *l dgy . å*<u>*t*</u>*rt* *CTA* 3 vi 10'
22) *mǵ . l qdš . åmrr* *CTA* 3 vi 11'
23) *i̇dk . ål . ttn* *CTA* 3 vi 12'
24) *pnm . tk . ḥqkpt* *CTA* 3 vi 13'
25) *i̇l . klh . kptr* *CTA* 3 vi 14'
....

Translation

[1] ["...] a gift (for) the Great Lady, ʾA<u>t</u>iratu of the [2] Sea,
a present (for) the Progenitress of the Gods,
[3] That she may grant a house to Baᶜlu like [4] the
(other) gods' (houses),
a court like (the courts of) the sons of [5] ʾA<u>t</u>iratu."
Aloud to his lads [6] does Baᶜlu cry:
"Look, Gapnu-[7]wa-ʾUgāru:
In darkness is the sea [8] enveloped,
in obscuri[ty] [9] the highest peaks.
...[...] [10] are dried up ...
[11] clouds under [...]
[12] ... [...]
[I]n [13] driving showers (is) the bond of your heads,
[14] lightning bolts (are) on your foreheads.
[15] O men, [traverse] a thousand [16] *ši̇*[*r*-measures in]
the sea,
ten thousand [17] [X-measures] in the rivers.
[18] [Cr]oss the mountain, cross [19] the peak,
cross the shores to [20] the heavenly height.
Draw nigh [21] unto the fisherman of ʾA<u>t</u>iratu,
[22] go to Qudšu-ʾAmrur.
[23] Then (all of you) are to head [24] off
to Memphis, [25] (to) the god of it all,
(To) Crete...

[14] The text resulting from the join of RS 3.364 with *CTA* 3 vi provides a salutary warning against textual reconstructions that are not based on clearly parallel texts: in Dietrich, Loretz, and Sanmartín 1995:15, one finds a reconstruction of *CTA* 3 vi 1'–4' that has nothing to do with the text provided by the join with RS 3.364 and this nonexistent text is the basis for the authoritative German-language translation in Dietrich and Loretz 1997:1150.

[15] The sign partially visible at the end of *CTA* 3 vi 1' is certainly {b,d}.

Implications of the Join of RS 3.364 with CTA *3*

Literarily speaking, the most important result of the join is that it assures that *CTA* 3 and *CTA* 4 appeared in that sequence in ʾIlîmilku's version of the Baᶜlu story: the reference to gifts for ʾA<u>t</u>iratu in RS 3.364 belongs perforce to a stage of the story leading up to the manufacture of the gifts as recounted in *CTA* 4 i. Precisely the same technical terms for the gifts are used, *mgn* and *mǵẓ*, and the rarity and technical nature of the terms leave no doubt that the reference is to the very same gifts and to an identical function for these gifts as in *CTA* 4. A long-standing debate is thus resolved (the history of the discussion is laid out in Smith 1994:2–19) and the literary arguments for various other arrangements of the tablets may now be laid to rest. This new certainty regarding the ordering of *CTA* 3 and *CTA* 4 offers little, of course, for the question of the place of *CTA* 1 and *CTA* 2 in the cycle; but it does provide two solid blocks of text, *CTA* 3–*CTA* 4 and *CTA* 5–*CTA* 6 (the sequence of these two tablets is assured by a continuous text from the one to the other) and it must be said that the broad scholarly consensus for seeing the last two tablets as completing the cycle is only reinforced by the joining of the first two. What might be described as a minor experiment in the Aleppo museum thus has far-reaching consequences for the definition of the Baal Cycle as conceived by its Late Bronze Age redactor (and poet?), ʾIlîmilku.

Descending from the heights of macrostructure to the foothills of plot line, the new composite text requires a modification of our views of the role of two characters named in *CTA* 3 vi. The real question that needed to be asked when this text stood on its own was why the messengers named therein as being dispatched by Baᶜlu are best known as ʾA<u>t</u>iratu's messengers (Qudšu-ʾAmrur, associated with the "fisherman[16] of ʾA<u>t</u>iratu")—something in which recent commentators, including myself, appear to have been supremely uninterested.[17] Unfortunately, the very presence in the text of Baᶜlu as the sender is uncer-

[16] I follow the convention of translating the term as singular, though it may be dual—cf. *CTA* 4 ii 32, where there is no word divider after {bdk} and the following sign could be {m} (only the right portion of a horizontal wedge is preserved).

[17] There is no comment on the difficulty in Pardee 1997: 255 (cf. n. 116, where a positive spin is put on the fact that Baᶜlu is the sender), Smith 1997:119, or Wyatt 1998:90. In a rapid overview of the major translations, I have not found anyone since Ginsberg's mention of the problem (1950:138 n. 18) who has attempted a literary explanation of the event.

tain, based as it is on two partially preserved signs in *CTA* 3 vi 24', which have been taken as the first two signs of *åliyn*, the standard title of that divinity, giving the reading/restoration {⌈ål⌉[iyn bˁl]}, "Mighty Baˁlu." De Moor, who places *CTA* 3 in first position in the cycle, proposes to read {⌈åd⌉} instead of {⌈ål⌉}, to restore the word as {⌈åd⌉[ty]}, "my lady," and to see in it an address to ˀAṯiratu (de Moor 1987:18 n. 97; followed by Dietrich and Loretz [1997:1150], without comment, but who translate the Baal Cycle in the order adopted in *CTA*, i.e., with this text as the third in the cycle). The reading proposed by de Moor is certainly possible because the bottom of the second sign is broken away and it may be read as {l}, {ů}, or {d}; but *ådt*, "lady," is, according to present attestations, a prose word, never occurring in a well-preserved poetic text. It appears preferable, therefore, to retain the traditional restoration and to explain the presence of ˀAṯiratu's messengers in col. vi as somehow related to Baˁlu's appeal to ˀAṯiratu for a house as voiced by ˁAnatu in *CTA* 3 v 44–45 (lines 36–37 in Dietrich, Loretz, and Sanmartín 1976/1995). But here also the precise chain of events between ˁAnatu's speech before ˀIlu and the events of RS 3.364 + *CTA* vi is obscured by a lacuna of at least twenty lines between columns v and vi of this tablet. However that may be, the join of RS 3.364 to *CTA* 3 vi leaves little doubt that the imperatives in *CTA* 3 vi 7'–11' (lines 18–22 of the composite text) were in fact addressed to Baˁlu's messengers Gapnu-wa-ˀUgāru and that the particle *l* in *CTA* 3 vi 10'–11' (lines 21–22 of the composite text) is not vocative, as has been generally accepted in recent scholarship,[18] but the preposition with the translation value of "at, to," etc. In the context as visible now, Baˁlu can only be telling his personal messengers to go to ˀAṯiratu's personal attendants. This command is followed immediately by the standard formula for sending messengers to a deity and the deity is identified as Kôṯaru-wa-Ḫasīsu || Hayyinu—there is no transition explaining the relationship to be observed between the two sets of messengers. This absence of explication of the role of ˀAṯiratu's messengers might be interpreted as meaning that they are to accompany Baˁlu's messengers in their journey to the abode of Kôṯaru-wa-Ḫasīsu || Hayyinu, but that is, of course, only a conclusion from silence. If such is the case, the function of ˀAṯiratu's attendants would have been to bear witness to their lady of the origin and hence of the quality of the gifts that will eventually be prepared by the craftsman deity. In a very broken passage in *CTA* 4 ii, situated between the arrival of Baˁlu and ˁAnatu at ˀAṯiratu's dwelling and their formal reception therein (lines 29 and following—the extent of the speech is uncertain because of the state of the tablet here), ˀAṯiratu addresses commands to her "fisherman," the same *dgy* as in *CTA* 3 vi 10' = composite text line 21. It has not been previously suspected that her "fisherman" may in fact have arrived with Baˁlu and ˁAnatu as they come bearing gifts, but that must now be considered at least a possibility.

Another important literary question to be discussed in terms of the join is the similarity between this new text and *CTA* 4 vii 5–57. It may be recalled that RS 3.364 was first published by Virolleaud as helpful in explaining the passage in the tablet that has since come to be commonly identified as the fourth in the cycle. The principal problem is that the passage in *CTA* 4 has to do with Baˁlu sending his messengers to Môtu and the damaged passage has been partially reconstructed on the basis of RS 3.364, with some seeing the peculiar vocabulary of the two texts as expressive of the projected encounter with the god of death (e.g., Wyatt 1998:111–12; Mazzini 1999:82). The new text resulting from the join of RS 3.364 with *CTA* 3 vi eliminates the latter interpretation, for the new continuous text leads directly to an encounter with the craftsman deity Kôṯaru-wa-Ḫasīsu || Hayyinu. The first thing to be stated is that the identity/similarity of the passages extends only to *CTA* 4 vii 57, usually reconstructed to read {[ṣḥrrm . ḥblm . b] ˁrpt} on the basis of RS 3.364:10–11. But even this reconstruction is in part hypothetical because the end of line 10 has disappeared and the even more fragmentary nature of the two texts thereafter precludes any reconstruction of the last three lines of *CTA* 4 vii and of RS 3.364:11–12—the signs and words that do remain do not, however, line up neatly and a common reconstruction may be judged unlikely. It would appear, therefore, that the terms in RS 3.364:6–11 and *CTA* 4 vii 53–57 could precede the dispatch of Baˁlu's messengers to any deity and that the terms proper for a visit to Môtu, if present at all, would have followed the preserved passage of *CTA* 4 vii. (For treatment of a specific problem in the comparison of RS 3.364 and *CTA* 4, see comment below to lines 7–8.)

Finally, there is an intriguing concentration of words in lines 13–14 that occur also in RS 24.245:1–7 (Virolleaud 1968:text 3), a literary depiction of the god Baˁlu, who sits as solidly as a mountain, who crouches as broadly as the waters below. He is said to have seven thunderbolts, his head is in the heavenly showers (*rišh b glṯ b šm*[*m*]) while his daughters

---

[18] In addition to the recent translations cited in the previous note, see del Olmo Lete and Sanmartín 1996:239 (interpretation retained in the English translation: 2003:486).

Dewy and Misty groom his head and his forehead (*rišh tply ṭly bn ˁnh* [*bt rb*]).[19] The motifs are distributed differently in RS 3.364, but it appears legitimate to interpret the parallels with the description of the weather deity as meaning that his messengers are to bear their master's insignia in a manner that makes them instantly recognizable as his envoys. Perhaps the most distinctive of these terms is *gl*ṯ, for it appears only in these two texts and in *CTA* 4 iv–v 69–71 (v 7–9). This third passage presents ˀAṯiratu as describing the effects of Baˁlu receiving permission to construct a palace in the following terms:

wn åp ˁdn mṭrh bˁl
*yˁdn ˁdn ṯkt b gl*ṯ
w tn qlh b ˁrpt
šrh l års brqm

For now Baˁlu can send his rain in due season,
can send the season of driving showers,
can shout aloud in the clouds,
shoot lightning bolts to the earth.

Though there has been a good deal of uncertainty regarding the precise meaning of *gl*ṯ, there can be little doubt that it depicts one of the weather deity's prime productions and that in RS 3.364/*CTA* 3 vi the term functions as a symbol by which his servants may be recognized.

(Brief) Commentary

Line 1. The first word was certainly formed of three signs, not two, as the editor proposed (Virolleaud 1932:158 {[ì]k}), followed by Herdner (1963:47) and by Dietrich, Loretz, and Sanmartín (1976:30; 1995: 30): the first word divider in line 2 is situated just under the junction of the first two preserved signs of line 1 and that word divider was preceded by two full signs—the conclusion is unavoidable that the first sign partially preserved in line 1 must have been preceded by another.[20] No trace of the lower tip of an {ì} is visible (contra Dietrich, Loretz, and Sanmartín 1976:30; 1995:30); quite to the contrary, both the tip of a lower horizontal wedge and the upper right corner of a vertical wedge are visible and the second sign can only have been {b}, {d}, or {ù}. Because the closest parallel to this verse contains a verb that cannot be restored here (*CTA* 4 i 21 *šskn mˁ*, "do prepare"), the restoration of the first sign here belongs to the realm of pure hypothesis. The terms *mgn* and *mǵẓ* are the technical terms in *CTA* 4 for the gifts prepared for ˀAṯiratu in the hope of inducing her to plead Baˁlu's case to ˀIlu. There can be very little doubt that they are nouns here[21] because the root of *mǵẓ* is ǴẒY (cf. *ǵẓtm*, "you offered presents," in *CTA* 4 iii 31).

Line 3. The editor read/restored line 3 as {[l] ttn},[22] but Gordon proposed that the first horizontal wedge should be taken as the right wedge of {w}: his reading was {⸢w⸣ tn} (1947:144). This reading was followed Herdner (1963:47), by Dietrich, Loretz, and Sanmartín (1976:30; 1995:30), and subsequently by most commentators.[23] The problem with Gordon's

[19] For this interpretation, see Pardee 1988:ch. 3.

[20] I first studied and prepared a copy of this text in 1995; a new digital photograph was done in 2003 and I went back to the fragment in 2005 and prepared a new copy traced from a printout of the digital photograph. Between the first and the second of these dates, a small chip disappeared from the upper left corner, removing the traces of the first sign that was previously partially visible and the left part of the {k}. The copy provided here (see figure 1) and my textual remarks reflect the state of the fragment as I saw it in 1995 and as it is visible in the photograph in Herdner 1963; the sign traces in question are not, of course, visible on the new photograph provided here. My attention was drawn back to this fragment in 2005 by R. Hawley, who was studying it in the context of his intention to reedit all the Ugaritic school texts—after close analysis of the fragment, we are in agreement that everything goes against that classification, as I have argued here above. My thanks to Hawley for his remarks offered while I was collating the fragment and for a close reading of preliminary forms of this manuscript (his reading improved my presentation at several points, but it is I, not he, who must bear the brunt of any criticisms thereof).

[21] As Ginsberg (1950:131) saw immediately and as has been the recent trend (Wiggins 1993:79; Smith 1997:179; Merlo 1998:97; Wyatt 1998:152) in translations of RS 3.364. Gordon (1949:38; 1977:102) translated both forms as verbs (cf. Driver 1956:119; Binger 1997:8), having earlier supported this interpretation by the remark that "*mǵẓ*... might be the D participle 'entreater, intercessor (with)'" (Gordon 1947:260). Though much more plausible than Mullen's (1980:67) vocalization as a G-stem participle of a root MǴẒ, this solution must be considered far less likely than the analysis as a *m*-preformative noun, certainly in the case of *CTA* 4 i 21–23, where *mgn* || *mǵẓ* function as direct objects of a transitive verb meaning "to prepare," because participles normally denote animate entities, which would require that the gifts be considered as personified (as indeed is implied in Gordon's literal translation in 1947:260).

[22] Montgomery and Harris (1935:72) transcribed {. . ttn}, as though two signs could be missing (they only indicate one dot before {k mgn} in line 1); Bauer (1936:57) transcribed {-ttn}, that is, with a dash but no square brackets.

[23] Even Wyatt (1998:152), who, however, believing the text to be a student's exercise, proposes to see the text as faulty for {w in}.

reading is that the verbal form *tn* should normally be an imperative, but the subject would here be unknown. The grant must ultimately come from ʾIlu, and the presence of this form here might lead to the conclusion that this verse is the last of a message that is to be transmitted either directly or indirectly to ʾIlu. On the other hand, the form *tn* is attested in another passage where it cannot function as the imperative (*CTA* 4 iv–v 70 [v 8]), and some have analyzed it there as a verbal substantive.[24] The same solution might be adopted here.[25] Ginsberg, however, followed the editor's lead in identifying the verbal form as *ttn*, which would have been preceded by a particle ("(So) [she] will give" [1950:131]), as did Driver ("[that] she may give" [1956:119]). This makes good sense following the reference to gifts for ʾAṯiratu, the only problem being that "give" would have, if the fragment is properly situated in the flow of the narrative, the pregnant meaning of "induce ʾIlu to do the actual granting," for there is never any hint that ʾAṯiratu herself has the authority to grant a palace to Baʿlu.[26] The head of the first horizontal wedge is not preserved and there is thus no certain criterion for determining whether it was {t} preceded by another sign or the last wedge of a {w}. Comparing the space available at the beginning of the line with the preceding and following lines leaves no doubt that there is sufficient room to reconstruct another sign before this wedge if the reading {⌈t⌉tn} is preferred: the sign {i} occupies a roughly equivalent space in the following line and a {y} and part of a {m} the same space in the preceding line. Virolleaud suggested that the additional sign would have been {l} because the asseverative particle *l* is attested several times before {ttn}. That occurs, however, only in the formula for sending messengers, YTN + *pnm*, "to head off" (lit. "to set the face"). Thus the restoration {[w] ⌈t⌉tn} might be preferable, though this {w} would have been a bit shorter than the only other two in the text (lines 4 and 7, the latter example appearing at the beginning of the line and extending further to the right than would have been the case in line 3). Also possible is the restoration of {l}, as Virolleaud supposed, and the possibility of a very long {w} followed by {tn} cannot be ruled out. Any of these solutions makes of ʾAṯiratu the addressee and requires that this fact be interpreted as a pregnant usage, as was suggested above, or conceivably as a sort of misunderstanding on the part of Baʿlu (and ʿAnatu), as was suggested by Mullen (1980:67–68).

Lines 7, 8 *bn . . . bn*. The crux of this passage is whether to favor the parallel, where the corresponding forms are *b . . . bn* (*CTA* 4 vii 54, 55) and the expression appears to be prepositional,[27] or this text, where the two tokens of *bn* could represent the common noun meaning "son."[28] In either of these ap-

[24] For the history of discussion, see de Moor 1971:150; this solution has been admitted by Tropper (2000:257 [§51.41h], 489 [§73.526], 638 [§75.516c]). Herdner 1963: 26 emends to {<y>tn}.

[25] Gordon 1949:48 (and 1977:102) and Smith 1997:179 translate as a passive. Mullen 1980:67 translates as an imperative and vocalizes the form as f.s.; Merlo 1998:97 as an imperative, but with no comment on the addressee.

[26] Mullen (1980:67) vocalized the form as f.s. impv., taking it as addressed to ʾAṯiratu, a solution that is literarily credible, but assumes a very long {w} before {tn}—see following epigraphic remarks.

[27] So Virolleaud, in the *editio princeps* of RS 3.364: "Il s'agit de la préposition בֵּין, puisqu'il y a *b* dans II AB, à cette place" (1932:158 n. 1). Other interpreters who have taken *CTA* 4 vii 54–55 as containing parallel prepositional phrases (many have translated *CTA* 4, few RS 3.364, and it is thus rarely possible to compare a given scholar's rendition of both texts): Gaster 1934:710; Driver 1956:101, 121 (both texts); Gibson 1978:66; Aartun 1978:25–26; del Olmo Lete 1983:210; Day 1985:147; Segert 1980:296; Pardee 1997:263; Tropper 2000:584, 823.

[28] Among early interpreters, Barton (1935:57) appears to have been the first to take RS 3.364 as providing evidence for the interpretation of *CTA* 4 vii 54–55: "The variant text (Syria, XIII, 158), reads *bn*, 'son,' which, in the context, gives a much better reading"; nearly a decade later, Ginsberg (1944:28 n. 13; cf. 1950:131, 135) adopted the same position; Gordon (1949:37, 38; cf. 1977:101, 102, and 1947:219) did the same but he did not believe it necessary to emend. Indeed, with this interpretation, two explanations have been offered for the form {b} in *CTA* 4 vii 54: it would represent (1) a scribal error for {bn} (Barton 1935: 57; Ginsberg 1944:28 n. 13; 1950:135; Gray 1957:n. 4; Segert 1958:198; Herdner 1963:30; de Moor 1971:164, 165; Caquot and Sznycer 1974:219; Dietrich, Loretz, and Sanmartín 1976:20; 1995:21; Margalit 1980:68; Dietrich and Loretz 1994:37, 41; Smith 1997:172 n. 148; Wyatt 1998:111 n. 171; Mazzini 1999:82; Loretz 2000:276), or (2) the assimilation of the /n/ to the following word (Gordon 1947:219 "the short prefixed form"; 260 "biǵǵalmat- < bin + ǵalmat-"; Dahood 1960:195; Virolleaud 1953:43 "On écrit . . . *bǵlmt* pour *bn ǵlmt*"; Lipiński 1981:385 "l'assimilation ou l'aphérèse du *n*"; Rendsburg 1989:108; Tropper 2000:144; Tsumura 2005:149). And two syntactic divisions have also been proposed: (1) the word "son" would modify the messengers, who would be "sons of ǴLMT/ẒLMT" (Barton 1935:47; Ginsberg 1944:29 n. 13; 1950:131, 135; Gordon 1949:37, 38; 1977:101, 102; Gray 1957 n. 4; Fensham 1966:63; Caquot and Sznycer 1974:219; Lipiński 1981:385; Dijkstra 1983:29; Smith 1997:138, 179); (2) the word "son" begins a new syntactic unit, so that "the son(s) of ǴLMT/ẒLMT" is/are the one(s) who bring(s) darkness (de Moor 1971:164; 1986:8; 1990:87; Margalit 1980:68 [only *ẓlmt*]; Dietrich and Loretz

proaches, the terms *ǵlmt*/*ẓlmt* have been taken either as variant forms of a word for "darkness"[29] or as words designating young females.[30] The parallel passage is also damaged but, as we have seen, the terminology of lines 7–11 cannot refer specifically to Môtu or his realm. Unfortunately, the state of this fragment precludes any certainty as to the meaning of lines 9b–12 and the interpretation of *bn ǵlmt* || *bn ẓlmt* is thereby rendered problematic.

Lines 9–12. Given the state of these lines and of the parallel text in *CTA* 4 vii, as well as the absence of any good parallel, a plausible reconstruction of this passage appears beyond reach at present. The multiple possibilities behind ᵓBR (one form of which means "pinion") and ḤBL (one form of which means "flock [of birds]"), as well as the difficulty of taking {mᶜṣrm} as related to the Ugaritic word *ᶜṣr*, "bird,"[31] render any interpretation of these lines as having to do with avian congregations uncertain.[32]

Line 13 {ỉs⸢r⸣}. The reading of the last sign as {r} must be classed as epigraphically likely (the only possible readings are {k,w,r} and the height of the upper corner of the right-most preserved wedge makes {r} the most likely of the alternatives) and as philologically probable (neither {ỉs⸢k⸣} nor {ỉs⸢w⸣} would provide an intelligible text). Imperative forms of I-ᵓ roots are poorly attested in Ugaritic (see Tropper 2000:425–26), but the analysis as an imperative (Dijkstra 1983:30—the only one of the authors cited above in footnote 1 to propose a translation for the term) may not be judged obvious: because there is no reason to doubt that ᵓSR had /u/ as the theme vowel in the imperative and the /YQTL/ forms, one might expect {ủsr}. Perhaps, therefore, {ỉsr} is either a noun designating a "binding," a "bond," or a D-stem perfective, "he has affixed."[33]

Line 16 {šỉ[-]}. Though previously unattested in one of the literary formulae expressing distance to be traveled and indeed of uncertain origin, *šỉr* functions in prose to express a surface measure of fields and vineyards and is hence the only plausible restoration here. It is more difficult to say whether *kmn*, the standard parallel to *šd* as a surface measure in poetry, is the proper restoration at the beginning of the next line, though the reading is certainly plausible from a purely epigraphic perspective (see remark above on the reading of {t} in previous editions).

Summary

The join of RS 3.364 to *CTA* 3 vi is an epigraphic reality that is confirmed by the neat solution that it provides to the apparent disparity between the forms {⸢r⸣ỉšk} and {ᶜnkm} in *CTA* 3 vi 2'–3'. The new text provided by the join shows Baᶜlu ordering his messengers Gapnu-wa-ᵓUgāru to join forces with ᵓAṯiratu's personal attendants Daggāyu[34] || Qudšu-ᵓAmrur in forming an embassy to the craftsman deity Kôṯaru-wa-Ḫasīsu || Hayyinu for the purpose of requesting the latter to prepare a set of handsome gifts for ᵓAṯiratu. This sequence of events can only precede the actual production of the gifts and their presentation to ᵓAṯiratu as recounted in *CTA* 4 and the original sequence of the tablets *CTA* 3 and *CTA* 4 in this order is thereby firmly established.

1997:1170; Wyatt 1998:111–12, 152; Loretz 2000:276–77).

[29] Barton 1935:57; Gaster 1934:710; 1935:42–43; Gordon 1947:233, 260; Ginsberg 1950:131; Driver 1956:101, 121; Gray 1957 n. 4 (*ẓlmt*, perhaps *ǵlmt*); de Moor 1971:164, 172; 1986:8; 1990:87; Caquot and Sznycer 1974:219; Gibson 1978:66; Margalit 1980:68 (only *ǵlmt*); del Olmo Lete 1983:210; Day 1985:147; Segert 1988:296; del Olmo Lete and Sanmartín 1996:157; Pardee 1997:263; Wyatt 1998: 111–12, 152; Loretz 2000:276–77.

[30] Gordon 1947:233, 260; Gray 1957 n. 4 (*ǵlmt* only); Aistleitner 1964:46; Lipiński 1981:385; Dijkstra 1983:29; Smith 1997:179 (with hesitation expressed in n. 6, p. 180).

[31] Given the various related but different forms of this word in the Semitic languages (the cognates are indicated in the various dictionaries), a Ugaritic form showing the root ᶜṢR and with *m*-preformative would almost have to be an inner Ugaritic denominative. It is just as likely that we are dealing here with the first attestation in Ugaritic of the Semitic root ᶜṢR of which the derivatives express notions of "restraining, retaining," etc.

[32] This was the line taken by Ginsberg 1944; 1958; Gordeon 1949; 1977; Driver 1956; Fensham 1966; Dijkstra 1983.

[33] On the writing of the D-stem /QTLa/ perfective with {ỉ}, see Bordreuil and Pardee 2004:(I) 66–67.

[34] As was indicated above (note 16), there is as yet no certain basis for the analysis of this term as singular or dual (or plural).

BIBLIOGRAPHY

Aartun, K.
1974 *Die Partikeln des Ugaritischen*. Part 2, *Präpositionen, Konjunktionen*. AOAT 21/2. Kevelaer, Germany: Butzon and Bercker.

Aistleitner, J.
1964 *Die mythologischen und kultischen Texte aus Ras Schamra*. Bibliotheca Orientalis Hungarica 8. Budapest: Akadémiai Kiadó.

Barton, G. A.
1935 The Second Liturgical Poem from Ras Shamra: A Liturgy for the Festival of the God Alein. *JAOS* 55:31–58.

Bauer, H.
1936 *Die alphabetischen Keilschrifttexte von Ras Schamra*. Kleine Texte für Vorlesungen und Übungen 168. Berlin: de Gruyter.

Binger, T.
1997 *Asherah: Goddesses in Ugarit, Israel and the Old Testament*. JSOTSup 232. Sheffield, England: Sheffield Academic Press.

Bordreuil, P., and D. Pardee
1989 *La trouvaille épigraphique de l'Ougarit*. Vol. 1, *Concordance*. Ras Shamra–Ougarit 5/1. Paris: Éditions recherche sur les civilisations.
2004 *Manuel d'ougaritique*. 2 vols. Paris: Geuthner.

Clines, D. J. A.
1974 The Etymology of Hebrew *ṣelem*. *Journal of Northwest Semitic Languages* 3:19–25.

Cunchillos, J.-L., and J.-P. Vita, eds.
1993 *Banco de datos filológicos semíticos noroccidentales*. Part 1, *Datos ugaríticos*: I. *Textos ugaríticos*. Madrid: Instituto de Filología.

Dahood, M.
1960 Review of Segert 1958. *Biblica* 41:194–95.

Day, J.
1985 *God's Conflict with the Dragon and the Sea: Echoes of a Canaanite Myth in the Old Testament*. University of Cambridge Oriental Publications 35. Cambridge: Cambridge University Press.

Dietrich, M., and O. Loretz
1994 Rasuren und Schreibfehler in den keilalphabetischen Texten aus Ugarit: Anmerkungen zur Neuauflage von KTU. *UF* 26:23–61.
1997 *Mythen und Epen*. Vol. 4. Texte aus der Umwelt des Alten Testaments 3/6. Gütersloh: Güterloher Verlagshaus.

Dietrich, M., O. Loretz, and J. Sanmartín
1976 *Die keilalphabetischen Texte aus Ugarit*. AOAT 24/1. Kevelaer, Germany: Butzon and Bercker.
1995 *The Cuneiform Alphabetic Texts from Ugarit, Ras Ibn Hani and Other Places (KTU: 2nd, enlarged edition)*. Abhandlungen zur Literatur Alt-Syrien-Palästinas und Mesopotamiens 8. Münster: Ugarit-Verlag.

Dijkstra, M.
1980 *Gods Voorstelling: Predikatieve expressie van zelfopenbaring in Oudoosterse teksten en Deutero-Jesaja*. Dissertationes Neerlandicae, series theologica 2. Kampen: Kok.
1982 Review of Margalit 1979. *BiOr* 39:147–53.
1983 Contributions to the Reconstruction of the Myth of Baᶜal. *UF* 15:25–31.
1987 Epigraphic Evidence for the Determination of the Column-Order in the Tablets KTU 1.1 and KTU 1.20–22. *UF* 19:49–60.

Driver, G. R.
1956 *Canaanite Myths and Legends*. Old Testament Studies 3. Edinburgh: T. and T. Clark.

Fensham, F. C.
1966 Winged Gods and Goddesses in the Ugaritic Tablets. *Oriens Antiquus* 5:157–64.

Gaster, T. H.
1934–35 The Combat of ᵓAleyân-Baᶜal and Mōt, a Proto-Hebrew Epic from Ras-Shamra: The Second Tablet, Transliterated from the Cuneiform Original with Introduction, Provisional Translation, Argument, and Commentary. *Journal of the Royal Asiatic Society* 1934:677–714; 1935: 1–44.

Gibson, J. C. L.
1978 *Canaanite Myths and Legends*. 2d ed. Edinburgh: T. and T. Clark.

Ginsberg, H. L.
1944 Baal's Two Messengers. *BASOR* 95:25–30.
1948 Review of Obermann 1948. *JCS* 2:139–44.
1950 Ugaritic Myths, Epics, and Legends. In *Ancient Near Eastern Texts Relating to the Old Testament*, ed. J. B. Pritchard, 129–55. Princeton, N.J.: Princeton University Press.

Gordon, C. H.
1947 *Ugaritic Handbook: Revised Grammar, Paradigms, Texts in Transliteration, Comprehensive Glossary*. AnOr 25. Rome: Pontifical Biblical Institute.
1949 *Ugaritic Literature: A Comprehensive Translation of the Poetic and Prose Texts*. Rome: Pontifical Biblical Institute.
1965 *Ugaritic Textbook: Grammar, Texts in Transliteration, Cuneiform Selections, Glossary, Indices*. AnOr 38. Rome: Pontifical Biblical Institute.

1977 Poetic Legends and Myths from Ugarit. *Berytus* 25:5–133.

Herdner, A.
1963 *Corpus des tablettes en cunéiformes alphabétiques découvertes à Ras Shamra-Ugarit de 1929 à 1939*. Mission de Ras Shamra 10. BAH 79. Paris: Geuthner.

Lipiński, E.
1981 Review of Aartun 1978. *BiOr* 38:383–86.

Loretz, O.
2000 "Schwarze Magie" des Tages in Hi 3,8 und KTU 1.6 VI 45b–53; 1.14 I 19–20; 1.4 VII 54–56. *UF* 32:261–87.

Margalit, B.
1980 *A Matter of "Life" and "Death": A Study of the Baal-Mot Epic (CTA 4–5–6)*. AOAT 206. Kevelaer, Germany: Butzon and Bercker.

Mazzini, G.
1999 On the Meaning of *ṣalmāwet:* A Discussed Word in the Old Testament. *SEL* 16:79–83.

Merlo, P.
1998 *La dea Ašratum–Aṯiratu–Ašera: Un contributo alla storia della religione semitica del Nord*. Rome: Pontificia Università Lateranense.

Montgomery, J. A., and Z. S. Harris
1935 *The Ras Shamra Mythological Texts*. Memoirs of the American Philosophical Society 4. Philadelphia: American Philosophical Society.

Moor, J. C. de
1971 *The Seasonal Pattern in the Ugaritic Myth of Baᶜlu according to the Version of Ilimilku*. AOAT 16. Kevelaer, Germany: Butzon and Bercker.
1986 The Crisis of Polytheism in Late Bronze Ugarit. *Oudtestemntische Studiën* 24:1–20.
1987 *An Anthology of Religious Texts from Ugarit*. Nisaba: Religious Texts Translation Series 16. Leiden: Brill.
1990 *The Rise of Yahwism: The Roots of Israelite Monotheism*. Bibliotheca Ephemeridum Theologicarum Lovaniensium 91. Leuven: Leuven University Press.

Mullen, E. T.
1980 *The Divine Council in Canaanite and Early Hebrew Literature*. HSM 24. Chico, Calif.: Scholars.

Obermann, J.
1948 *Ugaritic Mythology: A Study of Its Leading Motifs*. New Haven, Conn.: Yale University Press.

Olmo Lete, G. del
1981 *Mitos y leyendas de Canaan: segun la tradicion de Ugarit*. Madrid: Ediciones Cristiandad.

Olmo Lete, G. del, and J. Sanmartín
1996 *Diccionario de la lengua ugarítica*. Vol. 1. Aula Orientalis Supplementa 7. Sabadell (Barcelona), Spain: Editorial AUSA.
2003 *A Dictionary of the Ugaritic Language in the Alphabetic Tradition*. Translated by W. G. E. Watson. Handbuch der Orientalistik [Section One: Near and Middle East] 67. Leiden: Brill.

Pardee, D.
1988 *Les textes para-mythologiques de la 24ᵉ campagne (1961)*. Ras Shamra–Ougarit 4. Paris: Éditions recherche sur les civilisations.
1997 The Baᶜlu Myth. In *The Context of Scripture*, vol. 1, *Canonical Compositions from the Biblical World*, ed. W. W. Hallo and K. L. Younger, 241–74. Leiden: Brill.
2000 *Les textes rituels*. Ras Shamra–Ougarit 12. Paris: Éditions recherche sur les civilisations.

Rendsurg, G.
1989 Sabaic Notes to Hebrew Grammar. *Abr-Nahrain* 27:106–19.

Segert, S.
1958 Die Schreibfehler in den ugaritischen literarischen Keilschrifttexten in Anschluß and das textkritische Hilsbuch von Friedrich Delitzsch klassifiert. In *Von Ugarit nach Qumran: Beiträge zur alttestamentlichen und altorientalischen Forschung Otto Eissfeldt zum 1. September 1957 dargebracht von Freunden und Schülern*, ed. W. F. Albright et al., 193–212. BZAW 77. Berlin: Töpelmann.
1988 The Ugaritic Voiced Postvelar in Correspondence to the Emphatic Interdental. *UF* 20:287–300.

Smith, M. S.
1994 *The Ugaritic Baal Cycle*. Vol. 1, *Introduction with Text, Translation and Commentary of KTU 1.1–1.2*. VTSup 55. Leiden: Brill.
1997 The Baal Cycle. In *Ugaritic Narrative Poetry*, ed. S. B. Parker, 81–180. SBL Writings from the Ancient World 9. Atlanta: Scholars.

Tropper, J.
2000 *Ugaritische Grammatik*. AOAT 273. Münster: Ugarit-Verlag.

Tsumura, D. S.
2005 "Misspellings" in Cuneiform Alphabetic Texts from Ugarit: Some Cases of Loss or Addition of Signs. In *Writing and Ancient Near Eastern Society: Papers in Honour of Alan R. Millard*, ed. P. Bienkowski, C. Mee, and E. Slater, 143–53. New York: T. and T. Clark.

Virolleaud, C.
1932 Un nouveau chant du poème d'Aleïn-Baal. *Syria* 13:113–63.
1953 Additions au lexique ugaritique. *Comptes rendus du groupe linguistique d'études Chamito-Sémitiques* 6:43–44.

Wiggins, S.
1993 *A Reassessment of "Ashera": A Study According to the Textual Sources of the First Two Millennia* B.C.E. AOAT 235. Kevelaer, Germany: Butzon and Bercker.

Wyatt, N.
1998 *Religious Texts from Ugarit: The Words of Ilimilku and His Colleagues*. The Biblical Seminar 53. Sheffield, England: Sheffield Academic Press.

39. L'INSCRIPTION PHÉNICIENNE DU PITHOS D'AMATHONTE ET SON CONTEXTE

par Émile Puech

DANS le dépôt de céramique du Chypro-Archaïque dégagé en 1979 dans un bothros à l'intérieur du sanctuaire d'Aphrodite, sous les fondations d'une chapelle d'époque romaine sur l'acropole d'Amathonte,[1] fut repérée une inscription phénicienne peinte à l'encre sur le col d'un pithos de fabrique locale *Plain White IV*, dont furent retrouvés de nombreux fragments, AM 3151 (voir figure 1).[2] L'inscription court parallèlement au rebord inférieur de la lèvre du pithos (diam. d'ouverture 34,8 cm, hauteur restituable 110–120 cm).[3] Les fouilleurs ont donné les premières remarques que l'épigraphiste, M. Sznycer, leur transmit:[4]

> L'inscription contient six lettres phéniciennes, admirablement tracées avec des pleins et déliés, pouvant dater, d'après les critères paléographiques, de la fin du VIIe siècle av. J.-C. Ces six lettres sont, d'une manière sûre, de droite à gauche (transcription en lettres latines de gauche à droite): LʾMRYK. La première lettre, un *lamed* (L), est une préposition d'appartenance "pour," "à," "appartenant à," suivie, comme c'est courant dans de petites inscriptions sur vase, d'un nom propre, très probablement un nom de personnage. Cependant, tout indique que ʾMRYK ne peut constituer un nom phénicien valable, ni même ouest-sémitique. Plutôt qu'à un nom grec, qui serait lui aussi bien curieux, on penserait à un nom autochtone, en l'occurrence étéo-chypriote, dont on aurait ici une transcription en lettres phéniciennes.

C'est là l'essentiel de la note de l'épigraphiste parue aussi ailleurs mais où il a quelque peu nuancé: "La lecture des cinq premières lettres paraît sûre; en ce qui concerne la dernière lettre, on pourrait sans doute hésiter entre un *kaph* (*K*) et un *noun* (*N*)" (Sznycer 1999:197 et fig. 3 et 4).

Mais la lecture proposée *lʾmryk* paraît impossible au premier coup d'œil, car on ne connaît aucun tracé de *mem* phénicien qui corresponde à celui identifié par l'épigraphiste: une tête en "v" avec retour de calame fendu comme dans le tracé de la haste du *ʾaleph*, et une haste à droite et non à gauche comme on l'attendrait pour un *mem*, qui plus est, dans une écriture à l'encre dite cursive (voir photographie 1 et figure 1).[5] En revanche, ce ductus correspond parfaitement au tracé du *waw*, particulièrement à l'époque du Fer II ou Chypro-archaïque I précisément. Or S. Fourrier, qui a étudié la céramique archaïque du dépôt du sanctuaire d'Aphrodite, attribue "l'immense majorité des vases du dépôt à la classe IV, soit 750–600 av. J.-C."[6] La sixième lettre qui est moins claire sur les reproductions, est aussi de lecture un peu moins assurée. L'éditeur hésitait entre *kaph* et *nun*. Il semble que l'hésitation puisse porter entre *kaph* et *mem*, mais un *nun* est certainement ici exclu. On a affaire soit à la tête d'un *mem* au zigzag gauchement tracé, soit bien mieux à un *kaph* à la tête en "v" renversé touchant le haut de la hampe mais dont une écaille de la surface semble avoir endommagé le départ de la hampe. Dans ce cas, les six lettres ont toutes un tracé cohérent et parfaitement connu dans la deuxième moitié du VIIIe siècle et la première moitié du VIIe siècle. On peut leur comparer la graphie de l'inscription de la statue de Séville datée de la deuxième moitié du VIIIe siècle,[7] celle des

---

[1] Voir Hellmann et Hermary 1980, spéc. p. 812 où il est noté: "aucune importation grecque n'y est mêlée. Le reste du matériel est constitué de quelques terres cuites, dont un dromadaire fragmentaire (fig. 14), type unique à Chypre, semble-t-il, à l'époque archaïque, et des lampes-coupelles, dont une à sept becs (fig. 15): cette forme, répandue dans le monde sémitique, est fort rare à Chypre." Dans un chantier distinct de celui du sanctuaire, Aupert 1980 signale (p. 814) la découverte d'"une anse d'amphore d'un type très peu fréquent (fig. 21), qui attesterait des relations entre Amathonte et la Judée aux environs de 700 av. J.-C." Voir encore Aghion 1984 qui note (p. 657–58) la présence de bols et de coupes à bandes rouges et des plats à rebord évasé et à lèvre oblique, dont les uns (les bols) sont d'origine chypriote mais les autres proviennent certainement de centres extérieurs à l'île, et elle les estime comme des importations de Palestine, type céramique dite de Samarie. On a repéré le même type de céramique phénicienne par exemple à Tell Keisân aux niveaux 5 et 4, voir Briend et Humbert 1980, et Bikai 1978.

[2] Voir Hermary, Fourrier et Schmid 2000:542–45 et fig. 31. Les fouilleurs, S. Fourrier et A. Hermary que je remercie, me signalent la parution prochaine de leur étude *Le sanctuaire d'Aphrodite: Des origines à la construction du temple* (Amathonte 7; École française d'Athènes).

[3] Je remercie chaleureusement S. Fourrier pour toutes ces précieuses indications.

[4] Hermary, Fourrier et Schmid 2000:544–45, citant une note de M. Sznycer.

[5] Photographie de Ph. Collet, École française d'Athènes, aimablement communiquée par S. Fourrier.

[6] Voir Hermary, Fourrier et Schmid 2000:544, et pas uniquement *Plain White IV*, ainsi que me le précise S. Fourrier.

[7] Voir Puech 1977:89: deuxième moitié ou même troisième quart.

Figure 1. Inscription phénicienne du pithos d'Amathonte
Photographie par Ph. Collet et dessin par E. Puech.

inscriptions lapidaires de Karatepe datées peu après 700 dans les premières décennies du VIIe siècle,[8] mais leur tracé est un peu plus évolué que celui des coupes en bronze de Chypre vers le milieu du VIIIe siècle,[9] ou de la coupe de Kition,[10] et certainement de l'inscription archaïque de Chypre (voir Puech 1979: "inscription Honeyman"). La position penchée "en avant" du *yod*, la tête du *waw* et surtout la tête du *kaph* avec le petit trait attaché au-dessous et à l'extrémité du trait oblique gauche de la tête de la lettre sont les caractéristiques les plus fiables pour la datation proposée ici. Mais l'écriture à l'encre est généralement plus évoluée qu'une graphie gravée sur pierre, alors qu'une graphie incisée se rapproche davantage d'une écriture à l'encre.

Ainsi la lecture *lʾwryk*, compris comme "A(ppartenant à) *ʾwryk*," paraît-elle de loin la plus vraisemblable, préférable à "Pour *ʾwryk*." Mais l'anthroponyme *ʾwryk* ne répond à aucune forme connue de l'onomastique phénicienne où, à cette haute époque, l'usage de pures *matres lectionis* est certainement exclu. En effet, nulle racine sémitique n'est sous-jacente ou apparente, et la racine *ʾr* "lumière" qui se retrouve en *ʾrmlk*, "Urimilk," dans l'inscription de Yeḥawmilk de Byblos par exemple ne peut être

[8] Bron (1979:163–69) les date de la deuxième moitié ou même du deuxième quart du VIIIe siècle, mais les tracés sont un peu plus variés que ceux du tableau, p. 231. Voir aussi Niehr 2003:56 entre 720 et le début du VIIe siècle, et Hawkins 1979:156s.: début du VIIe siècle.

[9] Coupes généralement désignées comme "les inscriptions de Baʿal du Liban," datées vers le milieu du VIIIe siècle, entre 773 et 738, voir Peckham 1968:14–15 et 115, et planche 7, p. 104–5, voir *infra*.

[10] Voir Puech 1976, l'inscription incisée montre des influences de la cursive.

orthographiée avec *waw*, tout comme le *yod* ici ne peut être analysé comme une *mater lectionis*.[11] Il faut donc chercher dans une autre direction.

Vient alors à l'esprit le nom du roi des Danuniens, *Awarikus*, le roi de Qué en Cilicie, des inscriptions hiéroglyphiques louvites, le roi d'Adana qui promut Azatiwatas sur une partie du royaume, ainsi que le révèle ce dernier dans la narration de ses hauts faits sur les stèles bilingues de Karatepe.[12] Le nom *Awarikus* comprendrait un élément hourrite *awar-k*, "seigneur/roi *-k*."[13] Si, comme il semble, cet Awarikus est à identifier à Urîkki des sources cunéiformes assyriennes, celui-ci régnait sur Qué en 739/38, en 734-732 et en 729/28, puisqu'il payait tribut à Téglat-Phalasar III, et il est encore mentionné en 710/09 sous Sargon II, même si, à cette date, Qué était devenue une province assyrienne, depuis déjà au moins 713 ou même 715 et jusqu'en 705[14] (voir ci-dessous). Urîkki – *ʾwrk* et sa dynastie semblent bien avoir survécu pendant cette période de troubles, comme le suggèrent les inscriptions phéniciennes de Karatepe, puisque Azatiwada dit avoir "rétabli la maison de son seigneur dans le bonheur et avoir installé la descendance d'Urîkki sur le trône royal" à Adana.[15] Azatiwada semble donc avoir assuré une régence au royaume de Qué.

Le même Urîkki est encore connu par l'inscription phénicienne de Hassan Beyli à une quinzaine de kilomètres à l'ouest de Zincirli, sur les contreforts de l'Amanus en direction de Karatepe, mais le contexte est moins facile à saisir.[16] Cette inscription qui est certainement antérieure à celles de Karatepe par Azatiwada, fait du royaume de Qué une province assyrienne. Cela transparaît d'une lecture correcte des lignes 3 à 6,[17] où, au lieu de *]rym wbʾrṣ hmlk ʾšr wybʾ* ". . .] et dans le pays du roi d'Ashour et il vint [. . .," avec une construction impossible en phénicien, on doit lire, ligne 4: *ʾš]rym wbʾrṣ hmlk ʾš yšb ʾ[šr(ym)*, "les Assy]riens et dans le pays du roi où habite(nt) l'A[ssyrie/[les] A[ssyriens . . . ," ce qui répond aux traces visibles des lettres, supprime les impossibilités grammaticales et se coule dans la suite de ces lignes même fragmentaires; ligne 5: "tout le te]rritoire aux mains d'Urîkki, et il fit la [pai]x à Alep et [. . . "; ligne 6: "le ro]yaume d'Assour et le royaume de ce roi (devinrent) un [seul] royaume." Ainsi l'inscription décrit-elle explicitement, sous le règne même d'Urîkki, le royaume de Qué comme une province du grand royaume d'Assyrie. Mais elle n'explicite pas sous quel roi assyrien: Téglat-Phalasar ou Sargon II, ce dernier paraît le plus vraisemblable, mais sans certitude toutefois.[18]

À Çineköy à quelque 30 kilomètres au sud d'Adana, a été découverte fortuitement une autre inscription bilingue portant mention de *Warikas*, roi hiyawéen (= Qué; voir Tekoğlu et Lemaire 2000). Le louvite a orthographié le nom du roi Warikas (*wa/i+ra/i-i-ka-sá*) avec aphérèse du A- qui peut être considéré comme une voyelle prosthétique dans Awarikus de Karatepe calqué sur le phénicien *ʾwrk*; la réduction *wa* du hiéroglyphique au son *u-* de l'assyrien Urîkki est déjà connue pour des noms de personnes.[19] Mais dans cette inscription la graphie porte une autre variante *Warikas*, et comme l'alternance *u/a* est inconnue en hittite et dans les autres langues anatoliennes, l'éditeur suggère de la considérer comme une confusion scribale des signes *ku* et *ka*. Dans la partie phénicienne, le nom commence

---

[11] Ainsi par exemple Dupont-Sommer 1948:80: "homme puissant, illustre" l'expliquant par *ʾwr*, "lumière," mais Dunand 1944–45:93: de la racine *ʾrk* "qui accroît la durée."

[12] Voir Hawkins and Morpurgo Davies 1978, et Hawkins 1979:153–55.

[13] Voir Goetze 1972 et Gröndahl 1967:224s. et p. 234 pour l'élément *-k/-kki* du hourrite.

[14] Voir Hawkins 1979:154–57; Bron 1979:161; Elayi et Cavigneaux 1979:70; Tadmor 1994:54–55, 68–69, 89, 108–9, 170–71, et 265–68, 293; Garelli 1981; et Lanfranchi 2004.

[15] Voir Bron 1979 et ci dessous les inscriptions de Çineköy où le roi Warikas (= Urîkki) dit expressément que "l'Assyrie est devenue pour lui un père et une mère."

[16] Voir Lemaire 1983. Le contexte évoqué semble être antérieur à celui de la tablette de Nimrud, ND 2759, sous Sargon II en 710/09, voir Postgate 1973:21–34 "Sargon's letter referring to Midas."

[17] Déjà Lipiński (1986:87 et note 18) a justement relevé que "la traduction de *ʾrṣ hmlk ʾšr* par 'le pays du roi *d'Ashour*' est grammaticalement impossible, car *hmlk* ne peut être un état construit. L'emploi de l'article ne permet pas de douter que c'est le nom propre du roi qui fait suite à *hmlk*. Bien que les lettres *rdn* soient incertaines, la hampe du *nun* semble bien apparaître sous le *I* de l'inscription byzantine. . . ." Cet auteur veut y lire le nom d'Assarhaddon, *ʾrṣ hmlk ʾšrdn*. Mais cette lecture est aussi totalement exclue.

[18] On ne peut suivre Lemaire (2004:309), qui fait du royaume de Qué une province assyrienne lors de la campagne de Sennachérib en 796, avec la disparition de la dynastie de Mopsos du trône de Qué, du fait de l'absence du nom du descendant d'Urîkki dans l'inscription d'Azatiwada, alors que ce dernier dit avoir assuré la pérennité de la descendance royale sur le trône de Qué. La provincialisation du royaume ne supprime pas automatiquement le monarque avec sa lignée, ainsi que l'atteste le "traité" entre Assur et Qué dans l'inscription de Hassan Beyli bien comprise.

[19] Voir Tekoğlu et Lemaire 2000:974, renvoyant à Laroche 1960:14 nos. 19 et 20. On peut ajouter ici la graphie *su-ra/i-ia-sa* aussi avec aphérèse, et ailleurs *á-sú+ra/i-wa/i-(ni-ti)* pour l'Assyrie (voir Tekoğlu et Lemaire 2000:980).

cette fois certainement par *waw*, et est donc à restaurer *W*[*r*(*y*)*k bn* ---] d'après le louvite. Cette orthographe, probablement "pleine" *W*[*ryk* (?) dans cette inscription,[20] est celle du texte de l'inscription phénicienne de Çebel Ires Daği (8A) *Wryk* (voir ci-dessous), toutefois cette inscription ajoute un *ʾaleph* prosthétique devant une sifflante dans le mot *ʾšpḥ*.[21] Cette inscription, qui fait mention de l'agrandissement du territoire (louvite § II, phénicien lignes 3–4) et de la soumission d'Urîkki à l'Assyrie (§§ VII–VIII et lignes 7–10), suppose que le pays de Qué est déjà, de fait, une province assyrienne, très probablement sous Sargon II, et sans doute quelque temps avant 715 (voir ci-dessus). La paléographie daterait cette inscription quelque peu après celle de Hassan Beyli,[22] et quelques décennies avant l'inscription phénicienne de Karatepe, laquelle se place au mieux dans les premières décennies du VIIe siècle (voir ci-dessus). Cette dernière reprend une série d'expressions de l'inscription de Çineköy qui, à son tour, semble reprendre des formules de l'inscription de Hassan Beyli, à moins que ces deux inscriptions soient plus ou moins contemporaines et disposées en deux points opposés du royaume, à l'est et à l'ouest, comme rappel de la nouvelle situation politique.

Une trilingue en louvite hiéroglyphique, néo-assyrien et phénicien a été découverte en 1995 à Incirli, elle est déposée au Musée de Gaziantep. D'après les premières indications fournies, elle mentionne Awarikku, roi de Qué, et daterait des environs de 730.[23]

À Çebel Ires Daği à quelques kilomètres à l'est d'Alania, a été trouvée une inscription phénicienne portant le nom d'un roi *Wryk*–Urîkki avec aphérèse du *ʾaleph*[24] comme à Çineköy. A la ligne 3b, le graveur orthographie *Wryky*–Urîkkaya,[25] le nom de la localité fondée par le roi *Wryk*–Urîkki (ligne 8a–b), dans une construction identique à *ʾztwdy*–Azatiwadaya, bâtie par *ʾztwd*–Azatiwada des inscriptions phéniciennes de Karatepe (B 10). Cette inscription trouvée hors contexte archéologique dans les ruines de Çebel Ires Daği (= Laertes) devrait, par la paléographie, dater environ du dernier quart du VIIe siècle, soit un siècle après celle de Hassan Beyli. Elle atteste, dans une certaine mesure, la survivance de la descendance ou d'une branche de la dynastie d'Urîkki, roi de Qué en Cilicie Trachée, puisque ce dernier se dit lui aussi roi, *mlk wryk* (ligne 8a–b).[26]

Un sceau provenant de la région de Karaman, à l'est de Karatepe, porte gravé la séquence *lwr*/*kby*/*šhbr*, à lire sans doute comme "à Urikkibiyaš, le bén(i)" (voir Lemaire 1997). L'orthographe *wrk*, réduite à sa plus simple expression, vient sans doute de ce que l'espace réservé est très limité, réduction qui n'a cependant pas permis de graver la dernière lettre *-k* de *hbrk*, lettre somme toute plus importante pour la lecture, mais la formule est aussi bien connue.[27] Une datation paléographique situerait le sceau vers 600 avant J.-C., peu après l'inscription de Çebel Ires Daği. L'anthroponyme *wrk* et le qualificatif *hbr*(*k*) semblent rattacher ce sceau à la même région, le royaume de Qué, et au "clan" d'Urîkki, où son propriétaire devait avoir le rang d'un notable ou d'un haut dignitaire tout au moins.

Quoi qu'il en soit, dans les quatre à cinq graphies à présent connues, le nom du roi en phénicien est orthographié *ʾwrk* sans le *yod* (Hassan Beyli et Karatepe), et dans un (ou deux?) cas *wryk* (Çebel Ires Daği et peut-être Çineköy) avec le *yod* mais sans le *ʾaleph* tout comme dans le toponyme *wryky*, et dans un cas simplement *wrk* (sceau) sans *ʾaleph* ni *yod*. C'est dire l'inconstance et l'hésitation de la transcription d'un anthroponyme d'origine non sémitique. Mais cette même hésitation se retrouve aussi en hiéroglyphique louvite: *Awarikus*–*Warikas* et dans l'écriture cunéiforme: *Ú-ri-ik-ki*, *Ú-ri-ia-ik*, *Ú-ri-ia-*

[20] Voir l'écriture du louvite *ra/i-i* qui suppose in /i/ long.

[21] Contrairement au graveur de l'inscription de Çebel Ires Daği, voir ci-dessous.

[22] La graphie de l'inscription de Çineköy paraît un peu plus évoluée que celle de Hassan Beyli, mais on doit aussi laisser à chaque graveur son idiosyncrasie et sa liberté qui transparaît clairement dans l'exécution des tracés des *kaph* et des *mem* en particulier à Çineköy, lettres qui seraient en faveur d'une datation un peu postérieure, et particulièrement encore dans la transcription du nom (*ʾ*)*wr*(*y*)*k*.

[23] En attendant la publication, voir Kaufman 1997:107, S119: "highly-eroded trilingual inscription (Luwian hieroglyphs, Neo-Assyrian, and Phoenican) of Awarikku, King of Que (Cilicia) from ca. 730 B.C.E. The first two are essentially unreadeable. The latter has been revealed through the unmatched photographic skills of Bruce and Ken Zuckerman." On ne peut que suspecter une graphie *ʾwr*(*y*)*k* sur le schème Awarikku du louvite en attendant confirmation. Pour la bilingue louvito-phénicienne de Ivriz, voir Dinçol 1994 et Röllig 1992, spéc. p. 98, mais on attend toujours la publication du texte.

[24] Voir Mosca et Russell 1987. Mais le graveur a bien orthographié *špḥ* (ligne 6b) sans le *ʾaleph* prosthétique devant une sifflante comme à Çineköy.

[25] On doit certainement lire *bwryky*, non *bwrykly* avec les éditeurs, Mosca et Russell 1987:12s.—le *lamed* n'est pas tracé.

[26] Avec Mosca et Russel 1987:20, "it is tempting to suggest that they belonged to the same royal house, which would thus have continued to survive for over a century in Rough Cilicia, if not in the Cilician plain."

[27] Voir Lemaire 1977, sceaux provenant de ces régions, formule connue aussi à Karatepe.

ik-ki, Ú-ri-ik.[28] La graphie assyrienne suggère, à sa manière, une graphie avec *yod* pour transcrire ce son /*î*/, ce que laisse aussi entendre le louvite *wa/i+ra/i-i-ka-sá* à Çineköy. Dans ce cas, la graphie *ʾwryk* de l'anthroponyme sur le pithos d'Amathonte ne saurait surprendre, puisque ni le *waw* ni le *yod* ne sont alors de pures *matres lectionis* de la langue phénicienne, mais ils servent uniquement à transcrire phonétiquement aussi bien que possible un nom d'origine étrangère.[29]

Dans ce dossier faudrait-il encore rapprocher des anthroponymes bibliques, le roi *ʾrywk*–Ἀριώχ d'Ellasar en Gen. 14:1 et 9, ou les personnages homonymes de Dan. 2:14s et 24s et Jdt. 1:6? Si en *Daniel* et *Judith*, on peut invoquer un emprunt à l'onomastique iranienne *ariy-uka*, cette explication est plus difficile en *Genèse* 14 où une origine hourrite ne peut être exclue, étant donné le récit et les parallèles de Mari, *ar-ri-wu-uk*, et de Nuzi, *ar-ri-uk-ki*. Il est intéressant de relever que Symmaque et Jérôme (Vulgate) ont compris le pays "Ellasar" comme "Le Pont," que le manuscrit qumranien 1QApGn XXI 23s l'a interprété de la Cappadoce (*kptwk*) au nord de Qué, tout comme une inscription bilingue gréco-araméenne, trouvée en Asie mineure à Aghatchakale au sud-ouest de Divrighi à l'est du Halys, atteste des anthroponymes Ἀριούχης.[30] Il est assez surprenant que le texte qumranien ait gardé des connaissances assez précises des quatre "royaumes" dans son adaptation de *Genèse* 14: Kodorlaomer (l'élamite) en Elam, Amraphel (le sémite, voir Ammourapi?) à Babylonne, Aryôk (le hourrite) en Cappadoce et *Tidʿal* (= Tudḫalia le hittite) en Haute Mésopotamie. Quoi qu'il en soit du rapprochement de ces anthroponymes, Aryôk avec *ʾwryk* dans la sphère hourrite, confusion ou rapprochement par des scribes de deux noms proches en *Genèse* et *Daniel–Judith*, on note que l'hébreu comme l'araméen de Qumrân ont transcrit par *reš-yod* le son *-ri-* de la langue d'emprunt.

Ne faudrait-il pas enfin rapprocher le nom d'un roi d'Amathonte sur des tétroboles datés vers 450 avant J.-C., retrouvés dans une nécropole à quelque distance à l'est d'Amathonte, à "Limenia Bay"?[31] La légende est rédigée en étéo-chypriote à l'aide de quatre signes syllabiques en sinistrograde: *wo-ro-i-ko* qu'on explique généralement comme le génitif mycénien *wo-ro-ko-jo*. Le nom du roi *Wroïko(s)* écrit avec le *digamma* au Vᵉ siècle aurait donné (?) Rhoïkos–Ῥοικος, le nom d'un roi d'Amathonte au IVᵉ siècle; il pourrait alors être considéré comme l' "ancêtre ou du moins presque l'homonyme du dynaste" du siècle suivant, considéré d'origine grecque.[32] Toutefois, il est notable que la graphie *wo-ro-i-ko*–Wroïko(s) du milieu du Vᵉ siècle à Amathonte corresponde parfaitement à celle du phénicien *wryk* à Çebel Ires Dağı en Cilicie à la fin du VIIᵉ siècle, et dans ce cas l'origine de l'anthroponyme pourrait être différente.

Telles sont présentement les données onomastiques concernant la graphie *ʾwryk–wryk–wrk* en phénicien en Cilicie aux VIIIᵉ–VIᵉ siècles, correspondant au louvite *Awarikku*, à l'assyrien *Urîkki* et très vraisemblablement, semble-t-il, à l'étéo-chypriote *wo-ro-i-ko–Wroïko(s)* à Amathonte au Vᵉ siècle. On doit maintenant ajouter la même graphie *ʾwryk* en phénicien à Amathonte même au VIIIᵉ siècle. Et il est fort probable que ce même nom est à l'origine des noms dynastiques *Wroïko(s)* (et *Rhoïkos*?) du Vᵉ (et IVᵉ?) siècle, soit sur quelque quatre siècles au moins, et que, même sans la mention de roi, *mlk* ou de *skn*, cet ʾUrîkki écrit sur le pithos d'Amathonte comme offrande à Aphrodite–ʿAštart occupait une haute fonction.

Il n'est pas sans intérêt de noter que cet anthroponyme est caractéristique de "la maison de Mopsos" régnant à Adana dès le VIIIᵉ siècle jusqu'à la

---

[28] Voir Laroche 1966:199, no. 1444 avec des références; Tadmor 1994:54, 68, 86, 89, 170.

[29] On peut leur comparer les graphies *ḥy* et *ḥyʾ* de l'inscription phénicienne de Kilamuwa de Zincirli, *msnzmš* et *msnʾzmš* à Çebel Ires Dağı, sans oublier les formes *ʾšpḥ* à Çineköy à côté de *špḥ* à Çebel Ires Dağı, (*ʾ*)*dn* et *dnnym* (Karatepe et Hassan Beyli) et les formes plurielles en phénicien de *qryt* et *qrhty* (Hassan Beyli), *qṣyt, ḥmyt, šḏyt* où le *yod* transcrit la troisième radicale faible à côté des singuliers *qrt, qṣt, ḥmt* et *šdt*.

[30] Voir Grelot 1975 avec toutes les références; *Répertoire d'épigraphie sémitique*, vol. 2/3 (Paris: Klincksieck, 1912), no. 954: une famille de satrapes, grand-père et petit-fils d'origine perse (?), au IIIᵉ siècle, voir *Daniel* et *Judith*, et aussi de Vaux 1971:208–12.

[31] Voir Masson 1982:150–51, avec bibliographie.

[32] Voir Masson 1982:151, où sont cités les quelques autres attestations du nom Rhoïkos: à Samos au VIIᵉ siècle, à Athènes au Vᵉ siècle, à Naucratis et Milet au IVᵉ siècle et à Cymé d'Eolide au IV–IIIᵉ siècle, et il ajoute que la forme du nom "avec le *digamma* initial conservé et noté, est très satisfaisante: c'est la forme archaïque du nom qui a été postulée par les étymologistes, et se trouve probablement déjà dans le génitif mycénien *wo-ro-ko-jo*. . . . C'est le degré *o* **wroiko-* d'un thème **wreik-* . . ." Mais ces exemples anciens ou plus récents ne portent pas le *digamma*. Masson donne (p. 152s) d'autres indications sur le monnayage à Amathonte. Voir aussi Amandry 1984:58. Je laisse aux spécialistes une appréciation de ces remarques, mais il serait surprenant que le roi d'Amathonte *Wroiko* soit, au Vᵉ siècle, un vrai grec.

fin du VIIe siècle tout au moins.[33] À ces mêmes époques le phénicien y était une langue officielle à côté du louvite, certainement adoptée parce que plus facile à écrire et à lire, le néo-assyrien devant être réservé à l'administration centrale de la province. En était-il de même à Amathonte à ces mêmes époques où, à côté de la langue vernaculaire, le phénicien pouvait y être une langue locale reçue et servant aussi à la communication internationale? On peut alors se demander si les deux dynasties ont une origine commune, rattachées par quelque lien de parenté? Quoi qu'il en soit, les données archéologiques retrouvées sur l'acropole attestent des relations avec le monde phénicien par des importations de la côte levantine.[34] Si des relations fortes et anciennes sont connues entre le royaume de Qué et sa région d'une part et la côte phénicienne, jusqu'en Samarie et Judée (voir les chevaux et la cavalarie d'après les données bibliques) d'autre part, on ne peut être surpris qu'il en ait existé entre la Cilicie et Amathonte d'une part[35] et entre Amathonte et la Phénicie, d'autre part.

En effet, en dehors des témoignages céramiques, on en a au moins une preuve écrite à cette même époque avec les deux coupes en bronze trouvées dans la région d'Amathonte et achetées à Limassol.[36] Elles témoignent de relations priviligiées avec le roi de Sidon. On lit ainsi ces deux inscriptions incomplètes:

A. …]*s*(?) *skn qrtḥdšt ᶜbd ḥrm mlk ṣdnm ᵓz ytn lbᶜl lbnn ᵓdny brᵓšt nḥšt ḥr*[*šm*

…]*s* gouverneur/roi de Qartḥadašt, serviteur de Ḥirom, roi de Sidon(. Il) a donné ceci au Baᶜal du Liban, son seigneur, en prémices du cuivre des fon[deurs[37]

B. *ks . . . bn ᵓḥ*(?)]*ṭb skn qrtḥdšt ᵓ*[*z ytn lb*]*ᶜl lbnn ᵓdny* [. . .

(Coupe de) X, fils de *Aḥi*(?)]ṭub, gouverneur/roi de Qartḥadašt(.[Il) a donné] ce[ci au Ba]ᶜal du Liban, son seigneur [en prémices du cuivre des fondeurs(?).[38]

Ces nouvelles lectures des deux coupes inscrites donnent de précieux renseignements. D'une part, le rang du dédicant: un *skn* dont le sens est large, depuis "gouverneur, roi(telet)" à "ministre-préfet-administrateur,"[39] et ici il peut revêtir aussi bien le sens de "gouverneur" que de "roi" local dépendant de la métropole Sidon.

[33] Sur ce nom, voir un aperçu dans Bron 1979:172–76: en Lydie-Pamphilie-Cilicie, à Cnossos et Pylos (linéaire B), et en Anatolie dans l'empire hittite.

[34] Voir note 1. Les fouilleurs me signalent parmi les importations levantines de la céramique fine *Plain White* et, pour l'essentiel, des jarres torpilles, mais ce pourcentage est infime comparé à la production locale. Ces mêmes rapports existaient déjà entre Kition, sa voisine orientale, avec la Phénicie, Tyr en particulier, mais la céramique phénicienne y est bien plus abondante, voir *Kition IV* et *V*.

[35] D'autres découvertes attestent les relations avec la Cilicie, par exemple l'anthroponyme Kilikas, si fréquent à Chypre, voir Masson 1961:413, ou Egetmeyer 1992:70, et Egetmeyer 2001:18–20 (je remercie S. Fourrier pour cette indication).

[36] Voir par exemple Masson et Sznycer 1972:77–78, au lieu-dit Mouti Sinoas, à 10 km environ au nord d'Amathonte, a-t-on supposé, et Masson 1985.

[37] Voir *CIS* I 5, planche IV, et Sznycer 1985 avec de nouvelles photos, pl. IV–V. La première lettre paraît devoir être lue *samek* de préférence à *ᵓaleph* mais très difficilement *waw* (à la suite du *CIS* et de Sznycer 1985, p. 49), et peut être pour *k*]*s skn* attendu "Cou]pe du gouverneur..." ou encore être la fin du patronyme "(Coupe de) X fils de Y, en l'occurrence *ᵓšmnpl*]*s*, mais voir l'inscription B. La finale doit être lue *ḥr*[*šm* avec *ḥet* certain et la partie droite du *reš* (longueur de la haste et partie de la tête) au lieu de la simple lecture *h*[retenue par la plupart des auteurs (voir encore Gibson 1982:67). Sznycer (1985:50) lirait *dalet* ou *bet*. La lecture *ḥr*[*šm* s'impose ici et le mot signifie "forgeron, fondeur, sculpteur, artisan ou orfèvre" en relation avec le travail d'un métal, voir 1 Sam. 13:19; Deut. 27:15; Isa. 40:19; 41:7; 44:12; 54:16; Jer. 10:19; Os. 8:6; 1 Chron. 29:5; 2 Chron. 24:12. De ce fait l'inscription est directement en relation avec les mines de cuivre des pentes du Troodos–Tamassos. Il est concevable que le roi-gouverneur de la ville offre les prémices de cuivre à la divinité pour le succès des mineurs et des fondeurs et la prospérité de tous.

[38] *CIS* I. Sur la planche du *CIS* on lirait des traces possibles de *ḥet* à la première cassure et sans doute des restes de *ᵓaleph* à la deuxième cassure. Le premier mot serait un anthroponyme, sans doute le patronyme du dédicant. Il est probable qu'il faille compléter la finale comme sur la coupe précédente. Si, comme il n'est pas impossible, on avait affaire à un même dédicant, le graveur aurait incisé une fois le nom avec le patronyme du dédicant sur la coupe B, et sur la coupe A, il aurait omis ses nom et patronyme mais incisé le nom de son maître et sa dépendance (selon la longueur de la ligne autour de la coupe[?], la question pouvait se poser pour une coupe A d'au moins 12 cm de diamètre), et A commencerait alors par *K*]*s*... "Cou]pe de . . ."

[39] Voir par exemple l'inscription araméenne de Fekherye où Hadadyisiᶜ se dit "roi (*mlk*) de Gôzan" alors que le texte parallèle assyrien le qualifie de "gouverneur de Gôzan" (*sakin mati Guzani*). Le mot *skn* désigne un gouverneur dans l'inscription phénicienne du sarcophage d'Ahiram de Byblos, intercalé entre la mention de roi (*mlk*) et de commandant d'armée (*tmᵓ mḥnt*). Sur un sarcohage de Kition (?) au musée de Nicosie, on lit *lᵓšmnᵓdn bn ᵓšmnᵓdn skn ṣr* "À Eshmounadon, fils d'Eshmounadon, gouverneur de Tyr," voir Masson et Sznycer 1972:69–75, qui renseigne encore sur la dépendance de Kition de la métropole Tyr au IVe siècle tout comme déjà auparavant.

D'autre part, le toponyme, Qarthadašt–Carthage–Villeneuve de Chypre, doit désigner la ville où siège le gouverneur, serviteur de Ḥirom II, vers 740–730 av. J.-C., ainsi que probablement Urîkki peu après, et ce paraît être Amathonte avec l'arrière-pays riche en minerai cuprifère. Cette dépendance du gouverneur-roi de Carthage de son suzerain, Ḥirom de Sidon, correspond à celle de ses contemporains, les rois de Kition vis-à-vis de leur suzerain de Tyr, et probablement aussi pour les mêmes motifs géo-politiques, essentiellement commerciaux, le minerai de cuivre en premier lieu. Enfin, "le Baᶜal du Liban" en question ne saurait être autre que Baᶜalshamem, le chef du panthéon de Tyr par exemple, divinité que l'on retrouve dans les inscriptions phéniciennes de Cilicie, où il vient en tête dans les invocations d'Urîkki (Hassan Beyli, Çineköy) et d'Azatiwada à Karatepe (attesté encore plus tard en araméen à Gözne), et de même à Byblos où, au Xe siècle, il est cité avant Baᶜalat Gebal et toute l'assemblée des dieux de Byblos (inscription de Yeḥimilk). Ce Baᶜal parèdre d'Astarté–Aphrodite, la divinité poliade à Tyr et à Sidon aux côtés de Melqart et d'Eshmoun respectivement, plus tard assimilé à Zeus *Hypsistos*, est ici explicitement invoqué pour la réussite des opérations minières dans l'arrière montagne de Chypre,[40] et en conséquence, pour la prospérité de la ville et la satisfaction de son suzerain.[41] L'offrande d'Urîkki dans le sanctuaire d'Aphrodite à Amathonte devait répondre à cette même fin.

On comprend alors mieux le développement spectaculaire d'Amathonte au Chypro-Archaïque I d'une part.[42] Et d'autre part, les données convergentes de l'archéologie, de l'épigraphie et de la géo-politique locale sont nettement en faveur de l'identification d'Amathonte avec Qarthadašt, la Carthage de Chypre, mais très difficilement avec Kition, ainsi qu'on l'a soutenu, laquelle aurait alors reçu deux dénominations *kt* et *qrtḥdšt*, cette dernière désignant un quartier périphérique, ce qui ne se justifie guère.[43] Comme la graphie de l'inscription sur le pithos semble un peu plus évoluée que celle des coupes de bronze provenant très vraisemblablement d'un sanctuaire dédié à Baᶜalshamem à Amathonte ou environs,[44] non loin de celui d'Astarté–Aphrodite sur l'acropole, rien n'indique cependant que le dédicant de ces coupes soit à identifier à *ᵓwryk*–ᵓUrîkki, ni que ce dernier soit un *skn* "gouverneur/roi" du lieu, du moins la courte inscription ne le dit pas, elle n'indique même pas son patronyme. Toutefois, étant donné la lignée royale homonyme, à la même époque en Cilicie, l'onomastique royale étéo-chypriote par la suite, à côté des très rares inscriptions phéniciennes retrouvées sur l'acropole d'Amathonte,[45] ce dernier point ne peut être totalement exclu.[46]

[40] Voir Petit 1996, en particulier p. 101s, où l'auteur rappelle qu'"ailleurs dans l'île, des découvertes indiquent que le travail du cuivre était placé sous la protection de la déesse, comme à Tamassos et à Kition, où des ateliers métallurgiques fonctionnaient à proximité immédiate des sanctuaires. . . ." Il en était déjà ainsi au IIe millénaire avec les dédicaces à Baᶜalat-Ḥathor aux mines de Sérabit el-Khadim au Sinaï, voir Puech 2005, ou encore Puech 2002.

[41] Voir Niehr 2003:36–88, mais p. 43, on serait moins négatif que l'auteur au sujet d'une telle présence à Tyr-Sidon, tout comme ce culte est aussi attesté à Kition et à Carthage, filiales de Tyr (p. 60–66).

[42] Voir en particulier les importantes remarques du fouilleur, Hermary 1987, spécialement p. 378-81: "...il est légitime de se demander . . . si des Phéniciens ne sont pas responsables de la croissance rapide de la ville au VIIIe siècle et si Amathonte n'était pas alors la 'Carthage de Chypre'," et Hermary 2000. Et on ne connaît rien de comparable à cette époque pour sa voisine Limassol. Toutefois Katzenstein 1973, spécialement p. 207–10, est en faveur de Carthage–Limassol, de même Lipiński 1983:212, 218s, qui refuse aussi l'identification avec Kition en faveur d'une identification de Carthage avec Limassol, suivant des traditions postérieures, byzantines pour la plupart.

[43] Malgré les remarques dernièrement encore de Yon 1987, spéc. p. 366–69, et de Coldstream 2005:183. Entre autres, la plaque de Kition à double inscription qui connaît encore vers 400 avant J.-C. les toponymes distincts de *kt* et *qrtḥdšt* (B 6 et 8) n'est pas non plus en faveur d'une telle identification. Lipiński (1995:140s) estime qu'à cette époque ancienne "la région d'Amathonte se trouvait sous la mouvance tyrienne," mais les sarcophages anthropoïdes tout comme le trône vide ont beaucoup plus d'affinités avec Sidon. En outre, l'occupation continue depuis le XIe siècle à Kition n'est pas en faveur d'un double toponyme à cette époque.

[44] Ont été trouvés à Phassoula à 10 km à l'ouest de Mouti Sinoas, lieu supposé de la découverte des coupes en bronze, une dizaine d'ex-votos dédiés à *Zeus Labranios*, et juste au sud du village, sur la colline de Kastro, à 10 km au nord de Limassol et à une douzaine de km au nord-ouest d'Amathonte, un sanctuaire qui devait lui être consacré, voir Lipiński 1983:210s. Ce culte gréco-romain pourrait être une déformation de celui à *bᶜl lbnn*–Baᶜal du Liban des coupes en bronze. Si on retenait Carthage = Limassol, il faudrait montrer que le site est un royaume important aux VIIIe-VIIe siècles tout à côté d'Amathonte dont les restes archéologiques attestent son importance, alors qu'il est absent des listes assyriennes.

[45] Pour les deux autres inscriptions phéniciennes retrouvées: voir Sznycer 1982, AM 570 inscription gravée sur une amphore, datée du Ve siècle(?), mais à lire ainsi: *[ᵓšmnᶜz]r bn ᵓlpᶜl* "A Eshmounazo]r(?) fils de Elipaᶜal," haste et trace de la barre de *ᵓaleph*, pied du *lamed*, *pe* couché à gauche, puis traces de *ᶜaïn* et du pied de *lamed* probable, nom connu par ailleurs en phénicien et particulièrement à Sidon, continuant ainsi à souligner les liens

Quoi qu'il en soit de Carthage à Amathonte, bien préférable à Limassol sa voisine, mais cela reste à confirmer par d'autres découvertes, cette courte inscription phénicienne sur le col d'un pithos au Chypro-Archaïque I à Amathonte apporte des renseignements fort précieux pour cette époque, puisqu'elle est la plus ancienne trouvée sur le site même. Elle rappelle une forte présence phénicienne dans le secteur,[47] dans la ligne d'une relation privilégiée avec Sidon à la suite des coupes de bronze déjà connues comme provenant de la même région et attestant un important toponyme phénicien, Qartḥadašt.[48] Cette présence y est attestée sur plusieurs siècles, le phénicien y étant parlé à côté de l'étéo-chypriote ou mieux l'amathousien.[49] Cette présence pourrait s'inscrire dans la ligne des influences hurro-urartéennes sur l'amathousien, via la Cilicie, à une époque bien antérieure.[50]

Il m'est agréable de présenter cette note dans un volume en hommage à un distingué collègue, Larry Stager, qui a tant labouré dans ce secteur du Proche-Orient à cette même époque.

Post-scriptum

Depuis la rédaction de cette contribution ont paru des notes touchant au sujet traité :

Lemaire (2007:137) propose de lire "LʾWRYM, probablement à dater vers le début du VIIe ou même dans la seconde moitié du VIIIe s." Mais cette lecture ne répond à aucun anthroponyme connu et elle n'est donc pas à retenir.

Fourrier (2004–5:67–118) signale la présence d'un certain nombre d'objets et inscriptions phéniciennes, dont insc. 22 incisée après cuisson et insc. 21 incisée avant cuisson (numéros 55 et 56) que Sznycer a lues respectivement LŠʿ comme début d'un anthroponyme, et ML (?). Cette dernière lecture est plus que douteuse. La présentation du tesson (p. 113) "d'amphore *Plain White* à anses de panier de fabrication locale" montre que le tesson ne peut se situer vers le fond du vase et donc qu'il n'a pas à être lu à l'envers (p. 91). Étant donné les cassures, un déchiffrement assuré est impossible.

Durand (2005:59–70) essaie de montrer qu'Arriyuk, roi de Kalhu–Ellasar (= Al-šarri–Larissa) et contemporain d'Amraphel [= Amut-pâ-El (?)] roi de Qaṭna, a été un allié des Élamites. Ainsi les anciennes traditions amorrites ont pu passer au récit biblique de la *Genèse*.

En conséquence, l'anthroponyme Arriyuk du hourrite *ar(r)i* "donner" devrait être distinct du hourrite Awarikus–ʾUrîkki, du hourrite *awar-k* "seigneur/roi" (voir *supra* et note 13), même si les deux noms sont contemporains au VIIIe s. dans la région.

avec la métropole phénicienne, et l'inscription incisée sur la base d'une coupe à vernis noir, AM 817, datée du début du ve siècle, Sznycer 1987:133–35 ou 1987a:389–90 mentionnant *lyknšm*[*š*.

[46] Avec l'identification d'Amathonte à Qartḥadašt, on connaîtrait un autre nom de roi de la cité qui a payé tribut à Assarhaddon en 672 et à Assurbanipal en 667 en compagnie de dix autres rois de Chypre, "Damusi/u, roi de Qartiḥadasti," copies du prisme d'Assarhaddon et des listes assyriennes, voir Aupert, "Les auteurs anciens," *Amathonte I. Testimonia I, op. cit.*, p. 12, voir aussi Lipiński 1983, où l'auteur essaie d'expliquer la forme *Damusi* comme hypocoristique de Tammuz-Adonis, onomastique sémitique d'une ville au nom sémitique.

[47] Voir en ce sens Petit 2005:167.

[48] S'il en est bien ainsi, alors que Tyr qui avait déjà une tête de pont en Chypre à Kition, fondait une "Carthage" sur le continent africain, Sidon fondait aussi à la même époque peu avant la fin du IXe siècle une "Carthage" en Chypre.

[49] Voir Hermary et Masson 1990:207, inscriptions syllabiques de la première moitié du VIIe siècle. Elles seraient d'une génération au moins plus récentes que l'inscription phénicienne.

[50] Voir Petit 1997–98, spécialement p. 249.

Bibliography

Aghion, I.
1984 Un dépôt de céramique archaïque chypriote dans le sanctuaire d'Aphrodite à Amathonte. *BCH* 108:655–67.

Amandry, M.
1984 Le monnayage d'Amathonte. In *Amathonte*, vol. 1, *Testimonia*, part 1, *Auteurs anciens, monnayage, voyageurs, fouilles, origine, géographie*, ed. P. Aupert and M. C. Hellmann, 57–76. Études chypriotes 4. Paris: Éditions Recherches sur les Civilisations.

Aupert, P.
1980 Chantier B nord. Rapport sur les travaux de la mission de l'École française à Amathonte en 1979. *BCH* 104:812–14.
1984 Les auteurs anciens. In *Amathonte*, vol. 1, *Testimonia*, part 1, *Auteurs anciens, monnayage, voyageurs, fouilles, origine, géographie*, ed. P. Aupert and M. C. Hellmann, 11–56. Études chypriotes 4. Éditions recherches sur les civilisations "Mémoires" 33. Paris: Éditions recherches sur les civilisations.

Bikai, P.
1978 The Late Phoenician Pottery: Complex and Chronology. *BASOR* 229:45–56.

Briend, J., and J.-B. Humbert, eds.
1980 *Tell Keisân (1971–1976): une cité phénicienne en Galilée.* OBO Series Archaeologica 1. Fribourg, Switzerland: Éditions universitaires.

Bron, F.
1979 *Recherches sur les inscriptions phéniciennes de Karatepe.* Hautes Études Orientales 11. Genève: Droz.

Coldstream, J. N.
2005 Phoenicians in Crete, North and South: A Contrast. *Atti del V Congresso internazionale di studi Fenici e Punici*, vol. 1, ed. A. S. Giammellaro, 181–87. Palermo, Italy: Punto Grafica.

Dinçol, B.
1994 New Archaeological and Epigraphical Finds from Ivriz: A Preliminary Report. *Tel Aviv* 21:117–28.

Dunand, M.
1944–45 Les inscriptions phéniciennes de Karatépé. *BMB* 7:81–97.

Dupont-Sommer, A.
1948 Inscriptions phéniciennes récemment découvertes à Karatépé (Cilicie). *CRAIBL* 1948:76–83.

Durand, J.-M.
2005 De l'époque amorrite à la Bible: le cas d'Arriyuk. Memoriae Igor M. Diakonoff. *Babel und Bibel: Annual of Ancient Near Eastern, Old Testament, and Semitic Studies*, vol. 2, ed. L. Kogan, N. Koslova, S. Loesov, and S. Tishchenko, 59–70. Winona Lake, Ind.: Eisenbrauns.

Egetmeyer, M.
1992 *Wörterbuch zu den Inschriften im kyprischen Syllabar.* Kadmos Supplement 3. Berlin: de Gruyter.
2001 Sceau chypriote. In "Sceaux du Musée d'Adana," by H. Poncy et al. *Anatolia Antiqua* 9:9–37.

Elayi, J., and A. Cavigneaux
1979 Sargon II et les Ioniens. *Oriens Antiquus* 18:59–75.

Fourrier, S.
2004–5 Le dépôt archaïque du rempart Nord d'Amathonte: III. Les petits objets. *BCH* 128–29:67–118.

Garelli, P.
1981 Remarques sur les monuments de Karatepe: III. Les données assyriennes. *RA* 75:54–60.

Gibson, J. C. L.
1982 *Textbook of Syrian Semitic Inscriptions.* Vol. 3, *Phoenician Inscriptions*. Oxford: Clarendon.

Grelot, P.
1975 Ariok. *VT* 25:711–19.

Goetze, A.
1972 Cilicians. *JCS* 16:48–58.

Gröndahl, F.
1967 *Die Personennamen der Texte aus Ugarit.* Studia Pohl 1. Rome: Pontifical Biblical Institute.

Hawkins, J. D.
1979 Some Historical Problems of the Hieroglyphic Luwian Inscriptions. *Anatolian Studies* 29:153–67.

Hawkins, J. D., and A. Morpurgo Davies
1978 On the Problems of Karatepe: The Hieroglyphic Text. *Anatolian Studies* 28:103–19.

Hellmann, M.-C., and A. Hermary
1980 Sommet de l'acropole: le sanctuaire d'Aphrodite; Rapport sur les travaux de la mission de l'École française à Amathonte en 1979. *BCH* 104:805–12.

Hermary, A.
1987 Amathonte de Chypre et les Phéniciens. In *Phoenicia and the East Mediterranean in the First Millennium* B.C.*: Proceedings of the Conference Held in Leuven from the 14th to the 16th of November 1985*, ed. E. Lipiński, 374–90. Studia Phoenicia 5. OLA 22. Leuven: Peeters.

2000 Nouveaux documents phéniciens à Amathonte (Chypre). In *Actas del congresso internacional de estudios fenicios y púnicos*, ed. M. E. Aubet and M. Barthélemy, 1047–60. Cádiz, Spain: University of Cádiz.

Hermary, A., S. Fourrier, and M. Schmid
2000 Le sanctuaire d'Aphrodite. Rapport sur les travaux de l'École française à Amathonte en 1999: II. Préparation de publications. *BCH* 124: 542–45.

Hermary, A., and O. Masson
1990 Deux vases inscrits du sanctuaire d'Aphrodite à Amathonte (1865–1987). *BCH* 114:187–214.

Katzenstein, H. J.
1973 *The History of Tyre*. Jerusalem: Schocken Institute for Jewish Research.

Kaufman, S. A.
1997 American Academy of Religion–Society of Biblical Literature Annual Meeting Abstracts.

Lanfranchi, G. B.
2004 The Luwian-Phoenician Bilingual of Çineköy and the Annexation of Cilicia to the Assyrian Empire. In *Von Sumer bis Homer: Festschrift für Manfred Schretter zum 60. Geburtstag am 25. Februar 2004*, ed. R. Rollinger, 481–96. AOAT 325. Münster: Ugarit-Verlag.

Laroche, E.
1960 *Les hiéroglyphes hittites*. Part 1, *L'écriture*. Paris: Éditions du Centre national de la recherche scientifique.
1966 *Les noms des Hittites*. Paris: Klincksieck.

Lemaire, A.
1977 Essai sur cinq sceaux phéniciens. *Semitica* 27: 29–40.
1983 L'inscription phénicienne de Hassan Beyli reconsidérée. *RSF* 11:9–19.
1997 Sceau phénicien provenant de la région de Karaman (Turquie). *Epigraphica Anatolica* 29:123–26.
2004 "Maison de David," "Maison de Mopsos," et les Hivvites. In *Sefer Moshe: The Moshe Weinfeld Jubilee Volume; Studies in the Bible and the Ancient Near East, Qumrân, and Post-Biblical Judaism*, ed. C. Cohen, A. Hurvitz, and S. M. Paul, 303–12. Winona Lake, Ind.: Eisenbrauns.
2007 Épigraphie sémitique. *Transeuphratène* 33:135–37.

Lipiński, E.
1983 La Carthage de Chypre. In *Redt Tyrus = Sauvons Tyr; Histoire phénicienne = Fenicische Geschiednis*, ed. E. Gubel, E. Lipiński, and B. Servais-Soyez, 209–34. Studia Phoenicia 1–2. OLA 15. Leuven: Peters.
1986 Guadalhorce: Une inscription du roi d'Éqron? *Aula Orientalis* 4:85–88.
1995 *Dieux et déesses de l'univers phénicien et punique*. Studia Phoenicia 14. OLA 64. Leuven: Peeters.

Masson, O.
1961 *Les inscriptions chypriotes syllabiques*. Études chypriotes 1. Paris: Broccard.
1982 Variétés chypriotes: III. Une nouvelle monnaie d'Amathonte au nom du roi Wroikos. *Report of the Department of Antiquities of Cyprus* 1982: 150–55.
1985 La dédicace à Baᶜal du Liban (CIS I, 5) et sa provenance probable de la région de Limassol. *Semitica* 35:33–46.

Masson, O., and M. Sznycer
1972 *Recherches sur les Phéniciens à Chypre*. Hautes Études Orientales 3. Genève: Droz.

Mosca, P. G., and J. Russell
1987 A Phoenician Inscription from Cebel Ires Dağı in Rough Cilicia. *Epigraphica Anatolica* 9:1–28.

Niehr, H.
2003 *Baᶜalšamem: Studien zu Herkunft, Geschichte und Rezeptionsgeschichte eines phönizischen Gottes*. Studia Phoenicia 17. OLA 123. Leuven: Peeters.

Peckham, J. B.
1968 *The Development of the Late Phoenican Scripts*, HSS 20. Cambridge, Mass.: Harvard University Press.

Petit, T.
1996 Religion et royauté à Amathonte de Chypre. *Transeuphratène* 12:97–120.
1997–98 La langue étéocypriote ou l'"amathousien": Essai d'interprétation grammaticale. *AfO* 44–45: 244–71.
2005 Les origines du royaume d'Amathonte (Chypre) et les Phéniciens. In *Atti del V Congresso internazionale di studi Fenici e Punici*, vol. 1, ed. A. S. Giammellaro, 165–70. Palermo, Italy: Punto Grafica.

Postgate, J. N.
1973 Assyrian Texts and Fragments. *Iraq* 35:13–36.

Puech, É.
1976 Le rite d'offrande de cheveux d'après une inscription phénicienne de Kition vers 800 avant notre ère. *RSF* 4/1:11–21.
1977 L'inscription phénicienne du trône d'Astart à Séville. *RSF* 5/1:85–92.
1979 Remarques sur quelques inscriptions phéniciennes de Chypre. *Semitica* 29:19–43.
2002 Notes sur quatre inscriptions protosinaïtiques. *RB* 109:5–39.
2005 Les inscriptions proto-sinaïtiques 346 et 357. In *Atti del V Congresso internazionale di studi*

Fenici e Punici,vol. 1, ed. A. S. Giammellaro, 27–41. Palermo, Italy: Punto Grafica.

Röllig, W.
1992 Asia Minor As a Bridge between East and West: The Role of the Phoenicians and Arameans in the Transfer of Culture. In *Greece between East and West: 10th–8th Centuries B.C.*, ed. G. Kopcke and I. Tokumaru, 93–102. Mainz am Rhein: Zabern.

Sznycer, M.
1982 Une inscription phénicienne fragmentaire sur un tesson d'Amathonte. *BCH* 106:243–44.
1985 Brèves remarques sur l'inscription phénicienne de Chypre, CIS I 5. *Semitica* 35:47–50.
1987 Une inscription phénicienne d'Amathonte. *BCH* 111:133–35.
1999 Une nouvelle inscription phénicienne d'Amathonte (Chypre). *Semitica* 49:195–97.

Tadmor, H.
1994 *The Inscriptions of Tiglat-Pileser III King of Assyria*. Jerusalem: Israel Academy of Sciences and Humanities.

Tekoğlu, R., and A. Lemaire
2000 La bilingue royale louvito-phénicienne de Çineköy, avec le concours de I. Ipek et A. Kazim Tosum. *CRAIBL* 2000:961–1006.

Vaux, R. de
1971 *Histoire ancienne d'Israël*. Vol. 1. Paris: Gabalda.

Yon, M.
1987 Le royaume de Kition. Époque archaïque. In *Phoenicia and the East Mediterranean in the First Millennium B.C.: Proceedings of the Conference Held in Leuven from the 14th to the 16th of November 1985*, ed. E. Lipiński, 357–74. Studia Phoenicia 5. OLA 22. Leuven: Peeters.

40. A Fragmentary Text from Tel Aphek with Unknown Script

by Itamar Singer, with an appendix by Yuval Goren

In the first excavation seasons at Tel Aphek, an inscribed clay fragment (reg. no. 47111.10) was found in an early Iron Age context, Stratum X10, above Late Bronze Age strata.[1] Stratum X10 is characterized by pits and thick layers of ashes containing organic material and a mixture of Middle Bronze, Late Bronze, and early Iron Age sherds, including some Philistine pottery and "Ashdoda"-type figurines. This extensive burned layer, lacking recognizable evidence of occupation, was identified by the excavators as a threshing floor covering the entire surface of the higher mound. It is sandwiched between Late Bronze Age fills and Iron Age II silos, and is roughly dated to the eleventh century B.C.E. (Beck and Kochavi 1985:30). Despite its clear stratigraphic situation, the fragment was not found in a sealed context, and therefore it might also be residual from an earlier level. Petrographic analysis performed by Yuval Goren indicates that its clay probably originated in Philistia (see appendix).

Description of the Tablet Fragment

The ca. 35 × 30-mm fragment (figure 1) is probably the upper left corner of a rectangular clay tablet that was fired either deliberately or by accident when the threshing floor was scorched. The broken section reveals the method by which the tablet was modeled (figures 1c, 2c). A sheet of light-brown clay was folded over and pressed together to form a plano-convex tablet ca. 12 mm thick. The inscribed obverse has a slightly convex surface, whereas the uninscribed reverse is flat. The writing continues on the partly preserved left edge and is cut abruptly (figures 1d, 2d). From the break to the preserved part of the reverse there is an eroded surface ca. 7 mm wide, which must have contained one or two more signs in each line. The flat reverse is coarse and bears traces of fingerprints (figure 1d).

On the upper edge, there is a series of wedge-like incisions (figures 1b, 2b). This could be simply a decoration, or perhaps some kind of "tallying"—a rough summing up of units prior to writing a total on the tablet itself. Such a counting method has been noted, for example, on Linear B tablets (Bennett 1955:117). The three preserved lines of the inscription are divided by two guidelines. The first was drawn on the tablet, ca. 15 mm from its upper edge, before writing was begun. This is clearly shown by the word-divider, which cuts into the first guideline, separating the first and second compartments. Whether the second guideline was also drawn before writing, or only after the first line was already written, cannot be established. Both guidelines continue to the edge, not as simple prolongations of the long lines, but rather as subsequently added extensions.

The vertical word-dividers take up the whole width of the line and divide it into rectangular compartments of varying size. Six compartments can be distinguished (numbered from I to VI), only one of which (IV) is fully preserved (figure 2d).

The signs, numbered from 1 to 15 (see figure 2d), are written close to the upper margin of the compartment, and one of them, no. 11, actually cuts into the guideline. Some of the signs nearly touch others, but unfortunately none of them actually cuts into a neighboring sign (which could have helped in establishing the direction of writing).

The characters were impressed or punched into wet clay with a thin stylus. Consisting of short strokes without any curved lines, they resemble cuneiform signs more than linear scripts.[2] This observation is best demonstrated by the configuration of the composite signs, the trident-shaped no. 6 and the cross-shaped nos. 2 and 11. Both were executed by four impressions of the stylus rather than by dragging two long intersecting lines. A wedge-like form is typical mainly for signs that may conceivably be identified as numerals (nos. 8 and 12); less so in the remaining characters, which lack a thickened head of a wedge.

It is impossible to determine the original size and shape of the tablet, but the fact that it contained at

[1] The fragment was mentioned in preliminary publications (Kochavi 1981:80–81; Singer 1983:26) and a partial drawing was published in the catalogue of the Aphek exhibition at the Israel Museum (Kochavi 1990:xxiv). The publication of the fragment was first assigned to Prof. David Owen, who participated in the Aphek excavations, and he later passed it on to me, for which I am grateful to him and to Prof. Kochavi. The photographs were made by Pavel Shrago and the drawings by Rodica Penchas, both of the Institute of Archaeology of the Tel Aviv University. This article will also appear in the forthcoming Tel Aphek final report volume, *Aphek 2*.

[2] This observation supersedes the preliminary reports, in which the fragment was described as "linear."

a

b

c

d

e

Figure 1

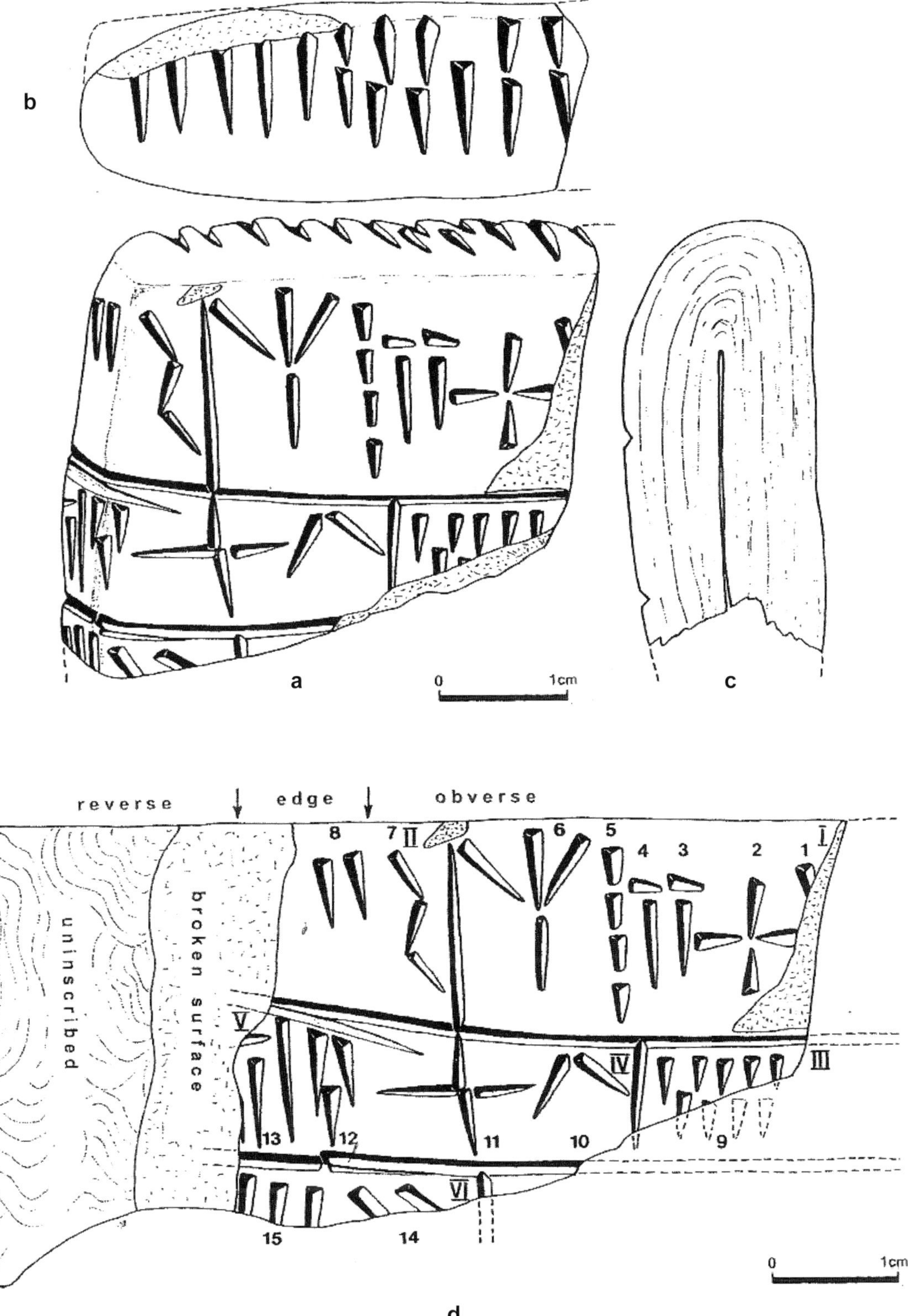
b
a
0
1cm
c
reverse
edge
obverse
uninscribed
broken surface
8
7
II
6
5
4
3
2
1
I
V
IV
III
13
12
11
10
9
VI
15
14
0
1cm
d

Figure 2

least three lines seems to indicate a "page-shaped" tablet rather than an elongated "leaf-shaped" ("bar-shaped") tablet (to use Linear A/B terminology). The latter form, which is found in the Aegean region and is also represented by the Tell Deir ᶜAlla tablets and some of the Ugaritic tablets (including those from Beth-Shemesh and Tell Taᶜannek), usually contains only one or two lines.

Orientation and Direction of Reading

How the tablet should be held for reading, whether as portrayed in the figures or upside down, is not obvious. Several observations prompted me to opt for the first possibility: (1) the wedge-like incisions on the edge of the tablet (figures 1b, 2b), whatever their purpose, would be more "in place" on the upper side of the tablet; (2) the first inscribed line has a guideline under it, but not above it—this is quite normal in ruled tablets, wherein the last line is usually followed by a guideline; (3) in impressed scripts, such as cuneiform, characters are closer to the upper edge of the register, whereas in linear scripts, such as ruled Linear B tablets, characters sit at the bottom of the register; since, as noted above, the characters on this tablet are impressed and not drawn, the inscription looks more natural in this position than it does upside-down; (4) the sharpened ends of the wedge-like signs would normally face downwards rather than upwards. In conclusion, I am quite confident that the fragment is the upper left corner of a tablet and not the lower right corner.

Establishing the direction of reading is more difficult. As noted above, I have painstakingly sought (by means of a stereoscopic microscope) evidence for overlapping (signs cutting into each other), but none of the marginal cases seems to be sufficiently convincing.[3] My preference for a right-to-left direction is based mainly on the continuation of the writing at the left edge. Except in cases of later additions,[4] I am not aware of any examples in which a scribe would deliberately begin his lines at the edge of a tablet. On the other hand, continuing a line at the edge (or even on the reverse) is commonplace in cuneiform writing, and is also found occasionally on Cypro-Minoan tablets from Ugarit (RS 20.25; Masson 1974:31). In Aegean scripts, there is no spilling over to the edges of a tablet. If an entry turned out to be too long for the available space, scribes preferred to add missing words in smaller characters above the line where they did not fit (Ventris and Chadwick 1973:111–12).

The Characters

Only fifteen characters are fully or partially preserved on the fragment. Discounting repeated signs and some uncharacteristic traces, we are left with only nine different signs, three of which (or possibly four) are most probably numerals. Obviously, there remains very little to start with in searching for the origins of the script of this tablet. But before we set out on this unpromising venture, it is expedient to add some brief observations on the graphic properties of each character and to attempt some tentative restorations.

No. 1 is the head of a vertical stroke. It could in fact be the beginning of a word-divider, but since it is almost on the same level as no. 2, it seems more likely that it belonged to a sign.

Nos. 2 and 11 are probably identical. As noted above, the four arms of this cross-shaped sign were executed separately by impressing the stylus, rather than drawing two intersecting lines, as in linear scripts. On no. 11, one can discern that the scribe drew the arms in a clockwise direction, with the upper vertical arm cutting into the left horizontal one.

Nos. 3 and 4 are two identical T-shaped characters. Their heads are almost touching each other, producing a Π-shape. However, a close examination shows that they fall short of actually touching each other, and appear to be two identical but separate characters. No. 13 is probably the same sign, but the horizontal and the vertical are more distanced from each other than in nos. 3 and 4. Left of the vertical of no. 13, it is possible to discern the trace of another vertical (which does not show up well in the photograph, figure 1e). If so, we may have here a "double-T" sign similar to nos. 3 and 4.

No. 5 is composed of four short strokes in a vertical line. It could be the numeral 4, but such a configuration would be most unusual. Perhaps it should be considered a non-numerical sign, an equally unusual configuration.

The trident-shaped no. 6 consists, as do cross-shaped nos. 2 and 11, of four separate impressed strokes. Once again, this differs from similar signs in linear scripts, where a central axis is drawn in one continuous line.

The "outstretched" Z-shaped no. 7 is followed by two vertical strokes, presumably standing for the numeral 2. The damaged surface to its left could have

[3] For example, no. 10 comes short of actually cutting into the word-divider to its right.

[4] As, for example, on a cuneiform fragment from Tell Keisan, in which the number "one" was added as an afterthought at the edge (Sigrist 1982). I am grateful to Wayne Horowitz for this reference.

accommodated another character, perhaps even two, if pressed together.

No. 9 in the second line appears to be a numeral consisting of two superimposed rows: five short strokes in the upper row and two heads preserved in the lower one. This configuration could only belong to the numeral 9, as restored in figure 2d. For parallels to this configuration, which may perhaps have some diagnostic value, see the discussion of numerals below.

The two right-angled bars forming no. 10 come short of touching each other. At first, I considered the possibility of separating them, combining the right one with the bar to its right. However, this long vertical is almost certainly a word-divider since, like other word-dividers, it cuts into the guideline above it.

No. 11 is identical to no. 2, though a bit larger. No. 12 consists of three vertical bars, the middle one lower than the others. This could perhaps represent a regular sign, but the numeral 3 seems a more likely interpretation.

Compartment V has been described under nos. 3–4 above. The worn-away surface following it could have accommodated one, or possibly two, signs.

Compartment VI in the third line has the heads of five strokes all together. The two on the right are bent, the three on the left are vertical. It is difficult to say how many and what kind of characters they represent, but a numerical sign is quite likely. Here, too, as in the previous lines, one or two characters may be missing.

General Observations and Comparisons

The Signary

With only a half-dozen signs at our disposal (discounting the numerals, see below), it would be preposterous to attempt an identification of the script, not to mention a "decipherment." What is more, even these few signs are schematic and simple, a "cross," a "trident," a "T," an "outstretched Z"—all basic geometrical forms that are found in most writing systems around the world. Take, for example, the cross-shaped nos. 2 and 11, which could represent a West Semitic *taw*, a Ugaritic *h*, a cuneiform *ti*, a Linear B *lo/ro*, a Cypriot *lo*, an Egyptian *wn*, a Hieroglyphic Luwian CRUX, and so on. The fallacy of futile "resemblance hunting" has duly been emphasized by specialists in ancient scripts and their decipherment.[5]

What may complicate speculation over the form of the signs on this fragment even more is the distinct possibility that wedge-like characters are in fact derived from linear shapes of some primary script, in which case the signs may be distorted in relation to their original forms.[6]

In short, I prefer to heed the warning of many experienced epigraphers "against placing too great a reliance on formal similarities between characters in attempting to trace the relationships among different writing systems" (Palaima 1989:38). A more useful approach would, I believe, be to consider carefully the internal traits of the inscription, such as orientation, word-dividers, numerical notation, and structure. Cumulative evidence from such observations, combined with appropriate comparisons, may lead to more reliable results than could be achieved by a mechanical comparison of a few isolated signs.

Word-Dividers

The practice of word-division is normal in the majority of ancient Near Eastern and Aegean writing systems (Millard 1970; Naveh 1973; Duhoux 1999). In most scripts, the units are separated by a space (cuneiform), a dot (West Semitic), or a vertical stroke (Hieroglyphic Hittite, Ugaritic, South Arabian, Aegean, and Cypriot). In rarer cases, three vertically placed dots function as word-dividers (archaic Greek, Lycian, Phrygian, and on the Proto-Canaanite Lachish ewer [see Millard 1970:12; Naveh 1973:206]).

Division by means of long vertical lines that traverse the entire width of a ruled register, as in the Tel Aphek fragment under discussion, seems to be quite rare. In fact, the only close parallels known to me are on the unique disc from Phaistos on Crete (Naveh 1982:19), with its spiral inscription, and on tablets from the Jordan Valley site of Tell Deir ᶜAlla (ibid., p. 22). Long word-dividers also appear on a single-line inscription from Qubur el-Walayda in Philistia (ibid., p. 36) and on the Gezer Calendar (ibid., p. 63), but these Semitic inscriptions do not have a division of space into compartments. The Phaistos Disk and the Tell Deir ᶜAlla tablets have not yet been deciphered, despite numerous attempts, and are therefore of little help in our quest for defining the script on the Aphek fragment.[7]

[5] See, e.g., Gelb 1963:144 (and fig. 77 on p. 142) in which he compared the signs of Semitic writing with signs of seven other scripts picked at random from around the world.

[6] Such a development has been claimed, for example, for the Ugaritic script (Dietrich and Loretz 1999).

[7] I suppose that some might claim a Philistine origin for all three scripts, referring to the biblical evidence for a Cretan origin of the Philistines (e.g., Amos 9:7). However, as most scholars have observed, the unique Phaistos Disk is intru-

Direction of Reading

Sinistroverse writing prevails in the Near East only towards the end of the second millennium B.C.E. Most earlier writing systems are either dextroverse (cuneiform, Linear A and B, Cypro-Minoan) or boustrophedon (Hieroglyphic Hittite). Hieratic Egyptian, written as a rule from right to left, constitutes a notable exception, and its influence must have been dominant in the development of new writing systems in the Egyptian-controlled Levant. Byblos, for example, the main Egyptian outpost on the Levantine coast, developed its own writing system, written as a rule from right to left. The linear alphabet, which slowly evolved in Egyptian Canaan, fluctuated between the directions from which it was written, and eventually settled on right to left. That became the standard direction in most Semitic scripts (Naveh 1982:42).

The influence of sinistroverse writing in the Egyptian-controlled parts of the Levant can even be felt in the rare Aegean-type inscriptions recently discovered in Israel (Singer 2000:25). Whereas an earlier inscription from Tel Haror maintained an invariable tradition of the Aegean region by being written from left to right (Oren et al. 1996),[8] by the time a later inscription from Lachish was written, it was from right to left (Finkelberg et al. 1996). A similar development occurred in Iron Age Cyprus, where second-millennium B.C.E. Cypro-Minoan was written from left to right,[9] while its first-millennium B.C.E. descendant, Cypriot Syllabic, changed direction, probably under Phoenician influence.

The situation at Ugarit, outside of the Egyptian-controlled zone, is more complex. Under the prevailing influence of Akkadian cuneiform, a standard 30-letter Ugaritic alphabet was written from left to right. In the late thirteenth century B.C.E., however, a reduced 22-letter Ugaritic alphabet developed that was written from right to left (Bordreuil and Pardee 1995). The few Ugaritic inscriptions discovered outside the kingdom of Ugarit are either sinistroverse (Beth-Shemesh, Mount Tabor) or dextroverse (Sarepta, Kamid el-Loz, Tell Ta^cannek).

This brief summary demonstrates that in Late Bronze Age and early Iron Age contexts along the Levantine coast, one may encounter inscriptions written in either direction. However, under Egyptian influence, a right-to-left direction gradually prevailed for local scripts, and in this respect the Tel Aphek fragment and the Deir ^cAlla tablets, both written, in my opinion, from right to left, fit well into the general picture of late second millennium B.C.E. scripts.

Numerals

On first inspection, it was obvious that some of the characters on the Tel Aphek fragment probably represent numerals, indicating some sort of administrative tablet (Singer 1983:26). This is quite clear with regard to nos. 8, 9, and 12; it is less clear in the case of the traces preserved in Compartment VI. The group of three verticals (no. 15) could belong to a numeral, and perhaps also the two slants preceding them (no. 14).[10] As for the peculiar sign no. 5, an unusual configuration of the numeral 4 is not impossible, but does not seem to be very likely.

Short vertical bars represent units in most scripts. Thus, no. 8 should be a 2 and no. 12 a 3. There may be some hesitation with regard to the latter interpretation because the middle bar is lowered, but such a disposition of the numeral 3 is occasionally found in inscriptions.

The numeral in Compartment III, which can only be restored as a 9, was probably preceded by some noun, now lost. Quite surprisingly, this numeral turned out to be more diagnostic than other signs on the fragment. In scripts that do not use a special sign for 5 (e.g., hieratic), the nine strokes of 9 can theoretically be drawn in six different configurations: nine strokes in a row; 8+1, 7+2, 6+3, or 5+4 in two rows; or 3×3 in three rows.[11] The most popular dis-

sive among the Cretan scripts and was perhaps imported from elsewhere. As for the Deir ^cAlla tablets, their alleged "Sea Peoples" connection has not been convincingly demonstrated, and many (including myself) doubt it altogether.

[8] Sinistroverse or boustrophedon writing is not extant in Linear B, and is very rare in Linear A (see references in Finkelberg, Uchitel and Ussishkin 1996:198). However, as Tom Palaima informs me (personal communication), all such cases in Linear A have to do with the way an inscription is placed upon dedicatory objects, as on four-sided libation tables, where inscriptions run continuously around four sides so as to suggest that it is boustrophedon.

[9] Including the eleventh-century B.C.E. inscribed obelos (T 49.16) from Palaepaphos-Skales (Karageorghis 1983:411–15; Palaima 1991:451–54; 2005:38).

[10] For example, a slanted line represents 100 in Hieroglyphic Cretan (Dow 1954:12).

[11] For a convenient, though not entirely accurate presentation of notations for nos. 1 to 9 around the world, see Ifrah 1985:137–41. I strongly object to Ifrah's statement (p. 136) that the reason for breaking up a row of single units after four strokes is "because the people who used those notations were unable to read a row of more than four identical signs at a glance."

positions are 9×1,[12] 5+4,[13] and 3×3,[14] while some scripts use all three.[15] Remarkably, Linear A and Linear B of the Aegean[16] differ in their notation of 9, and, as far as I can see, this distinction has not been noted in the past.[17] With few exceptions, Linear A writes 5+4,[18] whereas Linear B writes 3×3.[19] I have no idea what might have caused this difference, but even if it were purely accidental and trivial, it could be useful in tracing down possible origins of related scripts.

Structure of the Script

The inscription is neatly segmented into its structural sections by dividers defining rectangular compartments. Most of them, including the only fully preserved compartment, IV, contain numerals. The numerals 2 and 3 in Compartment IV are preceded by non-numerical signs that must stand for nouns indicating some type of commodity, personnel, or the like. If I am right in assuming a right-to-left direction of reading, the numerals follow a modified noun, as is customary in Aegean scripts (Ventris and Chadwick 1973:36; Olivier 1986:379; Bennett 1999:161), for example, "oxen 2," "sheep 3," etc. The same order is probably also found in Cypro-Minoan (Palaima 1989:44). By contrast, the cuneiform tradition usually has the opposite order, "2 oxen," "3 sheep," etc.,[20] and the same applies to cuneiform Ugaritic.[21]

In Compartment IV, the numeral 3 is preceded by two signs, nos. 10 and 11. These probably represent phonetic signs, syllabic or alphabetic, but a logographic compound cannot be ruled out entirely. On the other hand, the numeral 2 in partly preserved Compartment II is preceded by a single sign, the "outstretched Z"-like no. 7. This probably represents a logogram, or perhaps a phonetic abbreviation, as found in Aegean scripts (Ventris and Chadwick 1973: 48–50; Palaima 1989:41; Bennett 1996:128–29) and probably also in Cypro-Minoan (Palaima 1989:43). Ideograms are a rarity in West Semitic scripts (except for symbols for weights), but we do find, for example, the abbreviation *š*, probably signifying *šeqel* (*š 30*) on an inscription from Tell Qasile (Cross 1980:3).

The first compartment, with five fully preserved signs, seems to be different from the rest. It is longer and apparently does not end with a numeral. If it contains a numeral at all, it must be the sign no. 5 with its oddly superimposed four bars. The T-shaped sign preceding it resembles the Linear B fractional measure "T" (Ventris and Chadwick 1973:50, no. 112), but this should not be duplicated, as in this inscription. In short, we must reckon with the possibility that this compartment does not have a numeral at all, at least not in the preserved segment. If so, the five or six signs in this compartment could all be phonological, alphabetic or syllabic, perhaps even word-syllabic. Also, one must reckon with the possibility that all the signs in the compartment do not belong to

12 For example, Phoenician and Aramaic (Pettersson 1996: 801). Ancient Hebrew usually employs hieratic Egyptian numerals, but note the rare occurrence of nine strokes (followed by a hieratic 5) on an ostracon from Arad (Aharoni 1981:102, Inscription 87). Quite often in West Semitic writing, numbers are spelled out phonetically.

13 For example, Proto-Elamite, Sumerian, and Linear A (see below).

14 For example, Hieroglyphic Egyptian, Akkadian cuneiform, and Linear B (see below). In Hieroglyphic Egyptian there are also some rare configurations, such as 6+3 in the writing of the "Nine Bows" (Gardiner 1957: 566), or 5+4 on a potsherd from Kahun (Gelb 1963:127, fig. 65).

15 For example, Hieroglyphic Luwian (Laroche 1960:212, no. 395) and Ugaritic (Gordon 1965:42, §7.2; Pardee 2001: 252, recto ii, lines 20 and 31).

16 For Cypro-Minoan there is, unfortunately, not enough evidence. See Palaima 1989:42–52 for a collection of data on Cypro-Minoan numerical ideograms. Since this script developed primarily out of Linear A (ibid., p. 53), I would expect the 5+4 configuration to be prevalent in Bronze Age Cyprus.

17 In a table of Linear B numerals in Deroy 1962:34, the numeral 9 is inaccurately drawn.

18 Fourteen of fifteen occurrences of the numeral 9 are written as 5+4 (Godart and Olivier 1976–1985, vol. 1: HT 1; 13; 14; 24a; 26b; 27a; 58; 104; 109; 114b; KN 28a; vol. 3: ARKH 4b; KH 30; ZA 6a). The only exception is HT 10b with nine consecutive strokes in the last line, probably conditioned by lack of space. A similar configuration appears on a Hieroglyphic Cretan tablet from Malia (Olivier and Godart 1996:172).

19 Out of some eighty occurrences of the numeral 9 in the Linear B inscriptions from Knossos, only three tablets have 5+4 (Chadwick et al. 1986:vol. 1 no. 298, vol. 3 nos. 138 and 164); the remainder are all 3×3. At Pylos, 26 cases are written 3×3 and only two (Eb 297; Ua 25 rev) as 5+4 (Bennett 1955). The sole example from Mycenae is written 3×3 (Bennett 1958:no. Oe 107). I did not find any examples of 9 on tablets from Tiryns and Thebes (Melena and Olivier 1991; Aravantinos, Godart, and Sacconi 2001).

20 For example, in the various administrative tablets found in Israel: Aphek (Rainey 1975:128), Hazor (Horowitz and Shaffer 1992; Horowitz and Oshima 2002:183–84), Hebron (Anbar and Naʾaman 1986–87), and Tell Keisan (Sigrist 1982). For the cuneiform accounting system in general, see, e.g., Nissen et al. 1993.

21 See Gordon 1965:42, §7.2. There are, however, exceptions, for example, texts 65 and 110, where the numbers indicating quotas or taxes follow the names of the respective towns. In ancient Hebrew we encounter both orders (Renz 1995:50–51).

one vocable, but rather to a *compositum* or *scriptio continua* that combines several grammatical elements (for *scriptio continua* in Mycenean Greek, see Duhoux 1999:232–35).

Despite the aberrant appearance of the first compartment, it seems likely that the text is of the accounting type, listing some enumerated entities such as personnel or commodities. It is not easy to add anything more on the nature of this small fragment, except to recall that another tiny fragment from Aphek has an administrative text (Rainey 1975:128). On that cuneiform Akkadian fragment, however, the quantities (of some unknown commodity) are counted in hundreds and thousands.

Conclusions

To speculate excessively on a tiny fragment written in an unknown script in an unknown language is both unwarranted and unwise. Still, it is worthwhile to sum up the few observations made over the course of the preceding examination.

Generally speaking, some of the features of this inscription are more in line with Near Eastern writing traditions, whereas others seem to point towards Aegean and Cypriot traditions. To the former category belong its "cuneiform appearance" (the way the writing was applied by punching short strokes into the clay) and the continuation of the writing at the edge of the tablet. Such spillover from the face of the tablet is totally foreign to Aegean traditions, though it is occasionally found on Cypro-Minoan tablets from Ugarit, probably due to local cuneiform influence.

Closer to Aegean tradition is the "noun + numeral" order of accounting. The sign forms are not sufficiently distinctive to justify a meaningful comparison with other scripts. The only exception could be the 5+4 configuration of the restored numeral 9, which is the common form in Linear A, but which is very rare in Linear B. (In Cypro-Minoan, there are simply not yet enough examples to establish its preference for one form or the other.) If this distinction be considered significant, it could perhaps indicate a Cretan-derived influence on the script of the Aphek fragment.[22]

Line-by-line ruling is a feature often found on Near Eastern tablets, and also in late Mycenean texts, but only sporadically in Linear A (Brice 1991:42). Long word-dividers partitioning the register into neat compartments are a rarity in this region. In this respect, the closest parallels to the Aphek fragment are found in the Tell Deir ᶜAlla tablets, and indeed, in preliminary reports (Singer 1983:26) excessive weight was put on this resemblance. On closer examination, however, the Aphek fragment differs considerably from the Deir ᶜAlla tablets, both in shape (the former is page-shaped, the latter is bar-shaped), and in the forms of the signs (punched strokes on the former, curving linear signs on the latter). Judging by their outward appearance, I doubt the two are written in the same script.

The direction of writing from right to left (provided that my conclusion is correct) is foreign to the Linear A and Linear B, Cypro-Minoan, and cuneiform writing traditions. It becomes, however, increasingly widespread in the Late Bronze Age Levant, probably under the influence of Hieratic Egyptian.

All in all, the conflation of affinities with both eastern and western writing traditions is probably the most typical feature of the Tel Aphek fragment. Cypriot writing is also characterized by multiple sources of influence, from east and west,[23] but in other respects, the script of the Tel Aphek fragment can hardly be associated with any of the writing systems of Cyprus.

The turbulent transition period from the Bronze Age to the Iron Age saw various writing experiments in the Levant, or to use the words of a leading authority in grammatology, there were "many attempts to create systems which everywhere in this period began to spring up like mushrooms after the rain" (Gelb 1963:27). Tel Aphek, where various Near Eastern writing systems met,[24] may well be one of the places where a new venture was begun, adapting Aegean and Cypriot elements to Near Eastern writing traditions. Unfortunately, without additional evidence it is impossible to establish just how, when, and by whom this new experiment was initiated. Taking into ac-

[22] This would be in line with the Cretan tendency to disseminate scripts to other areas in the Aegean region and to Cyprus. It is also worthwhile to note that the two inscriptions from the Aegean region recently discovered in Israel (at Tel Haror and Tel Lachish) are closer to Cretan than to Mycenean writing traditions (see Finkelberg, Uchitel and Ussishkin 1996:204–5; Finkelberg 1998:267–69).

[23] For affinities of Cypriot scripts with Near Eastern scripts, see, e.g., Palaima 1989:42; Smith 2003:277, 284; Sherratt 2003:227, but note Palaima's recent reservations with regard to the alleged "cuneiformization" of Cypro-Minoan signs (Palaima 2005:36).

[24] For the Late Bronze Age inscriptions from Aphek, which include cuneiform Akkadian, Hieroglyphic Egyptian, and Hieroglyphic Hittite, see Kochavi (1978:15–17; 1981:79–81), Kochavi et al. 1978; Singer 1983; Owen et al. 1987). See also Yasur Landau and Goren (2004) for a Cypro-Minoan potmark incised on a pot handle from Tel Aphek.

count the traits of the fragment, its stratigraphic context and its petrographic analysis, the Philistines (or one of the other "Sea Peoples") are plausible candidates as creators of this inscription, but no more than that.

The Aphek Fragment and the Problem of Philistine Writing

The sparse results achieved in identifying the script of the Aphek fragment are in sharp contrast to its potential importance. *If*, as noted in the last sentence of the conclusions, the script *could* tentatively be identified as Philistine, then it would arguably constitute the best evidence for the very existence and character of a Philistine (or Sea Peoples) script. This statement requires a brief justification.

Whatever view one follows concerning the possible lands of origin of the Sea Peoples, there is no doubt that literacy existed there during the Late Bronze Age. Thus, it is logical to assume that the Sea Peoples were using some kind of script when they came to the Levant. If so, they must have abandoned it quite early in favor of the local alphabetic script (Singer 1994:335). It is difficult to establish when this cultural shift might have occurred, since most inscriptions found in Philistia are dated rather later (Naveh 1985; Kelm and Mazar 1990:56; Gitin 1993: 250–53; Gitin et al. 1997). However, the fact that, despite extensive excavations in the large Philistine cities, no early Philistine inscriptions (from the late second millennium B.C.E.) have been found, may indicate that the adoption of the local alphabet occurred shortly after their settlement in Philistia.

In addition to the Aphek fragment, the only inscriptions for which an early Philistine script has been suggested are the Tell Deir ᶜAlla tablets and two seals from Ashdod. The ᶜDeir Alla tablets, the number of which has recently doubled (Ibrahim and van der Kooij 1997:108; 2001), should probably not be considered in this context because of lack of supporting evidence that they are related in any way to the Philistines. This is not the place to dwell upon these highly intriguing inscriptions, but in passing it should be noted that there is nothing in the archaeological record that requires a Sea Peoples connection, nor is the script itself intrinsically Aegean or Cypriot.[25]

Two objects from Ashdod, a cylinder seal and a pyramid-shaped seal, which allegedly bear "Philistine" characters resembling Cypro-Minoan script,[26] have been referred to in various publications, most recently in a brief paper by T. Dothan (2000) dedicated to the first appearance of writing in Philistia. In her widely cited publications, Dothan disregards other viewpoints on the subject, notably, M. Shuval's convincing demonstration that the stamp seal bears schematic representations of animals rather than characters of a script.[27] The same may apply to the cylinder seal portraying three seated figures. In the spaces between them, some incised linear symbols have been interpreted as script signs. On closer examination, however, the resemblance of these schematic symbols to any known Aegean or Cypriot signs is superficial at best. Indeed, in the last excavation report of Tel Ashdod, D. Ben-Shlomo suggested a more convincing iconographic interpretation of these symbols (Dothan and Ben-Shlomo 2005:166).

In the last analysis, the Aphek fragment remains in its splendid isolation as the sole unquestionable inscription with an actual claim to represent an early Philistine (or other Sea Peoples) script. However, faced with the paucity of evidence from other, much larger Philistine sites, we must retain a healthy degree of skepticism concerning this interpretation.

APPENDIX: PROVENANCE STUDY OF THE TEL APHEK FRAGMENT

by Yuval Goren

The fragmentary tablet with an unknown script from Tel Aphek was subjected to petrographic examination in order to disclose its possible provenance. The analysis followed sampling and examination procedures that have been presented by Goren, Finkelstein, and Naᵓaman (2004) in their study of the Amarna tablets.

Petrographically, the fragmentary tablet is typified by the following features: the matrix is carbonatic, tan in PPL and optically active with speckled b-fabric, with some foraminifers. The silt (~10 percent) contains essentially quartz but with the addition of

[25] The prudent study of Weippert (1966) sheds serious doubts on the various "decipherments" and merely suggests that in this period and location one should probably expect some Northwest Semitic script (ibid., p. 302). See also Knauf (1987:15), who defines the script as "Proto-Canaanite" in a loose sense pertaining to various second-millennium local scripts used for early, local Canaanite dialects.

[26] For references, see Dothan and Ben-Shlomo 2005:166. The Cypro-Minoan comparisons have been credited to R. A. Stieglitz apud Dothan and Porath (1993:81, n. 84; stamp seal) and to J. Faucounau apud Dothan and Ben-Shlomo (2005:166; cylinder seal).

[27] Given in Keel, Shuval, and Uehlinger 1990:157, no. 79. This conclusion has meanwhile been supported by specialists, such as O. Masson apud Keel (1997:672, no. 27).

calcite and opaque minerals and rarely muscovite, zircon, and hornblende. The inclusions are made of moderately sorted sand (f:c ratio$_{\{0.062mm\}}$=~90:10) including subrounded to subangular quartz, up to 300µm, sometimes with undulose extinction and mineral inclusions, foraminiferous chalk, subrounded, up to 800µm, nari containing clay and some quartz silt, rounded and up to 600µm, and some fossilized mollusc shell fragments.

The matrix of this tablet combines the petrographic properties of loess (silty-carbonatic wind-blown, clay loam) and brown rendzina soil. The inclusions contain chalk and nari from the mother-rock of the rendzina soil, and some wind-blown quartz sand. This combination is typical of pottery assemblages from the southern lower Shephelah region of Israel. In the study of the Amarna tablets, it was found to characterize the tablets of Shuwardatu, the ruler of Gath, which is identified as Tel Zafit (Goren, Finkelstein, and Naʾaman 2004:279–86). Therefore, the origin of this tablet may be sought in this general area.

Bibliography

Aharoni, Y.
1981 *Arad Inscriptions*. Jerusalem: Israel Exploration Society.

Anbar, M., and N. Naʾaman
1986–87 An Account Tablet of Sheep from Ancient Hebron. *Tel Aviv* 13–14:3–12.

Aravantinos, V. L., L. Godart, and A. Sacconi
2001 *Thèbes: Fouilles de la Cadmée*. Vol. 1, *Les tablettes en linéaire B de la Odos Pelopidou, édition et commentaire*. Pisa: Istituti editoriali e poligrafici internazionali.

Beck, P., and M. Kochavi
1983 A Dated Assemblage of the Late Thirteenth Century B.C.E. from the Egyptian Residency at Aphek. *Tel Aviv* 12:29–42.

Bennett, E. L.
1955 *The Pylos Tablets: Texts of the Inscriptions Found in 1939–1954*. Princeton, N.J.: Princeton University Press.
1958 *The Mycenae Tablets*. Vol. 2. Philadelphia: American Philosophical Society.
1996 Aegean Scripts. In *The World's Writing Systems*, ed. P. T. Daniels and W. Bright, 125–33. New York: Oxford University Press.
1999 Minos and Minyas: Writing Aegean Measures. In *Floreant Studia Mycenaea: Akten des X. Internationalen Mykenologischen Colloquiums in Salzburg vom 1.–5. Mai 1995*, ed. S. Deger-Jalkotzy, S. Hiller, and O. Panagl, 159–75. Vienna: Österreichischen Akademie der Wissenschaften.

Bordreuil, P., and D. Pardee
1995 Un abécécedaire du type sud-sémitique découverte en 1988 dans les fouilles archéologiques françaises de Ras Shamra-Ougarit. *CRAIBL* 1995:855–60.

Brice, W. C.
1991 Notes on Linear A. *Kadmos* 30:42–48.

Chadwick, J., L. Godart, J. T. Killen, J.-P. Olivier, A. Sacconi, and I. A. Sakellarakis
1986 *Corpus of Mycenaean Inscriptions from Knossos*. 4 vols. Cambridge: Cambridge University Press.

Cross, F. M.
1980 Newly Found Inscriptions in Old Canaanite and Early Phoenician Scripts. *BASOR* 235:1–20.

Deroy, L.
1962 *Initiation a l'épigraphie Mycénienne*. Rome: Ateneo.

Dietrich, M., and O. Loretz
1999 The Ugaritic Script. In *Handbook of Ugaritic Studies*, ed. W. G. E. Watson and N. Wyatt, 81–89. Handbuch der Orientalistik: Erste Abteilung, der Nahe und Mittlere Osten 39. Leiden: Brill.

Dothan, M., and D. Ben-Shlomo
2005 *Ashdod*. Vol. 6, *The Excavations of Areas H and K (1968–1969)*. Israel Antiquities Authority Reports 24. Jerusalem: Israel Antiquities Authority.

Dothan, M., and Y. Porath
1993 *Ashdod*. Vol. 5, *Excavation of Area G*. Jerusalem: Israel Antiquities Authority.

Dow, S.
1954 Minoan Writing. *AJA* 58:77–129.

Duhoux, Y.
1999 La séparation des mots en Linéaire B. In *Floreant Studia Mycenaea: Akten des X. Internationalen Mykenologischen Colloquiums in Salzburg vom 1.–5. Mai 1995*, ed. S. Deger-Jalkotzy, S. Hiller, and O. Panagl, 227–36. Vienna: Österreichischen Akademie der Wissenschaften.

Finkelberg, M.
1998 Bronze Age Writing: Contacts between East and West. In *The Aegean and the Orient in the Second Millennium: Proceedings of the 50th Anniversary Symposium, Cincinnati, 18–20 April*

1997, ed. E. H. Cline and D. Harris-Cline, 265–72. Liège, Belgium: Université de Liège.

Finkelberg, M., A. Uchitel, and D. Ussishkin
1996 A Linear A Inscription from Tel Lachish (LACH ZA 1). *Tel Aviv* 23:195–207.

Gardiner, A.
1957 *Egyptian Grammar*. 3d ed. London: Oxford University Press.

Gelb, I .J.
1963 *A Study of Writing*. 2d ed. Chicago: University of Chicago Press.

Gitin, S.
1993 Seventh-Century B.C.E. Cultic Elements at Ekron. In *Biblical Archaeology Today, 1990: Proceedings of the Second International Congress on Biblical Archeology, Jerusalem*, ed. A. Biran and J. Aviram, 248–58. Jerusalem: Israel Exploration Society.

Gitin, S., T. Dothan, and J. Naveh
1997 A Royal Dedicatory Inscription from Ekron. *IEJ* 47:1–16.

Godart, L., and J.-P. Olivier
1976–85 *Recueil des inscriptions en Linéaire A*. 5 vols. Paris: Geuthner.

Gordon, C. H.
1965 *Ugaritic Textbook*. Rome: Pontifical Biblical Institute.

Goren, Y., I. Finkelstein, and N. Naʾaman
2004 *Inscribed in Clay: Provenance Study of the Amarna Letters and other Ancient Near Eastern Texts*. Tel Aviv: Institute of Archaeology, Tel Aviv University.

Horowitz, W., and A. Shaffer
1992 An Administrative Tablet from Hazor: A Preliminary Edition. *IEJ* 42:21–33.

Horowitz, W., and T. Oshima
2002 Two More Cuneiform Finds from Hazor. *IEJ* 52:179–86.

Ibrahim, M. M., and G. van der Kooij
1997 Excavations at Tall Dayr ʿAllā: Seasons 1987 and 1994. *ADAJ* 41:95–114.
2001 Excavations at Deir Alla. *Newsletter of the Institute of Archaeology and Anthropology of Yarmouk University*. Irbid, Jordan: Yarmouk University.

Ifrah, G.
1985 *From One to Zero: A Universal History of Numbers*. New York: Viking.

Karageorghis, V.
1983 *Palaepaphos-Skales: An Iron Age Cemetery in Cyprus*. Konstanz: Universitätsverlag Konstanz.

Keel, O.
1997 *Corpus der Stempelsiegel-Amulette aus Palästina/Israel: Von den Anfängen bis zur Perserzeit*. Vol. 1, *Von Tell Abu Farağ bis ʿAtlit*. Orbis Biblicus et Orientalis, Series Archaeologica 13. Freiburg: Universitätsverlag Freiburg Schweiz.

Keel, O., M. Shuval, and C. Uehlinger
1990 *Studien zu den Stempelsiegeln aus Palästina/Israel*. Vol. 3. Freiburg: Universitätsverlag Freiburg Schweiz.

Kelm, G. L., and A. Mazar
1990 Tel Batash (Timnah) Excavations: Third Preliminary Report, 1984–1989. BASORSup 27:47–67.

Knauf, E. A.
1987 The Tell Deir ʿAlla Tablets. *Newsletter of the Institute of Archaeology and Anthropology of Yarmouk University* 1:14–16.

Kochavi, M.
1978 Canaanite Aphek: Its Acropolis and Inscriptions. *Expedition* 20:12–17.
1981 The History and Archeology of Aphek-Antipatris. *BA* 44:75–86.
1990 *Aphek in Canaan: The Egyptian Governor's Residence and Its Finds*. Jerusalem: Israel Museum.

Kochavi, M., A. F. Rainey, I. Singer, R. Giveon, and A. Demsky
1978 *Aphek-Antipatris 1974–1977: The Inscriptions*. Tel Aviv: Institute of Archaeology, Tel Aviv University.

Laroche, E.
1960 *Les hiéroglyphes hittites*. Paris: Éditions du Centre national de la recherche scientifique.

Masson, E.
1974 *Cyprominoica: répertoires, documents de Ras Shamra, essais d'interprétation*. Göteborg: Åströms.

Melena, J. L., and J.-P. Olivier
1991 *Tithemy: The Tablets and Nodules in Linear B from Tiryns, Thebes and Mycenae*. Minos supplement 12. Salamanca: Ediciones Universidad de Salamanca.

Millard, A. R.
1970 *Scriptio Continua* in Early Hebrew: Ancient Practice or Modern Surmise? *JSS* 15:2–15.

Naveh, J.
1973 Word Division in West Semitic Writing. *IEJ* 23:206–8.
1982 *The Early History of the Alphabet*. Jerusalem: Magnes.
1985 Writing and Script of Seventh-Century B.C.E. Philistia: The New Evidence from Tell Jemmeh. *IEJ* 35:8–21.

Nissen, H. J., P. Damerow, and R. K. Englund
1993 *Archaic Bookkeeping: Early Writing Techniques of Economic Administration in the Ancient Near East*. Chicago: University of Chicago Press.

Olivier, J.-P.
1986 Cretan Writing in the Second Millennium B.C. *World Archaeology* 17:377–89.

Olivier, J.-P., and L. Godart
1996 *Corpus Hieroglyphicarum Inscriptionum Cretae*. Paris: Broccard.

Oren, E., J.-P. Olivier, Y. Goren, P. P. Betancourt, G. H. Myer, and J. Yellin
1996 A Minoan Graffito from Tel Haror (Negev, Israel). *Cretan Studies* 5:91–117.

Owen, D. I., W. W. Hallo, I. Singer, P. Beck, and M. Kochavi
1987 *Aphek-Antipatris 1978–1985: The Letter from Ugarit*. Tel Aviv: Tel Aviv University.

Palaima, T. G.
1989 Ideograms and Supplementals and Regional Interaction among Aegean and Cypriote Scripts. *Minos* 24:29–54.
1991 The Advent of the Greek Alphabet on Cyprus: A Competition of Scripts. In *Phoinikeia Grammata: lire et écrire en Méditerranée: Actes du Colloque de Liège, 15–18 novembre 1989*, ed. C. Baurain, C. Bonnet, and V. Krings, 449–71. Namur: Société des études classiques.
2005 *The Triple Invention of Writing in Cyprus and Written Sources for Cypriote History*. Nicosia: A. G. Leventis Foundation.

Palaima, T. G., and E. Sikkenga
1999 Linear A > Linear B. In *Meletemata: Studies in Aegean Archaeology Presented to Malcolm H. Wiener*, ed. P. P. Betancourt et al., 599–608. Aegaeum 20. Liège: Université de Liège.

Pardee, D.
2001 Épigraphie et structure dans les textes administratifs II: RS 19.017. *Orientalia* 70:250–82.

Pettersson, J. S.
1996 Numerical Notation. In *The World's Writing Systems*, ed. P. T. Daniels and W. Bright, 795–806. Oxford: Oxford University Press.

Rainey, A. F.
1975 Two Cuneiform Fragments from Tel Aphek. *Tel Aviv* 2:125–29.

Renz, J.
1995 *Die althebräischen Inschriften*. Part 2. Darmstadt: Wissenschaftliche Buchgesellschaft.

Sherratt, S.
2003 Visible Writing: Questions of Script and Identity in Early Iron Age Greece and Cyprus. *Oxford Journal of Archaeology* 22:225–42.

Sigrist, R. M.
1982 Une tablette cunéiforme de Tell Keisan. *IEJ* 32: 32–35.

Singer, I.
1983 Inscriptions from Aphek [in Hebrew]. *Cathedra* 27:19–26.
1988 The Origin of the Sea Peoples and Their Settlement on the Coast of Canaan. In *Society and Economy in the Eastern Mediterranean (c. 1550–1000 B.C.): Proceedings of the International Symposium Held at the University of Haifa from the 28th of April to the 2nd of May, 1985*, ed. M. Heltzer and E. Lipinski, 239–50. OLA 23. Leuven: Peeters.
1994 Egyptians, Canaanites and Philistines in the Period of the Emergence of Israel. In *From Nomadism to Monarchy: Archaeological and Historical Aspects of Early Israel*, ed. I. Finkelstein and N. Naʾaman, 282–338. Jerusalem: Yad Izhak Ben-Zvi and Israel Exploration Society.
2000 Cuneiform, Linear, Alphabetic: The Contest between Writing Systems in the Eastern Mediterranean. In *Mediterranean Cultural Interaction*, ed. A. Ovadiah, 23–32. Tel Aviv: Ramot.

Smith, J. S.
2003 Writing Styles in Clay of the Eastern Mediterranean Late Bronze Age. In *Sea Routes: From Sidon to Huelva; Interconnections in the Mediterranean 16th–6th c. B.C.: Proceedings of the International Symposium Held at Rethymnon, Crete, September 29th–October 2nd 2002*, ed. N. C. Stampolidis and V. Karageorghis, 277–89. Athens: Museum of Cycladic Art.

Ventris, M., and J. Chadwick
1973 *Documents in Mycenaean Greek*. 2d ed. Cambridge: Cambridge University Press.

Weippert, M.
1966 Archäologischer Jahresbericht: 3. Tell dēr ʿĀllā. *ZDPV* 82:299–310.

Yasur Landau, A.
2003 Why Can't We Find the Origin of the Philistines? In Search of the Source of a Peripheral Aegean Culture. In *The Periphery of the Mycenaean World, Lamia 1999*, ed. N. Kyparissi-Apostolika and M. Papakonstantinou, 587–98. Athens: Ephoreia Proistorikōn kai Klassikōn Archaiotētōn.

Yasur Landau, A., and Y. Goren
2004 A Cypro-Minoan Potmark from Aphek. *Tel Aviv* 31:22–31.

41. Camels in Ur III Babylonia?

by Piotr Steinkeller

An Ur III tablet from Puzriš-Dagan (modern Drehem),[1] dating to the tenth month of the forty-fourth regnal year of Šulgi, records deliveries of the animal GÚ.URU×GU:

1) ⸢8⸣ GÚ.URU×GU nita
2) 1 GÚ.URU×GU nita mu-3
3) 1 GÚ.URUxGU nita mu-2
4) 1 GÚ.URU×GU nita mu-1
5) 3 GÚ.URU×GU munus
6) libir-⸢àm⸣
7) ki Šu-^{d}Adad-ta
8) 10 lá 1 GÚ.URU×GU nita
9) 4 GÚ.URU×GU munus
10) Ià-ab-ra-at Šimaški(LÚ.SU)

rev. 11) 2 GÚ.URU×GU nita
12) Hu-un-da-hi-še-er lú An-ša-an^{ki}

(...)

17) [m]u-DU iti ezen-an-na
18) [mu Si-mu]-ru-um^{ki} / [Lu-l]u-bu^{ki} a-rá / [10 lá 1-ka]m-aš ba-hul
19) ud 13-kam (left edge)

Translation:

1) 8 male GÚ.URU×GU,
2) 1 three-year-old male GÚ.URU×GU,
3) 1 two-year-old male GÚ.URU×GU,
4) 1 one-year-old male GÚ.URU×GU,
5) (and) 3 female GÚ.URU×GU,
6) being an earlier (delivery),
7) from Šu-Adad.
8) 9 male GÚ.URU×GU
9) (and) 4 female GÚ.URU×GU
10) (from) Yabrat, a Šimaškian.
11) 2 male GÚ.URU×GU
12) (from) Hundah(i)šer, the man of Anšan.

(...)

17) The delivery. 10th month.
18) Year Šulgi 44.
19) 13th day.

The twenty-nine GÚ.URU×GU listed in this text, twenty-two of which were male and seven female, reappear as a single entry (30 lá 1 GÚ.URU×GU) in a balanced account of a man named Našag, the head of Puzriš-Dagan's Receiving Office, in an account that covers the period from the twelfth month of the year Šulgi 44 until the tenth month of the year Šulgi 46.[2] The conclusion that one and the same group of animals is involved is borne out not only by the identical number of GÚ.URU×GU in both cases and by the close correspondence between the dates of both texts, but equally by the fact that this animal is otherwise completely unknown in cuneiform documentation. It is particularly striking that, after their single appearance at Puzriš-Dagan in the year Šulgi 44, and their further occurrence in Našag's summary account, GÚ.URU×GU are never again mentioned in the Puzriš-Dagan corpus, which otherwise preserves an exceptionally detailed record of the animals that were brought to Babylonia from her periphery in lieu of taxes and as booty and diplomatic gifts (Steinkeller 1995:49–50). This uniqueness of GÚ.URU×GU makes it virtually certain that the importation of these animals to Babylonia in the year Šulgi 44 was a completely singular event that was never repeated, at least not in Ur III times.

But what can be surmised about the zoological identity of the GÚ.URU×GU? The name itself is of little help because even its reading is uncertain. Most likely, the signs are to be analyzed as gú-gur$_5$ or ^{gú}gur$_5$, but neither reading provides any truly convincing etymology, whether in Sumerian or in Akkadian (but see below for some possibilities). Much more informative in this respect are the identities of the parties who delivered these animals. As we have seen, one of them was Yabrat of Šimaški, who, based on various other data, can confidently be identified as Ebarat/Ebarti I, the third ruler of the so-called Šimaškian dynasty (Steinkeller 2007). Another supplier of the GÚ.URU×GU was Hundah(i)šer of Anšan, who, if not a king of Anšan himself, must have been an Anšanite official of considerable importance. Since Šimaški and Anšan occupied the central and

[1] Hilgert 1998:pl. 13 no. 171 (copy), pp. 141–42 (transliteration). This document was discussed already by Calvot (1969:110) based on the information provided by M. Civil.

[2] Calvot 1969:102 AO 19548:4, 19 (Šulgi 48/x). The GÚ.URU×GU are listed twice, first among the deliveries/assets (sag-níg-gur$_{11}$-ra-kam), and for the second time among the expenditures and the animals held in trust (zi-ga ù é-šu-sum-ma).

eastern portions of the Iranian plateau respectively,[3] it follows, therefore, that the GÚ.URU×GU's home must have been in the east, either on the Iranian plateau itself or in one its neighboring regions, such as Afghanistan, Bactria, Makran, or the Indus Valley.

As for Šu-Adad, the third supplier of the GÚ.URU×GU, he is otherwise known to have been a "herder (sipad) of GÚ.URU×GU."[4] This professional designation and the fact that his name is Akkadian indicate that Šu-Adad was merely a functionary under whose care the GÚ.URU×GU in question had been put after their delivery to Babylonia. Importantly, however, Šu-Adad also had a connection with Šimaški, since in the year Šulgi 46 he acted as a conveyor of sheep for the residence of Dala, the envoy/ambassador of the Šimaškian ruler named Barbanazu.[5] It is possible, therefore, that Šu-Adad enjoyed a professional relationship with Dala (or perhaps even with Barbanazu himself), and that the GÚ.URU×GU in question had ultimately been provided by Barbanazu.[6]

Since the animals supplied by Šu-Adad are designated as an "earlier" or "old" (libir) delivery, it appears that this particular group of GÚ.URU×GU arrived prior to the animals supplied by Yabrat and Hundah(i)šer. We can speculate that the former herd was entrusted to Šu-Adad without having first been entered into the delivery (mu-DU) records (as the usual procedure would have been). Presumably, it was only when the other GÚ.URU×GU arrived that Šu-Adad's herd was finally recorded. Although the text says that these animals "came from Šu-Adad," it appears certain that, rather than having been transferred to a Puzriš-Dagan official at that point, they continued to remain in Šu-Adad's care. Less obvious is the fate of the GÚ.URU×GU delivered by Yabrat and Hundah(i)šer. Chances are, however, that they too were entrusted to Šu-Adad, who subsequently incorporated them into his herd.

Next to its place of origin, another important indication of the GÚ.URU×GU's identity is the relative placement of these animals in the above-mentioned account of Našag. There, the GÚ.URU×GU are listed following oxen (gud), red deer (lulim), and fallow deer (šeg$_9$-bar),[7] but before horses (anše-zi-zi), mules (anše-kunga$_2$), and donkeys (dusu$_2$). This classification makes it highly certain that the GÚ.URU×GU was a large, hoofed herbivore. Further corroboration of this is provided by the fact that, in the text recording the delivery of the GÚ.URU×GU, the age of some of these animals is specified, an administrative practice otherwise documented only for cattle, equids, and deer.[8]

Given all these facts, a strong possibility arises that the herbivore in question was none other than the two-humped Bactrian camel (*Camelus bactrianus*), which, as its name indicates, is indigenous to Bactria, Turkmenistan, and Central Asia more generally. While this hypothesis cannot be proven conclusively at this time, various considerations speak in favor of it. First, there is the fact that, by the late third millennium, this animal was widely accessible to the inhabitants of Turkmenistan, Bactria, Margiana, and Seistan, very likely having being fully domesticated by that time. This is shown not only by the frequent depictions of Bactrian camels on the artifacts associated with the so-called "Bactrian-Margiana Archaeological Complex" (broadly dated to the late third

[3] For the basic geopolitical map of Iran at the end of the third millennium B.C.E., see Steinkeller 1982; 2006b; Potts 2004b. For Šimaški specifically, see Steinkeller 2007.

[4] Durand Documents 274:7—Šulgi 46/i/6; PDT 594:27—Amar-Suen 1/iii/4). While sipad (Akk. *rēʾû*), usually means "shepherd," i.e., a keeper of sheep and goats, it also carries a more general sense of "animal-keeper," as in, for example, sipad ur-gir$_{15}$-ra, "dog-keeper." Accordingly, its use in connection with the GÚ.URU×GU is of no help in determining the zoological classification of this animal.

[5] 3 udu niga é Da-la lú-kin-gi$_4$-a Ba-ar-ba-na-zu Šimaški (LÚ.SU.A)-šè gìr Šu-^{d}Adad sipad GÚ.URU×GU (Durand Documents 274:5–7—Šulgi 46/i/6). Quite possibly, Dala is identical with the envoy Duliya (Du-li-a), who, some years later, represented the Šimaškian ruler Yabrat. See 1 udu Du-li-a lú-kin-gi$_4$-a Ab-ra-ad Šimaški(LÚ.SU)^{ki} (Archi-Pomponio Drehem 254:2—Amar-Suen 7/vi/12); 1 udu niga Du-li-a lú-kin-gi$_4$-a Ià-ab-ra-ad Šimaški(LÚ.SU)^{ki} (Delaporte 1911:191 no. 12:1–2—Amar-Suen 7/vi/13).

As for Barbanazu (also known as Barbarazi), several other envoys of his are documented beside Dala/Duliya. They are Pušudu, Kuzuzu, and Šublud: animals é-⌈muhaldim⌉ [m]u Pù-šu-du ⌈lú-kin-gi$_4$-a⌉ Ba-ar-ba!-na-zu Šimaški(LÚ.SU)^{ki} (BIN 3 502:23–25—Šulgi 46/v/27); 1 udu 1 máš Ku-zu-zu lú-kin-gi$_4$-a Ba-ar-ba-ra-zi!(GI)) (TCL 2 5508 ii 2–3—Amar-Suen 4/i/6), Šu-ub-lu-ud lú-kin-gi$_4$-a Ba-ar-ba-ra-zi LÚ.SU.A(Šimaški) (YBC 15413—[-]/iii/2; unpublished, courtesy of M. Sigrist).

[6] Šu-Adad also conveyed sheep for the envoy of Huntiba, the ruler of Duduli, an Iranian principality situated in the general area of Šimaški and Anšan: 1 udu niga 1 máš-gal niga lú-kin-gi$_4$-a Hu-un-ti-ba lú Du$_8$-du$_8$-lí^{ki} gìr Šu-^{d}Adad sipad GÚ.URU×GU (PDT 594:25–27; collated by S. Picchioni 1975:166).

[7] For the zoological identification of šeg$_9$-bar, see Steinkeller 1995:50.

[8] In this connection, note also the later (since the late second millennium B.C.E.) usage of anše, "donkey/equid," to describe camels, as in anše-a-ab-ba and anše-gam-mal, for which see below. See also di-bi-id, "the 'donkey' of Anšan," discussed below in n. 14. Accordingly, it may not be by accident that the GÚ.URU×GU are listed immediately before the equids in Našag's account.

through the early second millennium),[9] but also by the actual finds of camel skeletal remains, as well as of camel dung and hair, in secure archaeological contexts dating from 3500 to 2000 B.C.E.[10]

Second, we know that, during the late third millennium, and particularly during Ur III and early Old Babylonian times, the Iranian polities such as Anšan, Šimaški, and Marhaši remained in close economic—and perhaps even political—contact with the lands of Bactria, Margiana, and Seistan, as demonstrated by the unmistakable and manifold influences of Elamite civilization on the culture of those regions (Steinkeller 2006a). This assures that the Bactrian camel must have been known to the peoples of the Iranian plateau during the time frame in question. Accordingly, nothing contradicts the possibility that a couple of camel herds made their way to Babylonia during the reign of Šulgi, either directly from Bactria or from some intermediate place on the Iranian plateau, where a local camel-breeding operation may already have been under way.

Although our sources do not spell it out, it is virtually certain that the GÚ.URU×GU were brought to Babylonia as a gift for Šulgi. This is affirmed by the high rank of their donors, at least one of whom (Yabrat) was definitely a royal figure. If these indeed were camels, it is difficult to think of a better and more original gift that a Šimaškian or Anšanite ruler could have sent to the king of Ur.[11] When paraded through the streets of Ur or Nippur, these animals and their exotic attendants would have caused as much excitement and commotion as the famed elephant Abul-Abbas, which was presented by Haroun al-Rashid to Charlemagne.[12]

This scenario is corroborated by the fact that our documentation mentions only the delivery of the GÚ.URU×GU. What happened, apparently, is that after they had been transported to and processed by Puzriš-Dagan's Receiving Office, these animals were then moved to some unknown location (a royal animal park?), where, apparently, they were cared for by Šu-Adad. This may explain the absence of any further information about them. As for their subsequent fate, we can only speculate. Since Šu-Adad was still identified as a "herder of GÚ.URU×GU" in the year Amar-Suen 1 (that is, three years later; see note 4 above), the herd seems to have lived for some time. But, since no further mentions of these animals are made in Ur III sources, camel breeding—if the GÚ.URU×GU indeed is a camel—obviously did not take root in Babylonia at that time. Many centuries would pass before camels would again make their way to Babylonia, this time to stay there permanently.[13]

Finally, let us revisit the question of the reading of GÚ.URU×GU to see whether any further insight into this problem can be gained, especially in view of the proposed zoological identification. As noted earlier, the most likely interpretation is that the signs are to be read gú-gur$_5$. If so, the term could be connected with the Sumerian verb gú-gúr(GAM), corresponding to Akkadian *kanāšu*, "to bend down, to bow down, to bend (something)" (see *CAD* K p. 144, lexical section of *kanāšu*). This would result in the meaning "the one who bends down," which would be a pretty good characterization of the camel and its behavior. Conceivably, gú-gur$_5$ could even mean "the humped one," by analogy with English "hump," which derives from the Indo-European root **kumb-* < **keu-*, "to bend, to curve." All of this, however, is simply speculation, since gú-gur$_5$ could equally well be a foreign word (Elamite?), whose form was **ku(r)kur* or something similar.[14] At any rate, gú-gur$_5$ cannot be

[9] See, especially, the set of silver and gold vessels excavated at Gonur-depe, all of which bear representations of Bactrian camels. Particularly striking among them is a tall silver vase, which is decorated with a procession of camels in high *repoussé* (Sarianidi 2005:234–38 and figs. 94–97, 252). For other examples, see Sarianidi 2002:139 (upper two figures), 302 (lower figure); Pittman 1984:40, 42 figs. 10 and 11. The Bactrian camel is also depicted on a shard from Sialk III$_4$ (Ghirshman 1938:pl. 79 A$_2$), which appears to be the only such example from Iran in early periods (before 2000 B.C.E.). Dating to ca. 3500 B.C.E., it is also the earliest representation of the Bactrian camel on record. For still further examples, see Potts 2004a:149–50.

[10] Such finds are documented at a number of sites in southern Turkmenistan, at Shahr-i Sokhta in Seistan, at Shah Tepe on the Gorgan Plain, and at Gonur-depe in Margiana. See Compagnoni and Tosi 1978; Hiebert 1994:134; Sarianidi 2005:215; Potts 2004a:148–50.

[11] Here it seems significant that the delivery of the GÚ.URU×GU by Yabrat in the year Šulgi 44 is the *earliest* known record of this ruler and his diplomatic contacts with the House of Ur, which were to last through the year Šu-Suen 8 (see Steinkeller 2007). Very likely, this gift was part of a diplomatic overture, by which Yabrat meant to introduce himself to Šulgi and to establish friendly relations with Babylonia.

[12] For other examples of exotic animals presented as gifts to Ur III kings by eastern powers, see Potts 2002.

[13] For the history of the camel, see Bulliet 1975:141–75, where the two-humped camel and its history in Iran and neighboring regions are discussed. This discussion is now surpassed by an excellent study by D. T. Potts (2004a:146–53). For the camel in Babylonia specifically, see also Heimpel 1976–80.

[14] Another, but less likely, solution would be to connect GÚ.URU×GU with the animal designation di-bi-id, which occurs in an Old Babylonian bilingual proverb: di-bi-id An-

connected with any of the known designations of "camel" in Sumerian and Akkadian, all of which are later than the Ur III period. Beginning with Sumerian, those terms are am-si-kur-ra, "mountain 'elephant,'" am-si-har-ra-an, "road/caravan 'elephant,'" and anše-a-ab-ba, "'horse' of the sea," all three of which appear only in lexical sources, where they are equated with Akkadian *ibilu*, "dromedary, Arabian camel."[15] Apart from *ibilu*, Akkadian also knows *gammalu*/*gamlu* (ANŠE.GAM.MAL, also ANŠE.A.AB.BA), "dromedary" (*CAD* G pp. 35–36), and *udru* (a loan from Old Iranian *uštra*), "Bactrian camel" (*AHw* 1401b), attested in Assyrian since the reign of Assur-bel-kala (1074–1057 B.C.E.).*

ša$_4$-an^{ki}-na = *i-mi-ir An-ša-ni-*[*im*], "the 'donkey' of Anšan" (Lambert 1960:272–73, pl. 71 N-3395:5; Alster 1997:288–89; collated and discussed by M. Civil 1998:11 and n. 6). This designation is otherwise unique, except for its occurrence in Izi C iv 35 (*MSL* 13:179), where it figures as an equivalent of *imēru*, "donkey": di-bi-da = *e-me-ru*. As suggested by Civil (1998:11), chances are that this "donkey" of Anšan is yet another early designation of the camel. Apart from the fact that camels were often identified as various types of "donkeys" in later periods (see above n. 8 and the discussion below), this interpretation is strongly supported by the context of the proverb in question, which, in the following lines, names three other exotic animals from the east: dìm-šáh Mar-ha-ši^{ki} = *ma-ar-gi*$_4$ *Pa-ra-aḫ-*[*ši*], "the bear?/crocodile? of Marhaši," gul-lum Me-luh-ha^{ki} = *šu-ra-an Me-luḫ-*[*ḫa*], "the 'cat' (probably the leopard) of Meluhha," til-lu-ug sa$_{12}$-ti-um^{ki} = *pi-i-ir ša-ad-di-*[*im*], "the Eastern elephant" (cf. Steinkeller 1980:9). However, a hypothetical reading /dibid(a)/ of GÚ.URU×GU finds no support in any data.

[15] See *PSD* A/3 p. 187, lexical section of am-si; p. 188, lexical sections of am-si-har-ra-an and am-si-kur-ra; *CAD* I/J p. 2, lexical section of *ibilu*. An am-si(-)kur-ra is mentioned already in a Pre-Sargonic (Fara) literary text (Jestin Šuruppak pl. 183 no. 46 i 1′-2′), but it is highly doubtful that "camel" is meant there; the sense "elephant of the mountains/foreign lands" seems much more likely. The earliest attestation of am-si-har-ra-an is found in an Old Babylonian literary text, where the meaning "camel" appears more plausible: ^{d}Dumu-zi ga ⸢am-si⸣-har-ra-⸢an⸣-[na se$_{12}$-a-ma-ab] ⸢am-si⸣-har-ra-an-na ga-bi [zé-ba-àm], "Dumuzi, [ferment] the ⸢camel?⸣ milk for me, the milk of the ⸢camel?⸣ [is sweet]" (Sefati 1998:221, Dumuzi-Inana P iii 24–24, pl. 28 Ni 9602).

* I am delighted to be able to present this little offering to Larry, my dear friend, colleague, and comrade-in-arms (in defense of mostly lost causes…).

Abbreviations used are those of the *Assyrian Dictionary of the Oriental Institute of the University of Chicago* (*CAD*) and/or the *Sumerian Dictionary of the University Museum of the University of Pennsylvania* (*PSD*).

Bibliography

Alster, B.
1997 *Proverbs of Ancient Sumer: The World's Earliest Proverb Collections*. Vol. 1. Bethesda, Md.: CDL.

Bulliet, R. W.
1975 *The Camel and the Wheel*. Cambridge, Mass.: Harvard University Press.

Calvot, D.
1969 Deux documents inédits de Ṣelluš-Dagan. *RA* 63: 101–14.

Civil, M.
1998 Adamdun, the Hippopotamus, and the Crocodile. *JCS* 50:11–14.

Compagnoni, B., and M. Tosi
1978 The Camel: Its Distribution and State of Domestication in the Middle East during the Third Millennium B.C. in Light of Finds from Shahr-i Sokhta. In *Approaches to Faunal Analysis in the Middle East*, ed. R. H. Meadow and M. A. Zeder, 91–103. Peabody Museum Bulletin 2. Cambridge, Mass.: Peabody Museum of Archaeology and Ethnology, Harvard University.

Delaporte, L.
1911 Tablettes de Drêhem. *RA* 8:183–198.

Ghirshman, R.
1938 *Fouilles de Sialk près de Kashan 1933, 1934, 1937*. Vol 1. Paris: Geuthner.

Heimpel, W.
1976–80 Kamel. *RLA* 5:330–32.

Hiebert, F. T.
1994 *Origins of the Bronze Age Oasis Civilization in Central Asia*. American School of Prehistoric Research Bulletin 42. Cambridge, Mass.: Peabody Museum of Archaeology and Ethnology, Harvard University.

Hilgert, M.
1998 *Drehem Administrative Documents from the Reign of Šulgi*. OIP 115. Chicago: Oriental Institute of the University of Chicago.

Lambert, W. G.
1960 *Babylonian Wisdom Literature*. Oxford: Clarendon.

Picchioni, S.
1975 Miscellanea Neo-Sumerica, II. *Oriens Antiquus* 14:153–68.

Pittman, H.
1984 *Art of the Bronze Age: Southeastern Iran, Western Central Asia, and the Indus Valley*. New York: Metropolitan Museum of Art.

Potts, D. T.
2002 Total Prestation in Marhashi–Ur Relations. *Iranica Antiqua* 37:342–57.
2004a Camel Hybridization and the Role of *Camelus Bactrianus* in the Ancient Near East. *JESHO* 47: 143–65.
2004b Exit Aratta: Southeastern Iran and the Land of Marhashi. *Nāme-ye Irān-e Bāstān* 4:41–51.

Sarianidi, V.
2002 *Margush: Ancient Oriental Kingdom in the Old Delta of the Murghab River*. Ashgabat, Turkmenistan.
2005 *Gonur-depe: City of Kings and Gods*. Ashgabat, Turkmenistan: Miras.

Sefati, Y.
1998 *Love Songs in Sumerian Literature: Critical Edition of the Dumuzi-Inanna Songs*. Ramat Gan, Israel: Bar-Ilan University Press.

Steinkeller, P.
1980 The Old Akkadian Term for Easterner. *RA* 74:1–9.
1982 The Question of Marḫaši: A Contribution to the Historical Geography of Iran in the Third Millennium B.C. *ZA* 72:237–65.
1995 Sheep and Goat Terminology in Ur III Sources from Drehem. *Bulletin on Sumerian Agriculture* 8:49–70.
2006a Beyond Marḫashi: Thoughts about Intercultural Connections in Greater Elam during the Third Millennium B.C. Unpublished paper read at the meeting "Countries and Lands on the Magan Sea, March 25–27, 2006, Ravenna, Italy."
2006b New Light on Marhaši and Its Contacts with Makkan and Babylonia. *Journal of Magan Studies* 1:1–17.
2007 New Light on Šimaški and Its Rulers. *ZA* 97: 215–232.

42. A Persian-period Hoard of Bullae from Samaria

by Ephraim Stern

A hoard of forty-four bullae was acquired by the late Dr. Reuben Hecht many years ago from a Jerusalem antiquities dealer. Twenty-seven of the bullae, which apparently originated from the Samaria area, are now in the Reuben and Edith Hecht Museum in Haifa (Stern 2002).[1]

None of the bullae in the collection bears an inscription, with the exception of two identical stamps (figure 1:1; plates 1:1, 3:1): a kneeling winged griffin inscribed with the name Ishmael written in *plene* (from left to right); and another incomplete impression (figure 1:6; plate 3:2), which originally was apparently stamped with a similar griffin; behind it is an illegible motif and the single letter *yod* (from left to right).

Another collection of bullae from this hoard, now in the Israel Museum,[2] contains seventeen bullae (two of them duplicates).

General Background

The hoard of bullae is of great interest for the study of the period because of its close similarities to impressions on bullae that sealed fourth-century B.C.E. papyri discovered earlier in the Wadi ed-Daliyeh cave in Samaria, in which a number of Samaritans had sought refuge after fleeing the city to escape the army of Alexander the Great in 332 B.C.E. Some of these papyri have already been published: those uncovered in the excavations and others previously purchased from Bedouin (cf. Lapp and Lapp 1974:17–29; Cross 1963; 1985:7*–17*; Gropp 1986). In addition to the documents that were written and sealed at *šmryn qiryata zi bšmryn medinta* ("in the city of Samaria in the province of Samaria"), numerous bullae were found, some still attached to papyri, which belonged to witnesses whose names were among the signatories of the documents. Among these names were high-ranking officials, such as Sanballaṭ, governor of Samaria, and Yoḥanan *sagna* (cf. the *ḥōrîm* and *s*[e]*gānîm* in Neh. 4:8). Whereas all the names appearing in the Wadi ed-Daliyeh documents were of local residents, the stamps on the bullae themselves can be divided into three categories:

1. Local motifs that continued ancient Israelite-Phoenician traditions.
2. Persian-Achaemenian motifs, most of them depicting the Persian king in various activities, as well as Achaemenian cult symbols.
3. A large number of impressions are in true Greek style. Some of them were published by F. M. Cross, who noted that they were engraved with "familiar Attic motifs" and went on to say: "One is particularly struck with the vivacity of Attic-Greek influences in the glyptic art of Samaria in the era before the coming of Alexander" (Cross 1963: 115).

A careful examination of the finds uncovered in the excavations of the city of Samaria revealed a number of impressions on bullae of the same type: local, Achaemenian, and Greek, as well as a glass seal (Crowfoot et al. 1957:fig. 92:80, pl. 15 Reisner et al. 1924:pl. 57; and see Stern 1983).

In recent times, numerous coins have begun to appear on the antiquities market that are impressed with dozens of motifs, some identical with those on the above-mentioned bullae, and others that can also be classified as local, Achaemenian, and Greek. On some of these coins appears the name Shomrin in *plene* or shortened form; others bear personal names, of which coins with the name Jeroboam (*yrbᶜm*) have been published (Spaer 1979:218). Other names on these coins include *yšmᶜˀl hym*, *ḥnnyh*, *bˀdyhbl*, *yhwˀnh*, *ᶜbdˀl*, *snblṭ*, *dlyh*, and *mzdy* (see Meshorer and Qedar 1999:14–31).

After even a cursory examination it is clear that there is a close correspondence, and even full agreement, between some of the impressions on the bullae under discussion and those on the coins from Samaria, with all their peculiarities and unique characteristics. In this connection, the writer some time ago suggested—and again repeats—that all the extremely diverse groups of Palestinian coins from the end of the Persian period (namely, the Yehud coins and the city coins of Samaria, Ashdod, Gaza, and Ashkelon and the uninscribed coins bearing personal names, now being uncovered in ever-increasing numbers) should be interpreted as coins of treasury offi-

[1] The bullae of this part of the hoard were photographed by Zeev Radovan and drawn by Natalie Masika. I wish to thank Hecht Museum director, Ms. Ofra Rimon, for allowing me to publish this material.

[2] The bullae in the Israel Museum were entrusted to me for publication by the late Prof. Y. Meshorer. They were drawn by Sarah Halbrein. Since the two collections were drawn by different artists, they naturally display a number of stylistic variations.

cials who served in the various provinces of Palestine in this period and used their private seals for stamping the coins (Stern 1982: 221–224).

As for the bullae: several hoards have already been found in Israel, some dating to the end of the Iron Age and others to the Persian period (Aharoni 1975: 19–25, pls. 20, 21; Shoham 2000; Avigad 1976; 1986). All of these bullae, however, included the names of their owners and rarely bore decorative designs. As was noted above, the assemblage with the closest affinity to our subject found in Israel are the bullae sealings of the Samaria papyri found at Wadi ed-Daliyeh, several of which were published already by F. M. Cross in 1974, and all of them when the papyri were opened by M. J. W. Leith (1997). More than seventy bullae were recently found (in 2006) in a "rock-cut pool" under the City of David (Reich, in Baruch et al. 2006:19–20).

Aside from the above assemblages, many sites in Israel have yielded—in strata from the Persian period—single impressions stamped on bullae, handles of clay vessels, and clay jar stoppers. Mention should be made, for example, of the finds from Tell Keisan, Atlit, Dor, Tel Michal, Samaria, Shechem, Gibeon, Ramat Rahel, Beth-zur, and En-Gedi; these will be discussed below.

In several cases, as at Atlit, Dor, Shiqmona, Samaria, Tel Michal, Gibeon, etc., the seals themselves were discovered, made of various materials: silver and gold, bronze and iron, semiprecious stones, but mainly faience and glass. Their shapes, like the motifs impressed on them, also fall into three types: local scaraboid seals, pyramidal seals in Mesopotamian style, and oval seals in Greek style (Stern 1982: 199–200).

In contrast to the rather meager finds of this type in Palestine, large hoards of bullae from the Persian period have been discovered in other countries: in Egypt, Phoenicia, Anatolia, Mesopotamia, and, of course, in Persia itself (Stern 1982:196–197). These hoards have been interpreted as remains of archives of officials serving in the Persian administration, and several are considered the archives of governors. It should be noted that in all the hoards from these countries, the eastern Achaemenian style formed only one component of the hoard and other styles were also represented, although all the hoards were the remains of royal archives directly related to the Persian administration. The hoard from Memphis, for example, included, alongside Achaemenian motifs, Egyptian impressions of different styles and periods, and others in a distinct archaic-Greek style. The same can be said of sealings of papyri from Elephantine, which were executed in Achaemenian and Egyptian styles. An assemblage from Dascylium in Anatolia, which may be the largest of its type (consisting of more than 300 impressions) also included two types: Achaemenian and Greek, some bearing Persian and Aramaic inscriptions. The collection of bullae from Ur contained so diverse an assortment of styles (Achaemenian, Babylonian, Greek, Phoenician, and Egyptian) that Woolley called it "a collector's treasure." However, in light of the other finds at this site, these impressions were probably produced by seals that were in use in a single office of the administration (Legrain 1951).

The Motifs

In general, the bullae in the hoard under discussion can be divided into local eastern-style bullae and western Greek bullae. It seems that there were no Achaemenian-style motifs whatsoever in the hoard (see below).

The Eastern Group

The following motifs are represented in the hoard of bullae: griffins (figure 1:1–6; plate 1:1–5, 3:1–2), lions (figure 1:7–13; plates 1:6, 3:3–8), horses and riders (figure 2:1–7; plate 3:9–13), a bird (figure 2:8; plated 3:14), and, lastly, apparently the lotus flower (figure 2:9; plate 3:15), which is found on the only seal in the assemblage. Among these motifs were a number of examples which, despite their eastern style, may have been executed by a Greek artist (in Greek-Phoenician style).

The entire assemblage contains only an insignificant number of the eastern motifs known from this period at other sites in Israel. We have already mentioned the total absence of Babylonian-Achaemenian motifs, which are very common on bullae of Samaria and Wadi ed-Daliyeh and on Samarian coins and Palestinian coins in general from this period, as well as (and primarily) on Phoenician coins. These popular themes include the Babylonian "Scorpion King" motif. Motifs such as the Persian king fighting a lion, a griffin, or a bull, shooting arrows, lifting lions and griffins by their hind legs, being driven in his chariot, going on a hunt, standing in front of a god, are all accompanied by emblems of the Babylonian and Persian gods. All of these motifs and others were discovered on bullae, seals and coins from the above-mentioned sites.

Also missing here are the numerous Persian-period motifs found on bullae, seals, and coins whose origins can be traced to the traditional repertoire in use by Palestinian-Phoenician and Transjordanian carvers already in the Israelite period: the figure of a king seated on his throne, a seated goddess, human faces; and numerous figures of animals stamped on coins, seals, bullae, and weights: a cow suckling a calf, rams flanking the "tree of life," sheep, gazelles, antelope and deer, bulls, cocks, various types of birds, locusts, fish, frogs, hedgehogs, and scorpions. The bullae also lack the numerous scenes of battles frequently found on ivories, such as a lion devouring a human, bull, ram, etc.; a griffin trampling a man, etc. (Avigad 1954; 1964; 1966; 1970; 1975; 1978; 1979; 1981; 1982; 1989; 1992; Avigad and Sass 1997; Tadmor 1972; Barkay 1992; Barnett 1982; Crowfoot and Crowfoot 1938; Stern 1976).

The Western Group

The western group of motifs appear on approximately half of the bullae (and, as was noted above, this group is also well represented in the finds from Wadi ed-Daliyeh and the city of Samaria). Like the eastern repertoire, the variety of its subjects is also extremely limited; among them are figures of nude or clothed men, identifiable by their accompanying attributes (see below), and figures of women in Greek dress, one of whom is seated on a stool holding a bird.

Greek figures are especially popular on seals and impressions from the Persian period discovered in Israel. Dozens have been encountered on rings or stamped on bullae, pottery vessels, clay jar stoppers, etc. They have been uncovered at Tell Abu Hawam, Atlit, Dor, Tel Michal, Beth-zur, Ramat Rahel, En-Gedi, and other sites, and, of course, as was noted above, they also appear in all the remains of Achaemenian archives outside of Palestine. They are especially widespread on coins of the period: on Samarian coins, Yehud coins, and coins of other Palestinian cities, and also—and primarily—on Phoenician coins. All of these reflect the especially rich repertoire that was derived for the most part from the world of Greek mythology. Exceptionally popular in this period are the motifs of Zeus as ruler, Heracles and the Persian king fighting animals and monsters, the figures of Hermes, Athena, a hippocampus and triton, and the heads of satyrs and medusas and of Janus. Figures from daily life are also represented, such as warriors (especially noteworthy is a Greek hoplite phalanx depicted on a bulla from the Persian period found at Dor [Stern 2000:192]) and animals not previously encountered: a pig, water buffalo, owl, hawk, an eagle fighting a snake, and others. It should also be noted that in this period, some of the local inhabitants—mainly Phoenicians—use Greek names (Avner and Eshel 1996).

The Impressions in Local Eastern Style

Griffins

The Hecht Collection contains seven impressions of griffins (figure 1:1–6; plates 1:1–5, 3:1–2), which are depicted in different forms. Two are represented as a couchant winged gazelle with an undefined floral motif in front of it. Both of these impressions bear the name Ishmael in mirror writing. On another fragmentary bulla (figure 1:6), in which only the griffin's back has been preserved, is inscribed the single letter *yod*, also in mirror writing. It was probably also inscribed with the name Ishmael. This bulla, which also seems to have been decorated with the griffin motif, is not identical with the others.

The other four bullae differ from one another. On the first bulla (figure 1:2; plate 1:2) appears a winged griffin, with the body of a lion and the head of a bird, leaping onto the back of an ibex with long branching horns, which is shown being forced to the ground during an attempt to flee. The second bulla (figure 1:3; plate 1:3) depicts a similar griffin, that is, with the body of a winged lion and the head of a bird fleeing with its two forelegs raised forward. The third bullae is similar (figure 1:4; plate 1:4) and also represents a galloping griffin, but this time with a winged body and the head of a bull. The fourth bulla is more difficult to decipher (figure 1:5; plate 1:5), but it, too, appears to display the front part of a griffin with the head of a bird standing upright. The forelegs and wings are clearly distinguishable.

The griffin motif has deep roots in Palestine and its widespread use in local glyptic art is evident as early as the Iron Age, as, for example, in the numerous ivories found in the city of Samaria, in which griffins are depicted with the head of a bird, ram, or bull, etc. Other motifs frequently represented in the ivories are the beast of prey—a griffin or a lion—attacking another animal (Crowfoot and Crowfoot 1938:pls. 6:2, 8:1, 14:4) and especially the griffin (or sphinx) trampling a human being. The griffin motif is also very common in all the Phoenician ivory assemblages uncovered at every site (Barnett 1957:pl. 66; 1982:pls. 47:b, 49:c). The motif of the predator and its prey is also portrayed on seal impressions of the First Temple period, of which the most beautiful example may be of a lion attacking and leaping onto the back of a deer on the uninscribed impression from Ramat Rahel (see Barkay 1992; Aharoni 1962:35, pl. 7:40).[3] This motif also appears in the well-known

[3] Among the uninscribed impressions and seals in the Hecht Museum in Haifa is one that also depicts a lion attacking an ibex with a bird above it.

scene in the ivories described above of a griffin trampling a man (Reisner et al. 1924:1:378; 2:pl. 1:57; Crowfoot et al. 1957:189, pl. 15:46).

In the Persian period, the griffin became a very popular motif in Palestine and adjoining countries and appeared frequently on seals (as, for example, on the scaraboid seal from Dor [Stern 2000:191, fig. 124]) and bullae of the period in all possible variations: with the head of a bird, bull, or deer, and in the familiar scenes of griffins leaping onto prey.

Because of the close resemblance between the impressions on seals and bullae, on the one hand, and the impressions on coins, on the other, the popularity of the motif and its appearance on all types of coins minted in Palestine in the Persian period is not surprising. It is frequently found on Samarian coins (Meshorer and Qedar 1999)[4] and on coins of the province of Judah, in which winged griffins with lion heads are portrayed—some not inscribed and some bearing the name *Yehizkiyo (*Meshorer 2001:7–17, pls. 1–3). The griffin is common on other uninscribed Palestinian coins, where it appears in many variations and also as beasts of prey (and see, e.g., Lambert 1932:nos. 45, 47, 48, 50–51; Kindler 1963:nos. 30–31, 33, 46, 55–56).

Later, the Greek-style griffin was adopted into the traditional repertoire, as, for example, in the form of a flying horse (hippocampus) which appears on seal impressions of the Persian and Hellenistic periods (Sellers 1933:62, fig. 11:56) and on Samarian and other Palestinian coins (Kindler 1963:no. 54) and, above all, on Phoenician coins (Lambert 1932:nos. 39–40).

Concurrently with the above appears the triton (half man, half fish) on seals and impressions and on Phoenician and local coins of the period (Herzog et al. 1989:335, fig. 1:28; Tufnell 1953:pl. 123:44; Lapp and Lapp 1974:pl. 80:4).

Lions

Lions of various types are depicted on a total of seven bullae (figure 1:7–13; plates 1:6, 3:3–8). Y. Meshorer (1992) has already noted the large number of lions on Samarian coins and offered his own explanation for this phenomenon. In our assemblage, two of the impressions depict a lion, bent over, and seen from the side (figure 1:7–8; plate 3:3–4); a lion devouring the thigh of a bull (figure 1:9; plate 1:6); and four versions of the head and upper part of a roaring, standing, or leaping lion (figure 1:10–13; plate 3:5–8). On two impressions, unidentified objects appear in front of the lion. Their unsophisticated portrayal seems to indicate that they were locally produced, with the possible exception of the lion feeding on the bull's thigh (figure 1:9; plate 1:6), which is of excellent workmanship; its motif was apparently copied from a Greek coin (as was noted above, it also appears on Samarian coins).

The lion motif was very common in Palestinian art beginning in the First Temple period, both on seals of officials—such as the famous seal of Shema Servant of Jeroboam (Tadmor 1972:30)—and on seals bearing personal names (as, for example, the seals of Ashne'l and Ashna, and the seal of Neri (Avigad 1992:33*–36*). Avigad, in his publication of the Ashna seal, observed: "The rarity of the lion in the iconography of the Hebrew seals is surprising; the Hebrew carvers apparently did not realize its symbolic significance" (Avigad 1979:125). In the opinion of the writer, however, this conclusion was based on chance finds. For example, the seal from this period from Ramat Rahel, mentioned above in connection with the griffins, portrays a lion leaping onto the back of an ibex (Aharoni 1962:35, pl. 7:40), and Palestinian copies of Assyrian seals exist on which lions are shown fighting, and also—and above all—lions are depicted on objects produced by local carvers and artists of the First Temple period. There are also many instances of lions on the Samarian ivories, on cast metal weights (Crowfoot and Crowfoot 1938:pls. 9–10; Avigad 1992; Avi-Yonah and Stern 1975:84; other lion weights are on display in a permanent exhibition at the Hecht Museum in Haifa), and also as figurines.[5]

In the Persian period, the lion motif increased in popularity and appears frequently on ordinary uninscribed seals and seal impressions (Stern 1982:200, fig. 326) as the principal motif on a group of seals from the province of Judah, and also as the main animal fighting the Persian king or other hero (Bes, Heracles, etc.; see Stern 1982:209–213, and, for a detailed discussion of the subject, Heltzer 1993:111–22). The figure of the lion on coins of the Persian period is even more widespread than on the seals: on coins of Samaria, Phoenician coins (Meshorer and Qedar 1999; Mildenberg 1987),[6] and on the many

---

[4] One of these depicts a galloping winged bull and another a lion leaping onto a deer and bearing the inscription *Shomrin.* This coin is very similar in shape to the impression from Ramat Rahel. Another coin depicts a griffin with a bird's head attacking a ram, almost identical to our impression (figure 1:2; plate 1:2). This coin is not inscribed.

[5] Three clay lion figurines are on display at the Hecht Museum in Haifa: one represents a roaring lion and the other two apparently served as a base for figurines of gods.

[6] Lion figures are very common on these coins, and appear in all possible variations: walking, couchant (and even in a

uninscribed coins of the Persian period throughout Palestine (Lambert 1932:nos. 45–61; Kindler 1963: nos. 1–11, 24–25, 31–35).

Horses and Riders

Horses and riders are another common motif in the group of impressions under discussion. At least seven bullae in the hoard depict horses (figure 2:1–7; plates 2:7, 3:4–13): five of them galloping, one showing a horse and rider (figure 2:1; plate 3:9), and the last (figure 2:6) a double impression of two horses in opposite directions. All are executed in a simple style and were locally made, with the possible exception of figure 2:2 (plate 1:7), which may have been carved by a Greek craftsman.

Horses in Palestinian art, especially the galloping horse, are very common from the Iron Age onward. Numerous figurines of horses and their riders (Tufnell 1953:pl. 29:17–18) have been uncovered in Iron Age strata at most sites in the country, and numerous horses are also depicted on seal impressions and seals. Examples of uninscribed impressions with galloping horses have been found at En-Gedi, Tel Zakariya, and Jerusalem (Mazar 1990; Barkay 1992); a fourth, similar impression is in the Hecht Museum.

From the Babylonian period there is an example of a seal of a rider hunting a ram with the assistance of a dog, from Tell el-Mazar in Transjordan—undoubtedly a local imitation of a Mesopotamian prototype (Yassine 1984:fig. 6:9).

In the Persian period, especially towards the end, this motif becomes increasingly popular and appears in numerous variations; many are found as figurines of horses and riders (Stern 1982:165–68) and on impressions and seals at various sites in the country, for example, on bullae from Tel Michal, a seal from Beth-zur, and a gold ring from Gibeon (Herzog et al. 1989:336–37, fig. 28:1, 5–6; Sellers 1933:60, fig. 10:53; Stern 1982:199, fig. 322). A great number of images of horses, in both Achaemenian and Greek style, were also stamped on bullae in archives of the Persian period found outside Palestine (Legrain 1951:pl. 41, nos. 766–74). The horse was also a popular motif on all types of coins minted in Palestine throughout the Persian period. Although not yet encountered in the archive of Wadi ed-Daliyeh, except for the horses drawing Athena's quadriga (Lapp and Lapp 1974:29, no. 46), on a great number of coins from the city of Samaria itself are depicted riders on horses in both Greek and Persian style, horses being led by their halters, galloping horses, and protomai of galloping horses. The names Shomrin or Jeroboam were inscribed on several of these coins. On the city coins of Samaria can also be found couchant horses and horses drawing the Persian king's chariot.

The horse and rider was also the principal motif on city coins of Sidon, and it also appears on a glass seal from Dor. The figure of a horse—in all possible variations—is a very common motif on uninscribed Palestinian coins in the Persian period (cf. Stern 1983; Baramki 1945:pl. 20; Mildenberg 1987:nos. 11, 14; Lambert 1932:no. 58; Kindler 1963:nos. 20, 25, 37, 40).

Birds

A bird appears in only one impression in our assemblage: a songbird is represented with outspread wings, with a lily above it (figure 2:8; plate 3:14).

The birds most frequently portrayed on seals from the First Temple period are those symbolizing strength and courage: the fighting cock and the hawk. The fighting cock appears on seals of the highest-ranking officials of the kingdom: Ya'azanyahu servant of the king and Yehoahaz son of the king. A hawk is depicted on the seal of *ʾbgd*. It is also apparently engraved on another seal, alongside the name of a person called *Orev* ("crow"; Tadmor 1972:nos. 31, 33; Avigad 1981:305, pl. 57:3).

In the Persian period, numerous birds are depicted on bullae, on seals, and on coins of the period. These are mostly birds of prey: the owl—the emblem of the goddess Athena—was engraved on Phoenician coins, on coins of Samaria and Judah, and on uninscribed Palestinian coins. Often found on these coins is a falcon or hawk with outspread wings (Meshorer 1966:217–19, pl. 25; 2001:pl. 2:15–16), or standing on the outstretched hand of a god or king. This western motif, which also occurs in our hoard (figure 4:5; plate 2:9) was apparently adopted into the local Palestinian coin repertoire, including the coins of Samaria and Judah (see further below).

At present, no definite parallels can be found for the songbird in our Persian-period assemblage.

Lily

The motif of the lily appears on Hebrew seals as a common decorative element, as well as on the ivories dating from this period (Crowfoot and Crowfoot 1938:pl. 23:2; Avigad 1989:94–95, no. 14).

rare frontal view), a protome of a lion leaping with open mouth, and jumping onto various animals: bulls, gazelles, etc. There is even a lion feeding on the thigh of a bull that is almost identical with the lion on our seal. It is most common, however, on Samarian coins, where it appears on its hind legs in a classical rampant attitude in combat with the Persian king, a motif that was adopted into Palestinian glyptic art as early as the Assyrian period.

Lotus Flower

The only seal in the hoard (figure 2:9; plate 3:15) has a scaraboid shape; its upper part is smooth and the surface is engraved with a lotus flower between two palm branches(?). Whether or not the seal was originally found together with the hoard of bullae is unknown; in any event, it was included among the objects of the hoard.

A similar motif from the First Temple period appears in the seal repertoire of the period, although it was still quite rare at that time. A similar flower, slightly more complex in form, was engraved on another scaraboid seal that bore the inscription *l'Padiyahu Shafal*. This seal was published by Avigad, who noted: "This is one of the rare seals in which the lotus flower serves as the main motif; on both its sides are two additional knobs" (Avigad and Sass 1997:144, no. 329). A very similar flower appears on the Peshhur seal (Avigad and Sass 1997: 146, no. 335) between lilies, of the type appearing in our collection, above the head of the bird (figure 2:8; plate 3:14). The lotus flower also appears on a third Hebrew seal, also published by Avigad. Another Hebrew seal, on which two similar flowers are carved, bears the inscription *Lelisur*; it is part of the permanent exhibition of the Hecht Museum in Haifa (Avigad 1970:307–308, pl. A:6; 1989:94, nos. 13–14).

This motif became especially popular in the Persian period, both on local impressions and on the various types of Palestinian coins. It was the sole decorative element on a Yehud coin published by Meshorer (2001:pl. 2:14–16).

Additional eastern motifs also appear in the collection of impressions from Wadi ed-Daliyeh published by Leith (several of which were discussed in the excavation report: Leith 1997). Aside from the group of impressions exhibiting classic Achaemenian motifs—totally absent in our assemblage—these themes include the king and the hero in combat with lions and other creatures, some of which are familiar, such as the flying bull, pairs of sphinxes, pairs of the "Scorpion King," as well as animals, among them lions, a number of which are indistinguishable from our lions (for some reason, Leith assigned them to the group of western motifs), and other, unknown motifs and numerous impressions of galloping horses, alone or in intersecting pairs.

Western Greek-Style Impressions

Male Figures

A large number of the bullae in our collection, thirteen in all (one is double), depict male figures in western Greek style (figure 3:1–13). Eight are impressed with an identical image of a nude young man with his hand extended in front of him and his left hand behind his back. In three of the bullae, a triangular-shaped form appears in front of the figure (figure 3:2–8; plate 3:7–12).

One of the bullae (figure 3:10; plate 2:2) depicts a partially clothed youth with a nude torso; another (figure 3:11; plate 2:3) represents a nude figure of a young man stooping; and on another (figure 3:12; plate 3:23) appears a warrior with a nude torso carrying a bow on his shoulder and a drawn sword in his right hand. The bottom part of the last bulla is missing, and the continuation of the scene is unknown. Another bulla (figure 3:1; plate 2:4) depicts a male nude(?) figure, holding the caduceus staff in his right hand with his left hand, like the young man in the first eight bullae, resting on his back. Another bulla (figure 3:13; plate 2:1) depicts an elderly man wearing a chiton and himation and holding in his hand the symbols of thunder and lightning; his head is damaged but he appears to have been bearded.

It is not difficult to identify the figures accompanied by emblems: the figure holding the symbols of thunder and lightning is undoubtedly Zeus and the figure with the caduceus is Hermes. The figure who is bent over and fastening his sandals also represents Hermes, and the warrior is Heracles, but these two figures can also be interpreted as an athlete preparing for a race and a soldier, respectively.

The figure of the nude youth with outstretched hand was discussed by F. M. Cross in his treatment of an almost identical impression on a bulla from the Wadi ed-Daliyah cave (Lapp and Lapp:28, no. 14, pl. 62d, no. 14). The youth on the Wadi ed-Daliyeh bulla is represented in the same position as the figure on our bulla but is not nude. Cross vacillated between identifying him as Jason or Hermes (cf. other parallels cited by Cross). In our opinion, the resemblance between the standing position of the youth on all our bullae and the figure holding the caduceus indicates that it is Hermes.

The depiction of the figures of Greek gods and of Greek scenes of daily life on private seal impressions of the Persian period is not unique to our hoard; it also occurs on bullae and impressions from Wadi ed-Daliyeh and the city of Samaria itself. The group of bullae from Wadi ed-Daliyeh also includes a reversed-double impression of a figure, like the double impression in our hoard; these two bullae may have been produced by the very same seal. There were also two impressions portraying Heracles struggling with a lion and Athena driving her chariot drawn by four horses—the quadriga (Lapp and Lapp

1974:28, pl. 63:4; p. 29, nos. 26, 42, 46). In the excavations conducted in the city of Samaria, two impressions with a similar motif were found on handles of clay vessels: an oval stamp bearing the nude figure of Hermes holding the caduceus in his right hand (Reisner et al. 1924:1:378; 2:pl. 57f:2–3).

The assemblage from Wadi ed-Daliyeh published by Leith contains numerous western motifs that are faithfully duplicated in the bullae under discussion, mainly the figures of Heracles and Hermes, young men either nude or wearing a himation, figures of warriors, etc. There are also motifs derived from the world of the Dionysiac cult and numerous animals, some mentioned above, such as an eagle, deer, and a hippocampus, and some animals not previously encountered, such as a winged pig.

The figure of Hermes, apparently a particularly favored motif in the Persian period, also decorates a seal from Tell Keisan and is stamped on a pottery vessel from Beth-zur. A stamp from Ramat Rahel depicts the figure of Athena; she is also apparently portrayed on a similar impression from En-Gedi (Briend and Humbert 1980:pl. 33:90; Sellers 1933: 62, fig. 56:6, 8; Aharoni 1962:pl. 7:9; Stern 1982: 198, fig. 319).

An interesting example of a scene of daily life is a bulla from Tel Dor that depicts a phalanx of Greek hoplites (Stern 2000:192, fig. 125).

The figure of Heracles was especially favored by the Greek-Phoenician carvers in the Persian period by virtue of his identification with the Tyrian god Melqart and also because in this period he replaced the Persian and Assyrian kings and ancient heroes in fighting a variety of animals—lions, bulls, rams, griffins, and other creatures (as is evidenced on bullae from Wadi ed-Daliyeh). Heracles is also portrayed brandishing his club, shooting arrows, etc. (Johns 1933:71, figs. 31, 75; Stern 1982:200, fig. 325; and see also the detailed discussion in Leith 1997).

It should be pointed out that the figures of Zeus, Hermes, Heracles, and Athena were as widespread in this period (or even moreso) on all the types of coins common in Palestine. Many Greek motifs, for example, are found on Samarian coins. In addition to the figure of Hermes with his right hand resting on a caduceus staff and the nude and muscular figure of Heracles, there are also images of Zeus holding a falcon in his outstretched right hand, the head of the goddess Athena or her emblem, the owl, heads of men wearing Greek helmets, heads of Janus, and heads of Gorgons.

Numerous Greek motifs also appear on Yehud coins: Zeus seated on his throne and holding a falcon (see further below), the heads of men wearing Greek helmets, the head of Athena and her owl, heads of gorgons, etc. Identical motifs were frequently stamped on regular, uninscribed Palestinian coins (Meshorer 2001:7–17, pls. 1–3; Lambert 1932; Kindler 1963).

Female Figures in Western-Greek Style: Figures of Standing Women

Four impressions of standing women in western, Greek style (figure 4:1–4; plate 2:5–8) are included in the Hecht hoard. All of them represent the same motif: the figure of a clothed female figure. Two of them (figure 4:3–4; plate 2:7–8) may have been stamped with an identical seal; the woman is depicted in profile standing next to a pillar, at the top of which is apparently a cock, her left hand behind her back and her right hand raised. On a third bulla (figure 4:2; plate 2:6) there is no pillar, but the stance is the same; on the fourth bulla (figure 4:1; plate 2:5), she faces front.

The identity of the women is difficult to establish, as their attributes are unclear. One woman (figure 4:2; plate 2:6) very likely represents Nike proffering a wreath, and another (figure 4:1; plate 2:5) may represent Tyche-Isis (Hamburger 1968:10–11), but their original identity is uncertain. These figures, moreover, served decorative purposes only and had lost their original significance.

The figures of women in Greek style also occur frequently on the various coins of the Persian period, as well as on the Samarian city coins, where they appear in a number of variations (singly, in pairs, standing, and seated). Especially widespread are heads of women with different headdresses and wearing various types of hats; similar figures are also found on uninscribed Palestinian coins of the period (Kindler 1963:nos. 10–12, 20).

A Seated Woman

An unusual motif occurring on the bullae in the hoard is the figure of a woman seated on a footstool and holding a falcon in her outstretched hand (figure 4:5; plate 2:9). In Phoenician-Israelite glyptic art of the Iron Age, a common theme was the figure of a goddess (or god) seated on a throne and holding the various symbols of government: the lotus flower or a chalice; the hand is occasionally outstretched in blessing. These figures are depicted on ivories, seals, stamped on pottery vessels, drawn on pottery, and, on a larger scale, also carved on stone orthostats. This motif continued into the Persian period in the traditional eastern version of Isis or the local goddesses such as Baalat of Byblos, in its new western version, and also on the various types of Palestinian coins

(Avigad 1978; Stern 1982:16, fig. 2; 200, fig. 324; Herzog et al. 1989:335–36, fig. 28.1.4).

The motif of a bird (falcon or hawk) standing on the outstretched hand of a ruler or god (or goddess) entered the Palestinian repertoire only in the Persian period. It was most likely adopted from the city coins of Cilicia, and especially of the province of Cilicia (interpreted as depicting the figure of Zeus).

A standing male figure with a hawk on his outstretched hand is also depicted on a seal found at Tell Qasile (not in stratigraphic context). It is unusual in its square shape. The seal is made of limestone and its face is engraved with a figure of a bearded man with extended hand holding a hawk; surrounding the figure is an inscription read by B. Mazar as "Ashanyahu servant of the king" (Maisler [Mazar] 1951:69, fig. 25). Based on its close resemblance to a scene on a Yehud coin (see below), Mazar attributed the seal to the Persian period. In his opinion, the seal belonged to an official in the service of the Persian king and the title, "servant of the king," which is known from the First Temple period in Israel and Judah, continued in use in this period (like the title of Tobiah, "the Ammonite servant," Neh. 2:10). Mazar dated the seal to the beginning of the Persian period; in the opinion of the writer, however, this motif, which, as was noted, also appears on Yehud coins, attests to a date in the fourth century B.C.E.

Only after much consideration could this seal be attributed to the group of seals from the province of Yehud (Judah), because Tell Qasile in this period belonged to the territory of the Sidonian kings (the province of Dor). The title "king" can perhaps be understood here as referring to the Persian king (Stern 1982:207, fig. 345). After this motif was adopted, it became very common on the various types of Palestinian coins from the end of the fifth century B.C.E. onwards, both on the coins minted in the provinces of Yehud and Samaria and on those Persian-period coins from Palestine that did not mention the name of the province (Meshorer 2001; Lambert 1932: pl. 1:1).

Seal impressions of standing and seated Greek woman figures have also been discovered in other assemblages from the Persian period in Palestine, such as those from Wadi ed-Daliyeh and Samaria (Crowfoot et al. 1957:88, pl. 15:43; Lapp and Lapp 1974:28, pl. 62a+b).

Conclusions

There is no doubt that the hoard under discussion comes from a single source, most likely from the city of Samaria (or its close surroundings—perhaps Wadi ed-Daliyeh?), because of the many common features it shares with the bullae and seals published so far from these two sites. It is also certain that from the standpoint of the style of the impressions and the inscriptions, they belong to the fourth century B.C.E. Decisive in this matter is the similarity of the motifs in this assemblage with those stamped on the Samarian coins published by Meshorer and Qedar (1999).

In light of this, it is perhaps possible to reach two conclusions. First, the bullae in the Hecht hoard contain relatively few emblems (in contrast with the extreme diversity of motifs on coins), and they include, on the one hand, figures of griffins, lions, and horses in eastern style and, on the other, Greek-style male and female figures that correspond very closely to other figures in their group. These impressions appear to represent a small number of seal owners, who probably possessed several seals bearing the same motif (as is evidenced by the fact that several seals have been found that are inscribed with the name of the same person), or else the motifs were family emblems and belonged to different members of the same family. We should recall here the name Ishmael on two identical stamps, and also the letter *yod*—perhaps part of the same name—on a seal bearing the same motif (griffin), but differing in details.

The correspondence between a certain motif and a family name was noted long ago by Avigad and again by G. Barkay (Avigad 1966; 1982; Barkay 1992). It may therefore be possible to explain the relative sparseness of the motifs and the differences between them and the dominant motifs at Wadi ed-Daliyeh, such as a hero in combat with a lion, etc., by suggesting that all our bullae came from the archives of a few families from Samaria that were not the same families represented in the family archives of the Wadi ed-Daliyeh cave.

The second conclusion, proposed some time ago by the writer, is that the close affinity between the stamps on the bullae from Wadi ed-Daliyeh and from our hoard and the stamps on the Samarian coins derives from the fact that coins and bullae were both stamped with seals of private individuals—the coins probably with the seals of treasury officials of the province of Samaria, as were the Yehud coins and the uninscribed Palestinian coins (Meshorer 1992:7*–14*; Stern 1982:221–224; Ornan 1991).

In any event, this hoard of bullae complements that of Wadi ed-Daliyeh and the Samarian coins, and constitutes an important contribution to the cultural background of Palestine in the fourth century B.C.E.

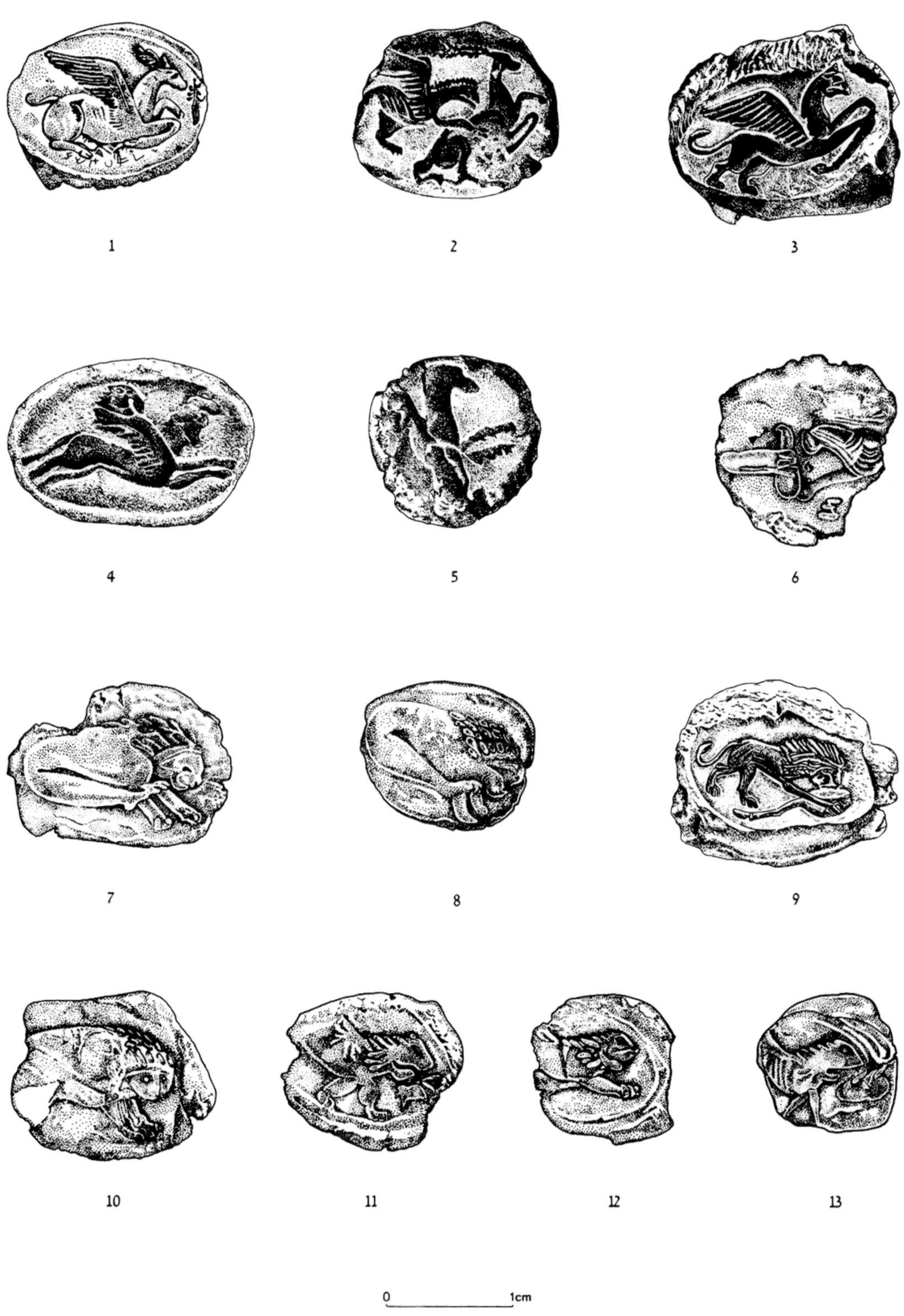

Figure 1

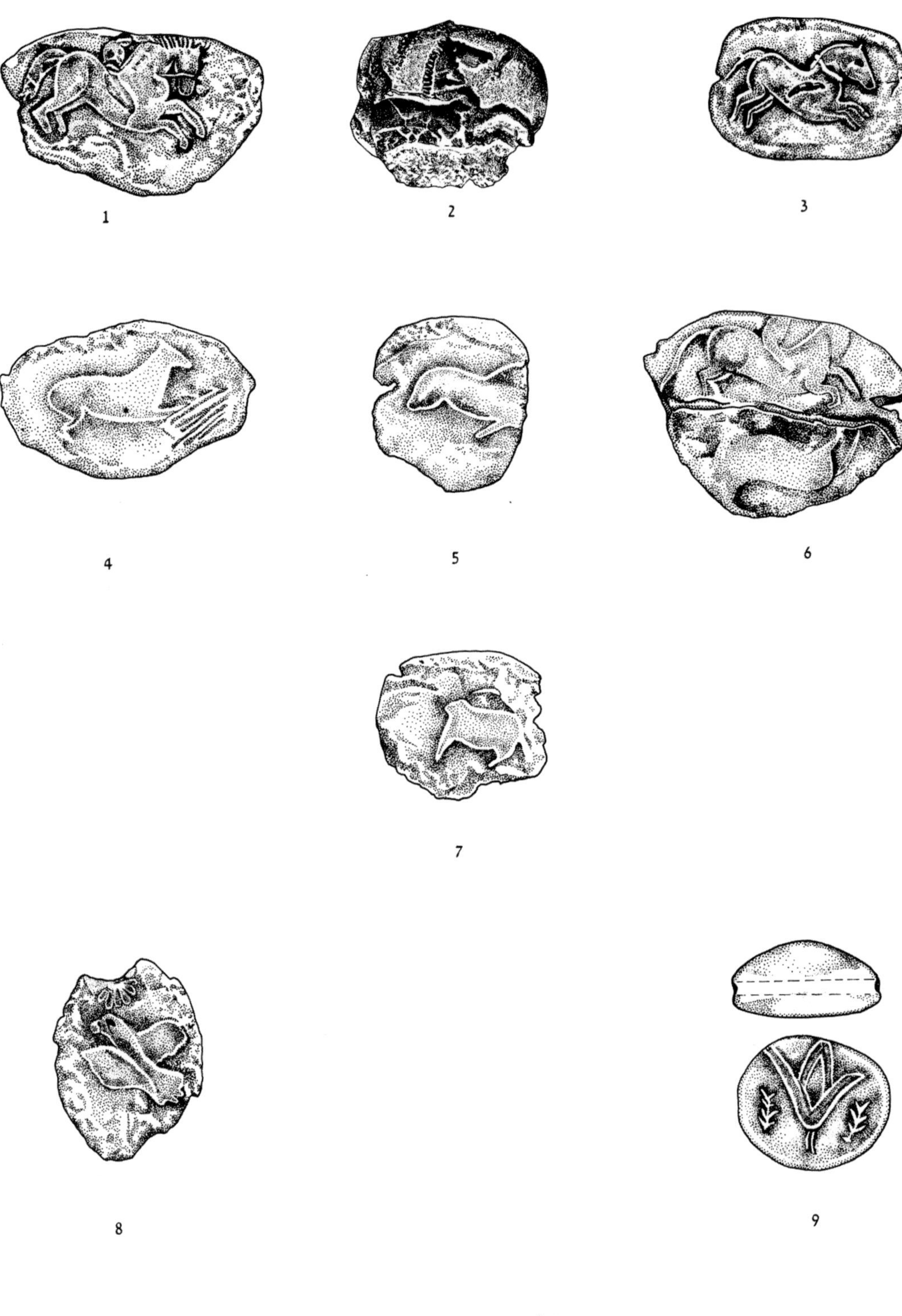

Figure 2

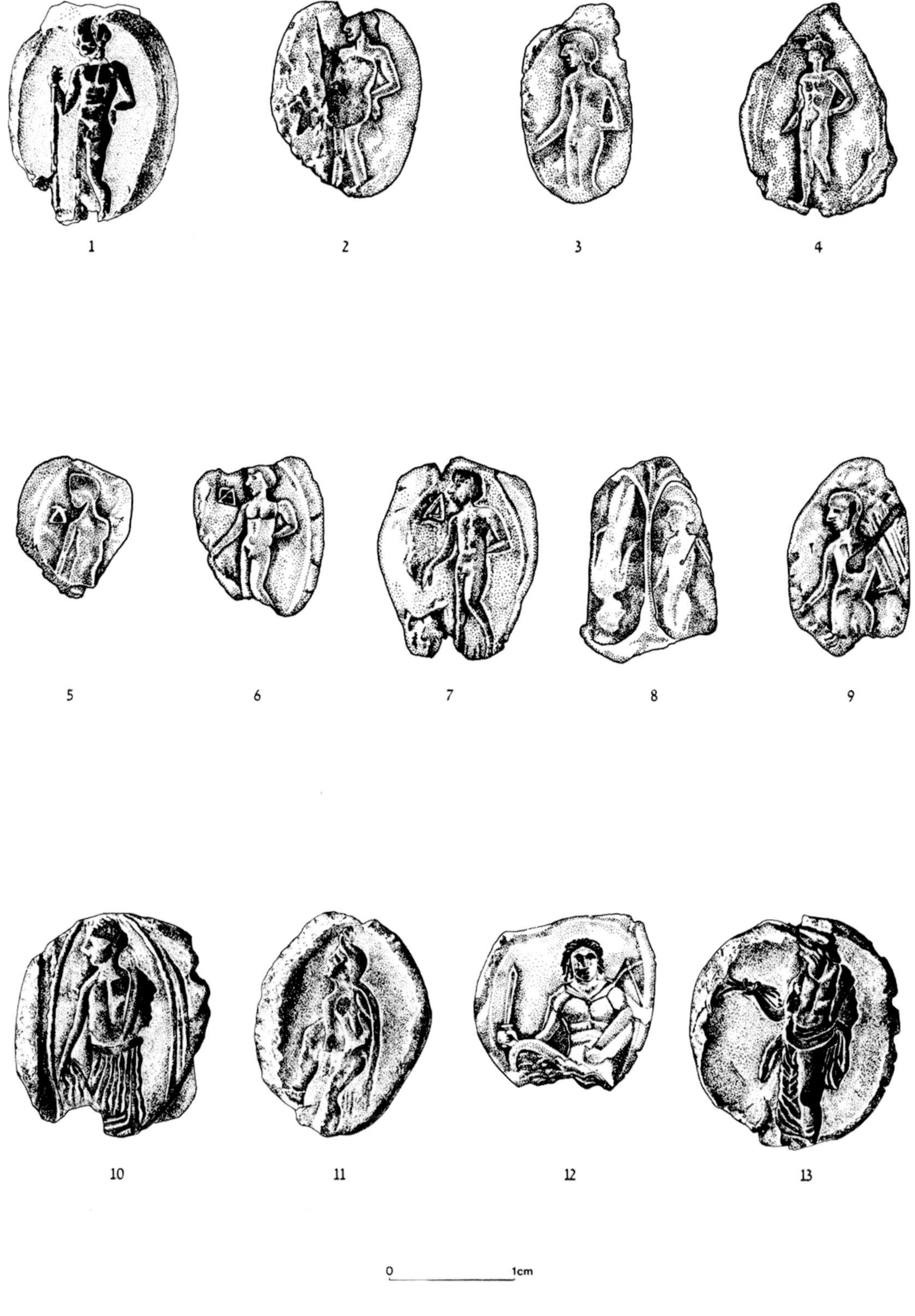

Figure 3

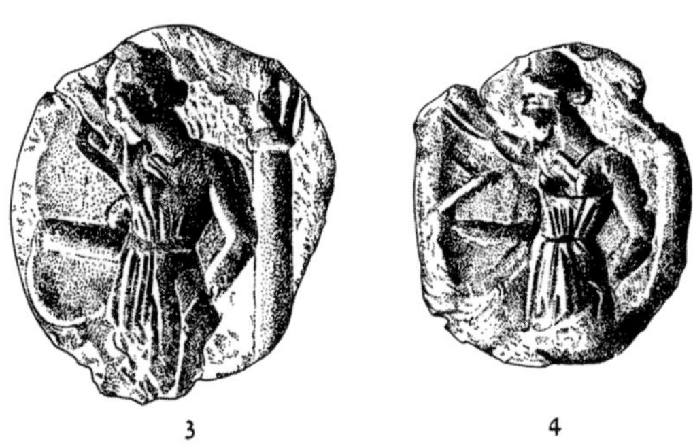

0 1cm

Figure 4

Plate 1
Photographs by Zeev Radovan

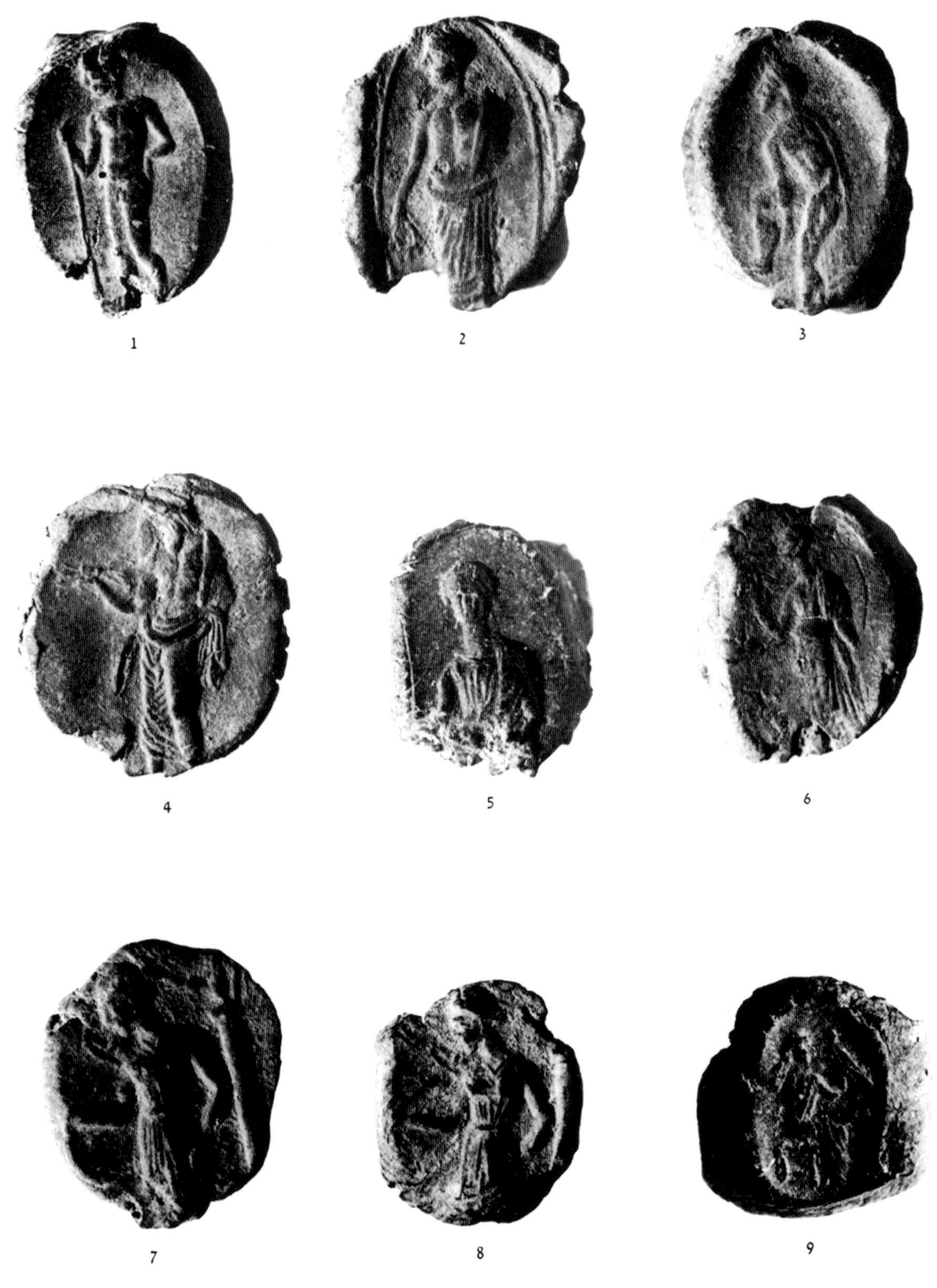

Plate 2

Photographs by Zeev Radovan

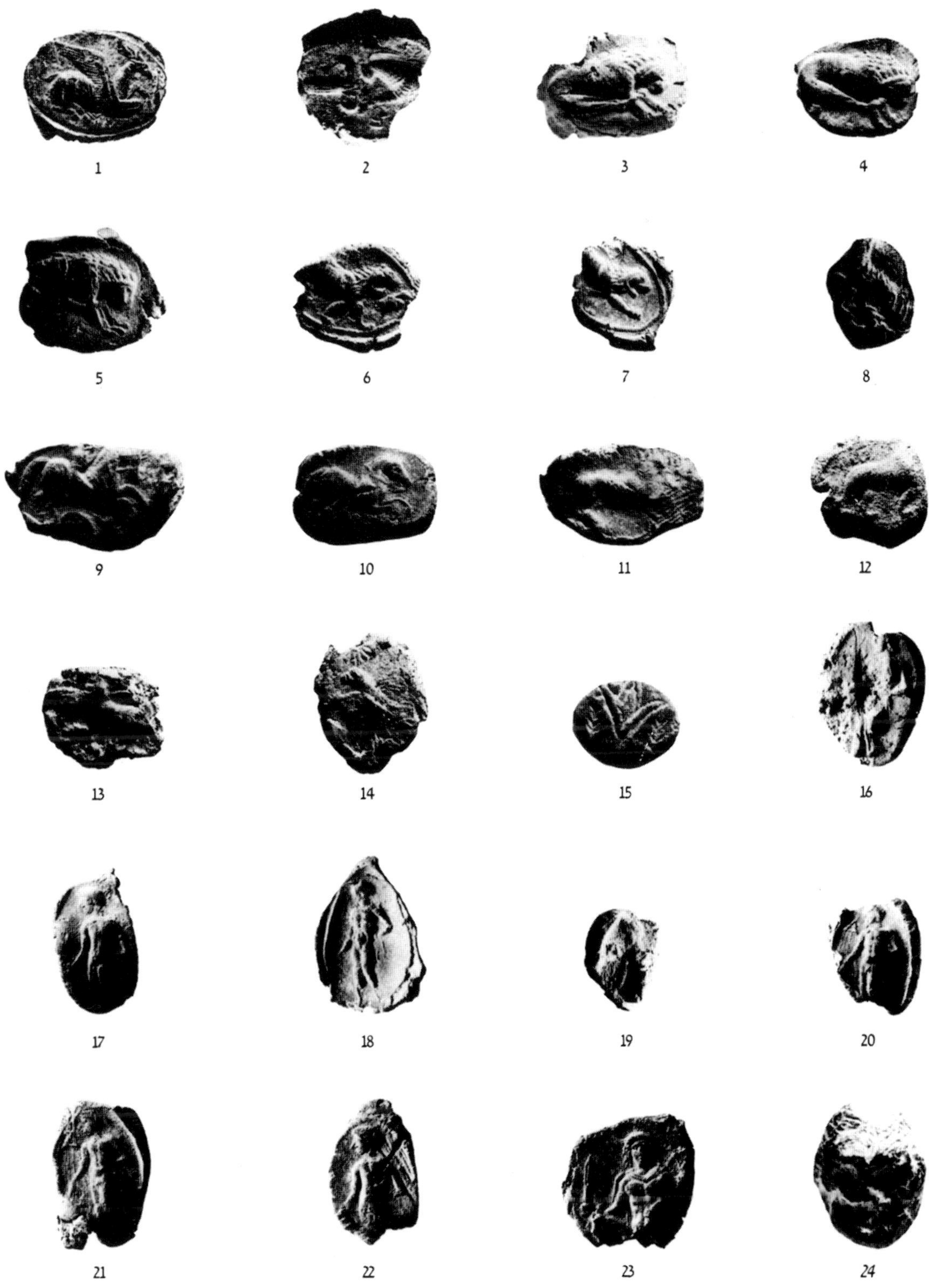

Plate 3

Photographs by Zeev Radovan

Bibliography

Aharoni, Y.
- 1962 *Excavations at Ramat Rahel: Seasons 1959 and 1960.* Rome: Centro di Studi Semitici.
- 1975 *Investigations at Lachish: The Sanctuary and the Residency (Lachish V).* Tel Aviv: Gateway.

Avigad, N.
- 1954 Three Ornamented Hebrew Seals, *IEJ* 4:236–38.
- 1964 Seals and Sealings. *IEJ* 14:190–94.
- 1966 A Hebrew Seal With a Family Emblem, *IEJ* 16: 50–53
- 1970 Six Ancient Hebrew Seals [in Hebrew]. In *Sefer Shmuel Yeivin*, ed. S. Abramski et al. Tel Aviv.
- 1975 The Priest of Dor. *IEJ* 25:101–5.
- 1976 *Bullae and Seals from a Post-Exilic Judean Archive.* Qedem 4. Jerusalem: Institute of Archaeology, Hebrew University.
- 1978 The King's Daughter and the Lyre. *IEJ* 28:146–51.
- 1979 A Group of Hebrew Seals from the Hecht Collection. In *Festschrift: Rëuben R. Hecht*, 119–26. Jerusalem: Korén.
- 1981 Titles and Symbols on Hebrew Seals [in Hebrew]. *EI* 15:303–5.
- 1982 A Hebrew Seal Depicting a Sailing Boat. *BASOR* 246:59.
- 1986 *Hebrew Bullae from the Time of Jeremiah: Remnants of a Burnt Archive.* Translated by R. Grafman. Jerusalem: Israel Exploration Society.
- 1989 Two Seals of Woman and Other Hebrew Seals [in Hebrew]. *EI* 20:90–96.
- 1992 A New Seal Depicting a Lion. *Michmanim* 6: 33*–36*.

Avigad, N., and B. Sass
- 1997 *Corpus of West Semitic Stamp Seals.* Jerusalem: Israel Academy of Sciences and Humanities.

Avi-Yonah, M., and E. Stern
- 1975 *Encyclopedia of Archaeological Excavations in the Holy Land.* Vol. 1. Jerusalem: Israel Exploration Society.

Avner, R., and E. Eshel
- 1996 A Juglet with a Phoenician Inscription from a Recent Excavation in Jaffa, Israel. *Transeuphraténe* 12:59–63.

Baramki, J.
- 1945 A Hoard of Silver Coins of Sidon and Alexander from Khirbet el-Kerak. *QDAP* 11:86–90.

Barkay, G.
- 1992 "The Prancing Horse": An Official Seal Impression from Judah of the Eighth Century B.C. *Tel Aviv* 19:128–29.

Barnett, R. D.
- 1957 *A Catalogue of the Nimrud Ivories with Other Examples of Ancient Near Eastern Ivories in the British Museum.* London: Trustees of the British Museum.

Barnett, R. D.
- 1982 *Ancient Ivories in the Middle East.* Qedem 11. Jerusalem: Institute of Archaeology, Hebrew University.

Baruch, E., Z. Greenhut, and A. Faust, eds.
- 2006 *New Studies on Jerusalem* [in Hebrew]. Vol. 11. Ramat Gan, Israel: Ingeborg Center for Jerusalem Studies.

Briend, J., and J.-B. Humbert, eds.
- 1980 *Tell Keisan (1971–1976): Une cité phénicienne en Galilée.* Orbis Biblicus et Orientalis, Series Archaeologica 1. Fribourg, Switzerland: Éditions universitaires.

Cross, F. M.
- 1963 The Discovery of the Samaria Papyri. *BA* 26: 110–21.
- 1985 Samaria Papyrus 1: An Aramaic Slave Conveyance of 335 B.C.E. Found at Wadi Ed-Daliyeh. *EI* 18:7*–17*.

Crowfoot, J. W., and G. Crowfoot
- 1938 *Samaria–Sebaste.* Vol. 2, *Early Ivories from Samaria.* London: Palestine Exploration Fund.

Crowfoot, J. W., G. Crowfoot, and K. M. Kenyon
- 1957 *Samaria–Sebaste.* Vol. 3, *The Objects from Samaria.* London: Palestine Exploration Fund.

Gropp, D. M.
- 1986 The Samaria Papyri from Wadi Ed-Daliyeh: The Slave Sales. Ph.D. diss., Harvard University.

Hamburger, A.
- 1968 *Gems from Caesarea Maritima.* ᶜAtiqot 8 [English series]. Jerusalem: Israel Department of Antiquities and Museums.

Heltzer, M., A. Segal, and D. Kaufman, eds.
- 1993 *Studies in the Archaeology and History of Ancient Israel in Honor of Moshe Dothan* [in Hebrew]. Haifa: Haifa University Press.

Herzog, Z., G. Rapp, and O. Negbi
- 1989 *Excavations at Tel Michal, Israel.* Minneapolis, Minn.: University of Minnesota Press.

Johns, C. M.
- 1933 Excavations at Atlit (1930–1931): The South Eastern Cemetery. *QDAP* 2:41–104.

Kindler, A.
- 1963 The Greco-Phoenician Coins Struck in Palestine in the Time of the Persian Empire. *INJ* 1:2–6.

Lambert, C.
1932 A Hoard of Phoenician Coins, *QDAP* 1:10–20.

Lapp, P. W., and N. L. Lapp, eds.
1974 *Discoveries in the Wâdī ed-Dâliyeh*. AASOR 41. Cambridge, Mass.: American Schools of Oriental Research.

Legrain, L.
1951 *Ur Excavations*. Vol. 10, *Seal Cylinders*. London: Oxford University Press.

Leith, M. J. W.
1997 *Wadi Daliyeh*. Vol. 1, *The Wadi Daliyeh Seal Impressions*. DJD 24. Oxford: Clarendon.

Maisler [Mazar], B.
1951 Excavations at Tell Qasile [in Hebrew]. *EI* 1:45–72.

Mazar, E.
1990 A Horseman's Tomb at Akhziv [in Hebrew]. *Qadmoniot* 23:104–9.

Meshorer, Y.
1966 A New Type of YEHUD Coin. *IEJ* 16:217–19.
1992 The Coins of Samaria in the Persian Period. *Michmanim* 6:7*–14*.
2001 *A Treasury of Jewish Coins from the Persian Period to Bar Kokhba*. Jerusalem.

Meshorer, Y., and S. Qedar
1999 *Samarian Coinage*. Jerusalem: Israel Numismatic Society.

Mildenberg, L.
1987 Preliminary Studies of the Local Coinage in the Fifth Satrapy. *EI* 15:28*–35*.

Ornan, T.
1991 Studies of the Glyptic Remains from Palestine and Transjordan. M.A. thesis, Hebrew University of Jerusalem.

Reisner, G. A., C. S. Fisher, and D. G. Lyon
1924 *Harvard Excavations at Samaria, 1908–1910*. 2 vols. Cambridge, Mass.: Harvard University Press.

Sellers, O. R.
1933 *The Citadel of Beth-zur*. Philadelphia: Westminster Press.

Shoham, Y.
2000 Hebrew Bullae. In *Excavations at the City of David, 1978–1985: Directed by Yigal Shiloh*, vol. 6, *Inscriptions*, 29–57. Qedem 41. Jerusalem: Institute of Archaeology, Hebrew University.

Spaer, A.
1979 A Coin of Jeroboam? *IEJ* 29:218.

Stern, E.
1976 New Types of Phoenician-Style Decorated Pottery Vases from Palestine. *PEQ* 110:11–20.
1982 *Material Culture of the Land of the Bible in the Persian Period, 538–332 B.C.* Warminster, England: Aris and Phillips.
1983 A Phoenician Art Center in Post-exilic Samaria. In *Atti del I Congresso internazionale di studi fenici e punici: Roma, 5–10 novembre 1979*, pp. 211–212. Collezione di studi fenici 16. Rome: Consiglio nazionale delle ricerche.
1994 Notes on the Development of Stamp Glyptic Art in Palestine during the Assyrian, Babylonian and Persian Periods. In *Uncovering Ancient Stones: Essays in Memory of H. Neil Richardson*, ed. L. M. Hopfe, 135–46. Winona Lake, Ind.: Eisenbrauns.
2000 *Dor, Ruler of the Seas*. Jerusalem: Israel Exploration Society.
2002 A Hoard of Persian-period Bullae from the Vicinity of Samaria [in Hebrew]. In *The Samaritans*, ed. E. Stern and H. Eshel. Jerusalem: Yad Ben Zvi.

Tadmor, M., ed.
1972 *Inscriptions Reveal*. Israel Museum Catalogue 100. Jerusalem: Israel Museum.

Tufnell, O.
1953 *Lachish (Tell ed-Duweir)*. Vol. 3, *The Iron Age*. London: Oxford University Press.

Yassine, K.
1984 *Tell el-Mazar*. Vol. 1, *Cemetery A*. Amman: University of Jordan.

43. Trade and Power in Late Bronze Age Canaan

by Michael Sugerman

The Late Bronze Age (1500—1150 B.C.E.) in Israel and Palestine has been a focus of research for over a century. A wealth of data from numerous archaeological and philological investigations creates the illusion that the cultures of the period are well known and understood. In reality, our interpretations of the period are based on (1) ceramic chronologies based largely on imported fine wares from the Aegean and Cyprus, (2) stratigraphic descriptions of a number of sites with LB phases, and (3) political and economic reconstructions extrapolated from texts found primarily in Egypt and Syria. Very few researchers have undertaken a detailed study of material culture from multiple sites to investigate sociocultural processes in the region. Instead, scholars of LB Canaan have relied on historical, rather than archaeological, methodologies to develop a framework for understanding the cultures of this period.

Modeling Political Society in LB Canaan

Many analyses begin with the supposition that the region was part of an Egyptian province in Asia (see references in Naᵓaman 1999:31), although there is some debate over the extent and coherence of this province (Lemche 1991; 1996; 1998). In a recent synthesis, one scholar describes the entire 350-year span almost exclusively in terms of hypothesized Egyptian political and military activity in the region (Gonen 1992). She concluded her analysis with a survey of artifactual and architectural typologies, with little discussion of the cultures, economies, or political structures of the region. In numerous other studies of the period, changes in settlement patterns, population density, and material culture have also been explained as results of historical events described in Egyptian or biblical texts (e.g., Aharoni 1967; Helck 1971; Naᵓaman 1975; 1981).

Paralleling the debate over Egyptian activities in LB Canaan, there has been some disagreement over how to determine the political boundaries of the "city-states" or "kingdoms" that filled the territory of Canaan in the latter half of the second millennium B.C.E. In recent years, the debate over the structure of politics and economy in LB Canaan has been argued mainly by two scholars, Israel Finkelstein (1993; 1996) and Nadav Naᵓaman (1986; 1992; 1997; 1999), and has been based on the classic works of Albrecht Alt (1939; 1953; 1954) and Wolfgang Helck (1971). Finkelstein and Naᵓaman differ slightly in their interpretations of certain aspects of the Amarna letters (e.g., Finkelstein 1996:222; Naᵓaman 1997:603), and more significantly, in their predispositions toward seeing "city-states" as centered on cities of different sizes. Thus, Finkelstein (1996:223) posits fewer city-states with larger urban centers and Naᵓaman (1997:605) suggests more city-states with smaller centers. Each of them, however, uses a similar set of assumptions to interpret the textual sources from Amarna, which are so often called upon to buttress arguments about LB society in Canaan. Both Finkelstein and Naᵓaman state that the writers of all of the Amarna letters sent from Canaan must have been rulers of city-states (Naᵓaman 1997:601). Finkelstein also presents a corollary to this argument: that the Amarna archive is representative enough to enable "a full, or almost full reconstruction of the territorial map of Late Bronze Canaan" (Finkelstein 1996:224).

In order to build such a territorial map, Finkelstein divides the region into Thiessen polygons (figure 1). Each polygon is centered on a large, theoretically urban, site and contains the hinterland that he considers necessary to support the center (Finkelstein 1996:228, 230, 241). Though he recognizes that there were areas that could not be effectively controlled by the city-state rulers, and that nonsedentary segments of society were also important in this period, Finkelstein (1996:226) argues that control of the whole region comprising modern Israel and Palestine was divided among thirteen or fourteen neighboring polities with abutting boundaries.

Naᵓaman opposes Finkelstein's interpretation and argues that hinterland territory is not a necessary feature of an independent city-state. Using Egyptian texts to support his arguments, Naᵓaman contends that during the Thirteenth Dynasty (eighteenth century B.C.E.), there were as many as four kingdoms within the limited geographical confines of the Akko Valley, none of which could have controlled the hinterland that Finkelstein claimed was necessary to support an urban center (Naᵓaman 1997:605). Economic resources, including staples, could be obtained by the inhabitants of settlements in key zones, who therefore did not have to rely on local agricultural production. Port cities and settlements situated on major trade routes—most notably those on the junctions of trade routes—fit this description. Another important implication of Naᵓaman's argument is that, given the smaller sizes of his proposed political units, many small cities and towns would have existed outside the control of any city-state. If that was the case, not all politically independent polities were states or even cities.

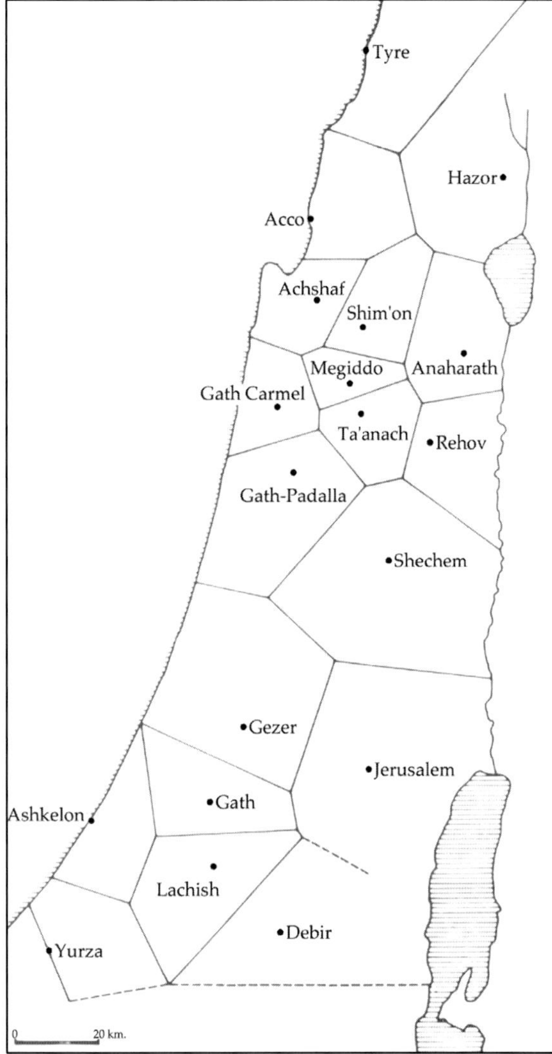

Figure 1. Thiessen polygons defining proposed Late Bronze Age city-states in Canaan

Naʾaman's critique highlights an important flaw in Finkelstein's model: the issue of control. Although Finkelstein acknowledged that there would have been "marginal" areas outside the control of the city-states in a practical sense, he considered all of the territory to be under the "jurisdiction" of the nearest ruling Canaanite city (1996:225–26). No mention is made of the structure of this control or how this "jurisdiction" was maintained. Stager (1985) and Bunimovitz (1994a) have argued that the LB in southern Canaan was characterized by a shortage of manpower after many settlements were abandoned in favor of pastoral lifeways. Given the lack of surplus labor—as discerned by the absence of major building projects during this period—it is difficult to hypothesize that the urban elites were able to muster militias of the size necessary to enforce their proposed jurisdictions. Textual descriptions of the military forces gathered in Canaanite cities on military maneuvers list dozens or hundreds, rather than thousands, of fighters (*ANET*[3] p. 237). It appears that large standing military forces were not an integral part of LB urban politics.

Beyond the issue of local "jurisdiction" there is, as noted above, some debate over the question of regional dominance as well. Thus Finkelstein (1996: 225–26) argues that the populations in Canaan were all under the jurisdiction of the ruling Canaanite elites, while Naʾaman (1997:619) argues that "Egypt governed Canaan and the real power was in the hands of the Egyptians." Neither of these arguments defines the nature of the governance nor the means by which the proposed rulers were supported.

City-States Problems

Underlying these omissions is a methodological problem. These scholars use, as have many others in the past, the model of the "city-state" to characterize the urban-centered polities that they propose comprised the LB political landscape of Canaan. The city-state model links the phenomenon of the state with a particular kind of settlement pattern that together form "small, territorially based, politically independent state systems, characterized by a capital city or town, with an economically and socially integrated adjacent hinterland" (Rihll and Wilson 1991: 60; Charlton and Nichols 1997:1). Other definitions of city-states include the concept that the polity is economically self-sufficient and perceived as being ethnically distinct from other, similar systems (Trigger 1993:8–14; 2003:92–103). It has been argued that, historically, city-states frequently occurred in groups of somewhat evenly spaced units that were all of similar sizes (Renfrew 1975:12–20).

The city-state construct has been the target of criticism in recent years. In many of the cases where the term has been applied, one or more core features of the model's definition have been changed to fit the case. In some cases, researchers have reinterpreted the data to fit the model (D'Altroy 2000:851; Yoffee 2004:42–62). In the case of Canaan, the model has been used so often to describe so many different conditions that it has very little utility for characterizing any particular political or economic situation. By using a poorly defined model and applying it uncritically across a widely variable social, political, and geographical map, Finkelstein, Naʾaman, and others who use the city-state model obscure the heterogeneous nature of political society in LB Canaan.

In two recent surveys of archaeological incarnations of city-states in many cultures, perhaps the most useful result was the argument that researchers need to explore the variability within the model and explain significant divergences from the model when they are encountered in the archaeological or historical data (Nichols and Charlton 1997; Yoffee 1997: 256; Hansen 2000). Although there may be evidence in LB Canaan for city-states of the type defined above, the range of variation in settlement size and type in the region was great. No understanding of the society of the LB is complete without an exploration of the way urban and nonurban settlements, as well as nonsedentary segments of the population, were integrated into the political and economic systems extant during this period.

Modeling the LB Local Economy

The apparently conflicting archaeological and textual data used to investigate LB Canaan have led to two schools of thought, in which scholars choose to emphasize their interpretations of the texts, on the one hand, or the archaeological data, on the other—but not both. The archaeologically based interpretation proposes that the combination of Egyptian military occupation and internal conflicts caused a long process of economic decline in Canaan, until it reached a low point during the thirteenth century B.C.E. (Knapp 1989a; 1989b; 1992). The alternative, textually supported interpretation, is that the rulers of the Eighteenth Dynasty received rich tribute from the kings of Canaanite city-states, which led to intensification of Egyptian military and economic activities there, which in turn caused the local Canaanite economies to expand so that by the thirteenth century the region was flourishing (Bienkowski 1989; Naʾaman 1981: 185).

Other recent syntheses have attempted to harmonize these conflicting points of view with only slight success. Gonen (1984; 1992) downgraded some of the textual evidence from Amarna in favor of archaeological data that indicate the presence of depleted urban settlements. Bunimovitz (1993; 1994b; 1995) used settlement-pattern studies and models of peer-polity interaction together with the textual evidence from Amarna to identify multiple responses to Egypt's impact on Canaan during the LB. He argued that the collapse of the socioeconomic system at the end of the Middle Bronze Age and the imperialistic designs of Egypt during the following centuries led to a response in which the diminished urban elite indulged in orgies of conspicuous consumption in an attempt to maintain power within an impoverished and unstable region (Bunimovitz 1995:326). At the same time, the rural inhabitants of the country, previously the productive foundation of the region's wealth, responded to the rising demands of the elites and the instability of the political structure by "voting with their feet." Agrarian populations shifted to nonsedentary lifestyles in which their produce could not easily be taxed by the urban authorities (Bunimovitz 1995:327–28; also Braudel 1972:85–101; Marfoe 1979). In this model, the wealth listed in Egyptian tribute texts is explained by the activities of the urban elite, while the pattern of depletion, destruction, and poverty indicated by the region's archaeological record is attributed, in part, to a large-scale shift from sedentary agriculture to nomadic lifeways.

Both of these syntheses deal differently with the evidence for concentrations of wealth as described in Egyptian records and apparent in some aspects of LB Canaanite material culture. While arguing that an Egyptian occupation brought about "the decline of the Canaanite city," Gonen also argued that, in the LB, Canaan was producing large quantities of high-prestige products, including monumental stone sculpture, richly dyed textiles, ornamental jewelry, carved ivory figurines, and inlaid furniture and boxes. In support of this apparent dichotomy between "decline" and wealth, Gonen (1992:247) asserted only that Canaan was an active participant in the broader eastern Mediterranean economy, without explaining how such an economically depleted region played an active economic role. Bunimovitz's (1995:326) explanation is more instructive, implying that the activities of the urban elite in concentrating wealth, both for themselves and as tribute gifts to Egypt, were short term in nature and could not have been supported for an extended period. Indeed, their activities were curtailed in the thirteenth century, at the end of the LB.

Unfortunately, neither synthesis presents a satisfying approach to the political economy of the LB because they both ignore the patterns of production and distribution of goods within the region during that period.

Lateral Directions in Bronze Age Trade

Recent analyses of the archaeological data available for the Early and Middle Bronze Age have identified settlement patterns in which sites are oriented along drainages running east-west from the inland highlands to the Mediterranean coast (Harrison 1993; Ilan 1995; Marcus 1991; 1995; Raban 1985). Although this pattern has been related to the significance of maritime trade in the economy of Bronze Age Canaan (Stager 1992; 2000), it is notable that this orientation was already in existence in the Chalcolithic period (4500–3500 B.C.E.), when maritime trade was less important (Levy 1995:229). Ilan (1995:302) has argued that the drainage systems, with estuarine ports, large inland urban sites, and small rural productive sites, comprised a unified polity. Although such a model might explain the distribution of goods among the coastal and inland sites, it does not go so far as to explain how the economy worked, and why it worked. It also fails to address the same key issue inadequately addressed in the political models presented by Finkelstein and Naʾaman, namely, control.

Ilan's model assumes a great deal of coercive control over the areas of rural production and less habitable areas of resource collection in the hill country. In the Middle Bronze Age, the period about which Ilan wrote, the population sizes may have been large enough to allow for the kind of coercive control that is indicated by his arguments (Ilan 1995:309). However, in the subsequent Late Bronze Age, with its pronounced reduction in sedentary population and thus in workforce, it is unlikely that the rulers of the urban centers were able to coerce the hinterland populations into providing goods for their markets by force. Rather, the centers had to have something to offer that would have brought the nonurban segments of the population into the system by choice.

In the 1970s, economists developed a model that describes these "dendritic market systems" as a variation on classical central place models. The dendritic model was initially used to investigate long-distance wholesale trade in America during the sixteenth through twentieth centuries (Vance 1970). The model was almost immediately applied to market systems in developing economies (Johnson 1970) and then to historically known cases, such as the political and economic structures of early coastal states in southeast Asia (Bronson 1977; Hall 1985). More recently, Stager (2000) adapted Bronson's work to develop an understanding of Early and Middle Bronze Age Canaan that he calls the "port power" model.

Coastal Approaches to Trade Networks

A dendritic model is useful for the purposes of this study for several reasons: (1) it is designed to explain the relations between sites in a networked trade system; (2) in most cases, it describes intersite relations that are noncoercive and do not necessitate extensive military forces; and (3) it situates the individual dendritic systems within a larger context in which they are competing for the attention of an "overseas" market (Bronson 1977:44–45). In the case of southeast Asia, those markets were in China and Java. In the case of LB Canaan, those markets were found in Egypt, the northern Levantine coast, and Cyprus.

Bronson's model focuses on a subset of dendritic models, an exchange network along a drainage that opens to the sea with the following elements (see figure 2):

A	the "center" at the mouth of the drainage
B and **C**	second- and third-order centers located upstream from A and at the junctures of other drainages
D	the most distant upstream center in the system; a concentration point for goods
E and **F**	the ultimate producers or collectors of the products that are concentrated at D; they may be centers in a different kind of nonmarket exchange system involving goods of which only part are involved in the A-based system
X	an overseas center that serves as the main consumer of A's exports and the main supplier of its imports
$\mathbf{A^1}$ $\mathbf{A^2}$	other coastal centers some distance away, dominating systems similar to A's

Aside from these elements, this model also operates under three other constraints: (1) X, the overseas center, is economically stronger than A, has a larger population, and a more productive economy; (2) the countryside between the drainages is such that movements of goods outside of the drainages is not feasible; and (3) the drainage basin cannot support its population based solely on agriculture, thus making the profits derived from trade of central importance (Bronson 1977:43–44).

In the case of LB Canaan, the first constraint is applicable. New Kingdom Egypt to the south—and even Ugarit to the north—was wealthier and more populous than any coastal city in Canaan. The second constraint is not as good a fit in that the land between the drainage systems does not preclude the passage of goods. Rather, the geography simply makes the use of the drainages the easiest choice in many areas, though it allows producers and traders to cross-cut

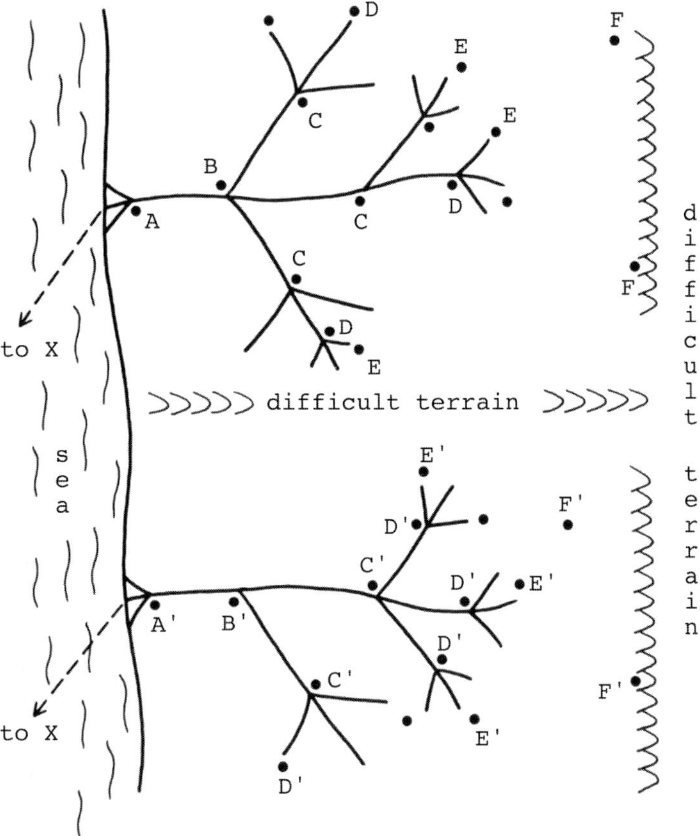

Figure 2. Idealized depiction of a dendritic trade system anchored in a port center (after Bronson 1977)

the drainage-based economic systems. This flexibility puts certain pressures on the centers (especially B, C, and D) to make themselves as attractive as possible to the upstream groups to avoid losing their patronage.

The third constraint can only be applied to Canaan in a limited manner. While the spring-fed lowlands of southern Canaan can be successfully dry-farmed, the risk of drought and starvation has more than once led sedentary populations to abandon agriculture and take up a pastoral lifestyle dependent on a more heterogeneous set of resources (Finkelstein 1988; Ilan 1995:314; Marfoe 1979:9). Thus, while it was possible for the urban elite in the coastal plain to support themselves by extracting produce from a farming population, such a state of affairs was unlikely to last for an extended period. Slight variations in the climate, population growth, disease, or changes in other aspects of the socioeconomy of the region continually undermined the possibility of developing a true peasant culture in Canaan. As a result, as Bronson's model would predict, the revenues derived from trade became extremely important to the urban centers that controlled the flows of goods both into and out of Canaan.

Hierarchies of sites have been identified in this region by other scholars, though they have not been set into this type of economic system. Gittlen (1993: 367–68) defined a three-tiered LB hierarchy of site types consisting of walled cities, baronial estates, and unfortified settlements. Ilan's MB hierarchy contained regional centers and gateways, subregional centers and/or loci of specialist production or service (e.g., cult), villages, and farmsteads (Ilan 1995:305). Knapp, in characterizing a similar economic system for Middle and Late Bronze Age Cyprus, defined a hierarchy in which he assigned a variety of functions to each type of site: primary coastal centers (commercial, ceremonial, administration, production); secondary inland towns (administration, production, transport); tertiary inland sites (ceremonial, production, transport, storage); and mining sites, pottery-producing villages, and agricultural support villages (production, storage, transport) (Knapp 1997:56–61).

The variety of functions that Knapp attributes to each type of site provides a more detailed image of the human activities taking place throughout the networks of production and exchange, but the relationships among the sites in his model are no more well defined than in other models that have been proposed for Canaan. Knapp's primary and secondary centers somehow "control" production of inland agricultural and mineral resources, and transport the products from the production centers out to the coastal capitals. Knapp (1997:62) hints at the possibility of a "king" overseeing the entire system, and of a governing elite, but again the nature of that dominance is not defined.

In each of these models, what is missing is the impetus for the hinterland communities to take part in the exchange network. Contrary to political or economic models that assume coercive relations between high- and low-order centers within a state-level system, dendritic models consider relations between sites on either end of the system to be somewhat egalitarian (Bronson 1977:44). Since D-level sites are simply concentration points for goods often produced by mobile populations, military solutions to problems in the trading relationships would be impractical. One method to bring peripheral populations into the network would be to offer manufactured or exotic goods that are otherwise unavailable and that might induce "D" to enter the network voluntarily.

Tracing the Networks

It is clear that exotic goods were transferred from the coastal centers to the upstream sites in LB Canaan, as demonstrated by Leonard's work on the distribution of Mycenean pottery in the Levant (Leonard 1976; 1981; 1987). Of the sixty-nine sites discussed by Leonard, six produced more than one hundred Mycenaean vessel lots (or minimum number of vessels). Of those six, three are important coastal centers where such finds would be expected: Ugarit, Byblos, and Tell Abu Hawam. Two more sites are secondary centers on major trade routes: Kamid el-Loz and Megiddo. The sixth site is Amman, east of the Jordan River. While this might be seen as an unexpected addition to the previous five, perhaps it illustrates the high status of such goods when they were moved inland away from the coastal centers, because all 150 items at that site were excavated in the temple discovered on the site of the Amman airport (Hankey 1974; for other arguments on the status of Mycenean ceramics in Levantine sites, see also Leonard and Cline 1998; van Wijngaarden 1999; 2002).

Fourteen sites on Leonard's list produced between ten and one hundred vessel lots, and again these are not surprising sites: the coastal centers Tell Sukas, Sarepta, Ashdod, Ashkelon, and Gaza, and the inland sites Alalakh, Hazor, Taᶜanach, Beth Shean, Shechem, Gezer, Beth Shemesh, Lachish, and Tell Beit Mirsim. Each of the southern sites are B- or C-level sites in the trade networks of the LB.

While the A-level sites were probably trading these imports upstream to the B- and C-level partners, it is the third segment of Leonard's data that best supports the argument that these secondary centers were using exotic goods to entice upstream inhabitants into the network. At forty-eight sites (70 percent of the sample), ten or fewer examples of Mycenaean pottery were found. In Canaan, these sites range from Tel Dan in the north to Tell el-Farᶜah (South). This class of sites also includes six sites in Jordan, indicating, along with the Amman finds, that there was an eastern overland extension to the networks that ran from the sea to the Jordan Valley (Leonard 1976:465).

Leonard's analysis of Mycenean ceramic imports undermines the economic arguments of the city-state model by showing that the majority of these elite artifacts were found at port centers. In fact, these artifacts are present in much smaller numbers at many of the settlements that have been proposed as centers of city-states (Leonard 1976; 1987). The pattern of distribution identified by Leonard runs counter to the argument that symbols of wealth were amassed by the rulers of urban city-states in shows of conspicuous consumption (Bunimovitz 1995:326). A recent comprehensive study of Mycenean pottery in the Levant argues the opposite: in urban economic centers, these imports are found in residences associated with a wide range of socioeconomic groups. Their distributions at smaller centers are less clear, in part because of the lack of data about these smaller sites, but these imports seem to be limited to elite social contexts at lower-order inland sites (van Wijngaarden 2002:109–24).

The routes upon which imports were carried are conspicuous archaeologically because the colorfully decorated Aegean sherds can be seen easily among the plain wares common to LB Canaan. But were these same routes used to carry goods in the opposite direction? The dendritic model posited here focuses primarily on the "bulking" of goods: the increasing concentration of goods at successive notes along the network. In order to support this side of the argument, we must be able to identify that process archaeologically. While exotic goods may be seen as one method of enticing lower-order sites into the network, utilitarian goods and raw resources are the likely objectives of those in the higher-order sites downstream. Utilitarian—or staple—goods include those that are (1) found in a range of socioeconomic contexts, indicating that they were common artifacts used in daily life; (2) found at many sites, indicating a role as an item of trade; and (3) suitable for provenience analysis, making it possible to map the routes of that trade.

Canaanite jars, one of the most common artifact types excavated at LB sites in Israel and Palestine, are one type of artifact that conforms to all of these criteria. By identifying the proveniences of Canaanite jar samples collected from many sites, it should be possible to ascertain the routes over which these transport and storage jars were carried. The patterns of distribution and the directionality of trade should reflect these jars' role in the economic system of the LB.

The two models already discussed here each posit different types of trade relations among sites and regions within Canaan. City-states are characterized as having "a capital city…with an economically and socially integrated adjacent hinterland" (Charlton and Nichols 1997:1). The capital city thus accumulates goods produced in a number of dependent settlements—possibly a very large number of settlements, depending on the extent of the hinterland controlled by the capital. As a result, ceramic samples collected from capital cities should exhibit a wide variety of production sources (reflecting both regional differences in the composition of the clays and technical choices on the part of the potters), while samples from satellite settlements should show less variation. In addition, trade among capital cities should not be limited to any particular direction.

Alternatively, the port-centered, dendritic trade model posits a process in which the transport of local goods and resources is largely a one-way journey. Goods collected in the hinterlands are consolidated at small settlements far upstream. Those goods are then joined to shipments from similar sites and funneled downstream through higher-level nodes until they reach the port center that dominates the economy of the network. As a result, ceramic samples collected from downstream sites should indicate a large variety of proveniences, and samples from the port center should show the greatest amount of variation. Conversely, samples collected from upstream sites should indicate fewer production sources. In contrast to the city-state model, local ceramics should indicate a strong directionality in their distribution. Samples from downstream production centers should not be found in large quantities at upstream sites.

In a recent project, I collected samples of Canaanite jars from Deir el-Balaḥ, Lachish, Ashdod (south shore), Tel Miqne-Ekron, Tel Batash, Tel Taᶜanach, Tel Nami, Tel Megadim, Tell Abu Hawam, Hazor, and Tel Dan. This sample includes large urban inland settlements, small inland settlements, large port centers and small coastal settlements. The political, economic, and geographic diversity of the sites provided the basis for a comprehensive test of the city-state and dendritic models. The detailed results of my petrographic analyses of those samples have been presented elsewhere and strongly support the predictions of the dendritic model (Sugerman 2000). In each of the 273 samples of Canaanite jars that were analyzed, the provenience of the sample was identified as either east of its archaeological findspot or—in the case of some coastal sites—to the north. The great majority of the ceramic groups were distributed within bounded ranges that, with the exception of the samples found at coastal sites, did not spread far to the north or south of the latitude in which they were produced (Sugerman 2000:122).

Further Investigations of LB Economic Structures

The sources of data most often used to model the political and economic structures of LB Canaan are elite artifacts and architecture, and documents from royal or other elite contexts. The city-state model commonly used as a baseline for modeling Canaanite political economy can be supported only by restricting the types of data used in one's analysis. The documentary support for this model is based largely on the assumption that "each person who wrote either to Pharaoh or to his officials was a city-state ruler" (Naᵓaman 1997:602), even though only a small number of the archaeologically known LB settlements can be identified in the Amarna archives. Most scholars are willing to assume that all of the other known settlements must have been subordinate to the settlements documented in the archives (for example, Finkelstein 1996:224).

The Amarna archive has also been used to support the argument that Canaan was an extension of imperial Egypt during the New Kingdom and that the rulers of the city-states were largely governing on behalf of the pharaoh. Along with these documents, scholars have suggested that Egyptian artifacts excavated in Canaan—pottery, scarab seals, alabaster vessels, and jewelry—are evidence for New Kingdom domination or outright military occupation of the region (Weinstein 1981:20–22). The presence of these high-prestige Egyptian artifacts at a given site is often argued to be evidence for Egyptian governance (Bietak 1993; Dever 1985; Hoffmeier 1989:189). But the evidence in support of this model of Egyptian political domination is actually quite weak; I will address the issue in a forthcoming article titled "Competition or Colonization? Disruption and Destruction in the Late Bronze Age Levant."

The limitations and assumptions noted above have made it difficult to model the political economy of Canaanite society coherently, and have led archaeologists to construct conflicting and inconsistent models based on either limited textual sources or limited archaeological datasets. The belief common among archaeologists that the LB is one of the "best illuminated" periods (Gonen 1992:211) results from ignoring these constraints. The absence of investigations of the staple economy of Canaan has created a bias toward seeing economic behavior and power reflected only in an artificially constrained range of artifact types and data sources. The majority of the data used to support the city-state model for LB Canaan is drawn from documentary sources. Data resulting from archaeological assessments of elite goods do not unambiguously undermine the city-state model, but they do support a dendritic systems model, with networks anchored in wealthy port centers (Leonard 1976; 1987). When archaeological data that reflect the staple economy are brought into the mix, the evidence for a dendritic system increases greatly. In order to test further the utility of either model for explaining the economy of LB Canaan, archaeologists need to continue to add to the range of data available, and to shift our economic focus from urban centers and eye-catching exotic goods to the archaeology of ordinary things.

Bibliography

Aharoni, Y.
1967 *The Land of the Bible: A Historical Geography.* Philadelphia: Westminster.

Alt, A.
1939 Erwägungen über die Landnahme der Israeliten in Palästina. *Palästina-Jahrbuch* 35:8–63.
1953 *Kleine Schriften zur Geschichte des Volkes Israel.* Munich: Beck.
1954 Neue Berichte über Feldzüge von Pharaonen an der phönikischen Küste und im syrischen Binnenland. *Zeitschrift des Deutsches Archaeologisches Vereins* 70:97–133.

Bienkowski, P.
1989 Prosperity and Decline in LBA Canaan: A Reply to Leibowitz and Knapp. *BASOR* 275:59–61.

Bietak, M.
1993 The Sea Peoples and the End of the Egyptian Administration in Canaan. In *Biblical Archaeology Today, 1990: Proceedings of the Second International Congress of Biblical Archaeology*, ed A. Biran and J. Aviram, 292–306. Jerusalem: Israel Exploration Society.

Braudel, F.
1972 *The Mediterranean and the Mediterranean World in the Age of Philip II.* Translated by Siân Reynolds. 2 vols. New York: Harper and Row.

Bronson, B.
1977 Exchange at the Upstream and Downstream Ends: Notes Toward a Functional Model of the Coastal State in Southeast Asia. In *Economic Exchange and Social Interaction in Southeast Asia: Perspectives from Prehistory, History, and Ethnography*, ed. K. L. Hutterer, 39–52. Ann Arbor, Mich.: Center for South and Southeast Asian Studies, University of Michigan.

Bunimovitz, S.
1993 The Study of Complex Societies: The Material Culture of Late Bronze Age Canaan As a Case Study. In *Biblical Archaeology Today, 1990: Proceedings of the Second International Congress of Biblical Archaeology,* ed A. Biran and J. Aviram, 443–51. Jerusalem: Israel Exploration Society.
1994a The Problem of Human Resources in Late Bronze Age Palestine and Its Socioeconomic Implications. *UF* 26:1–20.
1994b Socio-political Transformations in the Central Hill Country in the Late Bronze–Iron I Transition. In *From Nomadism to Monarchy: Archaeological and Historical Aspects of Early Israel*, ed. I. Finkelstein and N. Na'aman, 179–202. Jerusalem: Israel Exploration Society.
1995 On the Edge of Empires—The Late Bronze Age. In *The Archaeology of Society in the Holy Land*, ed. T. E. Levy, 320–31. New York: Facts on File.

Charlton, T. H., and D. L. Nichols
1997 The City-state Concept: Development and Applications. In *The Archaeology of City-States: Cross-Cultural Approaches*, ed. D. L. Nichols and T. H. Charlton, 1–15. Washington, D.C.: Smithsonian Institution Press.

D'Altroy, T. N.
1999 Review of *The Archaeology of City-States: Cross-Cultural Approaches*, by D. Nichols and T. Charlton. *AA* 101:850–52.

Dever, W. G.
1985 Relations between Syria-Palestine and Egypt in the "Hyksos" Period. In *Palestine in the Bronze and Iron Ages: Papers in Honour of Olga Tufnell*, ed. J. N. Tubb, 69–87. London: Institute of Archaeology, University of London.

Finkelstein, I.
1988 *The Archaeology of the Israelite Settlement.* Jerusalem: Israel Exploration Society.

1993 The Sociopolitical Organization of the Central Hill Country in the Second Millennium B.C.E. In *Biblical Archaeology Today, 1990: Proceedings of the Second International Congress of Biblical Archaeology; Supplement: Pre-Congress Symposium*, ed. A. Biran and J. Aviram, 119–31. Jerusalem: Israel Exploration Society.
1996 The Territorial-Political System of Canaan in the Late Bronze Age. *UF* 28:221–55.

Gittlen, B. M.
1993 Response to "Trade and its Renewal in the Iron Age." In *Biblical Archaeology Today, 1990: Proceedings of the Second International Congress of Biblical Archaeology*, ed A. Biran and J. Aviram, 367–69. Jerusalem: Israel Exploration Society.

Gonen, R.
1984 Urban Canaan in the Late Bronze Period. *BASOR* 253:61–74.
1992 The Late Bronze Age. In *The Archaeology of Ancient Israel*, ed. A. Ben-Tor, 211–57. Translated by R. Greenberg. New Haven, Conn.: Yale University Press

Hall, S. R.
1985 *Maritime Trade and State Development in Early Southeast Asia*. Honolulu: University of Hawaii Press.

Hankey, V.
1974 A Late Bronze Age Temple at Amman. *Levant* 6: 131–78.

Hansen, M. H., ed.
2000 *A Comparative Study of Thirty City-State Cultures: An Investigation.* Historik-filosofiske skrifter 21. Copenhagen: Kongelige Danske Videnskabernes Selskab.

Harrison, T. P.
1993 Economics with an Entrepreneurial Spirit: Early Bronze Trade with Late Predynastic Egypt. *BA* 56:81–93.

Helck, W.
1971 *Die Beziehungen Ägyptens zu Vorderasien im 3. und 2. Jahrtausand v. Chr.* 2d ed. Ägyptologische Abhundlungen 5. Wiesbaden: Harrassowitz.

Hoffmeier, J. K.
1989 Reconsidering Egypt's Part in the Termination of the Middle Bronze Age in Palestine. *Levant* 21: 181–93.

Ilan, D.
1995 The Dawn of Internationalism—The Middle Bronze Age. In *The Archaeology of Society in the Holy Land*, ed. T. E. Levy, 297–319. New York: Facts on File.

Johnson, E. A. J.
1970 *The Organization of Space in Developing Countries*. Cambridge, Mass.: Harvard University Press.

Knapp, A. B.
1989a Complexity and Collapse in the North Jordan Valley: Archaeometry and Society in the Middle–Late Bronze Ages. *IEJ* 39:129–48.
1989b Response: Independence, Imperialism, and the Egyptian factor. *BASOR* 275:64–68.
1992 Independence and Imperialism: Politico-economic Structures in the Bronze Age Levant. In *Archaeology, Annales and Ethnohistory*, ed. A. B. Knapp, 83–98. Cambridge: Cambridge University Press.
1997 *The Archaeology of Late Bronze Age Cypriot Society: The Study of Settlement, Survey and Landscape*. University of Glasgow, Department of Archaeology Occasional Paper Series 4. Glasgow: University of Glasgow.

Lemche, N. P.
1991 *The Canaanites and Their Land: The Tradition of the Canaanites*. JSOTSup 110. Sheffield, England: JSOT Press.
1996 Where Should We Look for Canaan? A Reply to Nadav Na᾽aman. *UF* 28:767–72.
1998 Greater Canaan: The Implications of a Correct Reading of EA 151:49–67. *BASOR* 310:19–24.

Leonard, A.
1976 The Nature and Extent of the Mycenaean Presence in the Southeastern Mediterranean during the Late Bronze Age. Ph.D. diss., University of Chicago.
1981 Considerations of Morphological Variation in the Mycenaean Pottery from the Southeastern Mediterranean. *BASOR* 241:87–101.
1987 The Significance of the Mycenaean Pottery Found East of the Jordan River. In *Studies in the History and Archaeology of Jordan*, vol. 3, ed. A. Hadidi, 261–66. Amman: Department of Antiquities of the Hashemite Kingdom of Jordan.

Leonard, A., and E. Cline
1998 The Aegean Pottery at Megiddo: An Appraisal and Reanalysis. *BASOR* 309:3–39.

Levy, T. E.
1995 Cult, Metallurgy, and Rank Societies—Chalcolithic Period (ca. 4500–3500 B.C.E.). In *The Archaeology of Society in the Holy Land*, ed. T. E. Levy, 226–44. New York: Facts on File.

Marcus, E.
1991 Tel Nami: A Study of a Middle Bronze Age IIA Period Coastal Settlement. M.A. thesis, Haifa University.
1995 A Petrographic Analysis of Storage Jars from Tel Nami, Israel: Ceramic Production and Trade Networks of the Middle Bronze Age IIA period

(ca. 2000–1750 B.C.). *Materials Issues in Art and Archaeology* 4(352):597–603.

Marfoe, L.
1979 The Integrative Transformation: Patterns of Sociopolitical Organization in Southern Syria. *BASOR* 234:1–42.

Naʾaman, N.
1975 The Political Disposition and Historical Development of Eretz-Israel according to the Amarna Letters. Ph.D. diss., Tel Aviv University.
1981 Economic Aspects of the Egyptian Occupation of Canaan. *IEJ* 31:172–85.
1986 The Canaanite City-States in the Late Bronze Age and the Inheritances of the Israelite Tribes [in Hebrew]. *Tarbiz* 55:463–88.
1992 Canaanite Jerusalem and Its Central Hill Country Neighbours in the Second Millennium B.C.E. *UF* 24:275–92.
1997 The Network of Canaanite Late Bronze Kingdoms and the City of Ashdod. *UF* 29:599–625.
1999 Four Notes on the Size of Late Bronze Age Canaan. *BASOR* 313:31–37.

Nichols, D. L., and T. H. Charlton
1997 *The Archaeology of City-States: Cross-Cultural Approaches*. Washington, D.C.: Smithsonian Institution Press.

Raban, A.
1985 The Ancient Harbours of Israel in Biblical Times. In *Harbour Archaeology: Proceedings of the First International Workshop on Ancient Mediterranean Harbours, Cesarea Maritima 24–28.6.83*, ed. A. Raban, 11–44. BARIS 257. Oxford: British Archaeological Reports.

Renfrew, C.
1975 Trade as Action at a Distance: Questions of Integration and Communication. In *Ancient Civilizations and Trade*, ed. J. A. Sabloff and C. C. Lamberg-Karlovsky, 3–59. Albuquerque: University of New Mexico Press.

Rihll, T. E., and A. G. Wilson
1991 Modeling Settlement Structures in Ancient Greece: New Approaches to the Polis. In *City and Country in the Ancient World*, ed. J. Rich and A. Wallace-Hadrill, 59–95. London: Routledge.

Stager, L. E.
1985 Response to "Archaeology, History, and Bible. The Israelite Settlement in Canaan: A Case Study." In *Biblical Archaeology Today: Proceedings of the International Congress on Biblical Archaeology, Jerusalem, April 1984*, ed. J. Amitai, 83–86. Jerusalem: Israel Exploration Society.
1992 The Periodization of Palestine from Neolithic through Bronze Age times. In *Chronologies in Old World Archaeology*, 3d ed., ed. R. W. Ehrich, 1:22–41. Chicago: University of Chicago Press.
2000 Port Power in the Early and the Middle Bronze Age: The Organization of Maritime Trade and Hinterland Production. In *Studies in the Archaeology of Israel and Neighboring Lands in Memory of Douglas L. Esse*, ed. S. Wolff, 625–38. SAOC 59. Chicago: Oriental Institute, University of Chicago.

Sugerman, M.
2000 Webs of Commerce: The Archaeology of Ordinary Things in Late Bronze Age Israel and Palestine. Ph.D. diss., Harvard University.
n.d. The Petrographic Proveniences of Some Canaanite Jars in Cyprus.

Trigger, B. G.
1993 *Early Civilizations: Ancient Egypt in Context*. Cairo: American University in Cairo Press.
2003 *Understanding Early Civilizations: A Comparative Study*. Cambridge: Cambridge University Press.

Vance, J. E.
1970 *The Merchant's World: Geography of Wholesaling*. Englewood Cliffs, N.J.: Prentice-Hall.

Weinstein, J. M.
1981 The Egyptian Empire in Palestine: A Reassessment. *BASOR* 241:1–28.

Wijngaarden, G. J. van
1999 An Archaeological Approach to the Concept of Value: Mycenaean Pottery at Ugarit (Syria). *Archaeological Dialogues* 6/1:2–46.
2002 *Use and Appreciation of Mycenaean Pottery in the Levant, Cyprus and Italy (ca. 1600–1200 B.C.)*. Amsterdam: Amsterdam University Press.

Yoffee, N.
1997 The Obvious and the Chimerical. In *The Archaeology of City-States: Cross-Cultural Approaches*, ed. D. L. Nichols and T. H. Charlton, 255–63. Washington, D.C.: Smithsonian Institution Press.
2005 *Myths of the Archaic State: Evolution of the Earliest Cities, States, and Civilizations*. Cambridge: Cambridge University Press.

44. East of Ashkelon: The Setting and Settling of the Judean Lowlands in the Iron Age IIA

by Ron E. Tappy

In a recent article that embraces both the historical and comparative methods of the *Annales* school (see Braudel 1972; 1980:25–54; Bloch 1953; 1974; 1995),[1] Lawrence Stager (2001) has convincingly adapted models developed for the study of trade and statecraft in Southeast Asia during the first millennium and a half C.E. (Bronson 1977; Hall 1985) to the economic and political role of Ashkelon during the third and second millennia B.C.E. (Early–Middle Bronze Age).[2] He has further indicated his intention to apply aspects of this Asian riverine- and rice-plain model to the Phoenician colonization of the Mediterranean world in the first millennium B.C.E. (2001: 629, 635). Although the political organizations in each of these contexts differ in important ways, valuable insights into the economic, interregional, and transcultural relationships in southern Canaan in the various historical periods emerge from the analogy.

But since the use of this "port-power" system in the coastal plain and highlands of Canaan during the first millennium B.C.E would have entailed commercial exchanges across oftentimes volatile political borders (a circumstance not as prominent among the ports and upland rivers of Southeast Asia), special consideration of relations between coastal sites and those in the lowlands and the inland valleys they protected becomes necessary.[3] Toward this end, I shall (I) outline some basic characteristics of the riverine and port-power models of exchange, (II) review Ashkelon's place within such a system in the light of the geography to its east, and (III) raise a few points related directly to Iron Age settlements in two of the principal valleys there, namely, Tel Zayit in the Naḥal Guvrin and Lachish in the Naḥal Lachish.

I

The so-called "riverine network" outlined in the Southeast Asian studies became the "port-power economic system" in Stager's analysis. Within both concepts, the coastal plain and hinterland valleys of a given region represent two ends of a trading continuum (not two opposing economic poles) that ultimately connects the local clusters of small, highland villages with international networks via foreign trade outlets at coastal ports such as Ashkelon. A well-organized, multitiered hierarchy of exchange existed from hill country to coast. While the hub of the overall network lay at the seaside emporium, with its large-scale merchants and access to international markets, other significant sites located in the valley lowlands (or, in the case of Southeast Asia, at primary and secondary river junctions; Hall 1985:13, fig. 1) served as crucial transition points where market-based middlemen received the flow of goods from upper valley and highland sources and facilitated their movement out to the port city.

Besides forwarding goods to the coastal port, these pivotal lowland cities that lay near the valley mouths in Canaan/Israel also produced valuable commodities, such as olive oil and wine, from as early as the late fourth millennium B.C.E. (Stager 2001:627). Behind the higher-order merchants of these borderland towns, various tiers of traders and peddlers occupied sites situated still farther up the valley, closer to the highland producers themselves. These vendors organized the collection of various trade items drawn from local, nonmarket, upland villages perched along or near the watershed, and they also began the transporting of goods down the valley-related rivers or roadways to the transition points (see Hall 1985:16, fig. 2, for the vendor-merchant hierarchy in Asia; for that of southern Canaan, see Stager 2001:625).[4] In cases where cultural and political borders were crossed within this inland network, it seems reasonable to look for these "fulcrum markets" in the outlying frontier of the inland culture, where the lower valleys open onto the inner coastal plain.

---

[1] For further references and appraisals of the *Annales* school, see Bunimovitz 1994:179–81, n. 3.

[2] It is a personal pleasure to offer this study in honor of Larry Stager, whose extensive fieldwork at Ashkelon and insightful research into the region at large helped form my own interest in the Shephelah.

[3] In the port-power model, Stager proposes that "power was exercised through economic ties and that this integrated, hierarchical network can and often did develop outside of or beyond a state exercising coercive political-military force over the hinterland" (Stager 2001:628–29).

[4] For the recognition and study of a similar network of economic zones connecting Judah and Philistia in the seventh century B.C.E., see Faust and Weiss 2005.

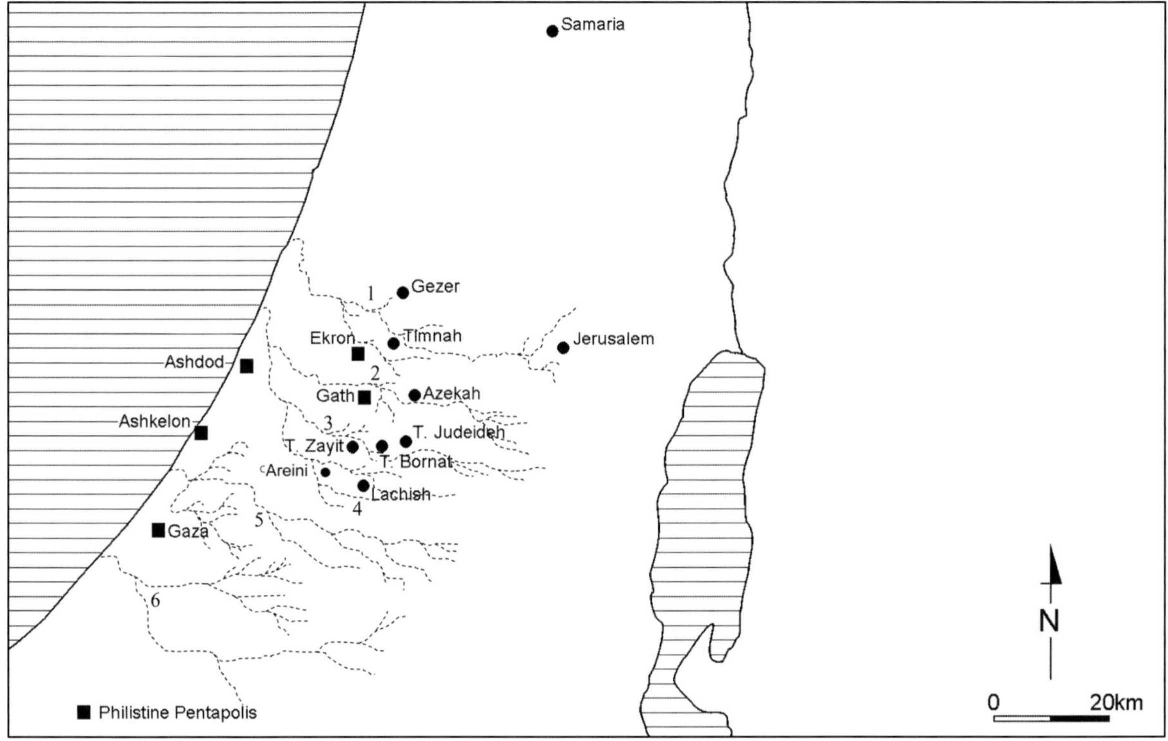

Figure 1. Map of selected sites in the Judean Shephelah and Philistine plain
1 Naḥal Sorek/Refaᶜim **2** Naḥal HaElah (Shephelah District 2) **3** Naḥal Guvrin/Libnah (Shephelah District 4) **4** Naḥal Lachish (Shephelah District 3) **5** Naḥal Shiqma/Adorayim **6** Naḥal Besor/Gerar

In any event, the larger, integrated system ultimately worked to benefit all those participating in the venture—from the small-scale, village-based peddlers in the mountains down through the various vendors to the large-scale, port-based merchants on the coast—even though the more insulated towns and villages of the hill country may have felt only minimal political or cultural loyalty to the port city that organized and ultimately dominated the overall economic network (Hall 1985:13–14).

One can hardly imagine a better topo-geographical setting—anywhere in Canaan, at least—for such a market system to take root than in the southern highlands, lowlands, and coastal plain areas of biblical Judah and Philistia, where multiple east-west valley systems exist and ancient roadways connected the various tiers of exchange (figure 1). Moreover, the large port at Ashkelon seems, in certain ways, perfectly situated to serve in all historical periods as a large-scale entrepot that drew many of its trade resources from sites lying in the lowlands and hinterland to its east. The city is nestled at the center of a series of drainage systems—Nahar Rubin and Wâdī Suqreir to its north, with Wâdī el-Ḥesi and Wâdī Ghazzeh to its south (see Stager 2001:627–28, figs. 31.2–31.3)—that descend from the mountain range stretching south from Jerusalem. Unlike other large, Iron Age municipalities along the southern coastal plain that might otherwise have become rival depots (e.g., Gaza, Ashdod), Ashkelon enjoyed a position directly on the shore of the Mediterranean Sea and therefore likely dominated the southern coast as a "favored port."[5]

Ironically, however, Ashkelon itself did not lie at the effluence of any one of the wadis that left the hill country and eventually fed into the Mediterranean.

[5] O. W. Wolters (1979:35–36) has employed the term "favored coast" to describe the unique benefits accrued by the southeastern coast of Sumatra because of its geographical proximity to the western end of the island of Java, where principal international routes through the Sunda Strait connected the Java Sea to the Indian Ocean. It seems likely, even prior to the full publication of pottery from Ashkelon and Ekron, that the ceramic assemblages from these two sites will resemble that already published from Ashdod, but with at least one notable exception: the Ashkelon repertoire appears to include a much wider array of imports throughout the Iron II period than do the other Philistine capitals (see Stager 1996:62–67; Gitin 1998:165). This situation undoubtedly reflects Ashkelon's role as the principal port outlet to the international markets.

Consequently, the import-export merchants at Ashkelon, unlike the river-mouth rulers in Southeast Asia, would have had to redirect goods and commodities (which, in their setting, moved by caravan and not by water) from the closest wadi branches that skirted the coastal plain in the immediate environs of their city. This situation underscores the need for the harbor princes who hosted the merchants at Ashkelon to have made and maintained agreements with key towns representing the intermediate markets that lay 25–30 km inland and along the transition from the highlands and foothills to the interior coastal plain, that is, at precisely the point where the various wadis mentioned above began to veer away from approaching Ashkelon directly. Judging from recent surveys of Iron Age roads and highways in the region (e.g., Dorsey 1991:183, 194, maps 13–14), the rulers of Ashkelon had little difficulty in this effort. Major east-west roadways connected Ashkelon with sites such as Shawafir, Tell eṣ-Ṣâfi, Tel Zayit, Tell el-ᶜAreini, Lachish, and Tell el-Ḥesi, some of which undoubtedly served as gateways into the valleys behind them during the Iron Age.

Such borderland sites would, of course, have found it necessary to interact economically not only with centers on the coastal plain, and specifically with the principal port city, but also with the towns and villages reaching into the hill country to their east. The reality of a political border, with differing local cultures and ethnic groups on each side, adds a dimension to the political and economic landscape of the Levantine port-power model that apparently did not often arise in the Southeast Asian riverine networks. If a port-power model is appropriate to a setting in the Iron Age, a large sector of the trade network would have owed primary allegiance to its own capital, Jerusalem, high up in the mountains behind most of the tiers of exchange, and the vicissitudes of politics and culture may often have jeopardized an uninterrupted flow of goods out to the port. Stager (2003) has described this emergent highland capital as a regal-ritual city (see Fox 1977) that headed up a rather localized patrimonial kingdom.

But regardless of how restricted the capital's political sway might have been in the early Iron II period, it surely would have constituted a center of consumers more than of producers, and its own economic needs would have placed a considerable drain on the same set of highland villages and valley towns from which the coastal port simultaneously sought to draw the same goods and commodities. The integrated economic landscape, not only the divergent cultural and political climates, would have pulled these hinterland sites in different directions. The terminus port at Philistine Ashkelon existed under a political and cultural organization that differed considerably from the make-up of most of the inland sites crucial to its larger network. In this context, the westernmost towns of Judah would undoubtedly have accrued additional status as they felt pressured to accept more enhanced roles and to display dual or sometimes conflicting loyalties. Two such towns—Lachish and Tel Zayit—lay along and helped define the highland kingdom's western border and could also have served as the strategic transition points to the outside trade system.

These internal stresses on the interior network, however, do not preclude the aptness of the strategy overall, since the emphasis in such an economy lies on integration, not domination and political centralization, and on controlling people, not political boundaries (see Hall 1985:2–4). Economic hegemony across the larger network required direct rule only over the coast and its port outlet(s), not a homogeneous political-cultural matrix throughout the entire system—one designed to transcend the political, cultural, and even religious boundaries it transected. The viability of such a policy received ample demonstration in the successful implementation of the same basic principle by the Neo-Assyrians in their western campaigns of the eighth century B.C.E., when their leaders clearly understood that to control the economies of the principal trade outlets (such as Tyre and Sidon) meant significant power over the entire trade route, even without military intervention, not only back into the hinterland and highlands, but also far beyond (for example, to South Arabia; see Tappy 2001:542; Gitin 1998:176–79).

II

The Brook of Kana plus the Valley of Ayalon (Wâdī Selmān) and their related feeder streams drain the hills of Ephraim between Jerusalem and the area south of Shechem. From Jerusalem south, six additional transverse valleys or basins descend from the hill country to the inner coastal plain. Besides the Naḥal Sorek-Refaᶜim system (*Nahar Rubin*), which bisects the hills immediately west of Jerusalem, the Naḥal HaElah (Wâdī eṣ-Ṣunt), Naḥal Guvrin (Valley of Zephatha), Naḥal Lachish (Wâdī Qubeibeh), Naḥal Shiqma-Adorayim (*Wâdī el-Ḥesi*), and Naḥal Besor-Gerar (*Wâdī Ghazzeh*) accommodate the runoff on the seaward slopes of the Judean highlands as far south as the Beersheba Basin. Once the network of capillary streams in each natural regime leaves the inland areas and reaches the inner coastal plain, the various tributaries merge into single, independent outlets (shown in italics in the previous list) before proceeding to the shoreline and emptying into the Mediterranean. The three principal streams from the HaElah-Guvrin-Lachish valleys likewise converge sequentially in the Wâdī Suqreir before it reaches the shore roughly 22 km north of Ashkelon. In this sequence, the Naḥal Guvrin first meets the Naḥal Lachish just north of Sapheir (modern Merkaz Shapira). From there, the two continue as a solitary stream until approaching the main coastal route slightly northeast of Ashdod. Here the Elah Valley effluence also joins this stream as it continues on a northward course for only a short distance more before turning toward the west, flowing past Tel Mor, and finally reaching the Mediterranean only 14 km south of the Sorek. (In a similar manner, the Shiqma and Adorayim branches of the Wâdī el-Ḥesi also approach the coast as one trunk channel approximately 7.5 km south of Ashkelon, and the Wâdī Ghazzeh outlet for the Besor and Gerar streams lies even farther to the south.) Thus, as noted above, none of these natural drainage routes actually reaches the shoreline at Ashkelon.

In light of the relative positions of these topographical features, the valleys that would have allowed the most direct access to the highland markets and, consequently, would have proven most relevant to the development of port power at Ashkelon include, from north to south, the HaElah, Guvrin, and Lachish systems. While roadways through the Vale of Elah provided access from the Ashkelon area to the Judahite highlands immediately north and south of Jerusalem and in the direction of Bethlehem, those in the Guvrin valley led into the hill country between Bethlehem and Hebron. Still others in the Lachish system connected the inner coastal plain east of Ashkelon to the hill country around and south of Hebron. Next to these passageways, the Naḥal Shiqma also undoubtedly proved useful, since it ran from Tell el-Ḥesi out to the coastal area south of Ashkelon.

Within these parallel networks, the two most central valleys (Naḥal Guvrin and Naḥal Lachish) led into inland areas directly east of Ashkelon and, in my judgment, constituted two of the most important access routes to the small- and large-scale traders in the highlands. These drainage systems followed (and helped carve) parallel valleys in which important sites flourished in the Bronze and Iron Ages. The Naḥal Guvrin, together with feeder streams such as the Naḥal Dikrîn and Naḥal ᶜUzzar to the north plus Naḥal Pôl to the south, drained from the Beth-tappuah area down to Mareshah and on past the unexcavated site of Tell Bûrnah before reaching Tel Zayit.

The centrality of this valley and the towns established there is reflected later in the selection by the Romans (and then by Eusebius in his *Onomasticon*) of Eleutheropolis (Beit Jibrîn = modern Bet Guvrin) as a reference point from which to gauge distances and locate towns throughout the general region.[6] The nearly 30-dunam site of Tel Zayit lay just over 6 km farther west from the Eleutheropolis-Mareshah area, on the border of Judah, and 26.96 km almost due east (only 0.74 km south) of Ashkelon, at the lower entrance to the strategic Beth Guvrin valley. This town, therefore, guarded the access from the southern coast to highland interchanges from Gedor to Hebron. Just over 5 km to the south, the Naḥal Lachish siphoned numerous tributaries in vicinities from Khirbet el-Qom (Makkedah, west-southwest of Hebron) to Tel ᶜEton (Eglon), Lachish, and Tell el-ᶜAreini, before continuing just north of modern Qiryat Gat and then assuming a northwesterly course through the Tell Zippor area en route to the Mediterranean. Since it remains uncertain whether Tell el-ᶜAreini—situated slightly more than 7 km northwest of Lachish, between the Naḥal Lachish and one of its southern tributaries, the Naḥal Noᶜam—officially belonged to the lowland districts of Judah (see Rainey 1983:7–9), Lachish itself appears to have constituted the westernmost Judahite town of significant political and economic import in this valley.

Only a short distance separated Lachish and Tel Zayit and the valleys to which they belong. (Tel Zayit lay 7.06 km north and 1.76 km west of Lachish.) In the Iron Age, east-west roadways followed the drainage patterns (described above) down from the hill country to the inner coastal plain via the Lachish and Guvrin valleys and then proceeded due west to the large trading emporium at Ashkelon (see Dorsey 1991:182, 194, maps 13–14). Through the central (Guvrin) valley, the road from Ashkelon advanced almost due east and passed by Tel Zayit, Tell Bûrnah (ancient Ether?—see note 36), Tell Judeidah (modern Tel Goded = ancient Moresheth-Gath, home of the prophet Micah), and both Adullam and Khirbet el-Beida as it ascended to Khirbet Jedur (biblical Gedor) and Beth-zur south of Bethlehem, near where it connected with the main north-south passageway stretching along the watershed ridge from Beersheba to Jerusalem. Not far to the south, another route from Ashkelon split at Tell el-ᶜAreini on the inner coastal

[6] The *Tabula Peutingeriana*, a somewhat schematized presentation of the road network during the Roman Empire, placed this town "32 Roman miles [approximately 53 km] from Jerusalem on the way to Ashkelon" (Kloner 1993: 195).

plain and continued through the valley both to Lachish and Mareshah (Tell Ṣandaḥannah, farther east through the Naḥal Mareshah) and then into the hill country, with the Lachish branch running through Khirbet el-Qom and Adorayim before reaching the Jutta-Ziph area south of Hebron. (Similarly, a more northerly road connected the port center at Ashkelon with Tell eṣ-Ṣâfi and proceeded past Azekah[7] before forking, with one branch leading up to the Judahite highlands between Bethlehem and Jerusalem.)

When considering these lateral roads and highways through the Elah, Guvrin, and Lachish valleys, a picture emerges that seems quite consistent with the topography and archaeological history of these regions and that correlates well with the outline given in Joshua 15:33–44 of the districts and cities belonging to Judah. The author(s) of that text organized the settlements of the Shephelah, or "Lowlands" area, into three geographical groups that follow roughly the Elah (vv. 35–36 = District 2), Lachish (vv. 37–41 = District 3), and Guvrin (vv. 42–44 = District 4) systems.[8] Just prior to this section—that is, from v. 33 through the first site listed in v. 35 (Jarmuth)—the roster names eight sites in the Sorek and related valleys before moving to the Naḥal HaElah, for which it lists seven sites, though an eighth town, Beth-Shemesh, may somehow have dropped from the line-up (Rainey 1983:7).

At any rate, this district list appears to identify each physical environment by naming its principal (and, in the case of District 4, westernmost) municipality together with some of its satellite sites. In District 4, Libnah clearly seems to represent the most significant (and very likely the westernmost) town in the Guvrin valley. In fact, one may reasonably refer to this area as the "Libnah District," just as the next valley to the south became the "Lachish District." From the Tel Zayit–Bûrnah area, the terrain rises from around 175–200 m above sea level to an elevation of just over 300 m near the Mareshah area. From there, the Naḥal Mareshah siphons the landscape as it declines again toward the Naḥal Lachish and the city of Lachish. Since Joshua 15 includes Mareshah in the Libnah District, the road from Lachish to Mareshah (mentioned above) must have run along or near the border between Districts 2 and 4, which basically followed the local watershed separating the southern tributaries of Guvrin (for example, Naḥal Pôl and Naḥal Ṣapûn) from the northern ones in the Lachish system (for example, Naḥal Gath, Naḥal Šaḥariyah, Naḥal Rôk, and Naḥal Mareshah).

Overall, the cities named in the Elah, Guvrin, and Lachish districts include seven of the eight sites listed elsewhere as constituting the western edge of Rehoboam's defensive network of fortresses: Lachish (in District 3); Mareshah (District 4); Adullam, Socoh, Azekah, Zorah (District 2); and, just north of District 2, Aijalon; only Moresheth-Gath in the Libnah District 4 is not included in Joshua 15 (see 2 Chron. 11:5–12 and the discussion in Aharoni 1979:330–33 and map 25). In District 4, only Libnah and Ether lay west of this line of forts (in the general area of Tel Zayit and Tell Bûrnah; see note 36). In addition, Judah's two most westerly Levitical cities (Joshua 21; 1 Chron. 6:39–66 [6:54–81]), Beth-Shemesh and Libnah, were located in the frontier of Districts 2 and 4, respectively. These cities apparently served both cultic and royal functions during the period of the United Monarchy (B. Mazar 1960:193–205; but see Naʾaman 1986:206–7; cf. Japhet 1993:163–65). The question germane to this study, however, asks whether any of these more westerly cities ever served as mediators in the economy between Ashkelon and the upper inland areas.

Regional survey data have also shown that in the Iron Age the east-west roadways through the lowlands of Judah intersected at least three converging north-south routes somewhere in the Tel Zayit–Lachish area (see Dorsey 1991:58, map 1; 67–70; also 182, map 13; 189–92, 196; and 195, map 14). These longitudinal routes connected Egypt and the northern Sinai Peninsula with the southernmost Philistine capital at Gaza and the lowland area of Judah by running roughly parallel to, but east of, the main coastal route. They proceeded through important Iron Age centers such as Tell Jemma (likely ancient Yurza) and Tell el-Farʿah (S)—major sites that, together with other mostly unidentified towns, protected the southern accesses around Philistia and into Judah and established the Besor Basin area as a natural border (Dorsey 1991:67–70). Importantly, the series of Iron Age sites leading northward from these checkpoints shows that these alternative routes actually began to merge near the Lachish–ʿAreini–Zayit area before continuing northward as a single highway to urban centers at Tell eṣ-Ṣâfi (Philistine Gath) and Tel Miqne (Philistine Ekron).[9]

[7] At Azekah, yet another road branched off to the northeast and led toward the Ramah-Mizpah area, north of Jerusalem.

[8] For detailed studies of these districts, see Rainey 1980: 194–202 and 1983:1–22.

[9] Other longitudinal routes to their east lay farther up in the hill country of Judah and connected such sites as Tell Ḥalif, Tell Beit Mirsim, and Tell Eitun, or still farther east, Khirbet Rabud (biblical Debir), Hebron, and Beth-zur (see Dorsey 1991:152, map 9).

The Lachish–ᶜAreini–Zayit triangle, then, constituted a crucial transitional area, as it represented the place where major latitudinal and longitudinal routes intersected. Goods arriving here from nearly all directions could easily make their way over the short run from the Naḥal Guvrin and Naḥal Lachish outlets to the coastal port at Ashkelon. This communication network connected the highland culture(s) of Judah to the Canaanite and Philistine city-states located near the hilly western flanks, along the Mediterranean seaboard, and toward the principal gateways into Egypt. Thus to ensure that goods moving through this region proceeded to Ashkelon and not elsewhere, trade agreements with sites either in the Libnah or Lachish area would have proven vital to the success of port power at Ashkelon, and an archaeological reflex should emerge in the material culture of these transitional sites if they, in fact, developed such connections with the coast.

The physical setting of Tel Zayit, for example, at a strategic location along a geographical and cultural interface in the Shephelah, accents the ease with which that town could have involved itself both in Philistine commercial and cultural activity to the west and in the political, cultural, economic, and religious affairs of the emergent kingdom of Judah to the east during the Iron Age IIA period. Since Tel Zayit is the westernmost site in the Guvrin Valley that has shown clear affinities with highland culture in levels dating from the tenth century B.C.E., and since it lies roughly halfway between Philistine Gath and Israelite Lachish (7.06 km north of Lachish and 8.09 km south of Gath), it seems reasonable to assume that a political-cultural border ran somewhere through this very area. This marginal zone lay between the southern coastal plain of Philistia and the lowland districts of Judah recorded in Joshua 15:35–44. Importantly, Tel Zayit also lies approximately 1.7 km *west* of both Lachish and Gath (but still approximately 2.25 km north*east* of Tell el-ᶜAreini) and therefore offers one of the best sites by which to evaluate the transitional-market phenomenon within the rise and success of a port-power mode of exchange based at Ashkelon.

III

Though subdividing the Judean hill country into smaller, discrete tracts of land presents a difficult task, a recent survey (Ofer 1994) parsed the area into six geographical units, with each unit claiming its own set of topo-ecological traits, accessibility (or lack thereof) to perennial water sources, and ancient settlement patterns. The geographical zones (starting just south of Jerusalem and moving southward) include: the northern central range, central range plateau, southern springs, southern central range, and, flanking the eastern edges of these four areas, the northern and southern desert fringes (Ofer 1994:94–95, fig. 1). From the inner coastal area, roadways through the Libnah and Lachish Valleys, respectively, led from the western lowlands directly up to two of these areas—the central range plateau around and north of Hebron, and the southern springs lying between Hebron and Khirbet Rabud (biblical Debir) to the south. Alternative routes through the Lachish Valley also connected indirectly to the southern central range, which extended southward from Khirbet Rabud.

The primary east-west road from Ashkelon entered the Libnah Valley at Tel Zayit and continued past Tell Bûrnah before branching to the north through Goded–Beidha–Adullam and south through Mareshah and proceeding up to the high ground of the central plateau between Gedor (T. Judeidah), Beth Zur (Khirbet Tubeiqa), and Hebron (Tell er-Rumeideh) (Dorsey 1991:182, map 13). Hebron nearly always constituted the principal site not only on the plateau but also for the entire highland region, except during the Late Bronze Age, when virtually no occupation occurred in the hill country and Khirbet Rabud became the major site. As soon as substantial settlement returned to the hills in the early Iron I period, however, the center shifted back to Hebron (Ofer 1994:96).

The Ashkelon–ᶜAreini–Lachish road, on the other hand, led through Khirbet el-Qom and Adorayim before approaching the hill country roughly halfway between Hebron and Khirbet Rabud. This route gave direct access to Ofer's "southern springs" portion of the hill country, a smaller unit that marked a transition from the higher ground of the central plateau to the southern desert fringe. Though this region receives less rainfall than the central range plateau, its two concentrations of springs allowed for significant settlement in the Sil el-Dilbe and Dura Valleys (Ofer 1994:94). Otherwise, the remainder of the area proved less suited to occupation. Roughly halfway between Lachish and el-Qom, another Iron Age road diverged from the main route and ran through Tell Eitun on its way directly to Khirbet Rabud itself, i.e., into the hills lying just south of the southern springs and toward the southern central range.

Thus, despite the sometimes steep pitch of the seaward slopes from these highland areas down to the Shephelah, the Libnah/Guvrin and Lachish drainage systems allowed for adequate movement between the coastal plain and lowlands and the two or three most densely populated sectors of the Judean hill country in the Iron Age I–II periods (see Ofer 1994:103–5, figs. 4–6).[10] Moreover, the heaviest concentration of sites and the largest sites consistently lay in the Hebron area of the central range plateau, i.e., near the source of the Libnah Valley,[11] where "the connection to routes [was] stronger than in the preceding [i.e., LBA] period" (Ofer 1994:104).[12] Moreover, a strong political, cultural, and religious connection appears to have existed between Hebron and Libnah at least from the time of the United Monarchy, when these places assumed a central role among the Levitical cities (see Naʾaman 1986:230–33) and either took their names from or gave them to certain Levitical families (e.g., Num. 26:58). By the Iron I–II transition, then, and certainly by the early ninth century B.C.E., the highlands of Judah became "a substantially settled land" and "part of a more extensive settlement system" (Ofer 1994:105–6), and the principal valleys that descended from the most populated sectors of the hill country ultimately led through the developing lowland sites of Lachish and Tel Zayit and then straight out to Ashkelon on the coast.

Despite a rise in the number of highland settlements in the Iron I period, however, the depositional history revealed through excavations at both Lachish and Tel Zayit shows that neither site could have served a transitional, market-based role in a port-power economy during that time, since both sites were then unoccupied. Only during the tenth and ninth centuries could such a network have grown new roots in the lower valleys of southern Canaan.[13]

The relative stratigraphic sequences at Tel Zayit and Lachish help refine our understanding of the settlement process in the Judean Shephelah and the potential role of the region as a vital link in such a trade network during the Iron Age II period. These two sites share a similar historical development, with both places showing significant occupations during the Late Bronze Age (when the highlands were sparsely settled), occupational gaps throughout most of the Iron Age I period (when hill-country settlements increased dramatically), and renewed occupations sometime during the tenth and ninth centuries B.C.E. (when the founding of hilltop villages accelerated

[10] Several other important observations have emerged from survey work pertaining to the settlement patterns within these three particular zones that bear on their viability as participants in a larger, port-power economic network. For example, the settlement of the hill country that began, to any traceable degree, in the Chalcolithic period suffered at least three periods of severe demographic decline or total occupational gap—during the Early Bronze Age II, Intermediate Bronze Age, and the Late Bronze Age (Ofer 1994: 99–100). Thus when Stager's purported port-power network at Ashkelon drew heavily on the Arad trade during the EB II period, the Judahite hills suffered their first major occupational decline or abandonment. As suggested by Stager, the southern valleys of the Naḥal Shiqma and Naḥal Besor would undoubtedly have proven more vital to Ashkelon's emergent economic design during this time. Following a revival in the EB III period and another decline in the Intermediate Bronze Age (Stager's MB I), occupation of the hill country resumed and strengthened during the Middle Bronze Age (Stager's second period of study), when settlement and plantation agriculture strengthened in the central range plateau sector, where Hebron served as the principal social center (Ofer 1994:100). But, alas, another virtual settlement gap occurred during the Late Bronze Age, when it appears that only Khirbet Rabud managed to occupy an area of around two hectares.

[11] Ofer believes that the hill country now "constituted part of a more extensive unit, with its center outside the region—in Jerusalem" (Ofer 1994:104), and he seems to attribute this rise in Jerusalem's status to David's having established the capital city there (see his comments on p. 114). He also concludes, however, that this demographic growth "did not have an immediate influence on its [that is, the hill country's] political development" and that the area remained a kind of "dimorphic state, comprised of the royal city and the tribal elements around it" (Ofer 1994:121).

[12] While many analysts have understood the impetus for this settlement and unification of the hill country as stemming only from "the appearance of common enemies" (e.g., Ofer 1994:117), the emergence of a regional political kingdom with its capital at Jerusalem, plus the development and integration of towns and villages that would have derived from shared economic ties within a port-power economic network, offers a fuller, perhaps equally realistic stimulus for the opening of the hill country in general.

[13] Recently, Faust (2003) has argued that the few highland sites that have undergone actual excavation seem to reveal that most of the rural settlements there were either abandoned or destroyed sometime near the late eleventh or early tenth century B.C.E. and that few, if any, of the Iron I highland villages maintained their settlements in the tenth century or were themselves resettled in the ninth century B.C.E. Instead, he claims, excavation data suggest that the tenth century witnessed a shift toward greater urbanization, with perhaps fewer but more fortified settlements (compare the discussion below of Tel Zayit in the tenth century B.C.E.). Further, the return of a significant number of interspersed rural villages occurred mainly during the ninth century. For a detailed response to this article at levels of both theory and method, see Finkelstein 2005. (Recently, scholars have appealed to both scenarios—that is, a continuous existence of rural villages throughout the tenth and ninth centuries B.C.E. vs. a decline in rural villages in the tenth century and their replacement by a few, more fortified towns—to argue for the formation of Israelite statecraft [with Jerusalem serving as the capital city] in the highlands of Judah during the tenth century B.C.E. [compare Ofer 1994 and Faust 2003]. In general, scholars now seem to have a renewed acceptance of greater urbanization and political centralization in the hill country region in the tenth century B.C.E. than they did only a decade ago.)

further). A comparative stratigraphic analysis based on the latest understanding of remains from Lachish, however, appears to indicate that Tel Zayit actually led the way in opening the Shephelah region on behalf of the kingdom of Judah in the tenth century B.C.E. and anticipated by at least half a century the burgeoning occupation of Lachish IVd-a. The larger site of Lachish came to dominate the lowlands area only in the ninth century, when Tel Zayit established stronger ties to the coastal culture.

The Tenth Century B.C.E. Although the full-scale, official excavation report from Lachish (Ussishkin 2004) presents a wealth of information about the site and the region, it also raises many vexing questions for such a comparative stratigraphic study. Lachish Level V, in particular, remains poorly defined and quite confusing, with the report itself showing signs of significant internal tension between its various contributors regarding the extent, character, date, and nature of the end of this stratum.[14] Ussishkin (2004:1: 44) describes this level, which followed the long period of abandonment,[15] as a sparsely populated, unfortified settlement marked by the arrival of "a new people bearing a new material culture" (evidenced by red-slipped, irregularly hand burnished pottery; see n. 15). This resettlement of the site constituted "part of the process of the crystallization of the Judean kingdom and the settlement of the Shephelah by the Judeans" (Ussishkin 2004:1:76). Yet according to the official report, the principal architecture recovered by the excavators included only a small house on the upper shoulder of Area S,[16] some poorly preserved walls and pits below the subsequent Judean palace-fort, and Level V pottery (mixed with fragments from the Middle and Late Bronze Ages) in the construction fills of the Level IV monumental architecture. Judging from discussion elsewhere in the report, however, it seems that traces of other Iron Age floor levels with pottery lying on them appeared *below* the Level V house floors and also beneath Walls 85–86 and the Enclosure Wall 27 (Ussishkin 2004:2:412, 416)—a fact that may indicate a longer lifespan (with at least two distinct phases) for Level V. But this possibility is not stressed in the report, and the contributors themselves remain divided as to whether the stratum ultimately suffered destruction by fire.

In addition, Ussishkin now reverses some of his earlier interpretations concerning Level V and lowers its chronology from the tenth to the ninth century by removing two key features that previous excavators had assigned to this stratum. First, he now sees no central palace-fort at Lachish in either Level V or the tenth century. Instead, he presents the so-called Podium A (which he originally believed constituted a second building phase in Level V that served as a foundation for Palace A [Ussishkin 1978:1–78]) as the first construction phase of Podium B, that is, the support system for Palace B in Level IV. In short, the purported Palace A never existed, and the Level IV construction of Podium A occurred, for unspecified "technical considerations," separately from the construction of Podium B (Ussishkin 2004:1:77). Second, neither did the "cult-room" and "high place" exist in Level V. These features were originally excavated by Y. Aharoni (1975:12, 26–32), who assigned them to Level V and understood them to represent a Judahite sanctuary that suffered destruction at the end of that stratum. Rather, the stone altar and cultic vessels that falsely led Aharoni to conclude a sanctuary lay here were merely dumped into a pit located in this area sometime during Level IV—a pit that, according to Ussishkin, Aharoni's team simply failed to identify (Ussishkin 2004:1:107).[17] After disassembling the various architectural elements of the so-called sanctuary, the new analysis concludes that none of the component parts actually originated together. Instead, Ussishkin sees eight distinct features that apparently ranged over "at least four stratigraphic phases" (Ussishkin 2004:1:107). Yet he does not clearly explain how these four phases fit between Levels V and IV or in Level IV alone.

If one accepts the revised views expressed by the excavator in his final report from Lachish, therefore, Level V becomes a rather ephemeral stratum somewhere in the early ninth century B.C.E. that is treated

[14] For example, compare the divergent positions of Ussishkin and Barkay in vol. 1, chapters 3 and 8, and in vol. 2, chapter 9.

[15] Except for a few sherds from a supposed workshop in Cave 4034, workers recovered no Philistine pottery at Lachish during the course of large-scale excavations. The few Bichrome sherds from Cave 4034 were followed by "the presence of a number of red-slipped and burnished Iron Age sherds [which show] that the cave was not abandoned following the destruction of this level" (Ussishkin 2004:1: 72).

[16] Excavations located portions of at least four rooms (with Building 3665 representing the largest room) with olive pits and carbonized grain on their surfaces (Ussishkin 2004:2: 413).

[17] Ussishkin believes that the ancient inhabitants dug this pit no later than the construction of Palace C (Level III), since the constructional fills and the floor of Palace C covered the pit; he therefore dates the cultic items contained in the pit to Level IV. In the detailed stratigraphic discussion, however, he takes a somewhat less dogmatic view by stating that these features "*could* date to Level IV" (Ussishkin 2004:2:412, emphasis added).

almost as a brief prelude to the first significant construction and settlement in Level IV. While Ussishkin concludes that "pottery typology is presently the only available indicator that can be used for dating Level V" (Ussishkin 2004:1:78), he in turn insists that this tool alone remains inconclusive. Yet he proceeds to argue for a ninth century dating of the level based solely on the pottery whose overall value he himself has questioned.[18] In the end, then, his report espouses that Level V (with however many subphases it might include), the four discernible stratigraphic phases of the sanctuary, and the four major building phases of Level IV (see below) should all squeeze into the ninth century (though the final phases of IV did continue into the early eighth century).[19] Undoubtedly, the overall nature and date of Level V will generate much discussion in the future. For now, however, the official report leads one to believe that Judahites may indeed have settled Lachish to some small degree in the early ninth century B.C.E. but that the site did not represent a significant center in the Shephelah prior to that time.

Tel Zayit, on the other hand, clearly came to life again during the early-to-mid-tenth century, after its own two-hundred-year gap in occupation following a fiery destruction of its large Late Bronze Age city.[20] Six seasons of excavation have revealed occupational levels from the early Iron Age II period in a 300 m^2 area on the eastern shoulder of the mound, in Squares N20, O20, and O19. These remains lie directly on those from the final stages of the Late Bronze Age occupation. No levels have emerged that could date to the interim between these two periods, and the ceramic repertoire has produced only a meager selection (roughly two dozen fragments) of Philistine Bichrome ware, mostly recovered from scattered and unrelated findspots. It seems clear, then, that a gap occurred in the occupation of Tel Zayit during the Iron Age I period (when settlements began to reappear in the highlands), and this depositional history matches closely that of Levels VI–V at nearby Lachish and suggests similar historical-cultural evolutions for the two cities at least through the Iron I–Iron II transition period.

Although later deposits at Tel Zayit have partly eroded down the steep eastern slope of the tell, the tenth-century (Local Level III) and most of the ninth-century (Local Levels II–I) levels have remained intact across the eastern summit and shoulder of the site. A well-built stone structure, whose construction date belongs in the early-to-mid tenth century B.C.E. and which suffered heavy destruction by fire sometime toward the close of that century,[21] constitutes the principal architectural feature in Local Level III. Multiple deposits that subsequently sealed the destruction debris and accumulated to a depth of over one meter represent two distinct building levels and several related subphases ranging from the early ninth through the early eighth centuries B.C.E. (For a full discussion of the depositional history, see Tappy et al. 2006.)

The destruction of the tenth-century building produced a 0.75-m-thick accumulation of heavily burnt debris that smothered the structure's principal components (figure 2), which include two parallel, stone-built walls (2307/2389 and 2314) joined by a well-built, 2.10-m-wide flagstone floor (2317), and a crosswall (2371) along the southwestern edge of both this room and at least one more chamber to the east (Surface 2378). The debris yielded only a small ceramic assemblage, but fragments from bowls, juglets, and thick-walled kraters typically display a dark-red slip (much darker than that witnessed in subsequent ninth-century deposits) and coarsely spaced, irregular, and discontinuous hand burnishing as well as pattern burnishing on the interior base of some bowls. Importantly, Wall 2307/2389 incorporated a heavy (17.33 kg) limestone boulder with two lines of letters clearly incised on one side and a large, bowl-shaped hollow ground into the other side (Tappy et al. 2006). The twenty-two-letter abecedary dates, on both archaeological and paleographic grounds, to the mid-tenth century and displays the linear alphabetic script of central and southern Canaan at the beginning of the first millennium B.C.E.—a transitional script that developed from the Phoenician tradition of the early Iron Age and anticipated the distinctive features of the mature Hebrew national script of the ninth century B.C.E.

A large monolith (measuring 1.60 m in height and 2.25 m in circumference) that formed part of Wall 2314 undoubtedly belonged to a series of at least nine other such elements, whose exposed tops encircle the perimeter of the summit at an elevation of 172 m. Near Crosswall 2371, a doorway in the monolith wall connected the southeastern corner of the flagstoned chamber to a room with a hard, beaten-earth surface

[18] See the comments on Ussishkin's presentation and analysis of the pottery from Lachish in Dever 2005:83–86.

[19] The report suggests that the final phase of Level IV ended as the result of an earthquake during the reign of King Uzziah, ca. 760 B.C.E. (Ussishkin 2004:1:83).

[20] Excavations have thus far exposed over six vertical meters of remains from the Late Bronze Age I–II periods.

[21] The historical background to this destruction remains uncertain (see Tappy et al. 2006:n. 33).

Figure 2. Tenth-century B.C.E. structure with monolith at Tel Zayit, Square O19 (arrow indicates location of the Tel Zayit abecedary)

(2378). It appears, then, that in the tenth century a tandem series of multiroom structures, punctuated by large upstanding monoliths, encircled the mound and constituted a coherent settlement plan designed, among other possible reasons, for defensive purposes.[22] This belt of houses or small buildings likely enclosed the upper part of the Iron Age IIA town at Tel Zayit in a manner perhaps comparable to the Stratum XII enclosure at Arad, now dated to the pre-fortress period in the second half of the tenth century B.C.E. While these and other "enclosed settlements" may reflect the final stage in a transition from pastoral-nomadic to sedentary lifestyles (see Herzog 2002:18–21, fig. 7; also 86–89), they might also relate to the rise of regional, fortified centers during the Iron I–Iron II transition period in strategic areas such as the Beersheba Valley,[23] the highlands around Jerusalem,[24] and now the Shephelah (as witnessed at Tel Zayit but apparently not at Lachish). Whatever their primary purpose, such sites clearly constituted more than rural villages (Faust 2003:156), and they could easily have assumed significant economic roles both within their respective regions and as part of a larger, transcultural network that benefited from the power of the port outlets. This possibility seems particularly apt for borderland sites such as Tel Zayit, which lay slightly farther west than even Lachish and at the

[22] See the discussion of the origin of this design for fortification purposes and its possible relationship to the evolution of pillared houses in Finkelstein 1988:250–63.

[23] For other possible comparisons at sites in the Beersheba Valley, see Tell Esdar (Stratum III, eleventh century), Beersheba (Stratum VII, late eleventh–tenth centuries), and even Tel Masos (Stratum II, mid-twelfth–mid-eleventh centuries), whose cultural affiliations remain less certain.

[24] Compare Khirbet ed-Dawwara, located northeast of Jerusalem in the territory of Benjamin (see Finkelstein 1988: 64, 262–63; 1990:162–208).

mouth of an important central valley that led down from the most populated portion of the hill country and out to the southern coastal plain.

***The Ninth Century* B.C.E.** According to Ussishkin, not until the period represented by Level IV did Lachish become a strong fortress city, which at its height (Phases b–a) covered ca. 20 acres and reflected "a fully developed kingdom of Judah" (Ussishkin 2004:1:82).[25] That Ussishkin himself, in his expanded discussion of the stratigraphy, allows for the possibility that Level IV had begun already by the late tenth century B.C.E. (Ussishkin 2004:2:417) underscores the tension with his desire elsewhere to lower the date of Level V out of the tenth century. In any event, the construction processes that gave rise to Level IV appear complex and, according to the final report, involved at least four distinct phases (*d*, *c*, *b*, *a*). Although "little is known about the development of Level IV, and most of the information is derived from Area S . . . " (Ussishkin 2004:1:82), the building sequence appears to have unfolded in the following manner. In the initial Phase *d*, a lime-plaster rampart was laid between the palace-fort and the city wall (both of which, therefore, must also have appeared at the very outset of Level IV if, as the report now espouses, they had not already emerged in Level V),[26] but no houses existed in Area S. In Phase *c*, which yielded "the first habitation remains in the area" (Ussishkin 2004:1:83), a debris layer accumulated on the rampart along with some pits. This phase, therefore, seems to reflect some level of occupation but no further significant building projects. In Phase *b*, domestic housing finally appears on top of the debris and adjacent to the city wall. Finally, Phase *a* gave rise to another group of domestic structures. Judging from this proposed sequence, the official buildings appeared first at Iron Age Lachish, and the domestic quarters subsequently grew up around these larger structures during the latter part of Level IV (*b*–*a*). So it seems reasonable to allow some time for Phases *d*–*c* to have developed, especially if the rampart in *d* was laid between an already existing palace-fort and city wall not yet constructed in Level V (according to Ussishkin's interpretation).

Despite "the unusual strength and monumentality of the Level IV fortress city," all the principal structures consisted mostly of roughly dressed blocks and not of fine ashlar masonry, homogeneous but moderate quality mudbricks, beams made of local (olive) wood but not from the cedars of Lebanon, etc. (Ussishkin 2004:1:81–82). In other words, the royal city that emerged gradually over the course of the ninth century boasted impressive fortifications (including a city-gate complex) and a centrally located palace that undoubtedly housed a governor or commander appointed from Jerusalem, but it did not display the kind of cross-cultural contact (either in materials or techniques) seen in other cities (e.g., Gezer, Megiddo, Dan) or in the capitals at Jerusalem and Samaria. In this respect, the planning and construction of Lachish Level IV in the ninth century B.C.E. seems to reflect a strictly regional project that utilized nearby resources and was coordinated from Jerusalem rather quickly and without substantial financial drain. Nevertheless, when considering the founding of Iron Age Lachish in the light of contemporary changes in the material culture at Tel Zayit, it appears that these building projects occurred during a time of significant political change in the principal east-west valleys of the Judean Shephelah.

Following the destruction of Tel Zayit in the late tenth century B.C.E., the city was rebuilt sometime around the turn of the century, and two major building levels ensued over the course of the ninth century B.C.E. The pottery repertoire recovered from the early ninth-century rooms (which lay up to 0.66 m below the late ninth-century levels) fits perfectly into this time period.[27] Importantly, the coastal traditions that appear at Tel Zayit in the late ninth century have not emerged from these early ninth-century deposits, even though some traditions (such as the Ashdod Ware; one-handled jugs) might easily have done so had Tel Zayit already established strong ties to the

[25] Opinions as to the date of the rise of this royal city range from the reign of Rehoboam (Yadin; Dever) to that of Asa (Tufnell) or possibly either Asa or Jehoshaphat (Ussishkin, see 2004:1:79 for references).

[26] Note that this plastering seems related to a similar work along the Outer Revetment Wall, where the plaster covered the foundation trench fills of the wall (Ussishkin 2004:1:79); thus if these plasterings occurred during the first phase of Level IV, it would seem that the walls must also be placed near the outset of this stratum.

[27] Small- to medium-sized red-slipped and hand-burnished bowls, with carination on the upper portion of their sidewalls and with a slight concavity between rim and carination, represent a typical class in this level and parallel Zimhoni's Type B-16 from Level V at Lachish (Zimhoni 1997:96–97, fig. 3.21:9, 11; cf. Tufnell's [1953: 271–72] Class B.5: Types 42–43, 55). At Lachish, the prevalence of this form waned during Level IV. In addition, rounded bowls with thickened, flattened, and slightly inverted rims also appear at both Tel Zayit and Lachish (cf. Zimhoni 1997:fig. 3.11:1, from Lachish Level V), with the red slip extending over the rim and just below the vestigial handles and a combination of irregular and horizontal hand burnishing appearing on the interior and upper exterior portions of the vessels—attributes that likely moved from inland (Judahite/Israelite) sites to the coastal area.

coast during this period. A subsequent repaving of certain areas with cobblestone flooring yielded fragments of short-necked coastal amphora (see below; also Tappy et al. 2006:pl. 1:1) alongside other high-necked storage jars with plain or bulbous rims and drooping shoulders.[28]

Above this cobblestone paving, another significant building period (Local Level I) that dates to the second half of the ninth century appeared across a 100-m² area of Squares N20–O20. The entire area suffered heavy destruction by fire sometime around the last quarter of that century. The principal architectural elements from this stratum consisted in a small room with two storage bins on its northern side (Square N20) and two well-sealed storage pits or cellars built into additional rooms to the east (Square O20). All these features yielded not only numerous restorable vessels that display a mix of inland and coastal forms, but also large deposits of carbonized grain, for which radiocarbon testing at two independent laboratories confirms the late ninth-century date for the destruction of this level. Pottery derived from inland industries and reflecting many attributes that descended from the tenth century B.C.E. includes straight-sided bowls with two handles, smaller bowls with red-to-orangish slip and chordal-horizontal hand burnishing, various juglet forms, a small four-handled krater with numerous large calcite grits, and a globular jar with wide throat, two handles from central neck ridge to shoulder area, rounded bulbous rim, and coarse vertical burnishing (for a fuller discussion, see Tappy et al. 2006). These same contexts, however, also yielded a series of one-handled jugs[29] and well-preserved examples of Ashdod Ware—traditions that reflect a clear increase in coastal connections. Another storage area in O20 held more than twenty whole or partial clay fermentation stoppers similar in design to those found at other sites in Israel starting as early as the late tenth century B.C.E.[30] These items hint at Tel Zayit's ability to produce and contribute wine to any economic network with which it became involved.[31]

The matrix (sub-Phase 1) that lay directly above the destruction of Local Level I belongs to the late ninth and early eighth centuries. It yielded a large, globular-shaped jug and multiple whole examples of the large, oval-shaped amphorae mentioned above. Though these jars appear at other inland sites,[32] they clearly have a coastal origin (see Zimhoni 1990:3–52, esp. 25–26 and fig. 17:4, Group IIID; also Gitin 1998:171, fig. 5:4) and are prominent in late Iron II levels at Ekron, Ashdod, and Ashkelon. Medium-sized, deep cooking pots with sharply protruding ridges on the exterior of their rims represent other diagnostic coastal attributes attested at Tel Zayit in the late ninth and early eighth centuries[33] (Tappy et al. 2006:pl. 2:4).

The overall assemblage from the second half of the ninth century B.C.E., then, is not exclusively inland or coastal in this period; rather, it shows connections in both directions—a situation that would surely characterize a mid-level, transitional-market town functioning in a port-power economic system. It is historically significant that this opening of exchange with the coastal area occurs at a time when Tel Zayit appears to have experienced strained relations with Judah. According to 2 Kings 8:22 (cf. 2 Chron. 21:10), Libnah along with Edom revolted against Judah during the reign of Jehoram (848–841 B.C.E.), son of Jehoshaphat. This realignment may have had many root causes, including local reaction against the perceived negative impact of the recent reforms made by Jehoshaphat (see Tappy 2000:332–33); the current

[28] The latter form resembles Zimhoni's SJ-1 class, which is heavily attested in Lachish V–IV but which disappears by Level III (see Zimhoni 1997:131, fig. 3.46).

[29] These jugs find close parallels in type JG-11 at Tel Batash. (See A. Mazar and Panitz-Cohen 2001:110–12 for a full discussion and comparative evidence from Ashdod Strata X–VII and Tel Batash Strata IV–II.) They represent a coastal tradition that appeared in the tenth and ninth centuries B.C.E., experienced a floruit in the eighth century, and remained a common form in the seventh century (though with noticeable nuances in both body and rim styles). For parallels from Tell eṣ-Ṣâfi, see Shai and Maeir 2003:110, 112, fig. 2. Compare also Gitin 1998:170, fig. 4:6–7.

[30] Compare the tenth-century examples from Ḥorvat Rosh Zayit and Tell el-Ḥammeh (Gal 1989:281–83; Cahill, Tarler, and Lipovich 1989:36–37 [Hebrew]) with later ones from Ashkelon (see Weiss and Kislev 2004:36). See also the comments regarding stoppers from Lachish Level III in Ussishkin 2004:4:1791.

[31] The overall assemblage recovered from this late ninth-century destruction layer finds excellent parallels in the contemporaneous destruction level at Tell eṣ-Ṣâfi (see Maeir 2001). Both events may have constituted part of a broader drive through this region by Hazael (2 Kings 12: 17–18) following the relaxation of Assyrian pressure against Damascus from the mid-830s on (see above for several other options). For a summary of the campaigns against Syria and the West by Shalmaneser III between 853 and 834 B.C.E., see Tappy 2001:507–16.

[32] E.g., Lachish (Y. Aharoni 1975:SJ 230, pl. 48:9, 16; Level II) and Arad (M. Aharoni 1981:181–204, fig. 9:5; Stratum XI). At Arad, these jars do not continue past Stratum XI.

[33] Gitin 1998:170, fig. 4:12. Compare A. Mazar and Panitz-Cohen 2001:pl. 103:18(?) (Stratum III); pls. 34:8, 12; 43:2–7; 65:11; 72:5; 96:14; 104:11 (Stratum II); see also their discussion of type CP 10 on pp. 86–87.

conflict between Jerusalem and Edom and the ensuing deployment of the Judahite army to the battle at Zair (see Cogan and Tadmor 1988:96–97); the resultant and opportunistic assault against Judah's western frontier by the Philistines and Arab tribes from Ethiopia (2 Chron. 21:16–17; cf. 2 Chron. 17:11; see Japhet 1993:814–16);[34] even the recent preference shown by Jerusalem for the development of Lachish to the south; or Tel Zayit's own economic interest in participating in the larger trade network managed by the coastal sites.[35] In any event, circumstances during the last half of the ninth century clearly provided a historical occasion for Tel Zayit to cultivate new avenues of contact, and if this site itself is not ancient Libnah,[36] it surely lay close enough to Libnah to have followed its lead in cultural, political, and economic matters.

The material culture recovered thus far from this period at Tel Zayit provides a clear example of a borderland site that maintained appreciable, although perhaps somewhat compromised, contacts with its political center to the east, while simultaneously associating itself with the open, international markets and ports to the west. Even though Tel Zayit was reestablished in the early-to-mid-tenth century B.C.E. and, presumably, was then capable of participating in a port-power type of economic network with the now fewer but larger highland towns, the site shows no signs of coastal contact until the mid-ninth century, when an appreciable number of Iron II rural villages that could contribute to such a network had reappeared in the hill country of Judah. The renewed settlement at Iron Age Lachish, on the other hand, reveals a "drastic reduction in commercial and cultural connections with the Coastal Plain" (Ussishkin 2004: 1:93) throughout the ninth and eighth centuries B.C.E., when the pottery assemblage displays very few coastal forms or traits. Ussishkin attributes this decline (which contrasts with the situation during the Late Bronze Age) to the fact that "during Levels IV–III the city-states of Philistia dominated the coastal area, while Judean Lachish was politically and economically oriented towards Jerusalem" (ibid.). Whatever the case, the decline certainly suggests that Lachish, even during its heyday, made no attempt to play a key role in Ashkelon's broader economic network, while Tel Zayit did. Not until Level II in the seventh century does the pottery assemblage from Lachish show an appreciable number of coastal-type vessels, but even then the data are too meager to confirm the existence of clear trade relations between this Judahite city and the coastal region (Ussishkin 2004:1:94).

The analysis of excavation data from Tel Zayit remains in the early stages, and the final report from Lachish will surely generate further discussion, particularly regarding the current interpretation of Level V.[37] Yet a comparison of the material culture from these two sites, an understanding of the terrain in the Shephelah and the access routes leading through the region, and an analysis of settlement patterns in the Judean hill country based on both survey and excavation data combine to give the impression that the centrally located Libnah Valley (Naḥal Guvrin)—even more than the Lachish Valley to the south—held the greatest potential to serve as a facilitator in any port-power economic system that may have arisen at Ashkelon during the Iron Age II.

---

[34] The possible historical connection between the Arab tribes and the army under the command of Zerah the Ethiopian (2 Chron. 14:9–15) a century earlier is tantalizing but impossible to confirm.

[35] It seems less likely that Libnah had "kept its Canaanite character [from the Late Bronze Age] and was not absorbed into the Judaean kingdom," with the consequence that its Iron II occupants considered "Judaean rule as foreign" (see Japhet 1993:811).

[36] The only other viable option in the Guvrin Valley for ancient Libnah is Tell Bûrnah, located ca. 4 km east of Tel Zayit (see Aharoni 1979:86, 279, 332, 353, 403, 439; for a brief survey of proposed identifications, see J. L. Peterson 1992:322–23). But Bûrnah has not undergone excavation, so reliable data are not currently available. Tel Zayit, on the other hand, has now revealed over six vertical meters of Late Bronze Age remains followed by important occupational levels and artifacts (including a fully developed alphabet) starting in the tenth century B.C.E. Judging from the site's unexpectedly large size, strategic location at the outer reaches of a recorded political district (Josh. 15:42–44), and far-reaching commercial ties, Tel Zayit now presents a viable candidate in the search to locate ancient Libnah. If further excavation and research support this suggested identification, it seems possible that Tell Bûrnah represents ancient Ether and that the name itself shifted to nearby Khirbet el-ᶜAtr—located only 1.5 km south and 0.5 km east of Bûrnah—at some later period (personal communication with A. Rainey). (For the common occurrence of the transferring of names from late villages in the Shephelah to nearby tells, see Rainey 1980:197.) Libnah and Ether head the city list for District 4 in Josh. 15:42 in a way that accords with Tel Zayit's and Tell Bûrnah's leading into the Guvrin Valley from the west.

[37] Compare, for example, King 2005:36–47 and Dever 2005:83–86. Both authors prefer to keep Level V, with the first Judean palace-fort, in the tenth century B.C.E. and to attribute the destruction of this stratum to the invasion by Pharaoh Sheshonq (Shishak) around 925 B.C.E. (cf. Mazar and Panitz-Cohen 2001:275).

Bibliography

Aharoni, M.
1981 The Pottery of Strata 12–11 of the Iron Age Citadel at Arad [in Hebrew]. *EI* 15:181–204.

Aharoni, Y.
1975 *Investigations at Lachish: The Sanctuary and the Residency (Lachish V)*. Tel Aviv: Gateway.
1979 *The Land of the Bible: A Historical Geography*, Translated by A. F. Rainey. 2d ed. Philadelphia: Westminster.

Bloch, M. L. B.
1953 *The Historian's Craft*. Translated by P. Putnam. New York: Knopf.
1974 *Apologie pour l'histoire ou Métier d'historien*. Paris: Colin.
1995 *Histoire et historiens*. Paris: Colin.

Braudel, F.
1972 *The Mediterranean and the Mediterranean World in the Age of Philip II*. Translated by Siân Reynolds. 2 vols. New York: Harper and Row.
1980 *On History*. Translated by S. Matthews. Chicago: University of Chicago Press.

Bronson, B.
1977 Exchange at the Upstream and Downstream Ends: Notes Toward a Functional Model of the Coastal State in Southeast Asia. In *Economic Exchange and Social Interaction in Southeast Asia: Perspectives from Prehistory, History, and Ethnography*, ed. K. L. Hutterer, 39–52. Ann Arbor, Mich.: Center for South and Southeast Asian Studies, University of Michigan.

Bunimovitz, S.
1994 Socio-Political Transformations in the Central Hill Country in the Late Bronze–Iron I Transition. In *From Nomadism to Monarchy: Archaeological and Historical Aspects of Early Israel*, ed. I. Finkelstein and N. Naʾaman, 179–202. Jerusalem: Israel Exploration Society.

Cahill, J., D. Tarler, and G. Lipovich
1989 Tell el-Hammah in the Tenth Century B.C.E. [in Hebrew]. *Qadmoniot* 85–86:33–38.

Cogan, M., and H. Tadmor
1988 *II Kings: A New Translation with Introduction and Commentary*. AB 11. New York: Doubleday.

Dever, W. G.
2005 Review of *The Renewed Archaeological Excavations at Lachish (1973–1994)*, by D. Ussishkin. *BASOR* 340:83–86.

Dorsey, D. A.
1991 *The Roads and Highways of Ancient Israel*. Baltimore: Johns Hopkins University Press.

Faust, A.
2003 Abandonment, Urbanization, Resettlement and the Formation of the Israelite State. *NEA* 66: 147–61.

Faust, A., and E. Weiss
2005 Judah, Philistia, and the Mediterranean World: Reconstructing the Economic System of the Seventh Century B.C.E. *BASOR* 338:71–92.

Finkelstein, I.
1988 *The Archaeology of the Israelite Settlement*. Translated by D. Saltz. Jerusalem: Israel Exploration Society.
1990 Excavation at Khirbet ed-Dawwara: An Iron Age Site Northeast of Jerusalem. *Tel Aviv* 17:163–208.
2005 [De]formation of the Israelite State: A Rejoinder on Methodology. *NEA* 68:202–8.

Fox, R. G.
1977 *Urban Anthropology: Cities in Their Cultural Settings*. Englewood Cliffs, N.J.: Prentice-Hall.

Gal, Z.
1989 Loom Weights or Jar Stoppers? *IEJ* 39:281–83.

Gitin, S.
1998 Philistia in Transition: The Tenth Century B.C.E. and Beyond. In *Mediterranean Peoples in Transition: Thirteen to Early Tenth Centuries B.C.E.*, ed. S. Gitin, A. Mazar, and E. Stern, 162–83. Jerusalem: Israel Exploration Society.

Hall, K. R.
1985 *Maritime Trade and State Development in Early Southeast Asia*. Honolulu: University of Hawaii Press.

Herzog, Z.
2002 The Fortress Mound at Tel Arad: An Interim Report. *Tel Aviv* 29:3–109.

Japhet, S.
1993 *I and II Chronicles: A Commentary*. The Old Testament Library. Louisville, Ky.: Westminster/John Knox.

King, P. J.
2005 Why Lachish Matters: A Major Site Gets the Publication It Deserves. *BAR* 31/4:36–47.

Kloner, A.
1993 Beth Guvrin. In *The New Encyclopedia of Archaeological Excavations in the Holy Land*, ed. E. Stern, 1:195–201. New York: Simon and Schuster.

Maeir, A. M.
2001 The Philistine Culture in Transformation: A Current Perspective Based on the Results of the First Seasons of Excavations at Tell eṣ-Ṣâfi/Gath [in Hebrew]. In *Settlement, Civilization and Culture: Proceedings of the Conference in Memory of David Alon*, ed. A. M. Maeir and E. Baruch, 111–29. Ramat-Gan, Israel: Bar-Ilan University.

Mazar, A., and N. Panitz-Cohen
2001 *Timnah (Tell Batash)*. Vol. 2, *The Finds from the First Millennium B.C.E.* 2 vols. Qedem 42. Jerusalem: Institute of Archaeology, Hebrew University.

Mazar, B.
1960 The Cities of the Priests and the Levites. VTSup 7:193–205. Leiden: Brill.

Naʾaman, N.
1986 *Borders and Districts in Biblical Historiography: Seven Studies in Biblical Geographic Lists.* Jerusalem Biblical Studies 4. Jerusalem: Simor.

Ofer, A.
1994 "All the Hill Country of Judah": From a Settlement Fringe to a Prosperous Monarchy. In *From Nomadism to Monarchy: Archaeological and Historical Aspects of Early Israel*, ed. I. Finkelstein and N. Naʾaman, 92–121. Jerusalem: Israel Exploration Society.

Peterson, J. L.
1992 Libnah. In *The Anchor Bible Dictionary*, ed. D. N. Freedman, 4:322–23. New York: Doubleday.

Rainey, A. F.
1980 The Administrative Division of the Shephelah. *Tel Aviv* 7:194–202.
1983 The Biblical Shephelah of Judah. *BASOR* 251:1–22.

Shai, I., and A. M. Maeir
2003 Pre-*LMLK* Jars: A New Class of Iron Age IIA Storage Jars. *Tel Aviv* 30/1:108–23.

Stager, L. E.
1996 Ashkelon and the Archaeology of Destruction: Kislev 604 B.C.E. *EI* 25:*61–*74.
2001 Port Power in the Early and the Middle Bronze Age: The Organization of Maritime Trade and Hinterland Production. In *Studies in the Archaeology of Israel and Neighboring Lands in Memory of Douglas L. Esse*, ed. S. R. Wolff, 625–38. SAOC 59. Chicago: Oriental Institute, University of Chicago.
2003 The Patrimonial Kingdom of Solomon. In *Symbiosis, Symbolism, and the Power of the Past: Canaan, Ancient Israel, and Their Neighbors from the Late Bronze Age through Roman Palaestina*, ed. W. G. Dever and S. Gitin, 63–74. Winona Lake, Ind.: Eisenbrauns.

Tappy, R. E.
2000 The Code of Kinship in the Ten Commandments. *RB* 107:321–37.
2001 *The Archaeology of Israelite Samaria.* Vol. 2, *The Eighth Century B.C.E.* HSS 50. Winona Lake, Ind.: Eisenbrauns.

Tappy, R. E., P. K. McCarter, M. Lundberg, and B. Zuckerman
2006 An Abecedary of the Mid-Tenth Century B.C.E. from the Judaean Shephelah. *BASOR* 344:5–46.

Tufnell, O.
1953 *Lachish.* Vol. 3, *The Iron Age*. London: Oxford University Press.

Ussishkin, D.
1978 Excavations at Tel Lachish, 1973–1977: Preliminary Report. *Tel Aviv* 5:1–97.
2004 *The Renewed Archaeological Excavations at Lachish (1973–1994).* 5 vols. Tel Aviv: Institute of Archaeology, Tel Aviv University.

Weiss, E., and M. E. Kislev
2004 Weeds and Seeds: What Archaeobotany Can Teach Us. *BAR* 30/6:32–37.

Wolters, O. W.
1979 Studying Srivijaya. *Journal of the Malaysian Branch of the Royal Asiatic Society* 52/2:1–38.

Zimhoni, O.
1990 Two Ceramic Assemblages from Lachish Levels III and II. *Tel Aviv* 17:3–52.
1997 *Studies in the Iron Age Pottery of Israel: Typological, Archaeological, and Chronological Aspects.* Tel Aviv: Institute of Archaeology, Tel Aviv University.

45. The Books of the Hebrew Bible As Material Artifacts

by Karel van der Toorn

Most of us think of the Bible as a book, or a collection of books. Naturally so: the very name of the Bible goes back to the Greek word for "books" (*biblia*).[1] Jewish writers refer to the Hebrew Scriptures as "the books" (Dan. 9:2) or "the holy books" (1 Macc. 12:9) from the second century B.C.E. onward.[2] This has since become the accepted view of the Bible. It informs rabbinical discussions on the order and the authors of the biblical books, and explains our custom of speaking of the "Book of Genesis," the "Book of Isaiah," and the "Book of Job."

However old and widespread the notion of the Bible as a series of books may be, though, it is a misleading concept. The books of the Bible are not books in the modern sense of the word; to see them as such distorts the historical reality. There were no books in ancient Israel. Books are a Hellenistic invention, born in a time of increasing literacy as schools and libraries spread around the Mediterranean and in the Near East. Since the bulk of the Bible predates the Hellenistic era, calling it a collection of books is an anachronism.

In this tribute to Larry Stager—once one of my masters admired from a distance, now for many years an esteemed colleague to be honored as a friend—I will look at some material aspects of the production of the biblical books.

The Cost of Written Texts

To most modern-day readers, a book is a physical object that you buy in a bookstore, carry home in a bag, read, and put on a bookshelf together with your other books. A book can cost less than a good meal and be manageable enough to hold in one hand even if it is 500 pages long. The differences between books nowadays and writing in antiquity are important to identify because they affect our idea of the Bible as a book. Two differences are particularly important: the first concerns the labor involved in text production; the second pertains to the nature of the writing materials.

The origins of the modern book culture go back to the advent of the printing press. Until then, books were made by hand; they were labor intensive, so the production costs were high. Since writing materials were expensive, too, books were beyond the reach of an ordinary individual reader. Only when books came to be mass-produced did they become a relatively cheap commodity. The offer created the demand and triggered the development of a new reading culture. As long as written texts were relatively rare, there was little incentive for literacy.

Quite instructive of the situation before the invention of the printing press are the production circumstances of medieval books (Rousse and Rousse 2000).[3] A copyist in Paris needed, as a rule, one day for every two pages (or four columns) he wrote, which amounted to about four months for a substantial book (Shooner 1988:19–20). Book prices varied widely depending on the manuscript in question: the richly illuminated luxury books were at one end of the continuum; excerpts for the use of students at the other. By modern standards, however, prices were often prohibitive; a book was indeed a treasure. To the extent that the high cost of books failed to prevent a robust and flourishing trade, the latter was confined to the upper social classes. The possession of manuscripts was a sign of affluence and learning.

Compared to the prices of medieval books, the cost of written texts in the ancient Near East was low. Let us first look at the situation in ancient Mesopotamia. The clay the scribes wrote on was free; the production costs of works like the Epic of Gilgamesh were simply labor costs. In the ancient Near East, there were no books as we know them today, but scribes did produce book-length texts. The standard version of the Epic of Gilgamesh is about 3,000 lines long. Modern experiments by Assyriologists who have tried writing cuneiform themselves suggest that the ancient scribes would have needed less than a minute per line. This means that copying the entire Gilgamesh text would have taken no more than fifty working hours—probably less.

---

[1] From *biblion*, derived from *biblos*, originally the Greek name for the papyrus plant; hence "papyrus roll," hence "book."

[2] 1 Macc. 12:9 uses the expression *ta biblia ta hagia*; 2 Macc. 8:23 speaks about *hē hiera biblos*, "the holy book," presumably in reference to the Pentateuch. Note also the reference to "the ancestral books" (*tōn* [...] *patriōn bibliōn*) in the Prologue to Ben Sira (ca. 140 B.C.E.). Around 100 C.E., Josephus speaks about "our books (*biblia*)" (*Contra Apionem* 1.38).

[3] For a useful introduction to the subject, see Bataillon et al. 1988.

An actual indication of the time involved in writing cuneiform tablets can be gleaned from the colophons of the Old Babylonian copies of Atraḫasis from Sippar. One Nūr-Aya copied the tablets while he was a junior scribe: tablet two on Shebat 28 in the eleventh year of Ammiṣaduqa; tablet one on Nisan 21, the next year; and tablet three in the month Iyyar of that same year (Lambert and Millard 1969:31–32; Hunger 1968:nos. 13–15). He probably wrote the copies in his spare time, since the twenty-first and the twenty-eighth of the month were holidays (Landsberger 1915:119–26). It demonstrates that a single day was all that was needed to produce a tablet of over 400 lines (Lambert and Millard 1969:32). Based on this evidence, a copy of Gilgamesh would require less than two weeks of work.

Since colophons often indicate the total number of lines on a tablet, it has been speculated that copyists were paid by the line (Hunger 1968:2). However, there is no attendant evidence to support this assumption. In the third millennium B.C.E., scribes received the same monthly wage as other male workers. By the first millennium, their social status had risen and their remuneration was above average. Assuming that work as a scribe paid about twice as much as most other professions, a complete copy of Gilgamesh would have cost a month's wages of an average worker. The fact that scribes sometimes donated a copy to the temple library as a votive gift shows that these tablets were regarded as valuable; however, these tablets were not beyond the means of a well-to-do citizen.

It may come as somewhat of a surprise, therefore, to find that the Babylonians were unfamiliar with the phenomenon of a trade in books—or a trade in written tablets, if we want to avoid anachronistic terms. Some scribes did have private libraries, but they acquired their texts by copying them from mother copies in the temple library. Such copying was traditionally left to the younger members of scribal families. Tablet collectors did not purchase texts for money. The case of Nūr-Aya, patiently copying Atraḫasis tablets in his spare time, is exemplary. Even Aššurbanipal, to whom we owe the largest cuneiform library of the past, did not accumulate his tablets by purely commercial means. He had his servants confiscate tablets and ordered copies from his scribes (Lanfranchi 1998; Fincke 2003–2004; Fincke 2004; Frame and George 2005). The latter acquisition method might be called a form of buying—after all, scribes were entitled to an income—but the tablet production was on command. A free market in cuneiform tablets did not exist.

The situation in respect to the Hebrew Bible differs only in the later periods. The earliest references to the buying and selling of Hebrew scrolls are from the Roman period (Blau 1902:188–94). Price is rarely mentioned. However, one rabbinic tractate from the late Second Temple period states that the price of a Torah scroll was 100 mineh, which equals 10,000 pieces of silver (Zlotnick 1966:70, lines 45–47). Considering the fact that the average laborer earned one piece of silver a day, this price is exorbitant (Matt. 20:2; b. ᶜAbod. Zar. 62a; Sperber 1991:101–2). This could just be an exaggeration, as in the Book of Acts, where the author values the books of the magicians at Ephesus at 50,000 pieces of silver (Acts 19:19).

Reference to a more reasonable price for a written scroll is found in the Talmud story about a widow whose only possessions were "a woolen blanket, one Psalms scroll, and a tattered scroll with Job and Proverbs" (*b. Giṭṭin* 35a)—estimated value: 5 mineh, which equals 500 pieces of silver. Judging by this anecdote, a brand new scroll of Isaiah would have a cost about 200 pieces of silver—more than six months' income. Another Talmudic tale tells about a thief selling a stolen Torah (referred to in the story as "the book," *sprᵓ*) for 80 pieces of silver; the receiver sells it to a third party for 120 pieces, thus pocketing over 30 percent profit (*b. Baba Qamma* 115a). This price seems realistic.

If the rabbinic references are of limited value in determining the price of written scrolls, they do show that there was a modest trade in written texts by the beginning of the Common Era. Because Jewish scribes used leather, papyrus, or parchment as writing material, scrolls were likely to be more costly than cuneiform tablets. Papyrus was the least expensive writing material, although the practice of recycling written scrolls indicates that none of the writing materials was cheap.[4] The cost of a papyrus scroll in antiquity is estimated to be equivalent to one to two weeks' wages of an ordinary worker (Lewis 1974: 129–34, esp. 133).[5] This means that the cost of the writing material was higher than the cost of writing (Skeat 1982:175). In Roman times, the price of papyrus fell once the state monopoly on papyrus ended and Palestine was able to control its own papyrus

---

[4] As Černý (1952:23) remarks: "These frequent palimpsests can best be explained if we assume that papyrus was relatively expensive material."

[5] On the cost of papyrus, see also Hans-Joachim Drexhage (1991:384–89), Lewis (1986:51, 54–55); Hezser (2001: 132–33). Cribiore (1996: 59) argues that papyrus was not very costly in Roman Egypt—witness the fact that writing exercises often have blank areas.

production (Préaux 1939:187–96; Theophrastus, *Historia Plantarum* 4.8.4; Josephus, *Bellum Judaicum* 1.130 = *Aniquities of the Jews* 14.33). On the other hand, the Qumran scrolls show that, for the classic texts, scribes would use the more expensive parchment.

The income of a Jewish copyist was above average. In *Ecclesiastes Rabbah* (*Midrash Qohelet* 2.17), Rabbi Meir states that a good scribe could earn two pieces of silver a day, which was twice the average wage of an ordinary worker. Add to this the cost of the writing material, previously estimated at two weeks' wages, and the production costs of an Isaiah scroll would have been about a month's wages (30 pieces of silver)—assuming a trained scribe would need one week to copy the text. Thirty pieces is considerably less than the 200 pieces of silver estimated on the basis of the Talmud passage discussed earlier. Is the difference to be explained by the use of a more costly writing material? We know nothing of the margins of profit, but it may have constituted a considerable part of the price. The eunuch reading Isaiah on his way back to Ethiopia probably purchased the scroll during his visit to Jerusalem (Acts 8:26–40); what he paid, we do not know.

It seems highly improbable that there should have been a trade in scrolls before the Hellenistic era. The evidence at our disposal only documents a book trade from the Roman period onward. Even then, however, written scrolls were not cheap. The duty for each Jewish man to own a Torah copy was a stimulus to the process of copying, but it did not lead to the widespread acquisition of texts; it was not until the third century C.E. that private possession of a Torah became common among Jews. For most of them, a Torah scroll was the only written text they possessed and was acquired at considerable cost. The trade in texts other than the Torah was confined to scribal circles and to the upper strata of society in which literacy had become a matter of course.[6]

The Codex and the Scroll

There is another aspect of writing in ancient Israel which illustrates that the books of the Bible cannot be seen as books in the modern sense of the word. The format of the modern book goes back to the codex. A codex consists of a group of papyrus or parchment sheets, folded in the middle, and stitched at the back to hold them together. It was invented in late antiquity; the first example is from the late first century C.E. (Skeat 1969:71). By 300 C.E., the codex became as common as the scroll and then took over as the use of the latter rapidly diminished (Roberts and Skeat 1983:35–37).

Modern editions of the Hebrew Bible are in the form of a book and thus display the format of a codex. In fact, the success of the codex was due in large part to its use in recording the sacred scriptures of Christianity (Skeat 1969:69–72). In the period of the Second Temple, however, the Bible was still a collection of scrolls—not a codex. One might conceivably argue that the difference is merely one of physical format. Although the Bible started as a series of scrolls, it could still be considered as a single book with regard to its content. But was it? This immediately raises the problem of the order of the books of the Bible. If the books were originally scrolls, their order in the codex is arbitrary to some degree. Unless their sequence was indicated by the use of catchlines, in conformity with Mesopotamian practice, the decision to put Lamentations right after Jeremiah or to relegate it to the Writings belonged to the editors of a particular codex.[7]

More important, perhaps, than the sequence of the scrolls are the constraints imposed by the use of papyrus and scrolls on writers, editors, and readers. Three observations are in order: the first concerns the writers of the time; the second, the editors; and the third, the readers and users of the text.

(1) Among modern writers, we can distinguish those who conceive their text while writing as opposed to those who only write once they have their text in mind. The former category has increased since the introduction of the electronic word processor. In antiquity, authors normally composed their text before they wrote it down. There is evidence of the use by Hebrew scribes of potsherds for making notes and rough drafts (see, e.g., Renz 1995:57–59). Mesopotamian scribes used clay tablets and wax-covered boards for a similar purpose (Weidner 1932–33:176; Jacobsen 1982:134; Cogan 1991:125–27). On the whole, however, scribes were trained to produce stock phrases from memory and to compose their text before they committed it to papyrus. The scroll served as the repository of a completed text. The

[6] On private possession of scrolls among Jews in the Roman period, see also the insightful observations by Günter Stemberger (1996).

[7] The earliest illustrations of a conventional order of the biblical books are extant in the canonical lists from the second century C.E. onwards. Nahum M. Sarna (1971) argues that the order of the biblical books in *b. Baba Batra* 15a mirrors the arrangement of the scrolls on the shelves of a library. In fact, the order follows the presumed chronology by author, as Louis Jacobs (1991:34) has shown.

composition of a text normally preceded its fixation in writing.[8]

(2) The use of papyrus scrolls as writing material has yet another consequence for its written content. If the codex corresponds to a book, the scroll corresponds to a storage room. In the first case, the length of the composition determines the size of the book; in the second, the volume of the scroll sets limits on the volume of text that can be accommodated. The standard scroll had twenty sheets of papyrus, which meant an average length of 340 cm. A longer scroll required forty, sixty, or even more sheets; the gain in volume was to the detriment of user-friendliness. A scroll of ten meters (sixty sheets) was at the limit of practicability (Skeat 1982:170; Hicks 1983:62–65). A scroll of that size was not long enough for Samuel, Kings, or Chronicles. The reason that we now have a first and second book of Samuel, Kings, and Chronicles, respectively, is because these texts were too long for one scroll. Conceptually, Samuel and Kings belong together as one work—or a single collection. Their division into four scrolls—or four "books" in our Bibles—is directly related to the constraints of the writing material. The same is true for Chronicles, Ezra, and Nehemiah.[9]

The division of a larger work over two or more scrolls is one consequence of the size of a scroll; but the reverse also applies. Scribes used to write down a number of smaller compositions on one scroll for purposes of economy. A case in point is the scroll of the Twelve Minor Prophets; in the rabbinic tradition, the twelve compositions came to be known as one book rather than as twelve (though they kept being referred to as "the Twelve"). These examples of division and combination illustrate scribal procedures that may lie behind other books of the Bible as well. Thus, the conjunction of the First and the Second Isaiah (conventionally referred to as "Deutero-Isaiah"), to give an example, could have been inspired for reasons of economy more than by putative authorship. To sum up: the boundaries of the literary composition are not by definition coterminous with the boundaries of the scroll. A scroll is not a book.

(3) The scroll differs from the book in yet another sense. To us, books are not merely works of entertainment, instruction, and meditation, but also works of reference. We are accustomed to quotations that are precise, with reference to author, title, and page. Scrolls do not easily lend themselves to such references. Unwinding a whole scroll to find a single passage is cumbersome and accelerates the process of wear and tear. That is why quotations in biblical literature, as among Greek and Roman authors, are often from memory. Inaccuracies are not uncommon, and the reference to the author or the scroll (assuming the two are distinguished) is very general.[10] The scroll served as a deposit-box of the text; for daily use, people consulted their memory.

To speak about the books of the Bible is misleading on more than one account. Historically, the Hebrew Bible is a collection of scrolls, and scrolls cannot be simply equated with books. The difference between the two is not merely a matter of form, but affects the mode of writing, editorial strategies, and the way in which readers use the text.

The Stream of Tradition

In his *Introduction to the Greek Tragedy*, Ulrich von Wilamowitz defines a book as a text published by its author through the medium of an organized book trade for the benefit of an expectant public (Wilamowitz-Möllendorff 1907:121–28). By this definition, the term "book" is an anachronism when applied to the Hebrew Bible.

Prior to the advent of Hellenism, the only text that was disseminated by means of "an organized book trade" was the Egyptian Book of the Dead. This text, however, was not written by a single author. Moreover, to speak of "an expectant public" is something of a euphemism. A copy of the Book of the Dead was purchased in order to place it in the tomb alongside the mummified deceased so that the latter might be protected from harm and reach the hereafter unscathed. This "book" was not meant for reading. In other words, the only ancient Near Eastern "book" for which there was a real market, in fact, served as an amulet (Černý 1952:26–27). In this respect, it is comparable to the Song of Erra, which served a somewhat similar purpose in warding off pestilence. No other text from Mesopotamia was copied as often as Erra—not because it was in

[8] Compare the oral creation of written texts in Egypt, for which see the illuminating observations by Donald B. Redford (2000:205).

[9] Note the use of a "catch-line" in 2 Chron. 36:22–23 = Ezra 1:1–2 to signal the fact that the separate scrolls belong to one work (see Blau 1902:58 and Haran 1985: 5–11).

[10] See Reynolds and Wilson (1974:2): "It is not difficult to imagine that an ancient reader faced with the need to verify a quotation or check a reference would rely if possible on his memory of the passage rather than go to the trouble of unwinding the roll and perhaps thereby accelerating the process of wear and tear. This would certainly account for the fact that when one ancient author quotes another there is so often a substantial difference between the two versions."

demand by a reading public, but because a carefully positioned copy would keep all sorts of evil at bay (Reiner 1960).

Aside from the Book of the Dead, then, there was no "book" trade in the ancient Near East; nor was there a reading public of any substance; nor were there books as we know them. One might, for the sake of argument, qualify Gilgamesh and Isaiah as the books of antiquity, but they are books only in a manner of speaking. Not only are the tablets of Gilgamesh and the scroll of Isaiah dissimilar in form to books, the text they contain does not conform to the concept of literature that is implied by the modern notion of a book. These book-length texts come from an oral culture and retain the characteristics of that culture. No one wrote books the way people write books in the modern age. The first books are only from the Hellenistic era.[11]

[11] Compare the statement of Pfeiffer (1968–76:1:102): "[T]he book is one of the characteristic signs of the new, the Hellenistic world."

Bibliography

Bataillon, L. J., B. G. Guyot, and R. H. Rouse, eds.
1988 *La production du livre universitaire au Moyen Age: Exemplar et pecia; Actes du symposium tenu au Collegio San Bonaventura de Grottaferrata en mai 1983*. Paris: Éditions du Centre national de la recherche scientifique.

Blau, L.
1902 *Studien zum althebräischen Buchwesen und zur biblischen Literaturgeschichte*. Budapest: Landes-Rabbinerschule in Budapest.

Černý, J.
1952 *Paper and Books in Ancient Egypt*. London: Lewis.

Cogan, M.
1991 A Plaidoyer on Behalf of the Royal Scribes. In *Ah Assyria...: Studies in Assyrian History and Ancient Near Eastern Historiography Presented to Hayim Tadmor*, ed. M.Cogan and I. Eph^c^al, 121–28. Scripta Hierosolymitana 33. Jerusalem: Magnes.

Cribiore, R.
1996 *Writing, Teachers, and Students in Graeco-Roman Egypt*. American Studies in Papyrology 36. Atlanta: Scholars.

Drexhage, H.-J.
1991 *Preise, Mieten/Pachten, Kosten und Löhne im römischen Ägypten bis zum Regierungsantritt Diokletians*. Vorarbeiten zu einer Wirtschaftsgeschichte des römischen Ägypten 1. St. Katharinen: Scripta Mercaturae.

Fincke, J. C.
2003 The British Museum's Ashurbanipal Library Project. *Iraq* 66:55–60.
2003–4 The Babylonian Texts of Nineveh: Report on the British Museum's Ashurbanipal Library Project. *AfO* 50:111–49.

Frame, G., and A. R. George
2005 The Royal Libraries of Nineveh: New Evidence for King Ashurbanipal's Tablet Collecting. *Iraq* 67:265–84.

Haran, M.
1985 Book-Size and the Device of Catch-Lines in the Biblical Canon. *Journal of Jewish Studies* 36:1–11.

Hezser, C.
2001 *Jewish Literacy in Roman Palestine*. Texte und Studien zum antiken Judentum 81. Tübingen: Mohr Siebeck.

Hicks, R. L.
1983 *Delet* and *m^e^gillāh*: A Fresh Approach to Jeremiah xxxvi.*VT* 33:46–66.

Hunger, H.
1968 *Babylonische und assyrische Kolophone*. AOAT 2. Kevelaer, Germany: Butzon and Bercker.

Jacobs, L.
1991 Rabbinic Views on the Order and Authorship of the Biblical Books. In *Structure and Form in the Babylonian Talmud*, by L. Jacobs, 31–41. Cambridge: Cambridge University Press.

Jacobsen, T.
1982 Oral to Written. In *Societies and Languages of the Ancient Near East: Studies in Honor of I. M. Diakonoff*, ed. M. A. Dandamayev, I. Gershevitch, H. Klengel, G. Komoróczy, M. T. Larsen, and J. N. Postgate, 129–37. Warminster, England: Aris and Phillips.

Lambert, W. G., and A. R. Millard
1969 *Atra-Ḫasīs: The Babylonian Story of the Flood*. Oxford: Clarendon.

Landsberger, B.
1915 *Der kultische Kalender der Babylonier und der Assyrer*. Leipziger Semitistische Studien 6/1–2. Leipzig: Hinrichs.

Lanfranchi, G.
1998 The Library at Nineveh. In *Capital Cities: Urban Planning and Spiritual Dimensions. Proceedings of the Symposium Held on May 27–29, 1996, Jerusalem, Israel*, ed. J. G. Westenholz, 147–56. Bible Lands Museum Jerusalem Publications 2. Jerusalem: Bible Lands Museum.

Lewis, N.
1974 *Papyrus in Classical Antiquity*. Oxford: Clarendon.
1986 *Greeks in Ptolemaic Egypt: Case Studies in the Social History of the Hellenistic World*. Oxford: Clarendon.

Pfeiffer, R.
1968–76 *History of Classical Scholarship*. 2 vols. Oxford: Clarendon.

Préaux, C.
1939 *L'économie royale des Lagides*. Brussels: Édition de la Fondation égyptologique Reine Élisabeth.

Redford, D. B.
2000 Scribe and Speaker. In *Writings and Speech in Israelite and Ancient Near Eastern Prophecy*, ed. E. Ben Zvi and M. H. Floyd, 145–218. Society of Biblical Literature Symposium Series 10. Atlanta: Scholars.

Reiner, E.
1960 Plague Amulets and House Blessings. *JNES* 19: 148–55.

Renz, J.
1995 *Die althebräische Inschriften.* 2 vols. Handbuch der Althebräischen Epigraphik 1. Darmstadt: Wissenschaftliche Buchgesellschaft.

Reynolds, L. D., and N. G. Wilson
1974 *Scribes and Scholars: A Guide to the Transmission of Greek and Latin Literature.* 2d ed. Oxford: Clarendon.

Roberts, C. H., and T. C. Skeat
1983 *The Birth of the Codex.* London: Oxford University Press.

Rousse, R. H., and M. A. Rousse
2000 *Manuscripts and Their Makers: Commercial Book Producers in Medieval Paris, 1200–1500.* 2 vols. London: Harvey Miller.

Sarna, N. M.
1971 The Order of the Books. In *Studies in Jewish Bibliography, History and Literature in Honor of I. Edward Kiev*, ed. C. Berlin, 407–13. New York: Ktav.

Shooner, H. V.
1988 La production du livre par la pecia. In *La production du livre universitaire au Moyen Age: Exemplar et pecia; Actes du symposium tenu au Collegio San Bonaventura de Grottaferrata en mai 1983*, ed. L. J. Bataillon, B. G. Guyot, and R. H. Rouse, 17–37. Paris: Editions du Centre national de la recherche scientifique.

Skeat, T. C.
1969 Early Christian Book-Production: Papyri and Manuscripts. In *The Cambridge History of the Bible*, G. W. H. Lampe, 2:54–79. Cambridge: Cambridge University Press.
1982 The Length of the Standard Papyrus Roll and the Cost-Advantage of the Codex. *Zeitschrift für Papyrologie und Epigraphie* 45:169–75.

Sperber, D.
1991 *Roman Palestine, 200–400: Money and Prices.* 2d ed. Ramat-Gan, Israel: Bar-Ilan University Press.

Stemberger, G.
1996 Öffentlichkeit der Tora im Judentum: Anspruch und Wirklichkeit. *Jahrbuch für Biblische Theologie* 11:91–101.

Weidner, E. F.
1932–33 Assyrische Beschreibungen der Kriegs-Reliefs Aššurbânaplis. *AfO* 8:175–203.

Wilamowitz-Möllendorff, U. von
1907 *Einleitung in die griechische Tragödie.* Berlin: Weidmann.

Zlotnick, D.
1966 *The Tractate "Mourning."* Yale Judaica Studies 17. New Haven, Conn.: Yale University Press.

46. The Temple Mount in Jerusalem during the First Temple Period: An Archaeologist's View

by David Ussishkin

A discussion of the Temple Mount, the royal acropolis and religious center of biblical Jerusalem, is a most difficult task for the archaeologist because—apart from some initial surveys conducted in the nineteenth century—hardly any fieldwork could be carried out in the area of the Haram esh-Sherif. However, based on topographical data, circumstantial evidence, archaeological evidence retrieved in other parts of Jerusalem, comparable archaeological material, and finally the data contained in the biblical text, some suggestions concerning the character and history of the Temple Mount during the First Temple period can be crystallized. These suggestions are summarized in the present study, to be published in a book dedicated to Larry Stager, my esteemed colleague and personal friend of many years.

Jerusalem of the late eighth century B.C.E., that is, Jerusalem during the reign of Hezekiah and Sennacherib's campaign, is the starting point of our discussion (figure 1). It seems clear that by that time Jerusalem extended over the Southeast Hill, that is the "City of David" (figure 1:2), as well as over the Southwest Hill (figure 1:6), where the "Mishneh" quarter was built, thus becoming the largest city in Judah. The city was heavily fortified, and segments of its walls have been uncovered along the eastern slope of the "City of David" by Kenyon (Steiner 2001:89–92), Shiloh (1984:8–10, 28; figs. 30, 33), and Reich and Shukrun (2000; see also Shanks 1999), as well as further to the north in the area of the "Ophel" by Eilat Mazar (Mazar and Mazar 1989:1–48). On the Southwest Hill, segments of the fortifications were uncovered in the Jewish Quarter by Avigad (1983:46–60; Avigad and Geva 2000; Geva and Avigad 2000), possibly also in Hagai Street by Kloner (1984), and in the Ottoman citadel near Jaffa Gate (Geva 1979; 1983:56–58). It can be safely concluded that during this period the Temple Mount formed an integral part of the metropolis and served as the royal acropolis or compound of the kings of Judah. It can also be safely assumed that by that time the Temple Mount was surrounded by a wall that was incorporated into the city's fortifications. The acropolis was situated at the edge of the city, and therefore part of its surrounding wall formed a segment of the city wall, while another part separated the Temple Mount from the "City of David" and from the "Mishneh" quarter on the Southwest Hill.

In reconstructing the plan of the royal compound extending over the Temple Mount, all scholars agree that it was smaller than the later Herodian compound, the shape of which is preserved to the present day in the Haram esh-Sherif. Many graphic reconstructions depict the outlines of the rectangular Herodian compound, with the smaller Iron Age compound marked by curving lines inside (e.g., Avigad 1983:58, fig. 36). On the other hand, other scholars, among them Kenyon (1974:111–14, fig. 22) and Ritmeyer (1992), believe that the Herodian walls follow, at least in part, the lines of the Iron Age walls, and hence the walls of the earlier compound must have extended in straight rather than curved lines.

Wightman (1993:29–31) compared the Solomonic compound with that of Omride Samaria (figure 2), also reconstructing its walls in straight lines. Following this line of thought, we can assume that the royal compound of the kings of the House of David in Jerusalem was based in plan and character on the same model as the royal Omride compounds at Samaria (Crowfoot, Kenyon and Sukenik 1942) and Jezreel (Ussishkin and Woodhead 1997:11, fig. 4). These compounds have much in common, thus representing a crystallized model and concept. At both Samaria and Jezreel, the compound was founded on the summit of a hill, with bedrock constituting much of the surface. In both places, the compound is rectangular, surrounded by a casemate wall that was based on bedrock. The lower parts of the casemates served as foundations or revetments, which supported large amounts of soil and debris dumped as constructional fills. Due to the fills, the enclosed area was turned into a rectangular podium, its surface almost horizontal. At Samaria, several buildings were found inside the compound, which also had large open courtyards. The excavations barely touched the inner parts of the Jezreel compound, but it seems to have had similar open spaces.

The architectural concept of the compounds at Samaria and Jezreel must have been imported from the north. Similar compounds can be found in Urartian fortresses in eastern Anatolia. A good example is the compound of Lower Anzaf, built by Ishpuini king of Urartu in the ninth century B.C.E. (figure 3; Belli 1999). Rectangular in plan, it forms a horizontal podium based on constructional fills, situated on the summit of the hill.

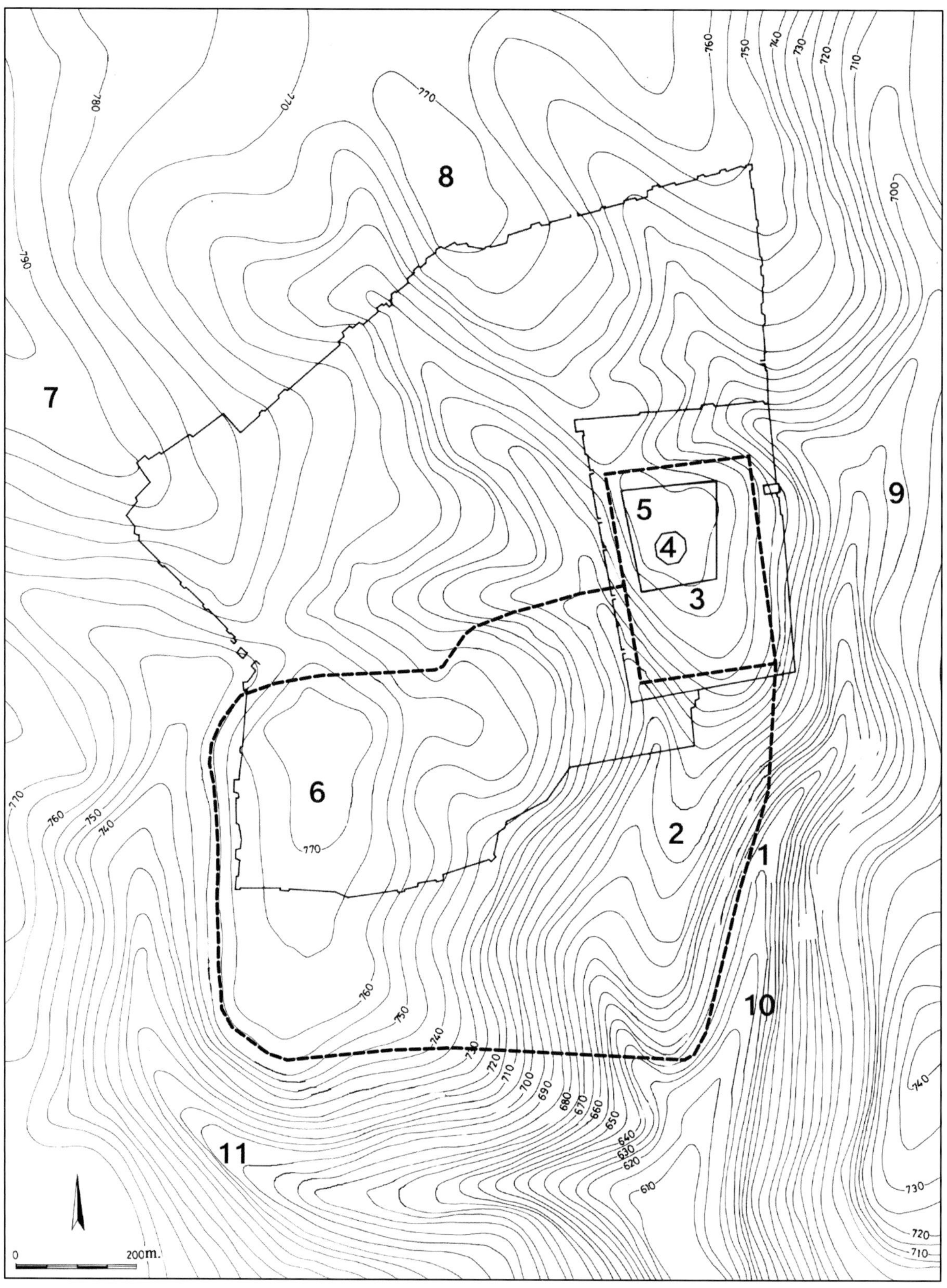

Figure 1. Jerusalem during the eighth and seventh centuries B.C.E.—a schematic reconstruction

1 Gihon Spring **2** "City of David" **3** Temple Mount **4** the temple **5** the royal palace **6** Southwest Hill **7** Northwest Hill **8** Northeast Hill **9** Mount of Olives **10** Kidron Valley **11** Hinnom Valley

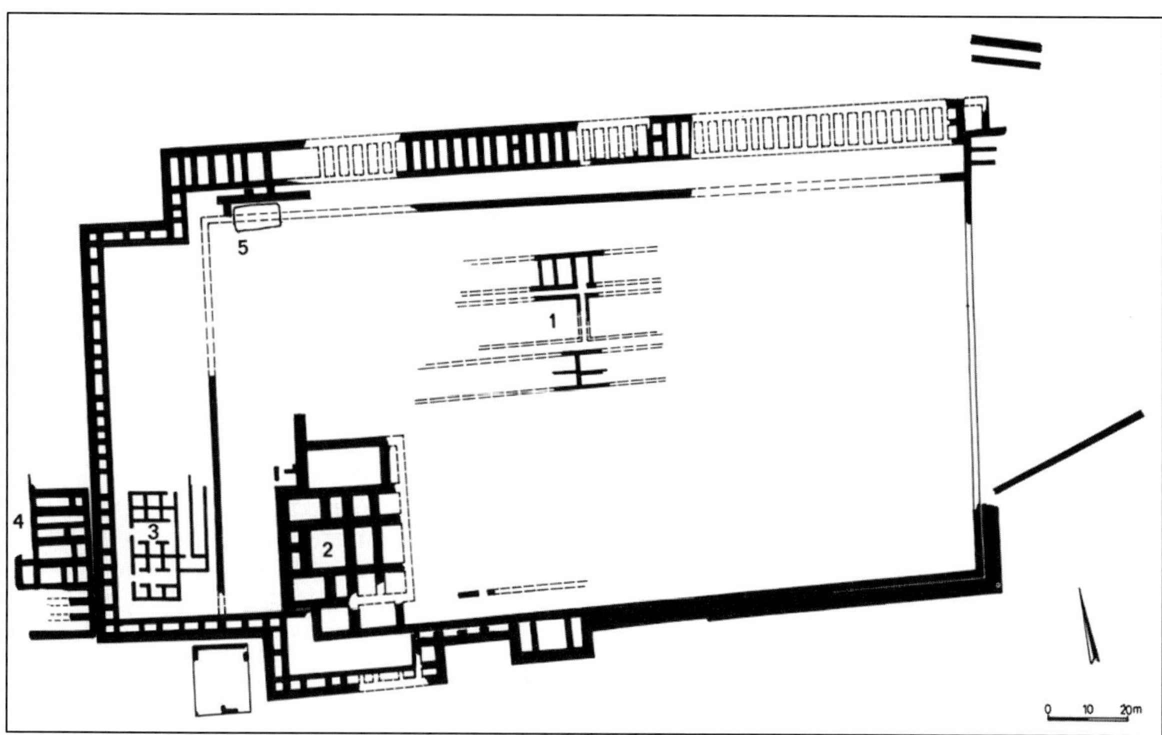

Figure 2. A plan of the Omride acropolis in Samaria (after Herzog 1997:230, fig. 5.22)
1 the "Ivory House" **2** the palace **3** the "Ostraca House"

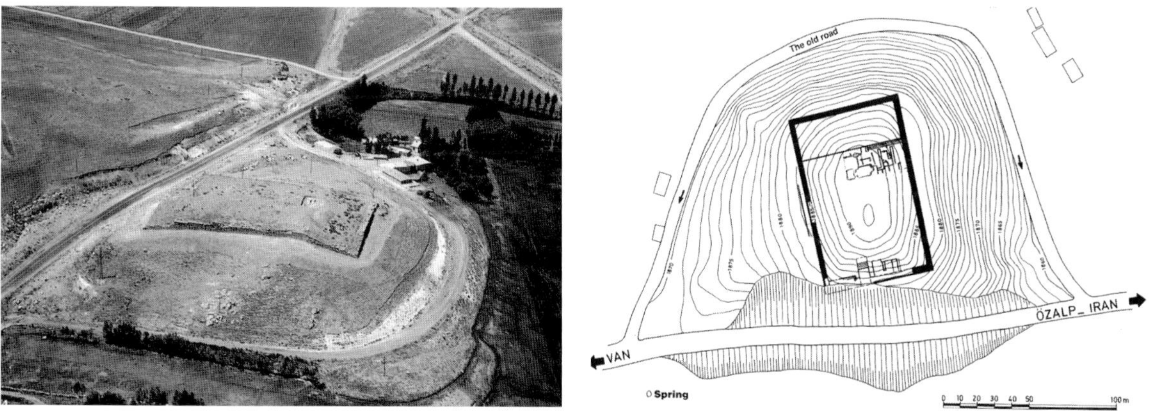

Figure 3. Aerial view and plan of the Urartian fortress of Lower Anzaf in eastern Anatolia (after Belli 1999:fig. 1 and pl. 1:4)

In Jerusalem, the Temple Mount was surrounded on three sides by a steep slope, but on the northwestern side it was connected by a topographical saddle to the hill running farther to the northwest, known as the Northeast Hill (figure 1:8). This saddle constituted the topographical weak point in the defense of the Temple Mount. Wilson and Warren surveyed the exposed rock surface in this area in 1864, and concluded that a deep ditch was cut at this point into the rock. In their own words: "Between the corner and the platform the ridge of Moriah must have been in one place very narrow; and here . . . the rock gives place to turf, and there are other indications which would lead us to believe that there was at one time a ditch cut in the solid rock" (Wilson and Warren 1871: 13). Ottosson (1989) and Oredsson (2000:92–95) have also recently suggested that a moat was cut in the rock across the saddle in the First Temple period.

The idea of cutting a deep moat in the rock also originates in the north. In Jezreel, three sides of the rectangular compound were protected by a deep, rock-cut moat (Ussishkin and Woodhead 1997:11, fig. 4). There was no need for such a moat on the fourth side, which faced a steep slope. Good comparisons to the assumed moat at the northwestern edge of the Temple Mount can be found in eastern Anatolia. In Van, in the central fortress of the kings of Urartu (figure 4), as well as in the fortress of Çavuştepe dated to the seventh century B.C.E. (figure 5), the sausage-shaped fortress was protected by a deep rock-cut moat on both of its ends, separating the fortress from the continuation of the hill.

According to the biblical text, the royal acropolis in Jerusalem contained two major buildings, the royal palace and the temple. At the time of its construction, the royal palace was almost certainly the main edifice of the compound, being much larger in size than the temple. In later periods, however, the temple gained in importance, while the royal palace was nearly forgotten. The best comparison to a contemporary temple *vis-à-vis* the royal palace is the eighth-century B.C.E. temple of Tell Taᶜyinat in northern Syria, built adjacent to the larger *bīt ḫilāni* palace in the royal acropolis of the kings of Kunulua (Haines 1971:pl. 103).

Assuming that the temple stood on the summit of the hill, exactly at the spot where the Dome of the Rock is presently situated (figure 1:4), all scholars reconstruct the royal palace to the south of the temple, where the ground is lower (e.g., Galling 1937: 411; Simons 1952:436; Vincent and Stève 1954:pl. 129; Wightman 1993:31, fig. 9). This reconstruction is based on several indications in the biblical text that one had to ascend from the palace to the temple (e.g., 2 Kings 22:3–4; Jer. 26:10; 36:10–12), and, more importantly, on the references to the royal palace in the descriptions of the rebuilding of Jerusalem's city walls in Nehemiah 3:25–29 and 12:37. The descriptions of Nehemiah's wall and its relationship to the palace, however, can be interpreted in different ways.

In my view, it is reasonable to assume that the palace stood on the lower ground to the north of the temple, an area spacious enough to accommodate such a large complex (figure 1:5). If located to the north of the temple, the royal palace of Jerusalem would have been ideally situated: the royal acropolis of Jerusalem was at the northeastern edge of the city and the palace was at the northern end of the acropolis, adjacent to the edge of the fortified city. This way, the palace would have been more secure and isolated, while if located to the south of the temple, everybody approaching the temple from the direction of the "City of David" would have had to pass near it.

This suggestion is based on the location of many palaces of rulers during the Bronze and Iron Ages. In many cities, we find the acropolis built at the edge of the city and the ruler's palace built at the edge of the acropolis, for example, at Hittite Hattusha (figure 6), Late Bronze Ugarit and Megiddo, as well as Assyrian Calah, Nineveh, Dur-Sharrukin, Til-Barsib, and Megiddo. There are, of course, other cases, notably Israelite Samaria and Neo-Hittite Zincirli-Samᵓal, in which the acropolis was located in the middle of the city, but in both these cities also, the royal palace was located at the edge of the acropolis.

The temple and its suggested reconstruction, analyzed in innumerable studies, will not be discussed here, but the palace warrants a brief description. The magnificent royal palace in Jerusalem, ascribed in the biblical text to King Solomon, is briefly described in 1 Kings 7:1–12 and can be partly reconstructed on the basis of archaeological comparisons (see Ussishkin 1973; King and Stager 2001:202–4). The edifice contained a ceremonial wing, residential quarters, and "the house of the Forest of Lebanon"—a separate unit as big as the temple, which probably functioned as the royal treasury. The palace complex was enclosed within its own large courtyard.

The large, magnificent ceremonial wing is of special interest. The biblical text informs us that it contained "the hall of columns, fifty cubits long and thirty cubits broad, and a hall and columns with a cornice in front of them" as well as "the hall for the throne," that is, "the hall of judgment"—the largest and most luxurious unit in the edifice.

The description of the ceremonial wing fits the model of the contemporary Syrian palace type known as *bīt ḫilāni*. A good example can be seen in Tell Halaf, in the ruler's palace of Aramean Gozan, dated to the tenth–ninth centuries B.C.E. (figure 7; see Langenegger et al. 1950). An impressive entrance with a portico led to an entrance hall, that is "the hall of columns"—the "columns" apparently being the columns of the entrance portico. The entrance hall opened to the throne room, the main hall of the edifice, where the throne of the king was placed on a dais built adjacent to one of the side walls.

Several archaeological comparisons can be found for details of the biblical descriptions of the throne room. This magnificent hall "was paneled in cedar from one side of the floor to the other" (1 Kings 7:7). Similar paneling can be seen in the walls of the entrance hall and the throne room of Barrakib's *bīt ḫilāni* palace at Zincirli-Samᵓal, dated to the third quarter of the eighth century B.C.E. (figure 8; von Luschan and Jacoby 1911:299). The magnificent throne, ascribed to Solomon, is described in detail in the biblical text (1 Kings 10:18–20). Almost certainly made of wood, it was lavishly decorated with ivory and gold, and flanked by lions. Similar thrones are portrayed on Canaanite ivories, Assyrian reliefs, and the sarcophagus of Ahiram, king of Byblos (figure 9). Finally, Jeremiah 36:22 informs us that Jehoiakim, king of Judah, "sat in the winter house in the ninth month, and there was a fire on the hearth burning before him." The ninth month, that is Kislev, falls about December, in mid-winter, and it is not surprising that a fire was lit in the hearth. Remains of a hearth were found in front of the throne dais in Zincirli, in the palaces of Kilamuwa and Barrakib, kings of Samʾal (von Luschan and Jacoby 1911:278–79, 296–98, pl. 49), and a metal brazier, shaped like a cart with wheels, was uncovered in the throne room in the Tell Halaf palace (figure 10; Langenegger et al. 1950:45–48, taf. 12).

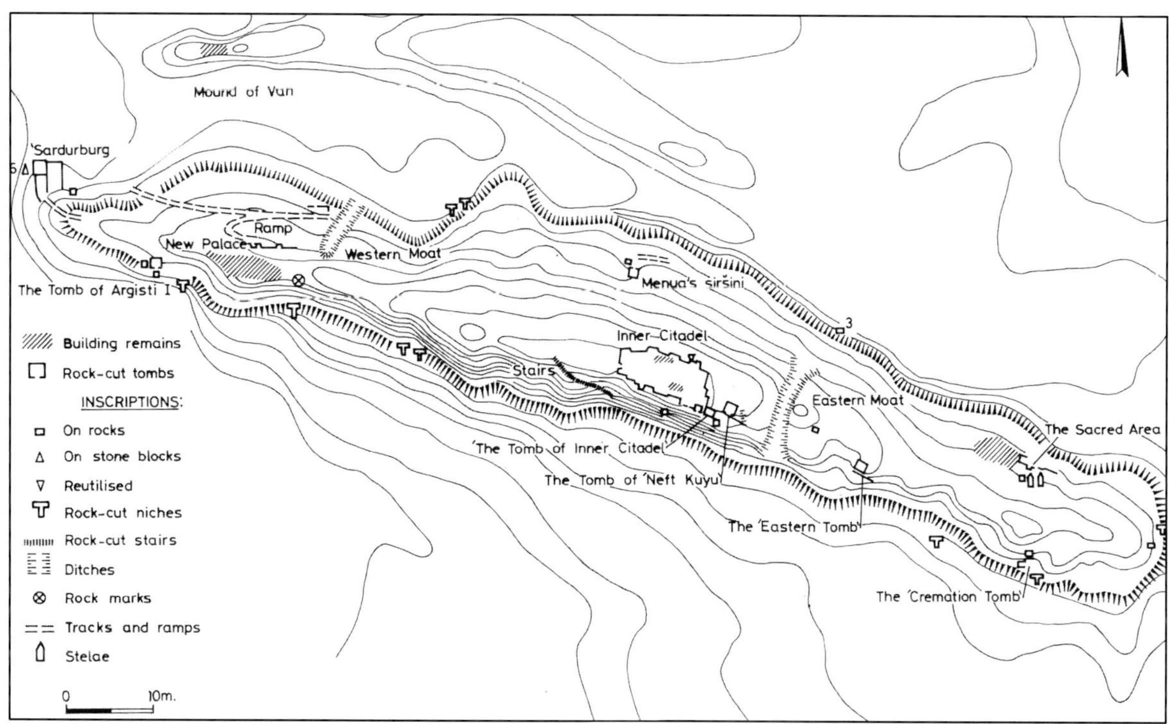

Figure 4. The Urartian fortress at Van (after Tarhan 1994:fig. 3)

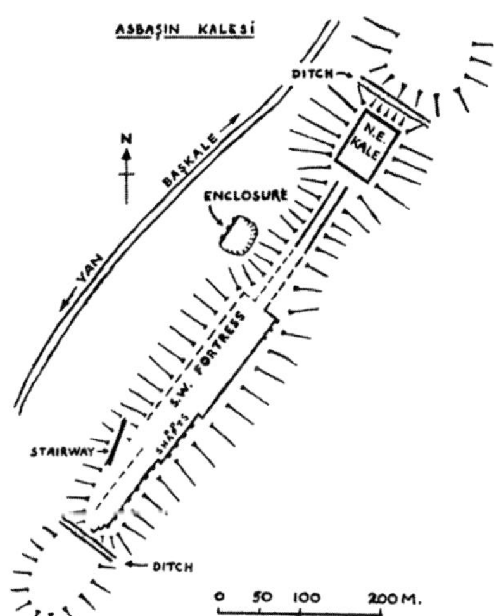

Figure 5. The Urartian fortress at Çavuştepe (after Erzen 1988:3, fig. 3)

Each rock-cut moat is marked as "ditch."

Figure 6. A plan of Hattusha during the period of the Hittite Empire (after Bittel 1970:26, fig. 3)

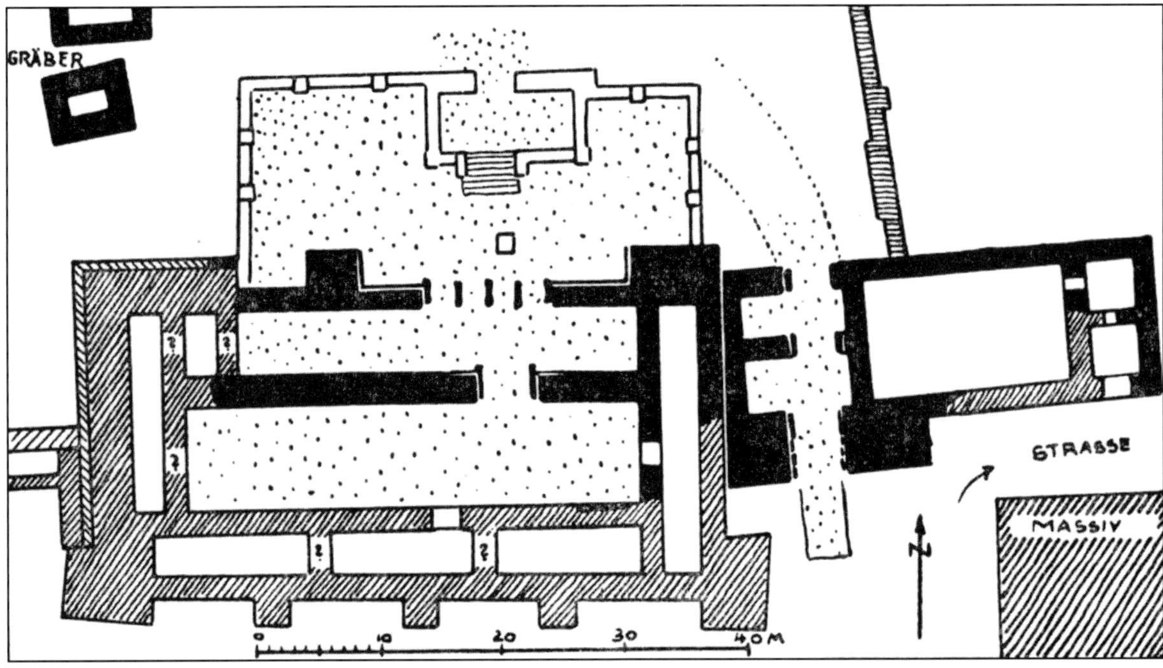

Figure 7. The *bīt ḫilāni* palace at Tell Halaf, plan and reconstruction (after Langenegger et al. 1950:fig. 6 and plan 5)

Figure 9. ► King Ahiram of Byblos seated on his throne; a relief carved on the king's sarcophagus (after Montet 1928:pl. 131)

◄ *Figure 8.* Reconstructed wooden paneling of the walls in Barrakib's Palace K at Zincirli (after von Luschan and Jacoby 1911:299, fig. 209)

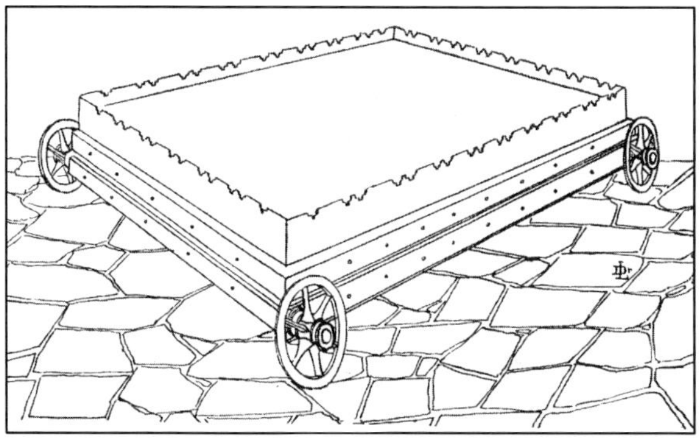

Figure 10. A cart-shaped metal brazier found in the throne room of the palace at Tell Halaf (after Langenegger et al. 1950:Abb. 15)

There is another matter which should be emphasized. In his descriptions of the Roman siege of Jerusalem in 70 C.E., Flavius Josephus twice mentions a place known as the "Camp of the Assyrians." The data brought by Josephus is sufficient to identify the site of the "Camp of the Assyrians" on the Northeast Hill, to the northwest of the Temple Mount (figure 1:8; Ussishkin 1979; 1995:290–92). We can safely assume that this place marks the very place where the Assyrian task force sent by Sennacherib to Jerusalem in 701 B.C.E. pitched its camp. A schematic view of such a camp is portrayed in the Lachish reliefs (see Ussishkin 1982:92–93, fig. 73). Apparently, the appearance of the Assyrian army at the gates of Jerusalem left a strong impact on the population of the city, and hence the site of the camp retained its name for nearly 800 years.

From the Assyrian point of view, the Northeast Hill was the optimal place for pitching the camp. Camping on the spacious summit of the hill, the Assyrian task force faced the Temple Mount extending on lower ground. The presence of the Assyrian army at this place directly threatened the center of the Judean government—the royal compound and, in particular, the royal palace, if it were located, as assumed above, on its northern side. The saddle and the area of the assumed moat was the most suitable place for conducting negotiations with Hezekiah, negotiations which eventually resulted in Hezekiah's *de facto* surrender to the king of Assyria.

Once we move backwards from the latter part of the eighth century to the tenth and ninth centuries B.C.E., the archaeological picture becomes problematic and obscure, in particular with regard to the Temple Mount, and the meager archaeological evidence has been interpreted in different ways.

Many scholars, for example recently Cahill (2003; 2004), believe that the archaeological evidence allows a reconstruction of the Solomonic city as described in the biblical text. On that basis, as can be seen in various reconstructions, such as those published by Shanks (1995:74–75) and Cahill (2004: 22), Jerusalem is shown as sausage-shaped. The city includes the "City of David" and the Temple Mount, the latter crowned by the prominent building of the temple. Based on 1 Kings 9:15, the city is shown surrounded by a massive city wall.

It seems, however, that the archaeological evidence presents a different picture of the Solomonic city (Ussishkin 2003a; 2003b). Intensive and systematic archaeological investigations have been carried out in different parts of biblical Jerusalem for more than 150 years, and sufficient data were recovered to give us some idea of the extent and character of the

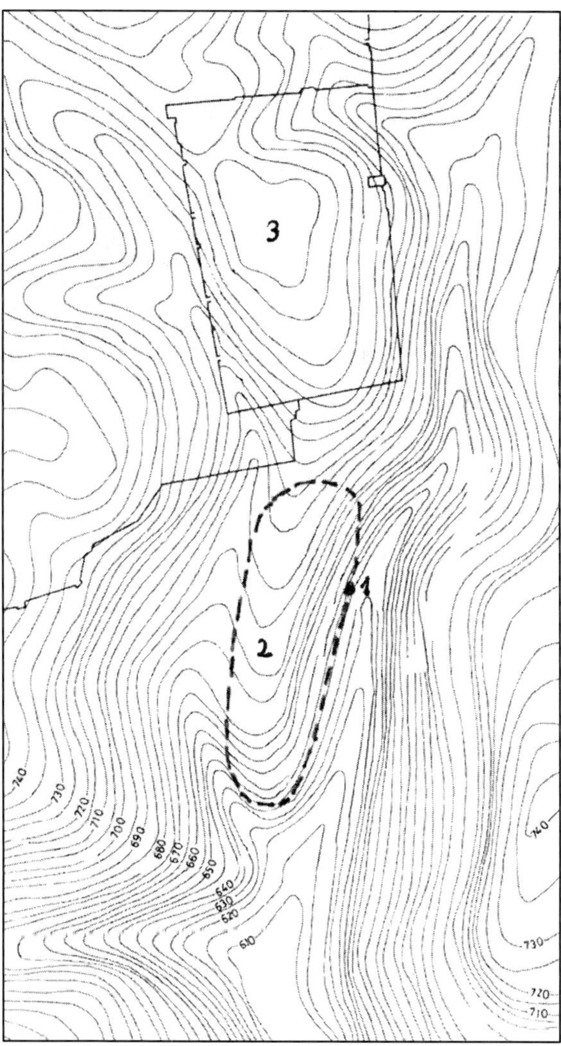

Figure 11. Jerusalem during the tenth century B.C.E.: a schematic reconstruction

1 Gihon Spring **2** "City of David" **3** Temple Mount

city during the tenth and ninth centuries B.C.E. The picture is unlikely to change drastically in the future. It appears that the settlement of this period extended solely along the central parts of the "City of David" (figure 11) and it was not protected by a city wall. The fortifications uncovered near the southeast corner of the Haram esh-Sherif (Mazar and Mazar 1989: 1–48) date to the eighth and seventh centuries B.C.E. city and not earlier, as recently suggested by Eilat Mazar (2006b) on the basis of the biblical text. In my view, the theory advocated by Kenyon (1974:81–83, 89–91) and Cahill (2003:21–23) that the city wall of the Middle Bronze Age settlement continued to be in use at that time cannot be accepted.

Most significant for our discussion are the results of the large-scale excavations carried out by Benjamin Mazar, and later by Eilat Mazar, to the south of the Temple Mount. Only a few pottery pieces earlier than the eighth century B.C.E. were recovered here, out of stratigraphical context (Mazar and Mazar 1989; E. Mazar 2006b:784 and fig. 3), and it seems that the entire area was not settled at that time. A similar, complementary picture is gained from the sifting of earthen fills originating in the southern parts of the Haram esh-Sherif: while later Iron Age pottery is well represented, very few Iron Age hand-burnished pottery pieces dated to before the eighth century B.C.E., as well as sherds dating to earlier periods, have been recovered here (Barkay and Zweig 2006:219–20). It thus appears that the settlement of the United Monarchy period did not reach the Temple Mount.

A few words must be added at this point on the enigmatic and unique "Stepped Stone Structure," a kind of retaining wall supporting the steep rocky slope above the Gihon Spring and on the underlying terraces. The structure, the underlying terraces, their function and their date, have been extensively studied in recent years (see Shiloh 1984:16–18, 29, figs. 16–19; Steiner 2001:36–39, 43–52; 2003; Cahill 2003: 33–54; Finkelstein 2003:84–86; A. Mazar 2006). Used and rebuilt for many generations, it seems that this structure or parts of it originates at the end of the Bronze Age and was in use, at least partly, until the Second Temple period.

It is usually assumed that the "Stepped Stone Structure" supported a public building or fort on the summit of the ridge. Recent excavations at this spot by Eilat Mazar revealed substantial structural remains, which she dated to this general period and—on the basis of the biblical text—identified as parts of King David's royal palace (E. Mazar 2006a; see also A. Mazar 2006:269–70). Different stratigraphical and chronological conclusions have recently been reached by I. Finkelstein, Z. Herzog, L. Singer-Avitz, and D. Ussishkin (2007).

Turning back to the problems of the Temple Mount, the above topographical and archaeological data leave us with four options for reconstructing the Temple Mount during the tenth century B.C.E.

First option: Based on the proposal of Knauf (2000), the Temple Mount formed the cultic and secular center of the city already during the Late Bronze Age and the earlier part of the Iron Age. However, there are no textual or archaeological indications to support this theory.

Second option: Based on the biblical tradition, Solomon built a small, modest temple on the Temple Mount, which formed the basis for later reconstruction and extension of the buildings here. In that case, the large compound and the monumental royal palace were added, and the temple was enlarged or rebuilt, in the eighth century B.C.E., when the Temple Mount was incorporated into the extended city. This is the view of Naʾaman, who argued that Solomon built a temple on the Temple Mount, "though on a much smaller scale than the one built in the late monarchical period" (Naʾaman 1996:23).

Third option: The royal acropolis was built as a separate entity by Solomon, as described in the biblical text, and it was incorporated in the expanding city during the late eighth century B.C.E.

Fourth option: The royal acropolis was built as described in the biblical text, but in the late eighth century B.C.E., when the modest tenth-century settlement became a large, fortified city and the Temple Mount was incorporated in it.

There is one strong argument in support of the first and second options. One would expect the planners of the city to have built the royal compound at the highest and most strategically located place in the city. The northern part of the Southwest Hill (figure 1:6), at an elevation of ca. 773 meters above sea level, is clearly the optimal place for the location of the acropolis, rather than the Temple Mount at ca. 743 meters (figure 1:4). And indeed, during the Second Temple period, the Hasmonean kings, and later Herod, shifted their royal palaces to the Southwest Hill. This is a clear indication that the Temple Mount had already been a significant cultic place before the extension of the city in the eighth century B.C.E., so that the royal acropolis was built at this spot.

A similar case can be observed in Hattusha, the Hittite capital (figure 6; see, e.g., Bittel 1970; Neve 1992). Settlement started here in the Early Bronze Age on the hill known as Büyükkale. During the Middle Bronze Age, the "Lower City" was added to the west and northwest, and in this way the Büyükkale became the acropolis. Later, during the period of the Hittite kingdom, the city was further extended, and the "Upper City" was added to the south of the Büyükkale and the "Lower City." The Büyükkale remained the acropolis of the extended city, and here was built the central palace of the Hittite kings, although the southern part of the "Upper City" was much higher than the Büyükkale.

The Temple Mount was the religious and political center of the kings of the House of David during the First Temple period. It is a great pity that it cannot be properly investigated archaeologically, although since the Temple Mount was built or destroyed extensively in later periods, it is doubtful whether archaeological investigations could retrieve significant data related to the First Temple period. However, as shown above, it is still possible to reconstruct in part its character and history during this important period.

N.B.: This article is an expanded version of a paper presented in the annual conference of the Society of Biblical Literature in Washington, D.C., in November 2006.

Bibliography

Avigad, N.
1983 *Discovering Jerusalem.* Nashville, Tenn.: Nelson.

Avigad, N., and H. Geva
2000 Iron Age II Strata 9–7. In *Jewish Quarter Excavations in the Old City of Jerusalem*, vol. 1, *Architecture and Stratigraphy: Areas A, W and X-2, Final Report*, ed. H. Geva, 44–82. Jerusalem: Israel Exploration Society.

Barkay, G., and I. Zweig
2006 The Project of Sifting Soil from the Temple Mount—Preliminary Report [in Hebrew]. *New Studies on Jerusalem* 11:213–37.

Belli, O.
1999 *The Anzaf Fortresses and the Gods of Urartu.* Istanbul: Arkeoloji ve Sanat Yayınları.

Bittel, K.
1970 *Hattusha: The Capital of the Hittites.* New York: Oxford University Press.

Cahill, J. M.
2003 Jerusalem at the Time of the United Monarchy: The Archaeological Evidence. In *Jerusalem in Bible and Archaeology: The First Temple Period*, ed. A. G. Vaughn and A. E. Killebrew, 13–80. Atlanta: Society of Biblical Literature.
2004 Jerusalem in David and Solomon's Time. *BAR* 30/6:20–31, 62–63.

Crowfoot, J. W., K. M. Kenyon, and E. L. Sukenik
1942 *Samaria-Sebaste.* Vol. 1, *The Buildings at Samaria.* London: Palestine Exploration Fund.

Erzen, A.
1988 *Çavuştepe.* Vol. 1, *Urartian Architectural Monuments of the Seventh and Sixth Centuries* B.C. *and a Necropolis of the Middle Age.* Publication of the Turkish Historical Society Series 5/37. Ankara: Türk Tarih Kurumu.

Finkelstein, I.
2003 The Rise of Jerusalem and Judah: The Missing Link. In *Jerusalem in Bible and Archaeology: The First Temple Period*, ed. A. G. Vaughn and A. E. Killebrew, 81–101. Atlanta: Society of Biblical Literature.

Finkelstein, I., Z. Herzog, L. Singer-Avitz, and D. Ussishkin
2007 Has King David's Palace in Jerusalem Been Found? *Tel Aviv* 34:142–64.

Galling, K.
1937 *Biblisches Reallexikon.* Tübingen: Mohr.

Geva, H.
1979 The Western Boundary of Jerusalem at the End of the Monarchy. *IEJ* 29:84–91.
1983 Excavations in the Citadel of Jerusalem, 1979–1980: Preliminary Report. *IEJ* 33:55–71.

Geva, H., and N. Avigad
2000 Area W—Stratigraphy and Architecture. In *Jewish Quarter Excavations in the Old City of Jerusalem*, vol. 1, *Architecture and Stratigraphy: Areas A, W and X-2, Final Report*, ed. H. Geva, 131–97. Jerusalem: Israel Exploration Society.

Haines, R. C.
1971 *Excavations in the Plain of Antioch.* Vol, 2, *The Structural Remains of the Later Phases: Chatal Hüyük, Tell al-Judaida, and Tell Taʿyinat.* OIP 95. Chicago: University of Chicago Press.

Herzog, Z.
1997 *Archaeology of the City: Urban Planning in Ancient Israel and Its Social Implications.* Monographs of the Institute of Archaeology of Tel Aviv University 13. Tel Aviv: Institute of Archaeology, Tel Aviv University.

King, P. J., and L. E. Stager
2001 *Life in Biblical Israel.* Louisville, Ky.: Westminster John Knox.

Kenyon, K. M.
1974 *Digging Up Jerusalem.* London: Ernest Benn.

Kloner, A.
1984 Reḥov Hagay. *ESI* 3:57–59.

Knauf, E. A.
2000 Jerusalem in the Late Bronze and Early Iron Ages: A Proposal. *Tel Aviv* 27:75–90.

Langenegger, F., K. Müller, and R. Naumann
1950 *Tell Halaf.* Vol, 2, *Die Bauwerke.* Berlin: Walter de Gruyter.

Luschan, F. von, and G. Jacoby
1911 *Ausgrabungen in Sendschirli.* Vol. 4. Mittheilungen aus den Orientalischen Sammlungen 14. Berlin: Georg Reimer.

Mazar, A.
2006 Jerusalem in the Tenth Century B.C.E.: The Glass Half Full. In *Essays on Ancient Israel in Its Near Eastern Context: A Tribute to Nadav Naʾaman,* ed. Y. Amit, E. Ben Zvi, I. Finkelstein, and O. Lipschits, 255–72. Winona Lake, Ind.: Eisenbrauns.

Mazar, E.
2006a Did I Find King David's Palace? *BAR* 32/1:16–27, 70.
2006b The Solomonic Wall in Jerusalem. In *"I Will Speak the Riddles of Ancient Times": Archaeological and Historical Studies in Honor of Amihai Mazar on the Occasion of His Sixtieth Birthday,* ed. A. M. Maeir and P. de Miroschedji, 2:775–86. Winona Lake, Ind.: Eisenbrauns.

Mazar, E., and B. Mazar
1989 *Excavations in the South of the Temple Mount, The Ophel of Biblical Jerusalem.* Qedem 29. Jerusalem: Institute of Archaeology, Hebrew University.

Montet, P.
1928 *Byblos et l'Égypte: Quatre campagnes de fouilles à Gebeil.* BAH 11. Paris: Geuthner.

Naʾaman, N.
1996 The Contribution of the Amarna Letters to the Debate on Jerusalem's Political Position in the Tenth Century B.C.E. *BASOR* 304:17–27.

Neve, P.
1992 Hattuša—Stadt der Götter und Tempel. *Antike Welt* 23:2–88.

Oredsson, D.
2000 *Moats in Ancient Palestine.* Old Testament Series 48. Stockholm: Almqvist and Wiksell.

Ottosson, M.
1989 Topography and City Planning with Special Reference to Jerusalem. *Tidsskrift for Teologi og Kirke* 4:263–70.

Reich, R., and E. Shukron
2000 Jerusalem, City of David. *ESI* 112:82*–83*.

Ritmeyer, L.
1992 Locating the Original Temple Mount. *BAR* 18/2: 24–45, 64–65.

Shanks, H.
1995 *Jerusalem, An Archaeological Biography.* New York: Random House.
1999 Everything You Ever Knew about Jerusalem Is Wrong (Well, Almost). *BAR* 25/6:20–29.

Shiloh, Y.
1984 *Excavations at the City of David.* Vol, 1, *1978–1982; Interim Report of the First Five Seasons.* Qedem 19. Jerusalem: Institute of Archaeology, Hebrew University.

Simons, J.
1952 *Jerusalem in the Old Testament: Researches and Theories.* Leiden: Brill.

Steiner, M. L.
2001 *Excavations by Kathleen M. Kenyon in Jerusalem, 1961–1967.* Vol. 3, *The Settlement in the Bronze and Iron Ages.* Copenhagen International Series 9. London: Sheffield Academic Press.
2003 The Evidence from Kenyon's Excavations in Jerusalem: A Response Essay. In *Jerusalem in Bible and Archaeology: The First Temple Period,* ed. A. G. Vaughn and A. E. Killebrew, 347–63. Atlanta: Society of Biblical Literature.

Tarhan, T.
1994 Recent Research at the Urartian Capital Tushpa. *Tel Aviv* 21:22–57.

Ussishkin, D.
1973 King Solomon's Palaces. *BA* 36:78–105.
1979 "The Camp of the Assyrians" in Jerusalem. *IEJ* 29:137–42.
1982 *The Conquest of Lachish by Sennacherib.* Publications of the Institute of Archaeology of Tel Aviv University 6. Tel Aviv: Institute of Archaeology, Tel Aviv University.
1995 The Water Systems of Jerusalem during Hezekiah's Reign. In *Meilenstein: Festgabe für Herbert Donner zum 16. Februar 1995,* ed. M. Weippert and S. Timm, 289–307. Ägypten und Altes Testament 30. Wiesbaden: Harrassowitz.
2003a Jerusalem as a Royal and Cultic Center in the Tenth–Eighth Centuries B.C.E. In *Symbiosis, Symbolism, and the Power of the Past: Proceedings of the Centennial Symposium, W. F. Albright Institute of Archaeological Research and American Schools of Oriental Research, Jerusalem, May 29–31, 2000,* ed. W. G. Dever and S. Gitin, 529–38. Winona Lake, Ind.: Eisenbrauns.
2003b Solomon's Jerusalem: The Text and the Facts on the Ground. In *Jerusalem in Bible and Archaeology: The First Temple Period,* ed. A. G. Vaughn and A. E. Killebrew, 103–15. Atlanta: Society of Biblical Literature.

Ussishkin, D., and J. Woodhead
1997 Excavations at Tel Jezreel 1994–1996: Third Preliminary Report. *Tel Aviv* 24:6–72.

Vincent, L. H., and M. A. Stève
1954 *Jérusalem de l'Ancien Testament: Recherches d'archéologie et d'histoire.* Paris: Gabalda.

Wilson, C., and C. Warren
1871 *The Recovery of Jerusalem: A Narrative of Exploration and Discovery in the City and the Holy Land.* London: Richard Bentley.

Wightman, G. J.
1993 *The Walls of Jerusalem: From the Canaanites to the Mamluks.* Mediterranean Archaeology Supplement 4. Sydney: Meditarch.

47. The Israelite *Mišpāḥâ*, the Priestly Writings, and Changing Valences in Israel's Kinship Terminology

by David S. Vanderhooft

The Priestly Writings (P) refer to terms in Israel's semantic field of kinship far more often than any other source or book in the Hebrew Bible.[1] Scholars remain ambivalent, however, about the value of evidence in P for understanding Israelite kinship organization. The problem is not simply that P was codified long after the period it purports to describe. Rather, many scholars agree that P projected a rigid, idealized social system onto Israel's post-Exodus past; such a social system, they argue, does not resemble the reality of any period.[2] Despite this widespread scholarly ambivalence, however, I contend that P remains a valuable source of data for analysis of Israelite kinship organization under the monarchy. To demonstrate this will depend on proving that P did not reconstruct Israel's post-Exodus social organization in a fantastical or capricious way. Rather, P presents a logical and internally consistent model of social organization, a model that derives from an accurate appreciation of Israel's social structure under the monarchy. P offers, in short, an elite perspective on the predominant familial patterns that shaped the lives of Israelites and Judeans in the era of the monarchies, a model that is not without value for being elitist.

The argument below proceeds in three parts: it highlights several assumptions undergirding negative scholarly assumptions about P; it shows that an inadequate "devolutionary" model of Israel's social development must be discarded on the basis of archaeological data; and it demonstrates that the Priestly representation of kinship organization, particularly the use of the term *mišpāḥâ*, corresponds with the monarchic era, not the Persian or early Hellenistic periods.

The idea that P provides a fabricated or idealized reconstruction of post-Exodus Israelite society derives in part from the nineteenth-century development that culminated in Wellhausen's representation of P as an ideologue of the exilic era. Wellhausen laid out his view as follows:

> The Priestly Code . . . tries hard to imitate the costume of the Mosaic period, and, with whatever success, to disguise that of its own. . . . [It] guards itself against all reference to later times and settled life in Canaan.
>
> . . . it keeps itself carefully and strictly within the limits of the situation of the wilderness, for which in all seriousness it seeks to give the law. It has actually been successful, with its movable tabernacle, its wandering camp, and other archaic details, in so concealing the true date of its composition that its many serious inconsistencies with what we know, from other sources, of Hebrew antiquity previous to the exile, are only taken as proving that it lies far beyond all known history, and on account of its enormous antiquity can hardly be brought into any connection with it. [Wellhausen 1958:9–10][3]

Wellhausen's theory about P—especially the chronological location of P in the late sixth century—commanded wide assent through much of the twentieth century, even when scholars criticized his view that P had reified Israelite religious traditions.[4] As a

[1] It is a great pleasure for me to contribute this paper to a festschrift honoring Larry Stager, whose seminal work on the Israelite family, and ancient social history more generally, helped shape and further the research of many scholars. I have been fortunate to have him as a teacher and friend. I would like to thank Dexter Callender, Jeffrey Geoghegan, Avi Faust, Baruch Halpern, Phil King, Oded Lipschits, Gary Knoppers, Daniel Master, Pheme Perkins, and David Schloen for their generosity in discussing issues addressed in this paper. None of these individuals is responsible for the shortcomings which remain.

[2] Williamson has succinctly summarized the problem in treating the Priestly kinship terminology. He notes that it is not simply a question of whether P is preexilic or not, since "even those who date the material late generally agree that it contains reflections of earlier material. . . . So of which period, if either, does it reflect the social reality?" (Williamson 2003:470–71).

[3] See, for further discussion, Milgrom 1991:3–13; and for discussion of negative scholarly evaluations of P, see Pola 1995:17–19.

[4] I will not deal here in a systematic way with the problem of the date of P. My purpose is not to assign a specific date to the entire corpus attributed by scholars to P. Indeed, as many others have noted, it is a mistake to think of P emerging out of whole cloth at a specific moment. The basic arguments for placing P in an exilic context were articulated by Wellhausen, as noted above. Efforts to rebut such arguments include the work of Y. Kaufmann (1960). R. E. Friedman (1981) has argued that Deuteronomy knew P, and that the initial promulgation of P came before the Exile. J. Blenkinsopp (1996:495–497) has laid out the contours of the debate, together with a review of major contributions, although he does not find the case for an early date for P

result of Wellhausen's legacy, scholars have often denigrated or ignored P's use of kinship terminology. N. Gottwald, for example, in his important study of Israel's premonarchic society, writes that "P . . . is unable to employ the device of pseudo-kinship in any consistent and thorough way to bring order into the ancient traditions about social organization" (Gottwald 1979:290). N. P. Lemche, in his extensive critique of Gottwald, is harsher yet, and doubts whether P ever accurately reflects the sociological content of such terms as *mišpāḥâ*[5] and *bêt ʾāb*, "house of the father" (Lemche 1985:262–63). P. McNutt has suggested, precisely in connection with the term *mišpāḥâ*—the term of main interest in the present dicussion—that "the stereotypical use of *mišpāḥâ* in the Priestly lists . . . may be a Priestly systematization of kinship units that is secondary and has no relation to the social reality the term may at one time have been associated with" (McNutt 1999:89). McNutt does not explain why or how P's presumed secondary "systematization" might be without a relationship to "social reality." In this respect, her argument typifies the dismissive view of P's representation of Israelite social organization.

Not all scholars dismiss P's ability to comprehend or accurately reconstruct Israel's past, but many still presume that P is an archaizer. B. Levine, for example, argues that P revived ancient, defunct terms in the kinship semantic field, such as *nāśîʾ*, "chieftain," and even *bêt ʾāb*, to describe Israel's early society. The purpose, Levine has suggested, was "to lend [P's] later projections an atmosphere of presettlement or premonarchic Israel" (1993a:132; see also idem 2003:445–53). Levine's view is more compelling than those quoted above, because he takes seriously the possibility that what he calls P's "later projections" may have been well informed. In other important respects, too, as this study will show, Levine's views of the *mišpāḥâ* conform to those presented below.

Nevertheless, both perspectives about P's reconstruction of Israelite social structure—that P is incapable of accurately reflecting the past, and that P shows a penchant for archaizing—rest in turn on the assumption that the monarchy eclipsed the tribal, kin-based society of early Israel. On this assumption, the kin-based, putatively egalitarian, social organization of the premonarchic era was a dim memory in P's time. Blenkinsopp's study of the Israelite family under the monarchy articulates this devolutionary view: "The process of political, economic, and military centralization [under the monarchy], even though never fully carried through, had a direct and negative impact on the typical rural household. . . . The net result was the erosion . . . of peasant freehold—and therefore the kinship and family structure dependent on it" (Blenkinsopp 1997:87–88).[6]

Thus, three basic scholarly views—the negative assessment of P; the assumption that an exilic or postexilic date for P means that the Priestly reconstruction of the past is inaccurate or anachronistic; and the devolutionary reconstruction of Israelite social history—supported the widely held conclusion that P projected onto early Israel only the debased social organization of the late monarchy, or, at best, an idealized reconstruction of it. New approaches and data, however, warrant a more constructive approach to the problem.

Numerous scholars have decisively attacked what I have called the devolutionary paradigm, which asserts that the centralization of governmental authority under the monarchy eradicated a presumed tribal and egalitarian social organization. The most important challenges derive from archaeological reconstructions of Israelite social structure. Prior to analyzing P's use of the term *mišpāḥâ*, therefore, I offer a brief discussion of developments in the reconstruction of Israel's social history on the basis of archaeology.

Stager's essay on the archaeology of the family represents a watershed in this research; it is a definitive demonstration of the inadequacy of the devolutionary model and a call for more careful social-historical research than was found in the older view

persuasive; J. Milgrom (1999:10–22) offered a rebuttal. B. Levine, like Blenkinsopp, has long sought to counter the linguistic arguments for an early date for P; a representative example may be found in his commentary on Numbers 1–20 (Levine 1993a:101–109). D. Sperling (1999:373–85) takes a different approach, and argues that decisive evidence from art history and the evolution of garment types exists to place P in the Achaemenid era.

[5] The term is variously translated, so I will use it in its original form throughout this paper to avoid ambiguity.

[6] This basic perspective owes much to the legacy of A. Alt (1959). Many variations of this basic view have appeared in the literature. Examples include: de Vaux 1961:23; Bright 1962:564; Donner 1963:229–245; Chaney 1986:68; Gottwald 1986:84; Davies 1989:358; and Matthews and Benjamin 1993:158. Matthews and Benjamin, for example, still accept a village-state dichotomy and the concept of linear evolution from tribe to state: "[b]y the end of Solomon's reign sometime after 925 B.C.E., the evolution of Israel as villages into Israel as a state became complete" (ibid.). McNutt (1999) allows the possibility that the monarchy may have coexisted with a "tribal" social organization, but she continues to see the two as fundamentally in opposition. In this she follows S. Bendor (1996). Bendor provides a summary of earlier views about the eclipse of kinship under the monarchy (Bendor 1996:207–15).

represented, for example, by Alt. Stager concluded that the inauguration of monarchy in Israel did not result in the eradication of Israel's kinship structures, and that if the Israelite kingdom were understood according to Max Weber's patrimonial model, then no necessary conflict need have existed between the king's domain and those of the local kin groups (Stager 1985:24; see also King and Stager 2001). Several of Stager's students have furthered this critique, as the following discussion will show (Bloch-Smith 1992; Tappy 2000:175–204; Master 2001:117–31; and especially Schloen 2001). J. S. Holladay also produced several important analyses of the form, function, and evolution of the typical Israelite house, which, together with Stager's work, helped bring the analysis of domestic architecture in Israel to a new level (1992:308–318; 1995:368–98; 1997a:337–42; 1997b:94–114). Others made key contributions to the analysis of Israel's social history, including B. Halpern, who composed several syntheses of the historical and archaeological data. Halpern attacked the devolutionary model both by reinterpreting the contribution of royal authority in the context of the debate, and also by asserting the persistence of traditional kinship patterns through the monarchic era (1991:11–107; 1996:291–338). Archaeologists, meanwhile, produced new analyses that denied any simple argument that Israel's premonarchic social organization quickly eroded after the rise of the monarchy (see the early work of Shiloh 1970:180–90; also Braemer 1982; Hopkins 1985; Netzer 1992:193–201; C. Meyers 1997:14–16; 2003:425–44; Herr 1997: 126; Bunimovitz and Faust 2003:411–23; and Lehmann 2004:141–93). As Schloen has put it, behind "attempts to restrict functioning kin-groups to the premonarchic period lies the evolutionist assumption that kin-based social organization is incompatible with the territorial organization of a centralized 'bureaucratic state'" (2001:153; also 63–90; 136; 183). Stager's work was instrumental in exploding that assumption.

The archaeological research just described focuses on domestic residence patterns in the Iron Age I through the Iron Age II and furnishes an interpretation of the physical correlates of Israelite kinship organization. In particular, these studies focus on the well-known three- and four-room pillared buildings and their subtypes, which constitute the most common form of domestic architecture excavated in Iron Age Israel and Judah. Archaeologists have recognized that the form and functions of the pillared houses—inside and outside of large towns and cities—represent a successful adaptation to farm life and the economic and environmental constraints of village life in Palestine. These structures had space for domestic food processing, storage, small craft production (e.g. weaving), oil pressing, and stabling, which is often indicated, as Holladay and Stager both argued, by cobbled surfaces in the side rooms (Holladay 1992:308–18; 1997a:338–339; 1995:386–391; Stager 1985:11–17; also Netzer 1992:195–199; for some of the gender-based differences in space utilization, see King and Stager 2001; and C. Meyers 2003: 425–44). Moreover, these houses frequently cluster in groups of two to five, often sharing party walls, and form compounds within both smaller and larger settlements. Stager (1985:17–23) made a compelling demonstration that a correspondence exists between such housing compounds and Israelite ideas of kinship: the compounds would have housed the synchronic patrilocal lineage, in biblical terminology, the *bêt ʾāb*. Schloen (2001:147–83) further refined this research and has provided a detailed analysis of the shape and structure of the typical household. Several studies by A. Faust have contributed to the discussion by highlighting differences in size between the pillared buildings in larger and smaller settlements. Faust concludes that the size of pillared buildings in larger towns and cities averages about 70 m^2, while those in what he calls smaller, "rural" settlements average about 110 m^2 (Faust 1999:233–52; 2000:17–39). However, his conclusion that this difference is a result of different family structures in urban versus rural settlements—"nuclear" families in urban contexts versus "extended" families in rural ones—is overly schematic. Faust raises but dismisses a more probable explanation: that circumvallation and settlement density in the larger settlements of Iron II Israel and Judah account in large measure for the differences in relative house size (compare the similar critique of Schloen [2001:140–41]). Here consideration of the philological evidence (see below) also provides a corrective, since the terminology (including *mišpāḥâ*) used in biblical sources to refer to family groups does not depend on the size of the settlement district or town. A relative difference in size between pillared buildings in the two environments, moreover, does not negate the fact that compounds of contiguous pillared buildings exist in both contexts and are homologous.

No doubt the daily lives of compound residents intertwined closely in myriad ways, as King and Stager have demonstrated (2001). The material record indicates this for both larger and smaller settlements, in large measure because of the evidence for residential propinquity. In addition, many of the compounds share ovens in common. Such ovens often appear in exterior locations or in the forecourts or annexes of the pillared buildings.[7] As ethnoarchaeological parallels suggest, groups resident in extended family compounds processed and consumed food together (Kramer 1982:120–30). Such physical arrangements, moreover, persisted for a long time. The archaeological record of Israel and Judah through the end of the Judean kingdom in the early sixth century points to a powerful conservatism in such arrangements.

The research of the scholars cited above undermines the devolutionary view of social development under the monarchy. As Stager and Holladay have showed, house size, layout, and function remained basically static between the Iron I and the late Iron II periods. Distribution of the houses naturally differed: in the Iron I they predominate in the small, unfortified villages, while in Iron II they appear in such small settlements but also, increasingly, in or near densely built-up administrative centers such as Megiddo and Beersheba (Holladay 1995:386–93; Schloen 2001:passim). The overall point, as Stager argued, is that the pillared house was a highly effective and durable adaptation to subsistence requirements in Palestine (Stager 1985:17). Holladay too stresses that the pattern of domestic residence—and the domestic subsistence economy undergirding that pattern—does not vary much from the early Iron Age down into at least the seventh century. Holladay writes:

> The basic architectural unit initially devised (or adapted) for the highly successful, highly individualistic, agro-economic exploitation of the highland frontier . . . was (a) the basic nuclear family's standard residence . . . . (b) . . . that same plan, with no substantive alteration, persisted as the standard rural and dominant urban residence for the entire period of the Hebrew monarchies. [Holladay 1995:393; see, too, Stager 1985:17, 22; Halpern 1991; Mazar 1990: 437; Meyers 2003:426]

Only in the Persian period does the pillared house and its subtypes disappear. This conclusion undermines another pillar of the devolutionary hypothesis: namely, that a sharp dichotomy existed between urban and rural lifeways in ancient Israel and Judah. Compounds composed of several pillared houses dominated the entire landscape of Iron Age Israel and Judah. The assumption that the (urban) state undermined the (rural) kinship structures depends on the a priori view that there was a fundamental distinction between urban and rural life ways. There is, however, little to recommend such a view, as D. Schloen has argued in his discussion of the patrimonial household in the Bronze and Iron Age Near East (2001:140–41 and ch. 13). The analyses of the material evidence for Israel's social organization briefly surveyed here, therefore, vitiate the simplistic idea that the introduction of a monarchy eradicated Israel's basic kinship organization.

What does this rough sketch of some of the material correlates of Israel's kinship organization have to do with P? Israel's domestic residence patterns and their underlying social and economic configurations were conservative and remained stable throughout the monarchic period. The same is true, I would argue, for the semantic fields of Israel's kinship terminology, although it remains true that the kinship terms possess an inherent flexibility. If, then, P's representation of Israelite kinship organization conforms with other demonstrably monarchic portrayals, why should scholars conclude that this represents a successful effort at archaizing? It is just as likely that P was knowledgeable about the dynamics of that kinship organization and perhaps originated during its floruit, which, in view of the arguments presented above, extended from the Iron Age I down through the Iron Age II. This argument finds additional support in analysis of the semantic range and evolution of a key kinship term in and beyond the P corpus: *mišpāḥâ*.

The term *mišpāḥâ* occurs some 303 times in the Hebrew Bible; more than half of these appear in P or related sources, 159 in Numbers alone. To determine how P's use of the term compares with that of other corpora, it will be useful first to survey nonpriestly texts in the Pentateuch, in the Deuteronomistic History, and in the Latter Prophets. A profile emerges from these sources which reflects the term's semantic range in the monarchic period.[8] *Mišpāḥâ* in these

[7] For representative examples in Iron II of ovens that probably were shared among several structures in a compound arrangement, see, e.g.: Beersheba Stratum VII Locus 2313—associated with Buildings 2524 and 2060 (Herzog 1984:26); and Tell Beit Mirsim Stratum A2 (Albright 1943: pl. 6, NW 31–32). At Tel Batash-Timnah, the excavators uncovered an excellent example of an oven (Locus 917) in the annex of a pillared building (Locus 909), which abuts several other such buildings; this example appears in the seventh-century Stratum II of Area E. A. Mazar and G. Kelm suggest that the room "probably served as a roofed cooking and baking area" for residents of the several adjacent pillared structures (Mazar and Kelm 1997:215 and plan 85).

[8] Naturally, not all scholars would agree that these corpora give a reliable indication of the term's semantic range in the monarchic era, since the constitutive books were subject to complex processes of authorship and redaction prior

texts refers often, but not exclusively, to a patrilateral association of kin that shares common title to a particular plot of land or region. The demographic extent of the *mišpāḥâ* can vary. What is clear is that *mišpāḥâ* is not simply the designation for an aggregation of extended families in a strict hierarchy of terms used to measure demography (see already Pedersen 1926:1:47–48, although his larger analysis of the *mišpāḥâ* is antiquated). Rather, the *mišpāḥâ* is normally a geographically defined entity, as the following discussion shows.

Mišpāḥâ is commonly used in reference to landholding. This point is emphasized in the Deuteronomistic border lists of Joshua 13–19, where the term appears 29 times.[9] In these lists, land is allotted *lĕmišpāḥôt*, "according to *mišpāḥôt*." The summary of the territory of Judah, which is typical of the lists, reads: *zeh gĕbûl bĕnê-yĕhûdâ sābîb lĕmišpĕḥōtām*, "this is the border of the Judahites all around according to their *mišpāḥôt*" (Josh. 15:12).[10] The term appears twelve more times in Joshua 21, where it is claimed that the twelve tribes assigned towns to the *mišpāḥôt* of the Levites. The text reads, for example, *kol-ʿārê haggēršūnnî lĕmišpĕḥōtām šĕlōš-ʿeśrēh ʿîr ûmigrĕšêhen*, "all of the towns of the Gershonites according to their *mišpāḥôt*: thirteen towns with their pasture land" (Josh. 21:33). This text clearly reflects the idea that towns and their adjacent lands were occupied "according to *mišpāḥôt*," the decisive landholding entities.

The relationship between *mišpāḥâ* and land tenure appears in other texts, and not only in connection with Israel and Judah. We read, for example, of the chiefs (*ʾallûpîm*) of Edom settled "according to their *mišpāḥôt* in the land of their possession" (Gen. 36:40; compare v. 43). A single man and his *mišpāḥâ* settle the town of Luz (Judg. 1:25–26), which demonstrates that a *mišpāḥâ* and a town were sometimes coextensive; such a town would have possessed arable and pasture lands, and occasionally "daughter" settlements (for the identity of a town with a *mišpāḥâ* see Schloen 2001:154–61, with additional literature). The tribe of Dan is reported to have consisted at first of a single *mišpāḥâ*, whose eponymous ancestor is called *ḥūšîm*, "Hushim" (Gen. 46:23), or *šûḥām*, "Shuham" (Num. 26:42).[11] Judges 17–18 locate the single *mišpāḥâ* of Dan in the two towns of Zorah and Eshtaol (Judg. 18:11), although Judges 1 and other texts know of additional towns associated with Dan in the Shephelah (thus Josh. 19:40–46; Naʾaman 1991:17–25). Nevertheless, Judges 17–18 narrate the migration of the single Danite *mišpāḥâ* northward to the town of Laish. Coincidentally, this description of the original location of the lone *mišpāḥâ* of Dan in Zorah and Eshtaol fits, conceptually if not literally, with a late-monarchic oracle of Jeremiah, in which YHWH promises to bring his rebellious brood to Zion, "one from a town (*ʿîr*) and two from a *mišpāḥâ*" (Jer.

to final codification in the Persian period and after. Here I make the assumption that the corpora selected largely originated before the Persian period, even if on occasion redaction-historical analysis might prove otherwise. I leave the book of Ruth out of the discussion, given the thorny issue of determining its date of composition. To include it would, in any case, buttress the arguments offered (see Levine 1983:95–106).

[9] Literature pertaining to this section of Joshua in particular and the historical geography of the "tribal" territories generally is extensive. The pioneer of research into the historical significance of these lists and territories was A. Alt (1953a:276–288; 1953b:193–202). Kallai, following the initial intentions of Alt to show that the lists were based on practical administrative realities of the monarchic era, argues that "these descriptions constitute a picture of a once-existing reality and are not the fabrications of an ancient writer, nor a prophetic vision or theory, for they clearly bear the stamp of reality . . . . [the] descriptions were recorded in accordance with a given historical reality, which they reflect, irrespective of whether the descriptions were originally composed in their present form, or whether the passages show signs of subsequent redaction or revision" (Kallai 1986:16, 279). Lemche demurs, arguing that "unless we can determine with certainty the level within the Israelite tribal system to which the actual 'living' usage of the term *mišpāḥâ* refers, its use . . . in the allocation-of-land traditions in the Book of Joshua must be regarded as secondary in relation to the original meaning of the term" (Lemche 1985:262–63). Lemche's demurral fails to appreciate that the geographical and spatial usage of *mišpāḥâ* is original, and that the term does not simply denote "a level" in an otherwise stable hierarchy of terms describing the "tribal system." N. Naʾaman offered a thorough review of the problem of the date, unity, and function of the lists and made a compelling case in support of Alt's effort to connect them to the late seventh century (1991:3–71, with extensive literature).

[10] Compare the phrase *zōʾt naḥălat maṭṭēh bĕnê-yĕhûdâ lĕmišpĕḥōtām*, "this is the patrimony of the tribe of the Judahites according to their *mišpāḥôt*" (Josh. 15:20); the formula is typical of the Deuteronomistic allotment texts in Joshua and occurs also for Reuben (13:23), Gad (13:28), Ephraim (16:8), Benjamin (18:20, 28), Simeon (19:8), Zebulun (19:16), Issachar (19:23), Asher (19:31), Naphtali (19:39), and Dan (19:48).

[11] The two texts probably refer to the same individual, with metathesis of the first two consonants in Genesis (Knoppers 2003:454). The Chronicler, perhaps dependent on Gen. 46:23, may preserve reference to Hushim as the only son of Dan; Japhet reads: *bĕnê dān ḥūšîm bĕnô ʾeḥad*, "the sons of Dan, Hushim, his one son" (1 Chron. 7:12; Japhet 1993:174).

3:14). All of these uses emphasize not purely the demographic extent of the *mišpāḥâ*, but rather its spatial aspect. Gottwald's functionalist definition of the *mišpāḥâ* as "a protective association of families" is not entirely wrong, but it overemphasizes the legal functions and demographic size of the unit.[12] Levine (2003:445), on the other hand, rightly emphasizes the spatial aspect: in "the economic context . . . the term relates to land ownership or land tenure in a predominantly agrarian community." Tappy (2000:180) makes a similar observation, as does Lehmann (2004:174), who concludes that "in the case of the *mišpāḥâ* the kinship system is connected to land tenure and territoriality." This is in fact the primary connotation of the term in the majority of its attestations.

This also explains why the Hebrew Bible gives relatively little explicit evidence of judicial, cultic, or other social functions associated with the *mišpāḥâ*. In a few cases, the texts connect blood vengeance for homicide (2 Sam. 14:7) and annual sacrificial celebrations with the *mišpāḥâ* (1 Sam. 20:6, 29; compare Exod. 12:21 [J]; see Wilson 1983:59–75; Tappy 2000). These examples focus on the retention of patrimonial lands within the *mišpāḥâ*, or on celebration of the productive resources of the land—a focus consistent with the spatial, title-holding, and hence agricultural associations of the *mišpāḥâ*, as Halpern (1996:296–302) has also emphasized. In monarchic Israel, patrilineal succession and virilocal residence, if not strict endogamy (on which see recently Lehmann 2004), also helped maintain patrimonial holdings within the *mišpāḥâ*. The spatial character of the *mišpāḥâ*, the fact that it is often a geographically defined entity, also explains why the term was sometimes used as a synonym for *gôy* (nation), which is a political entity located in a specific territory (Speiser 1960:157–63). This use of *mišpāḥâ* in parallel with *gôy* is thus not a secondary development; the same usage appears in the Yahwistic source (compare Gen. 12:3 and 28:14 with Gen. 18:18), and in prophetic oracles dealing with foreign nations beginning with Amos (e.g., Amos 3:1–2; Nah. 3:4; Jer. 1:15; 3:14; 10:25; 33:24; compare Ps. 96:7). The texts thus rarely link the *mišpāḥâ* with specific social functions. Neither do they directly associate the *mišpāḥâ* with leadership roles—e.g., *rōʾš* "head," *nāśîʾ* "chief," or *zāqēn* "elder"—except for rare occasions in texts originating in the Persian era (see below) or describing non-Israelite groups (e.g., Gen. 36:40, above; Lemche 1985:261–72).

Halpern (1991:53–60; 1996:296–303) has argued on the basis of the material evidence that corporate tomb groups in Iron Age Israel and Judah would have served the *mišpāḥâ* (for tomb typology, see Bloch-Smith 1992). He argues, too, that the *zebaḥ hayyāmîm*, "annual sacrifice," or *zebaḥ mišpāḥâ*, "sacrifice of the *mišpāḥâ*," which David claims as his alibi for not sitting at Saul's table (1 Sam. 20:6, 29), pertains to funerary rites associated with the group (Halpern 1996:297). Bloch-Smith (1992:125), in her survey of Judahite burial practices, makes a similar argument, and notes in particular the practice of offering tithes at such celebrations. If the identity of the *mišpāḥâ* derives in the first place from its connection to land tenure, then it makes eminent sense that funerary celebrations characterized by tithing appear within the *mišpāḥâ* (see Brichto 1973:1–54). Halpern and Bloch-Smith are no doubt correct in thinking that the ancestor cult—reverence of ancestors who shared the productive resources of lands held by the *mišpāḥâ*—would have been a feature of the ritual life of the *mišpāḥâ*, even if this must be inferred. Brichto (1973) already established how ownership of real estate by the kinship group was validated through the mechanism of burial. The conclusion follows, therefore, that during the monarchic era the *mišpāḥâ* was defined by the territory it occupied and the economic activity and familial rites associated with that territory.

Demonstrably postexilic texts, excluding P for the moment, evince a dramatic reduction in the number of attestations and a sharp change in the semantic field of the term *mišpāḥâ* (Levine 2003:451–52; Williamson 2003:472). The term appears twenty times in Chronicles; only one of these, a quotation of Ps. 96:7 in 1 Chron. 16:28, occurs outside of the genealogies in 1 Chronicles 1–9. Six of the other nineteen instances in Chronicles parallel the list of Levitical cities in Joshua 21. Furthermore, in each of these six parallel texts, the Chronicler alters the reading in Joshua, rendering a singular where the Joshua text uses the plural.[13] Both the scarcity of the term in

[12] Although Gottwald considered this definition basic, he did also recognize that the *mišpāḥâ* could be a topographically defined unit (Gottwald 1979:257–84, 316); the point was emphasized by Halpern (1983:242–43) and reiterated by Meyers (1997:13). A critique of Gottwald's view may be found in Lemche 1985 and Bendor 1996:82–86.

[13] 1 Chron. 6:39 parallels Josh. 21:10; 1 Chron. 6:46 || Josh. 21:5; 1 Chron. 6:55 || Josh. 21:26; 1 Chron. 6:56 || Josh. 21:27; 1 Chron. 6:51 || Josh. 21:20. In each case, Chronicles reads differently from Joshua: the first four read the construct singular of *mišpāḥâ* instead of the plural in Joshua, so that Chronicles reduces the number of Levitical *mišpāḥôt* given in Joshua. In 1 Chron. 6:51, the Chronicler has completely altered the context and meaning of the text in Joshua (Japhet 1993:159, 162). 1 Chron. 6:45 reads *bĕmišpĕḥôtêhem*, where Josh. 21:19 has *ûmigrĕšêhen*; the

Chronicles and the writer's reinterpretation of earlier sources suggest that Israel's kinship organization, and hence the semantic range of the term, had changed by the time of the Chronicler. Proof of this appears in several cases where the Chronicler uses *mišpāḥâ* as no preexilic source did. Twice Chronicles refers to guild-like institutions: once in a reference to the "the *mišpāḥôt* of the scribes residing in Jabez" (1 Chron. 2:55);[14] and once in "the *mišpāḥôt* of the house of linen workers of Beth-Ashbea" (1 Chron. 4:21). This usage may stem, as Knoppers (2003:351) has suggested, from emergent structures of kinship in relation to economic specialization in the Persian and Hellenistic eras.[15] Even if that is so, it has no precedent in monarchic sources. The Chronicler also furnishes the lone exception to the rule that leadership roles otherwise do not pertain to *mišpāḥôt* in preexilic usage: he identifies Simeonite "*nĕśîʾîm* [chieftains] in their *mišpāḥôt*" (1 Chron. 4:38). The Chronicler, thus, feels no constraint to use the term as his preexilic sources do, and on occasion alters his sources' conception of the term. Meanwhile, *mišpāḥâ* occurs only once in Ezra–Nehemiah, where it refers to temporary military units conscripted in defense of the wall-building project in Jerusalem (Neh. 4:7), which also suggests that the semantic range of the term had shifted. Moreover, the genealogies and border lists of Ezra–Nehemiah do not use the term at all. The reduction and alteration of the use of the term *mišpāḥâ* in Chronicles and Ezra–Nehemiah suggest that in the Persian period it lost its concrete associations with the spatial dimension of Israel's earlier kinship organization.[16] It is likely that the political disruptions of the sixth century, which upset the territorial distribution of the kinship groups that had prevailed through the end of the Judahite monarchy, helped to undermine the older geographical associations of the *mišpāḥâ*, and that this process accelerated with the territorial and demographic diminution of the Persian province of Yehud.[17]

P, however, does not reflect this dissociation of terminology and social organization. P demonstrates an understanding of *mišpāḥâ* that is fully compatible with other monarchic texts. In the Table of Nations in Genesis 10, the Priestly passages assume that the inhabited world consists of *gôyîm*, "nations," which reside in specific *ʾărāṣôt*, "lands," that in turn subdivide according to their constitutive, territorial *mišpāḥôt* (Gen. 10:5; cp. 10:20, 31; see also Speiser 1960). The model here presents larger polities composed of territorially defined *mišpāḥôt*, the same model by which P and other monarchic-era sources understand Israel's social and spatial organization. This model, to repeat, does not inform the usage of Chronicles and Ezra–Nehemiah. Several passages in the Holiness Code in Leviticus, which may antedate P, likewise identify the *mišpāḥâ* as a kin group that is defined by title to land.[18] Leviticus 25 states that in the year of the Jubilee any Israelite slave "will go out . . . he and his sons with him, and he will return to his *mišpāḥâ* and to the property of his fathers" (*ʾăḥuzzat ʾăbōtāyw*; Lev. 25:41; see Levine 1993:134–39 on *ʾăḥuzzāh*). The *mišpāḥâ* holds title to property. The ordinance in Leviticus, irrespective of whether it was ever enforced, existed to preserve Israel's kinship structure, which is centered in the land. The same logic undergirds the law about redemption (*gĕʾullâ*) of an indebted Israelite in Leviticus 25, where the redeemer must come from within the *mišpāḥâ*: alienation of patrimony subverts the social organization of the nation (Lev. 25:48–49; cf. Milgrom 1995:67). In Numbers, where the term *mišpāḥâ* appears most often in the P corpus, land allotment cannot be the explicit focus, since according to the narrative framework the Israelites had not yet settled the land. And Levine (2000:334) rightly notes that, in terms of ety-

latter is evidently the original summation for the list of cities "and their pasture lands," although the phrase is also lacking in the LXX of Josh. 21:19 (see Knoppers 2003:433).

[14] The emendation of *sōpĕrîm*, "scribes", to *siprîm*, "Siphrites" has sometimes been suggested (note, e.g., *BHS*). Japhet (1993:90) and Knoppers (2003:301) have argued convincingly for *sōpĕrîm*.

[15] Scholars should be wary of making the same mistake for the Persian and Hellenistic periods as they long made for the early Iron Age by arguing that centralization of political authority (in this case, the Persian imperial authority) has necessary and deleterious consequences for kin-based social organization. Social organization in the reconstructed Jewish community did undergo changes in the fifth and fourth centuries; some of these are noted by Weinberg (1973:400–14; see also Weinberg 1992). Weinberg's views, however, have been criticized by, among others, Williamson (1998:145–163). Nevertheless, social and political structures centered in the village and the extended family persisted. See the excellent survey of Collins (1997:103–62).

[16] Here I disagree with Bendor (1996:228), who argues for consistency in usage through the postexilic period.

[17] On the geographical extent of Yehud in the Persian period, the most thorough discussion is now Lipschits 2005: 154–84; cf. Carter 1999.

[18] The relationship between P and the Holiness Code has been the subject of extensive debate. Two significant studies have reconfigured the debate, those of Knohl (1995) and Milgrom (1991:13–35). A recent overview with literature may be found in Olyan 2005.

mology, "there is nothing in the meaning of the term *mišpāḥâ* that implies ownership of land or real property." Yet the model upon which P relies associates the *mišpāḥâ* with territory. Thus, even in Numbers, Moses informs the people that when they do finally cross over the Jordan, they are to "apportion the land by lot according to your *mišpāḥôt*" (Num. 33:54).[19] The geographical association of the *mišpāḥâ* in P texts in Numbers—it occupies specific territory—conforms with Joshua 13–19, the land-allocation lists in the Deuteronomistic History. In all of these contexts, then, the Priestly (and Holiness Code) use of the term basically matches the other monarchic attestations examined above. P reconstructs the social organization of early Israel spatially on the basis of the monarchic model.

Additional evidence shows that P's use of *mišpāḥâ* conforms to the monarchic reality of the term as a geographically defined entity. The P census of Numbers 26 enumerates the individual tribes according to their *mišpāḥôt*. In the case of Manasseh, P's genealogy (Num. 26:29–34) has connections with three other sources: Josh. 17:1–3; 1 Chron. 7:14–19; and, indirectly, the Samaria Ostraca.[20] Joshua and Numbers preserve substantially the same structure—and purpose—for the genealogy of Manasseh, except that "the remaining sons of Manasseh" in Joshua become his great-grandsons in Numbers. The genealogy in Chronicles, by contrast, bears little resemblance to the other two. The Chronicler may have used unknown sources to fashion his genealogy (Demsky 1982:70–75; Edelman 1991:179–201; Japhet 1993: 174–179; Knoppers 2003:454–56; 461–63), but it clearly concerns problems different from those in Joshua and Numbers. The genealogy in Joshua pertains explicitly to allotment of land, while Numbers, describing the period prior to the settlement in Canaan, treats the allotment proleptically. Even so, Joshua and Numbers share the same rationale for tracing Manasseh's sons, or *mišpāḥôt*, to the fifth generation: there was an anomaly in the settlement of the territory of Manasseh, such that Zelophehad's daughters inherited land because he had no sons (Albright 1931:241–44; Lemaire 1972:13–20; Aharoni 1979:356–68). The notion of genealogy as charter clarifies this situation (Wilson 1977; Levine 2000: 355–61), since the genealogical tradition reflected in Joshua and Numbers explains the anomaly that several Manassite *mišpāḥôt* in the heart of the tribal allotment descended from female eponyms. This exceptional arrangement and the accompanying legal amendments serve to insure that land would not be alienated from Zelophehad's descendants as a consequence of exogamy.

Data from the Samaria Ostraca also illuminate the genealogy of P. The ostraca consist of a series of dockets that record deliveries of wine and oil to Samaria from regions surrounding the capital. They evidently represent payments in kind, either to the crown or to officials residing in Samaria (an excellent analysis appears in Schloen 2001:155–65). What is important here is that the place names preserved in the ostraca refer to places from which the wine and oil originated. The toponyms thus illuminate the spatial distribution of productive agricultural units surrounding Samaria. Ostraca from the fifteenth year of an unnamed king, presumably Jeroboam II, mention seven names that are identified in Numbers and Joshua as *mišpāḥôt* of Manasseh: Heleq, Abiezer, Shemida, Shechem, Asriel, Noah, and Hoglah. The appearance of Noah and Hoglah as toponyms in the ostraca verifies that the *mišpāḥôt* of the daughters of Zelophehad did lend their names to agricultural districts of Manasseh near the northern capital. The *mišpāḥôt* of Manasseh thus represented agricultural districts in the first third of the eighth century B.C.E. within that tribal territory (and the same was likely true elsewhere; Aharoni 1979:367). Stager (1985:24) estimates that the seven Manassite *mišpāḥôt* occupied an area of ca. 700 km^2, or 100 km^2 per *mišpāḥâ*. It follows from this that the genealogical data preserved by P in Numbers 26 (and by the Deuteronomist in Joshua 17) reflect the concrete territorial and kinship organization of the monarchic era, even if, as Schloen (2001:162–63) has argued, P's data are not comprehensive.

Thus Stager could already conclude in his seminal study that "the Samaria ostraca indicate that at least some of the old clan and lineage divisions retained their integrity until much later. They survived as viable socioeconomic (and probably political) units" (Stager 1985:24). I would add that this is why P properly recognized that the *mišpāḥâ* was fundamen-

[19] Levine (2000:524) takes this to mean that the land "is to be allocated to the Israelites by lot according to clans commensurate with the population of each clan." I would suggest it rather means that the land will be allocated to the units that occupy space. Borders, after all, are not drawn according to the number of people occupying a territory, but rather by the extent of the territory they circumscribe.

[20] There is a large literature on the Samaria Ostraca and on the historical-geographical problems pertaining to the territory of Manasseh. The *editio princeps* of the ostraca is Reisner et al. 1924:1:227–46; a palaeographic study can be found in Kaufman 1966. See also, e.g., Aharoni 1979:356–69; Cross 1961; Lemaire 1977; Kallai 1986:50–55; and Rainey 1988:69–74. For discussions of the economic organization of the kinship groups reflected in the ostraca, see Halpern 1996:305–6 and Schloen 2001:155–65.

tally a social entity defined according to its spatial aspect.

In the foregoing analysis, I have concurred with other scholars who argued that a devolutionary model misrepresents the influence of the monarchy on Israelite society and should be abandoned. From a philological perspective, P's use of terms in the semantic field of kinship, specifically *mišpāḥâ*, conforms to that of other monarchic sources. To fix a date for the composition and codification of the P corpus, whether before or after the demise of the monarchy, requires evidence of a different kind, but the present analysis shows that P successfully structured early Israel's kinship organization according to concrete realities of the monarchic era. The Samaria Ostraca, in particular, demonstrate that P's retention and use of the term *mišpāḥâ* in genealogies conform neatly with organizational realities of the Iron II era. Contrary to its literary conceit, P does not, of course, provide an unfiltered view of the premonarchic era. Nevertheless, the reputation of P as falsifier, archaizer, or ideologue, even if it can be supported on other grounds, cannot be used as an argument against the accuracy of P's presentation of Israel's social organization. A priori assumptions about the character of P must not preclude investigation and use of P materials as data for social-scientific analysis of Israelite society under the monarchy, particularly if other evidence corroborates the essential accuracy of the Priestly model.

The present analysis therefore shows that in the case of P, the elite perspective conforms to externally received data on the social organization of ancient Israel during the monarchy. Cross has similarly credited P with a serious effort to reconstruct the social realities of an earlier era, and asserts that the Priestly writers "were more successful in their reconstructions of the covenantal institutions of early Israel than we critical scholars have supposed, and . . . their traditionalist approaches are often less doctrinaire and closer to historical reality than the unilinear historical schemes imposed by scholars of yesteryear" (Cross 1998:21). Thus, to gain access to information on Israel's rural population, there is no justification for ignoring data in sources that emanate from the sophisticated cadre of priests who compiled P.

Bibliography

Aharoni, Y.
1979 *The Land of the Bible.* Translated by A. F. Rainey. 2d ed. Philadelphia: Westminster.

Albright, W. F.
1931 The Site of Tirzah and the Topography of Western Manasseh. *JPOS* 11:241–54.
1943 *The Excavation of Tell Beit Mirsim.* Vol. 3, *The Iron Age.* AASOR 21–22. New Haven, Conn.: American Schools of Oriental Research.

Alt, A.
1953a Israels Gaue unter Josia. In *Kleine Schriften zur Geschichte des Volkes Israel*, by A. Alt, 2:276–88. Munich: Beck.
1953b Das System der Stammesgrenzen im Buche Josua. In *Kleine Schriften zur Geschichte des Volkes Israel*, by A. Alt, 1:193–202. Munich: Beck.
1959 Der Anteil des Königtum an der sozialen Entwicklung in den Reichen Israel und Juda. In *Kleine Schriften zur Geschichte des Volkes Israel*, by A. Alt, 3:348–72. Munich: Beck.

Bendor, S.
1996 *The Social Structure of Ancient Israel: The Institution of the Family* (beit ʾab) *from the Settlement to the End of the Monarchy.* Jerusalem: Simor.

Benjamin, D., and V. Matthews
1993 *The Social World of Ancient Israel, 1250–587 B.C.E.* Peabody, Mass.: Hendrickson.

Blenkinsopp, J.
1996 An Assessment of the Alleged Pre-Exilic Date of the Priestly Material in the Pentateuch. *ZAW* 108: 495–97.
1997 The Family in First Temple Israel. In *Families in Ancient Israel*, ed. L. G. Perdue, 48–103. Louisville, Ky.: Westminster John Knox.

Bloch-Smith, E.
1992 *Judahite Burial Practices and Beliefs about the Dead.* JSOTSup 123. Sheffield, England: Sheffield Academic Press.

Braemer, F.
1982 *L'architecture domestique du Levant à l'âge du Fer.* Paris: Éditions recherche sur les civilisations.

Brichto, H.
1973 Kin, Cult, Land and Afterlife—A Biblical Complex. *HUCA* 44:1–54.

Bright, J.
1962 Hebrew Religion. In *The Interpreter's Dictionary of the Bible*, ed. G. A. Buttrick, 2:560–70. Nashville, Tenn.: Abingdon.

Bunimovitz, S., and A. Faust
2003 Building Identity: The Four-Room House and the Israelite Mind. In *Symbiosis, Symbolism, and the Power of the Past: Canaan, Ancient Israel, and Their Neighbors from the Late Bronze Age through Roman Palaestina*, ed. W. G. Dever and S. Gitin, 411–23. Winona Lake, Ind.: Eisenbrauns.

Carter, C. E.
1999 *The Emergence of Yehud in the Persian Period: A Social and Demograhic Study*. JSOTSup 294. Sheffield, England: Sheffield Academic Press.

Chaney, M.
1986 Systemic Study of the Israelite Monarchy. *Semeia* 37:53–76.

Collins, J. J.
1997 Marriage, Divorce, and Family in Second Temple Judaism. In *Families in Ancient Israel*, ed. L. G. Perdue, 103–62. Louisville, Ky.: Westminster John Knox.

Cross, F. M.
1961 Epigraphic Notes on Hebrew Documents of the Eighth-Sixth Centuries B.C.: I. A New Reading of a Place Name in the Samaria Ostraca. *BASOR* 163:12–14.
1998 Kinship and Covenant in Ancient Israel. In *From Epic to Canon: History and Literature in Ancient Israel*, by F. M. Cross, 3–21. Baltimore: Johns Hopkins University Press.

Davies, E. W.
1989 Land: Its Rights and Privileges. In *The World of Ancient Israel*, ed. R. E. Clements. Cambridge: Cambridge University.

Demsky, A.
1982 The Genealogies of Manasseh and the Location of the Territory of Milkah, Daughter of Zelophehad [in Hebrew]. *EI* 16:70–75.

Donner, H.
1963 Die soziale Botschaft der Propheten im Lichte der Gesellschaftsordnung in Israel. *Oriens Antiquus* 2:229–45.

Edelman, D.
1991 The Manassite Genealogy in 1 Chronicles 7:14–19: Form and Structure. *CBQ* 53:179–201.

Faust, A.
1999 Differences in Family Structure between Cities and Villages in Iron Age II. *Tel Aviv* 26:233–52.
2000 The Rural Community in Ancient Israel. *BASOR* 317:17–39.

Frick, F.
1977 *The City in Ancient Israel*. SBLDS 36. Missoula, Mont.: Scholars.

Friedman, R. E.
1981 *The Exile and Biblical Narrative*. HSM 22. Chico, Calif.: Scholars.

Gottwald, N. K.
1979 *The Tribes of Yahweh: A Sociology of the Religion of Liberated Israel, 1250–1050 B.C.E.* Maryknoll, N.Y.: Orbis.
1986 The Participation of Free Agrarians in the Introduction of Monarchy to Ancient Israel. *Semeia* 37:77–106.

Halpern, B.
1981 *The Constitution of the Monarchy in Ancient Israel*. HSM 25. Chico, Calif.: Scholars.
1983 *The Emergence of Israel in Canaan*. Chico, Calif.: Scholars.
1991 Jerusalem and the Lineages in the Seventh Century B.C.E.: Kinship and the Rise of Individual Moral Liability. In *Law and Ideology in Monarchic Israel*, ed. B. Halpern and D. W. Hobson, 11–107. JSOTSup 124. Sheffield, England: Sheffield Academic Press.
1996 Sybil, or the Two Nations? Archaism, Alienation, and the Elite Redefinition of Traditional Culture in Judah in the Eighth–Seventh Centuries B.C.E. In *The Study of the Ancient Near East in the Twenty-First Century*, ed. J. S. Cooper and G. Schwartz, 291–338. Winona Lake, Ind.: Eisenbrauns.

Herr, L. G.
1997 The Iron Age II Period: Emerging Nations. *BA* 60/3:114–51,154–83.

Herzog, Z.
1986 *Beer-Sheba*. Vol. 2, *The Early Iron Age Settlements*. Tel Aviv: Institute of Archaeology, Tel Aviv University.

Holladay, J. S.
1986 The Stables of Ancient Israel: Functional Determinants of Stable Construction and the Interpretation of Pillared Building Remains of the Palestinian Iron Age. In *The Archaeology of Jordan and Other Studies Presented to Siegfried H. Horn*, ed. L. Geraty and L. G. Herr, 103–65. Berrien Springs, Mich.: Andrews University.
1992 House, Israelite. In *The Anchor Bible Dictionary*, ed. D. N. Freedman, 3:308–18. New York: Doubleday.
1995 The Kingdoms of Israel and Judah: Political and Economic Centralization in the Iron IIA–B (ca. 1000–750 B.C.E.). In *The Archaeology of Society in the Holy Land*, ed. T. E. Levy, 368–98. New York: Facts on File.
1997a Four-Room House. In *The Oxford Encyclopedia of Archaeology in the Near East*, ed. E. M. Meyers, 2:337–42. New York: Oxford University Press.
1997b Syro-Palestinian Houses. In *The Oxford Encyclopedia of Archaeology in the Near East*, ed. E. M. Meyers, 5:94–115. New York: Oxford University Press.

Hopkins, D.
1985 *The Highlands of Canaan: Agricultural Life in the Early Iron Age*. Sheffield, England: Almond.

Japhet, S.
1993 *I and II Chronicles*. Old Testament Library. Louisville, Ky.: Westminster John Knox.

Kallai, Z.
1986 *Historical Geography of the Bible*. Leiden: Brill.
1998 The System of Levitic Cities and Cities of Refuge: A Historical-Geographical Study in Biblical Historiography. In *Biblical Historiography and Historical Geography*, by Z. Kallai, 51–62. Beiträge zur Erforschung des Alten Testaments und das antiken Judentums 44. Frankfurt: Lang.

Kaufman, I. T.
1966 The Samaria Ostraca: A Study in Ancient Hebrew Palaeography. Ph.D. diss., Harvard University.

Kaufmann, Y.
1960 *The Religion of Israel*. Translated by M. Greenberg. Chicago: University of Chicago Press.

Knohl, I.
1995 *The Sanctuary of Silence: The Priestly Torah and The Holiness School*. Minneapolis: Fortress.

Kramer, C.
1982 *Village Ethnoarchaeology: Rural Iran in Archaeological Perspective*. New York: Academic.

Lehmann, G.
2004 Reconstructing the Social Landscape of Early Israel: Rural Marriage Alliances in the Central Hill Country. *Tel Aviv* 31:141–93.

Lemaire, A.
1972 Le "Pays de Hépher" et les "Filles de Zelophehad" à la lumière des ostraca de Samarie. *Semitica* 22:13–20.
1977 *Inscriptions hebraïques*. Vol. 1, *Les ostraca*. Paris: Éditions du Cerf.

Lemche, N. P.
1985 *Early Israel: Anthropological and Historical Studies on the Israelite Society before the Monarchy*. VTSup 37. Leiden: Brill.

Levine, B.
1983 In Praise of the Israelite *Mišpāḥâ*: Legal Themes in Ruth. In *The Quest for the Kingdom of God: Studies in Honor of George E. Mendenhall*, ed. H. B. Huffmon, F. A. Spina, and A. R. W. Green, 95–106. Winona Lake, Ind.: Eisenbrauns.
1993a *Numbers 1–20*. AB 4A. New York: Doubleday.
1993b On the Semantics of Land Tenure in Biblical Literature: The Term *ʾaḥuzzāh*. In *The Tablet and the Scroll: Near Eastern Studies in Honor of William W. Hallo*, ed. M. E. Cohen, D. C. Snell, and D. B. Weisberg, 134–39. Bethesda, Md.: CDL.
2000 *Numbers 21–36*. AB 4B. New York: Doubleday.
2003 The Clan-Based Economy of Biblical Israel. In *Symbiosis, Symbolism, and the Power of the Past: Canaan, Ancient Israel, and Their Neighbors from the Late Bronze Age through Roman Palaestina*, ed. W. G. Dever and S. Gitin, 445–53. Winona Lake, Ind.: Eisenbrauns.

Lipschits, O.
1999 The History of the Benjamin Region under Babylonian Rule. *Tel Aviv* 26:155–90.
2005 *The Fall and Rise of Jerusalem: Judah under Babylonian Rule.* Winona Lake, Ind.: Eisenbrauns.

Master, D. M.
2001 State Formation and the Kingdom of Ancient Israel. *JNES* 60:117–31.

Mazar, A.
1990 *Archaeology of the Land of the Bible, 10,000–586 B.C.E.* New York: Doubleday.

Mazar, A., and G. Kelm
1997 *Timnah (Tel Batash)*. Vol. 1, *Stratigraphy and Architecture*. Qedem 37. Jerusalem: Institute of Archaeology, Hebrew University.

McNutt, P.
1999 *Reconstructing the Society of Ancient Israel.* Louisville, Ky.: Westminster John Knox.

Meyers, C.
1997 The Family in Early Israel. In *Families in Ancient Israel*, ed. L. G. Perdue, 1–47. Louisville, Ky.: Westminster John Knox.
2003 Women's Culture in Agrarian Households of the Iron Age. In *Symbiosis, Symbolism, and the Power of the Past: Canaan, Ancient Israel, and Their Neighbors from the Late Bronze Age through Roman Palaestina*, ed. W. G. Dever and S. Gitin, 425–44. Winona Lake, Ind.: Eisenbrauns.

Milevski, I.
1996–97 Settlement Patterns in Northern Judah during the Achaemenid Period, according to the Hill Country of Benjamin and Jerusalem Surveys. *Bulletin of the Anglo-Israel Archaeological Society* 15:7–29.

Milgrom, J.
1991 *Leviticus 1–16*. AB 3. New York: Doubleday.
1995 The Land Redeemer and the Jubilee. In *Fortunate the Eyes That See: Essays in Honor of David Noel Freedman*, ed. A. Beck, A. Bartelt, P. R. Raabe, and C. A. Franke, 66–69. Grand Rapids, Mich.: Eerdmans.
1999 The Antiquity of the Priestly Source: A Reply to Joseph Blenkinsopp. *ZAW* 111:10–22.
2000 *Leviticus 17–22*. AB 3A. New York: Doubleday.
2001 *Leviticus 23–27*. AB 3B. New York: Doubleday.

Naʾaman, N.
1991 The Kingdom of Judah under Josiah. *Tel Aviv* 18: 3–71.

Netzer, E.
1992 Domestic Architecture in the Iron Age. In *The Architecture of Ancient Israel*, ed. A. Kempinski and R. Reich, 193–201. Jerusalem: Israel Exploration Society.

Noth, M.
1984 *The Laws of the Pentateuch and Other Studies*. London: SCM.

Olyan, S. M.
2005 Exodus 31:12–17: The Sabbath according to H, or the Sabbath according to P and H? *JBL* 124: 201–9.

Pedersen, J.
1926 *Israel: Its Life and Culture*. 2 vols. London: Oxford University Press.

Pola, T.
1995 *Die Ursprüngliche Priesterschrift: Beobachtungen zur Literarkritik und Traditionsgeschichte von* P^g. Wissenschaftliche Monographien zum Alten und Neuen Testaments 70. Neukirchen: Neukirchener.

Rainey, A. F.
1988 Toward a Precise Date for the Samaria Ostraca. *BASOR* 272:69–74.

Reisner, G. A., C. S. Fisher, and D. G. Lyon
1924 *Harvard Excavations at Samaria, 1908–1910*. Vol. 1. Cambridge, Mass.: Harvard University Press.

Reviv, H.
1989 *The Elders in Ancient Israel*. Jerusalem: Magnes.

Schloen, J. D.
2001 *The House of the Father As Fact and Symbol: Patrimonialism in Ugarit and the Ancient Near East*. SAHL 2. Winona Lake, Ind.: Eisenbrauns.

Shiloh, Y.
1970 The Four-Room House: Its Situation and Function in the Israelite City. *IEJ* 20:180–90.

Speiser, E. A.
1960 "People" and "Nation" of Israel. *JBL* 79:157–63.

Sperling, D.
1999 Pants, Persians, and the Priestly Source. In *Ki Baruch Hu: Ancient Near Eastern, Biblical, and Judaic Studies in Honor of Baruch A. Levine*, ed. R. Chazan, W. W. Hallo, and L. H. Schiffman, 373–85. Winona Lake, Ind.: Eisenbrauns.

Stager, L. E.
1985 The Archaeology of the Family in Ancient Israel. *BASOR* 260:1–35.

Tappy, R. E.
2000 Lineage and Law. *RB* 107:175–204.

Vaux, R. de
1961 *Ancient Israel: Its Life and Institutions*. New York: McGraw-Hill.

Weinberg, J. P.
1973 Das *Beit ʾAbôt* im 6–4. Jh. v.u.Z. *VT* 23:400–14.
1992 *The Citizen-Temple Community*. Translated by D. L. Smith-Christopher. JSOTSup 151. Sheffield, England: JSOT Press.

Wellhausen, J.
1958 *Prolegomena to the History of Ancient Israel*. New York: Meridian.

Williamson, H. G. M.
1998 Judah and the Jews. In *Studies in Persian History: Essays in Memory of David M. Lewis*, ed. M. Brosius and A. Kuhrt, 145–63. Achaemenid History 11. Leiden: Nederlands Instituut voor het Nabije Oosten.
2003 The Family in Persian-period Judah: Some Textual Reflections. In *Symbiosis, Symbolism, and the Power of the Past: Canaan, Ancient Israel, and Their Neighbors from the Late Bronze Age through Roman Palaestina*, ed. W. G. Dever and S. Gitin, 469–85. Winona Lake, Ind.: Eisenbrauns.

Wilson, R. R.
1977 *Genealogy and History in the Biblical World*. New Haven, Conn.: Yale University.
1983 Enforcing the Covenant: The Mechanism of Judicial Authority in Early Israel. In *The Quest for the Kingdom of God: Studies in Honor of George E. Mendenhall*, ed. H. B. Huffmon, F. A. Spina, and A. R. W. Green, 59–75. Winnoa Lake, Ind.: Eisenbrauns.

48. Two New Hellenistic Lead Weights of the Tanit Series

by Samuel R. Wolff and Gerald Finkielsztejn

Thanks to his association with Larry Stager, Samuel Wolff has been encountering Tanit throughout his archaeological career, first at Carthage (Stager and Wolff 1983) and later at Ashkelon (Stager 1991:37). It is his pleasure to offer this modest contribution on Tyrian lead weights of the Tanit series to Larry Stager in appreciation of the years he spent with him as a student (in his first class as a lecturer at the University of Chicago in 1973) and as an excavation staff member (Carthage 1975–1979 and Ashkelon 1985–1990).

Gerald Finkielsztejn, who was kindly invited by Wolff to study the weights discussed here, is very pleased to have this occasion to further his research on weights from the Levant, especially on the Tanit series attributed to Tyre, the mother city of both Carthage and Ashkelon.

Two weights are discussed below. One weight was recently discovered in the renewed excavations at Tel Gezer; the second, a surface find from Ashdod-Yam, was partially published many years ago.

The Gezer Weight

The lead weight from Tel Gezer was discovered in the 2006 season of excavations, which concentrated on the casemate wall system attached to the western portion of the so-called Solomonic Gate.[1] It came from Field A, Square A-8, Locus 11001, which was a surface locus containing Iron II and Hellenistic pottery. The excavations yielded some *in situ* remains that are dated to the Hellenistic period, including a wall fragment that overrides an earlier Iron II wall in Square Y-8, and much Hellenistic pottery *ex situ*. But there is no question that a significant Hellenistic settlement existed in the immediate vicinity. In Field VII, excavated by the Hebrew Union College team in the early 1970s, located just dozens of meters from Square A-8, two Hellenistic strata were revealed: Stratum 3, dating to the late third/early second centuries B.C.E., and Stratum 2A–B/C, dating to the early second to mid-first centuries B.C.E. (Gitin 1990; cf. also Reich 1981). This excavation, by the way, also yielded a lead weight, albeit not of the same type discussed here, rather one of the *agoranomos* series (Seger 1976:144). Two stamped Rhodian amphora handles were also found in the 2006 Gezer excavations, preliminarily dated by Finkielsztejn to the second century B.C.E. Thus, while the lead weight was not found in a secure context, strata which have been excavated nearby provide a general local context.

Description of the Gezer Weight (figure 1)

Dimensions: 5.3 × 5.8 × 0.8 cm
Weight: 216.52 g

Obverse: Thick frame of schematic eggs (half outlined dots) separated by beads (most of the frame is worn). The inner field is divided in three parts:

Palm branch to left
(Winged?) club to right
L AΟ̣Ρ̣

The second letter cannot be read as a *delta* because it is clear that there is no line at the bottom; the bar of the *alpha* is faint but most probably there. In any case, it cannot be a *lambda* in the context of a date. Although the upper loop of the *rho* is faint, the reading is not in doubt. There seems to be a circular sign at the end of the line but it is not clear at all. There is no sign of a lug on any side. The club is that of Heracles-Melqart, the main god of Tyre. The orientation of the stamp and some restoration of the symbols are based on known similar weights (see discussion below) and on what can be seen of the letters below. The club may have been intended to be winged, as evidenced by two thick short lines to the left, at the tip of the narrow end. The symbol L generally introduces a date (Seyrig 1950) or very rarely the value of a weight (see Finkielsztejn 2006:21, table 2, lower part; 2007). Here the former is most probably the case. The date should comprise units, tens, and hundreds; that can only be L AΟ̣Ρ̣ (Year 171).

On known Tyrian weights, the symbol L was normally used to introduce dates according to the Seleucid era. Generally, and especially in Tyre, the dates according to the local calendars were introduced by the Phoenician word *št*, "year," followed by the year, either in Phoenician or Greek numerals. When there is only a unit- or a tens-letter, it may refer rather to a

[1] The 2006 excavations at Gezer were codirected by Dr. Steven Ortiz, representing New Orleans Baptist Theological Seminary, and Dr. Samuel R. Wolff of the Israel Antiquities Authority. We are grateful to Dr. Ortiz for allowing us to publish this object here. We also thank Stephen Rives for his useful remarks.

Figure 1. Lead weight from Gezer (obverse and reverse)
Photograph by C. Amit

date according to a local calendar. However, in one series described here as "Year 12 Ago(" (see below and table 1), it is most probable that the symbol L introduces a date according to a Tyrian calendar. Year 171 would correspond to 142/1 B.C.E. according to the Seleucid era.[2]

Reverse: Large sign of Tanit on a network of lozenges. No frame.

The use of a network of lozenges (to prevent intentional scratching to reduce the weight) is known in the Hellenistic period, down to the first century B.C.E. The designs on both sides are molded and not incised.

The Ashdod-Yam Weight

The discovery of a lead weight found in the sand dunes at Ashdod-Yam (OIG 1143/1320) was first published by Moshe Dothan (1964:18).[3] A photograph of one side, the reverse depicting the sign of Tanit, was published in Ephraim Stern's synthesis of the Persian period (Stern 1973:214, fig. 353; 1982: 216, fig. 363) and in a recent catalogue of Phoenician weights (Elayi and Elayi 1997:pl. 27, 363). Stern called it a "Punic (?) lead weight of the fourth century" (1973:217). A drawing of the obverse was never published, nor was it described, other than briefly in Elayi and Elayi (1997:131–32, no. 363), where a reading of the Phoenician inscription and a terse description of the symbols were offered.[4] The late Avraham Eran, a specialist in ancient metrology, wrote a paper on this weight in 1973, which he kindly put at our disposal.

Description of the Ashdod-Yam Weight (figure 2)

Dimensions: 3.14 × 3.36 × 0.85 cm
Weight: 63.48 g

Obverse: Frame made of two parallel rounded lines. The inner field is divided in three parts:

Palm branch to left
Winged club to right
g m/š ᵓ n/l (from right to left)

---

[2] Considering that there are only 149 years between the first year of the era of the "People of Tyre" (275 B.C.E.) and that of the new era of the "Freedom of Tyre" (126 B.C.E.), 171 could refer only to the latter era, i.e., corresponding to 44 C.E. The aspect of the weight is definitely that known for the Hellenistic period and a date in the first century C.E. is not likely.

[3] The object is in the possession of the anonymous finder. He allowed A. Eran to examine the object soon after its discovery. The late Moshe Dothan provided S. Wolff with the finder's name and address. He kindly allowed Wolff to photograph the object in 1992. Note that the object was found before the date (1970) of the adoption of the UNESCO Convention on the Means of Prohibiting and Preventing the Illicit Import, Export and Transfer of Ownership of Cultural Property. The question of whether or not to publish this object was discussed in late January and February 1994 on the Ancient Near East (ANE) web list, which is archived and available to the reader. Pros outnumbered cons, but since the object was found prior to the UNESCO code mentioned above, was in the hands of a private individual who is not a collector *per se*, was already published (albeit partially), and provides us with valuable information, we decided to proceed with its publication. It is our hope that the object will ultimately reach the Israel Antiquities Authority or an accredited museum, but it is clear from discussing this with the finder (11 December 2006) that this is clearly not his intention.

[4] Elayi and Elayi (1997:177, n. 117) incorrectly acknowledge L. Stager and A. Lemaire for this information; it should have read S. R. Wolff and A. Lemaire.

The club is that of Heracles-Melqart, the main god of Tyre. The orientation of the stamp and some restoration of the symbols are based on known similar weights (see discussion below) and on the letters below. The palm branch is complete. The wings are represented by two parallel lines protruding from the narrow end of the club. Four letters in Phoenician script appear on the obverse. Eran (unpublished report), who was not trained in epigraphy, read these letters as *gimel-mem-taw-nun*. P. Mosca (personal communication, December 17, 1992) read *gimel-mem-aleph-nun*, noting that the *mem* could be read as a *šin* and that the *aleph* is missing its lower vertical and may be an intrusion from the cursive series. Lemaire (see Elayi and Elayi 1997:131–32, no. 363) also read *gimel-mem-aleph-nun*, noting also that the *mem* could possibly be read as a *šin*. None of these scholars could propose a convincing meaning for the word *gm/šˀn*. Note that the first sign is also similar to that representing the number 100, but that does not seem to fit with the other letters.

Reverse: Large sign of Tanit on a network of lozenges. No frame.

The designs on both sides are molded and none are incised. There is a well-preserved lug on the left side of the weight.

Figure 2. Lead weight from Ashdod-Yam (obverse and reverse)
Photograph by S. R. Wolff

The Hellenistic Weights from Tyre

The two weights under discussion belong to a series that can be attributed to Tyre because of the use of the sign of Tanit—long since demonstrated as belonging to the religious and national iconography of that Phoenician city (Bordreuil 1987)—and the club of Heracles-Melqart, the main god of the city. The group can be described as the Winged Club series, comprising weights made from different molds, displaying variants of all sorts listed below. On all the examples, the designs on both sides are molded and not incised.

The third known example was found in Umm el-ᶜAmed (Elayi and Elayi 1997:no. 405). The frame is made of half-egg-and-dart motifs. It has a palm branch at the top and the club is rather cylindrical, with only the lower wing visible. Nothing is visible of an inscription below, if there was any. On the reverse, the sign of Tanit is quite carefully molded and centered on the network of lozenges. There is a lug to the left.

The fourth example, of unknown provenance, has a frame of half-outlined dots/eggs without any separating motif. The club is clearly winged, as on the Ashdod-Yam weight, and the parallel lines join to round the tip of each wing. The top of the field is plain, missing the palm branch, and two signs that look like a repeated unclear letter are located below the club. There is simply a network of lozenges in the reverse without the sign of Tanit. There is a pierced lug on the left side (Elayi and Elayi 1997:no. 344).

The fifth example, also of unknown provenance, has a much-worn frame of probably half-outlined dots/eggs and a club that may have somehow been designed as winged (but that is not clear at all); the upper and lower registers are only two thick lumps of lead. On the reverse there is a sign of Tanit on a network of lozenges. There is no trace of a lug (Elayi and Elayi 1997:no. 407).

The sixth example was very recently sold at an auction (Spear Collection 2007:15–16, no. 410). It is very close to the fifth one, with a much-worn thick frame, displaying almost no traces of the outlined dots/eggs of the other examples, the club being cylindrical and narrow and the two upper and lower registers being also two thick lumps of lead. One of these (the upper rather than the lower one, according to the description) displays faint traces of letters. Considering the location (based on the form of the club), these may rather be traces of the palm branch. On the reverse there is a very large sign of Tanit on a network of lozenges, which is tangent to three of the edges of the weight. No lug is visible on the picture nor mentioned in the commentary.

Interestingly, the sign of Tanit is "off flan" on the fifth example, and the "head" and right "arm" are partly missing. Similarly, that device is set to the right edge of the weight in the same manner on both the weights from Gezer and Ashdod-Yam, but it is most unlikely that they were made from the same mold. However, the relatively large size of the device is an additional link between all the weights of that series. In addition, when there is a lug, it is set on the left side of the weight, when the latter is oriented according to the inscription, that is, when the club is oriented to the right. This is also evidence for a common production for these weights, considering that the lug is often added along any of the sides, notwithstanding the orientation of the inscriptions or devices. The purposes of the lug seem to be for handling and hanging the weight and probably, first and foremost, to adjust the weight.

The Winged Club series is indirectly linked to a better known one, which can be described as the Year 12 Ago(series, based on the common inscriptions they bear. One of the weights of the latter series (two or three examples from the same molds are known: Elayi and Elayi 1997:nos. 392–94) has a clear frame of the egg-and-dart motif and the inner field is outlined by a thin linear frame. The field is divided into three registers, with a prow in the center. The top is a mere thick lump of lead, and below the boat, one reads the inscription: L BI ΑΓΟ(. ΑΓΟ(stands for the beginning of the word referring either to the magistrate, the *agoranomos*, or to the institution of the *agoranomia*. On the reverse, there is a network of lozenges with a sign of Tanit in the middle of the field. To this series belong several examples with different devices and of different weight denominations, summarized in Table 1, where the examples of the Winged Club series are also listed. The weights of the "Year 12 Ago(" series are all of a much better workmanship than those of the Winged Club series under discussion, and appear to have been made under the supervision of an anonymous *agoranomos* of Tyre of a Year 12.[5] Considering the fact that only Greek is used, it should probably be dated according to the era of the Freedom of Tyre, starting in 126 B.C.E., i.e., 115/4 B.C.E. However, in case it would date according to the era of the People of Tyre, which starts in 275 B.C.E., the date would be 264/3 B.C.E. In view of the similarity beween the dated series of Year 12 Ago(and the Winged Club series, the determination of the era would help in understanding their significance (see below).

Metrology

As we can see, the Year 12 Ago(series was quite well organized as far as metrology is concerned. Each of the four denominations was represented by a different device: no device for the eighth of a mina, a "club" for the fourth, "palm tree" for the half, and "prow" for the full mina. This is not the case for the Winged Club series, which, besides being of lesser workmanship, uses only one symbol for each of the denominations. In addition, the discrepancies to the calculated theoretical standard may be much greater, which is not so surprising considering their state of preservation.[6] In any event, it is clear that these weights are according to the Tyrian standard of ca. 455–470 g (depending on various authors). We know that the minas of the Levant were based on traditional shekels, which could fit the central power's Syrian mina or not (Finkielsztejn 2007). There were 50 shekels to a mina, thus a shekel corresponded to a didrachm, because a Greek mina was divided into 100 drachms. In Tyre, the shekel was determined as weighing ca. 9.1 to 9.4 g, that is, a theoretical mina of 455–470 g.[7]

[5] Misled by the readings in Elayi and Elayi 1997 of some examples of the Year 12 Ago(series, which I (G. Finkielsztejn) did not check carefully enough, I listed some as L B instead of L BI (as actually already seen for some of them by the author of their *editio princeps*). This led me to be quite confused and I unfortunately published that confusion in Finkielsztejn 2004 and 2007. Now the solution is much simpler due to the homogeneity of the weights of the series, all made during the same year (see discussion here). The reason for the wrong readings lays in the fact that the *iota* is sometimes mixed with the right edge of the *beta*.

[6] The effect of lumps of lead on some of the Winged Club series, as well as on the "prow" example of the Year 12 Ago(series, may give the impression that the mold was re-engraved or that a previous inscription was erased. However, considering that these are systematically found, this cannot be considered for the time being, until we find an example molded before that supposed alteration. This, however, is a quite unlikely possibility because the lead of old weights was most probably recycled.

[7] Finkielsztejn's basic calculations led to a weight closer to 465 g, but that may be due to the general state of conservation of the examples (Finkielsztejn 2007). Fortunately, none of the main standards of the Hellenistic Levant overlap; as a result, the lack of knowledge of the precise value in grams of each of them does not prevent us from drawing historical and economic conclusions.

The main challenge of the Winged Club series concerns the inscriptions on the various examples, which, although generally unclear, appear to be different in almost all of them.

There are other series of weights which can be attributed to Tyre and each of them appears original. They cannot be presented here in detail, but it seems useful to summarize them (Table 2) for general information and further research based on similar future (or unpublished) finds. The variants also concern the weights, which may be quite different from the main standard. This may have been due to necessary (apparently rare) instances of adjusting to other main standards to facilitate trade, as is known elsewhere in the Levant (Finkielsztejn 2006:20–21, tables 1 and 2; Finkielsztejn 2007).

One sees that the first two groups in Table 2—that of the weights in the shape of an astragalus (i.e., caprine knucklebone) and that of those simply linked by the sign of Tanit—follow the standard of Tyre of ca. 465 g. The astragalus series is represented by three denominations and is dated with mixed Phoenician-Greek letters to a Year 29. Here, again, the era is not ascertainable. The shape and the material, bronze instead of lead, are reminiscent of an unpublished example from an Iron Age tomb at Akhziv and of others from the Persian period, depicting animals or other objects. Thus it could be dated early, according to the era of the People of Tyre, to 247/6 B.C.E., a period when tradition may not have been disturbed by Greek influence. However, the use of Greek letters (especially for the number of years) seems to fit better the late Hellenistic period, giving a date of 98/7 B.C.E. according to the era of the Freedom of Tyre (Finkielsztejn 2003; 2004; 2007). The question remains open.

In the second group, only the weight from Umm el-ᶜAmed was found in an excavation. It is of excellent quality while the others are very poorly made, but the two illustrated by Elayi and Elayi 1997 show that they belong to a same series.

The last group in Table 2 comprises weights that bear features definitely linking them to Tyre. It is identified as the "heavy mina" group because most of them weigh much more than ca. 465 g, and the suggested standards are roughly twice that value. It is not an actual series as they were certainly not made by the same engraver, nor with any common design. This seems to indicate that they were made for specific rare occasions. Elayi and Elayi's (1997) no. 404 is not illustrated; no. 333, which is dedicated to Melqart of Tyre and is stylistically linked with the Year 12 Ago(series, is definitely Tyrian. The two following weights are related by their weights, and the Beth Shean one is also definitely Tyrian, as evidenced by the club of Heracles-Melqart and the double dating according to both the Seleucid era and the era of the People of Tyre. This dating system may also be that of no. 391 (as Finkielsztejn 2003 contends, in the appendix). Their weights are related, the first one being half of the second one. Actually, no. 333 seems to be an overweight example of a quarter of the Beth Shean one and an eighth of no. 391. Although, in the first study of the Beth Shean weight it was suggested that it may be related to a Syrian mina of ca. 500 g, no. 333 seems rather in favor of an actual heavy mina of ca. 700–800 g (750 g in Beth Shean) known in late-Hellenistic Syria (see Finkielsztejn 2003), of which no. 333 would be a quarter (overweight), that of Beth Shean a standard mina, and no. 391 a double-mina, like others known in first-century B.C.E. Syria (Seyrig 1947–48). The use of that heavy mina would be an adaptation to Syrian standards, like others known in Arados or Marathos, for example (always rare, as in this case). This may have facilitated trade in the region under particular conditions unknown to us. The use of both Phoenician and Greek, and, above all, a double-dating, may support that suggestion. However, the case of no. 333, being written only in Phoenician and clearly associated with the national god, weakens the suggestion (but compare with other written items from Tyre in Finkielsztejn 2004). Even in the Winged Club series, we have two examples showing discrepancies in both directions with the Tyrian standard (nos. 363 and 407), which cannot be fully explained, if only by the state of preservation.[8] The dates of the three last weights are 169/8 B.C.E. (the Beth Shean example), 97/6 B.C.E. (no. 391) and either 266/5 or, more likely, 117/6 B.C.E. (no. 333; see below).

The Contexts of the Gezer and Ashdod-Yam Weights

The contexts of discovery of the two weights presented here provide interesting data that may contribute to a better understanding of (1) the dating of the series they belong to, and (2) the circulation of weights. Considering that these weights may not have been used by Judeans, who were using their own stone weights in Judea proper, and that we do not have any evidence so far of any Hasmonean metal weight being used in the territories conquered by the Judean dynasty (or even in Judea proper), the two

[8] Note that lead may develop either lighter or heavier chemical components with time, depending on the preservation conditions (Seyrig 1946–48).

Tyrian lead weights may bear some historical significance.[9]

We have deduced that the date of the Gezer weight can only be according to the Seleucid era. For that period, if the Seleucid era was used, one would expect it to be part of a double dating, the second one being according to the local era. However, two amphora stamps from Tyre are (for one of them, seems to be) dated according to the Seleucid era only (Finkielsztejn 2004). The study of the many Rhodian amphora stamps found at Gezer by Macalister showed that none were imported during the period of occupation by Simon the Hasmonean, ca. 142–134/132 B.C.E., and that activities ceased there around 125 B.C.E. (Finkielsztejn 1995:286, 290–92). If our reading is right and 142 B.C.E. is indeed the date of the Gezer weight, one may suggest that it was brought to the city long after it was manufactured, about ten years later, at least. Would a lead weight be in use for so long? This is probable if it was not damaged and its weight was checked regularly. Furthermore, the Tyrian Winged Club weight from Gezer is an additional evidence for the circulation of weights far from their city of origin (and not only along the coast), together with the examples from Beth Shean, Dor (Stern 2006), and Ashdod-Yam, as well as those (non-Tyrian) weights found underwater off Atlit (probably connected with a shipwreck; see Galili et al. forthcoming).[10]

The latest dated Rhodian amphora found in Ashdod by M. Dothan is dated ca. 114 B.C.E. It was found intact with several other containers, both imported and local, and other pottery (from Locus 18, eponym Hestieios; Dothan 1971:48–50, fig. 13:2, pl. 15:4–5; Finkielsztejn 2001:195). It was probably *in situ* and the end of the phase may be related to the struggle for power between the half-brothers Antiochus VIII and Antiochus IX, which took place in part in the area. Actually, the last Greco-Macedonian coin found in Ashdod is also dated to 114 B.C.E. (Dothan 1971:206, no. 3). The Winged Club weight found at Ashdod-Yam does not appear to be dated, but its similarity to those of Gezer and the Year 12 Ago(series (which can, thus, be dated in 115 B.C.E.), together with the context in Ashdod, confirm that they were contemporaneous, dating to the twenties and teens of the second century B.C.E.

P. Bordreuil (1987) summarized the occurrence of the sign of Tanit in the East some years ago. His list was updated by D. Ariel and J. Naveh (2003:62–64), including nine bullae from Tel Kedesh dated to the middle of the second century B.C.E. A handful of recent discoveries can be added to his list: two bronze and one bone object from Ashkelon dated to the Persian period (mentioned above); and a lead weight from Dor of the Year 12 Ago(series, dated (correctly, as it appears now) by Y. Meshorer to 115/4 B.C.E. (Stern 2006; for a summary on inscribed and dated *instrumentum* from Tyre, see Finkielsztejn 2004). These new finds demonstrate that Tanit was still well regarded in the second century B.C.E. in her eastern homeland and not just in the Punic sphere, especially in the Phoenician province of Tyre, and, indirectly also in Arados and Marathos, where the Tyrian standard was used for weights that also bore a stylized sign of Tanit (Finkielsztejn 2007).

---

[9] It is only during the Herodian dynasty that such weights are known in the annexed territories surrounding Judea, including Ashdod (Stein 1995).

[10] That the weight was brought by a Phoenician merchant from the coast with one of the last deliveries of Rhodian wine is a pleasant thought, but nothing more.

Table 1. The Tanit Year 12 Ago(and Winged Club series of Tyrian weights
(divided according to denominations and then to the actual weights of each example)

*Reference** *(with provenience, if known)*	*Description*	*Dimensions* (cm)	*Weight* (g)	*Value in shekels*	*Weight of the shekel* (g)	*Value in minas*	*Weight of the mina* (g)
Dor Stern 2006	O: frame of eggs and darts; club / ΑΓΟ(L BI R: sign of Tanit on network of lozenges	?	?	12?	?	¼?	?
Ashkelon Elayi and Elayi 1997: no. 402	O: frame of eggs and darts; L BI R: sign of Tanit on network of lozenges	3.0×2.7×?	55	6	9.17	⅛	440
Beirut Elayi and Elayi 1997: no. 401	O: frame of eggs and darts; L BI R: sign of Tanit on network of lozenges	3.1×2.8×0.65	57.98	6	9.66	⅛	463.84
No provenience Elayi and Elayi 1997: no. 400	O: frame of eggs and darts; club / ΑΓΟ(L BI R: sign of Tanit on network of lozenges	4.0×3.7×0.9	110.71	12	9.23	¼	446.84
Syro-Phoenician coast Elayi and Elayi 1997: no. 399	O: frame of eggs and darts; club / [/ ΑΓΟ(L BI] R: sign of Tanit on network of lozenges	?	111	12	9.25	¼	444
No provenience Elayi and Elayi 1997: no. 398 = no. 397	O: frame of eggs and darts; club / L BI ΑΓΟ(R: sign of Tanit on network of lozenges	5.3×4.0×0.7	111.74	12	9.31	¼	446.96
No provenience Elayi and Elayi 1997: no. 397 = no. 398	O: frame of eggs and darts; club / L BI ΑΓΟ(R: sign of Tanit on network of lozenges	3.7×3.5×0.7	116	12	9.67	¼	464
No provenience Elayi and Elayi 1997: no. 395	O: frame of eggs and darts; palm tree / L BI ΑΓΟ(R: sign of Tanit on network of lozenges	6.4×5.4×0.8	220.47	25	8.82	½	440.94
No provenience Elayi and Elayi 1997: no. 394 = no. 392, 393?	O: frame of eggs and darts; prow to left / L BI ΑΓΟ(R: sign of Tanit on network of lozenges	7.3×7.3×1.4	450	50	9.0	1	450
No provenience Elayi and Elayi 1997: no. 393 = no. 392?, 394?	O: frame of eggs and darts; prow to left / L BI ΑΓΟ(? R: sign of Tanit on network of lozenges	square	475	50	9.5	1	475
Tyre Elayi and Elayi 1997: no. 392 = no. 394, 393?	O: frame of eggs and darts; prow to left / L BI ΑΓΟ(R: sign of Tanit on network of lozenges	7.0×7.0×0.8	478	50	9.56	1	478
Ashdod-Yam this article; Elayi and Elayi 1997: no. 363	O: frame of eggs and darts; palm branch / winged club / *g/p m/š ʾ n/l* R: sign of Tanit on network of lozenges	3.5×3.1×0.85	63.48	6	10.58	⅛	507.84

Table 1 *continued.* The Tanit Year 12 Ago(and Winged Club series of Tyrian weights

*Reference** *(with provenience, if known)*	*Description*	*Dimensions* (cm)	*Weight* (g)	*Value in shekels*	*Weight of the shekel* (g)	*Value in minas*	*Weight of the mina* (g)
No provenience Elayi and Elayi 1997: no. 407	O: frame of eggs and darts; plain? / winged club / plain? R: network of lozenges	4.0×3.7×0.8	99.44	12	8.29	¼	397.76
No provenience Spear Collection 2007: 15–16, no. 410	O: frame of eggs and darts; plain? / winged club / letters R: sign of Tanit on network of lozenges	4.2×3.7×?	110.58	12	9.22	¼	446.32
No provenience Elayi and Elayi 1997: no. 344	O: frame of eggs and darts; plain / winged club / letters R: network of lozenges	5.1×3.9×0.9	117	12	9.75	¼	468
Gezer this article	O: frame of eggs and darts; palm branch / winged club / L AỌP̣. . R: sign of Tanit on network of lozenges	5.3×5.8×0.8	216.52	25	8.66	½	433.04
Umm el-ᶜAmed Elayi and Elayi 1997: no. 405	O: frame of eggs and darts; plain? / winged club / plain? R: sign of Tanit on network of lozenges	6.7×6.7×?	466	50	9.32	1	466

*References are only to Elayi and Elayi 1997 when the example is listed there. References to previous publications of a given item appear there and are not repeated in the table.

Table 2. Other Series of Weights That May Be Attributed to Tyre

*Reference** (*with provenience, if known*)	*Description*	*Dimensions* (cm)	*Weight* (g)	*Value in shekels*	*Weight of the shekel* (g)	*Value in minas*	*Weight of the mina* (g)
	ASTRAGALUS-SHAPED						
No provenience Elayi and Elayi 1997: no. 123	F1:H (⅛)	3.5×2.3×2.0	67.78	6	11.30	⅛	542.24
No provenience Bordreuil 1996: 56, fig. 5	F1:*št* KΘ Δ (Year 29, ¼; countermark with club) F2: *lṣr* (of Tyre)	5.0×2.5×2.1	117.2	12	9.77	¼	468.8
No provenience Elayi and Elayi 1997: no. 126	F1:*št* KΘ Δ (Year 29, 1; countermark with club) F2:*lṣr* (of Tyre)	8.2×3.7×4.2	455	50	9.1	1	455
	SIGN OF TANIT						
Syro-Phoenician coast Elayi and Elayi 1997: no. 416	O or R: sign of Tanit; hatching	rectangular	12.70	2?	6.35	1/32?	406
Syro-Phoenician coast Elayi and Elayi 1997: no. 413	O or R: sign of Tanit	square	60.10	6?	10.02	⅛?	480.80?
Tyre Elayi and Elayi 1997:no. 412	O or R: sign of Tanit	square	61	6?	10.17	⅛?	488?
Umm el-ᶜAmed Dunand-Duru 1962: 175, pl. 68:1	O: frame of bead-and-reel inside a plain frame; prow to left with Nike R: caduceus and sign of Tanit intermingled	circular diam. 6.5	225.5	25	9.02	½	451
	HEAVY MINAS?						
No provenience Elayi and Elayi 1997: no. 333	O: frame of egg-and-dart; caduceus; *lmlqrt* / *št* ^ / *bṣr* (To Melqart / Year 10 / of Tyre) R: network of lozenges	5.1×5.1×1.0	197.70	12.5 or 18.75 or 25?	7.91 or 10.5 or 15.8?	¼ or ⅛ or 1.5/4?	1,581.6 or 790.8 or 527.2?
Beth Shean region Finkielsztejn 2003	O: L ΔMP (144 S.E.) / club to right / *št* I IIIIII Δ (Year 106/7) / < A R: plain	square	750	50 or 75 or 100?	7.5 or 10 or 15?	1 or ½ or 1½?	1,500 or 750 or 500?
Syria Elayi and Elayi 1997: no. 391; Finkielsztejn 2003	O: ΣIZ or ς (217/6 S.E.) *št* / Λ P (Year 30 and 100 shekels?)	10.1×9.5×1.6	1,497	100 or 150 or 200?	7.49 or 9.98 or 14.97?	1 or 2 or 3?	1,497 or 748.5 or 499?
Syro-Phoenician coast Elayi and Elayi 1997: no. 404	O or R: sign of Tanit	square	830	100?	8.30	2 or 1?	415 or 830?

*References are only to Elayi and Elayi 1997 when the example is listed there. References to previous publications of a given item appear there and are not repeated in the table.

Bibliography

Ariel, D. T., and J. Naveh

2003 Selected Inscribed Sealings from Kedesh in the Upper Galilee. *BASOR* 329:61–80.

Bordreuil, P.

1987 Tanit du Liban (Nouveaux documents religieux phéniciens III). In *Phoenicia and the East Mediterranean in the First Millennium B.C.: Proceedings of the Conference Held in Leuven from the 14th to the 16th of November 1985*, ed. E. Lipiński, 79–85. Studia Phoenicia 5. OLA 22. Leuven: Peeters.

Dothan, M.

1964 Punic Weight [in Hebrew]. *Ḥadashot Arkheologiyot* 10:18.

1971 *Ashdod.* Vols. 2–3, *The Second and Third Seasons of Excavations, 1963, 1965, Soundings in 1967.* ᶜAtiqot English Series 9–10. Jerusalem: Israel Department of Antiquities and Museums.

Elayi, J., and A. G. Elayi

1997 *Recherches sur les poids phéniciens.* Supplément à Transeuphratène 5. Paris: Gabalda.

Finkielsztejn, G.

1995 Chronologie basse des timbres amphoriques rhodiens et évaluation des exportations d'amphores. *Acta Hyperborea* 6:279–96.

2001 *Chronologie détaillée et révisée des éponymes amphoriques rhodiens de 270 à 108 av. J.-C. environ: Premier bilan.* BARIS 990. Oxford: Archaeopress.

2003 Administration du Levant sud sous les Séleucides: Remarques preliminaries. In *La Syrie hellénistique (Tours, octobre 2000)*, ed. M. Sartre, 465–84. Supplément à Topoi orient-occident 4. Lyon: Maison de l'orient méditerranéen.

2004 L'économie et le roi au Levant sud d'après les sources textuelles et archéologiques. In *Le roi et l'économie: Autonomies locales et structures royales dans l'économie de l'empire séleucide (Lille 23 juin, 2003, Orléans, 29-30 janvier, 2004)*, ed. V. Chankowski and F. Duyrat, 241–65. Supplément à Topoi orient-occident 6. Lyon: Maison de l'orient méditerranéen.

2006 Production et commerce des amphores hellénistiques: récipients, timbrage et métrologie. In *Approches de l'économie hellénistique*, ed. R. Descat, 17–34. Entretiens d'archéologie et d'histoire 7. Saint-Bertrand-de-Comminges, France: Musée archéologique de Saint-Bertrand-de-Comminges.

2007 Poids de plomb inscrits du Levant: une réforme d'Antiochos IV? In *Productions et échanges en Syrie hellénistique et romaine (Tours, juin 2003)*, ed. M. Sartre, 35–60. Supplément à Topoi orient-occident 8. Lyon: Maison de l'orient méditerranéen.

Galili, E., D. Syon, G. Finkielsztejn, V. Sussman, and G. Stiebel

forthcoming A Hoard of Late Ptolemaic Bronze Coins and Weights from a Wreck off ᶜAtlit, Israel. Jerusalem: Israel Antiquities Authority.

Gitin, S.

1990 *Gezer.* Vol. 3, *A Ceramic Typology of the Late Iron II, Persian and Hellenistic Periods at Tell Gezer.* Annual of the Nelson Glueck School of Biblical Archaeology 3. Jerusalem: Hebrew Union College.

Reich, R.

1981 Archaeological Evidence of the Jewish Population at Hasmonean Gezer. *IEJ* 31:48–52.

Seger, J. D.

1976 The Search for Maccabean Gezer. *BA* 39:142–44.

Seyrig, H.

1946–48 Poids antiques de la Syrie et de la Phénicie. *BMB* 8:39–77.

1950 *Notes on Syrian Coins.* Numismatic Notes and Monographs 119. New York: American Numismatic Society.

Spear Collection

2007 *The Arnold Spear Collection of Hellenistic and Roman Lead Weights and Byzantine and Crusader Lead Bullae.* Auction no. 40 part 2, 4th of April 2007. Tel Aviv.

Stager, L. E.

1991 Why Were Hundreds of Dogs Buried at Ashkelon? *BAR* 17/3:26–42.

Stager, L. E., and S. R. Wolff

1984 Child Sacrifice at Carthage: Religious Rite or Population Control? *BAR* 10:30–51.

Stein, A.

1995 An Inscribed Lead Weight from Ashdod: A Reconsideration. *ZPE* 105:81–84, pl. 10.

Stern, E.

1973 *Material Culture of the Land of the Bible in the Persian Period 538–332 B.C.* [in Hebrew]. Jerusalem: Bialik.

1982 *Material Culture of the Land of the Bible in the Persian Period 538–332 B.C.* Warminster, England: Aris and Phillips.

2006 Goddesses and Cults at Tel Dor. In *Confronting the Past: Archaeological and Historical Essays on Ancient Israel in Honor of William G. Dever*, ed. S. Gitin, J. E. Wright, and J. P. Dessel, 177–80. Winona Lake, Ind.: Eisenbrauns.

49. BEHAVIORAL PATTERNS IN TRANSITION: ELEVENTH-CENTURY B.C.E. INNOVATION IN DOMESTIC TEXTILE PRODUCTION

by Assaf Yasur-Landau

FOLLOWING the fall of the Late Bronze Age polities in the thirteenth and twelfth centuries B.C.E., which was accompanied by the Philistine migration and the first formation of proto-Israelite identity in the twelfth century, there was, in the cultural horizon of the eleventh century, ending with the destruction of sites such as Megiddo VIA and Tell Qasile X, a period of accelerated growth and innovation.[1]

Mazar (1994:54) describes the period as one of intensive change: "Many of the conventions of the Late Bronze Age disappeared during the eleventh century. The freedom from earlier concepts enabled the people of the country to develop their own way of life and their own cultural traits."

Indeed, nearly every element of culture was transformed. Trade, having nearly ceased in the twelfth century,[2] was beginning to revive, with an active role played by the coastal polities of the Phoenician coast (Sherratt 2003:51–53). Iron was used as a material for the manufacture of tools and weapons, making the eleventh century a true Iron Age (Mazar 1994:49; Sherratt 1994:90–91; Dothan 2002:14–22). Much of the iron was probably imported, in the form of luxurious iron knives, such as those from Tel Miqne-Ekron and Tell Qasile. Pottery from Cyprus and even from the Aegean, such as luxurious drinking wares intended for elite consumption, was also imported (Gilboa 1989; 2001:349, 352; Mazar 1994:51–53; 2004; Sherratt 1994:74; Coldstream 1998; Fantalkin 2001). Commercial ties with Egypt were renewed after the end of Egyptian domination in Canaan (Weinstein 1998:191–92). Seals, both locally made and imported, became abundant (e.g., the "Philistine anchor seals"; see Keel 1994), and pottery decoration was transformed: from painted pottery in the twelfth–eleventh centuries to the widespread use of red slip (Mazar 1998).

The Rise of the Elite in the Eleventh Century

Most of these changes may be explained by the demands of the social elite for luxury products, enabling them to define themselves in contrast to the less privileged. Further strong evidence for the rise of such a social elite is evident in the mobilization of resources for constructing grand houses. Indeed, after the middle and late twelfth century, in which monumental buildings were not built, elite architecture reappeared in the eleventh century in new forms. The courtyard palaces of the Late Bronze tradition (Oren 1993), and even the twelfth-century Aegean-inspired large hearth-halls in Philistia, were replaced by what appear to be oversized versions of the contemporary three- and four-room houses, with a broadroom at the back, enclosed by solid walls, with two long-rooms and an inner court facing it (Netzer 1992:193). The main structure in ᶜIzbet Ṣarṭah Stratum II, Structure 109b (Finkelstein 1986:14), is an extremely large, 11.9 × 16.6-m four-room building, built on top of the less impressive one- or two-room buildings of Stratum III. Dozens of storage silos surrounding it display its important economic role in the storage of quantities of grain that far exceeded the needs of the inhabitants of the house, further demonstrating the economic power of the members of the elite who resided in this house.

In Philistia, the rectangular freestanding hearth, by far the most characteristic of all Aegean-inspired architectural elements in Philistia,[3] went out of use in the eleventh century, suggesting that more than a hundred years after their arrival, the Philistines' Aegean architectural traits were gradually being abandoned. At Tell Qasile Building 335 in Area C, Stratum XII, there was a large hall, centered around a keyhole hearth (Mazar 1986:fig. 2). This was the last structure to retain Aegean features. Building 495, built on the same spot later in Stratum XI (Mazar and Harpazi-Ofer 1994) does not have a hearth, and its

---

[1] For the sake of convenience, the term "eleventh century" is used here to describe the major part of the Iron IB, according to the middle chronology. However, absolute chronology has little bearing on the social processes described here.

[2] With the exception of the Late Helladic IIIC-style imports to northern Israel (D'Agata et al. 2005).

[3] For example, Tel Miqne-Ekron, Field IV, Stratum VII and VI Building 357 (Dothan 2003:fig. 4; Dothan and Zukerman 2004:fig. 2); Ashdod, Area G, Strata XIII–XII (Bunimovitz and Yasur-Landau 2002; Dothan 2003:fig. 12); Ashdod, Area H, Stratum XII, Building 5337 (Dothan and Ben-Shlomo 2005:26–30; Dothan 2003:fig. 10); Ashkelon, Grid 38 Phases 19–18 (Master 2005:fig. 20.7, 20.8).

blueprint may reflect an original three-room plan. Another building with a layout resembling the three- or four-room plan rather than an Aegean plan, and erected over remains of houses with rectangular hearths, is monumental Building 350 at Tel Miqne-Ekron Stratum V (Dothan 1998:155–57; Dothan 2003:194–96). It had four rooms in its eastern wing and an unroofed space in the western wing. This building may have included a very untypical round hearth in its early stage, yet it went out of use in Stratum IV, thus reflecting the decline of Aegean traditions: "By the second half of the eleventh century, with the Aegean heritage fading into the past, the people of Ekron no longer used the hearth" (Dothan 1998:158).

Similar structures were built in the northern littoral and valleys: for example, Structure 2072 in Stratum VIA at Megiddo may also be viewed as an elaboration of the four-room building. Interpreted as the residence of a Philistine governor by Kempinski (1989: 93) and Harrison (2004:18 and fig. 7), the structure displays a long broad room (2075) and a row of rooms on its west side (2068–2071) separated by a corridor (2072) from a complex of three rooms on its east side (including 2077, 2101). Similar large complexes are the building at Area B in ᶜEn Ḥagit by Wadi Miliq (Wolff 1998:451–52), and possibly the building complex at Tell Keisan, Area B, Stratum 9a, which was only partially preserved (Briend and Humbert 1980:figs. 51–52).

The newly formed elite at the above-mentioned sites were of remarkably varied ethnic backgrounds: Philistines, Proto-Israelites, Phoenicians, and Canaanites, all enjoying access to new types of materials and luxury items. The introduction of iron and imported pottery certainly changed elite fashions with respect to consumption and social display; but did these social changes affect domestic behavioral patterns? It will be argued here that even the most basic activities in the houses of the elite underwent profound changes, with innovations in both cooking and textile production. The new types of cooking pots and the new forms of loom weights will be presented, as well as their social context.

Barriers to Innovation in the Domestic Sphere

The eleventh-century innovations in the domestic arena had powerful barriers to overcome. Basic "traditional" domestic activities such as food preparation and textile production are of immense importance in preserving group identity.[4] The domestic arena, inseparable from concepts of family and kinship, is where socialization starts. By participating in group activity, observing the behavior of others, and assimilating behavioral patterns, one establishes some of the most important elements of one's identity, among them kinship (lineage), a sense of place, and language.[5] Burmeister (2000:542), discussing migrant societies, argues for a dichotomy in the identity-elements of migrant society: some elements belong to the external public sphere, in which there is much interaction with the local population, and some belong to the internal domain. The *habitus* is affected by changes occurring in the external sphere that are imposed by the social and economic environment of the society. It is likely to persist in its original form in the internal domain, which is less exposed to external conditions. Therefore, according to Burmeister, the social system of family and household, as well as the organization of private life, are less prone to change than behavioral patterns connected with the outside world.

Ironically, while domestic activities are essential for maintaining identity, and thus less likely to change, they often suffer from lower status in comparison to activities carried on outside the house, as a result of a gender bias. The necessary duties of everyday life such as cooking, cleaning, child care, and domestic activities such as textile production are often undertaken by women and are considered household maintenance activities (Hendon 1996:49–55; Picazo 1997; Damm 2000:114–15). Thus they suffered from male bias both in antiquity and in modern research, which is seen, for example, in the use of the term "full-time specialists" to refer mostly to men (Damm 2000:114–15). Furthermore, the timing of these domestic activities is often determined by the male schedule of work. Although tasks such as cooking and textile production require many skills, knowledge, and experience, they are not continuous tasks and can easily be interrupted. Women's labor time is thus often doubled as they perform several tasks simultaneously. Men, on the other hand, are free to concentrate on one continuous task.

It is possible that such bias, causing household activities to be regarded as nonprestigious, made

4 For the role of homemade textiles in conveying messages of identity, see Washburn 1994 (on women of southern Laos); for the concept of "ethnic dress" as a non-fashionable "traditional" manifestation of identity, see, e.g., Eicher and Sumberg 1995:300–4 (general observations), Walters 1995 (ethnic dress in Greece), Renne 1995 (Yoruba-Bunu handwoven marriage dress).

5 These elements are evidently so important for establishing group identity that they appear in "old," "primordial" definitions of ethnicity noted by Jones (1997:65–66), as well as in the latest ones (ibid., p. 84).

these activities less susceptible to change in response to new fashions, new technology, or new definitions of prestigious activity.

A final barrier for innovation is set by the people who create the vessels and by those who use them. Both strongly demonstrate traditionalism in their behavioral patterns, that is, "habitual postures, actions, and ways of doing things" (Rice 1987:462). Behavioral patterns are manifested in the way vessels are formed through the motor habits of potters or other artisans (Arnold 1989:224; Shanks and Tilley 1992: 141), and have a deep effect on the style of objects, which reflect the "style of action" (Dietler and Herbich 1998:236)—the *chaîne opératoire* that determines the "material style." The conflict between innovation and conservatism in traditional pottery production has been studied by Nicklin (1971:31–33) and Arnold (1989:221–24), who conclude that the acceptance of innovations may depend on the motor habits of the potter. The well-embedded behavioral patterns are also related to the way vessels are *used* by the consumer; they "are resistant to change because they are related not only to the positions in which implements are used, but to the shapes and sizes of the implements themselves" (Rice 1987:462).

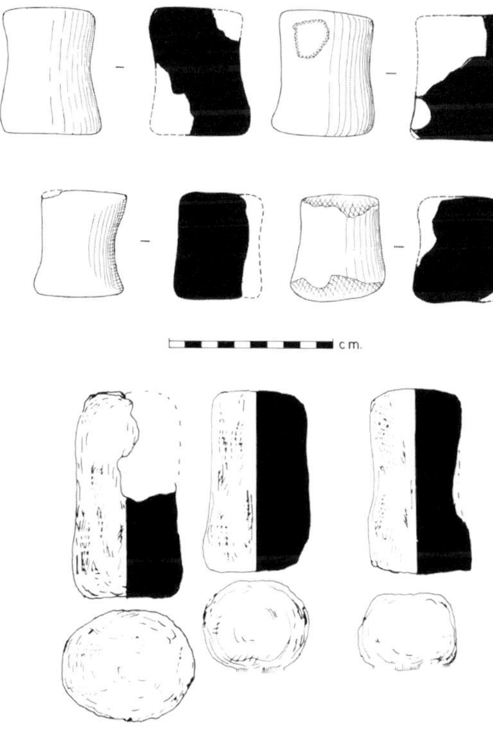

Figure 1. Nonperforated spool-shaped loom weights

Top: Loom weights from Maa-Palaeokastro (after Karageorghis and Demas 1988:pl. 189). *Bottom:* Loom weights from Ashdod (after Dothan and Porath 1993:fig. 24:3–5).

The Aegean-style Loom Weights

Nonperforated reel- or spool-shaped objects, made of unfired clay, made their first appearance in twelfth-century assemblages in Philistia, at Tel Miqne-Ekron, Ashkelon, and Ashdod (figure 1). It has been suggested that these are loom weights of Aegean origin, common in Late Helladic IIIC sites on the Greek mainland and in the islands (Stager 1995:346; Bunimovitz and Yasur-Landau 2002; Yasur-Landau 2002; 2003; Rahmstorf 2003). Similar loom weights were found in twelfth-century LC IIIA assemblages in Cyprus, such as those of Kition (Karageorghis and Demas 1985a: 266, pl. 5.6:2; 1985b:pl. 195; Karageorghis 1985:125–26)[6] and Maa-Palaeokastro (Karageorghis and Demas 1988:pls. 56, 64, 111). These were a novelty in both the Levant and Cyprus, where pyramidal, conical, and rectangular perforated loom weights had traditionally been used since the Middle Bronze Age.[7]

The most telltale find comes from Ashkelon, where a public building in Grid 38 yielded more than 150 of these weights dated to both phases of its existence (Stager 1995:14–15). These weights, in several cases found lying in a row along a wall together with linen fibers, established the identification of these objects as loom weights.[8] At Ashdod, the monumental residency in Area G, Stratum XIIIa, produced a few weights of this type (Dothan and Porath 1993:fig. 24:3–5). At Tel Miqne-Ekron Field X, Stratum VIIb, they were discovered possibly in the context of Cultic Room F (Bierling 1998:pl. 7b). Later, the northern room of eleventh-century Building 350 in Field IV,

[6] Area II, in LC IIIA contexts (Karageorghis and Demas 1985a:266, pl. 5.6:2; Karageorghis 1985:125–26; Karageorghis and Demas 1985b:pl. 195.

[7] See Barber 1991:300–1 on the first appearance of perforated conical loom weights in the Levant, and Friend 1998:35 on the LB weights from Taᶜanach.

[8] Barber (1991:107 nn. 16, 17), referring to "spools" earlier than the Late Bronze Age, rejects the association of spools with the textile industry, claiming that "they are awkwardly heavy, breakable, and much too fat to hold thread efficiently." The linen fibers recovered at Ashkelon, however, satisfactorily support the connection of spools to the textile industry. Several circumstances support their use as loom weights. No other type of loom weight was found in Ashdod, Area G, nor was any other form found, according to published material, at Ashkelon and Tel Miqne-Ekron. In Maa-Palaeokastro, only a few perforated weights were found, in contrast to many dozens of reels. If these weights were not used for weaving, we are left with very few, if any, objects that can be identified as loom weights. Spools were found in a row along a wall in Ashkelon, thus providing strong indication that they had been attached to a loom.

Stratum V (Stager 1995:346) yielded dozens of spool-shaped loom weights.

The use and production of the spool-shaped weights reflect a set of motor habits entirely different from those associated with the use of pyramidal or conical loom weights. The spool-shaped loom weights do not seem to have any technical advantage over the perforated ones. In fact, the opposite may be true: they are crude objects, and tying thread to them is a more complicated procedure than tying thread to perforated weights. Moreover, their unbaked and muddy composition could not have contributed to the neatness of the fabric. But the production of spool-shaped loom weights was extremely easy and cheap, and thus fits a domestic mode of production perfectly. Nothing but simple mud was required; there was no need for a specific type of clay or an investment of energy for firing. A broken loom weight was easily replaced in a short time.

Since typology is a reflection of behavioral patterns, we may conclude that the spool-shaped loom weights represent a cognitive concept of loom weights that is entirely different from previous perceptions. This sudden innovation in textile production could not have been initiated by the local Canaanite population of Philistia. On one hand, the absence of a local ancestry for this type of loom weight and the Aegean prototypes both point to an exogenous source for the innovation. On the other hand, the lack of trade in any such items during the thirteenth century (or indeed the twelfth century) eliminates the possibility that local production was initiated by previous imports from the Aegean. Thus the introduction of spool-shaped loom weights to Philistia has been attributed by most of the scholars cited above to the migration of people of an Aegean origin—the Philistines—who brought with them domestic behavioral patterns significantly different from the local ones.

Eleventh-Century Innovative Forms

While spool-shaped loom weights were the predominant type in twelfth-century Philistia, new forms of loom weights appeared in the northern border of Philistia already in the eleventh century.

Excavations by A. Mazar at Tell Qasile uncovered the remains of a large house in Strata XI–X (Building 495) that had been destroyed by a violent fire (Mazar and Harpazi-Ofer 1994:16). This Iron IB building was exceptionally well built; its elite status is shown by its ashlar façade and courtyard paved with large *kurkar* slabs (ibid., pp. 12–13). The width of its walls suggests that they supported two stories.

Major destruction deposits were found in Room C451, the paved western room of this house (deposits C444 and C443; Mazar and Harpazi-Ofer 1994:13). They included 64 loom weights, of which 22 are doughnut shaped and 42 have the shape of a perforated cylinder (Shamir 1994:35).[9] The crude doughnut-shaped weights were the most common type of loom weight during the Iron Age II, with numerous parallels from sites ranging from Tell el-Hama in the north to Beer-sheba in the south (Shamir 1994:37; figure 2 below). The perforated cylinder-shaped weights are less common by far, as noted by Shamir (figure 3). Their diameter varies from 6.8–9.9 cm, their length from 3.7–7 cm, and their weight from 271.2–403 g. Some of them have an hourglass shape.

Figure 2. Perforated cylinder-shaped and doughnut-shaped weights from Tell Qasile, Room C451
Courtesy of A. Mazar

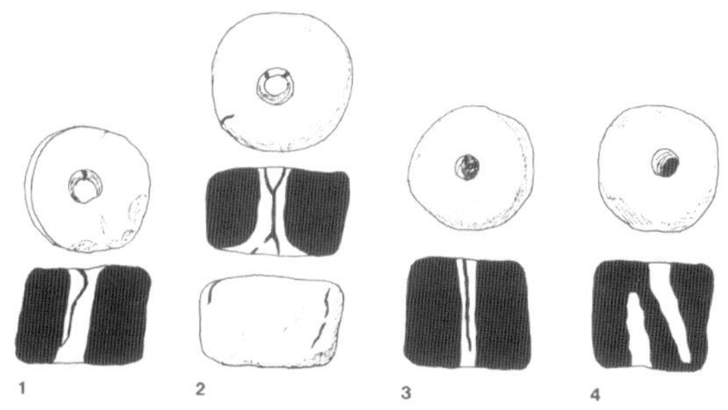

Figure 3. Perforated cylinder-shaped weights from Tell Qasile, Room C451
Courtesy of A. Mazar

The weight and diameter of the perforated cylinder-shaped weights do not differ substantially from those of the doughnut-shaped weights, which had a diameter of 6.2–9 cm and a weight of 264.8–366.9 g.

[9] Additional disc-shaped loom weights were found in B. Mazar's excavations (Maisler 1951:pl. 7:4, first weight to the right), but the exact findspot is not indicated in the report.

Both types were sun-dried and made of the same locally available *ḥamra* soil (Shamir 1994:36–37). This similarity strongly suggests that the two types of loom weight were functionally similar and could have been used on the same loom. Shamir also noted the appearance of nonperforated spool-shaped loom weights of Aegean origin at Tel Miqne-Ekron and Ashkelon. But what was the relationship between the perforated and nonperforated weights in Philistia?

A possible key to the solution of this problem comes from the contemporaneous Iron IB Stratum VIA at Megiddo. A large concentration of perforated cylinder-shaped loom weights was found in the monumental elite Building 2072 (Harrison 2004:fig. 33), attributed to Stratum VIA (see figure 4). A group of weights were found together in the base of a vessel. The similarity of these weights to the nonperforated spool-shaped loom weights from Philistia was observed by Harrison (2004:105; 2003:35), who identified them as Philistine. He used them, together with the architectural style of Building 2072 and its two-handled cooking-pots and anchor seals, to argue for a Philistine presence in Megiddo. However, unlike any of the spool-shaped loom weights from Philistia, Cyprus, and the Aegean, these weights are perforated.

The connection between these perforated, short, cylinder-shaped loom weights and the Philistine and to Aegean traditions of textile production is manifested by a single nonperforated loom weight from the same stratum (Loud 1948:pl. 170:26; Paice 2004: 59–60). This nonperforated loom weight, 6.8 cm in diameter and 7.4 cm in length (figure 5), is rightly compared by Paice (2004:60) to Aegean-style spool-shaped loom weights from Ashdod, Ashkelon, Tel Miqne-Ekron, and Beth Shean.

Figure 4. Perforated cylinder-shaped weights from Megiddo, Stratum VI, Building 2072

Courtesy of the Oriental Institute of the University of Chicago

Figure 5. Nonperforated spool-shaped weight from Megiddo, Stratum VI

Courtesy of the Oriental Institute of the University of Chicago

The perforated cylinder-shaped weights seem to combine qualities typical of both the eastern and the Aegean traditions. Their general shape was without doubt derived from the spool- or cylinder-shaped Aegean weight of the twelfth century. Their smooth appearance indicates a more careful finish than that of most of the spool-shaped loom weights, probably intended to make them more appealing and aesthetically pleasing. Their perforation, however, reflects a return to Near Eastern and Cypriot traditions of perforated loom weights. These new, almost cylinder-shaped weights were manufactured using motor habits formerly employed in the making of the Aegean-style nonperforated spool-shaped weights; but unlike its predecessor, this new variant provided a solution to the technical problem of attaching the weights to the warp or to the shed bars.

The Mechanism of Innovation

The spatial distribution of the perforated cylinder-shaped weights provides a clue to the identity of those who created this innovation and employed it. In addition to Megiddo and Tell Qasile, weights of this type were found also in Tell Keisan (Nodet 1980:pl. 97:28), Tel Batash (Shamir 1994:37), and Tell Qasile Stratum X. Although the shape of the weights was inspired by Philistine forms, the lack of published examples from any of the four Philistine Pentapolis sites excavated to date is probably not coincidental. Indeed, a cache of nonperforated spool-shaped loom weights found in Building 350 at Tel Miqne-Ekron indicates that the original Aegean tradition was maintained at the site well into the eleventh century B.C.E. (Dothan and Gitin 1993:1054–55; Stager 1995:346). Similarly, nonperforated spool-weights had a 150- to

200-year history in Ashkelon Grid 38, being used continuously in Phases 20–17 (Master 2005:346). Evidently, the similarity between the perforated cylinder-shaped weight and the Aegean-style loom weight was not enough to facilitate the acceptance of the innovative shape in the heart of Philistia.

It is likely, therefore, that the source of the innovation was a population that was, on the one hand, aware of the peculiar Aegean/Philistine nonperforated loom weights, and, on the other hand, was not bound by a strong tradition of motor habits associated with Aegean-style textile production. A population of this nature existed on the periphery of Philistia and in the lowlands of Canaan in the eleventh century. Following the territorial expansion of Philistia north of the Yarkon River (Gadot 2006), intercultural contact was renewed between people originating from Philistia, who maintained some form of the Aegean behavioral pattern, and those who had, until that moment, not been exposed to it. To many of the latter, the Philistine material culture may have seemed rich and its products prestigious, as indicated by the trade in high-quality Philistine Bichrome pottery, which was exported to and imitated in sites as far from Philistia as Dor (Stern 1994:96, fig. 47, attributed to the "Sikils" Sea People; Gilboa 2001:402–3) and Dan (Biran 1994:126, 127, fig. 87:3; Ilan 1999:93–94, pls. 25:3; 59:1, 7, 8; 62:1; 65:6). Closer interaction with the Philistine population must have exposed the population in the area of the Yarkon River to other Philistine behavioral patterns such as cooking and textile production. In a previous article (Yasur-Landau 2005), it was argued that the use of Aegean closed cooking pots with handles and a flat base by people from the heart of Philistia had likely triggered a process resulting in new forms of cooking pots in the Yarkon area. Some forms, existing only in Iron IB, were failed experiments attempting to maximize the qualities of the Aegean cooking jugs. Other forms combined the qualities of both Canaanite and Aegean cooking pots, creating a cooking jug that was closed like the Aegean form but had the rounded base of the Canaanite one. These served as the base for the creation of the standard closed Iron II cooking pot. It was suggested that one vehicle for the creation of these innovative forms was intercultural marriage, which is common in migration situations and can thus be postulated for the Aegean immigration to Cyprus and Israel (Yasur-Landau 1999; Bunimovitz and Yasur-Landau 2002). Resulting bicultural households are a natural arena for acquiring behavioral patterns via socialization carried out within the family home.

A similar explanation may be suggested with regard to weaving and the use outside the Philistine heartland of Aegean-style nonperforated spool-shaped weights, which were subsequently used as a starting point for innovative loom-weight forms. Alternatively, it is possible that the use of the Aegean-style nonperforated loom weight and the innovative forms stemming from it was adopted by people without Aegean ancestry because this type was associated with elite technology—the weights being a part of a complete *chaîne opératoire* for the production of elite garments. The findspots of perforated cylinder-shaped loom weights within the patrician buildings at Tell Qasile and Megiddo suggest that they were used for the production of prestigious fabrics alongside plain ones. This possibility finds support from the blue paint marks found on seven of the perforated cylinder-shaped loom weights (Shamir 1994:37). Shamir suggests that they were marked by a weft dyed in indigo, very likely used for the making of expensive colored garments. Coincidentally, the imprint of a linen fabric dyed in blue, to which red wool was possibly added, was found at Tell Qasile itself. It was recovered in the northwestern corner of Temple 200, Stratum XI (Sheffer 1985), placing it earlier than the loom weights of Building 495, yet nonetheless providing further evidence for the existence of prestigious garments at the site during the eleventh century.

However, the conservatism demonstrated by the shape of the perforated cylinder-shaped disc-weights, while probably facilitating the innovation process and neutralizing some of the resistance to its acceptance, resulted in a very short-lived form, persisting throughout the Iron IB only. Once the barrier to innovation in weight forms was lifted, the short cylinder-shaped weights were added to the repertoire in the eleventh century alongside the doughnut-shaped weights, as seen at Tell Qasile, completely replacing the latter by the tenth century. In fact, the doughnut-shape design was so successful and suitable for household production of textiles that weights of similar shape became the dominant Iron II form in Israel (Shamir 1994:37; 1996:140–46). These weights were more robust; their resilient structure and crude form meant that they were easier to produce and less likely to break than the short cylindrical weights.

Such weights were also adopted by the Philistine inhabitants of Tel Miqne-Ekron (Dothan and Gitin 1993:1057; Shamir 1996:142) and Ashkelon (King and Stager 2001:fig. 75) in the seventh century, the nonperforated loom weights having gone out of use sometime in the late eleventh or tenth century B.C.E. The discovery of the two forms together at Tell Qasile demonstrates how short was the period in which they were used together.

Bibliography

Arnold, D. E.
1989 *Ceramic Theory and Cultural Process.* Cambridge: Cambridge University Press.

Barber, E. J. W.
1991 *Prehistoric Textiles: The Development of Cloth in the Neolithic and Bronze Age.* Princeton, N.J.: Princeton University Press.

Bierling, N.
1998 *Tell Miqne Ekron: Report on the 1995–1996 Excavations in Field XNW: Areas 77, 78, 79, 89, 101, 102, Iron Age I; Text and Data Base (Plates, Sections, Plans).* Tel Miqne-Ekron Limited Edition Series 7. Jerusalem: W. F. Albright Institute of Archaeological Research.

Biran, A.
1994 *Biblical Dan.* Jerusalem: Israel Exploration Society.

Briend, J., and J.-B. Humbert
1980 *Tell Keisan (1971–1976): Une cité phénicienne en Galilée.* Orbis Biblicus et Orientalis, Series Archaeologica 1. Fribourg, Switzerland: Éditions universitaires.

Bunimovitz, S., and A. Yasur-Landau
2002 Women and Aegean Immigration to Cyprus in the Twelfth Century B.C.E. In *Engendering Aphrodite: Women and Society in Ancient Cyprus*, ed. D. Bolger and N. Serwint, 211–22. CAARI Monograph 3. Boston: American Schools of Oriental Research.

Coldstream, J. N.
1998 The First Exchanges between Euboeans and Phoenicians: Who Took the Initiative? In *Mediterranean Peoples in Transition: Thirteenth to Early Tenth Centuries B.C.E.* ed. S. Gitin, A. Mazar, and E. Stern, 353–60. Jerusalem: Israel Exploration Society.

D'Agata, A.-L., Y. Goren, H. Mommsen, A. Schwedt, and A. Yasur-Landau
2005 Imported Pottery of LH IIIC Style from Israel: Style, Provenance, and Chronology. In *Emporia: Aegeans in the Central and Eastern Mediterranean; Proceedings of the Tenth International Aegean Conference, Athens, Italian School of Archaeology, 14–18 April 2004*, ed. R. Laffineur and E. Greco, 371–79. Liège: Université de Liège.

Damm, C. B.
2000 Time, Gender and Production: A Critical Evaluation of Archaeological Time Concepts. In *Gender and Material Culture in Archaeological Perspective*, ed. M. Donald and L. Hurcombe, 110–22. New York: St. Martin's.

Dietler, M., and I. Herbich
1998 *Habitus*, Techniques, Style: An Integrated Approach to the Social Understanding of Material Culture and Boundaries. In *The Archaeology of Social Boundaries*, ed. M. T. Stark, 232–63. Washington, D.C.: Smithsonian Institution Press.

Dothan, M., and D. Ben-Shlomo
2005 Ashdod. Vol. 6, *The Excavations of Areas H and K (1968–1969).* IAA Reports 24. Jerusalem: Israel Antiquities Authority.

Dothan, M., and Y. Porath
1993 *Ashdod.* Vol. 5, *Excavations of Area G: The Fourth–Sixth Season of Excavations 1968–1970.* ᶜAtiqot 23. Jerusalem: Israel Department of Antiquities and Museums.

Dothan, T.
1998 Initial Philistine Settlement: From Migration to Coexistence. In *Mediterranean Peoples in Transition: Thirteenth to Early Tenth Centuries B.C.E.*, ed. S. Gitin, A. Mazar, and E. Stern, 148–61. Jerusalem: Israel Exploration Society.
2002 Bronze and Iron Cultic Objects at Ekron. *IEJ* 52: 1–27.
2003 The Aegean and the Orient: Cultic Interactions. In *Symbiosis, Symbolism and the Power of the Past: Canaan, Ancient Israel and Their Neighbors from the Late Bronze Age through Roman Palaestina*, ed. W. G. Dever and S. Gitin, 189–221. Winona Lake, Ind.: Eisenbrauns.

Dothan, T., and S. Gitin
1993 Miqne, Tel (Ekron). In *The New Encyclopedia of Archaeological Excavations in the Holy Land*, ed. E. Stern, 1051–59. New York: Simon and Schuster.

Dothan, T., and A. Zukerman
2004 A Preliminary Study of the Mycenaean IIIC:1 Pottery Assemblages from Tel Miqne-Ekron and Ashdod. *BASOR* 333:1–54.

Eicher, J. B., and B. Sumberg
1995 World Fashion, Ethnic and National Dress. In *Dress and Ethnicity: Changes Across Space and Time*, ed. J. B. Eicher, 295–306. Oxford: Berg.

Fantalkin, A.
2001 Low Chronology and Greek Protogeometric and Geometric Pottery in the Southern Levant. *Levant* 33:117–25.

Finkelstein, I.
1986 *ᶜIzbet Ṣarṭah: An Early Iron Age Site near Rosh Haᶜayin, Israel.* BARIS 299. Oxford: B.A.R.

Gadot, Y.
2006 Aphek in the Sharon and the Philistine Northern Frontier. *BASOR* 341:21–36.

Gilboa, A.
1989 New Finds at Tel Dor and the Beginning of Cypro-Geometric Pottery Import to Palestine. *IEJ* 39:204–18.
2001 Southern Pheonicia during Iron Age I–IIA in the Light of the Tel Dor Excavations: The Evidence of Pottery. Ph.D. diss., Hebrew University of Jerusalem.

Goldman, H.
1956 *Excavations at Güzlü Kule–Tarsus*. Vol. 2. Princeton, N.J.: Princeton University Press.

Harrison, T. P.
2003 The Battleground: Who Destroyed Megiddo? Was It David or Shishak? *BAR* 29/6:28–33, 60–62.
2004 *Megiddo*. Vol. 3, *The Final Report on the Stratum VI Excavations*. OIP 127. Chicago: Oriental Institute, University of Chicago.

Hendon, J. A.
1996 Archaeological Approaches to the Organization of Domestic Labor: Household Practice and Household Relation. *Annual Review of Anthropology* 25:45–61.

Ilan, D.
1999 Northeastern Israel in the Iron Age I: Cultural, Socioeconomic and Political Perspectives. Ph.D. diss., Tel Aviv University.

Jones, S.
1997 *The Archaeology of Ethnicity: Constructing Identities in the Past and Present*. London: Routledge.

Karageorghis, V., and M. Demas
1985a *Excavations at Kition*. Vol. 5, *The Pre-Phoenician Levels, Part I*. Nicosia: Cyprus Department of Antiquities, Republic of Cyprus.
1985b *Excavations at Kition*. Vol. 5, *The Pre-Phoenician Levels (Plates)*. Nicosia: Department of Antiquities, Republic of Cyprus.
1988 *Excavations at Maa-Palaeokastro 1979–1986*. Nicosia: Department of Antiquities, Republic of Cyprus.

Keel, O.
1994 Philistine "Anchor Seals." *IEJ* 44:21–35.

Kempinski, A.
1989 *Megiddo: A City-State and Royal Centre in North Israel*. Munich: Beck.

King. P. J., and L. E. Stager
2001 *Life in Biblical Israel*. Louisville, Ky.: Westminster John Knox.

Loud, G.
1948 *Megiddo*. Vol. 2, *Seasons of 1935–39*. OIP 62. Chicago: University of Chicago Press.

Maisler, B.
1951 The Excavations at Tell Qasile. *EI* 1:45–72.

Master, D. M.
2005 Iron I Chronology at Ashkelon: Preliminary Results of the Leon Levy Expedition. In *The Bible and Radiocarbon Dating: Archaeology, Text and Science*, ed. T. Levy and T. Higham, 337–48. London: Equinox.

Mazar, A.
1986 The Excavations at Tell Qasile, 1983–1984: A Preliminary Report [in Hebrew]. *Israel—People and Land* 2–3:9–20.
1988 Some Aspects of the "Sea Peoples" Settlement. In *Society and Economy in the Eastern Mediterranean (c. 1500–1000 B.C.)*, ed. M. Heltzer and E. Lipiński, 251–60. Leuven: Peeters.
1994 The Eleventh Century in the Land of Israel. In *Proceedings of the International Symposium: Cyprus in the Eleventh Century B.C.*, ed. V. Karageorghis, 39–58. Nicosia: University of Cyprus.
1998 On the Appearance of Red Slip in the Iron Age I Period in Israel. In *Mediterranean Peoples in Transition: Thirteenth to Early Tenth Centuries B.C.E.*, ed. S. Gitin, A. Mazar, and E. Stern, 368–78. Jerusalem: Israel Exploration Society.
2004 Greek and Levantine Iron Age Chronology: A Rejoinder. *IEJ* 54:24–36.

Mazar, A., and S. Harpazi-Ofer
1994 The Excavations at Tell Qasile from 1988 to 1991 [in Hebrew]. *Israel—People and Land* 7–8:9–34.

Netzer, E.
1992 Domestic Architecture in the Iron Age. In *The Architecture of Ancient Israel: From the Prehistoric to the Persian Periods*, ed. A. Kempinski and R. Reich, 193–201. Jerusalem: Israel Exploration Society.

Nicklin, K.
1971 Stability and Innovation in Pottery Manufacture. *World Archaeology* 3/1:13–48.

Nodet, É.
1980 Fusaïoles et Penons, 1980. In *Tell Keisan (1971–1976): Une cité phénicienne en Galilée*, ed. J. Briend and J.-B. Humbert, 315–21. Orbis Biblicus et Orientalis, Series Archaeologica 1. Fribourg, Switzerland: Éditions universitaires.

Oren, E. D.
1993 Palaces and Patrician Houses in the Middle and Late Bronze Age. In *The Architecture of Ancient Israel: From the Prehistoric to the Persian Periods*, ed. A. Kempinski and R. Reich, 105–20. Jerusalem: Israel Exploration Society.

Paice, P.
2004 The Small Finds. In *Megiddo*, vol. 3, *Final Report on the Stratum VI Excavations*, ed. T. P. Harrison, 58–108. OIP 127. Chicago: Oriental Institute, University of Chicago.

Picazo, M.
1997 Hearth and Home: The Timing of Maintenance Activities. In *Invisible People and Processes: Writing Gender and Childhood into European Archaeology*, ed. J. Moore and E. Scott, 59–67. London: Leicester University Press.

Rahmstorf, L.
1998 Clay Spools from Tiryns and Other Contemporary Sites: An Indication of Foreign Influence in LHIIIC? In *The Second International Interdisciplinary Colloquium: The Periphery of the Mycenaean World, 26–30 September, Lamia 1999*, ed. N. Kyparissi-Apostolika and M. Papakonstantinou, 397–415. Athens.

Renne, E. P.
1995 Becoming a Bunu Bride: Bunu Ethnic Identity and Traditional Marriage Dress. In *Dress and Ethnicity: Changes across Space and Time*, ed. J. B. Eicher, 117–37. Oxford: Berg.

Rice, P. M.
1987 *Pottery Analysis: A Sourcebook*. Chicago: University of Chicago Press.

Shamir, O.
1994 Loomweights from Tell Qasile [in Hebrew]. *Israel—People and Land* 7–8:35–42.
1996 Loomweights and Whorls. In *Excavations at the City of David 1978–85 Directed by Y. Shiloh*, vol. 4, ed. D. T. Ariel, 135–70. Qedem 35. Jerusalem: Institute of Archaeology, Hebrew University of Jerusalem.

Shanks, M., and C. Tilley
1992 *Re-Constructing Archaeology: Theory and Practice*. London: Cambridge University Press.

Sheffer, A.
1985 Dyed Textile from Temple 200. In *Excavations at Tell Qasile*, vol. 2, *Various Objects, The Pottery, Conclusions*, ed. A. Mazar, 151. Qedem 20. Jerusalem: Institute of Archaeology, Hebrew University of Jerusalem.

Sherratt, S.
1994 Commerce, Iron and Ideology: Metallurgical Innovation in Twelfth–Eleventh Century Cyprus. In *Proceedings of the International Symposium: Cyprus in the Eleventh Century* B.C., ed. V. Karageorghis, 59–107. Nicosia: University of Cyprus.
2003 The Mediterranean Economy: "Globalization" at the End of the Second Millennium B.C.E. In *Symbiosis, Symbolism and the Power of the Past: Canaan, Ancient Israel and Their Neighbors from the Late Bronze Age through Roman Palaestina*, ed. W. G. Dever and S. Gitin, 37–62. Winona Lake, Ind.: Eisenbrauns.

Stager, L. E.
1995 The Impact of the Sea Peoples in Canaan (1185–1050 B.C.E.). In *The Archaeology of Society in the Holy Land*, ed. T. E. Levy, 332–48. New York: Facts on File.

Stern, E.
1994 *Dor, Ruler of the Seas*. Jerusalem: Israel Exploration Society.

Walters, L.
1995 Ethnicity in Greek Dress. In *Dress and Ethnicity: Changes across Space and Time,* ed. J. B. Eicher, 53–77. Oxford: Berg.

Washburn, D. K.
1994 The Property of Symmetry and the Concept of Ethnic Style. In *Archaeological Approaches to Cultural Identity*, ed. S. J. Shennan, 157–73. One World Archaeology 10. London: Routledge.

Weinstein, J. M.
1998 Egyptian Relations with the Eastern Mediterranean World at the End of the Second Millennium B.C.E. In *Mediterranean Peoples in Transition: Thirteenth to Early Tenth Centuries B.C.E.*, ed. S. Gitin, A. Mazar, and E. Stern, 188–96. Jerusalem: Israel Exploration Society.

Wolff, S. R.
1998 An Iron Age Site at ᶜEn Ḥagit (Northern Ramat Menashe). In *Mediterranean Peoples in Transition: Thirteenth to Early Tenth Centuries B.C.E.*, ed. S. Gitin, A. Mazar, and E. Stern, 449–54. Jerusalem: Israel Exploration Society.

Yasur-Landau, A.
1999 The Daughters of Philistia: Towards a Methodology of Gender and Migration in Archaeology [in Hebrew with English summary]. In *Material Culture, Society, and Ideology: New Directions in the Archaeology of the Land of Israel*, ed. A. Faust and A. Maeir, 67–75. Ramat-Gan, Israel: Bar-Ilan University.
2002 Social Aspects of the Aegean Migration to the Levant in the End of the Second Millennium B.C.E. Ph.D. diss., Tel Aviv University.
2003 Why Can't We Find the Origin of the Philistines? In Search of the Source of a Peripheral Aegean Culture. In *The Second International Interdisciplinary Colloquium: The Periphery of the Mycenaean World, 26–30 September, Lamia 1999*, ed. N. Kyparissi-Apostolika and M. Papakonstantinou, 578–98. Athens.
2005 Old Wine in a New Vessel: Intercultural Contact, Innovation and Aegean, Canaanite and Philistine Foodways. *Tel Aviv* 32:168–91.

50. Bedhat esh-Shaᶜab: An Iron Age I Enclosure in the Jordan Valley

by Adam Zertal and Dror Ben-Yosef

The site of Bedhat esh-Shaᶜab (Israel Grid 1988/1742; UTM Grid 7272/5612) was discovered on November 11, 1989. It was partially published ten years ago (Zertal 1998:245–47 and fig. 8) and then fully published in the fourth volume of the Manasseh Survey (Zertal 2005a:site 65). This survey was begun in 1978 and has continued ever since. It covers approximately 3,000 km^2 of the northern and central parts of Israel/Palestine. To date, the six survey volumes published—four in Hebrew (Zertal 1992; 1996; 2005a; Zertal and Mirkam 2000) and two in English (Zertal 2004; 2008)—provide a detailed database of more than 1,500 sites, 85 percent of which are newly discovered.[1]

The survey of the western Jordan Valley (part of our Manasseh Survey), conducted since 1985, has produced more than 150 new Iron Age I sites. This "wave" follows an almost complete absence of settlement during the Early, Middle, and Late Bronze Ages in the western Jordan Valley (Zertal 2005a:56–85). The new sites described above, to which more were added during Iron Age II, represent a settlement revolution. The site discussed in this paper is just one facet of this revolution.

Bedhat esh-Shaᶜab (figure 1), was excavated over two one-week periods in the winters of 2002 and 2003, under the direction of Dror Ben-Yosef and on behalf of the Zinman Institute of Archaeology, Haifa University, Israel. The results of the dig were fully published in Hebrew (Ben-Yosef 2005a);[2] the present paper comprises their first publication in English.

Setting and Shape

Bedhat esh-Shaᶜab is located in and alongside a narrow wadi valley, the outlet of Wadi el-Kharrubeh to the western Jordan Valley (figures 2 and 3). It is situated about 1 km southwest of Moshav Argaman, about 3 km northwest of the Damiyeh Bridge, and 600 m west of the Beth Shean–Jericho main road (figure 1). Being situated in the narrow valley with its deep wadi (figure 2), its setting has no strategic advantages. Quite the contrary: it is located in a low position, dominated by all the hills around (figure 4). Thus, it seems that the builders of the site did not consider any tactical features in determining its location.

The site is situated at the foot of a long and stony slope, part of the high Ras el-Kharrubeh range (whose peak is 24 m below sea level, while our site is 266 m below sea level; see figures 2 and 4). This slope, naturally shaped in a pattern of long stone "bleachers," was used to supply the site with building material for construction. At the same time, from these "bleachers" there is an excellent view of the place (figure 2).[3]

Already at the time of discovery, the special shape of this large site (169 m long [maximum] by 88 m [widest point], encompassing an area of some 12,500 m^2 within the enclosure) was apparent. When first surveyed and measured by an alidade, and later when photographed from the air, the site was called by us "sandal-" or "shoe-shaped" (figure 2). It consists of a narrow southern side (the "heel" of the foot, Area B; figures 3 and 5) and the wider northern one (the "forefoot," Area A; figures 3 and 5), with the entrance at the narrow "heap," Area C. The five main areas of the site, A–E, descend from the south to the north in three main "steps," with a height difference of a couple of meters between them (Area A is the lowest part; figure 5).

Description of the Various Areas

The unusual shape, together with the fact that the Jordan Valley was practically unknown archaeologi-

[1] Among other features of its methodology, the Manasseh Survey team combs by foot the entire area under inspection, produces plans when possible, and continues the "characteristics" computerized method, first presented by Zertal and Greenberg (1983; see also Zertal 2004:17–22).

[2] The dig took place February 10–15, 2002 (first season) and February 2–7, 2003 (second season). The area supervisors were Oren Cohen (Areas A, A4), Haim Cohen (Areas A1–A3, B), Sharon Guleh (Area D), Na'amah Yahalom (Area A2), and Murad Tabar (Areas B, E). Students of the premilitary school in Argaman, headed by Mati Hai, participated in the dig. The Jordan Valley Regional Council helped with the dig, as did the Zinman Institute of Archaeology, the IDF, Gil Cooper (Argaman), and Avraham Kopilevic (Meholah). Adam Zertal was the scientific adviser. In the winter of 2007–2008, the excavation was continued and completed, with parts of the site reconstructed, under Zertal's direction. The results of the final season, similar to those here, are to be published soon.

[3] Inside the "heel" of the site (Area B), an additional, rectangular courtyard can be seen in the air photograph. This is a modern courtyard, presumably built by a military commander (Israeli or Jordanian).

cally, led the Manasseh Survey team to decide to excavate the site in order to determine its date and various features. As an enclosure in an arid region, the site was very well preserved. In addition, there were in fact no strata, and the place seems to have been used with few alterations or additions. This situation facilitated the dig and left few points to be clarified.

Five areas, A–E, were opened (figure 5). In each of these, several 5×5-m squares were picked to check the stratigraphy and dating. In this manner, an overall picture was achieved, the results of which are described here.

Enclosure and Enclosure Wall

The site is an open enclosure (figures 2 and 4) surrounded by a 370-m-long enclosure wall built of medium-sized local stones. The wall, some 1.5 m wide on average, is generally composed of two rows of stones, and along a 20-m-long strip (U-W/11-15 in figure 5) it has three rows. The lack of fallen stones around the wall (figure 2), and the smoothed tops of the stones, show that the shape and the present height of the wall (ca. 50 cm above the surface) are the original ones. The long western wall (W25002 in figure 5) stretches along and at the bottom of the stony slope.

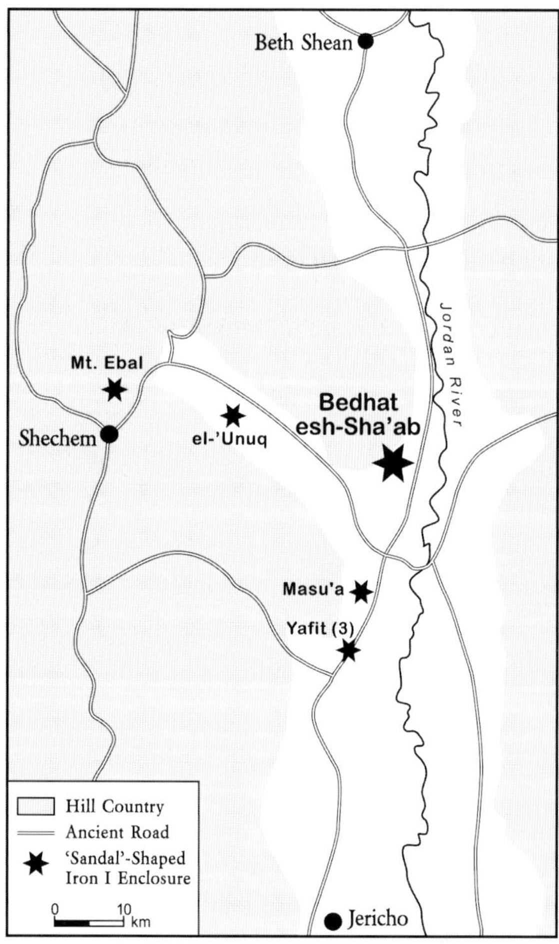

Figure 1. Map of eastern Manasseh showing the location of Bedhat esh-Shaᶜab and other "sandal-shaped" Iron I sites

The entire main enclosure wall (W21024 in figure 5) examined in Areas A–C produced an identical picture. The wall consisted of a single course of medium-sized stones, mostly flat and smooth on their upper side and taken from the neighboring wadi bed. During construction, they were laid in a trench dug in the natural or imported soil. In the soil and below the patches of pavement, Iron Age I potsherds dating to the thirteenth–twelfth centuries B.C.E. were collected.

During the construction process, the enclosure wall seems to have been built first. Then, to level up the area, quantities of soil were brought and put inside the frame, in order to fill up the enclosure.

Entrance C (no. 2 in figure 4)

The wide entrance (5 m; Q-T/24-26 in figure 5)[4] is funnel-shaped, with the widest side connected to the enclosure wall (figure 4). The edge of the enclosure wall coming from Area A (W21024) turns inwards and the facing wall W13002 departs from the other side of the enclosure wall (W13003). Although not fully preserved, the remaining parts of the entrance clearly point to its function. The entrance opens onto all three main areas of the site: Area A (the "forefoot"), B (the "heel"), and D (the central courtyard; figure 5). All these were excavated to determine their dating and architectural relationship, showing that the entrance was an organic part of the system.

Area A (the "Forefoot")

This is a large, open, relatively flat and partially paved area. It is the largest and the lowest part of the site, 75 m long (north-south) and 88 m wide (east-west; figures 2, 4, 5).

Area A is divided by thin walls, presumably built to prevent erosion. Here and there, patches of pavement made of small stones can be detected (figure 4). In its eastern part, some 11 m from the enclosure wall, stands round construction U10 (figures 5, 9, 10). This stone building (P-Q/8-9) was excavated during the two seasons to determine its date and function. U10 seems to have been built together with the

[4] From here on, all references to walls and loci in this paper relate to the plan in figure 5.

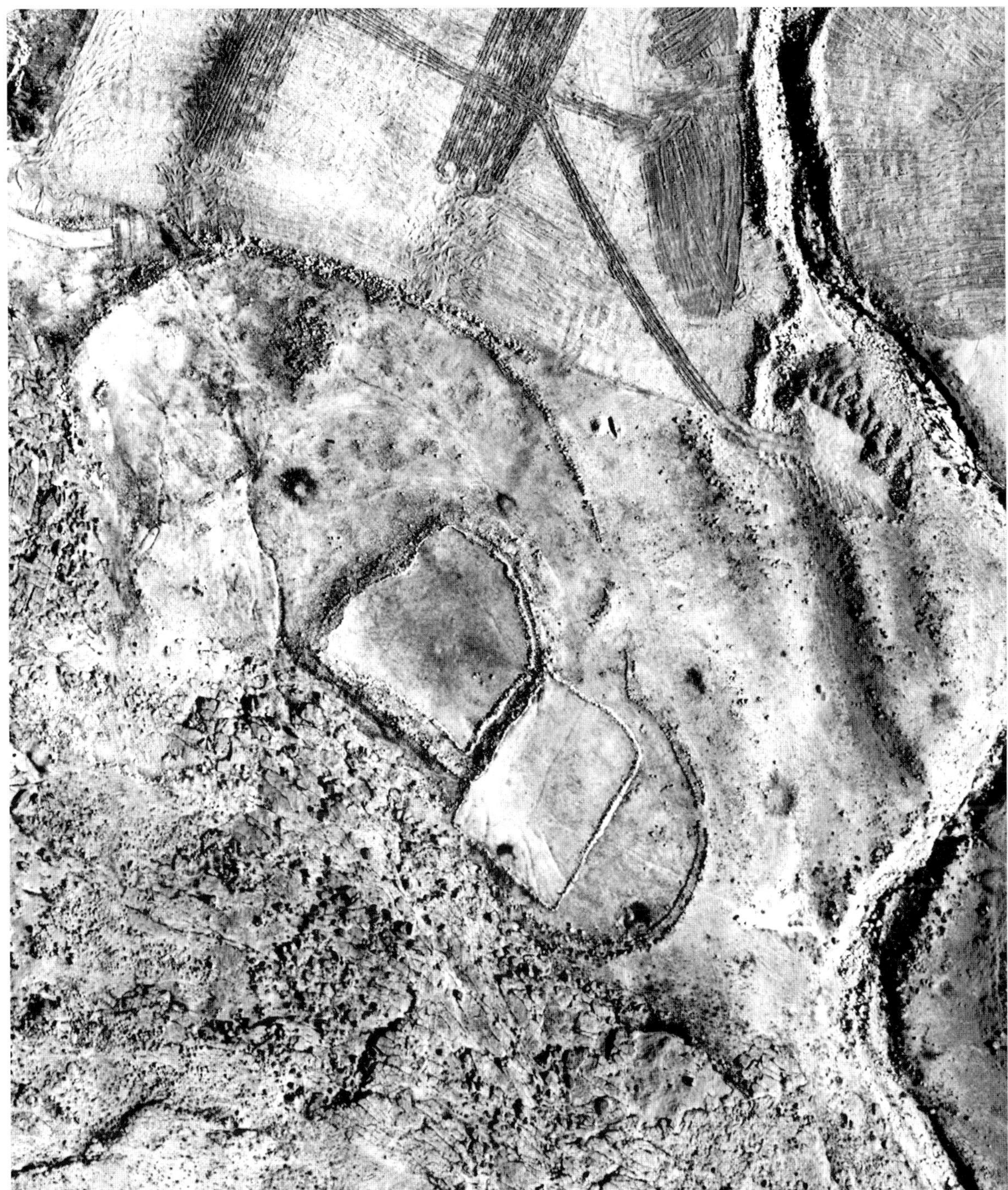

Figure 2. Bird's-eye view of the site of Bedhat esh-Sha[c]ab, looking east.
The photograph was taken before excavation by the Israeli Mapping Service (1986).

whole site: W21003, connected to the construction, points toward the enclosure wall on the same level and was beyond doubt connected to it (figure 5). Although no physical connection was achieved, they both belong to the same design and plan.

Construction U10 is built of relatively large field stones (figure 10). The outer row of stones is laid in the header method, that is, the narrow side of the stones is directed outwards (fig. 9). The stones inside the outer row are jumbled, probably the result of the

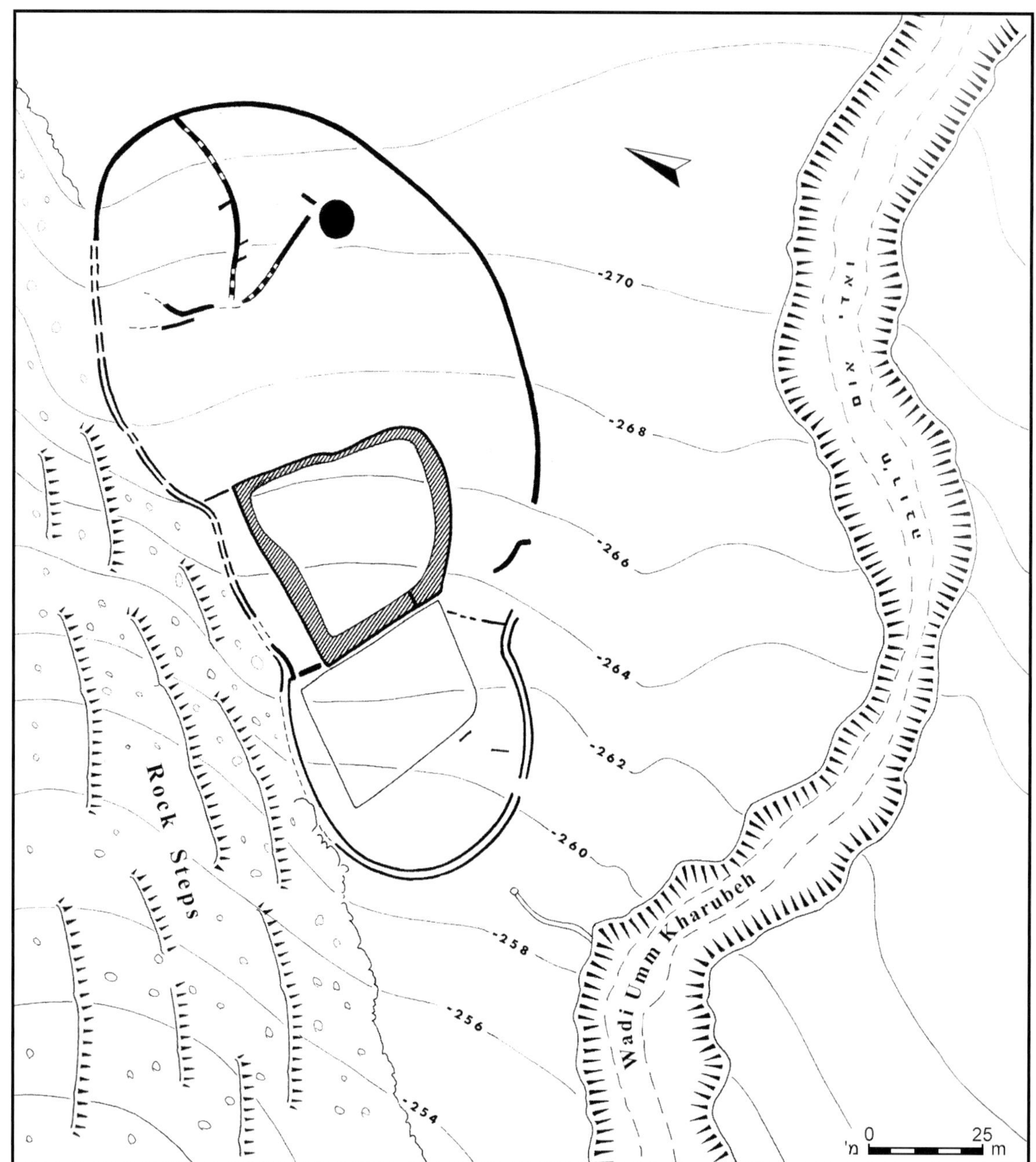

Figure 3. General plan of the site with its immediate surroundings

collapse of the construction. Judging by the quantity of stones around U10 before excavation, it seems that two more courses stood upon the present building: the height of it was, according to this, some 1.5–2 m above the surface of the site.

U10 was surrounded, at least on three sides, by a rough pavement (F11004; figure 9). The construction technique here is identical to the enclosure wall and the "procession road," U11. The pavement was laid upon a mixture of virgin and imported soil that had been put in a shallow trench. In this imported soil below F11004, pure Iron Age I sherds were found. Here, again, it seems that U10 was established together with the other components of the site and as an organic part of its design.

Close to U10 and on the pavement, twenty-two animal bones were collected, among them sheep, goat, and cattle bones and one donkey bone (Bar-Oz and Raban 2005).

The function of U10 is not completely clear. Round, separate constructions are unknown in the Iron Age. Round "Ammonite" towers of the "Malfuf"

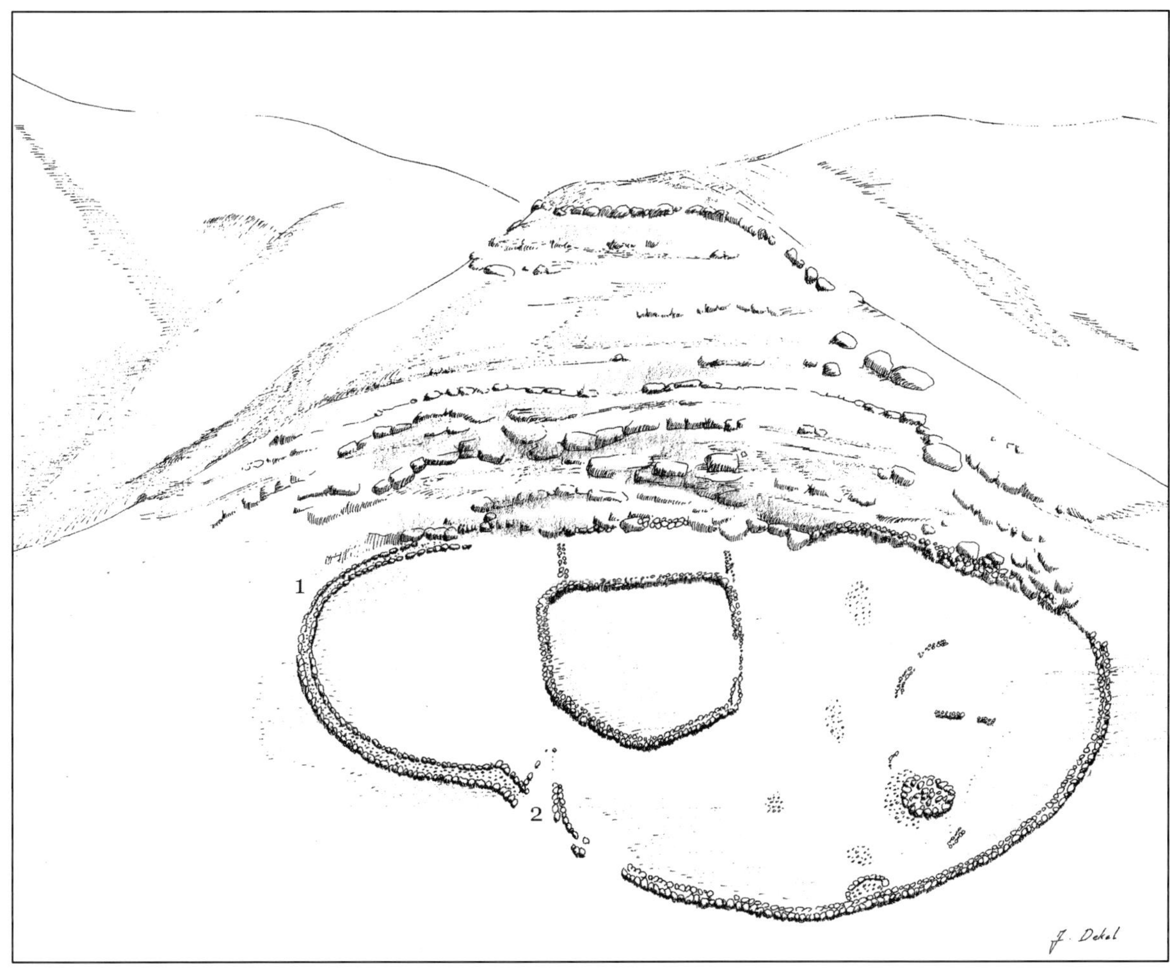

Figure 4. A reconstruction of the site in its topographical setting
Drawing by Judith Dekel

type for defense are known only from Iron Age II (Glueck 1937:18–21; Landes 1961:72; Boraas 1971; Zertal 1995), but they are much larger in diameter and are not filled with stones. The closest parallels are the Early Bronze altars from Megiddo Stratum XV (Loud 1948:78–84) and Khirbet Zeraqun in Transjordan (Ibrahim and Mittman 1991). U10 cannot be explained as a tower: it is too low and commands nothing around it. Since other functions seem impossible, a cultic use, similar to that of Megiddo and Zeraqun, seems to be a reasonable option.

Area B (the "Heel"; no. 1 in figure 4)

This flat area, oval on its outer side and measuring 50 × 50 m, is entered through Area C (figures 2, 4, 5). Its perimeter, except for wall W14005 of the central court D, is enclosed by the built "road" U11 (Area B, W12000A–B; figures 6–8). This "procession road" deserves special mention. It begins at Entrance C (R/27) and ends close to its connection to Area D (the western corner of Courtyard D, HJ/26-27). It is slightly elliptically shaped, some 85 m long and 2–2.5 m wide (figures 2, 6). The "road" is composed of two rows of stones 2–2.5 m apart, an inner row (W12002B) and an outer one (W12002A; figures 6, 8). While the stones of the inner row lie mostly parallel to the surface in a bench-like manner, most of the outer ones are standing. Between the two rows is what seems to be the remains of a rough pavement, raised some 20–30 cm above the surface. Thus, a special "road" or passage was created, paved, and slightly raised above the surface of Area B. Between the stones of the outer and the inner rows there are spaces, which clarify that it was not made for the passage of animals.

The function of this "road" is hard to determine because of the lack of any parallels known to us.

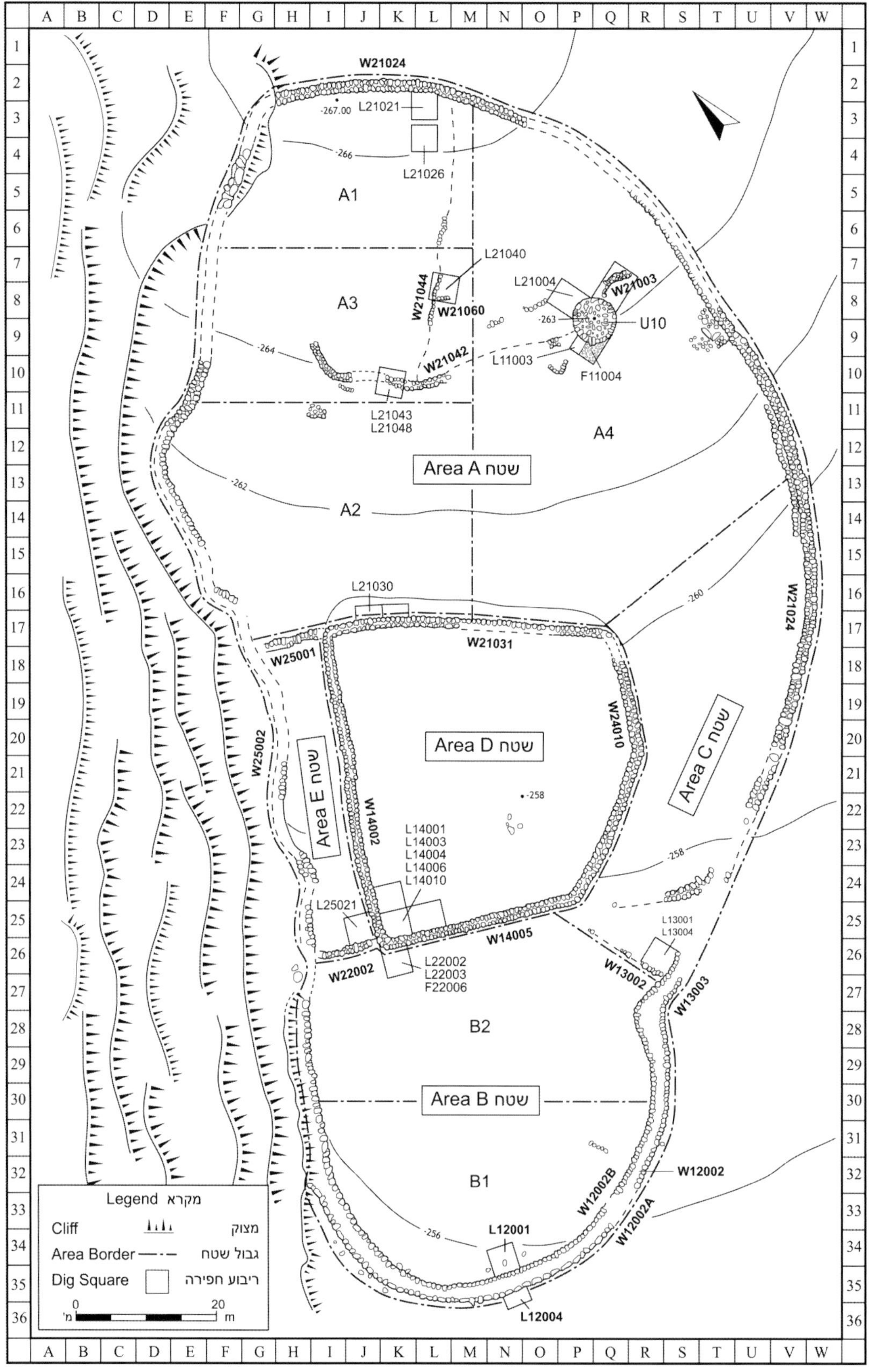

Figure 5. A detailed plan of the site showing excavation areas and loci

Figure 6. "Procession road" U11, surrounding Area B, looking to the southwest

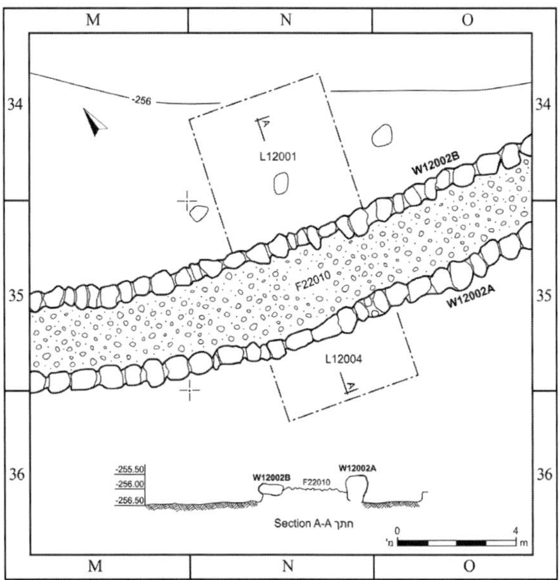

Figure 7. Plan and section of "procession road" U11

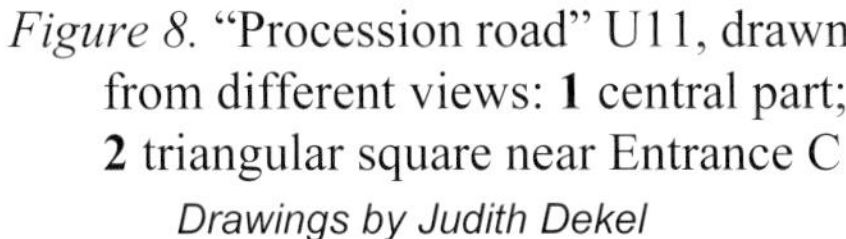

Figure 8. "Procession road" U11, drawn from different views: **1** central part; **2** triangular square near Entrance C ▶
Drawings by Judith Dekel

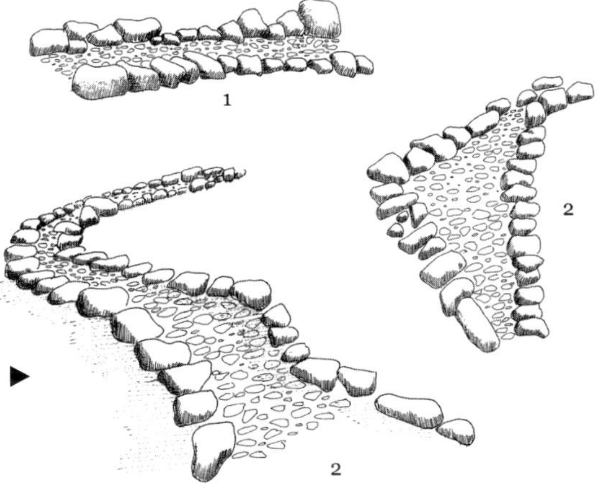

Nevertheless, some points can be offered. (1) The "road" cannot have been used for protection or defense. It is an open construction with relatively large spaces between the stones. (2) As a part of the enclosure wall, it must have been used together with the latter. Here again, the squares dug facing the outer and inner sides of the "road" presented the same picture as the other parts of the site: stones were dug into the natural (and partly imported) soil, which contained pure Iron Age I sherds. (3) The special construction cannot have been accidental, it cannot have been used for animals, and the best use suggested is ceremonial or cultic. In other words, the "road" was used to enclose the "heel" of the "sandal."

Area D (the Central Courtyard)

This closed unit is surrounded by a well-built 1-m-wide wall and is irregularly shaped (figures 2, 4, 5). It is 46 × 30 m in size, with a flat, empty surface inside it. Its western wall (W24010) is arranged parallel to the enclosure wall W21024, with a distance of 6–7 m between the two (figures 2, 4–5).

The courtyard does not stand in the middle of the site. Rather, it is located between the "heel" (Area B) and the "forefoot" (Area A; figure 5). Its two western corners connect to the enclosure wall W25002 (in I/26 and G/17–18). This connection demonstrates that the whole system was designed and built at the same

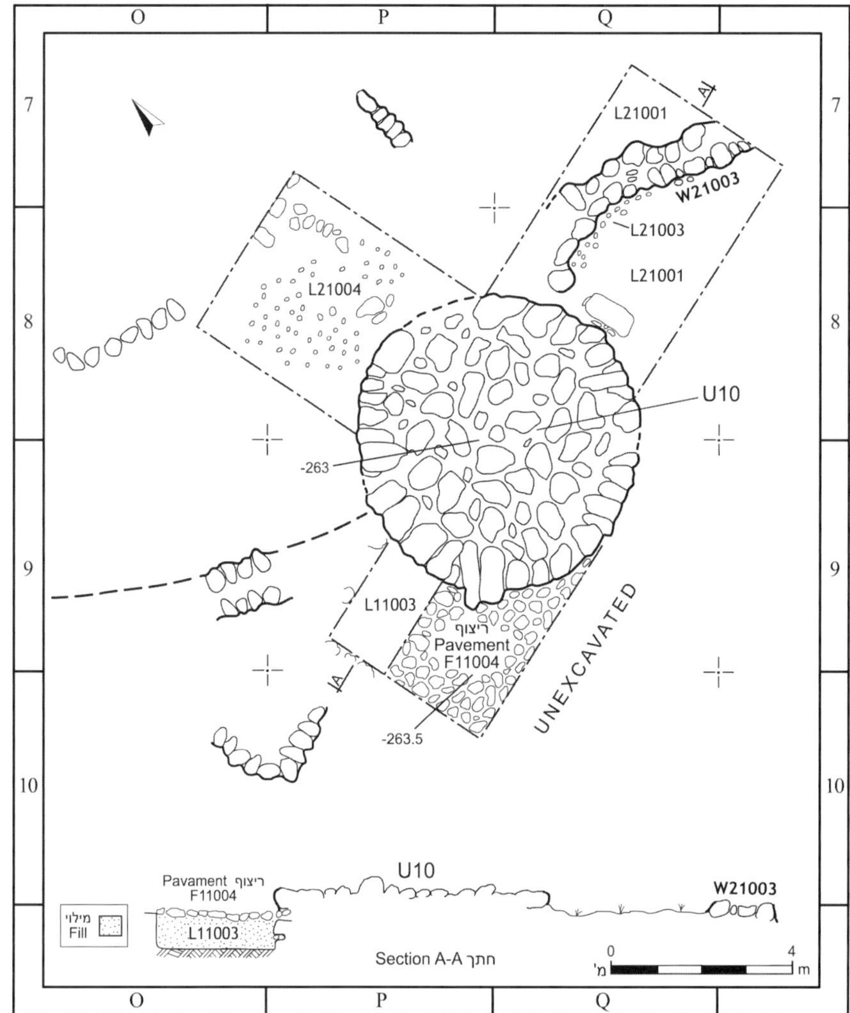

Figure 9. Plan of round construction U10

Figure 10. Round construction U10 after excavation, looking north (note the stony slope in background)

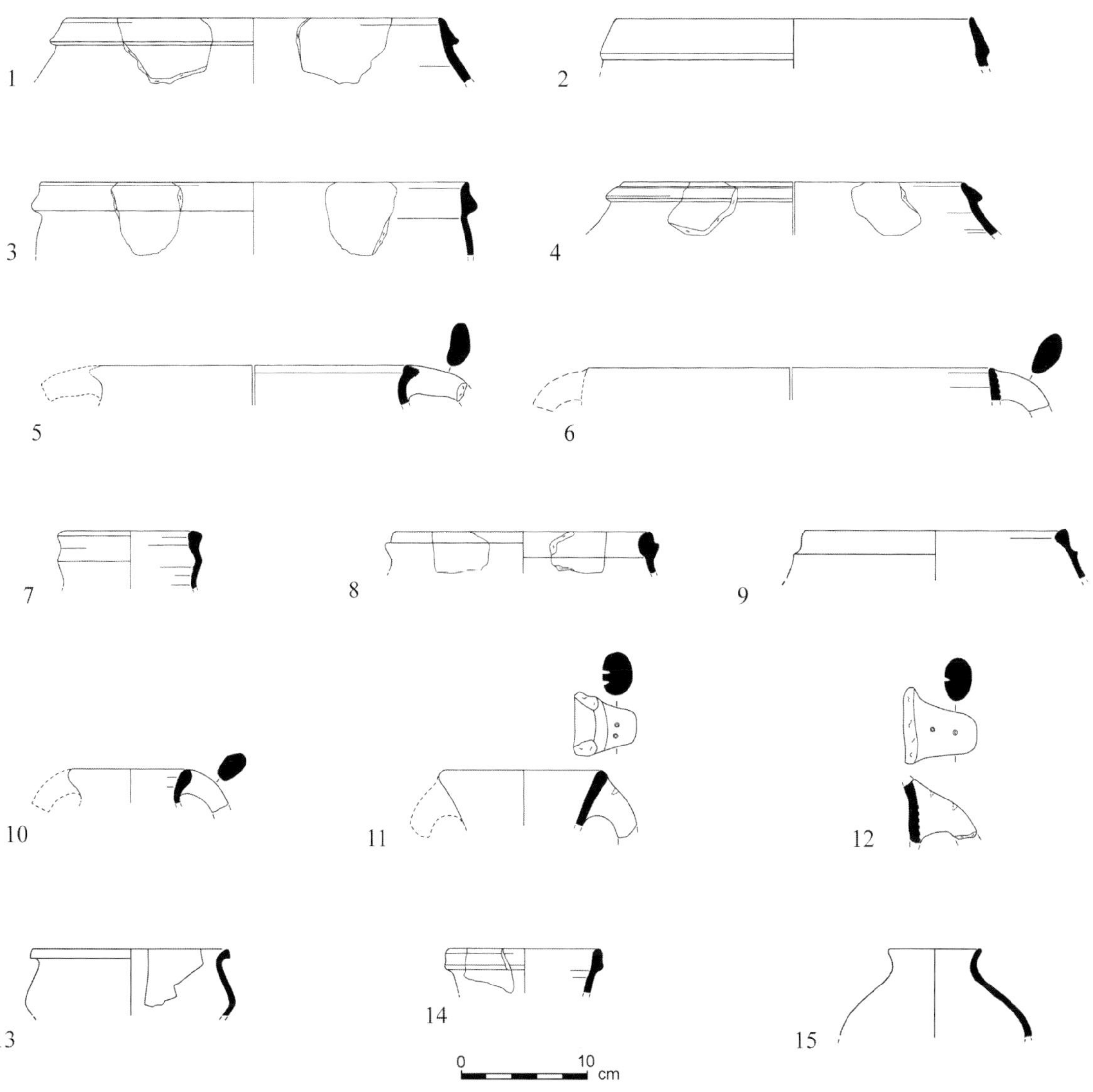

Figure 11. Iron Age I–II pottery from Bedhat esh-Shaᶜab

1–4 Cooking pots Types B–C, dark brown or black, many grits **5** Bowl, light-brown, well fired **6** Open krater, light brown, few grits **7** Jug, brown-yellowish, well fired **8–9** Cooking pots Types D–C, dark brown, many grits **10–12** Jugs, light brown or gray, grits, well fired, indentations on the handles **13** Cooking pot Type A, black, many grits **14** Jug, brown-yellowish, well fired **15** Jug, light brown, well fired

time, and that wall W14002 of Courtyard D suits the enclosure wall.

Courtyard D is surrounded by a stone wall, consisting of two rows of medium-sized stones with filling inside. A cut in its western corner (L14001, 14003–4, 14006, 14010) revealed that this wall was laid in the same manner as the other walls of the site. However, in contrast to the latter, it is the only wall that stands to a height of 1 m and that created a closed unit. The inner space of the courtyard, unexcavated so far, is now covered by eroded soil.

Pottery and Date

Already during the survey, Iron Age I pottery comprised 60 percent of the overall sherd finds (Zertal 2005a:241), a fact that led us to conclude that the site was founded in this period. This date was definitively confirmed with the excavations. Additional indirect evidence supporting this assumption comes from two other excavated "shoe-shaped" enclosures that have been dated to the same period, namely, Yafit (3) (Zertal 2005a:site 103) and Mount Ebal.[5]

Of the 904 sherds uncovered during the excavation, 139 (15 percent) were found to be indicative of the Iron Age I period (figure 12). Of these, 3 percent are bowls, 53 percent cooking pots, 5 percent kraters, 13 percent jars, 22 percent jugs, and 3 percent juglets (Zertal 2005b:chart 13). The others are pithoi and miscellaneous types. The large percentage of cooking pots and jugs originated mainly in Areas A–A1, near round construction U10. This construction was apparently used as a center for cooking and/or eating, since a large percentage of the potsherds was found there.

The site was founded, according to the pottery, in the thirteenth century or the beginning of the twelfth century B.C.E. This date is generally similar to Ebal Stratum II (Zertal 1986–1987:109–11 and 125–38) and Shiloh Stratum IV–V (Bunimovitz and Finkelstein 1993). The dating is indicated by the Type A cooking pot (Mazar 1981; Zertal 1991:39), the "Manassite Bowl" (Zertal 1986–87:125–26; Bunimovitz and Finkelstein 1993:155), and the jug handles with indentations (figure 11:11–12; Cohen 2005). The site continued to exist during the Iron Age II period, but from the tenth century B.C.E. onwards the activity there diminished gradually, until it was completely abandoned in the eighth century B.C.E.

Other Small Finds

The site is relatively poor in small finds. In addition to the bones, seventy flint items were detected. They present, according to Winter (2005), not a sedentarized society but a sporadic one, where groups of people used to meet on special occasions. Most of the twelve stone artifacts (not flint, mostly made of basalt) that have been published (Ben-Yosef 2005b) were used generally for grinding and were found broken. This phenomenon typifies sites where no constant grinding activity or food preparation was executed, like the site on Mount Ebal (Ben-Yosef 2006). A "Cassid Lip" shell (Ben-Yosef 2005c) could be interpreted as cultic, according to Reese (1989).

[5] The excavations at Yafit (3) took place in the winters of 2005 and 2006, and the material is in preparation for publication. For the excavations of Ebal, see Zertal 1986–1987.

Discussion and Conclusions

With the absolute lack of parallels known to us in the southern Levant, our analysis is based mostly upon independent considerations.

Setting

The place is located in a narrow valley, not suitable for animal husbandry. It is isolated from the surrounding area by the deep wadi and the slope. Its situation on the foot of this stony slope can be interpreted as chosen for crowds to observe the enclosure (a "proto-theater"; figure 4). This situation is repeated in another "sandal-shaped" site, Yafit (3), which is likewise located on the foot of a stony slope, but not in other sites of this type.

Bedhat esh-Shaᶜab, like the other "sandal-shaped" enclosures, is surrounded by other Iron Age I sites, located ca. 0.5–1 km away from it, whose populations could have attended events at this center.

Architecture

The site is an open space enclosed by a low temenos wall with few constructions inside. There is a great-disproportion between the investment in the outer architecture (the temenos wall and the "procession road") and the constructions inside. The site was designed according to a pattern that must have originated from a symbolic, ideological, and/or religious meaning. This is the most logical explanation for the special "sandal" or "shoe" shape. This conclusion derives from two considerations: first, the uniqueness of the shape; and, second, the independence of the design from any topography—the shape has no connection to local topography. Moreover, it repeats itself in the other five instances of the same shape and period.[6] The lack of alterations or additions through hundreds of years of existence points to the nature of the place as a center of periodic visitation and/or pilgrimage.

In addition, its principles seem not to have changed over hundreds of years. "Procession road" U11 was presumably used for the movement of people around the "heel" (Area B), most probably in the form of a procession. Round construction U10 could theoretically have been used for several activities. Similar constructions are unknown during Iron Age I,

[6] These are Masua (4) (Zertal 2005a:site 92), Yafit (3) (Zertal 2005a:site 105), el-ᶜUnuq (Zertal 1996:site 160), and the inner and outer enclosures at Mount Ebal (Zertal 1986–87:fig. 2).

while in Iron Age II—much later—the round "Ammonite" towers of the "Malfuf type" appear, some 20 m in diameter and much different in their contents. Our construction was surely not a tower, with its 1.5–2 m of height, nor can another use be supposed. The concentration of animal bones and cooking pots around it imply a feasting center. The function of Courtyard D, an open area surrounded by a well-built 1-m-wide, high wall, is unknown. No entrance to it has been found so far.

Finds

The scarcity of potsherds again points to sporadic activity. While the general inventory of vessels is similar to that of the central hill country in the Iron Age I, the complete lack of collared-rim pithoi merits attention. Since this phenomenon is typical of all the Jordan Valley sites, it may be interpreted according to the model suggested by Zertal (1988; 1994:59–61). This model explains the early stages of the Israelite penetration into western Palestine from Transjordan in accordance with the water factor. The entire eastern part of the central hill country (the "Samarian Desert"), from Beth Shean to the Dead Sea, enjoys a free water supply via the five perennial wadis that irrigate eastern Manasseh: the wadis Malih, Farᶜah, Rashash, Aujeh, and Qelt. These were used to water the animals (mainly sheep) without taking into consideration the autochthonous population. This situation changed with the entrance of the new populace into the hilly area in the west. There, the water supply was dependent upon springs controlled by the remaining Canaanite city-states of the Late Bronze Age. The result was the need for new coexistence with the Canaanites, so that the Israelites could bring water from the springs and store it in their collared-rim pithoi.

The animal bones found imply sheep breeding, with the addition of the donkey and cattle. Cattle were not well known in the arid climate of the Jordan Valley, and their bones may indicate winter activity. The place was partly used for food preparation in a limited quantity. The "Cassid Lip" shell presumably points to cultic practice.

Function and History

The lack of buildings inside the enclosure and the relative scarcity of potsherds and animal bones remove the option of a dwelling place. By elimination, a pen for animals seems highly improbable as well. The place is too large and too well built for this possibility. In addition, animal pens are well known during Iron Age I and later, having been found in a great percentage of the settlements in the Jordan Valley overall (around 70 percent of the total; see Zertal 2005a:chart 5). In most cases, they are composed of a stone circle 25–40 m in diameter around which tents stood (as indicated by the sherd scatter and the analogy of contemporary Bedouin tents).

The special shape, the architecture, the "procession road," and the other features point to a special type of site in the Iron Age I–II. It seems to have been used for seasonal gatherings, most probably of a cultic or religious character. The population involved was nomadic or seminomadic, as emerges from the evidence of the Jordan Valley in general: most of the sites in that period were enclosures of various kinds (Zertal 2005a:64–69). The population that lived in these enclosures was either sedentary in the valley and/or they used to pass into the inner hill country to the west.

We may conclude, therefore, that during most of the Iron Age, people would gather in this place and perform ceremonies of various kinds, the nature of which we know little. It seems that the "procession road" U11 was used to enclose and circle part of the site (the "heel," Area B). Magical surrounding and enclosing were an important part of ancient cultic practice (Josh. 5:14–16; Ps. 48:13; etc.).[7] Sites of this kind are mentioned in the Hebrew Bible as *gilgalîm* (Deut. 11:30; Josh. 5:9; 9:6; 1 Sam. 7:16; see Sellin 1917; Kotter 1992). The *gilgal*, as emerges from the biblical accounts, was a camp used for gatherings and religious activities.[8]

Although much discussed in the literature (see, among others, Kraus 1951; Muilenburg 1955; Bennett 1972; Landes 1975), no *gilgal* was defined archaeologically until 1991, when Zertal (1991; 1996:site 160; 1998:fig. 8) suggested the site of el-ᶜUnuq in Wadi Farᶜah as the first archaeological *gilgal*. To this category, we now add the new "sandal-shaped" sites in the Jordan Valley.

---

[7] In Hebrew, Arabic, and other Semitic languages, the word for "feast," "celebrations," etc., is חג, which derives from the verb חוג—"to enclose, surround, walk in a circle around."

[8] It should be noted that the term *gilgal*, according to its Semitic root, suggests a circular shape.

Bibliography

Bar-Oz, G., and N. Raban-Gerstel
2005 The Animal Bones [in Hebrew]. In *The Manasseh Hill Country Survey*, vol. 4, *From Naḥal Bezeq to the Sartaba*, ed. A. Zertal, 762–64. Haifa: Haifa University.

Bennett, B. M.
1972 The Search for Israelite Gilgal. *PEQ* 104:111–22.

Ben-Yosef, D.
2005a Bedhat esh-Shaᶜab: An Early Iron Age I Enclosure in the Jordan Valley, Excavations 2002–2003 [in Hebrew]. In *The Manasseh Hill Country Survey*, vol. 4, *From Naḥal Bezeq to the Sartaba*, ed. A. Zertal, 724–70. Haifa: Haifa University.
2005b The Stone Artifacts [in Hebrew]. In *The Manasseh Hill Country Survey*, vol. 4, *From Naḥal Bezeq to the Sartaba*, ed. A. Zertal, 755–58. Haifa: Haifa University.
2005c A Shell ("Cassid Lip") from Area B2 [in Hebrew]. In *The Manasseh Hill Country Survey*, vol. 4, *From Naḥal Bezeq to the Sartaba*, ed. A. Zertal, 758–61. Haifa: Haifa University.
in preparation The Stone Artifacts. In *Mount Ebal: An Early Cultic Center and Altar from the Beginning of the Iron Age, Excavations 1982–1989, Final Report*, ed. A. Zertal.

Boraas, R. S.
1971 A Preliminary Sounding at Rujm el-Malfuf, 1969. *ADAJ* 16:31–45.

Bunimovitz, S., and I. Finkelstein
1993 The Iron Age I Pottery. In *Shiloh: The Archaeology of a Biblical Site*, ed. I. Finkelstein, 153–96. Monograph Series of the Institute of Archaeology 10. Tel Aviv: Institute of Archaeology, Tel Aviv University.

Cohen, O.
2005 Indentations and Incisions on Pottery in the Iron Age I Period in the Central Hill Country of Canaan [in Hebrew]. M.A. thesis, Haifa University.

Glueck, N.
1937 Explorations in the Land of Ammon. *BASOR* 68: 13–21.

Ibrahim, M., and S. Mittman
1991 Excavations at Kh. ez-Zeraqun, 1991. *Newsletter of the Institute of Archaeology and Anthropology, Yarmouk University* 12:3–5.

Kotter, W. R.
1992 Gilgal. In *The Anchor Bible Dictionary*, ed. D. N. Freedman, 2:1022–24. New York: Doubleday.

Kraus, H. J.
1951 Gilgal: Ein Beitrag zur Kultusgeschichte Israels. *VT* 1:181–99.

Landes, G. M.
1961 The Material Civilization of the Ammonites. *BA* 24/3:66–86.
1975 Report on an Archaeological "Rescue Operation" at Ṣuwwānet eth-Thaniya in the Jordan Valley North of Jericho. In *Report on Archaeological Work at Ṣuwwānet eth-Thanīya, Tananir, and Khirbet Minḥa (Munḥata)*, ed. G. M. Landes, 1–22. BASORSup 21. Missoula, Mont.: Scholars.

Loud, G.
1948 *Megiddo*. Vol. 2, *Seasons of 1935–1939*. OIP 62. Chicago: University of Chicago Press.

Mazar, A.
1981 Giloh: An Early Israelite Settlement Site near Jerusalem. *IEJ* 31:1–36.

Muilenburg, J.
1955 The Site of Ancient Gilgal. *BASOR* 140:11–27.

Reese, D. S.
1989 On Cassid Lips and Helmet Shells. *BASOR* 275: 33–39.

Sellin, E.
1917 *Gilgal: ein Beitrag zur Geschichte der Einwanderung Israels in Palästina*. Leipzig: Deichert.

Winter, H.
2005 The Flint Artifacts [in Hebrew]. In *The Manasseh Hill Country Survey*, vol. 4, *From Naḥal Bezeq to the Sartaba*, ed. A. Zertal, 753–54. Haifa: Haifa University.

Zertal, A.
1986–87 An Early Iron Age Cultic Site on Mount Ebal: Excavation Seasons 1982–1987, Preliminary Report. *Tel Aviv* 13–14:105–65.
1988 The Water Factor during the Israelite Settlement Process in Canaan. In *Society and Economy in the Eastern Mediterranean (c. 1500–1000 B.C.)*, ed. M. Heltzer and E. Lipinski, 341–52. OLA 23. Leuven: Peeters.
1991 Israel Enters Canaan—Following the Pottery Trail. *BAR* 17/5:28–50.
1992 *The Manasseh Hill Country Survey*. Vol. 1, *The Shechem Syncline* [in Hebrew], ed. A. Zertal. Haifa: Haifa University.
1994 "To the Land of the Perizzites and the Giants": On the Israelite Settlement in the Hill Country of Canaan. In *From Nomadism to Monarchy: Archaeological and Historical Aspects of Early Israel*, ed. I. Finkelstein and N. Naᵓaman, 47–70. Jerusalem: Israel Exploration Society.
1995 Three Iron Age Fortresses in the Jordan Valley and the Origin of the Ammonite Circular Tower. *IEJ* 45:253–73.
1996 *The Manasseh Hill Country Survey*. Vol. 2, *The Eastern Valleys and the Fringes of the Desert* [in

Hebrew], ed. A. Zertal. Haifa: Haifa University.

1998 The Iron Age I Culture in the Hill Country of Canaan—A Manassite Look. In *Mediterranean Peoples in Transition: Thirteenth to Early Tenth Centuries* B.C.E., ed. S. Gitin, A. Mazar, and E. Stern, 238–50. Jerusalem: Israel Exploration Society.

2004 *The Manasseh Hill Country Survey*. Vol. 1, *The Shechem Syncline*. 2d ed. Leiden: Brill.

2005a *The Manasseh Hill Country Survey*. Vol. 4, *From Naḥal Bezeq to the Sartaba* [in Hebrew], ed. A. Zertal. Haifa: Haifa University.

2005b The Pottery [in Hebrew; in D. Ben-Yosef, "Bedhat esh-Shaᶜab: An Early Iron Age I Enclosure in the Jordan Valley, Excavations 2002–2003"]. In *The Manasseh Hill Country Survey*, vol. 4, *From Naḥal Bezeq to the Sartaba*, ed. A. Zertal, 743–52. Haifa: Haifa University.

2008 *The Manasseh Hill Country Survey*. Vol. 2, *The Eastern Valleys and the Fringes of the Desert*. 2d ed. Leiden: Brill.

Zertal, A., and M. Greenberg

1983 Methodical Problems in Survey Conducting and Data Processing. In *The Tenth Archaeological Congress in Israel, May 26–27th 1983*, p. 3. Jerusalem: Israel Exploration Society.

Zertal, A., and N. Mirkam

2000 *The Manasseh Hill Country Survey*. Vol. 3, *From Naḥal ᶜIron to Naḥal Shechem* [in Hebrew]. Haifa: Haifa University.

INDEX OF AUTHORS

INDEX OF BIBLICAL AND UGARITIC SOURCES

Biblical Texts

Ugaritic Texts

INDEX OF SITES